Barbarous Antiquity

BARBAROUS ANTIQUITY

Reorienting the Past in the Poetry
of Early Modern England

MIRIAM JACOBSON

PENN

UNIVERSITY OF PENNSYLVANIA PRESS

PHILADELPHIA

Published by
University of Pennsylvania Press
Philadelphia, Pennsylvania 19104-4112
www.upenn.edu/pennpress

Printed in the United States of America on acid-free paper
10 9 8 7 6 5 4 3 2 1

Library of Congress Cataloging-in-Publication Data
Jacobson, Miriam Emma.
Barbarous antiquity : reorienting the past in the poetry of
early modern England / Miriam Jacobson. — 1st ed.
    p. cm.
Includes bibliographical references and index.
ISBN 978-0-8122-4632-2 (hardcover : alk. paper)
1. English poetry—Early modern, 1500-1700—History
and criticism. 2. English language—Early modern, 1500-
1700—Diction. 3. English literature—Classical influences.
4. English literature—Foreign influences. 5. Great Britain—
Commerce—Middle East. 6. Middle East—Commerce—
Great Britain. 7. Commerce—Terminology. 8. Commercial
products in literature. I. Title.
PR535.L3J33 2014
821'.309357—dc23

                                            2014004922

For my parents

Contents

Illustrations

Introduction

Trafficking with Antiquity: Trade, Poetry, and Remediation

In the poetry of late sixteenth-century England, writers struggled with ambivalence toward ancient Greek and Latin poetic paradigms. Classical antiquity was already estranged: as a fragmented, partially obscured, and lost "golden age," it was only partly accessible through its literary remains. Though they wrote in vernacular English, most early modern writers were nevertheless schooled in Latin from childhood. As they wrestled with this literary legacy, writers turned to contemporary mercantile trade for new models and metaphors. Much of this trade was located in the Levant, the same space occupied by the classical myths that inspired much of early modern poetry. In this way, the classical antiquity represented in early modern English poetry became newly barbarous.

The growing appetite for foreign goods and England's increased diplomacy with the Ottoman Empire had an impact not only on early modern drama but on poetry as well, and this can be traced, in part, through philology. In 1581, the Turkey Company was founded, the first successful English trade company to begin importing goods into England directly from Turkey (previously the Russia Company traded with the East, attempting trade with Persia). In 1593, the Turkey Company officially became the Levant Company. The first English ambassadors to the Ottoman Empire were merchants; thus, Anglo-Ottoman diplomatic relations were from the start bound up with trade. And with trade came new imports and new, imported English words for such things, words for things that, though they must have been known to the ancient classical world, did not have Greek or Latin names.[1] And these words were quickly adopted and assimilated by English poets, figuring prominently in poetry that still paid homage to ancient Greek and Roman models.

It would be a Herculean task to document the number of newly assimilated late sixteenth-century English words that describe goods and practices imported from the Far East and North Africa by way of the Ottoman Mediterranean, a task that no one has accomplished thus far.[2] As the appetite for imported luxury goods continued to grow in this period, words for exotic spices and pharmaceuticals—including *sugar, candy, syrup, julep, marzipan,* and *eryngo*—enhanced the vocabularies of English writers, dyers, and culinary artists. Although words for some of these objects were in use in English in the late Middle Ages, the *Oxford English Dictionary* reveals that their English meanings shifted and expanded greatly in the middle of the sixteenth century. A variety of words connected with artists' pigments and the dyed textile trade were introduced into the English language in this period, words like *crimson* (from Turkish *kirmiz,* a beetle crushed to create the scarlet dye), *turquoise, indigo,* and *ultramarine* (from their places of origin in Turkey, India, and a place "beyond the sea," the Lapis mines of Afghanistan).[3] The terms for the different types of flowering bulbs imported from Turkey—including *tulip,* which takes its name from the Persian word for turban—were so numerous that they took up twenty-five additional pages between the first and second editions of Gerard's *Herball* in 1597 and 1633.

In early modern English, the word *import* functioned only as a verb, not as a noun in the sense that I am using it.[4] The terms *merchandise, wares,* and *goods* described what we now call imports. By the middle of the seventeenth century, English writers were already describing imported words as if they were merchandise. A dedicatory poem states this boldly in the front matter of Thomas Blount's English lexicon *Glossographia: or a Dictionary, Interpreting all such Hard Words, Whether Hebrew, Greek, Latin, Italian, Spanish, French, Teutonick, Belgick, British or Saxon; as are now used in our refined English Tongue* (1656): "And, as with Merchandize, with terms it fares, / Nations do traffic Words, as well as Wares."[5] Blount's address to his readers emphasizes the abundance of imported foreign words assimilated into English, depicting each culture's contribution almost as a plundering of treasure.[6]

We can draw a parallel between these imported words' currency in English and the way the goods they refer to were imported through early modern mercantile markets. These words might be seen as global versions of what Pierre Bourdieu has termed the "economy of linguistic exchange."[7] A similar collection of Eastern (Turkish, Sanskrit, Persian, and Semitic) words and imports began to function as *poetic currency* in the texts that this book examines, mirroring and mimicking the way that the materials they signified functioned as global commodities within the Ottoman Mediterranean. Jonathan Gil Harris has recently noted the correlation between the migration of pepper as an Indian import to Europe and to the New World, and then back to Asia, and the way the words *pepper* and its cognate, *pimiento*, similarly moved from Indian through European, American, and Oriental vocabularies.[8] To clarify, then: foreign words come into England with foreign trade, and many of them describe the new goods that have entered the country. But unlike the imports they denote (the material objects signified), these words were not exchanged for money or other words within the English language: they circulated freely. More important, these words circulated *associatively*, forming a web or network of meanings and associations rather than corresponding one to one with the object they signified. Thus, an early modern reader might encounter the word *orient* while reading Marlowe's *Hero and Leander* and associate the word with any number of different things—the East, a sunrise, a bright light, a nacreous pearl. The formulation of early modern language proposed by Foucault, which has been adopted by other scholars of early modern material textuality and philology[9] serves as a useful model here. Foucault imagines early modern language as a web of associations, with meanings "renewed in every interval, which combines here and there with the forms of the world and becomes interwoven with them."[10] Each of the words this book examines forms a point in this web composed of many different associative strands. The meaning of the word thus fluctuates throughout the early modern text, just as it fluctuates throughout early modern culture.

Just as the imported goods in question did not supplant established commodities, these words augmented English vocabularies. As poetic currency, new words did not replace existing imagery; they enhanced it. Even in English translations of Latin, new words amplify the original text: the early modern English word *cipher* (zero, imported from the Middle East) shows up in Marlowe's translation of Ovid's *Amores* 3.6 to describe impotence, and the word *orient* (nacreous) appears several times in Philemon Holland's translation of Pliny's *Historia Naturalis*, describing the luminescent quality of pearls.[11] Though *orient* is of Latin origin, starting in the middle of the sixteenth century, this word was used to refer to a pearl's shine. Though they may have encountered these concepts, neither Pliny nor Ovid had access to any of these *words*; they came to Europe by way of mercantile exchange but were only naturalized when European traders began to adopt them in practice. *Zero* was adopted through contact with Arab and South Asian mathematical culture, and jewel merchants brought back pearls from the Persian Gulf and Sri Lanka, utilizing the term *orient* as a way of grading and valuing a gem.

The central premise of *Barbarous Antiquity* is that the growing English appetite for strange things and stranger words extended to literary production: poets and printers of the period responded to the same allure by incorporating foreign words and images into their poetry—texts that simultaneously paid homage to ancient Greek and Roman writers and styles. These words and images inaugurate a new poetic economy, reconfiguring cultural attitudes toward ancient and modern, East and West, and redefining what it meant to write and publish poetry in English during the Renaissance. Often imported words or names for imported things appear only a few times within a poetic text, but what matters is their placement at key moments of the narrative, not their frequency. Working together with imagery, as verbal representations of foreign merchandise, words and things create new networks of associations with early modern overseas trade.

Although early modern global trade and Anglo-Ottoman relations have been a popular topic in early modern literary scholarship, few studies have turned from analyses of drama to poetry.[12] This is partly because the early modern stage was prime space for negotiating issues of cultural and religious identity, and with the exception of Spenser's *Faerie Queene*, we rarely find representations of Turks, Muslims, and Saracens in early modern poetry modeled on classical narrative and lyric. The majority of stage depictions of Ottoman characters engage with negative representations of the powerful, early modern Ottoman Empire as bloodthirsty, idolatrous, sybaritic, and overly militaristic, representations that can also be found in the multiplicity of meanings for the word *Turk* in the period, many of which point to uncouth and barbaric behavior.[13]

As Jonathan Burton has demonstrated, early modern English poetry is fairly uninterested in Turkish racial or religious identity, other than to stereotype it.[14] In looking for representations of Turks themselves in poetry, Burton finds no evidence of the Turks as "trading partners as allies."[15] But what if we turn our attention away from Ottoman identity and look for Ottoman imports? We do find references to mercantilism and non-Western commodities in poetry. And as Roland Greene has demonstrated in his analysis of Petrarchism, many early modern English poetic forms, like the sonnet, were themselves imports, originating in Persian and Arab literary culture and making their way into Britain through Italy by way of Mediterranean trade routes.[16]

As this book will show, early modern poetry depicted England's exchanges with trading partners to the East and South differently from drama, through language and imagery of imported commodities rather than through positive or negative representations of Ottoman identity. Commodities imported from the eastern Mediterranean were often ornate luxury goods, which had much in common with early modern metaphors for poetic ornament as oriental gemstones, imported cosmetics, pigments, and dyes.

Trafficking with the East

Engaging directly with the Ottomans for the first time, the English disrupted and reoriented the flow of trade around the Mediterranean. Up to this period, goods originating in the Ottoman and Islamic Middle East and North Africa had come into England by way of the Catholic European West (Italy, France, Portugal, and Spain). Once the English began offering British woolen "kersies" and English-mined tin and lead directly to Turkey, Venetian and French middlemen could no longer offer English wool to the Turks at higher cost. The flow of traffic no longer moved east to west along a horizontal axis; it now moved north to England and south to North Africa, in widening circles and arcs.

The word *East* serves here as a fragile placeholder for a number of different global coordinates and cultures (among them eastern Europe, central Asia, Anatolia, the Maghreb, Persia, India, and Indonesia). The Ottoman Empire is only "the East" when viewed from the European perspective. *East* implies a division between Europe as West, Asia and North Africa as East, but this bilateral division was not clear in sixteenth-century cartography. Where was the line drawn, when the Ottoman Empire's borders were liquid and flexible? Equally useful to understanding early modern English global geography is the notion of North and South, where the South encompasses not only the Italian Mediterranean, but Spain and North Africa as well.[17] To early modern readers and writers on all sides of the Mediterranean, the late sixteenth-century Ottoman Empire was more than simply the "East," a diachronic space in the history of dialogue between East and West. That empire held a uniquely polychronic space, not only because of the multiple temporalities it encompassed, as the current occupant of the lands formerly part of ancient Greece and Rome, but because it constructed its own space in a more malleable, fluid way. Its lands and seas stretched from the Greek islands across the Mediterranean and south to North Africa, east to Jerusalem, and up into central Asia. As Palmira Brummett's and Halil Inalcik's histories of early modern Ottoman expansion have shown, the Ottoman Empire's boundaries were defined by sea trade more than by land conquest, and they were almost always subject to change.[18] On the one hand, the Ottomans redefined empire by blending trade with diplomacy, seafaring with conquest, creating something new and different from the Western empires of the classical past. On the other hand, sixteenth-century Ottoman rulers themselves were aware of the layered temporal landscapes they inhabited, redefining themselves as new Roman rulers. Both the Ottoman sultans and the Hapsburg emperors in the sixteenth century "would aspire to resurrect the Roman Empire."[19]

Because of the fluidity of the Ottoman Empire's borders and its translation of diplomacy into trade, early modern engagements between England and the Ottoman Empire thus participate in something different from a linear discourse of East and West; they create multitemporal and transglobal configurations. As Jerry Brotton's analysis of sixteenth-century cartography reveals, early modern European travelers and explorers also viewed the classical world and the lands occupied by the Ottoman Empire as one and the same: "The supposedly 'western' world of Europe actually defined itself as coextensive with, rather than in contradistinction to, the classical world of the east, whatever its intellectual and cultural dimensions."[20] We can join Brotton's analysis of a coextensive East and West with Jonathan Gil Harris's multilayered approach to history, which entails moving beyond diachronic and synchronic models of narrative space in favor of multitemporal, or "polychronic" strata.[21] In other words, for English eyes, the lands of the early modern Ottoman Empire were in the process of becoming the "East" but were not fixed in space or time. They were also, at the same time, lands of classical antiquity and ancient Greek myth. The site of ancient Troy, near ancient Abydos, was also the site of an Ottoman military garrison: both places were coextensive and equally present for early modern readers and travelers.

One such traveler and writer was George Sandys, who is known for his English translation of Ovid's *Metamorphoses* (1632). Sandys wrote an extensive and richly illustrated narrative documenting his travels across Europe to the Ottoman Empire in 1610.[22] As an antiquarian, he was "curious in the search of Antiquities," keen to explore the monumental relics of ancient European empires and to learn as much as he could about the history of the current cultural groups that controlled and occupied those lands and waterways.[23] For an English antiquarian like Sandys, the ancient classical past might have felt more vivid and alive than either the medieval Orthodox past or the Muslim present. As he travels through the Mediterranean and farther east into central Asia, Sandys must find a way to reconcile his familiar but extinct classical antiquity with the unfamiliar yet jarringly contemporary cultures and religious groups of the early seventeenth-century Ottoman Empire.

As Sandys remarks in his dedicatory epistle to King James, the lands and artifacts of classical antiquity so precious to English literary history were now sadly in the possession of the Ottoman Empire, the "barbarous Tyrant posessing the thrones of ancient and iust dominion."[24] *Barbarous* was originally a classical Latin term for invading northerners, but in early modern English, it came to mean non-European and sometimes Levantine.[25] Sandys laments the destruction and disappearance of classical antiquity at the hands of a conquering Muslim empire, but it is clear that what he is mourning is not so much the Ottoman occupation of these lands as the loss of the past itself. The Greek islands are desolate and deteriorated, "so highly celebrated by the ancient Poets: but now presenting nothing but ruines, in a great part desolate, it groneth vnder the Turkish thraldome."[26] Smyrna is now an early modern Ottoman city with new mosques filled with practicing Muslims: "now violated by the *Mahometans*, her beautie is turned to deformitie, her knowledge to barbarisme, her religion to impietie."[27]

What Sandys experiences in these encounters is a kind of temporal and spatial dislocation between the ancient, classical past in the early modern English humanist imagination, the Byzantine Empire in the early modern Christian thinking, and contemporary, early modern Ottoman culture.[28] Eliding the lost beauty of ancient myth with the more recent loss of Eastern Christianity, Sandys's temporality might be seen even to classicize or antiquate medieval history. What does it mean for Western antiquity to be repossessed by "barbarous" Ottoman foreigners? How does this change the early modern English project of reclaiming Roman antiquity as its own? This book argues that early modern English poetry occupies a space in which English writers negotiated their vexed relationship to classical antiquity by engaging with and appropriating non-Western culture through words and imagery associated with Mediterranean and Asian imports. By trafficking with imagery and vocabularies of imported commodities, early modern English poets also trafficked with, or exchanged, the past, replacing an already fraught vision of classical antiquity with a further estranged and exoticized one. When words and things from the East began to be imported into English, the poets of England revised their attitude toward ancient Greece and Rome. Just as exotic luxury goods, scientific theories, and decorative styles were brought into England from Italy, Persia, and the countries under Ottoman control, so too were foreign, nonnative words absorbed into English. Once these new, imported words started infiltrating poetic texts ostensibly modeled on classical literary traditions, the already complicated status of classical "antiquity" was thrown further into flux. With the addition of these new concepts, imported neologisms, and imaginary things circulating associatively through early modern culture and texts, antiquity itself took on the characteristics of Levantine and Asian cultures, becoming "barbarous."

Trafficking with the Past

Latin literature was the staple for an early modern humanist grammar school education, where boys learned to write, speak, and orate in Latin in imitation of Virgil, Horace, Ovid, Cicero, and Seneca. Yet although early modern English writers acknowledged and paid homage to the literary authority of classical antiquity, by the sixteenth and early seventeenth centuries, there were signs of strain in English writers' relationship to ancient Greek and Roman culture. The English had recently broken away from the Roman Catholic Church, and they viewed the ancient Romans as both ancestors (via the Troy myth) and conquerors (via the narrative of the Four Empires: Roman, Danish, Saxon, and Norman).[29] Latin had been banished from the Anglican Church and was preserved only at the courts and schoolrooms. And the English language was rapidly expanding to include new Latinate forms of English words alongside words imported from England's growing global encounters with non-Western cultures.[30] Leonard Barkan, Sean Keilen, and Jonathan Gil Harris have exposed fissures in the early modern cultural elevation of classical antiquity.[31] In his analysis of broken ancient Roman monuments and sculpture, Barkan argues that early modern Europeans viewed classical antiquity itself as a collection of fragments, and Keilen notes that early modern English depictions of the classical past as a "golden age" allowed writers to question and critique the practice of classical imitation and the authority of the ancients. Harris encourages us to read the layered landscape of early modern London with its ancient Hebrew mural inscriptions as a temporal palimpsest that impresses an occidental present onto an oriental past.

The alternately familiar and vexed relationship of early modern English writers to classical antiquity derives in part from the authority that the

Elizabethan education system vested in Latin authors, grammar, and language. For Jeff Dolven, "skepticism and self-doubt smolder at the roots of English humanism," which is why English writers turned to Romance (a genre excluded from classical hierarchies).[32] The violent discipline that characterized classical humanist education may have made the authority of the ancients seem savage and barbarous itself: Dolven and Lynn Enterline note that corporal punishment of children was at the heart of classical humanist education of schoolboys.[33] Some of this violence characterizes the speaker's frustration in Philip Sidney's sonnet sequence *Astrophil and Stella*. In the first sonnet, the poet struggles with writer's block and characterizes his creative capacity as a boy exposed to corporal punishment: "Invention, Nature's child, fled stepdame study's blows" (*AS*, 1.10). Later, the speaker rails against his humanist education in moral virtue, claiming that Cato's philosophy is better suited to "Churches or Schooles" (*AS*, 4.6) and the poet's mouth "too tender for thy hard bit" (*AS*, 4.8). Throughout the sequence, Astrophil describes himself as Stella's shackled, tortured slave and in several instances speaks of the failure of his humanist education to help him in love.[34]

Even Ben Jonson, famous for his classical learning and his adoption of the Roman poet Horace's ideals in the creation of his own literary "plain" style, acknowledges the ambivalence early modern writers felt when confronted with authority of classical antiquity. "*Non nimium credendum antiquitati*" ("not particularly believing in the ancients") he wrote in *Timber* (1641), his published commonplace book and *ars poetica*.[35] Jonson explains that as much as writers ought to acknowledge and emulate ancient Greek and Roman erudition, they must also move past it, "not to rest in their sole authority, or take all upon trust from them." Demonstrating his mastery of Latin commonplacing, Jonson peppers this ambivalent passage with quotations. Classical writers should act "*Non domini nostri, sed duces fuere*" ("not as our leaders but as our guides"). He concludes with a combination of English and Latin slightly paraphrased from Seneca: "Truth lies open to all; it is no man's several. *Patet omnibus veritas; nondum est occupata. Multum ex illa, etiam futuris relicta est.*" The English phrase that opens this commonplace, "Truth lies open to all," and so on, appears in the first Latin sentence, but Jonson leaves the second sentence untranslated: "And there is plenty of it [Truth] left even for posterity to discover."[36] The phrase is found in Seneca's epistle 33 (line 11). In his combination of Latin and English *sententiae*, Jonson is able to ground his idea about departing from classical authority in Roman literary authority itself, both paying homage to his classical humanist education and inviting others to transcend it.

The early modern ambivalence to Greek and Latin antiquity also may have been bolstered by the representation of British and northern Europeans themselves as barbarous tribes in classical Latin texts. Some writers, like Spenser and Harvey, attempted to reclaim this native English "Gothish" behavior by linking it to the innocence of Ovid's Golden Age (*Metamorphoses* I. 89–112). Both Thomas Campion and Samuel Daniel describe English as a barbarous language, but they dispute whether it is suited to classical hexameters, with Daniel arguing that the imposition of Latin hexameters onto English forces it to seem even more uncouth.[37] But the experience of reading about one's own ancient ancestors as the very barbarians that Roman writers denigrate must have further complicated the early modern view of Britain's inherited and imposed Roman literary legacy.

One way early modern poets responded to this frustrated bond with the literary authority of classical antiquity was by emulating a Roman poet whose writings were perceived as "counter-classical" (to borrow W. R. Johnson's and Heather James's terminology). That poet was Ovid.[38] Shakespeare and the poets of the 1590s preserve an early modern interest in classical poetics only by appropriating the work of a "classical" poet who was anything but classical. For James, this means that the kind of classicism that early modern poets located in Ovidian narrative and elegy made classicism itself commensurate with early modern poetic experimentation and innovation. The task of early modern humanism, which, as Enterline teaches us was physically beaten into schoolboys in the Latin grammar schools, was to imitate the ancients.[39] Yet the fragmented material remains of Roman culture made antiquity seem both foreign and incomplete.[40] Perhaps this is why so many poets turned to Ovid, whose writing unravels the threads of his own classical literary culture from within. If Ovid is "counter-classical" for early modern English readers, it is not simply because his poems are violent, erotic, and fantastical; he is "counter-classical" because these aspects of his poetry align themselves with foreignness in a period when Britain was encountering and engaging with exogamous cultures to a greater extent than ever before.

In their appropriations of Ovid's poetry, early modern English poets not only engaged in a process of rewriting the classical in early modern England; they constantly augmented these Ovidian appropriations with new imported words and concepts from contemporary eastern Mediterranean trade as a way of dealing with the challenges presented by a fragmented, outdated literary inheritance. In this instance, it might be useful to think about the reliance of English poets on classical sources moving beyond *imitatio* (replicating the

arguments, methods, and style of classical authors) to a version of remediation. As defined by the digital media scholars Jay Bolter and Richard Grusin,
remediation involves both a material refashioning and a dialectic between
older forms of media and newer ones; it is "that which appropriates the techniques, forms, and social significance of other media and attempts to rival or
refashion them in the name of the real."[41] Thus, we might see printed English
verse translations or appropriations of stories taken from Ovid's *Metamorphoses* (poems that we now call epyllia) and dramatic performances incorporating
his writings (such as Shakespeare's *Titus Andronicus*) as textual remediations
of first-century classical Latin codices, of illuminated manuscripts and the
fourteenth-century *Ovide Moralisé*, of sixteenth-century printed, woodcut-
illustrated vernacular translations, and everything in between. Though Bolter
and Grusin readily point out that written texts can be remediated in the same
way that visual images are, and that this process is an ancient one, I find that
early modern poetry calls for a modified version of their initial theoretical
model. Each new version of early modern printed and manuscript literature
did not necessarily struggle to provide what Grusin and Bolter call "immediacy" (the vanishing or supplanting of the media itself by its content).[42] In
contrast, early modern English textual and linguistic conventions continually
forced readers and writers to confront the textual medium's material shape and
the space it occupied.[43] Early modern textual remediation drew attention *to*
the material text, not away from it. It was a process that involved both translation and appropriation but highlighted rather than ignored the newness of
the material media in which it worked: media that included the printed and
illustrated text, poetic and rhetorical ornament, and new English vocabularies
derived from imported words and things.[44]

　　Early modern poetic remediation is Ovidian in nature: the writers of this
period described the processes of translation and the adoption of figurative
language as metamorphosis.[45] And Ovid was the Roman poet most widely
translated from Latin into the vernacular in England and Europe—the vast
number of European vernacular editions of Ovid's texts printed in the sixteenth century attests to his immense popularity.[46] Therefore, it could be said
that Ovid's *Metamorphoses* was the most appropriate text for early modern
writers to remediate, given that it contained numerous tales of characters
whose bodies and thoughts were remediated into other material forms. Another aspect of early modern Ovidian remediation occurs when English poets
reconfigure a poem by introducing nonclassical vocabularies and concepts
into Ovidian narrative. Arthur Golding's "Englished" Ovid, which replaces

nymphs with fairies, dryads with elves, and Hades with Hell, serves as one such example.[47] The poems that this book examines are another: they incorporate other, nonclassical elements, from Arabic arithmetic to Turkish bulbs and dyed textiles. Thus, I maintain that it was not only Ovid's popularity in print and his rejection of Augustan decorum that made him so appealing a poet to early modern imitators; it was also his preoccupation with strangeness and otherness, and his own history of exile and marginalization to the Black Sea, the limits of the Roman Empire, that made his poetry an ideal crucible for the early modern experimental importation of new media, including foreign words and ornament.

Ornamentalism

As Georgia Brown and Gordon Braden have demonstrated, the highly rhetorical and elaborately structured Ovidian narrative poems of the 1590s—three of which (*The Rape of Lucrece, Venus and Adonis*, and *Hero and Leander*) take up the largest part of this book's attention—are self-conscious of their own ornamental form.[48] To some extent, the ornate style of Renaissance English narrative verse has its origins in late classical minor epics attributed to the school of Nonnos, of which Grammaticus Musaeus's poem *Hero and Leander* is the most well known today.[49] Yet the extravagance of early modern English epyllia cannot be attributed solely to the ancient origins of the poems' form. Poetic and rhetorical handbooks compare poetic ornament to luxury goods imported from the East like precious stones, colored textiles, and cosmetics— the same imagery of Eastern imports that I am arguing populates sixteenth-century English verse.

Drawing on a classical metaphor (color as figurative language), George Puttenham claims that poetry comprises "a manner of vtterance more eloquent and rhetoricall than ordinarie prose . . . because it is decked and set out with all maner of fresh colours and figures, which maketh that it sooner inueglieth the iudgement of a man."[50] The phrases "decked out" and "fresh colors" suggest fancy dress, freshly rouged cheeks, and a painted canvas. Several times in his treatise, Puttenham draws on the language of bodily decoration to describe poetic tropes, particularly in the third book of the treatise, "Of Ornament." There, Puttenham compares poetic ornament to embroidered clothes, judiciously applied facial cosmetics, highly polished marble, and painted miniatures (222). Thomas Wilson places an equally materialistic emphasis on rhetorical ornament, comparing it to exotic, scintillating gemstones. With the use of exornation (poetic and rhetorical figures), "our speech may seeme as bright and precious, as a rich stone is faire and orient."[51]

The late Elizabethan connection between poetry and ornament was not contained to figurative language alone. Poems themselves were conceived of as having an ornamental material form, and this is evidenced by the way that individual poems and verses, described as "flowers," were stored and copied into commonplace books. Poetic anthologies (from the Greek *anthos* or flower) emphasized this further, highlighting the material and linguistic connection between poems and posies (both deriving from the Greek word *poieisin* [ποιείσιν], "to fashion").[52] Indeed, for Juliet Fleming, poems together with inscriptions are all part of a larger, more fluid material form known as *posy*: "To contemplate a song of pearl, or a 'poysee' ('posy', 'poesie') 'made of letters of fine gold'—or, alternatively, a miniature book in an ornamental binding designed to be worn at the waist—is to be unable to distinguish between a poem, a jewel, an acoustical structure and a feat of embroidery."[53] In Fleming's view, early modern writing has an "ostentatious materiality" that makes poetry indistinguishable from real, material objects.[54] I would extend this analogy further by noting that each of the inscribed objects Fleming describes—embroidered letters in seed pearl and gold filament, enameled girdle books like Elizabeth's tiny prayer book—are both ornamented and ornamental. These objects not only seem to comment on the ornamental nature of early modern poetry, but to remediate and embody it. Puttenham depicts poetic form as gem-like, when he presents his readers with poems in geometric shapes that he insists are reproductions of poems originally fashioned out of inlaid gemstones. The poems take the shapes of carved jewels in lozenges and diamonds, reproduced on the pages in print, first just as lined shapes and then as fully worded poems. According to Puttenham, these shaped poems, like the gemstones they represent, have Ottoman origins, which I will discuss in more detail in Chapter 2.

It is no accident, then, that many late sixteenth-century poems are also rich with imagery associated with the traffic in Near Asian and Levantine luxuries, whether they are the literal gemstones and "Orient" pearls Marlowe uses to describe Hero's virginal virtue and bodily fluids, which I examine in the first half of Chapter 5, or the cryptic ciphers and zeros (arithmetic was a recent Eastern mercantile import, too) that inscribe and scar the bodies of Shakespeare's Tarquin and Lucrece, as I will discuss at length in Chapter 3.[55] References to the trade with the East create their own verbal and associative economies within each text, expanding and remodeling England's view of itself as an emerging player in the global market. This book explores what it means for English writers to have a materially inflected Eastern poetics at the dawn of the seventeenth century, long before the British Empire's colonization of and infatuation with the Orient.[56] Early modern English poets, I argue, turned to Levantine and Asian imports as a way of renegotiating their ambivalent relationship to classical poetry.

Words and Things

If overseas exchange helped English poets adapt and remediate stories and themes from classical poetry, the active mediators that reshaped ideas about the ancient world and the contemporary Near East were words. And words in early modern England had more materiality than they do for us. By this I mean that words had a physical presence, that they possessed textual materiality—as figures of ink pressed into a page, as graffiti on a wall, or as an inscription on a monument—and also that they could be considered objects or "merchandise," as the dedicatory poem in Blount's dictionary attests, when they entered the English language from foreign tongues. In those cases, words functioned as imports.[57]

What happens when a word that signifies a thing, maybe even an imported, luxurious thing such as a pearl, takes up residence in the imaginary world of a poem? The circulation of words-as-things and things-as-words must necessarily shift, and the word-as-thing must undergo another metamorphosis once it is placed within a fictional and poetic register. An early modern reader may not have had access to an orient pearl, a Turkey red carpet, or an Arabian horse, but poetry made imaginary versions of these things graspable. My reading of early modern English poetic space as an arena of possibility owes something to Giorgio Agamben's idea that poetry necessarily occupies a "topology of the unreal" in order paradoxically to appropriate reality.[58] For Agamben, words play an integral role in conjuring inaccessible things: "the phantasm generates desire, desire is translated into words, and the word [la parola] defines a space wherein the appropriation of what could otherwise not be appropriated is possible."[59] This is not so different from Sidney's definition of poesy as occupying a conditional, synchronic space outside the linear past and present of historical reality. For Sidney, proper poets "borrow nothing of what is, hath been, or shall be; but range, only reined in with learned discretion, into the divine consideration of what may be and should be."[60] For Sidney, poetry has the ability to effect social change, but only because it engages not with past, present, or future but with conditional possibility.

Things, Bill Brown reminds us, draw attention to their existence only when they cease to function as we expect them to: we are supposed to look *through* a window, but when the window is begrimed, we find ourselves looking *at* its surface.[61] I want to draw attention to the "thingness" of words and imagery in early modern poetry, to what the reader is not supposed to see.[62] Although poetry is always drawing attention to its sinews and musculature, today we are supposed to wrestle *through* this infrastructure to arrive at a poem's meaning, to bypass the words and metaphors in favor of uncovering the significance, stories, form, and arguments of a poem, not to pause and contemplate the individual words themselves. But early modern language was neither transparent nor fixed in meaning, nor was composition distanced from the physical exertion of writing and printing as much as it is in our digital age. Though this could be said about all poetry, early modern writers and readers in particular demonstrated a heightened awareness of the "thingness" of words, not only as building blocks of text but also as marks on a page and as imports from other countries and cultures. Each of the individual words I examine in this book is a tiny axis of associations that is incorporated into a larger network of images of imported things within a poem.

In many cases in this book, an imported word appears only a few times within a poem I examine. Statistical frequency, however, does not determine the resonance or significance of a given word within a text, especially when the word is found to participate in a larger network of imagery throughout the poem. The word *cipher*, for example, appears thrice in Shakespeare's *Lucrece*, but each instance marks a turning point in the narrative, and each instance is accompanied by a succession of circles, Os, windy exhalations, and illustrations of written negations that together form a network of zero-like associations. *Orient* appears twice in Marlowe's *Hero and Leander*, but the pearls it describes are everywhere, dripping from Hero's eyes, twined around Cupid's arm, at the bottom of Neptune's aquatic bower.

Uncovering networks of imported words and things necessarily entails asking my readers to shift their gaze from the dominant imagery and narrative of a poem to images less apparent. By uncovering new networks of images, I deliberately reorient a poem around early modern global trade networks and networks of association between words, objects, metaphor, and imaginary things. Queer theory performs a similarly disorienting gesture, allowing canonical writers like Shakespeare, as Madhavi Menon puts it, to "break out of the boundaries within which he has been confined."[63] As Menon argues, queer readings are no longer limited to explorations of same-sex subjects and gender; they include other forms of textual dislocation. My own reorientations of poems around an axis of imported goods can then be read as queer "disorientations."[64] The notion of reorientation within a poem can be extended to a larger, global cultural model: early modern English trade with Asian and Arab cultures participated in a kind of reorientation itself, in which European cultural assumptions about the East (or the Orient) were reevaluated and revised, and the European Renaissance understanding of classical history had to be reconceived as well.

To understand the agency of imported oriental words and imagery in a remediated ancient occidental poem, I will borrow two terms from Bruno Latour: *intermediaries* and *mediators*.[65] According to Latour, the circulation of objects creates social networks; these objects can be either intermediaries, which do not reshape networks and only serve to convey meaning in a symbolic manner, or mediators, which connect and transform these networks. The distinction between a mediator and an intermediary is one of materiality: whereas an intermediary indicates a change through an abstract, symbolic relationship, there is something in the material infrastructure of a mediator that fundamentally changes or creates a social network.[66] For example, in 1930s American culture, silk stockings (intermediaries) symbolized upper-class luxuries, until the newly invented chemical structure of nylon made sheer stockings affordable and available to all classes, thus reconfiguring both the social network and its meanings. A similar argument might be made about the technological transition from a literary culture based on book publication (intermediary) first through manuscripts and next through moveable type (mediator), which reconfigured social networks by making books more affordable and readily available.

If we accept that language and poetry contribute to the fabric of social networks, then early modern imports and the words associated with them can be read both as intermediaries and mediators, transforming and revising early modern understanding of classical antiquity by their etymologies and material presence, and creating new symbolic vocabularies to describe these acts of exfoliation and revision. Words and vocabularies are intermediaries—they will always be a part of language and culture. New and imported words, on the other hand, are mediators, introducing a way of discussing exotic, new things and changing the landscape of language itself by making it more global and diverse. In each of the chapters of this book, I explore a different set of imported things: words, sugar, zero, horses, bulbs, pearls, dyes, and ink. Each of these imports can function as a mediator in an early modern global economy due to its material nature (even zero has a material counterpart, a mark on a page that indicates absence—it made double-entry bookkeeping possible by allowing merchants to indicate a negative balance in writing), but when these things are introduced into English poetry and transformed into words, metaphors, and material textual objects, poetry itself becomes the agent for change, mediating between the ancient classical past and the contemporary mercantile present.

As an example of a word and poetic image as mediator, I want to consider Edmund Spenser's use of the word *antique* in his translation of Joachim du Bellay's sonnet sequence and dream visions *Les Antiquitez du Rome*, which appeared in English as two poems: *The Ruines of Rome: by Bellay* and *Visions of Bellay* in Spenser's *Complaints* of 1591. *Antique* mediated between traditional and newer notions of classical antiquity, furthering the estrangement of classical antiquity in early modern England, a process that increased during the Reformation as England found itself at odds with Rome. Depending on its context, the early modern English word *antique* (accented on the first syllable and also spelled *anticke*, *antic*, and *antike*) could mean either ancient or wild and savage. Today, we distinguish between these words by spelling them differently as *antique* (ancient) and *antic* (grotesque). But since both words had interchangeable orthography in the sixteenth and seventeenth centuries, it is difficult to tell if early modern English writers and readers considered them distinct. The modern word *antic* derives from the Italian term *stila antica*, or "ancient style," first used to describe the grotesque designs found on the walls of the baths of Nero's Domus Aurea in Rome, first appearing in English in 1548 (according to the *Oxford English Dictionary*).[67] As decorative grotesques, *antics* were foreign imports, entering England from Italy and ancient Rome. But in early modern England, *antic* could also indicate all sorts of barbarous things and behavior, including the capering skeletons in the wild *danse macabre*, and dark-skinned foreigners and blackness. The fact that *antic* and *antique* were orthographically indistinguishable further emphasized their connections to death and decay.[68] For example, in Spenser's *The Ruines of Rome*, ancient Rome, and by extension antiquity itself, is rendered barbarous and foreign— even oriental—through the repeated use of the semantically fluid early modern term *antique/antic*. It is the plasticity of early modern orthography and the fluidity of its associative polysemia that make this word a Latourian mediator in the fabric of early modern English literary culture.

Du Bellay's poems are elaborate meditations and dream visions that describe the fall of the Roman Empire. Spenser's English versions of these poems are more than translations: they are also remediations in which the visions become even more estranged, exotic, and "counter-classical."[69] The original poems were composed by a French Catholic writer during an extended stay in Rome in 1550, but in Spenser's translation, they acquire English Protestant resonances. When Rome is not only the ancient seat of culture and learning but also, to Elizabethans, the contemporary location of the popish antichrist, Rome's credibility as the seat of classical learning begins to tarnish. Spenser's translation of du Bellay attempts to negotiate this oscillating identity through his use of the equally multivalent term *antique*.[70]

The opening poem in Spenser's sonnet sequence *Ruines of Rome: by Bellay* is both antic and antique in character.[71] Like the *antic* Dance of Death, the invocation resembles a ritualistic summoning, as the speaker tries to raise the ashy phantoms of ancient Roman poets to help him tell his tale. And like the mystical rituals performed by Odysseus and Aeneas on the boundary between the living and the dead, it evokes *antique* classical epic: "Thrice vnto you with lowd voyce I appeale" (11). The summoning has a terrible echo, full of "shrilling voyce" (5) and "shrieking yell" (8). And though he intends to sing their praises, the poet's resurrection of these ancient buried "heavenly spirites" is fraught with "sacred horror" (13). Exactly whose corpses are Spenser and du Bellay reanimating? Unlike du Bellay, who calls his classical ghosts up heroically from the underworld, Spenser summons demons and tortured souls from the "depth of darkest hell" (6).[72] In addition to ancient Roman poets, the sonnets invoke the very architectural ruins themselves ("Arcks, spyres" in Sonnet 7), along with something more primitive, the spiritual and mythological forces of Rome itself: Sonnet 5 imagines the shade (ghost) of Rome as a female "corse drawne forth out of the tombe" (63). No matter what phantom form these reanimated ashes of ancient poetry will take, it is their "*antique* furie" that the poet most desires:

> Thrice vnto you with lowed voyce I appeale,
> And for your antique furie here doo call,
> The whiles that I with sacred horror sing
> Your glorie, fairest of all earthly thing. (11–14)

Does Spenser mean *antic* fury or *antique* fury? I want to propose that he means both. The rage of these resurrected, fallen spirits is no doubt wild and savage, but it is also ancient, an old grudge left buried in ruins for centuries. Finally, of course, these are *antique* "ashie cinders" (1) quite literally, as they are the dead material ruins of ancient Rome.

Spenser uses *antique* in this poem in all of its *antic* senses, to signify death, destruction, and monstrous, outlandish behavior as much as to signify the ancient Roman past.[73] In other words, Spenser's use of *antique* encapsulates the seeds of ancient Rome's own destruction, even as it moves beyond du Bellay's Catholic poem to imagine Catholic Rome's corruption from an English Protestant perspective. All of Spenser's uses of *antique* appear in French as *antique* in du Bellay's French text, which after all bears the title "Antiquities of Rome."[74] Spenser's choice to translate du Bellay's title *Antiquitez* as "Ruines" is therefore surprising, but it suggests that for Spenser, *antiquities* themselves *are* ruins, "dusty reliques" (200), real physical traces of a lost and destroyed past. In French, there is no equivalent to early modern English ambiguity of *antic/antique*. It is worth noting that the early modern French word *antique* may have had a similar double valence: it was defined as both "auncient, old, stale" and as "cut with Antickes" or material decorated with grotesques, in Randall Cotgrave's 1611 English-French dictionary.[75] This suggests that du Bellay's own use of the term may have also suggested a Rome both ancient and grotesque, though Spenser's English translation estranges his readers from Rome even further, since the English word *anticke* could also indicate decaying corpses, demons, clowns, and foreigners.

When the adjective *antique* appears in the poem to indicate Roman antiquity, it represents not simply the ancient past but Rome's physical material remains: the literal ashes of its people, its broken spires, its mountains like "th'antique Palatine" (52), and its charred remains. Spenser's use of *antique* here finds a corollary in his use of the word *relique*. Antic ashes are Rome's material relics. Thus, the material sense of *antique* in the poem becomes most closely tied to ruins and corpses. Sonnet 25 opens with a vain wish to awake "Those antique *Caesars*, sleeping long in darke" (339). Sonnet 19 imagines that the sins of ancient Rome (luxuriousness) are still buried in its architectural foundation: "Vnder these antique ruines yet remaine" (266), which indicates that from Spenser's Protestant perspective, the same sins will reappear all over again as Catholic idolatry.

In other instances, *antique* comes to represent not only Rome's material remains but its twofold destruction at the hands of foreign invaders (Goths) and its decline into the "cancring leisure" (312) of luxury and sensuality, which is illustrated through the language of rich material goods imported from the East.[76] In Sonnet 17, Jove's eagle flying too close to the sun becomes both an omen and a metaphor for Rome's fall to northern European (Gothic) invaders, here described as "the Germane Rauen in disguise" (233).[77] When the eagle catches fire and falls burning from the sky, the earth gives birth to Rome's destruction: "The earth out of her massie wombe forth sent / That antique horror, which made heauen adredd" (231–32). The "antique horror" here is the "Germane Rauen," in other words, the foreign invaders. Rome's inflated sense of pride informs the next use of *antique*, in Sonnet 27, which urges early modern visitors to Rome to find the same extravagance that led to ancient Rome's downfall in "Rome from day to day" (373). Rome's ruined architectural monuments are "haughtie heapes" (367), evidence of "The antique pride, which menaced the skie" (366). "Antique pride" finds a parallel in the "ruin'd pride / Of these old *Romane* works" (208–9) in Sonnet 15, which asks the "ashie ghoasts" of ancient Romans whether they still mourn the fall of Rome. This, along with the transposition of du Bellay's title, suggests that for Spenser, *antique* and *ruin* are almost interchangeable. Thus, we might read "antique pride" as "ruined pride."

The combination of *antique/ruin* with "pride" also hints at (Eastern) luxuriousness. The sonnet juxtaposes the ruined "haughtie heapes" with present-day Rome's "buildings rich and gay" (375) to show that early modern Rome is rebuilding ancient Rome anew. For Catholic du Bellay, this may be hopeful, but for Protestant Spenser, it is ominous, and ancient Rome's ghost as "the *Romaine Daemon*" (*demon romain* in du Bellay's text) takes on new meaning as the Catholic pope, who will "with fatall hand enforce, / Againe on foote to reare her pouldred corse" (378). The reanimated dusty ("pouldred") corpse of Rome resembles the resurrected antic skeletons of the *danse macabre*. Du Bellay's Sonnet 27 contains a second use of *antique*: "*Regarde après, comme de jour en jour, / Rome, fouillant son antique séjour, / Se rebâtit de tant d'oeuvres divines.*" But Spenser replaces du Bellay's *antique séjour* with "decayed fashion": "Then also marke, how Rome from day to day, / Repayring her decayed fashion, / Renewes herself with buildings rich and gay" (373–75). Like his translation of *antiquitez* in the poem's title into "ruines," Spenser's translation of *antique* here into "decayed" suggests that there is a more material, physical presence to antiquity, one of putrefaction and loss.

In both *Ruines of Rome* and *Visions of Bellay*, Spenser and du Bellay attribute Rome's fall to the monstrous growth of its empire. Rome becomes a female mythological beast, a "*Hydra*" (*Ruines* 10.132; *Visions* 10.136), and the seven-headed beast of Revelation—the seven heads are the seven hills of Rome, a convenient trope for Puritan polemicists (*Visions* 8). In *Ruines* Sonnet

23, Rome embodies the grotesque, as the poet compares it to "a vicious bodie" poisoned and distended by the "grose disease" of luxury, "cancring leisure" (*Ruines* 23.312) brought about by Rome's defeat and colonization of the North African kingdom of Carthage: "That *Carthage* towers from spoile should be forborne" (310). Carthage's plunder makes Rome's inhabitants grow lazy: "people giuen all to ease" (317), and fat: "swolne with plenties pride" (321). And in Sonnet 28, Rome becomes a "half disbowel'd" (383) oak with a rotten, vermiculated trunk, and "barbarous troupe of clownish fone" (*Visions* 5.64).

The subtle differences between du Bellay's French and Spenser's English reveal in the latter text an anxious and distanced relationship to Rome and antiquity. Sonnet 3 opens with an address to the Roman tourist, "*Nouveau venu, qui cherches Rome en Rome.*" In Spenser's translation, the addressee is not simply a tourist but someone wrenched out of his or her own world: "Thou stranger, which for *Rome* in *Rome* thou seekest" (*Ruines* 3.1). Although it is a convention of early modern English printing to present proper nouns in italics, in Spenser's text, the italicization of *Rome*, coupled with "stranger" in place of du Bellay's "newcomer," serves to emphasize the cultural difference between the addressee and Rome. Who is this "stranger," this foreigner, and what does it mean to be a "stranger" to Rome? Leonard Barkan has characterized the genealogy of early modern Roman ruins poetry as a "descendancy of displaced persons," moving from Florentine Dante and Petrarch to French du Bellay and finally to English Spenser.[78] Thus, the addressee could be the reader, estranged by the process of reading Spenser's translation. But what if this addressee is Spenser himself, struggling to transpose du Bellay's "strange" French text, already twice removed from Rome? The distance is more powerfully felt in Spenser's translation than in du Bellay's French. In a single word, Spenser's translation distances itself from its own genealogy, demonstrating exactly how removed from ancient and contemporary Rome early modern English readers and writers felt.

In the chapters that follow, I will show how antiquity is reoriented in the East through the fluctuating imagery of imports within a material poetic text. What ultimately happens in these texts is that the classical poetry of the past becomes reanimated by the eastern Mediterranean mercantile present, which helps the English conceive of a new, global poetics. The imported words I examine could be seen as engaging in a small-scale version of Bakhtinian "interanimation." For Bakhtin, the polyphonic interplay of multivalent languages that was strongest in the Renaissance eventually led to a new literary form, the novel.[79] However, Bakhtin categorically dismisses poetry from being capable of interanimation; he insists that poetry depends upon linguistic and authorial individuality, which closes it off to dialogic registers.[80] As I hope this book will demonstrate, such is not the case for the poetry of early modern England, where the language itself was becoming polyvalent and interanimated, and writers were constantly shifting registers by appropriating classical poetic voices. In the chapters that follow, I will attempt to show how a single word or image can interanimate a poetic text through a network of metaphors and associations.

Each chapter focuses on an early modern Eastern import or set of imports, along with the words, metaphors, and associations that define it. Seven of these will be considered: newly coined loanwords, sugar, zero, horses, bulbs, pearls, and dyes. They include both material commodities (like pearls) and immaterial ones (like words and zero), though each of these things—even zero—finds an embodied material form in the text. Given my emphasis on the relationship between words and things, each chapter takes a similar shape, beginning with the material history or historical philology of an imported object, followed by a close reading of how the import initiates a dialogue with the classical past within the selected poetic text or texts.

Part I, "Barbarian Invasions," addresses texts in which barbarous linguistic imports challenge and supplant the venerated status of ancient Greek and Roman literary culture—from the introduction of barbarous imported neologisms in ancient Rome to the Middle Eastern and Indian inflected language of sugar, which replaces classical metaphors of honey to describe poetic production. The first chapter examines the status of imported and manufactured words as commodities in early modern literary culture and in Jonson's Horatian poetics. Jonson's play *Poetaster* fuses early modern literary London with Augustan Rome, dramatizing a classical society purging its language of outlandish neologisms. In the comedy's climax, a young upstart poet is given an emetic and vomits inkhorn terms into a bucket, which in turn are taken out, read, and passed around to the other characters. The play imagines ancient poetry contorted into a grotesque by modern linguistic imports, arguing for the establishment of a new, plain style uncorrupted either by Eastern imports or ornate Latinate neologisms. In this way, Jonson subtly both celebrates and ridicules new-made words and imported luxury goods, showing neologisms and archaisms to be two sides of the same, overly ornate coin.

The second chapter argues that as the language of poetic sweetness changes from honey to sugar in the early modern period, this shift also indicates a rejection of classical poetic models in favor of new, imported language located in new English words for confectionary deriving from Arabic, Persian, Indian, and Ottoman languages. The connections between English poetry and sugar not only are found in descriptions of poetry as sugared sweets but extend to the culinary uses to which sugar was put in the period. Sugar was a favored culinary and artistic medium because, like poetry, it could be transformed and shaped in a myriad of ways. Just as metaphors of sugar begin to dominate early modern writers' descriptions of poetry, pushing classical models of honey into the back seat, so do discussions of English poetry like Puttenham's begin to turn toward Asian poetic models and away from classical ones. At the heart of my analysis of Puttenham's *Arte* is an interpretation of his jeweled pattern poems as parallels to and patterns for inscribed sugar-plate and lozenges. Though Puttenham insists that his poems are real translations from Turkish and were originally written with colorful gemstones, the patterns he presents to his audience mirror patterns suggested for sugared sweets found in early modern cookbooks.

Part II, "Redeeming Ovid," posits that the addition of imagery and new English words for Asian and Levantine imports makes it possible for Shakespeare's narrative poetry to strive toward and propose alternatives to the pain of violation and thwarted union depicted in Ovid's poetry. In my readings of Shakespeare's two narrative poems, *The Rape of Lucrece* and *Venus and Adonis*, the Levantine and Asian imports of zero, horses, and bulbs allow this poet to provide alternative endings to two violent Ovidian poetic tragedies. *The Rape of Lucrece* contains an abundance of O-shaped images, from Lucrece's punctuated cries of desperation ("O!") to the suicide that circumscribes her body in a "watery rigoll" or circle of blood. Chapter 3 contends that the circular imagery and rhetoric of *ciphers* (zero) in *The Rape of Lucrece* enacts a poetic transformation of rape from an invisible, "unseen shame" into a figure for publication and agency, lending Ovid's tragic heroine pen and print, as well as a voice. In Chapter 4, I argue that the inclusion of imported Arabian stallions and Turkish tulips in *Venus and Adonis* presents readers with a productive alternative ending concurrent with the poem's tragically unproductive Ovidian genealogy. Shakespeare makes many significant changes to Ovid's story, namely choosing to represent Venus as older and physically larger than Adonis. But this chapter looks at two other Shakespearean additions: Adonis's horse and the "chequered" purple flower into which he transforms. Though Venus is not successful in her courtship, Adonis's horse is. Its position on display in the poem may hint at the wished for breeding of fame and fortune for its new author, counterbalancing the poem's tragic narrative outcome. The metamorphosis of Adonis into a purple flower checkered with white presents readers with another image of an imported object, a Turkish tulip or fritillary bulb. Bulbs were unique botanical specimens because they contained within them the promise of their own reproduction. If Adonis transforms into a bulb, then all is not entirely lost. As a bulb, the Adonis flower would be able to reproduce as well as regenerate, just as the poem holds the hope of the poet's success in publication.

In Part III, "Reorienting Antiquity," the classical mythology of the Hellespont works together with the language of early modern Ottoman mercantile geography to create a new, global form of English poetry that addresses both the excitement and the precariousness associated with Anglo-Ottoman traffic. For early modern English writers, the Hellespont was a geographical and historical intersection of East and West, Ottoman and classical. It was where Hero and Leander drowned, where a Byzantine Christian princess betrayed her father to a Muslim general, and where early modern Ottoman Janissaries conducted routine customs inspections of merchant ships. In Marlowe's and Chapman's *Hero and Leander* (1598), the landscape of the Hellespont is a space of dynamic and contested boundaries, infused with and informed by the English mercantile trade with the Ottoman Empire in luxury goods.

Marlowe's poem and Chapman's continuation and translation negotiate the boundaries and commodities of empire differently. For Marlowe, the narrow watery space separating Europe and Asia becomes a dynamic "free trade zone" where anything can happen and jeweled treasure lies buried at the bottom of the sea, free for anyone to discover. Marlowe's imagery of *orient* pearls represents freedom from Western mores, and the dynamic and protean space of the Hellespont becomes a body of water that queers its subjects as much as it divides East from West. For Chapman, on the other hand, the Hellespont is a heavily policed and regulated space, characterized by betrayal and dissimulation. Imported crimson dyes and paint pigments configure the protagonists' sexual concealment and dissimulation, which must be rooted out and punished by the gods. Unlike Jonson, Puttenham, or Shakespeare, Marlowe and Chapman incorporate the imagery of Ottoman and Asian imports back into classical poetic models: for Marlowe, pearls represent Ovidian *libertas*, and for Chapman, oriental pigments and dyes exemplify the colors of rhetoric and poetic dissimulation. Just as the Hellespont represents a palimpsestic space, *Hero and Leander* is a palimpsestic form of poetry.

In the book's Epilogue, I examine how the very imported things that became poetic currencies in sixteenth-century England were translated back into commodities in two seventeenth-century texts, thus assimilated into a global poetic economy that extended north and west as well as further east. Sir John Beaumont's poem *The Metamorphosis of Tabacco* (1600) translates the American commodity tobacco back into classical narrative, giving it not one but two Ovidian metamorphic myths of origin. Beaumont's representation of trade as a new Pantheon is global, rather than located in one place: tobacco is just one of a host of imports coming from the East, West, North, South, earth, sky, and sea. In contrast, Richard Ligon maps early modern poetic metaphors of the eastern Mediterranean onto the body of an African woman. His fantastical description of the mistress of the Portuguese governor of the Canary Islands simultaneously fragments her body into a collection of imported commodities and into an anthology of early modern poetic and literary references. Ligon's portrait of the governor's mistress reveals that just as early modern poems themselves were ornamented with imported words and things, so could foreign bodies be ornamented with poetry itself. Far out in the Canary Islands, with North Africa behind and the Caribbean ahead, early modern poetic artifacts assume the roles of foreign imports themselves, mediating this time between a familiar Mediterranean oriental world and an unfamiliar New World.

PART I

Barbarian Invasions

Chapter 1

Strange Language: Imported Words in Jonson's *Ars Poetica*

Inky Words

Peter Burke notes that the hybridization of all European languages increased in the early modern period, a process he attributes to diaspora, trade, and imperial conquest.[1] According to Bryan Garner and Paula Blank, between 1500 and 1650, at least 20,000 new words entered the English vocabulary and nearly 8,000 in the period between the defeat of the Spanish Armada and Queen Elizabeth's death (1588–1603).[2] Many of them were newly coined words combining Latin or Anglo-Saxon roots, like *consanguineous*.[3] Others, like *damask* and *tulip*, came from the East because embroidered cloth, attar of roses, and tulip bulbs came from Damascus and Turkey. These words participated in the early modern Levantine mercantile network.[4] English writers could not ignore these neologisms, which, to the great dismay of certain poets who nevertheless made extensive use of them, began to be called *inkhorn terms*. This chapter examines how English poets conceived of inkhorn terms—neologisms, manufactured archaisms, and imported language—as an invasion of England by strange and foreign things. I read Ben Jonson's play *Poetaster* as a dramatic staging of the project of a community of English poets crafting, consuming, and purging themselves of these immigrant words. By attempting to banish such language from the classical empire of English poetry, the poets in this play are actually acknowledging the futility of their project. Yet Jonson did not simply stage the banishment of Ovidian, counter-classical, imported words: he struggled to come to terms with the tension between newness and classicism in his own poetic theory of plain style, which I locate in his published commonplace book *Timber: or, Discoveries Made upon Man and Matter* (1641) and in his careful, marginal annotations in his private copy of the printed text of George Puttenham's *The Arte of English Poesie* (1589). Philologically speaking, this chapter deals with words in general, rather than individual words with specific Eastern origins or mercantile associations. In this, it is unlike the successive chapters of the book, each of which explores a particular set of English words (often of non-Western derivation) describing imports of Eastern origin. As I will demonstrate here, early modern English writers placed Latinate neologisms, English archaisms, and new words of imported, Eastern origin on the same plane: all were barbarous foreigners to English. Thus, for my reading of *Poetaster* and Jonson's translation of Horace's *Ars Poetica*, the actual origins of such barbarous words matter less than the fact that they are made to seem (in Jonson's text and staging) distended, obscure, grotesque.

The *Oxford English Dictionary* (*OED*) defines *inkhorn term* as "learned or bookish language" and *inkhornism* as "a learned or pedantic expression."[5] The words were presumably so named because they were thought to have originated with scholars and to have been first inscribed on paper with ink from a scholar's inkhorn, a small, portable receptacle for ink often worn attached to the belt by means of a chain.[6] Borrowed words and neologisms may have also been labeled *inkhorn* because, Puttenham guesses, a lot of ink would need to be expended in writing long compound words. Puttenham identifies inkhorn words of Latinate origin as part of a larger group that includes imported words: "some words of exceeding great length, which have been fetched from the Latin inkhorn or borrowed of strangers."[7] Puttenham's phrase "Latin inkhorn" conjures a ridiculous image of different languages being written in different types of ink and stored in different receptacles: Latinate neologisms come out of Latin inkhorns; French, Italian, and more exotic ones are "borrowed" from foreigners, but at what cost? These words supplement and augment English vocabularies; they are not exchanged for other words or for commodities. And yet the materiality posited in the phrase "inkhorn term" reminds the reader or listener of the liquidity of ink and the carved receptacle that contains it and keeps it from spilling out all over the page. Inkhorn terms draw attention both to the material scene of writing and to the deliquescent nature of early modern English. Particularly long bouts of neologistic activity were described with the verb *inkhornize*, and inkhorn terms themselves were also known as *inkhornisms*. This points to the ironic playfulness of the term itself: *inkhornize* and *inkhornism* are the very kind of neologisms that the critics of inkhorn terms seem to disparage, as a new word was needed in order to identify a new linguistic phenomenon. The coiners of such phrases were called *inkhornists*, though the dictionary cites only Gabriel Harvey in this instance, which suggests that the writer may have created the appellation himself in a brilliant bout of his own *inkhornizing*, for a text whose title contains a lengthy Latinate inkhorn term, *Pierces Supererogation*: "I haue seldome read a more garish, and pibald stile in any scribling Inkhornist."[8] Like many of his contemporaries with whom he collaborated and playfully disparaged, here Harvey both criticizes and celebrates the neologistic style.

The *OED* gives no extensive etymology for *inkhorn* as a neologism other than saying that it is a compound of *ink* and *horn*, a premodern inkwell made out of bone. An early modern synonym for *inkhorn term* is *inkpot word*.[9] But in their evocation of writing materials, *inkhorn* and *inkpot terms* reveal that what distinguishes inkhorn terms from other words is their textual materiality: inkhorn terms materialize out of ink; they are graphic and text based, rather than vocal or aural. George Pettie writes, "It is not unknown to all men . . . how many words we have fetcht from hence within these few yeeres, whiche if they should all be counted inkepot tearmes, I know not how we shall speake any thing without blacking our mouthes with inke."[10] Even when they are conceived of as spoken, these words are inky. When they are spoken on stage, as in Jonson's *Poetaster*, they nevertheless retain their written materiality, manifesting themselves as slips of paper read aloud to the players and audience or as words in poems recited from a scroll. Thomas Nashe's encomium to Pietro Aretino in *The Vnfortunate Traveller* (1594) suggests that late Elizabethan minds also connected the creation and adoption of new and imported words with the materials of textual production:

> If out of so base a thing as inke there may be extracted a sprite, he writ with nought but the sprite of inke and his stile was the spiritualtie of artes, and nothing else, where as all others of his age were but the lay temporaltie of inkhorne tearmes. For indeed they were mere temporizers, & no better. His penne was sharpe pointed like a ponyard. No leafe he wrote on, but was like a burning glasse to sette on fire all his readers. With more then musket shot did he charge his quill, where he meant to inueigh.[11]

In a fantastical description of the writing process, Nashe characterizes Aretino as a poet so witty that his writing goes beyond the mere "inkhorne tearmes" of the "lay temporaltie," or the common writers of his time. Aretino himself becomes a kind of alchemical warrior with writing materials: he is born out of ink; his pages are burning mirrors, or instruments designed to "sette on fire all his readers"; his quill is charged not with ink but with the recent Asian import, gunpowder. Harvey's response to Nashe and Spenser furthers the connection between ink and explosives in the creation of inkhornisms by alluding directly to Nashe's Aretino passage:

> they haue termes, quoth a maruellous doer, steeped in *Aqua Fortis*, and Gunnepouder, that shal rattle through the skies, and make Earthquakes in such pesauntes eares, as shall dare to sende them awaie with a flea in their eare: (howe might a man purchase the sight of those puissant, and hideous termes?) they can lash poore slaues, and spurgall Asses mightily, they can tell parlous Tales of Beares and Foxes, as shrewdlye as mother Hubbard, for her life: they will dominiere in Tauernes, and Stationers shops, to die for't: they will be as egregiouslly famous, as euer was *Herastratus*, or *Pausanias*, or *Kett*, or *Scoggin: Agrippa*, and *Rabelays* but Ciphers to them they haue it onely in them.[12]

Inkhorn terms have the power to animate and provoke anyone and any-thing they encounter, functioning as thunder, earthquakes, whips, and spurs, but ultimately resulting in spreading and securing the fame of their authors (which includes Spenser, the author of "mother Hubbard"). Embedded in Harvey's encomium to inkhornisms is a metaphor of these words as com-modities, the parenthetical phrase "howe might a man purchase the sight of those, pouissant, and hideous termes?" Though the question is rhetorical—these words are priceless—the notion of inkhorn terms as commodities, as *things* that might be bought or sold, suggests that early modern writers were already thinking of words not only as weapons or implements but as objects of value, and new words, like luxury goods, were the most desirable and the most expensive.

Charting the growing critical anxiety over the changing language, Paula Blank shows us how what historical philologists call the "inkhorn controversy" began to sharply delineate social differences, for inkhorn terms were turning English into a foreign tongue, only comprehended by a select, educated few (i.e., those with Latin, Greek, Italian, and other foreign languages under their belts).[13] More important, Blank reveals that people were aware that many of these words were imports and associated them with foreign trade:

The fear that an unregulated foreign trade might ultimately devalue English wares was . . . common enough in economic treatises of the period. The idea was that many foreign words and borrowings were merely "trifles," the sense that the new trade in words did not represent enrichment but a kind of cultural bankruptcy.[14]

Indeed, the language describing both neologisms and borrowed words seems to support Blank's premise. The words most frequently employed to describe such words are *strange, forrein,* and *outlandish,* all of which point to the fact that these words are not indigenous.[15] In other words, these words are treated literally as exotic others, or as aliens. In his *Arte of Rhetorique* (1553), Thomas Wilson advises his readers to steer clear of borrowed words and phrases:

> Emong al other lessons, this should be first learned, that we never affect any straunge ynkehorne termes, but so speake as is commonly received. . . . Some seke so farre for outlandishe English, that thei forget altogether their mothers language. . . . Somme farre jorneid jentelmen at their returne home, like as thei love to go in forrein apparell, so thei will pouder their talke with oversea language.[16]

Wilson uses metaphors of cosmetics and apparel to describe the importation of foreign words and phrases, repeating the word *farre.* Like courtiers bringing new styles of doublets and scented powders to England from France and Italy, these "farre jorneid jentelmen" powder their talk, as well as their bodies, with foreign imports.[17] Wilson inserts an example of an "ynkhorne letter" after this caveat. The letter is also identified in the margin of the text and seems to be repetitive as well as neologistic: "Ponderying, expending, and reuolutying with my self your ingent affabilitie, and ingenious capacitee, for mundane affaires: I cannot be celebrate and extolle your magnificall dexteritee."[18]

Shakespeare's plays are full of examples of courtiers mocked for their continental affectations and adoption of neologisms. Don Armado in *Love's Labour's Lost* affects a number of Italian, French, and Spanish malapropisms much to the laughter of the other characters and the scorn of his beloved, Jaquenetta, and Nathaniel and Holofernes produce an equally ridiculous number of Latinate inkhornisms.[19] Hamlet makes fun of Osric's inkhorn terms by throwing them back to Osric in a convoluted conversation: "Sir, his definement suffers no perdition in you . . . But, in the verity of extolment, I take him to be the soul of great article and his infusion of such dearth and rareness as, to make true diction of him, his semblable is his mirror, and who else would trace him his umbrage, nothing more."[20]

Donne's first satire contains one the most well-known dissections of a composite continental courtier.[21] In the poem, the speaker is cajoled by his friend, a "fondling motley humorist" (1) to leave the speaker's study and walk through the city streets (a map of vices) to court.[22] The poet mocks his companion for idolizing courtiers affecting the latest imported fashions, behaviors, and turns of phrase. Both the companion and the courtier over whom he swoons are compared to imported, exotic animals—the companion to an "elephant or ape" (81), the courtier to a "many-colored peacock" (92). The companion imitates the courtier in dress and manner, as his dress is "motley" or multicolored as well. What the ignorant companion admires most about the courtier is how exotic and un-English he appears in dress and speech: "He hath traveled. Long? No, but to me / (who understand none) he doth seem to be / Perfect French and Italian" (102–3). The companion imagines that travel to the continent and back to England has transformed the body of the courtier, turning him into a composite of foreignness. The poet demotes this foreign affectation with a single, simple English phrase: "So is the pox" (104). In Donne's urban satire, imported words and phrases are vices, corrupting and infecting the public like venereal diseases.

In a section of *The Scholemaster* (1570) describing the proper use of epitomes, Roger Ascham finds a way of circumventing inkhorn terms, insisting that his readers translate any imported or inkhorn terms into simple English: "a wise man would take Halles Cronicle, where moch good matter is quite marde with Indenture Englishe, and first change strange and inkhorne tearmes into proper, and commonlie vsed wordes."[23] Ascham compares "strange and inkhorne tearmes" to the "Indenture Englishe" of Hall's Chronicle, which presumably means a kind of primitive English that is still under thrall to Latin or to Norman French and has not yet come into its own.

A similar description of inkhorn terms as bearing the marks of Britain's early colonizers crops up in Samuel Daniel's *Defense of Rhyme*. Like Ascham, Daniel wishes to liberate the English language from any colonizers, past or future, and inkhorn terms continue to threaten to control the language. Daniel urges poets to resist "disguising or forging strange or unusuall wordes," because such contortions turn poetry into another language entirely. Daniel proceeds to critique the "strange presumption of some men, that dare so audaciously adventure to introduce any whatsoever forraine wordes, be they never so strange, and of themselves, as it were, without a Parliament, without any consent or allowance, establish them as Free-denizens in our language."[24] Daniel writes of the threat of foreign words entering England as if they were Jesuit priests or illegal aliens. His repeated use of the language of foreignness highlights this: *strange* appears three times in the passage, as do the words *forraine*, *unusuall*, and *adventure*. Early modern English writers felt ambivalent about new-made words, whether they were crafted by British wordsmiths or introduced into English vocabularies by means of trade and conquest. Either way, all neologisms and new words were rebranded as strange and foreign.

Puttenham suggests that new-made words and foreign terms were thought of as one and the same in early modern English, as he lumps inkhorn terms together with borrowed and obscure words. Furthermore, Puttenham, like many early modern poetic and rhetorical theorists, personifies foreign and new-made words, comparing them to illegal immigrants. He describes all such writing as "strange" and "darke":

> & ye shall see in some many inkhorne termes so ill affected brought
> in by men of learning as preachers and schoolemasters: and many
> straunge terms of other languages by Secretaries and Marchaunts
> and travailors, and many darke wordes and not vsuall nor well
> sounding, though they be dayly spoken in court.[25]

The picture here is of "straunge" and "darke" words entering the country like foreigners, "brought in" by scholarship and by trade. Puttenham's use of "darke" here means obscure and difficult to understand, but by being placed with "straunge," the word may carry a racial association as well. Though Puttenham seems to disparage the infiltration of his language by strange and dark words, he also acknowledges that he is as culpable as the preachers, schoolmasters, secretaries, merchants, and courtiers he describes: "And peradventure the writer hereof be in that behalf no less faulty then any other, using many strange and unaccustomed words and borrowed from other languages."[26] This is the central duality of inkhorn terms: they are both mocked and disparaged as pedantic and as foreign, while at the same time created and celebrated by the same writers that profess to revile them.[27]

There were some, however, who went further than Puttenham's modest admission of fault, or Nashe's and Harvey's witty dual neologistic disparagement and display, and wholeheartedly embraced the use of foreign words.[28] Richard Carew describes the augmentation of English with foreign words as an international trade profitable to England:

Seeing then we borrow (and not shamefully) from the Dutch, the
Britain, the Roman, the Dane, the French, the Italian, and Span-
iard; how can our stock be other than exceeding plentiful? . . . For
our own parts we employ the borrowed ware so far to our advantage, that we raise a profit of new words from the same stock, which
yet in their own Countrey are not merchantable.[29]

Neologisms and words imported into English from Asian and Semitic languages were not the only English words described as strangers and aliens by
early modern writers: archaisms, or Anglo-Saxon words no longer in use in
early modern England, also played this role. As Blank illustrates, there was an
increasing interest in rehabilitating Anglo-Saxon words as a way of opposing
outlandish foreign terms and neologisms. Yet I have found that the language
some writers and poets use to describe archaisms is very much the same language that they use to discuss foreign inkhorn terms, and this suggests that an
early modern archaism might be indistinguishable from a neologism.

Though Blank gives us several examples of antiquarians and lexicogra-
phers who prefer Anglo-Saxon to Latinate neologisms and borrowed words,
the former are themselves frequently described as "strange" by poets and
rhetoricians. The best examples of English archaisms can be found in E. K.'s
glosses for *The Shepheardes Calender* (1579); E. K., as Blank correctly notes,
first opposes "true and auncient english woords" to deplorable inkhorn terms
but then feels the need to qualify and gloss each word that represents "the
antiquitie of our mother tongue," which will appear unfamiliar to most readers: "Hereunto have I added a certain Glosse or scholion, for th'exposition of
old wordes and harded phrases: which maner of glosing and comenting, well
I wote, wil seeme straunge and rare in our tongue."[30] Though Blank contends
that the Northern archaisms Spenser employs, and his alter ego E. K. glosses
in the *Shepheardes Calender*, do not appear again in *The Faerie Queene* (1596),
I would argue that Spenser's description of allegory as a "darke conceit" in the
Preface to his epic might be seen as an extension of his glosses of "strange"
archaisms in the *Calender*.[31] Moreover, the "ancient" poetic diction of *The Faerie Queene* is primarily manufactured, rather than based on real Anglo-Saxon
words as it is in the *Calender*. In this sense, Spenser's diction in *The Faerie
Queene* might be seen as embracing the concept of archaism, while wielding
neologisms, placing both on the same plane.

Wilson calls archaisms "ouer old and ouer strange words" in an anecdote
about the ancient philosopher Phauorinus, who "did hit a yong man over the

Thumbes very handsomely" for using archaisms.[32] He further elides archaisms with neologisms through analogy, when he compares the importation of Italian words into English to a Latin orator using words from an unidentified, more ancient language: "An other chops in with English Italienated, and applieth the Italian phrase to our English speaking, the which is, as if an Oratour that professeth to vtter his mind in plaine Latine, would needes speake Poetrie, and farre fetched colours of straunge antiquitie."[33] The final phrase, "farre fetched colours of straunge antiquitie," marries the implication of foreign travel and trade carried by inkhorn terms ("farre fetched . . . straunge") with words so archaic that they, too, appear foreign ("straunge antiquitie").

If Latinate inkhorn neologisms, foreign words, and English archaisms were all considered "strange," and both deplored and appreciated, what might this tell us about early modern English attitudes toward foreign trade and antiquity? As I explained in the Introduction, both European antiquity and the contemporary Ottoman Empire were in flux in the early modern English imagination. The fact that both new words could be constructed from Latin roots and older English words needed interpreters greatly contributed to the vexing of the status of literary classical antiquity. When these imported words and archaisms are introduced into poetic texts that derive from classical sources or traditions, antiquity must necessarily change. And since none of the texts I am examining has an E. K. well versed in neologisms to explain what these strange, new words mean, their status is much more fluid and yields a number of intriguing associations. What if early modern English neologisms— inkhorn terms—function as mediators in Latour's actor-network theory of social change? As new words introduced into English, they augment vocabularies and catalyze social discourse such that most writers both disparage and employ them. By comparing such words to illegal immigrants and foreign invaders, English writers are acknowledging the capacity of these words to enact social change, to transform the by no means pure English language further, creating a language enmeshed in British culture's emergent global identity.

Ben Jonson's own attitude toward inkhorn terms reveals the same paradox expressed by prolific neologizers like Harvey, Spenser, Nashe, and Puttenham (that inkhorn terms are both desirable and reviled), but Jonson's writing for different genres and audiences attempts to bifurcate the two sides of the problem: in his own poetic theory, the cult of the plain style that he inaugurated, Jonson sets out to expurgate such convoluted, newly coined words from English poetic vocabularies; in his plays, however, Jonson delights in the grotesque humor such words produce, even as he exorcises them from the stage. In Jonson's play *Poetaster*, which I read as a dramatization of his poetic theory, the playwright grounds his linguistic celebration of monstrous, grotesque bodies in an indictment of Roman (early modern English urban) society's taste for foreign imports, ultimately reveling in and banishing both.

Jonsonian Classicism

Jonson's classical poetics is usually located in two texts: his reflections on style and the art of poetry in *Timber*, a printed commonplace book, and in his translation of Horace's poem the *Ars Poetica*, first published posthumously in the 1640 edition of *The Works of Ben Jonson*. A third space that reveals Jonson's emergent championing of classical Greek and Roman poetry over contemporary European and non-Western models is in his careful manuscript annotations to his copy of Puttenham's *The Arte of English Poesie* (1589), now housed in the British Library, to which I will return in more detail in the conclusion of this chapter. As I have proposed above, a fourth text that articulates Jonson's theory of poetry, and therefore one that we ought to read as a dramatic *ars poetica*, is his play *Poetaster*.[34]

Victoria Moul has read Jonson's translation of Horace's *Ars Poetica* as a commentary on the role of Latinity in early modern English poetry. For Moul, Jonson's translation of Horace's poem—which is about translation itself— places translation, and not composition, at the center of Jonson's classical poetics.[35] Indeed, Jonson translates Horace's Latin phrases freely, frequently preferring simple, English words to Latin cognates derived from the words Horace employs. Instead of directly translating Horace's Latin phrase "*Aut prodesse volunt, aut delectare Poetae, / Aut simul & iucunda, & idonea dicere vitae*" (Poets desire either to benefit or to amuse, or to speak words both jocund and helpful to life), Jonson carefully juxtaposes two Latinate words with two native English ones: "Poets would either profit, or delight, / Or mixing sweet, and fit, teach life the right" (477–78).[36] The first two verbs Jonson uses, "profit" and "delight," derive from the Latin words *profitere* (to make a profit) and *delectare* (to delight), while the second two, "sweet" and "fit," have Anglo-Saxon origins in *swoete* and *fitta*.[37] The first line's Latin cognates are thus prominently juxtaposed with the second line's much freer translation.

Both lines describe possible roles for poetry: poetry for personal or financial success, poetry for entertainment, and poetry as a moral way of life. Clearly, the third option is the most desirable, and Jonson's use of plain,

Anglo-Saxon–derived English words highlights his view that this is what English poetry, or English translations of Latin poetry, ought to attempt to do. In order to enforce the juxtaposition between the two lines further, Jonson subtly replaces Horace's original *prodesse* (bring forth) with *profit*, derived from *profectus* (progress, success), the past participle of *proficere*, which also means to bring forward, but with the added sense of gaining advantage. The difference is between being a productive poet (Horace) and being a *profitable* or successful one (Jonson).

Jonson associated himself with Horatian poetics not only in his translation of the *Ars Poetica*, in his taste for hexameter, and in the short lyrics that comprise his *Epigrammes*—he also projected himself onto the Roman poet in his drama. The character of Horace, whom most scholars identify as Jonson, appears in *Poetaster* to help the poet Virgil and the emperor Augustus police the state, partly through his judgment of good and bad poetry. One of the reasons Jonson emulated Horace lies in both poets' awareness of the way language refused to remain static. Jonson the writer is as much concerned with stylistic vocabulary as Horace is in the *Ars Poetica*. Where Horace writes that poets must keep a translation alive by both reinvigorating forgotten words and introducing new ones, Jonson's translation echoes a sentiment he expresses in *Timber*, the notion of heeding the wisdom of antiquity while nevertheless departing from it:[38]

As woods whose change appears
Still in their leavs, throughout the sliding yeares,
The first borne dying; so the aged Fate
Of words decay, and phrases borne but late
Like tender Buds shoot up, and freshly grow.
Our selves, and all thats ours, to death we owe. (85–90)[39]

Words are like woods for both Horace and Jonson, who gave the title *Underwood* to a collection of his poetry, and *Timber* (a more seasoned, ancient wood) to his prose. Old, outdated words are dying leaves (with a pun on leaves as pages in a book), whereas fresh new ones are tender shoots. Jonson's translation elegizes Horace's ancient, decaying old words, drawing attention to the colorful, autumnal display that heralds the leaves' departure ("whose change appears / Still in their leavs," 85–86). Jonson transforms Horace's prescient acknowledgment of his own text's antiquity into Jonson's own plain, English monosyllables that work both as accentual (pentameter) and syllabic prosody: "Our selves, and all thats ours, to death we owe" (90).

In *Timber*, Jonson presents his musings on poetic style in more detail,
paying close attention to language and style. *Timber* associates new-made and
imported phrases with impure and foreign speech: "Pure and neat Language
I love, yet plaine and customary. A barbarous Phrase has often made mee out
of love with a good sense, and doubtfull writing hath wracked mee beyond
my patience" (118). A "barbarous Phrase" indicates an ill-formed, unclear sentence, but the word *barbarous* suggests that it involves foreign or inkhorn
terms. Jonson's preference for "pure and neat" extends from words to figurative language. Metaphors must be simple, rather than "far-fetched" and difficult to understand, which renders them "deformed." Finally, Jonson warns
against the dangers of creating and using too many inkhornisms or archaisms,
despite the popularity of both: "a man coynes not a new worde without some
perill, and lesse fruit" (118), he warns. Word coining is as dangerous as counterfeiting money:

> *Custome* is the most certain Mistresse of Language, as the public
> stampe makes the current money. But wee must not be too frequent
> with the mint, every day coyning. Nor fetch words from the ex-
> treme and utmost ages; since the chiefe vertue of a style is perspi-
> cuitie, and nothing so vitious in it as to need an Interpreter. Words
> borrow'd of Antiquity doe lend a kind of Majesty to style, and are
> not without their delight sometimes; for they have the Authority of
> yeares, and out of their intermission doe win themselves a kind of
> grace like newnesse. But the eldest of the present, and newnesse of
> the past Language is the best. For what was the ancient Language,
> which some men so doate upon, but the ancient Custome? (118–19)

Jonson plays on the notion of "coyning" a word by connecting new-made
words to the early modern English economy through the metaphor of minting
currency. Just as "Custome" influences language, so are current coins stamped
with the same images, but just because it is customary to "fetch words from
the extreme and utmost ages" does not mean that poets should turn such difficult words into common currency. Though Jonson acknowledges the "majesty" of words "borrowed of antiquity," which suggests that such words are on
loan to English and ought to be returned to their own time and place eventually, he cleverly argues for a conservative approach to language situated in the
present, eschewing both extremes of new (imported, inkhornized) and old
(archaic) words, preferring instead "the eldest of the present, and the newness

of the past." *Timber* contains its own textual complexities and contradictions. Because it is Jonson's commonplace book, *Timber* includes statements that contradict his own behaviors: "nothing so vitious in it as to need an Interpreter" above seems to fly in the face of the lengthy textual glosses and authorial explications "To the reader" that frame his masques and plays—the 1616 Folio edition of *Poetaster*, for example, concludes with two addresses to the reader, the first a prose paragraph and the second a closet dialogue (possibly performed once) between a character called "Author" and two critics. In its fixed, printed form of 1640, *Timber* can appear less like a working repository for *sententiae* and meditations and more like a posthumous biographical document elaborating Jonson's worldview. Though I want to claim that *Timber* contains the closest thing we have to a prose statement of Jonson's own *ars poetica*, I also must acknowledge here that as a collection of interpretations of commonplaces, it functions more as an index than a theory.

Poetaster and the Arraignment of Language

Although Jonson's prose and poetry champion his classical Horatian poetics, the stage is where his critique of imported language and inkhornisms takes fullest shape, and this is partly because Jonson uses the mechanics of performance—properties, physical actions, vocalizations—in order to dramatize the massive materiality of inkhorn terms. His play *Poetaster* can be read as a performance of his own *ars poetica*, better equipped than a text to comment on the material nature of new-made words. At the height of the dramatic action in *Poetaster, or the Arraignment*, Ovid is exiled from Rome for inviting all his friends to a fancy dress banquet in which he and his mistress, the emperor's daughter Julia, pretend to be the gods, issuing a mock-edict permitting adultery in direct opposition to Augustan morals. At this moment, Ovidian poetic sensual excess is forced out of Augustan Rome, pushed to its outer limits on the Black Sea. The play's subplot mirrors this act of banishment by staging a purgation of language in which the eponymous poetaster, an appalling would-be poet called Crispinus, is brought before the Roman authorities accused of plagiarism and bad poetry (in this case these authorities include the poets Horace and Virgil) and forced to vomit his neologisms, thus purging the empire of bad poetry and banishing made-up foreign words.

Though this book is about imported things in early modern poetry, not in drama, I think it is fitting to start with Jonson's play, since it deals with how early modern poets work with words. As part of a larger group of plays exchanged between Marston, Dekker, and Jonson known as the *poetomachia* ("war of the poets"), *Poetaster* is unique in its dramatization of writers writing, poets composing. The play's poets enact the struggle of early modern English poetry to pay homage to ancient classical literature while remaining attuned to the fast growth of the English language and culture, due in large part to global trade. Jonson's Crispinus is widely associated with Marston; Horace is clearly a version of Jonson, and Ovid has been tied to Marlowe.[40]

Leaving aside the roman à clef aspect of the play, critics have wondered why Jonson would be interested in banishing Ovid, the dominant poet of early modern classical imitation.[41] For some, the play is Jonson's attempt to put to rest the vogue for Ovidian appropriation that dominated the late sixteenth-century verse of his rivals Marlowe, Shakespeare, and Beaumont.[42] Yet this does not account for the tenderness the play shows toward the character of Ovid, whom Jonson sympathetically chooses to present as an infatuated youth with an excess of talent, forced by his unsympathetic father to study law. (The actual Ovid was close to fifty at the time of his banishment). In the reading that follows, I will demonstrate how Jonson's play problematizes what is happening to the language of early modern English poetry by depicting a cosmopolitan culture as enamored with Eastern foreignness and linguistic inventiveness as it is anxious about these qualities' power to destabilize the integrity and authority of classical poetry. This analysis sets the stage for closer readings of imported words at play in poetry. In the chapters that follow, I will show how imported words and things enact the very destabilization, remediation, and relocation of antiquity that *Poetaster* simultaneously fears and accepts has happened.

Despite its setting in Augustan Rome, Jonson's play belongs to the genre he perfected—English city comedy full of references to the cosmopolitan luxuries imported from the Ottoman Empire, Asia, and North Africa that made London rich, and replete with satirical critiques of such urban vices. Yet far from seeming a jarringly anachronistic mashup of ancient Roman and urban early modern, the play's bitemporality draws attention to the connection between Augustus's empire, which was in the process of eastward expansion, and early modern England, which longed for it. Luxurious imported goods feature prominently in the opulent household of the jeweler and merchant Albius and his young prodigal wife Chloe (today she would be labeled a trophy wife and a shopaholic).[43] Like many ambitious Jonsonian city comedy characters, Albius and Chloe belong to a wealthy merchant-artisan class that interacts with nobility but can never cross over into aristocracy. Unlike Albius, Chloe is a "gentlewoman borne," who has lowered her class by becoming "a citizen's wife" (2.1.28). Like many early modern goldsmiths, Albius is both an artisan and a merchant, as evidenced by Chloe's condescending description of his warehouse, which bears the signs of labor and trade, things with which she would rather not associate: "Because you can marshall your pack-needles, horse-combes, hobby-horses and wall-candlestickes in your ware-house better than I; therefore you can tell how to entertaine ladies, and gentle-folkes better than I?" (2.1.48–51).[44] Despite her inability to comprehend her newfound merchant class status—she has married Albius because he is wealthier than most gentry and she believes she has the upper hand in the marriage (2.1.29–32)— Chloe longs to reascend to the rank of noblewoman, and she believes this will happen if she takes a lover who is also a poet (she chooses a bad one— Crispinus, the poetaster).

Over the course of the play, Albius and Chloe participate in at least two banquets at which their riches—rare, exotic gemstones—are on display, and marveling at the jewels is part of the evening's anticipated entertainment, as Julia herself remarks: "but when shall wee see those excellent iewells you are commended to haue?" (2.2.84). The first banquet takes place in Albius's house (2.2 and 2.3), the second at court, where he and his wife have been invited to participate in the feast-of-the-gods banquet that is Ovid's and Julia's undoing (4.1 to 4.6). Most of the imports on display in each situation find pride of place in bawdy jokes linking jewels and cosmetics to women's bodies and male and female genitalia, often showing the fruits of empire to be nothing but a grotesque body. For example, on their way to the second banquet, the lady Cytheris remarks to Chloe that the jeweler's wife is "as well iewelled as any" of the noblewomen in attendance (4.1.7), describing Chloe's glittering ornaments without and within her body. Earlier, Crispinus has warned Albius to keep an eye on the jeweler's easily seduced fashion-obsessed wife: "Ieweller, looke to your best Iewel yfaith" (2.3.212). Later, meeting Horace in the street, Crispinus describes one of his ridiculous poems, strengthening the connection between Chloe's ornamented body, her husband's profession as goldsmith and merchant, and her sexuality: "I composed e'en now of a dressing, I saw a ieweller's wife wear, who was indeed a iewell herselfe" (3.1.45). Part of the joke here is that the connection between women as jewels and a woman who is a real jeweler's wife is too much of a cliché to make a good poem. More important, Crispinus is so steeped in commodity culture that his poetic subjects are all superficial—later in the same scene, he composes a poem extempore about a *"sweet, deintie cap"* (3.1.85). Rather than focus his poem on the woman, as Ovid does with his Julia, Crispinus has composed an ode on Chloe's *dressing*, a word that in the early seventeenth century described not only a woman's clothing but her jewelry, cosmetics, and perfume, all of which, as we shall see, comprise foreign imports from Asia, the Mediterranean, and North Africa.[45] *Dressing* also figured as a culinary term, as it does today on North American Thanksgiving tables, describing the sauce, stuffing, or garnish used in preparing a dish of meat.[46] Crispinus's panegyric on Chloe's *dressing* is doubly uncouth: not only does it transform a woman into a collection of decorative, imported ornaments but it also depicts her as a seasoned slab of flesh.

Ovid plays more deftly with the double entendre of "jewel" and "Julia" in 1.2: "Iulia the gemme and iewell of my soule / Takes her honours from the golden skie / As beautie doth all lustre, from her eye" (1.3.38–40). Although Julia ornaments Ovid's soul, and not his body, the lines twice link her name to precious gemstones ("gem and jewel"), suggesting a more dangerous corporeal union is at hand for Ovid and Julia, whose "jewel" is also her virginity, according to the early modern commonplace famously set in verse by Marlowe (Jonson's model for Ovid, whom the audience first encounters reciting Marlowe's English translation of the *Amores*): "Jewels being lost are found again, this never; / 'Tis lost but once, and once lost, lost forever" (*Hero and Leander*, 2.85–86). At the end of the play, Ovid will lose both his Julia and his home forever.

There is no place more packed with imported commodities than Chloe's boudoir. Albius uses the language of precious imported pharmaceuticals, cosmetic ointments, and perfumes to praise his wife: "I am mum, my deare mummia, my balsamum, my *spermacete*, and my verie citie of —— shee has the most best, true, faeminine wit in Rome!" (2.1.66–70). This is a dirty pun: Albius is calling his wife a "sperma city," or city of sperm, a pun made even clearer in the 1602 Quarto by an added space between *Sperma* and *Cete*.[47] Since the fourteenth century, *sperm* has been the word for the male generative seed of animals and humans, and as Tom Cain notes in his edition of the play, *spermaceti* was also the word used in seventeenth-century England for whale fat made into candles and cosmetic ointments.[48] Yet *spermaceti* might equally allude to expensive perfumes here, since *The Grete Herball* (1576) suggests that the highly valued perfume ingredient ambergris comes from whale sperm (though today we know that ambergris is a petrified anal glandular secretion): "Ambre is hote and dry . . . some say that it is the Sparme of a whale."[49] The other ingredients in Albius's list are the names of cosmetics and pharmaceuticals imported from North Africa and the Middle East. *Mumia* or "mummy" was a powdered pigment and medicinal ingredient taken from the bitumen-laced bodies of ancient Egyptian mummies (and later pilfered or prepared from any dead body). It was consumed to ward off death, seizure, and heart attacks, and mixed with liquid it became a dark pigment in dyes, paints, and facial cosmetics. It was also believed to be an aphrodisiac.[50] Balsam, or balm, was a highly prized perfume ointment imported from the Middle East.[51] Branding Chloe with these imported words, Albius turns her into a messy smear of expensive, imported pigments, ointments, perfumes, and aphrodisiacs all deriving from bodily and seminal fluids.

In her consumption of these imports, Chloe figures as a monstrous body, a Leviathan: not only is her skin coated in *spermaceti* and her bodily cavity full of men's sperm, but she physically resembles a whale, as she draws attention to the fact that she is wearing whalebone stays under her bodice. The stays are items imported by her husband: "Nor you nor your house were so much as spoken of before I disbast myself from my hood and my fartingall, to these bumrowles and your whale-bone-bodies" (2.1.65), Chloe exclaims. The pronoun "your" suggests not only that Albius has provided the whalebone stays for Chloe through his mercantile activities, but that the confining undergarments themselves are indicative of his ownership of her. Kept in Albius's whalebone bodice, Chloe envisions herself as one of his luxurious commodities. But the Folio's unusual spelling of *farthingale* (a wide petticoat frame also fashioned from whalebone) as "fartingall" extends the metaphor of Chloe as a grotesque body by underlining the activity in the vicinity of her bumrolls: flatulence. With backdoor neologistic puns, Jonson transforms Chloe into an *arse poetica*. *Fartingall* indicates either continuous flatulence, "farting all," or an intensified gust of flatulence, "farting gale."[52] The spelling of *bumrolls* (bustles) as "bumrowles" furthers the aural quality of the wind beneath Chloe's skirts: according to the *OED*, *rowles* indicated particularly loud and continuous thunder in 1602.[53] The spelling of *bodice* or stays as "bodies" further emphasizes her monstrousness; not merely confined in a whalebone bodice, Chloe *is* a collection of "whale-bone-bodies."

Smeary messes of new, imported things figure prominently in this play, not only in words for jewels, perfumes, and ointments but also in the imagery of the neologisms that appear in Crispinus's and Demetrius's terrible poems, and the words that Crispinus is later forced, literally, to expurgate. Many of the words in these hilarious examples of bad poetry describe foamy, viscous fluids and low bodily functions. In Crispinus's abysmally verbose poem, the terms "glibbery," "lubricall," "spurious snotteries," "barmy froth," "bespaules," and "fome" (5.3.287–301) evoke drool and phlegm, while the words "puffy," "inflate," "turgidous," and "ventosity" (5.3.515), which Crispinus throws up, summon images of distended flesh that culminate in farting and burping. Topping this off, Demetrius's shorter poem contains the line "a critic that all the world *bescumbers*" (5.3.313), referring to the action of a dog befouling an object with excrement. Jonson affords equal treatment to imported words and Latinate neologisms. Whether the words indicate imports, like *spermaceti*, or are imports themselves, like *balsam* and *mumia*, or Latinate inkhorn terms, like *furibund, fatuate, stenuous,* and *prorumped* (5.3), they all ooze, froth, and seep out of the body's orifices with equally revolting zest.

Horace strengthens the connection between neologism and the bodily grotesque by way of the insults he directs at Crispinus, words that take the shape of serpentine monstrosities, recalling the monstrous figure of envy, Lictor, that delivers the play's prologue (1.1). Horace calls Crispinus a "Python" and a "Hydra" (3.1.295–99), a "Land-Remora" (3.2.6), a "poore and nasty Snake" (5.3.319), a "viper" that devours its parents, and a monstrous birth or "Prodigy" (3.2.28). He also compares the poetaster to an African slave: "These be blacke Slaues; *Romanes*, take heede of these" (5.3.333). It is impossible to confront the phrase "blacke Slaues" with modern eyes and not read it as a description of a dark-skinned foreigner pressed into slavery by Europeans; the exploitation of human life was as much a part of the Roman Empire as it would later be a part of the British colonial project. Horace's move from the metaphor of monsters to black slaves further links neologisms to non-Western imported words, demonstrating that grotesque or monstrous inkhorn terms could also easily be seen as dark-skinned African, Middle Eastern, or Asian foreigners. Using the language of the monstrous to describe dark-skinned foreigners was not unusual to early modern English writers; as I noted in the Introduction, the same word that described blackness and the grotesque, *antic*, was nearly indistinguishable from the word that indicated classical antiquity, *antique*.[54] Though the words *antic* and *antique* do not appear in *Poetaster*, the barbed insults of Jonson's Horace echo the Roman poet's description of bad poetry as a dark grotesque chimera in the opening lines of the *Ars Poetica*, which in Jonson's English translation emphasizes bodily distention and ridiculousness through carefully placed enjambment:[55]

If to a woman's head a painter would
A horse neck joyn, & sundry plumes o'erfold

On every limb, ta'en from a several creature,
Presenting upwards a fair female feature,
Which in a blacke foule fish uncomely ends:
Admitted to the sight, although his friends,
Could you contain your laughter? Credit me,
That book, my *Piso's*, and this piece agree
Who shapes like sick men's dreams are form'd so vain,
As neither head nor foot one forme retain: (1–10)

The first phrase snakes through the poem's first three lines like a grotesque illustration, combining leaves and vines with feet, claws, and wings. It is as if the chimera is being painted before our eyes, each hybrid animal part added on as the lines progress. The restless description does not come to a final stop until the end of line 5 at the phrase "uncomely ends" (5), and this is not a full stop but a colon, preparation for the irrepressible derision featured in the following lines, also depicted with a disruptive, misplaced caesura and further enjambment: "Could you contain your laughter? Credit me, / That book, my *Piso's*, and this piece agree" (7–8). The ridiculous chimera is not only a mismatched hybrid figure—a woman's head, horse's neck, bird's feathers, and mermaid's tail—she is also hideous ("uncomely," 5), dark colored ("blacke," 5), and filthy ("foule," 5), the product of delusional fantasy ("sick mens dreams" 9). Lictor (Envy), the monster that delivers the prologue to *Poetaster*, is similarly grotesque, describing itself as entwined with snakes: "Cling to my necke and wrists, my louing Wormes; / And cast you round, in soft, and amorous folds" (1.1.6–7). Like Horace's fish-woman, Lictor is also associated with darkness, shunning light in the first lines uttered on stage: "Light, I salute thee, but with wounded nerues: / Wishing thy golden splendour, pitchy darknesse" (1.1.1–2).

Echoing the physical darkness in Lictor and in Jonson's translation of Horace's painted woman ending in a "black, foule, uncomely fish" (5), *Poetaster's* Horace frequently uses the ambivalent language of darkness to describe poetic abuses, which come from "path-lesse, moorish minds" (5.1.84). Though Cain glosses *moorish* as "swampy," the word hints at racial difference.[56] Likewise, Horace commends Virgil's refined spirit for its removal "from all the tartarous Moodes of men" (5.1.103), where *tartarous* can either mean dark and gloomy like the Roman underworld Tartarus or dark-skinned like a Tartar. Moors and Tartars feature prominently in the scenes performed by boy actors in the Roman streets in the middle of the play: all are excerpts from popular

English plays about Ottoman and North African conquest. The most popular character to appear in Jonson's play is the "Moor" Muly Mahomet from
Thomas Peele's *The Battle of Alcazar*, whose speech is reproduced by Jonson
(2.3.468–78, omitting 469–71). Other plays featured are "King Darius' dole-
ful strain" (3.4.211–16), a parody of the *Pretie new Enterlude . . . of the Story of
Kyng Daryus* (1565); Chapman's *Blind Beggar of Alexandria* (3.4.245–46); and
Thomas Kyd's *Spanish Tragedy* (which includes a performance of Kyd's Ottoman play-within-a-play *Soliman and Perseda*).[57]

Aside from being parodies of popular drama, these plays are the favor-
ites of Tucca, a character known for his uncouth, neologistic speech. Tucca's
speech is distinguished not merely by its neologisms but by the outrageous
uses to which his words are put. It includes the word *glavering* or sycophantic
(3.4.306) and the verbal form of *twang* to signify speaking: "The oracle never
twanged clearer" (1.2.46) and "Thou twang'st right, little Horace" (5.3.334).
These are the only two instances of the verb *twang* denoting speech that appear in the *OED*. Tucca's use of *mangonizing* (trafficking in slaves) is also novel
in its redundancy: "No, you mangonizing slave" (3.4.277). Cain's note tells
us that Tucca's usage carries "the suggestion of prostitution."[58] In *Poetaster*,
Jonson presents us with a picture of Roman antiquity reworked into a monstrous body by means of outlandish and imported words, commodities, and
theatrical subjects. The transformation of metaphors of bad poetry (spurred
on by envy) from serpentine chimeras into black slaves also calls to mind the
spilling of black ink onto a page. Only the "whitest Hellebore" (5.3.385–86)
administered as an emetic will relieve Crispinus of the dark, grotesque, and
foreign poetry that invades his body and his writing.

Crispinus's words take literal, material shape on stage in three ways. First,
they appear on a scroll of poetry that Tibullus reads "alowd" (5.3.266) at Virgil's command to Augustus's court audience (5.3.311–30). Then, when Crispinus takes Horace's pill, they spill aurally from his mouth with painful moans.
Finally, they appear in the basin into which Crispinus vomits as little scraps
of paper for Horace to hold up and read aloud a third time (5.3.479–521). This
way, each word resonates aurally three times with the audience and materially
at least twice:

> *Crisp.* O—*Retrograde—Reciprocall—Incubus.*
> *Hor. Retrograde, Reciprocall,* and *Incubus* are come up.
> *Gall.* Thanks be to *Iupiter.*
> *Crisp.* O—*Glibbery—Lubricall—Defunct—O!*

Hor. Well said, here's some store.

Virg. What are they?

Hor. Glibbery, Lubricall, and *Defunct.* (5.3.483–90).

The audience has already heard each of these words in the poems of Crispinus and Demetrius that Tibullus read aloud at Virgil's request. But here, the audience hears each word twice more, first in Crispinus's groans and second in Horace's enunciation to the gathered court of poets. Although the Folio and Quarto texts do not contain stage directions indicating that strips of paper be placed in the basin, because the words are being collected on stage in such a property, it seems likely that they would be placed in the receptacle prior to the vomiting scene for the actor playing Horace to retrieve, read out, and display to his on-stage and off-stage audiences. Though many of these words no longer seem like neologisms today (particularly words like *retrograde, reciprocal,* and *defunct*), they were new in early modern England. Interestingly, when the words in the poetasters' poems do not pertain to bodily fluids and functions (*glibbery, lubricall, snotteries, incubus*), they pertain to time that is out of joint, whether turning back on itself (retrograde), repeating itself unnecessarily like the triple refrain of neologisms in the scene (reciprocal), or no longer in use (defunct). Perhaps we can read them as a melancholy comment on the nature of Roman antiquity in early modern English literary culture: though writers seek to reciprocate the styles of the ancients, this task may already be becoming retrograde and defunct.

Despite Horace's wish to cleanse Rome of such language, Jonson delights in these words, which are repeatedly read out and presented as material texts on stage. Augustus's banishing Ovid to the Black Sea is mirrored in Horace's purging Crispinus of words; the guardians of Rome desire to send these foreign words and counter-classical, metamorphic verse back to the East, where they supposedly belong. But this does not happen: the purging of Crispinus's language dredges these words up on stage, where it is impossible to escape them. There is also self-mockery in this parody: many of the inkhorn terms that Jonson ridicules are his own creations.[59] And the play would not be witty without Jonson's expert Rabelasian display and manipulation of these words. It is one thing for Jonson to write a bad poem using made-up words but quite another to write a riotously funny one that pokes fun at his critics poking fun at him for poking fun at them (Demetrius's "critic" is clearly meant to be Jonson) and then to unwrite it, as it were, in Crispinus's physical purging of words. As much as *Poetaster* mocks the invasion of new and foreign words into the English language, it also celebrates them by putting them on display.

His cult of plain style and his warnings against barbarous words in *Tim-ber* notwithstanding, Jonson was remembered in death for his own neologistic creations. In his "Funeral Elegie" (1637) for Ben Jonson, the poet John Taylor writes that all surviving poets are "Vnfit to beare the Inkhorn after Ben" (10), alluding primarily to the materials of literary production, but also subtly, to the words Jonson created, ridiculed, banished, and ultimately celebrated in his plays. One reason why Taylor may be thinking of inkhorn terms here, rather than just writing implements, can be found in Taylor's other writings, which include "An Inkehorne Disputation, or Mungrell Conference, between a Law-yer and a Poet" (1630). This poem depicts a poet "boldly" (39) holding his own in battle with a lawyer and using inkhornisms and "pickled words" (46) as weapons: "The Poet boldly yet maintaines the field, / And with his Inkhorne termes disdaines to yeeld" (39–40). Once the lawyer sees how many "pickled words" the poet holds, the lawyer gives up the fight.

Coda

The next chapter deals with sugar, an import that reconfigured classical ideas about the sweetness of poetic language in another early modern English *ars poetica*, George Puttenham's *The Arte of English Poesie* (1589). As a coda to this chapter, it is interesting to note that Jonson not only read Puttenham's book but consumed and responded to it with fervor, if his marginal annotations on the British Library's copy are indications of active reading, as William Sher-man tells us they are.[60] Jonson annotated a number of printed texts composed by his poetic forbears, including an edition of Chaucer now housed at the Folger Library. But his annotations in Puttenham's text are, in Sherman's eyes, the "most emphatic."[61] When you open Jonson's copy of Puttenham, you are immediately confronted with a personalized title page, carefully ornamented in Jonson's italic hand. The top of the page bears his name, "Ben: Jonson," in bold italic lettering. On either side of Puttenham's title sit two symmetrical biblical quotations in Latin. Two more appear below, the first underneath the subtitle ("Contrived into three bookes . . .") and the final quotation placed beneath the printer's name and date. The quotation on the top left is from John 8: "*Sic Abrahamus Christum*" (just as Abraham was to Christ) and the one on the right from Psalm 42: "*Ut Cervus fontem*" (As a deer to the fountain).[62] The two below derive from Ephesians ("*Introite: Nam hic bii sunt Heraclit,*" or "come in, for the gods are here") and Genesis 15 ("*Noli timere Abrahame: Ego*

Protector suus sum," or "do not fear me O Abraham: I am your protector"). As David Riggs intimates in his biography of Jonson, these challenging citations suggest that Jonson's attitude toward poetry "borders on religious awe."[63] Yet this annotated title page not only tells us how Jonson read his Puttenham but also how Jonson performed and displayed his reading of Puttenham: devoutly, maybe even typologically. Jonson's biblical references create an analogy between Puttenham and Abraham, positioning Jonson as Puttenham's heir, a Christian reader and creator. Jonson's annotations transform this printed book into a hybrid of print and manuscript, a uniquely private copy that held an important place in Jonson's library.

Jonson's copy of Puttenham has been published in facsimile by Scolar Press (1968), but the facsimile's black and white ink does not accurately reproduce the many colors of ink Jonson used in his copy of Puttenham, which include different blacks now faded to brown and periodic cloverleaf-shaped flowers and crosshatches in red.[64] Throughout the text, Jonson underlines and marks out salient passages using a system of signs (yet to be fully deciphered) including quotations in English, Latin, and Greek; underlining; brackets; asterisks; trefoils (three-petal flowers); quatrefoils (four-petal flowers); hatch signs; dashes; and elaborate pointing hands or *manicules*, as Sherman calls them.[65]

Jonson's manicules are notable not only for their visual detail—the hand marking off a passage about Homer bears fingernails and a lace cuff—but for their scarcity relative to the rest of his markings. If Jonson's manicules leap off the page for current readers, it is because they are larger than his other marginal markings and appear to have taken longer to illustrate. We can deduce from this evidence that the manicules point to the parts of the text Jonson wanted most to retain or felt were the most important at the time of his reading. Jonson's manicules appear only five times in the volume: they ornament Puttenham's description of Homer (2), his attribution of the barbarian invasions to the corruption of Greek and Latin meter (8), his definition of the classical Greek epithalamion (41), an elaborate description of Queen Elizabeth's poem "The Doubt of Future Foes" as an example of poetic gorgeousness (207), and finally Puttenham's anecdote about Henry VIII's wittily flatulent manservant, Andrew Flammock (224). Jonson was a careful reader, indexing many of the features that set Puttenham's poetics apart from his classical forbears and early modern contemporaries like Sidney, Campion, Daniel, and Wilson. Puttenham is the only poetic theorist of the late sixteenth century to cite and publish Queen Elizabeth's verse, and his historical narrative of the origin of

epithalamia is probably the longest and most unusual in this field. The reference to Flammock, who recovers his initial faux pas of farting inappropriately
with an appropriately deferential witticism, speaks to Jonson-the-dramatist's
delight in grotesque bodily functions and *arse poetica*.

Jonson's manicules and annotations reveal much about his own classicism: he read his Puttenham with acute attention to the role of the ancient
Greeks and Romans in shaping poetic form and meter, choosing to index
three passages addressing the classical roots of English verse. The passage comparing Homer and later the queen (marked marginally by Jonson's trefoil) to
"creating gods" (2) links the archaic Greek poet with the present Elizabethan
period. Puttenham's discourse on the epithalamion is lengthy and contradictory, and from it Jonson plucks out the one paragraph that mourns the loss of
classical meter to foreign invaders (see Figure 1).

As further evidence of Jonson's classicism, his marginalia sometimes appear to contradict Puttenham's own movement away from classical form and
meter. At one point, when Puttenham criticizes the use of syllabic meter in
English poetry, particularly lines containing nine or eleven syllables, declaring
that they force the poem to sound "ill favouredly and like a minstrell's mu-
sicke" (59), Jonson counters with a marginal quote in English from Thomas
Tusser in dactylic meter: "what carrie we then, but a sheet to ye grau[e] / to
couer this carkas, of all that we haue- Tuss[er]" (K4r).[66] Each line is composed
of eleven syllables. Though we can view this as a marginal example as well
as a rebuttal, it remains a reader's response as much as an annotation. Many
of Jonson's marginal quotations are in Latin or Greek. By comparison, his
quotation of Tusser's plain, English lines contrasts starkly with Jonson's veiled
biblical citations on the title page, reminding future readers of the transience
of human life and material possessions. Jonson did not merely annotate his
copy of Puttenham; he argued with it, transformed it, and made it his own.

The next chapter takes up where Jonson has left us. Caught between the
ancient classical past and the contemporary global present, Puttenham's poetical
manual moves away from classical models, favoring exotic, foreign ones verging on
anti-Horatian strangeness. In Jonsonian Rome, foreign words and commodities
are smeared on bodies, regurgitated or excreted from bodies to pollute, stain, and
poison the language and the state. In Puttenham's text, the foreign word serves as
a sweetener, figuratively, materially, and sensually. For Puttenham, exotic imports
are sweet and malleable substances, not foul excretions, and they take the form of
epigrams printed into sugar-plate and elaborate jewel-shaped poems that call to
mind the colored, perfumed sugar lozenges consumed at court.

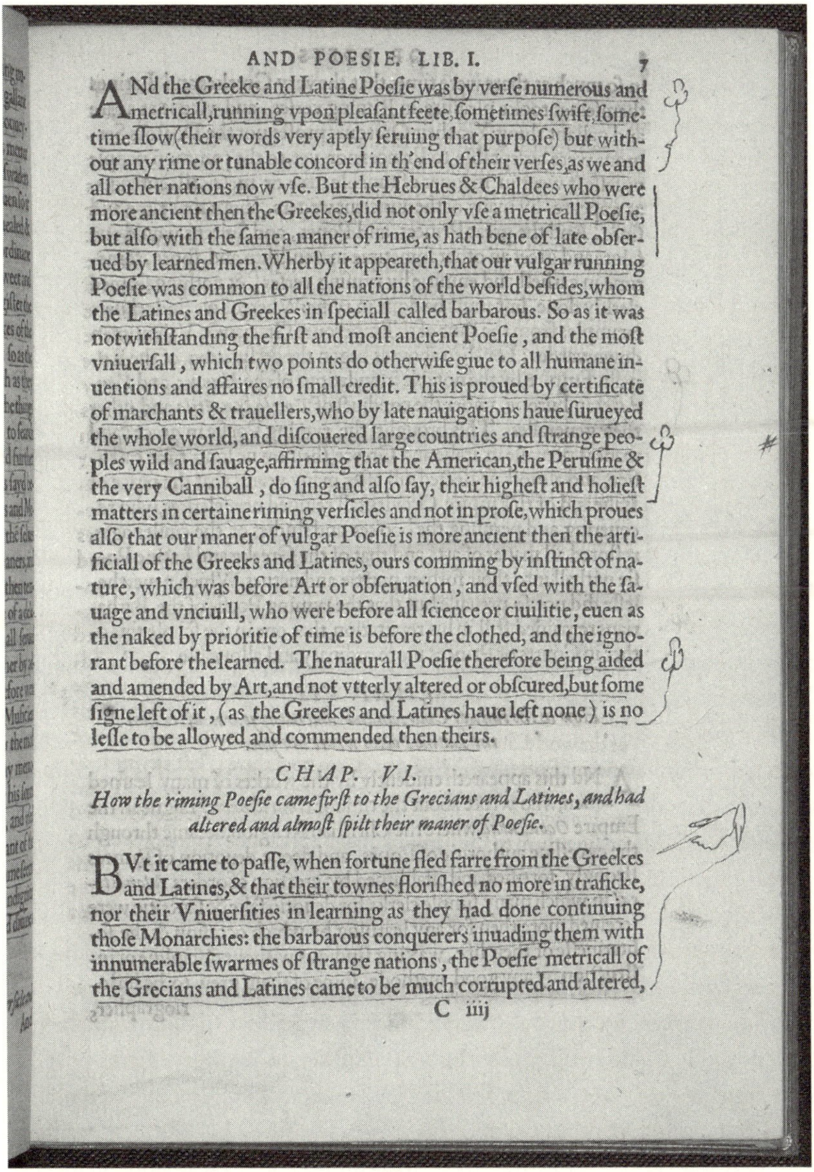

ANd the Greeke and Latine Poesie was by verse numerous and metricall, running vpon pleasant feete, sometimes swift, sometime slow (their words very aptly seruing that purpose) but without any rime or tunable concord in th'end of their verses, as we and all other nations now vse. But the Hebrues & Chaldees who were more ancient then the Greekes, did not only vse a metricall Poesie, but also with the same a maner of rime, as hath bene of late obserued by learned men. Wherby it appeareth, that our vulgar running Poesie was common to all the nations of the world besides, whom the Latines and Greekes in speciall called barbarous. So as it was notwithstanding the first and most ancient Poesie, and the most vniuersall, which two points do otherwise giue to all humane inuentions and affaires no small credit. This is proued by certificate of marchants & trauellers, who by late nauigations haue surueyed the whole world, and discouered large countries and strange peoples wild and sauage, affirming that the American, the Perusine & the very Canniball, do sing and also say, their highest and holiest matters in certaine riming versicles and not in prose, which proues also that our maner of vulgar Poesie is more ancient then the artificiall of the Greeks and Latines, ours comming by instinct of nature, which was before Art or obseruation, and vsed with the sauage and vnciuill, who were before all science or ciuilitie, euen as the naked by prioritie of time is before the clothed, and the ignorant before the learned. The naturall Poesie therefore being aided and amended by Art, and not vtterly altered or obscured, but some signe left of it, (as the Greekes and Latines haue left none) is no lesse to be allowed and commended then theirs.

CHAP. VI.
How the riming Poesie came first to the Grecians and Latines, and had altered and almost spilt their maner of Poesie.

BVt it came to passe, when fortune fled farre from the Greekes and Latines, & that their townes florished no more in traficke, nor their Vniuersities in learning as they had done continuing those Monarchies: the barbarous conquerers inuading them with innumerable swarmes of strange nations, the Poesie metricall of the Grecians and Latines came to be much corrupted and altered,

C iiij

Figure 1. Ben Jonson's copy of George Puttenham, *The Arte of English Poesie* (London: Richard Field, 1589), 7. By permission of The British Library Board.

Chapter 2

Shaping Subtlety: Sugar in *The Arte of English Poesie*

Sugared Words and English Poetry

In the late sixteenth century, something changed in how people wrote about poetry. No longer content with metaphors of honey, sweet fruit, and wine, poets began to employ words that described a newer, more far-fetched import, sugar, to articulate the idea of poetic sweetness. Over the course of this chapter, I will document this shift in order to show how sugar offered English poets and poetic theorists a new, material medium for talking about poetry. As I hope my reading of Puttenham's *Arte of English Poesie* will demonstrate, sugary language and imagery made it possible for writers to conceive of poetry as something both exotic and non-European and as a material that lent itself to malleability and reproducible patterns.

Francis Meres praised Shakespeare's poetry in his commonplace book of 1598, connecting it to the language of a newly affordable commodity of Asian and Levantine provenance, sugar. Meres's comparison also refers to honey, the culinary commodity that sugar would largely replace in the following centuries, not only in kitchen cabinets but, as I will argue, in poetic metaphors:

> As the soul of Euphorbas was thought to live in Pythagoras, the sweet, witty soul of Ovid lives in mellifluous and honey-tongued Shakespeare: witness his *Venus and Adonis*, his *Lucrece*, his sugar'd sonnets among his private friends.[1]

If we are to believe in Pythagorean metempsychosis, Meres suggests, then surely Shakespeare is Ovid reincarnated. Following the convention that

Pythagoras ate nothing but honey, Meres describes Shakespeare's poetry (as opposed to his drama), both published and unpublished, with metaphors of sweet-tasting things like honey ("honey-tongued" and "mellifluous") and sugar ("sugar'd sonnets").[2] The poetic works are listed in the order of their publication and circulation: *Venus and Adonis* first, followed by *Lucrece*, and then the tightly guarded *Sonnets*.[3] But the list also draws a distinction between the two classically influenced narrative poems and the intimate sonnets shared only with Shakespeare's "private friends." Meres's wording appears to associate the published, more classically influenced poems *Venus and Adonis* and *The Rape of Lucrece* (heirs to Ovid's *Metamorphoses* and *Fasti*) with a classical sweetener, honey, and the newer, more experimental *Sonnets* with a newer, more precious substance, sugar.[4] The English sonnet is an early modern invention, begun in the 1530s in translations of Petrarch and further refined in the Elizabethan period. There is nothing classical or Ovidian about a sonnet's form. Meres's phrasing hints that it was not only in their kitchens that his culture began to replace the older sweetening agent, honey, with the newer and foreign imported spice, sugar; classical forms of poetry were also being replaced with innovative (or imported Italian) Elizabethan ones. Shakespeare's "sugar'd sonnets," not yet available to the public, were the fresh poetic commodity of the future.

Sugar was closely associated with poetic language, eloquence, and style during the sixteenth and seventeenth centuries, a relatively new phenomenon.[5] Noting that the root of the Latinate *persuade* is the Indo-European *swad*, which means sweet, Sidney Mintz maintains that the takeover of sugar imagery in early modern English poetic language mirrored the rise of this commodity in European markets, "competing with and supplanting honey imagery among the terms of endearment and affection."[6] Jeffrey Masten, spinning this into an elegant argument about male friendship and beyond, analyzes *sweet* as a form of address.[7] But sugar imagery did not simply characterize terms of endearment. Like honey and other sweet-tasting substances that came before, sugar characterized poetic language and acquired a reputation as an exotic import. Sugar was at first so rare and desirable a commodity (only accessible to nobility, sampled at courtly banquets in the form of sugar paste and marzipan structures) that using sugary imagery to describe poetic language and eloquence served the function of providing, through words, what most people experienced only infrequently through taste, sight, or touch. Following Mintz, one might say that the language of sugar helped achieve the project of Renaissance self-fashioning and upward mobility.

Describing verse and figurative language as sweet has a long history. Perhaps the earliest known reference to the sugariness of words occurs in the *Atharva-Veda*, a Sanskrit poem written during the Mantra period between 1000 and 800 BCE. The poem takes the form of a magical love spell, which compares the beloved's "voice and words" to honey, and ends with the speaker circumscribing his beloved with "a zone of sugar-cane."[8] In Europe, however, from ancient Greece up to the Middle Ages, the material metaphor for sweetness remained constant: honey. Although sugar was present in the ancient Greco-Roman world (the earliest culinary use of sugarcane occurred in ancient Egypt), it was neither refined nor accessible to the populace at large.[9] Honey was what Pythagoras ate and Pindar drank; according to Plato, honey was what the Muses gave to poets, and Lucretius rimmed his cup with honeyed verses to sweeten the medicine of his philosophy.[10]

Until sugar became widely available, there really wasn't anything sweeter than honey. Only in the fourteenth century, when sugar began to be a major commodity imported into Europe from the Arab world, and later in the sixteenth and seventeenth centuries, when sugar refineries were built in all the major ports of Europe and candying methods developed and improved, did the dominant material metaphor for sweet words change from honey to sugar. The Song of Songs indicates sweetness with honey and fruit ("comfort me with apples" [3:5]; "honey and milk are under thy tongue" [4:11]); classical Greek and Latin texts use honey to describe sweet words, but early modern English writers prefer sugar.[11] An allusion to sugar appears in the King James version of the Song of Solomon in the form of a banqueting house, a building created in the seventeenth century and designed chiefly for consuming sweets: "Hee brought me to the banketting house, and his banner ouer mee, *was* loue. / Stay me with flagons, comfort me with apples, for I am sick of loue," sighs the female speaker of the song.[12] Banqueting houses were small structures located at some distance from the main house, in the garden, and used for dessert and postprandial entertainment.[13] Around this time (c. 1600), the word *dessert* also entered English from French, describing the action of clearing the table of dishes from the main meal in preparation for the final course (from French *desservir*, to remove what has been served), though early modern English folk may have heard it as *deserting* the main table for the banqueting house.[14]

In earlier English translations of the Song of Songs beginning with Wycliffe (1395) and including the Coverdale (1535), Geneva (1576), and Douay-Rheims (1582, 1609) Bibles, the female speaker is brought to a "wine cellar," which is called a *Weinkeller* in Luther's German translation (1545) and *cellam vinarium* in the Latin Vulgate. In the original Hebrew, it is *Beit ha-yayin*, literally "the house of wine." But by 1611, the metaphor for sensual excess had shifted from wine to sugar and from sour to sweet. The wine sipped during the dessert course of a meal (*hippocras*) was sweetened and spiced. In a "banketting house," one might consume vast amounts of sugary desserts while watching and participating in masques and musical entertainments. As Patricia Fumerton points out, at Renaissance banquets, even the plates and cups were made out of sugar and meant to be either consumed or shattered.[15] By the seventeenth century, the ancient house of wine of the Hebrew Scriptures had been replaced by an early modern banqueting house, the wine and apples replaced with sweets known collectively as banqueting stuff: *hippocras*, suckets (preserved fruits in sugar syrup or dry and coated in sugar crystals), comfits (seeds and spices coated with hardened sugar), lozenges (jewels made from sugar), and elaborate sculptures called "subtleties," all made out of sugar.

Sweetness of poetic language is often understood synaesthetically, not only describing sweet-tasting words but sweet-sounding and sweet-smelling phrases as well. The noun *sweet* entered the English language in the mid-sixteenth century, referring to sweet-tasting delicacies and beverages. It was only at the end of the century that it acquired a sense of smell, and *sweets* began to refer to flowers, herbs, perfumes, and, in rare cases, to sounds.[16] And therefore, in many cases, especially in late sixteenth- and early seventeenth-century literature, it is difficult to tell whether *sweet language* means perfumed, melodic, or mellifluous. Words carried on the air, issuing from someone's mouth, might indeed seem to bear a sweet or noxious perfume. Words of courtship whispered by a lover might even seem to taste sweet if uttered before a kiss. Given current scholarship on the permeability of the body and the confusion of the senses in the period, *sweet* may have referred to all three at once: though refined white sugar has no smell today, early modern English recipes for sugar included sugar scented with rose petals, violet, and ambergris.[17] Sugared sweets were most frequently enjoyed by the nobility at banquets accompanied by poetic recitations, singing, dancing, masques, and musical performances, all of which were designed to produce a sweet sensory experience. Orsino's speech in the opening lines of *Twelfth Night* mixes sweet taste, sound, and scent, giving us an example of the way an early modern banquet might mingle the different senses of sweet:

If music be the food of love, play on;
Give me excess of it, that, surfeiting,

The appetite may sicken, and so die.
That strain again! It had a dying fall:
O, it came o'er my ear like the sweet sound,
That breathes upon a bank of violets,
Stealing and giving odour! Enough; no more:
'Tis not so sweet now as it was before. (1.1.1–8)

Though synaesthesia of sound and taste is common in early modern poetry, Orsino's speech plumbs the depths of sweet, directly connecting music to the excessive consumption of sweets and sugar that characterized early modern banquets. He calls for "excess of it" (2), hoping to surfeit from the music the way someone might overeat at a banquet. The idea is that by hearing too much sweet music (or eating too much sugar), Orsino's desire for sweetness will wane, as it predictably does at the end of the passage: "'Tis not so sweet now as it was before" (8). In the second half of the passage, Orsino moves from sweet sounds and tastes to sweet scents, comparing the strain of music to "a bank of violets" (6). Violets were frequently used in early modern confectionery to scent and give color to candied fruits, lozenges, and marzipan. They were also candied themselves and used to decorate cakes, sugar plate, and other confections. The phrase "a bank of violets" (6) also hints phonically at a similar word, a *bankett* (or banquet) of violets.

Twelfth Night was intended for performance during Christmastime festivities, when festival banquets were held throughout London. In early modern England, the word *banquet* increasingly referred to what we would today call the dessert course, a separate meal served after the main, savory dishes were cleared in the garden's banqueting house, a course that consisted primarily of sweet cakes, sugared preserved fruits, spices, cordials and *hippocras*.[18] As Fumerton has noted, it was also called a *void* and involved not only consuming sweet, dainty, dissolvable delicacies like spiced sugar candies but "voiding" the room by literally breaking plates and glasses, themselves frequently fashioned out of sugar.[19] But *Twelfth Night*'s opening banquet of sweet senses also points to the exotic source of sweetness in the early modern era. *Twelfth Night* is set in Illyria, an eastern European country on the coast of the Mediterranean (present-day Bosnia) that permits certain freedoms from traditional gender and relationship distinctions. It is surrounded by a body of water in which traditional laws are frequently ignored and lawless pirates sail the seas. Illyria was all Ottoman in the early seventeenth century, and part of the appeal of the play is the freedom to which this exotic, northern Mediterranean locale lends itself.[20] In the early seventeenth century, some of the primary sources of sweetness (not only sugar but also per-fumed balsams and spices) were the Mediterranean islands of Crete and Cyprus, alternately under Venetian and Ottoman control. The opening of *Twelfth Night* calls up not only the sensory overload of the dessert course at an early modern festival banquet but the outlandish and exotic lineage of sugar itself.

The English word *sugar* derives from Arabic *sukkar* and may be related to ancient Greek *sakcaron* and Sanskrit *sarkara*, ground or candied sugar, origi-nally meaning pebbles or gritty sand. It first appears in English around 1300, when sugar first entered European markets, but the majority of new defini-tions and compound words originate in the sixteenth and early seventeenth centuries, when sugar importation and cultivation became more common.[21] Although the production and early industrialization of sugar moved from North Africa and the eastern Mediterranean to include South America by the end of the sixteenth century, English words for the commodity and for confectionary held onto their Eastern associations. *Sugar* meaning a commod-ity, as in "cargoes or stocks of sugar," appears for the first time around 1570.[22] During the seventeenth century, *sugar* also referred to the botanical substance of sugarcane itself.[23] By the late sixteenth century, English writers had a whole host of new words for sweet-tasting things, many of them of South Asian and Middle Eastern derivation. In addition to the well-used *honey* (Old English *hunig*, from Old Frisian) and its Latinate derivative *mellifluous* (flowing with honey), they had at least six new English words of Asian etymology: *candied* (Persian *qand*; Sanskrit *khanda*), meaning "sugar in crystalline pieces"; *march-pane* (*marzipan*, a word and delicacy of unknown origin but probably an East-ern provenance); and *julep* (Persian *gulhab*) from the Persian word for *rose*, which lent its petals and fragrance to confections.[24] The Arabic word *sharhab*, a cold, sweet drink, gave us not only *syrup* but also *sherbet* and *sorbet*. English also developed the new nouns *sweetmeat* (c. 1500) and *sweet* (c. 1540), which meant a sweet-tasting food or drink.[25] They also had *lozenge*, not only the word for a diamond-shaped figure or gemstone but, from the late sixteenth century onward, increasingly the word for a jewel-like, diamond-shaped con-fection of molded or cut sugar paste. Tim Richardson posits that the English word for *lozenge* is related to the Arabic word *lauzinaj*, "a kind of almond paste cake that is mentioned in a cookery book written in Baghdad in the twelfth century."[26] If Richardson is correct, then *lozenge* as a shape and gemstone cut has its origins in confectionary. Though all of these words were in use by the sixteenth century and, in some cases, as early as the fourteenth, their figurative uses and connection to poetry began in the sixteenth.[27]

Like the words that described them, sugar, candy, syrups, juleps, and marzipan were all spices, confections, and recipes that came into Europe from the East, transmitted from India to Persia to the Arab world, and from the Arab conquest of the Mediterranean in the thirteenth and fourteenth centuries to Italy and Spain. In the Elizabethan and Jacobean periods, the majority of sugar imports came from the eastern Mediterranean and North Africa.[28] Over the course of the sixteenth century, the Ottoman Empire conquered much of the Mediterranean, which caused the decline of Spanish, Italian, and Portuguese sugar plantations in North Africa and the Mediterranean, eventually leading Europeans to carry the sugar industry to South America and the West Indies.[29] Although some early modern readers and sweet-toothed consumers might have associated sugar with New Spain as early as the mid-sixteenth century, it was equally associated with the Barbary Coast and the eastern Mediterranean islands. As Wendy Wall and Kim Hall have noted, it was not until the middle of the seventeenth century that Atlantic sugarcane plantations took over the production and distribution of sugar to the rest of the world, due in part to the European (first Spanish and Portuguese, then French, English, Dutch, and Danish) colonialist expansion in the West Indies and exploitation of African slave labor.[30] According to Mintz, this happened between 1625, when England established its first sugar plantations and colonies in Barbados, and 1650, when sugar from Barbados began flooding British and European markets.[31]

Between 1598 and 1609, when Shakespeare was writing, circulating, and publishing his "sugar'd sonnets," England was importing sugar from three places: North Africa and the Spanish Canary Islands ("Barbary sugar"), Spain's and Portugal's Atlantic plantations, and the Mediterranean islands of Crete and Cyprus.[32] The Venetian colony of Crete was known as *Candia* (called "Candy" in sixteenth-century English) from 1212 until its Ottoman occupation in 1645 and then as *Kandiye*. Originally the name for Crete's capital city, *Candia* has an Arabic origin meaning "castle of the moat," but it might also refer to the Arabic word for rock sugar (*qandi*), an allusion to the medieval sugar refineries there. Either way, English readers must have associated *Candy* with *candy*. In the mid-sixteenth century, Cypriot sugar was considered the finest in the world, even though its industry had already begun to decline, and Barbary sugar was considered the poorest.[33] But the sugar that arrived on British shores was not the crystalline white grains found in supermarkets today; it was only partially refined, packaged in large brown lumps ranging in color from tan to orange-brown (it was sometimes described as "red"), called *cassonade* for the boxes in which it was transported and sold (*cassone* in Italian).[34] The sugar was further clarified in sugar refineries in the major European ports—London's first sugar refinery was created in 1544—and then refined some more in professional and household kitchens. By the late 1580s, London had already become the largest sugar port in Europe.[35]

Though they did not abandon the use of honey as a real sweetener for food and a figurative one for words, early modern English people augmented their vocabulary to include all sugary imports and culinary practices. Thus, in *Hamlet*, we have Ophelia returning Hamlet's love tokens, accompanied by sugary or perfumed language "of so sweet breath composed / As made the things more rich" and lamenting having "suck'd the honey of [Hamlet's] music vows" (3.1.165) and, in the very next scene, Hamlet assuring Horatio that neither one of them engages in the materialistic rhetorical pose of flattery: "Let the candied tongue lick absurd pomp / And crook the pregnant hinges of the knee" (3.2.54).[36] Though Shakespeare's language of candy melting has long been known thanks to image clusters identified and interpreted by Caroline Spurgeon and Edward Armstrong, both of *Hamlet's* uses of *candied* are metaphors for rhetoric and speech.[37] In both instances, the language of culinary sweetness translates readily into the language of *language*, though the newer import appears to suggest something untrustworthy, obsequious flattery, whereas the older one is both true (the honey of Hamlet's courtship) and already lost. For Masten, the language of sweetness in *Hamlet* indicates a rhetoric of interchangeability, a wish to dissolve the boundaries between oneself and one's friend or lover in the same way that a sugary sweet dissolves upon the tongue. This incorporation and dissolution is not without danger, as Hamlet makes clear when he warns against flattery as a "candied tongue."[38]

Early modern English poetry is replete with metacommentaries on verse as sugar: no aspect of poetry escapes its shiny, sweet coating. Not only are words, phrases, rhymes, speeches, and sentences described as candied, sugared, and dripping with syrup, even the materials of writing must receive a dusting of sugar.[39] Pens, quills, and styluses are described as dipped in sugar, converting Plato's conceit of poetry as honey from the muses into this strange, new commodity. Most intriguingly, early modern English writers anachronistically gloss the writing utensils of the great ancient Greek and Roman poets with such sugary metaphors, even inserting sugar into English translations of Roman authors like Seneca and Virgil.[40] In Sir John Beaumont's poem *The Metamorphosis of Tabacco*, the poet uses sugar to introduce his readers to American tobacco, to "paint the praise of sugred smoke" invoking a pantheon of classical poets from Apollo to Homer: "Nor had Anacreon with sugared

glose / Extol'd the virtues of the fragrant rose."[41] Here sugar, a valuable commodity that is both Ottoman and newly South American, converts smoky,
insubstantial Western tobacco into a more legible commodity. For Thomas
Churchyard, both ancient Roman writers and contemporary English ones
coated their pens and words in sweet white crystals: in *The Worthiness of Wales*,
Churchyard begs for half the eloquence of Cicero's "sugred tonge," and in *A
Commendatory Poem*, he begs his readers to take seriously "The workes and
sugred verses fine" of English poetry, despite its being written in a "barborus
language rued."[42] Churchyard's description of early modern English as "barbarous" and rude has as its necessary counterpart the refined languages of Latin
and Greek. Yet Churchyard's poem elevates English verse to the same level
as the ancients, which as I will argue below is George Puttenham's project as
well. Churchyard's comparison suggests that in the 1580s—as far as poetry was
concerned—English was still a foreign-inflected language. English was changing fast; Latin and Greek were static. This may sound strange, but not if you
take into account the great number of words being imported into England
from "barbarous" non-European countries, along with the commodities they
signify, like sugar from the barbarous Barbary Coast.

Sugar Subtleties and Ekphrasis

Sugar has a number of remarkable properties, each of which made it a more
desirable culinary, pharmacological, and decorative substance than honey.
The chief of these properties is its malleability: sugar can be molded, pressed,
printed, and sculpted. Because of its fine crystalline structure, which makes it
whiter the more it is refined, sugar accepts colors better than almost any other
artistic medium.[43] And sugar is an excellent preservative as well in its ability to
expel moisture.[44] In short, sugar can be shaped into an almost limitless number of representations of other, nonsugary things, which will maintain their
shape a long time, and these characteristics must have made it appear to carry
almost magical, alchemical properties in early modern England. In her history of confectionery, Laura Mason discusses how early modern people must
have thought of sugar's marvelous protean properties: sugar "was transformed
according to rules: grained, pulled into ropes, cut, molded and modeled. If
things didn't work the first time, it could be dissolved back into syrup to try
again. Sugar boiling must have seemed akin to magic."[45] If we follow Bruno
Latour's description of mediators as material changes (frequently chemical

discoveries) that reshape social and economic networks, sugar qualifies as an early modern mediator.[46] Not only did an understanding of sugar's properties reshape how early modern Europeans produced, thought, and wrote about food culture, but it also gave them a new way of talking about poetry: not only did they have access to an entire vocabulary for sweet things imported from Turkey, Persia, India, and the Arab world, but they also acquired new shapes and forms for verse. If, like sugar, verse could be molded, stretched, and spun fine, then poetry had remarkable abilities to animate and move readers and listeners in the same way.

Sugar's culinary malleability meant that the substance could take any possible shape, from hardened, diamond-cut lozenges ornamented with gold leaf mimicking precious jewels, to elaborate ships and fountains of pressed and molded sugar plate that spouted water and wine. As a material medium, sugar held near limitless possibilities. This made it akin to early modern poetry as well, where as Philip Sidney proposed, poets discussed neither history ("what hath been") nor the future ("what shall be") but the *possible* ("what may be").[47] Both sugar and poetry went further toward representing the *impossible*, creating fantastical, imaginary structures and worlds for the delight of their consumers. In early modern England, both the material of sugar and the material of poetry simultaneously embraced both possibility and impossibility, enacting what Giorgio Agamben has defined as the primary role of poetry, to represent a "topology of the unreal."[48]

Elaborate and fantastical sugar structures known as *subtleties* embodied more of a topography of the unreal, mimetically reproducing an animated world in miniature. In the sixteenth century, *subtlety* could indicate any "ingenious contrivance; craft or cunning device" or artifice, but also, starting in the fifteenth century, it specifically referred to ornamental sugar sculptures.[49] The source of the term is uncertain: it could derive from the mystery and ingenuity of such creations, or it could derive from the process of powdering, boiling, and refining sugar until it was thin ("subtle"), comparable to the word's use to describe the process of alchemical distillation.[50] *Subtleties* were so called because they were cunning in conceit and constructed from a light and highly refined substance, according to the *OED*, which defines *subtle* as skillful, abstruse (when applied to an object), cleverly contrived, and fine or delicate.[51] Prose descriptions of subtleties make these confections appear to function like classical poetry in their detailed representation. Subtleties lent themselves to ekphrasis. In *Thomas Wolsey, Late Cardinall, his Lyffe and Deathe* (written in 1558 and published in 1641), the biographer George Cavendish describes the cardinal's lavish feasts in great ekphrastic detail, singling out the extraordinary intermediary dishes brought out between courses, called *entremets* by the French and *subtleties* by the English. These were elaborate, three-dimensional structures made from various sweet concoctions, primarily sugar plate (a sugar paste made of refined sugar and gum tragacanth pressed into wooden molds) and marzipan (a white paste made of fine sugar and ground almonds):

> Anon came vppe the Second Course, w^t so many disshes, subtilities,
> & curious devysis, w^{che} ware above an Cth in nomber of so goodly
> proporcion and Costly / that I suppose the ffrenchemen neuer
> sawe the lyke / the wonder was no lesse than it was worth in deade
> / there ware Castelles w^t Images in the same / powlles Chirche
> and steple in proporcion for the quantitie as well counterfeited as
> the paynter should haue painted it vppon a clothe or wall / There
> ware beastes, byrdes, fowles of dyuers kyndes And personages most
> lyvely made & counterfet in dysshes / some fightyng (as it ware)
> w^t swordes / some w^t Gonnes and Crosebows / Some vaughtying
> and leapyng / Some dauncyng w^t ladyes / Some in complett harnes
> Iustyng w^t speres / And w^t many more devysis than I ame able w^t
> my wytt to discribbe.[52]

Like a scene from an early modern poetic romance, these sugar sculptures and miniature buildings are a source of "wonder," full of "curious devices." Cavendish's prose also captures the amazement of the banqueters: the description is divided into choppy lines that look to postmodern eyes like free verse, though from an early modern perspective, it is simply an itemized list. Cavendish's description of sugar subtleties is not merely ecstatic; it is poetic and ekphrastic. The sugar is "as well counterfeited as if a painter had painted it upon a wall." The variety of movement captured in the sculptures invests them with the qualities of an ekphrastic microcosm found in classical, medieval, and early modern descriptions of visual works of art, from Achilles's shield to Lucrece's wall hanging.[53] Cavendish even adopts the language of early modern poetics to describe the ingenuity of the sculptures, returning to the careful "proporcioun" of the sculptures three times in the full passage. This sugar is not just food; it is art. And more than art, it is poetry.

The English professional cook Robert May, who prepared banquets during most of the seventeenth century, highlights the similarities between sugar sculpture and poetic mimesis: his description of the elaborate subtleties he designed is animated and ekphrastic, making use of the poetic technique of classical mimesis to describe his confectionery artifice. Like Achilles's shield, the sugar banquet May describes, replete with belching dragons, firing castles, and bleeding stags, is a fantastical reproduction of a miniature world:

> Make the likeness of a ship in pasteboard, with flags and stream-
> ers, the guns belonging to it with kickses, binde them about with
> packthred, and cover them with coarse paste proportionable to the
> fashion of a Canon with Carriages . . . then in another Charger have
> the proportion of a stag made of coarse paste, with a broad arrow in
> the side of him, and his body filled up with claret wine. In another
> charger at the end of the stag have the proportion of a Castle with
> battlements, Percullices, gates, and drawbridges made of pasteboard,
> the Guns of kickses, and covered with coarse paste as the former.
> Place it at a distance from the ship to fire at each other . . . being all
> placed in order upon the table, before you fire the trains powder,
> order it so that some of the Ladies may be persuaded to pluck the
> Arrow out of the Stag, then will the Claret wine follow as blood
> being run out of a wound.[54]

The banquet includes pies full of living frogs and birds and little eggshell cups filled with rosewater to diffuse the sulfurous stink of the gunpowder. May's description of the festivities ends with the sugar ship blowing off a side of the castle, the ladies throwing rosewater at one another and shrieking at the avian and amphibian surprises. According to May, this is how nobles used to enjoy themselves in the Elizabethan and Jacobean periods, "before good housekeeping had left England" with the interregnum. May's fantastical description of sugar plate action figures and castles ushers in a nostalgic return to such luxury with the Restoration. His description of sugary pageantry is full of play and animation. In addition to the gushing of the claret blood through the wound of the stag and the gunpowder exploding through the castle's and ship's cannons, there is the movement of the ladies throwing water, skipping and shrieking, the hopping of frogs, and the beating of wings.

The art in creating such a display is dedicated to achieving precision, based on careful organization, size, and position. The word *proportion* and the phrase *in order* recur throughout the passage, suggesting an attention not only to detail but to scale and form, as in a poem. Proportion is an important concept to early modern poetic theory: Puttenham dedicates the middle book of his treatise *The Arte of English Poesie* to poetic structure, calling it "Of Proportion Poetical" (153–219).[55] Puttenham includes in his text several wood-cut diagrams to illustrate line and stanza length, just as May includes woodcuts of sugar shapes and molds in his recipe book, which is subtitled *The Art and Mystery of Cookery*, which insists that learning to cook is a secret craft, available only to select initiates—and the consumers of the book.[56] Given the way that both treatises discuss the creation of poetry and cookery as complicated artisanal practices, available only to a select few, it is therefore not surprising that both May and Puttenham should use the same word, *proportion*, to talk about sugar sculpture and poetry.

The practice of displaying opulent sugar subtleties at royal banquets originated, with sugar, in India and the Arab world and was adopted by Europeans in the Middle Ages.[57] The travel writer Al-Guzuli (d. 1412) describes a mosque built entirely of sugar, into which beggars were invited and allowed to destroy and consume at the end of the festivities.[58] This persisted in Turkey and the Arab world well into the early modern period. In Istanbul in 1582, specialized artists known as *sukker nakkasarli* created a life-sized sugar bestiary to celebrate the circumcision of the Sultan's son.[59] By the fifteenth century, the English were serving *sotelties* at the coronation banquet for Henry VI, to which John Lydgate composed explanatory verses.[60] In 1562, Queen Elizabeth received a marzipan model of St. Paul's Cathedral in miniature.[61] Subtleties could be constructed from sugar plate, sugar paste, and marzipan, and by the late sixteenth century were not confined to aristocratic households. Following the first printed recipe for sugar paste in English, Girolamo Ruscelli's *The Secretes of the Reverend Maister Alexis of Piedmont* (1558), John Partridge, Gervase Markham, and Hugh Plat all offered instructions for creating sugar and marzipan sculptures in their household manuals directed at discerning and upwardly mobile gentlewomen.[62]

The connection between early modern sugar subtleties and poetry is not merely an associative one; it is also medicinal and material. Sugar was believed to enhance the mind as well as the body. According to Pliny and Dioscorides, sugar helped settle stomach ailments.[63] By the early modern period, sugar was believed to cure a cold, eliminate gas, stimulate the sex drive, and sharpen the wit. Apothecary shops were stocked with *Manus Christi* (gold-leafed rosewater sugar lozenges for colds), candied eryngo root (aphrodisiacs), and even *Saccharum Tabulatum Perlatum*, which according to Ivan Day was a pill composed of "crushed pearls, gold leaf and boiled sugar" used for "cooling and comforting the heart."[64] According to Richardson, *Manus Christi* was reputed to harness sugar's miraculous healing power, and this was reflected in its name ("hand of Christ") as well as the precious materials included in its preparation: "There was a strong belief that flakes of gold and silver, or even crushed gemstones, would prove medicinally efficacious in most circumstances," Richardson writes, though he is quick to remind us that such confections were reserved for the extremely wealthy.[65]

John Marston mocks these confections in his satirical court comedy *The Malcontent* (1602), when an old procuress named Maquerelle proffers a sugary aphrodisiac to Bianca, the lowborn, young wife of an elderly courtier named Bilioso. This confection is a miniature map of exotic ingredients:

seauen and thirtie yelkes of *Barbarie* hennes egges, eighteene
spoonefulles and a halfe of the iuyce of cockesparrow bones, one
ounce, three drammes, foure scruples, and one quarter of the sirrop
of *Ethiopian* dates, sweetned with three quarters of a poond of pure
candide *Indian Eringos*, strewed ouer with the powder of pearle of
America, amber of *Cataia*, and lambe stones of *Muscouia*.[66]

Maquerelle calls the sugar pill a "prettie pearle," visually connecting sugar to semiprecious gems and white Barbary sugar to oriental pearls from Bahrain and Sri Lanka. New World pearls are an ingredient in the concoction as well, further conflating one imported substance with another. As another court lady, Emilia, attests, such sugar pills were thought to sweeten the speech as well as the breath: "By my troth *I* haue eaten but two spoonefulls, and me thinkes I could discourse most swiftly and wittily alreadie."[67] This belief that sugar had the power to enhance speech is mocked in Johnson's satire *Poetaster*. The would-be poet Crispinus has a terrible sweet tooth and is nearly hauled off to prison for defaulting on his apothecary's bill, which is for "sweet meates" (3.1.162 and 3.3.26).[68] Begging for some respite from his debt, Crispinus addresses everyone who might help him as "sweet" as if the sugar had migrated into his speech.[69] When Captain Tucca finally bails him out, Crispinus promises to repay the captain with verse, converting sugar into poetry. Crispinus's taste for candied sweets is tied to his mistaken belief in sugar's power to enhance his literary skill. In this city comedy about talentless aspiring poets, Jonson satirizes sugar as both substance and metaphor: as an expensive imported commodity that can lead to penury and tooth rot, sugar is an urban vice. And as an epithet for pretty poetry, sugar can be misconstrued and abused by would-be writers hoping for a shortcut to literary excellence and fame.

The practice of making sugar plated subtleties had much in common with printing. Sugar was made into malleable paste with gum tragacanth, called "gum dragon" in early modern recipe books, a mucilaginous gum from the Middle Eastern *Astragalus* plant, similar to gum arabic, used as a binding agent in ink.[70] Gum arabic was also employed in confectionery, in the production of rock candy and of comfits (seeds and spices coated with colored, molten sugar). As Mason points out, gum was useful to confectioners because it enhanced sugar's malleability and preservative capabilities so that it "could be modeled like clay, dried, and kept indefinitely."[71]

Pressing sugar into molded shapes was called "printing" and sugar molds "prints," as this recipe for "Walnuts Artificial" reveals: "take seared sugar, and Cinnamon . . . work it up into a paste, print it in a mould made like a walnut shell."[72] Today, we have returned to the notion of the process of forming three-dimensional molded replicas as "printing" with the patented invention of 3D printing machines, which digitally scan any object, producing solid three-dimensional plastic replicas of them, though the machines "print" using a process of digital layering, rather than creating and pressing plastic into a mold.[73] In early modern England, sugar was molded into alphabets to make "faire capitall Romane letters."[74] And, as Fumerton reminds us, it was also inscribed with words in verse.[75] The cast sugar "walnuts artificial" that appear in W. M.'s *The Queen's Closet Opened* (1655), along with the walnut posies from the earlier *A Closet for Ladies and Gentlewomen* (1608), were frequently filled with slips of paper bearing brief poems and mottoes, early modern precursors to fortune cookies, "that when you cracke it, you shall find . . . a prettie Posey written."[76]

Shaping Sugar and Poetry in Puttenham's *Arte*

George Puttenham's *The Arte of English Poesie* includes these sugary graphic shapes and writings—in his list of poetic forms: "There be also other like epigrams that were sent usually for New Year's gifts or to be printed out or put upon their banqueting dishes of sugar plate, or of marchpane, and such other dainty meats as by the courtesy and custom every guest might carry from a common feast home with him to his own house, and were made for the nonce" (146). According to Puttenham, such sugar plated poems derive from the ancient Greek and Roman forms *nenia* and *apophoreta* but in English are called *posies*. In Puttenham's narrative, these *posies* are in turn appropriated by the English as "devices in rings and arms and about such courtly purposes" (146). Sugary posies belonged to the larger category of confectionary sculpture known as *subtleties*. Recipes for sugar subtleties abound in trickery, not only deceiving the senses into taking sweet for savory (as in a sixteenth-century recipe for marzipan bacon) but also bitter for sweet. Gervase Markham's *The English Huswife* sandwiches a recipe for "wormwood water" between recipes for cinnamon and sugar waters. As Elizabeth Spiller notes, the authors of early modern culinary books of secrets considered sugar a substance "not quite *of* nature, but rather to be used *on* nature."[77] Thus, sugar and marzipan could be said to contain the transformative power of art in the early modern sense of craft and artifice. They also have much in common with the transformative powers of figurative language. Sugar was more than a sweetener; it was a spice, a medicine, an artistic medium, and a powerful tool of material transformation and manipulation.

Puttenham's description of sugar plate poetry, read alongside Cavendish's ekphrastic depiction of Wolsey's subtleties' *proporcion*, suggests a vivid material connection between sugar and poetry in the early modern imagination. This is furthered by Puttenham's frequent use of the word *sweet*, which appears forty-seven times, and more powerfully with *subtlety* (spelled in some instances *subtilitie*) throughout his poetic treatise. *Subtlety* appears eighteen times in the full text of the *Arte*, followed by eight instances of *subtle* and one of *assubtiling*. Puttenham places sweetness beside subtlety in his description of the queen as the consummate English poet: "last in recital and first in degree is the Queen, our Sovereign Lady, whose learned and delicate muse easily surmounteth all the rest that have written in her time or since, for sense, sweetness, and subtlety" (151). These three categories, "sense, sweetness, and subtlety," might be describing a sugary early modern banquet of the senses as much as they describe the queen's meaning, elegance, and wit. Though Puttenham does not directly refer to sugar sculptures in his use of *subtlety*, his fascination with poetry that could be shaped or molded or turned into a witty inscription or written in sugar suggests a deeper connection, which the text bears out.

In early modern English, the word *subtlety* meant also mental acuity, which frequently carried a negative connotation, indicating not only craftiness but guile and deception; it was not until the late seventeenth century that *subtlety* took on positive connotations of refinement.[78] Richard III, for instance, admits proudly that he is "subtle, false, and treacherous" (1.1.37), and the *Boke of Common Prayer* begs for deliverance from "those evyls, which the

crafte and subteltie of the devyll or man worketh against us" in the litany.[79]
It follows therefore that Puttenham should reappropriate the term *subtlety*
for his own poetic theory, which, like an elaborate subtlety crafted out of
sugar, depends upon harnessing rhetorical dissimulation and metamorphoses
of sense for the sake of art. Puttenham's *subtlety* is thus a virtue, not a fault,
and describes poetry that is clever and witty, involves some degree of wordplay,
and can be difficult or opaque. Puttenham's subtleties are not sugar sculptures,
but they are so much *like* sugar sculptures that early modern readers would
certainly have made this connection.

For Puttenham, the most subtle poetry is that which is the most deceptive
and fancifully wrought, playing tricks with the reader the same way that sugar
subtleties tricked and surprised viewers and tasters. This means that word
games like anagrams and witty mottoes—the same things Puttenham says
would be inscribed upon sugar plate or marzipan (146)—count as poems, and
these contain the highest degree of subtlety. Throughout the text, Puttenham
reveals the trick of wordplay in each of his poetic examples by showing where
its subtlety can be found: "the subtlety lieth not in the conversion, but in the
sense in this" (on the Ptolemaic anagram *apomelitos*, 196), or: "and the subtlety
lay in the accent and orthography of these two words" (219). Puttenham's description of the figure for obscure speech, *Noema*, is an example of this poetic
ingenuity "whereof we do not so easily conceive the meaning, but as it were by
conjecture, because it is witty and subtle or dark" (316). Poetic subtlety reaches
its highest density in two places in the *Arte*: first, in the analysis of emblems
and anagrammatic devices in Book II, "Of Proportion," and second in the
final discussion of poetic *sprezzatura* in Book III, "Of Ornament." This is no
coincidence: for Puttenham, both poetic form and style were highly ornamental and material.

Imperial mottoes, devices, and anagrams count as forms of poetry, all of
which have the power through their imagery and shape to keep subjects in
check. The device Puttenham singles out demonstrates a high degree of what
Puttenham calls "subtlety," or secret meaning. It is also the most exotic and
foreign, "that of the king of China in the farthest part of the Orient" (194):

> I could not forbear to add this foreign example to accomplish our
> discourse touching devices, for the beauty and gallantness of it,
> besides the subtlety of the conceit and princely policy in the use,
> more exact than can be remembered in any other of any European
> prince, whose devices I will not say but many of them be lofty and

ingenious, many of them lovely and beautiful . . . but that any of them be comparable with it . . . in my conceit there is not to be found. (195)

The emblem, Puttenham goes on to describe, depicts two snakes, twisted together, devouring one another's heads, "two strange serpents intertangled in their amorous congress, the lesser creeping with his head into the greater's mouth, with the words purporting *ama et time*, 'love and fear'" (194). Further, the emblem decorates the garments of the imperial court, "embroidered upon the breast and the back with silver or gold or pearl or stone, more or less richly according to every man's dignity and calling" (196). It is possible that Puttenham is correct in his understanding of how the Chinese imperial court used ornamental symbolism to enforce its ideology: surcoats bearing the circular and imperial "five-clawed" dragon medallion were worn by the Chinese royal family during the Ming dynasty (1368–1644), and though they were not jewel encrusted, the medallions were often made of gold-wrapped silk filaments.[80] These robes were also presented as gifts to foreign visitors from "tribute-bearing nations" to prevent invasion and increase trade, which suggests that European merchants and courts might have had such robes in their possession. Puttenham might well have seen or read a description of one.[81]

We need to suspend our disbelief if we are to imagine that the Chinese court was not only familiar with classical Latin mottoes and popular early modern emblems but also adopted them. But Puttenham appears to believe, or to want his readers to believe, that classical humanism extended even to the Far East and that the king of China was a good early modern humanist, using emblems ideologically, the same as early modern Europeans might. His *ama et time* is a foreign sibling to Elizabeth I's *video et taceo* ("I see and am silent"), a European emblem, not a Chinese one. The image of two serpents—vipers, usually—was a popular one in early modern emblem books, though not traditionally bearing Puttenham's motto of "love and fear." Its roots are classical at least: Pliny's *Historia Naturalis* states (erroneously) that the female viper bites off the head of the male during copulation.[82] It makes sense that Puttenham might use this emblem to describe "love and fear," given that the congress of the vipers represents a lethal combination of conjugal bliss and murder (another emblem, from Alciato, uses a viper courting a moray eel to depict marital bliss).[83] The choice of serpents for an emblem of incomparable subtlety is no accident, given the biblical associations of serpents with subtle craft in the period. Serpents feature in emblem books as representatives of subtlety itself, as in the emblem "*subtilite vaut mieulx que force*" in Gilles Corozet's *Hecatomg-raphie*.[84] Puttenham exports a well-known early modern emblem with classical roots, transplanting it to China, reassigning it a "strange" (194) East Asian origin, and imports it back into England to represent foreign subtlety. That the image and motto are lettered in gemstones suggests that the East has a definite material form for Puttenham, just as sugar plate verses sent as New Year's gifts do. These materialized words will become a pliable medium in his description of Turkish figured poetry, reinforcing their connection to sugar subtleties.

Puttenham's championing of "Chinese" *imprese* and his reworking of a classical theme as Asian demonstrate his predilection for foreign ornament that runs throughout the *Arte* and finds its lengthiest expression in the section on Ottoman figured poetry, which, unlike the Chinese king's Latin motto, Puttenham claims to have translated "word for word" (180) out of Turkish or Italian. As I hope to demonstrate, Puttenham's shaped Turkish poems have much in common with the subtlety of Asian devices, as well as with shaped sugar. He introduces the poems by creating a narrative account of his encounter with an Italian traveler: "But being in Italy conversant with a certain gentleman, who had long traveled the Oriental parts of the world, and seen the courts of the great princes of China and Tartary . . . I being very inquisitive to know of the *subtleties* of those countries, and especially in matter of learning and of their vulgar poesy, he told me that they are in their inventions most witty … and therefore when they utter any pretty conceit they reduce it into metrical feet and put it in form of a lozenge, or a square, or other such figure" (180, emphasis added). Like sugar, the poetry that is most foreign and imported is the most valuable. Like Puttenham's description of posies that are written on sugar, it is a "pretty conceit." And like sugar, this kind of poetry is malleable and can be "reduced" or refined, then sliced or molded into numerous geometric shapes.

The various forms of figured poetry are reproduced first as a table of blank geometric shapes run through with lines like notepaper, each one labeled and each one inverted (181), and next as individual poems (182–88).[85] The left page (see Figure 2) with its cut-out shapes resembles the pages of shaped sugar designs that one might find in an early modern book of secrets or a culinary manual.[86] By including hand-drawn illustrations of his figures (one of which, the "pyr" or pyramid, comes from Egyptian sources), Puttenham demonstrates the plasticity of this verse form. His fascination with the different ways these poems can be opened up or turned inside out into mirror images, "displayed" (181) and "rabbetted" (181), is echoed by early modern recipe manuals extolling the adaptability of sugar. As Jennifer Summit reminds us, Puttenham's audience was composed of educated court ladies and the queen, and so it makes sense that the craft represented here should have much in common with confectionery, which, as Wendy Wall and Kim Hall have shown, was considered an early modern woman's art.[87]

Puttenham's fascination with creating an oriental origin for pattern poetry reveals how Puttenham privileges contemporary global forms over ancient classical ones, an atypical move for an early modern English poetic theorist, and possibly the reason why Jonson—a writer who favored classical Greek and Latin models above others—read his Puttenham so assiduously, with pen in hand.[88] Puttenham's choice of global over classical becomes clearer in Book III, "Of Ornament," in which he compares figurative poetic ornament to rich garments decorated with precious pearls and gold, and to miniatures painted with "orient colors" (222), presumably costly pigments made from crushed ultramarine lapis, cochineal (carmine), and cinnabar. Puttenham's Turkish figured poems embody his ornamental poetics literally, supposedly originating as exotic, far-fetched ornaments themselves. In order to show how poetic language is *like* rubies and pearls, Puttenham imagines poems physically constructed from the same materials.

The Turkish pattern poems take printed shape in italic typeface, as Puttenham's figured verse blossoms into diamonds, inverted triangles, pillars, and spires, just as sugar might blossom into these shapes on a banqueting table. There are Greek shaped poems that might easily have served as Puttenham's originals, such as those found in the *Greek Anthology* (central to Renaissance lyric), which saw many translations into Latin, Italian, French, and English.[89] As Susan Stewart notes, the work of Ernst Robert Curtius links Hellenistic pattern poetry to Persian calligraphic poems.[90] But Puttenham chooses to argue that the highest number of pattern poems is to be found not in ancient Greece or Persia but in contemporary, sixteenth-century Ottoman Turkey: "I find not this proportion used by any of the Greek or Latin Poets, or in any vulgar writer, saving of that one form which they call *Anacreon's egg*" (180). Puttenham mistakenly ascribes ancient Greek shaped poems by Simmias of Rhodes to Anacreon, a different poet featured in the *Anthology*.[91] In other words, instead of locating figured verse in classical Greek poetry, Puttenham situates the birthplace of figured verse in the Muslim East, roughly the same place where sugar subtleties appear to have originated.[92]

The first pair of figured poems takes the shape of "lozenges" (182) or diamonds, which Puttenham states is "a most beautiful figure, and fit for this purpose" (182) of shaped verse. The pair, the first supposedly composed of topaz and diamonds and the second of emeralds and amethysts, illustrates the romance between the Tartar Emperor named Temir Cutzclewe (the great Tamerlane) and his beloved, the lady Kermesine (Figure 2, right).

The second set of poems, inverted triangles of blue sapphire and topaz (183), documents the pursuit of the lady Selamour by the Persian sultan Ribuska and Selamour's refusal. These examples emphasize poetry as an exchange of gifts. The only other example of poetry as a gift exchange in the *Arte* occurs in Puttenham's discussion of sugar plate and marzipan posies sent as New Year's gifts (146).[93] An early modern reader would have associated poetic gift exchange with verses inscribed or hidden in sugar (walnut posies).

Ottoman jeweled inscriptions were ubiquitous in the Turkish courts, especially on the walls of the palaces, and men and women in the sixteenth-century Ottoman Empire engaged in witty poetic exchanges.[94] But Puttenham's "transcriptions" translate the poems into the global language of early modern Romance: *Selamour* appears to possess an allegorical name (*seul amour*, only love), and the great adjoining kingdom of *Corasoon* is indeed a Turkish name (Khorasan was a well-known place in sixteenth-century Persia, now in Afghanistan), but it sounds and looks on the page remarkably like the Spanish word for heart, *corazón*.[95] The name *Kermesine* is in fact related to the Turkish word for red, *kırmızı*, which is also the Ottoman root of the English word *crimson*. Crimson grain beetles, or *kermes*, first produced in the Ottoman Empire, gave a scarlet stain to paint pigments, textiles, cosmetics, and food, producing the bright "orient colors" (222) on the painter's palette that Puttenham compares to poetic ornament in Book III. Crimson grains were also used in confectionary to dye comfits (sugar-coated seeds and spices) a brilliant red, rubbed into the lips to enhance their color, and treated as a spice alongside sugar. Recipes for cosmetics made with crimson grains frequently appear in the same books of recipes alongside those for sugar subtleties.[96] I will discuss the role of crimson in early modern Mediterranean mercantilism further in Chapter 5.

Crimson lips appear quite frequently as epithets in early modern amorous verse, and they also play a part in Puttenham's discourse on ornament when he compares poetic tropes to the judicious use of cosmetics, suggesting that misusing ornament is like putting lipstick on your chin: "the crimson taint, which should be laid upon a ladies lips, or right in the center of her cheeks should by some oversight or mishap be applied to her forehead or chin" (222). Puttenham underlines the exotic, strange nature of these poems only to

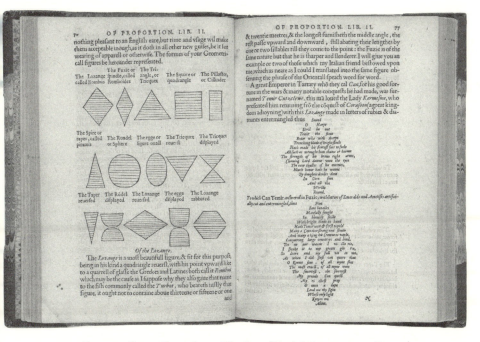

Figure 2. George Puttenham, *The Arte of English Poesie*, 76–77. By permission of the Folger Shakespeare Library.

familiarize them as Romance. Yet *seul amour, crimson*, and *corazón* do more than enhance the allegorical nature of these gem-like poetic exchanges: they also sweeten them with the language of early modern love poetry exchanged as sweet and pretty gifts.

Scholars have been routinely drawn to and puzzled by the shaped poetry that appears in Puttenham's *Arte*. Are they authentic Ottoman poems, a precolonialist, philo-Orientalist fantasy, or simply voguish French and Italian models made to appear as imports even more luxurious and even more foreign? Does it matter? Frank Whigham and Wayne Rebhorn, the editors of the modern critical edition of *The Arte of English Poesie* that I cite throughout this chapter, suggest that the poems' shapes as delineated by Puttenham's bare lines have more in common with popular early modern geometry textbooks and heraldry than with any real Asian imports.[97] Likewise, Henry Turner locates Puttenham's pattern poems in a larger poetics of patterned thinking about language, which he associates with the role practical geometry played in early modern cognitive processes.[98] Following the research of Margaret Church, A.

L. Korn attempted to uncover an oriental origin for Puttenham's poetry, and though he found numerous examples of verse written in the shapes of flowers and stars in medieval and early modern Persian manuscripts, Korn correctly notes that none of these calligraphic examples (all of them religious poetry) resembles the rigid geometric shapes of Puttenham's *fuzies*, *triquets*, and *pyrs*.[99] John Hollander makes this difference clearer, noting that Persian scribes would often simply "calligraph" a prewritten text into a given shape rather than compose poetry with a shape in mind.[100] Juliet Fleming[101] reads them as an orientalist fantasy that provides Puttenham with the chance to demonstrate the "thingness" of early modern English writing. These poems, when conceived of as jeweled letters, possess a heavy, material nature that brings us closer to understanding the way early moderns conceived of language and poetry as objects and artifacts, focusing more on the form, substance, and tangible surface of it than the abstract concepts that the words imparted. In a way, they are more literal than figural.

Susan Stewart takes up this idea of language as material in her examination of shaped poetry. Stewart calls pattern poems such as Puttenham's "objectlike or artefactual."[102] For Stewart, pattern poetry is distanced from sensory experience, removed as it is from bodies and voices. But Puttenham's pattern poems do, in fact, engage the senses, not only in his materialist description of these poems taking tangible form as inlaid gems, jewelry, and missives but because of their affinity with sugar lozenges, which were frequently gilded, mixed with crushed pearls, inscribed with verse, and passed from aristocratic hand to aristocratic hand and from finger to mouth.

Whether it came from the East or simply from France and Italy, figured poetry was all the rage in late Elizabethan England, so much so that in *Have with you to Saffron Walden* (1596), Thomas Nashe mocked Gabriel Harvery for indulging in this vogue, claiming that Harvey had been "writing verses in all kinde, as the forme of a paire of gloues, a dozen of points, a paire of spectacles, a two-hand sword, a poynado, a Colossus, a Pyramide, a painter's eazill, a market crosse, a trumpet, an anchor, a paire of pot-hooks, etc."[103] Needless to say, none of these figured poems apparently exists in printed or manuscript form. This is not to suggest that Harvey refrained from indulging in this literary fashion and that his poems were not lost to the sands of time, but Nashe's copious, Rabelasian list makes the poems themselves seem unlikely if not impossible.

What makes Nashe's list interesting are its far-fetched analogies: how can a poem form a "paire of spectacles"? The arbitrary range of images that Nashe attributes to Harvey's verse mocks and mimics the range of objects fashioned into banqueting stuff described by culinary authors like Plat, Partridge, Murrell, and Markham. Nashe's list of shaped poems is nearly identical to a list of subtleties appearing in Hannah Wooley's *Accomplisst ladys delight*: "Buttons, Beakes, Charms, Snakes, Snails, Frogs, Roses, Chives, Shooes, Slippers, Keyes, Knives, Gloves, Letters, Knots, or any other Iumball for a banquet quicklie."[104] Plat's word "Iumball" suggests the haphazard nature of this collection; like Nashe's list of made-up figure poems, it is simply a random pile of things. Nashe further belittles figured poetry's confectionary connections by concluding his list with a kitchen tool, "a paire of pot-hooks." According to the rules of early modern sugar plate sculpture, the more ridiculous and incongruous the item (marzipan bacon and eggs, for example), the more subtle and witty it was. Nashe's pot-hooks takes this paradigm to extremes, selecting an item that is as mundane as it is incongruous. Nashe's use of culinary terminology to mock figured poetry suggests not only that writers like Nashe made the connection between sugar posies and shaped poems but that some of them found such forms of poetry, like cookery, demeaning, even menial.

Puttenham's patterned Turkish verse would have been legible to early modern readers as models for jewels constructed from words and from pressed and molded sugar, given that sugar itself was cut and decorated to resemble jewels and treated in much the same way. Puttenham's Turkish figured poems take on familiar early modern shapes, shapes familiar not only to goldsmiths and jewelers but to anyone with access to household manuals (sometimes known as books of secrets) that included recipes for making sugar candies into shapes. The most familiar shape of candied sugar in the period was the lozenge, and based on the *OED*'s entry for *lozenge*, it is not entirely clear which came first, the sugar candy or the gemstone. From 1430 onward, a lozenge was a quadrilateral-shaped ornament employed by cooks to garnish a dish, whether sweet or savory.[105] But this meaning changed in the sixteenth century, when *lozenge* began to refer specifically to something made out of sugar, a piece of hard candy in the shape of a diamond.[106] Just as lozenges garnished dishes, so do Puttenham's visual patterns for poems ornament his printed treatise as illustrations. In this way, Puttenham represents poetic form ("proportion") as a kind of ornament, paving the way for his materialist interpretation of figurative language in Book III, "Of Ornament."

Popular with apothecaries (these are precursors of the cough drops of today, still referred to as lozenges) and with fancy confectioners, early modern recipes for lozenges emphasize the jewel-like nature of these confections, urging readers to decorate them with gold leaf and to color them with rose petals and crimson dyes. Partridge directs readers to decorate lozenges, here spelled *losings*, so that they resemble jewels: "Lay on your Golde leaf . . . cut your Losings [1627 Loosings] Diamonde fashion, and so keepe them."[107] Partridge and other authors of books of secrets frequently admonish their readers to "keepe" or preserve their hard candies, in other words, to store them in closed boxes, much the way early modern people stored their precious jewels and miniatures. As Fumerton convincingly demonstrates, jewels and painted miniatures were not so indistinguishable from sparkling, brightly colored sweets in early modern England: all were wrapped in paper, placed in pretty boxes, kept in cabinets, carried around, and presented as lavish gifts.[108]

Several scholars of the early history of sugar connect early modern confectionery even more closely with gemstones, jewels, and miniatures, suggesting to me that there was less distinction between jewels and sweets in early modern England than there is now. Mintz notes that the presentation of sugar sweets at a banquet involved surrounding them with precious materials: "Plain spices were passed about on gold and silver spice plates, filigreed and engraved with coats of arms and often jewel encrusted. . . . With them went the drageoirs, as richly decorated and as costly as the spice plates, but filled with sugared confections."[109] Fumerton takes this point further, revealing how the figurative language of early modern confectionary manuals reveals sweets designed to mimic exotic, imported jewels: jellies are "Chrystall" or "orient as a Rubie"; candied sprigs of rosemary "seeme to be couered with sparks of diamonds"; pancakes "looke as yellow as golde."[110] Like rubies, diamonds, and pearls, sugar was an exotic import, traveling to Britain's shores from the East. Sugar was also frequently mixed with real precious materials, like pearls and gold leaf in *Manus Christi*, making it nearly indistinguishable from gemstones.

Art and Nature

Puttenham's poetics depends upon a *sprezzatura*-like artifice: good poetry is all about cloaking one's artifice with the appearance of natural behavior. This is where *subtlety* in behavior becomes a virtue: "we do allow our courtly poet to be a dissembler only in the subtleties of his art; that is, when he is most artificial, so to disguise and cloak it as it may not appear, nor seem to proceed from him by any study or trade of rules, but to be his natural" (Puttenham, 382). Subtle poetic behavior resembles sugar subtleties that contain secrets to be unlocked, tricking and confounding the senses. Over the course of his treatise, Puttenham compares poetry to several different crafts or "mechanical arts" (222), many of which have corollaries in early modern culinary science. Although Puttenham does not explicitly include culinary artifice in his list of crafts with which he compares poetry, sugar sculpture haunts this list, as its artistry involves combining many of the crafts Puttenham does mention. As Jennifer Montagu has suggested, many of the same molds used for casting bronze in seventeenth-century Italy must have been reused to cast sugar sculptures.[111] Marble sculpture, which molded sugar subtleties imitate, appears in his discussion of the *Gorgeous* (333–35), along with woodcarving and gardening (also part of culinary cultivation) in the book's conclusion. In the opening chapter to Book III, "Of Ornament," Puttenham compares poetic artistry to two ornamental crafts, both of which deal with precious materials: "a Poet setteth upon his language by art, as the embroiderer doth his stone and pearl, or passements of gold upon the stuff of a Princely garment, or as the excellent painter bestoweth the rich Orient colors upon his table of portrait" (222). As I have shown, candied lozenges were wrapped in organza and displayed in embroidered boxes. They were also painted and decorated using the same natural pigments—rose petals, violets, crimson grain beetles, gold leaf—miniaturists used to limn their portraits.[112] It is not inconceivable that some portraits might have been done in sugar for a banquet. In other words, confectionery is the only art that—like poetry—imitates or accompanies each of the crafts Puttenham adumbrates.

I have compared Puttenham's imagined audience of court ladies to the aspiring household comfitmakers to whom Plat addressed his *Delights for Ladies*. Numerous instructional manuals on various crafts were available to early modern readers in print and in manuscript. Thomas Hilliard's manuscript *A Treatise Concerning the Arte of Limning* (1598–99) presented itself as a teaching guide to miniature painting, though painting miniatures must have been an elaborate fantasy for all but the most talented and wealthy gentlemen and women.[113] The crafts that Puttenham describes were exclusively for men, with only a few exceptions. Though most expensive embroideries were guild creations done by men, women were encouraged to embroider at home.[114] There were also few female miniaturists working in early modern England: Levina Teerlinc was a notable one.[115] Women were encouraged to pursue crafts that took place in the kitchen or the lady's closet: embroidering, preserving fruit, perfuming, and candying. Valuable, foreign, and new, sugar offered women a modicum of artistic possibility, the chance to create something clever and marvelous. By championing Queen Elizabeth as the quintessential English poet and addressing his audience as women, Puttenham's text could be read as a ladies' manual for poetry alongside Plat's or Murrell's housewives' manuals for confectionary.

Puttenham concludes his treatise by comparing his courtly poet to painters, sculptors, and gardeners:

> In that which the poet speaks or reports of another man's tale or doings . . . he is as the painter or carver that work by imitation and representation in a foreign subject. In that he speaks figuratively, or argues subtly, or persuades copiously and vehemently, he doth as the cunning gardener, that, using nature as a coadjutor, furthers her conclusions and many times make her effects more absolute and strange. (385)

Like the gardener who manipulates nature through bulb mutation, grafting, and cross-pollination, the poet creates something strange and artificial (figurative language) out of something natural (human speech). The poetic artistry Puttenham describes resembles early modern confectionery not only because it involves sculpture and painting but because it achieves effects both familiar and unfamiliar, English and exotic. Puttenham's extended simile of the poet as "painter or carver" blurs the distinction between poetic imitation and material transposition. Both poets and painters imitate. Painters—whether muralists or miniaturists—sculptors, and woodcarvers all find their designs "in a foreign subject" and proceed to copy it into their chosen media. To an artisan, "foreign" primarily means different types of media, a material different from the page on which the pattern is printed. But it could also indicate imported material, either in shape, such as an arabesque or an Italian grotesque, or in substance, such as crimson pigments, oriental pearls, Carrera marble, and sugar. A "foreign subject" (385) suggests Puttenham's demotion of Latinate rhetoric and promotion of Eastern ornamental poetic forms in the making of English poetry. By tying poetic imitation to artistic pattern transposition, Puttenham advises his readers to imitate poetically more in the practical manner of artisans than the cerebral manner of rhetoricians. They should trace patterns into their commonplace books rather than memorize tenets of style.

Puttenham has already provided his readers with empty patterns for Eastern figured poems that look like shapes cut out of lined writing paper. These "forms of your geometrical figures" (180) offer themselves to readers as blueprints for future application, like the printed arabesques, ornamental columns, facades, and antics of early modern pattern books or like the shapes used by confectioners to size and cut out lozenges of hardboiled sugar. Mason even suggests that sugar paste was used to mimic marble.[116] Like the elaborate designs in the "foreign" pattern books, out of which English painters, sculptors, and confectioners realized their work, Puttenham's English poetry strives to attain a stylistic identity apart from the ancients, defining itself precariously through other influences: far-fetched English names, Italian court culture, Turkish jewelry, medieval French romance. And to this catalogue we can surely add sugar subtleties.[117]

Coda: Puttenham's Global Model for Poesy

Puttenham's use of oriental shapes and the sugary metaphors of "sweetness, and subtlety" to destabilize classical poetry's authority is part of a larger project that continually privileges and upholds outlandish, foreign behavior and material artifacts as representative of English poetry. Puttenham conceives of poetry itself as an exotic import like sugar, something that comes from far away but takes root in the early modern English poetic landscape, allowing itself to be shaped and fashioned by English writers. Puttenham's poetic project is designed to augment sixteenth-century English reliance on Latin and Greek poetic models with "foreign subjects" (385) from the Mediterranean courts of Italy and Spain and the Asian courts of China and Turkey. In Book I, Puttenham's ancient genealogy of poetic kings is dominated by European rulers who are Moroccan, Egyptian, Persian, Hebrew, Spanish, and Arab (112). Puttenham repeatedly recommends the estrangement and hybridization of poetic language as part of his project to export poetry from the schools to the court, revealing a predilection for the outlandish over the normative classical models for poetry. This can be accomplished by composing poems pirated from Turkish engraved jewels and by rejecting Greek and Latin syllabic meters in favor of accentual verse and rhyme, which Puttenham derives not from medieval Europeans but from the Middle East and the New World: "the Hebrewes and the Chaldees" as well as "Peruvians" and Native Americans (99–100). It is also accomplished by translating familiar Greek and Latin rhetorical tropes into far-fetched English names (Book III). For example, Puttenham translates the Greek trope *metalepsis* into the English "far fetched" (267–68), which, rather than familiarize these classical rhetorical tropes, makes them seem even more outlandish. By the end of his treatise, Puttenham represents poetic (and courtly) decorum, contra Horace, as a paradoxical exercise in outlandish behavior.

Summit, Rebhorn, and Richard Helgerson acknowledge that Puttenham finds alternatives to Greek and Latin models in contemporary English poetry, though each critic finds Puttenham championing a different alternative model: for Helgerson, Puttenham rejects Latin and Greek models in favor of French and Italian court Romance; for Rebhorn, Puttenham recasts Latin rhetoric as outlandish and foreign;[118] and Summit finds that Puttenham's eschewal of Latin and Greek literary influences carves out a space for women's poetry.[119] Puttenham's references, direct and indirect, to the subtlety of sugar as an Eastern ornament serve as another of Puttenham's overwriting of classical poetic models. If we read Puttenham's allusions to sugar plate, subtlety, and (sugar) lozenges as early modern women's work, this supports Summit's reading of the *Arte* as directed at a female readership less interested in classical precepts and more in what an early modern Englishwoman could fashion with her hands and with what was accessible to her in her own household. Puttenham seems to be saying that both sugar and poetry are things a woman can make, empowering his female readership.

For Puttenham, poetic ornament distances itself from ordinary speech, alluring its readers and listeners with its otherwordly strangeness. Book III opens with a discussion of ornament as strange and foreign: "so is there yet . . . another manner of exornation, which resteth in the fashioning of our makers language and style, to such purpose as it may delight and allure as well the minde as the ear of the hearers with a certain novelty and strange manner of conveyance, disguising it no little from the ordinary and accustomed" (221). In the latter half of the sixteenth century, the adjective *strange* referred to faraway places and alien cultures.[120] Puttenham's "novelty" and "strange manner of conveyance" (221) can be found in his outlandish habit of importing Eastern stylistic figures into English verse. If for Puttenham, poetic ornamentation rests in making language "strange" through poetic figures, then these very figures conversely make the English language look "foreign" and even non-Western.[121]

By validating the Elizabethan notion of outlandish and foreign (Eastern) and valorizing ancient primitive rhyme against the familiarities of Greek and Latin pedagogy, *The Arte of English Poesie* does more than back warily away from classical poetic models: it antiquates Latin and Greek poetics so far as to make them appear outmoded.[122] Introducing his Turkish pattern poems, Puttenham claims to have translated them "word for word and as near as I could both the phrase and the figure" (180) and adds that they may seem discordant at first, "nothing pleasant to an English ear, but time and usage will make them acceptable enough, as it doth in all other new guises, be it for wearing of apparel or otherwise" (180). Here Puttenham acknowledges the difficulty of supplanting well-worn classical models with unfamiliar and new Ottoman ones but expresses a wish that the new Ottoman poems will become as well worn as classical verse models, in effect replacing occidental antiquity with an antiquity anticipated for oriental futurity.

PART II

Redeeming Ovid

Chapter 3

Publishing Pain: Zero in
The Rape of Lucrece

Remediating Ovid

In the previous two chapters, I have discussed how early modern English poetry came to be filled with verbal and figurative references to imported merchandise, including nonnative English words, that threatened to supplant,
destabilize, and undermine the status of classical poetry. But metaphors for
Levantine and Asian imports combined with their corresponding newly imported English words also could allow poets to represent ancient civilization
in a new (early) modern light. In this section of the book, I explore how these
imports, functioning as metaphors and as rhetorical devices, may have offered
alternative resolutions to the violent discourse of Ovidian metamorphosis that
early modern writers transported from the humanist schoolroom into their
adult writing. This chapter on Shakespeare's *Lucrece* and the one that follows
on *Venus and Adonis* examine how an associative early modern discourse that
included Arab and Turkish imports can be put to work to translate, adapt,
and remediate Latin poetry in order to revise and resolve the violent conflicts
and tragedies represented by Ovid in his *Fasti* and *Metamorphoses*. Because the
readings in this section trace early modern resonances of newly assimilated
English words through Shakespeare's poems, the arguments in these chapters
travel along the associative networks I uncover in each poem, so that their
force builds with the evidence of accruing associations rather than through
rational or empirical formulae.

Uncovering and following an imported word through a well-known
Shakespearean poem can feel a little dislocating, as the reading of the poem

reorients itself around a set of resonating words, images, and tropes. But this is my object: to read discontinuously, much as an early modern reader might have done, if we follow Peter Stallybrass's argument about early modern reading practices.[1]

The project of Ovidian revision established Shakespeare's reputation as a writer and paved the way for the transposition of Ovidian narratives onto the early English stage. His first tragedy, *Titus Andronicus* (Q1, 1594), makes great use of Ovid, remediating the story of Philomela for the stage, using the stage property of the book of the *Metamorphoses* as a surrogate tongue to speak for the raped and mutilated Lavinia. Not surprisingly, the play also informs its audience that Shakespeare is the author of that soon-to-be released smash hit poem, *The Rape of Lucrece*, published later that year, a poem cited three times in the play (2.1.109, 4.1.62–63, and 4.1.90), each in reference to Lavinia's chastity and subsequent rape.[2] The previous chapter opened with a brief discussion of Francis Meres's 1598 epigram on Shakespeare as Ovid reincarnated. In that chapter, I focused my attention on Meres's depiction of Shakespeare's more modern sonnets as "sugared," in order to highlight the difference between the ancient metaphor of honey for poetry and the early modern English metaphor of sugar. In the first part of the passage, Meres singles out the two classical epyllia *Venus and Adonis* and *Lucrece* as evidence that "mellifluous and honey-tongued" Shakespeare follows in Ovid's footsteps, giving life to the Roman poet's "sweet, witty soul."[3] Meres goes on to compare Shakespeare's dramatic talent to that of Plautus and Seneca, concluding by analogy that just as Epius Stolo claimed the muses would speak Latin by Plautus, so does Meres claim they would speak English by Shakespeare. In other words, Shakespeare is the early modern English amalgamation of any number of Latin *auctores*, but it is from Ovid that he gets his poetic voice.

As Meres makes clear, Shakespeare is not simply Ovid's heir or incarnation; he may have Ovid's soul, but the character of his writing is decidedly English (and early modern): "the Muses would speak with Shakespeare's fine filed phrase, if they would speak English." And for many readers, the changes Shakespeare makes to Ovid's stories are what define the English poet's reworkings of Ovid as early modern and English. Both *Venus and Adonis* and *The Rape of Lucrece* are much longer, more detailed versions of stories found in Ovid's *Metamorphoses* and *Fasti*. In each of them, Shakespeare makes a number of significant changes, increasing the disparity between Venus and Adonis by age and size, adding a long description of Adonis's erotically charged horse, replacing Ovid's tale of Atalanta to Venus's fable of Wat the Hare, and entering the traumatized consciences of both Tarquin and Lucrece. Shakespeare's formal transposition of these stories into iambic pentameter and *rime royale* (the same poetic form used for complaints) further converts Ovid's classical tales into a new early modern English genre. Some of the ways that Shakespeare revises and remediates Ovid are less obvious to today's readers, perhaps because the resonances of early modern words and metaphor have faded or changed over the past several centuries. For me, finding new Shakespearean revisions of Ovid entails reorienting each of the poems around an early modern English imported word or metaphor, words for Asian imports that have no Latin or Ovidian counterpart, and following these words associatively through the poem as an early modern reader might have done.

In this chapter, I investigate the enabling role that a particular Asian import (from India, the Arab world, Persia, and the Ottoman Empire), the cardinal number zero, O, or *cipher* as it was called in early modern England, plays in Shakespeare's Ovidian epyllion *The Rape of Lucrece*. There is no word for zero in Latin. Though ostensibly Ovid and Livy knew of the concept, it did not figure in Roman numerals or mathematics. But by the late sixteenth century in England, *zero* was a relatively well-assimilated Eastern import. Rather than disrupt or destroy the poem's vision of ancient Rome, the poem's Os, circles, zeros, and ciphers allow the poem discursively to liberate Ovid's heroine from her sentences of invisible evidence, silence, and death, supplying a voice for her in print. My argument therefore runs counter to Joseph Ward's recent reading, which positions Lucrece as a victim of rhetoric rather than as a rhetorician; I side instead with Lynn Enterline, who interprets Lucrece as finding agency in her suffering and proposes that Shakespeare gives his heroine not one voice but many.[4] Yet whereas Enterline argues that Shakespeare makes use of Ovidian ventriloquism, I find Shakespeare's poem looking past Ovid to the imported notion of the *cipher* or zero, newly available to English writers because newly available *in English*, which helps his text redeem Lucrece's shameful death and rescue her from silence by giving to her rape a graphic habitation and a sign.[5] The poem's many written Os, zeros, and cryptic ciphers also give the poet a chance to out-Ovid Ovid, by offering both his heroine and his readers an alternate and perhaps more satisfying ending to the tragedies of sexual violence and control that they were forced to confront (and, if we agree with Enterline, to embody and perform) as children in the Latin grammar schools. Shakespeare's poem offers his readers a chance to experience a more heroic Lucrece, whose honor is, if not fully recuperated, at least published and partially redeemed through the figure of the cipher. Though many readers would argue that it is Shakespeare's psychological humanizing of Lucrece and Tarquin that makes this poem distinctly English and early modern, I want to suggest that it is paradoxically the incorporation of an imported Asian concept, word, and image that defines this poem's early modern Englishness, especially if we view early modern English literary culture as increasingly and aggressively global and cosmopolitan.[6] An early modern understanding of zero as a mathematical import imbues the graphic shape of Lucrece's violation and pain (O and o) with added meaning, giving testimony and evidence to her rape, while elevating her silent suffering to material textual status that can be printed, reproduced, and circulated. In effect, Shakespeare's poem ultimately anticipates and celebrates its own participation in the printing and circulation of English poetry.

Zero as Mediator

Zero and arithmetic were brought to Europe by Italian merchants who learned them from Persian and Arab merchants on the Silk Road, as the mathematical historian Brian Rotman has revealed.[7] Although Italian merchants introduced the Arabic numerals into Europe in the thirteenth century, zero and Arabic arithmetic did not fully replace Western methods of calculation until the sixteenth and, in England, the seventeenth centuries. Before the introduction of zero, merchants had no way of graphically representing bankruptcy or a negative balance, and double-entry bookkeeping was not possible. Zero changed the early modern mercantile economy, and since it was employed first and primarily by medieval merchants, the early modern English word for zero, *cipher*, retains oriental and mercantile associations in early modern texts. Like the concept of zero, the English word *cipher* derives from Middle Eastern languages. The Semitic etymology of *cipher* is found in the Arabic word *sifra* (number) and today informs the modern Hebrew word *sefer* (book).[8]

Rosalie Colie has taught us that *nothing* was frequently utilized in Elizabethan literature as a philosophical paradox, the physical presence (a mark on a page) that indicated absence.[9] This paradox is augmented by the way in which zero worked in Renaissance arithmetic and mercantile economics. Standing alone like an empty "O," zero marks the space taken up by nothing. However, when it appears to the right of a numeral, it indicates a multiplication by ten, increasing exponentially with each place to the right. In Bruno Latour's actor-network theory, mediators change and renegotiate social infrastructures through innovations in their own material structure.[10] Over the course of this book, I have been discussing the way that foreign imports entering early modern England from mercantile trade with the Near East (the Ottoman Empire, central Asia, and North Africa) function as cultural mediators, changing the way people do business, make things, and write poetry. Their figurative presence in poetry often turns poetry itself into a mediator, allowing late Elizabethan writers to adapt and reconfigure the classical past in the language of contemporary global trade. Inkhorn terms and imported words are mediators, augmenting and reconfiguring English vocabularies, allowing writers like Nashe, Harvey, and Jonson the linguistic agility to make use of them as well as the chance to criticize them, along with England's expanding global economy. Sugar changed not only how sweetness was valued, produced, and shaped but also how writers conceived of poetry. Unlike sugar, but more similar to words, zero was a concept, not a commodity, and it was immaterial. Nevertheless, zero was also a mediator, and its mediating structure lay in its interplay between abstraction and materiality.

Materially speaking, zero has no substance: as an idea, even as a technology, it is an abstraction; it describes something that is not. And yet what makes zero conceptually unique is the way its graphic, material textuality communicates its conceptual lack: the ability to make a mark on a page, a circle that circumscribes emptiness, offers zero a material presence from which we can infer absence. Zero's material paradox is what makes it a mediator; once merchants could indicate a zero sum balance, they could conceive of a negative balance. The European mercantile economy would never be the same. And neither would early modern poetry: zero both conceptually and graphically (as O) helped poets write about absence and loss. Zero helped Shakespeare's narrative poetry remediate the classical past: by populating his poem with images of nothing, Os, circles, and holes, Shakespeare is able to represent something invisible and unspeakable (rape) with proliferation. This ultimately allows his heroine to speak without speaking, giving her a graphic, textual vehicle with which silently to publish Tarquin's crime. I do not mean to imply that Shakespeare was fully aware of all of zero's Eastern connotations and implications within his own poem, nor that he intentionally placed ciphers and Os all around Lucrece's rape deliberately to solve the problems of Ovid's tale. Instead, I am suggesting that attending to the presence of all the zeros, Os, and ciphers in the poem can lead us to a deeper understanding of how Shakespeare revises Ovid and transforms Lucrece into a legendary heroine. Reorienting Shakespeare's poem around the web of associations between zero, nothing, O, printing, ciphering, and deciphering is partly an experiment in inhabiting an educated early modern reader's mind. Each of these connections constitutes an associative link in zero's global philological network, links that an early modern reader might have formed himself or herself in reading the poem.

The Fluidity of O

In early modern printed books, zero enjoyed more semantic fluidity than it does today, functioning as both a numeral (a *figure*, in sixteenth-century English) and a letter, represented by a circle drawn around an empty white space: O.[11] This means that we can read references to zero in empty circles and the letter O in early modern texts, as writers and printers had yet to create a separate type for zero that distinguished it from the letter O or a circle. It also figured in sixteenth-century typographical and arithmetic treatises as a foreign, Arab import. Zero appears as both an Arabic letter and a number in *Champfleury*, Geoffroy Tory's 1529 illustrated treatise on the graphic proportion of the Roman alphabet. Tory concludes his book with a series of ornamental typefaces and foreign alphabets. The final letter of Tory's Arabic alphabet is not an Arabic letter at all but a quasi-circular figure (more of an oval) that Tory labels *nulla* in the accompanying text.[12] It appears in the bottom left-hand corner of Figure 3.

Reading this alphabet in the Arabic order as Tory advises, right to left, top to bottom, places an ovoid figure at the very end. However, *nulla* is one of the Latin words for nothing, which suggests that the circular symbol also represents the Renaissance symbol for zero. Tory grounds his argument about the proportion of Roman lettering on the perfection of the circular letter O, but nowhere in his text does a comparison between the letter O and the number zero arise. The only evidence of zero's presence and its resemblance to O lies hidden in the back of Tory's book in a non-Western alphabet.

Embedding the Latin word for nothing and the circular zero in an Arabic alphabet in a Renaissance printed book collapses three categories relatively new to Renaissance Europe—printing, imported language, and arithmetic—into one space. There is also evidence suggesting that Renaissance typesetters used the letter O to represent zero: the Italian mathematician Picinelli, writing in the late seventeenth century, described zero as a figure that functioned "either arithmetically or grammatically."[13] The conflation of the imported Arabic figure zero and the Roman letter O in Renaissance printed books and poetry

Figure 3. Persian, Arabic, and Chaldaic letters. From Geofroy Tory, *Champfleury* (Paris: Tory, 1529), 180. Courtesy of the United States Library of Congress.

emphasizes the cipher's physicality and paradoxical productivity. *The Rape of Lucrece* draws on this convergence by depicting the aftermath and legacy of rape as a proliferation of spoken, written, and embodied Os.

Rotman points out that in late sixteenth-century England, Roman and Arabic numerals were used simultaneously for different functions, including book pagination, account keeping, and itemization as well as monetary pricing: "[Shakespeare and Jonson] wrote their plays at the historical point of transition between two methods of writing down monetary accounts: when the new Hindu numerals based on zero and the traditional abacus-based Roman ones about to be ousted by them existed, briefly, side by side."[14] Perhaps this explains why Tory might relegate the O-shaped figure for zero to the Arabic alphabet but give it a Latin name. *Nulla*'s appearance at the end of Tory's Arabic alphabet further suggests that it is a zero: Tory was a printer, and zero occupies the last place in an early modern printer's case of letters and numerals, which proceed from "a, b, c" to "1, 2, 3, 4, 5, 6, 7, 8, 9, 0."[15]

Though Tory gives zero an Arab provenance, he also transforms it from a numeral into a letter.[16] And the Arabic word for zero is *sifra*, not *nulla*. Why should Tory confuse a numeral with a letter? Tory's Arabic symbol points to a semantic and material slippage between the letter O and the number o in Renaissance printed texts. Renaissance printers did not employ different typefaces for zeros, making O and o indistinguishable on the page.[17] Zero is further Westernized by the hollowness of the O. Arabic numbering represents zero not as an O but as a filled in circle or a solid point, so the original Arabic mathematical symbol when Westernized took the form of a European letter.[18] Consigned to the final pages of Tory's treatise on Western lettering, this little symbol illustrates zero's relative newness in Western culture.

In late sixteenth-century English, the Latin word *nulla* would have been translated into *cipher* (variants *cypher*, *cifer*, and *ciphre*) and represented on the page with the letter O.[19] The word *cipher* came into English in the Middle Ages, but its meanings shifted and expanded in the sixteenth century with the advent of moveable type and the popularity of arithmetic manuals like Robert Recorde's book *Arithmeticke, or the Ground of Artes*, which was reprinted 45 times between 1543 and 1700.[20] Bruno Latour's mediators can only be capable of transforming cultural value when something changes in their material structure, and intermediaries indicate that transformation. Though the concept of nothing had always existed, zero's role as both mediator and intermediary was cemented in sixteenth-century printing houses and arithmetic manuals. Once nothing had a material presence as a mark on the page, zero became both an indicator of value (or lack) and an embodiment of that lack.

Like the concept of zero, the polysemia of the word *cipher* was an innovation in sixteenth-century English: *cipher* could mean a cryptic symbol, a heraldic crest, the letter O, nothing, and a zero. Elizabethan and Jacobean lexicons do not agree on how to define *cipher*. Though many, like John Barrett, refer to its non-Western origins, others emphasize the visual ambiguity of the sign: Recorde's treatise states that a *cipher* "is made lyke an O," and Henry Cockeram's 1623 dictionary omits *cipher*'s mathematical value as nothing entirely, describing it as "a circle in Arithmetique, like the letter (o)."[21] Though Cockeram mentions "Arithmetique," he does not explain what zero represents. Robert Cawdrey's lexicon defines the cipher mathematically as "a circle in numbering, of no value of it selfe, but serveth to make up the number, and to make other figures of more value."[22] Thus, when the Fool declares that Lear is "an O without a figure" (*King Lear F*, 1.4.183), he is suggesting that without Lear's title and his lands, the king has become a physical nothing with no capability to add value, a zero rather than a 10.[23] Though the prologue to *Henry V* (1600) contains perhaps the most famous Shakespearean use of *cipher*, *The Rape of Lucrece* (1594) predates the performance and publication of *Henry V* by six years and contains not one but three uses of *cipher*.[24] All three represent a form of writing and occur at crucial dramatic moments in the poem, when Tarquin contemplates violating Lucrece, when Lucrece imagines the rape writing itself on her body, and when Lucrece confronts her inability to have foreseen the rape by examining a painted wall hanging of the Trojan War. And in all three instances, *cipher* is used as a verb, "to cipher," meaning to write cryptically, and to mark with a zero. The three verbal appearances of *cipher* are only part of a larger network of images, shapes, and figures: the poem is replete with graphic and nonverbal references to zero.

In *The Rape of Lucrece*, zero in all its early modern semantic plasticity—as O, circles, nothingness, and cryptic ciphers—is inextricably linked with rape. Despite the fact that rape leaves no mark on the body of a married woman, in Shakespeare's poem, rape writes itself on Lucrece's and Tarquin's faces, contorts Lucrece's body into both a secret cipher and a zero, and publishes streams of Os in its wake, not only on the page but in the hollow, windy cries that echo through Lucrece's body afterwards.[25] Tarquin's tyrannical attempt to silence Lucrece backfires. The knowledge of the rape surfaces repeatedly throughout the text in circular and cryptic ciphers, configuring Lucrece's body as a succession of Os and as a secret text that constantly reveals itself. The many senses of *cipher* in the poem—to embody absence, to suggest a mercantile economy, to multiply, to signify cryptically, and to generate meaning—combine with imagery of circular figures to demonstrate that rape, like murder, "will out," in this case profusely, productively. Moreover, by making Lucrece the author and publisher of this plethora of ciphers, the poem dissolves the tawdry Renaissance commonplace that compares a woman's body and genitalia to a nothing or an empty O: *this* woman's body is productive, generative, and will not stop until its story of violation is told.[26] Unlike Ophelia's voiceless body, which represents, according to Elaine Showalter, "the cipher of female sexuality to be deciphered by feminist interpretation," Lucrece's body and speech decipher themselves.[27]

Ciphering Lust

Each time the image of a circle, an O, or the word *cipher* appears in *The Rape of Lucrece*, it indicates an imagined, embodied inscription.[28] Circles, zeros, and ciphers figure prominently in the poem as emblems of Tarquin's bodily lust, as inscriptions marking faces, as ink circling bodies, and as wind whistling through opened mouths and empty bodily cavities. Tarquin's incendiary lust for power takes the form of cryptic circles. As the first stanza narrates Tarquin's galloping away from the siege of Ardea and toward Colatium to seduce Colatinus's famously chaste wife, Tarquin's tyrannical desire is hidden and invisible to the naked eye like cryptic cipher, a "lightless fire / Which in pale embers hid, lurkes to aspire" (4–5).[29] His lust is also a circular ring of flames that will soon encircle, or "girdle with embracing flames" (6), Lucrece's waist. While this image appears to be the physical reverse of rape—an encircling rather than a penetration—it is important to note that rape in this poem is characterized both as penetration (inscription) and as encirclement. Tarquin's desire is both "trustlesse" and "false," suggesting that it is not lust that motivates him but power.

When Lucrece encounters him, Tarquin's "false desire" is well concealed. He craftily hides this "base sin" in "pleats of Maiestie" (93). "Pleats of Maiestie" signifies both folded cloth concealing an object and rhetorical pleas. Like his carefully modulated speech, Tarquin's eyes will not offer up a clear reading of his intent to Lucrece: they are placeholders for something more sinister, like mathematical ciphers symbolically standing in for nothing. On top of this, they brim with arcane figures:

> But she, that neuer cop't with straunger eies,
> Could pluck no meaning from their parling lookes.
> Nor read the subtle shining secrecies,
> VVrit in the glassie margents of such bookes,
> Shee toucht no vnknown baits, nor feard no hooks,
> > Nor could shee moralize his wanton sight
> > More than his eies were opend to the light. (99–105)

The "straunger eies" (99) and "parling looks" (100) suggest that Tarquin is gesturing or speaking ("parling," from the French *parler*) in a foreign tongue. Tarquin's lust is ciphered not because it is hidden in pleats of majesty but because it appears *straunge* (foreign) and thus untranslatable to Lucrece. Tarquin's "straunger" eyes (also a pun on *ayes*) seem like books filled with ciphers or strange symbols ("subtle shining secrecies") appearing as marginalia ("in the glassie margents") that Lucrece cannot decipher. As I explained in Chapter 2, one kind of *subtlety* was a crafty, elaborate, and deceptive conceit, often sculpted from sugar and enjoyed sensually at a banquet. As they dine, Tarquin offers Lucrece the chance to taste figurative sweet, delicate *subtleties* of sexual pleasure with his eyes, but she is too chaste to recognize them as a sensual dish. These secrets may shine, but they challenge Lucrece to unravel their meaning. "Such books" glistening with open secrets puts us in mind of Renaissance illuminated texts containing arcane marginalia, perhaps pornographic references; "glassie" (102) is thus also *glossy*.[30] *Glossy* indicates the shiny black ink of printing or even the shiny sizing (made from alum and gelatin) with which printers treated the paper. The most popular printed text in the sixteenth century to contain arcane ciphers in its margins was the *Corpus Hermeticum*, printed in John Harvey's English translation in 1583.[31] John Dee's *Monas Hieroglyphica* (1564) concludes with a Latin motto that states, "Here the vulgar eye will see nothing but Obscurity and will despair considerably."[32] Another widely popular printed book filled with enigmatic symbols was the erotic dream vision *Hypnerotomachia Poliphili*, part of which was printed in English translation in 1592, two years before the first printing of *Lucrece*. The *Hypnerotomachia*'s narrator Poliphilo is as much sexually titillated by indecipherable architectural symbols as he is by gossamer-clad maidens.[33] As marginal glosses in fancy printed books, Tarquin's veiled predatory eyes publish their secrets to the poem's readers by way of dramatic irony but remain closed to Lucrece.[34]

More than taking the forms of a ring of fire and cryptic eyes, Tarquin's surfeit of lust forces his honor to assume the value of zero in the early modern mercantile economy. A bankrupt balance, Tarquin's cupidity figures as a superfluous expenditure that leaves coffers empty and devoid of profit:

Those that much couet are with gaine so fond
That what they haue not, that which they possesse
They scatter and vnloose it from their bond,
And so by hoping more they haue but lesse,
Or gaining more, the profite of excesse
  Is but to surfet, and such griefes sustaine,
  That they proue bankrout in this poore rich gain. (134–40)

The key word in this stanza is "bankrout" (140). By pursuing the object of his lust, Tarquin will gain Lucrece but end up bankrupt of honor. Seeking to possess and ruin Lucrece, Tarquin neglects to preserve his good name, which he must "scatter and vnloose" (136). Bankruptcy is only possible with an understanding of zero, an ability to represent loss through a graphic sign. Tarquin's lust is only superfluous ("surfet," 139) if it has a negative balance, if it can also be imagined as something *less* than zero. Zero's presence in an early modern mercantile economy haunts this stanza, suggesting that honor can be stored (in a figurative bank) or pawned like a valuable textile or piece of jewelry. Like a merchant who assumes great risk with each ship ventured, Tarquin risks his reputation for a few moments of sexual dominance, "pawning his honor to obtaine his lust" (156). It is as if Tarquin-the-merchant has overloaded his ship with cargo and destined it to sink and make him bankrupt, indebted to others. Tarquin's sexual excesses will eventually nullify his honor, as the couplet of a previous stanza warns, substituting "wealth" hypothetically for lust: "Honor for wealth, and oft that wealth doth cost / The death of all, and altogether lost" (146–47). The wealth here is also Lucrece's chastity, doomed cargo from the outset to the end of the poem: she is the "vnlocked treasure" (16) and "rich jewel" (34) Collatine has accidentally set loose on the world by advertising her chastity; Collatine is the "hopeless Merchant of his loss" (1660). Here, Tarquin's lust indirectly figures as a line of zeros in a merchant's account book.

Marked Bodies and Faces

Even as it takes the form of cryptic, encircling ciphers, Tarquin's rape graphically reproduces itself by inscribing Lucrece's body with ciphers. As Tarquin and Lucrece each argue in turn for and against the future rape, the narrative itself dilates like a widening O, and for 200 lines, the action of the poem takes a back seat to rhetoric. The violent act of rape encircles, enfolds, and writes itself upon Lucrece's body, marking her with circles, Os, and ciphers. The poem represents rape as writing that immediately hides itself: rape "entombs" Tarquin's penis in Lucrece's labia, Lucrece in her curtained bed, and her screams in her head. In an image derived from Ovid's *Fasti*, Lucrece is compared to an innocent lamb and Tarquin to the wolf trespassing on the pasture: "The wolfe hath ceazed his pray, the poor lamb cries, / Till with her own white fleece her voice controld, / Intombs her outcrie in her lips sweet fold" (677–79). "Fold" describes three circular enclosures: a sheepfold for the innocent lamb, the enclosing ("intombs") of Lucrece's cries inside her mouth, and her forced open labia, the "lips soft fold." The comparison of Lucrece to a lamb enhances the material textual metaphor if (thanks to Michael Finlay and Jonathan Goldberg), we think of her innocent, lamb-like skin as the vellum onto which Tarquin's phallic pen is scraping and writing its brutal message.[35] Though in English, *pen* and *penis* are not etymologically linked, they are partial homophones and connected associatively by their elongated shape and penetrative motion.

Tarquin stifles Lucrece's screams by encasing her head in her inverted nightgown: "For with the nightlie linen that she wears / he pens her piteous clamours in her head" (680–81). The pun on "pens" indicates that Tarquin is simultaneously fencing (penning in) Lucrece like a lamb enclosed in a "fold" (679) and writing on her body. We can read this scene as a version of what Goldberg calls "the violence of the letter."[36] As Goldberg explains, early modern writing practices begin with the material and metaphorical linking of pens with knives and end with the pen or pencil (an English word related to Latin *penes* or penetrator) assuming a violent, phallic force. The knife shapes the quill and shaves the page; the quill in turn molds the hand into a knife that penetrates as it writes. The English word for pencil, which in the early modern period meant a small paintbrush, also constructed with a knife, derives not from Latin *penna* (wing) as pen does but from *penis* (tail) and is thus even closer, etymologically, to *penes*.[37] But Shakespeare modifies this; instead of the pen imagined as a penis, the *penes*/penis is imagined as a pen that writes a secret (invisible) mark onto a woman's body.

Circular faces figure as sites of inscription wrought by rape throughout the poem. Both Tarquin and Lucrece worry about whether their acts will be inscribed in enigmatic figures or "ciphered" in their faces, and Lucrece vandalizes the face of a figure in a painting (Hecuba) because like Tarquin, the painting has so effectively camouflaged (ciphered) the deceit of its depicted traitor (Sinon). Knowledge of the rape reproduces itself rampantly, ironically taking the place of the real outcome of sexual intercourse, progeny. Mimicking the exponential increase indicated by zero's placement to the right of a number, Lucrece's and Tarquin's shame will reproduce itself like a printed text. Hesitating on his way to raping Lucrece, Tarquin berates himself for lacking "true valour" (201) and not turning back.[38] Tarquin acknowledges that he is setting himself up for failure; his own lack of respect "is so vile, so base, / That it will liue engrauen in my face" (202–3). Tarnishing his family arms with a "loathsome dash," rape will mark his heraldic crest, invalidating his family's honor, "To cipher me how fondlie I did dote" (207). *Cipher* functions here as a verb; it both indicates and cancels: honor is still invoked on the shield, but the heraldic strikethrough blots it out.

Despite Tarquin's fears, his shame lives engraven on Lucrece's face, not his own, configuring her as a printed emblem. Railing against the approaching dawn, which will illuminate the loss of chastity she believes all (but Collatine) will see, Lucrece compares herself to an engraved book illustration. Her tears will carve shame into her face: "And graue like water that doth eate in steele / Vppon my cheeks, what helplesse shame I feele" (755). Lucrece's tears do not simply write on her face; they "graue," (754) like the marks aqua fortis (nitric acid) makes biting into copper to fashion an engraving. As a copper plate engraving, Lucrece's graven face less resembles a text than a picture or an emblem that even "the illiterate that know not how / To cipher what is writ in learned bookes" (810–11) will comprehend. By comparing herself to a printed picture, Lucrece metonymically links herself to the emblems of Lucretia that abounded in early modern English printed books. Expensive engravings of Lucretia, several based on drawings and paintings by Raphael and Parmigianino, could also readily be found in Renaissance books.[39] Two prolific sixteenth-century English printers employed woodcuts of Lucretia for their signatures. Thomas Berthelet, the court-appointed printer to Henry VIII, chose Lucretia as his printer's mark (Figure 4), as did Thomas Purfoote (Figure 5).

Both printers operated in Fleet Street under "The signe of the *Lucrece*," and there is some indication that Purfoote inherited the shop sign from Berthelet.[40] Purfoot's books bear three different Lucrece devices, two in a square with Lucrece in Italianate Renaissance dress and a third in an oval medallion with Lucrece in more classical garb.[41] In all three, Lucrece plunges a sword into her bosom. As Katherine Duncan Jones and H. R. Woudhuysen note in their Arden edition of Shakespeare's poems, the square Lucrece device opens a children's Latin-English dictionary printed in 1594.[42] They imagine a young early modern reader encountering the device and associating it with Latin humility and virtuous Roman suicide. But it might also warn of the violent and passionate stories the child is about to decipher. In fact, Purfoot's Lucretia device appears in several editions of John Withals's *Dictionarie of Latine and English for Young Beginners*, on both the first and final leaves of the book (the one pictured here is from the 1608 edition he printed for the bookseller Nathaniel

Figure 4. Printers' device
of Thomas Berthelet.
From Richard Sampson, *Regii
sacilliae decani oratio*
(London: Tho. Bertheleti, 1535).
By permission of the
Folger Shakespeare Library.

Figure 5. Printer's device of
Thomas Purfoot.
From John Withals,
*A Dictionarie in English and Latine
for children and yong beginners*
(London: Thomas Purfoot, 1608).
By permission of the
Folger Shakespeare Library.

Butter).[43] His oval Lucretia device also appears at the end of Purfoot's 1597 and 1608 editions of Claudius Hollyband's *The Italian schoole-maister*, furthering the connection between Lucrece and early multilingual literacy.[44]

Once inscribed, Lucrece fears she will become a text that even the illiterate can decipher. She begins to think that everyone can see her shame:

> The light will shew characterd in my brow,
> The storie of sweete chastities decay,
> The impious breach of holy wedlocke vowe.
> Yea the illiterate that know not how
> To cipher what is writ in learned bookes,
> Will cote my lothsome trespasse in my lookes. (807–12)

Shame "characterd" on Lucrece's forehead, perhaps physically as worry lines, will be so legible that even those incapable of parsing or "ciphering" texts will easily decipher the figures in her face. The word *character'd* is also telling as it suggests letters, numbers, or symbols, all of which would have been called *ciphers* in late sixteenth-century English. Reading her face like a picture, everyone will "cote" Lucrece's "lothsome trespasse" in her "lookes" (812). Modern editions of the poem modify *cote* to *quote*, which suggests a metamorphosis in illiterate picture-book readers, from uneducated masses to commonplace book-toting courtiers. Lucrece's shame publishes itself not only as an engraving in a printed book but as an epigram in a commonplace book. But the five editions published before 1616 have *cote*. In Elizabethan England, *cote* means to overtake or to surpass: Lucrece's readers have instantly grasped her secret before it is even out. *Cote* is also a homonym for *coat*, which suggests a heraldic coat of arms, connecting Lucrece with Tarquin's fantasy of an "engrauen" face and *bâton sinistre* (207). Finally, *cote* as *coat* may indicate covering up (cloaking) or inking over (coating). Like an inked etched plate, Lucrece's face is coated in guilt, ready to print her rape.

The ciphered forehead that Lucrece believes is indelible and legible is also an agent of publication. Lucrece's fear that everyone can decipher the secret of her rape reproduces itself further when she comes into contact with her maid and her messenger. In each case, her shame is so great that it reproduces itself on the face of her servants, proliferating silently through ignorant gesture. The maid has no knowledge of Lucrece's violation, and yet she sees her mistress crying and immediately begins to cry herself, marking her own face with watery Os: "Even so the maid with swelling drops 'gan wet / Her circled eyne" (1228–29). Salty tears inscribe the maid's face with ciphers, encircling her eyes. Eventually, Lucrece, who knows her maid is ignorant of the rape, describes the maid as "the poor counterfeit of her complaining" (1269), suggesting another kind of textual reproduction, whether an inscription or a printed or stamped image. Instead of tears, the "silly groom" (1345) of a messenger paints his face red, reproducing Lucrece's blushes. This causes Lucrece to redden even more violently, blushes multiplying between them: "The more she saw the blood his cheeks replenish, / The more she thought he spied in her some blemish" (1357–58). In both instances of weeping and blushing, Lucrece's shame silently publishes by transferring itself onto other bodies, marking them with tears and color.

Lucrece's face and the faces of her servants are not the only marked or ciphered faces in the poem. As she reads the painted wall hanging depicting the fall of Troy, Lucrece imagines inscriptions upon the faces of Greek heroes Ajax and Ulysses. So skillfully rendered, the hanging captures the warriors' sentiments in their facial expressions. The poem's use of *cypher* emphasizes the graphic way emotions write themselves onto circular faces; each hero's face is inscribed with his heart: "The face of eyther cypher'd eythers heart / Their face their manners most expressly told" (1396–97). The anaphora of "face" across both lines indicates a topical ambiguity: it is not clear whether Ajax's face is inscribed with his own heart or with Ulysses's (and vice versa). If the faces of Ajax and Ulysses contain or reveal one another's hearts, then the text imagines their historic loathing as a kind of intuitive preternatural sympathy visible on the painted faces of the heroes. And though these are faces inscribed with hearts, the syntax of the line hints at a further inversion—hearts inscribed with faces—that calls to mind the Elizabethan practice of examining autopsied murder victims' hearts for the names of their killers.[45]

Because they figuratively bear their hearts inscribed in their faces, the painted Ulysses and Ajax possess something Tarquin lacks. Tarquin's face before the rape, and the painting of Sinon that Lucrece encounters afterward refuse to offer up their true faces to Lucrece; she cannot decipher them. This, I would argue, is why she rends the painted hanging with her nails; it is in a knowingly futile attempt literally to open the picture up to meaning. Unique to this description of Ajax and Ulysses is that it is impossible for this painting literally to show their hearts "cyphered" onto their faces, unless the figures were painted symbolically with hearts above their brows, and even then such emblems would not necessarily be able to "tell their manners" so "expressly." What the painting represents visually—the heroic nature of these characters and their hidden, intuitive rivalry—the poem represents verbally. This moment of the poem speaking when the painting cannot expresses the larger function of ciphers throughout the poem, which is to reveal something that cannot literally be shown or discussed. Rape is a known, invisible secret to which Lucrece and the text eventually give (poetic) form and (material) shape.

In addition to faces, privities, mouths, and voices are also forced and scarred into visible and invisible Os in this poem. Rape invisibly marks Lucrece's genitalia, but the words of the text make it visible and copious: "O vnseene shame, inuisible disgrace, / O vnfelt sore, crest-wounding priuat scarre!" (827–28). The repeated double negative of "O vn-" supplemented by "in-" and "dis-" illustrates how Lucrece's shame resembles the inversion of zero: instead of something indicating nothing, here is absence insisting upon presence. Though the "crest-wounding priuat scarre" may refer to Collatine's invisible cuckold's horns, a "priuat scarre," "vnseene shame," and "vnfelt sore" also allude to Lucrece's vagina, her secret "nothing" invisibly bruised by rape.[46] Both the material text's Os and Lucrece's metaphors of hidden wounds produce an abundance of circular images. Though these marks are imagined and invisible, both the poem and Lucrece call them into being.

Tarquin's violating inscription forces Lucrece's mouth into O-like shapes that allow her agonized breath to escape the confines of her body. The poem refuses to reproduce Lucrece's muffled cries; nevertheless, the narrator apostrophizes at the end of the rape, "O that prone lust should stain so pure a bed" (684). Though the text withholds Lucrece's tortured "Os," it accompanies the description of the rape with the circular figure of a mouth's moan ("O!") in the narrator's words. In the lament that follows, Lucrece may already be thinking of her body as a zero when she exclaims, "But when I feared I was a loyal wife / So am I now, ô no that cannot be" (1049). The circumflex appears in the 1594 text, but subsequent editions add a comma to the phrase "O no, that cannot be," to suggest that Lucrece is correcting herself in mid-sentence: "But when I feared I was a loyal wife, / So am I now—O no, that cannot be": she is no longer a "loyal wife."[47] But when we read it without the comma, Lucrece herself as a raped wife is a "no" that "cannot be."

Marked Breath: Windy Os

To illustrate the wordless cries that fly from Lucrece's O-shaped lips, the text contains numerous printed Os, which may seem common in a Shakespearean dramatic text but function in this poem to show how rape in its aftermath becomes a repeated sound issuing forth from Lucrece's body. Neither letters nor numerals, these Os are pure expressions of emotion. They have, in Bruce Smith's words, a "semantic emptiness."[48] As Joel Fineman's reading of "O" in *Othello* and Colin Burrow's reading of the last stanza of *A Lover's Complaint* demonstrate, the material presence of repeated dramatic Os on a page of text registers as emotion that moves beyond language.[49] O is a visual representation of the sound and motion of breath, the image of air being pushed out. And as Renaissance thinkers associated breath and voice with wind, Lucrece's Os might be seen as expressions of wind moving through her body.[50] Early modern "O" expletives indicate the vocative case, the sense that one is calling out. Yet they are singular to English: the Latin vocative has so such exclamation, expressing address in the elongated vowel at the end of the noun (usually a long *e*, as in Julius Caesar's accusation, "*Et tu, Brute?*").[51] Thus, Lucrece's Os reveal another level to Shakespeare's project of Ovidian remediation, supplementing the original text's classical Latin with an English exclamation that, in this period, continually calls to mind an identical imported Arab numeral.

For early modern readers of Ovid, the wind could be a violent, rapacious, and generative force. Even Zephyrus, the warm and gentle west wind, was responsible for raping and inseminating young women: his rape of Chloris and her transformation into the goddess Flora occur in Book Four of Ovid's *Fasti* (published in Latin in England in 1583). The *Fasti* is the same poem that describes the rape of Lucrece (Book Two), a text with which Shakespeare was undoubtedly familiar from his Latin grammar education and the commentaries of others.[52] Raping Chloris as a hot breeze, Zephyrus transforms her into the fecund goddess Flora, who fertilizes the earth with flowers, their offspring.[53] In the writings of Pausanias, Quintus Smyrnus, and Homer, Zephyrus is also credited with the rape of the Harpy Podarge, which produces Asian tigers as offspring, and the attempted rape of Hyacinthus.[54]

Zephyrus is both violently rapacious and prodigiously generative. His reproductive capacity is what characterizes his role in English literature[55] and in Renaissance geohumoral theory.[56] Zephyrus may be a source of insemination, but in classical poetry, wind is also a source of dissemination. As Virgil describes it, wind drives the many-tongued monster rumor, or *Fama*, across the world. Shakespeare resurrects this character to deliver the induction to *Henry IV, Part II*: "I from the orient to the dropping west, / Making the wind my post-horse, still unfold / The acts commenced on this ball of earth" (Induction, 1–5).[57] The tale of the rape of Chloris was also a productive story in Renaissance Europe, reproduced in painting and woodcuts—its combination of violent rape and floral fecundity is the subject of Botticelli's painting *La Primavera*.[58]

Zephyrus also plays an intermediary role in the etymology of *zero*: Fibonacci, a medieval Italian arithmetician writing in Latin, first attempted to translate the Arabic word *sifra* into Latin by renaming it *zephirus* in his manuscript treatise on Hindu-Arabic numerals, *Liber Abacci* ("The Book of the Abacus," 1202).[59] After Fibonacci's *zephirus*, European arithmeticians alternately employed the terms *zephyr, zefirum, zeverum*, and its early printed dative form *zeuero*. By abbreviating *zeuero*, we get zero. By translating the Arabic word *sifra* into Latin *zephirus, zephyr*, and *zefirum*, Fibonacci and his followers recast zero's Eastern ancestry as ancient Roman. Though we can only guess at their reasons for doing so, a contemporary French lexicon theorizes that the renaming of *sifra* as *zephirus* deliberately combines the Latin word for the western wind, Zephyr, with the Arabic word for zero, perhaps in order to give *cipher* an allegorical or mythological identity. Furthermore, as a homonym for the *west* wind, zero loses its Eastern roots entirely.[60]

In the nonstandardized spelling of Elizabethan English, it is a small step from *zephirus* to *Zephyrus*.[61] Given the associative nature of early modern English, the homophonic similarity of *Zephyr* and *cipher* calls forth a number of interpretive possibilities. Zephyrus is wind, a movement and force that is felt but not seen. Moreover, his rapacious acts result in propagation and publication, much in the same way that early modern zero functions mysteriously to multiply by tens and in the way that ciphers and Os write themselves all over the body of Shakespeare's violated heroine.

The expletive O creates a different kind of breath, the rapacious and invisible breath of Zephyrus/zero that issues into Lucrece's body as she is raped, and out of it as a kind of pneumatic publication afterward.[62] That there are so many expletive Os (ten in a speech of 300 lines) may appear obvious to modern readers: Lucrece is distressed; "O" is a dramatic prompt for an explosive emotional release. But if we read these Os as zephyrs and zeros, they aurally and materially publish Lucrece's rape. Rape ultimately marks women's bodies with pregnancy, which Lucrece imagines in lines 1058 to 1064. But rape leaves no literal mark on a married woman (no blood on the sheets and, according to some early modern theories, even no bastard children).[63] The poem counters this by supplying an abundance of aural and graphic ciphers, effectively marking the textual corpus, when Lucrece's physical corpus remains unreadable. Lucrece herself compares her speech both to wind and childbirth when pleading with Tarquin to spare her: "my sighs like whirlwinds labour hence to heave thee" (586). After the rape, Lucrece's body is compared to a volcano, her breath the smoke. Suicide would allow the wind better to escape her body, "to make more vent for passage of her breath, / Which thronging through her lips so vanisheth / As smoke from Etna, that in air consumes" (1040).

Lucrece's lament has three rhetorical shifts, railing first against the darkness of night (764–833), second against the opportunity Tarquin has seized (834–924), both of which, it turns out, depend upon a third category: time (925–41). Each of the three sections is introduced by an O-shaped wail, and in this case, the Os might serve as oratorical markings, separating the three paragraphs of her oration into three subjects.[64] When day draws near, Lucrece rejects her argument against night and time: "But cloudie LVCRECE shames her selfe to see, / And therefore still in night would cloistred be" (1084–85). Since Lucrece ultimately jettisons her argument, the grounding of each new idea with a cipher appears to accentuate the airy futility of her cries, which she calls "This helpless smoake of words" (1027). Lucrece's words evaporate in the face of the pain and shame of her violation, but the printed Os on the page ground them in material reality.[65]

Ciphering as Publication

The final moments of the poem configure the legacy of Lucrece's rape as multiple acts of publishing. Ciphers abound in all their forms, as numerals, shapes, zeros, and Os, flowing together to produce a layered image of Lucrece as zero, O, jewel, and printed impression. Stabbing herself, Lucrece physically produces a longed-for hole in her body, turning herself into an O shape through which her soul can escape: "if in this blemish'd fort I make some hole / through which I may convey this troubled soul" (1175–76). The stabbing in turn releases a halo of blood that encircles her body, turning her corpse into a cryptic symbol. Her confession, together with Junius Brutus's subsequent unmasking, illustrates moments of private publishing—(de)ciphering or di/ delation. As Lucrece reveals her rape before husband, father, and Lucius Junius

Brutus, she stabs herself, extinguishing her voice, her shame, and her existence but publishing her secret. From her body flows blood that enacts the paradox of remaining chaste while being defiled: part of it is red and pure, untainted, whereas the rest of it is black, stained by shame: "the crimson blood / Circles her body in on every side. . . . Some of her bloud still pure and red remain'd, / And som look'd black, & that false Tarquin stain'd" (1742–43). Continuing the analogy the poem establishes between Lucrece's body and a besieged castle, the blood surrounds her like a moat.[66] A "wat'ry rigol" draws an "O" around her twice nullified body. Empty of life, Lucrece's corpse is a mathematical nothing. But it is also a fertile O, gushing blood. Lucrece's blood takes on the colors and properties of ink, flowing like water in red and black, the two colors used in the Renaissance for printing. Lucrece's red and black blood circumscribes her body like ink around an emblem. It is the black, stained blood that, like an inkblot, is impure, "putrified" (1750). The red blood, like the red ink that denotes a red-letter day in an early modern printed Bible calendar, commemorating the death of a martyr, announces Lucrece's chastity in death. In death, Lucrece renews herself as a printed cipher. Framed by a circle of blood, she is both a numerical figure for a nothingness and an emblem or miniature portrait of martyred chastity.

The publication of Lucrece's rape coincides with Brutus's decision to reveal himself as a leader. No longer masquerading as an empty fool (another kind of cipher), Brutus casts off "That shallow habit. . . . Wherein deep policy did him disguise" (1814–15). But Brutus's revelation is inverted, described as a remasking: "Brvtvs . . . Began to cloath his wit in state and pride, / Burying in Lvcrece wound his follies show" (1807–10). Rather than throw off his cloak of idiocy, revealing his wit, Brutus begins to "cloath his wit" with powerful oratory. This inverted revelation implies that every speech is a kind of masking; every text is a kind of cipher. Brutus does not only clothe his own wit with rhetoric; he also substitutes the living Lucrece's questionable chastity with the emblem of "chaste Lucrece" (1840):

> Now by this Capitol that we adore,
> And by this *chaste* blood so uniustlie stained, . . .
> And by *chaste* Lucrece soul that late complained . . .
> We will reuenge the death of this true wife. (1835–41)

Brutus replaces living, tainted Lucrece with "chaste Lucrece soul that late complained," and "chaste Lucrece" becomes a fresh cipher, an emblem (made up of image, word, and the text of the poem itself) standing in for a former person.

The historical result of the rape of Lucrece is the birth of the Roman republic, the transition from tyrannical rule to constitutional government, but the product of rape in Shakespeare's poem is publication. As Lucrece's bloody body is paraded throughout the streets of Rome, her rape is published, which eventually brings about the downfall of the Tarquinian kings. The narrative of the poem is bookended by two accounts of publishing: Collatine's verbal publication of his wife's chastity and Brutus's physical proclamation of Lucrece's death with her corpse. From the opening of the poem to its end, Lucrece figures as a printed text. Collatine's announcement of Lucrece's chastity takes the form of a printed book: "Why is Colatine the publisher / Of that rich jewell he should keepe unknown, / From theevish eares because it is his owne?" (33–35). As a published "rich jewell," Lucrece is metaphorized as three material objects: a sexualized body, a jeweled miniature, and, most important, as the title or frontispiece of a printed book of secrets, many of which allude to treasures, store holds, and jewel boxes.[67]

Jewels representing Lucrece were popular in the sixteenth century. Many were O-shaped, often in more than one dimension (a circular ring could display a circular cameo). They were also frequently carved in relief, either cast bronze or cameos, which made them tools for printing themselves: a sixteenth-century ring engraved with Lucrece is found in the collection of Lord Londesborough, now housed in the British Museum. Albrecht Dürer and his contemporaries designed bronze medallions of Lucrece, and a number of oval and round cameos depicting Lucrece at the moment of her suicide date from the mid to late sixteenth century. Jan Vermeyen surrounds Jacopo da Trezzo's cameo of Lucrece with an enamel O decorated with rubies that look like little drops of blood. The cameo's setting is a black-and-white enamel "O" that resembles a printed letter, calling to mind Shakespeare's image of Lucrece's corpse encircled by ink-like blood (Figure 6).

The Elizabethan text of *The Rape of Lucrece* itself has a legacy of proliferation through publication. Shakespeare's poem was reprinted multiple times in the first half of the seventeenth century.[68] Through her reproduction in woodcuts and engravings and the repetition of the name "Lucrece" on the title pages and upper margins of editions of *The Rape of Lucrece*, the word and emblematic image of "Lucrece" begin to stand in for an often printed story of rape and regime change. As "the impression of Lucrece" repeatedly surfaces in woodcuts, relief medallions, and signet rings, it becomes both literally and

Figure 6. Lucretia cameo, by Jacopo da Trezzo and Jan Vermeyen, c. 1582–1602.
By permission of the Kunsthistoriches Museum, Vienna.

figuratively a tool for printing and publishing in the English Renaissance. In most woodcuts, engravings, and medallions, Lucrece points a knife at her breast, about to annihilate herself. This enacts the paradox of zero that both embodies absence and proliferation: Lucrece points the sword at her heart, emphasizing her sacrifice, but the sword (pen) points back at Lucrece, marking her as a well-known and often circulated emblem of chastity. Like her poetic counterpart, the "Lucrece" of early modern pendants and printers' marks embodies the paradox of the early modern cipher: she is ubiquitous absence, a legible secret, and a defiantly productive O. Zero transforms the classical Lucretia, whose own capabilities of reproduction and generation have been doubly silenced, into Shakespeare's early modern English Lucrece, a woman able to publish and reproduce her legacy through Arabic arithmetic and early modern European print. Current critical analyses of *The Rape of Lucrece* tend to emphasize the poem's investment in metaphors of reading, writing, and rhetoric.[69] As a numeral that shares its shape with a letter, and as a mark on paper signifying nothing, zero is part of this investment. The cipher's Eastern genealogy is occluded by its use in a "Roman" poem, but the very presence of this foreign import is what allows for *The Rape of Lucrece* to transcend Ovid's and Plutarch's destinies for Lucrece by imagining rape as a force that repeatedly writes Os onto violated bodies and texts, in effect, as a kind of violent printing press.[70] It is almost as if Shakespeare's poem, with its circling, inscribing, imprinting imagery, anticipates its own success as a printed text or at least acknowledges its insertion in a continuity of printed and printing Lucreces.

Remediating Shakespeare

Why did early modern English writers feel the need to redeem Ovid's tragic narratives, and why empower or rehabilitate Lucrece by lending shape and figure (if not voice) to her suffering? As Enterline suggests, the Latin humanist classroom probably created a violent, traumatic environment for small boys who feared the constant threat of corporal punishment that went hand in hand with what she calls the "theater" of imitation that the students performed.[71] This upbringing may have made Ovid's more violent tales loom large and threatening in former schoolboys' eyes. Early modern responses to Ovid's version of the rape of Lucretia in the *Fasti* are not limited to Shakespeare's. They include Thomas Heywood's tragedy *The Rape of Lucrece* (1608) and Thomas Middleton's narrative poem *The Ghost of Lucrece* (1600). Each of these texts attempts, much more explicitly than Shakespeare's, to exorcise the Ovidian legacy of rape and suicide in different ways. In Heywood's text, comic love songs interspersing the dramatic action were sung by the character Valerius to familiar tunes, invitations for the audience to join in singing with the actors on stage and momentarily transform the shocking violence of the narrative into communal moments of emotional release.[72]

Middleton's poem exorcizes the rape more demonstrably, choosing the genre of complaint over epyllion, as a demonic Lucrece returns fury-like from the grave to avenge her death by murdering Tarquin. Middleton's ghostly Lucrece has more in common with Seneca's vengeful Medea than with the silent victim of the *Fasti*. She is much more Lady Macbeth than Lucrece, calling upon supernatural forces to do her vengeful bidding: "Medea's Magic, and Calypso's drugs, / Circe's enchantments, Hecate's triform / Weans my soul sucking at Revenge's dugs, / To feed upon the air."[73] In Middleton's poem, an angry, blood-soaked, vengeful ghost recounts the story of her rape and suicide, bloodied sword in hand, all the time calling for Tarquin's brutal death.

In making his phantom Lucrece more vocal and vengeful, Middleton revives and appropriates Shakespeare's cipher imagery as Lucrece declaims: "Lo, under that base tip of Tarquin's name, / I cypher figures of iniquity" (337–38). In Shakespeare's poem, both Lucrece and Tarquin imagine rape as spectral writing on their faces, bodies, and characters, but in Middleton's poem—despite its ectoplasmic heroine—this graphic zero seems more visceral, material, and vivid. This Lucrece is not simply going to imagine Tarquin's name destroyed; she is going to put in the "loathsome dash" herself. Instead of inserting a *bâton sinistre* onto Tarquin's coat of arms, she will "cypher figures of iniquity" onto his physical body. An act of ciphering implies inscribing a circle, which suggests that the shameful figures that Lucrece is adding to Tarquin's name could be seen as a circumcision or castration of his "base tip," which would nullify him just as he did her. Remarkably swiftly, Middleton appropriates Shakespeare's use of the figure of the cipher as an instrument of Lucrece's liberation, translating it into a tool that exercises violent, vengeful justice. At the end of Shakespeare's poem, Lucrece transforms herself into a publishing zero; at the end of Middleton's, she takes this further, converting Tarquin into an empty, partly legible text by ciphering/castrating him. In Middleton's hands, the cipher's legacy of redemption and publication is reinscribed with violence and punishment. Yet it is Shakespeare's use of the imported oriental *cipher* to redeem Ovid's Roman Lucrece through writing and publication that makes it possible for later writers like Middleton to carry this image further and

avenge her death. Middleton's complaint actively incorporates and appropriates Shakespeare's epyllion's imagery, rather than Ovid's metaphors, in order
to lend further agency to Lucrece. Middleton's follow-up poem secures Shakespeare's *Lucrece*'s place in the emergent canon of early modern English poetry,
not by making reference to the Romanness of this poem but by attending to
the poet's *English* imagery of newly assimilated Asian technology.

Chapter 4

Breeding Fame: Horses and Bulbs
in *Venus and Adonis*

Failure and Its Counter-Narrative

Near the end of Shakespeare's narrative poem *Venus and Adonis*, the goddess Venus, enraged and grief stricken by the death of her unrequited love Adonis, bestows upon lovers a universe of pain for all future generations. Foreshadowing Adonis's corporeal metamorphosis into an ephemeral blossom, Venus converts love from something that gives pleasure into a force for sorrow: "'It shall be fickle, false, and full of fraud, / Bud and be blasted in a breathing-while'" (1141–42).[1] In this passage, Shakespeare draws attention to Ovid's description of the anemone into which Adonis transforms, a flower that takes its Greek name from the winds that violently rend its petals into pieces (*Metamorphoses* 10.1189). And yet Shakespeare's description of Adonis's transformation into a flower a little later strays far from Ovid's anemone. Shakespeare's Adonis flower droops its head on a thick, tubular, and sappy green stalk. Its petals are decorated with a purple and white checkerboard pattern (1168–75). Just how close to and how far is Shakespeare's poem from Ovid's?

In its emphasis on incompatibility and unrequited desire, Shakespeare's poem is often read as augmenting the tragic ending of Ovid's version of the myth.[2] As Madhavi Menon has elegantly demonstrated, in its rejection of a happy conclusion and emphasis on failure, the poem resists teleological readings, refuting normative sexuality.[3] This resistance to teleology and union is compatible with Ovid's rendition of the tale that closes Book 10 of the *Metamorphoses*. Venus and Adonis's relationship comes last in a lineage of thwarted and nonnormative couplings (human-doll, father-daughter, human-tree) that

Arthur Golding, in the moral preface to his English translation of 1567, called "most prodigious lusts" (214).[4]

On one hand, Shakespeare's poem is a showcase for unfulfilled desire, evidenced by the great rhetorical lengths to which Venus goes to convince Adonis to make love to her. In Shakespeare's version, the heroes are more at odds than their Ovidian counterparts: Shakespeare makes Venus a rapacious older woman, a giantess, and Adonis an indifferent prepubescent boy of "unripe years" (524), more interested in horses and hunting than in sex and love. In Ovid's version, Adonis is a young but fully mature man: "*iam iuvenis, iam vir, iam se formosior ipse est / iam placet et Veneri matrisque ulciscitur ignes*," which Golding translates as, "Anon a stripling hee became, and by and by a man, / And every day more beawtifull than other he becam" (10.602–3).[5] Ovid's Adonis willingly allows Venus to rest her head in his lap under a poplar to tell him the love story of Atalanta and Hippomenes, interrupted by frequent kisses, "and in her tale she bussed him among" (645–47).

On the other hand, I want to argue, Shakespeare's ending to *Venus and Adonis* is more ambivalent than Ovid's. Embedded in Shakespeare's poem about unrequited, unconsummated love and the origins of amorous loss, I contend, are the seeds of a movement in an opposite direction. Underneath the great unresolved frustration, grief, and loss that Shakespeare attaches to his protagonists thrives a poetic economy of images that posits an alternative productive outcome, not perhaps for Venus or Adonis, but for English poetry, and even for the young poet Shakespeare, who hoped to establish himself next to Ovid in the literary pantheon with his first poem. I am not discounting the enormous sense of loss and failure that pervades Shakespeare's retelling of Ovid's tragic tale; instead, I would like to show what kind of possibilities and new routes for interpretation open up when we reorient the poem around two of the major changes Shakespeare makes to Ovid's narrative: the narrative digression that describes Adonis's erotically charged steed and the description of the flower into which Adonis transforms as checkered in purple and white. My argument is that Shakespeare's inclusion and extended focus on two Levantine imports in the poem—an Arabian horse and a Turkish bulb—present an alternative narrative of generation, productivity, and publication within a poem about incompatibility, failure, and loss in love.

If, as Giorgio Agamben states, poetry can unite possibility with impossibility, or appropriate "what must in every case remain unappropriable," I would like to uncover nodes of possibility (in this case, images of fecundity and flourishing) within a poem primarily about a love that remains impossible.[6]

Following two networks of words and images for imported things—Arabian horses and Turkish bulbs—I will briefly reorient the poem around these images in order to uncover how *Venus and Adonis* remediates Ovid's version of a classical myth through two extended metaphors for Levantine merchandise. In so doing, the poem becomes not only a discourse on English poets paying homage to classical writers while attempting to surpass them but an opportunity to reconfigure elements of Ovid's ancient Mediterranean landscape as a global, cosmopolitan English one, made fruitful by overseas Mediterranean trade.

In the previous chapter, I followed the associative network of ciphers, circles, and graphic Os through Shakespeare's *Lucrece*, positing that attending to early modern philological associations with zero in the poem allows us to see the devastated heroine giving graphic shape to her shame, thus empowering Lucrece to publish her shame not only to future Roman Republicans but to future early modern English audiences. If, through the cipher, Lucrece commands her early modern appropriators to redeem her story by publishing her sorrow (or exorcizing her trauma or avenging her rape), what do Venus and Adonis call for? Even as Shakespeare's epyllion thwarts the union of Venus with Adonis, it presents its readers with images of generation, not only in Shakespeare's inclusion of imported Arab equine and Turkish floral imagery but in the way Shakespeare ties this imagery to his own poetic techniques of translation, description, and representation. In other words, Adonis's Arabian horse and the checkered purple flower, which may well be a fritillary or tulip, both bulbs newly imported into England from Turkey, stand out against the poem's classical landscape as Shakespeare's inventions and additions, as Shakespeare's global *imports*. Whereas in *Lucrece* the poet offers early modern readers and writers like Middleton a sense of vindication in its metaphoric and rhetorical use of the newly assimilated Eastern import of zero, in *Venus and Adonis* the poet presents an alternative narrative that runs alongside his emphasis on the Ovidian characters' aborted and severed sexual union: the possibility of gaining and generating a literary text. And it is chiefly through contemporary imagery of imported horses and bulbs that *Venus and Adonis* draws attention to the remediation of Ovid's tale, not just in the translation from one language (Latin) to another (English) but in the transition of setting from Ovid's Mediterranean landscape to Shakespeare's England, where imported horses and bulbs were becoming naturalized.

Naming and Renaming

Two remarkable additions to Ovid's story are Shakespeare's eleven-stanza-long description of horse mating, which occurs in the first quarter of the text, and the extended description of the metamorphosis of Adonis into a multicolored flower that concludes the poem (1165–89). There is no hint of horses in Ovid. Though Ovid's Venus pursues Adonis as he hunts rabbits, stags, bucks, boars, wolves, bears, and lions (10.622–25), horses never appear in the tale. Ovid has the goddess magically transform Adonis's blood into an anemone, a small, garnet-red flower with petals so frail that they are almost instantly shaken and shed by the wind (10.861–63).[7] Shakespeare's flower, on the other hand, is different. It is "purple . . . chequered with white" (1168) and releases a viscous green substance when cropped (1175). Yet both poets name their flowers slyly, through allusion, metaphor, and descriptive adjectives.

In previous chapters, I have discussed how the names and descriptive words given to imported things can reorient a reading of poem or an *ars poetica* around a network of imported *objects*: it matters that the word *subtlety* could equally be applied to English poetic ingenuity and to sugar sculptures inherited from Arab culinary culture and that the word *cipher* and the symbol O indicated forms of writing that represented something immaterial or otherwise invisible. The names of imported objects are also of crucial importance in *Venus and Adonis*. Adonis's horse is called a *courser*, a term typically applied to horses imported from North Africa and the Middle East. It runs off in hot pursuit of a Spanish *jennet*, a naturalized European horse bred from both Middle Eastern and European stock. But both Shakespeare's and Ovid's texts name the Adonis flower more discretely and indirectly, through metaphor and allusion. Ovid's pomegranate-red Adonis flower is named as anemone only indirectly, when the poet states that the winds that tear the flower's petals apart bestow on it a name. Ovid names his flower by alluding to its etymology. Shakespeare, on the other hand, indirectly names his flower (most likely the snake's head fritillary or *Fritillaria meleagris*) through description, "purple . . . chequered with white" (1168). Though flower petals bearing checkerboard patterns may seem fantastical, one or two floral candidates decidedly match Shakespeare's description: the remarkable fritillary and perhaps a patterned tulip (as I will show, a secondary meaning for the early modern English word *chequered* was spotted or streaked). The fritillary's strikingly geometric pattern of purple and white checkered squares would have been recognizable to an early modern reader, as fritillaries and tulips were, along with other bulbs like the crown imperial, recent exotic imports to English gardens from Turkey. Such brightly patterned specimens stood out in the Dutch and Flemish still lives that began to appear at the beginning of the seventeenth century.

These flowers were so new to England that when they first appeared in print in an English-language book (Henry Lyte's translation of Dodoens in 1578), they lacked a common English name. Lyte can only define the flower with its newly acquired Latinate name: "it is called . . . *Flos Meleagris* . . . some do also cal this flower *Fritillaria*," and by hybridizing two other flower names into "lily narcissus." Throughout the late sixteenth and early seventeenth centuries, the fritillary had no standard English name; horticulturalists kept inventing new names for it, and none of them stuck.[8] There was no fixed English word for fritillary in 1594 when *Venus and Adonis* was published. The flower could only be defined and described by pointing out its checkerboard pattern. We could attribute Shakespeare's poem's lack of reference to the anemone to Golding's English translation, which simply leaves the reference out. But as Jonathan Bate has demonstrated, Shakespeare was a keen reader of Ovid's Latin text.[9] Thus, Shakespeare's choice to rename the flower adjectivally with *chequered*—a word that describes not only an imported flower but also a game imported from the Arab world—seems deliberate. It is Shakespeare's subtle recasting of the Adonis flower as *chequered* that allows us to read the flower as something non-European and counter-classical. Further, unlike Ovid's ephemeral wind-flower, this new checkered flower has the potential to regenerate. The winds do not make an appearance at the end of Shakespeare's poem to shed the flower's petals as they do in Ovid's version; instead, the flower first withers but then feeds in Venus's bosom (1182).

Living Imports

Unlike the graphic, windy ciphers in *The Rape of Lucrece*, the imports in *Venus and Adonis* are living, breeding things: horses and flowers. The inclusion of Arabian horses and Turkish bulbs in the latter poem allows Shakespeare to imagine two possible productive outcomes to a story that, for its protagonists, is decidedly unproductive.[10] Indeed, though in Ovid's poem, Venus wins Adonis's love, the tale itself ends with the hero's death and the end of procreation, not to mention the cutting off of Adonis's genealogical line. In what would seem like an even more unproductive conclusion, Shakespeare's Adonis leaves his Venus unsatisfied, and he ends up impaled on a boar's tusk. Yet despite its tragic and unfruitful outcome, the poem is rich with references to reproduction and procreation—just not Venus and Adonis's.

Part of the reason the poem blossoms with animal and floral generation is that Venus is using the springtime setting to convince Adonis of the ubiquity of procreation. If we read Shakespeare's Venus as a conflation of Ovid's powerful goddess of love and Lucretius's Venus, an embodiment of growth and nature, her connection to a fruitful and productive landscape makes sense.[11] Lucretius invokes Venus at the opening of Book One of *De Rerum Natura*: "*tibi suavis daedala tellus / summitit flores*" ("For you, that sweet artificer, the earth, submits her flowers," 1.7–8).[12] Part of Venus's rhetoric in wooing Adonis, then, is to call forth fecundity from the landscape—to provoke the flora and fauna around her to do her bidding when Adonis refuses to yield to her desires. Ovid's Venus is powerful, too, but her strength lies in bestowing normative love upon couples who pray for her help: midway through Book 10, she turns Pygmalion's ivory doll into a woman for him to marry (300), and as she tells Adonis, she devises a plan for Hippomenes to win Atalanta in marriage (755). When her subjects fail to offer thanks, she punishes them by transforming them into wild beasts. Her tale to Adonis seems to be a warning of her wrath but also a caveat to Adonis to beware the rapacious lions (Hippomenes and Atalanta) out for revenge, who might seek to harm her through his death.

Shakespeare's Venus is more similar to Lucretius's creative goddess than that of Ovid, who demands mortals' respect. Shakespeare's Venus elicits desire from every living thing around her, except from Adonis. And once Adonis dies, she calls forth a new flower from the earth. The carefully bred Arabian courser that is eager to procreate with a Spanish jennet when Adonis refuses Venus, along with the imported bulb that replaces Adonis's bleeding corpse, makes it possible for Shakespeare to offer readers an alternative narrative of generation and reproduction—a Lucretian one—in spite of, or alongside, the failures of his (and Ovid's) protagonists. As I hope to show, the imagery of horses and bulbs in the poem capitalizes on itself by linking Shakespeare's poetic remediation of Ovid with the imagery of valuable and fungible Levantine imports. Venus fails to win Adonis's love or body, but the horses rush off the page, eager to breed in the springtime. Adonis dies, is given new life as a flower, and then just as quickly is killed off again, when Venus "crops the stalk" (1175). But the thing about flowers is that they come back every spring. And bulbs do more than return in March: because they contain within them the embryo of the flower, they can self-generate and spread on their own, even after the flowers are cut.[13] If Shakespeare's Venus has connections to Lucretius's

goddess of nature, then this has profound implications for the poem's emphasis on failure and loss. For Lucretius, Nature-as-Venus cannot allow anything
to disappear or be obliterated; Nature is cyclical and regenerative: "*quando
alit ex alio reficit natura nec ullam / rem gigni patitur nisi morte adiuta aliena*,"
or "Nature from one thing brings another forth, / And out of death new life
is born" (263–64).[14] If we imagine Shakespeare's Venus carrying some of the
power of Lucretius's goddess of nature, her powerlessness in the face of loss,
articulated in her painful curse to love, is only temporary, and the subsequent
transformation of Adonis into a flower that can go on living even when the
blossom is cut seems like a regenerative act.

Arabian Horses

Shakespeare's poem contains a great number of allusions to Renaissance hunting and horsemanship, all deployed to convey sexual desire and many deriving
from the popular English hunting and riding manuals by George Gascoigne
(previously thought to be George Turbervile) and Thomas Blundeville.[15] The
poem's lengthy description of Adonis's stallion breaking free of bit and bridle
to court a young mare as a metaphor for unbridled sexual desire is a commonplace; as Colin Burrow states in a note to the Oxford edition, it was "as
old as Plato's *Phaedrus* 253d, and was a commonplace of Renaissance iconography."[16] Nevertheless, the language and imagery of horsemanship and hunting
in the poem call to mind a foreign mercantile economy that stretched across
the Middle East from North Africa to the Ottoman Empire and Persia: that
of breeding, trading, and depicting Arabian steeds. As Lisa Jardine and Jerry
Brotton's analysis of the early modern Mediterranean horse trade reminds us,
"the horse inevitably carried powerful associations with the East which are
largely lost on us today . . . familiarity has de-exoticized them for us, and we
can no longer retrieve their highly specific 'orientalism.' "[17]

Heinrich Bünting's figurative map of Europe, Asia, and Africa (1581, 1595)
illustrates this visually, depicting all of Asia, from the sixteenth-century Ottoman Empire to India and the Far East, as a winged horse, combining the
classical image of Pegasus with an Arabian steed.[18] In ancient Greek mythology, Pegasus is intimately connected to the East through the figure of Perseus, mythological ancestor of the emperors of Persia, having sprung from the
Gorgon Medusa's head when Perseus decapitated her.[19] The map was printed
several times in several European cities (Hannover, Magdeburg, Prague, and

Stockholm) during the late sixteenth and seventeenth centuries, both in woodcut and copper plate, from 1581 to 1648 (Figure 7).

In Bünting's map, Persia is depicted in the saddle-cloth draped across the horse's back and belly, perhaps alluding to the carpets and silks Europeans imported from that region. Playfully prancing forward, the horse's front knees nudge North Africa, while it reaches out with an eager tongue, trying to bite or taste Constantinople, the seat of Ottoman trade (and sensual luxury goods), with its teeth. The map seems to suggest that Asia is about to take over the world through global trade; Asia breathes new life into Europe.

The complex global trade that linked Arabian steeds with political advancement and inheritance ultimately reconfigures the poem's preoccupation with reproduction and generation, so that Venus's enchantment of Adonis's horse serves not only as her *exemplum* on the necessity of procreation and generation; it is also the author's attempt to generate publicity and economic success. And, as I will demonstrate, the metamorphosis of Adonis's corpse into a purple and white checkered flower references another highly productive global economy, the bulb trade. Both imported horses and flowers function in the poem as alternative modes of production and generation, which seem to counteract the poem's themes of thwarted love and halted genealogy.

Historical animal studies have contributed richly to early modern scholarship in recent years, and as a result, there has been a small but significant outpouring of recent work on the cultural role of imported livestock in the premodern European economy, particularly horses.[20] Many of these studies, including important work by Erica Fudge and Bruce Boehrer, have also begun to historicize animals as part of a spectrum of emerging philosophies of humanity, as sub- or posthuman.[21] Although I find such philosophical investigations compelling and relevant to early modern scholarship, in this chapter I am primarily interested in the Levantine associations that horse and flower imagery may have projected to early modern readers, as I argue for horses and bulbs as living luxury objects capable of self-generation in a global economy.

Along these lines, Donna Landry has revealed how the English thoroughbred—the mark of refined Englishness for eighteenth-century gentry—derived from the trade in Arabian and Turkish horses, and Bruce Boehrer locates exotic birds at the center of early modern global trade and empire building.[22] Both scholars argue that the living nature of these imported commodities had a more profound and complex effect on Western culture than imported inanimate objects did. However, I would add that just as animal and posthuman studies has now expanded to include plants and plant

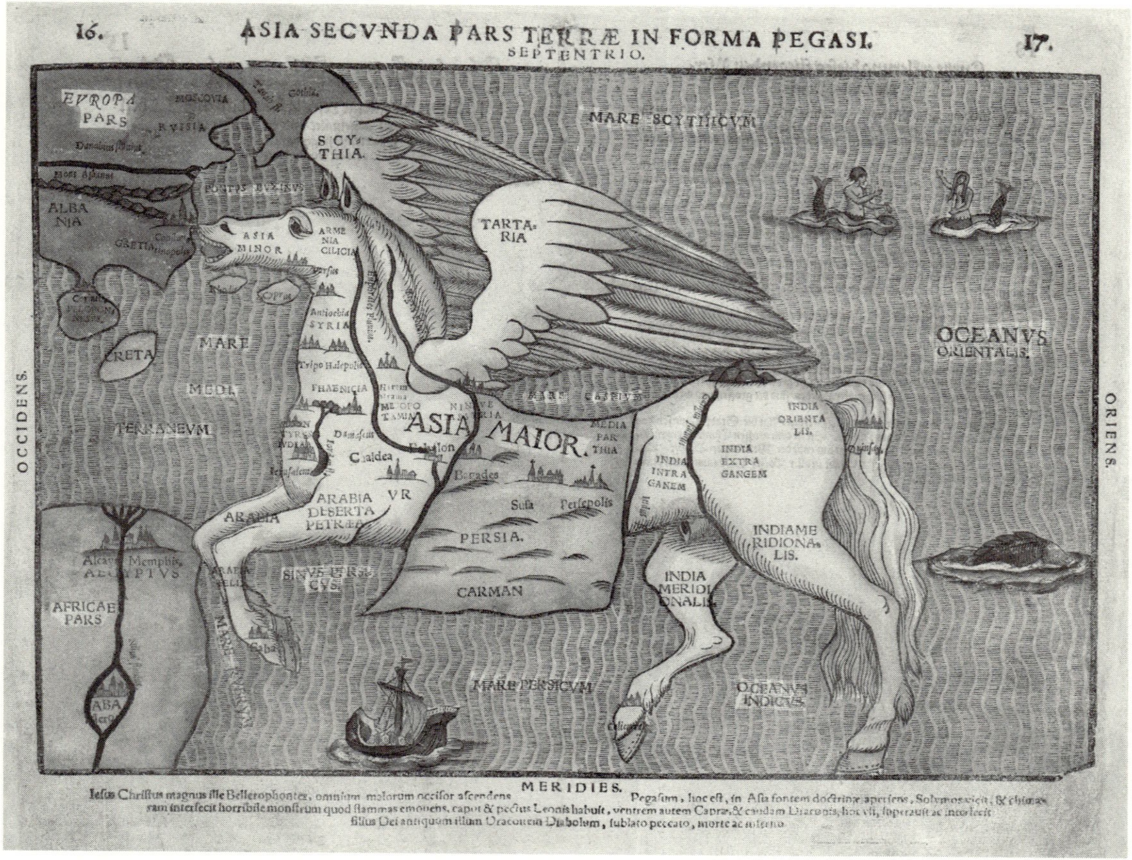

Figure 7. Heinrich Bünting, "Asia Secunda Pars Terrae in Forma Pegasi," hand-colored facsimile of *Itinerarium Sacrae Scripturae* (Magdeburg: 1581), 16–17.

life, so too the field of early modern animal economies can be augmented to include botanical commodities. Flowers and bulbs were living imports, too, things that also lent themselves to breeding and naturalization. In the same way that the second and third generations of Arabian steeds became English thoroughbreds in the eighteenth century (as Landry demonstrates), Turkish tulips and daffodils became Dutch tulips and English jonquils. In Shakespeare's time, however, prized coursers could still be Barbary (the name of Richard II's favorite horse), and bulbs could still be exotic Turkish imports.

Early modern books on horsemanship demonstrate the significant role Turkey had begun to play in early modern English mercantile and political imaginations. In his popular and often reissued manual on horse breeding, *The Fower Chiefyst Offices Belongyng to Horsemanship* (London: 1597), Thomas Blundeville places two Levantine breeds of horses, the "Turkey" and "Barbary," before European and British horses in his catalogue of breeds.[23] Blundeville mentions Ottoman horses first not only because Turkey is furthest from England but because of the Ottoman Empire's impressive strength and size.[24] Gervase Markham's late Elizabethan tracts on horsemanship were frequently reprinted and collated throughout the seventeenth century.[25] Like Blundeville, Markham prefers Levantine horse breeds to European. Markham praises the Arabian courser above all others as the most "peerelesse" stallion, which "hath in him the puritie and vertue of all other Horses." Markham's Arabian courser travels from "a parte of Arabia called *Angelica* to *Constantinople*, and from thence to the higher-most partes of Germanie by lande, and so by Sea to Englande, yet was hee so couragious and lyuely, (hauing no fleshe on his backe) that by no meanes hée coulde bée ruled."[26] Markham's description of the Arabian courser borders on ecstatic. Coming from a realm called "Angelica," the horse seems to have descended from heaven. This horse is a luxury object, his coat so fine that "it is not possible almost in any parte of him but his mane and tayle, to catch holde to pull of one hayre."[27] Moreover, the horse's tawny hide conjures comparisons to precious commodities like fine silk and gold: "a most delicate bay, whom if you viewe in the Sunne, you will iudge him eyther like changeable Satine or cloth of Gold."[28] This horse is a living, breathing, sentient thing, and though inanimate objects are occasionally described with gendered pronouns in early modern English, this horse is a "him," not an "it," which, even as it complicates his commodification, makes him more easily appropriated as sensuous, erotic imagery in art and poetry.

In Shakespeare's poem, when the unrequited goddess of love compels

Adonis to stay and hear her out, he tries to ride away on his horse. But no such luck—the horse, a stallion, falls in love with a Spanish mare (a "jennet") nearby, breaks out of his tethering and saddle, and rushes off to mate with her. Jilted by his horse and only means of transportation, reluctant Adonis must remain with Venus an interminable while longer. Although the poem never explicitly describes Venus enchanting Adonis's horse, it does seem plausible that this is exactly what happens. Despite her ironic inability to capture Adonis's reciprocal affection and desire, Venus is still the goddess of love and desire, and her presence ought to compel those around her to engage in amorous pursuits. Though she never confesses to having bewitched his courser, Venus too conveniently makes Adonis's horse the subject of a pretty *exemplum* about yielding to desire physically and naturally.

In its physical blazon as "Round-hoofed, short-jointed, fetlocks shag and long, / Broad breast, full eye, small head, and nostril wide" (295–96), Shakespeare's courser not only resembles Blundeville's ideal stallion—"let him have short and slender head, a wide mouth, and wide nostrils, slender jaws, great eyes and black"—as Colin Burrow and John Roe have noted,[29] but also Markham's Arabian courser:

> hys head is small, leane and slender, hys nostrell (if he be angred) wonderfull wide, hys eyes like fire, readie to leape out of hys heade, hys eares sharpe, small, and some-what long, hys chaule thinne and wide, his thropell large, hys necke long, hys crest high, thinne and firme, his back short, hys chyne a handfull broade and more, hys buttocke long, vpright and cleane.[30]

Markham's description of an Arabian courser seems more animated, passionate, and alive than Blundeville's ideal stallion. Markham's horse is a living, breathing animal, with eyes "like fire, readie to leape out of hys head," and a wide nostril especially when "he be angered." Unlike Blundeville's technical anatomy of a horse, Markham describes an animal that is sentient and passionate. In this sense, his Arabian courser much more closely resembles Adonis's inflamed steed, whose "nostrils drink the air, and forth again / As from a furnace" (273–74), and whose eyes are also fiery: "His eye which scornfully glisters like fire / Shows his hot courage and his high desire" (275–76). Both Markham's and Shakespeare's steeds express emotion with a widening of their nostrils; Shakespeare's expresses scorn, "courage," and "desire," whereas Markham's is capable of being "angered."

Unlike Blundeville's generic stallion, Markham's courser is continually marked as Eastern and exotic, as the text repeatedly calls him a "horse of Arabia" and an "Arabian"; compares his coat in the sun to taffeta and cloth of gold, both luxury goods imported from the East; and gives him an origin in "a parte of Arabia called Angelica" and "Constantinople."[31] *Angelica* seems a fitting name for the fictive point of origin of an early modern Arabian horse, since Angelica, the heroine of Ariosto's verse romance *Orlando Furioso* and the title character's unrequited beloved, is an Indian princess from Cathay who marries the Moorish knight Medoro. John Harington's English translation of *Orlando Furioso* was published by Richard Field in 1591, and Robert Greene's tragicomedy appeared in 1594, a year after Shakespeare's *Venus and Adonis* and Markham's text.[32]

Like Markham, Shakespeare orientalizes Adonis's steed. In addition to sharing physical and emotional characteristics with Markham's Arabian courser, Adonis's horse is hot-blooded, with fiery eye revealing his "hot courage," and uncontrollable, breaking free of his reins, saddle, and bit, which is exactly how Blundeville and Markham describe Turkish and Arabian horses. As Brotton and Jardine note, even horse breeding participated in early modern racialist stereotypes: Levantine breeds were considered "hot-blooded," whereas Europeans were "cold-blooded."[33] According to Blundeville, "Turky" horses, prized for their speed, are extremely difficult to control:

> they neuer be ridden (as I haue learned) until they be ten or
> twelve years old, whereby they be so headstrong, as they be not
> easily brought to make a good stop: yea, if when you runne him
> at his setting forth you say but this word (Braie) vnto him, he will
> neuer leave running so long as his breath will serve him, shun-
> ning nothing that shall stand in his way, if he may go ouer the
> same by any meanes possible: for they be of nature verie coura-
> geous, and wil do more by gentil meanes than by stripes or great
> threatening."[34]

Markham cites Blundeville to support this, noting that Levantine breeds are best employed in creating swift breeds: "Also, Maister *Blandauill* aduiseth . . . him that will bréede Runners, a Barbarie or a Turke."[35] Whether a Turkish, Barbary, or Arabian courser, Adonis's stallion has all the qualities of the "headstrong" and exceedingly swift oriental horse, popping out of his restraints one by one as he rushes to pursue his tantalizing jennet:

> The strong-necked steed being tied unto a tree
> Breaketh his rein, and to her straight goes he . . .
> And now his woven girths he breaks asunder . . .
>> The iron bit he crusheth 'tween his teeth,
>> Controlling what he was controlled with. (264–70)

As he shreds his bit between his incisors, Adonis's horse dominates the trappings of his oppression, overpowering his (already too delicate) rider, "controlling what he was controlled with." Rushing after his sexy mistress, he is as unstoppable as Blundeville's Turkish horse, deliberately ignoring Adonis's commands: "What recketh he his rider's angry stir, / His flatt'ring 'Holla' or his 'Stand, I say!' / What cares he now for curb or pricking spur...?" (283–85). Blundeville insists that Turkish horses are more easily controlled with gentle whisperings than with violence, and though not physically intimidating, Adonis's "angry" calls to his horse are increasingly aggressive. "Holla" is a loud cry used to stop a horse in its tracks, though Adonis presumably utters it as sweetly as possible, since the horse finds it "flatt'ring" (284), but "Stand, I say!" reveals increased ire and urgency.[36] In Blundeville's description, the Turkish horse cannot be stopped—he will run until he dies: one soft word "Braie" sets the Turkish horse running "so long as his breath will serve him, shunning nothing that shall stand in his way." If the horse is Turkish or Arabian, Adonis fights a losing battle.

Furthering Nature's Conclusions

Adonis's Levantine horse rushes away to mate with a Spanish mare—a good equine coupling, Blundeville and Markham might say. Markham, in particular, notes that Arabian stallions are so rare and such good breeding stock that whoever is lucky enough to possess such a horse should breed it immediately, preferably in the early spring.[37] Not coincidentally, *Venus and Adonis* is set in the springtime, and the poem contains a plethora of references to various early spring flowers, most notably the imported checkered white and purple flower (probably a snake's head *fritillary*, which blooms in early spring) into which the dead Adonis transforms at the end of the poem, and which I will discuss in more detail below.[38] Roses, violets, primroses, and lilies figure prominently in the poem's imagery, ornamenting both the grass on which Venus struggles to keep Adonis and the figurative language the poet employs to describe Adonis's cheeks (like roses and lilies) and hands (like lilies).

At the poem's outset, Venus immediately addresses Adonis as "The field's chief flower" (7), suggesting that they are discoursing in a springtime field of flowers, all of which Adonis outshines in beauty. During her courtship of Adonis, Venus makes reference to violets underfoot—"These blue-veined violets whereon we lean / Never can blab, nor know not what we mean" (125–26)—and to reclining on a "primrose bank" (151) where the delicate yellow flowers magically "like sturdy trees support me" (153). Attempting to allure Adonis with her magical weightlessness, Venus notes that though she is enormous (in lines 31–36, she tosses Adonis under one arm and his horse under the other), when lying upon a bank of flowers, she crushes not a single one. Later in the poem, when she searches for Adonis after the hunt, Venus treads so lightly that "the grass stoops not" (1028). What Venus's weightlessness also tells us is that it is springtime, when violets and primroses blossom and soft grass grows. A third floral allusion to the season might be located in Venus's warning to Adonis not to become too much like Narcissus (161–62), immortalized in a flower of the daffodil family, which blooms from late winter to mid-spring.

Though Burrow posits that the poem's allusion to primroses sets it in early spring, March or April, the imagery of roses and lilies that embellish Venus's and Adonis's bodies suggests a slightly later springtime setting, late April or May, when those flowers bloom in Britain. In the opening stanza, the sun's purple face is paralleled in "rose-cheeked" Adonis (3). Venus, too, has rosy cheeks that blanch when Adonis mentions the boar, "Like lawn being spread upon the blushing rose" (590). Venus traps Adonis in her hands, "locks her lily fingers one in one" (228), and when she takes Adonis by the hand, his white skin encircled in her white skin appears as "A lily prisoned in a gaol of snow" (362). When Venus finds Adonis's body gored by the bore, his once "lily white" (1053) side is purpled with blood. As embodiments of roses and lilies, Venus and Adonis become gardenlike inhabitants of the springtime landscape of Shakespeare's poem. This is furthered by Venus's description of herself as Adonis's deer park (229–40), which imagines the goddess's sexualized body as an eroticized landscape populated with "Sweet bottom grass, and high delightful plain" (236) quite similar to Lucretian Venus's connection to the springtime. In *De Rerum Natura*, Lucretius associates Venus with springtime procreation and generation: "*nam simul ac species patefactast verna diei / et reserata viget genitabilis aura favoni, / aeriae primum volucris te, diva, tuumque / significant initum perculsae corda tua vi*" (1.10–13) ("Ah, goddess, when the spring / Makes clear its daytime, and a warmer wind / Stirs from the west, a procreative air, / High in the sky the happy-hearted birds, / Responsive to your coming do call and cry").[39] In addition to comparing Venus and Adonis to roses and lilies, Shakespeare's poem associates Adonis's young age with the immature, green buds of spring: Venus notes that "The tender spring upon thy tempting lip / Shows thee unripe" (127–28), despite launching into a carpe diem argument in favor of Adonis gathering "fair flowers . . . in their prime" (131), an age he has not yet achieved. Adonis is not yet in his prime, and the poem's springtime setting advances this point, so that when Adonis describes himself as an "orator too green" (806), we are reminded not only of his rhetorical immaturity but also of the greenness of unripe fruit (he is compared to a green plum, 527) or an unopened flower bud (416).

Whether by Lucretian Venus's chthonic powers or sheer coincidence, Adonis's Arabian stallion is spontaneously driven to breed at precisely the right time for horse breeding. The concept of equine breeding involves combining two species in order to fashion a new one. It is a gentle manipulation of the natural world, similar to the horticultural hybridization and bulb "breaking" techniques that created multicolored and patterned varieties of flowers and bulbs. As Perdita's discourse on striped carnations or "streaked gillyvors" (4.4.82) in *The Winter's Tale* demonstrates, the forced couplings and grafting of plants and animal husbandry were sometimes described as artificial and against nature in early modern England, as much as they were admired for harnessing nature to create new plants and species. Perdita highlights this controversy when she compares planting flowers whose colors are changed by hybridization to cosmetic face painting, finding cross-bred gillyflowers as false as painted ladies.[40] The new technology of hybridization and bulb "breaking" presented gardeners and investors with new opportunities on the markets, and the scientific experimentation involved in developing new species eventually led to the creation of the Royal Society in the later seventeenth century.

The imported objects and technologies discussed in each chapter of this book function as social mediators, reconfiguring the markets and culture into which they were imported. Uncovering the presence of these objects in poetry, whether through language or imagery, in turn exposes a larger network of images that remediate the poems' classical sources. In this case, breeding Arabian and Ottoman steeds with Spanish, Italian, and English horses and the hybridization and breaking of plants and bulbs can both be thought of as early modern social mediators in Bruno Latour's actor-network theory.[41] While new material artifacts (foreign horses and bulbs) were introduced into England, it was what breeders and horticulturalists did with them that changed how people thought about flora and fauna. In the late sixteenth century, we can see this thinking at work in early modern discourses about Nature as a painter or craftswoman and gardeners as craftspeople who manipulate the natural world.

As I mentioned in Chapter 2, Puttenham connects gardeners' grafting of new plants to poets' interpolation of new, foreign subjects, finding the way gardeners manipulate plants a fitting management and metamorphosis of nature. He praises "the cunning gardener, that, using nature as a coadjutor, furthers her conclusions and many times makes her effects more absolute and strange" (385). And yet Adonis's courser seems compelled to breed all on his own, without human encouragement or intervention. The mare he hotly pursues is already in heat, described as "a breeding jennet" (260), a "fair breeder" (282), and eventually an "unbacked breeder" (320), which indicates that the mare is incomplete without a stallion to mount her. Though invisibly spurred on by Venus's power over the fertile landscape (if we read her in Lucretian terms), the horses' desire to rut seems autonomous, not engineered by any outside forces. But in Shakespeare's decidedly counter-classical addition to Ovid's narrative, the horse's desire is spurred on by the poet. If horse breeding and flower hybridization are Latourian mediators reshaping early modern social understanding of plants, animals, and nature, then poetic adaptation is another kind of mediator that reconfigures how early modern readers think about Ovid. Grafting, hybridization, and breeding all describe the process of poetic remediation in which Shakespeare engages when he adapts Ovid's source text. Like Puttenham's gardener, he merely "furthers" Ovid's "conclusions," making the story's effects more "strange" with the addition of living imports. The strangeness brought on comes not merely in the horses' exoticism but in the way both the horses and the flower at the end present the possibility of fruitfulness in the face of the poem's dominant tragedy of loss.

As Venus explains to Adonis, the Arabian courser's reckless pursuit of his Spanish jennet represents an idealization of unbridled sexual passion, the pursuit and fulfillment of erotic desire lacking in Adonis, despite Venus's urgings that "by law of nature thou art bound to breed" (171). The horse's base animal instinct to breed should instruct Adonis in surrendering to Venus's desire: "Though I were dumb, yet his proceedings teach thee. / O learn to love: the lesson is but plain" (406–7). Venus pleads, didactically. It is not enough to say that the horse-as-unbridled desire is an early modern erotic commonplace, because this is an oriental horse. Thus, it follows that Venus rhetorically orientalizes and seeks to fashion or manipulate (to breed or hybridize) erotic desire as much as she locates it in the natural landscape, Lucretian Venus's purlieu.

The fashioning of desire occurs several times throughout the poem, not only in Venus's rhetorical entrapments but in her discourse of Nature as a craftsperson, painter, or sculptor of desirable bodies. Venus notes that when Nature made Adonis, she was "with herself at strife" (11) and later on imagines that Nature stole statue molds from the gods to fashion Adonis's body (730). At Adonis's first rejection, Venus brands him a lifeless statue for being so stony-hearted: "Well painted idol, image dull and dead, / Statue contenting but the eye alone, / Thing like a man, but of no woman bred" (212–14). This last statement is partly true, because according to Ovid, a tree incubated and gave birth to Adonis. But Adonis's arboreal birth (in Ovid's text) makes him more a child of the natural landscape than an artificially constructed statue like a "painted idol" (212). Adonis is not the only living body compared to a work of art in Shakespeare's poem. The sexualized stallion resembles an expensive, imported art object, a painting of a horse. Nowhere is this clearer than when the poem's rhetorical *enargeia*, or pictorial aspect, outstrips Plutarch's dictum that "*poema pictura loquens*" ("poetry should be a speaking picture") by comparing Adonis's horse to a painting of a horse:[42]

> Look when a painter would surpass the life
> In limning out a well-proportioned steed,
> His art with nature's workmanship at strife,
> As if the dead the living should exceed:
>   So did this horse excel a common one
>   In shape, in courage, colour, pace, and bone. (289–94)

This simile compares the way an idealized painting of a horse outstrips a real horse. The painting is not alive, not animated, but it "exceeds" the living horse in beauty: it is a deception, a *trompe-l'oeil*, because it tricks the viewer into believing that it can "surpass life" (289). Like the painting, which dulls the luster of reality, Adonis's steed outshines all common horses. The phrase "a common one" (293) reminds us that this is no ordinary horse, further distinguishing Adonis's horse from native or "common" horses as an imported Arabian courser, a rare example of perfected breeding, perfectly proportionate "In shape, in courage, colour, pace, and bone" (294). The list of attributes that concludes the stanza sounds like a veterinary or mercantile evaluation of the animal, noting its build, aspect, movement, and structure. But there is something else going on in this simile as well: by drawing attention to the way a painting can represent an object as more beautiful than its model, Shakespeare draws the reader's attention to his own poetic technique and reminds us that

Adonis's horse is also not a real one; it's the creation and addition to the story of a new poet who is not Ovid. Just as the physical description of the horse might resemble a veterinary inventory of features, it is also a humorous poetic blazon, enumerating and fragmenting the horse's features. The painter's craft or "art" in the passage is described as "at strife with" "nature's workmanship" (291), just as Venus describes Adonis's fashioning by Nature "with herself in strife" (11). Like breeding horses or hybridizing flowers, this creator strives to improve the horse, but unlike a gardener or breeder, he works *against* nature's craft hoping to outdo nature, exactly as the poet attempts to outshine Ovid by the addition of breeding imported horses to the narrative.

The simile is formally classical: Roman poets like Ovid and Virgil adapted epic similes from archaic Greek poets like Homer. Its subject matter, however, is the role of painting in early modern global exchanges. Landry makes the important point that, unlike copper or cloth, "a horse can never be a commodity," and Brotton and Jardine show how prized horses were traded individually and never in groups.[43] Horse *imagery*, whether in material or poetic form, as paintings, coins, or metaphors, circulated more widely than horses themselves. As Brotton and Jardine note, medallions, tapestries, paintings, frescoes, and pen-and-ink drawings of real, individual Turkish and Arabian horses (each owned by a nobleman and represented by name) proliferated in the fifteenth and sixteenth centuries.[44] Pisanello's paintings and portrait medals memorialize Byzantine Emperor John VIII Paleologus alongside his favorite horses, and the Gonzaga family, synonymous in the fifteenth century with the Levantine horse trade and breeding, decorated their palaces with *trompe-l'oeil* frescoes of specific breeds they had developed.[45] Like the Arabian horses these Italian nobles imported, *trompe-l'oeil* decoration was an Ottoman import as well.[46]

Shakespeare's analogy of Adonis's horse to an idealized painted portrait reminds us that the circulation of horse imagery in the period could function as its own economy, and such decorative objects might function like currency on the market for horse aficionados. To return to Latour's social networks: if horse-breeding technology was an early modern mediator, then the parallel circulation of horse imagery served as its intermediary, expressing the material changes orchestrated by breeders in a symbolic medium. Perhaps the poet is offering up his own eleven-stanza representation of a fictional Arabian stallion as part of this intermediary network of horse images, comparing his skill as a poet to the skill of the imaginary horse painter in the simile. The poem's imagery of Arabian horse trade and breeding also suggests that there is an anticipated economic value in something as weightless and illusory as poetry.

Throughout the poem, Venus dons various poetic guises, adopting a Renaissance schoolboy's handbook of poetic and rhetorical techniques in her attempt to seduce Adonis. Perhaps in the horse blazon, Shakespeare pits his own poetic technique not just against Ovid's but against Venus as a compendium of classical poetic and rhetorical devices.

For Catherine Belsey, Shakespeare's poem makes use of *trompe l'oeil* imagery to express the illusion of constantly unfulfilled desire: she compares Adonis to Zeuxis's tantalizing grapes, a painted representation so mouthwateringly convincing that it is mistaken for the real thing.[47] For Belsey, deception is at the heart of Venus's misunderstanding of desire. Venus does indeed use deceptive rhetoric to entice Adonis, switching gears frequently whenever it fits her cause. The episode in which Adonis loses his horse can be read as part of Venus's elaborate deception aimed at capturing Adonis, since it easily makes such an elegant rhetorical example in her following speech. Venus begins that hermeneutic exercise by lowering and then building up again the status of Adonis's horse. The horse begins Venus's discourse as Adonis's "palfrey" (385), a mild, effeminate saddle horse, who once tethered transforms into the much inferior breed used for farm work "like a jade . . . tied to the tree" (391). That Venus has herself plucked the horse out from under Adonis and "nimbly" fastened him to the tree (38) hardly matters now. Only the unfettered pursuit of sexual desire elevates the horse from servile breed back to exalted Arabian courser: "Let me excuse thy courser, gentle boy, / And learn of him, I heartily beseech thee, / To take advantage on presented joy" (403–5). Adonis's Arabian courser therefore metamorphoses from Levantine luxury good to painted artistic deception, and finally from palfrey to jade back to courser, a tool for Venus's schoolboy rhetoric of seduction.

Turkish Bulbs

The horse breeding in the opening of the poem finds a counterpart in the horticultural image that ends the poem. After Venus has delivered her powerful lament and curse, metamorphosing love into something inseparable from suffering (this is also Shakespeare's contribution to the story), a second metamorphosis takes place. The poem's description of Adonis's metamorphosis into a striped or speckled flower that Venus cradles in her bosom suggests an alternative ending to this tale of thwarted union and a possible antidote to Venus's curse. Adonis's metamorphosis may carry its own kernel of reproduction because, I would like to argue, the flower Shakespeare describes is not just any flower, root, or seed: it is very likely a bulb, more specifically a marbled tulip or checkered fritillary. Both of these bulbs entered European markets and gardens in the middle of the sixteenth century as Turkish imports, and both, unlike flowers born from seeds, contained their own embryos and were thus well designed for cultivation, transport, and replication. In my reading, the flower that springs up at the end of Shakespeare's poem cannot be an anemone as it is in Ovid's text, because anemones are not variegated (multicolored), and they bloom in the summer, not the spring. The fact that Shakespeare refuses to give the flower a Greek name and instead presents his readers with a different flower, one that is purple and white instead of red, also attests to the poet's decision to transform Ovid's flower into something entirely new.

As the historian Anne Goldgar demonstrates, the European economy was flooded with botanical imports from the middle of the sixteenth century to the middle of the seventeenth.[48] Perhaps the most famous of these imports were Turkish and Persian bulbs, and the most famous bulbs were tulips. What made bulbs so valuable as imports was their hardy, compacted form. Unlike seeds, which need water, soil, and nutrients in order to germinate, producing blooms at the end of this process, bulbs (like corms and tubers) are geophytes: each bulb is its own storage organ that, even when dormant, already contains its embryonic bloom. They are easily propagated, and because they require a long, cold dormancy, they were easy to trade and store when introduced into northern Europe. By the end of the sixteenth century around the first printing of *Venus and Adonis*, a number of bulb species had been introduced into Europe from the Ottoman Empire and Persia, primarily by the Flemish horticulturalist Rembert Dodoens, whose works were translated into French by the botanist Carolus Clusius (Charles de l'Ecluse). By 1597, three years after the first printing of Shakespeare's poem, John Gerard mentioned several bulb species in his *Herball*, including tulip, narcissus, fritillary, ranunculus, and the crown imperial, though Gerard is at times uncertain of their origin and frequently states that he can find no account of these flowers in his classical sources. Henry Lyte's translation of Dodoens's *Herball* from 1578 also mentions the tulip, the fritillary, and the crown imperial, the last two of which had been recently introduced into the gardens of European royalty.[49] According to Goldgar, all of these bulbs first came into Europe in the 1550s from Turkey, and many of them are mentioned for the first time in Clusius's correspondence.[50] Thus, it seems plausible that an early modern reader or writer would read a description of a tulip, fritillary, iris, hyacinth, or crown imperial as a description of an exotic Turkish flower. By 1629, when John Parkinson published his first botanical encyclopedia, *Paradisi in Sole*, most bulbs were considered exotic; Parkinson refers to all bulbs as "Out-Landish plantes."[51]

When Adonis dies, his body evaporates into a mist and from his blood springs a variegated flower, speckled crimson and white, "a purple flower . . . chequered with white, / Resembling well his pale cheeks, and the blood / Which in round drops upon their whiteness stood" (1168–70). The flower might also be purple and red, as the spelling in the Quarto edition reads "check*red*" (emphasis added), and dark red blood is frequently described as purple in Latin texts, owing to the reddish hue of Tyrian purple.[52] In sixteenth-century English, *purple* denoted a color somewhere between violet and red. Yet Ovid uses the word *sanguine* (blood red) to describe the Adonis flower, not *purpureis*, a word he employs to describe Hyacinthus's flower and Atalanta's blushes (*Metamorphoses* 10.213 and 596).[53] What kind of flower is Adonis? Though Burrow maintains that Shakespeare's flower might be an anemone like Ovid's (citing Gerard's *Herball*, which labels red chamomile "false anemone" and "Adonis flower"), Shakespeare refuses to give his flower a Greek or a Latin name, which suggests that his flower is new and not ancient. Ovid, too, is coy about providing Adonis's name as a flower, yet he indicates that the flower has already been named. Instead of including the word *anemone* in his text, Ovid buries the flower's Greek name in a Latin reference to the wind ravaging the flowers' petals: "*namque male haerentem et nimia levitate caducum excutiunt idem, qui praestant nomina, venti*" (10.738–39; "for the winds, which gave a name to the flower, shake off the petals too early, doomed to fall too easily," my translation). The Greek word for wind is *anemos*, which is related to *anemone*.[54]

Most modern English translations of the poem (Humphries, Mandelbaum) insert the word *anemone* somewhere in the last two lines of Book 10, for clarity. Ovid's Latin and Golding's English do no such thing.[55] Ovid names the flower only through metaphoric allusion, employing the Latin word *venti* (winds) to describe the naming of the flower, expecting his readers to be literate in Greek etymology and in the etiology of how the *anemone* became red. Golding's translation is even more obscure about the flower's name than Ovid's, referencing the winds, but not etymologically: "As that the windes that all things perce, with every little blast / Doo shake them off and shed them so as that they cannot last" (10.862–63). Though Golding has the winds shaking off the flower's petals, dooming Adonis to a short life even in his metamorphosed state, Golding's flower remains anonymous. It is therefore possible that Shakespeare's refusal to name the Adonis flower stems from his close reading of Golding's English translation or perhaps from his small knowledge of Greek etymology. But given that he attended a Latin grammar school as a boy (Stratford Guildhall), Shakespeare was surely as familiar with Ovid's Latin text as he was with Golding's English version, so his refusal to mention the flower's Greek name or its name givers (the winds) makes his own Adonis flower something distinct from Ovid's. This is a moment in which we can see Shakespeare deliberately breaking away from Ovid. The refusal to give the flower a Greek or Latin name can be read as a refusal to continue to uphold the story's classical inheritance. At the end of Shakespeare's poem, Adonis does not transform into Ovid's (or Greek myth's) anemone but into something newer and imported from central Asia.[56]

Only two types of flower were described as "checkered" or speckled in early modern English botanical writing, and both were Turkish bulbs.[57] As Burrow notes, a purple or "snake's head" fritillary is the most likely candidate for a checkered flower, its drooping petals most closely resembling a checker-board of dark and pale violet.[58] This peculiarly marked flower has an equally peculiar and unfixed collection of early names. Just as botanists began hybridizing flowers in this period (like Perdita's "pied . . . gillyvor"), so did they hybridize the names of newly imported flowers. Early modern botanists create composites out of two names in naming the fritillary. Henry Lyte's translation of Dodoens calls the fritillary a "lily-narcissus," and Gerard and John Parkinson both call it a "checquered daffodil" as well as labeling it the "Turkie or Ginny-Hen Floure" because of its speckled appearance.[59] Gerard describes the blossom as if it were a painting itself:

> six small leaues checquered most strangely: wherein Nature, or
> rather the Creator of all things, hath kept a very wonderfull order,
> surpassing (as in all other things) the curiousest painting that Art
> can set downe. One square is of a greenish yellow colour, the other
> purple, keeping the same order as well on the backside of the floure,
> as on the inside, although they are blackish in one square, and of a
> Violet colour in an other; insomuch that euery leafe seemeth to be
> the feather of a Ginny hen, whereof it tooke his name.[60]

Like Shakespeare's Adonis flower, this is a "purple" flower whose petals bear a strange checkerboard pattern, as the middle figure in Parkinson's later illustration clearly demonstrates (Figure 8).

Gerard's description of the fritillary unwittingly alludes to the bulb's

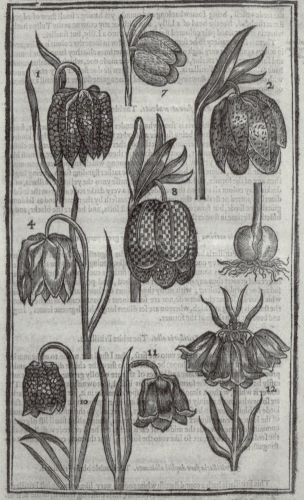

Figure 8. Fritillaries. From John Parkinson, *Paradisi in Sole*
(London: Humfrey Lownes and Robert Young, 1629), 41.
By permission of the Folger Shakespeare Library.

Ottoman origin in naming the bulb the "Turkie or Ginny-Hen" flower. Though here Gerard clearly means turkey the bird, the word *Turkie* cannot help but simultaneously conjure up connotations with the country from which the bird takes its English name. The word *fritillary* most accurately describes the chessboard pattern on the flower's petals, deriving from the Latin name for a Roman dice game, as John Parkinson illustrates: "It is now generally called *Fritillaria,* of the word *Fritillus,* which diuers doe take for the Chesse borde or table whereon they play, whereunto, by reason of the resemblance of the great squares or spots so like it, they did presently referre it."[61] In his enthusiasm over the flower's classical etymology, Parkinson connects its name with another Eastern import, the Persian game chess, which Europeans brought back from the Crusades. The Roman game fritillus had a tall, rectangular dice box perforated with a lattice pattern, not a checkered board.[62] In his poem, Shakespeare replaces this Latin botanical name, deriving from a Roman game, with an English adjective deriving from an Eastern game: *chequered.*

The purple fritillary is like a work of craftsmanship or a decorative object, "the curiousest painting that Art can set downe," in other words a curiosity within nature's cabinet, one that upsets the distinction between art and nature. As late sixteenth-century bulb propagation itself involved playing around with nature—producing more and more vibrant, painterly displays from tulips through "breaking" bulbs (actually introducing a virus into the bulb, a technique first attributed to Clusius) and cross-breeding carnations or gillyflowers—even naturally occurring patterns on bulbs themselves might have seemed like a strange mixture of natural and artificial. The *trompe l'oeil* Arabian courser's formal perfection makes it more like an idealized painting than a living horse, and it makes sense that Shakespeare would choose a natural flower that looks like a painting for Adonis's metamorphosis: the fritillary appears artificial in its natural state, just like Adonis, who is "the curious workmanship of nature" (734).

Another indication that Adonis may be metamorphosed into a fritillary is Venus's prophetic vision of Adonis's bleeding corpse, "Whose blood upon the fresh flowers being shed / Doth make them droop with grief and hang the head" (665–66). Like fritillaries, these flowers are speckled with red and have drooping heads. This prophecy comes to pass, and as Adonis lies bleeding on the ground, "No flower was nigh, no grass, herb, leaf, or weed, / But stole his blood and seem'd with him to bleed" (1055–56). More than mourning Adonis's death as Venus predicts, the flowers bleed with him in sympathy. And although Adonis's body has yet to begin its vapory metamorphosis, he has

already begun to resemble a flower: his skin is "wonted lily white" drenched
"with purple tears" (1053–54). Like fritillaries, daffodils, tulips, and narcissi,
lilies are bulbs.

Perhaps it is no accident that Adonis's body is both "lily white" and "purple." As Burrow notes, *Venus and Adonis* is "haunted" by another Ovidian
character changed into a flower, Narcissus, and, we might add, Hyacinthus.[63]
As an Ovidian poem dedicated to Wriothsely, *Venus and Adonis* was preceded
in 1591 by Henry Clapham's Latin poem *Narcissus*.[64] Like Shakespeare's *Venus
and Adonis*, Ovid's tale of Echo and Narcissus is a story about gender ambiguity
and unfulfilled desire. Adonis's transformation into a purple "lily-narcissus,"
Lyte's name for the fritillary, might be seen to further his connection to Ovid's
other tale of thwarted sexual union and metamorphosis. Though if this is the
case, Adonis is doubly or triply bulb-like, since narcissus and hyacinth are also
bulbs, and thus Adonis's metamorphosis into a Turkish bulb suggests that this
unproductive disunion nevertheless has a lucrative and productive future on
early modern markets. Unlike perennial seeds, unplanted bulbs were capable
not only of self-regeneration but of reproduction, because each bulb was a
storage organ, housing its own embryo.[65] This meant that they were both
transportable and contained the potential to double and triple their yield.
Perennial flowers like anemones come back year after year, but bulbs like fritillaries and tulips come back and multiply. My argument here is not simply that
as a bulb, Adonis-as-flower can regenerate but that he also holds the potential
to *reproduce*, though not in physical, human form.

If not a snake's head fritillary, Adonis might also be a streaked tulip, a
flower whose name alludes to its Ottoman origin. As Charles Evelyn noted
in *Gardening Improv'd* (1717), the fritillary is very closely related to the tulip.
Both bulbs have bell-shaped blossoms made up of six petals, though the fritillary's blossoms are droopier and the tulip's more upright. According to Evelyn, "Their [the fritillaries'] seasons and management is not unlike that of the
Tulip." He renames the fritillary a "*chequer'd Tulip*," which makes more sense
than Gerard's and Parkinson's "chequered daffodil" and "chequered lily."[66]
Gerard's woodcuts of tulips resemble his and Parkinson's fritillaries: both are
variegated and bell shaped (Figure 9).

Since early modern tulips were as capable of variegated color as fritillaries
(though this was expressed in vertical and horizontal stripes and streaks, rather
than checks), it is possible that Adonis's metamorphosis is into a tulip. The
English word *tulip* comes from *tulband*, a Turkish translation of the Persian
word for turban, *dulband*.[67] Indeed, in the late sixteenth century, the words

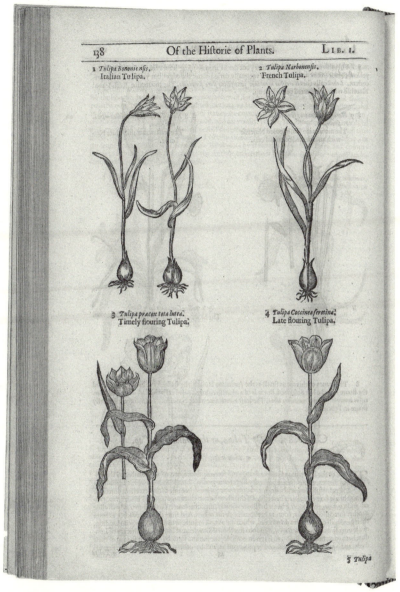

Figure 9. Tulips. From John Gerard, *The herball or Generall historie of plantes* (London: Adam Islip, Joice Norton, and Richard Whitakers, 1633), 139. By permission of the Folger Shakespeare Library.

turban and *tulip* were closer than they are today. For instance, Thomas Washington's translation of Nicolas de Nicolay's description of Turkey calls turbans "tulibants," and Samuel Purchas describes the green turbans worn by Islamic clerics as "Tulipans."[68]

The tulip's tightly folded overlapping petals lend it the appearance of a miniature turban, but this name also marked it as a flower of difference, coming from the East, a place where elaborate dome-shaped headdresses distinguished Ottoman Turks from European travelers.[69] Gerard tightens the connection between tulips and Turkish dress in his description of the flower and its etymology: "the points and brims of the flower turne backward, like a Dalmatian or Turkes cap, called *Tulipan, Tolepan, Turban*, and *Turfan*, whereof it tooke his name."[70] In tulips, an early modern English person could possess the dazzling colors of Ottoman dress in one small flower. In Shakespeare's poem, Venus plucks the flower from its stem, causing it to gush a seminal "Green-dropping sap" (1176), and proceeds to fold it into her bosom as if she were nursing a child: "Here was thy father's bed, here in my breast . . . Lo in this hollow cradle take thy rest" (1183–85). The stalks of bulbs like tulips and fritillaries are dense with viscous fluid like the "Green-dropping sap" that leaks from the stalk of the Adonis flower.[71] Swaddling the flower with her breasts, Venus and the metamorphosed Adonis together resemble a tulip blossom's overlapping turban-like petals. And if Venus is indeed an embodiment of the landscape (Adonis's deer park or Lucretius's Nature), then here she transforms her body into a garden plot where she will plant a flower, with a play on "thy father's bed" (1183). Venus's breast is where Adonis has rested his head, but it is also where she buries the flower, planting it there as if in a garden bed.

According to Gerard and Dodoens (by way of Lyte), tulips came in a mind-boggling variety of color combinations and were noted primarily for their exoticism.[72] Solid-colored tulips existed, but as Gerard maintains, striped and streaked tulips whose petals looked as if they had been spattered with paint, much like Adonis's petals are spattered with blood, were the most popular in the period. Describing multicolored tulips, Gerard states that the petals are "commonly of one ouer-worne colour or other, *Nature seeming to play more with this floure than with any other that I do know*" (emphasis added).[73] If he were transformed into a tulip, Adonis would probably have white petals "over-worne" with blood red, a color that appears frequently in Gerard's descriptions of tulips.

Gerard's descriptions of both tulip and fritillary ought to remind us of Puttenham's "cunning gardener," who makes nature "more strange," and of

Shakespeare's description of Adonis's courser as surpassing a painting of horse. Here, however, Nature, not a human gardener, is the artist who paints the flowers. And according to Lucretius, Venus *is* Nature. By transforming Adonis into a flower, Venus fulfills her role as the force that conjures blossoms and fertility from the earth. But as the goddess Nature, she also paints the flower, noting how Adonis's blood speckles the ground and replicating these spots in the flower's petals itself. The metamorphosis of Adonis into an exotic bulb painted or played with by Nature echoes Shakespeare's earlier metamorphosis of the Arabian courser into an image that transcends a painting.

Nature's "own sweet and cunning hand" (*Twelfth Night*, 1.5.240) may lay paint on tulips, but it is also Shakespeare's poetic hand that paints the bloody speckles and checks onto Adonis's white petals, since Ovid's version of the flower is quite different.[74] Ovid compares the flower's color to a pomegranate, recalling the fatal fruit that instigates Persephone's half-death: "*cum flos de sanguine concolor ortus, / qualem, quae lento celant sub cortice granum, / punica ferre solent*" ("a blood-red flower rose up, similar in color to those pomegranates bear, which hide their seeds underneath an unyielding rind," 10.735–37). Golding's mistranslation of *ferre* (tenacious, unyielding) removes Ovid's emphasis on the harshness of the fruit's rind: "Even like the flower of that same tree whose frute in tender rynde / Have pleasant grayness inclosde" (10.859–60). Whether in Ovid's Latin or in Golding's English, the flower into which Ovid's Adonis transforms is blood red all over, like a pomegranate fruit and blossom, like a red anemone. Shakespeare rejects both pomegranate and anemone, choosing to represent Adonis as a streaked, dotted, or checkered bulb, his petals spattered with blood rather than saturated with it. This emphasizes both Venus-as-Nature's artistic hand as painter of Nature and Shakespeare's poetic one, as remediator of Ovid.

Among the many types of tulip blossoms that Gerard lists, two in particular most closely resemble Adonis's pale cheeks spattered with drops of blood. These are the fourth and fifth tulips Gerard lists, a late-blooming red and white-speckled tulip and the blood-red "apple blossom" tulip. The speckled tulip has red spots all over its heart-shaped white center: "The middle part is like vnto a hart tending to whitenesse, spotted in the same whitenes with red speckles or spots."[75] Like this tulip's white heart, the flower that takes Adonis's place has red or purple speckles that are set off against the background of his white skin, "Which in round drops upon their whiteness stood" (1170). And given that the flower contains the imprint of Adonis's blood, it is interesting Gerard describes the red of an "apple blossom tulip" as sanguine: "The floure consisteth of six small leaues ioyned together at the bottome: the middle of which leaues are of a pleasant bloudy colour, the edges be bordered with white, and the bottome next vnto the stalke is likewise white; the whole floure resembling in colour the blossomes of an Apple tree."[76] Not only are these tulip petals compared to blood; they can also be associated with human cheeks, since cheeks were figuratively described as "apples" in sixteenth-century English.[77]

Cheeks have figured as flowers earlier in the poem, when Venus weeps out of frustration, "Wishing her cheeks were gardens full of flowers, / So they were dew'd with such distilling showers" (65–66). It seems that Venus gets her wish with a heavy dose of irony, as it is Adonis's cheeks and not her own that become a garden, speckled not with dew but with blood.[78] Despite this dark resolution, and in spite of Venus's powerful curse that bequeaths pain to love, if we read Adonis's transformation into a flower as one into a bulb, his death still contains the chance of regeneration into a larger garden like a bulb's inner embryo or its ability to split to form other bulbs, especially if we interpret Venus enfolding the flower into her bosom (its father's "bed," 1183) as the planting of a garden into her already floribund and earthbound body as Lucretius's goddess.[79] Early modern collections of verse frequently described themselves as gardens and posies (a word that has as its root the same root for *poetry*, the Greek word *poieisin*, "to make"), such as George Gasgoine's *A Hundreth sundrie Flowres bounde up in one small Poesie* (1573) and Isabella Whitney's *Sweet Nosegay, or Pleasant Poesy Containing a Hundred and Ten Philosophical Flowers* (1573). Given that *Venus and Adonis* was Shakespeare's first published poem, we might see its ending as a promise to his audience that there will be more poetic "flowers" to come. The choice to turn Adonis into an exotic bulb, whether a fritillary or a variegated tulip, might then be seen as a calculation on the part of Shakespeare in order to generate literary currency in the same way that bulbs in sixteenth-century Europe generated speculative currency. For ballast to this claim, we need only to turn to Lisa Jardine's description of how the demand for exact copies made the sixteenth-century printed book trade mirror the Turkish bulb market: when people saw bulbs growing in others' gardens or books in booksellers' stalls, they wanted the same specimens for themselves.[80] Venus herself describes the flower as Adonis's offspring, "Sweet issue of a more sweet-smelling sire" (1178), adopting it as her own, simulating nursing when she places it at her breast, "Here was thy father's bed, here in my breast" (1183). The transformation of Adonis into an imported bulb therefore embodies Shakespeare's hopes for the poem's printed success, the "hopeful expectation" for theoretical offspring that concludes the prefatory epistle. Adonis has been killed and Venus left unsatisfied, but the garden of his remains will propagate as (the poet hopes) it is printed in successive copies and editions.

The fritillary or tulip springs up from Adonis's blood, but the rest of his body "Was melted like a vapour" (1166). If Adonis's blood transforms into a flower that holds the possibility of regeneration, then what happens to his body gestures toward a different kind of floral production: perfume, in the form of liquid or smoke. Shakespeare's depiction of the vaporization of Adonis's flesh recalls Ovid's image of Venus conjuring a mist of tiny bubbles from Adonis's blood. In Ovid's text, Venus sprinkles nectar on the blood, causing it to vaporize like a mist on a lake, in Golding's translation "like bubbles sheere that rise in weather cleere / On water" (856–87). In both Ovid's and Shakespeare's poems, the image is of Adonis dispersing into a fine mist, though in the latter, Adonis's entire body dissolves into the air, suggesting that total bodily loss is necessary in order for regenerative transformation to occur within the blood. This mist is fragrant, not only because Ovid has Venus apply nectar to the blood but because the early modern English word *perfume* indicated a scented vapor or smoke (from Latin *per fumare*, to suffuse with smoke).[81] Adonis's fleshly dispersal into a mist calls to mind two imported scented vapors fashioned from botanicals: cannabis or tobacco smoked in nargiles and flowers distilled into perfume.[82]

Much of the poem's emotional action is characterized by metaphors of deliquescence, as Jonathan Gil Harris observes.[83] Most of these images of liquefaction are also fragrant ones: Adonis's breath is like "steam" (63) on which Venus feeds, sucking in his breath as one "drinks" smoke, wishing her cheeks gardens of flowers "So they were dewed with such distilling showers" (66). The mingling of Adonis's vaporous breath with Venus's imagined floral cheeks produces a distillation, the very act required to transform a flower's scent into perfume. Venus clarifies the image of Adonis's breath as perfume further when she compares Adonis's breath to perfume: "From the stillatory of thy face excelling / Comes breath perfumed, that breedeth love by smelling" (443–44). Here, Adonis's face becomes an alembic that distills flowers into a misty, productive essence that "breedeth love." As Holly Dugan notes, the image of breeding here plays with early modern metaphors of poetic reproduction as a productive distillation of beauty.[84] Even Adonis's horse produces hormonally scented steam, "As from a furnace, vapours doth he send" (274). And when Venus's tears begin to fall more slowly, they become a valuable, imported substance: "Yet sometimes falls an orient drop beside, / Which her cheek melts"

(981–82). As I will discuss in the next chapter, in sixteenth-century English, the word *orient* came to mean "pearly" as well as Eastern; the image of Venus's tears sitting in her eyes can therefore be understood as "pearls in glass." But an "orient drop" could also indicate a drop of precious oriental balsam or attar of roses, or any number of expensive perfumes imported from the Arab world (as most of them were), "All the perfumes of Arabia" (*Macbeth*, 5.1.51). It is true, as Dugan observes, that not all perfumes were exotic and oriental—many had been "produced, distributed, and represented" in England since 1400.[85] But an "orient drop" is certainly not a local perfume, if we interpret *orient* as meaning "Eastern," just as Cleopatra's "strange invisible perfume" (*Antony and Cleopatra*, 2.2.217) cannot be English, if we read *strange* in its early modern sense as "foreign."

The anxious anticipation of a fruitful poetic harvest appears most clearly in the dedicatory epistle that prefaces the poem. Shakespeare christens *Venus and Adonis* "the first heir of my invention," his patron the earl of Southampton its "godfather," and its anticipated reception a "harvest." Though this language of generation, legacy ("heir"), and yield ("harvest") can be taken as a subtle suggestion to the unwed Southampton to marry and preserve his lineage, the phrasing of the epistle remains ambiguous. The poem is not yet a success, the result only a "hopeful expectation," like a father awaiting the birth of his first son, too cautious to accept praise. What the epistle suggests is not fruition but the potential of fruition, the possibility of generation, just as the images of horses and bulbs in the poem hint at the possibility for regeneration in the face of rejection, loss, and grief. As Burrow verifies, the poem succeeded in this enterprise, launching Shakespeare's literary career, seeing at least sixteen editions by 1640, so few of which survive today that Burrow surmises that "many eager readers read their copies to pieces."[86] Adam Hooks's extensive study of the marketing of *Venus and Adonis* by contemporary booksellers also lends credence to the poem's literary success in its own time.[87] As I mentioned in my chapter on sugar, it was this poem along with *The Rape of Lucrece* that earned Shakespeare the epithet "Hony-Tongued" from Francis Meres, through which Meres portrays Shakespeare as the reincarnation of Ovid. Thus, Shakespeare, Ovid's poetical offspring, is born out of the Latin poet's text of marred and disrupted sexual union.

In her cultural history of thoroughbred horses in the long eighteenth century, Landry demonstrates how sixteenth- and seventeenth-century European aristocrats acquired Ottoman and Arabian horses in order to naturalize and dominate the Ottoman imperial power they envied.[88] Though *Venus and*

Adonis could easily be said to participate in this "imperial envy" (a concept Landry shares with Gerald MacLean), not only in its incorporation of an Arabian horse and a Turkish bulb but in its reworking of a Roman poet and subject, Shakespeare takes this naturalization process further, using the language and imagery of new, living imports from the Ottoman Empire and Arab world, implanting in his verse an alternative ending to his own, more comic and tragic reworking of Ovid's poem. Shakespeare's imagery of living Levantine imports may not counteract Adonis's coldness and death or Venus's legacy of suffering in love, but it will engraft new growth onto Ovid's truncated genealogy that ends *Metamorphoses* 10. In so doing, Shakespeare transplants Ovid's ancient Mediterranean into an English countryside where Levantine imports are taking root, replacing one ancient empire with the fantasy of a new, more powerful one. This new empire is not the Ottoman Empire but England's imagined global mercantile and linguistic one. Shakespeare's poem builds a new, global English landscape of imported words and things, reformulating Spenser's wish to "have the kingdom of our own language."[89] Shakespeare's participatory global poetics thus runs somewhat counter to Jonson's later desire to construct an English plain style that cautiously draws from ancient classical sources but remains more firmly rooted in native English, as discussed in Chapter 1. Yet though Jonson objects to distended, barbarous, invented language, he also longs for a poetic and linguistic economy that is England's own in a widening world. As the following chapter and epilogue will demonstrate, perhaps it was English poetry itself, a poetics inflected with both ancient classical and contemporary Mediterranean language and imagery, that allowed early modern readers and writers to make sense of this new and expanding world.

PART III

Reorienting Antiquity

Chapter 5

On Chapman Crossing Marlowe's Hellespont: Pearls, Dyes, and Ink in *Hero and Leander*

Over the course of this book, I have described the effect that Ottoman and Asian imports, in their verbal and visual representation, had on early modern English poetry, how they disrupted and reconfigured early modern attitudes to literary classical antiquity. Both the imports (words, sugar, zero, horses, bulbs) and the network of poetic images representing them within a given literary text functioned as mediators and intermediaries, reshaping how people thought about language, style, poetry, nothing, writing, hybridization, and textual reproduction. In this chapter, I will examine a final set of Middle Eastern and Asian imports: pearls and pigments. Like the imported words and things examined in the previous chapters, these two commodities reconfigured Elizabethan culture in complex and different ways. Pearls functioned as intermediaries in premodern narratives of chastity and purity, figuratively representing virginal whiteness and impenetrability. Once pearls acquired the adjective *orient*, they were marked as non-Western, and yet they continued to represent female sexual purity and whiteness symbolically. Marlowe's poem *Hero and Leander* inverts this symbolic vocabulary, reconfiguring—and remediating—pearl imagery into its opposite: sexual fluidity and freedom. The trade in pigments and recipes for colorfast dyes was regulated by the Ottoman Empire, and the recipes for Turkey Red and Tyrian Purple were closely guarded secrets. Dye technology was thus a cultural mediator, but one that the sixteenth- and seventeenth-century English were unable to retrieve. However, English merchants were adept in the use of *figurative* pigments: the colors of rhetorical and mercantile dissimulation. Both types of coloring surface in

Chapman's poem, which transforms dyes and ink into images of failure, and poetry into a mediator between mortals and gods, as well as East and West.

This concluding chapter synthesizes the several actions I have attributed to imported words and things. Previously, I have examined the semantic disruptions that foreign imports create in such literary representations of classical antiquity as the Roman state (Jonson) and *ars poetica* (Jonson and Puttenham), as well as the way that networks of imagery and words representing imported things allow poets like Shakespeare to imagine more redemptive and productive legacies to Ovidian narrative poetry. Here, in the Hellespont of Marlowe's and Chapman's *Hero and Leander*, I find an early modern literary depiction of classical antiquity not at odds with the contemporary Ottoman Mediterranean but coterminous with it. In Marlowe's *Hero and Leander*, the imagery of oriental pearls liberates the characters in the classical source narratives (by Musaeus and Ovid) from their tragic condition, just as the imagery of zero and O, horses and bulbs allows Shakespeare to recuperate and rehabilitate the tragic loss he locates in Ovidian epyllia. Unlike Shakespeare's epyllia, which I argued use imagery of Middle Eastern and Asian merchandise to depart from classical source narratives, Marlowe's poem cycles back to his classical sources, reorienting Asian pearl imagery to celebrate Ovidian sexual freedom, or *libertas*. And though Chapman's view of empire is more anxious and precarious than Marlowe's, Chapman's references to Ottoman pigments, paints, dyes, and inks allow his characters to negotiate across the precarious and heavily policed Hellespont, mirroring the way rhetorical dissimulation worked in the same space within early modern Anglo-Ottoman diplomacy. In Chapman's continuation of *Hero and Leander*, vocabularies and imagery of imported things do not simply disrupt and reconfigure attitudes toward classical poetry; the colors of the East merge with the colors of classical rhetoric, working together to advance the power of figurative language and poetic dissimulation not only within the poem but in the early modern Hellespont as well. In both Marlowe's and Chapman's versions of the poem, Asian and Middle Eastern commodities complement the poem's Greek and Roman inflections. Much of this is accomplished geographically, by locating the story in and around the Hellespont, a layered, palimpsestic landscape that is also fluid and shifting because it is a body of water.

The two sets of imports I will examine here—Marlowe's pearls and Chapman's pigments—appear in each poet's version of *Hero and Leander* as both words (names for colors) and images. Much of Marlowe's poem is characterized by jewel-encrusted imagery—Hero's clothing is gilded and ornamented with "hollow pearl and gold"; she cries streams of pearl; the temple of Venus, where she is a priestess, is a monument of sculpted semiprecious stones and minerals; and Neptune's palace below the sea brims with shipwrecked treasure. Additionally, Hero's virginity is repeatedly referred to as a precious jewel. All of this gemstone imagery makes more sense when we locate Marlowe's poem in the Hellespont, the center of European and Ottoman trade, straddling the Aegean and the Black Sea, separating Europe from Asia Minor, and central Asia from the Mediterranean. In the early modern period, these gems were primarily Middle Eastern and South Asian imports, and their role, as I will argue, is to reconfigure Western ideas about sex and chastity. Chapman's continuation is similarly shot through with imagery, but in his case, the imagery is of colors, many of which derived from imported valuable pigments and dye-stuffs from eastern Europe, central Asia, and the Far East: pigments like *alkermes* (the scarlet grain beetle and the source of the English word *crimson*), *Rubia tinctorum* or madder, and Syrian oak galls for producing black dyes and ink. In Chapman's poem, black dyes transfer onto skin, and characters drown in floods of ink. Brilliant colors imported from the East mask the truth, representing poetic dissimulation, which the poem both warns against and advocates. Both poets draw upon the language and imagery of precious natural and mineral imports in a commercial Ottoman-inflected landscape, reorienting an ancient classical myth through poetry.

Two *Hero and Leanders*

Published in 1598, five years after Christopher Marlowe's death, *Hero and Leander* narrates an ancient Greek myth of lovers living on either side of the Hellespont (now called Dardanelles, located in western Turkey). *Hero and Leander* is usually treated as a narrative poem—a playful Ovidian epyllion, or *erotopaignon*—written by Christopher Marlowe. But for early modern readers, it was a longer poem with a tragic outcome, as stated on the title page of the second edition of 1598: "begun" by Marlowe and "finished" by George Chapman.[1] Marlowe's poem, first printed alone in 1598, tells the story of ancient lovers separated by the Hellespont, a story that ends after their second parting but before their watery deaths. It was assumed unfinished, but later that year, Paul Linley printed an edition of the poem appending George Chapman's continuation (twice the length of Marlowe's original text), and the eight editions that followed until 1637 continued to be printed as a Marlowe-Chapman joint effort. By 1609, the poems were printed as one continuous text, omitting Chapman's dedicatory material that broke the text in two. And Chapman continued his work with *Hero and Leander*, publishing the first English translation of the sixth-century Byzantine poet Grammaticus Musaeus's version of the Hero and Leander story under the title *The Divine Poem of Musaeus* (1616).[2]

At first glance, the two parts of the epyllion contrast starkly: Marlowe's rhetorically playful pansexual comedy of young love seems unprepared for Chapman's somber moral tragedy. Where Marlowe celebrates insouciant desire, Chapman has the gods brutally chastise his protagonists for indulging in premarital sex. In Marlowe's text, Hero's nakedness lights her chamber like a second sunrise; in Chapman's, her shameful blushes darken the room. In Marlowe's part, the god Neptune courts Leander; in Chapman's, heterosexual deities fiercely regulate morality: while the goddess Ceremony lectures Leander on the social necessity of marriage, a sadistic Venus frightens the chastity back into Hero by whipping one of her swans senseless.

Nevertheless, both Marlowe's and Chapman's poems reconfigure the classical literary past in early modern geographic and mercantile terms. In both texts, the bodies and spaces of the characters are charged with references to England's newly established but precarious mercantile trade in the East. For Marlowe, the boundaries of empire are permeable and dynamic. Marlowe's Hellespont is a fluid, synchronic space, at once ancient and modern, European and Eastern. The dominant imagery of historical and geographical fluidity in Marlowe's poem is also that of sexual fluidity, illustrated by a symbolic vocabulary of nacreous, *orient* pearls. In Marlowe's Hellespont, the bottom of the sea glitters with gold, abalone, coral, and pearl, available for anyone to seize—anyone who can reach them without drowning, that is. Marlowe's amorous Neptune treats water-borne Leander as one such gem, making this free-trade zone a bit more like a "rough trade" zone. For Chapman, the boundaries between West and East and past and present are similarly fluid and shifting, but they are also consistently contested and renegotiated.

Chapman's use of exotic imports presents a more anxious view of empire than Marlowe's. The imagery of Middle Eastern and Asian luxury goods—in this case, that of Turkish and Persian dyes, pigments and colored cloth—is employed to represent the lovers' attempts to conceal their premarital activities from the gods. The gods here respond as if the boundaries of their empire have been contested, attempting to colonize and contain the lovers' heedless sexual misdemeanors against the background of a shifting commercial and political landscape in which slippage and indeterminacy reign supreme. For Chapman, rich crimsons, dense blacks, and purples indicate the lovers' loss and betrayal by bleeding and staining their bodies.

Furthering the analogy this book has made between Bruno Latour's intermediaries, mediators, and early modern imported words and things, pearls and dyes function as modified mediators and intermediaries in early modern English mercantile culture and in Marlowe's and Chapman's texts.[3] Marlowe converts an early modern English symbolic vocabulary of pearls-as-chaste into an argument for sexual freedom, emphasizing pearls' fluidity. Part of this transformation depends upon new, early modern uses of the word *orient* to mean pearly. In this way, Marlowe remediates a Western early modern cultural commonplace—the pearl-as-blazon—relocating it at the crossroads between East and West. Within his poem, pearly imagery and words work as intermediaries, where the nacreous, watery nature of the substance of pearls comes to symbolize a longed for social change, in this case a change in sexual mores. Chapman's text, on the other hand, dramatizes English and European anxieties and fantasies about a longed- for mediator—Ottoman colorfast dye technology—while at the same time revealing an expanded social network that connects mercantile and diplomatic practices of deception to classical rhetoric and early modern poetics. Therefore, Chapman's use of colors and dyes suggests that rhetorical tropes, and poetry itself, could function as a mediator, changing the fabric of late Elizabethan culture.

Three Hellesponts

Marlowe's *Hero and Leander* opens with a geographic description. We enter the story in a liminal space, the body of water that divides the lovers from one another:

> On *Hellespont* guilty of true loues blood,
> In view and opposite, two Cities stood,
> Seaborders, disioined by *Neptune's* might:
> The one *Abydos*, the other *Sestos* hight. (1–4)

The Hellespont divides more than Hero from Leander, Sestos from Abydos, and the Mediterranean from the Black Sea: it also separates Europe and Asia Minor. Here, "On Hellespont," is where the early modern Ottoman Empire begins to encroach on the world of classical mythology and where, in the sixteenth and seventeenth centuries, European merchant companies clashed, competing for the right to import fine cloth, jewels, medicine, and spices. An Italian faience plate (1525) shows that Marlowe was not the only artist to transpose the myth of Hero and Leander into the world of early modern seafaring and trade. Set against a background of a busy Renaissance port, the lovers court amid ships and canons (Figure 10).

When Ovid wrote his *Heroides* (the earlier of Marlowe's two source texts) between 25 and 16 BCE, the Emperor Augustus had already planned the eastward expansion of the Roman Empire. This was later completed during the reigns of Nero and Trajan in the first century CE, with both sides of the Hellespont (Thrace and Asia Minor) formally added to the Roman Empire. By the fifth century, the time of the Byzantine poet Grammaticus Musaeus (and author of Marlowe's second source), Thrace and Asia Minor were firmly established as part of the Roman Empire. The space became a zone of conflict between East and West as early as the First Crusade at the end of the eleventh century, when at the bequest of Pope Urban II, Catholic Europeans came to the aid of Byzantine Christian Emperor Alexios I Komnenos to help him repel the Muslim Seljuk Turks invading from Anatolia. And in early modern England, the Hellespont belonged to another Empire: though the Dardanelles remained Orthodox until the 1380s, from the 1450s onward, they formed the center of the Ottoman Empire. And very near to the Dardanelles was the prized capital Constantinople or Byzantium, which the Eastern Christians lost to the Ottoman (Muslim) Turks in 1453. Mercator's Atlas of 1595 depicts the vastness of the Ottoman Empire in the early modern period. It easily encompassed all the parts of Asia Minor that the Romans had conquered.

To early modern English eyes, the Hellespont might have appeared as a geographical palimpsest, a text written over a partially obscured earlier text, a space layered with ancient loss, medieval betrayal, and early modern commercialism. In the Introduction, I discussed the English antiquarian and Ovidian scholar George Sandys's perception of the Ottoman Empire as characterized by ambivalence, combining grief with discovery. Sandys struggled to make sense of the multiple temporalities that infused the landscape. Finding the layers of the ancient classical world, which must have appeared so vivid in his well-read humanist mind, fragmented and in ruins, Sandys was instead confronted with the rich and colorful, multiethnic and multireligious hustle and bustle of contemporary Ottoman sea trade and urban life. A similar ambivalence infuses his experience of the Hellespont, and his narrative of the seascape

Figure 10. Plate with Hero and Leander, artist unknown. Italian Faenza ware (tin-glazed earthenware), c. 1525. Courtesy of the J. Paul Getty Museum, Los Angeles.

is a chorography layered with loss and control. Sandys describes three histories of the Hellespont, the first history classical, the second a medieval romance, and the third an early modern, commercial account.

First, Sandys characterizes the Hellespont as the site of several Greek myths of tragic loss. Sandys contends that the Hellespont takes its name from the tragic fate of the maiden Helle, "the daughter of *Athamas* King of *Thebes*, and sister of *Phryxus*, who, flying the stratagems of their step mother *Ino*, was drowned therein."[4] The ancient city of Troy was located on the Asian side, but rather than describe the Greek encampment and the destruction of Troy (as Fynes Moryson did two years later), Sandys dwells on Chersonesus, the peninsula jutting out into the Hellespont, which he links to the story of

Hecuba's postwar captivity and demise. Hecuba was supposedly buried on this peninsula in a tomb called *Cynossema*. The other stories of loss tied to this landscape include "the vnfortunate loues of *Hero* and *Leander*, drowned in the vncompassionate surges," and the Persian king Xerxes' bridge of boats built across the water to (unsuccessfully) invade Thrace (on the European side). The general, who famously whipped the Hellespont in a futile attempt to make it obey him like a horse, rows back across the same waters broken and disgraced (here Sandys quotes Lucan, in Sandys's own English translation): "But how return'd? Dismaid, through bloud-stain'd seas, / With one boate, stopt by floting carcasses."[5]

For his second tale, Sandys jumps ahead to the Middle Ages, noting that both sides of the Hellespont have been under Ottoman control since the mid-fourteenth century, "in the reign of *Orchanes*," or Orhan I (1326–59). For Sandys, the loss of the Hellespont foreshadows the later Eastern Christian "loss" of Constantinople to the Muslim Ottoman Empire in 1453. Sandys recounts that the defining moment of the loss of the Hellespont came when a Byzantine Christian woman living in Abydos (the city on the Asian side of the Hellespont) betrayed her people for the love of a Muslim Turkish general. The daughter of the general of Abydos dreams that she falls into a ditch and is rescued by a gorgeously clothed gentleman who gives her rich garments. She then spots the Turkish general, believes he is her dream lover, and helps him take her castle by stealth. This story is actually Turkish in origin—and early modern.

This exogamous romance derives from the chronicles of Hoca Sadeddin Efendi (Sad'ud'din, 1536–99), the court historian for Sultan Murad III, who was the first sultan to allow the English to trade on Ottoman soil.[6] Sadeddin's original history of this siege located it not in Abydos, but in Aydos, a city in northern Anatolia near Iznik, but early modern English readers continued to associate the romance with the Hellespont, certainly up to and after Robert Stapylton's translation of Musaeus in 1646.[7] Sandys probably read a paraphrased version of the tale in Richard Knolles's *Generall Historie of the Turks*, published in 1603.[8] Here the Hellespont has begun to be associated with trade, as the Byzantine lady is enticed by the material riches of the Ottoman Empire, the heavy damasks, and precious gemstones found along the Silk Road.[9] In a sense, this account recasts the tale of Hero and Leander, the lovers from European Sestos and Asian Abydos, as an exogamous romance of religious difference and Muslim conquest. This is not an unusual way for an early modern to think about the Hellespont. As Sujata Iyengar has pointed out, in early modern drama, the Hellespont is a metaphor for a cuckholded husband who separates a European lady from her Eastern lover.[10]

Sandys's classical and medieval narratives characterize the Hellespont as treacherous and unstable, but his third narrative catapults his readers into the Hellespont of 1610, a busy commercial customs port, heavily policed and guarded on both sides by the Turkish military. This echoes descriptions made by earlier French travelers André Thevêt and Nicolas de Nicolay.[11] On the sites of ancient Sestos (Thrace) and Abydos (Asia Minor), the Turks have built two castles, each of which is more like a military garrison than a palace, "nothing lesse then inuincible, by reason of the ouer-peering mountaines that bracket the one, and slender fortification of the other to land-ward."[12] These edifices are illustrated in the engraving accompanying the text (Figure 11).[13] The "castles" operate as customs gatekeepers, detaining the flow of European merchant ships, calling for passports and searching the commodities on board: "All ships are suffered to enter, that by their multitude and appointment to threaten no inuasion; but not to returne without search and permission."[14] So strict is the Ottoman control over the water and both banks of the Hellespont that Sandys describes it as imprisoning the landscape: "the *Turke*, as it were, chaineth vp the *Propontick* Sea: so that none passe in or out, without his allowance, and discharge of duties."[15]

Fynes Moryson's journey across the Hellespont (published two years after Sandys's) corroborates and augments Sandys's description, emphasizing the military precision and rigor of the Turkish customs searches:

> For the ships that come from *Constantinople*, vse to bee detained
> here some three daies. . . . Besides, these searchers and Customers
> looke, that they carry no prohibited wares, neither can the ship, nor
> any passenger be suffered to passe these Castles, except they bring
> the Pasport of the great Turke, which the chiefe Visere or Basha
> vseth to grant vnto them. Thus when no ship without the knowl-
> edge of the chiefe Visere can either passe these Castles leading to the
> *Mediterranean* Sea, or the two Castles aboue leading into the *Euxine*
> Sea, noted with (D E), surely these foure Castles are the greatest
> strength of *Constantinople* by Sea.[16]

Moryson's text is illustrated with a woodcut map of the Hellespont and its edifices, one of which looks like a fortified wall of connected towers to the west of the channel, more of a military complex than a castle (Figure 12).

their orisons, and from thence ascend the mountaine to open the veine from whence they produce it:which they do with great preparations and solemnities, accompanied with the principall *Turkes* of the Iland. That which couereth it being remoued by the labour of wel-nigh fiftie pioners, the Priests take out as much as the *Cadee* doth thinke for that yeare sufficient, (lest the price should abate by reason of the abundance) to whom they deliuer it: and then close it vp in such sort, as the place where they digged is not to be discerned. The veine discouered, this precious earth, as they say, doth arise like the casting vp of wormes; and that onely during a part of that day: so that it is to be supposed rather that they gather as much as the same will affoord them. Certaine bags thereof are sent to the great *Turke*: the rest they sell (of which I haue seene many cups at *Constantinople:*) but that which is sold to the Merchants, is made into little pellets, and sealed with the *Turkish* character. The ceremonies in the gathering hereof were first inducted by the *Venetians*.

And now we entred the *Hellespont*,

A. *Mount Ida.*	D. *Abidos.*	G. *Zenhenic.*	K. *Cape Ianizary.*
B. *Tenedos.*	E. *Sestos.*	H. *Hellespont.*	L. *Ruines of Alexandria.*
C. *Seate of old Troy.*	F. *Mayto.*	I. *Gallipolis.*	M. *Mouth of Simois and Scamander.*

so called of *Helle* the daughter of *Athamas* King of *Thebes*, and sister of *Phryxus*: who, flying the stratagems of their step-mother *Ino*, was drowned therein. Bounded on the left hand with the *Thracian Chersonesus* (vulgarly called *S.Georges* arme) a *peninsula* pointing to the Southwest: whereon stood the Sepulcher of *Hecuba*, called *Cynossema*, which signifieth a Dog: fained to haue bene metamorphosed into one, in regard of her impatiencie. She in the diuision of the *Troian* captiues, contemned, derided, and auoided of all, fell to the hated share of *Vlysses*: when to free her selfe from shame and captiuitie, shee leapt into the *Hellespont*. But *Dictus Cretensis* saith, that distracted with her miseries, and execrating the enemy, she was
slaine

Figure 11. Map of the Hellespont. From George Sandys, *A Relation of a Iourney begun an: Dom: 1610* (1615), 24. By permission of the Folger Shakespeare Library.

iects as others, so as no man sayleth into these parts, but vnder the Banner of *England*, *France*, or *Venice*, who being in league with the great Turke, haue their Ambassadours in this Citie, and their Consuls in other Hauens, to protect those that come vnder their Banner, in this sort sending them a Ianizare to keepe them from wrongs, so soone as they are aduertised of their arriuall.

My selfe lodged in the house of Master *Edward Barton*, the English Ambassadour, who gaue me a Ianizare to guide and protect me, while I went to view the City, round about the whole circuit whereof I went on foot and by boat in foure houres space, the forme of the Citie being triangular, and containing nine miles by Sea towards the North and East, and fiue miles by land towards the West. I professe my selfe to haue small skill in the art of Geography, yet will I aduenture (though rudely) to set downe the forme and situation of this City, so plainely, as I doubt not but the Reader may easily vnderstand it; howsoeuer in the same (as in other cities formerly described) I acknowledge that I vse not the rule of the scale, in the distance of places, nor other exquisite rules of that Art, hauing no other end, but to make the Reader more easily vnderstand my description.

The description of the City of Constantinople, and the adiacent Territories and Seas.

The great lines or walles shew the forme of the City, and the single small lines describe the Territory adioyning. (A) In this Tower they hang out a light of pitch and like burning matter, to direct the Saylers by night, comming to the City, or sayling along the coast out of the Sea *Euxinus* (which they say is called the Black Sea of many
                                                                              shipwracks

Figure 12. Map of the Hellespont. From Fynes Moryson, *An Itinerary* (1617), 260. By permission of the Folger Shakespeare Library.

The Hellespont was the only way merchant ships could reach both Constantinople on the Black Sea, the capital and busiest port of the Ottoman Empire, and the Greek islands, responsible for many of the most valuable commodities to the Mediterranean: Candia, or Crete, supplied olive oil and flour to the Ottomans, while Zante (Zakynthos) and Cephalonia supplied the tiny dried raisins—currants—that kept the European economy rich. By policing the Hellespont, the Ottoman Empire ensured that it controlled access to international mercantile trade, which in turn strengthened its empire. In the Introduction, I have drawn on Palmira Brummett's portrayal of the early modern Ottoman Empire as an institution built not around land battles but trade routes. It is worth returning to her depiction of the sixteenth-century Ottoman Empire. It is a merchant state in which conquest and commercialism are atemporal and inseparable, "not fixed in time and space," and "negotiable, like commerce."[17] This meant that the boundaries of the Ottoman Empire were unfixed and fluid, located in the seas along trade zones, rather than delineated on maps or patrolled territories, and that these spaces carried their histories with them.[18]

The early modern Hellespont was an important Ottoman boundary and trade zone. By regulating the flow of ships and goods through the Hellespont, the Ottoman Empire maintained its imperial hold on the countries and nations on either side of the channel, as well as the goods that were traded between them. Materially, bodies of water function differently from landscape, as Steve Mentz points out in his reading of Shakespeare's oceans.[19] In the water, says Mentz, our senses are warped and reconfigured; we see, hear, taste, and feel things differently; we are forced to move more slowly.[20] Marlowe's and Chapman's Hellespont is as much about the water as it is about the Asian and European towns on either side. Pearls are found at the bottom of the ocean and characterized by jewelers and merchants by their *water*, a term used alongside *orient* to describe their shine and nacre. From the Middle Ages to the late seventeenth century, it was believed that pearls were made from water, formed when oysters rose to the surface of the ocean at night to receive seminal dew from the moon. For Marlowe, it is the water's transformative properties, which he associates with pearls, that allow his young lovers to cross the threshold from innocence into sexual maturity. Water is also a necessary ingredient in dye baths and ink. As much as it can wash bodies clean, it combines with pigments to darken and mark them. For Chapman, the waters of the Hellespont both obscure the truth by gilding Leander's limbs when he swims home and reveal it as Hero's shameful salty tears wash the black dye from her veil and onto her cheeks.

Water's transformative and unstable properties make it an effective vehicle for understanding how seafaring European merchants conducted themselves around the Mediterranean Sea. Alison Games's historical analysis of early modern English mercantile travelers' experience in the Ottoman Mediterranean provides a frame of reference for my reading of the poetic Hellespont. Games reveals that the English who trafficked in the Ottoman Mediterranean viewed the seascape and its peoples as both alluring and dangerous and, in order to establish themselves as legitimate traders in this unstable space, engaged in tactics of disguise, dissimulation, and role-playing.[21] In other words, they adopted the fluid, shape-shifting qualities of water in their behaviors on land, sometimes darkening their skin to blend in. To the English setting out on their mercantile ventures, the Ottoman Mediterranean was an unstable space in which one might encounter riches, piracy, and alternative sexualities, much as Marlowe characterizes the rough currents of the Hellespont governed by Neptune. As Games notes, "Travelers were interested in cloistered communities, polygamy, the harem, eunuchs, and homosexuality, and so, it seems, were their readers . . . In their manuscript and published accounts of the Mediterranean . . . Scots and English visitors described it as a place where all sorts of appetites could be satisfied and all sorts of domestic living and sexual arrangements could be sanctioned."[22] Marlowe also connects water to nonnormative sexualities. Across the Hellespont from his home in Anatolia, Leander is courted by "the barbarous Thracian soldier" (1.81) and embraced by the god Neptune as he swims across it (2.167).

In order to succeed in their ventures, English merchants in Ottoman lands had to engage in rhetorical and visual deception and equivocation, just as Chapman describes Hero doing with imagery of colors and dyes in his continuation of Marlowe's poem. In addition to adopting native dress and gesture as soon as they arrived, English traders were advised to keep a low profile and not to admit to being English, for self-preservation as well as for political reasons: "For those who journeyed in the Mediterranean, deceit was important both for minor advantages—better sightseeing—and for major considerations—saving life and limb."[23] Engaging in Mediterranean trade had much in common with navigating the treacherous currents of the Hellespont. It was sink or swim, and English traders learned to swim by swiftly disguising and adapting themselves to other cultures.

Though Sandys's and Moryson's Hellespont is a precarious space, Sandys's three histories stress a continuity, rather than abrupt shifts from Roman to Christian to Ottoman. The same cultural expansion and proliferation of imports that Ovid describes in his poetry might be seen to apply to the early modern European view of the Ottoman Empire. As a body of water, the Hellespont is also a space of fluid borders rather than strict boundaries and must therefore be policed and guarded carefully by the Turks in order to ensure their continued commercial and imperial success. The early modern Hellespont, then, can be read as a *liquid* palimpsest. As Jonathan Gil Harris has argued, the tension between temporal layers in palimpsests creates an additional temporality of disruption, one that "allows [the] past to speak back."[24] This chapter explores how the ancient Hellespont "speaks back"—or, rather, across—both to the early modern commercial Hellespont and to early modern English readers of poetry. Marlowe's and Chapman's *Hero and Leander* overwrites its classical literary past with early modern English mercantilism. Marlowe's text functions as a linguistic and poetic palimpsest as well, weaving contemporary English words associated with Eastern sea trade into classical epic similes. The bodies and spaces of his characters are charged with references to England's newly established and uncertain mercantile trade in the East. Here, the boundaries of empire are permeable and dynamic. Marlowe's Hellespont is a fluid, synchronic space, the intersection of East and West, antique and modern, English and Ottoman. It is finely layered, like a pearl.

Liberating Orient Pearls

Marlowe's poem is replete with pearly imagery. Adding to this copia or net of pearls, the word *orient* appears twice in Marlowe's poem, referring to bodies as pearls and thus oriental imported objects. In late sixteenth-century English, *orient* was an adjective and a noun that described not only the East but the glittering nacre of pearls; according to the *OED*, it meant "the color or special lustre of a pearl of great quality."[25] Both appearances of *orient* in Marlowe's poem are significant as each configures Hero's and Leander's bodies as erotic objects—imported luxury goods—rather than as subjects, but these bodies are also desired for their pearly white skin. Worshipped for his near-feminine beauties, Leander possesses Narcissus's "Orient cheeks and lips" (1.73), which can indicate either central Asian facial features (Abydos, where Leander lives, is in Anatolia) or shining, pearlescent skin. When Hero disrobes, she lights up the room like a sunrise "from an Orient cloud" (2.320). So the "Orient cloud" to which Hero is compared can be both a cloud brightened by an eastern sunrise and a white, pearlescent cloud.

By the end of the sixteenth century, Europe had become infatuated with the riches of the Ottoman Empire, Persia, the Maghreb, and Asia. As John Florio's 1603 translation of Montaigne put it, "The richest, the fairest, and best part of the world [was] topsiturvied, ruined and defaced for the traffick of Pearles and Pepper."[26] The word *orient* was bound up with pearls and precious goods originating in the Middle East, India, and Africa. It had a range of intersecting meanings, all of which create a network of associations linking precious gems and minerals with the geographical space from which they were imported. Here is how those meanings operated: *orient* derives from Latin *oriens*, the east and the place in the sky where the sun rises. Thus, the deponent form of *oriens*, *orior*, is the root of the word *origin*. But because in the sixteenth and seventeenth centuries, pearls were imported into England and Europe from Sri Lanka and Bahrain, *orient* designated not only a geographical direction (east) but bright and shiny things like pearls and gold. This range of overlapping meanings can be found in Florio's definition of the same word in Italian, *oriente*. His Italian-English dictionary *Queen Anna's New World of Words* (1611) defines the Italian cognate *oriente* as "the east part of the world. Also the East-winde. Also shining, bright, glistering and oriant, sun-shining. Also Gold among alchemists."[27] Adding to *orient*'s scintillating quality, the *OED* also notes that around 1573, *orient* was used to indicate a "sparkle of the eyes."[28] Though pearls can be found across the globe, and many early modern jewel merchants did find them in North and South America as well as in the Middle East, the primary ports where pearls of superior quality were traded and imported (and still are today) were in Bahrain and Sri Lanka. These Eastern or "oriental" locations can also be tied etymologically to the adjective and noun *orient* that described highly valuable pearls in medieval and early modern English.[29]

Orient as lustrous and white was a new meaning for an older, Latinate word, and writers and translators began to use it to supplement classical Latin texts about pearls. In the first complete English translation of Pliny's *Natural History*, published in 1601, Philemon Holland supplies the new English word *orient* several times (six) over four pages to describe the bright luster of the most nacreous pearls, whereas Pliny's Latin text (composed around 77 CE) has only *candor* (whiteness), *clarior* (clarity), and *vigor* (liveliness)[30]: "In the very whitenesse it selfe, there is a great difference among them. That which is found in the red sea, is the clearest and more orient. . . . The most commendation that they have is in their colour, namely, if they may be truly called Exaluminati, *i.* orient and cleare as Alume."[31] In early modern English as today, the word *union* meant a joining together of more than one thing: a political alliance, a marriage, or a sexual consummation. But for Pliny's Romans as for early modern Europeans, *union* was also another word for pearl. This is because, as Pliny states, no two pearls are alike. Pearls are unique, "singular, and by themselves alone."[32]

If *orient* could mean bright and glistering, the phrase *orient pearl* comes to seem a bit redundant, given that pearls are already shiny. But orient pearls were the pearliest pearls: merchants with the Goldsmith's company in London frequently used the term *orient* to indicate a pearl particularly high in nacre and thus high in value; thus, *orient* may be closer in meaning to another technical term Elizabethan and Jacobean goldsmiths drew on to describe a pearl's luster: *water*.[33] The latter definition held true for Ralph Fitch, an Elizabethan merchant who traveled to the Middle East in 1583 with the jeweler William Leedes. In an account published in the 1600 edition of Hakluyt's *Principall Navigations*, Fitch reports seeing "many Ilandes, and among others the famous Ilande Baharim from whence come the best pearles which be round and Orient."[34] Fitch pairs *orient* with *round*, which suggests that he is using the word to describe the pearls' visual characteristics. One of the two primary ports in the early modern pearl business, Bahrain was controlled by the Portuguese from 1507 to 1602 (the other, Sri Lanka, was under Dutch control from 1517 to 1658). Later passing through Sri Lanka, Fitch notes that the pearls there are of a lesser quality, "not so orient as the pearle of Baharim in the gulfe of Persia."[35] In Fitch's sentence, the word *orient* cannot mean *Eastern* since from his perspective, Sri Lanka lies further east than the Persian Gulf, so *orient* here must indicate the pearl's quality and value, its nacre.[36] The Dutch merchant John Huyghen van Linschoten traveled to Goa and the Persian Gulf between 1579 and 1592. In his *Itinerario*, translated into English in 1598, van Linschoten attests in a play on words that the most *orient* pearls are also Eastern in origin: "The principal and the best that are found in all the Oriental Countries and the right Orientale pearles, are between Ormus and Vassora in the straights, or Sinus Persicus, in the places called Bareyn, Catiffa, Julfar, Camaron."[37] Most of these travelers also observed how pearls were laboriously harvested by skilled and overworked Arab laborers in the Persian Gulf, and South Asian natives poorly paid in leftover pearls.[38] Marlowe's poem gives us some indication of the laborious challenges of fishing for pearls when Leander is dragged, thrashing, to the bottom of the Hellespont by Neptune, where "underwater he was almost dead" (2.170). In the Hellespont, Leander becomes Neptune's pearl, just as Hero will become Leander's in their bed (2.260–80). Fishing for both bodies and pearls, the poem acknowledges, is life-threatening work.

In the early modern world, pearls were associated with dew, tears, and seminal fluids as much as they represented the opposite, serving as emblems of chastity and sexual imperviousness. The dominant belief (inherited from ancient India, Greece, Persia, and the Arab world) was that pearls were generated when their shells were impregnated by the rain or dew. This was the view held by Pliny, Marbode of Rennes (twelfth century), Albertus Magnus (thirteenth century), and Bartolomaeus Anglicus (fourteenth century).[39] Early modern writers citing this etiology included Stephen Batman in his translation of Camillus Leonardus (1516), Olaus Magnus (1555), William Camden (1587), and John Frye in his *Newe Account of East India and Perisa* (1672–81).[40] Though in 1555 Guillaume Rondelet suggested that pearls were the products of disease, formed by layers of the same substance that lines the mussel's shell, the dew theory of pearl generation remained prevalent in Europe until Filippo di Filippi correctly identified parasitic pearl nuclei in 1852.[41]

In the symbolic vocabulary of medieval and early modern English poetry, orient pearls are metaphors for female chastity, purity, and impenetrability. We can find the *locus classicus* of this metaphor in the Middle English poem *Pearl* (c. 1380–1400), in which the speaker mourns the premature death of his little girl, whom he describes as a lost pearl: "Perle, plesaunte . . . Oute of oryent I hardyly saye, Ne Proued I neuer here precios pere" (3). He falls asleep on a bank of flowers and in his dream vision beholds his daughter as a fully grown maiden in Paradise, clothed in pearls and married to Christ. The poem frequently repeats that the speaker's lost pearl was "withouten spot," untainted by sin. Two hundred years later, Queen Elizabeth I, the royal "virgin," was depicted in gowns, necklaces, and headdresses adorned with pearls to symbolize her sexual purity. Even her effigy in Westminster Abbey is decorated with marble pearls.[42] In Elizabethan romances, pearls represented virgin purity.[43] Marlowe's use of pearl imagery, however, converts this commonplace into a new symbolic vocabulary.[44]

Women—and by extension their unblemished bodies, virgin tears, and impenetrable chastity—appear as "orient pearls" so frequently throughout early modern writing that it is tempting to dismiss the pearly bodies of Hero and Leander as commonplaces, an extension of the blazon tradition. But there is more to an orient pearl than meets the eye. As jewels, pearls are valuable, fungible imports. Furthermore, orient pearls are simultaneously bright white (which, in reference to skin color, marks one as Western) *and* foreign. In the figure of the orient pearl, the Western ideal of spotless virginity gets reconfigured as an Eastern material object. And, in line with Shakespeare's ironic uses of pearls, Marlowe's orient pearls turn chastity on its head. In the poem, Hero's chastity is consistently compromised and easily won. Leander craftily makes it seem a rhetorical "nothing" (another Eastern import, as we have seen, is the notion of zero). And as a priestess of Venus, the Roman goddess of love and sexual desire, Hero's virginity is already a joke. I maintain that Marlowe's poem reconfigures orient pearls not as emblems of feminine purity but as indicative of a kind of sexual fluidity and freedom from Western mores, a freedom that can only take place in the layered landscape of an Ottoman-inflected mythological Hellespont. Patrick Cheney characterizes Marlowe as the Elizabethan poet who celebrates Ovidian *libertas*, or freedom from traditional authority.[45] I will draw on Cheney's characterization in order to demonstrate how orient pearls in *Hero and Leander* lay claim to antique *libertas*, but only through the contemporary language of Eastern and Mediterranean trade. For Cheney, Marlowe's use of Ovidian *libertas* allows the poet to engage with Spenser in an opposing rhetoric of counter-nationhood, one that "subverts Elizabethan royal power . . . in order to represent 'the poet' as the 'true nation.'"[46] But what happens to counter-nationhood when it is transported to the Ottoman-inflected Mediterranean? Marlowe locates *libertas* not only in the classical past, I would argue, but in the English mercantile present.

Marlowe compares the bodies of both lovers to precious stones and jewels, especially those associated with water and Eastern sea trade. These allusions turn Hero and Leander into fungible commodities on the Mediterranean market and emphasize the transformative properties of their pearly nature. Hero is decked with jewels culled from the sea: "About her neck hung chaines of pebble stone, / Which lightned by her necke, like Diamonds shone" (1.25–26). Her boots, or "buskins" (1.31), are embroidered with "shells al siluered" (1.31) with abalone or mother-of-pearl, and "blushing corall to the knee, / Where sparrowes percht, of hollow pearle and gold" (1.31–33). Though there is evidence of early modern clothing and accessories adorned with mother-of-pearl—for instance, a sixteenth-century etched purse in the collection of the Victoria and Albert Museum—Hero's is a fantastical costume. The sparrows become miniature water organs, filled by her handmaid. This hyperbolic costume immediately constructs Hero as a valuable, Eastern commodity, not only because she is covered in precious materials from the sea but because of the handiwork that has gone into creating her dress and boots—which is also Marlowe's poetic handiwork.[47] With her mechanical mother-of-pearl and coral boots, Hero's clothes are best suited to a Renaissance cabinet of curiosities containing the marvels of world travel, like one of Wenzel Jamnitzer's coral Daphnes, which took up residence in aristocratic wonder-cabinets in the early seventeenth century.[48] Hero's blue "kirtle" or petticoat is stained, "Made with the blood of wretched lovers slaine" (1.16). The line's enjambment halts at the rhyme "whereon was many a stain" (1.15), suggesting that the blood of the line that follows stands in for stains made by other bodily fluids, blood and semen being frequently interchangeable in Renaissance physiology. Compare this stain to the first line of the poem, "On Hellespont, guilty of true love's *blood*" (1.1): the Hellespont is laced with the lovers' blood and, presumably, the fluids of their lovemaking. Given the early modern associative fisherman's net linking pearls, dew, water, and seminal fluids, it is understandable that there would be pearls—and a great many of them—littering the floor of Marlowe's Hellespont, which Virgil in his *Georgics* calls *ostriferi* or oyster breeding.[49] Pearls were valued by the early modern English Goldsmith's company not just for their size and clarity but for their water, a term that surfaces frequently in Hannibal Gamon's *Gouldesmythe's Storehowse*.[50] For English goldsmiths, *water* is almost indistinguishable from early modern inflections of *orient* as shiny whiteness: it describes the fineness and amplitude of a pearl's nacre, but it also locates the pearl more transparently as a precious mineral coming from the sea, and we can almost imagine that an early modern goldsmith or noble in possession of pearl high in water would believe the pearl to carry something of the sea with it, as when we hold conch shells up to our ears to hear the roaring of the waves. Marlowe's orient pearls do not merely evoke the sea but embody its fluidity and transformative powers.

The jewels that ornament and stand in for Hero's body and virginity in Marlowe's poem are numerous. When Leander follows her into the temple of Venus (built of "green sea agate," sporting a crystal roof and silver altar, 1.138), he launches into a speech to persuade her to yield her virginity (a "faire Iemme," 1.247) to him. Hero responds with tears, which Marlowe metaphorizes as pearls:

Foorth from those two translucent cisterns brake
A streame of liquid Pearle, which downe her face
Made milk-white paths, whereon the gods might trace
To Loues high Court. (1.296–99)

The speaker compares Hero's tears not only to precious pearls but also to the celestial *Via Lactea*, as if she were a mythological heroine immortalized in a constellation. As a sexual commodity (a virgin), Hero is a living, breathing, secreting pearl. When she finally capitulates and accepts Leander, Hero weeps a second time. In this instance, Marlowe playfully has Cupid transform Hero's tears to pearl, wind them on his arm, and attempt to bribe the Fates into preventing her tragic death (it doesn't work). Why is Hero's surrender to Leander—her admission that he is right, that virginity is a nonentity—then turned into a tangible, material artifact of pearls? This string of pearls might contradict Leander, serving as a relic to Hero's virginity, but it also functions to illustrate the rhetorical brilliance of his reasoning. Early modern English had a term for pithy, quotable arguments: *pearls of rhetoric*. Over the course of the poem, Hero, who begins as an impenetrable string of perfectly matched pearls, will be converted into a baroque pearl, one whose sexual fluidity exceeds its bounds.

Hero is not the only pearl in the poem: Leander's body is also an Eastern precious commodity possessing Narcissus's "orient cheeks and lips" (1.73) and "ivory skin" (2.153), as is Neptune, who is "Saphyr-visaged" (2.155). The epithet "Saphyr-visaged" does not merely paint Neptune's face blue; it also makes it seem carved out of gemstone, just like the gods carved out of jasper, agate, and crystal (1.136–141) in Venus's temple on Sestos. Neptune resembles an elaborate early modern gem in the shape of a triton or nereid, many of which incorporated baroque or oddly shaped pearls, providing a meta-commentary on the riches of the sea. Unlike the tiny, round, and perfectly matched pearls one might find in a Hilliard miniature of Queen Elizabeth, which emphasize her uniqueness and virgin purity, baroque pearls are oddly shaped, and their form dictated the shapes and frames that jewelers chose for them, not the other way around.[51] Perhaps it is no accident that so many early modern jewelers chose to frame baroque pearls as erotic, metamorphic, and monstrous figures like nereids, sirens, serpents, and dragons. Where the miniature round pearl implies impenetrable purity, the baroque pearl suggests sexual fluidity and perversity in excess.[52]

Like the sea god's body, Neptune's palace is full of gemstones, only these are neglected, sunken treasure:

> the ground
> Was strewd with pearle, and in low corrall groues,
> Sweet singing Mermayds sported with their loues,

On heapes of heauy gold, and took great pleasure,
To spurne in carelesse sort the shipwracke treasure:
For here the stately azure palace stood. (2.160–65)

Here classical mythology encounters the early modern East, only to snub it. The sea floor of the Hellespont is littered with "shipwracke treasure" (2.164) and "heapes of heauy gold" (2.163), treasure for which some seafaring merchants or corsairs may have paid dearly with their lives. But the sea god's nereids willfully ignore the lost spoils of the present in favor of Neptune's mythological "azure palace" (2.165). Although Neptune is obviously besotted with Leander, the god treats Leander like a possession, dragging the youth (who cannot breathe underwater) down to the bottom of the sea. Ivory-skinned Leander seems in danger of becoming a sunken treasure himself. This is the sexual freedom of Marlowe's Hellespont: in the wrong hands, it can become dangerous. Therefore, the watery currents of the Hellespont where Neptune encounters Leander could be read as a queering space, its pearl-strewn bottom and powerful waves emphasizing sexual fluidity and metamorphosis, despite Leander's struggle to resist it and conform to heteronormative desire. Shakespeare would later draw on this transformative power of the sea in *The Tempest*, when he has Ariel sing about a corpse with pearls for eyes sea-changing into "something rich and strange" (1.2.405). Rubens's nearly identical paintings *Hero and Leander* (1605 and 1606) similarly incorporate elements of sea nymphs and sunken treasure (Figure 13). As a marginalized Hero flings herself from her tower (on the right), a tangle of nymphs adorned with coral and pearl carries Leander's body to a pearl-and-shell-strewn shore. The painting depicts the Hellespont as a conflicted space, overpopulated with bodies, sea monsters, and roiling waves. Its title, *Hero and Leander*, seems almost ironic, as it is difficult to identify which of the fifteen bodies is Hero and which Leander. In Rubens's painting as in Marlowe's poem, pearls are transformed from emblems of sexual purity into markers of sexual freedom and excess. Rubens was twenty-one when Marlowe's poem was published. Given Marlowe's connections with the Netherlands, it would not be too far-fetched to imagine the classically educated teenaged painter encountering or at least learning of the poet in Antwerp in 1590s and reading his final masterpiece eight years later.[53]

Neptune threatens to depose Leander's precious chastity much as Leander will later conquer Hero's, for as Hero knows, "Iewels been lost are found againe, this neuer. / 'Tis lost but once, and once lost, lost forever" (2.85–86).

Figure 13. *Hero and Leander*, by Peter Paul Rubens, 1606. By permission of the Gemäldegalerie Alte Meister, Dresden.

This narrative interjection is Marlowe himself making a rhetorical "pearl" or commonplace out of a figurative pearl (Hero's virginity) and thus mocking both Hero's soon-to-be-lost pearl and the practice of extracting "pearls" of wisdom itself. Once he arrives at Sestos, Leander struggles with Hero, mirroring Neptune's struggle with Leander: "Ne're King more sought to keepe his Diademe, / Than *Hero* this inestimable gemme" (2.77–78). Hero's bed sheets become billowy waves as Leander attempts to chart this territory, fishing for Hero:

> His hands he cast vpon her like a snare:
> She ouercome with shame and fallow feare,
> Like chaste *Diana* when *Acteon* spide her,
> Being sodainly betraid, diu'd down to hide her
> And as her siluer body downeward went,
> With both her hands she made a tent. (2.259–64)

Tent and silver body suggest a silver ship with sails, mirroring an elaborate pearl ship pendant or salt-cellar *nef* of the period.[54] The tent-ship then becomes an ivory mountain and finally a globe "with azure circling lines empal'd" for Leander to navigate: "Much like a globe (a globe may I tearme this / By which loue sailes to regions full of blis)" (2.275–76). The imagery of navigation, trade, and conquest intersect as Leander tries to lay claim to Hero's pearly body. When Leander finally succeeds, Hero slips from his grasp, flopping "Mermaid-like vnto the floore" (2.315). Sex transforms our heroine: once a virgin who cried tears of perfectly round, impervious pearls, she is now a watery, animated baroque pearl jewel, becoming one of the numerous mermaids and sirens that jewelers constructed around these oddly shaped marine minerals.

Like the Hellespont, Hero's bed and, by extension, her body becomes another fluid space where borders must be negotiated and crossed, sometimes violently. When she finally disrobes, Leander has charted the globe and conquered the East. Hero becomes "a kinde of twilight" (2.319) breaking "from an Orient cloud" (2.320), and as the lovers embrace, Apollo plays his "golden harpe" (2.327), and Marlowe's poem ends in the Orient with the sun rising and driving night far away and "downe to hell" (2.334). Although the last lines of the poem, "danged down to hell her loathsome carriage" (2.334), foreshadow darkness to come, and Chapman will take up this dark thread in his follow-up to Marlowe, the image we are left with is one of night being swallowed up by the underworld, so that the brilliant, shimmery light of the

Eastern sun can refract off Hero's skin, emphasizing her pearliness once more. As the lovers begin to consummate their desire, they are surrounded by a pearly sunrise. Hero's chastity may be lost, but the orient pearls and gold of the poem's afterglow appear to commend rather than punish Hero for having sex. Though Hero is warned against losing her "inestimable gemme" (2.78), the poem repeatedly reassures us that she will continue to shine. Her pearly tears suggest not one gem to lose but a whole string of them to barter with. At the end of the poem, it is not Hero's virgin pearl that is lost but Hero and Leander's sexual *union*, a pearl itself, that the poem validates.

Dyes and Dissimulation in Chapman's Hellespont

Where Marlowe celebrates the dangerous *libertas* afforded by his Ottoman-inflected landscape in the watery figure of the orient pearl, Chapman emphasizes the treachery and political dissimulation of Anglo-Ottoman trade in his use of color and textile. Chapman's rich crimsons, dense blacks, and purples indicate the lovers' loss and betrayal by bleeding and staining their bodies. Chapman employs classical rhetorical devices to highlight such betrayals, simultaneously imitating and undoing much of Marlowe's dominant imagery. Marlowe's poem opens famously "On Hellespont, guilty of true love's blood" (1.1). Chapman's continuation returns to the same space but opens with a shift: "new light brings new directions" (3.1). Chapman hastens to pin the "guilt" on Leander rather than on Hellespont, punning guilt with gilding and inverting Marlowe's description of Hero and Leander's "true love" (1.186) by transforming it into impulsive sin: "The God of gold of purpose guilt his lims / That this word guilt including double sense / The double guilt of his *Incontinence*" (3.24–26). The word *limbs*, spelled here *lims*, draws attention to the way the golden light upon the water paints or "limns" Leander's limbs. Thus, Chapman's poem opens by transposing Marlowe's bloody, guilty Hellespont onto Leander, whose guilt is masked with gold paint.

Chapman's Hellespont is instantly a space where disguise and concealment can occur. Games's analysis of early modern English mercantile travelers' role-playing and disguise emphasizes the practicality of mercantile deception.[55] As it appeared to the English setting out on their mercantile ventures, the Mediterranean (and by extension the Hellespont and Black Sea) was a volatile waterway in which one might encounter riches, piracy, and alternative sexualities, much as Marlowe characterizes Neptune's Hellespont.[56] In order to succeed in their ventures, English merchants in Ottoman lands had to engage in rhetorical and visual deception and equivocation, just as Chapman describes Hero doing in his continuation of Marlowe's poem. As Games has observed, deception was both pragmatic and life preserving for merchants: "deceit was important both for minor advantages—better sightseeing—and for major considerations—saving life and limb."[57]

In addition to disguising Leander's guilt with gilt, Chapman also has Hero's loss of innocence transform her into a foreigner. As soon as Hero realizes she has lost her "inestimable iemme" (2.78) and remains unwed, she becomes "even to her selfe a straunger" (3.203). Not only does Chapman compare Hero in her defiled state to a foreigner in a strange land, but he goes on to compare her to Cádiz, the Spanish city that the English army (led by Essex) sacked in 1596:

> [Hero] was much like
> Th' *Iberian* citie that wars hand did strike
> By English force in princely *Essex* guide
> Whence peace assur'd her towers had fortifide
> And golden-fingered *India* had bestowd
> Such wealth on her, that strength and Empire flowd
> Into her Turrets, and her virgin waste
> The wealthy girdle of the sea imbraste. (3.203–10)

The port from which Columbus set sail for his second and fourth voyages, Cádiz was the site of many Spanish imperial successes. Its ships were constantly under attack, sometimes successfully (for example, by Francis Drake in 1587), sometimes unsuccessfully, by numerous Barbary corsairs. Hakluyt's *Principall Navigations* contains an account of Drake's voyage to Cádiz.[58] Rich with the wealth of eastern sea trade (in this instance), Hero is a valuable foreign city plundered too soon, desired by Leander (as Essex) too impetuously. To describe Hero's body as Cádiz is to contain her sexuality as a captured and spent commodity. The epic simile also invokes a sense of English inferiority and anxiety about its Spanish and Portuguese mercantile and imperial competition. Though the English were sometimes successful in plundering Cádiz and defeated the armada, they could not hold a candle to the Spanish and Portuguese for imperial and mercantile control of Southeast Asia and the New World in the sixteenth and early seventeenth centuries.

Some of the most valued commodities Europeans imported from the Ottoman Empire were color pigments and dyes, especially reds, purples, and blacks. Colorfast dyes were prepared using guarded, ancient formulae. After Constantinople fell to the Turks in 1453, Europeans lost the recipes for imperial (Tyrian) purple and colorfast crimson. Crimson "grains" (kermes beetles) and madder were imported from eastern Europe and central Asia to dye European textiles, but even these reds were likely to fade and bleed. The Ottoman recipes for making reds colorfast were guarded from European merchants until 1750.[59] Ottoman dye recipes might be read as Latourian mediators: material and chemical changes to dye baths meant a less costly but technologically more advanced way of producing textiles. If a European nation could get its hands on this technology, it would be able to reproduce vibrant, durable color on British wool without having to import foreign predyed cloth from Turkey. But because such technology was out of reach, the early modern English imagined Ottoman dye recipes as fantasy mediators that would ostensibly reconfigure their own culture and make them more powerful players in global markets.[60] Searching out new dye ingredients and formulae, particularly the coveted shades of deep crimson and purple, was a competitive and secretive mission for early modern European merchants. Hakluyt's *Principall Navigations* published an itemized list of secrets to obtain from the Turks, written by Hakluyt the elder, under the title "Remembrances for master S."[61] Among the list of techniques and materials to be gathered from the Turks is "to learne of the Diers to discerne all kind of colours; as which be good and sure. . . . Then to take the names of all the materials and substances used in this Citie or in the realme, in dying of cloth or silke."[62] Documents sent by Walsingham to Levant Company officers include lists of commodities from the East like indigo, *Rubia* (or madder), kermes (tiny beetles mistaken for "grains"), gum-lac (similar beetles, used for lacquer), and sal ammoniac and alum, all materials used in the dyeing process.[63] Red and purple dyeing pigments mentioned in Leonard Mascall's practical household book of dye recipes from 1583 include "grening weed" and "berries," "crimisine" (dried kermes beetles), "Brasill" (a cheap alternative to kermes, derived from an Asian wood producing a watery red or pink color), "Lack" (gum-lac), and gall nuts.[64] None of these recipes were colorfast, though judging by the brown, spattered condition of the 1588 edition in the Folger Shakespeare Library, the recipes were probably widely used.

In Chapman's poetry, such dyed textiles are simultaneously text and textile, subject to the same problems of masking and bleeding. Chapman invokes the imagery of exotic eastern imports—jewels, damask cloth (named for Damascus), and silk—to describe Hero's precious beauty and virginity. Chapman invokes red textiles to describe Leander musing on his love for Hero:

> Through whose white skin, softer than the soundest sleep
> With damaske eies the rubie bloud doth peep
> And runs in branches through her azure veins
> Whose mixture and first fire his love attains; (3.39–42)

"Damaske" (3.40) describes a cloth woven or embroidered with flowers and named for Damascus and its famous roses, but here it illustrates the patterns of red blood running through blue veins and evokes also the branched pattern of a bloodshot eye. The liquid "rubie bloud" (3.40) peeping through her veins suggests both gemstone rubies and *Rubia tinctorum*: madder red dye. It also conjures up an image of a cloth that has been dyed with red and blue to create an artificial purple, the red dye already beginning to show.

Chapman's 1616 translation of Musaeus goes further, bathing Hero and Leander in red during their first encounter even when the Greek text calls for blue: "And as he saw the Russet clouds increase / He strain'd her Rosie hand" (*Divine Poem [DP]*, 169–70).[65] Musaeus's Greek describes the coming twilight as a blue cloak of darkness, "κυανοπεπλων ομιχλειν" (Mus., 114–15), but Chapman modifies this to "Russet clouds."[66] Modestly blushing, Hero becomes "the rubi-color'd maid" (*DP*, 193), where Musaeus simply describes Hero as "fragrant" (Mus., 133). Though Musaeus does utilize the Greek word for ruddy "ερευθοσαν παρειην" (Mus., 161), which derives from the word for madder, to describe Hero's bashful glances, Chapman augments Musaeus's madder reference from one to three types, as Hero's "Rosy eyes: hid in Vermilion hew" are "Made red with shame" (*DP*, 229–31).[67]

As Chapman's continuation progresses, red turns to purple and to black. Hero and Leander's desire and shame have begun to mark and seep into their bodies. After Leander departs, Hero's shameful blushes darken the room in direct opposition to Marlowe's description of her nakedness as a "false morne": "And all the aire she purpled round about, / And after it a foule blacke day befell, / Which euer since a red morne doth fortell" (3.176–78). The color purple here, designating her blush, calls to mind the highly expensive dye from the Murex mollusk, found and cultivated in the Greek islands, Tyrian purple. Iyengar has argued that Hero's blushes function here to "color" her as racial Other through her sin. If we read this poem as an exogamous romance, with Hero on the European side and Leander on the "orient" side of the Hellespont, we might see Hero as having crossed over to the other race, physically colored by her union with the Asian Leander.[68]

Chapman's Hero is transformed. No longer a *marguerite* or pearl (as Marlowe conceives of her), Hero is tarnished, her tears stained black by her mourning veil: "How fast her cleere teares melted on her knee / Through her black vaile, and turned as black as it, / Mourning to be her tears" (3.308–10). We have seen tragic poetic heroines' bodies streaked with black before: The corpse of Shakespeare's Lucrece is encircled with blood and a "watery rigol," some of her blood stained black by sin (*Lucrece*, 1594). As I interpreted it in Chapter 3, the O of blood around Lucrece's leaky corpse betrays a truth, serving as mystical evidence of rape, which, in an era long before rape kits and DNA analyses, leaves no physical mark on an ordinary married woman. What truths do Hero's sooty tears betray? As a European cloth cheaply dyed with unfixed pigments that seep out at the merest hint of water, the veil does more than point out Hero and Leander's sexual transgressions; it also highlights the precariousness of English mercantile commercial ventures in the Ottoman Empire. Hero drapes herself in her black veil to cover and conceal her shame, but the veil is poorly dyed, and ends up staining her face. The black tears also resemble liquid ink, suggesting that this is alternately a moment of shameful if inadvertent publication of the knowledge that she and Leander have physically consummated their love, too prematurely for the likes of Chapman's hypocritical custodial gods.[69]

English merchants trading for the first time with the Ottomans were urged to conceal their missions. In a private letter to the first members of the Levant Company in 1581, Elizabeth's secretary and spymaster Sir Francis Walsingham urges merchants to let "lies be given out" rather than reveal the reason for their journey.[70] If a European competitor gained any knowledge of Anglo-Ottoman trading, he could endanger the whole English enterprise, as William Harborne, the first English merchant and ambassador to the Ottoman Empire, discovered. Harborne boasted too freely about English trading rights, engaged in some indiscreet piracy off the coast of Rhodes, and subsequently lost a number of ships. He was accused of spying and working to ruin the Ottoman Empire. The company nearly lost its trafficking privileges, and Queen Elizabeth wrote the sultan a formal apology.[71] Elizabeth describes the affair itself as a deception: "whether it were true or fained, we knowe not . . . but under the colour thereof they have done that, which the trueth of our dealing doeth utterly abhorre."[72] Feigning an activity "under the colour thereof" suggests disguising or mistaking one thing for another, but in the sixteenth century, *colouring* also referred to the shady mercantile practice of forging signatures in order to avoid paying a particular country's customs fees. As Alan Stewart explains, to *colour* was to pass off your own goods as those belonging to another merchant by signing someone else's mercantile mark on the bill of lading.[73] *Colouring* thus resembles some early modern descriptions of poetic ornament or rhetorical dissimulation (all figurative language in effect) as cosmetic painting.[74] In *The Arte of English Poesie* (1589), Puttenham describes allegory, which he dubs the ringleader of all the other tropes as "a dissimulation under covert and dark intendments."[75] Because metaphor, allegory, and all other figurative tropes "draw" language "from plainness and simplicity to a certain doubleness," all figurative language is thus "foreign and colored talk."[76] Colors and, by extension, paints and dyes thus become associated with forgery, disguise, and rhetorical dissimulation.

Chapman directly connects deception with colored textiles and Eastern dyes. While violently chastising Hero for attempting to conceal lascivious behavior, Venus—clad in a "scarlet" robe, wearing a "black" headdress (4.240)—conjures a winged, scorpion-tailed, allegorical monster, Eronusis, "Architect of all dissimulation" (4.312). Eronusis has dazzlingly colorful wings: "Cloth had neuer die, / Nor sweeter colours neuer viewed eie, / In scorching *Turkie, Cares, Tartarie,* / Then shined about this spirit notorious" (4.297–300). As Iyengar reminds us, these colors can also be read as expensive Eastern cosmetics, like the coral, vermillion, and carmine (kermes and cochineal) pounded into powder and rubbed into the cheeks to produce false blushes.[77] The same red pigments that were imported for cosmetic use (kermes, brazilwood, gumlac, coral) were used for paints and dyes. Yet these colors represent not only material cosmetics but rhetorical ones as well, since, taking their cue from the Latin grammar school handbook of classical rhetoric *Rhetorica ad Herennium,* early modern writers described rhetorical tropes with cosmetic metaphors.[78] Eronusis personifies the *colores,* or the colors of rhetoric described by Geoffrey of Vinsauf in the *ad Herennium,* but these are foreign rather than familiar colors.[79] The marvelous cloth, dye, and pigments produced by the cultures of the East thus mix with the classical colors of rhetoric to create the warning figure of dissimulation. This allegorical figure's polychromatic dress also might suggest sinfulness, as throughout the sixteenth and early seventeenth centuries, the wearing of various forms of polychromatic textiles was strictly regulated by sumptuary laws. At one point, striped fabric was considered the devil's cloth.[80]

Venus uses dissimulation as a notorious *exemplum* to frighten Hero into owning up to her mistake (pretending to remain a virgin), but Venus's own multicolored language goes further, branding Hero as a counterfeit coin still in circulation:

> Loue makes thee cunning, thou art currant now,
> By being counterfait. Thy broken bow,
> Deceit with her pyde garters must reioyne, ["pide" 1598]
> And with her stampe thou count'nances must coine,
> Coyne, and pure deciets for purities. (4.250–54)

Deceit (most likely Eronusis herself, though possibly yet another allegorized concept) is a whorish woman dressed in multicolored clothes, in this case "pyde garters" or bicolored stocking laces. As a counterfeit coin still "currant," a loose woman circulating as a virgin, Hero upsets the social economy. In this way, she is like a forged merchant's mark, passing herself off as a virgin when she is no longer one. But this is also a larger, less stable global mercantile economy, one whose currency might easily be swept away by the sea's currents. *Currents* is also an Elizabethan word for news or gossip, which ties Hero even closer to dissimulation and rumor.[81] Currents are linked homophonically and orthographically here to *currants* (the dried "Corinth" grape from Zakynthos), which further highlights Hero's mercantile connections: for the early modern English, currants were practically the gold standard of Mediterranean commodities.[82] Venus's anti-dissimulation lecture reveals anxieties not only about the circulation of women but about England's risky economic trading position in the Mediterranean, Aegean, and Black Sea, one that depended upon lying and dissimulative rhetoric and, in so doing, unleashed the real possibilities of counterfeiting and mercantile "colouring."

Dissimulation has close ties to Virgil's *Fama* or Rumor, the multioptic, many winged beast that spreads lies throughout the land in Book Two of the *Aeneid* and delivers the prologue to Shakespeare's *Henry IV, Part Two*. But unlike Eronusis, *Fama* is colorless (like Chapman's transparent goddess Ceremony, who visits Leander to educate him on the importance of marriage rites). Chapman extends Virgil's classical image of Rumor to blend the classical rainbow of Iris (messenger to the gods) with rich, contemporary Ottoman pigments. The connection to dyes also implies a connection to ink, made with many of the same imported ingredients, suggesting that Chapman's reworking of Virgil's *Fama* into Eronusis has ties to the vagaries of the printing process.

False gossip and rumormongering take on a similar, multihued shape in the landscape of Chapman's Hellespont, embodied in the character of an overly chatty teenage maiden named Adolesche, who appears in the story of Hymen, which briefly interrupts the main narrative. Jealous of Hymen's success, Adolesche perpetuates false rumors of his failure and death. The gods punish her with metamorphosis, transforming her into a parrot:

> lightning from aboue,
> Shrunk her leane body, and for meere free loue,
> Turnd her into the pied-plumed *Psittacus*,
> That now the Parrat is surnamed by vs,
> Who still with counterfeit confusion prates,
> Naught but newes common to the commonst mates. (5.419–24)

Like Dissimulation, the "Parrat" is ornamented with colors, and like Fama, she is covered with "pied-plumed" feathers (5.421). This multicolored plumage represents her deceitful, misleading speech of "counterfeit confusion" (5.423). Of course, parrots are also exotic imports, reaching England from the New World, Africa, and Asia. Like Hero's circulating counterfeit virginity, Adolesche's rumors are "common." The challenge for early modern merchants, then, is to deceive and dissimulate without being labeled "common," like whores (4.424).[83]

Dissimulation's counterpart in Chapman's poem is the goddess Ceremony, sent to punish Leander for his impetuousness but also to give him hope by urging him to marry Hero. Unlike Dissimulation's multicolored coat, ceremony's body is "cleere and transparent as the purest glass" (3.118). Though she holds a "Mathematicke Christall" (3.130) in her right hand, which, when touched with fiery rays from her eyes, abolishes confusion, even Ceremony dissimulates. Clad in a robe embroidered with "strange characters," Ceremony possesses a face so "changeable to every eye" that "one way looked ill / Another graciously" (3.124–25).

As the tragic outcome gathers force, Chapman's epic similes gather references to ships, cargo, the vagaries of the weather, and mercantile loss. Chapman's poem is dominated by imagery of deceitful coloring, but his conclusion connects the lovers' tragic deaths to English mercantile risk taking. As Hero struggles internally between truthful love and acknowledged shame, her veins become miniature Hellesponts, conduits on which her emotions toss like ships:

> the red sea of her blood
> Ebb'd with Leander, but now turn'd the flood,
> And all her fleet of spirits came swelling in
> With child of sayle, and did hot fight begin,
> With those seuere conceits, she too much markt,
> And here Leanders beauties were imbarkt.
> He came in swimming, painted all with ioyes. (3.323–29).

Leander's physical beauties resemble a ship laden with merchandise, "painted all with joys" (3.329), one of an entire "fleet" of emotions (3.325), beginning a sea battle with Hero's morals. Hero's resolution to this conflict is a wish to dissolve the physical limits separating the bodies of the two lovers entirely: "Hero Leander is, Leander Hero" (3.356). But this is Chapman's deceitful Hellespont, not Marlowe's watery, pearly one. In the early modern Hellespont, where both Sestos and Abydos were heavily policed, such border dissolution would be impossible. Likewise, in Chapman's mythological Hellespont, the gods will not permit the dissolution of such boundaries either. The real tragedy of the poem is not that Hero and Leander have engaged in premarital sex but that the gods cannot maintain consistent order over the Hellespont. Once Hero and Leander agree to marry, the gods are appeased, but the lovers die anyway.

When the poem nears its tragic conclusion, Chapman compares Leander's false confidence in swimming the Hellespont on a stormy night to an "empty Gallant full of form" (6.108), a Dutch merchant who inflates his inexperience with boasting. The Dutch merchant is then compared to an English merchant's ship in a double epic simile:

> A Ship with all her sayle contends to fly
> Out of the narrow Thames with winds vnapt
> Now crosseth here, then there, then this way rapt,
> And then hath one point teacht, then alters all,
> And to another crooked reach doth fall,
> Of halfe a Burd-bolts shoote, keeping more coile,
> Then if she danc't vpon the Oceans toyle,
> So serious is his trifling company,
> In all his swelling Ship of vacantry. (6.122–32)

Trapped in the narrow, overpopulated Thames, this ship is unable to reach open water and can only turn around, bumping into other ships. And though inflated with wind, it is empty of cargo. Like the ship struggling to navigate the Thames, overly confident with all its sails raised, "swelling" with "vacantry," Leander inflates himself with false confidence before plunging into the Hellespont, where, in a return to the language of coloring, he will drown in a literary dye-bath of "floods of inck" (6.133) from Chapman's pen.

Chapman's figurative use of ships to describe the hero's tragic death converts a traditional European poetic reference, the Petrarchan image of the lover as a storm-tossed ship, into a reference to English and European mercantile ventures in the Ottoman-controlled Mediterranean. A number of nations and geographies converge in Chapman's image of Leander as a ship: Turkey, Italy, Holland, and Britain. Anatolian Leander caught between the Aegean and Black Seas becomes a seafaring Dutchman who inflates his lack of experience with boasting, which metamorphoses into a wind-tossed ship wedged in the narrow London Thames and a Petrarchan simile. Chapman's conversions are part of a double epic simile, an ancient Greek and Roman poetic technique, which Chapman deftly translates into the imagery of global trade. Metaphors and similes, as Puttenham tells us, are figures of "transport," shifting meaning from one frame of reference to another. This double epic simile (perhaps triple, if we add the Petrarch reference) literalizes the notion of metaphor as conveyance, as Chapman transports Leander like a ship or imported cargo from Asia Minor to London, by way of Italy and the Netherlands.

Chapman's simultaneous drowning of Leander in the fictional waves of the Hellespont and in the material textual "floods of inck" (6.133) ties the waters of the Hellespont back to the materials of coloring, staining, and writing. *Floods* suggests a deluge of tears or spilt ink, and a river, as the Latin root of *flood* is *fluvus*, or river. This Hellespont is not only a dark and impenetrable body of water; it also marks its bodies, gilding Leander's limbs and blackening his skin. If Leander drowns in "floods of inck," his body will be painted, stained with pigments and resins imported from the East, an emblem of the perils of dissimulation. Though dissimilar in formula (dyes needed a mordant; inks a resinous binding agent), paints, dyes, and inks were all concocted from the same pigments: oak galls for black paint, dye, and ink; kermes, gum-lac, brazilwood, and cinnabar for red. [84] Chapman's "floods of inck" connect the watery and transformative Hellespont to the equally transformative fluid of watery, gray manuscript ink, which will eventually be converted into printer's ink, the glossy mixture of linseed oil, iron oxide, gum arabic, and Syrian oak galls (the last two ingredients imported from Turkey) that coated the rollers that printed the poem. Chapman's success means prolonging and reiterating Leander's death: Leander will also die/dye over and over again in "floods of inck" (6.133) used in the printing process. Just as Leander drowns in the unstable Hellespont, so he is reborn, dyed in ink, to die again in the early modern printing process. Chapman transforms imported commodities of dyes and ink into poetic images that expose the rhetorical and poetic nature of England's dealings with the East, but he also returns to classical form in order to celebrate them, championing the colors of rhetoric in his poetry, even as his vengeful goddesses warn against them, and converting Homeric and Virgilian similes into contemporary, global ones.

Secret Ottoman dye recipes may have seemed like a panacea to England's mercantile economy, but this was a fantasy; poetry and rhetoric are the true Latourian mediators in this story. Reading the rhetorical posturing in the correspondence of Queen Elizabeth and Sultan Murad published in Hakluyt's *Principall Navigations*, Jonathan Burton illuminates how both rulers engaged in the political rhetoric of dissimulation, stylistically buffing over the differences between Islam and Protestantism in order to unite commercially against their Catholic foes. Ostensibly, both Elizabeth and Murad engaged in the same kind of deception Walsingham calls upon his merchants to do: "from its foundation, England's policy on trade with the Ottoman Empire depended upon saying one thing and doing another."[85] Games's historical analysis supports this, viewing the necessary deception of the English in the Mediterranean as strategy that eventually helped the English begin functioning as a global empire.[86] What is missing from both Burton's and Games's excellent close readings of strategic dissimulation, however, is its connection to early modern literary practice.[87] Games's discussion of English adaptation and disguise has parallels in theatrical role-playing and poetic *imitatio*, both of which came naturally to poets educated in the Latin grammar schools where imitation and ventriloquism of classical authors were the chief forms of instruction.[88] Both Marlowe and Chapman engage in textual *imitatio* in their versions of *Hero and Leander*. Marlowe mimics Ovid's witty sexual puns—Hero is "Venus's nun" (1.45 and 1.316) and Marlowe's "rude pen / Can hardly blazon forth the loves of men" (1.69–70), but it does a pretty good job of eroticizing the hidden parts of Leander's body through *enarratio*, rhetorical withholding. The most obvious examples of Marlowe's and Chapman's *imitatio* can be found in their uses of double epic similes, which convert Homeric, Virgilian, and Ovidian *technopoesis* into examples of early modern English virtuosity. Marlowe packs them in, one after another. Over the course of twenty lines, his poem runs through four different epic similes illustrating the dreadful power of Hero's beauty (1.100–20), comparing it to

Phaeton's solar chariot, the songs of nereids, the moon, and nymphs chasing centaurs over hill and dale. Chapman's epic similes are layered and enfolded, rather than successive. His comparison of Leander to a Dutch gallant, a London ship, and a Petrarchan simile encloses one simile within another, like a matryoshka.

Though Chapman's goddesses appear to rail against dissimulation and rumormongering, perhaps they protest too much; perhaps they are merely dissimulating. Dissimulation, gossiping, and inflating one's speech may be morally wrong, but they are also necessary and unavoidable, not only for early modern English traffic in the Ottoman Mediterranean but for English poets who wish to engage with classical authors and themes.[89] In addition to his use of rhetorical coloring, Virgilian *Fama*, and epic simile, Chapman engages in a deeper act of poetic dissimulation: like an early modern merchant, he "colors" his poem with Marlowe's mark, slipping his Sestiad divisions and introductions into Marlowe's text as if they were the first poet's own and inserting himself in the narrative without directly indicating to readers where Marlowe's poem ends and Chapman's begins, except in a hidden elegy. Chapman's recycling of Marlowe's imagery between the end of the first poem and the beginning of his own—the play on Marlowe's "guilty" Hellespont in describing Leander's gilded limbs, the inversion of Marlowe's "orient cloud" into Hero's sunset of purple blushes—"colors" his text as Marlowe's. Chapman's only acknowledgment of Marlowe occurs in the unnamed elegy he embeds in his poem, aligning the deceased poet with Leander. Chapman describes the poem as a melding of his spirit with Marlowe's after death, but he buries this information, enfolding it in the middle of the narrative action:

> Now (as swift as Time
> Doth follow Motion) finde th' eternal Clime
> Of his free soule, whose liuing subject stood
> Vp to the chin in the Pyerian flood,
> And drunke to me halfe this Musæan storie,
> Inscribing it to deathles Memorie:
> Confer with it, and make my pledge as deepe,
> That neithers draught be consecrate to sleepe;
> Tell it how much his late desires I tender
> (If yet it know not), and to light surrender
> My soul's dark offspring, willing it should die
> To loues, to passions, and societie. (3.187–98)

Such a moment of epic poetic inspiration ought to appear at the beginning of Chapman's poem, not hidden in the middle of the story, right after Leander has vowed to obey the rites of the Goddess Ceremony by seeking his father's blessing and before Hero's chastisement by Venus and Eronusis. Chapman further conceals this transaction by refusing to draw attention to Marlowe's name: Marlowe is simply "his free soule" (3.187) and "it" (3.198, 199). The imagery of drinking and drowning furthers the connection between Marlowe and Leander, as Marlowe half drowns in poetic inspiration, "Up to the chin in the Pyerean flood" (3.190). Linking Marlowe to Leander, Chapman characterizes the Muses' Macedonian Pierean spring of inspiration as a "flood" (from the Latin word for river, *fluvius*) more like the Hellespont than a small river. Marlowe has "drunke to me" (3.191) his tale, a curious phrase that suggests both that Marlowe offered Chapman the poem as one might proffer a drink and that Marlowe has taken too deep a quaff of inspiration, choking on the waters of his own tale. Chapman refers to both poems as "draught(s)" (3.194), drunk ritualistically to seal a contract, his "pledge" (3.196) with the poet's ghost. Yet the passage also wistfully longs for Marlowe's absent poetic guidance: "Tell it how much his late desires I tender / (if yet it know not)" (3.197–98), Chapman shyly admonishes. In this striking passage, Chapman imagines becoming one with his dead muse in a watery poetic marriage of inspiration.

The child of this marriage is Chapman's poem, his "soul's dark offspring," which will, if lucky, assume its father Marlowe's role and "die / To loues, to passions, and societie" (3.197–98). This passage is echoed later when Chapman admits that his dolorous task is to drown Leander in "floods of inck" (6.133). Drowning Leander necessarily entails drowning Marlowe. There are connections to printing's fluctuating peregrinations here as well: Chapman characterizes his poem as "dark offspring" (3.197), adopting the language of laborious birth that Elizabethan poets conventionally use to illustrate their manuscripts' migrations into print. The passage is full of allusions to printer's ink: "dark" (3.197) evokes Chapman's inky deluge where Leander drowns, and there is a play on the verb "to die / To loues" (3.198), which indicates not only a sexual consummation but also a thick, black dye-bath of ink. Chapman's textual coloring highlights the numerous routes a printed text can travel, just like a ship laden with imported goods. Like a merchant ship navigating the currents of the Hellespont, the early modern printed text must travel a watery, uncertain way, always subject to "textual drift."[90] The same challenges that imported commodities faced in the eastern Mediterranean, of plundering, counterfeiting, smuggling, and coloring, are faced by Chapman's appropriation of Marlowe's poem in print.

Do Marlowe and Chapman engage in a kind of cultural and historical syncretism? Yes and no. Though both poems embrace historical and geographic synchronicity, neither Marlowe's nor Chapman's view of the Ottoman Empire presents an ideal of intercultural cooperation between East and West. As much as they make use of Eastern imports to interrogate Western mores, these poets also emphasize the danger, uncertainty, effort, and deceit involved in England's Ottoman mercantile enterprises. As several recent scholars of early modern Ottoman history and global trade have suggested, there is a dark underbelly to cultural syncretism in the period: for every example of religious toleration under the Ottoman Empire, there is another one of imperial subjugation.[91] Chapman's and Marlowe's Hellesponts are precarious waterways. In Chapman's poem, lies and dissimulation color Hero and Leander's bodies until they drown in murky waters. In Marlowe's, Leander nearly drowns when Neptune mistakes him for immortal Ganymede, dragging Leander down to ornament his palace full of plundered, sunken "shipwreck treasure," which calls to mind early modern descriptions of the arduous labor and scant oxygen experienced by early modern pearl fishers. Yet despite the dangers of the Hellespont's transformative waters, which suggest the conversion from breathing human into pearly ornament (Marlowe) and masking the truth with lies and dissimulative rhetoric (Chapman), both poems allow the imagery of early modern global imports from Asia and the Middle East to rework classical poetic technique and form in new ways. For Marlowe, oriental pearls allow a celebration of Ovidian *libertas*, and for Chapman, dyed textiles and texts and mercantile practices of deception are appropriated as the colors of rhetoric, necessary both to early modern Mediterranean mercantile diplomacy and to English poetry. For both poets, the space of the Hellespont is not populated by angry Turkish janissaries, renegados, or Barbary corsairs; the only indication of the presence of early modern global trade is in the poems' references to Eastern imports. Pearls and dyes were oriental and Mediterranean imports in Musaeus's Byzantine Greece, as they were in Ovid's Augustan Rome. But in early modern England, they acquired geographical and material associations with the East through the importation of words associated with their trade, *orient* and *crimson* (from Persian and Arabic).

These imports do not disrupt the poems' classical mythological setting, but the new, early modern global network of associations they create is layered on top of an already layered landscape. The layering of contemporary Orient upon ancient Occident continues when Chapman remediates classical poetics through the rhetoric of Mediterranean mercantile dissimulative practices and the material imagery of inks and dyes. On top of this exoskeleton or hardened pearl, Chapman adds a final layer: his own remediation or coloring of Marlowe's text.[92] Though he ambivalently embeds his invocation of Marlowe's spirit as his muse deep inside his poem, linking Marlowe's and Leander's premature deaths, this can also be read as Chapman's attempt at textual seamlessness. In the sixteenth- and seventeenth-century printed editions of *Hero and Leander*, we cannot see the seams or layers separating Chapman's from Marlowe's text unless we read closely. Some of those layers have hardened with time: most modern editions of *Hero and Leander* retain Chapman's division of the poem into sestiads; most are also printed with Chapman's continuation, despite their placement in anthologies under Marlowe's name.[93] Today, Chapman's continuation has been absorbed into Marlowe's poem. If we read *Hero and Leander* as a palimpsest or pearl composed of layered times, spaces, and authors, even Chapman's anxious views of imperial global competition are smoothed out.

Marlowe and Chapman were both writers invested in the project of reconstructing England's classical literary past with critical regard to the cultural and economic present.[94] In *Hero and Leander*, that present is located not in urban London but at the crossroads of Europe and the Ottoman Empire, on either side and deep within the unpredictable currents of the narrow body of water that keeps them apart. As a growing naval and mercantile power, Britain struggled to compete against far more successful cultures for the right to trade in Asia and the Middle East. Richard Helgerson teaches us that, linguistically at least, English writers saw themselves as a conquered culture struggling to establish their own literary empire, to have, as Spenser wished, "a kingdome of their own language."[95] For Helgerson, early modern English writers achieve this by assembling a composite culled from other European literary traditions and imagined elements of native, pre-Roman "Gothish" culture. Ian Smith, too, contends that even as English writers began the process of defining themselves as culturally superior to "barbarous" non-Western languages and cultures, they were haunted by a past in which their own language was perceived of as "barbarous," through the lens of classical rhetoric.[96] But an alternative composite can be found in Marlowe's and Chapman's reworking of classical mythology interspersed with references to early modern Eastern geography and trade. Here, *orient* pearls, ornaments like rhetorical coloring, and imagery of imported jewels and pigments work alongside classical mythology and poetics, halting and reorienting *translatio imperii* (the spread of knowledge through empire), which traditionally moves between East and West, by placing the literary authority of the ancient Greco-Roman world on the same plane as late sixteenth-century global trade. Even as English writers looked to escape their own barbarous past, they reframed Roman and Greek literary models with an Ottoman-inflected classical poetics. In the end, Marlowe's and Chapman's Hellespont is just as fluid and shifting as imperial Ottoman boundaries and trade routes, affirming the larger Mediterranean as a fruitful palimpsest, while at the same time acknowledging the deceptive rhetorical and poetic practices necessary to engage with it.

Epilogue

The Peregrinations of Barbarous Antiquity

In each of this book's chapters, the East emerges from the graphic space of the material page. Latour's model of mediators and intermediaries as instigators of cultural change depends upon a tangible, physical metamorphosis occurring in the material structure of the mediator itself. The malleable, protean nature of the material text is therefore what makes this transformative process possible in early modern poetry and poetics. The imported, newly minted words that *Poetaster*'s characters expel materialize as strips of paper, as vocalizations, and as italicized commodities on the pages where they appear. Though the play was popular in contemporary performance, this process was amplified by print, which then allowed further staged performances. The analogies I have made between Puttenham's shaped Turkish poems and sugar lozenges would not be possible without the reproduction of the lozenge shapes in the printed text of *The Arte of English Poesie* and in printed and manuscript culinary manuals. Shakespeare's two narrative poems also draw on the conventions of printing, drawing, and writing—their ability to make visible and legible, to reproduce an otherwise invisible mark, and to illustrate newly imported botanical commodities like the "chequered" fritillary. And Chapman uses a second printing and metaphors of ink to subsume Marlowe's poem within his own.

Over the course of this book, imported words and metaphors have reconfigured notions of classical antiquity within early modern poetic texts, and writers have wrestled with developing a nuanced, globally inflected, definitive English poetic style, remaining keenly aware of classical models while experimenting with new words, imagery, and rhetorical practices. English poetry itself has become a mediator for past and present, East and West. Since Latour's mediators effect change through changes in their material, chemical structure, we can imagine late sixteenth-century English poetry and poetic theory as a laboratory where writers concocted and compounded new poetic formulas, measuring ancient Greek and Latin methods with and against modern imported concepts, words, and things. If we follow *Poetaster*, Jonson's translation of Horace, and his annotations to Puttenham, we can deduce that Jonson's recipe for English poetry contains a higher percentage of one type of classical model (Horatian) than another (Ovidian) but at the same time judiciously strains out classical archaism and Latinate neologisms, bolstering his cocktail with a balance of plain, English words. Puttenham's potion is stronger and thicker when it comes to imported Ottoman and Asian forms and tropes; it's also sweeter and harder, containing as it does a super-concentrated amount of sugar, ready to be pressed into new forms and molds resembling oriental gemstones.

Shakespeare's global, Ovidian poetry takes the form of a perfume's accord: the bright, vibrant top notes are his early modern English additions to Ovid's tragic tales—the humorously large Venus, Adonis's horse as poetic blazon, the empowered and intelligent Lucrece. The strong base note remains his debt and homage to Ovid, which can even be seen in his poetry's desire to match or outstrip the poet in inventive variety. The middle notes are the most subtle. They begin to emerge as the potion begins to dry down, as we contemplate the texture of the poem: they are the spices that tie the scent together. Shakespeare's inclusion of imported Ottoman, Levantine, and Asian words and objects balances ancient with modern, English with Roman. Marlowe's and Chapman's poetic quintessence might resemble a vial of seawater taken from the Hellespont or the Persian gulf at the height of Anglo-Ottoman trade and diplomacy. Floating in its inky depths are traces of sediment, fine layers made up of ground pearl, a purple swirl of dissolved Asian inks and dyes, some crumbled sand from Troy, or a few threads of cloth from Xerxes' or Hecuba's gown. Once the sediment settles on the bottom of the bottle, we have a liquid palimpsest of ancient mythological past and contemporary mercantile present; shake it up, and you get Marlowe's and Chapman's imaginary poetic space.

What is the afterlife of the process of remediating classical poetry through Mediterranean trade? At the beginning of the seventeenth century, English traders began to pursue mercantile ventures west to the New World and further east to the East Indies, partly to compete with Spain and Portugal, which were moving west, and partly to avoid competing in Ottoman markets, which were becoming too expensive an investment.[1] What, then, happens to Puttenham's Eastern-inflected model of poetry as sugar, when sugar is no longer an Eastern import but a New World one, or to Chapman's oriental dye imagery when crimson *alkermes* beetles are replaced with sturdier and less expensive South American cochineal? When early modern mercantile geography shifted from the eastern Mediterranean to a larger, global market, I want to suggest, the interplay between the contemporary East and the ancient Mediterranean reoriented itself again. As American commodities like tobacco and cochineal entered the English market (and with them unfounded hopes of British mercantile success), so did their metaphoric and linguistic counterparts take up residence in English poems, but in at least one case, instead of the New World remediating classical antiquity, the inverse happens: classical poetic techniques work to reorient the New World.[2] Sir John Beaumont's satirical panegyric *The Metamorphosis of Tabacco* (1602) creates not one but two metamorphic Ovidian etiologies for the North and South American import tobacco, reinscribing this New World import onto a Mediterranean-inflected, mythological landscape. Opening in mock-heroic mode, the poet imitates Homer and Virgil to "sing the loves of superior powers, / with the faire mother of all fragrant flowers" (275).[3] Tobacco is the muse that literally inspires the poet (by drawing its smoke into his lungs) to write his paean. Over its course, the poem creates two Ovidian etiologies for tobacco, first reinserting it into the cosmogony that opens Book One of Ovid's *Metamorphoses* (277–86) and second imagining the transformation of the maiden who lives in "the valleys of *Wingandekoe*" (Virginia) into the plant by a jealous Juno (286–304). Here, Ovidian myth makes tobacco weightier, both in the English imagination and in English markets, as North American colonial and mercantile investments continued to fail.

Tobacco is not the only non-European imported commodity to receive a retroactive classical inflection in Beaumont's poem. As I have mentioned in Chapter 2, sugar—by 1602 both a Mediterranean and a New World commodity—also takes up residence in the poem, mediating between the more familiar eastern Mediterranean and the exotic New World. Throughout the poem, tobacco is referred to as "sugred" and "sweet," lending the vaporous substance more weight and value. The poem's references to sugar participate in a larger, global landscape of imports that includes oriental gemstones, African gold, and Asian spices, all of which the poet weds to classical imagery in order to validate and familiarize this New World import. Not only is tobacco sweet and sugary, but it is also a "precious gemme." The poem's expansive representation of global imports culminates in its description of a divine summit in which each of earth's waterways converges to bestow their material gifts upon Ops, the Earth, as she labors to bring forth tobacco. The "Magellanick sea" brings pearly "unions," the Iberian river Tagus brings gold, the British seas offer "holesome coral" (punning on coral's perforations and its use as an early modern pharmaceutical ingredient), the "Danish Gulf" amber, and the Po river electrum, a naturally occurring alloy of silver and gold (284). Though it can be disputed whether these commodities are properly matched to their geographical sources (perhaps Beaumont is alluding to small, cold water reefs off the coast of Scotland), here we have a fantasy in which all the watery global trade routes across Europe and the Mediterranean produce their commodities to help inaugurate the production of yet one more. With the exception of the "Magellanick" sea, which draws attention to contemporary early modern cartography, Beaumont's waterways and their products bear classical, Latinate names. Amber is "Succinum," the Po river "Euridinus." Beaumont's poem widens the early modern English poetic landscape into global dimensions, while at the same time narrowing and containing imported commodities sharply within a classical, Ovidian frame. As Jeffery Knapp's reading of the poem points out, it is not tobacco alone that stakes out an imaginary imperial claim for England but something equally insubstantial yet powerful, English poetry.[4] Noting the way Beaumont's poem plays with tobacco's smoky insubstantiality, Knapp argues for both tobacco and poetry as *immaterial* commodities that have the potential to conjure British imperial success fantastically out of thin air.[5] Just as the material qualities of text and words provide transformative, remediating power in the Eastern-inflected texts I have examined, so does the fantastical, immaterial nature of imaginative, Ovidian poetry bolster England's as-yet insubstantial imperial and colonial fantasies in Beaumont's satire.

If English poetry could mediate between the ancient classical past and the sixteenth-century Mediterranean present in a printed poem, how did it fare on a ship? Did merchants and travelers read poetry with a similar understanding of the sympathies between language and commodities, and between Western antiquity and the early modern East? I want to suggest that they did and that the early modern English poetic dialogue between antiquity and the East became a global currency that traveled farther than the Mediterranean and beyond the limits of formal poetry. The plays of Shakespeare had a significant role in shaping the British colonial project.[6] But before this happened on a large scale—before nineteenth-century British missionaries, for example, distributed copies of Shakespeare's plays in India and Africa to "civilize" their indigenous colonial subjects—early modern poetry found its way into early transatlantic travel narratives, just as foreign words found their way into translations and adaptations of classical texts. And, in at least one example, it is the kind of poetry exposed in this book that seems to have been most readily appropriated: poems that remediate classical antiquity through the imagery of Ottoman, Arab, and Asian mercantilism. The passage that I will discuss below comes from an account associated with the violent and dehumanizing seventeenth-century Atlantic slave and sugar trade. But it narrates an encounter that takes place off the coast of North Africa, on Portuguese Cape Verde, before the author reached the West Indies. It is therefore well positioned to give us a glimpse into the afterlife and travel of early modern English classical-mercantile poetry. It can also tell us how English poetry may have helped early modern merchants translate and interpret their own increasingly unfamiliar travels into a more familiar literary discourse. When transported across the Atlantic, the barbarous antiquity of early modern English poetry becomes its most distinctly English feature.

Richard Ligon, an English merchant who set up sugar plantations in Barbados in the early seventeenth century, first traveled past the northwest coast of Africa in order to observe the sugar plantations in the Canary Islands and Cape Verde, where he developed a crush on the Portuguese governor's African mistress, whom he met at a banquet.[7] His description of her dark beauty is full of literary references, ancient and modern. She is Shakespeare's Dark Lady from *The Sonnets*; she is the dark bride from the King James Bible's version of the Song of Solomon; she is more graceful than Queen Anne dancing in one of Ben Jonson's court masques. As Jane Stevenson's reading of this passage makes clear, we are meant to think of Queen Anne's role in Jonson's masques of *Blackness* and *Beauty*, both of which featured the queen and her ladies in exotic costume and blackface as daughters of the Niger.[8]

What is most remarkable about Ligon's description of the mistress, however, is the way it appropriates the eastern Mediterranean textiles found in Marlowe's and Chapman's descriptions of Hero. Although Ligon's text is in prose, his description of the mistress begins much like Marlowe's poem, immediately concentrating on a woman's remarkable, ornate, outlandish dress (Ligon, 12; *Hero and Leander* [*H&L*], 9–36). Like Marlowe's Hero, she is clad in layered clothes rich with color, embroidery, and patterns, so luxuriant as to be outlandish. The colors Ligon uses to describe this lady's dress correspond almost exactly to Marlowe's description of Hero: white, green, purple, gold, blue. Her green and white silk turban calls to mind Hero's embroidered green sleeves and white lawn dress (*H&L*, 9–11). Hero's dress is lined with purple silk, dotted with gold stars (*H&L*, 10); the mistress has the same purple and gold, "a mantle of purple silke, ingrayld with straw Colour," this time covering her dress (Ligon, 12). The word *engrailed* ("ingrayld") derives from heraldry and is defined by the *OED* as a border "ornamented with a series of curvilinear indentations."[9] This suggests a woven hem of contrasting color adding figural texture to the garment, though *engrailed* may also indicate variegated color produced with contrasting threads.[10] Like Hero's "kirtle blue," the mistress has a linen petticoat of "Skye Colour," though here it is patterned "Orange Tawny ... not done with Straite stripes, but wav'd" (Ligon, 12). Channeling Marlowe, Ligon draws attention to the mistress's silver boots, using the same word to describe them, "buskins" (Ligon, 12). These are real boots, not fantastical hydraulic ones, but they resemble Hero's in that they are lavishly decorated with silver, replacing shells with silk. Hero's buskins are made of "shells al siluered" decorated with a lacy pattern, "branched with blushing corall to the knee" (*H&L*, 1.31), and Ligon's lady has "buskins of wetched Silke, deckt with Silver lace, and Fringe" (Ligon, 12). *Wetched* is a pale, gray-blue color that echoes the silvery sheen of the buskins' lace. Marlowe's description of Hero's dress turns his poem's protagonist into a textual artifact, a cunning depiction of poetic artifice, complete with mechanical birds and artificial flowers prettier than the real thing.[11] Ligon's appropriation of Marlowe's Hero appears at first to turn a real woman into an artifact, a conglomeration of imported commodities. What serves as a bravura display of poetic technique in Marlowe's poem becomes, when mapped onto the body of a spectacularly dressed African woman in Ligon's description, a poetic key to deciphering non-European physical beauty.

Like Hero, the dark mistress is associated with orient pearls: "about her neck and on her armes, fayre Pearles" (Ligon, 12). This phrase echoes Marlowe's diction ("about her neck") in his description of Hero's necklaces. Hero has round pebbles on her neck, made rarer in the way they are magically illuminated by the bright white of Hero's skin: "About her neck hung chains of pebble-stone, / Which lightened by her neck, like diamonds shone" (*H&L*, 1.25–26). Though these shiny, white stones are not valuable, their whiteness and luminescence makes them sound a lot like pearls. As I argued in Chapter 5, Hero becomes an orient pearl in Marlowe's poem; similarly, in Ligon's description, the mistress's body becomes indistinguishable from the jewels she sports. Despite her black skin, Ligon metaphorizes her eyes into pearls: "But her eyes were the richest Iewells: for they were the largest, and most oriental, that I have ever seene" (Ligon, 12). Just as Hero is a living, secreting pearl, the Padre's mistress is a jewel box of treasures. Like Hero, who in Marlowe's inversion of the pearl-as-virgin cliché is just as pearly after she has lost her virginity as she was before, this lady's treasure lies in her sexual availability, not in her chastity. She is already the mistress of the Padre running the town, and Ligon hopes rather futilely that she will entertain his advances, too.

The mistress also resembles Chapman's female characters. Like his Hero, she wears a veil and drapes herself in purple and black; and like Eronusis, her clothes are remarkable for their variety of shifting, changeable color: green, purple, orange, and blue, in fluid stripes that shimmer like waves. She is also dark-skinned like Teras, Chapman's female bard who tells the Ovidian tale of multicolored Adolesche's transformation into a parrot. Ligon also compares the African mistress to a "black swan" (Ligon, 13), which inverts the image of the white swan Leucote, "pure brightness" (*H&L*, 4.236) that black-clad Venus whips in Chapman's text for speaking eloquently in Hero's defense (*H&L*, 4.285–86). Like Leucote and Hero, Ligon's black swan is both eloquent and resists interpretation. Despite the "gracefull delivery" of her language, which unites and confirms "a perfection in all the rest" (her skin color and costume), Ligon depends upon a Spanish-English interpreter to convey his gift of colored silk ribbons to her (Ligon, 13). And though in return for his gift Ligon receives one of her lovely smiles (a kind of erotic mercantile transaction), his attempt at courtship fails miserably: "Other addresses were not to be made" (Ligon, 13). The mistress is clearly a figure of sexual freedom for Ligon as Hero is for Marlowe, yet in her artfulness, the Padre's mistress represents eloquence coupled with obscurity and inaccessibility, like Chapman's female characters, and by extension like early modern merchants engaging in global trade for the first time.

Hero and Leander is not the only poetic currency in this description. The black mistress also has sympathies with Shakespeare's Dark Lady ("In the old age black was not counted fair . . . But now is black beauty's successive heir," Sonnet 127, 1–3) and with Sidney's Stella. Despite the darkness of her skin, the Padre's mistress's black eyes shine brightly like jewels, "the largest and most oriental that I have ever seen," which calls to mind Sidney's Petrarchan image of Stella's eyes as "seeming jet blacke yet in blacknesse bright" (*Astrophil and Stella* [*AS*], 91.8) and "in collour blacke" wrapped in "beames so bright" (*AS* 7.1–2).[12] She also allows Ligon to play the role of courtly sonneteer: Ligon briefly challenges an early modern European commonplace, that dark-skinned people have whiter teeth than pale-skinned Westerners, when he claims that their teeth are as "yellow and foul" as anyone's and only appear whiter because they are offset by dark skin (Ligon, 12–13). This momentary refusal to surrender the poetic convention of the "rich Jewel in an Ethiop's ear" (*Romeo and Juliet*, 1.5.47) echoes Shakespeare's terrestrial Sonnet 130, which brings all such poetic commonplaces crashing to the ground: "My mistress' eyes are nothing like the sun ... / If snow be white, why then her breasts are dun" (Sonnet 130, 1–3).[13] But no sooner does Ligon voice this Shakespearean skepticism than he tosses it aside and waxes lyrical about the lady's pearly teeth: "And then she shewed her rowes of pearls, so clean, white, Orient, and well shaped, as Neptune's Court was never pav'd with such as these; & to shew whether was whiter, or more Orient, those or the whites of her eyes, she turn'd them up, & gave me such a look, as was a sufficient return for a far greater present" (Ligon, 13). In this new simile, the mistress resembles both the pearly Hero and the ivory-skinned Leander, who risks becoming an orient jewel paving the sea bottom of "Neptune's Court," where, in Marlowe's text, "the ground was strewed with pearl and gold" (*H&L*, 2.644). Ligon confuses the dual senses of the word *orient* here: this is not an oriental lady but an African one, geographically located south and west of Ligon's England. She is also not white but dark-skinned. The only white part of her is her teeth, which are nacreous and jewel-like. By describing her teeth as *orient* pearls, Ligon continues the inversion of pearls that Marlowe initiates in his poem, associating pearls with this woman's sexual availability and desirability, not with her chastity or purity.

The description of the lady's teeth also invokes another figure from early modern English poetry, the beautiful bride from the Song of Solomon in the King James Bible, a woman whose white teeth are compared to a flock of young goats: "Thy teeth are like a flock of sheep that are even shorn, which came up from the washing; whereof every one bear twins, and none is barren among them" (4: 2–4).[14] Ligon has already connected the mistress to biblical antiquity by noting that before her entrance, the company listened to an ancient song, an "Antique piece . . . that was in fashion in King Davids daye" (12). Rich in color and pattern and radiant like gems, Ligon's description of the governor's mistress distances itself from her black skin color, focusing instead on her whiteness, the orient pearls of her eyes and teeth. Like the biblical bride, whose black skin only appears twice in the song, the lady's blackness is partially obscured by her other, more colorful attributes. Her head swathed in a turban of green taffeta, her white leather shoes laced with blue and fashionably serrated or "pinkt" (12), she seems more an image of an Ottoman lady in native dress, such as one might find in woodcut from the pages of Nicolas de Nicolay's *Peregrinations* to Turkey (1585), than a West African woman.[15]

The presence of biblical antiquity in Ligon's description of the lady, rather than Greek or Roman culture, is telling, since the land of the Bible was under Ottoman rule at the time. With his description of her pearly teeth as *orient* and his reference to Solomon's beautiful black bride, Ligon both orientalizes and antiquates this West African lady. Ligon locates this Cape Verdean lady in the discourse of the ancient and contemporary East as a way of distinguishing her from "barbarous" savages. Ian Smith has demonstrated how early modern English writers used their understanding of classical rhetoric to convert (or deliberately misread) the Latin word for Northern invaders, *barbarian*, into the English word used to describe Moors and Africans, which coincidentally linked them geographically through a homonym to the North African Barbary Coast.[16] But the descriptions of barbarous Turks that appear in Sandys's and Nicolay's accounts have a civilizing influence on Ligon's description of an African lady. Like Marlowe's Thracian Hero and oriental Leander, this woman's physical racial difference is commodified and translated into valuable silks and pearls, her African identity reconfigured as an antique oriental and contemporary Ottoman one. But as a body composed of precious stones, she is also poetry commodified, a living blazon.

What are Shakespeare's *Sonnets*, the Song of Solomon, and *Hero and Leander* doing in the prologue to Ligon's ventures in the Atlantic sugar trade? The poems examined in this book upset the literary authority of ancient Greece and Rome, but in Ligon's narrative, it is English poetry that upsets and rewrites the narrative of European colonialism. Much of the rest of Ligon's account describes, in far less favorable terms, the African slave women who labor on the sugar plantations, though at one singular moment, Ligon stops to admire the beauty of two Cape Verdean sisters carrying water from a well on the island of Jago. These women are local laborers, not wealthy courtesans like the governor's mistress. And yet Ligon is just as attracted to them as he is to the mistress and pursues them in identical fashion, first trying to converse with them and then presenting them with love tokens in the form of silk ribbons. In his description, Ligon compares the women's bodies to contemporary European visual arts, fixing the image in his prose as an engraving might fix his subjects:

Creatures, of such shapes, as would have puzzelld *Albert Durer,*
the great Mr of Proportion, but to have imitated; and *Tition,* or
Andrea de Sarta, for softnes of muscles, and Curiositie of Colouring,
though with a studied diligence; and a love both to the partie and
the worke. To express all the perfections of Nature, and Parts, these
Virgins were owners of, would ask a more skillfull pen, or pencill
then mine; Sure I am, though all were excellent, their motions were

the highest, and that is a beautie no painter can expresse, and therefore my pen may well be silent.[17]

Adopting the same classical rhetorical trope of withholding (*enarratio*) that allows Marlowe to suggestively explore Leander's naked backside with his silent
"rude pen" (1.69), Ligon somewhat overplays this technique, calling for his
unskilled pen to be silent one too many times. His references to Dürer, Titian,
and del Sarto transport these black women away from Africa and Portugal,
relocating them in the European art scene. But Ligon does not stop there—he
continues to sing their praises, comparing their curled hairs to "wiers," recalling
the "black wires" growing on the Dark Lady's head in Shakespeare's Sonnet 130.

Comparing these younger, lower-class women with the Padre's mistress,
Ligon cites another English poet, John Donne: "But I found the difference
between young fresh Beauties, and those that are made up with the addition
of State and Majesty: For though they counsell and perswade our Loves; yet,
young Beauties force, and so commit rapes upon our affections" (Ligon, 17).
Here Ligon paraphrases almost word for word the lines in Donne's "Autumnall" elegy that elevates middle-aged beauties above impetuous youthful ones:
"Young beauties force our love, and that's a rape, / This doth but counsel, yet
you cannot scape" (Donne, 3–4).[18] Ligon reverses Donne's argument, claiming that he prefers having his affections seized by these young maidens to the
quiet counsel of an older, wealthier woman. Donne's elegy is full of references
to classical antiquity, locating the older woman's beauty in Ovid's golden age:
"she's gold oft tried, and ever new" (Donne, 8).[19] The poem—and the woman's
approaching old age—is threatened throughout with more menacing images
of corporeal Death, culminating in the speaker's attempt to arrest the inevitable convergence of these images: "Name not these living deathsheads unto
me / For these not ancient but antique be" (Donne, 43–44).[20] The wrinkled,
"winter faces" (Donne, 37) of truly old women Donne associates with antics,
which, as I demonstrated in the Introduction, could indicate both skeletons
and dark-skinned foreigners. Perhaps Ligon's reversal of Donne's argument in
the "Autumnall" operates on a deeper level here, deliberately choosing antics
over ancients, while reconfiguring antics *as* ancients.

In the canon of early modern English descriptions of black women, the
Padre's beautiful mistress and the elegant water carriers stand apart.[21] Ligon's
descriptions of these women are remarkable not for their commodification of
a racialized female body, which is typical of an early modern travel narrative,
or for the grace and nobility of the characters, but for the way they retranslate

those commodified bodies back into the language and imagery of early modern English poetry. Ligon's passage shows how an early modern English *poem* (*Hero and Leander*, *Astrophil and Stella*, the "Autumnall" elegy, the "Song of Songs") can operate within an Atlantic travel narrative in the same way that the imported words I have been examining operate within individual poems, to upset and revise a dominant literary paradigm. Just as Middleton's vengeful phantom Lucrece reveals that Shakespeare's language of imported *ciphers* operated outside its own text as a kind of counter-classical literary currency, Shakespeare's Dark Lady, the dark bride in the of Song of Solomon, and Marlowe's Hero begin to function on a larger, more global scale, translating bodies and cultural difference into both merchandise and texts, relocating them in the classical-oriental antiquity of Herodotus, Alexander, and the Bible as well as in the Mediterranean, Ottoman, and Persian present.

As a seventeenth-century Atlantic travel narrative, the title of Ligon's account, *A True and Exact History of Barbados*, leads us to expect an almost scientific description of the indigenous peoples of Cape Verde and the West Indies as if they were flora and fauna and not people. Instead, we get a description of an African woman dressed like an Ottoman lady, laced with references to biblical poetry and early modern English erotic verse. In Ligon's account of the Padre's mistress, it is English poetry and translation that transform this woman into an Eastern commodity and an antique text. Returning once more to Latour's actor-network theory, we can see poetry—*English* poetry—operating as intermediary, drawing on an established network of images and associations about "the East" and foreign women that allow Ligon to read a West African woman as an ancient, Eastern treasure. But English poetry mediates this cultural transaction as well: the new, contemporary Eastern references in English poetry are what allow Ligon to change the symbolic language of blackness, converting the mistress from a barbarous savage into an ancient, Eastern beauty.

This book contends that the longing of late sixteenth-century English poets for their own literary empire involved implanting new metaphors drawn from Britain's Eastern mercantile ventures into poetic texts modeled on classical themes and precedents. What I hope to have uncovered in Jonson's poetics, Puttenham's sugary shape poems, Shakespeare's counter-classical Ovidian narratives, and Marlowe's and Chapman's Hellespont are multiple models for a global English poetics that was portable and transferrable, even when Anglo-Ottoman trade relations no longer dominated English, or even early modern English culture. By the end of the seventeenth century, the Ottoman

Mediterranean was no longer a productive real and imaginary space where early modern English merchants and poets practiced dissimulative rhetorical practices; imported flowers, horses, sugar, and jewels; and learned Arabic accounting and arithmetic. Britain was imagining a proximate colonial future to the west of Europe while simultaneously investing in mercantile ventures in South and East Asia. However, for a brief moment in the late sixteenth and early seventeenth centuries, the flourishing of mercantile exchange between England and the Near East also happened in English poetry. Included in this exchange was a chance to reimagine and reorient poetic discourse about classical antiquity onto a new landscape and, in so doing, develop more globally and materially inflected forms of English poetry.

We can therefore read the moments before the creation of the colonial British Empire as an early or intermediate stage in Britain's cultural development, full of possibility and open to the incorporation of new, imported ideas as part of a larger cultural exchange between East and West. Ligon's amorous encounter with the governor's scintillating mistress occupies a liminal geographic and oceanic space. In Ligon's own geographic confusion between the Canary Islands and Cape Verde—he initially states that St. Iago (on Cape Verde) is in the Canaries—the island where these cross-cultural amorous encounters occur loses its coordinates, floating somewhere between Europe, Africa, and the West Indies. Ligon's description of this woman likewise occupies an indeterminate, intermediate space along the way to the literary establishment of British colonial rule, a space that allows us to glimpse, if only briefly, a moment in which a female colonial subject can be translated into a literal blazon more beautiful than the queen, a glimpse facilitated by the circulation of imported words in English poetry.

Though they did not travel as far as Ligon did, the poets he read were reading the printed accounts of merchants and travelers, whether those printed in Hakluyt's hugely popular volumes or in individual itineraries. Some, like George Sandys, traveled figuratively back in time to ancient Greece and Rome and literally southeast to the Ottoman Empire to write their own literary and historical accounts. Jonson, Puttenham, Shakespeare, Marlowe, and Chapman travel to both places and times imaginatively, as each poet exposes the parallels between the circulation of merchandise, words, and poetic ornament by attending to the conveyance of the material text as a medium for circulation and imaginative travel. What Mediterranean and Near Eastern traffic gave to English poetry was not only the opportunity and vehicles for the remediation and reevaluation of the authority of classical poetry but the possibility of imagining a national literature that was fluid and unmoored by space (Europe) and time (antiquity). We might even locate one vector of such a desire for unmooring half a decade later in the stirrings of independent consciousness that appear in the first book of Milton's *Paradise Lost*. Addressing his band of fallen angels, Satan professes to bring "a mind not to be changed by place or time" (I.251). At first glance, this seems a statement of stalwart fixedness, until Satan upends the notion of anything being grounded, championing the ability of thought to make landscape and history malleable: "The mind is its own place, / And in itself can make a heaven of hell, a hell of heaven" (I.252–53). By placing exotic currencies into dialogue with ancient Greek and Roman form, late sixteenth-century English poetry made time and space malleable, too.

Notes

1. Ancient Greeks and Romans traded with cultures all over Asia and Asia Minor, most famously via the Silk Road. They must have come into contact with spices like sugar, dyes like *alkermes*, and concepts like zero. But there were no words for these things in Latin or Greek, which suggests to me that these commodities and concepts, though they existed, were not embraced by Europeans until the Middle Ages and early modern period.

2. John Frederick Stanford and Charles Augustus Maude Fennell's *The Stanford Dictionary of Anglicized Words and Phrases* (Cambridge: Cambridge University Press, 1892) is the only text that comes close to noting the volume of imported and adopted words in English, though this lexicon does not always include English words that were newly anglicized in the Middle Ages or the sixteenth century. For example, there are no entries for *sugar* (from Sanskrit *sakhara*) or *zero* (Arabic *sifra*), though *sherbet* (Persian *sharbat*), *crimson* (Arabic *qirmis*), and *alkermes* (the insect and dye that produces the crimson color) do appear. Though more challenging to navigate because it is organized by roots, Joseph Twadell Shipley's *The Origins of English Words: A Discursive Dictionary of Indo-European Roots* (Baltimore: Johns Hopkins University Press, 1984) is also useful in locating how far-fetched words find their way from Persian and Sanskrit into English, though I have found it most helpful as a searchable online text, despite the fact that Hamitic-Semitic words (from Arabic, Hebrew, Egyptian) are not included.

3. See Linda Levy Peck, *Consuming Splendor: Society and Literature in Seventeenth Century England* (Cambridge: Cambridge University Press, 2005); Alison V. Scott, *Languages of Luxury in Early Modern England* (Burlington, VT: Ashgate, 2013). See also Lisa Jardine, *Wordly Goods: A New History of the Reniassance* (New York: Norton, 1998), and Jerry Brotton and Lisa Jardine, *Global Interests: Renaissance Art Between East and West* (Ithaca, NY: Cornell University Press, 2000).

4. *import*, v. and n., *OED*.

5. J.S., "To His Honored Friend Mr. *T.B.* Upon his *GLOSSOGRAPHIA*," in Thomas Blount, *Glossographia* (London: Thomas Newcombe, 1656), A7v.

6. Notably, Turkish words appear at the top of a list of cultures, nations, fields of knowledge, and professions: "For example, in the Turkish history I met with Janissaries, Mufties, Tinariots, Basha's, Seraglio's, Shashes, Turbants, &c.," Blount, *Glossographia*, "To the Reader," A2r.

7. Pierre Bourdieu, *Language and Symbolic Power* (Cambridge: Cambridge University Press, 1991), 35; also cited in Peter Burke, *Languages and Communities in Early Modern Europe* (Cambridge: Cambridge University Press, 2004), 122.

8. Jonathan Gil Harris, "Introduction," in Harris, ed., *Indography: Writing the Indian in Early Modern England* (New York: Palgrave Macmillan, 2012), 5–6.

9. Juliet Fleming, *Graffiti and the Writing Arts of Early Modern England* (Philadelphia: University of Pennsylvania Press, 2001), 26–27.

10. Michel Foucault, *The Order of Things: An Archeology of the Human Sciences* (New York: Vintage Books, 1994), 34.

11. I discuss each word and import (zero/*cipher* and pearl/*orient*) in more detail in Chapters 3 and 5.

12. For analyses of Turks, Moors, Islam, and non-Western cultural Others on the Renaissance stage, see Ania Loomba, *Shakespeare, Race, and Colonialism* (Oxford: Oxford University Press, 2002); Jonathan Burton, *Traffic and Turning* (Cranbury: University of Delaware Press, 2005); Jane Degenhardt, *Islamic Conversion and Christian Resistance on the Early Modern Stage* (Edinburgh: University of Edinburgh Press, 2010); Emily Bartels, *Speaking of the Moor: From Alcazar to Othello* (Philadelphia: University of Pennsylvania Press, 2008), and *Spectacles of Strangeness: Imperialism, Alienation, and Marlowe* (Philadelphia: University of Pennsylvania Press, 1993). Even books on poetry and Romance still tend to emphasize drama and racial difference. See Benedict Robinson, *Islam and Early Modern English Literature: The Politics of Romance from Spenser to Milton* (New York: Palgrave, 2007); Kim F. Hall, *Things of Darkness: Economies of Race and Gender in Early Modern England* (Ithaca, NY: Cornell University Press, 1995); and Sujata Iyengar, *Shades of Difference: Mythologies of Skin Color in Early Modern England* (Philadelphia: University of Pennsylvania Press, 2005).

13. *Turk*, 3a, 4a, 5b, *OED*.

14. Burton, *Traffic and Turning*, 28.

15. Ibid., 28.

16. See Roland Greene, *Post-Petrarchism: Origins and Innovations of the Western Lyric Sequence* (Princeton, NJ: Princeton University Press, 1991).

17. Mary Floyd-Wilson has noted that early modern geohumoral racial discourse of North and South was employed not only by British writers to describe Italians, Spaniards, Arabs, and Jews but also within Britain to describe the Irish, the Scottish, and the inhabitants of southern Britain, in *English Ethnicity and Race in Early Modern Drama* (Cambridge: Cambridge University Press, 2006).

18. Palmira Brummett, *Ottoman Seapower and Levantine Diplomacy in the Age of Discovery* (Albany, NY: SUNY Press, 1994), 2–3; Halil Inalcik, *The Ottoman Empire: The Classical Age, 1300–1600* (London: Phoenix Press, 2000) and with Donald Quataert, *An Economic and Social History of the Ottoman Empire Vol. I 1300–1600* (Cambridge: Cambridge University Press, 1994).

19. Suleiman the Magnificent, who reigned from 1520–66, challenged the Hapsburg emperor's claim to title of "caesar," and sultans also set as their goal the task of finishing

Alexander's enterprise and conquering the Indian Ocean and Persian Gulf (which they never accomplished). Brummett, 5

20. Jerry Brotton, *Trading Territories: Mapping the Early Modern World* (Ithaca, NY: Cornell University Press, 1998), 34. Brotton's analysis sits well with the term John Archer coins, *para-colonial*, to describe early modern English engagements with the Middle East, one that takes into account this sense of continuity between Old World and New World: "A proper consideration of Europe amidst the Old World in the early modern period requires a concept like *para-colonial* studies, where the Greek prefix means 'along side of' without precluding either 'before' or 'beyond' and can suggest both 'closely related to' and 'aside from' as well," John Archer, *Old Worlds: Egypt, Southwest Asia, India, and Russia in Early Modern English Writing* (Palo Alto, CA: Stanford University Press, 2001), 16–17.

21. Harris's project is to uncover the ancient oriental past in the early modern English (occidental) present. Mine might be seen as the inverse: to examine how early modern oriental trade exfoliates the layers of occidental antiquity in the early modern English poetic imagination. See Jonathan Gil Harris, *Untimely Matter in the Time of Shakespeare* (Philadelphia: University of Pennsylvania Press, 2008), 19, 24.

22. George Sandys, *A Relation of a Iourney begun anno dom. 1610* (London: Printed by Richard Field for W. Barrett, 1615).

23. Ibid., 4.

24. Ibid., A2r.

25. As Ian Smith argues, the English term *barbarous* was mapped onto Ottomans and North Africans in the sixteenth century, encouraged by a coincidental homophony with the *Barbary* Coast. See Ian Smith, *Race and Rhetoric in Early Modern England: Barbarian Errors* (New York: Palgrave Macmillan, 2009).

26. Ibid., 9.

27. Ibid., 15.

28. Sandys's sense of dislocation echoes Petrarch's in the letters the poet wrote to Cicero, Seneca, and Virgil and in his famous letter VI.2 to Giovanni Colonna, which describes walking through Rome as if ancient history were unfolding in real time. In their attempts to bridge space and time to reconnect with a lost literary culture, both writers articulate a profound sense of loss. See Francesco Petrarca, *Letters on Familiar Matters (Rerum familiarum libri)* Vols. 1 and 3, trans. Aldo S. Bernardo (Baltimore: Johns Hopkins University Press, 1975–2005), VI.2 and XXIV. For more discussions of letter VI.2, see Angus Vine, *In Defiance of Time: Antiquarian Writing in Early Modern England* (Oxford: Oxford University Press, 2010), 3–4, and Leonard Barkan, *Unearthing the Past: Archeology and Aesthetics in the Making of Renaissance Culture* (New Haven, CT: Yale University Press, 1999), 24–25.

29. Margreta de Grazia draws on the myth of the Four Rules in her reading of the title page of Drayton's *Polyolbion* in relation to *Hamlet*. The four figures on Drayton's title page include both imagined ancestors (Trojan Brutus) and Roman, Saxon, and Norman conquerors. See Margreta de Grazia, *Hamlet without* Hamlet (Cambridge: Cambridge University Press, 2008), 57–59.

30. On the expansion of the English language to include borrowed words from trade,

see Burke, *Languages and Communities*. On neologisms, see Bryan A. Garner, "Shakespeare's Latinate Neologisms," *Shakespeare Studies* 25 (1982): 149–70, and Paula Blank, *Broken English: Dialects and the Politics of Language in Early Modern Writings* (London: Routledge, 1996).

31. Keilen locates early modern literary ambivalence to classical antiquity in Nashe's and Lyly's linking of the myth of the "golden age" to Ovid's tale of Midas, in "English Literature in Its Golden Age," in Leonard Barkan, Bradin Cormack, and Sean Keilen, eds., *The Forms of Renaissance Thought: New Essays in Literature and Culture* (New York: Palgrave Macmillan, 2008), 46–74. See also Barkan, *Unearthing the Past*, and Harris, *Untimely Matter*.

32. Jeff Dolven, *Scenes of Instruction in Renaissance Romance* (Chicago: University of Chicago Press, 2007), 3.

33. Dolven notes that punishment was a part of classical education as well as humanist, though Quintillian and Plutarch disparaged it, *Scenes of Instruction*, 216. See Lynn Enterline, *Shakespeare's Schoolroom: Rhetoric, Discipline, Emotion* (Philadelphia: University of Pennsylvania Press, 2012), 35–36, and "Rhetoric, Discipline, and the Theatricality of Everyday Life in Elizabethan Grammar Schools," in Peter Holland and Stephen Orgel, eds., *From Performance to Print in Shakespeare's England* (New York: Palgrave, 2006), 173–90.

34. Sir Philip Sidney, *Sir P.S. his Astrophel and Stella* (London: Printed for Thomas Newman, 1591). References to slavery and torture appear in *AS* 2, 29, 35, 47, 53, 57, 58, 86, and Songs 5 and 9. In Sonnet 63, the poet contorts the authority of Lady Grammar to misinterpret Stella's double negative as affirmation.

35. Ben Jonson, *Timber, or Discoveries Made upon Men and Matter* (London: 1641), 89.

36. Jonson slightly bungles the Latin here, as the first word of the epigram ought to read "*Multis*," not "*Multum*."

37. Thomas Campion, *Observations in the Art of English Poesie* (London: Printed by Richard Field for Andrew Wise, 1602); Samuel Daniel, *A Panegyricke congratulatorie deliuered to the Kings most excellent Maiestie … with a defence of ryme heretofore written, and now published by the author* (London: Printed for Edward Blount, 1603). See also Richard Helgerson, *Forms of Nationhood* (Chicago: University of Chicago Press, 1992), 25–39.

38. See W. R. Johnson, "The Problem of Counter-Classical Sensibility and Its Critics," *California Studies in Classical Antiquity* 3 (1970): 123–51, especially 136–48. Drawing on the opening of Ovid's *Amores*, James characterizes Ovid as a nonconformist, a poet who chose the "strange and wondrous" shifting shapes of metamorphosis and desire over the balance and proportion of classical decorum dictated by Augustan Roman society. See Heather James, "Shakespeare's Classical Plays," in Margreta de Grazia and Stanley Wells, eds., *The New Cambridge Companion to Shakespeare* (Cambridge: Cambridge University Press, 2010), 154–55. Georgia Brown also addresses the popularity of Ovid as counter-classical in *Redefining Elizabethan Literature* (Cambridge: Cambridge University Press, 2004), 36–37.

39. Enterline, *Shakespeare's Schoolroom*, 33–61.

40. See, for example, Leonard Barkan's argument about the fragmented nature of classical antiquity in the early modern European imagination, in *Unearthing the Past*.

41. Jay David Bolter and Richard Grusin, *Remediation: Understanding New Media* (Cambridge: MIT Press, 2000), 65. Bolter and Grusin discuss how new media forms carve out their own cultural space by appropriating, remaking, and revising older forms (like painting, film, and television), arguing that each new media form always emerges from a dialogue with an older form (photography from painting, for example). It is therefore not too much of a leap to suggest that remediation has been going on for centuries and is present not only in transitions from manuscript to print but in translations of poetry from Latin into English, and from one poetic form into another (or from poetry into theater). Literary scholars like Richard Menke and Maureen McLane have already appropriated (and modified) Bolter's and Grusin's theory in their readings of information technology in Victorian novels and ballads in English Romantic poetry, respectively: see Richard Menke, *Telegraphic Realism: Victorian Fiction and Other Information Systems* (Palo Alto, CA: Stanford University Press, 2007), 5, 103–4; Maureen McLane, *Balladeering, Minstrelsy, and the Making of British Romantic Poetry* (Cambridge: Cambridge University Press, 2011), 30.

42. Bolter and Grusin argue that remediations are all "attempts to achieve immediacy by ignoring or denying the presence of the medium and the act of mediation," *Remediation*, 11. Later on in their work, the authors expand their definition to include refashionings "in the name of the real," *Remediation*, 65.

43. Late sixteenth-century sonnet sequences are a particularly rich locus of self-conscious attention to materiality, from the opening sonnet of Sidney's *Astrophil and Stella*, which demonstrates a profound awareness of the difficult process of early modern manuscript composition ("Biting my truant pen," *AS*, 1.13), to Shakespeare's *Sonnets*, which urge the youth to procreate, or "print more, not let that copy die" (11.14), comparing faithful, human reproduction with the unfaithful vagaries of the printing press. See *William Shakespeare: The Complete Sonnets and Poems*, ed. Colin Burrow (Oxford: Oxford University Press, 2002).

44. A number of theorists agree that language functions as a mediator and as a form of media. For Frederic Jameson, visual media challenge older linguistic media, whereas for Bruno Latour, language actively mediates between nature and society. For Bolter and Grusin, language "operates just as visual media operate in their tasks of remediation." See Bolter and Grusin, *Remediation*, 57 and 57n.4.

45. The verb *translate* was often used to signify metamorphosis, as when in *A Midsummer Nights Dream*, Peter Quince notices Bottom's transformation into an Ass's head: "Bottom, Thou art translated" (3.1.118). George Puttenham describes figurative language as transportation and metamorphosis: metaphor entails wresting a word from one sense and forcing it into another. See Puttenham, *The Art of English Poesy by George Puttenham: A Critical Edition*, ed. Frank Whigham and Wayne A. Rebhorn, (Ithaca, NY: Cornell University Press, 2007), 262.

46. According to the University of Virginia's online *Metamorphoses* project, there were at least thirty-five printed editions of Ovid's *Metamorphoses* in circulation in England and on the continent between 1497 and 1632, many of them illustrated. These were both Latin texts and vernacular translations, including Arthur Golding's (1567) and George Sandys's (1632) English verse translations. See *The Ovid Collection*, http://etext.virginia.edu/latin/ovid/index.html.

47. See Arthur Golding and Ovid, *The XV Bookes of P. Ovidius Naso, entytled: Meta-morphosis. Translated oute of Latin into English meeter by Arthur Golding Gentleman, a worke very pleasaunt and delectable.* (London: William Seres, 1567).

48. Brown contends that the early modern epyllion constructs a poetic voice that is self-consciously associated with ornament and excess and thus well poised to interrogate transgression, in *Redefining Elizabethan Literature*, 48. Gordon Braden traces a larger European epyllion craze to the school of Nonnos, which included Musaeus, known for his "self-consciously elaborate" verse, in *The Classics and English Renaissance Poetry: Three Case Studies* (New Haven, CT: Yale University Press, 1978).

49. See Braden, *The Classics and English Renaissance Poetry*, 75–85. Braden demonstrates how the followers of Nonnos remediated epic form, fracturing it and rebuilding it anew; he also points out that early modern literary critics like J. C. Scaliger valued poets like Nonnus and Musaeus precisely for their elaborate rhetorical displays, 83.

50. George Puttenham, *The Arte of English Poesie* (London: Richard Field, 1589), 5.

51. Here, as in Holland's translation of Pliny the Elder, *orient* indicates both an Asian or Middle Eastern origin and a white nacreous surface. Wilson includes other material ornaments in his metaphors for exornation, including cosmetics, flowers, and tapestry. Employed sparingly as a single flourish, a figurative trope stands apart "as starres stande in the Firmament, or flowers in a garden, or pretie deuised antiques in a cloth of Arras," Thomas Wilson, *The Arte of Rhetorique* (London: Richard Grafton, 1553), 90ff.

52. George Gascoigne's poetic anthologies draw attention to poems as material ornament by grouping his poems into *A Hundreth sundrie Flowers Bound up in One Small Poesie* (London: R. Smith, 1573), *Poesies* (London: Christopher Barker, 1575), and *Flowers, Herbs, and Weeds* (London: R. Smith, 1587). Isabella Whitney's poetic transposition of Hugh Plat's *The Floures of Philosophie* (London: Henry Bynneman, 1572) makes this connection between poesy and posy as *fashioned* floral ornament clearer in its title *A Sweet Nosgay or Pleasant Posye: Contayning a Hundred and Ten Phylosophicall Flowers* (London: R. Jones, 1573).

53. Fleming, *Graffiti and the Writing Arts of Early Modern England*, 10.

54. Ibid., 13.

55. This discussion also appears in my article "The Elizabethan Cipher in Shakespeare's Lucrece," *Studies in Philology* 107.3 (Summer 2010): 336–59.

56. For Edward Said, this process began in the eighteenth century. Several scholars of early modern England have revised that thesis. See Said, *Orientalism* (New York: Vintage Books, 1979, 1994); Daniel Vitkus, *Turning Turk: English Theatre and the Multicultural Mediterranean* (New York: Palgrave, 2003); Richmond Barbour, *Before Orientalism: London's Theatre of the East, 1576–1626* (Cambridge: Cambridge University Press, 2003); Nabil Matar, *Islam in Britain* (Cambridge: Cambridge University Press, 1998), *Turks, Moors, and Englishmen in the Age of Discovery* (New York: Columbia University Press, 1999), and *Britain and Barbary* (Gainesville: University Press of Florida, 2005).

57. J. S., "To his honored friend Mr. T. B.," *Glossographia* A7v. In an article that calls to mind the French title of Foucault's *The Order of Things* (*Les mots et les choses*, or "Words and Things"), de Grazia argues that words may very well have been more thing-like before the

seventeenth century, when language began to be conceived of as transparent and abstract. See Margreta de Grazia, "Words as Things," *Shakespeare Studies* 28 (2000): 231–35.

58. Giorgio Agamben, *Stanzas: Word and Phantasm in Western Culture* (Minneapolis: University of Minnesota Press, 1993), xviii.

59. Ibid., 129.

60. Philip Sidney, *Sir Philip Sidney's An Apology for Poetry (or the Defense of Poesy)*, 3rd ed., ed. R. W. Maslen (Manchester: Manchester University Press, 2002), 68. Sidney further states that "The poet . . . nothing affirmeth . . . In truth, not laboring to tell you what is, or is not, but what should, or should not be," 98. In his Introduction to the *Apology*, R. W. Maslen reads Sidney's statement about the conditional space poetry occupies as a call for poetry to instigate change, 41.

61. Bill Brown, "Thing Theory," *Critical Inquiry* 28.1 (Autumn 2001): 1–22.

62. In exploring the associative nature of words, I am following the descriptions of early modern English as material and unstable proposed by scholars such as Judith H. Anderson, Patricia Parker, Margreta de Grazia and Peter Stallybrass, and Jeffrey Masten, all of whom chart the relationship of philology to the material text. See Anderson, *Words that Matter: Linguistic Perception in Renaissance English* (Palo Alto, CA: Stanford University Press, 1996); Parker, *Shakespeare from the Margins: Language, Culture, Context* (Chicago: The University of Chicago Press, 1996); de Grazia and Stallybrass, "The Materiality of the Shakespearean Text," *Shakespeare Quarterly* (Fall 1993): 255–83; Jeffrey Masten, *Queer Philologies: Language, Sex, and Affect in Shakespeare's Time* (Philadelphia: University of Pennsylvania Press, 2014).

63. Madhavi Menon, "Introduction: Queer Shakes," in Madhavi Menon, ed., *Shakesqueer: A Queer Companion to the Complete Works of Shakespeare* (Durham, NC: Duke University Press, 2011), 1–27.

64. Ibid., 3.

65. See Bruno Latour, *Reassembling the Social: An Introduction to Actor-Network Theory* (Oxford: Oxford University Press, 2008), and "The Berlin Key or How to Do Words with Things," trans. Lydia Davis, in P. M. Graves-Brown, ed., *Matter, Materiality, and Modern Culture,* (London: Routledge, 2000), 18–19.

66. See Latour's discussion of silk and nylon in *Reassembling the Social*, 40.

67. According to the *OED*, antic first appeared in the second half of the sixteenth century and was used to describe the wild designs of decorative grotesques. In his chapter on Henry VIII, Edward Hall describes "A fountayne of embowed woorke . . . ingrayled with anticke woorkes," *The Union of the Two Noble and Illustrate famelies of Lancastre and Yorke* (London: Richard Grafton, 1548), f. lxxiij. Fifty years later, John Florio used the adjective *anticke* to define the Italian word *grottesca* (grotesque) in his Italian-English dictionary *A Worlde of Wordes* (London: 1598). Both cited in *OED, antic*, n. 1a.

68. *antic*, adj. and n., *OED*. For antics and the *danse macabre* in early modern drama, see Michael Neill, *Issues of Death: Mortality and Identity in English Renaissance Tragedy* (Oxford: Clarendon Press, 1997), 51–89, 274; James Midgely Clark, *The Dance of Death in the Middle Ages and the Renaissance* (Glasgow: Jackson, 1950). For Patricia Parker, the different

inflections of *antic* in Shakespeare's plays, from grotesque to Death to foreignness, "suggest the blackface familiar from mumming, morris dancing and other theatricals, as well as the *antic* masks of carnival inversion" in *"Black* Hamlet: *Battening on the Moor," Shakespeare Studies* 31 (2003): 127–64. Dark-skinned foreigners are described as *antics* in Shakespeare's *Antony and Cleopatra* (2.4.280) and *Much Ado About Nothing* (3.1.63–64), Jonson's *Masque of Oberon* (1616), Dekker's *Troia-nova Triumphans* (1612), and Middleton's *The Triumphs of Honor and Vertue* (1622). See Iyengar, *Shades of Difference*, 123–30. For antics as stage clowns and demons, as well as their connection to "antique Romans," see de Grazia, "Hamlet the Intellectual," in Helen Small, ed., *The Public Intellectual* (Oxford: Blackwell Publishing, 2002), 89–109; George Walton Williams, "Antique Romans and Modern Danes in *Hamlet* and *Julius Caesar*," in Vincent Newey and Ann Thompson, eds., *Literature and Nationalism* (Liverpool: Liverpool University Press, 1991), 41–55; John Cox, *The Devil and the Sacred in English Drama, 1350–1642* (Cambridge: Cambridge University Press, 2000).

69. Spenser's translations of du Bellay appeared in his *Complaints* in 1591, though an earlier selection of translations from du Bellay and Petrarch appeared alongside emblematic woodcuts in Jan van der Noot's *Theatre for Worldlings* in 1569. Du Bellay's *Antiquitez* was published with both sets of poems, but in Spenser's *Complaints*, they are separated into *Ruines* and *Visions*. Edmund Spenser, *Complaints* (London: William Ponsonby, 1591); Jan van der Noot, *A Theatre for Worldlings* (London: Henry Bynneman, 1569).

70. In his third "ruins" poem, *The Ruines of Time*, Spenser mourns the death of Philip Sidney in the form of a lament for the lost ancient Roman British city of Verulamium, personified as a weeping woman. All three poems contemplate tragedies of loss, but Spenser's translations of du Bellay in the *Ruines of Rome* and *Visions of Bellay* are mainly concerned with the fall of Rome.

71. The text I am quoting is from *Edmund Spenser: The Shorter Poems*, ed. Richard A. McCabe (New York: Penguin Classics, 2000), which preserves the spelling from the 1591 edition of Spenser's complaints but counts all the sonnets together as one long text in its line-numbering scheme.

72. Hassan Melehy demonstrates admirably how Spenser's translation of du Bellay's *Antiquitez* is both more archaic English and more Christian than du Bellay's (early) modern French and classical original, in "Spenser and du Bellay, Translation, Imitation, Ruin," *Comparative Literature Studies* 40.4 (2003): 415–38.

73. The word *antique* appears seven times in *Ruines of Rome*, which is composed of thirty-two sonnets and an *envoy*. This is a rather high number, given that the word only appears thirty-seven times in the entire *Faerie Queene*. We cannot ascribe too much agency to the choice of employing the word seven times, tempting as it may be to connect it to the seven hills of Rome, because we know that Spenser is translating from du Bellay's French text, and du Bellay himself uses the French word *antique* nine times.

74. See Joachim du Bellay, *Les oeuvres francoises de Ioachim Du-Bellay, gentil homme Angeuin, & poëte excellent de ce temps* (Paris: Frederic Morel, 1569), 52.

75. "*Antique. Taillé à Antiques*," Randall Cotgrave, *A Dictionarie of the French and English Tongues* (London: Adam Islip, 1611).

76. *The Ruines of Rome* is not the only Spenserian text to indicate both sinful Eastern luxuriousness and the ancient world through use of the word *antique*; Spenser does this in *The Faerie Queene* as well, most notably in Book IV, where tapestries and relics of the fall of "antique Babylon" decorate the palace near the gates of hell where Ate lives (4.1.22), and a chariot is decorated "With gold and many a gorgeous ornament / After the Persian monarks antique guize" (4.3.37). See Edmund Spenser, *The Faerie Queene* (London: William Ponsonby, 1596).

77. Shakespeare's *Cymbeline* contains at least two references to eagles flying into the sun in the West: first a soothsayer misinterprets it (4.2.350–54) and then correctly reads it at the end as a positive image for the unification of Britain and Rome (5.6.470–76). See Stephen Greenblatt, Walter Cohen, Jean E. Howard, and Katherine Eisaman Maus, *The Norton Shakespeare* (New York: W. W. Norton & Co., 1997–2008).

78. Barkan argues that the poems stage the early modern "narrative of history," in which Rome serves as an *exemplum* and floating signifier for understanding both past and present. Despite the cultural rift created by the Protestant Reformation in Europe and England, this seems to work well for both Catholic du Bellay and Protestant Spenser. In Barkan's analysis, Rome becomes an inaccessible key to the past, a kind of palimpsest overwritten by contemporary fantasy. Leonard Barkan, "Ruins and Visions: Spenser, Pictures, and Rome," in Jennifer Klein Morrison and Matthew Greenfield, eds., *Edmund Spenser: Essays on Culture and Allegory* (Aldershot: Ashgate, 2000), 30–31.

79. Mikhail Bakhtin, "From the Prehistory of a Novelistic Discourse," in Michael Holquist, ed. and trans., *The Dialogic Imagination* (Austin: University of Texas Press, 1981), 41–83, esp. 68.

80. Ibid., 264.

CHAPTER 1

1. Peter Burke, *Languages and Communities in Early Modern Europe* (Cambridge: Cambridge University Press, 2004), 112–13.

2. Bryan A. Garner, "Shakespeare's Latinate Neologisms," *Shakespeare Studies* 25 (1982): 149–70; Paula Blank, *Broken English: Dialects and the Politics of Language in Early Modern Writings* (London: Routledge, 1996), 18.

3. *Consanguineous* appears in *Twelfth Night* (2.3.77). It is one of some 630 Shakespearean Latinate neologisms that Garner identifies. See Garner, 159.

4. Burke lists a number of "linguistic imports" that entered English from non-Western cultures in the early modern period, but this book examines a different set of words. Burke correctly notes that African and American terms enter European languages as evidence of European imperialism, but that such is not the case with the Ottoman Empire. See Burke, 122–24.

5. *inkhorn term*, n. and *inkhornism*, n., *OED*.

6. *inkhorn*, n., *OED*.

7. Frank Whigham and Wayne A. Rebhorn, eds., *The Art of English Poesy by George Puttenham: A Critical Edition* (Ithaca, NY: Cornell University Press, 2007), 169.

8. Cited in *inkhornist*, n., *OED*. Gabriel Harvey, *Pierces Supererogation or A new prayse for an old asse* (London: John Wolfe, 1593), 181.

9. *inkhorn*, n., *OED*.

10. George Pettie, *The Ciuile Conversation of M. Stephen Guazzo . . .* (London: Richard Watkins, 1581), iiir.

11. Thomas Nashe, *The Vnfortunate Traveller* (London: Printed for Cuthbert Burbie, 1594), 55.

12. Gabriel Harvey, *Fovre Letters, and certaine sonnets: Especially touching Robert Greene, and other parties by him abused: But incidentally of divers excellent persons, and some others of note* (London: John Wolfe, 1592), 37–38.

13. Blank, 40–41.

14. Ibid., 46.

15. In the sixteenth century, *strange* (also spelled *straunge*) meant foreign, from another country or land, and unknown, as well as distinctly different, since it derived from the French word *étrange*, from *étranger*, stranger. See the *strange*, adj. I. 1–3, *OED*.

16. Thomas Wilson, *The Arte of Rhetorique* (London: Richard Grafton, 1553), yiir, v.

17. Sujata Iyengar notes that the pigments and powders used in most early modern facial cosmetics themselves were composed of precious exotic imports from the Ottoman Empire, India, and the Spice Islands. Iyengar mentions henna, vermillion, and ivory, but rouge was also fashioned from carmine (*alkermes* beetles), cinnabar, and brazilwood; powders were made from alum and lead mined from the same places. See Iyengar, *Shades of Difference: Mythologies of Skin Color in Early Modern England* (Philadelphia: University of Pennsylvania Press, 2005), 111.

18. Ibid., yiiv.

19. Blank argues that this play turns words into commodities and the academy into a market of wit. See Blank, 46–52.

20. William Shakespeare, *The Tragicall Historie of Hamlet, Prince of Denmark* (Q2; London: Printed for Nicholas Ling, 1604), 5.7.110–12.

21. John Donne, *Poems by J.D.* (London: John Marriot, 1635).

22. Quotations are taken from John Carey, ed., *John Donne: The Major Works Including Songs, Sonnets, and Sermons* (Oxford: Oxford University Press, 2009).

23. Roger Ascham, *The Scholemaster or plaine and perfite way of teachyng children, to vnderstand, write, and speake, the Latin tong but specially purposed for the priuate brynging vp of youth in ientlemen and noble mens houses, and commodious also for all such, as haue forgot the Latin tonge . . . By Roger Ascham*, Book II (London: John Daye, 1570), 111–12.

24. Samuel Daniel, *A Panegyricke congratulatorie deliuered to the Kings most excellent Maiestie at Burleigh Harrington in Rutlandshire. By Samuel Daniel. Also certaine epistles, with a defence of ryme heretofore written, and now published by the author* (London: Printed for Edward Blount, 1603), 1r.

25. George Puttenham, *The Arte of English Poesie* (London: Richard Field, 1589), 121.

26. Ibid.

27. "Early modern 'inkhornism' is a game in which each player makes up his own rules and then legitimizes those rules—most often, by proscribing those of others. For those authors, including William Shakespeare, who exploited the new trade in words, profits depended, crucially, on regulating the linguistic ventures of others." Blank, 44. See also 43–52.

28. In her book *Uncommon Tongues: Eloquence and Eccentricity in the English Renaissance* (Philadelphia: University of Pennsylvania Press, 2014), Catherine Nicholson adroitly argues that "eccentric" or foreign speech became the defining feature of English writing, despite rhetoricians and poets' ambivalence about strangeness.

29. Carew's speech is cited in William Camden's *Remaines Concerning Britain* (London: Printed for Simon Waterson, 1614), 47–48, and in Blank, 45.

30. E. K., *The Shepheardes Calender* (London: Hugh Singleton, 1579), cited in Blank, 104.

31. Edmund Spenser, *The Faerie Queene* (London: William Ponsonby, 1596), Preface.

32. Wilson, *The Art of Rhetorique*, xxxi.

33. Ibid., 162.

34. Norbert Platz has described *Poetaster* as Jonson's *ars poetica*, but not with attention to imported words and things. See Norbert H. Platz, *Jonson's Ars Poetica: An Interpretation of Poetaster in Its Historical Context* (Salzburg: Salzburg Studies in English Literature, 1973).

35. Jonson's translation of Horace's *Ars Poetica* was not published until 1640. See Victoria Moul, "Translation as Commentary? The Case of Ben Jonson's *Ars Poetica*," *Palimpsests* 20 (2007): 59–77; and Ben Jonson, *Q. Horatius Flaccus: His Arte of Poetry Englished by Ben. Jonson. With other Workes of the Author, never Printed before*, ed. Sir Kenelm Digby (London: 1640).

36. Jonson, *Q. Horatius Flaccus* (1640), 20.

37. *sweet*, adj., and *fit*, adj., etymologies, *OED*.

38. "*Non nimium credendum antiquitati*," which can be translated as "Not believing entirely in the ancients," Jonson, *Timber: or, Discoveries Made upon Men and Matter*, ed. Sir Kenelm Digby (London: 1641), 89.

39. Jonson, *Q. Horatius Flaccus* (1640), 4, B2v.

40. The opening lines that Ovid speaks are taken directly from Marlowe's translation of the *Amores*: Christopher Marlowe, *All Ovid's Elegies, 3 Books, by C. M.* (London: 1603).

41. Tom Cain reads the play's banishment of Ovid as an indirect topical reference to the Essex rebellion of 1601. Ben Jonson, *Poetaster*, ed. Tom Cain (Manchester: St. Martin's Press, 1995), 41.

42. Cain maintains that Jonson turns his back on Ovid deliberately in order to argue for a new kind of poetics that demanded a break from the "fashionable Ovidian poetry and drama of the years immediately preceding *Poetaster*," Ibid., 23. For Joan Carr, Jonson is banishing part of himself, his youth. Horace and Virgil may be projections of Jonson's hopes, but Ovid is a "projection on Jonson's fears." Joan Carr, "Jonson and the Classics: The Ovid-plot in Poetaster," in *English Literary Renaissance* 8 (1978): 311. In the introduction to her edition of the play, Margaret Kidnie suggests that Ovid's poor judgment requires

that he "be abandoned by a judicious state," though she does admit that the play makes it uncertain as to whether "these limitations on the imagination" are being dramatized as proper or problematic. See Ben Jonson, *The Devil Is an Ass: And Other Plays*, ed. Margaret Jane Kidnie (Oxford: Oxford University Press, 2009), xiv.

43. Chloe alludes to her role as a trophy second wife in 2.1: "Alas, man; there was not a gentleman came to your house i'your tother wiues time, I hope, nor a ladie?" (2.1.61–62).

44. All following citations from the play in this chapter derive from F, *The Workes of Beniamin Jonson* (London: William Stansby, 1616), unless otherwise noted.

45. *dressing*, n. 4b, *OED*.

46. *dressing*, n. 4a, *OED*.

47. Jonson, *Poetaster, or the Arraignment* (London: Printed for M. Lownes, 1602), C2r.

48. *sperm*, n. 1a, *OED*.

49. *The Grete Herball* (London: Peter Treveris, 1526), xxviii, Bv.

50. See Louise Noble, *Medicinal Cannibalism in Early Modern English Literature and Culture* (New York: Palgrave, 2011); and Richard Sugg, *Mummies, Cannibals, and Vampires: The History of Corpse Medicine from the Renaissance to the Victorians* (London: Routledge, 2011).

51. Benedict S. Robinson examines how Milton uses balsam to transform Eden into an ancient oriental paradise in *Islam and Early Modern English Literature: The Politics of Romance from Spenser to Milton* (New York: Palgrave, 2007), 151–56.

52. Cain draws attention to this spelling as well, noting that "J deliberately chooses the unusual spelling 'fartingall,'" 107n.64–66.

53. *roll*, n. 2, *OED*.

54. See the Introduction to this book.

55. Jonson, *Q. Horatius Flaccus* (1640), 1, Br.

56. Cain, 260.

57. See Cain, 153 n.212–16.

58. Cain, 156 n.277.

59. According to Cain, not all of these neologisms are Marston's; some are coined by Jonson himself to suggest "the flatulence of Marston's style"; others come from Harvey and "one or two from Shakespeare," Cain, *Poetaster*, 26.

60. See William H. Sherman, *Used Books: Marking Readers in Renaissance England* (Philadelphia: University of Pennsylvania Press, 2008); George Puttenham, *The Arte of English Poesie*, STC 20519, The British Library, G. 11548. All following quotations are from this volume.

61. Sherman, *Used Books*, 45.

62. In his *Remaines Concerning Britain*, William Camden claims that these two inscriptions are actually elaborate ciphers representing a different annotator's name: the "Gentleman scholler" Abraham Hartwell. Camden, 173.

63. David Riggs, *Ben Jonson: A Life* (Cambridge, MA: Harvard University Press, 1989), 42.

64. Puttenham, *The Arte of English Poesie* (Menston, Yorkshire: Scolar Press, 1968).

65. Sherman, "Toward a History of the Manicule," *Used Books*, 25–52.

66. These lines appear in Chapter 21, "A Description of Life & Riches," from Thomas Tusser's *Five Hundreth Points of Good Husbandrie* (London: Richard Tottel, 1573), 28.

CHAPTER 2

1. Francis Meres, *Palladis Tamia, Wits Treasury* (London: Printed for Cuthbert Burbie, 1598), 281–82.

2. In his *Life of Pythagoras*, Porphyry claims the philosopher ate only honey and honeycomb (34); Diogenes Laertius, however, in his own biography of Pythagoras, suggests that the philosopher supplemented his bread and honey with vegetables (18). See Kenneth Sylvan Guthrie, eds., *The Pythagorean Sourcebook and Library* (Grand Rapids, MI: Phanes Press, 1987), 130, 146.

3. *Venus and Adonis* was published first, by Richard Field in 1594, after being registered at the Stationer's register in 1593, followed by *Lucrece* (London: John Harrison, 1594). Sonnets 138 and 144 were published in the miscellany *The Passionate Pilgrim* (London: William Jaggard, 1599), and the complete sequence of the *Sonnets* was published by Thomas Thorpe in 1609 with *A Lover's Complaint*.

4. In ancient Rome, the dominant sweeteners were honey and dates. Apicius's cookbook from the first century CE includes stuffed dates and a sort of hard bread or paste made from boiled flour smothered in honey. See Tim Richardson, *Sweets: A History of Candy* (London: Bloomsbury, 2002), 77–78.

5. Noel Deerr's history from 1949 remains one of the most thorough on the subject of sugar. Deerr dates the moment when sugar surpassed honey in English markets to around 1558, though its rise began around 1450. Noel Deerr, *The History of Sugar* (London: Chapman & Hall, 1949), 9.

6. Mintz writes, "From the seventeenth century onward—and it may be worth noting that Shakespeare died nearly half a century *before* sugar from Barbados, the first English 'sugar island,' began to reach England—sugar imagery became ever commoner in English literature . . . this imagery bridges the two very different 'meanings' we have discussed: the inside meaning as sugar became commoner, and its employment in social settings by even the least privileged and poorest of Britain's citizens; and the significance of sugar for the empire." Sidney Mintz, *Sweetness and Power: The Place of Sugar in Modern History* (New York: Elizabeth Sifton Viking Books, 1985), 154–55.

7. Jeffrey Masten, "Toward a Queer Address: The Taste of Letters and Early Modern Male Friendship," *GLQ: A Journal of Gay and Lesbian Studies* 10.3 (2004): 367–84.

8. See Deerr, *The History of Sugar*, 40. In Deerr's translation, the poem compares sugar to honey, but in Vedic mythology, ambrosia, another sweet substance (a kind of nectar) figures prominently as well, conferring immortality on the *Vedas* (divine beings).

9. See Deerr, 8; Richardson, 78.

10. Plato's *Ion*, 534b: "For of course poets tell us that they gather songs at honey-flowing springs," *Plato: Complete Works*, ed. John M. Cooper (Indianapolis, IN: Hackett,

1997), 942. Lucretius, *De Rerum Natura*: "To rim the lesson, as it were, with honey / Hoping this way to hold your mind with verses / While you are learning all that form, and pattern / Of the way things are" (1.947–50), trans. Rolph Humphries, *The Way Things Are: The De Rerum Natura of Titus Lucretius Carus* (Bloomington: Indiana University Press, 1968), 47. On further connections between ancient Greek poetry, honey, and bees, including Pindar, see Gregory Crane, "Bees Without Honey, and Callimachean Taste," *American Journal of Philology* (Summer 1987): 399–403, and Susan Scheinberg, "The Bee Maidens of the Homeric Hymn to Hermes," *Harvard Studies in Classical Philology* 83 (1979): 21ff. Along with metaphors of honey, Roman poets and writers were interested in how it was produced. Both Cato the Elder and Varro address apiculture, and Virgil's fourth *Georgic* is primarily concerned with honey production. See Deerr, *The History of Sugar*, 8.

11. See, for example, Song of Solomon, *The Holy Bible Conteyning the Old Testament, and the New* (London: Robert Barker, 1611), 2:3, which compares the beloved to an apple tree.

12. Song of Solomon, 2:4–5.

13. For descriptions and pictures of banqueting houses, see Patricia Fumerton, "Consuming the Void," in *Cultural Aesthetics: Renaissance Literature and the Practice of Social Ornament* (Chicago: University of Chicago Press, 1990), 113–22; Marc Girouard, *Robert Smythson and the Elizabethan Country House* (New Haven, CT: Yale University Press, 1983); and Stephen Orgel, *The Illusion of Power: Political Theater in the English Renaissance* (Berkeley: University of California Press, 1975).

14. *dessert*, n. a., *OED*.

15. Fumerton, *Cultural Aesthetics*, 111–68.

16. *sweet*, n. 1b, 5a, and 6, *OED*.

17. For the permeability of the body by air, fumes, and spirits, see Mary Floyd-Wilson, "English Epicures and Scottish Witches," *Shakespeare Quarterly* 57.2 (2006): 131–61; for an excellent analysis of early modern sensing and emotion as smelling and tasting, see Carolyn Sale, "Eating Air, Feeling Smells: Hamlet's Theory of Performance," *Renaissance Drama* 35 (2006): 145–70. In his analysis of the epithet *sweet* in male-male friendships, Masten appears to read the adjective as pointing both to taste and to smell, without distinction; Masten, "Toward a Queer Address," 367–84.

18. *banquet*, n. 3a and b, *OED*.

19. Fumerton argues that the practices of dissolution characteristic of early modern banquets and voids are indicative of early modern selfhood, in *Cultural Aesthetics*, 122–24.

20. Bruce Smith's edition of the play contextualizes Illyria as an Ottoman Mediterranean space. William Shakespeare, *Twelfth Night, or What You Will*, ed. Bruce Smith, *Texts and Contexts* (New York: Palgrave, 2001), 126–28.

21. *sugar*, n. 1a, *OED*.

22. *sugar*, n. 1b, *OED*.

23. *sugar*, n. 1c, *OED*.

24. *Marchpane* or *marzipan* has a confusing etymology, about which philologists continue to disagree: does it derive from *Martaban*, a Burmese city known for its decorative

boxes filled with confections as the *OED* suggests, or from the Arabic word *mauthaban* ("king who sits still and does not go off to war")? Or is it simply a Latinate word meaning pastry (*massa*) or bread (*pane*)? Among food historians, it appears that *marzipan* has a pick-and-choose etymology. I prefer the one put forth by John Cooper in his history of Jewish food because it emphasizes the materiality and Eastern origin of marzipan. Cooper contends that both the word and the confection come from the Arabic *matuapan*, which is related to the word for white, *uatapan*. Whatever its etymological history, the European confection of ground almonds and sugar known as marzipan originated in India and Persia. See John Cooper, *Eat and Be Satisfied: A Social History of Jewish Food* (Lanham, MD: Jason Aronson, 1993), 83.

25. *honey*, n.; *candied*, adj.; *sugar'd*, adj.; *marchpane*, n.; *julep*, n.; *syrup*, n.; *sweetmeat*, n.; and *sweet*, n., *OED*.

26. Richardson, *Sweets*, 123.

27. Cooper, *Eat and Be Satisfied*, 83.

28. In the Middle Ages, sugar from the Arabs was imported into Europe by Italian and Genovese merchants, and by the sixteenth and early seventeenth centuries, it was mostly imported from Spanish plantations on the Canary Islands, though according to Richard Eden's translation of Sebastian Munster's *Treatise of Newe India*, as early as 1553, the Spanish had already begun to plant sugarcane and set up presses on the island of Hispaniola. See Richardson, *Sweets*, 84.

29. The Atlantic sugar trade began in part as a way for European traders like the Spanish and Portuguese, and eventually the English, to circumvent the high taxes imposed on Mediterranean and Middle Eastern sugar from Crete, Cyprus, and Egypt by the Ottoman Empire in the late sixteenth century. See Mintz, *Sweetness and Power*, 28–30; Deerr, *The History of Sugar*, 78, 81, 83, 94.

30. Wendy Wall, "'Just a Spoonful of Sugar': Syrup and Domesticity in Early Modern England," *Modern Philology* 104.2 (2006): 149–72; Kim F. Hall, "Culinary Spaces, Colonial Spaces: The Gendering of Sugar in the Seventeenth Century," in Valerie Traub, M. Lindsay Kaplan, and Dympna Callaghan, eds., *Feminist Readings of Early Modern Culture: Emerging Subjects* (Cambridge: Cambridge University Press, 1996), 168–90.

31. Mintz, *Sweetness and Power*, 37–38, 60.

32. Mintz notes that despite the fact that Egypt was under Ottoman control after 1518, the price of sugar did not rise, unlike other Mediterranean commodities, and this suggests that the West Indies had already begun to enter the sugar market earlier than recorded, 159. See also 38–39; and Deerr, 73–99.

33. Deerr, 86–87.

34. Mintz, 83.

35. Ibid., 45; Laura Mason, *Sugar-Plums and Sherbet: The Prehistory of Sweets* (Blackhawton, Devon: Prospect Books, 2004), 37. J. E. Gillespie writes that "after 1585 London was the most important refining center for the European trade" in *The Influence of Overseas Expansion on England to 1700*, Columbia University Studies in History, Economics, and Public Laws, Vol. 91 (New York: Columbia University Press, 1920), 147.

36. Shakespeare, *The Tragicall Historie of Hamlet, Prince of Denmark* (London: Printed for Nicholas Ling, 1604).

37. Caroline Spurgeon famously identified the "dogs licking, candy melting" cluster of images in *Shakespeare's Imagery and What It Tells Us* (Cambridge: Cambridge University Press, 1935), which she attributed to Shakespeare's distaste for flatterers. In *Shakespeare's Imagination*, first published in 1946, Edward Armstrong read this image cluster as indicative of unconscious associations in the playwright's mind (Lincoln: University of Nebraska Press, 1963).

38. Masten, "Toward a Queer Address," 376.

39. For the sugared phrases, sentences, and speech, see Philip Sidney, *Sir P.S. his Astrophel and Stella*, Sonnets 12, 25, 100; Bernard Garter, *The tragicall and true historie which happened betweene two English lovers* (London: Richard Tottel, 1565); for sugared pens and quills, see Edmund *Elviden, The most excellent and plesant metaphoricall historie of Pesistratus and Catanea* (London: Henry Bynneman, 1570), line 3051. In his manuscript of epigrammatic poetry (c. 1600), Francis Thynne speaks of Spenser's "sugared Penn" in epigram 38 on the *Faerie Queene* (7) and in epigram 51 to Humphrey Waldron, and he describes Golding's "hawtie verse, with suggred words well knit" (17), Thynne, *Emblemes and Epigrames*, ed. Frederick James Furnivall (London: N. Trubner and Co. for the Early English Text Society, 1876). Roland Greene maps Sidney's use of sugar onto the language of early modern Spanish colonialism and trade. Just as Astrophil positions himself as a black slave, so is Stella the product of such labor, a sugary sweet. See Greene, *Unrequited Conquests: Love and Empire in the Colonial Americas* (Chicago: University of Chicago Press, 1999), 185–87.

40. See, for example, Richard Stanyhurst's translation of Virgil's *Aeneid* I: "Hee tames with sugred speeches theyre boysterus anger" (1.70), *The First Foure Bookes of Virgil his AEneid* (Leiden: John Pates, 1582); John Studley's translation of Seneca's *Medea* speaks of "tongue in sugar dept" (1.121), and in Seneca's *Hercules*, Studley's Chorus warns us that "treason lurkes amid the sugred wyne" (2.490), both from Seneca, *Seneca, His Tenne Tragedies, Translated into English* (London: Thomas Marsh, 1581). The talents of long-absent classical authors are frequently invoked, almost always with reference to sugar: John Sharrock's English translation of Christopher Ocland's Latin text *Anglorum proelia* modestly begs the reader to put up with his lowly verse, when it would be better told by a different author, "*Homer* . . . in sugred verse," John Sharrock, trans., Christopher Ocland, "To the gentle Reader" from *The valiant actes And victorious Battailes of the English nation* (London: Robert Waldegrave, 1585), line 5. Lodowick Lloyd longs to imitate both the style and *stylus* of ancient writers, "To write Demosthenes sugred stile, with noble Tullies quill," Lodowick Lloyd, "Had Greke Calisthenes silence kept, had Neuius spared speache," from *The Pilgrimage of Princes* (London: John Wolfe, 1573), line 178.

41. Sir John Beaumont, *The Metamorphosis of Tabacco* (London: Printed for John Flasket, 1602), 701–2.

42. Thomas Churchyard, "An Introduction for Breaknoke Shiere," from *The Worthines of Wales* (London: Printed for Thomas Cadman, 1587), 145; and "If slouth and tract of time," from "A commendatory poem" in *Pithy pleasaunt and profitable workes of maister Skelton* (London: Thomas Marsh, 1568), 43–45.

43. See Mason, *Sugar-Plums and Sherbet*, 195.

44. Mintz, 123; Mason, 195.

45. Mason, 52. Mason also notes the difference in the chemical structure of honey and sugar, concluding that honey cannot harden confections as sugar can, and therefore is a less effective preservative, 44.

46. Bruno Latour, *Reassembling the Social: An Introduction to Actor-Network Theory* (Oxford: Oxford University Press, 2008) and "The Berlin Key or How to Do Words with Things," trans. Lydia Davis, in P. M. Graves-Brown, ed., *Matter, Materiality, and Modern Culture* (London, 2000), 18–19.

47. Philip Sidney, *Sir Philip Sidney's An Apology for Poetry and Astrophil and Stella: Texts and Contexts*, ed. Peter C. Herman (Glen Allen, VA: College Publishing, 2001), 68. See also the Introduction to this book.

48. Giorgio Agamben, *Stanzas: Word and Phantasm in Western Culture* (Minneapolis: University of Minnesota Press, 1993), xviii.

49. *subtlety*, n. 5 and *subtle*, adj. and n. 10 and 11, *OED*.

50. Etymology, *subtlety*, *OED*.

51. *Sublte*, adj. and n., and *subtlety*, n., *OED*.

52. George Cavendish, *The Life and Death of Cardinal Wolsey*, ed. Richard S. Sylvester, Early English Text Society No. 243 (London: Oxford University Press, 1959), 70–71; British Library Egerton 2402, 38ff.

53. On ekphrastic objects representing the entire world mimetically, see Eric Auerbach, *Mimesis* (Princeton, NJ: Princeton University Press, 1953, 2003).

54. Robert May, *The Accomplisht Cooke, or the Art and Mystery of Cookery* (London: 1660), A3, A4v. See also Mintz, 93, and Maxime de la Falaise McKendry, *Seven Centuries of English Cooking* (London: Weinfeld and Nicholson, 1973), 62–63.

55. George Puttenham, *The Art of English Poesy by George Puttenham: A Critical Edition*, ed. Frank Whigham and Wayne Rebhorn (Ithaca, NY: Cornell University Press, 2007). All subsequent quotations in this chapter refer to this edition, unless otherwise noted. The illustrations refer to the first edition, titled *The Arte of English Poesie* (London: Richard Field, 1589).

56. See Puttenham, *The Art of English Poesy*, 181; May, *The Accomplished Cooke*, 253.

57. For a brief history of the fashion of sugar subtleties from medieval Persia and the Arab world to eighteenth-century Europe, see Richardson, *Sweets*, 150–53.

58. Mintz cites the eleventh-century Egyptian Caliph Zahir's banquet of sugar sculpture, as reported by Nasir-i-Chosrau, a Persian visitor to Egypt in 1040: 73,300 kilos of sugar were incorporated into the Caliph's Eid feast table celebrating the end of Ramadan, where there stood an entire tree made of sugar along with other large displays, 88.

59. These included giraffes, elephants, lions, fountains and castles, some of which were so large that they had to be carried by four people. See Ivan Day, *Royal Sugar Sculpture*, Bowes Museum, 2002, http://www.historicfood.com/Royal-sugar-Sculpture.htm (c. 2003); see also Peter Brown and Ivan Day, *The Pleasures of the Table: Ritual and Display in the European Dining Room 1600–1900* (York: York Civic Trust, 1997).

60. Richardson writes that subtleties employed symbolic devises both serious and

humorous, making "some serious point about the occasion, the guest of honour, or a date in the religious calendar, but they could be light-hearted, too . . . some subtleties were heraldic, religious, or descriptive devices—crowns, eagles, saints, military heroes, mythic figures, coats of arms, the Virgin and Child, a tiger looking in a mirror, a peacock with a golden beak—and some were even more elaborate: hunting scenes, skirmishes, dances, complex religious tableaux, church interiors, ships in full sail." Subtleties could also be meta-commentaries: "strangest of all were the miniature replicas of ceremonies which had just taken place and which the feast was celebrating." *Sweets*, 148.

61. Day, "The Art of Confectionary," online treatise at http://www.historicfood.com; see also Peter Brears, "Rare Conceits and Strange Delights," in C. Anne Wilson, ed., *Banquetting Stuffe* (Edinburgh: Edinburgh University Press, 1991), 61.

62. John Partridge, *The Treasurie of Commodious Conceits* (London: Richard Jones, 1573); Hugh Plat, *Delights for Ladies* (London: Peter Short, 1600); Gervase Markham, *Country Contentments in two books ... the second intitled, The English Huswife* (London: Printed for Roger Jackson, 1615).

63. Wendy Wall, "'Just a Spoonful of Sugar': Syrup and Domesticity in Early Modern England," 149–72.

64. Day, "The Art of Confectionary," 4.

65. Richardson, *Sweets*, 108.

66. On Eringo and other candied roots in the sixteenth and seventeenth centuries, see Richardson, *Sweets*, 115.

67. John Marston, *The Malcontent* (London: Printed by Valentine Simmes for William Aspley, 1604), 2.4.7–25.

68. Ben Jonson, *Poetaster* in *The Workes of Benjamin Ionson* (London: 1616).

69. "Sweet Horace, goe with me, this is my houre" (3.1.223–24); "Sweet master Minos. I am forfeited to eternall disgrace if you do not commiserate" (3.3.30); "By Iove, sweet captain, you do most infinitely endeare, and oblige me to you" (3.4.86), *The Workes of Benjamin Ionson*. Crispinus's overuse of the term *sweet* also appears in his terrible poetry and his addresses to just about everyone else in the play, even when he does not require their help.

70. Day, "The Art of Confectionary," 33.

71. Mason also notes that both gums were useful to apothecaries because they helped slow down the delivery system of drugs, *Sugar-Plums and Sherbet*, 139–40.

72. Anon., probably Hugh Plat, *A Closet for Ladies and Gentlewomen* (London: Printed for Arthur Johnson, 1608), 33.

73. See, for example, Hod Lipson and Melba Kurman, *Fabricated: The New World of 3D Printing* (Oxford: Wiley Blackwell, 2013).

74. John Murrell's "Cinnamon Letters" appear in *A Daily Exercise for Ladies and Gentlewomen* (London: Printed for the widow Helme, 1617), 89.

75. See Fumerton, *Cultural Aesthetics*, 138. Mason charts the vogue for written inscriptions in sweets from walnut posies in the anonymous *A Closet for Ladies and Gentlewomen* all the way to the nineteenth century, *Sugar-Plums and Sherbet*, 130, 145.

76. Plat, *A Closet for Ladies and Gentlewomen*, 33; W. M., *The Queens closet opened:*

incomparable secrets in physick, chyurgery, preserving and candying, and cookery (London: Printed for Nathaniel Brook, 1655), 263.

77. Elizabeth Spiller, "Introduction," in Betty S. Travitsky and Anne Lake Prescott, eds., *Seventeenth Century English Recipe Books: Cooking, Physic, and Chirurgery in the Works of Elizabeth Talbot Grey and Alethia Talbot Howard* (Aldershot: Ashgate, 2008), xvi.

78. *subtlety*, n., is defined by the *OED* as treachery in definitions 3 and 4, beginning c. 1430, and as "a refinement or nicety of thought, speculation, or argument" in definition 7, beginning c. 1654.

79. Church of England, *The Boke of Common Prayer* (London: John Daye, 1583), B5v.

80. In sixteenth-century China, lower-ranking court officials wore robes decorated with insignia badges depicting four-clawed dragons in squares, though most of the nine ranks of officials wore badges embroidered with a bird form fitting their rank. See the following three books by Valery Garrett: *Children of the Gods: Dress and Symbolism in China* (Hong Kong: Hong Kong Museum of History, 1990); *Chinese Dragon Robes* (Oxford: Oxford University Press, 1998); and *Chinese Clothing: An Illustrated Guide* (Oxford: Oxford University Press, 1994), 3–18, esp. 14. See also James C. Watt, *When Silk Was Gold: Central Asian and Chinese Textiles* (New York: Metropolitan Museum of Art in cooperation with the Cleveland Museum of Art, 1997).

81. Garrett, *Chinese Clothing*, 9.

82. Pliny, *Historia Naturalis* X. 62, trans. Philemon Holland (London: 1601).

83. Andrea Alciato, *Reverentium in Matrimonio Requiri* in *Livret des Emblemes* (Paris: Christian Wechel, 1543), B7v; Horapollo, *Hieroglyphica*, Jean Cousin, engraver (Paris: Jacques Kerver, 1543), 2.59; Hadrianus Junius, *Emblemata* (Antwerp: Christophe Plantin, 1565), 44; Pierre Coustau, *Le Pegme* (Lyons: Barthelemy Molin, 1560), 412; Guillaume Guerolt, *Le Premier Livre des Emblemes* (Lyons: Balthazar Arnoullet, 1550), 29.

84. Giles Corrozet, *Hecatomgraphie* (Paris: Denis Janot, 1540), H7r.

85. The images are taken from the first edition of *The Arte of English Poesie* (London: Richard Field, 1589), 76–77.

86. See, for example, the pattern for *marchpane* that May offers his readers in *The Accomplisht Cook*, 253.

87. Jennifer Summit, "A Ladies' Penne: Elizabeth I and the Making of English Poetry," in *Lost Property: The Woman Writer and English Literary History 1380–1589* (Chicago: University of Chicago Press, 2000), 173–74; Hall, "Culinary Spaces," 176–78; Wendy Wall, *Staging Domesticity: Household Work and English Identity in Early Modern Drama* (Cambridge: Cambridge University Press, 2002), 44–51.

88. No other late sixteenth-century poetic theorist chooses so many foreign and global models to discuss English poetry. Though Samuel Daniel celebrates barbarous native English rhyme, he does not draw from the larger global groups that Puttenham does, which include African, Arab, Hebrew, Chaldaic, Peruvian, Ottoman, Chinese, and Italian models. Sidney's models for poetry are all English or classical, and Campion produces the pro-quantitative English verse tract that prompts Daniel's anti-classical response. See Richard Helgerson, *Forms of Nationhood: The Elizabethan Writing of England* (Chicago: University

of Chicago Press, 1992), 36–40. Roland Greene reads Puttenham's "The roundel displayed" as emblematic of Puttenham's all-encompassing worldview that admits variety and tensions in poetic customs into its circle, replicated in an image of several worlds (cultures) contained within one large world, part of what Greene defines as a "fiction of immanence." See Roland Greene, "Fictions of Immanence, Fictions of Embassy," in Elizabeth Fowler and Roland Greene, eds., *The Project of Prose in Early Modern Europe and the New World* (Cambridge: Cambridge University Press, 1997), 186–87.

89. *The Greek Anthology* saw several editions in early modern Europe, including some by Aldus Manutius beginning in 1494.

90. Susan Stewart, *Poetry and the Fate of the Senses* (Chicago: University of Chicago Press, 2002), 34.

91. See Rebhorn and Whigham, 180n.4.

92. Puttenham does finally get around to mentioning classical Greek poetry's influence on egg-shaped verse, but he delegitimizes the classical influence, describing egg-shaped poetry as "a bastard or imperfect round" (190) and does not dignify it with an example.

93. Puttenham also frequently quotes from his own New Year's gift to the queen, a poetic manuscript called the *Partheniades*, but nowhere in the printed text does he mention that it was a gift. Whigham and Rebhorn suggest that the manuscript's title page describing its presentation at court may be embellishment on Puttenham's part. See Whigham and Rebhorn, 15.

94. Perhaps the most well-known inscribed jewel is the *Timur* ruby talisman, inscribed with the ornamental signatures of all the sultans that possessed it. Unlike Puttenham's geometric shapes, it is round and bumpy, and the names and inscriptions etched onto its surface do not obey the rules of symmetry. Its six inscriptions are Persian, written in Arabic script. See Diane Morgan, *Fire and Blood: Rubies in Myth, Magic, and History* (Westport, CT: Greenwood, 2008), 153–58. Suleiman the Magnificent and his successors wrote poems to their mistresses and received replies. Sulieman wrote some 3,000 poems and corresponded in poetry with his wife Hürrem Sultàn. The most famous fifteenth- and sixteenth-century Turkish women poets included Zeyneb (d. 1474) and Mihri Hatun (1460–1506), often linked with Prince Ahmed, and was also known as the "Turkish Sappho." See Sener Sufur, *Türc Safo'su Mihri Hatun: Belgesel Anlati* (Istanbul: AD Yayincilik, 1997).

95. I quote here from Field's 1589 edition of Puttenham's text in order to show how Puttenham, or else the printer Richard Field, succeeds in romanticizing and Europeanizing these names. Rebhorn and Whigham do away with the 1589 text's italicized proper nouns and, in modernizing the names, make them seem more Ottoman than they might have appeared to early modern English eyes: *Can* becomes *Khan*, and *Corasoon* is changed to *Khorason*. See Whigham and Rebhorn, 182.

96. See Giambattista della Porta, *Natural Magick* (London: Thomas Young and Samuel Speed, 1658), books 4 and 9.

97. Whigham and Rebhorn, 180n.5.

98. Turner identifies "the management of patterned language" as an important

component of early modern theories about the craft of poetry. Henry S. Turner, *The English Renaissance Stage: Geometry, Poetics, and the Practical Spatial Arts 1580–1630* (Oxford: Oxford University Press, 2006, 2011), 36, 118–47.

99. A. L. Korn, "Puttenham and the Oriental Pattern Poem," *Comparative Literature* 6 (1954): 289–303; Margaret Church, "The First English Pattern Poems," *PMLA* 61 (1946): 636–50. See also Dick Higgins, *Pattern Poetry: Guide to an Unknown Literature* (Albany: State University of New York Press, 1987), 11–13, 95–102, 165–66.

100. John Hollander, *Vision and Resonance: Two Senses of Poetic Form* (Oxford: Oxford University Press, 1975).

101. Fleming, *Graffiti and the Writing Arts of Early Modern England*, 18.

102. Stewart, *Poetry and the Fate of the Senses*, 34.

103. Thomas Nashe, *The Works of Thomas Nashe Edited from the Original Texts*, vol. 3, ed. Ronald B. McKerrow (London: Sidgwick and Jackson, 1905–10), 67.

104. Hannah Wooley, *The Accomplisht ladys delight in preserving, physic and cookery* (London: Printed for B. Harris, 1675), nos. 73–79, cited in Mintz as Plat, 92.

105. *lozenge*, n. 2b, *OED*.

106. *lozenge*, n. 2c, *OED*: "A small cake or tablet, originally diamond-shaped, of medicated or flavoured sugar, etc. to be held and dissolved in the mouth."

107. Partridge, *A Treasurie of Commodious Conceits*, xxvi. sig. D.j.

108. Fumerton, 125.

109. Mintz, 124.

110. Fumerton, 134.

111. Jennifer Montagu, *Roman Baroque Sculpture: The Industry of Art* (New Haven, CT: Yale University Press, 1989), 220n.107.

112. Mason, 111, 195.

113. Arthur F. Kinney and Linda Bradley Salomon, *Nicholas Hilliard's Art of Limning* (Boston: Northeastern University Press, 1983).

114. See Susan Frye, *Pens and Needles: Women's Textualities in Early Modern England* (Philadelphia: University of Pennsylvania Press, 2010).

115. Frye devotes a chapter to Teerlinc's work in *Pens and Needles*, 75–115.

116. Mason, 143.

117. For an analysis of imported pattern books and their uses in early modern artisanal crafts, see Katherine Acheson, "Gesner, Topsell, and the Purposes of Pictures in Early Modern Natural Histories," in Michael Hunter, ed., *Printed Images in Early Modern Britain: Essays in Interpretation* (Farnham: Ashgate, 2010), 127–44; and Gill Saunders, "'Paper Tapestry' and 'Wooden Pictures': Printed Decoration in the Domestic Interior before 1700," in Michael Hunter, ed., *Printed Images in Early Modern Britain*, 317–36.

118. In *Forms of Nationhood*, Helgerson posits that Puttenham's text destabilizes itself by relying not on Greek and Roman precedents but Medieval French and Italian ones, 26–34. See also Wayne A. Rebhorn, "Outlandish Fears: Defining Decorum in Renaissance Rhetoric," *Intertexts* 4.1 (2000): 3–24.

119. Summit, *Lost Property*, 163–202.

120. *strange*, adj., *OED*.

121. James Biester argues that early modern English poetic manuals aimed to produce wonder through tropes of condensed amplification in *Lyric Wonder: Rhetoric and Wit in Renaissance English Poetry* (Ithaca, NY: Cornell University Press, 1997), 9. For Biester, this is an ancient Greek trope on which Puttenham, Peacham, and Wilson draw, 107. My analysis counters this, finding Puttenham rejecting ancient Greek and Roman models in favor of a different kind of wonder, one associated with new commodities coming into England from the East.

122. For Rebhorn, Puttenham makes Latin "outlandish" in comparison with the vernacular. I add to these claims the point that Puttenham not only counters antiquated Latin with vernacular English verse but embraces the poetry of outlandish and "strange" Eastern cultures to a similar effect. Wayne A. Rebhorn, "Outlandish Fears: Defining Decorum in Renaissance Rhetoric," 234.

CHAPTER 3

1. Peter Stallybrass, "Books and Scrolls: Navigating the Bible," in Jennifer Andersen and Elizabeth Sauer, eds., *Books and Readers in Early Modern England* (Philadelphia: University of Pennsylvania Press, 2011), 42–79.

2. According to the editors of the *Norton Shakespeare*, *Titus Andronicus* was published after it was entered in the stationer's register in January of 1594. *The Rape of Lucrece* was entered in the register in May of 1594 and appeared in print later in the summer of that year. See Katherine Eisaman Maus, "Textual Note," Introduction to *Titus Andronicus* and "Textual Note," Introduction to *The Rape of Lucrece*, in Stephen Greenblatt, Walter Cohen, Jean Howard, and Katherine Eisaman Maus, eds., *The Norton Shakespeare* (New York: Norton, 1997), 378, 640. Thus, it is possible that *Titus* predates *Lucrece* and might have served to advertise it, but it is more likely that the poem was already being advertised in bookshops, functioning as a sort of soft release to generate publicity before it appeared in print. For more on booksellers' roles in launching Shakespeare's dramatic career through the selling of his poems, see Adam Hooks, "Shakespeare at the White Greyhound," *Shakespeare Survey* 64 (2011): 260–75.

3. Francis Meres, *Palladis Tamia, Wits Treasury* (London: Printed for Cuthbert Burbie, 1598), 282.

4. Enterline teases out Lucrece's many Ovidian voices and registers, which include Orpheus, during Lucrece's dilatory argument with Tarquin against rape, and Philomela's missing tongue, in her "duet" with Philomela post-violation. Lynn Enterline, *The Rhetoric of the Body from Ovid to Shakespeare* (Cambridge: Cambridge University Press, 2000); Joseph B. Ward, *Violence, Politics, and Gender in Early Modern England* (New York: Palgrave, 2008), 69.

5. In this way, Shakespeare is able to capitalize on the popularity of Lucrece, but as Enterline suggests, he does so ambivalently by riding on the coattails of a dead and violated

woman: "if I give Lucrece a voice, I can be 'just like' her insofar as she is author to a famous publication and an undying name." See Enterline, *The Rhetoric of the Body from Ovid to Shakespeare*, 186.

6. See, for example, Margaret C. Jacob, *Strangers Nowhere in the World: The Rise of Early Modern Cosmopolitanism* (Philadelphia: University of Pennsylvania Press, 2008), and Linda Levy Peck, *Consuming Splendor: Society and Culture in Seventeenth-Century England* (Cambridge: Cambridge University Press, 2005).

7. Brian Rotman, *Signifying Nothing: The Semiotics of Zero* (Palo Alto, CA: Stanford University Press, 1993). See also Robert Kaplan, *The Nothing That Is: A Natural History of Zero* (Oxford: Oxford University Press, 1999); and Charles Seife, *Zero: The Biography of a Dangerous Idea* (New York: Viking, Penguin Books, 2000).

8. In Modern Hebrew, the noun for *number* is מספר (*mispar*), from the same root as *book*, ספר (*sefer*). Another related word is *saper*, which means both to tell a story and to count, much like the early modern English *tell* for counting and telling a story, and modern English *recount*. Although there are a number of Greek and Semitic homonyms for *sifra* (the Greek word for sphere, σφαῖρα, and the Hebrew word for sapphire, *sapir*, for example), according to Ernest Klein's *Comprehensive Etymological Dictionary of the Hebrew Language*, these words are unrelated to the Hebrew root ספר; Hebrew apparently does not possess the same semantic fluidity as early modern English. Like Klein, the *OED* stresses that *sapphire* likely derives from a Sanskrit root word, *sanipriya* ("dear to Saturn"). The origin of *sphere* is unknown, but Klein's dictionary claims a Greek origin for the Hebrew word for *sphere*, not the other way around. Renaissance Jewish mystical texts list the *sefirot*—from ספירה, *sefira*, a feminine version of *sefer* (book), a masculine noun—as the divine enumerations, or numbered aspects, of God. This is an example of Hebrew, like Latin, feminizing a normally masculine noun in order to signify an abstract entity. Although *sefirot* occasionally appear in Kabbalistic diagrams as circles, it is unclear whether the *sefirot* are at all etymologically related to *sphere*—Klein certainly does not make this connection. If they are, they would have a Greek, rather than Hebrew, origin. See the entires for *sapphire* and *sphere* in the *OED*; σφαῖρα in H. G. Liddell, R. Scott, and Henry Stuart Jones , *Greek-English Lexicon* (Oxford: Clarendon Press, 1996); and ספר and ספיר in Ernest Klein, *A Comprehensive Etymological Dictionary of the Hebrew Language* (Haifa: University of Haifa Press, 1987).

9. Rosalie Colie, *Paradoxica Epidemica: The Renaissance Tradition of the Paradox* (Princeton, NJ: Princeton University Press, 1966).

10. Bruno Latour, *Reassembling the Social: An Introduction to Actor-Network Theory* (Oxford: Oxford University Press, 2008) and "The Berlin Key or How to Do Words with Things," trans. Lydia Davis, in P. M. Graves-Brown, ed., *Matter, Materiality, and Modern Culture* (London: Routledge, 2000), 18–19.

11. *figure*, n. 19a, *OED*.

12. Geofroy Tory of Bourges, *Champfleury*, ed. and trans. George B. Ivies (Paris, 1529, repr., New York: The Grolier Club, 1927), 179–80.

13. Picinelli, *Mundus Symbolicus*, ed. and trans. August Erath (1694; repr., New York: Garland, 1976), col. 143. Eugene Ostashevsky supports this reading of Picinelli. See Eugene

Ostashevsky, "Crooked Figures: Zero in Hindo-Arabic Notation in Shakespeare's *Henry V*," in David Glimp and Michelle Warren, eds., *Arts of Calculation: Quantifying Thought in Early Modern Europe* (New York: Palgrave, 2004), 207.

14. See Rotman, *Signifying Nothing*, 78.

15. Printer's cases held uppercase letters on top and lowercase letters and symbols on the bottom. Zero appeared at the end, after the numerals 1 to 9. This practice of representing zero after 9 continues on computer keyboards and calculators today. For images of a Renaissance printer's case and model typefaces, see Joseph Moxon, *Mechanic Exercises on the Whole Art of Printing* (1683 repr., eds. Herbert Davis and Harry Carter [New York: Dover, 1978], 32 and 124–26).

16. In early modern Europe, zero was assigned multiple origins in Asia and the Middle East. The mathematician Robert Recorde attributes Arabic numbering to the Sumerians, but earlier Latin and Italian texts like Leonardo (Fibonacci) Pisano's *Liber Abacci* and Philippi Calandri's *De Aritmetica Opusculum* (Little Work on Arithmetic) contend that the system originated in India. See Michele Sharon Jaffe, *The Story of O: Prostitutes and Other Good-for-Nothings in the Renaissance* (Cambridge, MA: Harvard University Press, 1999), 33.

17. In English printing, zeros first appear as publication dates on the title pages of texts around 1530 and as pagination around 1535, but throughout the period I am examining, the late sixteenth and early seventeenth centuries, they are always indistinguishable from the letter O. It was not until the late seventeenth century that printers began to differentiate between zero and the letter O with serifs (presumably zero gained its italic typeface o much later). Moxon's *Mechanic Exercises* was the first printed text to reveal the technical details and guild secrets of printing.

18. As Jaffe, Louis Karpinski, and David Eugene Smith note, the Hindu-Arabic numbering system from which we have borrowed the zero never uses an empty circle to indicate zero. Jaffe, 50–51, Louis Charles Karpinski and David Eugene Smith, *The Hindu-Arabic Numerals* (Boston: Ginn and Company, 1911), 53.

19. Until the middle of the sixteenth century, the English words for *nothing* were *null* (from the Latin *nihil* and *nulla*), *naught*, *aught*, *void*, and *not*. When the novelty of Arabic numbering became part of English everyday usage, these words were joined by a new, imported term from the Arabic language, *cipher*. See the *OED*, *cipher*, *not*, *naught*.

20. Stephen Johnson, "Robert Recorde (c. 1512–1558)," *Oxford Dictionary of National Biography* online (Oxford: Oxford University Press, 2004–13).

21. Henry Cockeram, *The English Dictionary, or an Interpreter of Hard English Words* (London: Printed for Edmund Weaver, 1623), Dr; Robert Recorde, *The Grōnd of Artes Teachyng the Worke and Pra-ctise of Arithmetike* (London: R. Wolfe, 1543), 43. John Barrett's *An Alvearie or Quadruple Dictionarie* (London: Henry Denham and William Seres, 1580) describes a "ciphre" as a character that "is no Significative figure of it selfe, but maketh the other figures wherewith it is joined, to increase more in value by their places, as 10.20.30, &c, which be called Digit numbers" (unnumbered treatise inserted between Aiiiv and Br). It has a Semitic origin ("this science of Arythmetike was first inuented

among the Hebrewes and Chaldeis") as well as two names: "o" and "cipher." John Florio's Italian dictionary *A Worlde of Words* (London: Edward Blount, 1598) describes the word *Zifrare* as "to cifre or cast account," indicating calculations made with Arabic numerals, 461. Claudius Hollyband's *Dictionarie of French and English* (London: Thomas Woodcock, 1593) illustrates *chiffre* with a French phrase, "avoir le chifre d'un prince pour entendre les secrets," which he translates as "to have the bill, scrole [scroll], or memorandum of a prince, to know his secrets," G3v. This leads to a second inflection: ciphering as intimate, secret writing. Cooper's Latin-English *Thesaurus* (London: Thomas Berthelet, 1565) provides the Latin synonym for "to cipher" as "*Notis Scribere*" or to write notes, Mmmm 3v, s.v. "Notae."

22. Robert Cawdrey, *A Table Alphabeticall* (London: Edmund Weaver, 1604), 39.

23. English translations also employ *cipher* to enhance Latin phrases. For example, Christopher Marlowe wrestles with the new term in his translation of Elegy 6, in Book 3 of Ovid's *Amores*. Describing the narrator's impotence as "like a dull cipher, or a rude block I lay" (3.6), Marlowe inserts *cipher* as a supplement to the Latin phrase *truncus iners* (3.7). Christopher Marlowe, *Epigrammes and elegies. By I.D. and C.M.* (London: 1599).

24. As Eugene Ostashevsky demonstrates, the famous use of cipher in the prologue to *Henry V* (Q1) explores the paradox of O as a figure of emptiness and generation. See Ostashevsky, 205–28, 4; and Shakespeare, *The chronicle history of Henry the fift* (London: Printed for Thomas Millington and John Busby, 1600).

25. Joel Fineman illuminates how *The Rape of Lucrece* enacts the metaphors it produces through the circular figure of chiasmus. Like Fineman, I am interested in how a graphic figure (in this case, the cipher in all its forms) dominates the poem. Unlike Fineman, I focus on material and associative linguistic registers rather than rhetorical and psychoanalytic import. See Joel Fineman, "Shakespeare's Will: The Temporality of Rape," *Representations* 10.20 (Autumn 1987): 25–76. The chiastic movements Fineman uncovers in the poem are not Xs but Os, an "imagery of encirclement," Fineman, 40.

26. Two such puns on vaginas and "nothing" occur in *Hamlet* (3.2.107) and in the title of *Much Ado About Nothing*. See David Wilbern, "Shakespeare's 'Nothing," in Murray M. Schwartz and Coppélia Kahn, eds., *Representing Shakespeare: New Psychoanalytic Essays* (Baltimore: Johns Hopkins University Press, 1981), 244–63; Mary C. Williams, "Much Ado About Chastity in *Much Ado About Nothing*," *Renaissance Papers*, 41 (1984): 37–45; Thomas Pyles, "Ophelia's Nothing," *Modern Language Notes* 64 (May 1949): 322–23; and John Arthur Harris, "Ophelia's Nothing: It Is the False Steward That Stole His Master's Daughter," *Hamlet Studies: An International Journal of Research on the Tragedie Hamlet, Prince of Denmark* 19.1–2 (Summer–Winter 1997): 20–46.

27. Elaine Showalter, "Representing Ophelia: Women, Madness, and the Responsibilities of Feminist Criticism," in Patricia Parker and Geoffrey Harman, eds., *Shakespeare and the Question of Theory* (New York: Methuen, 1985), 78.

28. The *Oxford English Dictionary* cites Shakespeare's poem twice as one of the first texts to use the verb *to cipher* meaning "to delineate," and as the only text to use it expressly to describe an act of deciphering. *OED, to cipher*, v., 3 and 4.

29. William Shakespeare, *The Rape of Lucrece* (London: Richard Field, 1594). All subsequent citations are from this text unless otherwise noted in the body of the chapter.

30. Sexually suggestive marginalia appeared in both sixteenth-century manuscripts and printed texts. See Richard Rambuss, *Spenser's Secret Career* (Cambridge: Cambridge University Press, 1993).

31. John Harvey, *his translation of the learned worke, of Hermes Trismegistus, intituled, Iatromathematica...* (London: Richard Watkins, 1583).

32. John Dee, *Monas Hieroglyphica* (Antwerp: William Silvis, 1564), 28. See also *Monas Hieroglyphica*, ed. and trans. C. H. Josten, *AMBIX* 12 (1964): 221.

33. Robert Dullyngdon's English translation of first two thirds of Colonna's *Hypnerotomachia Poliphili* appeared under the English title *Hypnerotomachia. The Strife of Loue in a Dreame* (London: Printed for Simon Waterson, 1592). See Francesco Colonna, *Hypnerotomachia Poliphili: The Strife of Love in a Dream*, trans. Jocelyn Godwin (London: Thames and Hudson, 1999).

34. Sanders argues that Lucrece cannot read such books because she is a woman but that rape makes her literate in a new way. I am less interested in a "before-after" model of female literacy than I am in the symbolism of Tarquin's circular eyes as open ciphers. Eve Rachele Sanders, *Gender and Literacy on Stage in Early Modern England* (Cambridge: Cambridge University Press, 1996), 139.

35. See Michael Finlay, *Western Writing Implements in the Age of the Quill Pen* (Wetheral, Scotland: Plains Books, 1990); and Jonathan Goldberg, *Writing Matter: From the Hands of the English Renaissance* (Palo Alto, CA: Stanford University Press, 1990), 59–107.

36. Goldberg, 73.

37. Goldberg contends that both *pencil* and *penis* are "cognate with *penes*, penetrator," *Writing Matter*, 99. Actually, there are a few more steps to retrieving this etymology: the Latin preposition *penes*, meaning "in the possession of," derives from the adverb *penitus*, meaning "inwardly," which in turn derives from the verb *penetrare*, "to penetrate." *Pencil* and *penis* both derive from *penis*, the Latin for "tail." See the entries for each word in D. P. Simpson, *Cassell's Latin Dictionary* (New York: Macmillan, 1959, 1968).

38. Olga Valbuena has suggested to me that this moment teaches us to read as Lucrece cannot—turning back would be cowardly, and Tarquin is a military tyrant who must forge on ahead, so although he berates himself, he perversely goes forward toward what is wrong.

39. For an analysis of the cultural impact of Renaissance images of Lucretia, see Ian Donaldson, *The Rapes of Lucretia: A Myth and Its Transformations* (Oxford: Clarendon Press, 1982); and A. Robin Bowers, "Iconography and Rhetoric in Shakespeare's *Lucrece*," *Shakespeare Studies* XIV (1981): 1–19, esp. 9.

40. According to Sir Sidney Lee, Purfoot inherited the sign from Berthelet in 1512. Sidney Lee, Introduction, *Shakespeare's Lucrece: Being a Reproduction in Facsimile of the First Edition 1594* (Oxford: Clarendon Press, 1905), 12. See also Ronald B. McKerrow, *Printers' & Publishers' Devices in England & Scotland 1485–1640* (London: Chiswick Press for the Bibliographical Society of London, 1913), 80, 151.

41. McKerrow, 151, 161, 173.

42. Katherine Duncan Jones and H. R. Woudhuysen, eds., *Shakespeare's Poems* (London: Arden Shakespeare, Third Series, 2007), 37–39.

43. John Withals, *A short dictionarie most profitable for young beginners* (London: Thomas Purfoot, 1568) and *A dictionarie in English and Latine for children, and yong beginners* (London: Thomas Purfoot, 1608).

44. Claudius Hollyband, *The Italian Schoole-maister* (London: Thomas Purfoot, 1597, 1608).

45. David Hillman describes Elizabethan coroners searching entrails for such inscriptions in "Visceral Knowledge: Shakespeare, Skepticism, and the Interior of the Early Modern Body," in his collection edited with Carla Mazzio, *The Body in Parts: Fantasies of Corporeality in Early Modern Europe* (New York: Routledge, 1997), 81–105.

46. Smith's book begins by noting how the shape of the mouth mirrors the mark on the page of an "O": "[o:] is O because the lips make an O." This could also be applied to the labia. Smith, *The Acoustic World of Early Modern England: Attending to the O-Factor* (Chicago: University of Chicago Press, 1999).

47. Greenblatt et al., eds., *The Norton Shakespeare*, 665.

48. For Smith, the dramatic utterance of "O" defines the boundaries of physicality: "A cry from within, [o:] seeks resonance without." Smith, *The Acoustic World of Early Modern England*, 14.

49. Joel Fineman, "The Sound of O in *Othello*," in *The Subjectivity Effect in Western Literary Tradition: Essays Towards the Release of Shakespeare's Will* (Cambridge: MIT Press, 1991). Colin Burrow notes the ecphonesis of the stream of five Os in Shakespeare's *A Lover's Complaint*, Colin Burrow, ed., *William Shakespeare: The Complete Sonnets and Poems* (Oxford: Oxford University Press, 2002), 144.

50. The ancient Greek word *pneuma* (πνεῦμα) meant both breath and wind. This is true in Elizabethan English as well, where wind specifically refers to breath drawn in order to produce sound. The connection between wind and breath persists today when we characterize a tedious speech as "long winded." See Shigehisa Kuriyama, *Expressiveness of the Body and the Divergence of Greek and Chinese Medicine* (New York: Zone Books, 1999), 236, 246; *OED*, *wind*, n. 1, 11a, b. In Renaissance England, wind was also considered the basis for music; see *OED*, *wind*, n. 1, 12a.

51. Many thanks to the meticulous anonymous reader for the University of Pennsylvania Press who reminded me of this point.

52. Jonathan Bate writes, "T. W. Baldwin has shown that all the details in the poem which are derived from Livy and not Ovid would have been available in the commentary by Paulus Marsus in Shakespeare's copy of Ovid, but the fact that Shakespeare's main source was Ovid rather than the historian's version is a first indication that he was not primarily interested in the political significance of the story," Jonathan Bate, *Shakespeare and Ovid* (Oxford: Oxford University Press, 1993), 67. See also T. W. Baldwin, *On the Literary Genetics of Shakespeare's Poems & Sonnets* (Urbana: University of Illinois Press, 1950), 108–10.

53. "I was Chloris, Nymph of the happy fields, the homes of the blessed (you hear) in earlier times. To describe my beauty would mar my modesty: it found my mother a son in

law god. It was spring, I wandered; Zephyrus saw me, I left. He pursues, I run: he was the stronger; and Boreas gave his brother full rights of rape by robbing Erechtheus' house of its prize. But he makes good the rape by naming me his bride, and I have no complaints about my marriage. I enjoy perpetual spring: the year always shines, trees are leafing, the soil always fodders. I have a fruitful garden in my dowered fields, fanned by breezes, fed by limpid fountains." P. Ovidius Naso, *Fasti*, 5. 197, English translation by A. J. Boyle and Roger D. Woodward (New York: Penguin Classics, 2000).

54. The travel writer Pausanias, whose description of Greece was translated into Latin and published widely in the sixteenth century, alludes to Zephyrus's struggle with Apollo over Hyacinthus, *Graecae Descriptio* (Florence, 1551; and Xylander & von Silberg, 1583); see also *Description of Greece*, ed. and trans. W. H. S. Jones and H. A. Omerod, vol. 2 (Cambridge, MA: Harvard University Press, 1918), 121. In Homer's *Iliad*, Zephyr's hot breezes blow east as well as west; he rapes the harpy Podarge, who thereafter produces three powerfully fast Arabian horses, Xanthos, Balios, and Arion. In some texts, these sons are not steeds but Asiatic tigers, *Iliad*, 16.149–51, trans. Richmond Lattimore (Chicago: University of Chicago Press, 1961). Quintus Smyrnaeus's fourth-century Latin epic *The Fall of Troy* and Colluthus Trythiodorus Oppian's third-century *Cynegetica* also mention Zephyrus having fathered Asiatic animals, *The Fall of Troy*, 3.743 and 4.569, trans. A. S. Way, Loeb Classical Library (Cambridge, MA: Harvard University Press, 1962); Oppian, *Cynegetica*, 1.320 and 3.350, trans. A. W. Mair, Loeb Classical Library (Cambridge, MA: Harvard University Press, 1928).

55. The *locus classicus* for Zephyrus is the General Prologue of Chaucer's *Canterbury Tales*, which describes the warm, gentle breezes of springtime invisibly stirring the earth into production: "Whan *Zephirus* eek with his sweete breeth / Inspired hath in every holt and heeth / The tendre croppes. . . ." Geoffrey Chaucer, "The General Prologue," *The Canterbury Tales*, in *The Riverside Chaucer*, gen. ed. Larry D. Benson, 3rd ed. (Oxford: Oxford University Press, 2008), Fragment I (Group A), lines 5–7.

56. Cool, humid breezes from the west (Zephyrus) inspire growth, as stated in Batman's 1582 translation of Agrippa: "But Zephyrus ye West winde, which is also called Fauonius, is verye light, bloweth from ye west, & brething pleasantly, is cold and moist, thawing frosts, and snow, & bringing forth grasse & flowers. {marginal note: A breeder of caterpillars, and wormes that growe}." Bartholomaeus Anglicus, *Batman upon Bartholomaeus his booke de Proprietatius rerum* (London: Thomas East, 1582). For more wind in classical medicine, see Kuriyama, *Expressiveness of the Body and the Divergence of Greek and Chinese Medicine*, 233–70.

57. See Virgil, *Aeneid* IV. 173, VIII. 554; *Georgics* II. 44 in *I. Eclogues, Georgics, Aeneid*, trans. Rushton Fairclough, Loeb Classical Library (Cambridge: Harvard University Press, 1916).

58. The *Primavera* depicts a dark and stormy Zephyrus seizing a pale, androgynous Chloris as a stream of flowering vines escapes from her mouth. The month of April in Spenser's *Shepheardes Calender* invokes Elizabeth I as Flora, a virgin who miraculously mothers her many subjects. Edmund Spenser, or E. K., *The Shepheardes Calender* (London: Hugh Singleton, 1579).

59. *Fibonacci's Liber Abaci*, trans. L. E. Sigler (Springer, 2002).

60. The entry on *zéro* in the *Dictionnaire historique de la langue francaise* (Paris: Le Robert, 1998) posits that the French word *zéro* derives from eliding the wind Zephyrus with *sifra*: "*zéro* est directement emprunté de l'Italien *zero* qui est une contraction de *zefiro*, du latin médiéval *zephirus*, vent doux et tiède." ("Zero is directly borrowed from the Italian *zero*, which is a contraction of *zefiro* and the medieval Latin *zephirus*, the warm and gentle wind.")

61. This premise depends upon the associative nature of Renaissance English homonyms, a theory that I describe in Chapter 1. See also Patricia Parker in *Shakespeare from the Margins: Language, Culture, Context* (Chicago: University of Chicago Press, 1996); and Margreta de Grazia and Peter Stallybrass in "The Materiality of the Shakespearean Text," *Shakespeare Quarterly* 44.3 (Fall 1993): 255–83.

62. In this reading, I differ from Enterline, who connects breath, wind, and music with Lucrece's empowered voice rather than with Tarquin's rapacious act. Enterline, *The Rhetoric of the Body*, 191.

63. See, for example, Thomas Lacquer, *Making Sex: Body and Gender from the Greeks to Freud* (Cambridge, MA: Harvard University Press, 1990), 162.

64. Later editions attempt to organize the poem into chapters: Roger Jackson's "newly revised" edition of 1616 contains a table of contents, and John Stafford's 1655 edition of *The Rape of Lucrece* supplies ornamental lines throughout the body of the text, dividing the body of the poem explicitly into the same twelve chapters Jackson specified in his table of contents. Stafford anchored the appearance of each new chapter with an Arabic numeral and an ornamental border. See Katherine Duncan-Jones, "Ravished and Revised: The 1616 Lucrece," *Review of English Studies* 52.208 (2001): 516–23.

65. Lucrece's rhetorical Os might document what Stephanie Jed has called the attempts of the chaste hand to chastise (base) subject matter into good form. Stephanie Jed, *Chaste Thinking: The Rape of Lucretia and the Rise of Humanism (Theories of Representation and Difference)* (Bloomington: Indiana University Press, 1989).

66. "Vnder that colour am I come to scale / Thy neuer conquered Fort" (477–82). For more on heraldry in the poem, see Nancy Vickers, "This Heraldry in Lucrece' Face," *Poetics Today* 6.1–2 (1985): 171–84.

67. Hugh Plat's *The iewell house of art and nature* (London: Peter Short, 1594) is one such title, printed the same year as Shakespeare's poem. See Deborah Harkness, *The Jewel House: Elizabethan London and the Scientific Revolution* (New Haven, CT: Yale University Press, 2007); and William Eamon, *Science and the Secrets of Nature* (Princeton, NJ: Princeton University Press, 1996).

68. Often bearing a one-word title, "Lucrece," Shakespeare's poem appeared in eight editions between 1594 and 1655, six in quarto (1594, 1600, 1607, 1616, 1624, and 1632), and three in octavo (1598, 1600, and 1655). The poem was first printed by John Harrison under Richard Field and then independently by Harrison until 1632, although editions printed by T. S. for Roger Jackson appeared in 1616 and 1624.

69. Wendy Wall discusses the material ambiguity of ink and paper in Lucrece's writing

of the letter in "Reading for the Blot: Textual Desire in Early Modern English Literature," in David M. Bergeron, ed., *Reading and Writing in Shakespeare* (Newark: University of Delaware Press, 1996), 131–59. In *Gender and Literacy on Stage in Early Modern England*, Eve Sanders stresses that rape makes Lucrece literate. Joyce Green has written about Lucrece as a silent orator in a poem obsessed with rhetoric, in "Speech, Silence, and History in *The Rape of Lucrece*," *Shakespeare Studies* 22 (1994): 77–103. More recently, Amy Greenstadt has argued for Lucrece as an empowered, rather than silenced, orator, in "'Read It in Me': The Author's Will in *Lucrece*," *Shakespeare Quarterly* 57.1 (Spring 2006): 45–70.

70. Wayne Rebhorn and Margreta de Grazia each discuss the sexual imagery of the Renaissance printing press. For Rebhorn, printing itself is a kind of rape. Margreta de Grazia, "Imprints: Shakespeare, Gutenburg, Descartes," in Terence Hawkes, ed., *Alternative Shakespeares 2* (New York: Routledge, 1996), 63–94; and Wayne Rebhorn, "Petruchio's Rape Tricks: *The Taming of the Shrew* and the Renaissance Discourse of Rhetoric," *Modern Philology* 92.3 (1995): 294–327.

71. The notion that children who learned Ovid in the humanist classroom experienced trauma deriving both from reading and imitating the poet's violent, erotic tales at an early, prepubescent stage and from being constantly beaten is more fully established by Enterline in her book *Shakespeare's Schoolroom: Rhetoric, Discipline, Emotion* (Philadelphia: University of Pennsylvania Press, 2012) and in her chapter "Rhetoric, Discipline, and the Theatricality of Everyday Life in Elizabethan Grammar Schools," in Peter Holland and Stephen Orgel, eds., *From Performance to Print in Shakespeare's England* (New York: Palgrave, 2006), 173–90.

72. Thomas Heywood, *The Rape of Lucrece* (London: Printed for I. Busby, 1608). The tragedy was hugely successful, reprinted five times in the early seventeenth century: twice in 1609, 1614, 1630, and 1638. The full lyrics of comic songs of Valerius were appended to the play in an appendix. For a contextualization of the tragedy's bawdy and comic songs in Jacobean popular culture, see Richard Rowland, *Thomas Heywood's Theatre, 1599–1639: Locations, Translations, and Conflict* (Aldershot: Ashgate, 2010), 5–7.

73. Thomas Middleton, *The Ghost of Lucrece* (London: Valentine Simmes, 1601), 1–4

CHAPTER 4

1. All references to *Venus and Adonis* come from Colin Burrow's Oxford edition of Shakespeare's poems.

2. See Heather James, "Shakespeare and Classicism," in Patrick Cheney, ed., *The Cambridge Companion to Shakespeare's Poetry* (Cambridge: Cambridge University Press, 2007), 210.

3. Madhavi Menon, "Spurning Teleology in Venus and Adonis," *GLQ: A Journal of Gay and Lesbian Studies* 11.4 (2005): 491–519.

4. The violently tragic myth of Venus and Adonis that ends Ovid's *Metamorphoses* 10 is the final severed knot in a long and increasingly aberrant string of mismatched couplings and births: Adonis's parents are the incestuous couple Myrrha and Cinyras; his grandparents

the idolatrous Pygmalion and his ivory doll. Ovid, *Metamorphoses*, trans. Arthur Golding, ed. Madeleine Forey (Baltimore: Johns Hopkins University Press, 2002), 312–19.

5. Arthur Golding, *The XV bookes of P. Ouidius Naso, entytuled Metamorphosis, translated oute of Latin into English meeter by Arthur Golding Gentleman* (London: William Seres, 1567).

6. Giorgio Agamben, *Stanzas: Word and Phantasm in Western Culture* (Minneapolis: University of Minnesota Press, 1993), xviii.

7. *"namque male haerentem et nimia levitate caducum excutiunt idem, qui praestant nomina, venti"* (10.738–39).

8. See my discussion of Gerard, Lyte, and Parkinson later in this chapter. Each botanist invents a new English name for the flower, usually a combination of several words, as in Gerard's "Turkie or Ginny Hen Flower."

9. Jonathan Bate, *Shakespeare and Ovid* (Oxford: Oxford University Press, 1994), 48–82.

10. Spenser's two versions of the same tale, appearing in Book Three of *The Faerie Queene* London: William Ponsonby, 1590, 1596) are, like Shakespeare's, both unproductive and hyperproductive. In the tapestry that Britomart cannot interpret decorating the walls of Castle Joyeous (3.1), Venus cradles a bloodied Adonis in her arms, warning viewers about the hazards of unchecked female desire. In Amoret's nursery, the Garden of Adonis (3.6), however, Adonis lives, and his and Venus's love fertilizes an overly fecund place where time is cyclical and everything is reborn.

11. In suggesting that Shakespeare's Venus has something of Lucretius's Venus in her, I am following Gerard Passannante's convincing argument that Lucretian philosophy permeated much of early modern literary culture: *The Lucretian Renaissance: Philology and the Afterlife of Tradition* (Chicago: University of Chicago Press, 2011). Stephen Greenblatt also finds Lucretian thought to have been pervasive in early modern literary culture in *The Swerve: How the World Became Modern* (New York: Norton, 2012). Though neither Passannante nor Greenblatt discusses Shakespeare's *Venus and Adonis*, both books make a strong argument for the inclusion of Lucretian philosophy in any understanding of Renaissance writers. Many thanks as well to Tina Taormina for first introducing me to the idea of a Lucretian Venus during her talk at the Southeastern Renaissance Conference, October 2012 in Knoxville, TN.

12. Lucretius, *The Way Things Are: The De Rerum Natura of Titus Lucretius Carus*, trans. Rolph Humphries (Bloomington: Indiana University Press, 1968), 19.

13. Bulbs take much longer to reproduce (seven to twelve years) when grown from seed. Once planted, bulbs can generate more bulbs at a much faster rate, and this is what made them so valuable initially on the market and also what led to their devaluation: suddenly tulips were everywhere. Speculators entered the market in the 1630s, and the tulip bubble burst in February 1637. See Ann Goldgar, *Tulipmania: Money, Honor, and Knowledge in the Dutch Golden Age* (Chicago: University of Chicago Press, 2007).

14. Lucretius, *The Way Things Are*, 27.

15. George Gascoigne, *The Noble Art of Venerie* (London: 1565); Thomas Blundeville,

The Fower Chiefyst Offices Belongyng to Horsemanship (London: 1565). For an analysis of animals in this poem and Shakespeare in general, see Laurie Shannon, "The Eight Animals in Shakespeare; or, Before the Human," *PMLA* 124.2 (March 2009): 472–79.

16. Colin Burrow, ed., *The Oxford Shakespeare: Complete Sonnets and Poems* (Oxford: Oxford University Press, 2002) 190, n.263–70.

17. Jerry Brotton and Lisa Jardine, *Global Interests: Renaissance Art Between East and West* (London: Reaktion, 2000), 145.

18. See Heinrich Bünting, "*Asia Secunda Pars Tarrae in Forma Pegasir,*" from *Itinerarium Sacrare Scripturae* (Magdeburg: Printed by Ambrosius II Kirchner for Paul Donat 1584).

19. Hesiod, *Theogony*, 281; Pseudo-Apollodorus, *Bibliotheke* 2.42, both in Stephen L. Harris and Gloria Platzner, eds., *Classical Mythology: Images and Insights* (New York: Mayfield Publishing, 1998), 234.

20. See, for example, Peter Edwards's excellent work on economies, spaces, and the importance of horses in early modern English life, *The Horse Trade of Tudor and Stuart England* (Cambridge: Cambridge University Press, 2004), and *Horse and Man in Early Modern England* (Hambeldon: Continuum, 2007); see also Karen Raber and Treva Tucker, eds., *The Culture of the Horse: Status, Discipline, and Identity in the Early Modern World* (New York: Palgrave, 2005).

21. Erica Fudge's *Perceiving Animals: Humans and Beasts in Early Modern English Culture* (Champaign: University of Illinois Press, 2002) first came out in 1999, and its second printing was followed by her edited collection *Renaissance Beasts: Of Animals, Humans, and Other Wonderful Creatures* (Champaign: University of Illinois Press, 2004). Her philosophical work *Animal* (London: Reaktion, 2002) was followed more recently by *Pets* (London: Reaktion, 2008). Bruce Boehrer's *Shakespeare Among the Animals: Nature and Society in the Drama of Early Modern England* (New York: Palgrave/St. Martins Press, 2002) was followed by his cultural history of parrots, *Parrot Culture: Our 2500 Year Long Fascination with the World's Most Talkative Bird* (Philadelphia: University of Pennsylvania Press, 2004).

22. Donna Landry, *Noble Brutes: How Eastern Horses Transformed English Culture* (Baltimore: Johns Hopkins University Press, 2009), 104–25; Boehrer, *Parrot Culture*, 50–82.

23. Blundeville's *A Newe Booke containing the Art of Ryding and Breaking Great Horses* (London: William Seres, 1560), an English translation of Federico Grisone's *Gli Ordini di Cavalcare* (1550), was augmented and printed as *The Fower Chiefyst Offices Belongyng to Horsemanship*, which came out in six editions between 1565 and 1609.

24. Blundeville, *The Fower Chiefyst Offices Belongyng to Horsemanship* (London: William Seres, 1566) 3.

25. See, for example, Gervase Markham, *A discource of horsmanshippe Wherein the breeding and ryding of horses for seruice, in a breefe manner is more methodically sette downe then hath been heeretofore* (London: Printed for Richard Smith, 1593); *How to chuse, ride, traine, and diet, both hunting-horses and running horses* (London: Printed for Richard Smith, 1595); *Cauelarice, or The English horseman* (London: Printed for Edward White, 1607); and *Markhams faithfull farrier* (London: Printed for Michael Sparke, 1631).

26. Gervase Markham, *A discource of horsmanshippe*, A4r.

27. Ibid., A3v.

28. Ibid.

29. Burrow, 191n.295–300; John Roe, ed., *Shakespeare: The Poems* (Cambridge: Cambridge University Press, 2006), 103n.295; Blundeville, *Horsemanship*, 8v–9r.

30. Markham, A4v.

31. Ibid.

32. Lodovico Ariosto, *Orlando Furioso* (Ferrara: Giovanni Mazzoccho di Bondeno, 1516); John Harington, *Lodovico Ariosto's Orlando Furioso* (London: Richard Field, 1591); Robert Greene, *The History of Orlando Furioso* (London: Printed for Cuthbert Burbie, 1594).

33. Brotton and Jardine, 211n.80.

34. Blundeville, 4.

35. Markham, A3v.

36. See Burrow, 190n.284.

37. "Having gotten yourself a stallion of this Countrey, being young and lustie, which commonlie are the best, or for want of such, (because they bee rare), one of those which I have before mencioned, I woulde wish you to thus to breede, in the moneth of March or Aprill, or from midde March to midde May following," Markham, A3v.

38. Burrow argues that the poem alternates between spring and summer: "its seasonal setting consequently straddles the spring-time under-ripeness of Adonis *and* the full summer bloom of Venus." Burrow, 28. But he also attempts to pin down the poem's seasonal setting to the early spring, some time between March and April, through the reference to primroses on the ground. Burrow, 183n.151.

39. Lucretius, *The Way Things Are*, 19.

40. In her flower speech, Perdita speaks out against horticultural experimentation (*The Winter's Tale*, 4.4.82–103), disagreeing with Polixenes, who states that grafting is "an art / Which does mend nature" (4.4.95–96). Adopting a view similar to Polixenes's, Francis Bacon finds nature most interesting when most manipulated: "I mean it to be a history not only of nature free and at large . . . but much more of nature under constraint and vexed; that is to say, when by art and the hand of man she is forced out of her natural state, and squeezed and moulded," he states in his plan for *The Great Instauration*. See Francis Bacon, *The Great Instauration*, trans. James Spedding, Robert Leslie Ellis, and Douglas Denon Heath in *The Works*, vol. VIII (Boston: Taggard and Thompson, 1863); and Bacon, *Summi Angliae Cancellarii, Instauratio magna* (London: Bonham Norton and John Bill, 1620).

41. Latour, *Reassembling the Social*, and "The Berlin Key or How to Do Words with Things," 18–19.

42. Plutarch attributes this statement to Simonedes of Keos in *De Gloria Atheniesium*. See Alex Preminger, ed., *The Princeton Handbook of Poetic Terms* (Princeton, NJ: Princeton University Press, 1986), 288.

43. Landry, 109.

44. "The fifteenth and sixteenth centuries saw an escalation in the commissioning of visual representations of horses in all media, from frescoes to statuary, by the princes of Europe," Brotton and Jardine, 150.

45. Ibid., 29, 149.

46. The *trompe-l'oeil* technique originated in ancient Greece and Rome, but it could be found in Byzantine architecture all over the Ottoman Empire and experienced a revival during the European Renaissance from the fifteenth through the seventeenth centuries, which coincided not only with a renewed interest in classical art but in European commercial trade in antiquities with the Ottomans. See Marie-Louise d'Ortange Mastai, *Illusion in Art: Trompe-l'Oeil: A History of Pictorial Illusionism* (Norwalk, CT: Abaris Books, 1976).

47. Catherine Belsey, "Love as Trompe-L'Oeil: Taxonomies of Desire in Venus and Adonis," in Philip C. Kolin, ed., *Venus and Adonis: Critical Essays* (New York: Garland, 1997), 261–85.

48. Goldgar, *Tulipmania*. For a history of "tulipomania," see, for example, Charles Mackay, *Extraordinary Popular Delusions and the Madness of Crowds* (Hampshire: Harriman House, 2003); Mike Dash, *Tulipomania: The Story of the World's Most Coveted Flower and the Extraordinary Passions It Aroused* (London: Crown, 1999).

49. Henry Lyte, *A niewe Herball* (London: 1578). Rembert Dodoens's Herbal first appeared in Dutch as the *Cruijdeboeck* (Antwerp: Jan van der Loe, 1544) and was translated into French by Clusius as *L'histoire des plantes* (Antwerp: Jan van der Loe, 1557).

50. Goldgar, *Tulipmania*, 33. Clusius's letters are held at the University of Leiden, where they are being entered in a digital database.

51. John Parkinson, *Paradisi in Sole* (London: Humfrey Lownes and Robert Young, 1629), 8.

52. The word *purple* originally described a dark maroon color tending to violet obtained from the Murex mollusk on the Greek island of Tyre, whose secretions were used to create the famous Tyrian purple dye. It derived from the classical Latin name for the mollusk, *purpura*. See *purple*, n. and adj., *OED*.

53. The adjective *purpureus* appears three times in Book 10 of the *Metamorphoses*, first to describe the fanciful reins with which Cyparissus decks his beloved stag (10.125), second to describe the color of the flower into which Hyacinthus transforms (10.213), and finally mixed with white (*candida*) to describe Atalanta's blushes (10.596).

54. See Madeleine Forey, ed. and intro., *Ovid's Metamorphoses Translated by Arthur Golding* (Baltimore: Johns Hopkins University Press, 2002), 465n.862.

55. Humphries has "for the winds / Which gave a name to the flower, anemone, / The wind-flower, shake the petals off, too early, / Doomed all too swift and soon," *Ovid: Metamorphoses Translated by Rolphe Humphries* (Bloomington: Indiana University Press, 1955, 1983), 258. Mandelbaum's translation reads: "it clings too loosely to the stem, and thus is called / Anemone—"born of the wind"—because / winds shake its fragile petals and they fall." *The Metamorphoses of Ovid* (New York: Harcourt Brace, 1995), 356.

56. As Jonathan Gil Harris has shown, the story of Adonis has an ancient Mesopotamian corollary in the tale of Tammuz, of which Milton was aware, but probably Shakespeare was not. The Tammuz flower in Lebanon is a red anemone. See Jonathan Gil Harris, "Four Exoskeletons and No Funeral," *New Literary History* 2.4 (Autumn 2011): 615–39.

57. Burrow notes that a fritillary is a possible candidate for the Adonis flower, 235n.1168.

58. Burrow, *William Shakespeare: The Complete Sonnets and Poems*, 235n.1168. Burrow

also suggests Gerard's red chamomile or "Adonis flower" as a candidate, misreading it as a type of anemone, but despite the flower's highly suggestive name, I think this is unlikely, as there is nothing "checkered" about the red flower's appearance.

59. Henry Lyte, *A niewe Herball, or historie of plants* (London: Gerard Dewes, 1578); John Gerard, *The Herball, or Generall Historie of Plantes* (London: Printed for John Norton, 1597), 122; Parkinson, *Paradisi in Sole*, 40.

60. Gerard, *The Herball*, 122.

61. Parkinson, *Paradisi in Sole*, 28.

62. See Peneleope M. Allison, "Labels for Ladels: Interpreting the Material Culture of Roman Households," in Penelope Allison, ed., *The Archeology of Household Activities* (New York: Routledge, 1999), 62. In Thomas Johnson's 1633 enlargements to Gerard's *Herball*, Johnson corrects Parkinson's assumption that the *fritillus* board was checkered like a chess-board, citing Book 5 of Martial's Epigrams: "for *Martialis* seemeth to call *Fritillus, Abacus,* or the Tables whereat men play at Dice," Gerard, *The Herball or Generall historie of plantes. Gathered by Iohn Gerarde of London Master in Chirurgerie very much enlarged and amended by Thomas Iohnson citizen and apothecarye of London* (London: Adam Islip, Joyce Norton, and Richard Withers,1633), 97.

63. Burrow, Introduction, 22.

64. Ibid., 11.

65. In "'Sweets Compacted': Posies and the Poetry of George Herbert," in Christopher Hodgkins, ed., *George Herberts Travels: International Print and Cultural Legacies* (Newark: University of Delaware Press, 2011), I argue that the type of flower Herbert describes in his poem "The Flower" is also a bulb, which furthers Herbert's description of the flower underground as a house, 227–49.

66. Charles Evelyn, *Gardening Improv'd*, in "Making Gardens of Their Own: Advice for Women 1550–1750," in Jennifer Munroe, ed., *The Early Modern Englishwoman: A Facsimile Library of Essential Works: Series III: Essential Works for the Study of Early Modern Women, Part 3, Vol. 1*, general eds. Betty Travitsky and Anne Lake Prescott (Aldershot: Ashgate, 2007), 24.

67. *tulip*, n. *OED*.

68. Nicholas de Nicolay, *The navigations, peregrinations and voyages, made into Turkie by Nicholas Nicholay Daulphinois*, trans. Thomas Washington (London: T. Dawson, 1585), 108; Samuel Purchas, *Purchas, his Pilgrimmage* vol. 3 (London: Printed for Henry Featherstone, 1613), 267. For more early modern English uses of *tuliband* and *tulipant*, see *turban*, n., *OED*.

69. Benedict Robinson has argued that tulips themselves embodied the cultural problems of rapidly expanding early modern global economies. See Robinson, "Green Seraglios: Tulips, Turbans, and the Global Market," *Journal of Early Modern Cultural Studies* 9.1 (2009): 93–122.

70. Gerard, *Herball*, 116.

71. I should note here that anemones have thick stalks, but they are not full of viscous sap. Anemones are in the buttercup family, and though perennial, they are not bulbs.

72. Gerard writes that the tulip is "a strange and forreine floure" and that it would be impossible to name all the varieties of this flower because new varieties are continually being produced: "each new yeare bringeth forth new plants of sundry colours, not before seene: all which to describe particularly were to roll *Sisiphus* stone, or number the sands." Gerard, *Herball*, 116.

73. Ibid., 118.

74. The reference to "Nature's own sweet and cunning hand" comes from *Twelfth Night's* Viola, who has just heard Olivia boast that she wears no cosmetics (1.5.526).

75. Gerard, *Herball*, 118.

76. Ibid., 118.

77. The *OED* dates the phrase "apple of the cheek" to the middle of the sixteenth century. *apple*, n. 5a, *OED*: "1559 P. Morwyng tr. C. Gesner *Treasure of Euonymus* 207 To make ye apple of the chieck ruddy."

78. Shakespeare may be transposing another image from Ovid in his description of Adonis's blood-speckled cheeks and purple and white flower. In Ovid's version, Venus tells Adonis the tale of Atalanta and Hippomenes. When Atalanta runs, her body reddens, which Ovid compares to light filtering through a purple curtain onto a white wall: "*quam cum super atria velum / candida purpureum simulatas inficit umbras*" (10.596). In his English translation of this passage, Golding replaces Ovid's violet-red and white (*purpureum* and *candida*) with "scarlet" and "plastered" (10.694).

79. On an early modern connection between flowers and poetry, see my essay "'Sweets Compacted,'" 227–33.

80. "The eager [book] purchaser, by the mid-sixteenth century, required his copy of a work to look exactly like the one purchased by his neighbor . . . in this respect the trade in books, by the 1550s, closely resembled the trade in tulip bulbs at the same date. Once the bulbs of the exotic variegated flowers which the Low Countries' Ambassador had seen originally growing in the Ottoman sultan's garden in Adrianople had been acquired, they could be divided, and the blooms replicated precisely by the skilled bulb grower," Lisa Jardine, *Worldly Goods: A New History of the Renaissance* (New York: Norton, 1994), 165.

81. *perfume*, n. 1a and 2, *OED*.

82. George Sandys notes that besides being "incredible takers of Opium," the Turks also "delight in Tabacco," perhaps for the same reason, in *A Relation of a Iourney Begun An. Dom. 1610* (London: Printed by Richard Field for W. Barrett, 1615), 66. Before the introduction of tobacco from the New World in the early seventeenth century, smoking cannabis was also a popular recreational activity in Middle Eastern culture. See Sander Gilman and Zhou Yun, eds., *Smoke: A Global History of Smoking* (London: Reaktion Books, 2004), 20–21. The hookah was invented in India and central Asia in the sixteenth century with the spread of tobacco across the Ottoman Empire, and according to Rudi Matthee, references to nargiles appeared in Persian poetry by the middle of the sixteenth century, Gilman and Yun, *Smoke*, 13, 58.

83. Harris, "Four Exoskeletons and a Funeral," 631–33.

84. Holly Dugan observes that the poem and Shakespeare's sonnets draw on a

"ubiquitous" late sixteenth-century network of "damask roses, perfume, and eroticism," in *The Ephemeral History of Perfume* (Baltimore: Johns Hopkins University Press, 2011), 58.

85. Ibid., 21.

86. Burrow, 15; Burrow posits that there were several editions we may not know about today, "completely destroyed by eager consumers," 7.

87. Hooks demonstrates how booksellers connected Meres's epithet of Shakespeare as a honey-tongued reincarnation of Ovid with their marketing of *Venus and Adonis* in "Shakespeare at the White Greyhound," *Shakespeare Survey* 64 (2011): 260–75.

88. Landry, 72–73.

89. Edmund Spenser to Gabriel Harvey, 1580. See G. Gregory Smith, ed., *Elizabethan Critical Essays*, vol. 1 (Oxford: Clarendon Press, 1904), 99. Richard Helgerson has extracted this phrase from one of Spenser's letters to Gabriel Harvey and used it to underpin his argument that early modern English writers turned to continental sources in building their own linguistic nation, in *Forms of Nationhood: The Elizabethan Writing of England* (Chicago: Chicago University Press, 1994)

CHAPTER 5

1. Christopher Marlowe and George Chapman, *Hero and Leander, begun by Christopher Marlowe and finished by G. Chapman* (London: Paul Linley, 1598). All subsequent quotations are from this edition unless otherwise noted.

2. The only known copy of this duodecimo text is in the Bodleian library.

3. See Latour, *Reassembling the Social* and "The Berlin Key or How to Do Words with Things," 18–19.

4. George Sandys, *A Relation of a Iourney Begun An. Dom. 1610* (London: Printed by Richard Field for W. Barrett, 1615), 24.

5. Ibid., 24.

6. Sadeddin's chronicle, the *Taj-Ut-Tevarikh* ("The Crown of Histories") has never been fully translated into English, but a portion of it documenting the reign of Orhan I was translated by William Seaman in 1652 as *The Reign of Sultan Orchan Second King of the Turks. Translated out of Hojah Effendi, an eminient Turkish Historian. By William Seaman.* (London: T. R. and E. M., 1652). Seaman notes that earlier accounts have misread "Aydus" in Iznik as "Abydos" on the Hellespont, which means that the original location of the tale is not in the Hellespont at all but about 150 miles east and inland from the Black Sea. Perhaps ironically, the tale's association with the Hellespont has nonetheless stuck despite Seaman's attempts at clarification: a Victorian orientalist version by "G.W.N." appeared in an 1829 issue of *The Mirror* under the title "The Siege of Abydos," *The Mirror of Literature, Amusement and Instruction* 14: 382, 25 July 1829, 58–59.

7. John Stapylton, *Musaeus on The Loves of Hero and Leander with Annotations upon the Originall* (London: Humphrey Moseley, 1646).

8. Richard Knolles, *A Generall Historie of the* Turks (London: Adam Islip, 1603),

182–83. The earliest printed English versions of the tale appear in Knolles, Sandys, and in Staplyton's notes to his translation of Musaeus, *Musaeus on the Loues of Hero and Leander,* Biiv–Biiiv. In all of them, a Christian woman dreams that she is rescued from a ditch and clothed in rich garments by her beloved; she believes the Turkish general Abdurachman to be his living counterpart. She throws a message down to him from her tower asking him to withdraw his troops and seize the castle secretly that night. The Turks win, and the lady is given to the general as a prize for his conquest. For more on Sadeddin, see Jonathan Burton, *Traffick and Turning: Islam and English Drama 1579–1624* (Cranbury: University of Delaware Press, 2005), 41; and Brandon Beck, *From the Rising of the Sun: English Images of the Ottoman Empire to 1715* (New York: Peter Lang, 1987), 73–74. Linda McJannet reads this exogamous romance as a Muslim conversion story, the mirror image of a medieval Christian romance of conversion, what Geraldine Heng calls a "Constance Tale." See McJannet, *The Sultan Speaks: Dialogue in English Plays and Histories About the Ottoman Turks* (New York: Palgrave, 2006), 175–76; Gerladine Heng, *Empire of Magic: Medieval Romance and the Politics of Cultural Fantasy* (New York: Columbia University Press, 2003), 186.

9. Desire for rich silks and jewels from the East is typically gendered as feminine in early modern Europe. The clearest example of this occurs in Robert Wilson's play *The Three Ladies of London* (London: Roger Warde, 1584), where merchants poke fun at English ladies' desires for "trifles" (1.1.335, 337, 361). But when viewed from the Ottoman perspective, the lady's dream vision could equally be a metaphoric conversion ritual as she is first cleaned, then clothed with the grace of the Islamic faith.

10. Sujata Iyengar, *Shades of Difference: Mythologies of Skin Color in Early Modern England* (Philadelphia: University of Pennsylvania Press, 2005), 109.

11. André Thevêt, *Cosmographie du Levant* (Lyon: Jean de Tournes and Guillaume Gazeau, 1556), 66–67, and Nicholas de Nicolay, *The nauigations, peregrinations and voyages, made into Turkie by Nicholas Nicholay Daulphinois,* trans. Thomas Washington (London: T. Dawson, 1585), 43 verso–44.

12. Sandys, 26.

13. Ibid., 24.

14. Ibid., 26.

15. Ibid., 87.

16. Fynes Moryson, *An Itinerary* (London: J. Beale, 1617), 266–67.

17. Palmira Brummett *Ottoman Seapower and Levantine Diplomacy in the Age of Discovery* (Albany: SUNY Press, 1994), 4–5, 123.

18. "Conquest was defined not in terms of chunks of territory but in terms of routes defended and fortresses garrisoned. . . . Frontiers then were large and porous, the borders of one empire melding into those of another with many independent or semi-independent governors between." Ibid., 12–13. Instead of borders, Brummett identifies three trade zones, each one dealing in a different commodity. The Island Coast zone from the Aegean to the Adriatic was known for grain; the Anatolia-Syria zone for silk, spices and lumber; and the eastern Mediterranean–Indian Ocean for spices and copper.

19. Steve Mentz, *At the Bottom of Shakespeare's Ocean* (London: Continuum, 2009).

20. Ibid., 33–34.

21. Alison Games, *The Web of Empire: English Cosmopolitans in the Age of Expansion 1560–1660* (Oxford: Oxford University Press, 2008), especially Chapter 2, "The Mediterranean Origins of the British Empire," 47–79. Though the longer narrative accounts Games cites are primarily from early seventeenth-century travelers, many of the inventories and letters she references first appeared in the first and second editions of Richard Hakluyt's *Principal Navigations* in 1589 and 1599, bookending the publication of Marlowe's and Chapman's *Hero and Leander*.

22. Games, 58–60.

23. Ibid., 78.

24. Jonathan Gil Harris, *Untimely Matter in the Time of Shakespeare* (Philadelphia: University of Pennsylvania Press, 2008), 16.

25. *orient*, A n. 1b and 4, B adj. 1a and b, *OED*.

26. John Florio, *The Essayes of Michael of Montaigne* (London: William Barret, 1605).

27. John Florio, *Queene Anna's New World of Words* (London: Printed for Edward Blount and William Barret, 1611), "*oriente.*"

28. *orient*, n., *OED*.

29. *orient*, A1b, A4, B1a, *OED*.

30. Pliny, *The History of the World, Commonly called the Natural History of G. Plinius Secundus*, Book 9, Ch. 35, trans. Philemon Holland (London: Adam Islip, 1601), 254–58.

31. Ibid., 255.

32. Ibid., 255.

33. "A Pearle that is in all partes perfect, both of water, gloss and Beauty, without knobs or spots, or yellow, of fourme very round, or like a peare, being of the weight of one Caratt is wotth one Duckatt, And after this rate you are to make your reckoning," Hannibal Gamon, *The Gouldesmythe's Storehowse*, mss, 95ff (1606), The Folger Shakespeare Library.

34. Richard Hakluyt, *The Principall Navigations*, vol. III (London: George Bishop, Ralph Newberie, and Robert Barker, 1599–1600), 284.

35. Ibid., 312.

36. Other early modern European travelers describe pearl fishing in the Persian Gulf and Sri Lanka in more detail: André Thevêt's La *cosmographie universelle* of 1575 includes an illustrated map of a pearl fishery in Bahrain, and the Venetian trader Cesare Federici describes the pearl harvest on the Portuguese-controlled island of Mannar off the coast of Sri Lanka in his voyage of 1569. Thévet, *La cosmographie universelle* (Paris: Chez Guillaume Chaudière,1575); Thomas Hicock, trans., *The voyage and trauaile of M. Caesar Frederick, merchant of Venice, into the East India, the Indies, and beyond the Indies* (London: Richard Jones and Edward White, 1588), 14–15.

37. Jan Huygen Linschoten, *Iohn Huighen van Linschoten his Discours of Voyages into ye Easte & West Indies* (London: Printed for John Wolfe, 1598), 133.

38. According to R. A. Donkin, African slaves were employed as pearl divers primarily by the Spanish in the West Indies, and the divers in India and the Persian Gulf were a designated class of skilled workers. Donkin describes the hazards and rigor of diving for pearls

in the medieval Persian Gulf, 127, and cites Leonardo da Vinci's description of an elaborate diving contraption, which Donkin ascertains must be Chinese in origin, 159. R. A. Donkin, *Beyond Price: Pearls and Pearl Fishing: Origins to the Age of Discoveries* (Philadelphia: American Philosophical Society, 1998), 322.

39. Ibid., 1–21.

40. As Holland translates Pliny, "When the season of the yeere requireth that they should engender, they seeme to yawne and gape, and so doe open wide; and then (by report) they conceive a certaine moist dew as seed, wherewith they swell and grow bigge; and when time commeth, labour to be delivered hereof: and the fruit of these shell-fishes are the pearles," 254.

41. Donkin, 16.

42. Perhaps the most famous pearl-studded depiction of the Virgin Queen is the Ditchley Portrait (1592), in which she wears a dazzling white silk dress and white lace ruff. The dress carries a nacreous sheen, seeming to glow on its own. In addition to five long strands of pearls draped about her neck, the baroque pearl choker, and the gigantic pearl drop earrings, Elizabeth's dress, collar, and hair are strewn with pearls. Her shoes are round and white, and ten pearls decorate her fan. Only Elizabeth's pale skin is whiter than the pearly sheen of the dress.

43. English prose romance seems to contain the highest number of allusions to "orient pearls" as metaphors for female perfection and, by extension, chastity. Following the medieval tradition employed by poets like Froissart, Machaut, and Chaucer of representing a maiden's body as a *marguerite*, a pearl or daisy (a metaphor that also appears in *Pearl*), Renaissance writers of prose romance adopt the term *orient pearl* in their descriptions. For example, Thomas Lodge's *Rosalynde* invokes the *orient pearl* twice to describe its heroine, first her fragile perfection, second her chastity: "the more orient the Pearle is, the more apt to take a blemish," Alindas, the hero, warns his beloved. And later, another of Rosalynd's admirers contradicts this, arguing that her chastity is not precarious: "She is a Diamond, bright but not hard, yet of most chast operation: a pearle so orient, that it can be stained with no blemish." Thomas Lodge, *Rosalynde* (London: Printed for T. G. and John Bushie, 1592), D3r, G4r. Amphialus, the disguised hero of Sidney's *Arcadia*, sings the praises of his love, Philoclea, weighing pearl against oyster: "All things that earst I sawe, as orient pearles exceed / That which their mother hight, or else their silly seed," Philip Sidney, *The Countesse of Pembrokes Arcadia* (Oxford: Oxford University Press, 1999), 293.

44. Marlowe is not the first Renaissance poet to address the pure and pearly blazon in a new way: Shakespeare's uses of pearl imagery are frequently ironic: his hypersexualized Venus conjures pearly tears as "orient drops" in *Venus and Adonis* (979–90), and the dark-skinned foreigner Aaron, Shakespeare's most unrepentant and corrupt villain, uses the language of "pearl and gold" (1.2.519) to describe his ascension to power at Tamora's side. Later, Lucius sarcastically refers to Aaron's mixed-race bastard child as a "pearl" (5.9.42). Like *Hero and Leander*, Shakespeare's *Titus Andronicus* collapses all of Roman history into a period that is at once ahistorical and polychronic. See Jonathan Bate, "Introduction," *Titus Andronicus* (New York: Arden Shakespeare: Third Series, 1995), 17.

45. Patrick Cheney, *Marlowe's Counterfeit Profession: Ovid, Spenser, Counter-Nationhood* (Toronto: University of Toronto Press, 1997), 21–25, 273–74n.40–41.

46. Cheney, "Introduction," *The Cambridge Companion to Christopher Marlowe* (Cambridge: Cambridge University Press, 2004), 14.

47. Wendy Beth Hyman connects Hero's hydraulic boots to pneumatic organs designed by Hero of Alexandria, reading them as metaphors for Marlowe's *technopoesis*. For Hyman, Hero is an automaton, a simulacrum for poetry itself. See Wendy Beth Hyman, "Mathematical Experiments of Long Silver Pipes: The Early Modern Figure of the Mechanical Bird," in Wendy Beth Hyman, ed., *The Automaton in Renaissance Literature* (Burlington, VT: Ashgate, 2011), 156.

48. On Jamnizter and the Cabinet of Curiosities, see Arthur MacGregor and Oliver Impey, *The Origin of Museums: The Cabinet of Curiosities in Sixteenth and Seventeenth Century Europe* (Cornwall: House of Stratus, 2001).

49. Virgil, *Georgics*, I. 207. Although poetically evoked as a landscape full of pearls, the Hellespont was not known in the classical or early modern world as a place where pearls were harvested. That said, pearls could be found in the Mediterranean and even in Britain, though according to Pliny, British pearls are "small, dim of colour, and nothing orient." *Natural History* (1601), 256. Despite its lack of valuable pearls, the Mediterranean did yield a large amount of precious coral.

50. Gamon, *The Gouldesmythe's Storehowse*, 95ff.

51. I have Sarah van der Laan to thank for this excellent observation comparing Hilliard's miniatures to baroque pearl jewels. For more on the way pearls and lace function in miniatures to obscure and protect the Elizabethan self, see Patricia Fumerton, *Cultural Aesthetics: Renaissance Literature and the Practice of Social Ornament* (Chicago: University of Chicago Press, 1991), 67–110.

52. Like Marlowe's Neptune, the pearly sea-god in the late Elizabethan Canning Jewel (in the collection of the Victoria and Albert Museum) holds a "saphyr-visaged" shield in his left hand, brandishing a scimitar-shaped knife in his right that calls to mind a marauding Turkish pirate.

53. As the art historian Amy Golahny has shown, Rubens was trained in a European, classical humanist bent and would have been familiar with Musaeus's Greek version of the story: "Rubens left a well-marked trail of his reading. . . . His early canvas *Hero and Leander*, relied on Musaeus's epic for Hero's plunge from her tower, and Bion's lament for *Adonis* for the nymphs bewailing Leander's death," Amy Golahny, *Rembrandt's Reading* (Amsterdam: Amsterdam University Press, 2003), 210.

54. See, for example, the Burghley *Nef* in the Victoria and Albert Museum or the late sixteenth-century baroque pearl caravel brooch in the Hermitage Museum.

55. Games, 78.

56. Games, 58–60.

57. Ibid., 78.

58. Hakluyt, vol. I, 24–26.

59. Once chemical dyes overtook natural dyes, the secret was lost and the recipe only

recently discovered in 1998 by the British chemist John Edmonds. See Robert Chenciner, *Madder Red: A History of Luxury and Trade* (London: Routledge-Curzon, 2000), 293. The problem was not how to extract the purple dye from the Murex shell but how to dissolve the pigment into an alkaline solution.

60. Ottoman dye technology remained a fantasy mediator until the French discovered the recipe in the eighteenth century. Instead, the English looked west to the New World for innovations in textile dyes, importing the larger and plumper version of the kermes insect, *cochineal*, which yielded a higher volume of red dye more cheaply. *Cochineal* thus took the role of mediator while Turkey Red remained a fantasy.

61. Hakluyt, vol. V, 294.

62. Ibid., 233–34.

63. See S. A. Skilleter, "Lord Burghley's notes on towns and commodities of the Levant" (1582-ish) (177–) [BL Landsdowne MS 34, ff 178–79], in S. A. Skillerter, *William Harborne and the Trade with Turkey 1578–1582* (London: British Academy, 1977), Document 30.

64. Leonard Mascall, *A profitable booke declaring dyuers approoued remedies* (London: Thomas Purfoote, 1588).

65. George Chapman, *The Divine Poem of Musaeus. First of all Bookes. Translated according to the Originall by Geo: Chapman* (London: Isaac Jaggard, 1616).

66. Grammaticus Musaeus, *Musei opousculum de Herone & Leandro*, trans. Marcus Musurus (Venice: Aldus Manutius, 1517). Liddell, Scott, and Jones note that *kuanopeploV* is a Homeric word meaning "dark-veiled," in their *Greek English Lexicon* (Oxford: Oxford University Press, 1996), 1004.

67. Musaeus does utilize his own image of reddening dye to describe Hero modestly casting her eyes upon the ground, with "ερεύθοσαν παρειν" (Mus., 161). Ερεύθοσαν or *ruddy* derives from the Greek word for madder, ερεύθεδανον. In early modern bilingual editions, Marcus Musurus translates ερεύθοσαν into the Latin word *rubefactam*, furthering a connection to madder's Latin name, *Rubia tinctorum*.

68. In her chapter on "Heroic Blushing," Iyengar shows how, over the course of Marlowe's and Chapman's poem, Hero moves from purest white to darkest black, as a physical manifestation of shame for her union with Leander, *Shades of Difference*, 103–22.

69. Here is where I depart from Iyengar's reading of Hero's coloring. Where Iyengar contends that the veil turns Hero into a dark opacity that attempts to resist signification, I see it revealing and publishing her shame. *Shades of Difference*, 119.

70. Skilleter, *William Harborne and the Trade with Turkey*, Doc. 1A, 33. There was an important political need for the English to keep a low profile in these early ventures: as producers of wool ("kersies" appear in Walsingham's list of commodities), the English could trade directly with the Turks, eliminating the need for Venetian or French middlemen. The English also provided direct access to tin, pewter, and lead (sourced from Cornwall and even from dissolved monasteries as "bell metal") to the Turkish army. As Burton notes, the term "bell metal" soon meant all contraband England shipped to Turkey, for "English cargoes included "broken bells and images . . . iron and steel, lead [and] copper." Burton, 61.

71. See Skilleter, 154–58.

72. Ibid., 167.

73. See *OED, colour*, v., and Alan Stewart, "Come from Turkie: Mediterranean Trade in Late Elizabethan London," in Goran Stanivukovic, ed., *Remapping the Mediterranean World in Early Modern English Writings* (New York: Palgrave, 2007), 157–78.

74. Puttenham compares the judicious use of rhetorical figures to a painter's palette of "rich, orient colors" and to ladies' cosmetics. Improper use of figurative language is like tinting the chin or forehead with lipstick: "if the crimson taint, which should be laid upon a lady's lips or right in the center of her cheeks, should by some oversight or mishap be applied to her forehead or chin, it would make (ye would say) but a very ridiculous beauty." George Puttenham, *The Art of English Poesy by George Puttenham: A Critical Edition*, ed. Frank Whigham and Wayne A. Rebhorn (Ithaca, NY: Cornell University Press, 2001), 222.

75. Ibid., 239.

76. Ibid.

77. Iyengar, 120.

78. See Geoffrey of Vinsauf's *Poetria Nova* in the *Rhetorica ad Herennium* IV. xi. 16: *quae si rare disponentur distinctam sicuti coloribus*, which Jane Baltzell Kopp translates as "distributed sparingly, these figures set the style in relief, as with colors," in James J. Murphy, ed., *Three Medieval Rhetorical Arts* (Berkeley: University of California Press, 1971, 1985), 60. Geoffrey identifies thirty-five plain colors in the *ad Herennium* IV; see Murphy, 73n.76.

79. In his critique of Vinsauf's rhetorical colors, Alain of Lille compares them to a whore's makeup. See Holly A. Crocker, *Chaucer's Visions of Manhood* (New York: Palgrave, 2007), 98.

80. See Michel Pastoreau, *The Devil's Cloth: A History of Stripes* (New York: Columbia University Press, 2001).

81. *current*, n. 5 and adj. 6, *OED*.

82. Currants were one of the main commodities by which all other commodities were valued. A bright piece of damask cloth, for instance, might be valued in pounds of currants. Only members of the Levant Company were authorized to sell and import currants into England, and those who sold them under false pretenses paid dearly for it. Those who sold currants in the Mediterranean without a license also paid dearly: Sandys's visit to the island of Zante (Zakynthos, one of the largest exporters of currants in the period), where currants are the "chief riches," includes witnessing an English merchant killed for smuggling a bag of currants on board a ship "uncustomed" or without paying customs fees (clearly it was better to "color" your goods than to smuggle them). See, for example, Mortimer Epstein, "The Currant Trade and the Regulation of Trade in Other Commodities" in *The Early History of the Levant Company* (London: Routledge, 1908), 109–210; and Alfred Cecil Wood, *A History of the Levant Company* (Oxford: Oxford University Press, 1935).

83. Curiously, Bruce Boehrer's book on parrots in Western culture does not mention either Virgil's *Fama* or Chapman's Adolesche as early etiologies of the parrot. See Bruce Boehrer, *Parrot Culture: Our 2500 Year Long Fascination with the World's Most Talkative Bird* (Philadelphia: University of Pennsylvania Press, 2004).

84. Michel Pastoureau notes that oak galls were used in textile dye as well as in ink:

"to obtain a truly uniform, solid, black black, the medieval dyer knew of only one product: the oak gall. . . . This dye was an expensive product . . . it had to be imported from eastern Europe, the Near East, or North Africa," Michel Pastoureau, *Black: The History of a Color* (Princeton, NJ: Princeton University Press, 2009), 92. Most early modern recipes for manuscript ink depend upon oak galls as well. See James Daybell, *The Material Letter in Early Modern England: Manuscript Letters and the Culture and Practice of Letter-Writing, 1512–1635* (New York: Palgrave Macmillan, 2012), 38, 241n.58. See also Michael Finlay, *Western Writing Implements in the Age of the Quill Pen* (Wetheral, Scotland: Plains Books, 1990), 26–28.

85. Burton, 59.

86. Games, 79.

87. Burton dismisses early modern English poetry as representative of the complex relationship between England and its new mercantile allies, arguing that unlike drama and prose, English poetry "depends upon a denial of the emerging idea of Turks as trading partners and allies," Burton, 28.

88. On classical *imitatio* as theatrical performance in the Latin grammar schools, see Lynne Enterline, "Rhetoric, Discipline, and the Theatricality of Everyday Life in Elizabethan Grammar Schools," in Peter Holland and Stephen Orgel, eds., *From Performance to Print in Shakespeare's England* (New York: Palgrave, 2006), 173–90; and *Shakespeare's Schoolroom: Rhetoric, Discipline, Emotion* (Philadelphia: University of Pennsylvania Press, 2013).

89. I am not the first to make this observation, though I may be the first to tie it to Anglo-Ottoman diplomacy in the Mediterranean: Iyengar suggests that both Marlowe and Chapman make colorful deception "a necessary part of lyric or fictionality," 122.

90. Margreta de Grazia and Peter Stallybrass, "The Materiality of the Shakespearean Text," *Shakespeare Quarterly* 44.3 (1993): 261. In their article, de Grazia and Stallybrass characterize the instability of the early modern printed text with language of plasticity and fluidity.

91. The anthropological term *syncretism* is mostly used to discuss the melding and inclusiveness of two or more religions and cultures. See, for example, Charles H. Parker, *Global Interactions in the Early Modern Age* (Cambridge: Cambridge University Press, 2011), 130, 200–205; Tijana Krstic, *Contested Conversions to Islam: Narratives of Religious Change in the Early Modern Ottoman Empire* (Palo Alto, CA: Stanford University Press, 2011), 17–18; and Charles Stewart and Rosalind Shaw, eds., *Syncretism/Anti-Syncretism* (London: Routledge, 1994).

92. Drawing on the theory of Manuel de Landa, Jonathan Gil Harris reads some layered geographies as exoskeletons, not as palimpsests. In an exoskeleton, history builds up in hardened layers, much like the layers of a pearl or rock face. See Jonathan Gil Harris, "Four Exoskeletons and No Funeral," *New Literary History* 2.4 (Autumn 2011): 615–39.

93. See, for example, Stephen Orgel, ed., *Christopher Marlowe: The Complete Poems and Translations* (New York: Penguin Classics, 2007). To be fair, Orgel also includes Henry Petowe's less popular continuation of the poem in his edition.

94. Marlowe's fascination with non-Western religions and cultures in Asia and the

mercantile Mediterranean extends to his plays, particularly *The Jew of Malta* and *Tamberlaine* Parts I and II. Emily Bartels has examined this aspect of Marlowe's dramatic writing in *Spectacles of Strangeness: Imperialism, Alienation, and Marlowe* (Philadelphia: University of Pennsylvania Press, 1993), but few have written about it with regard to his poetry, with Sujata Iyengar's chapter in *Shades of Difference* being the notable exception.

95. Richard Helgerson, *Forms of Nationhood: The Elizabethan Writing of England* (Chicago: University of Chicago Press, 1992), 25.

96. Ian Smith, *Race and Rhetoric in Early Modern England: Barbarian Errors* (New York: Palgrave Macmillan, 2009), 16.

EPILOGUE

1. See Chapter 2, note 29.

2. On *cochineal* in early modern English poetry, see Edward M. Test, "Amerindian Eden: the Divine Weeks of Du Bartas," in Ken Hiltner, Stephanie LeMenanger, and Teresa Shewry, eds., *Environmental Criticism for the Twenty-first Century* (New York: Routledge, 2012), 121–34.

3. All citations from this poem are taken from *The Poems of Sir John Beaumont, Bart.*, ed. and intro. Rev. Alexander Grossart (Lancashire: Blackburn, 1869). The poem first appeared as Sir John Beaumount, *The Metamorphosis of Tabacco* (London: Printed for John Flasket, 1602).

4. Jeffrey Knapp, *An Empire Nowhere: England, America, and Literature from Utopia to The Tempest* (Berkeley: University of California Press, 1994), 165–74.

5. Knapp, 174.

6. See, for example, Gauri Viswanathan, *Masks of Conquest: Literary Study and British Rule in India* (New York: Columbia University Press, 1989); and Jyotsna Singh, "Post-colonial Criticism," in Stanley Wells and Lena Cowen Orlin, eds., *Shakespeare: An Oxford Guide* (Oxford: Oxford University Press, 2003), 492–507.

7. Kathleen Brown is one of the first critics to draw attention to Ligon's description of the governor's mistress as a positive account of black beauty, in "Native Americans and Early Modern Concepts of Race," in Martin Daunton and Rick Halpern, eds., *Empire and Others: British Encounters with Indigenous Peoples, 1600–1850* (Philadelphia: University of Pennsylvania Press, 1999), 97.

8. The African mistress moves with "far greater majesty, and gracefulness, than I have seen Queen Anne, descend from the Chair of State, to dance the Measures with a Baron of England, at a Maske in the Banquetting house." Richard Ligon, *A True & Exact History of the Island of Barbados* (London: Humphrey Moseley, 1657), 13. All subsequent quotations are from this edition. Ben Jonson wrote two masques in which the queen and her ladies appeared in blackface and they were published together as *The Characters of Two Royall Masques the one of Blacknesse, the other of Beautie* (London: Printed for Thomas Thorp, 1608). See Jane Stevenson, "Richard Ligon and the Theatre of Empire," in Allan

I. Macinnes and Arthur H. Williamson, *Shaping the Stuart World 1603–1714: The Atlantic Connection* (Leiden: Brill, 2006), 285–310.

9. *engrail*, v., 1, *OED*.

10. *engrail*, v., 4, *OED*.

11. See Wendy Beth Hyman, "Mathematical Experiments of Long Silver Pipes: The Early Modern Figure of the Mechanical Bird," in Wendy Beth Hyman, ed., *The Automaton in Renaissance Literature* (Burlington, VT: Ashgate, 2011), 156.

12. Philip Sidney, *Sir P.S. his Astrophel and Stella* (London: Printed for Thomas Newman, 1591), 38, 3.

13. Both plays cited in *The Norton Shakespeare*, ed. Greenblatt, Cohen, Howard, and Maus (New York: W. W. Norton & Company, 1997–2008).

14. Song of Solomon, *The Holy Bible Conteyning the Old Testament, and the New* (London: Robert Barker, 1611). Early modern English readers of the King James Version would have associated the female body described here with that of the black bride of 1: 5–6.

15. Nicolay's *Peregrinations* covers the Greek islands, eastern Europe, Constantinople and Anatolia, and Persia. It is interspersed with sixty woodcuts of men and women in regional dress (twenty-six are of women, including the first twelve images). See Nicholas de Nicolay, *The nauigations, peregrinations and voyages, made into Turkie by Nicholas Nicholay Daulphinois*, trans. Thomas Washington (London: T. Dawson, 1585).

16. Ian Smith, *Race and Rhetoric in Early Modern England: Barbarian Errors* (New York: Palgrave Macmillan, 2009).

17. Ligon, 15.

18. John Donne, *Poems by J.D. with Elegies on the Author's Death* (London: John Marriott, 1635), 84.

19. Ibid., 84.

20. Ibid., 85.

21. See Sujata Iyengar, *Shades of Difference: Mythologies of Skin Color in Early Modern England* (Philadelphia: University of Pennsylvania Press, 2005), 223; and Jennifer Lyle Morgan, *Laboring Women: Reproduction and Gender in New World Slavery* (Philadelphia: University of Pennsylvania Press, 2004), 13–15, 48–49

Bibliography

Acheson, Katherine. "Gesner, Topsell, and the Purposes of Pictures in Early Modern Natural Histories." In Michael Hunter, ed., *Printed Images in Early Modern Britain: Essays in Interpretation*. Farnham: Ashgate, 2010.

Agamben, Giorgio. *Stanzas: Word and Phantasm in Western Culture*. Trans. Ronald L. Martínez. Minneapolis: University of Minnesota Press, 1993.

Alciato, Andrea. *Livret des emblemes*. Paris: Christian Wechel, 1543.

Allison, Penelope M., ed. *The Archeology of Household Activities*. New York: Routledge, 1999.

Anderson, Judith H. *Words That Matter: Linguistic Perception in Renaissance English*. Palo Alto, CA: Stanford University Press, 1996.

Anglicus, Bartholomaeus. *Batman upon Bartholomaeus his booke de Proprietatius rerum*. London: Thomas East, 1582.

Anon. *The Grete Herball*. London: Peter Treveris, 1526.

Anon., probably Hugh Plat. *A Closet for Ladies and Gentlewomen*. London: Printed for Arthur Johnson, 1608.

Archer, John. *Old Worlds: Egypt, Southwest Asia, India, and Russia in Early Modern English Writing*. Palo Alto, CA: Stanford University Press, 2001.

Ariosto, Lodovico. *Orlando Furioso*. Ferrara: Giovanni Mazzoccho di Bondeno, 1516.

Armstrong, Edward. *Shakespeare's Imagination*. Lincoln: University of Nebraska Press, 1963.

Ascham, Roger. *The Scholemaster or plaine and perfite way of teachyng children, to vnderstand, write, and speake, the Latin tong . . .* London: John Daye, 1570.

Auerbach, Eric. *Mimesis*. Princeton, NJ: Princeton University Press, 1953, 2003.

Bacon, Francis. *Summi Angliae Cancellarii, Instauratio magna*. London: Bonham Norton and John Bill, 1620.

———. *The Great Instauration*. Trans. James Spedding, Robert Leslie Ellis, and Douglas Denon Heath. *The Works of Francis Bacon*. Vol. VIII. Boston: Taggard and Thompson, 1863.

Bakhtin, Mikhail. *The Dialogic Imagination*. Ed. and trans. Michael Holquist. Austin: University of Texas Press, 1981.

Baldwin, T. W. *On the Literary Genetics of Shakespeare's Poems & Sonnets*. Urbana: University of Illinois Press, 1950. 108–10.

Barbour, Richmond. *Before Orientalism: London's Theatre of the East 1576–1626*. Cambridge: Cambridge University Press, 2003.

Barkan, Leonard. *Unearthing the Past*. New Haven, CT: Yale University Press, 1999.

———. "Ruins and Visions: Spenser, Pictures, and Rome." In Jennifer Klein Morrison and Matthew Greenfield, eds., *Edmund Spenser: Essays on Culture and Allegory*. Aldershot: Ashgate, 2000. 30–31.

Barrett, John. *An Alvearie or Quadruple Dictionarie*. London: Henry Denham and William Seres, 1580.

Bartels, Emily. *Spectacles of Strangeness: Imperialism, Alienation, and Marlowe*. Philadelphia: University of Pennsylvania Press, 1993.

———. *Speaking of the Moor: From Alcazar to Othello*. Philadelphia: University of Pennsylvania Press, 2008.

Bate, Jonathan. *Shakespeare and Ovid*. Oxford: Oxford University Press, 1994.

Beaumont, Sir John. *The Metamorphosis of Tabacco*. London: Printed for John Flasket, 1602.

———. *The Poems of Sir John Beaumont, Bart*. Ed. Rev. Alexander Grossart. Lancashire: Blackburn, 1869.

Beck, Brandon. *From the Rising of the Sun: English Images of the Ottoman Empire to 1715*. New York: Peter Lang, 1987.

Bellay, Joachim du. *Les oeuvres francoises de Ioachim Du-Bellay, gentil homme Angeuin, & poëte excellent de ce temps*. Paris: Frederic Morel, 1569.

Belsey, Catherine. "Love as Trompe-L'Oeil: Taxonomies of Desire in Venus and Adonis." In Philip C. Kolin, ed., *Venus and Adonis: Critical Essays*. New York: Garland, 1997. 261–85.

Biester, James. *Lyric Wonder: Rhetoric and Wit in Renaissance English Poetry*. Ithaca, NY: Cornell University Press, 1997.

Blank, Paula. *Broken English: Dialects and the Politics of Language in Early Modern Writings*. London: Routledge, 1996.

Blount, Edmund. *Glossographia*. London: Thomas Newcombe, 1656.

Blundeville, Thomas. *A Newe Booke containing the Art of Ryding and Breaking Great Horses*. London: William Seres, 1560.

———. *The Fower Chiefyst Offices Belongyng to Horsemanship*. London: William Seres, 1566.

Boehrer, Bruce. *Shakespeare Among the Animals: Nature and Society in the Drama of Early Modern England*. New York: Palgrave, 2002.

———. *Parrot Culture: Our 2500 Year Long Fascination with the World's Most Talkative Bird*. Philadelphia: University of Pennsylvania Press, 2004.

Bolter, Jay David, and Richard Grusin. *Remediation: Understanding New Media*. Cambridge: MIT Press, 2000.

Bourdieu, Pierre. *Language and Symbolic Power*. Cambridge: Cambridge University Press, 1991.

Bowers, A. Robin. "Iconography and Rhetoric in Shakespeare's *Lucrece*." *Shakespeare Studies* 14 (1981): 1–19.

Braden, Gordon. *The Classics and English Renaissance Poetry: Three Case Studies*. New Haven, CT: Yale University Press, 1978.

———. "Ovid and Shakespeare." In Peter Knox, ed., *A Companion to Ovid*. Oxford: Wiley-Blackwell, 2009. 446–49.

Brears, Peter. "Rare Conceits and Strange Delights: The Practical Aspects of Culinary Sculpture." In C. Anne Wilson, ed., *Banquetting Stuffe: The Fare and Social Background of the Tudor-Stuart Banquet*. Edinburgh: Edinburgh University Press, 1991. 67–68.

Brenner, Robert. *Merchants and Revolution: Commercial Change, Political Conflict, and London's Overseas Traders, 1560–1630*. Princeton, NJ: Princeton University Press, 1993.

Brotton, Jerry. *Trading Territories: Mapping the Early Modern World*. Ithaca, NY: Cornell University Press, 1998.

———. *The Renaissance Bazaar: From the Silk Road to Michelangelo*. Oxford: Oxford University Press, 2002.

———. "St. George between East and West." In Gerald MacLean, ed., *Re-Orienting the Renaissance: Cultural Exchanges with the East*. New York: Palgrave, 2005. 50–65.

Brotton, Jerry, and Lisa Jardine. *Global Interests: Renaissance Art Between East and West*. London: Reaktion, 2000.

Brown, Bill. "Thing Theory." *Critical Inquiry* 28.1 (Autumn 2001): 1–22.

Brown, Georgia. *Redefining Elizabethan Literature*. Cambridge: Cambridge University Press, 2004.

Brown, Kathleen. "Native Americans and Early Modern Concepts of Race." In Martin Daunton and Rick Halpern, eds., *Empire and Others: British Encounters with Indigenous Peoples, 1600–1850*. Philadelphia: University of Pennsylvania Press, 1999.

Brown, Peter, and Ivan Day. *The Pleasures of the Table: Ritual and Display in the European Dining Room 1600–1900*. York: York Civic Trust, 1997.

Brummett, Palmira. *Ottoman Seapower and Levantine Diplomacy in the Age of Discovery*. New York: SUNY Press, 1994.

Bünting, Heinrich. *Itinerarium Sacrare Scripturae*. Magdeburg: Printed by Ambrosius II Kirchner for Paul Donat, 1584.

Burke, Peter. *Languages and Communities in Early Modern Europe*. Cambridge: Cambridge University Press, 2004.

Burton, Jonathan. *Traffic and Turning: Islam and English Drama 1579–1624*. Cranbury: University of Delaware Press, 2005.

Burton, Jonathan, and Ania Loomba, eds. *Race in Early Modern England: A Documentary Companion*. New York: Palgrave, 2007.

Camden, William. *Remaines Concerning Britain*. London: Printed for Simon Waterson, 1605.

Campion, Thomas. *Observations in the Art of English Poesie*. London: Printed by Richard Field for Andrew Wise, 1602.

Carey, John, ed. *John Donne: The Major Works Including Songs, Sonnets, and Sermons*. Oxford: Oxford University Press, 2009.

Carr, Joan. "Jonson and the Classics: The Ovid-plot in Poetaster." *English Literary Renaissance* 8 (1978): 296–311.

Cavendish, George. *The Life and Death of Cardinal Wolsey*. Early English Text Society No. 243. Ed. Richard S. Sylvester. London: Oxford University Press, 1959.

Cawdrey, Robert. *A Table Alphabeticall*. London: Edmund Weaver, 1604.

Chapman, George. *The Divine Poem of Musaeus. First of all Bookes. Translated accoring to the Originall by Geo: Chapman.* London: Isaac Jaggard, 1616.

Chaucer, Geoffrey. *The Canterbury Tales. The Riverside Chaucer.* Ed. Larry Benson et al. New York: Houghton Mifflin, 1986.

Chenciner, Robert. *Madder Red: A History of Luxury and Trade.* London: Routledge-Curzon, 2000.

Cheney, Patrick, ed. *Marlowe's Counterfeit Profession: Ovid, Spenser, Counter-Nationhood.* Toronto: University of Toronto Press, 1997.

———. *The Cambridge Companion to Christopher Marlowe.* Cambridge: Cambridge University Press, 2004.

Church, Margaret. "The First English Pattern Poems." *PMLA* 61 (1946): 636–50.

Church of England. *The Boke of Common Prayer.* London: John Daye, 1583.

Churchyard, Thomas. "A Commendatory Poem." In *Pithy pleasaunt and profitable workes of maister Skelton.* London: Thomas Marsh, 1568. 43–45

———. *The Worthines of Wales.* London: Printed for Thomas Cadman, 1587.

Clark, James Midgely. *The Dance of Death in the Middle Ages and the Renaissance.* Glasgow: Jackson, 1950.

Cockeram, Henry. *The English Dictionary, or an Interpreter of Hard English Words.* London: Printed for Edmund Weaver, 1623.

Colie, Rosalie. *Paradoxica Epidemica: The Renaissance Tradition of the Paradox.* Princeton, NJ: Princeton University Press, 1966.

Colonna, Francesco. *Hypnerotomachia. The Strife of Loue in a Dreame.* Trans. Robert Dullyngdon. London: Printed for Simon Waterson, 1592.

———. *Hypnerotomachia Poliphili: The Strife of Love in a Dream.* Trans. Jocelyn Godwin. London: Thames and Hudson, 1999.

Cooper, John. *Eat and Be Satisfied: A Social History of Jewish Food.* Lanham, MD: Jason Aaronson, 1993.

Cooper, Thomas. *Thesaurus.* London: Thomas Berthelet, 1565.

Cormack, Bradin. "Tender Distance: Latinity and Desire in Shakespeare's Sonnets." In Michael Schoenfeldt, ed., *A Companion to Shakespeare's Sonnets.* Oxford: Blackwell, 2010. 242–60.

Corrozet, Giles. *Hecatomgraphie.* Paris: Denis Janot, 1540.

Cotgrave, Randall. *A Dictionarie of the French and English Tongues.* London: Adam Islip, 1611.

Coustau, Pierre. *Le Pegme.* Lyons: Barthelemy Molin, 1560.

Cox, John. *The Devil and the Sacred in English Drama, 1350–1642.* Cambridge: Cambridge University Press, 2000.

Crane, Gregory. "Bees Without Honey, and Callimachean Taste." *American Journal of Philology* (Summer 1987): 399–403.

Crocker, Holly A. *Chaucer's Visions of Manhood.* New York: Palgrave, 2007.

Daniel, Samuel. *A Panegyricke congratulatorie deliuered to the Kings most excellent Maiestie … with a defence of ryme heretofore written, and now published by the author.* London: Printed for Edward Blount, 1603.

Dash, Mike. *Tulipomania: The Story of the World's Most Coveted Flower and the Extraordinary Passions It Aroused*. London: Crown, 1999.

Day, Ivan. "The Art of Confectionary," online treatise at http://www.historicfood.com

Daybell, James. *The Material Letter in Early Modern England: Manuscript Letters and the Culture and Practice of Letter-Writing, 1512–1635*. New York: Palgrave Macmillan, 2012.

Dee, John. *Monas Hieroglyphica*. Antwerp: William Silvis, 1564.

———. *Monas Hieroglyphica*. Ed. and trans. C. H. Josten. *AMBIX* 12 (1964): 84–221.

Deerr, Noel. *The History of Sugar*. London: Chapman and Hall, 1949.

Degenhardt, Jane. *Islamic Conversion and Christian Resistance on the Early Modern Stage*. Edinburgh: University of Edinburgh Press, 2010.

Dictionnaire historique de la langue française. Paris: Le Robert, 1998.

Dodoens, Rembert. *Cruijdeboeck*. Antwerp: Jan van der Loe, 1544.

———. *Histoire des plantes*. Trans. Carolus Clusius. Antwerp: Jan van der Loe, 1557.

Donaldson, Ian. *The Rapes of Lucretia: A Myth and Its Transformations*. Oxford: Clarendon Press, 1982.

Dolven, Jeff. *Scenes of Instruction in Renaissance Romance*. Chicago: University of Chicago Press, 2007.

Donkin, R. A. *Beyond Price: Pearls and Pearl Fishing: Origins to the Age of Discoveries*. Philadelphia: American Philosophical Society, 1998.

Donne, John. *Poems by J.D. with Elegies on the Author's Death*. London: John Marriot, 1635.

Dugan, Holly. *The Ephemeral History of Perfume*. Baltimore: Johns Hopkins University Press, 2011.

Duncan-Jones, Katherine. "Ravished and Revised: The 1616 Lucrece." *Review of English Studies* 52 (2001): 516–23.

Eamon, William. *Science and the Secrets of Nature*. Princeton, NJ: Princeton University Press, 1996.

Ebling, Florian. *The Secret History of Hermes Trismegistus: Hermeticism from Ancient to Modern Times*. Ithaca, NJ: Cornell University Press, 2007.

Edwards, Peter. *The Horse Trade of Tudor and Stuart England*. Cambridge: Cambridge University Press, 2004.

———. *Horse and Man in Early Modern England*. Hambeldon: Continuum, 2007.

Elviden, Edmund. *The most excellent and plesant metaphoricall historie of Pesistratus and Catanea*. London: Henry Bynneman, 1570.

Enterline, Lynn. *The Rhetoric of the Body from Ovid to Shakespeare*. Cambridge: Cambridge University Press, 2000.

———. "Rhetoric, Discipline, and the Theatricality of Everyday Life in Elizabethan Grammar Schools." In Peter Holland and Stephen Orgel, eds., *From Performance to Print in Shakespeare's England*. New York: Palgrave, 2006. 173–90.

———. *Shakespeare's Schoolroom: Rhetoric, Discipline, Emotion*. Philadelphia: University of Pennsylvania Press, 2012.

Epstein, Mortimer. *The Early History of the Levant Company*. London: Routledge, 1908.

Fineman, Joel. "Shakespeare's Will: The Temporality of Rape." *Representations* 10.20 (Autumn 1987): 25–76.

———. *The Subjectivity Effect in Western Literary Tradition: Essays Towards the Release of Shakespeare's Will.* Cambridge: MIT Press, 1991.

Finlay, Michael. *Western Writing Implements in the Age of the Quill Pen.* Wetheral, Scotland: Plains Books, 1990.

Fleming, Juliet. *Graffiti and the Writing Arts of Early Modern England.* Philadelphia: University of Pennsylvania Press, 2001.

Florio, John. *A Worlde of Wordes.* London: Edward Blount, 1598.

———. *The Essayes of Michael of Montaigne.* London: William Barret, 1605.

———. *Queene Anna's New World of Words.* London: Printed for Edward Blount and William Barret, 1611.

Floyd-Wilson, Mary. "English Epicures and Scottish Witches." *Shakespeare Quarterly* 57.2 (2006): 131–61.

———. *English Ethnicity and Race in Early Modern Drama.* Cambridge: Cambridge University Press, 2006.

Foucault, Michel. *The Order of Things: An Archeology of the Human Sciences.* New York: Vintage Books, 1994.

Frye, Susan. *Pens and Needles: Women's Textualities in Early Modern England.* Philadelphia: University of Pennsylvania Press, 2010.

Fudge, Erica. *Animal.* London: Reaktion, 2002.

———. *Perceiving Animals: Humans and Beasts in Early Modern English Culture.* Champaign: University of Illinois Press, 2002.

———. *Renaissance Beasts: of Animals, Humans, and Other Wonderful Creatures.* Champaign: University of Illinois Press, 2004.

———. *Pets.* London: Reaktion, 2008.

Fumerton, Patricia. *Cultural Aesthetics: Renaissance Literature and the Practice of Social Ornament.* Chicago: University of Chicago Press, 1991.

Games, Alison. *The Web of Empire: English Cosmopolitans in the Age of Expansion 1560–1660.* Oxford: Oxford University Press, 2008.

Gamon, Hannibal. *The Gouldesmythe's Storehouse* mss. The Folger Shakespeare Library V. a. 129. c. 1604.

Garner, Bryan A. "Shakespeare's Latinate Neologisms." *Shakespeare Studies* 15 (1982): 149–70.

Garrett, Valery. *Children of the Gods: Dress and Symbolism in China.* Hong Kong: Hong Kong Museum of History, 1990.

———. *Chinese Clothing: An Illustrated Guide.* Oxford: Oxford University Press, 1994.

———. *Chinese Dragon Robes.* Oxford: Oxford University Press, 1998.

Garter, Bernard. *The tragicall and true historie which happened betweene two English lovers.* London: Richard Tottel, 1565.

Gascoigne, George. *A Hundreth Sundry Flowers Bound up in One Small Poesie.* London: Printed for Richard Smith, 1573.

————. *The Posies of George Gascoigne Esquire*. London: Printed for Richard Smith, 1575.

————. *The Noble Art of Venerie*. London: Printed for Christopher Barker, 1575.

————. *The pleasauntest workes of George Gascoigne Esquyre newlye compyled into one volume, that is to say: his flowers, hearbes, weedes*. London: Printed for Richard Smith, 1587.

Gerard, John. *The Herball or Generall Historie of Plantes*. London: Printed for John Norton, 1597.

————. *The Herball or Generall historie of plantes. Gathered by Iohn Gerarde of London Master in Chirurgerie very much enlarged and amended by Thomas Iohnson citizen and apothecarye of London*. London: Adam Islip, Joyce Norton, and Richard Withers,1633

Gilchrist, Roberta. *Gender and Material Culture: The Archaeology of Medieval Women*. London: Routledge, 1994.

Gillespie, J. E. *The Influence of Overseas Expansion on England to 1700*. Columbia University Studies in History, Economics, and Public Laws, vol. 91. New York: Columbia University Press, 1920.

Gilman, Sander, and Zhou Yun, eds. *Smoke: A Global History of Smoking*. London: Reaktion Books, 2004.

Girouard, Marc. *Robert Smythson and the Elizabethan Country House*. New Haven, CT: Yale University Press, 1983.

Golahny, Amy. *Rembrandt's Reading*. Amsterdam: Amsterdam University Press, 2003.

Goldberg, Jonathan. *Writing Matter: From the Hands of the English Renaissance*. Palo Alto, CA: Stanford University Press, 1990.

Goldgar, Anne. *Tulipmania: Money, Honor, and Knowledge in the Dutch Golden Age*. Chicago: University of Chicago Press, 2007.

Golding, Arthur. *The XV bookes of P. Ouidius Naso, entytuled Metamorphosis, translated oute of Latin into English meeter by Arthur Golding Gentleman*. London: William Seres, 1567.

de Grazia, Margreta. "Imprints: Shakespeare, Gutenburg, Descartes." In Terence Hawkes, ed., *Alternative Shakespeares 2*. New York: Routledge, 1996. 63–94.

————. "Words as Things." *Shakespeare Studies* 28 (2000): 231–35.

————. "Hamlet the Intellectual." In Helen Small, ed., *The Public Intellectual*. Oxford: Blackwell Publishing, 2002. 89–109.

————. *Hamlet Without Hamlet*. Cambridge: Cambridge University Press, 2008.

de Grazia, Margreta, and Peter Stallybrass. "The Materiality of the Shakespearean Text." *Shakespeare Quarterly* (Fall 1993): 255–83.

Green, Joyce. "Speech, Silence, and History in *The Rape of Lucrece*," *Shakespeare Studies* 22 (1994): 77–103.

Greenblatt, Stephen. *The Swerve: How the World Became Modern*. New York: Norton, 2012.

Greene, Robert. *The History of Orlando Furioso*. London: Printed for Cuthbert Burbie, 1594.

Greene, Roland. *Post-Petrarchism: Origins and Innovations of the Western Lyric Sequence*. Princeton, NJ: Princeton University Press, 1991.

————. "Fictions of Immanence, Fictions of Embassy." In Elizabeth Fowler and Roland

Greene, eds., *The Project of Prose in Early Modern Europe and the New World*. Cambridge: Cambridge University Press, 1997.

——. *Unrequited Conquests: Love and Empire in the Colonial Americas*. Chicago: University of Chicago Press, 1999.

Greenstadt, Amy. "'Read It in Me': The Author's Will in *Lucrece*." *Shakespeare Quarterly* 57.1 (Spring 2006): 45–70.

Guerolt, Guillaume. *Le Premier Livre des Emblemes*. Lyons: Balthazar Arnoullet, 1550.

Guthrie, Kenneth Sylvan. *The Pythagorean Sourcebook and Library*. Grand Rapids, MI: Phanes Press, 1987.

Hakluyt, Richard. *The Principall Navigations*. London: George Bishop, Ralph Newberie, and Robert Barker, 1598–1600.

Hall, Edward. *The Union of the Two Noble and Illustrate famelies of Lancastre and Yorke*. London: Richard Grafton, 1548.

Hall, Kim F. *Things of Darkness: Economies of Race and Gender in Early Modern England*. Ithaca, NY: Cornell University Press, 1995.

——. "Culinary Spaces, Colonial Spaces: The Gendering of Sugar in the Seventeenth Century." In Valerie Traub, M. Lindsay Kaplan, and Dympna Callaghan, eds., *Feminist Readings of Early Modern Culture: Emerging Subjects*. Cambridge: Cambridge University Press, 1996. 168–90.

Harington, John. *Orlando Furioso in English Heroical Verse*. London: Richard Field, 1591.

Harkness, Deborah. *The Jewel House: Elizabethan London and the Scientific Revolution*. New Haven, CT: Yale University Press, 2007.

Harris, John Arthur. "Ophelia's Nothing: It Is the False Steward That Stole His Master's Daughter." *Hamlet Studies: An International Journal of Research on the Tragedie Hamlet, Prince of Denmark* 19.1–2 (Summer–Winter 1997): 20–46.

Harris, Jonathan Gil. *Untimely Matter in the Time of Shakespeare*. Philadelphia: University of Pennsylvania Press, 2008.

——. "Four Exoskeletons and No Funeral." *New Literary History* 2.4 (Autumn 2011): 615–39.

——. *Indography: Writing the Indian in Early Modern England*. New York: Palgrave Macmillan, 2012.

Harris, Stephen L., and Gloria Platzner, eds. *Classical Mythology: Images and Insights*. New York: Mayfield Publishing, 1998.

Harvey, Gabriel. *Fovre Letters, and certaine sonnets: Especially touching Robert Greene, and other parties by him abused: But incidentally of divers excellent persons, and some others of note*. London: John Wolfe, 1592.

——. *Pierces Supererogation or A new prayse of the old asse*. London: John Wolfe, 1593.

Harvey, John. *his translation of the learned worke, of Hermes Trismegistus, intituled, Iatromathematica . . .* London: Richard Watkins, 1583.

Helgerson, Richard. *Forms of Nationhood: The Elizabethan Writing of England*. Chicago: University of Chicago Press, 1992.

Heng, Gerladine. *Empire of Magic: Medieval Romance and the Politics of Cultural Fantasy*. New York: Columbia University Press, 2003.

Heywood, Thomas. *The Rape of Lucrece*. London: Printed for I. Busby, 1608.

Hicock, Thomas. *The voyage and trauaile of M. Caesar Frederick, merchant of Venice, into the East India, the Indies, and beyond the Indies*. London: Richard Jones and Edward White, 1588.

Higgins, Dick. *Pattern Poetry: Guide to an Unknown Literature*. Albany: SUNY Press, 1987.

Hillman, David. "Visceral Knowledge: Shakespeare, Skepticism, and the Interior of the Early Modern Body." In David Hillman and Carla Mazzio, eds., *The Body in Parts: Fantasies of Corporeality in Early Modern Europe*. New York: Routledge, 1997. 81–105.

Hollander, John. *Vision and Resonance: Two Senses of Poetic Form*. Oxford: Oxford University Press, 1975.

Hollings, Marion. "Romancing the Turk: Trade, Race, and Nation in Spenser's Faerie Queene." In Debra Johanyak and Walter S. Lim, eds., *The English Renaissance, Orientalism, and the Idea of Asia*. New York: Palgrave, 2010. 51–76.

Hollyband, Claudius. *Dictionarie of French and English*. London: Thomas Woodcock, 1593.

———. *The Italian Schoole-maister*. London: Thomas Purfoot, 1597, 1608.

The Holy Bible Conteyning the Old Testament, and the New. London: Robert Barker, 1611.

Homer. *Iliad*. Ed. and trans. Richmond Lattimore. Chicago: University of Chicago Press, 1961.

Hooks, Adam. "Shakespeare at the White Greyhound." *Shakespeare Survey* 64 (2011): 260–75.

Horapollo. *Hieroglyphica*. Paris: Jacques Kerver, 1543.

Hunter, Michael, ed. *Printed Images in Early Modern Britain: Essays in Interpretation*. Aldershot: Ashgate, 2010.

Hyman, Wendy Beth. "Mathematical Experiments of Long Silver Pipes: The Early Modern Figure of the Mechanical Bird." In Wendy Beth Hyman, ed., *The Automaton in Renaissance Literature*. Burlington, VT: Ashgate, 2011.

Inalcik, Halil, with Donald Quataert. *An Economic and Social History of the Ottoman Empire Vol. I 1300–1600*. Cambridge: Cambridge University Press, 1994.

———. *The Ottoman Empire: The Classical Age, 1300–1600*. London: Phoenix Press, 2000.

Iyengar, Sujata. *Shades of Difference: Mythologies of Skin Color in Early Modern England*. Philadelphia: University of Pennsylvania Press, 2005.

Jacob, Margaret C. *Strangers Nowhere in the World: The Rise of Early Modern Cosmopolitanism*. Philadelphia: University of Pennsylvania Press, 2008.

Jacobson, Miriam. "The Elizabethan Cipher in Shakespeare's Lucrece." *Studies in Philology* 107.3 (Summer 2010): 336–59.

———. "'Sweets Compacted': Posies and the Poems of George Herbert." In Christopher Hodgkins, ed., *George Herbert's Travels*. Newark: University of Delaware Press, 2011. 227–49.

Jaffe, Michele Sharon. *The Story of O: Prostitutes and Other Good-for-Nothings in the Renaissance*. Cambridge, MA: Harvard University Press, 1999.

James, Heather. "Shakespeare and Classicism." In Patrick Cheney, ed., *The Cambridge Companion to Shakespeare's Poetry*. Cambridge: Cambridge University Press, 2007. 202–20.

———. "Ovid in English Renaissance Literature." In Peter Knox, ed., *A Companion to Ovid*. Oxford: Wiley-Blackwell, 2009.

———. "Shakespeare's Classical Plays." In Margreta de Grazia and Stanley Wells, eds., *The New Cambridge Companion to Shakespeare*. Cambridge: Cambridge University Press, 2010. 154–55.

Jardine, Lisa. *Worldly Goods: A New History of the Renaissance*. New York: W. W. Norton, 1998.

Jed, Stephanie. *Chaste Thinking: The Rape of Lucretia and the Rise of Humanism*. Bloomington: Indiana University Press, 1989.

Johnson, W. R. "The Problem of Counter-Classical Sensibility and Its Critics." *California Studies in Classical Antiquity* 3 (1970): 123–51.

Jonson, Ben. *Poetaster, or the Arraignment*. London: Printed for M. Lownes, 1602.

———. *The Characters of Two Royall Masques the one of Blacknesse, the other of Beautie*. London: Printed for Thomas Thorp, 1608.

———. *The Workes of Beniamin Jonson*. London: William Stansby, 1616.

———. *Q. Horatius Flaccus: His Arte of Poetry Englished by Ben. Jonson*. Ed. Sir Kenelm Digby. London:, 1640.

———. *Timber, or Discoveries Made upon Men and Matter*. Ed. Sir Kenelm Digby. London: 1641.

———. *Poetaster*. Ed. Tom Cain. Manchester: St. Martin's Press, 1995.

———. *The Devil Is an Ass: And Other Plays*. Ed. Margaret Jane Kidnie. Oxford: Oxford University Press, 2009.

Johnson, Stephen. "Robert Recorde (c. 1512–1558)." *Oxford Dictionary of National Biography* online. Oxford: Oxford University Press, 2004–13.

Junius, Hadrianus. *Emblemata*. Antwerp: Christophe Plantin, 1565.

Kaplan, Robert. *The Nothing That Is: A Natural History of Zero*. Oxford: Oxford University Press, 1999.

Karpinski, Louis Charles, and David Eugene Smith. *The Hindu-Arabic Numerals*. Boston: Ginn and Company, 1911.

Keilen, Sean. "English Literature in its Golden Age." In Leonard Barkin, Bradin Cormack, and Sean Keilen, eds., *The Forms of Renaissance Thought*. New York: Palgrave, 2008. 47–50.

Kilgour, Maggie. "Eve and Flora." *Milton Quarterly* 38:1 (2004): 1–17.

Kinney, Arthur F., and Linda Bradley Salomon, eds. *Nicholas Hilliard's Art of Limning*. Boston: Northeastern University Press, 1983.

Klein, Ernest. *A Comprehensive Etymological Dictionary of the Hebrew Language*. Haifa, Israel: University of Haifa Press, 1987.

Knapp, Jeffrey. *An Empire Nowhere: England, America, and Literature from Utopia to The Tempest*. Berkeley: University of California Press, 1994.

Knolles, Richard. *A Generall Historie of the Turks*. London: Adam Islip, 1603.

Korn, A. L. "Puttenham and the Oriental Pattern Poem." *Comparative Literature* 6 (1954): 289–303.

Krstic, Tijana. *Contested Conversions to Islam: Narratives of Religious Change in the Early Modern Ottoman Empire*. Palo Alto, CA: Stanford University Press.

Kuriyama, Shigehisa. *Expressiveness of the Body and the Divergence of Greek and Chinese Medicine*. New York: Zone Books, 1999. 233–70.

Lacquer, Thomas. *Making Sex: Body and Gender from the Greeks to Freud*. Cambridge, MA: Harvard University Press, 1990.

Landry, Donna. *Noble Brutes: How Eastern Horses Transformed English Culture*. Baltimore: Johns Hopkins University Press, 2009.

Latour, Bruno. "The Berlin Key or How to Do Words with Things." In P. M. Graves-Brown, ed., *Matter, Materiality, and Modern Culture*. Trans. Lydia Davis. London: Routledge, 2000. 10–21.

———. *Reassembling the Social: An Introduction to Actor-Network Theory*. Oxford: Oxford University Press, 2008.

Lee, Sidney. "Introduction." *Shakespeare's Lucrece: Being a Reproduction in Facsimile of the First Edition 1594*. Oxford: Clarendon Press, 1905.

Liddell, H. G., R. Scott, and Henry Stuart Jones, *Greek-English Lexicon*. Oxford: Clarendon Press, 1996.

Ligon, Richard. *A True & Exact History of the Island of Barbados*. London: Humphrey Moseley, 1657.

Lim, Walter S. "John Milton, Orientalism, and the Empires of the East in *Paradise Lost*." In Debra Johanyak and Walter S. H. Lim, eds., *The English Renaissance, Orientalism, and the Idea of Asia*. New York: Palgrave, 2010. 203–36.

Linschoten, Jan Huygen. *Iohn Huighen van Linschoten his Discours of Voyages into ye Easte & West Indies*. London: Printed for John Wolfe, 1598.

Lipson, Hod, and Melba Kurman. *Fabricated: The New World of 3D Printing*. Oxford: Wiley Blackwell, 2013.

Lloyd, Lodowick. *The Pilgrimage of Princes*. London: John Wolfe, 1573.

Lodge, Thomas. *Rosalynde*. London: Printed for T.G. and John Bushie, 1592.

Loomba, Ania. *Shakespeare, Race, and Colonialism*. Oxford: Oxford University Press, 2002.

Lucretius. *The Way Things Are: The De Rerum Natura of Titus Lucretius Carus*. Trans. Rolph Humphries. Bloomington: Indiana University Press, 1968.

———. *De Rerum Natura*. Trans. Anthony M. Esolen, Baltimore: Johns Hopkins University Press, 1995.

Lyte, Henry. *A niewe Herball, or historie of plants*. London: Gerard Dewes, 1578.

MacGregor, Arthur, and Oliver Impey. *The Origin of Museums: The Cabinet of Curiosities in Sixteenth and Seventeenth Century Europe*. Cornwall: House of Stratus, 2001.

Mackay, Charles. *Extraordinary Popular Delusions and the Madness of Crowds*. Hampshire: Harriman House, 2003.

Mandeville, John. *The Travels of Sir John Mandeville*. Ed. C. W. R. D. Mosely. New York: Penguin, 1983.

Markham, Gervase. *A discource of horsmanshippe* ... London: Printed for Richard Smith, 1593.

————. *How to chuse, ride, traine, and diet, both hunting-horses and running horses.* London: Printed for Richard Smith, 1595.

————. *Cauelarice, or The English horseman.* London: Printed for Edward White, 1607.

————. *The English Arcadia.* London: Edward Alde, 1607.

————. *Country Contentments in two books ... the second intitled, The English Huswife.* London: Printed for Roger Jackson, 1615.

————. *Markhams faithfull farrier.* London: Printed for Michael Sparke, 1631.

Marlowe, Christopher. *Epigrammes and elegies. By I. D. and C. M.* London: 1599.

————. *All Ovid's Elegies, 3 Books, by C. M.* London: 1603.

————. *Christopher Marlowe: The Complete Poems and Translations.* Ed. Stephen Orgel. New York: Penguin Classics, 2007.

Marlowe, Christopher, and George Chapman. *Hero and Leander, begun by Christopher Marlowe and finished by G. Chapman.* London: Paul Linley, 1598.

Marston, John. *The Malcontent.* London: Printed by Valentine Simmes for William Aspley, 1604.

Mascall, Leonard. *A profitable booke declaring dyuers approoued remedies.* London: Thomas Purfoote, 1588.

Mason, Laura. *Sugar-Plums and Sherbet: The Prehistory of Sweets.* Blackhawton, Devon: Prospect Books, 2004.

Mastai, Marie-Louise d'Ortange. *Illusion in Art: Trompe-l'Oeil: A History of Pictorial Illusionism.* Norwalk, CT: Abaris Books, 1976.

Masten, Jeffrey. "Pressing Subjects, or the Secret Lives of Shakespeare's Compositors." In Peter Stallybrass and Nancy Vickers, eds., *Language Machines: Technologies of Literary and Cultural Production.* New York: Routledge, 1997. 75–107.

————. "Toward a Queer Address: The Taste of Letters and Early Modern Male Friendship." *GLQ: A Journal of Gay and Lesbian Studies* 10.3 (2004): 367–84.

————. *Queer Philologies: Language, Sex, and Affect in Shakespeare's Time.* Philadelphia: University of Pennsylvania Press, 2014.

Matar, Nabil. *Islam in Britain.* Cambridge: Cambridge University Press, 1998.

————. *Turks, Moors, and Englishmen in the Age of Discovery.* New York: Columbia University Press, 1999.

————. *Britain and Barbary.* Gainesville: University Press of Florida, 2005.

May, Robert. *The Accomplisht Cooke, or the Art and Mystery of Cookery.* London: Printed for Nathaniel Brooke, 1660.

McJannet, Linda. *The Sultan Speaks: Dialogue in English Plays and Histories About the Ottoman Turks.* New York: Palgrave, 2006.

McKendry, Maxime de la Falaise. *Seven Centuries of English Cooking.* London: Weinfeld and Nicholson, 1973.

McKerrow, Ronald B. *Printers' & Publishers' Devices in England & Scotland 1485–1640.* London: Chiswick Press for the Bibliographical Society of London, 1913.

McLane, Maureen. *Balladeering, Minstrelsy, and the Making of British Romantic Poetry.* Cambridge: Cambridge University Press, 2011.

Melehy, Hassan. "Spenser and du Bellay, Translation, Imitation, Ruin." *Comparative Literature Studies* 40.4 (2003): 415–38.

———. *The Politics of Literary Transfer in Early Modern France and England.* Burlington: Ashgate, 2010. 182–83.

Menke, Richard. *Telegraphic Realism: Victorian Fiction and Other Information Systems.* Palo Alto, CA: Stanford University Press, 2007.

Menon, Madhavi. "Spurning Teleology in Venus and Adonis." *GLQ: A Journal of Gay and Lesbian Studies* 11.4 (2005): 491–519.

———. "Introduction: Queer Shakes." In Madhavi Menon, ed., *Shakesqueer: A Queer Companion to the Complete Works of Shakespeare.* Durham, NC: Duke University Press, 2011. 1–27.

Mentz, Steve. *At the Bottom of Shakespeare's Ocean.* London: Continuum, 2009.

Meres, Francis. *Palladis Tamia, Wits Treasury.* London: Printed for Cuthbert Burbie, 1598.

Middleton, Thomas. *The Ghost of Lucrece.* London: Valentine Simmes, 1601.

Mintz, Sidney. *Sweetness and Power: The Place of Sugar in Modern History.* New York: Elizabeth Sifton Viking Books, 1985.

Montagu, Jennifer. *Roman Baroque Sculpture: The Industry of Art.* New Haven, CT: Yale University Press, 1989.

Morgan, Diane. *Fire and Blood: Rubies in Myth, Magic, and History.* Westport, CT: Greenwood, 2008.

Morgan, Jennifer Lyle. *Laboring Women: Reproduction and Gender in New World Slavery.* Philadelphia: University of Pennsylvania Press, 2004.

Moryson, Fynes. *An Itinerary.* London: J. Beale, 1617.

Moul, Victoria. "Translation as Commentary? The Case of Ben Jonson's *Ars Poetica*." *Palimpsests* 20 (2007): 59–77.

Moxon, Joseph. *Mechanic Exercises on the Whole Art of Printing.* Ed. Herbert Davis and Harry Carter. London: 1683; York: Dover, 1978.

Munroe, Jennifer, ed. *Making Gardens of Their Own: Advice for Women, 1550–1750.* In Betty S. Travitsky and Anne Lake Prescott, eds., *The Early Modern Englishwoman: A Facsimile Library of Essential Works: Series III: Essential Works for the Study of Early Modern Women, Part 3, Vol. 1.* Burlington, VT: Ashgate, 2007.

Murphy, James J., ed. *Three Medieval Rhetorical Arts.* Berkeley: University of California Press, 1971, 1985.

Murrell, John. *A Daily Exercise for Ladies and Gentlewomen.* London: Printed for the widow Helme, 1617.

Murrin, Michael. "Spenser and the Search for Asian Silk." *Arthuriana* 21.1 (2011): 7–19.

Musaeus, Grammaticus. *Musei opousculum de Herone & Leandro.* Trans. Marcus Musurus. Venice: Aldus Manutius, 1517.

Nashe, Thomas. *The Vnfortunate Traveller.* London: Printed for Cuthbert Burbie, 1594.

———. *The Works of Thomas Nashe Edited from the Original Texts.* Ed. Ronald B. McKerrow. London: Sidgwick and Jackson, 1904–10.

Neill, Michael. *Issues of Death: Mortality and Identity in English Renaissance Tragedy.* Oxford: Oxford University Press, 1997.

Nicholson, Catherine. *Uncommon Tongues: Eloquence and Eccentricity in the English Renaissance*. Philadelphia: University of Pennsylvania Press, 2014.

Nicolay, Nicholas de. *The navigations, peregrinations and voyages, made into Turkie by Nicholas Nicholay Daulphinois*. Trans. Thomas Washington. London: T. Dawson, 1585.

Noble, Louise. *Medicinal Cannibalism in Early Modern English Literature and Culture*. New York: Palgrave, 2011.

Ocland, Christopher. *The valiant actes And victorious Battailes of the English nation*. Trans. John Sharrock. London: Robert Waldegrave, 1585.

Oppian. *Cynegetica*. Loeb Classical Library No. 219. Trans. A. W. Mair. Cambridge, MA: Harvard University Press, 1928.

Orgel, Stephen. *The Illusion of Power: Political Theater in the English Renaissance*. Berkeley: University of California Press, 1975.

Ostashevsky, Eugene. "Crooked Figures: Zero in Hindo-Arabic Notation in Shakespeare's *Henry V*." In David Glimp and Michelle Warren, eds., *Arts of Calculation: Quantifying Thought in Early Modern Europe*. New York: Palgrave, 2004.

Ovid. *Ovid: Metamorphoses Translated by Rolphe Humphries*. Bloomington: Indiana University Press, 1955, 1983.

———. *Fasti*. Ed. and trans. A. J. Boyle and Roger D. Woodward. New York: Penguin Classics, 2002.

———. *Metamorphoses*. Trans. Arthur Golding. Ed. Madeleine Forey. Baltimore: Johns Hopkins University Press, 2002.

———. *The Metamorphoses of Ovid*. Trans. Allen Mandelbaum. New York: Harcourt Brace, 1995.

The Oxford English Dictionary. Oxford: Oxford University Press, 2011.

Parker, Charles H. *Global Interactions in the Early Modern Age*. Cambridge: Cambridge University Press, 2011.

Parker, Patricia. *Shakespeare from the Margins: Language, Culture, Context*. Chicago: University of Chicago Press, 1996.

———. "*Black* Hamlet: Battening on the Moor." *Shakespeare Studies* 31 (2003): 127–64.

Parkinson, John. *Paradisi in Sole*. London: Humfrey Lownes and Robert Young, 1629.

Partridge, John. *The Treasurie of Commodious Conceits*. London: Richard Jones, 1573.

Passannante, Gerard. *The Lucretian Renaissance: Philology and the Afterlife of Tradition*. Chicago: University of Chicago Press, 2011.

Pastoreau, Michel. *The Devil's Cloth: A History of Stripes*. New York: Columbia University Press, 2001.

———. *Black: The History of a Color*. Princeton, NJ: Princeton University Press, 2008.

Pausanias. *Graecae Descriptio*. Florence: Xylander & von Silberg, 1583.

———. *Description of Greece*. Vol. 2. Ed. and trans. W. H. S. Jones and H. A. Omerod. Cambridge, MA: Harvard University Press, 1918.

Peck, Linda Levy. *Consuming Splendor: Society and Literature in Seventeenth Century England*. Cambridge: Cambridge University Press, 2005.

Petrarca, Francesco. *Letters on Familiar Matters (Rerum familiarum libri)*. Vols. 1 and 3. Trans. Aldo S. Bernardo. Baltimore: Johns Hopkins University Press, 1975–2005.

Pettie, George. *The Ciuile Conversation of M. Stephen Guazzo* . . . London: Richard Watkins, 1581.

Picinelli, *Mundus Symbolicus*. Ed. and trans. August Erath. New York: Garland, 1976.

Plat, Hugh. *The iewell house of art and nature*. London: Peter Short, 1594.

———. *The Floures of Philosophie*. London: Henry Bynneman, 1572.

———. *Delights for Ladies*. London: Peter Short, 1600.

———. *A Closet for Ladies and Gentlewomen*. London: Printed for Arthur Johnson, 1608.

Plato. *Plato: Complete Works*. Ed. John M. Cooper. Indianapolis, IN: Hackett, 1997.

Platz, Norbert H. *Jonson's Ars Poetica: An Interpretation of Poetaster in Its Historical Context*. Salzburg: Salzburg Studies in English Literature, 1973.

Pliny. *The History of the World, Commonly called the Natural History of G. Plinius Secundus*. Trans. Philemon Holland. London: Adam Islip, 1601.

della Porta, Giambattista. *Natural Magick*. Trans. Anon. London: Thomas Young and Samuel Speed, 1658.

Preminger, Alex, ed. *The Princeton Handbook of Poetic Terms*. Princeton, NJ: Princeton University Press, 1986.

Purchas, Samuel. *Purchas his Pilgrimmage*. London: Printed for Henry Featherstone, 1613.

Puttenham, George. *The Arte of English Poesie*. London: Richard Field, 1589.

———. *The Art of English Poesy by George Puttenham: A Critical Edition*. Ed. Frank Whigham and Wayne A. Rebhorn. Ithaca, NY: Cornell University Press, 2007.

Pyles, Thomas. "Ophelia's Nothing." *Modern Language Notes* 64 (May 1949): 322–23.

Raber, Karen, and Treva Tucker, eds. *The Culture of the Horse: Status, Discipline, and Identity in the Early Modern World*. New York: Palgrave, 2005.

Raman, Shankar. *Framing India: The Cultural Imaginary in Early Modern England*. Palo Alto, CA: Stanford University Press, 2001.

Rambuss, Richard. *Spenser's Secret Career*. Cambridge: Cambridge University Press, 1993.

Rebhorn, Wayne A. "Petruchio's Rape Tricks: *The Taming of the Shrew* and the Renaissance Discourse of Rhetoric." *Modern Philology* 92.3 (1995): 294–327.

———. "Outlandish Fears: Defining Decorum in Renaissance Rhetoric." *Intertexts* 4.1 (2000): 3–24.

Recorde, Robert. *The Grõnd of Artes Teachyng the Worke and Pra-ctise of Arthmetike*. London: R. Wolfe, 1543.

Relihan, Constance C. "Barbaby Riche's Appropriation of Ireland and the Mediterranean World, or How Irish Is 'The Turk.'" In Goran Stanivukovic, ed., *Re-Mapping the Mediterranean World in Early Modern English Writings*. New York: Palgrave, 2007. 179–90.

Riggs, David. *Ben Jonson: A Life*. Cambridge, MA: Harvard University Press, 1989.

Richardson, Tim. *Sweets: A History of Candy*. London: Bloomsbury, 2002.

Robertson, Elizabeth. *Early English Devotional Prose and the Female Audience*. Knoxville: University of Tennessee Press, 1990.

Robinson, Benedict S. *Islam and Early Modern English Literature: The Politics of Romance from Spenser to Milton*. New York: Palgrave, 2007.

———. "Green Seraglios: Tulips, Turbans, and the Global Market." *Journal of Early Modern Cultural Studies* 9.1 (2009): 93–122.

Rotman, Brian. *Signifying Nothing: The Semiotics of Zero*. Palo Alto, CA: Stanford University Press, 1993.

Rowland, Richard. *Thomas Heywood's Theatre, 1599–1639: Locations, Translations, and Conflict*. Aldershot: Ashgate, 2010.

Said, Edward. *Orientalism*. New York: Vintage Books, 1979, 1994.

Sale, Carolyn. "Eating Air, Feeling Smells: Hamlet's Theory of Performance." *Renaissance Drama* 35 (2006): 145–70.

Sambucus, Johannes. *Les Emblemes*. Antwerp: Christophe Plantin, 1567.

Sanders, Eve Rachele. *Gender and Literacy on Stage in Early Modern England*. Cambridge: Cambridge University Press, 1996.

Sandys, George. *A Relation of a Iourney begun anno dom. 1610*. London: Printed by Richard Field for W. Barrett, 1615.

Saunders, Gill. "'Paper Tapestry' and 'Wooden Pictures': Printed Decoration in the Domestic Interior Before 1700." In Michael Hunter, ed., *Printed Images in Early Modern Britain*. Farnham: Ashgate, 2010.

Scheinberg, Susan. "The Bee Maidens of the Homeric Hymn to Hermes." *Harvard Studies in Classical Philology* 83 (1979): 1–28.

Scott, Alison V. *Languages of Luxury in Early Modern England*. Burlington, VT: Ashgate, 2013.

Seaman, William. *The Reign of Sultan Orchan Second King of the Turks. Translated out of Hojah Effendi, an eminient Turkish Historian. By William Seaman*. London: T. R. and E. M., 1652.

Seife, Charles. *Zero: The Biography of a Dangerous Idea*. New York: Penguin, 2000.

Seneca. *Seneca His Tenne Tragedies, Translated into English*. London: Thomas Marsh, 1581.

Shakespeare, William. *Lucrece*. London: John Harrison, 1594.

———. *Venus and Adonis*. London: Richard Field, 1594.

———. *The chronicle history of Henry the fift*. London: Printed for Thomas Millington and John Busby, 1600.

———. *The Tragicall Historie of Hamlet, Prince of Denmark*. London: Printed for Nicholas Ling, 1604.

———. *Titus Andronicus*. Ed. Jonathan Bate. New York: Arden Shakespeare: Third Series, 1995.

———. *The Norton Shakespeare*. Ed. Stephen Greenblatt, Walter Cohen, Jean Howard, and Katherine Eisaman Maus. New York: W. W. Norton & Company, 1997–2008.

———. *Twelfth Night, or What You Will. Texts and Contexts*. Ed. Bruce Smith. New York: Palgrave, 2001.

———. *William Shakespeare: The Complete Sonnets and Poems*. Ed. Colin Burrow. Oxford: Oxford University Press, 2002.

————. *Shakespeare: The Poems*. Ed. John Roe. Cambridge: Cambridge University Press, 2006.

————. *Shakespeare's Poems*. Ed. Katherine Duncan Jones and H. R. Woudhuysen. 3rd ser. London: Arden Shakespeare, 2007.

Shannon, Laurie. "The Eight Animals in Shakespeare; or, Before the Human" *PMLA* 124.2 (March 2009): 472–79.

Sherman, William H. *Used Books: Marking Readers in Renaissance England*. Philadelphia: University of Pennsylvania Press, 2008.

Shipley, Joseph Twadell. *The Origins of English Words: A Discursive Dictionary of Indo-European Roots*. Baltimore: Johns Hopkins University Press, 1984.

Showalter, Elaine. "Representing Ophelia: Women, Madness, and the Responsibilities of Feminist Criticism." In Patricia Parker and Geoffrey Harman, eds., *Shakespeare and the Question of Theory*. New York: Methuen, 1985.

Sidney, Philip. *Sir P. S. His Astrophel and Stella*. London: Printed for Thomas Newman, 1591.

————. *The Countesse of Pembrokes Arcadia*. Oxford: Oxford University Press, 1999.

————. *Sir Philip Sidney's An Apology for Poetry and Astrophil and Stella: Texts and Contexts*. Ed. Peter C. Herman. Glen Allen, VA: College Publishing, 2001.

————. *An Apology for Poetry (or the Defense of Poesy)*. Ed. R. W. Maslen. 3rd ed., Manchester: Manchester University Press, 2002.

Sigler, L. E., trans. *Fibonacci's Liber Abaci*. New York: Springer-Verlag, 2002.

Simpson, D. P. *Cassell's Latin Dictionary*. New York: Macmillan, 1959, 1968.

Singh, Jyotsna. "Post-colonial Criticism." In Stanley Wells and Lena Cowen Orlin, eds., *Shakespeare: An Oxford Guide*. Oxford: Oxford University Press, 2003. 492–507.

Skilleter, S. A. *William Harborne and the Trade with Turkey 1578–1582*. London: British Academy, 1977.

Smith, Bruce. *The Acoustic World of Early Modern England: Attending to the O-Factor*. Chicago: University of Chicago Press, 1999.

Smith, G. Gregory, ed. *Elizabethan Critical Essays*. Oxford: Clarendon Press, 1904.

Smith, Ian. *Race and Rhetoric in Early Modern England: Barbarian Errors*. New York: Palgrave Macmillan, 2009.

Smyrnaeus, Quintus. *The Fall of Troy*. Trans. A. S. Way. Loeb Classical Library. Cambridge, MA: Harvard University Press, 1962.

Spenser, Edmund. *The Shepheardes Calender*. London: Hugh Singleton, 1579.

————. *The Faerie Queene*. London: William Ponsonby, 1590.

————. *Complaints*. London: William Ponsonby, 1591.

————. *The Faerie Queene*. London: William Ponsonby, 1596.

————. *Edmund Spenser: The Shorter Poems*. Ed. Richard A. McCabe. New York: Penguin Classics, 2000.

————. *A View of the Present State of Ireland*. Ed. Andrew Hatfield and Willy Maley. Oxford: Blackwell, 2003.

Spiller, Elizabeth. "Introduction." In Betty S. Travitsky and Anne Lake Prescott, eds.,

Seventeenth Century English Recipe Books: Cooking, Physic, and Chirurgery in the Works of Elizabeth Talbot Grey and Alethia Talbot Howard. Aldershot: Ashgate, 2008. ix–li.

Spurgeon, Caroline. *Shakespeare's Imagery and What It Tells Us*. Cambridge: Cambridge University Press, 1935.

Stallybrass, Peter. "Books and Scrolls: Navigating the Bible." In Jennifer Andersen and Elizabeth Sauer, eds., *Books and Readers in Early Modern England*. Philadelphia: University of Pennsylvania Press, 2011. 42–79.

Stanford, John Frederick, and Charles Augustus Maude Fennell. *The Stanford Dictionary of Anglicized Words and Phrases*. Cambridge: Cambridge University Press, 1892.

Stanyhurst, Richard. *First Foure Bookes of Virgil his Aeneid*. Leiden: John Pates, 1582.

Stapleton, M. L. "Spenser, the *Antiquitez de Rome*, and the Development of the English Sonnet Form." *Comparative Literature Studies* 27.4 (1990): 259–74.

Staplyton, John. *Musaeus on the Loues of Hero and Leander*. London: Humphrey Moseley, 1646.

Stevens, Paul. "*Paradise Lost* and the Colonial Imperative." In J. Martin Evans, ed., *John Milton: Twentieth Century Perspectives*, vol. 4: *Paradise Lost*. London: Routledge, 2003. 193–211.

Stevenson, Jane. "Richard Ligon and the Theatre of Empire." In Allan I. Macinnes and Arthur H. Williamson, eds., *Shaping the Stuart World 1603–1714: The Atlantic Connection*. Leiden: Brill, 2006. 285–310.

Stewart, Alan. "Come from Turkie: Mediterranean Trade in Late Elizabethan London." In Goran Stanivukovic, ed., *Remapping the Mediterranean World in Early Modern English Writings*. New York: Palgrave, 2007. 157–78.

Stewart, Charles, and Rosalind Shaw, eds. *Syncretism/Anti-Syncretism*. London: Routledge, 1994.

Stewart, Susan. *Poetry and the Fate of the Senses*. Chicago: University of Chicago Press, 2002.

Sufur, Sener. *Türc Safo'su Mihri Hatun: Belgesel Anlati*. Istanbul: A D Yayincilik, 1997.

Sugg, Richard. *Mummies, Cannibals, and Vampires: The History of Corpse Medicine from the Renaissance to the Victorians*. London: Routledge, 2011.

Summit, Jennifer. *Lost Property: The Woman Writer and English Literary History 1380–1589*. Chicago: University of Chicago Press, 2000.

Test, Edward M. "Amerindian Eden: the Divine Weeks of Du Bartas." In Ken Hiltner, Stephanie LeMenanger, and Teresa Shewry, eds., *Environmental Criticism for the Twenty-first Century*. New York: Routledge, 2012. 121–34.

Thevêt, André. *Cosmographie du Levant*. Lyon: Jean de Tournes and Guillaume Gazeau,1556.

———. *La cosmographie universelle*. Paris: Chez Guillaume Chaudière, 1575.

Thynne, Francis. *Emblemes and Epigrames*. Ed. Frederick James Furnivall. London: N. Trubner and Co. for the Early English Text Society, 1876.

Tory, Geoffrey. *Champ Fleury by Geofroy Tory*. Ed. and trans. George B. Ives. New York: Grolier Club Press, 1927.

Turner, Henry. *The English Renaissance Stage: Geometry, Poetics, and the Practical Spatial Arts 1580–1630*. Oxford: Oxford University Press, 2006, 2011.

Tusser, Thomas. *Five Hundreth Points of Good Husbandrie*. London: Richard Tottel, 1573.

Van der Noot, Jan. *A Theatre for Worldlings*. London: Henry Bynneman, 1569.

Vickers, Nancy. "This Heraldry in Lucrece' Face." *Poetics Today*. 6.1–2 (1985): 171–84.

Vine, Angus. *In Defiance of Time: Antiquarian Writing in Early Modern England*. Oxford: Oxford University Press, 2010.

Virgil. *I. Eclogues, Georgics, Aeneid*. Loeb Classical Library. Trans. Rushton Fairclough. Cambridge, MA: Harvard University Press, 1916.

Viswanathan, Gauri. *Masks of Conquest: Literary Study and British Rule in India*. New York: Columbia University Press, 1989.

Vitkus, Daniel. *Turning Turk: English Theatre and the Multicultural Mediterranean 1570–1630*. New York: Palgrave, 2003.

W. M., *The Queens closet opened: incomparable secrets in physick, chyurgery, preserving and candying, and cookery*. London: Printed for Nathaniel Brook,1655.

Wall, Wendy. "'Just a Spoonful of Sugar': Syrup and Domesticity in Early Modern England." *Modern Philology* 104.2 (2006): 149–72.

———. "Reading for the Blot: Textual Desire in Early Modern English Literature." In David M. Bergeron, ed., *Reading and Writing in Shakespeare*. Newark: University of Delaware Press, 1996. 131–59.

———. *Staging Domesticity: Household Work and English Identity in Early Modern Drama*. Cambridge: Cambridge University Press, 2002. 44–51.

Ward, Joseph B. *Violence, Politics, and Gender in Early Modern England*. New York: Palgrave, 2008.

Watt, James C. *When Silk Was Gold: Central Asian and Chinese Textiles*. New York: Metropolitan Museum of Art in cooperation with the Cleveland Museum of Art, 1997.

Whitney, Isabella. *A Sweet Nosgay or Pleasant Posye: Contayning a Hundred and Ten Phylosophicall Flowers*. London: R. Jones, 1573.

Wilbern, David. "Shakespeare's 'Nothing.'" In Murray M. Schwartz and Coppélia Kahn, eds., *Representing Shakespeare: New Psychoanalytic Essays*. Baltimore: Johns Hopkins University Press, 1981. 244–63.

Williams, George Walton. "Antique Romans and Modern Danes in *Hamlet* and *Julius Caesar*." In Vincent Newey and Ann Thompson, eds., *Literature and Nationalism*. Liverpool: Liverpool University Press, 1991.

Williams, Mary C. "Much Ado About Chastity in *Much Ado About Nothing*." *Renaissance Papers* 41(1984): 37–45.

Wilson, Robert. *The Three Ladies of London*. London: Roger Warde, 1584.

Wilson, Thomas. *The Arte of Rhetorique*. London: Richard Grafton, 1553.

Withals, John. *A short dictionarie most profitable for young beginners*. London: Thomas Purfoot, 1568.

———. *A dictionarie in English and Latine for children, and yong beginners*. London: Thomas Purfoot, 1608.

Wood, Alfred Cecil. *A History of the Levant Company*. Oxford: Oxford University Press, 1935.

Wooley, Hannah. *The Accomplisht ladys delight in preserving, physic and cookery*. London: Printed for B. Harris, 1675.

Index

Page references in italics refer to illustrations.

Acknowledgments

Like an exotic import, this project has traveled long and far. First, I thank Margreta de Grazia for introducing me to early modern material philology and for instilling in me the discipline, focus, and patience required to write a book like this. I would also like to thank the following exemplary faculty and graduate students I encountered while at the University of Pennsylvania and Oxford, who lent me their ears and thoughts when I began to wonder what happened to classical antiquity in early modern English poetry: Rebecca Bushnell, Rita Copeland, Urvashi Chakravarty, Jane Degenhardt, Stephanie Elsky, Jennifer Higginbotham, Rayna Kalas, Sean Keilen, Erika Lin, Diane Purkiss, Matthew Niblett, Catherine Nicholson, Phyllis Rackin, Helen Smith, Peter Stallybrass, Emily Steiner, David Wallace, Elizabeth Williamson, and many others.

I, too, have traveled in the service of writing *Barbarous Antiquity*. At McGill University, Paul Yachnin and Canada's Social Sciences and Humanities Research Council–sponsored Making Publics project gave me, and my book project a warm, collaborative, and multidisciplinary home. I am grateful to Michael Bristol, Sara Coodin, Brian Cowan, Leslie Cormack, Kevin Curran, Nicholas Dew, Jen Drouin, Marlene Eberhardt, Wes Folkerth, Maggie Kilgour, Patrick Nielson, Monica Popescu, Fiona Ritchie, Angela Vanhalen, Bronwen Wilson, and Myra Wright for helping me think about imported words as mediators. Wake Forest University's Archie Fellowship, the University of Georgia's Sarah H. Moss Fellowship and Provost's summer research grant took me to the British Library and the Warburg Institute. A special note of thanks goes to Kathleen Lynch, Owen Williams, Georgiana Ziegler, and the overwhelmingly helpful and knowledgeable librarians, staff, and readers at the Folger Shakespeare Library and Institute, where I held a short-term fellowship in 2008 and participated in Michael Neill's invigorating National Endowment for the Humanities–funded summer institute on Global Shakespeare in 2011.

My colleagues at the University of Georgia seem to think supporting one another ordinary, but I know it is rare. Sujata Iyengar read my entire manuscript, while Christy Desmet, Channette Romero, Beth Tobin, Fran Teague, Chloe Wigston-Smith, and Elizabeth Wright guided me through the first book publication process with wisdom and humor. I have spent many long walks and work sessions trading ideas and untangling writing problems with Emily Sahakian. Graduate students in my English 8300 classes have shared their enthusiasm and insight, particularly regarding Shakespeare, Ovid, and Marlowe. At Wake Forest, Jessica Richard and Olga Valbuena provided valuable suggestions on earlier chapter drafts, and Randi Saloman generously shared her advice on revision and publication.

Not every academic monograph receives so much close attention. I am particularly grateful to Jerry Singerman and my anonymous readers at the University of Pennsylvania Press for recognizing what I was trying to do with this book while pushing me to take it further, make it clearer, and polish it *ad unguem*. I could not have found a better copy editor than Gillian Dickens, or a more supportive managing editor in Erica Ginsburg.

There are a number of scholars whose encouragement, support, and mentoring helped this book come to fruition. They include Heather Dubrow, Roland Greene, Jonathan Gil Harris, Lynne Magnusson, Michael Neill, Patricia Parker, and Maureen Quilligan. I also have the best extended peer cohort of early modernists a scholar could wish for; it includes J. K. Barrett, Gina Bloom, Brooke Conti, Lara Dodds, Holly Dugan, David Goldstein, Jenny Mann, Jim Marino, Ellen McKay, Lucy Munro, Vin Nardizzi, Ayesha Ramachandran, Benedict Robinson, Adam Smyth, Amy Tigner, Sarah Van der Laan, Jennifer Waldon, and Jessica Wolfe. No one understands my scholarly predilections better than Wendy Beth Hyman. I am lucky to call her my close friend and to look forward to future collaborations. My parents, Ellen and Richard Jacobson, nurtured in me a love of literature before I could speak. Richard sparked my interest in philology, and Ellen reminds me of the joy in writing and scholarship. Last, this book in its present form would not have been possible without the considerable amount of attention Ari Lieberman devoted to it and to me.

Two chapters in this book incorporate articles that have appeared in print elsewhere, although in different form. An earlier version of Chapter 3, "The Elizabethan Cipher in Shakespeare's *Lucrece*," appeared in *Studies in Philology* 104.3 (Summer 2010): 336–59. An earlier version of Chapter 4, entitled "The East as Poetic Commodity in *Venus and Adonis*," appeared in *Literature Compass* 8.1 (2011): 15–27. I thank the University of North Carolina Press and Wiley-Blackwell publishers for permission to reproduce them here.

Foundations in Human Development

SECOND EDITION

JERRY J. BIGNER, PH.D

Department of Human Development and Family Studies
Colorado State University

TROIANNE GRAYSON, M.A.

Department of Social and Behavioral Sciences
Florida State College at Jacksonville

BVT
PUBLISHING

THE PUBLISHER OF AFFORDABLE TEXTBOOKS

Foundations in Human Development, Second Edition

The views and opinions of each author do not necessarily reflect the views and opinions of the other authors or of the publisher and its affiliates.

Some ancillaries, including electronic and print components, may not be available to customers outside the United States.

ISBN: 978-1-60229-958-0

PRODUCT DEVELOPMENT MANAGER: Brae Buhnerkemper

PRODUCT DEVELOPMENT ASSISTANT: Brandi Cornwell

MANAGING EDITOR: Joyce Bianchini

SENIOR DEVELOPMENTAL EDITOR: Rhonda Minemma

PHOTO RESEARCHER: Della Brackett

COVER DESIGN: Brae Buhnerkemper, Dan Harvey

ILLUSTRATIONS: Dan Harvey

TYPESETTER: Della Brackett

TEXT AND COVER PRINTING: Worldcolor, Inc.

SALES MANAGER: Robert Rappeport

MARKETING MANAGER: Richard Schofield

COPY EDITOR: Susan Gall

PERMISSIONS COORDINATOR: Suzanne Schmidt

ART DIRECTOR: Linda Price

From J. J. Bigner:

For Duane—Partner, Mentor, Best Friend, my Hero,
The wind beneath my wings.

and

For Todd, Shannon, and Katy—
Once again with feeling!

From T. Grayson:

For Glenn, Whisper, Haley, Alexa, Lance, and my Lord
I couldn't have written this without your support, love, patience, and strength. Thank you!

TABLE OF CONTENTS

CHAPTER

2

The Dawn of Development 53

CHAPTER

3

Infancy 99

C H A P T E R

4

Early Childhood 141

CHAPTER

5

Middle Childhood   193

CHAPTER

6

Adolescence   235

CHAPTER

7

Early Adulthood   275

CHAPTER

8

Middle Adulthood   305

C H A P T E R

9

Late Adulthood   339

C H A P T E R

10

The Dusk of Life   375

PREFACE

Foundations in Human Development is a comprehensive and engaging introduction to life span development. With a unique blend of classical studies and cutting-edge research, the reader is provided a context in which he or she is able to appreciate the historical foundations of life span development, as well as current themes and findings. The reader is consistently encouraged to apply the text material to his or her own life, in order to encourage retention and increase interest.

After the first two chapters, which focus upon introducing the field of human development and biological beginnings, each chapter is organized into three parts. The first part of each chapter emphasizes biological development. The second part emphasizes cognitive development. The third part emphasizes socioemotional development. The central task of these chapters is to help students learn basic concepts that relate to developmental changes affecting individuals throughout each stage of the life span.

There are some important pedagogical features to the text that distinguish it from others as well. First, each chapter is written using the SQR3 (S-Q-R-R-R) method. This is a method designed by Dr. Francis Robinson to facilitate effective learning of written material. The first step in learning this material is to survey (S) each chapter. The second step is observed with questions (Q) that are raised as a result of reading a section. The third step is to read (R) each chapter carefully, one section at a time. The fourth step is recitation (R) where you may make notes, underline, or use the learning objectives or pause and process questions within each section to check for comprehension of main points. The final step is review (R) where you might test your comprehension by performing the self-quiz given at the end of a chapter, rereading your notes, or rereading a chapter, for example.

Second, learning objectives are given at the beginning of each chapter. Throughout the chapter, key terms and concepts appear in **bold face** print. These terms are defined in the glossary. At the end of each section of the chapter, pause and process questions are given so that a student may gauge his or her understanding for each segment of the chapter.

Third, a summary at the end of each chapter explains important concepts for that chapter. The summary could also be read prior to reading the whole chapter, in order to gain a preview of what the chapter contains.

Fourth, each chapter contains a self-quiz that may be used in the recitation and review steps of learning. It also may be interesting to test yourself prior to reading a chapter and also upon completing the steps in learning the material to observe your progress.

Finally, part of the human condition is that individuals can differ in their views on controversial issues. Because of this, a few controversial topics are discussed within the text. Research on these topics is presented and students are encouraged to think critically about these issues and form their own opinion. Some controversial topics discussed in the text include stem cell research, the cohabitation effect, whole versus partial-brain death, and euthanasia. Coverage of these societal controversies should pique the student's interest in the field of human development as a whole.

SUPPLEMENTS FOR INSTRUCTORS

1. **Study Guide**. The study guide is uniquely designed to encourage students to manipulate and apply the textbook material. KWL charts, graphic organizers, key term definitions, and matching exercises provide students with ample opportunities to master textbook material.

2. **Instructor's Manual**. In addition to providing the typical chapter outlines, website recommendations, and student handouts; this manual also provides suggested online tutorials and activities, blogs, online (free) videos, podcasts, and jigsaw activities for each chapter. Teaching life span development has never been so much fun!

3. **Test Bank**. An extensive test bank is available to instructors in both hard copy and electronic forms. Each chapter consists of a variety of multiple choice, true/false, short answer and essay questions.

4. **PowerPoints**. A set of PowerPoint slides covering the main concepts and ideas are available to instructors who adopt this textbook.

5. **Customize This Book**. If you have additional material you'd like to add (handouts, lecture notes, syllabus, etc) or simply rearrange and delete content, BVT Publishing's custom publishing division can help you modify this book's content, to produce a book that satisfies your specific instructional needs. BVT Publishing has the only custom publishing division that puts your material *exactly* where you want it to go, easily and seamlessly. Please visit www.bvtpublishing.com or call us at 1-800-646-7782 for more information on BVT Publishing's Custom Publishing Program.

SUPPLEMENTS FOR STUDENTS

BVT Publishing is pleased to provide students with a free, comprehensive online tutorial which can be found at www.bvtstudents.com. This website offers the following:

1. **eBook editions**. Save time, money and paper by purchasing an eBook version of this text directly from our convenient online store, located on our student website.

2. **Shopping Cart**. For the student's convenience and pocketbook, the student website also contains a shopping cart where they have the added option of purchasing the traditional paper textbook directly from the publisher if they prefer.

3. **Self Testing**. Students can test their knowledge of this book's content on our student website. The Self Test questions are designed to help improve students' mastery of the information in the book.

4. **Chapter Outlines**. Chapter outlines are available for students to use either on our website or they can be downloaded directly from our website. They are designed to serve as a helpful outline approach to getting an overview of each chapter's content.

5. **Flash Cards**. We also feature Flash Cards on our student website. The Flash Cards are

an easy way for students to spot-check their understanding of common and important terms, as well as effectively retain the information.

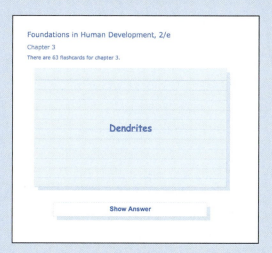
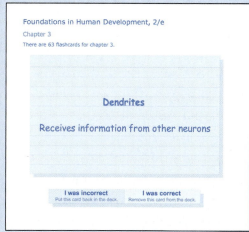

6. **Chapter Summaries**. The Chapter Summaries are another tool designed to give the students an overview of each chapter's content, further aiding the students in content comprehension and retention.

CHAPTER 1

The Field of Human Development

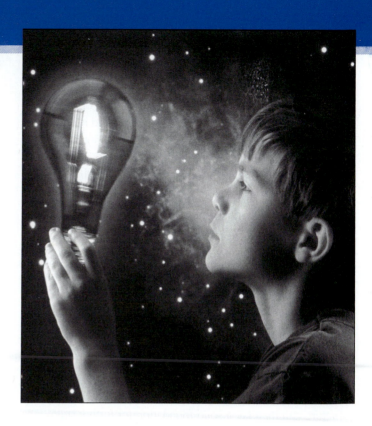

OUTLINE

THE LIFE SPAN PERSPECTIVE

- The field of human development
- The importance of studying life span development
- Historical perspectives on human development
- Domains and principles of development
- Phases of developmental change

DEVELOPMENTAL RESEARCH METHODS

- The foundation for research
- How are theories tested?
- Developmental considerations in research
- Widely used statistical approaches

THEORIES IN HUMAN DEVELOPMENT

- Theories that focus on biological processes
- Theories that focus on cognitive processes
- Theories that focus on socioemotional processes
- Theories that focus on the environment or context of development
- Comparing developmental theories

When does human life begin? What is a "typical life" versus an "abnormal life"? What causes one baby to develop into a Mother Teresa or Abraham Lincoln and another baby to develop into a Jeffrey Dahmer or Adolf Hitler? When does it become too late for a child headed down a dangerous path to be bumped onto a more optimal path? When does human life end?

All of these questions, and many others, form the core of the field of **human development.** The study of human development seeks to describe, understand, and explain human development, factors that promote or inhibit optimal development, and ways to help individuals struggling in their development (Galatzer-Levy & Cohler, 1993).

In college there are many courses in human development. Some focus on child development, others on prenatal development or adolescence, and still others on adulthood and aging. Why study life span development? It is a lofty goal indeed to study life from conception to old age; however, the study of life span development provides the "big picture" of how humans both change and stay the same from conception to death. Such a big picture can then lay a solid foundation for further study within particular phases of the life span, such as adolescence, during which you can learn the finer details of that period.

Life span encompasses the human development of all age groups.

Each of you reading this book is human and developing. You will never reach a time in your life when you are "done developing." Indeed, part of being human is continual development. Although we will soon see that there are many reasons to study life span development, perhaps the most important reason is for you to gain a better perspective of where you have been, where you are now, and where you are going in this journey through life. This book and this course will hopefully help you to better understand your own life and development, a lesson that will always be with you.

THE LIFE SPAN PERSPECTIVE

LEARNING OBJECTIVES:

1. *Understand how the field of human development is defined and know the focus of this field of study*
2. *Understand the reasons why it is important to learn about human development over the life span*
3. *Awareness of the historical issues that guide human development theories and research*
4. *Describe the domains and principles of development*
5. *Identify the stages and development and the conceptualizations of age*

THE FIELD OF HUMAN DEVELOPMENT

Interdisciplinary

What factors had the greatest influence on the person you are today? I typically ask my life span development students this question on the first day of class. I ask them to jot down

Human development begins at the earliest stages of life.

Human development

The changes that occur in individuals between conception and death.

their answers anonymously on a piece of paper and pass them forward. Then, as a class, we go through some of the answers. As you may have guessed, typical answers include family, friends, and genetics. Less often, answers will include religion, ethnicity, neighborhood, or some life-altering event. Seldom do answers include historical time period, geographical location, nutrition, prenatal environment, or special talents. However, all of the above have had a hand in the person you are today.

The point of the above discussion is that understanding **human development** takes more than just psychology. Don't get me wrong, psychology is important and will be the foundational discipline discussed in this textbook; however, the field of human development is a rich and diverse field that incorporates the research and theories of many disciplines (National Research Council & Institute of Medicine, 2000). Some of the disciplines that have greatly contributed to our understanding of human development include genetics, molecular biology, neuroscience, nutrition, embryology, medicine, computer science, cognitive science, psychology, sociology, gerontology, epidemiology, cultural studies, anthropology, philosophy, theology, linguistics, economics, and history. Although there is significant overlap between some of these fields, each has made unique contributions to our understanding of human development. Throughout this book research and theories from each of these disciplines, and more, will be woven into our discussion about human development.

Careers in Human Development

Now that you know that human development is interdisciplinary, you may be wondering what type of careers a person can pursue with a degree in human development.

Disciplines such as neuroscience have greatly contributed to the understanding of human development.

First, approximately 170 colleges and universities in the United States offer a major in either Human Development or Human Development and Family Studies leading to a bachelor's degree (College Board, 2008). A bachelor, master, or doctorate degree in human development can prepare you for a variety of careers. Some of the more obvious career choices include child care work, social work and human services, pre-K–12 teaching, college teaching, university teaching or research, and counseling. However, there are also some less obvious career choices for which a degree in human development can prepare you.

Many branches and departments at all levels of government entities engage in work on issues related to human development. For example, the Census Bureau, Department of Education, Department of Health and Human Services, Department of Housing and Urban Development, Department of Justice, and the Department of Labor all have offices that focus on family and/or child issues. In addition to government, many nonprofit organizations hire individuals with expertise in human development. Nonprofit organizations include research institutes, professional associations (such as the American Psychological Association), advocacy organizations, and foundations. Finally, a degree in human development could lead to a career in the private sector. Many management consulting firms and survey/evaluation research firms employ individuals from the human development field. If you are considering majoring in human development, consider visiting http://cfp.igpa.uiuc.edu/brseek/learnfields.asp. This website has a wonderful career guide for life span development majors, written by Chase-Lansdale and Gordon that is updated regularly. It is truly amazing the diversity of fields one can work in with a degree in human development. Of course, websites are continually created and dismantled, so a search on "careers in life span development" may lead you to some other insightful career guides available online. Your college counseling center can also provide a wealth of information on careers, not just in human development, but for any number of other majors as well.

Pause and Process:

1. What are some disciplines that are important in contributing to our understanding of human development?

2. What are some possible careers for a person pursuing a degree in human development?

THE IMPORTANCE OF STUDYING LIFE SPAN DEVELOPMENT

Although the introduction to this chapter alluded to the importance of studying development in order to gain a better understanding of your own life, there are also other important reasons for such study.

Social policy and **social norms** are both influenced—or should be influenced—by knowledge of human development (Galatzer-Levy & Cohler, 1993; National Research Council & Institute of Medicine, 2000). Should grandparents have visitation rights if parents divorce (or never marry)? What information should be on file from sperm donors in case their children someday have questions about their biological father? How should juvenile offenders be treated differently than adult offenders? Should taxpayers pay for parental leave, daycare, or elder care? Should kindergarten last half a day or a full school day? Should expectant parents be required to obtain a license prior to childbirth? How old is too old to have children? How young is too young to have children? What is the best age to get married? All of these questions are actively discussed in our society, some at official, legislative levels, and others around the office cooler. Regardless, the way we treat individuals and create social policy is largely based upon our knowledge of human development.

Psychopathology, which is our understanding of developmental delays, as well as therapy techniques are also based upon our knowledge of human development (Galatzer-Levy & Cohler, 1993; National Research Council & Institute of Medicine, 2000). Many preschool children have imaginary friends. Such imaginary playmates cause little concern in parents. However, parents would begin to raise their eyebrows if their nine-year-old had an imaginary friend. Professional intervention would probably be sought if a family's teenager had an imaginary friend. As you can see, the "normalness" of imaginary playmates depends upon a person's age and development. Normal and abnormal development often lie upon the same continuum, and our understanding of abnormal is dependent upon our understanding of normal development.

Intervention and therapy should also be based upon an individual's stage of development. A counselor would need to use different strategies and techniques for a five-year-

Social policy

Typically, a government policy regarding a social issue.

Social norms

Expectations in a given society about how an individual should behave, feel, and think.

Psychopathology

The branch of medicine dealing with the causes and processes of mental disorders.

old who underwent a traumatic event versus a twenty-five-year old. Along a similar line of reasoning, a bereavement counselor must consider a client's developmental understanding of death prior to ascertaining the best course of action in assisting in the grieving process.

Finally, studying human development provides a person with enormous understanding of the multiple pathways and timetables development can take (Galatzer-Levy & Cohler, 1993). Knowledge of human development allows us to place our own **life history** into a broader perspective and helps us to be more appreciative of others' life stories.

Life history

All the changes experienced by a living organism, from its conception to its death.

Pause and Process:

1. What is a social norm that you are aware of related to human development?

2. What do you think would be a good social policy in relation to human development?

HISTORICAL PERSPECTIVES ON HUMAN DEVELOPMENT

Philosophical Issues

Do all humans develop basically the same, regardless of where or when they live? How do humans acquire knowledge? Are some people born evil? What these questions touch upon are the historical philosophical issues that form the foundation for many of the theories in human development and psychology (Hergenhahn, 2005). Although a theory may not directly address all of the persistent philosophical issues we are going to discuss, the theorist or theorists that developed the theory had a point of view on each of these issues. You will be able to better appreciate each theory more deeply by understanding the impact these philosophical issues had in their development.

1. Which philosopher believed that humans are born basically good and that it is civilization that corrupts the human race?

THE NATURE OF HUMAN NATURE   Are humans born basically good, bad, or as a *tabula rasa* (blank slate)? Some philosophers, such as Jean-Jacques Rousseau, believed that people are born basically good, and that it is civilization that corrupts the human race. Other philosophers, such as John Locke, believed that people are born like blank slates and that it is our experiences that mold us into good or bad people. Still others see humans as nothing more than animals with instincts and drives that will lead to unacceptable, bad behaviors. In this case, it is civilization's job to teach humans during childhood acceptable behavior and to curb such bad, innate tendencies.

Human nature is really rather fascinating if you think about it. Every person that you have ever encountered has a perspective on the nature of human nature, whether they have thought about it consciously or not. Imagine how differently an emergency room nurse who believes people are basically good would treat a patient in pain than a nurse who

2. What are three views of human nature?

thinks that people are basically bad. Which nurse do you think would be more likely to assume that a patient is only after pain medication versus really in pain and in need of medication? How do you think teachers or parents may behave differently based upon their view of human nature?

What is your view of human nature? How has such a view impacted your interactions with others throughout your life? Have you always held this view of human nature, or did something happen that changed your view? Every theory that we will cover in this chapter will have a view of human nature, and we will highlight the importance of this persistent issue throughout the text.

NATIVISM VERSUS EMPIRICISM What are humans born preprogrammed with, and what must be learned? As we will see in Chapter 2, healthy babies are born with certain reflexes. These reflexes can assist in survival from the beginning or they may be precursors for later behavior that will assist in survival. Either way, these reflexes are inborn (native) not learned. Other behaviors must be learned via trial and error. For example, your mother may have told you repeatedly as a young child not to touch the hot stove. Still, the hot stove was so pretty and shiny and attractive that it seemed to call you to touch it. Those of you who did not heed your mother's advice and actually touched the shiny, hot stove probably learned really fast that it hurt. Therefore, not touching hot stoves is something we learn (either by listening to advice, observational learning, or trial and error). Such knowledge is not nativistic, but empirical. As we will learn throughout the book, some parts of human development seem largely preprogrammed in our genes, whereas others are largely learned through our experiences.

ACTIVE VERSUS PASSIVE KNOWLEDGE In college there were many late nights when I wished that the material in the textbook would magically be transferred to my brain while I rested my forehead on it. Unfortunately, knowledge is not typically acquired in such a passive manner. Instead, we now know that in order for information to be learned, we must be active in its acquisition. Philosophers, and even some modern theorists, weren't always so sure on this issue. Some, like Jung, believed that there is a collective unconscious which contains information to which all humans have unconscious (hence passive) access. The issue of active versus passive knowledge acquisition will be important when we discuss cognitive development.

CONTINUOUS VERSUS DISCONTINUOUS Think back to your childhood. Did you buy clothes and shoes before each school year started? If yes, did you buy these clothes because you needed a bigger size or because you wanted something new for the coming school year? You probably needed a bigger shoe size or pant size *and* wanted something new for the brand new school year. In fact, unless you came from a family that utilized hand-me-downs, you probably outgrew many of your nicer clothes and dress shoes before you wore them out. This is because physical growth throughout childhood is slow and steady. However, not everything in development happens so continuously. For example, Erik Erikson has a theory that describes socioemotional development as occurring in distinct stages. Areas of development that are slow and steady are viewed as continuous. Areas of development that happen in stages are viewed as discontinuous. Some of the theories and topics that we will discuss in this course will focus on continuous aspects of development, whereas others will focus on the discontinuous aspects of development.

UNIVERSALISM VERSUS RELATIVISM   Did you know that all healthy humans follow the same sequence of prenatal development regardless of ethnicity, geographical location, or gender? Nearly all healthy humans also follow a similar sequence in motor skill development. Such aspects of physical development are universal to the human race. However, other aspects of development are much more relativistic. Emotional expression, education, and death rituals are some examples of topics in human development that vary according to the culture upon which we are focusing.

The above was just a sampling of the persistent philosophical issues that guide theory and research in human development. Many others—such as determinism versus free will, the relationship between body and mind, and what makes humans unique—are also important and will be touched upon within the context of specific topics and/or theories throughout the book.

Pause and Process:

1. Do you believe that babies are born basically good, basically bad, or blank slates? Why?

2. Pick another of the above issues and state your perspective on it. How did you come to obtain this perspective? Do you expect your perspective to change during this class? Why or why not?

DOMAINS AND PRINCIPLES OF DEVELOPMENT

The previous section discussed historical perspectives on development. This section will discuss what we know about the domains and principles of development today. Some are going to echo back to the information covered in the previous section, as they should. (History is always guiding the present and future.) However, most of the information that will be introduced is new.

The Domains of Development

Development within a person can be conceptualized as occurring within different domains. A human undergoes biological changes (e.g., puberty or brain development), cognitive changes (e.g., memory development or language development), and socioemotional changes (e.g., per-

Physical (biological) domain

Changes in the body or physical appearance.

Cognitive domain

Changes in intellectual or mental functioning.

Socioemotional domain

Changes in emotion, personality, and relationships.

3. What are the three domains of human development?

sonality development or identity development) throughout life. Although nearly every human activity encompasses all three of these processes simultaneously, it is sometimes useful to separate these activities into their component parts to more easily understand developmental changes. It is important to keep in mind that the **biological**, **cognitive**, and **socioemotional** processes of development are intertwined and influence each other across the life span. Each broad domain has many subdomains within it. Can you think of some subdomains (or sub-areas) within biological development?

Principles of Developmental Change

There are several principles that characterize developmental change (Baltes, Lindenberger & Staudinger, 1998). Many of these principles have already been discussed in this chapter.

- *Lifelong*   Development is a lifelong process, from conception until death in old age.

- *Multidimensional*   Development occurs within the physical, cognitive, and socioemotional domains across the life span.

- *Multidirectional*   Human development does not simply involve growth. It also involves the processes of maintenance and decline. For example, bone density increases early in life, is (hopefully) maintained for a while in adulthood, and then shows decline in later adulthood. The rate of decline can depend upon diet and exercise. The principle of multidirectionality applies to all the domains of development, and the timetable for growth, maintenance, and decline can vary.

- *Multidisciplinary*   As mentioned at the beginning of this chapter, information from many fields is used to gain a comprehensive understanding of human development.

- *Continuity*   Early development is influential for later development; however, the connection is not always perfectly predictive. Although early development makes later outcomes more or less likely, development is way too complex to allow for a crystal ball vision of one's future.

- *Dance between nature, nurturing, and the individual*   Human development involves complex interactions between biological components, environmental influences, and individual actions. For example, a person may have the genetic propensity for developing schizophrenia. However, one can choose to avoid environmental triggers and thus prevent initiating the onset of the disease.

- *Context*   Development is embedded in an environment. These settings can be micro in nature, such as one's family, or macro in nature, such as one's culture or historical time period. We will discuss Bronfenbrenner's bioecological theory later in the chapter, which will explain one conceptualization of the levels in which development occurs. On a more general level than Bronfenbrenner's theory, developmentalists can focus on three specific contexts for influences on development (Baltes, 2003):

- *Normative age-graded influence*   These influences include experiences that most people experience around the same age within a given population of interest. For example, most healthy males experience puberty within a certain age range. Most children in the United States start school around the same age.

- *Normative history-graded influence*s   Individuals born within the same time-frame and location often experience life-influential events unique to their cohort. Some normative history-graded influences include the Great Depression, the JFK assassination, the *Challenger* space shuttle explosion, and the events of 9/11. Although individuals born after September 11, 2001, will be able to watch the Twin Towers destruction on video, it is not the same as having lived through that day.

- *Non-normative life event influences*   The above influences include events that most people of a given cohort will experience. They are common experiences that we share with most of our peers. However, non-normative life event influences are unique because they are events that most people do not experience. For example, it is estimated that more than one million children are currently homeschooled in the United States. Nevertheless, percentagewise, homeschooling is still relatively rare and could be considered a non-normative life event. A life-threatening illness in childhood, losing a parent in childhood, winning the lottery, or being able to travel the world in eighty days would all be considered non-normative life event influences.

Pause and Process:

1. Give an example of an activity that involves the biological, cognitive, and socioemotional domain.

2. List a non-normative life event that you have experienced. How has this event influenced your development?

PHASES OF DEVELOPMENTAL CHANGE

Although development is continuous and the timetable for development is unique to each person, developmentalists like to organize the human life span into distinct phases. Such distinctions allow for ease in discussing broad changes across the life span. We are going to discuss two ways of organizing developmental phases in this section: stages of the life span and conceptualizations of age.

Stages of the Life Span

The stages of the life span are a conceptual framework for organizing the transformations human beings experience between conception and death. These stages are necessarily culture bound. For example, the stages presented here (characteristic for the mainstream culture in the United States) are very different than the life span stages for the traditional Navajo culture (Rogoff, 2003).

It should be understood that the stages of the life span are categorized into approximate age ranges. Although most adolescents are between the ages of twelve and eighteen, it is possible to have a thirty-year-old adolescent. This is because, although chronological age is a factor in considering one's stage, each developmental stage of the life span has unique characteristics and tasks, and some individuals are considered developmentally off-time.

The unique characteristics and tasks that help define each stage are known as **developmental tasks** (Havinghurst, 1972) and are derived from both maturational and environmental sources. Each stage's characteristics and tasks are the accomplishments that a person is expected to achieve or master at that particular period. These expectations help to ensure that a person will function effectively in the present and be prepared for healthy development in subsequent stages.

Society tempers its expectations of people according to the developmental stage they are currently experiencing. Additionally, social norms are often tied to a person's developmental stage. For example, people typically tolerate young children throwing food at each other in a restaurant and use the occasion as a teachable moment for table manners. Conversely, people would typically stare in wonder if they saw a group of middle-aged women in a restaurant throwing food at each other. It is more likely they would think that the women had too much alcohol instead of seeing the occasion as a good time to enter a discussion on proper etiquette.

Developmental tasks

The unique characteristics and tasks that help define each stage of life span.

The stages of experience between conception and death seem to be culture bound.

Everyone is expected to experience each of the life stages in sequence, though the rate of development in each stage will differ from person to person. Still, many developmentalists contend that a person should resolve and accomplish the major developmental tasks at the appropriate stage in order to be considered healthy.

Eight stages are used in this text to delineate the developmental progress of human beings over the life span. These are described in greater detail in the chapters that follow. Here they are listed with approximate age ranges.

1. Prenatal (conception to birth)

2. Infancy (birth through two years)

3. Early childhood (three to six years)

4. Middle childhood (six to twelve years)

5. Adolescence (puberty to eighteen years)

6. Early adulthood (eighteen to thirty-nine years)

   a. Emerging adulthood is a term sometimes used to describe individuals eighteen to twenty-five years of age.

7. Middle adulthood (forty to retirement)

8. Late adulthood (retirement to near death)

   a. Centenarians are individuals one hundred years of age and older.

Conceptualizations of Age

When someone asks you how old you are, do you say it depends? Actually, it should depend because you may have more than one answer. Most of us give our chronological age when presented with this question. Our **chronological age** is the number of years that have passed since our birth (or conception in some cultures). You also have a biological age, psychological age, and social age (Hoyer & Roodin, 2003; Rogoff, 2003; Santrock, 2007).

Your **biological age** is how old your body is, based on health. You may be biologically older, younger, or the same as your chronological age based on lifestyle choices and other health factors.

Psychological age is based upon your adaptive capacities in relation to your chronological age. A mentally challenged individual may be chronologically twenty years of age; whereas psychologically, he or she may be only five years of age. Like biological age, you may be psychologically older, younger, or the same as your chronological age.

Social age is based upon social norms and expectations in relation to what an individual "should" be doing at a specific chronological age. These norms can vary by gender. For example, it is often expected for girls to be more socially mature than boys on the first day of kindergarten or during early adolescence. Although these norms may or may not be accurate,

Chronological age

The number of years that have passed since an individual's birth (or conception in some cultures).

Biological age

How old an individual's body is based on health.

Psychological age

Based upon an individual's adaptive capacities in relation to their chronological age.

Social age

Based upon social norms and expectations in relation to what an individual "should" be doing at a specific chronological age.

social age expectations can be powerful in guiding people's thoughts and behaviors. The comic strip "Cathy" used the main character's violation of the social age norm for marriage for years to engage readers.

Pause and Process:

1. What stage of development are you currently in? What tasks do you think you need to accomplish prior to progressing to the next stage?

2. Do you think your biological age is older, younger, or the same as your chronological age? Why?

Age is determined in various ways such as chronological, biological, psychological, and social.

DEVELOPMENTAL RESEARCH METHODS

LEARNING OBJECTIVES:

1. *Understand the importance of theory for research and the scientific method*
2. *Describe the basic approaches to research*
3. *Explain how the developmental aspect is incorporated into research designs*
4. *Awareness of some new and growing statistical approaches*

Statistically, most of you reading this book will one day be a parent or you already are. How will you know how to best raise your children? Will you simply raise your children the same way you were raised? Will you do the exact opposite of what your parents or caregivers did? Will you seek advice? Whose advice will you seek: family, friends, and/or expert opinions?

There are many ways of knowing how to raise a child. There is knowledge based on personal experiences, television shows, folklore, religious beliefs, wisdom from other people's lives, superstitions, and science (Cozby, 2001).

Science

The marriage of rationalism and empiricism that provides a mechanism allowing for understanding the world within a system of checks and balances.

What is science? **Science** is the marriage of rationalism and empiricism that provides a mechanism allowing for understanding the world within a system of checks and balances (Hergenhahn, 2005). Huh? Okay, let's try to explain this again using plain English. Science uses observations, guided by theory, to test ideas and understand the world. Of course, the scientific method is a little more complicated than that brief definition would allow, but it is a good place to start.

This section will help you to understand some of the more common research methods in human development. Much of the information in the chapters ahead is based upon findings using these research methods. This is why it is critical that you gain a good understanding of research methods early on in this course. You want to be a critical reader of the information that lies ahead. We don't have the time or space to teach you every single research method and technique out there, but you will have a good foundation from which to begin your studies in human development.

THE FOUNDATION FOR RESEARCH

The Scientific Method

Scientific method

A series of steps that scientists from any field use as a process to test theories and gain knowledge within their field.

The **scientific method** is a series of steps that scientists from any field use as a process to test theories and gain knowledge within their field (Cozby, 2001). The general steps in the scientific method include:

1. Making observations about some phenomenon (e.g., people's behavior).

2. Developing a theory to explain your observations.

3. Generating a hypothesis that can test your theory and either support or not support it. You need to identify variables in your hypothesis and operationally define these variables.

4. Selecting a method to test your hypothesis and carry out the research.

5. Review the results of the study.

6. Revise your theory, share your results, and start the cycle over.

Spotlight

11. What is the scientific method?

An important assumption embedded in the above steps is that the scientist is aware of the research within the field he or she is studying and use this past research as a guide in developing his or her current research (Cozby, 2001).

There are probably quite a few unfamiliar words within our scientific method steps. Hopefully, the next few sections will help clarify some of these terms and provide a better context for understanding these steps.

THEORY   Have you ever noticed that parents seem particularly stressed and short-tempered with their children at shopping stores and amusements parks? Why do you think this occurs? Have you ever noticed those individuals who play the radio so loud in their cars that the vibrations tell you something is coming before you can see them? Why do these people feel the need to pollute the air in this way? If you ventured any guesses to explain these behaviors, then you just used theories—in a very generic yet common way.

Theory

A collection of ideas used to explain observations.

People use theories everyday. A **theory** can be thought of as a collection of ideas used to explain observations. A good theory must be testable; hence, falsifiable (Cozby, 2001;

Hergenhahn, 2005). One of the biggest theories in human development faced its decline because it was largely untestable, at least in its heyday. We will talk about this more when we discuss psychoanalytic theory later in the chapter.

Let's go back to an earlier example. You may have observed that parents seem particularly stressed with their children at amusement parks. You may also have theorized as to why this may occur: heat, crowds, exhaustion, or overly excited kids. Well, in order to make this more manageable (and testable); you may want to break your theory down into smaller parts to test:

- If the weather is hot, then parents experience more stress.

- If the amusement park is crowded, then parents experience more stress.

- If parents are exhausted, then parents experience more stress.

- If children are excited, then parents experience more stress.

What we just did was take our more global theory (or collection of ideas about why parents seem more stressed with children at amusement parks) and broke it down into four testable hypotheses. The generic and ubiquitous definition of a **hypothesis** is that it means an educated guess. A hypothesis should come from a theory, be a statement (preferably in an if-then format), and be testable (Cozby, 2001).

Still, a hypothesis must be narrowed to a **prediction** in order to be tested. Choosing the first hypothesis above, we could develop the following prediction: it is predicted that as temperature increases, parental stress will increase. The difference is slight, nevertheless, we have moved from a general idea of hot weather, to the specific idea of temperature increases.

There is now one final piece of information that we must add to our above prediction in order to be able to test it: **operational definitions** of the **variables**. We have two variables (or things that vary) in our prediction, temperature and stress. The operational definitions will let everyone in the world know exactly how we plan to measure these two variables (Cozby, 2001). Are we going to measure temperature in Celsius or Fahrenheit? How are we going to measure parental stress? We could measure blood pressure, heart rate, self-report, or use some other observational measure.

You may be wondering why we should care if the world knows how we plan to measure temperature and stress. Not all variables in human development are as concrete as temperature. Most reasonable people could guess that you are going to either use Celsius or Fahrenheit when measuring temperature. However, other variables are much more conceptual and abstract in nature, like stress. Americans seem to be constantly talking about stress; we eat, sleep, and breathe stress day in and day out. Yet, what you consider stressful and how you experience stress may be completely different from someone else. Some people thrive on challenges, living on the edge, and standing in hour-long lines. Other people prefer quiet, predictable lives. This is why it is so important to be extremely precise in defining what we mean by conceptual, abstract variables, and how we plan to measure them; because, two reasonable people may have completely different conceptual ideas of what stress is and how to measure

Hypothesis

Generically, hypothesis means educated guess. A hypothesis should come from a theory, be a statement, and be testable.

Prediction

A statement of what somebody thinks will happen in the future.

Operational definitions

How a variable is defined in a measurable way.

Variables

Anything that can vary.

it—and both could be right. Also, good research must be replicable. A theory must be tested over and over again in order to have confidence in its tenets. Having good operational definitions allows for easy study replication (Cozby, 2001).

THE IMPORTANCE OF THEORY   Why is theory important to research? Couldn't you just have a question that you want to test? Good questions, if we must say so ourselves. Remember that a theory is an organized collection of ideas developed to help explain observations. Without theory, all you have are random observations without any reasoning or understanding behind these observations. In some ways, to borrow a favorite metaphor, you would see the tree but not the surrounding forest.

You could easily observe: "The baby is crying." However, what good is that observation? Why is the baby crying? Is there something that the baby needs? Is crying developmentally appropriate? What will help the baby stop crying? How long do babies typically cry? Can babies cry too much? What can happen if you don't respond when the baby cries? All of these follow-up questions bridge the gap between a simple observation and the larger, theoretical context in which the observation is embedded. Observations provide the "what," but theory provides the much more interesting "why."

Pause and Process:

1. What are the steps in the scientific method?

2. Why is theory important for research?

HOW ARE THEORIES TESTED?

Types of Questions

The method that a researcher uses is dependent upon the type of question that he or she seeks to address (Cozby, 2001). Some questions focus on describing a situation, some focus on understanding relationships between variables, and still others seek to understand cause-and-effect relationships. Although specific techniques can be used regardless of the type of question asked (e.g., laboratory research could address any of the above questions), each of these different foci requires a different approach.

Descriptive Research

Descriptive research

Research that seeks to describe a phenomenon.

Like its name, **descriptive research** seeks to describe human development. The basic tool and method of gathering information regarding descriptive research is observation. This method is useful in making generalizations about individuals, to test a new theory, and to collect data to support or reject hypotheses. Observation is also a method used to help students gain a better understanding of human behavior at various stages of the life span.

Naturalistic observation method

A method of conducting research on human development that usually occurs in the "real" world where behavior happens spontaneously.

Ethnographic research

A specific type of naturalistic research largely used in anthropology, education, and cultural studies.

Laboratory studies

Allow for better variable control and manipulation than naturalistic studies.

Observation may be used in either a natural setting or in a laboratory (Cozby, 2001). A **naturalistic observation method** for conducting research on human development usually occurs in the "real" world where behavior happens spontaneously. There may be no attempt to control the environment of the people being studied and observed. Among the places that can provide rich opportunities for observing people in a natural setting are shopping malls, fast food restaurants, or beaches, for example.

Sometimes, a naturalistic observational study is conducted because it would be impossible or unethical to try to recreate the situation in a more controlled way. For example, riot behavior is an interesting phenomenon to study, but no one would cause a riot for the sole purpose of research. Instead, it must be studied when it spontaneously occurs.

Ethnographic research could be considered a specific type of naturalistic research. Ethnographic research is largely used in anthropology, education, and cultural studies; however, other fields can also utilize this strategy. Although ethnographic research can vary in approach, it can broadly be defined as the use of systematic observation in order to understand a particular social or cultural group's way of life. Very often, though not always, the observer will become an active participant in the setting of interest. Such research takes an extended amount of time because the group must come to trust the observer and view them as an insider before trusting them with open access to their group (Vogt, 1993).

Many studies using observation as the primary method of data collection are conducted in a laboratory. In this setting, the researcher can control certain variables or conditions. These may be lighting levels, or excluding distractions such as the conversations of others, traffic sounds, or household noises, for example. **Laboratory studies** allow for better variable control or manipulation than naturalistic studies. However, what is gained in control is lost in generalizability. Although we have laboratory observational research under descriptive research, with enough control and a shift in focus, this type of research can be classified as experimental research (discussed later on in the chapter).

Observation is the basic tool of descriptive research. This method is useful in making generalizations about individuals.

Studies using observation data collection methods may be very valuable and provide the researcher with much information. However, is always a question about the validity and reliability of the data that are collected by observers. Scientists are careful to use several observers to collect the data they wish to analyze. The observers receive special training to help them recognize behaviors under investigation. Different accounts, however, often are given by people who observe the same event. This is called **observer bias** and constitutes a major disadvantage of this method of data collection.

Correlational Research

Correlational research seeks to study if a relationship exists between two or more variables (Cozby, 2001). How is information gathered for correlational research? Lots of ways! Surveys, physiological measurements, interviews, observations, and archival data sources are among the ways data can be collected for correlational research.

Let's work through a few examples in order to gain a better understanding of correlational research and types of correlations.

Example 1: Do you think that there is a relationship between the number of hours you spend studying for an exam and the score you earn on the exam? If yes, what is that relationship? Hopefully, you would say that as the number of hours studying increases, your score on an exam increases. This would indicate a **positive correlation**—as one variable increases, the other variable increases.

Example 2: Have you ever watched the reality show, *The Biggest Loser*? In this show, individuals that are extremely overweight are taught how to eat healthy and exercise. They then compete for a cash reward for losing the most weight. At the beginning of the competition, each individual is given a comprehensive physical examination. Often, the contestants suffer from high cholesterol, elevated blood pressure, and diabetes. Do you think that there is a relationship between weight loss and bad cholesterol levels? If yes, what is that relationship? Ideally, you would say that as a person's weight decreases, his or her levels of bad cholesterol decreases. What type of correlation would this indicate? If you answered positive correlation you are correct. Say what? How can a positive correlation characterize a relationship in which two variables are decreasing together? Well, the key idea behind a positive correlation is that both variables move in the same direction; that is, both variables increase together and decrease together. Spend some time thinking about this because it is a concept that many students struggle with for some time.

Example 3: Let's pretend that you start keeping a journal. In this journal, you keep track of the number of hours that you sleep each night and your level of irritability during the following day. Do you think there will be a relationship between these two variables (hours of sleep and daytime irritability)? It is possible that as hours of sleep increases, level of irritability decreases. What type of correlation would this be? It can't

Observer bias

Different accounts given by people who observe the same event.

Correlational research

The study of relationship existence between two or more variables.

Positive correlation

As one variable increases, the other variable increases.

be a positive relationship, because the variables are not going in the same direction. Instead, as one variable increases, the other decreases. This type of correlation is referred to as a **negative correlation**.

Positive and negative correlations are the two basic types of correlations examined in research. A correlation coefficient indicates how strong two variables are related (Cozby, 2001). A correlation coefficient of zero indicates that there is absolutely no relationship between two variables. A score of +1.00 indicates a perfect, positive correlation between two variables. A score of −1.00 indicates a perfect, negative correlation between two variables. Hence, correlation coefficients can range from −1.00 to +1.00. The closer to -1.00 or +1.00 a correlation coefficient is, the stronger the correlation. The closer to zero a correlation coefficient is, the weaker the correlation.

There are, of course, other types of correlations. When you take a statistics course or a research methods course, you will learn about all the possible types of correlations out there. Nonetheless, it is worth mentioning one other type of correlation—**the curvilinear relationship**. You can visualize this type of correlation as either a U-shaped curve or an upside-down, U-shaped curve. In this type of correlation, two variables increase or decrease together up to a point (i.e., exhibit a positive correlation), then switch to a negative correlation (i.e., as one variable increases, the other decreases). Can you think of something that increases with age up to a certain point, then starts to decrease with continued aging? If you can't think of an example at the moment, you should certainly know some examples by the end of this course.

We cannot complete this section without teaching you the most important mantra within all of research methods: "A correlation does not imply causation!", or something to that effect. What this mantra means is that just because two variables are related does not mean that one variable is causing the other variable. Going back to our *"Biggest Loser"* example, losing weight may very well cause a decrease in bad cholesterol. However, some third variable (such as an increase in exercise or healthy food) may be influencing both the weight loss and cholesterol level. Because correlational research is just measuring variables, and not manipulating or controlling any, we must avoid assuming any cause-effect relationship exists. Only experimental research, discussed in our next section, can hope to establish cause-and-effect relationships.

Experimental Research

Experimental research seeks to establish cause-and-effect relationships (Cozby, 2001). Up until now, we have used the word variables rather globally. However, there are different types of variables. In experimental research, the experimenter hypothesizes that the **independent variable** has a causal effect on the **dependent variable**. The independent variable is controlled and/or manipulated and the dependent variable is measured.

Let's start with a simple example. Dr. Doe has created a brand new drug and she is convinced that it will cure depression. She hypothesizes that if people with depression

---

Negative correlation

As one variable increases, the other decreases.

Curvilinear relationship

In this type of correlation, two variables increase or decrease together up to a point, then switch to a negative correlation where one variable increases while the other decreases.

Experimental research

Seeks to establish cause and effect relationships.

Independent variable

A variable that is controlled and/or manipulated.

Dependent variable

A variable that is measured in an experimental study; the outcome of an experimental study.

Sample

A subset of a population.

Randomly assigned

Assignment of research participants to groups in an experimental study by chance.

Experimental group

The group that receives the experimental treatment.

Control group

The group that receives the placebo.

Placebo

An inert or innocuous substance used especially in controlled experiments testing the efficacy of another substance (as a drug).

Double-blind study

An experiment where neither the researcher nor the participants are aware of who is receiving the actual treatment or who is receiving the placebo.

Experimenter bias

The influence of the experimenter's expectations or behavior in an experiment.

take her drug, then they will be cured of depression. The independent variable is her new drug and the dependent variable is depression. To test her hypothesis, she will need to find a **sample** of depressed people. The sample should resemble the entire population of depressed individuals in the world—meaning they should have similar ages, percentage of males and females, ethnicity, socioeconomic breakdowns, and other important characteristics. The sample participants should then be **randomly assigned** to one of two groups: the **experimental group** which will receive the new drug, or the **control group** which will receive a **placebo**. Neither Dr. Doe nor the participants should be aware of who is receiving the actual drug and who is receiving the placebo; it needs to be a **double-blind study** in order to avoid **experimenter bias**. After a specified amount of time, all of the participants will have their depression measured. If the experimental group shows a statistically higher rate of depression being cured than the control group, then Dr. Doe's hypothesis will have been supported.

That was a pretty dense example. Here are the key points. First, a researcher has a hypothesis that one variable (the independent variable) has an effect on the other variable (the dependent variable). Second, the researcher must be able to control or manipulate the independent variable. Third, the hypothesis must be tested with a sample of participants that resembles the population of interest. In the example above, we needed a sample that resembled all people with depression, not all people with schizophrenia. Fourth, the participants needed to be randomly assigned to either the experimental group or the control group. Fifth, neither the participants nor the researcher should know which group they are in or bias could occur. Finally, after the study and statistical analysis is complete, the hypothesis will either be supported or not supported.

As complicated enough as the preceding two paragraphs sound, true experimental research is usually even more complicated. Researchers must worry about confounding variables, the reliability and validity of measures, and ethical issues (Cozby, 2001). To avoid ethical issues, all participants should receive **informed consent** and be debriefed after the study. Additionally, the benefits of the study must outweigh any costs, deception of participants must be avoided, and the research must be judged as ethical by an **Institutional Review Board** (IRB).

Pause and Process:

1. What is the difference between a research technique and a research approach?

2. Explain the main ideas behind descriptive, correlational, and experimental research.

DEVELOPMENTAL CONSIDERATIONS IN RESEARCH

Because developmentalists are interested in change across time, they must include an additional layer to their research designs. There are three basic developmental designs (cross-

Informed consent

Providing research participants with enough information about a study that they can knowledgeably agree or disagree to participate.

Institutional Review Board

A committee that evaluates whether a research study is ethical and allowed to be conducted.

Cross-sectional research design

A research design that compares measurements or observations of some particular trait or behavior between groups of people of different ages at the same time.

Cohort

A group of individuals having a statistical factor (as age or class membership) in common in a demographic study.

sectional, longitudinal, and sequential) that are used by scientists when conducting research into developmental processes. Each of these designs attempts to capture the significance of developmental changes in relation to the passage of time.

Cross-Sectional Research

A **cross-sectional research design** compares measurements or observations of some particular trait or behavior between groups of people of different ages at the same time (Cozby, 2001). For example, maybe you are interested in how children's understanding of death changes throughout childhood. You could gather a sample of three-year-olds, seven-year-olds, and eleven-year-olds all at once and compare their understanding of death. This one-shot approach would allow you to obtain a broad understanding of how children change between ages three to eleven in their understanding of death. Cross-sectional designs offer the researcher efficient, quick, and economical means to survey the way in which a particular developmental process may occur.

Cross-sectional designs, however, present problems to researchers. First, it is important to use similar groups of people at the different age levels being investigated. In other words, it is essential to keep the people in all of the groups as similar as possible in their common characteristics. For example, these may include racial group membership, income levels, intelligence, and so on. This is a very difficult challenge to accomplish successfully. Second, researchers are challenged to ensure that their measurements are the same for each age group being investigated. It is a difficult problem to ensure that the test used to measure a three-year-old child's understanding of death is measuring the same equivalent quality in eleven-year-old children, because language must be simplified for a younger child. Third, these designs can present distorted evidence of the influence of age changes. Each **cohort** of children has experienced a decidedly different environment and it may be cohort differences instead of age differences that you are measuring. For example, children who were alive and aware of the events of 9/11 may have a very different perspective on death, not because of their age but because of the experience of living through that day.

Children who were aware of 9/11 have a different perspective of death.

Longitudinal Research

A study that makes repeated measurements or observations of the same individuals over an extended period of time

Longitudinal design

A study that makes repeated measurements or observations of the same individuals over an extended period of time.

Microgenetic studies

A study that only lasts a matter of days or weeks.

Sequential design

A compromise that minimizes the disadvantages of both cross-sectional and longitudinal designs.

uses a **longitudinal design** (Cozby, 2001). In the previous section, we were interested in how children's understanding of death changes across childhood. To study this longitudinally, we could find a sample of three-year-olds and survey them at the ages of three, seven, and eleven. This way, we can see the progression of death understanding as the same group of children develops across time.

How long a longitudinal study lasts can vary significantly. Werner and Smith (2001) have followed the same group of individuals in Kauai, Hawaii, for more than forty years. There have been a small number of such studies that have followed a group of individuals across the life span. However, **microgenetic studies** usually last only a matter of days or weeks. What aspect of development you are interested in and the time-frame during which it develops will help determine the length of the longitudinal study.

There are three advantages to the researcher in using this design: (1) direct analysis of changes is allowed in relation to increasing age; because the same people are being studied repeatedly over a period of time, only the time element changes in relation to the same group of individuals, (2) there are fewer problems with the sample of people being studied in that the same individuals are investigated at each age level that changes in relation to the passage of time, (3) the researcher can use powerful statistical tests with this design that reduce the problem of error and large variations in the data over the time period of the study (Nunnally, 1973).

Two major criticisms usually are mentioned about longitudinal studies: (1) there may be a "practice" effect present in the data in that any changes that are found can be traced to the effects of repeated performance on the same tests used over the period of the research study, (2) the feasibility of conducting such studies is limited due to the enormous expenses involved in supporting a group of researchers, keeping in touch with participants, and providing the same research facilities over the time period of the investigation (Nunnally, 1973).

Sequential Research

Studies may be conducted that use a **sequential design** based on the concepts of the cross-sectional and longitudinal designs (Cozby, 2001). The sequential design is a compromise that minimizes the disadvantages of both cross-sectional and longitudinal designs. The sequential design uses cohorts as participant groups. A cohort group represents a particular generation of individuals. Comparisons are made with generational groups rather than with age groups. The cohort sequential design has a strong advantage—it allows the researcher to obtain estimates of developmental changes by using an economized longitudinal strategy. Several different cohort groups are observed over a specified period of time.

This type of design is increasingly popular with researchers due to its ability to provide relatively quick longitudinal results. The design can determine fairly accurate age differences over time rather than cohort differences among participants.

Pause and Process:

1. What are the main differences between cross-sectional and longitudinal designs?

2. What is the sequential design?

WIDELY USED STATISTICAL APPROACHES

Up until now, we have covered three basic research approaches (descriptive, correlational, and experimental) and three basic developmental designs (cross-sectional, longitudinal, and sequential). Here, we will briefly introduce you to three statistical approaches that are increasingly used in developmental research. These approaches are complicated; however, if you can grasp the conceptual ideas behind them it will serve you well when discussing specific research findings in future chapters.

Multiple regression

A statistical method that allows researchers to predict one variable based on the values of other variables.

Multiple regression is one statistical method that allows researchers to predict one variable based on the values of other variables (Vogt, 1993). Going back, once again, to our *"Biggest Loser"* example, we could hypothesize that higher levels of exercise and fiber intake will predict lower levels of bad cholesterol. After data collection, a multiple regression could be used to analyze the data. Results would either support or not support our hypothesis. The advantage here is that more than one variable can be used to predict the outcome of another variable. Once again, a cause-and-effect relationship cannot be presupposed unless the experimental method was utilized.

Time-series analysis

A study of the same variable across time.

Time-series analysis typically studies the same variable across time (Vogt, 1993). Perhaps you are curious as to how ADHD rates have changed over the last fifteen years. A time-series analysis would allow you to track this information. Further, additional variables could be examined in relation to ADHD in order to ascertain if they seem predictive of ADHD rates.

Meta-analysis

The data from numerous studies on a particular topic are synthesized and analyzed.

Meta-analysis is another statistical method gaining popularity. It was mentioned earlier in this chapter about the importance of replicating studies in science. In meta-analysis, data from numerous studies on a particular topic are synthesized and analyzed (Vogt, 1993). For example, let's say that more than one thousand studies have researched the effect of toxin A on developmental disorder B. Meta-analysis is one statistical way of integrating the findings of these one thousand studies so that data from the studies can be analyzed and overarching outcomes identified.

Structural equation modeling

A model that is developed to explain patterns of relationships among variables.

Structural equation modeling (SEM) is the final statistical approach we will discuss here. In SEM, models are developed that help explain patterns of relationships among variables. Typically, multiple models are examined until the best fit (best theoretically and statistically) is found. These models are complex but helpful in testing complicated theories (Vogt, 1993).

This section describes a few statistical approaches. Please do not confuse these with research approaches or designs. Statistics are a way of analyzing data collected using a research approach. Said another way, a researcher's question determines the research approach (descriptive, correlational, or experimental). There are many research techniques (e.g., observation, surveys, biological measures, etc.) that can be used for any one research approach. An appropriate technique must be matched to the specific hypothesis. Because we are particularly interested in development across the life span, we have the additional layer of either a cross-sectional, longitudinal, or sequential design. Once data is collected, it must be analyzed using statistics. Once again, the appropriate statistical approach must be matched to the research approach. The results of the statistical analysis will either support the hypothesis or not.

Pause and Process:

1. What is multiple regression? How is multiple regression different than correlational research?

2. What is structural equation modeling?

THEORIES IN HUMAN DEVELOPMENT

LEARNING OBJECTIVES:

1. *Understand the major theories that focus on biological processes*
2. *Understand the major theories that focus on cognitive processes*
3. *Understand the major theories that focus on socioemotional processes*
4. *Understand the major theories that focus on the environment or context of development*
5. *Understand the similarities and differences between the major developmental theories*

As discussed in the previous section, theories are important because they help us to understand our observations. A good theory is a testable theory that can either be supported or not supported by research. This chapter is much longer than the rest of the chapters in this book (Did I just hear a groan or sigh?). Please keep in mind that we are summarizing a couple hundred years worth of the brightest minds and their thoughts in human development in these pages. A basic foundation in these theories is vital in order to have a common starting point for all of our future chapters. Take your time and learn these theories well, for you will be seeing many of them again in the near future.

The theories in this section are categorized into broad categories based upon whether their emphasis is on biological processes, cognitive processes, socioemotional processes, or the environment. However, you must keep in mind that such classifications have their shortcomings. Most of these theories cover multiple aspects of development; we simply grouped them upon where most of the theory focused. You may find that you absolutely hate some of these theories and love some of the others. You will find that the theories that share your basic assumptions about human nature are more likable than those that differ with you on this or any of the other philosophical issues discussed in the first section. Enjoy!

THEORIES THAT FOCUS ON BIOLOGICAL PROCESSES

Some theories emphasize the importance of biological processes on development. These theories may emphasize genetics, the process of maturation, or evolution; nevertheless, they all still understand the importance of the environment for development as well. This section will discuss some of the more commonly known theories of human development that emphasize the influence of biological processes.

Evolutionary Theory

Evolutionary theory

Those theories of developmental change that are founded on Darwin's theory of evolution; these theories stress the role of biological factors in the individual's adaptation to the environment.

Fitness

How well an individual is suited for his or her environment and the ability to survive and reproduce.

Adaptive features

Those features that are conducive to survival in a given environment, whatever those features may be.

Charles Darwin (1809–1882) is largely credited as the founder of **evolutionary theory**. Although many contributed to and shared his thoughts, he was the most thorough in presenting and documenting his theory (Desmond & Moore, 1991; Hergenhahn, 2005). In terms of human development, key concepts in evolutionary theory would include the ideas of adaptation and fitness. **Fitness** would be seen as how well an individual is suited for his or her environment and the ability to survive and reproduce. Adaptation is traditionally posed in terms of **adaptive features**. "Adaptive features are those features that are conducive to survival in a given environment, *whatever* those features may be" (Hergenhahn, 2005, p. 275). In purely Darwinian terms, adaptation does not imply progress, improvement, or anything

After Charles Darwin published On the Origin of Species *in 1857, scientists began to use animal studies to gain insight into human physiology and behavior.*

of the like. In Darwin's view, evolution lacks strategy or direction. This tends to run counter to what most of us think of when we use the terms adaptation or evolution. Evolutionary theory has been highly influential in the field of sociobiology—commonly referred to as evolutionary psychology—(Hergenhahn, 2005).

Sociobiology (or Evolutionary Psychology)

Sociobiology

The study of the biological bases of social behavior.

Sociobiology theorists believe that genetic makeup and functioning are the prime basis of social behavior (Hergenhahn, 2005). They recognize, however, that developmental changes result from the interaction of heredity with the environment. A species tends to resist the alteration of its basic genetic pattern from one generation to another. This resistance, called phylogenetic inertia, is the nature part of the developmental change equation in the sociobiological framework. Factors from the environment, however, force a species to undergo a change in its genetic pattern over several generations. This change happens because it is beneficial to survival. Some environmental factors that force genetic change upon a species are a shortage of shelter, floods that destroy food, and disease that incapacitates or kills many individuals of the species.

Sociobiologists propose that several levels of such factors explain why individuals behave as they do. The ultimate goal of all individual behavior and developmental change, in this theory, is the survival of genetic material. All behavior relates to this basic premise: life exists in order that genes may be replicated and survive from one generation of a species to another. All living organisms adapt their behavior to ensure the survival of these basic elements of life.

Sociobiologists have studied a variety of social behaviors to test their ideas: altruism (concern for the welfare of others), competition, socialization, mating behavior, and communication, for example. Their research attempts to uncover the genetic basis underlying these behaviors—in other words, to find the biological source of developmental change.

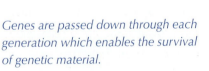

Genes are passed down through each generation which enables the survival of genetic material.

Ethology

25. What is ethology?

Ethology is the field of inquiry that studies the biological bases of behavior patterns in animals and humans. Several basic concepts that are used to explain behavior are briefly discussed here.

Ethology focuses on learning about the innate basis of behavior and the hereditary factors that influence developmental changes (Crain, 2005; Hergenhahn, 2005). Ethologists remind us of our animal origins. They believe that many of our behavior patterns are innate and are linked to past ancestral traits. Several researchers have stressed the role of genetic programming in the functioning of human behavior patterns. For example, Noam Chomsky (1957, 1965, 1968, and 1975) believes that the demonstrated ability of human infants to learn any particular language points to an inborn language-generating mechanism. He asserts that the human brain has evolved neuropsychological patterns that facilitate the learning and use of language, and this distinguishes us from lower animals (we will return to Chomsky's language theory later in the book).

Several researchers have suggested that certain human behavior patterns and features have undergone evolutionary adaptation and have endured because of their survival value. For example, Lorenz (1965) proposed that physical features in the young of many animal species stimulate mothering behaviors in the adults. Crying may serve this same purpose. Another researcher has confirmed Lorenz's findings in humans. Hess (1962), reports that the pupils of adult women enlarge significantly when they are shown pictures of babies. Pupillary dilation is a reflex that indicates interest in and curiosity about an object. Hess concludes that women, unlike men, may have a biological predisposition to respond to babies in ways that help to ensure the babies' survival.

The process by which a human infant becomes attached to its parents through emotional bonds is similar to the imprinting process found among some bird and animal species. Imprinting is an irreversible learning process that occurs within a relatively short time after the birth or hatching of the young. During this critical period, the young will attach themselves psychologically to anything that moves within their vision field. Researchers have found that the process of imprinting differs from other types of learning. It is influenced by genetic factors, and appears to have the function of ensuring the survival of the young.

Some developmentalists suggest that there are other critical (or sensitive) periods in other areas of human development. They have hypothesized that these periods exist at each stage of an individual's life. During these optimal times for learning, an individual is especially sensitive to mastering tasks that are necessary to healthy developmental progress (Colombo, 1982; Crain, 2005). The presence of such critical or sensitive periods at any stage of the life span is highly speculative and an area of active research.

Implications

Evolutionary theory, sociobiology, and ethology have proved helpful in filling out our understanding of the causes of developmental changes. Although these approaches raise many interesting issues for contemplation, critics point to a number of problems with each approach.

Sociobiology's main premise—that biological heritage shapes and limits human nature—is reminiscent of Freud's statement that "biology is destiny." Essentially, the theory proposes that what one is today is the result of past ancestral evolution. One's current developmental status has not been determined by intellect, social process, free choice, self-determination, learning, or other environmental factors.

Some ethologists insist there are critical or sensitive periods for optimal development. They believe that it is next to impossible for someone who has a developmental deficit to "catch up" at a later time (White, 1975). We will soon read about other theories that allow for flexibility in developmental milestones.

Pause and Process:

1. How do you think sociobiology theory would explain mating behavior in humans?

2. What is an area of human development for which you believe there may be a sensitive period?

THEORIES THAT FOCUS ON COGNITIVE PROCESSES

There are many theories that focus upon cognitive processes in development. However, one of the best-organized and most comprehensive explanations of how human beings acquire their thought processes and problem-solving abilities was proposed by Jean Piaget (1896–1980). We will discuss the foundation of Piaget's cognitive development theory in this section, laying the groundwork to discuss his stages in detail later in the book. Lev Semenovich Vygotsky (1896–1934) provided the framework for a social-historical theory of cognitive development before his life was cut short by tuberculosis at the age of thirty-eight. We will also be laying the foundation of his theory in this section. Finally, a number of theories fall under the blanket term "information-processing theory." Because the general assumptions and tenets of information-processing theory will be important when we learn about memory, problem-solving, and other cognitive processes later in the book, we will introduce some of its core concepts here.

Piaget's Cognitive Development Theory

Piaget's training was in biology, although he devoted most of his life to child psychology. His intent was to learn as much as he could about how intellect developed. Ultimately, he wished to explain how human knowledge was acquired, used, and limited in scope (Crain, 2005; Dixon, 2005).

Piaget based much of his theory of cognitive development on observations of, and interviews with, children (Crain, 2005; Dixon, 2005). He also intently observed his own children to learn about the mental development of infants. Although he began publishing his findings and thoughts in 1921, his work went largely unnoticed in the United States until the 1960s (although Vygotsky knew of Piaget's work and critiqued it). His works have probably stimulated more research and educational programming for children than those of any other theorist in this area of development (Beilin, 1994).

BASIC CONCEPTS   Several concepts are central to Piaget's thoughts about the development of the intellect. **Cognition** and cognitive development are terms that refer to the way in which people come to know and understand the world. A variety of related processes—perception, problem-solving, judgment, and reasoning, for example—are involved in how people organize their mental life.

Cognitive development also refers to the changes that take place as people acquire a general understanding of the world. Piaget proposed that individuals go through a series of four stages in infancy, childhood, and adolescence (Beilin, 1994; Crain, 2005; Wadsworth, 2004). These lead to more complex and sophisticated ways of understanding the world. The ages at which people proceed through these stages are somewhat variable, though the sequence of the stages is invariable (i.e., you must go through the stages in order and not skip any stages).

A **schema** (or scheme) is a building block in cognitive development. This term refers to any consistent, reliable pattern or plan of interaction with the environment. Schemas are usually goal-oriented strategies that help the person to achieve some type of intended result from his or her behavior (Wadsworth, 2004).

PIAGET PROPOSED TWO TYPES OF SCHEMAS: SENSORIMOTOR AND COGNITIVE   Sensorimotor schemas are formed during the years of infancy and early childhood. These are the first rudimentary ideas about how the world functions and how the young child may operate or act to make things happen. Sensorimotor schemas have a strong base in early reflexes and motor behavior. Sucking is an early sensorimotor schema, for example. This motor act is used by babies to define and understand their world as well as to receive nourishment. It satisfies some goal and can be initiated by babies even when they are not hungry.

Cognitive schemas are derived in part from sensorimotor schemas. Cognitive schemas refer to ideas or patterns that are based largely on the individual's experiences in operating upon the environment. They differ from sensorimotor schemas in having a strong basis in mental imagery. They reflect the person's ability to use symbolism and abstract reasoning or thinking. Cognitive schemas begin to be formed in early childhood, and are continually formed throughout life. Mathematical processes, for example, are a type of cognitive schema. Once you master the mathematical operation of addition, you are then able to perform the operation using imagery rather than needing to have concrete objects before you. Visualizing objects or symbols becomes automatic through trial-and-error learning and practice.

Piaget proposed that individuals use two processes to modify schemas (Dixon, 2003; Wadsworth, 2004). Assimilation is the process by which people acquire new knowledge or

Cognition

Those processes, such as perception, thinking, reasoning, and problem solving, by which one comes to know and understand the world.

Schema

Any consistent, reliable pattern or plan of interaction with the environment.

information and match it with or incorporate it into their existing schemas. Accommodation refers to the process of altering existing schemas in order to bring about congruence with reality. For example, infants modify or change a sucking schema by learning that they can suck not only on a nipple but also on thumbs. An infant who attempts to suck on someone else's thumb may find that this is not allowed. The sucking schema may then be restricted to nipples and the infant's own thumb. This illustrates how accommodation or experiences with reality modify an existing schema. The sucking schema is modified as an infant discovers what can be sucked on and what cannot. The processes of assimilation and accommodation function throughout life to provide the means for changing and modifying schemas.

Central to Piaget's theory is the idea that mental life is devoted to active organization of one's personal understanding of the environment (Crain, 2005; Dixon, 2003; Wadsworth, 2004). Progression through the stages of cognitive development does not occur automatically, either from biological maturation or from genetic programming. Rather, people progress cognitively as they learn to organize their understanding of the world in more complex ways. Experience in interacting with the environment is the cornerstone for producing changes as people grow older. Because of this factor, each person has his or her own unique interpretation of the environment. In essence, Piaget believed that we derive our own singular understanding of the world based on our personal experiences. It is these individual meanings that we attach to what we observe that give rise to the emotional reactions we experience (Burns, 1980).

Vygotsky's Social-Historical Theory of Cognitive Development

Vygotsky lived in Russia during the Communist Revolution and at a time when Marxist theory was a topic of active discussion. In fact, Vygotsky built his theory of development utilizing some of the key concepts of Marxism (Crain, 2005). This means that although Vygotsky valued both biological and environmental forces in development, he tended to spend more energy focusing on the environmental forces. Specifically, he appreciated the importance of social processes in guiding development and the value of culturally-based, psychological tools in cognitive processes (Crain, 2005; Vygotsky, 1978; Wertsch & Tulviste, 1994). Finally, Vygotsky believed that one absolutely must consider the social-historical context in which a human is developing in order to study cognitive development.

You may be wondering what on Earth culturally-based, psychological tools are. They are not nearly as esoteric as they sound. In fact, you use some everyday. Speech, writing, our number system, and memory aids are all psychological tools which we use to mediate our behavior in the world. Vygotsky felt that although intrinsic maturational processes are enough to motivate cognitive growth the first few years of life, these cultural systems are necessary to maintain cognitive growth after that (Crain, 2005). Therefore, one of the main ideas to take away from social-historical theory is that one must understand the historical and social context of development if thinking is to be understood. We will be returning to Vygotsky's theory when we learn about language development.

As interesting as the above discussion of Vygotsky's theory is, it is not what most Americans think about when they think about Vygotsky. Instead, it is his impact on the educational system with which most American's are familiar. Vygotsky proposed the idea of the zone of proximal development. The **zone of proximal development** is the range between what a child can accomplish alone and what they can accomplish with assistance. For example, a child may be able to "read" only a picture book on his or her own, but with some help sounding out words, he or she could read a beginning Dr. Seuss book.

Another important term to Vygotsky and modern education is **scaffolding**. Scaffolding provides a framework to assist a child learning a new skill initially through small steps. Initially, the parent or teacher provides a lot of support and assistance, then incrementally reduces the assistance as the child can complete more of the skill or task independently. For example, let's say that a child wants to learn to make a salad. Initially, the parent would probably gather and prepare all of the necessary ingredients and simply have the child toss everything into the salad bowl. Over time, maybe the child can gather the ingredients, the parent will do the necessary washing/cutting/cooking, and the child will combine the ingredients in the bowl. Ultimately, the child will take over the task in its entirety having been guided through the process time and again by the parent via a scaffolding process.

Zone of proximal development

The range between what a child can accomplish alone and what can be accomplished with assistance.

Scaffolding

Provides a framework to assist a child learning a new skill initially through small steps.

Information-Processing Theory

As mentioned at the beginning of this section, information-processing theory is actually an overarching term for a group of theories. We will learn about the specifics of memory, language, and problem-solving development across the life span. All we seek to do in this

Teaching a child a new skill through small steps is referred to as scaffolding.

section is provide you with the general framework all information-processing theories share. Below are the general assumptions in information-processing theory (Siegler, 1998):

Information-processing

How information is represented, processed, and applied in reference to memory constraints at any given age.

1. The term **information-processing** is synonymous with thinking. Thinking can be defined as how information is represented, processed, and applied in reference to memory constraints at any given age.

2. Information-processing researchers seek to understand the specific mechanisms that allow for cognitive development.

3. Cognitive development is guided by constant self-modification in thinking.

4. Although we can understand adult thinking by studying children, we can also understand child thinking by studying adults.

Future chapters will further illuminate the complexity of topics studied within information-processing theory. We will learn about types of memory, cognitive processes, and age-related changes in both of these areas.

Implications

Theories that focus on cognitive processes in development share much in common yet have some marked differences. All of these theories seek to understand how thinking develops across the life span. Piaget sees cognitive development as discontinuous, or occurring in stages. Vygotsky emphasizes the importance of the social and historical context in cognitive development. Information-processing theories view cognitive development as a continuous, self-modifying process.

The most important impact all of these theories have had in the United States would be upon education. For example, the sequence of learning in a curriculum, what topics should be covered at each grade level, how children's intelligence should be measured, how children learn best and through what types of teaching methods, and what information should be taught to children, have all been developed based upon research with these theories. Beyond education, these theories have also impacted parenting advice and psychotherapy approaches.

Pause and Process:

1. What is one main concept from Piaget's and Vygotsky's theories?

2. What is one main difference between Piaget's theory and information-processing theory?

THEORIES THAT FOCUS ON SOCIOEMOTIONAL PROCESSES

The theories discussed in this section address important issues regarding the nature of human beings. As such, they have had a significant impact on both researchers and practitioners in the field of human development. Psychodynamic and psychosocial theories laid the foundation for many contemporary methods of psychotherapy, for example, and parents and educators have applied these theories to child rearing. We will also briefly touch upon humanistic theory, attachment theory, and socioemotional selectivity theory.

Psychodynamic Theories

Few individuals had more influence on modern psychology than Sigmund Freud. To much of the public, in fact, "psychology" is synonymous with "Freudian psychoanalytic theory." Though Freud's ideas about human personality development are still controversial, they are widely known and drawn upon by mental health professionals.

Freud was a physician who spent most of his life in Vienna, Austria. As a young doctor working in France in the late 1800s, Freud became interested in people's emotional disorders. He began experimenting with hypnosis as a means to study emotions. He also was interested in the role and function of dreams as emotional expression. As a result of his investigations, Freud proposed a theory of personality development that he expounded on in various books and professional articles in the early 1900s (Crain, 2005).

Freud's theory centers on how the individual progresses through a series of stages during childhood and adolescence that shape adult personality (Crain, 2005). **Personality** in Freudian theory refers to inner behavior that represents the true inner self as well as to outward actions manifesting that inner self. Personality also refers to the collection of emotional traits that are unique to the person.

Personality

The inner behavior that represents the true inner self as well as to outward actions manifesting that inner self.

28. What is personality?

Freud used the term psychosexual in referring to the stages of personality development. He derived the characteristics and nature of these stages through a process called psychoanalysis, which involved using hypnosis and by asking people to recall their experiences when growing up. The majority of people Freud studied would today be diagnosed as emotionally ill. From his studies of these patients, Freud came to believe that events from a person's past determined that person's behavior in the present.

Another theme in Freud's writings about personality development relates to the basic nature of human beings. Freud believed strongly that children's behavior was rooted in basic animalistic instincts that came to be controlled as they matured. These instincts, which he

Sigmund Freud (1856–1939), an Austrian physician, proposed the progressive development of the personality in distinct but related stages of psychosexual development.

thought were irrational in content, became channeled into appropriate, acceptable behavior patterns as the individual grew up.

BASIC CONCEPTS   Freud was convinced that much human behavior is influenced by the unconscious mind, especially by the conflict between instinctual drives and social constraints against their expression. Basic personality structures are involved in mediating this conflict. Because the conflict is unbearable, people block off their awareness of their basic drives by repressing them in the unconscious part of their minds. Defense mechanisms are used to ward off the anxiety generated by conflict. But the drives do not disappear; they seek expression in some manner. Freud and others proposed that repressed drives are often expressed as physical symptoms, which the person finds to be more acceptable than the direct expression of forbidden emotions. Freud believed that the role of a psychoanalytic therapist was to help patients release these repressed emotions—to bring into the conscious (aware) mind what had been delegated into the unconscious (unaware) mind.

Early experience plays a prominent role in Freudian theory. The periods of infancy and early childhood are thought to be crucial for development in the later years of life. Interactions with parents during these years are especially important, according to Freud, in determining how healthy a person's personality development is in these years.

Freud thought that an individual's personality structure included three components. The first component of the personality is the **id**, which contains the person's life force. The id is composed of the drives that seek gratification of elemental needs for food, water, sex, and warmth, and contains the emotions basic to all human beings, such as anger, joy, love, and fear. The id is unconscious and operates according to the **pleasure principle**—that is, it is attracted to those things that are enjoyable and repelled by those things that produce discomfort. The id is largely illogical and very mysterious. Dreams are the best means for learning how a person's id functions, according to this theory. The id wishes to satisfy its needs, and does not care how it does so. If it is hungry, it doesn't care if the person buys the food or steals the food, as long as the food is obtained and eaten.

The second component of personality is the **ego**, which is responsible for contact with day-to-day reality. The ego emerges slowly and becomes noticeable only after a child's first birthday. This part of the personality is guided by the **reality principle**—that is, the ego analyzes reality in relation to past experiences, alternatives, and options for action. It also predicts probable outcomes of behavior choices. Although the ego operates fairly independently of the id, it also guides the expression of basic impulses that arise from the id.

The third part of the personality is the **superego**. This structure functions to control and override the id's attempts to express basic drives in ways that are socially unacceptable. It is similar to the traditional notion of conscience in that it contains information and decision-making processes that produce guilt when the person transgresses its standards. The superego is often likened to an internalized judge or parent figure guiding the person's behavior according to social and moral ideals. That is why the superego is said to operate according to the **perfection principle**.

Id

The drives that seek gratification of elemental needs for food, water, sex, and warmth.

Pleasure principle

Attraction to those things which are enjoyable and repelled by those things that produce discomfort.

Ego

The rational part of our psyche which tries to balance the needs of the id and superego.

Reality principle

According to Freud, the tendency to behave in ways that are consistent with reality.

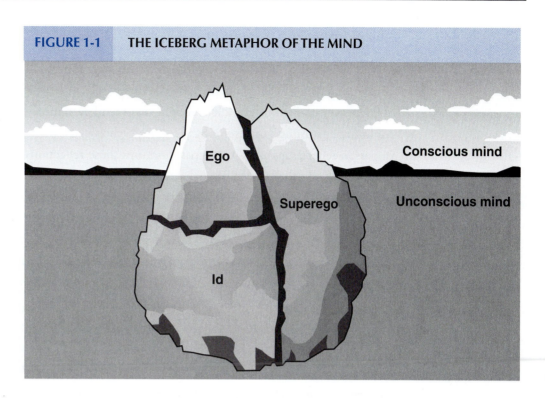

FIGURE 1-1   THE ICEBERG METAPHOR OF THE MIND

Superego

Functions to control and override the id's attempts to express basic drives in ways that are socially unacceptable.

Perfection principle

An internalized judge or parent figure guiding the person's behavior according to social and moral ideals.

Fixation

Occurs when attempts to satisfy needs at a certain stage of personality development are continually frustrated.

The interaction of these three structures as they seek to express themselves in an individual constitutes personality, according to Freud.

STAGES OF DEVELOPMENT   Freud described the progression of personality development through stages. These are experienced in the growing years of infancy, childhood, and adolescence. The role of sexual feelings or emotions is prominent in all the stages. Freud believed that much behavior in the early years of life was dominated by the struggle to bring the id under control of the other personality structures. Because the id operates on the pleasure principle, this means that children participate in behaviors that are sexually satisfying to them and only learn with time to control their expression.

As the person experiences each stage of development, the general sexual energy, or libido, becomes concentrated in a specific body region called an erogenous zone. Through the years of infancy and childhood, the principal erogenous zone shifts to different body locations. The sequence of the shift from one body area to another is determined by the maturation of the body as well as by experiences.

Freud also concluded that development can be retarded by **fixation**. A fixation occurs when attempts to satisfy needs at a certain stage of personality development are continually frustrated. When tensions are experienced later in life, the person will revert to behaviors that were effective in managing frustrations at an earlier time in life.

It is important to remember that Freudian theory has generated much interest in the developmental processes involved in personality changes. Freud emphasized the influences of the unconscious mind and early experience on later development. These are outstanding contributions to our understanding of developmental changes across the human life span.

Neo-Freudian Theories

Freud had many disciple's that built upon his psychodynamic theory, making changes where they saw fit (Hergenhahn, 2005). Alfred Adler (1870–1937) is one such theorist. Like many neo-Freudian's, Adler thought that Freud overemphasized the biological aspects of human nature and underemphasized the psychosocial aspects. He was interested in how a person reflects upon his or her past and uses those reflections to direct development in the future and other aspects of goal-directed behavior. The ideas of inferiority and striving for superiority run throughout his work. Adler is also well-known for his theories on birth order and sibling relationships (Corey, 1991; Fadiman & Frager, 1976).

Carl Jung (1875–1961) altered Freud's theory on the personality structure to include elements such as the collective unconscious, the persona, and the shadow. Beyond that, much of popular culture's ideas about a midlife crisis come from Jung's theory, and he discussed aging and late adulthood development. Additionally, he discussed the importance of archetypes and religiosity when facing death. Besides psychodynamic theory, Eastern philosophy was highly influential to Jung's ideas (Crain, 2005; Fadiman & Frager, 1976; Jung, 1964).

Erikson's Psychosocial Theory

Most modern development theories focus on the development of children. They offer extensive abstract explanations of how heredity and environment interact to influence the changes that take place during infancy, childhood, and adolescence. Our society considers the changes that occur during these periods to be the most significant life changes. Therefore, few developmental theories explain or interpret the changes that occur after adolescence. In fact, it is only within the last few decades that developmentalists have become convinced that changes do occur during adulthood.

The psychosocial theory of Erik Erikson (1950, 1964, 1982, and 1986) is a notable exception to this cultural belief. His approach is an exception also to the notion that individual development happens only under the influence of psychological and biological forces.

Erikson's theory recognizes that changes occur throughout the life span. His explanation of psychosocial development builds upon Freud's theory. Erikson expanded upon the ideas that Freud first presented, but differed from Freud in major ways about how changes are experienced, the forces that motivate changes, and the process by which changes are experienced.

Erikson's concept of development emphasizes the individual experiencing a "series of childhoods"—or changes—throughout life. Psychosocial changes occur as an evolutionary process, meaning one based on a sequence of stages involving biological, social, and psychological events that take place during life. A person enters each stage of psychosocial development with the goal of developing the specific skills and competencies considered appropriate for that time in life. Erikson sees the person as having a *dynamic* rather than a *static* personality. Thus an individual constantly experiences the reshaping and revising of personality configuration over the life span (Maier, 1965).

Psychosocial crisis

A central problem that the person is expected to master in order to make healthy progress to the next stage.

Each stage of psychosocial development has its own theme, which Erikson terms a **psychosocial crisis**. A psychosocial crisis is a central problem that the person is expected to master in order to make healthy progress to the next stage. Changes are enhanced or retarded by the way the person confronts and handles the central crisis of each particular stage of psychosocial development. If the person successfully deals with the crisis, she or he will experience "normal," healthy changes that lead toward happiness and personal fulfillment. If, however, the person has overwhelming difficulties in accomplishing what is expected at a particular stage, the result will be a failure to establish healthy changes not only at that particular stage but at future stages as well. As you can see, Erikson's theory incorporates epigenesis—the notion that development occurs in a stepwise manner.

Erikson's theory strongly refutes the idea that changes are triggered simply by some preset biological programming. Changes occur through interaction with social and psychological events as well as from biological programming. As the person grows older, he or she is influenced by an increasing number of people. Changes are fostered by interactions and relationships within the family context first, and then within an ever-expanding social radius (friends, the school environment, and so on). **Significant others** are those who are singularly important at each particular stage of a person's psychosocial development. These others influence the person's changes positively or negatively. Readiness to progress to a subsequent stage occurs when she or he is ready or has completed the requirements at a particular stage.

Significant others

Those people who are singularly important at each particular stage of a person's psychosocial development.

The psychosocial crisis at each stage of Erikson's theory is thought to challenge the person to acquire a corresponding psychosocial sense or attitude. Each psychosocial sense is an attitude or general feeling resulting from how adequately the person meets the crisis.

Erikson describes eight stages of psychosocial development. There are two opposing attitudes that are possible at each stage. Experiences lead the person to feel one attitude in the pair more predominantly than the other. Erikson acknowledges that it is unrealistic to expect no negative experiences at any stage. The desirable outcome is to resolve the overall developmental challenge of each stage so that more healthy than unhealthy attitudes are acquired over the life course.

It is this successful resolution that enables the person to progress in psychosocial development. In the early years of childhood, for example, children are thought to experience a psychosocial stage where they have the opportunity to develop a sense of autonomy (positive) or a sense of shame and doubt (negative). Healthy development, of course, requires the child to achieve a sense of autonomy. At each of the eight stages of psychosocial development over the life span, healthy progress depends on acquiring the positive rather than the negative sense in the pair of attitudes possible for that stage.

Erikson's theory is basically optimistic in that it provides for the possibility of redemption at each stage if unhealthy attitudes were acquired at earlier stages. Someone who failed to develop a healthy psychosocial sense at one stage is not condemned to an unhealthy path of change for the rest of his or her life. But failure or difficulty in meeting the developmental challenge of one stage does slow down healthy progress in the next stages. Still, Erikson believed that a person could transform negative attitudes acquired at one stage into positive attitudes later in life.

TABLE 1-1	ERIKSON'S TIMETABLE OF DEVELOPMENTAL STAGES			
STAGE	**PSYCHOSOCIAL CRISIS**	**SIGNIFICANT OTHER**	**THEME**	**PERIOD OF LIFE SPAN**
I.	Trust vs. Mistrust	Maternal person	To get; to give in return	Birth–18 months
II.	Autonomy vs. Shame and Doubt	Paternal person	To hold on ; to let go	18 months–3 years
III.	Initiative vs. Guilt	Family	To make; to make like	3–6 years
IV.	Industry vs. Inferiority	School	To make things; to make things together	6–12 years
V.	Identify vs. Role Confusion	Peers	To be oneself; to share being oneself	13–18 years
VI.	Intimacy vs. Isolation	Partners	To lose and find oneself in another	18–24 years
VII.	Generativity vs. Self-absorption	Life partner	To make be; to take care of	24–54 years
VIII.	Integrity vs. Despair	Humankind	To be, through having been; to face not being	54 years–death

Erikson's theory of psychosocial development is an extension of Freudian theory. Erikson's theory stresses (1) the discontinuity of psychosocial development over the life span; (2) the resolution of a central psychosocial crisis at each stage of the life span; (3) the establishment of an associated psychosocial attitude at each of his stages; and (4) the important influence "significant others" have on the individual's psychosocial development at each stage. Erikson described eight stages of psychosocial development that extend from birth until death. We will discuss each of Erikson's stages of psychosexual development when we discuss socioemotional development later in the book.

Humanistic Theory

Humanistic psychology describes the human experience differently than other theories (Crain, 2005; Hergenhahn, 2005). Some people consider this approach to be diametrically opposed to behavioral theory (discussed later in this chapter). Humanistic theory views the individual as a dynamic force who seeks self-fulfillment over the course of life. Continuity of change is therefore an ever-present reality in human beings. The individual seeks her or his own destiny by setting goals, attempting to meet inner-self needs, and expressing creative energies. Humanistic theory denies the exclusive influence of either the environment or unconscious drives. Self-understanding and fulfillment—the ultimate

TABLE 1-2	A COMPARISON OF CONCEPTS IN FREUDIAN AND ERIKSONIAN THEORY	
CONCEPT	**FREUD**	**ERIKSON**
Development	All behavior and change are determined by instinctual drives. Psychic energy propels change.	Changes occur as an evolutionary process according to a sequence of biological, social, and cultural events.
Dynamics of Change	Individual experiences a series of stages marked by certain characteristics.	Individual resolves psychosocial crises while progressing through a series of related stages.
Factors Influencing Changes	The unconscious mind; libidinal energy; the id, ego, and superego; nature of instinctual drives.	Experiencing the sequence of epigenetic stages; significant others.
Socialization	Maturing ego and superego gain increasing control over the id.	Establishment of identity; intrusive behavior; increasing radius of significant others.

goals of life span changes in this view—result from a conscious choice. Individuals willfully seek to maximize their experiences.

Maslow's Concepts

Abraham Maslow (1970) is probably the most prominent humanistic psychologist. Maslow's approach stresses that people are motivated to make changes in order to achieve their personal full potential. He called this the drive to **self-actualization**.

This state in the personal developmental path is at the pinnacle of a **needs hierarchy** common to all humans. Maslow proposed that people have to satisfy certain basic needs before they can attempt to realize self-actualization. The needs he describes are ranked in terms of priority. The most essential needs, those addressed first, relate to basic survival. These include the creature comforts of having food, warmth, shelter, safety, and so on. After these basic needs are satisfied, individuals then seek love and social contact with others. Once these needs have been satisfied, the individual turns to self-worth and self-esteem needs. These particular needs are satisfied by interactions with others that produce the conviction that the person is valued by peers, colleagues, and others. After all these needs have been fulfilled, the individual addresses the need for self-actualization. As the person experiments and learns to express his own unique nature, he may achieve self-fulfillment.

Maslow and others (Shaffer, 1978) believe that the process of achieving self-actualization is not usually begun until people reach middle or even late adulthood. Earlier in life, people tend to focus on fulfilling the lower-ranked needs. Adolescents, for example, are developmentally unready to do what is necessary to fulfill their self-actualization needs because the need for belongingness is typically addressed at this time in

Self-actualization

A person's drive to achieve their personal full potential.

Needs hierarchy

A person's need to satisfy certain basic needs before they attempt to realize self-actualization.

FIGURE 1-2   MASLOW'S HIERARCHY OF NEEDS

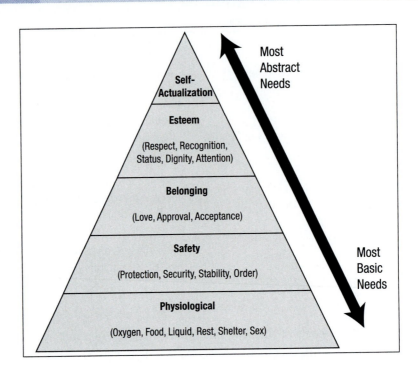

life. Early adulthood is the developmentally appropriate time for addressing self-esteem needs.

Making the changes in our thoughts and behaviors that lead us to be all that we can be is what life is all about, according to Maslow. Self-actualization can be a near-mystical experience. According to Maslow, the self-actualizing person has **peak experiences**. These are feelings of great joy, ecstasy, and cosmic identification with the whole universe.

Rogers' Concepts

Carl Rogers is another humanistic psychologist. In contrast to Freud, Rogers (1961) believed that human behavior is driven by impulses that are basically healthy and positive. Roger's concept of human nature is similar to Maslow's.

Unlike Maslow, though, Rogers was a practicing psychotherapist. His humanistic orientation led him to promote a style of interaction with clients termed **client-centered therapy**. Rogers' approach is less formalized than Maslow's; it has no stages. Rogers shared Maslow's conviction that reaching one's personal potential is the ultimate goal of developmental changes, but he saw the need for some people to turn to others for assistance in working through their problems. He created a style of psychotherapy that differed greatly from psychoanalysis. It stresses the attitude of the therapist. Rogers promoted a therapeutic attitude of **positive regard** toward clients. Positive regard is characterized as being warm, genuine, and giving total attention and acceptance to the client. Rogers felt that

Peak experiences

The feeling of great joy, ecstasy, and cosmic identification with the whole universe.

Client-centered therapy

Also known as person-centered therapy, it is a non-directive approach to therapy based upon humanistic theory. This approach believes that the client has the necessary inner resources to cope with his or her problems.

Positive regard

Characterized as being warm, genuine, and giving total attention and acceptance to the client.

Attachment theory

Intense emotional tie between two individuals, such as an infant and a parent.

Socioemotional selectivity theory

A theory that as age increases, so does the desire to be more selective in one's social relationships, optimizing positive interactions.

such an attitude would help the client to become more self-accepting and to achieve the greatest degree of personal growth possible (Shaffer, 1978).

Attachment Theory and Socioemotional Selectivity Theory

Two other theories that are of increasing interest in human development are attachment theory and socioemotional selectivity theory. We will discuss these theories at length when we discuss socioemotional development later in the text. For now, we just want to introduce these two theories.

John Bowlby developed **attachment theory** by integrating the psychodynamic, evolutionary, and ethological perspectives (Dixon, 2003). Mary Ainsworth greatly extended the theory through developing methodology to assess attachment and further research on the implications of attachment on development. This theory views the need for attachment as real as the need for food or water. Early in life, we develop mental models of attachment based upon caregiver behavior. As we shall see, these attachment models have life-long consequences.

Many times, older people are viewed as lonely because they do not seem to have as extensive friend networks as adolescents or young adults. Research, however, shows that older people are simply choosier in selecting relationships that are rewarding, and letting negative relationships fall to the wayside. **Socioemotional selectivity theory**, developed by Laura Carstensen, discusses this process and the developmental outcomes associated with social networks (Carstensen, Mikels, Mather, 2006).

Implications

Freud's psychodynamic theory of psychosexual development has generated much fruitful debate about the nature of humankind and the manner in which individual personality development occurs. However, there are difficulties with this theory that cast doubt on its validity in explaining personality development.

First, it is hard for scientists to test the concepts, principles, and propositions of Freud's theory. For instance, researchers have a hard time operationally defining some of Freud's key concepts, such as id, ego, or superego. Remember from the first section that any good theory must be a testable theory, and so far, it has been extremely difficult to test psychodynamic theory. However, new advances in neuroscience are making the testing of the unconscious mind more feasible (Galatzer-Levy & Cohler, 1993).

Second, psychodynamic theory may be biased in several ways. First of all, the theory is criticized as culture-bound and therefore limited in its application. Freud derived his concepts and principles from adults reminiscing about their past. Errors in memory are quite likely under these circumstances. It should be noted here as well that Freud drew his ideas about personality development from people who were emotionally maladjusted. His theory may better explain unhealthy personality development than normal development.

Beyond being culturally biased, psychodynamic theory has been accused of being gender biased (Crain, 2005; Hergenhahn, 2005).

Third, the theory is imprecise about the nature of personality development, making it difficult to predict how people will change over time. However, it did in many ways begin the psychological study of personality and development. Additionally, psychodynamic theory has great appeal because it is such a broad-based explanation of personality development. Despite its shortcomings, Freud's psychodynamic theory has done much to increase awareness of the importance of early life experiences on later development.

Erikson's psychosocial theory attempted to extend psychodynamic concepts and stages beyond adolescence. Psychosocial theory is also significant for its emphasis on the normal rather than the abnormal aspects of developmental changes. Erikson was optimistic about human nature. His psychosocial theory allows for the possibility of later resolution of problems and tasks left unresolved at a previous stage of development. His theory also acknowledges the impact of significant others who influence the individual's psychosocial changes for better or worse throughout life. Psychosocial theory is used extensively in the fields of psychology and education as a teaching device. It helps students to understand the course of human development from a social-psychological perspective.

One of the main criticisms of Erikson's theory is its vagueness (Crain, 2005). Its explanation of the role of maturation in adulthood, for instance, is neither clear nor specific. The theory does not fully mesh with Freud's ideas and concepts on some points. Finally, this theory has generated only limited research either substantiating or refuting it.

Humanistic explanations of development offer an important alternative to learning theory and psychosocial explanations. This approach encourages an examination and appreciation of individual differences in the course of developmental changes. It stresses that certain goals cannot be accomplished until certain fundamental needs are addressed. The humanistic approach has influenced educational programs for children.

Critics judge this approach to be as imprecise as psychoanalytic theory and equally difficult to test empirically. They regard concepts such as self-actualization, peak experiences, self-fulfillment, and positive regard skeptically. They insist on the need for objective measurement of both concepts and therapeutic outcomes.

Attachment theory and socioemotional selectivity theory are relatively new theories that are the focus of a plethora of research at the moment. Attachment theory has the potential to explain how the roots of adult relationships can be traced all the way back to infant-caregiver relationships. Socioemotional selectivity theory is a theory focusing on the positive aspects of adult social networks.

Pause and Process:

1. What is one main difference between psychodynamic theory and psychosocial theory?

2. Explain Maslow's hierarchy of needs.

THEORIES THAT FOCUS ON THE ENVIRONMENT OR CONTEXT OF DEVELOPMENT

Reflecting back on the philosophical issues discussed in the first section, the theories discussed in this section have two main assumptions. First, humans are born as blank slates that will be shaped by their environments. Second, empiricism (or learning by experience) is far more important in shaping human development than nativism. Although the degree of rigidness on these issues varies across the theories in this section, these basic assumptions are crucial in these theories.

Behavioral Theory

Behavioral theory is sometimes referred to as learning theory. The two terms will be used interchangeably in this text. Behavioral theory stresses the role of an individual's interactions with the environment in shaping developmental changes. Learning is thought to take place in several ways. Behavior is modified or changed as a result of experiences and interactions with factors external to the individual.

Classical conditioning

The pairing of a neutral stimulus with an unconditioned stimulus in order to achieve a desired response.

Operant conditioning

The use of reinforcers and punishers to control behavior.

There are two major ways learning is believed to occur in behavioral theory: **classical conditioning** and **operant conditioning**. Ivan Pavlov is the name associated with classical conditioning. He was a Russian physiologist who won the Nobel Prize in 1904 for his studies of the digestive system. Pavlov became involved in learning research unintentionally when he was using dogs as subjects in studying the digestive process. Whenever he placed meat powder on their tongues to stimulate salivation, the salivation reflex was automatically performed by the dogs. Then, Pavlov noticed that the salivation reflex was also initiated when the dogs heard their caretaker approach at mealtime, when they saw or smelled food, and when they heard noises associated with their meal preparation. The dogs had learned to respond to a new stimulus that had come to replace the original stimulus. This process of pairing a new stimulus with one that automatically produces a particular response is called classical conditioning. After this serendipitous finding with his dog subjects, Pavlov proceeded to investigate the development of classical conditioning techniques as a learning theory of behavior.

You may be thinking that although all this talk of dogs and meat and salivation is fascinating, what on earth does it have to do with human beings. Well, you have been classically conditioned and you probably don't even realize it. Put simply, classical conditioning builds new reactions built on pre-existing reflexes. Let's work through an example.

What would you feel if someone poked you with a needle? You would probably flinch or cringe and withdraw from the needle. You didn't need to learn this response; it was a reflex with which you were born. Now imagine that every time that you were poked with this needle you heard a particular sound. Eventually, just that sound alone would be enough to cause you to flinch or cringe in anticipation of the needle poke—that is, you would be classically conditioned to respond to a previously neutral stimulus in a way you responded to the original stimulus. If you don't believe this, imagine—right now—the sound of the dentist's drill (made

FIGURE 1-3   PAVLOV'S CONDITIONING APPARATUS

An apparatus similar to that used by Pavlov to study classical conditioning in dogs. (From An Introduction to Psychology, by Ralph Norman Haber and Aharon H. Fried, 1975. Copyright © by Holt, Rinehart and Winston. Reproduced by permission.)

you cringe). The first time you heard a dentist's drill, that sound meant nothing to you. However, because it has been paired with pain over and over again, just the sound of the drill is enough to cause a cringe reaction. The same can be said of food poisoning/food aversion or the smell of perfume/cologne your ex-girlfriend or ex-boyfriend wore. All of us have been classically conditioned at some point in life, and this conditioning impacted our development.

Okay, so that's classical conditioning. Let us now turn our attention to operant conditioning. Behaviorism received a great deal of attention in the 1950s and 1960s owing to the works of psychologist B. F. Skinner (1957). His contributions focus on the role and function of the consequences of behavior to learning. There are two broad categories of consequences to behavior: reinforcements and punishments. **Reinforcers** are meant to increase the behavior they follow, whereas **punishers** are meant to decrease the behaviors they follow. In general, reinforcers are more powerful in shaping behavior long-term. If you ever received praise (a reinforcer) for a good grade, or grounding (a punisher) for a bad grade, you have been operantly conditioned.

Reinforcers

Are meant to increase the behavior they follow.

Punishers

Are meant to decrease the behaviors they follow.

2050

2010 13

hypertension
hypertension
hypertension
Reagton

Stamina
coordination

Strength

presbyopia
presbyopia

Social Cognitive Theory

This theory is sometimes referred to as social learning theory. In some textbooks, it would have been discussed under behavioral theories, in other texts it would be discussed under cognitive theories. We will honor this theory with its own subsection, but please realize that not everyone will agree with our choice.

Social cognitive theory is an extension and application of behavioral theory. You see, hard core behavioral theory thought that all human behavior could be explained via external circumstances—that there was no need to consider a person's thinking. At the same time, the environment that directed a person's development had to be experienced first-hand. Social cognitive theory turned both of these assertions on their head. First, social cognitive theory recognized the importance of cognition. Second, social cognitive theory recognized that we could learn by observing the impact of the environment on others.

One of the proponents of this approach is psychologist Albert Bandura (1977). He agrees with Skinner that social learning occurs by reinforcers and punishers, but differs from Skinner in proposing that **observational learning** also shapes or changes social behavior (Bandura & Walters, 1963). **Modeling** and imitation are key ideas in social cognitive theory. Bandura believes that many kinds of behavior are acquired by watching the behavior of another person, and then coming to model one's own behavior on that of the others.

Research into this style of learning investigates how children learn to express such social behaviors as sharing, cooperation, and aggression by imitating role models in their environment. Role models include both real people and characters on television shows or video games. Research reveals that when children see a model being rewarded for aggressive behavior, for instance, they are more likely to demonstrate that same kind of aggressive behavior in their own play.

Social cognitive theory also explains how people acquire social values and attitudes as well

Observational learning

Learning that occurs through observing others.

Modeling

The process by which behavior is acquired and modified through observing and replicating the behavior of others.

A child playing dress up to imitate a mother is an example of modeling and imitation.

as occupation skills in adulthood. Social roles are learned by modeling. Children imitate behaviors they observe in adults and in other children they perceive as role models. Some aspects of human development are not so efficiently explained in social learning terms, however, as we will see throughout the book. Despite these limitations, social learning theory has significance in explaining how at least some of our different types of behavior are shaped and how learning occurs over the life span.

Other Contextual Theories

There are several other theories that focus upon the environment or context of development. Bioecological theory, sociocultural theory, and family systems theory are three examples that are currently receiving a lot of attention.

Bioecological theory
A theory by Bronfenbrenner that emphasizes the nested environments that influence human development.

Bioecological theory was developed by Urie Bronfenbrenner (Bronfenbrenner, 1979, 1995). This theory focuses on layers of development, much like the nested Russian dolls, that can be visualized as a series of circles. The innermost circle is the person and his or her biology (e.g., genetics, sex, age, etc.). The next circle is called the microsystem and it includes the person's immediate environment (e.g., family, friends, neighborhood, etc.). Now think briefly back to your teenage years. Did your parents and friends always get along? Interactions among the elements in your microsystem are referred to as the mesosystem, and that is the next level of context. Beyond the mesosystem is the exosystem. The exosystem involves elements that influence a person's life indirectly, such as parents' jobs or vacations. The macrosystem is the final, outside circle and includes the culture and society in which a person develops. Beyond all these circles, Bronfenbrenner includes the chronosystem, or historical time period in which an individual develops. We know this is a lot of circles and systems to wrap your brain around—the theory is dense and uses confusing terminology. Still, bioecological theory is comprehensive in tearing apart the numerous contexts in which we develop; hence, allowing researchers to zero in on the influence of specific layers of the environment on development. It may be helpful for you to sketch out your own bioecological context of development, listing influential factors to your development at each level.

Sociocultural theory
A theory that cognitive development is dependent upon social interactions.

Sociocultural theory is still evolving, largely due to the work of Barbara Rogoff. Although this theory could be viewed as neo-Vygotskian and included in the cognitive development section of this chapter, Rogoff's cross-cultural research has touched upon so many different aspects of human development (not just cognitive), that we felt it needed to be placed, on its own, in this section of the chapter. Rogoff (2003) believes that "Human development is a cultural process…people develop as participants in cultural communities. Their development can be understood only in light of the cultural practices and circumstances of their communities—which also change" (pp. 3–4). Rogoff's research not only seeks to investigate how culture creates unique patterns in human development, but also what is universal in development across cultures. She also explores the diversity of goals in human development.

Family systems theory describes the family as a social system. This approach theorizes that families operate as a system in the ways in which they make decisions and

Family systems theory

The approach that theorizes that families operate as a system in the ways they make decisions and take actions that govern behavior, help the group meet its goals, and enable the group to maintain stability over time.

take actions that govern behavior, help the group meet its goals, and enable the group to maintain stability over time. Maintaining dynamic equilibrium is a challenge to a family. It must adapt as a group to the changing nature of its members as each experiences different rates of developmental change. Several concepts describe the family as a social system: wholeness, interdependence, self-regulating patterns, equifinality, adaptation, open versus closed boundaries, relationships among members, and homeostasis (Becvar & Becvar, 1982; Galvin & Brommel, 1986; Olson et al., 1983; Olson, Sprenkle & Russell, 1979; von Bertalanffy, 1974a/1974b).

Implications

Theories that focus on the environment or context of development have generated a substantial amount of research into human development. Behavioral and social cognitive theories have had a broad impact on educational programs as well as on therapeutic methods for treating a variety of behavioral problems such as phobias, learning disabilities, and stress management.

Behavioral theory emphasizes the role of experience and environmental interactions that produce changes in behavior. Critics of behavioral theory have pointed out several limitations of these approaches. First, these theories emphasize the environment to the point of bias. Hereditary and biological factors also play important roles in shaping changes in behavior. Second, behavioral theory is limited to explaining specific types of behavior (neglecting cognitive processes and emotions). Third, behaviorism has been criticized for depicting the individual as rather like a machine whose performance can be controlled through conditioning. Fourth, research on behavioral theory is usually conducted in laboratory settings in which small segments of behavior are isolated, which makes the application of their findings to everyday life dubious. Critics also note that studies of

Under the family systems theory families operate as a system which enables the group to maintain stability over time.

behavioral theory have focused extensively on the behavior of lower animals and it is difficult to generalize these studies findings to humans. Despite all these criticisms, behavioral theory still provides some of the best approaches we know of in the treatment of autism and phobias.

The bioecological theory has led developmentalists to appreciate the nested environments that impact development, and sociocultural theory has enhanced our appreciation of the impact of culture on development. Family systems theory encourages us to see individuals as part of a system of mutual influences. All of these theories have impacted research in human development, social policy, and therapy.

Pause and Process:

1. Give an example of a time when your parents or caregivers used operant conditioning to modify or control your behavior.

2. Which factor in your microsystem do you think was most influential during your adolescent years?

COMPARING DEVELOPMENTAL THEORIES

Four broad categories of theories have been discussed in this chapter. Always remember that theories are not facts, but can change and are not all-inclusive. Theories provide a springboard for exploration, discussion, and debate about the many issues involved in explaining a complex process in a complex organism—developmental changes in human beings.

Some of you may feel confused and frustrated by the variety of developmental theories presented here. You may find it helpful to remember that each theory addresses different aspects of human functioning. As yet, we have no grand unifying theory of human development that explains everything in an integrated, concise manner.

Theories that focus on biological processes view us with at least some preprogramming in our genes that will guide our development. Reflecting back on the philosophical issues in the first section, these theories would be seen as largely nativistic in their approach. They also tend to focus on the universal aspects of development.

Theories that focus on cognitive processes typically view humans as having a positive human nature. These theories also emphasize the active nature of knowledge acquisition. Some cognitive theories see development as continuous (e.g., information-processing theories), whereas others see development as discontinuous (e.g., Piaget's theory of cognitive development). Piaget's theory of cognitive development and information-processing theories tend to focus on the universal aspects of development, and Vygotsky's social-historical theory emphasized the importance of context.

Theories that focus on socioemotional processes vary considerably in their stance of the philosophical issues. Freud's psychodynamic theory viewed humans as animalistic and instinct driven—hence, a negative view of human nature. Conversely, humanistic theory views human nature in a positive light. Most of these theories appreciate the biological propensities with which we are born, as well as the influence of our experiences and environment. Psychodynamic and psychosocial theory both view human development within a discontinuous, or stage-like framework.

Theories that focus on the environment or context of development tend to view human nature from the *tabula rasa* perspective. These theories also tend to emphasize the empirical view of human development. Behavioral theories would view learning as largely passive in nature.

Theoretical eclecticism

The approach of investigating the varied models and concepts and choosing the best to apply to a particular issue.

Although we did not discuss all of the philosophical issues for all of the theories, we did cover the ones most pertinent to each theoretical approach. You may be thinking, "What does all this mean for me? How can I, a student, apply this information?" Perhaps the most useful approach is to study and consider the many different theories and then construct your own explanation of developmental change. Most developmentalists do just this. They investigate the varied models and concepts and choose those they think best apply to each particular issue. This approach is termed **theoretical eclecticism**.

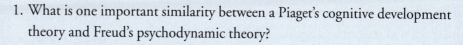

Pause and Process:

1. What is one important similarity between a Piaget's cognitive development theory and Freud's psychodynamic theory?

2. What is one important difference between a sociobiological theory and behavioral theory?

SUMMARY

1. Life span development involves the study of human beings from conception until death in old age. Understanding human development incorporates research and theories from a diversity of disciplines. A degree in human development can lead to a career in education, counseling, the government, nonprofit organizations, or the private sector.

2. There are persistent, philosophical issues that form the foundation of theory and research in human development. Not all theories share the same perspective on these issues. These philosophical issues will be revisited throughout the text.

3. The study of human development is important for several reasons. Social norms and social policy are guided by our understanding of human development. Therapy and intervention must consider development in order to be effective. Understanding the multiple paths that development can take gives perspective to our own development and broadens our awareness of human development across history and culture.

4. Development occurs in three broad domains: physical, cognitive, and socioemotional. Although nearly all human activities involve all three of these domains concurrently, it is sometimes easier to

research and understand development by categorizing it into these domains. Each domain consists of numerous smaller subdomains.

5. Principles of developmental changes guide our understanding about the process of development. Development is lifelong, multidimensional, multidirectional, multidisciplinary, contextual, and a dance between nature, nurture, and the individual. The life span can be categorized into eight periods of development: prenatal development, infancy, early childhood, middle childhood, adolescence, early adulthood, middle adulthood, and late adulthood. Age can be conceptualized into four types: chronological, biological, psychological, and social.

6. This chapter introduced you to the scientific method and research designs. Theories are an important part of research and can generate hypotheses. A good theory must be falsifiable; hence, testable.

7. One's research approach should depend upon the type of question being asked. If one wishes to describe behavior, cognitions, or emotions, then a descriptive approach should be taken. If one wishes to explore relationships among variables, then a correlational approach should be utilized. If one wishes to establish cause-and-effect, then an experimental approach should be used.

8. Because developmentalists are interested in change across ages and time, researchers must consider an additional layer in their work. Development may be studied utilizing cross-sectional, longitudinal, or sequential designs.

9. Thanks to advances in statistical theory and computer software, statistical approaches are increasingly discussed in developmental textbooks. It is helpful for students to have a conceptual understanding of multiple regression, time-series analysis, meta-analysis, and structural equation modeling. With such knowledge, students can understand the results of research studies more easily.

10. All research designs have their own strengths and weaknesses. Every theory must be tested and retested. Theories also must be modified based upon the results of research studies.

11. Theories provide a comprehensive framework from which to conduct research. A theory must be testable. Theories tend to focus on one aspect of human development: biological, cognitive, socioemotional, or environmental/contextual. They also differ on their stances on the historical, philosophical issues. There is no one theory that explains every aspect of human development. It can be helpful to select the most useful aspects of a variety of theories for addressing a particular question about developmental changes. This approach is known as theoretical eclecticism.

SELF-QUIZ

1. Which philosopher believed that humans are born basically good and that it is civilization that corrupts the human race?

2. What are three views of human nature?

3. What are the three domains of human development?

4. What is the principle that development involves growth, maintenance, and decline?

5. What is the principle that development is embedded in an environment?

6. What is the principle that early development is related to later development?

7. What are three specific contexts for influences on development?

8. What is the term used to refer to individuals 100 years of age and older?

9. What is the age range that refers to early adulthood?

10. What are the four conceptualizations of age?

11. What is the scientific method?

12. What is a theory?

13. Why are operational definitions important?

14. The method that a researcher uses is dependent upon the type of _____ that he or she seeks to address.

15. What are the three broad approaches to research?

16. What are two specific types of observational research?

17. What are three general types of correlations?

18. Which correlation is stronger, −.84 or +.62?

19. The _____ variable is controlled and/or manipulated and the _____ variable is measured.

20. What are three developmental designs?

21. What theories discussed in this chapter focus upon biological processes?

22. What theories discussed in this chapter focus upon cognitive processes?

23. What theories discussed in this chapter focus upon socioemotional processes?

24. What theories discussed in this chapter focus upon the environment or context of development?

25. What is ethology?

26. What is cognition?

27. What is a schema (or scheme)?

28. What is personality?

29. What are the three components of Freud's personality structure?

30. What are two main ways learning is believed to occur in behavioral theory?

TERMS AND CONCEPTS

The Dawn of Development

If I asked you to reflect upon your life and remember your most important moments, what would come to mind? You may recall your high school graduation, birth of a sibling, or other such monumental events. Did you think about your moment of conception? Arguably, this is your most important moment in life, because it is when you became a life. As you will learn in this chapter, the period of prenatal development is a magical time of incredible growth and development. We will also discuss genetics and the birth process.

GENETICS

LEARNING OBJECTIVES:

1. *To have a general knowledge of genetic terminology and processes*
2. *Awareness of some of the different types of genetic disorders*
3. *Appreciation for the field of behavior genetics within the context of studying life span development*

We know, we know—most of you just learned about genetics in your college or high school biology class. That's good! Some of the basic terminology and processes will simply be review for you. However, it is possible that you will learn some new material as well. We will explain some genetic disorders that are of interest to developmentalists in this section. Most of them are heart wrenching. We will also briefly touch upon the field of behavior genetics. In general, we will try to keep the focus on why genetics is important to the field of human development, hopefully providing a new perspective for you.

BIOLOGICAL FOUNDATIONS

What color are your eyes? How tall are you? What shape is your nose (before any breaks or plastic surgery)? Clearly, genetics play a role in how you answer each of these questions. Are you shy or outgoing? Do any of your relatives have schizophrenia? Are you smarter than a fifth grader? Did you also know that genetics play a role in answering these questions as well? Genetics, in conjunction with the environment, play a role in all aspects of your development: biological, cognitive, and socioemotional. In this section we will discuss some of the basic biological aspects of genetics.

The Basics in Genetics

Spotlight

1. What does the nucleus of all cells contain?

At the moment of conception a complex hereditary process is initiated. This allows for a new genetic blueprint of a human being who is similar to others but genetically unique. It has been estimated, for example, that there is the possibility of 17 million different genetic combinations available for the makeup of a human being when conception occurs

(Kowles, 1985; Patten, 1976). Genetics can be defined as "the study of how parents pass on characteristics to their offspring" (Jenkins, 1998, p. 16).

The nucleus of all cells contains **chromosomes**. The number of chromosomes typically found in a cell nucleus is species-dependent. For example, dogs and chickens have seventy-eight chromosomes, chimpanzees have forty-eight chromosomes, goldfish have ninety-four chromosomes, and alligators have thirty-two chromosomes (Jenkins, 1998). For a number of years in the past, humans were thought to have forty-eight chromosomes in each cell of their bodies. Investigations conducted in 1965 determined this to be an error. These reported only forty-six chromosomes per each normal human cell, which is widely accepted today as the accurate chromosome count. Therefore, you have twenty-three pairs of chromosomes, half from your mother and half from your father. Geneticists refer to the first twenty-two pairs of chromosomes as **autosomes**, and the twenty-third pair as your **sex chromosomes**.

Chromosomes are composed of **genes**, which are the basic agents of heredity from one generation of humans to the next. Genes are known today to be composed of chemical molecules. It is through genes that one's biological make-up is passed on to offspring. They also direct the daily functioning of individual cells as well as organ systems. The total genetic makeup of an individual is known as that person's **genotype**. The interactions of genes with one another and with the environment produce the person's **phenotype**. We cannot directly see a person's genotype (it's inside his or her genes); however, we can observe a person's phenotype in certain traits and characteristics such as hair color, skin color, and behavior.

Each gene contained within a chromosome package is a single but uniquely composed molecule of **deoxyribonucleic acid** (DNA). DNA molecules have a special structure

Chromosomes

A collection of genes contained within a cell nucleus; the total number per cell is constant for each species, with humans having forty-six in each cell, except for the gametes, which have twenty-three.

Autosomes

A single chromosome; any one of the forty-six chromosomes found in the nucleus of a human cell.

Sex chromosomes

The twenty-third pair of chromosomes, which determines a person's gender.

Gene

The basic agents of heredity from one generation of humans to the next.

FIGURE 2-1	A MODEL OF THE DNA MOLECULE

DNA molecules have a special structure called a double helix. DNA passes genetic material to the next generation.

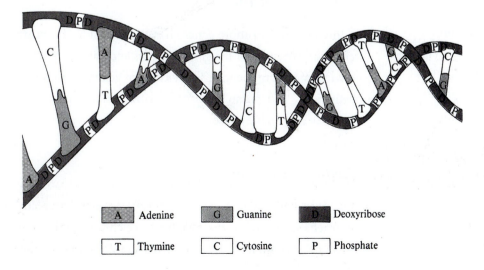

A	Adenine	G	Guanine	D	Deoxyribose
T	Thymine	C	Cytosine	P	Phosphate

Genotype

The total genetic makeup of an individual.

Phenotype

The traits and characteristics such as hair color, skin color, and behavior that can be observed.

Deoxyribonucleic acid (DNA)

A complex molecule composed of four basic nucleotides that is the carrier of genetic inheritance.

Mitosis

The splitting of each chromosome in the body cell to form a new pair.

Meiosis

The process by which the gametes (sperm and ova) are produced in the male testicles and the female ovaries.

Mutation

A change in the chemical structure of the gene or genes and can occur during cell division or as a result of environmental influences.

called a double helix (see Figure 2-1). It resembles a twisting ladder or a spiral staircase. There are two known functions for DNA: passing genetic material on to the next generation and the instructions for cells to make proteins (Werner, 2007). Any DNA molecule is formed of four basic nucleotides (commonly referred to as A, T, C, and G—see below). These are paired in repeated sequences to form a specific genetic code. These nucleotides are composed of a carbohydrate (deoxyribose), a phosphate, a purine (adenine or guanine), and a pyrimidine (cystocine or thymine).

It is important to distinguish between the replacement of other body cells and the manufacture of the sex cells responsible for fertilization. The average body cell is eventually replaced by new ones as growth and development occur over the life span. Through a process called **mitosis**, each chromosome in a body cell splits to form a new pair. The result is a new daughter cell containing forty-six chromosomes that are identical with those of the original cell. **Meiosis** is the process by which the gametes (sperm and ova) are produced in the male testicles and the female ovaries. Two cell divisions usually occur when the testicles (or ovaries) produce a new sperm cell (or ovum). The result is that the nucleus of the gamete contains only twenty-three rather than the usual forty-six chromosomes. At conception, the sperm and the ovum (produced via meiosis) join together. The process of mitosis is initiated and the new genetically constituted human being begins to grow.

As most of you know, your biological sex was determined at conception. The female ovum contains twenty-three chromosomes, one of which is known as the X sex chromosome. Every normal ovum contains only an X sex chromosome.

Sperm cells from the male also contain twenty-three chromosomes. Some sperm contain an X sex chromosome, like the one found in the female ovum, whereas other sperm cells contain a Y sex chromosome. When a sperm containing an X chromosome fertilizes an ovum (containing its own X chromosome), a biological female is created. When a sperm containing a Y sex chromosome unites with an ovum (containing its X chromosome), a biological male is created. Males have a genotype of XY and females have a genotype of XX. It is the type of sperm from the father, then, that determines the biological sex of the offspring.

Gene Mutation

Sometimes one or more genes change as a result of a **mutation**. A mutation changes the chemical structure of the gene or genes and can occur during cell division or as a result of environmental influences. Three types of gene mutations are insertion mutations, deletion mutations, and point mutations. Most mutations cause illness or death; relatively few result in a desirable outcome.

Genetic Processes

Okay, so half of your genetic material (twenty-three chromosomes) comes from your mother and half (the other twenty-three chromosomes) comes from your father. For each pair of chromosomes, the genes that you inherit may be the same (homozygous) or may be different (heterozygous). This is because the gene may have identical or different alleles (Jenkins, 1998, p.159). This sounds confusing, so maybe the following passage from a developmental biology textbook will help:

> "For each kind of a gene there is a position—a locus—where it is found along the length of a chromosome. The locus for most genes is found on two chromosomes—one inherited from our mother and one from our father. That is, we have two copies (alleles) of most genes. These copies may be identical or different. If they are different, they may both be expressed, or one copy (dominant) may mask the other (recessive)" (Dye, 2000, p. 16).

For example, you may have inherited an allele for five fingers from your dad and an allele for six fingers from your mom. Will you end up with five and half fingers? Or is one allele stronger than the other allele? We will see that some genes have a dominant/recessive process to determine how a genotype is expressed as a phenotype. Other genes have a polygenetic process to determine phenotype. Still others work by genetic processes that we are just beginning to understand. Things are much more complicated than Gregor Mendel (often called the father of genetics) may have imagined.

Dominant/Recessive Processes

Sometimes, one allele is stronger than another allele. For example, look at your fingers. Are they long and slender (let's call this L for its genotype) or are they short and clublike (let's call this S for its genotype)? The allele for short, clublike fingers is **dominant**, whereas the allele for long, slender fingers is **recessive**. This means that if you have long, slender fingers, both of your alleles are recessive (genotype LL). If just one of your alleles was S, you would have short, clublike fingers because it is a dominant allele. This means that people with either genotypes SL or SS have the phenotype of short, clublike fingers.

Gene dominance occurs when any two partner alleles are not identical for a gene. One allele is said to be dominant and the other recessive. The dominant gene of the pair acts to produce the trait this pair of genes is supposed to affect, and the activity of the recessive gene is repressed. However, sometimes there can be **incomplete dominance** (such as when a red flower and a white flower bred together can create a pink flower) and **codominance** or **intermediate inheritance** (such as when a white cow and a red bull will produce a calf with red and white hairs). Occasionally, a specific trait or characteristic may have more than one pair of alleles possible (multiple allelism). Blood type is an example of this (Dye, 2000; Jenkins, 1998).

Sex-Linked Inheritance

As mentioned earlier, there are two sex chromosomes that control the biological sex of a child (XX or XY). The X chromosome is larger than the Y chromosome and seems to carry more genetically rich information (Dye, 2000). Later in this chapter we will briefly discuss some sex-linked chromosome disorders. If a male inherits a recessive gene on his X chromosome,

Dominant

A gene from one parent that controls or suppresses the influence of the complementary (recessive) gene from the other parent in the offspring.

Recessive

A gene from one parent whose influence is repressed by the complementary (dominant) gene from the other parent in the offspring

Incomplete dominance

Occurs when one allele is not completely dominant over the second allele.

Codominance

Occurs when both alleles are fully expressed.

Polygenic process

The interaction of alleles from more than one gene.

Discontinuous variation

When a trait or variation can be placed into distinct categories.

Continuous variation

When a trait or variation is distributed on a continuum or spectrum.

Epigenetic information

A characteristic of developmental changes meaning that changes that are currently observed were determined by those that occurred earlier in time, and changes that follow will be influenced by the ones currently being observed.

Genetic imprinting

The repression or expression of a gene or chromosome in an offspring that is dependent upon which parent it is inherited from.

he will exhibit the recessive trait. However, if a female inherits a recessive gene on one of her X chromosomes, she will be a carrier of the gene, but may not exhibit the recessive trait if her other X chromosome has a dominate gene. This is why males are more likely to inherit certain sex-linked traits, characteristics, or disorders such as color-blindness, baldness, or hemophilia.

A pink flower is an example of incomplete dominance.

Polygenic Inheritance

Although some inherited traits and characteristics follow a dominant/recessive process, others involve a **polygenic process** (or the interaction of several genes). Intelligence, skin color, eye color, and height are just some of the human traits that involve polygenic inheritance (Dye, 2000; Jenkins, 1998). For instance, you may have been taught that eye color is a matter of dominant/recessive alleles; however, eye color is determined by the amount of melanin present in your iris. Light-colored eyes have lower amounts of melanin than dark-colored eyes. Skin color is the same way, and many geneticists believe that at least three genes interact to determine skin color.

Some human traits and characteristics are coded for an either/or presentation (i.e., **discontinuous variation**) driven by dominant/recessive processes. For example, either you have five fingers or six fingers, depending upon your genotype. However, other human traits and characteristics are coded for a **continuous variation** as seen with polygenetic inheritance. For example, an individual's intelligence or height is limited by a range set forth in the genotype, but it is the interaction of genes (and sometimes environmental influences) that ultimately determines that person's phenotype (Dye, 2000; Jenkins, 1998).

Beyond the Genes

A child receives three kinds of information during prenatal development: "genes, maternally derived substances, and differential chemical modification of parental genes" (Dye, 2000, p. 16). The first, the genes, we have already covered. The other two forms of information can be collectively referred to as **epigenetic information**. These mechanisms are still in the process of being understood, but some preliminary information is known.

Genetic imprinting can be considered one form of epigenetic information. It is the fascinating process whereby how genetic material is expressed is dependent upon from which parent it is inherited (Moore & Persaud, 1998). For example, some chromosome disorders will manifest as different syndromes dependent upon whether the chromosome deletion is carried by the mother or the father. Another form of epigenetic information is the cytoplasmic environment during ovum development (Dye, 2000). As stated, epigenetic information is a new area of research; however, some preliminary findings suggest that longevity, metabolism rates, and height may be influenced by epigenetic information from both the parents and possibly the grandparents.

In summary, each of us is endowed with a unique genetic make-up at the moment of conception. Sometimes, however, mistakes can happen in our genes and a genetic disorder is the result. The next section will discuss some ways in which our genetic process can go awry.

Pause and Process:

1. Distinguish between genotype and phenotype.

2. Explain the genetic processes of dominant/recessive genes and polygenetic inheritance.

GENETIC DISORDERS

There are different categories of genetic disorders (ACOG, 2005); we will discuss three broad categories here. Some disorders are caused by a single gene. Other disorders are caused at the chromosomal level (or by many genes). Still others are multifactorial in cause (or caused by genes and environmental factors). Below, we will briefly highlight several genetic disorders and then discuss a few of the more common ones at length.

Inherited Disorders

Inherited disorder

A disorder or disease that develops due to a gene mutation, chromosomal problem, or other genetic factor.

As mentioned above, some genetic disorders are initiated by a single gene. These are referred to as **inherited disorders**. They may originate from dominant genes, recessive genes, or sex-linked genes.

If a disorder is inherited from a dominant gene, then it can be given to a child by a single gene from one parent. These disorders can range from life-threatening to nonserious. See Table (2a-1) of some dominant-gene (or autosomal dominant) disorders (ACOG, 2005; Carlson, 1999).

If a disorder is inherited from a recessive gene, then both parents must be carriers of the gene in order for the child to have the disorder. If only one parent is a carrier, then the child may be a carrier but will not have the disorder. Many of these disorders have different prevalence rates for different ethnic groups. See Table (2a-2) of some recessive-gene (or autosomal recessive) disorders (ACOG, 2005; Carlson, 1999).

Sex-linked chromosome disorders are carried on the X chromosome; hence, they are sometimes referred to as X-linked recessive disorders. These disorders are much more common in males. This is because males have only one X chromosome; therefore, if there is a recessive gene on it, they will develop the disorder. On the other hand, females have two X chromosomes, so if one has a recessive gene, the other may have a dominant gene that prevents the disorder from materializing or will mitigate the materialization of the disorder. See Table (2a-3) of some sex-linked disorders (ACOG, 2005; Carlson, 1999).

TABLE 2A-1	DOMINANT-GENE DISORDERS
DOMINANT-GENE DISORDERS	**BRIEF DESCRIPTION**
Anchondroplasia	Dwarfism with short limbs
Aniridia	Incomplete iris
Crouzon syndrome	Abnormalities to the cranium structure
Huntington's disease	Degeneration of the nervous system
Neurofibromatosis	Pigmentation abnormalities and tumors on the skin
Polycystic kidney disease type III	Having cysts in the kidneys
Polydactyly	Having extra fingers or toes

Chromosomal Disorders

Chromosomal disorder

A disorder due to a chromosomal abnormality or defect.

Chromosomal disorders stem from a missing, duplicate, or damaged chromosome (ACOG, 2005). In this category of disorders, the problem typically originates during fertilization. The risk of having a baby with a chromosome disorder increases with the mother's age. For example, a twenty-five-year-old woman has a 1/476 chance of having a baby with any chromosomal disorder; conversely, a thirty-five-year-old woman has a 1/192 chance and a forty-five-year-old woman has a 1/21 chance of having a baby with

TABLE 2A-2	RECESSIVE-GENE DISORDERS
RECESSIVE-GENE DISORDERS	**BRIEF DESCRIPTION**
Albinism	Reduction or lack of pigmentation in the skin, eyes, and/or hair; eye problems
Bloom syndrome	Prenatal and childhood growth problems, cognitive deficits
Cystic fibrosis	Mucus build-up in the respiratory system, frequent respiratory infections
Polycystic kidney disease type I	Having cysts in the kidneys
Phocomelia syndrome	Deformities in the limbs
Sickle-cell disease	Misshapen red blood cells that cannot properly carry oxygen to all parts of the body and block white blood cells
Tay-Sachs disease	Nervous system degeneration and early childhood death

TABLE 2A-3	SEX-LINKED DISORDERS	
SEX-LINKED DISORDERS	**BRIEF DESCRIPTION**
Fragile X syndrome	Cognitive deficiencies possible, including learning disabilities or mental retardation
Hemophilia	Inability to clot blood normally
Hydrocephalus	Large cranium
Icthyosis	Skin disorder
Testicular feminization syndrome	Genetic male with a female phenotype

such a disorder (as cited by the ACOG, 2005). The two most discussed chromosome disorders are Down syndrome and trisomy 18.

Multifactorial Disorders

Multifactorial disorder

A disorder that results from the interaction of genetics with the environment.

Multifactorial disorders come from a combination of genetic and environmental causes. Often, doctors are never quite certain what the specific cause of such disorders is. Some examples of multifactorial disorders include neural tube defects and cleft palates.

Support for Families Coping with Genetic Disorders

Genetic disorders may be minor in nature or life-threatening. Regardless, the impact of learning that you or your loved one is facing such a disorder cannot be underestimated. Some of these disorders are widely known and have established support networks. Others are so rare, that finding support can be difficult. The genesis of the World Wide Web has offered individuals facing a genetic disorder a new hope in finding support. Information, support groups (online and in person), medical interventions, and research information are now available in an easy-to-use interface. Again, the rarer disorders may still be hard to find support for; however, families can reach out and try to find help in ways never thought possible.

Pause and Process:

1. What is the difference between inherited disorders and chromosomal disorders?

2. Why are males more likely to inherit some genetic disorders than females?

BEHAVIOR GENETICS

The field of behavior genetics seeks to understand how genetic and environmental factors interact to produce particular behaviors, characteristics, and traits. This is not the nature versus nurture argument of old; instead, it is an endeavor to truly understand the interactive dance between nature and nurture and their coactive influence on development. Environmental factors can be broadly conceptualized as external environmental factors and internal environmental factors that influence the expression of genes (National Research Council, 2000). This section will address some of the research designs used in behavior genetics and some of the ways in which genetics and the environment interact and influence one another.

Research Designs

Because developmentalists can neither ethically nor practically enact selective breeding programs to study behavioral genetics, they have heavily relied upon twin and adoption research. Both approaches have their strengths and their limitations.

In adoption research, a child's characteristics are compared with his biological and adoptive mothers' characteristics. For example, let's say you are interested in how musical preferences are influenced by genetics and environment. You could compare an adopted child's preference for classical music to his biological mother's like of classical music (where the child and mother share genes, but not the home environment). You could also compare the adopted child's preference for classical music to his adoptive mother's like of classical music (where the child and mother share a home environment, but not genes). What could you assume if the child's preferences closely resemble the adoptive mother's preferences but not the biological mother's preferences? One possible assumption could be that home environment is more important in the development of musical preferences than genetic endowment. This is an overly simplified example of the adoptive research design, but it gives you a general idea of what the approach is like. There are variations on this theme that may focus upon biologically related and unrelated siblings.

There are some potential problems with the adoption research design (National Research Council, 2000). Can you guess what they may be? First, adoption designs can neglect to consider the possibilities that adoption agencies are selective in their placements and how that may bias the research. Second, adoption studies may neglect to consider the impact of prenatal experiences on the child. Finally, a child is not a lump of clay when placed with an adoptive family. He or she comes with their own set of characteristics that may evoke certain responses and interactions from adoptive parents. This can also bias, or at least impact, the outcomes of any study.

Twin studies compare the traits/characteristics/behaviors of monozygotic (genetically identical—identical twins) and dizygotic (genetically similar, but not identical—fraternal twins) twins. What would you suppose if monozygotic twins were more alike in their music preferences than dizygotic twins? It would be easy to assume that music preference is at least somewhat influenced by genetics. Again, this is an overly simplified example, but it gives you the big picture of twin studies. Sometimes, twin studies compare twins that were raised together against those that were separated at birth and reared apart (think *The*

Spotlight

9. What are the two types of twins?

Twin studies compares the traits/characteristics/behaviors of monozygotic and dizygotic twins.

Parent Trap here). This allows researchers the additional layer of considering home environment influences.

Twin study designs also have some potential problems (National Research Council, 2000). It is possible that monozygotic twins and dizygotic differ in regards to how similar their home environments are. Perhaps parents are more likely to treat monozygotic twins more alike than dizygotic twins. If the twin study involves separation at birth and adoption, then we have the same issues mentioned earlier for the adoption studies. Additionally, maybe twin development is not the same as development in individuals who are not twins. In this case, the research findings are applicable only to twins, not people in general. Still, adoption and twin studies within the paradigm of behavior genetics have offered some interesting insights into the co-influence of genetics and environment.

Genetic/Environment Interactions

Evocative geno-type-environment correlation

An environment in which the child elicits certain environments or behaviors due to his or her genetics.

Passive genotype-environment correlation

An environment in which the child passively receives an environment.

How do genes and the environment interact? The answer is that it depends. There are a few different ways that we can see genes and the environment interact (Scarr, 1993). These are largely false categorizations, because in the real world, all of these different interactions are probably happening simultaneously and continuously.

One perspective on gene/environment interactions highlights the dynamic nature of such interactions. A child's genetic endowment may lead to some behavioral propensities, which in turn, evoke certain responses from the environment. For example, a child with impulsive behaviors may elicit impulsive behaviors from the parents. Hence, this type of relationship could be viewed as an **evocative genotype-environment** relationship (or correlation).

Another perspective on gene/environment interactions may focus upon the influence of the environment in activating genes. For example, a person may have the genetic propensity for developing bipolar disorder; however, whether those genes are activated depends upon environmental factors. This type of relationship is viewed as a **passive genotype-environment** relationship (or correlation).

A final perspective on gene/environment interactions may emphasize what is referred to as niche-picking. Within this perspective, attention is paid to the fact that people, influenced by their genetics, seek out environments that are in harmony with their genetic propensities. For example, a child who is, by nature, social and active may seek out sports that are social and active. Conversely, a child who is, by nature, quiet and introspective may seek out activities that mesh better with his or her nature. This type of a relationship is viewed as an **active genotype-environment** relationship (or correlation) in which individuals seek environments in tune with their biological preferences.

Active genotype-environment correlation

An environment that the child seeks due to genetic preferences.

Pause and Process:

1. What is the goal of behavior genetics?

2. Describe adoption and twin studies.

PRENATAL DEVELOPMENT

LEARNING OBJECTIVES:

1. *Understand and describe the nature of developmental changes occurring between conception and birth*
2. *Identify and describe various hazards that may be experienced during a woman's pregnancy*
3. *Discuss complications that may arise during pregnancy*
4. *Relate common prenatal care*
5. *Understand typical reactions to pregnancy*

The period before birth is perhaps the most crucial stage in the life span. During the average 280-day period, the biological foundations are established that are influential for the entire life span.

In earlier times, development before birth was surrounded by mystery. Because it is hidden from direct observation, the beginnings of life were largely misunderstood, even by scientists. In these less-informed times, folklore and superstition governed popular speculation about pregnancy. One folk belief held that everything a pregnant woman experienced affected the developing child within her uterus. Birthmarks on the baby's body, for example, were attributed to the mother's having a frightening or stressful experience, spilling wine at a meal, or eating too many strawberries during pregnancy. A newborn's harelip (a deformation of the upper lip and palate that produces a rodentlike appearance) was attributed to the mother's viewing a rabbit during pregnancy. On a more elevated plane, many women believed that if they listened to classical music, read fine literature, and thought "good" thoughts, their child would be born with an appreciation for music, high intelligence, and a good character.

These folklore beliefs were discarded in modern times as scientists gained information on how life begins, how the process of genetic transmission occurs, and how the internal and external maternal environments influence the individual's development during pregnancy. These advances in knowledge are discussed in this section. Other topics explored are the course by which these changes occur, the factors that critically influence how they occur, and the tools used by modern medical science to provide the kind of prenatal care that will enhance an individual's development.

STAGES OF PRENATAL DEVELOPMENT

The developmental changes that occur before birth are significant in many ways. Many experts consider this the most important stage of life. The changes an individual experiences during this time have a critical bearing on development in subsequent stages in the life span.

The time before birth is the shortest stage of the life span. The average length of pregnancy is 280 days (about nine calendar months or ten, twenty-eight-day lunar months). Although the length of pregnancy is somewhat variable, there are invariably many remarkable changes between conception and birth. Essentially, an individual develops from a genetically unique, one-celled human into a newborn with more than 200 billion cells during this relatively short time. As we will soon learn, the most rapid rate of growth and development of the entire life span occurs before birth! As we will also soon learn, this is a highly critical period in human development, in which the person is sensitive to many hazards and benefits to its development provided through the maternal environment.

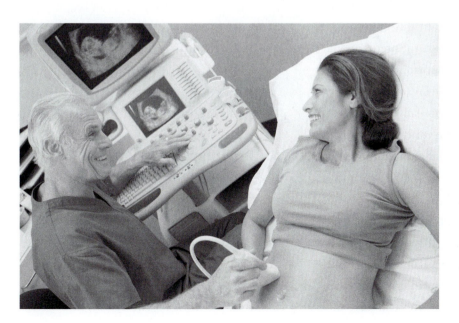

The average length of pregnancy is 280 days. During this time life begins with one cell and quickly grows into a newborn with more than 200 billion cells.

Stages versus Trimesters

When thinking about pregnancy, most people think about the three trimesters. The first trimester would be the first three months of pregnancy. Many women experience morning sickness, or all day sickness, during this time. The second trimester would be the second three months of pregnancy. This trimester is sometimes alluded to as the honeymoon trimester because morning sickness subsides for most women and the woman is still comfortable physically. The third trimester would be the final three months of pregnancy. This is the trimester when the baby gains weight rapidly and the woman can begin to have aches and pains due to the weight of the baby and shift in her center of gravity.

Developmentalists, however, view prenatal development as occurring in three periods that do *not* correspond with the three trimesters. These periods are based on biological milestones and are not broken into equivalent lengths. The germinal period is from conception to two weeks. The embryonic period is from three to eight weeks. The fetal period is from nine weeks until birth. As you will see, each of these periods is highlighted by unique developmental milestones during this prenatal stage of life.

Conception

Fertilization

The penetration of the ovum by a sperm cell.

Conception

The fertilization of an ovum by a sperm cell.

The development of an individual begins with **fertilization** of an ovum by a sperm cell. This is called **conception**. The sperm contained in the semen from the male are deposited by ejaculation into the vaginal tract. One ejaculation—about a teaspoon of fluid—normally contains about 300 million to 500 million sperm cells. Of this vast number, only several hundred survive to reach the fallopian tube that harbors the ovum.

Sperm cells are propelled on the journey by their long, whipping tails, which move them up the vaginal tract to the cervix. From this point, sperm are assisted through the uterus and fallopian tubes by small, weak contractions of these organs. The great majority of sperm fail to survive the journey to the ovum because of the highly acidic condition of the female reproductive tract, the immaturity of some sperm cells, breakage of tails, fatigue, and moving into the wrong fallopian tube.

Conception begins when the surviving sperm encounter the ovum in the upper end of the fallopian tube

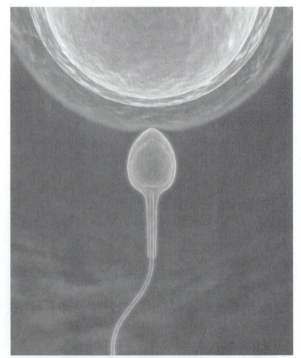

A sperm cell fertilizes an ovum. This is the point of conception and the beginning of an individual.

into which the ovum was deposited after ovulation. The sperm cells gather around the ovum with their head areas pointing toward the surface. The head region of the sperm cells releases an enzyme. A pathway may then be opened through the cellular matter surrounding the ovum.

When the head of one sperm comes into contact with the ovum's surface, a biochemical change occurs within the ovum that prevents the entry of other sperm cells. This process is not clearly understood. The sperm cell in contact enters the ovum, initiating a complex process leading to the completion of a fully constituted, single-cell human. If normal, this single cell now contains forty-six chromosomes, twenty-three from the sperm cell and twenty-three from the ovum. Hence, from the moment of conception, the human being has a unique, genetic composition (Moore & Persaud, 1998).

Germinal Period

Germinal period

The phase of prenatal developing lasting from conception until implantation in the uterus (around ten to fourteen days).

Zygote

The name of the developing individual during the germinal period.

The **germinal period** lasts from conception of the individual until his or her implantation into the uterus (about ten to fourteen days). We refer to the baby as a **zygote** during this period of prenatal development. From the moment of fertilization, the zygote's sex is already determined by the sperm (X-bearing or Y-bearing sperm). Fertilization also initiates cleavage—or cell division—in the zygote (Moore & Persaud, 1998).

The first two weeks following conception constitute a critical period for the developing individual. For the first three or four days after conception, cilia lining the fallopian tube move the zygote on his or her journey to the uterus. Again, the zygote experiences cleavage as he or she moves along the tube.

The one-celled zygote created at conception divides by mitosis into two genetically identical cells within twelve to fifteen hours. These cells reproduce themselves to make four, then eight, then sixteen, and so on. Cell division begins slowly, but then rapidly picks up speed. By the third day following conception, the cells have divided sufficiently through mitotic cleavage to form a small ball that is known as a blastocyst. It is in this form that the zygote enters the uterus. Attachment in the uterus begins about six days after conception, although the process of implantation takes some time to complete (Moore & Persaud, 1998).

The endometrial tissue has been prepared for accepting the zygote by hormones. The outer layer of the blastocyst, called the trophoblast, will develop into the support structures for the individual during prenatal development (e.g., placenta). The inner part of the blastocyst (or inner cell mass) is the part where the zygote resides.

Implantation

Occurs when the zygote burrows into the uterus.

Implantation occurs when the blastocyst sinks into the endometrium. With this event, an important process begins that serves to ensure the survival of the zygote. Through the action of hormones produced by the blastocyst, an intensive chemical exchange occurs between the blastocyst and the mother's tissue to signal his or her presence in the mother's womb. The exchange temporarily impairs the mother's immune system to prevent antibodies from attaching the blastocyst as foreign matter. Said in plain English, the baby has a unique genetic composition. As such, the mother's immune system would see the baby's body as foreign tissue and attack it. However, implantation triggers biochemical activity that is equivalent to the zygote saying, "I'm here! Please don't reject me!" If this biochemical reaction did not occur, all pregnancies would result in miscarriage due to the woman's body rejecting the baby.

While the blastocyst is implanting itself in the uterine wall, other changes are taking place within. During the second week after conception, the inner cell mass separates into three distinct layers that specialize and give rise to different organ systems and structures of the body.

The outer layer is known as the ectoderm. It gives rise to cells that form skin, hair, sweat glands, tooth enamel, salivary glands, and all the nervous tissue, including the brain. The middle layer, or mesoderm, forms the muscles, bones, blood, circulatory system, teeth, connective tissues, and kidneys. The inner layer, the endoderm, is the one from which most of the internal organs (stomach, intestines, liver, lungs, heart, and so on) are formed. The implantation process is usually completed by the second week after conception.

Embryonic Period

Embryonic period

The two weeks after conception until around eight weeks after conception.

Embryo

The name of the developing individual during the embryonic period.

The **embryonic period** spans from two weeks after conception until around eight weeks after conception. The individual is called an **embryo** during this time. Developmental changes during this crucial period are characterized generally by rapid cell growth and differentiation, the formation of the placenta, and initial organ functioning. While all the organs are formed and begin functioning at some level during this period, some organs are not fully mature until the person is in his or her early to mid-twenties.

Several important functional systems of pregnancy appear early in the embryonic period. These are the development of the placenta, the umbilical cord, and the amniotic fluid. Their function is to ensure the survival and proper development of the individual throughout the pregnancy.

The placenta has three primary functions: (1) metabolism; (2) transfer of gases and chemicals between the developing individual and the mother; and (3) hormone production. A wide variety of chemical and nutrient matter is exchanged across the placental tissue between the developing child and its mother. The blood of the two never mixes in this transfer process. Rather, exchanges are made through the chemical process of osmo-

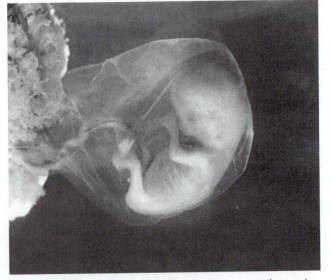

An individual is called an embryo from two to eight weeks after conception.

sis. The placenta acts as a barrier to many harmful substances that could enter the developing baby's body. However, it also can expose the child to many adverse environmental influences before birth.

The umbilical cord extends from the center of the placenta into the baby's abdomen. Two major arteries and one vein from the embryo's body lead into the placenta. The structure is twisted in a way that resembles a coiled rope or cord. It has no nerves.

The amniotic fluid is saline in nature. This material fills the amniotic sac during pregnancy. It cushions the developing child from jolts and bumps by allowing it to float freely and buoyantly within the cavity. It also maintains a constant temperature environment for the baby. Because it enables freedom of movement, it encourages muscle development. Amniotic fluid is swallowed by the developing child, which serves to prime the intestines and kidneys for functioning after birth. It is also useful in determining the health status of the child in a type of prenatal diagnostic test discussed later in this chapter.

The main body organs make their first appearance during the third week following conception. The central nervous system and the circulatory system are the first primary organ systems to appear. The heart begins to beat and circulate blood during this early time. By the eighth week, all of the organ systems are present in their early forms and functioning at some level. Although human since conception, the embryo now has a human appearance. **Organogenesis** is the term given to organ formation and it is the completion of organogenesis that marks the end of the embryonic period.

Fetal Period

The developing individual is known as the **fetus** from the beginning of the ninth week after conception until birth (around forty weeks). The **fetal period** of prenatal life is characterized by refinements in organs formed earlier, by reflexive actions, and by rapid increases in the weight and length of the developing individual.

Although the baby has been on the move since conception, the mother will usually feel the baby move for the first time around the fourth or fifth month of pregnancy, called the **quickening**. The baby's body also becomes covered with a fine downlike hair called **lanugo**.

Meanwhile, the skin begins to be covered with a substance called the **vernix caseosa** that is much like thick cold cream. It serves to protect the skin from chapping in the liquid environment of the uterus before birth. It also lubricates the fetus's passage through the birth canal and protects the infant from skin infections for a short time after birth.

The **age of viability** is the point in prenatal development where the baby stands a chance of surviving outside of the womb. This typically happens between the twenty-second and twenty-fourth week. Even though the baby may survive if born at this point in time, there can be serious complications and difficulties associated with premature birth. We will discuss this in more depth in the next section.

Organogenesis

The formation of organs during the embryonic period.

Fetus

The name of the developing individual beginning in the ninth week after conception until birth.

Fetal period

The phase of prenatal development that spans from eight weeks after conception to birth (at around forty weeks).

Quickening

The first detection by a mother of movements made by a fetus.

Lanugo

A fine down-like hair covering the baby's body.

Vernix caseosa

A thick, cold cream-like substance covering the baby's skin. It serves to protect the skin and lubricate the fetus for passage through the birth canal.

Age of viability

The point in prenatal development where the baby stands a chance of surviving outside of the womb.

During the seventh, eighth, and ninth months, there are continued refinements in the body and large gains in body weight. The lanugo is shed and the vernix covers the entire body by the end of this last trimester.

Pause and Process:

1. What are the three periods of prenatal development? How are they different than the three trimesters of pregnancy?

2. Which period of prenatal development is when the organ systems develop and begin functioning? When is organogenesis complete?

CRITICAL FACTORS IN PRENATAL DEVELOPMENT

The individual is exposed to many factors before birth that can influence his or her development positively or adversely. In this section, we will learn about some critical factors in prenatal development.

General Factors of Concern

One general risk factor during pregnancy is the age of the mother. Women younger than eighteen and older than thirty-five years of age have a higher probability of having a high-risk pregnancy—one that is characterized by complications that endanger the health and well-being of either the mother or child or both.

Adolescents are more likely to have problems during pregnancy or delivery than women in their twenties. However, proper nutrition and prenatal care can help prevent these problems. Older women seem especially prone both to miscarriage and to bearing children with a genetic disease. For example, the incidence of Down syndrome (a type of mental retardation cased by a genetic disorder) increases significantly among women older than thirty-five. Older women are also more likely to struggle with infertility.

Another general risk factor during pregnancy is poor nutrition. The

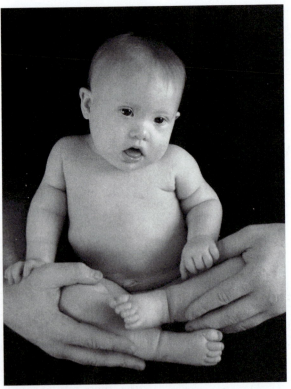

Women over thirty–five are more likely to have children with Down syndrome.

nutrition of the pregnant woman is an important influence on the quality of development of her child. This factor also strongly affects the mother's well-being and can influence the course of subsequent pregnancies.

One of the most significant aspects of nutrition in pregnancy is the association between adequate weight gains by the mother and the infant's weight (and health) at birth (Brazelton, 1987). Birthweight is related to the baby's ability to survive as well as to his or her susceptibility to certain health risks (Cassady & Strange, 1987). Most women of average weight should gain between 25 and 35 pounds during pregnancy. Underweight women should gain slightly more and overweight women should gain slightly less. Due to an increase in obesity among women of childbearing age, medical professionals are currently researching what a safe weight gain is for them. However, current research indicates that it is never advisable for a woman to diet and/or lose weight during pregnancy.

Beyond just weight gain, the quality of the food a woman eats is reflected in the health and well-being of her child. Adequate folic acid intake is critical early in pregnancy, as it can help prevent neural tube defects such as **spina bifida** (ACOG, 2005). Calcium and iron are also important for health and development. Most doctors recommend that a woman take a prenatal vitamin during pregnancy (if not before) in order to ensure proper levels of vitamins and minerals.

Teratogens

"**Teratology** is the branch of science that studies the causes, mechanisms, and patterns of abnormal development" (Moore & Persaud, 1998). Therefore, a **teratogen** is anything that can cause abnormal development: drugs, diseases, or environmental hazards. The influence of a teratogen depends upon the following:

- The genetics of the child
- During what stage of prenatal development exposure occurred
  - Germinal period—miscarriage or no effect
  - Embryonic period—major abnormalities in limbs, tissues, and organs
  - Fetal period—functional or morphologic abnormalities (especially in the brain or eyes)
- What the teratogen is
- Amount of teratogen the baby is exposed to in utero
- Impact may be first apparent during prenatal development, at birth, or years later

Drugs

Physicians generally urge their pregnant patients not to take any drugs without their advice. This warning is based on the knowledge that certain drugs can cause malformations and

---

Spina bifida

A birth defect in which the tissue surrounding the spinal cord does not properly close during prenatal development.

Teratology

A branch of science that studies the causes, mechanisms, and patterns of abnormal development.

Teratogen

Anything that can cause abnormal development.

16. What is a teratogen?

other related problems in the developing individual (Moore & Persaud, 1998). The effects of drugs vary widely, depending upon the factors listed above.

The list of drugs that can cause abnormal development is long. One of the most common is alcohol. No amount of alcohol consumption during pregnancy can be considered safe (Moore & Persaud, 1998). Alcohol consumption during pregnancy is one of the leading causes of mental retardation and even learning disabilities (ACOG, 2005). Moderate to heavy drinking during pregnancy can lead to **fetal alcohol syndrome** (FAS). FAS results in a baby with characteristic malformations to areas of the face, mild to severe mental retardation or lowered intelligence, severe growth disturbances, and heart malformation. However, even light drinking during pregnancy can cause cognitive deficiencies and behavioral troubles. It is really sad that the inability or unwillingness to give up alcohol during pregnancy can lead to a life-sentence of struggles for the baby.

Caffeine is widely consumed in the United States and abroad. It is not known, at this time, to cause any birth defects (Moore & Persaud, 1998). Heavy consumption may be associated with miscarriage early in the pregnancy or low birth weight at delivery. More research on the potential effects of caffeine is still needed.

Nicotine and cigarette smoking is a well-known teratogen. Cigarette smoking doubles the risk of premature birth (and all the complications that come with that). It is also a leading cause of low birthweight and the strongest predictor of infant death (Moore & Persaud, 1998). Lowered intelligence, heart defects, and limb defects are also related with smoking in both mom and dad. One of the reasons smoking is so detrimental to the child during prenatal development is that nicotine decreases the amount of oxygen in the blood. No amount of smoking is considered safe during pregnancy, by either mom or dad.

Entire chapters of embryology textbooks are devoted to the teratogenic effects of drugs. Certain antibiotics can lead to teeth discoloration and deafness. Aspirin may lead to cognitive and motor deficiencies. The effects of illegal drugs vary depending upon the type of drug, but common effects include low birthweight, irritability in the newborn, and cognitive and motor deficiencies (Moore & Persaud, 1998). In general, all drugs should be avoided unless a doctor gives the okay.

Diseases

Several types of infectious diseases are transmitted by the mother to the developing child through the placental membrane. The severity of their effects depends on when during the pregnancy the disease is contracted. Other diseases can damage the baby during delivery as it passes through the birth canal.

German measles (rubella) is one of the best known diseases that can harm a developing baby. Infection with this virus can result in deafness, blindness, heart defects, central nervous system damage, and mental deficiencies, or a combination of these, depending on when the virus enters the mother's body (Moore & Persaud, 1998).

Other viral agents that are known to damage the central nervous system during the prenatal period include the cytomegalovirus and toxoplasmosis. The cytomegalovirus

---

Fetal alcohol syndrome

A disorder that may include physical abnormalities and cognitive deficits due to a mother drinking alcohol during pregnancy.

is found in the vaginal tracts of many women. This virus enters the nasal and throat passages of the baby during delivery and quickly becomes established in the central nervous system. Infection can cause learning disabilities and related behavior problems in children later in life. Toxoplasmosis is a common parasite in cats and other animals. Women are typically tested for these two agents during pregnancy so that the proper precautions may be taken.

The HIV (human immunodeficiency virus) that causes AIDS (acquired immune deficiency syndrome) can also be passed by an infected pregnant woman to her developing child. Other STDs, such as syphilis and gonorrhea, can also cause permanent defects if passed from mother to child. Early detection and treatment is vital.

Environmental Hazards

We are just beginning to understand some of the dangers that environmental factors can pose to prenatal development. For example, pregnant women are now advised to avoid eating certain seafood due to mercury. Mercury can cause cerebral palsy, mental retardation, and growth deficiencies in a developing child. Exposure to lead can lead to miscarriage, growth deficiencies, mental retardation, and other abnormalities. Polychlorinated biphenyls (PCBs), found in some water and fish, can lead to growth deficiencies, skin discoloration, and cognitive deficiencies. X-rays can lead to leukemia, mental retardation, and growth deficiencies. Radiation is linked to mental retardation. The list could go on; however, the moral of the story is

Certain fish contain high levels of mercury.

for pregnant women to stay healthy, avoid toxins, and receive prenatal care. To do otherwise is to risk causing the developing child a lifetime of suffering.

Pause and Process:

1. What is a teratogen? What influences how a teratogen will impact a developing child?

2. Which teratogen surprised you the most and why?

COMPLICATIONS IN PREGNANCY

Most pregnancies proceed with little difficulty for the mother or child. Some, however, are complicated by one or more conditions that threaten the well-being of the mother or child or both. The purpose of prenatal care is to monitor the progress of a pregnancy to enhance the health and well-being of both mother and baby. Proper prenatal care improves the probability of detecting problems and treating them to minimize their effects.

Extrauterine Pregnancy

Ectopic pregnancy

A pregnancy that develops in a location outside the uterus.

An **ectopic**, or extrauterine, **pregnancy** is one that develops in a location outside the uterus. The individual may implant in the fallopian tube, on the ovary itself, or on the lining of the intestine. These pregnancies necessitate the surgical removal of the area on which the child has implanted. As of yet, there is no way to save the child and transplant him or her to the uterus for the duration of the pregnancy.

Loss of Pregnancy

Miscarriage

The unwanted ending of a pregnancy, usually within the first three months of pregnancy.

A **miscarriage** is the unwanted ending of a pregnancy, usually within the first three months of pregnancy (ACOG, 2005). Up to 15–20 percent of all pregnancies end in miscarriage, so it is far from uncommon. Generally, they are caused by abnormalities in the developing child, most frequently resulting from chromosome errors or acute infectious diseases. In addition to chromosome abnormalities and maternal illness, hormone imbalances, immune system disorders, and uterine problems can all lead to miscarriages. The loss of the child is devastating to most parents. We will discuss coping with the loss of a pregnancy and stillbirth in the last chapter of the textbook.

Toxemia

Toxemia

An acute hypertensive disease of pregnancy characterized by high blood pressure, retention of body fluids, and the presence of protein in the urine.

Maternal **toxemia** is an acute hypertensive disease of pregnancy. Typically, it is characterized by high blood pressure, retention of body fluids, and the presence of protein in the urine. It generally appears after the sixth month of pregnancy. Toxemia varies in severity but will become progressively worse if left untreated. This condition is highly dangerous to both the mother and child. It can be treated successfully with medication and diet.

Although these are clearly not all of the complications that can occur during pregnancy, they are some of the more common ones. They point toward the importance of early prenatal care, which is the topic of our next section.

Pause and Process:

1. Where in the woman's body can an ectopic pregnancy occur?

2. What are potential causes for a miscarriage? Why do you think that up to one in five pregnancies end in miscarriage?

PRENATAL CARE

Perinatology

Concerned with the detection and treatment of illness in developing individuals before birth.

Prenatal development is important for the health of the child and mother. **Perinatology** is concerned with the detection and treatment of illness in developing individuals before birth. This field was made possible by recent advances in diagnostic methods and intervention techniques in prenatal medical care. However, prenatal care is not simply the detection and treatment of medical problems. Prenatal care includes counseling, education, childbirth and parenting preparation, and identification of necessary community resources (ACOG, 2005).

Prenatal care is very important for preventing abnormalities in children. It includes: being in good health before conception; eating a balanced diet and getting a sufficient amount of the right kinds of exercise during pregnancy; ceasing all alcohol consumption, smoking, or other drug use; avoiding excessive stress while pregnant; and making regular visits to a health-care provider all through the pregnancy. Family health histories should also be given to the health-care provider.

Typical Prenatal Care

A woman's first prenatal visit usually takes longer than most of her subsequent visits. On this first visit, a health history will be taken, a physical exam will be conducted, lab work may be completed, an estimated due date is calculated, and the baby's heart beat will be heard for the first time (either by an external Doppler ultrasound device or an internal Doppler ultrasound device—depending on how far along the baby is in development). The baby's heart begins beating around the time a woman finds out she is pregnant (about eighteen to twenty-four days after conception); however, it takes several weeks to be able to be heard by an external Doppler device. Prior to that, an internal Doppler ultrasound device can detect the heartbeat.

Monthly visits are typically scheduled for the first thirty weeks, unless health concerns necessitate more frequent visits. During most of these visits, the expectant mother's weight and blood pressure is recorded, urine is tested, uterus height is measured (externally), the baby's heart beat is heard, and the woman can ask any questions she may have of her health-care provider.

Typical prenatal tests include various lab tests throughout the pregnancy. The first test a woman will receive will be a pregnancy test. This can be either a blood test or a urine test to check for the human chorionic gonadotropin (HCG) hormone. As mentioned above, urine checks are also conducted regularly to check for various issues such as infection or diabetes. At various points during the pregnancy, blood tests may be conducted to check for anemia, HIV, STDs, Rh factor, or thyroid levels. Additionally, lab tests from pelvic exams can check for various infections. Finally, a glucose screening test to check for gestational diabetes is normally done in the later part of pregnancy.

Beyond these typical prenatal tests, other forms of fetal assessment are possible—some are routine and others are need-based. During the third trimester, expectant mothers may be asked to chart their baby's kicks/movements each day as an easy check on fetal well-being. Ultrasounds are conducted for multiple reasons. The most common reason ultrasounds are conducted is to assess the age and sex of the baby, as well as to identify the placenta's location and baby's position. Ultrasounds can also monitor potential problems such as retarded growth or low amniotic fluid. Amazingly, ultrasounds can sometimes identify birth defects, some of which can be fixed prenatally or shortly after birth.

Prenatal Diagnostic Methods

Amniocentesis

The withdrawal of a sample of amniotic fluid (which includes the baby's sloughed off skin cells) from the mother's uterus.

One of the best known and most widely used prenatal diagnostic tools is **amniocentesis**, or the withdrawal of a sample of amniotic fluid (which includes the baby's sloughed off skin cells) from the mother's uterus. This procedure is done to help determine whether the child has a hereditary disorder. Amniocentesis is usually performed between the fifteenth and twentieth week of pregnancy. The positive part of this test is that if the baby has a disorder, such as hypothyroidism, medication can be provided during pregnancy to help correct the problem. If it is a disorder that cannot be treated or cured, the parents have time to become educated about the disorder prior to birth. Two negative possibilities associated with an amniocentesis are a false positive (i.e., the amniocentesis saying the child has a disorder, when in fact they do not) and an increased risk of miscarriage after the procedure (~0.5 percent) (ACOG, 2005).

Chorionic villus sampling

A procedure by which chorionic villi (hairlike structures that are the predecessors of the placenta) are removed and analyzed to determine if genetic disease is present.

Another procedure that is used to diagnose genetic disease is **chorionic villus sampling** (CVS). Chorionic villi are small hairlike structures that are the predecessors of the placenta. Ultrasound is used to locate the tissue, then a small catheter is inserted through the vagina into the cervix and a very small section of chorionic villi is removed from the uterine wall. CVS allows an earlier diagnosis of genetic disease than is possible with amniocentesis because it is typically performed between the tenth and twelfth week of pregnancy. CVS carries the same potential benefits and costs as an amniocentesis; except, the risk of miscarriage after the procedure is slightly higher (~ 1 percent) (ACOG, 2005).

Both the CVS and the amniocentesis are offered or recommended based upon the parents' genetic profiles and the mother's age. Women who conceive after the age of thirty-five have a higher probability of having a child with genetic abnormalities than younger women. Sadly, these tests have sometimes resulted in what some consider prejudicial outcomes. It is estimated that 88–92 percent of babies identified as having Down syndrome by these tests are aborted (Bristow, 2008). Hence, some feel that one potential outcome of these tests is discrimination against the disabled who have yet to be born.

Fetal medicine

Any medical intervention or care directed at the developing, in utero individual.

Fetal Medicine

Any medical intervention or care directed at the developing, in utero individual could be considered **fetal medicine**. For example, if an amniocentesis indicates a hormonal deficiency, medication may be able to be administered prenatally to help reduce or eliminate the consequences of such a deficiency.

Fetal surgery

Surgery that is conducted while the child is still developing prenatally.

Fetal surgery is also a growing, although still experimental, field. Fetal surgeries have been successful in correcting or lessening certain heart defects, spinal cord abnor-

FIGURE 2-2   AMNIOCENTESIS PROCEDURE

This procedure consists of inserting a needle through the woman's abdominal wall into the uterine cavity to draw out a sample of amniotic fluid (fluid surrounding the fetus). Fetal cells from the fluid are cultured for chromosomal analysis.

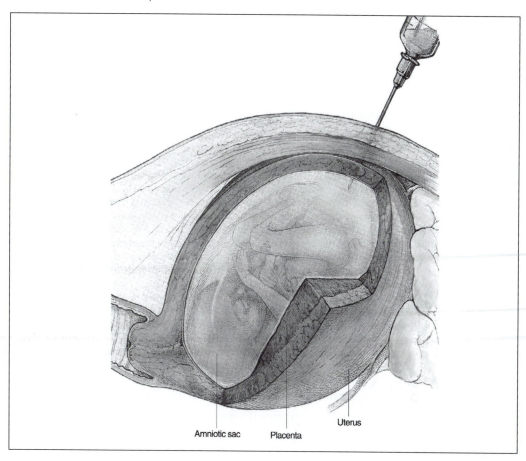

Amniotic sac   Placenta   Uterus

malities, vascular lung issues, and other organ problems. However, this is still a field in its infancy. Just as there are potential risks with any surgery, there are severe potential costs to fetal surgery. First, both the mother and fetus must be given pain medication and face the potential side effects inherent in such drug administration. Second, the mother could face such complications as infection, blood clots, or early labor. Third, the fetus could be accidentally injured by surgical instruments, be born prematurely, or die. Clearly, the potential benefits for such a potentially dangerous procedure must outweigh the costs. Still, these surgeries have already been credited with saving lives and reducing the need for surgery and drugs after birth for those in which the surgery was successful (Kalb, 2005).

Pause and Process:

1. What is prenatal care? Why is it important?

2. Compare and contrast amniocentesis and CVS.

REACTIONS TO PREGNANCY

There is a wise old saying that the reason pregnancy lasts nine months is to allow the expectant parents plenty of time to get used to the idea of being parents and to prepare. The initiation of a pregnancy can produce several reactions in a couple. Although the pregnancy has an impact on the mother and father, each may react differently.

Holmes and Rahe (1967) report that pregnancy is the twelfth most stressful life event during adulthood. The initiation of a pregnancy causes many reactions in the expectant mother. Among these are changes in her body image and a sense of physical and psychological well-being, feelings of uncertainty about what it is like to be pregnant (if this is her first pregnancy), and alterations in her mood. Many women and their partners react with excitement to the confirmation of pregnancy, especially if the pregnancy was planned and desired.

Pregnancy is a common human experience, but it carries many different meanings for couples. For some, it validates their sexuality. The woman proves her femininity by conceiving, and the man proves his masculinity by impregnating. For others, impending parenthood revives memories of childhood and anticipation of a happy future as a parent. For still others, expecting a child fulfills an expectation laid when they took their marriage vows. They now can share the excitement of bringing a life into the world that they created together.

Not everyone reacts with pleasure to the confirmation of a pregnancy, however. Less positive emotional reactions are often attributed to feelings of ambivalence about becoming a parent, marital difficulties, and lack of an adequate social network to provide emotional support during the pregnancy (Flemming et al., 1988). Pregnancy crisis centers are wonderful places to turn to in such circumstances. They can help an expectant couple prepare emotionally for the child's arrival, as well as provide social and financial support. Many can even provide sup-

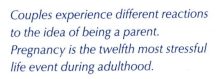

Couples experience different reactions to the idea of being a parent. Pregnancy is the twelfth most stressful life event during adulthood.

port after the birth of the child, or help find additional sources of support in the local community. We live in a society where no woman needs to face a pregnancy alone; there is always help to be found. Two websites that may be a good starting place are www.pregnancycenters.org and www.care-net.org. The Care-net offers a toll-free hotline at 1-800-395-HELP.

Pregnancy, especially a first one, focuses a couple's thinking on many new issues. They ponder what it will be like to be a parent or what kind of parent they will make. Some prepare for the immense change a baby will make in their lives—at least intellectually. Pregnancy lasts long enough to allow couples to do some preparation for parenthood—to begin transforming their identity from a couple without children to parents. Many couples prepare for first-time parenthood by attending childbirth preparation classes, reading books and articles about child development, and arranging for prenatal and birth care. They equip a nursery and enjoy getting gifts at baby showers. They may spend some time caring for babies and young children of relatives and friends. In all these ways, couples begin the process of accepting a radical change in their identities and lifestyles.

Pause and Process:

1. What are some common reactions to pregnancy?

2. What are the contributing factors to a negative reaction to pregnancy? What can be done to help in these circumstances?

BIRTH AND THE NEWBORN

LEARNING OBJECTIVES:

1. *Understand and describe the process by which birth occurs as well as the different types of birth experiences*
2. *Identify complications associated with the birth process*
3. *Describe the characteristics of newborns*
4. *Describe the transition that newborns and parents go through during this period*

Birth is obviously a major event in the life of an individual and the family into which he or she is born. This section will discuss the birth process, complications that can arise during birth, characteristics of the newborn, and the transitions that the newborn and family go through the first couple of weeks after birth.

THE BIRTH PROCESS

As you learned in the previous section, a pregnant woman waits around forty weeks to meet her baby face to face for the first time. Late in the third trimester, the expectant mother is probably both excited for this first meeting and a bit anxious about the birth process. First time mothers often wonder what this birth process will be like. How long will labor and delivery last? How painful is labor really? What are the options for medicated pain control? What techniques work best to control pain that do not involve medication? What can go wrong during labor and delivery? What will the little bundle of joy be like immediately after birth? How will life change after the baby is born?

This section will address all of these questions. Even if you (or your partner) never have a child, chances are that you will experience the birth of a child of a relative or close friend at some point in your life. The information you learn in this chapter will help you to know, at least somewhat, what to expect. It will also help you to be able to critically evaluate television shows and movies that depict birth and newborns. After all, you must have wondered at some point in time why shows that depict a person assisting a woman giving birth outside of a hospital are always in need of water, towels, and string of some sort.

Labor and Delivery

It's called **labor** for a reason, as we will see. Women often know that labor is getting close due to several preceding events. The woman will be visiting her doctor or midwife frequently toward the end of pregnancy. If the doctor or midwife believes that labor may be starting soon, he or she can check the condition of the woman's cervix. Certain physical changes to the cervix can let the doctor or midwife know that the body is preparing for labor. Other events can also occur as labor nears. **Braxton-Hicks contractions** will often increase in frequency and strength as the uterus starts practicing for the big event. Vaginal discharge may also increase and/or change in color as the body prepares for labor. Finally, the fetus may become less active and may drop into the pelvic cavity of the woman (**lightening**). Experts are still uncertain as to what actually initiates labor, but most believe it is the fetus that triggers its start (Hrdy 1999).

If you remember, prenatal development occurs in three stages. Well, labor occurs in three stages as well. Just like the periods of prenatal development, the stages of labor are not equal in length of time.

During the first stage of labor, the Braxton-Hicks contractions give way to real contractions. These real contractions typically come at regular intervals and increase in intensity, length, and frequency. The contractions help efface and dilate the cervix, and push the baby down. If the membranes did not rupture (i.e., water break) at the onset of labor, they will break (or be broken) sometime during this stage. Typically, the first stage of labor is the longest, lasting an average of six to twelve hours. The first stage is usually shorter in second and subsequent childbirths. This stage is over when the cervix has dilated to 10 centimeters and the baby is ready to be pushed out.

The contractions during the second stage of labor are paired with the urge to push down. The crowning of the baby's head signals that birth is imminent. Delivery is the actual birth or expulsion of the baby from the uterus and is the highlight of this stage of labor. This part of

Spotlight

22. How many stages of labor are there?

Labor

The process by which the cervix is opened prior to birth and the fetus is moved from the uterus through the birth canal; accomplished by means of contractions of the uterus, which increase in strength, duration, and frequency as delivery nears.

Braxton-Hicks contraction

Practice contractions by the uterus.

Lightening

Occurs when the fetus' head drops down into the pelvis.

Cephalic presentation

Head first delivery.

Breech

When a child is upside down for delivery, with the bottom being delivered first.

Transverse

When a child is sideways during labor (requires either that the child is physically moved to the head-down position, or delivered c-section).

Afterbirth

The final stage of labor which involves the expulsion of the placenta and the membranes as well as any remaining amniotic fluid from a woman's uterus.

the birth process typically lasts from twenty minutes to three hours (ACOG, 2005). In a normal delivery, the baby is delivered head first (known as a **cephalic presentation**). Once the head is out, the rest of the body is usually quick to follow. Sometimes the baby is not head down, which can cause complications during the delivery process. **Breech** and **transverse** presentations are often delivered via cesarean-section, which we will discuss later in the chapter.

You may think that labor is over after the birth of the child, but you would be wrong. The final stage of labor is referred to as the **afterbirth** phase. The afterbirth phase involves the expulsion of the placenta and the membranes, as well as any remaining amniotic fluid from a woman's uterus. This part of the birth process usually lasts less than twenty minutes (ACOG, 2005). The uterus continues to contract after the birth of the baby. These contractions and the assistance of a nurse or midwife manipulating the woman's abdomen help the uterus to cleanse itself of the debris of birth. The umbilical cord is cut when the doctor or midwife can no longer detect a pulse in the cord. The baby feels no discomfort because the cord does not contain nerves. The woman's husband or support person may cut the cord if all has gone well.

Approaches to Labor and Delivery

Now that we know the nuts and bolts of labor and delivery, we can take time to examine some of the finer details. Let's start with the well-known saying that "misery loves company." Now, of course, no one should consider giving birth to a beautiful child misery. Nonetheless, the fact of the matter is that labor is physically—well—uncomfortable to say the least. Pain is a very subjective experience, and the degree of discomfort or pain endured during labor and delivery varies greatly across women. However, research shows that women experience less pain and discomfort when they have a support person during the birth process (ACOG, 2005).

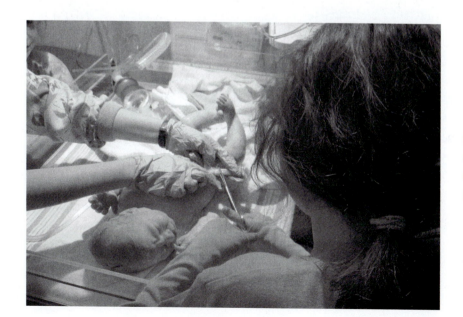

When a pulse can no longer be detected in the umbilical cord it can then be cut. The husband or support person may cut the cord if they wish.

FIGURE 2-3   BIRTH OF A FETUS

Illustration of birth of a fetus showing rotation of the head and trunk through the woman's pelvis.

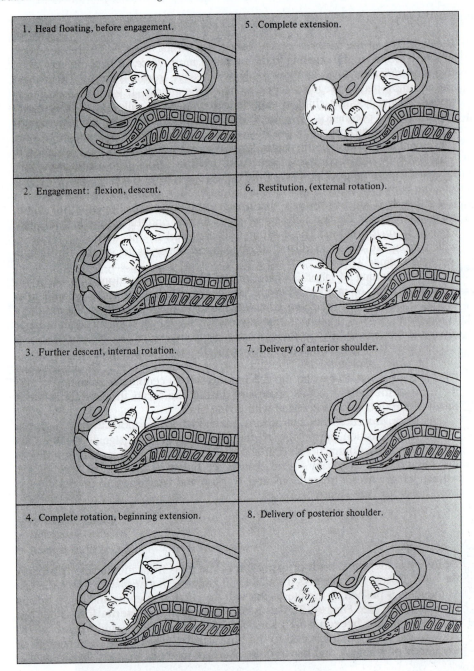

1. Head floating, before engagement.

2. Engagement: flexion, descent.

3. Further descent, internal rotation.

4. Complete rotation, beginning extension.

5. Complete extension.

6. Restitution, (external rotation).

7. Delivery of anterior shoulder.

8. Delivery of posterior shoulder.

The customary choice of a support person is the expectant woman's partner; except, this is not always possible for a number of reasons. A friend or relative can also be an excellent support person. Ideally, any support person should attend childbirth

Doula

A professional labor coach.

classes with the expectant mother in order to be best prepared to be a labor coach. An expectant mother may also want or need a professional support person. In that case, she may want to consider a **doula**. A doula is a professional labor coach. He or she can offer emotional, psychological, and physical support during the birth process; however, a doula cannot assist in any medical care. The doula can offer support to the woman alone or can work in partnership with the woman's support person to offer a support network.

Regardless of whom an expectant mother's support person is, this labor partner can be invaluable. According to the American College of Obstetricians and Gynecologists (2005), a support person can assist in many ways, including: timing contractions and talking the woman through them, monitoring room conditions (such as lighting), giving massages or assisting in various labor positions, coaching the woman through breathing techniques, and offering general encouragement and assistance.

Thus, one approach to lessen pain during the birth process is to have a support person. Another approach is commonly referred to as prepared childbirth. Although there are a few different, specific strategies that fall under this general umbrella (e.g., Bradley, Lamaze, Read, etc.), the general idea is the same. Prepared childbirth asserts that expectant mothers being educated as to what to expect during the birth process will lessen anxiety, and in turn, lessen pain. Specific strategies may include breathing techniques, labor postures, and other relaxation techniques. Having a support person is usually instrumental in prepared childbirth. Successful implementation of prepared childbirth includes minimal (if any) use of pain medication during labor, active participation of both the mother and support person in the birth process, and a reduction of fear and anxiety about labor and delivery.

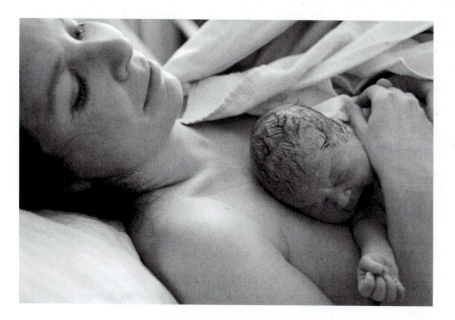

The pain and discomfort that is experienced during labor varies between women. However, studies show that the pain experienced is lessened when there is a support person present.

Even with support and preparation, some women opt for the use of pain medication during labor and delivery. There are two general classes of pain medications: analgesics and anesthetics. Systemic analgesics lessen pain by working on the entire nervous system. The woman will maintain consciousness, but may be tired. Regional analgesia numbs a specific area. Epidurals and spinal blocks are two examples of regional analgesics. After insertion of the epidural tube by an anesthesiologist, some hospitals now allow women to self-administer pain medication via their epidural using a hand held button control. There are pros and cons to using pain medication during labor and delivery, and these issues should be considered prior to the onset of labor.

There are numerous alternative or supplemental strategies for pain control not yet mentioned. For example, hypnosis is sometimes used in place of drugs to reduce pain during delivery. The technique is somewhat limited by the fact that not every mother can be trained to enter a hypnotic state. Also, it requires special training that not many physicians have. The use of birthing tubs is also increasing in popularity. Massages, acupuncture, and music therapy are also possible choices for pain management during the birth process. The thing to keep in mind is that all women will experience pain differently during labor and delivery, and there are a variety of options for pain management.

Settings for Labor and Delivery

For a healthy and uncomplicated vaginal birth, there are some options for labor and delivery (ACOG, 2005). Some women give birth at home with the assistance of a doctor or midwife. As long as the pregnancy has been healthy and there are no risk factors or complications, this is a viable choice for many women. There are also birthing centers. These are free-standing centers that are devoted to labor and delivery. Again, as long as the pregnancy has been healthy and there are no risk factors or complications, this is a viable choice. Birthing centers may offer labor options, such as tubs and massages, which a typical hospital may not offer. However, if complications arise during labor or delivery, precious time may be lost in transit to a hospital. Most American women choose to give birth in a hospital.

Many modern hospitals have entire wings devoted to labor and delivery. These wings can offer separate entrances (so women in labor do not need to come in through the emergency room), birthing rooms, and easy access to operating rooms in case an emergency cesarean-section is needed. Modern birthing rooms typically have a homelike atmosphere, with a sleeper sofa for dad, room for the baby after birth, soft lighting, and personal bathrooms with showers. The beds can be transformed from a typical bed one can sleep in, into a delivery bed, and back into a typical bed with a few easy maneuvers. This means that labor, delivery, and recovery can all occur in the same room. Most of the medical equipment can be strategically hidden from view until needed.

Of course, around one out of four births are not vaginal, but cesarean-sections (ACOG, 2005). What can cause a woman to need a C-section? Is it more dangerous than a vaginal birth? Our next section will address this topic.

pitched sounds as well as adults. These abilities will develop within the first couple of years after birth.

The senses of smell, taste, and touch are well-developed at birth. Newborns can recognize the smell of their own amniotic fluid and mother's milk. They prefer some smells, such as vanilla, over other smells, such as fish. Newborns also prefer the taste of sweet foods, over bitter or sour foods. Finally, newborns are sensitive to touch and pain. The American College of Obstetricians and Gynecologists (2005) advises parents to be certain that their sons receive pain medication prior to circumcision.

Sleep

Labor is not just hard on the mother; it is stressful for the baby as well. Newborns are often alert for a while after birth and then sleepy for the next several hours or days. All babies are born with their own unique personalities. Some babies like to sleep more than other babies. Some babies are more predictable in their sleep patterns than other babies. In general, newborns will sleep an average of fourteen to eighteen hours a day, in small stretches at a time (ACOG, 2005).

Newborn sleep cycles are different than adult sleep cycles. Interestingly, newborns will often begin their sleep cycle in the REM (rapid eye movement) stage. This is thought to be a stage where dreaming occurs. Adults begin sleep in a state of non-REM sleep. Additionally, newborns will spend around 50 percent of their sleeping hours in REM sleep, whereas adults spend only 20 percent of their sleep time in this stage. It is speculated that newborns, and infants in general, spend so much time in REM sleep due to the brain's need for stimulation, brain development, or learning.

Pause and process:

1. In what ways are newborns' health assessed?

2. Which senses are fairly well-developed by birth? What sense is the least-developed at birth?

TRANSITIONS

Every human being is unique in many ways. Any quality, trait, or characteristic that distinguishes one person from others is referred to as an **individual difference**. These individual differences are present from birth (and some prenatally). Just look through the window of a newborn nursery, some babies are quiet and content. Other babies cry a lot. All babies are born with mini-personalities. Some research suggests that activity level in the womb is predictive of activity level after birth.

One individual difference proposed in newborns is **temperament**. A temperament can be thought of as a baby's general approach to the world and behavioral orientation.

Tonic neck reflex

This reflex usually occurs when the neonate is placed on its back. The arms, legs, and head move to a characteristic "fencing" position in which the arm and leg on one side are extended, while those on the other side are flexed. The baby's head turns to one side, usually in the direction of its extended limbs.

Walking reflex

Step-like motions of the legs occur reflexively when the neonate is held in an upright position and allowed to touch a flat surface with its feet. The legs respond by flexing alternately as if the child is walking.

Swimming reflex

This unusual reflex occurs when the neonate is submerged on its abdomen in water. The baby holds its breath and makes swimming motions with both arms and legs.

Visual acuity

Sharpness or clarity of vision.

Individual difference

Any quality, trait, or characteristic that distinguishes one person from others.

Temperament

A baby's general approach to the world and behavioral orientation.

Difficult temperament

The resisting of physical handling, crying inconsolably, and showing irregular sleeping and eating patterns.

Slow-to-warm-up temperament

The display of quiet activity levels, somewhat fussy, and wary around others and situations.

Some see temperament as the foundation from which personality will grow. Because temperament is apparent so early in life, it is assumed that it is at least somewhat genetic in origin (Paludi, 2002).

Thomas and Chess (1987) suggest a temperament classification scheme in which neonates are described as **difficult** (resisting physical handling, crying inconsolably, showing irregular sleeping and eating patterns), **slow-to-warm-up** (quiet activity levels, somewhat fussy, wary around others and situations), and **easy** (adaptable, cheerful and happy, responsive to others and situations), or a mixture of these.

A critical issue is what effect these individual differences are likely to have on the adults who care for newborns. For example, a newborn classified as difficult is probably frustrating for his parents. This child may even be abused if his parents' frustration limits are exceeded. A newborn described as quiet or slow-to-warm-up may be equally frustrating to parents, but for different reasons. Caregivers may have to try hard to stimulate any type of response in a newborn with this type of temperament. An easy newborn has the type of temperament that most American parents want.

Thomas (1986) proposes that there is such a thing as "goodness of fit" between the personality of the parents' and the temperament of the child at birth. This fit may enhance development and growth among all family members. Conversely, lack of fit may make interactions in the family difficult.

All parents should realize that their offspring will be different in many respects from one or both of them. Furthermore, individual differences make using a "standard" child-drearing style for all one's children questionable (Bigner, 1989). The best approach is for family members to acquire an empathic understanding of the individual differences of each new member.

The birth of a couple's first child moves the family into a new stage of the family life-cycle. The couple must redefine their roles and develop new behaviors. This transitional period can

Thomas and Chess suggested a temperament classification. Thomas proposed the "goodness of fit" idea that exists between the personality of the parents and baby.

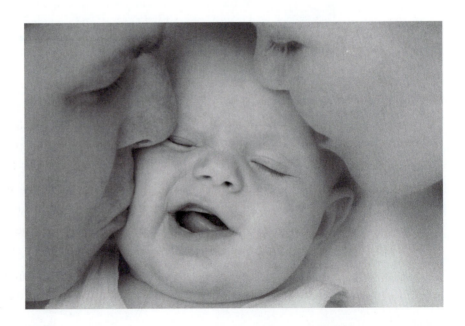

Easy temperament

A baby who is adaptable, cheerful and happy, and responsive to others and situations.

take time and may be difficult. The adjustments that couples make at this time constitute a transition to being parents as well as redefining their role in the marriage. It is important to still make time for each other during the hectic period of caring for a newborn.

The hospital will try to provide educational materials to new parents prior to discharge. New parents may be required to watch videos or attend short classes on newborn care. A lactation consultant will probably visit the mother to give tips on breastfeeding. Nurses or doctors will provide instructions on the first bath, belly-button care, diapering, feeding, and possible problems for which to watch. Nurses are also usually taught to watch for signs of bonding between the newborn and parents. Parents will also be provided with resource information for the road ahead.

Pause and process:

1. What are the three basic temperaments that newborns may be classified as?

2. How can a hospital help to prepare parents for taking home and caring for their newborn?

SUMMARY

1. Genetic information contained in the male and female gametes intermingles at conception, resulting in a new combination of chromosomes (and genes). The chemical basis of genetic inheritance is DNA. The genetic blueprint determined at conception will be identical in all cells that are produced during the individual's life span. Most cells reproduce themselves through a process known as mitosis. The production of sex cells, however, occurs through a process called meiosis.

2. Genetic processes include the dominant/recessive process, polygenetic inheritance, and epigenetic information. Some traits and characteristics behave according to the either/or nature of dominant/recessive genes, whereas others behave according to the continuous variation nature of the polygenetic process. Epigenetic information, such

as the cytoplasmic environment during ovum development and genetic imprinting are new areas of research that are just beginning to be understood.

3. One category of genetic disorders may be inherited by a single gene that may be dominant, recessive, or sex-linked. A second category of genetic disorders may be inherited at the chromosomal level. A third category of genetic disorders are multifactorial. Although it is often unknown what specifically causes a multifactorial genetic disorder, it is thought that an interaction of genetics and environmental issues give rise to the problem. An increasing number of organizations are available to offer support and information to individuals with genetic disorders and their loved ones.

4. The field of behavioral genetics investigates how interactions between genetic and environmental factors influence cognitive and behavioral

processes. Research designs in behavioral genetics have typically included adoption studies and twin studies. Gene/environment relationships can be viewed as passive, active, or dynamic in nature.

5. The prenatal stage is thought to be the most crucial stage of the life span. Changes experienced during this time have a critical bearing on development throughout the rest of the individual's life.

6. The individual can be exposed to many factors before birth that could positively or negatively affect his or her development. These include the age of the mother, maternal nutrition, and exposure to teratogens. The effects of teratogens depend upon genetics, dose, timing of exposure, and specific teratogen. Different teratogens target different parts of the body at different stages of prenatal development. In general, the embryonic period is the most vulnerable stage.

7. There are several common complications that can occur during pregnancy. Three include miscarriage, ectopic pregnancy, and toxemia. A miscarriage usually occurs during the first three months of pregnancy as a result of chromosomal abnormalities or other health factors. An ectopic pregnancy is a pregnancy that occurs outside the uterus. Toxemia can be life-threatening to the mother and child, but is treatable.

8. Adequate prenatal care is vital for preventing and/or treating birth defects and related problems of pregnancy. Prenatal tests provide a means for diagnosis of potential genetic and metabolic disease before birth. Fetal medicine offers hope for treating some medical disorders or diseases prior to birth.

9. Both partners react to the initiation of a pregnancy in the woman. Validation of one's sexuality, marriage vow fulfillment, changes in body image, and reassessment of personal well-being are among the more common reactions. Reactions may be largely positive or negative. Negative reactions are typically due to a lack of social support or marital difficulties. Pregnancy crisis centers are a wonderful place to receive emotional, social, and financial support throughout the pregnancy or even after the birth. Pregnancy provides time for couples to adjust to impending changes in their identities and lifestyles. A couple's preparation during their first pregnancy assists them to move to a new stage in their family life-cycle.

10. This chapter discussed birth, delivery, and the newborn. The birth process has three distinct phases of labor: stage one involves the effacement and dilation of the cervix; stage two involves the delivery of the baby from the uterus; stage three involves the expulsion of the placenta and other matter from the uterus. The length of time each phase lasts is variable. It usually depends partly upon whether or not the woman is having her first baby.

11. Birth can occur vaginally or via C-section. Pain management during a vaginal birth can include a support coach, prepared childbirth techniques, medication, or strategies such as hypnosis or massage. A C-section requires the use of general or regional anesthesia. A healthy woman who has had a healthy pregnancy with no risk factors can sometimes choose to give birth at home, in a birthing center, or in a hospital. A C-section should always be done in a hospital. Modern hospitals often have entire wings devoted to labor and delivery with birthing rooms that accommodate labor, delivery, and recovery.

12. Delivery and birth may be complicated by one or more conditions. Anoxia, or oxygen starvation, to the baby during delivery may occur for a variety of reasons. Low-birthweight and prematurity may give rise to many complications. Postpartum depression of the new mother may affect her ability to function adequately.

13. The average weight of a newborn is between five and one-half and nine and one-half pounds, and the average length is between eighteen and twenty-two inches. The appearance of the newborn reflects the nature of their existence before birth—their skin is

very wrinkled and is covered with vernix. The eyes are a prominent feature, and the head is large in proportion to total body length. Overall health of the newborn is assessed with the Apgar at birth.

14. Newborns must make some physical adjustments to ensure their survival following birth. They must establish independent respiration, regulate their body temperature, and initiate the process of digestion and elimination of body wastes. Newborns are also born ready to interact with the world with reflexes and senses functioning. They

are also born with mini-personalities commonly referred to as temperaments. Babies typically have one of three types of temperaments: difficult, slow-to-warm-up, or easy.

15. The period after birth is a period of adjustment for both newborn and parents. New parents will need to redefine their roles within the marriage. This adjustment period can be stressful, but at the risk of sounding like a hippy, this too shall pass. The hospital provides basic care information prior to discharge.

SELF-QUIZ

1. What does the nucleus of all cells contain?
2. How many chromosomes do humans have?
3. What do geneticists sometimes refer to as the first twenty-two pairs of chromosomes?
4. What is the process by which the gametes are produced?
5. What genetic process involves the interaction of two or more genes?
6. What is the term used to describe information passed on to offspring that is not genetic in nature?
7. What are the three different categories of genetic disorders?
8. What are two types of research designs in behavioral genetics?
9. What are the two types of twins?
10. What are three possible relationships between genotypes and the environment?
11. Are the three stages of prenatal development and the three trimesters of pregnancy the same?
12. What are the three stages of prenatal development?
13. By what week after conception are all the organs present and functioning at some level?
14. What is the age of viability?

15. How much weight should the average woman gain during pregnancy?
16. What is a teratogen?
17. What is it called when a pregnancy develops in a location outside the uterus?
18. About what percentage of known pregnancies end in a miscarriage?
19. What prenatal diagnostic tool involves the withdrawal and testing of amniotic fluid?
20. What is fetal surgery currently used to correct?
21. What is it called late in pregnancy when the fetus becomes less active and drops into the pelvic cavity?
22. How many stages of labor are there?
23. How long does the first stage of labor typically last?
24. During which stage of labor is the baby delivered?
25. What is delivered during the third stage of labor?
26. What are the two general classes of pain medications that can be administered during labor?
27. What are some possible reasons for a C-section?
28. What complications do pre-term infants possibly face?
29. What percentage of women experience the baby blues? What percentage of women experience postpartum depression?
30. What quick assessment is made of the newborn to determine the presence and/or extent of any injury?

TERMS AND CONCEPTS

CHAPTER 3

Infancy

OUTLINE

PHYSICAL DEVELOPMENT DURING INFANCY

- Physical growth
- Motor development
- Perceptual development
- Health issues

COGNITIVE DEVELOPMENT DURING INFANCY

- Piaget's cognitive development theory and the sensorimotor stage
- Information-processing in infancy
- Language development in infancy

GENETICS

- Emotional development
- Self and others
- Psychosocial development

They come out scrunched up and pink and spend most of their hours sleeping, and within no time at all they are running around full of energy. Infancy (birth through the second year) is a time of remarkable growth and change. In this chapter, we will see some of the amazing physical, cognitive, and socioemotional feats infants achieve during this short period of time.

PHYSICAL DEVELOPMENT DURING INFANCY

LEARNING OBJECTIVES:

1. *To have a general knowledge of genetic terminology and processes*
2. *Awareness of some of the different types of genetic disorders*
3. *Appreciation for the field of behavior genetics within the context of studying life span development*

PHYSICAL GROWTH

Physical changes in infancy are dramatic and rapid. We gain a stark impression of the drama of these changes when we compare the abilities and functioning of a newborn with those of the same child at the end of the infancy stage. Significant physical changes are observed in all aspects of the body. In this section, we will describe these dramatic physical changes during infancy.

Growth Patterns

Many significant physical milestones are reached before a child's third birthday. These include mastery of the basic motor competencies shared by all human beings: locomotor

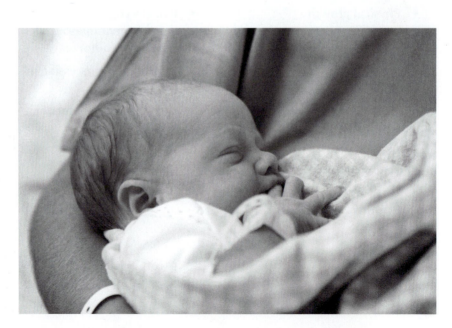

The physical changes and abilities of a newborn through the end of the infancy stage is dramatic.

(movement) and manual (hand) skills, perceptual skills, and coordination of sensory and motor activities. These basic competencies allow the individual to interact actively with the environment. They stimulate development in other areas as well.

Growth in infancy follows two basic patterns that began with the physical changes observed during the prenatal stage. The progression of these basic patterns can be observed in many physical changes that happen during infancy, especially in those associated with motor skill development and physical development. These patterns will continue throughout the growing years until the individual achieves full maturity.

The first basic pattern is that changes are **cephalocaudal** in direction. This means that changes in the head region of the body, both internally and externally, are in advance of those occurring toward the abdominal region. Maturation takes place in a head-to-foot direction. For example, developmental changes in motor performance and functioning occur first in the head region and last in the foot region of the body. The spinal cord, nerves, and muscles experience maturational changes in the head region earlier than in the pelvic region. For this reason, infants are able to rotate their heads from side to side long before they can sit up without support or walk.

The second basic pattern is that maturational and developmental changes occur in a **proximodistal** manner. This means that changes happen first in the center, innermost area of the body and then move outward to the ends of the extremities. This proximodistal pattern is also observed in prenatal development. For example, during the embryonic period, arms and legs appear containing finger and toe buds at their ends. Eventually, these buds give rise to the digits of the hands and feet.

Cephalocaudal growth pattern

Changes occur in the head region of the body, both internally and externally in advance of those occurring toward the abdominal region.

Proximodistal growth pattern

Changes happen first in the center, innermost area of the body and then move outward to the ends of extremities.

| FIGURE 3-1 | **CHANGES ARE CEPHALOCAUDAL IN DIRECTION** |

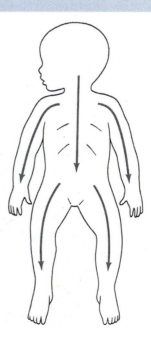

Generally, function follows form in growth trends throughout infancy (Timiras, 1972). The pattern of proximodistal changes predicts, for example, that infants will use their arms before they are able to use their hands or fingers to grasp an object accurately.

For the first six months following birth, growth is a continuation of the rapid changes begun during the prenatal stage. Thereafter, the rate of changes declines slowly for the remainder of infancy.

Weight and Height Changes

4. What does myelination of the axon accomplish?

Neuron

The information processing cell of the nervous system.

Cell body

Contains the parts of the cell to keep it alive and functioning (such as the nucleus).

Dendrites

Receives information from other neurons.

Axon

Takes information from the neuron away to be sent to other neurons.

Myelinated

A layer of fat that can surround the axon.

Neurotransmitters

Chemical messengers that carry information to other neurons.

Synapses

The tiny gaps between neurons.

Weight changes are much more dramatic than height changes during the first year. A normally developing baby doubles his or her birth weight by the fourth month and triples it by his or her first birthday. Newborns grow to about one and a half times taller by their first birthday. By the second year, an individual has reached about 50 percent of his or her potential adult height and 20 percent their adult weight (Tanner, 1990).

Brain Development

Before specifically discussing brain development during infancy, it is important to lay the foundation by describing some basic features of the brain. The neuron is the information-processing cell of the nervous system (Bransford, Brown & Cocking, 2000). Nearly all of your neurons were generated during your prenatal life and will continue to function into old age. In fact, neurons started being created within ten weeks after conception and production was pretty much complete by twenty-eight weeks after conception. These neurons were created at the astonishing rate of about 1,000 neurons per second, resulting in somewhere around 100 billion neurons.

The **neuron** has several important parts (Bransford, Brown & Cocking, 2000). The **cell body** contains the parts of the cell to keep it alive and functioning (such as the nucleus). The **dendrites** receive information from other neurons, whereas the axon takes the information from the neuron away to be sent to other neurons. The **axon** can be **myelinated** (or surrounded by a layer of fat). Myelination insulates the axon and speeds up message transmission (and it may possibly provide energy). At the end of the axon are the terminal buttons which can release neurotransmitters. **Neurotransmitters** are chemical messengers that carry information to other neurons. The tiny gaps between neurons are called **synapses**. We know this is brief and to the point, but most of you have probably already learned about the brain in general psychology, biology, anatomy, or health.

The outer surface of the brain (the wrinkled part) is called the cerebral cortex (called cortex for short). The cortex is where the magic called "human qualities or traits" occurs. Personality, problem-solving, language, purposeful movement, and emotional control are just some examples of important human behavior that are at least partially controlled by the cortex (Siegler, 1998). Areas of the cortex can be specialized for special processes—we will learn more about this with language development.

There are two hemispheres to the brain, the left and the right. Language ability is specialized in certain areas of the left cerebral cortex for most individuals (Siegler, 1998; Tanner,

1990). This specialization is evident in newborns as measured by brain activity in response to speech. It is theorized that such specialization may help prime the brain to learn language quickly in infancy. Spatial processing seems to be specialized in certain areas of the right cerebral cortex for most individuals. This specialization is evident during infancy.

Sometimes, babies are born with (or develop after birth) severe forms of epilepsy which necessitate removal of the left hemisphere of the brain. If this is done during infancy, language function is moved to the remaining right hemisphere with relatively little problem. Interestingly, when language processing moves in, spatial processing moves out (at least somewhat). It appears that it is within our genetic code to give language processing preference for any available healthy brain tissue over spatial processing. It is important to note that the earlier in life that such brain surgery is done, the better. The brain appears to lose some of it's plasticity with development, resulting in less optimal recovery at later ages (Siegler, 1998).

An adult brain is about three pounds. The brain achieves 25 percent of its weight by birth and 75 percent by the first birthday. Although the newborn is born with most of the neurons he or she will ever have, the number of dendrites (with corresponding synapses) increases significantly during infancy. No experience is lost on a newborn, as experiences build connections in the brain. Research shows that animals and humans reared in stimulating environments have bigger brains and more connections than animals and humans reared in barren or neglectful environments (National Research Council and Institute of Medicine, 2000).

Different areas of the brain develop at different times. Many are not complete until well into adolescence. In terms of infants, areas important for language, visual, motor, emotions, and planning all show development during infancy (National Research Council and Institute of Medicine, 2000).

Other Physical Changes

Three major areas of physical development would include muscle development, fat development, and bone development. Although nearly all of a person's muscle fiber is present at birth; it continues to grow, strengthen, thicken, and band together during infancy and throughout childhood. During the end of prenatal development, a layer of fat begins to be deposited below the skin. This layer of fat continues to develop during infancy and is important for body

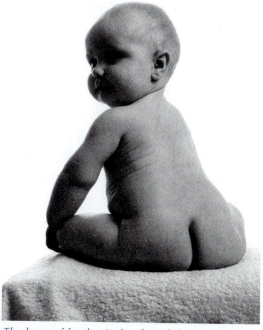

The layer of fat that is developed during infancy is important for body temperature control.

temperature control. Finally, bones begin as cartilage during prenatal development. It slowly hardens to bone in the center core during prenatal development and the outer ends (epiphyses) harden to bone near birth. The rest of the cartilage turns to bone slowly and, when complete, finishes growth of the skeleton (Tanner, 1990).

Pause and Process:

1. Describe the physical growth patterns discussed in this section.

2. In which hemisphere of the brain is language localized for most people? Why may the brain have such a specialized area?

MOTOR DEVELOPMENT

Basic motor, or movement, skills are developed in infancy. Changes or refinements in these skills are based on (1) maturation of structures such as nerves and muscles, (2) exercise of existing reflexes present at birth, and (3) experiences in practicing and refining the skills as they appear and change. In many respects, motor skill development reflects the interaction between genetic programming and environmental experiences more dramatically than any other developmental pattern.

The pattern of motor skill development in infancy illustrates many of Gesell's ideas regarding maturation (that development unfolds according to a preprogrammed, biological sequence). Gesell stressed that motor skills emerge in accordance with a predictable, inborn sequence that is highly organized and common to all humans. Babies do not acquire them before they are developmentally ready. Individual differences in the rate at which these skills emerge and become refined are apparent among infants.

Motor Skills

The achievement of upright locomotion is a milestone in human development. An infant's first steps reflect much developmental progress in motor skills from the time of birth. They set the stage for many related developmental events later in the life span.

Walking is a highly complex behavior. It involves the coordination of a large number of muscle groups working in association with sensory perception to maintain balance. Reflex activity in the neonatal period and movement behaviors in the early months of infancy prepare the individual to walk. Upright locomotion develops as a sequence of events that follows the cephalocaudal pattern. It is accompanied by maturation of muscle groups and nerve fibers involving the spinal cord and lower brain structures. Please note that although we are heavily emphasizing the importance of biological maturation in this section, keep in mind the importance of caregiving behaviors and infant experiences in promoting infant motor development. As always, nature and nurture both play a role in this developmental feat.

The sequence of events that culminates in walking illustrates the principle that changes in motor skills proceed from the general to the specific. The diffuse, largely uncoordinated behaviors of early infancy are brought under the control of the specific body parts involved in walking. The process involves orderly changes as an infant experiences the maturational pre-programmed responses that partially compose motor skill development.

The sequencing begins in association with the behavior of early infancy. The child first acquires the ability to lift its head and then its chest from a prone position. The ability to sit up with, and then without, support is attained next. This illustrates an infant's increasing control over the muscles and nerves of the trunk region of its body. By about seven months of age, most infants show the rapid increase in motor skill activity and changes that permit **crawling** (locomotion with the abdomen on a surface). This is followed by **creeping** (locomotion by moving the hands and knees with the abdomen off the surface). A variation in locomotion is **hitching**, or crawling or creeping backward using the buttocks rather than the hands and knees. Using various body parts in numerous combinations produces movement in all directions.

Toward their first birthday, many infants are able to pull to a standing position using crib sides, furniture, or walls for support. **Cruising**, or walking using the assistance of objects or people leads to upright, independent walking. Walking occurs for most American infants around the first birthday. Although we are giving approximate ages for these motor milestones, remember that infants can vary and have their own timetable.

One of Gesell's principal conclusions about the role of maturation was that none of these events will occur until an individual is ready developmentally. In other words, neither the appearance of these events nor their rate of development can be altered. His conclusion is questionable, however, because infants who have received special training have been shown to walk earlier than usual (Zelazo, 1983). What is controversial is the *purpose* of accomplishing this achievement earlier than typically expected.

Hand Skills

The human hand is an engineering marvel. Composed of several dozen

Crawling

Locomotion with the abdomen on a surface.

Creeping

Locomotion by moving the hands and knees with the abdomen off the surface.

Hitching

Crawling or creeping backward using the buttocks rather than the hands and knees.

Cruising

Walking using the assistance of objects or people.

By their first birthday many infants are able to pull themselves into a standing position by using the sides of their cribs.

Hand skills

The ability to explore and manipulate a wide variety of objects with the hands.

bones, the hands provide the means for exploring and manipulating a wide variety of objects. **Hand skills** let the developing infant take in rich sensory input from the environment and participate in much instrumental or goal-oriented behavior. They are as significant for active exploration as walking or locomotion.

Much of our understanding of the developmental changes in hand or manual skills come from observing the grasping activities and behaviors of infants (Frankenburg et al., 1981; Halverson, 1931; von Hofsten, 1983). The emergence and refinement of the ability to handle objects and use the hands with agility follows the proximodistal pattern and conforms to the trend of general to specific responses. Essentially, there is an orderly sequence of steps and refinements in this type of motor skill.

At birth, grasping is governed by reflexive action. By the second month, this behavior is random and clumsy as the infant attempts to reach and retain objects. Initially, a baby uses the entire hand to grasp or pick up something. Later an infant uses only the palm and the fourth and fifth fingers. This is referred to as the ulnar grasp.

By six months of age, a different problem emerges. The infant is able to grasp an object in a primitive manner, but is unable to let go of it. Willful letting go of objects is not possible until about eight months of age. At this age, the ulnar grasp is modified to include the middle fingers and the center of the palm (the palmar grasp). Next it is refined to include the index finger and the side of the palm (the radial grasp). The final refinement involves the use of the thumb with the forefinger, known as the pincer grasp. The pincer grasp becomes the preferred method of picking up all objects, large as well as very small in size. This final ability is achieved at twelve to fourteen months of age. From this point forward, an infant experiences great delight in this new mastery and becomes absorbed in searching for all kinds of objects to successfully transfer to its mouth.

Pause and Process:

1. How does walking develop?

2. How do hand skills develop in infancy?

PERCEPTUAL DEVELOPMENT

Perceptual Development

Perceptual skill development is closely associated with changes in motor skills development. This association is clearly observed in the emerging abilities of infants to use visual-motor skills in many activities. Infants learn to guide their movements and make adjustments in motor actions based on what they see.

Much of the change that takes place in grasping behavior reflects the increasing ability of an infant's brain to organize and interpret visual feedback. Up until they are four to five months of age, infants devote a great deal of their time to gazing at their

Perceptual skill

The ability to perceive through sight and sound; especially those skills related to motor skill development, such as depth perception and pattern perception, that emerge in infancy.

hands. Even while reaching for an object, an infant will become fascinated with watching his own hand. In fact, he will often lose sight of the object because he is so intent on examining the movements his hand is making (Bower, 1977; von Hofsten & Fazel-Zandy, 1984).

By the time a baby is about five to six months old; her hand movements are more controlled by visual feedback (Hatwell, 1987). The infant is now more motivated to grasp and manipulate objects and less fascinated by her own hand movements. This important achievement results from continual practice in hand gazing. Hand gazing apparently establishes neural circuits in the brain, and these provide information about where the hand is in space, which way the arms and legs are moving in space, and what happens as a result of such actions. The development of kinesthetic sense, or knowledge of where one's body is in space, how it performs when making certain movements, and what happens as a result—will become significant in learning to walk.

In learning about visual-motor coordination, researchers have studied two other related areas: the acquisition of depth perception and pattern perception.

Depth Perception

The ability to detect differences in surface depths and three-dimensional perception seems to be inborn in many animal species. These skills in depth perception are not innate in human beings but emerge very early in their development. Their early emergence may serve to protect infants from falling and injuring themselves.

Psychologists Eleanor Gibson and Richard Walk (1960) conducted a famous investigation called the visual cliff experiment to study depth perception in infancy. An apparatus was constructed using checkerboard patterns. One pattern was part of one end of the surface of the apparatus; the other was on the floor but could be seen through glass that extended across the apparatus' surface. This gave the appearance of a change in surface depth. A group of infants from six and one-half to fourteen months of age were placed individually at the shallow end of the apparatus and encouraged to crawl to their mother, who was at the other end. The reactions of the majority of infants showed that they detected the apparent change in

The differences in surface depths and three-dimensional perception protects infants from falling and injuring themselves.

depth of the surface. Some would approach the edge, touch the glass, and retreat back to the shallow end. Others cried in frustration at not being able to reach their mother. All of these infants clearly demonstrated avoidance of the apparent deep zone.

This experiment cleverly showed that stereoscopic or binocular vision appears by the time an infant is ready to begin actively exploring its environment by crawling and creeping. This is usually at about six months of age. Several studies have revealed that a rapid increase in this ability to perceive the world in a three-dimensional manner occurs between the age of three and six months as a result of the establishment of neural circuitry in the brain (Bertenthal & Camos, 1987; Yonas, Granrud & Pettersen, 1985). Other work has shown the importance of early visual experiences in the development of binocular vision (Hubel & Wiesel, 1970). The cells in the brain that are responsible for this ability apparently disappear if they are not stimulated with sensory signals from both eyes during the first few months of life. In effect, the brain will not establish the appropriate neural circuitry for this necessary visual ability unless the infant has adequate experience visually exploring his or her environment. This is a good argument in favor of providing visual experiences to infants during their alert periods.

Pause and Process:

1. Describe what is meant by perceptual skills.

2. What do we know about infant depth perception?

HEALTH ISSUES

Nutritional Needs

"Breast is best." Surely you have heard this mantra before. Overwhelming research indicates that breast milk provides the best nutrition for infants; it offers the perfect combination of carbohydrates, fats, and proteins. Breast milk also contains the mother's antibodies to help fight infections. In comparison to formula-fed babies, breastfed babies have lower childhood obesity rates, lower rates of illnesses and infections, lower rates of SIDS (sudden infant death syndrome), lower childhood cancer rates, lower rates of diabetes II, lower rates of allergies, and denser bones. Additionally, breastfeeding may be correlated to better cognitive development and visual acuity. Breastfeeding also provides benefits to the mother; including, lower stress levels, weight loss, and a sense of peace and bonding (thanks to hormones).

However, there are reasons as to why breastfeeding should be avoided. If the mother has a disease that can be transmitted through the breast milk (such as AIDS), breastfeeding should be avoided. Additionally, certain medications that may harm the baby may prevent a woman from breastfeeding.

Approximately two-thirds of women breastfeed while in the hospital, with about a third still breastfeeding six months later. Most medical professionals recommend breast-

Research has shown that breast milk has many benefits for infants. For example, breastfed babies have lower childhood obesity rates, lower rates of SIDS and denser bones. Breast milk also contains the mother's antibodies which helps fight infections.

feeding for at least the first year. Women with social support are more likely to continue breastfeeding than women without such support.

Baby foods (special infant cereal is usually first) are introduced typically between four and six months. Unfortunately, some uneducated parents mix formula with cereal in a bottle before this time with the thought of helping the infant sleep through the night. This practice is highly discouraged because the infant's digestive system is not yet developed enough to handle the cereal and the parents may cause some serious health issues. By the first birthday, the infant is usually ready to eat some finely cut or mashed table food. Pediatricians often assist parents in knowing when it is appropriate to introduce certain foods. If certain foods are introduced too soon, parents can risk triggering allergic reactions that may create sensitivities that will last a lifetime.

Safety Concerns

As motor skills advance from crawling and creeping to upright walking, the infant's perspective of the world changes. Now an infant can move about with increasing speed and has more freedom to explore the physical surroundings. To grow and develop adequately, they need these experiences. They need to learn they are distinct persons, separate from other people and things, yet also a part of their surroundings. As children act upon their environment, they discover how their environment acts.

Childproofing

Arranging and adapting housing and physical space (e.g., by capping electrical outlets) to meet safety concerns for infants.

Naturally, parents are concerned about the infant's physical safety at this time. It soon becomes obvious that a child's quest to discover the environment can lead to danger. Parents generally react by **childproofing** their home—that is, they adapt it to the needs and behavior of a small child (Duvall & Miller, 1985). Cleaning solutions are placed out of reach, accessories are moved from tables, tablecloths are put away, protective gates are placed across doorways, and electrical outlets are plugged with specially designed caps. Often the entire family's lifestyle must be modified to protect an infant's safety.

In recent years, numerous baby products and toys have been recalled because of lead paint or other toxins. Because babies have the tendency to put everything in their mouth, it is especially important to avoid anything that may have lead or lead paint. Although steps have been taken to ensure the safety of infant and child products, safety should not be taken for granted. It is important for parents to stay up to date on product recalls.

Promoting Wellness

Health should be closely monitored during infancy. Periodic visits to health-care professionals help to promote well-being and normal growth patterns during this stage.

Immunizations

Making sure that an infant is immunized against a variety of communicable diseases is an important aspect of health care. Most of the diseases that once killed people in infancy are now preventable by immunization. Although there is some debate in the general public as to whether a preservative in vaccinations may have triggered autism in chil-

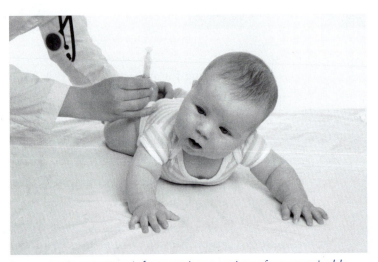

Immunizations protect infants against a variety of communicable diseases.

dren, medical professionals vehemently deny this assertion. Sadly, some once eradicated childhood illnesses are making a comeback because of parents not vaccinating their children. Parents who are concerned about vaccinations and potential health hazards should talk to their pediatrician.

Sleep

In the last cycle we spoke about infant sleep cycles. Although babies differ as to when they will actually start sleeping through the night, parents can rest assured that it should happen sometime before the first birthday (although one of the author's daughter's did not sleep through the night until around sixteen to eighteen months of age).

Sudden Infant Death Syndrome (SIDS) is a worry for parents of infants. What is SIDS? It is when an infant stops breathing during sleep and suffocates to death. SIDS claims approximately five thousand infant lives in the United States each year. The peak age for SIDS deaths is between two and four months of age.

Sudden infant death syndrome (SIDS)

A condition of unknown cause resulting in the sudden and unexpected death of an infant.

Doctors and researchers are not sure what causes SIDS. A genetic predisposition and brain defect are likely candidates; however, there are known environmental factors that can place infants at risk. For example, exposure to maternal smoking in the womb, second-hand smoke, low-birthweight, premature birth, co-sleeping, heavy blankets/sleepwear, and a sibling death due to SIDS increase the risk of SIDS. Breastfeeding, sleeping in the parents' bedroom (but in a separate bed), sleeping with a fan on, and sleeping on one's back seem to help prevent SIDS.

Co-sleeping

Parents and children sleep in the same bed.

Co-sleeping is a controversial issue in the United States. **Co-sleeping** is when parents and children sleep in the same bed. Many cultures accept co-sleeping as a natural way of life. Many parents enjoy the time of closeness with their infant and it facilitates breastfeeding. However, many U.S. medical professionals advise against co-sleeping because of the risk of rolling over on the infant and suffocating them. Some American parents are opting to have an infant room-in with them—the infant sleeps in the same room (making breastfeeding easier), but a separate bed.

Baby Exercise

Infants are typically active on their own. They work very hard, almost nonstop, toward reaching their next motor milestone (e.g., rolling, crawling, or walking). Free movement and playtime, while being supervised, is encouraged for infants. Structured exercise, however, is largely unnecessary and potentially dangerous. Because infants cannot directly communicate if a parent is going too far in helping them exercise, it is usually recommended that parents hold off on the structured exercise classes until the child is older. An obvious exception to this general rule is if the infant has a developmental disability that requires physical therapy.

Pause and Process:

1. Do vaccines cause autism?

2. What are risk factors for SIDS? What can help prevent SIDS?

COGNITIVE DEVELOPMENT DURING INFANCY

LEARNING OBJECTIVES:

1. *Understand the general progression of cognitive development during the sensorimotor stage*
2. *Describe infant information-processing skills*
3. *Identify milestones in infant language development*

We are going to begin this section by discussing Piaget's first stage of cognitive development: the sensorimotor stage. This stage lasts from birth until around the age of twenty-four months. Remember, Piaget posited that individuals go through four stages of cognitive development, each qualitatively different from one another. The stages must be gone through in order, and no stage may be skipped. However, in Piagetian theory, not all individuals reach the fourth stage of cognitive development, which we will discuss later in the book.

If you remember back to Chapter 1, Piaget's cognitive developmental theory saw assimilation and accommodation as two processes that help individuals adapt or change their schemas based upon their experiences in the world. This means that we can view cognitive development as driven by intellectual adaptation to the world.

This would be a good time to introduce two other key concepts in Piagetian theory: equilibrium and disequilibrium. There was probably a time back in your childhood when you believed in Santa Clause, the Easter Bunny, and the Tooth Fairy. When you accepted their existence without question, you were in a state of equilibrium. However, as you grew, you started to have some questions. Santa has a sleigh, but how does the Easter Bunny get around the world in one night? What does the Tooth Fairy do with all these teeth? Why does Tommy down the street keep saying that there is no Santa Claus? These, and many other doubts, started entering your mind. You entered a state of disequilibrium, an uncomfortable cognitive state in which your experiences and beliefs are no longer perfectly aligned. When this happened, you were forced to seek out answers and go through a process of equilibration, until your beliefs and experiences/observations were once again aligned.

Therefore, cognitive development is driven by adapting our thinking to our experiences in the world. When our thoughts and beliefs are no longer in equilibrium with our experiences, we are thrown into a state of disequilibrium. As we go through the equilibration process, we use the processes of assimilation and accommodation to adapt our schemas; hence, we grow cognitively.

After we finish discussing Piaget's sensorimotor stage, we will highlight information-processing and language development during infancy. Although the infancy period lasts from only about two weeks after birth until the age of two, cognitive development is astronomically quick. When you compare the cognitive abilities of a two-year-old child with a two-week-old child, the amount of growth seems incomprehensible. Yet, it is a task that occurs in all cognitively healthy infants and toddlers.

PIAGET'S COGNITIVE DEVELOPMENT THEORY AND THE SENSORIMOTOR STAGE

Piaget uses the term sensorimotor to describe the integration of sensory input (perceptions of sound, sight, taste, smell, and touch) with motor behavior during infancy. Motor skills that are quickly developed in infancy, such as walking, grasping, and manipulating objects, are increasingly guided by sensory input as the infant matures. In Piaget's view, self-differentiation is accomplished through sensory and motor activities. With adequate brain maturation, an infant can learn about the world, discover how to react to it, and develop schemes to solve problems in interactions with it. At first, the child is able to do this only through such sensory means as taste and touch and through motor actions. An infant's understanding of the world is therefore limited. However, it is through such means and level of functioning that lifetime mental development begins.

One of the infant's major accomplishments is learning that objects, people, and things are permanent. This enables an infant to realize that she or he is a distinct and separate entity from the things and people that populate the environment. This realization requires the construction of a concept known as **object permanence**—the understanding that something continues to exist even though it is hidden or removed from sight. The reason the game of peek-a-boo is so fascinating to young infants is that they do not yet understand this principle. As they develop and discover that things can be moved and manipulated, they master this cognitive skill.

One other accomplishment during this time of the life span is the elementary ability to represent the external world by internal, mental images. An infant takes the first step in this rather complicated process (which is not mastered until later in life) by understanding the world through sensory means. Things are known by how they feel, taste, look, and smell, as well as by how they can be manipulated. If it were possible for an infant to use language effectively and she was asked to define a ball, her likely answer would be in words noting sensory and motor characteristics: "It's something that's slick on my tongue, and rolls across the floor when I hit it." This is probably the only way a ball can be understood at this stage in life.

The cognitive changes during this period happen in a sequence Piaget describes as beginning with reflexes at birth and culminating in symbolic reasoning at eighteen to twenty-four months of age (see Table 3-1). They are facilitated by the acquisition of the ability to use language in communication with others. The next section discusses the order of this sequence.

Substages of the Sensorimotor Stage:

1. *Use of existing reflexes* to progress toward developing sensorimotor schemas occurs between birth and one month of age. Reflexes present at birth provide much of the basis for motor behavior at this time. The infant performs these reflex actions more efficiently with practice. As the infant's brain structures mature, the same actions come more under willful control. Searching for a nipple, for example, is first guided by the rooting reflex. Such behavior becomes learned rather than automatic as the reflex is replaced by willful action by virtue of the maturation process. In adapting from automatic to willful acts, infants gain more control over their interactions with the world.

2. *Primary circular reactions* are formed between one and four months of age. **Circular reactions** are actions that occur by chance and then are repeated and modified through practice. We will use the act of sucking to illustrate how primary circular reactions are formed. An infant accidentally happens to put a finger in her mouth. This stimulates sucking, an action based on a strong reflex present before birth. Because this is a pleasurable act, the baby repeats it. The repetition leads to learning how to suck on a thumb. As maturation proceeds, anything

Object permanence

The understanding that something exists even though it is not in sight or has been removed from the field of vision; accomplished between 18 and 24 months of age.

Circular reactions

Actions that occur by chance and then are repeated and modified through practice.

TABLE 3-1	SUMMARY OF THE SUBSTAGES OF THE SENSORIMOTOR STAGE
SUBSTAGE	**DESCRIPTION**
1. Use of reflexes (birth to one month)	Use of reflexes present at birth to adapt to the environment.
2. Primary circular reactions (one to four months)	Repetition of pleasurable acts that happen first by body acts; object permanence not yet developed.
3. Secondary circular reactions (four to nine months)	Focus shifts to environment as infant learns that chance, then deliberate, actions produce certain results.
4. Coordination of secondary schemas (nine to 12 months)	Coordination and integration of secondary schemas to achieve goals; increasing awareness of object permanence.
5. Tertiary circular reactions (12 to 18 months)	Purposive variation of behavior to experiment and vary schemas; trial-and-error used in solving problems and reaching goals.
6. Symbolic logic (18 to 24 months)	Primitive reasoning system used; object permanence achieved, symbol user.

the baby grasps is brought to her mouth to be sucked upon. These actions involve hand-eye and hand-mouth coordination. They are called primary because they occur first in reference to the infant's body. They are called circular because they are habitual actions based on continual repetition.

3. *Secondary circular reactions* are formed between four and nine months of age. In forming secondary circular reactions, the infant's reference shifts from the body (primary reactions) to the physical environment. The baby observes that random chance movements produce specific results and outcomes—for example, a particular kicking motion in his crib produces wild, swinging movements of the mobile hanging overhead. This pleases, delights, and fascinates the infant. He rapidly learns that willfully controlled actions of his body produce results in the physical environment. As this type of association between a personal action and its environmental result is repeated, a secondary circular reaction is formed. Later in the infancy stage, a baby may modify his physical actions to produce similar results with different objects. For example, the baby who formed a secondary circular reaction to make his crib mobile move learns to modify basic movements to make a similar piece of equipment move when placed in his playpen. It is in such simple ways that an infant learns to act in certain ways to make certain things happen. This is a very significant advance. The ability to make a connection between action and result (cause and effect) is the very foundation of human learning ability.

Object permanence, as far as we know, is not understood this early in infancy. Infants are mastering this skill, however, as they recognize and recover objects only partially hidden from their view. But they still will not try to discover an object's whereabouts if it is hidden from their view.

4. *Coordination of secondary schemas* occurs between nine and twelve months of age. If you can remember from Chapter 1, schemas (or schemes) are the basic building blocks of mental life. They are consistent, reliable patterns or plans for processing information, experiences, or perceptions of the world. Individuals change or modify their schemas with experience throughout life. Piaget suggests that the numerous schemas formed in interaction with the physical environment earlier are combined and coordinated at this particular time in infancy. New behavior patterns emerge from existing ones as an infant learns new ways to solve problems and interact with

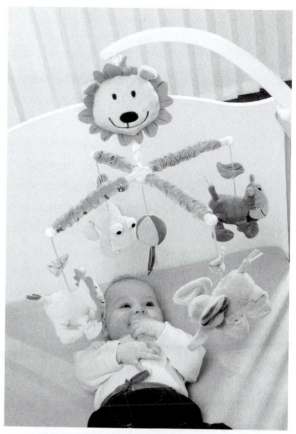

An example of secondary circular reaction is when a baby is able to make a mobile move by kicking his legs.

the surroundings. An infant may learn, for example, to search for an object that she saw hidden. She will grasp the object once she has located it. Piaget describes this as intentional behavior. The infant established a goal before acting and purposely tailored her physical actions to enable her to reach that goal. The infant can adapt behavior to attain goals effectively in the social and physical environment.

5. *Tertiary circular reactions* are formed between twelve and eighteen months of age. Piaget describes infants as true scientists now because of their incessant motivation to explore their environment, to discover new understandings, and to experiment with new approaches to solving problems and attaining goals. A new skill learned by the infant is the ability to make new events happen. These refinements in cognition are shown by the baby's first efforts to learn the cause-and-effect nature of bodily movements and physical acts. Toys are dropped or thrown repeatedly. This is because the infant observes that they always fall, make certain sounds, or produce particular actions when treated in this manner.

Infants' exploration of their environment is largely by trial-and-error. This is the hallmark of the type of change taking place in their mental functioning at this time. It explains their fascination with banging pots and pans, investigating waste cans, playing in the toilet, splashing water in the bath, and exploring everything in detail with their fingers. Childproofing the home is a necessity at this time.

6. *Symbolic (or elementary) logic* emerges between eighteen and twenty-four months of age. There are first indications of simple internalization as infants gradually develop mental images of objects and actions. Object permanence usually becomes fully established now. The first sign of symbolic thought processes is that infants require little or no experimentation to reach solutions to their problems. For instance, an

An example of tertiary circular reaction is when a baby repeatedly throws or drops a toy.

infant at this age may try to wake her father by placing eyeglasses on his face because she associates this feature with his being awake and seeing to her needs.

Infants this age engage in much imitation of others' actions and pretend play. As they learn to incorporate others' actions into their own range of behaviors, they learn other ways to solve problems and reach goals. Ways to solve future problems and reach goals are anticipated.

Characteristics of Sensorimotor Thought

In summary, sensorimotor thought is based largely on motor actions. Two important milestones are reached during this stage: object permanence and symbolic thought. During this stage, the infant already actively explores the environment and adapts his or her schemas based upon these experiences. By the end of the sensorimotor stage, the child is capable of symbolic thought, meaning he or she can use mental representations when thinking.

Critiques of Piaget's Theory

The critiques to Piaget's theory will seem familiar to issues discussed in Chapter 1. Piaget's theory allowed us to view infant thought as unique, not as simply a rudimentary form of adult thought. Indeed, infants do not think less than adults, they think differently (hence, the idea of qualitative changes).

Current research indicates that Piaget underestimated the cognitive abilities of infants. As developmentalists have created amazing research techniques that allow us a glimpse into an infant's mental world, it has become apparent that infants are far more cognitively capable than we previously thought. For example, there is some evidence that they achieve object permanence and deferred imitation earlier than Piaget thought (Crain, 2005). As we continue to progress in our research abilities it should be interesting to see what cognitive skills infants achieve far earlier than we ever dreamed.

Pause and Process:

1. What is object permanence? What would your life be like if you thought people and objects ceased to exist if they left your view?

2. Describe what sensorimotor thought is like.

INFORMATION-PROCESSING IN INFANCY

Although Piaget viewed cognitive development as occurring through qualitatively distinct stages, information-processing theories view cognitive development as a continuous process during which specific processes increase in efficiency to a certain point, and then, perhaps, decline.

Basic processes

"Frequently used, rapidly executed, memory activities such as association, generalization, recognition, and recall. They are among the building blocks of cognition, in the sense that all more complex cognitive activities are built by combining them in different ways."

Within the information-processing paradigm, **basic processes** are defined as "frequently used, rapidly executed, memory activities such as association, generalization, recognition, and recall. They are among the building blocks of cognition, in the sense that all more complex cognitive activities are built by combining them in different ways" (Siegler, 1998, p. 180). Basic processes are functional at birth, with some functional prenatally. Although infants lack knowledge structures, memory strategies, and such, their ability to use basic processes allow them to form and access memories.

Explicit memories

Conscious memories that can be visualized as well as provide a verbal account.

First, we should distinguish between the basic processes of explicit and implicit memories. **Explicit memories** are memories of which we are conscious. We can typically visualize these memories and provide a verbal account. **Implicit memories** are unconscious memories that influence our behavior. For example, most of you have probably been driving for a while. You do not need to (hopefully) consciously try to remember which pedal is for the gas and which is for the brake. You implicitly know this and this knowledge directs your behavior. This is an example of an implicit memory. However, if I asked you to recount your scariest driving moment, you would verbally relate the story to me as you consciously extricate it from your memory. This would be an example of an explicit memory. Both types of memory are important; yet, they have their own developmental timetable.

Implicit memories

Unconscious memories that influence our behavior.

It appears that infants are capable of forming implicit memories from birth, if not prenatally. However, it is not until around six to eight months that infants seem able to form explicit memories. Evidently, implicit and explicit memories utilize different parts of the brain that mature at different times (Siegler, 1998).

Association is the most fundamental of basic processes and it is the ability to form a connection between a stimuli and a response. **Recognition** is another basic process. Once

Association

The ability to form a connection between a stimuli and a response.

Recognition

Awareness or recollection of having seen something before.

Habituation/ dishabituation

An experimental technique that allows researchers to measure recognition in babies.

Imitation

The basic process of a newborn being capable of immediately imitating your behavior.

Recall

The basic process of a newborn being capable of recalling observed behavior experiences.

15. What are the two basic types of memories discussed in this chapter?

Infantile amnesia

The inability to remember much about the first two or so years of life after birth.

again, both of these are certainly present at birth and are most likely present prenatally. Association can be tested through the classical conditioning process discussed in Chapter 1. Recognition has been tested in preterm and full term infants using the **habituation/dishabituation** process. For example, newborns like to gaze at novel visual stimuli. Once a stimulus becomes familiar, their gazing time decreases. However, if you present a new, novel stimulus, gazing time increases again. This basic knowledge allows us to test both visual preferences and recognition. Using habituation/dishabituation, we know that two-month-olds recognize old visual stimuli for more than two weeks after initial exposure.

Have you ever stuck your tongue out at a newborn? I suppose most of you haven't, but guess what would happen if you did? The newborn would stick his or her tongue out at you in reply. The newborn isn't being rude; instead, they are imitating observed behavior. **Imitation** and **recall** are also basic processes present at birth. Not only is the newborn capable of immediately imitating your behavior, but they still recall the experience twenty-four hours later. Newborns that have observed tongue protrusion behavior are more likely to engage in such behavior for the twenty-four hours afterward than newborns who did not observe such behavior. This pattern holds true not just for tongue protrusion behavior, but also for opening and closing of mouth behavior. As infants grow older, the amount of time between observation and imitation/recall increases. Shortly after the first birthday, infants can demonstrate imitation and recall more than four months after the initial observation (Siegler, 1998).

Rovee-Collier (1995) demonstrated the memory capabilities of infants across a series of experiments utilizing infant mobiles (the circular things that hang above cribs with dangling toys that play music). Rovee-Collier would tie a string connected to a mobile to the ankle of an infant. If the infant kicked, the mobile would make sounds. The studies showed that three-month-olds would experience an "aha" moment in which they would learn that their kicking behavior caused the mobile's noise. Infants were able to recall and generalize their learning across similar situations if comparable experiences were provided within three days of each other.

In summary, infants are born with basic processes that allow for quick learning about the surrounding world. These basic processes provide the foundation for all information-processing throughout life. Future chapters will discuss the specifics of intelligence, attention, memory, and problem-solving development.

Infantile Amnesia

What is your earliest memory? How old are you in this earliest memory? Most of us do not remember much about the first two or so years of our life after birth. This is referred to as **infantile amnesia**. It used to be assumed that infants could not form long-term memories; however, we now know that is false. Experiences at the age of eleven months can sometimes be recalled a year later and some three-year-olds can remember experiences from when they were one. So why is it that we cannot remember our own birth? Why can't we remember our first steps, walks, or piece of birthday cake? These seem like worthwhile memories to keep, so where have they gone?

There are three leading theories in regard to the causes of infantile amnesia. The first theory is that the parts of the brain instrumental in storing long-term, explicit, retrievable memories continue to mature well past infancy. The frontal lobes seem to be particularly important for these memories (Siegler, 1998).

The second theory highlights the importance of practicing information in order to retain information (and access to that information) in long-term memory. For example, the more young children hear stories about their first birthday—and relate stories about their first birthday—the more likely it is that they will form enduring memories about their first birthday. Parents seem to naturally begin having these dialogues with their children around the age of three, which may be why some of our earliest memories are around that age (Siegler, 1998).

The third theory is in regard to how infants and older individuals may encode information differently. For example, when you try to remember something, how do you do it? Do you use words (verbal codes)? Do you use mental images (visual codes)? It has been theorized that infants are more likely to encode their memories using smells, tastes, and touches rather than our preferred verbal and visual codes. However, as children acquire language and begin using verbal codes to encode and retrieve information, they may lose the ability to access memories encoded in different modalities (Siegler, 1998).

In all likelihood, it is a combination of these three theories, and perhaps some other theories not considered here, that will eventually explain the phenomenon of infantile amnesia. But honestly, even if you could remember your own birth, would you really want to?

Pause and Process:

1. Give a description of information-processing abilities in infancy.

2. In your own words, explain the three explanations for infantile amnesia discussed above. Which explanation seems the most plausible to you?

LANGUAGE DEVELOPMENT IN INFANCY

One characteristic that is uniquely human emerges during infancy. This is the ability to use language to communicate information, ideas, feelings, and thoughts to others. Before individuals emerge from infancy, they are expected to be able to pronounce words so that others can understand them. They are also expected to learn meanings associated with words, so that they can understand others.

An infant's acquisition of communication skills is a very complex process and one that is not completely understood. Our human brain structure is extremely important to language development and seems to hint that aspects of language acquisition are innate with proper exposure. This means that humans are hardwired with the ability to learn language with

Language

"A system of abstract symbols and rule-governed structures, the specific conventions of which are learned."

Speech

Orally expressed language.

Phonemes

The simplest and most elementary sounds in speech, or the building blocks of speech.

Morphemes

Meaningful units of speech.

Syntax

The rules for making grammatical sentences.

Semantics

The ability to express meaning through language.

Pragmatics

The ability to adjust speech in socially and culturally appropriate ways.

Language Acquisition Device (LAD)

An innate brain structure proposed by Chomsky that regulates the means by which an individual learns language.

proper social interaction. Two basic areas of the brain appear to be responsible for speech and language skills. They are located deep within the left hemisphere.

Hulit and Howard (1997) define **language** as "a system of abstract symbols and rule-governed structures, the specific conventions of which are learned" (p. 3). Although language is related to speech, they are not one and the same. **Speech** is orally expressing language; however, language can be conveyed through modalities other than verbal speech. Both speech and language are important processes for communication.

Language has some basic components. **Phonemes** are the simplest and most elementary sounds in speech, or the building blocks of speech. **Morphemes** are meaningful units of speech. **Syntax** comprises the rules for making grammatical sentences. **Semantics** is the ability to express meaning through language. **Pragmatics** is the ability to adjust speech in socially and culturally appropriate ways. Each of these components is mastered at different points in development. They are typically understood before they are fully able to be mastered in speech production (Dixon, 2003; Hulit & Howard, 1997; Piper, 2003).

Mastering the complexities of language is important for several reasons. First, language permits communication. It is through the medium of language that an infant is given information about many things. Cognitive changes, which allow the developing individual to understand the world in which he lives, are motivated and based on language. Words are the means by which the individual is educated, not only about facts of the world, but also about the rules by which his family operates, what his parents expect of his behavior, how people in his community live, and how society, in general, functions on a daily basis.

Second, language permits individual expression. By using language, an individual is able to express her inner feelings, attitudes, and thoughts and to connect her personal experiences with those of others. That is why language is often viewed as the observable expression and extension of inner thought processes and seen as reflective of the individual's level of cognitive development (Galatzer-Levy & Cohler, 1993; Kolata, 1987; Piper, 2003).

Theories of Language Acquisition

In the first year following birth, an infant comes to understand others' speech and to use some speech in an elementary and limited fashion. The change from uttering incomprehensible sounds to making sounds that are given meaning by others happens dramatically. There are some basic avenues to this dramatic change, according to developmental researchers.

Some developmentalists believe that there is an innate language structure, or **language acquisition device (LAD)**, within the brain that regulates the means by which an individual learns language (Chomsky, 1959). This is a very nativistic theory, focusing on the biological innateness to language acquisition.

The LAD is theorized to be a deep brain structure which is identical in all human beings, and allows any infant to acquire the language of the family and culture into which she or he is born. The human brain appears to be sensitive to the sound of language. The LAD organizes these sounds into meaningful understandings according to the grammatical structure of the particular language the child is exposed to daily. This explanation rests on the proposition that humans are born with a predetermined ability to learn any language, and that this is what makes them distinctly different from every other species. It does not completely explain just how language acquisition takes place, however.

Language acquisition is also thought to be influenced by environmental factors (Hulit & Howard, 1997). Imitation, caretaker speech (i.e., **motherese** or **infant-directed speech**), and reinforcement appear to play some role in speech development. However, the behavioral principles of reinforcement and imitation are not enough to explain language acquisition entirely. For example, we will learn soon that the vocabulary explosion that occurs in early childhood happens too quickly to be explained by imitation and reinforcement alone.

Linguists currently seem to favor an interactionist approach to understanding language development. This approach appreciates both biological endowments and social interactions in the acquisition of speech (Hulit and Howard, 1997). Over time, research may clarify what aspects of speech are primarily genetically preprogrammed (or primed) and which are highly dependent upon social interaction.

The General Sequence

There is a general sequence to language learning during infancy. First, infants cry at birth to communicate with their caregivers. Around one to two months of age, infants begin to coo. Next, around three months of age, infants enjoy making consonant sounds. It is around six months of age that babbling begins. Babbling involves combining consonant and vowel sounds and repeating them. Typically, babies will mimic the intonation that

Infant-directed speech

Speech that is more accentuated and of a higher pitch.

Babies try to mimic the sounds of their caregivers, and by their first birthday they say their first word.

their caregiver is using in communicating with them. Babies appear to understand their first word around eight months of age. Finally, around the first birthday, infants say their first word (Siegler, 1998).

The typical age range for generating their first word is between ten and thirteen months. First words are usually focused upon people, objects, and actions. Vehicles and food are among their favorite objects to speak about.

After achieving their first word, infants quickly progress to speaking in one-word phrases, commonly referred to as **holophrases**. Speaking seems to tax their cognitive resources, so infants use the least amount of words (and simplest words) possible to get their message across (Siegler, 1998).

Between the ages of eighteen and twenty-four months, the average toddler will begin speaking in two-word sentences. These sentences, again, leave out the niceties of speech (e.g., adjectives, adverbs, prepositions, etc.), and focus on conveying meaning. There are some common errors that occur during this time in regards to word meanings.

Toddlers will often commit errors of underextensions, overextensions, and overlaps (Siegler, 1998). An **underextension** is when a child limits the meaning of the word too narrowly. For example, a child may think that the word chair can refer only to a dinner table chair, not to office chairs, recliners, rocking chairs, or other forms of chairs. An **overextension** is when a child applies the meaning of a word too broadly. For example, all flying insects may be called a fly, including butterflies, bees, hornets, and mosquitoes. **Overlaps** occur when a word is underextended on some occasions and overextended on other occasions. For example, the word dress may not be appropriately used to refer to a wedding gown (underextension), but may be used to refer to a bathrobe (overextension).

Vocabulary development begins slowly in early infancy and then speeds up substantially during toddlerhood. For example, it is estimated that a child has a vocabulary of three words at his or her first birthday. However, a vocabulary explosion begins between eighteen months (with a vocabulary of 22 words) and twenty-one months (with a vocabulary of 118 words). Then there is another major jump by twenty-four months (with a vocabulary of 272 words). Such **fast-mapping** of words continues through early childhood with five-year-olds having a vocabulary of more than two thousand words and ten-year-olds having a vocabulary of more than forty thousand words. Mathematically, this works out that between the ages of eighteen months and ten years of age, a child learns about ten words a day (Siegler, 1998). Can you imagine trying to achieve this at your current age? Flashcards, anyone? Yet, these children achieve this with little or no effort through basic, everyday social interactions and educational experiences. Amazing!

Sentence structure and grammar is understood before it is produced by children. Grammatical knowledge is connected with vocabulary development. Typical two-word sentences will typically follow basic grammar rules (e.g., subject/verb). We will discuss how grammar, semantic, and pragmatic skills continue to develop across childhood in future chapters. The important thing to realize is that by the end of the second year,

Holophrases

An early speech form used by infants in which single words convey a wide number of meanings.

Underextension

When a child limits the meaning of the word too narrowly.

Overextension

When a child applies the meaning of a word too broadly.

Overlaps

When a word is underextended on some occasions and overextended on other occasions.

Fast-mapping

A language skill used by young children; the meaning of a new word is acquired by comparing it with one that is familiar.

children can effectively communicate their intentions and messages. The children also enter the early childhood period with a basic grasp of the language rule systems.

Pause and Process:

1. What is the difference between language and speech?

2. Summarize language development between birth and two years of age.

GENETICS

LEARNING OBJECTIVES:

1. *Describe emotional development during infancy*
2. *Explain infants self-understanding, family influences, and societal influences*
3. *Understand psychosocial development during infancy*

Social and emotional development during infancy is a fascinating topic. What emotions can an infant feel? What purpose do these emotions serve? When does an infant realize that he or she is a person? How does an infant develop psychosocially? This section will attempt to answer these questions as we take a peek into socioemotional development from birth through the second year.

EMOTIONAL DEVELOPMENT

Emotions

Subjective feelings such as love or joy that help to define our existence as human beings.

22. What neural circuit in the brain seems important for emotional and social understanding?

Emotions are subjective feelings such as love or joy that help to define our existence as human beings. Without these feelings and the ability to express them our lives would be impoverished. Emotions are also among the earliest means of communication that infants have with their caregivers, allowing infants to learn about the world, themselves, and others (Galatzer-Levy & Cohler, 1993; Gallese, 2005).

Emotional development is dependent upon brain development. As the brain develops, we see emotion expression, emotion recognition, and emotion regulation evolve. One neural circuit in the brain that seems important for emotional and social understanding (among other things) is the mirror neuron system (Gallese, 2005; Keestra, 2008). The mirror neuron system (MNS) seems to allow for early imitation and empathy. The research on the MNS is new and complicated, but it appears that the brain is hardwired in a way that allows us to "feel" what certain motor behaviors and emotions in others feels like to them. Said another way, sports and movies can emotionally move us because we vicariously experience the athletes and actors emotions via these mirror neurons. Our brains mimic the athlete and actor brains, allowing us to empathize with their emotions. Thus, it is currently hypothesized (and actively being researched) that these mirror neurons play a key role in early emotional development. However, let's take a step back and take a slightly broader view of what research in emotions has entailed up to now.

Behavioral scientists have described emotions in various ways. Some descriptions focus on the physiological basis of emotional reactions—for example, the changes that occur in blood vessels, heart rate, kidney, and digestive system function when someone feels angry or frightened. Other descriptions focus on the subjective aspect of emotions—people's own words describing their feelings. Others focus on the ways that emotions are expressed—for example, crying when feeling sad or using physical force when angry. This means that behavioral scientists can focus on the *physiological, cognitive/subjective feeling,* or *behavioral* aspects of emotions.

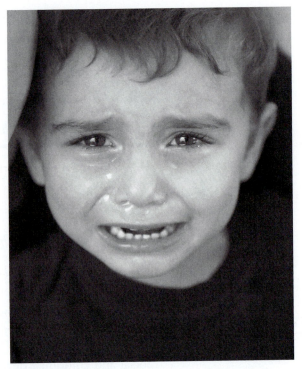

Crying when feeling sad is one way of expressing emotions.

Just as behavioral scientists can focus on different manifestations of emotion, developmentalists can have different theoretical viewpoints as to the importance and purpose of emotions. One notion is to view *emotion* as *communication.* Darwin was among the first to view human emotion as communication with the potential to provide us with an evolutionary advantage. For example, emotion communication (such as dominance and submission) can allow for the settlement of disputes without fighting to the death (Galatzer-Levy & Cohler, 1993). Such communication, within this viewpoint, greatly facilitates infant/caregiver interactions, allowing for sensitive, responsive, and appropriate caregiving behavior.

Just as the physiological manifestation of emotion can be the focus of research, it can also provide an overarching theoretical perspective into the study of emotion (Galatzer-Levy & Cohler, 1993). *Emotion as bodily change* is a perspective with a long and diverse history. One main idea that is of particular importance to emotions in infancy is that emotions learn to label and monitor their physiological states as emotions via interactions with caregivers. Although an infant may exhibit physiological arousal and accompanying stress, the parent may help label that bodily change as anger or frustration. Hence, it is through a caregiver's response to an infant's bodily change that an infant comes to recognize and label such changes as a particular emotion. It is theorized that if a child is raised by caregivers that are dismissive or repressive of emotional expression, the child may lack the ability to label and express emotions throughout life.

A third viewpoint is *emotion as a means to discharge tension* (Galatzer-Levy & Cohler, 1993). This viewpoint is largely based upon Freud's psychodynamic theory discussed in chapter one. From this perspective, emotion is energy that compels a person to action. In regards to emotion in infancy, caregivers can help infants to understand and channel their emotions into appropriate behaviors, as well as learn emotional control in general.

The fourth perspective that we will discuss here views *emotion as an indicator of importance* (Galatzer-Levy & Cohler, 1993). This position views emotion as a motivating system that is hardwired in all healthy people and allows for communication. Much like some of the other perspectives mentioned previously, this position views emotion as an important mechanism through which infants can hope to educe appropriate caregiving responses.

There are, of course, other perspectives on emotion; however, these four will serve as an excellent basis from which to begin our study of emotional development. Other perspectives will be introduced throughout the book as appropriate. In all likelihood, human emotion is complex enough to allow for all of the above perspectives to provide insight into emotional development. In summary, emotions probably provide humans with an evolutionary advantage by means of providing us with an early and effective communication system. Emotions are correlated with bodily changes that, when labeled correctly, enhance emotion communication. Emotions can motivate us, or distract and impair us. It is important for children to learn to understand, control, and channel emotions in adaptive ways.

As an example of how emotions enable communication, let's examine crying. Crying is one of the infant's most powerful means of communicating with others because it almost invariably brings someone to investigate his or her needs. Four basic patterns have been identified in infant crying. Hunger cries are a rhythmic series of cries associated with feeding needs. Angry cries are a loud series of rhythmic cries associated with distress. Frustration cries involve a long cry and holding the breath. Painful cries are loud, sudden cries that may be prolonged and are associated with injury.

Crying shows the strong effect a small child's behavior can have on adults' behavior. It is an infant's most powerful means of getting a caregiver's nurturing attention. It is never a good idea to ignore a young infant's cry. First, it is their only way of communicating many needs (such as a hurting ear or stomach). Second, when an infant has caregivers that are reliably responsive to his or her cries, the infant will learn to self-soothe sooner and more effectively, cry less, and trust their caregivers more. You will not spoil your child by responding to his or her cries, but you may harm your child by ignoring them.

Basics of Emotional Development

Primary emotions

Emotions which are present at birth or shortly thereafterwards. They are believed to be hardwired into the brain and serve an adaptive purpose.

Emotions can be broken into two main categories during infancy, primary (or basic) emotions and secondary (or self-conscious, discrete, or complex) emotions (Izard, 1991; Lewis, 2000; Saarni, Mumme & Campos, 1998). **Primary emotions** are present from birth or are evident shortly thereafter. The emotions appear to be universal, meaning that all healthy infants from anywhere in the world display these emotions early in life. Given the universality of these emotions and the early stage at which they develop, two theories emerge: one, these primary emotions are hardwired into the brain; two, these primary emotions must serve some evolutionary purpose. **Secondary emotions** are dependent

Secondary emotions

Emotions that develop during the second year or so after birth, as cognitive development advances. They can be a blend of two or more primary emotions, culturally-specific, or self-conscious/self-evaluative in nature.

upon cognitive development and the internalization of parental/societal standards and expectations. Secondary emotions can vary by culture.

Primary Emotions

Emotions in infancy are largely assessed via facial expressions, vocalizations, and other observable behaviors. Some primary emotions include pleasure, distress, joy, anger, and fear. Pleasure and distress are evident at birth; whereas joy, anger, and fear are measurable within the first six months. It is always important to be mindful that just because we fail to measure something until a certain age (such as a specific emotion), it is not the same as the infant lacking that skill or emotion (Galatzer-Levy & Cohler, 1993). Developmentalists are continually amazed at the emotions and cognitions that infants possess as we develop better ways to assess such emotions and cognitions. Therefore, at the moment, we believe that infants develop joy around two or three months of age. However, it is possible that a decade from now some bright young researcher will develop a new technique of assessing joy and find that it is present as early as one month or even one day of age.

One way researchers have ascertained that infants experience joy is by social smiling. The first **social smile**—smiling in response to social stimulation from others—is usually observed at about six weeks of age. Before that babies smile, but researchers assume that this is either a reflex activity seated in the brain, a random occurrence, such as gas, or by being about to fall asleep (Sroufe & Waters, 1976). Of course, many parents disagree with researchers on this particular issue.

Social smile

Smiling in response to social stimulation from others.

Smiling is a powerful method for eliciting caregiving. It reinforces nurturance from caregivers and forms the basis for positive interactions between the baby and his or her parents (Tautermannova, 1973). At about four months of age, babies begin to laugh to express their delight at positive experiences such as being kissed, or seeing interesting and

Infants seem to experience joy by social smiling. They smile in response to social stimulation from others.

unfamiliar things (Sroufe & Wunsch, 1972). One of the authors used to elicit the biggest belly laugh from one of their children by walking toward them like a big ogre with a silly face. Another good way of getting a laugh is by pretending to drink or eat the baby's food.

Developmentalists believe that anger emerges around four months of age and fear around six months of age. Anger expression can be provoked by thwarting goal directed behavior, such as preventing a baby from obtaining a desired toy. Fear is easily observable around six months of age because **stranger wariness** (or stranger anxiety) develops around this time. Stranger wariness can serve an adaptive purpose because it emerges around the same time that a child begins creeping or crawling; hence, it can prevent babies from straying too far from parents. Stranger wariness can also be mitigated by the environment (i.e., it is less likely in a familiar versus unfamiliar place) and stranger behavior. If the stranger gives an infant some space and interacts with the adults first, the infant will usually initiate some interaction in a few moments (after he or she has had a chance to see how mom or dad is interacting with the stranger). This means that Aunt Lucy from Omaha, who sees the baby only once a year, should wait for the baby to initiate contact instead of entering the room and swooping the fear-struck infant up immediately.

Social referencing, when infants look at their parents' faces and behavior for information about something, emerges around the first birthday (Dickson & Parke, 1988; Klinnert et al., 1986; Sorce et al., 1985). This is a valuable way for infants to obtain knowledge about the world. They use it to make decisions about acting as well as reacting. Apparently, the emotional reactions of our parents condition many of our own reactions in the early years.

Secondary Emotions

As mentioned earlier, secondary emotions are dependent upon cognitive development and the internalization of at least some parental expectations and/or societal norms. These emotions may vary by culture and may involve a blend of two or more primary emotions. Examples of secondary emotions include embarrassment, pride, guilt, and contempt. Secondary emotions begin to emerge around eighteen to twenty-four months, at the end of Piaget's sensorimotor stage of cognitive development. If you try to recall your earliest memory, there is a good chance that it will involve a secondary emotion (such as embarrassment over not making it to the potty in time or pride over writing your name correctly).

Emotion Regulation

Emotion regulation is also evident in infancy, although with limited strategies (Galatzer-Levy & Cohler, 1993; Saarni, Mumme & Campos, 1998). For a moment, imagine that you are lying in your bed, trying to catch some shut eye, and some strange giant keeps shaking a noisy rattle in your face. Also assume that you do not have very good control of

Stranger wariness

Or stranger anxiety, which is observable around six months of age.

Social referencing

When infants look at their parents' faces and behavior for information about something.

your speech, hands, arms, or legs at the moment. What would you do? What would you be feeling? Infants can become overstimulated when adults fail to read their body language. One way infants deal with their annoyance (i.e., regulate their emotion) is by withdrawing. Clearly, a young infant can't up and move away from the imbecile, so they use basic strategies such as closing the eyes or looking away. Infants also learn to regulate fear by moving close to loved ones when feeling afraid.

Revisiting Temperament and Goodness-of-Fit

Differences in temperament are an aspect of emotional and personality development in infancy (Thomas & Chess, 1984). About two-thirds of infants studied can be classified into one of three categories: easy, difficult, or slow-to-warm-up. Infants and children can be placed into these classifications based upon their behavior on nine dimensions: activity level, adaptability, approach/withdrawal, attention span/persistence, distractibility, intensity of reaction, quality of mood, rhythmicity, and threshold of responsiveness.

In general, easy babies are happy, have rhythmic bodily functioning, and are accepting of new experiences. These are the babies that have a predictable bodily schedule for when they will be hungry, tired, or in need of a diaper change. These are the babies that can go anywhere and will allow themselves to be admired and cuddled by just about anyone. These are the typical American parents' dream baby.

Difficult babies are generally irritable, have irregular bodily function, and show more intense emotional expressions. These are the babies that, biologically, struggle with feeding or sleeping schedules. It is best to feed them on demand (when their body tells them they are hungry) and be flexible with their other body functions.

Slow-to-warm-up babies have generally mild emotional expressions and are slow to adapt to new experiences. Although both the difficult and slow-to-warm-up infants have negative reactions to new experiences, the slow-to-warm-up infants' emotional reactions are lower in intensity and they will eventually accept the situation.

Temperament is assumed to have a genetic component, because it is observable so early in life. Interestingly, literature given to expectant mothers often suggests that an active baby in the womb will be an active infant, whereas a quiet baby in the womb will be a quiet infant. Talk about setting up parent expectations! Temperament also shows some stability during early childhood. However, temperament is not carved in stone.

Thomas, Chess, and Birch spent more than two decades studying temperament (among other developmental issues) in a longitudinal study known as the New York Longitudinal Study. One concept which they presented was that of goodness-of-fit. **Goodness-of-fit** can be defined as how adaptable a child's environment is to his or her temperament. For example, a difficult temperament child with a difficult-type parent would often clash heads and may result in adjustment problems. However, a difficult temperament child with an easy-going-type parent would be in a more flexible and responsive environment, allowing for optimal development. Hence, a good fit between child and parent can lead to good developmental outcomes. Alternatively, a poor fit

Goodness-of-fit

How adaptable a child's environment is to his or her temperament.

can place a child at risk for poor developmental outcomes, such as behavioral disturbances (Dixon, 2003). Future chapters will discuss the relationship between temperament and cognitive and socioemotional development in early and middle childhood. We will also see what aspects of temperament appear most likely to remain stable, and which are more malleable.

Attachment

Attachment

A strong affectional tie or emotional bond between two individuals.

What is attachment? Every healthy infant develops an attachment to someone. **Attachment** is a strong affectional tie or emotional bond between two individuals (Ainsworth, 1973). The attachment between an infant and his or her primary caregiver is one of the few psychological phenomena that is universal in human development. It occurs in every cultural setting known. Attachment appears to be essential to an infant's well-being. Without it, children suffer damage to their emotional, physical, social, and psychological functioning.

Infants have a strong drive to explore their environment that conflicts with their equally strong drive for security and comfort (Ainsworth, 1977). Attachment to an adult allows the baby to use his or her caregiver as a secure base for exploring the world. This helps the child to grow mentally and socially. In the long run, successful attachment in infancy generates greater competence throughout life. This is shown in a greater capacity to cope with novelty, handle failure, persist in problem-solving, participate in loving relationships, and maintain a healthy self-esteem (Sroufe, 1985; Galatzer-Levy & Cohler, 1993).

Attachment involves mutual interaction between an infant and his or her primary caregivers. If the infant is normal, he will behave in ways that signal his desire to be near those who provide for his care. These behaviors include crying, smiling, vocalizing, looking at the person(s), and active physical movements such as clinging, clutching, and touching. The caregivers react in nurturing ways that promote the attachment process. They smile at, gently handle, stroke, feed, and diaper the infant, for example.

27. What are the four developmental phases of attachment?

The attachment development process has four phases (Bowlby, 1982). The first, *undiscriminating social responsiveness*, occurs at about two to three months of age. This phase is characterized by an orientation to all humans. An infant visually tracks and explores, listens when being addressed, and relaxes when being held.

The second phase, *discrimination in social responsiveness*, occurs at about four to five months of age. An infant shows that it recognizes familiar as well as unfamiliar people. She does this by smiling and vocalizing when a familiar person comes into her view. She also is observed by exhibiting restless, crying behavior when this person leaves her field of vision. This is the age when stranger anxiety is a reaction to unfamiliar people.

In the third phase of the attachment development process, the infant *actively seeks physical proximity and contact* with familiar persons. This phase starts at about seven months of age. An infant clings to, crawls toward, and otherwise seeks active contact with the familiar person.

Goal-corrected partnership is the fourth and final phase of the attachment process. At about the age of three years, the child learns to predict his parent's movements and adjusts his own to maintain some degree of physical proximity.

Many factors influence the quality of the bonding between parents and infants. Responsive, dependable, warm caregiving that is flexible to the child's needs is critical in order for a secure attachment to develop. A lack of sensitive parenting can result in an insecure attachment.

How do we know what type of attachment infants have? It all goes back to Ainsworth's idea of infants using their parents as a secure base when infants go out to explore the world. Ainsworth and colleagues (1978) conducted a series of experiments utilizing what is now known as "the strange situation." Through a series of separations and reunions in a laboratory room, infants (around age one) and their mothers were observed. By observing the infants reactions to the mother's leaving and returning, their play behavior, and their interaction with the mother and a stranger, a few patterns of attachment emerged. These studies have been repeated over time by many researchers and four patterns are evident.

One attachment pattern is secure and the other three are considered insecure. All of these attachment patterns (or types/styles) are adaptive for the situation in which the child is being raised. Although the insecure patterns are not optimal, they are also not considered a disorder. Attachment disorders are different than having an insecure attachment pattern.

The **secure attachment style** is the most prevalent pattern (60–65 percent). These infants miss their mother when she leaves the room and greet her upon return. The **avoidant-insecure attachment style** is the second most prevalent pattern (20 percent). These infants do not seem to care if the mother leaves or returns. The **preoccupied-insecure attachment style** (a.k.a., resistant or ambivalent) is the third most prevalent pattern (10–15 percent). These infants are terribly upset when the mother leaves and are inconsolable when she returns. The **disorganized/disoriented attachment style** is the least prevalent pattern (5–10 percent). The infants seem to lack a cohesive strategy for interacting with their mother, or dealing with her departure and return. They may cling to the mother while leaning away or go through a series of approach/withdrawal behaviors.

It is important to remember that attachment is a process between two people. Attachment is important regardless of what type of relationship we are discussing. We will focus upon attachment between a child and caregivers in the childhood years. Later, we will examine attachment in friendships and romantic relationships during adolescence and adulthood. Attachment is of lifelong importance, and early attachments lay the foundation for later attachments.

You have just been introduced to the attachment styles and it can be easy to just start thinking about people in terms of their attachment "types." However, this would be a mistake. People tend to have a predominant attachment style; nevertheless, attachment is a dyadic process. This means that a person may have a secure attachment to his mother, brother, and sister, but an insecure attachment to his father. As you will learn, attachment does not just have important implications for emotional development, but also for social and cognitive development as well.

Secure attachment style

An infant misses their mother when she leaves the room and greets her upon returning.

Avoidant-insecure attachment style

An infant does not seem to care if the mother leaves or returns.

Preoccupied-insecure attachment

An infant is terribly upset when the mother leaves and is inconsolable when she returns.

Disorganized/disoriented attachment style

An infant that lacks a cohesive strategy in coping with the strange situation.

Attachment and Mental Models

Early parent-child interactions provide the early environment in which infants begin to develop mental models regarding themselves and others (Dixon, 2003; Galatzer-Levy & Cohler, 1993). If a caregiver is dependable, warm, and responsive, an infant will come to trust that the caregiver will be there when needed. The infant will also come to believe that they must be worthy of such care and attention and learn to love and trust him or herself. If, on the other hand, the caregiver is undependable, emotionally inept, and unresponsive, an infant will come to believe that the caregiver cannot be trusted to be there when needed. The infant may also begin to question whether they have any self-worth, and/or if he or she can trust him or herself. Of course, an infant neither verbally encodes this information, nor consciously has these thoughts. Nonetheless, these early experiences set mental expectations that can last a lifetime if not challenged or questioned. Future chapters devoted to social and emotional development will discuss how attachment impacts development.

Pause and Process:

1. What is the difference between primary and secondary emotions?

2. How does attachment develop?

SELF AND OTHERS

In this section, we will highlight the development of self-awareness, play behavior, and daycare.

Understanding of Self and Others

When does a baby know that they are a person, separate from the rest of the world? There is a cool experiment involving a baby, a mirror, and some make-up (rouge) that has tested this question. First, place the baby in front of the mirror and observe her behavior. Next, place some rouge on her nose (or other face location) without her noticing what you are doing. Then, place her back in front of the mirror and observe? Does she seem to notice the make-up on her nose? Does she touch her face as she views her reflection in the mirror? The mirror test is one research technique that has been used to assess when self-recognition emerges in infancy. Self-recognition is measurable around fifteen months of age.

Self-awareness

A child's use of self-referencing pronouns, using their own name, and occasionally labeling themselves by sex and age.

Between fifteen months and two years of age, a child's growing sense of **self-awareness** is evident in their use of self-referencing pronouns (i.e., me or I), using their own name, and occasionally labeling themselves by sex and age. Toddlers seem to have some awareness of how others see them and strive to please their caregivers (Galatzer-Levy & Cohler, 1993).

The mirror test is a technique used to assess when self-recognition emerges.

Not only do toddlers have a growing sense of self, but they also have a growing sense of others. Toddlers often spontaneously display **prosocial behavior**. They will try to offer comfort to others that seem to be sad or worried. Toddlers will often pat or hug someone or say in their telegraphic speech something like "It okay." Such early prosocial behaviors demonstrate early emotion recognition in others and empathy.

Prosocial behavior

A growing sense of others (e.g. comforting other children who seem sad or worried).

Family Influences

Play is another behavior that emerges during the toddler period. Between twelve and fifteen months, parallel play appears. **Parallel play** entails two toddlers playing side by side, occasionally observing each other, but not interacting with each other. It is not until around the age of two that children learn to **play cooperatively**. Parents with children this age will often arrange "play dates" so that their child can play with others and learn early social skills with peers.

Some research has examined mother-child play. Mother's who engage in exploratory play (object-oriented play) tend to have children who engage in **exploratory play**. Mother's who engage in **symbolic play** (using objects in a pretend fashion—like tea parties) tend to have children who engage in symbolic play. Hence, children seem to imitate the type of play modeled by their parents. That said, boys are more likely to engage in exploratory play, whereas girls are more likely to engage in symbolic play (Bornstein et al., 1999). Parent-child play interactions facilitate social and cognitive development in children.

Parallel play

The side by side playing of two toddlers who occasionally observe each other, but do not interact with each other.

Cooperatively play

The willingness to play with one another.

Exploratory play

Object oriented play.

Symbolic play

Using objects in a pretend fashion (e.g., tea parties).

The Outside World

The United States is one of only a few industrialized societies that do not offer paid parental leave after the birth of a child. At least partly for this reason, the majority of American infants are placed into some form of child care before their first birthday.

The developmental consequences of daycare depend upon the quality of the daycare, the number of hours spent there, and parent-child interaction when at home. High quality daycare on a part-time basis, coupled with sensitive parenting at home will either have no negative consequences for the child or even lead to positive cognitive and socioemotional outcomes for the child. Unfortunately, the majority of daycare is of low quality (NICHD Early Child Care Research Network, 2001). Low quality daycare, long hours, and inadequate parent-child interactions are all predictive of poor cognitive and/or socioemotional outcomes. Can daycare be harmful to infants? Yes. Is daycare always harmful for infants? No. However, many children do suffer suboptimal developmental outcomes because quality daycare is the exception in this country, instead of the rule.

Pause and Process:

1. How do researchers test for self-recognition in infants?

2. What is the difference between exploratory and symbolic play?

PSYCHOLOGICAL DEVELOPMENT

In Chapter 1, we were introduced to Erikson's psychosocial theory. We will discuss the first two stages of psychosocial development in this section.

Establishing Basic Trust

Basic trust

The sense that others are predictable and can be relied on.

Erikson (1950, 1964) describes the development of an attitude of **basic trust** as a primary task of psychosocial development in infancy. This sense usually is established between birth and eighteen months of age. It is believed to have long-range implications for a person's social and psychological adjustments throughout the life span.

Impressions of infants, gained both from informal observations and empirical study, suggest that the sense of basic trust emerges through numerous interactions and activities between the mother and the baby. The father becomes a significant force in the infant's development at a later time, according to Erikson's theory. Feeding situations provide ample opportunities for the infant to explore its caregivers both through vision and touch. Feeding is thought to be a significant event for the infant in encouraging attachment. It also assists to identify the caregiver as a primary source of physical and psychological nurturance.

A consistent caregiver who holds the infant consistently and who has a consistent pattern of behavior toward the infant in the feeding situation, for example, leads the child to learn to trust the integrity of others. This elementary attitude is based on the infant's discovery that there is predictability in his or her world. The early learning that there is consistency in life and in activities helps an infant to predict how it will be treated. It learns that certain events or sensations will occur if he or she behaves in particular ways. For example, a baby learns that a lusty cry will produce the appearance of the caregiver who attends to his or her needs. Other interactions with the physical environment contribute to an infant's learning that there is predictability or consistency in many things. The baby discovers, for example, that movement in the crib makes a mobile move in response. As babies gain better motor control, they learn that fingers and toes move in accordance with their will. Their behavior becomes instrumental or goal-oriented.

As the body matures, an infant learns that objects can be manipulated and that they can move their bodies from one location to another. In essence, they learn to experience and explore their physical setting. They actively reach out to interact with their environment.

An infant learns to trust the caregiver when held and fed consistently.

An attitude of mistrust may prevail if an infant learns that routines and the physical and social environment are unpredictable and inconsistent. This is especially true regarding people who are its primary caregivers. Infants who have been deprived of consistent nurturing show such a pervasive sense of mistrust regarding others' integrity. This attitude also is characterized by apathy, delayed developmental progress, poor appetite, and even illness. Such an attitude makes infants less vulnerable to emotional pain. It is devastating, however, in preventing the child from loving and being loved. This can adversely affect progress through other developmental stages.

Acquiring a Sense of Autonomy

Autonomy

Refers to establishing personal boundaries and self-differentiation from things and others.

Shame and doubt

Refers to the belief that one is unable to be autonomous and that one's inner self is basically flawed and defective.

Erikson proposes that individuals establish a sense of **autonomy** versus **shame and doubt** between eighteen months and three years of age. Parents may view interactions with their infant as a series of troublesome encounters. This is because so much of his or her behavior is directed toward developing an initial identity as a person independent of parents.

What may amaze and confound parents of a child this age is not so much that changes are experienced; rather, it is the rapid nature and intensity by which they occur. Stubborn insistence on having their own way and expressing their own point of view in interactions with parents are common. These are predominant behavioral patterns among many children who are in the process of developing an attitude about their autonomy. An emerging sense of self is shown for the first time in the swings from independent to dependent behavior and back again. The behavior and nature of the infant at these ages appears to be unpredictable in many ways. This relates to their attempts to develop a sense of autonomy.

From a family systems theory perspective, what are occurring for the infant at this period in its life are experiences that teach about personal boundaries. The attachment process in the early period of infancy apparently leads an infant to believe that there is a symbiotic relationship between him or her and the parents. This may be the case especially with the mother as she is very often the principal caregiver. The relationship is described as emotionally enmeshed. Both an infant and the mother may have difficulties in perceiving the personal boundaries that distinguish them as distinct individuals.

Both mothers and infants experience blurred personal boundaries because of the intense closeness and intimacy of their relationship. It is thought that an infant may have difficulty in perceiving that he or she is not an extension of the parent and vice versa. Lack of such distinctions between the self and others cannot continue indefinitely, however, as this is unhealthy psychologically. Self-differentiation from others begins when an infant learns to erect personal boundaries by behaving in ways that establish its autonomy.

For many infants, there is a change in personality at this time of their life span. The smiling, friendly, accepting child is replaced on many occasions by what seems to be a surly, whining, little demon. This child now is obstinate, gets into mischief, refuses to cooperate or obey parents' requests, and has only one apparent and very overworked word in his or her vocabulary: "NO!" This is the terrible two-year-old at his or her very worst, according to many parents. Yet, some parents can be very preoccupied or motivated with using power to gain control over their child's unacceptable actions. Many may be unaware that these difficult interactions are a very necessary part of the child's healthy psychosocial development.

The attitude of feeling ashamed and doubtful occurs when parents restrict or fail to encourage an infant's attempts to be autonomous. This is an unhealthy attitude that may stem in part from many parents' overreaction to negativistic behavior from an infant. However, such behavior is normal at this time in life. Many adults were raised by parents who used strict, rule-oriented methods. It is only to be expected that these methods are likely to be repeated in raising their own children. This is done unthinkingly because our society does so very little to train people to be parents.

Reliance on rules and rigid standards of acceptable behavior becomes imposed on children at this time as appropriate childrearing by such parents. This is likely because of the parents' belief that strict control is called for. It also is implemented because so much of a toddler's behavior appears to be acting out against parental authority. These attempts to control the rebelliousness of a child are seen as necessary and appropriate. However, many parents are apparently too successful and relentless in trying to achieve this end. The result is that many infants emerge from this period of their lives with the basic negative belief about the inner core of their self. This is the part that is basic to the self-concept and their essence as a human being. The belief is that they are bad, flawed, unacceptable, undesirable, and unlovable.

This is what Erikson calls an attitude of shame and doubt. For many children, the overwhelming majority of interactions with parents are corrective in nature. This relates to their behavior that is seen as problematic by parental standards (John-Roger & McWilliams, 1990). The focus of parental attention toward an infant shifts from unconditional and unadulterated adoration prior to this time, to being one of exasperation and punitiveness. Infants are more active now than ever before. They are more liable to do things that are dangerous and disruptive.

The challenge of parents who want to facilitate a child's healthy psychosocial development now is to focus on the behavior rather than on the child's character. Behavior that is appropriate deserves as much or more attention than behavior that is not. A parent may say, for example, "You're just the most rotten kid I've ever seen." This promotes feelings of shame and doubt by labeling the child's inner self negatively. It is more helpful to say, "I'm glad you're so interested in touching the cat but I can't let you pull its tail because it may scratch and you can get hurt." This promotes feelings of autonomy while teaching limits for the child's behavior.

Some biologically-oriented events contribute to preparing and assisting an infant to achieve the psychosocial attitude of autonomy. These include learning to walk and to feed oneself, controlling eliminations, and so on. Toilet training is an especially significant developmental event that assists in this endeavor.

Pause and Process:

1. What can assist in the development of basic trust?

2. What can assist in the development of autonomy?

SUMMARY

1. Many physical changes occur during infancy. First, there is a continuation of growth patterns established before birth, in that changes occur in cephalocaudal (head-to-foot) and proximodistal (inner-to-outermost) directions. Second there are significant increases in weight and height. The birthweight is doubled by four months of age, and tripled by the infant's first birthday. Height increases by about 50 percent the first year. The brain shows a rapid increase in connections during infancy. Fat, muscle, and bones all show growth during infancy as well.

2. Basic motor skills occur sequentially. Use of the hands in manipulating objects also progresses sequentially. It begins with use of the full hand in grasping objects, then proceeds to use of various

combinations of fingers, and culminates in the ability to use the forefinger and thumb with accuracy in picking up objects.

3. Perceptual skills advance with motor skill development. Perceptual changes at this stage primarily involve the ability to use eyesight to guide and make adjustments in motor behaviors. They may be observed in the ways infants use their eyesight in learning to judge depth or surface changes.

4. Health concerns for infants include meeting their nutritional needs, protecting them from diseases, and taking steps to prevent SIDS. Breastfeeding provides the best nutrition for infants. Vaccinations help prevent many childhood diseases and do not appear to cause autism. Infants should be kept away from second-hand smoke and put to sleep on their back in order to prevent SIDS.

5. A major stage in cognitive development, the sensorimotor period, is experienced during infancy. This period primarily involves changes that result in the integration of sensory input and perceptions with motor behaviors. Infants acquire an understanding of their environment through these means. A major accomplishment at this stage is understanding object permanence, or the notion that something continues to exist even though it has been removed from the child's field of vision. This understanding is part of the process of self-differentiation, according to cognitive development theory.

6. The changes observed during the sensorimotor period occur in a graduated sequence. It begins with an infant's use of reflexes present at birth and progresses to more complex circular reactions. These are habitual actions that are constructed through continual repetition. The process culminates in the use of symbolic logic and reasoning at the end of infancy. Sensorimotor schemas are rudimentary ideas about the nature of the world. They are constructed and modified through expe-

rience in interacting with the environment by sensory and motor actions.

7. Infants are born with some basic processes that allow for learning and information-processing. Many of these processes are evident prenatally, but we can test them more definitively after birth. Infants are capable of forming memories, association, recognition, imitation, and recall. These early basic processes pave the way for future problem-solving, memory strategies, and other information-processing development.

8. The ability to use language to communicate with others emerges in infancy in a series of gradual advancements. Infants are born with the ability to cry, then progress through cooing, babbling, understanding words, and producing their first word. Speech begins with one-word sentences, then progresses to two-word sentences. Infants typically understand the rules of language prior to being able to fully utilize these rules.

9. Developmental changes are observed in the emerging emotional expression of infants. Infants become gradually capable of expressing a wide range of feelings through facial gestures, vocalizations, and other behaviors.

10. An infant develops an emotional attachment to his or her primary caregivers. This attachment provides the infant with a sense of security and promotes his or her exploration of the environment. Attachment is believed to occur in four distinct phases: undiscriminating social responsiveness, discrimination in social responsiveness, active seeking of physical proximity and contact, and goal-corrected partnership.

11. Attachment can be assessed in infants by utilizing the strange situation paradigm. There are four patterns of attachment: Secure, avoidant, preoccupied, and disorganized/disoriented. Each attachment style has distinct mental models of self and others. Although a person may

have a predominant attachment style, attachment is a process between two people and can vary by relationship.

12. Self-awareness increases during the toddler period. Prosocial behavior and play behavior also emerge during this time. Parents can influence type of play behavior in infants and gender differences are apparent. Daycare can be correlated to positive or negative developmental outcomes, dependent upon quality of daycare, hours spent in daycare, and parent-child interactions.

13. Establishing a sense of basic trust as opposed to mistrust is the first of a series of psychosocial tasks the individual experiences during the life span. The optimal time for acquiring the healthy attitude of trust is between birth and eighteen months of age. It is derived principally from consistent, positive interactions with the maternal caregiver, according to Erikson. Favorable interactions with the physical environment also contribute to this attitude. According to psychosocial theory, the accomplishment of basic trust significantly improves the chances of healthy development at subsequent stages of the life span.

14. Acquiring a healthy sense of personal autonomy as opposed to an unhealthy attitude of shame and doubt is the principal psychosocial challenge for the individual between eighteen and thirty-six months of age. The behaviors leading to the acquisition of a healthy sense of autonomy are often quite troublesome to parents. They are necessary, however, if the infant is to accomplish self-differentiation and establish personal boundaries. An infant who feels comfortable in separating from primary caregivers is able to explore his or her environment. Certain developmental tasks of infancy, such as toilet-training, contribute to this healthy attitude. An unhealthy attitude of personal shame and doubt is promoted when infants are discouraged from becoming autonomous and made to feel that exploratory behaviors are inappropriate.

SELF-QUIZ

1. What are the two basic growth patterns?
2. How much do weight and height increase between birth and the first birthday?
3. What is the information-processing cell of the nervous system called?
4. What does myelination of the axon accomplish?
5. Which hemisphere of the brain is language localized in for most people?
6. What influences motor skill development in infancy?
7. When do most infants achieve walking?
8. What purpose do hand skills serve in infancy?
9. How do hand skills progress during infancy?
10. What classic study allowed for the investigation of depth perception in infancy?
11. Within Piaget's cognitive developmental theory, what two processes help individuals adapt or change their schemas based upon their experiences in the world?
12. When your thoughts and beliefs are no longer in equilibrium with your experiences, what cognitive state are you thrown into?
13. What is the term for Piaget's first stage of cognitive development?
14. How many substages are there within Piaget's first stage of cognitive development?
15. What are the two basic types of memories discussed in this chapter?
16. What are three theories about why we have infantile amnesia?
17. Is language the same as speech?
18. What are the five basic components of language discussed in this chapter?

19. What innate language structure is hypothesized to help us learn language?
20. What are three common errors toddlers make in word use?
21. What are emotions?
22. What neural circuit in the brain seems important for emotional and social understanding?
23. What are three aspects of emotion?
24. What are four viewpoints as to the importance or purpose of emotion?
25. What are the two main categories of emotions during infancy?
26. What is attachment?
27. What are the four developmental phases of attachment?
28. What are the four attachment styles?
29. What type of play emerges during infancy?
30. What two stages of psychosocial development are important during infancy and toddlerhood?

TERMS AND CONCEPTS

Early Childhood

Early childhood is a time of refinements in physical abilities. These not only allow greater personal freedom but facilitate mental and social changes as well. In fact, the interrelationship among physical, socioemotional, and cognitive skills is very evident at this time of the life span. There is a close relationship between these changes and the type of environmental experiences to which a child is exposed.

PHYSICAL DEVELOPMENT DURING EARLY CHILDHOOD

> ### LEARNING OBJECTIVES:
>
> 1. Describe physical growth during early childhood
> 2. Explain motor skill development during early childhood
> 3. Awareness of the unique health issues faced in early childhood

Physical changes occur rapidly in early childhood (ages three to six years), but not at the rate seen in infancy. Generally, the physical changes in early childhood are also less dramatic than those observed in infancy. Yet, they are impressive. The changes in hand skills, for example, allow a child to explore objects more easily, and new body skills permit greater investigation of the environment.

PHYSICAL GROWTH

Height and Weight Changes

Preschool-age children grow at half the rate they did during infancy. Height gains exceed weight gains. A typical preschool child grows about three inches each year. At age three, the average child is about thirty-eight inches tall, and by age five, has reached a height of about forty-three inches (Cratty, 1986; Tanner, 1978, 1990; WHO, 2007).

Weight increases follow a similar pattern of deceleration in early childhood. Children gain about four pounds a year during this stage. The average child weighs approximately thirty-one pounds at three years of age and forty pounds by age five (WHO, 2007). A rule of thumb is that children should be about seven times their birthweight by age six (Bloom, 1964).

There are individual differences in these trends related to sex, genetics, medical history, eating habits, and general nutrition (Eveleth & Tanner, 1976; Tanner, 1990). Height and weight changes during this stage are closely followed by health-care professionals to determine if the child falls within normal limits. Very slow or very rapid changes can signal the presence of certain abnormal conditions. Most of these conditions can be treated effectively if detected early.

Other Body Changes

The changes in body proportions and appearance in early childhood are very noticeable. As bone and muscle growth occur, there is a gradual lengthening of the body. A preschooler looks less like an infant and more like a child. At age four, most begin to lose the chubby appearance of a baby (Tanner, 1978, 1990). A child's abdomen is quite prominent at this age—almost a "pot belly"—and the head and face are still large in comparison to other body parts. But with continued growth in the extremities and trunk areas, a young child becomes leaner-looking. This change to a spindly appearance is also attributed to the metabolism of fatty tissue acquired in infancy. This material is consumed as a source of energy by the constantly active child.

Weight gains in infancy resulted from increases in fatty material deposited into adipose tissue. In early childhood, weight gains come more from increases in muscle and bone tissue. Muscle tissue is composed 72 percent of water and 28 percent of solids in early childhood (Timiras, 1972). Muscle fatigue occurs more easily among young children because of this high ratio of water to solids, as well as because muscles are not yet strongly attached to bone and skeletal material. A young child needs frequent rests and naps (although they may fight a nap every step of the way).

Ossification of bony tissue continues throughout this period. The long bones grow faster than the other bones of the body, accounting for the lengthening in arms and legs that gives the young child a lanky appearance by age six. Because the ossification process is not yet complete, the bones, joints, ligaments, and tendons are flexible. Injury and infection can result in severe damage to these tissues.

Teeth

Deciduous teeth

The primary or first set of 16 teeth that erupt when an infant is between five and seven and one half months of age.

Most of the primary or **deciduous teeth** have erupted by a child's third birthday. These teeth will remain in the gums until about age six or seven, when they are shed as part of the natural growth process.

Many parents and caregivers tend to overlook young children's need for dental care. Only 76 percent of children in the United States visit the dentist at least once a year (Federal Interagency Forum on Child and Family Statistics, 2008). Regular dental care (along with adequate nutrition and other factors) improves the quality of the secondary (permanent) teeth that are developing in the gums.

The Brain

The brain and central nervous system experience perhaps the most significant changes of any body system during early childhood. These follow the cephalocaudal trend that began during prenatal development and continued during infancy.

Most brain growth during early childhood takes the form of weight gain. By age three, the brain has attained about 75 percent of its total adult weight; by age six, it has reached almost 90 percent of adult weight. Because nearly no new neurons appear in the brain

Primary or deciduous teeth come in by the age of three. At about six or seven they will begin to be replaced by adult teeth.

after birth, most of these increases come from growth in neuron size, from slight increases in glial cells (which support the neurons), and from myelination of the axons.

Brain circuitry is established in early childhood in something like the manner in which a sculptor produces a final image from stone (Kolb, 1989). Excess neurons and unnecessary connections between millions of neuron cells are eliminated over time. This is referred to as **pruning**. In addition, brain circuit patterns governing particular functions become established in graduated sequences as myelination is accomplished in various areas of the brain between infancy and adolescence.

As noted earlier, myelination involves the deposit of fatty material called **myelin** around axons. Myelin facilitates the transmission of electrical impulses between neurons. Advancing myelination makes certain brain functions possible, rapid, and/or more efficient, such as speech, sensory perception, and logical thought. The myelination process will continue throughout childhood and adolescence. For example, the areas of the brain that are responsible for hand-eye coordination become fully functional (myelinated) by age four. Those that facilitate focused attention are fully functional by age ten, and those that regulate skilled language use mature by age fifteen (Tanner, 1978, 1990). Improvements in all these abilities, however, can be observed in early childhood as myelination progresses in the areas of the brain that govern them (Higgins & Turnure, 1984). Because of these improvements, most young children are ready for formal educational instruction around the age of six.

There are two other significant changes in the brain and central nervous system in early childhood. First, the brain continues to coordinate its parts to specialize in particular functions. The human brain has two sides, or hemispheres, that work together to control the functions of each side of the body. The organization format is unusual in that it is the right hemisphere of the brain that controls the left side of the body and the left hemisphere that controls the right side. The process that leads to hemispheric specialization begins early in life and continues for years, but marked changes are evident during early childhood. When the process is completed, the right hemisphere will govern a variety of

Pruning

The elimination of unnecessary excess neuron connections between millions of neuron cells over time.

Myelin

A fatty material deposited around axons.

visual and creative skills, as well as spatial perception, and the left hemisphere will govern language abilities and logical thought processes (Tanner, 1978, 1990). A channel for neural communication known as the corpus callosum connects both hemispheres, facilitating coordination of the various functions. Myelination in this structure is also significantly advanced during early childhood, which explains the improvements in mental and motor skill functioning observed in young children.

Second, the definitive preferential use of one hand over the other emerges during early childhood as another indication of brain specialization. As mentioned in the last chapter, the first hint of this appears very early in life. Fetuses that suck their right thumb in utero are more likely to become right-handed than those that suck their left thumb. Most infants orient their heads to the right, and these infants usually become right-handed (Gesell & Ames, 1947). As infants grow older, most tend to reach with their right hand, though there is much experimentation in manipulating objects with both hands throughout infancy and into early childhood. By age four, however, the majority of children have developed a preference for using one hand over the other (Tan, 1985).

Perceptual Skills

Visual and hearing abilities are firmly established by six months of age, but subtle refinements continue to unfold as a child progresses through early childhood (Siegler, 1986). Maturation of the brain accounts for some of these refinements.

Because the eyeball does not complete its growth until puberty, young children tend to be farsighted (Roberts & Rowland, 1978). The ability of the eye to accommodate or focus accurately improves during early childhood, but not enough to produce accurate vision. By age six, the visual acuity of most young children measures 20/30 rather than 20/20. So although their vision has vastly improved since infancy, young children still do not see things quite clearly. Corrective lenses or glasses may be needed, particularly if the child constantly squints when looking intently at something. About 5 percent of children begin to use glasses in early childhood (Siegler, 1986).

By the age of six a child may need to have corrective lenses or glasses.

Pause and Process:

1. How do height and weight change during early childhood?

2. Describe two ways that the brain continues to develop during early childhood.

MOTOR DEVELOPMENT

4. Define bilateral coordination.

Bilateral coordination

The coordinated, integrated use of both sides of the body in performing motor acts.

Gross motor skills

Those motor acts that require the use of large muscle groups.

Fine motor skills

Those motor acts that require the use of small muscle groups and hand-eye coordination.

Developmental changes in motor skills in early childhood follow the proximodistal and general-to-specific patterns that emerged earlier in life. Motor skills now become more refined. Activity and energy levels remain high during this period as well.

In many respects, the changes observed in motor skills in early childhood reflect maturation and changes in body metabolism. Parents often remark that young children are constantly on the move. This restlessness reflects a desire to learn about the environment and a quest for novel stimulation. Restlessness declines by the end of this period, however. Researchers note that children change their activities and physical location less and less as they grow older (Eaton & Ennis, 1986; Routh, Schroeder, & O'Tauma, 1974).

Maturation and environmental influences on motor skill improvement are also evident in the child's **bilateral coordination** (Williams, 1983). Bilateral coordination (e.g., symmetrical gait pattern) refers to the coordinated, integrated use of both sides of the body to smoothly and efficiently perform numerous actions. In early childhood, improvements are seen in climbing stairs, tying shoelaces, running, and using a tricycle—all skills that require use of both hands, both feet, or the arms and legs, and both sides of the body. Opportunity is an important environmental factor in these improvements. Young children not only profit from practicing these skills but also appear to gain much pleasure from doing so. Most children put a lot of effort into mastering these skills until they can perform them smoothly and efficiently (Bertenhal & Clifton, 1998).

There are significant improvements in both **gross motor skills** (those involving the large muscle groups of the body) and **fine motor skills** (those involving the small muscle groups) in this stage. Elementary motor skills that allowed for locomotion of the body and manipulation of objects emerged during infancy. Now children expand these basic skills into more specific actions (Bertenhal & Clifton, 1998). For example, the ability to run, hop, climb, and jump are specific gross motor skills that are mastered in early childhood. Cutting with scissors, drawing, turning pages in books, and manipulating small toys are among the fine motor skills that emerge at this stage.

Gender differences in motor skill performance show up in early childhood. Boys are generally more advanced than girls in performing quick and agile gross motor activities. Girls generally outshine boys at activities involving fine motor skills. Girls also perform better than boys at gross motor activities that require coordination, such as skipping, hopping, and balancing on one foot (Cratty, 1986). These differences are probably due to both inherent biological factors and socialization. For example, most parents still steer their children into sex-appropriate play activities—expecting boys, for instance, to be more physically active, especially outdoors, and girls to be less active and to play more indoors (Harper & Sanders, 1978).

Gross Motor Skills

Gross or large-muscle skills involve many muscle groups. These are the skills that are used in throwing objects, walking, running, climbing, and so on. By age four, children's level of performance at these skills resembles that of adults. Young children perform these skills awkwardly. But with the establishment of the necessary nerve circuitry and much practice, speed improves, balance becomes more automatic, and stride lengthens (Bertenhal & Clifton, 1998).

To illustrate how gross motor skills advance at this time of the life span, we will use the ability to catch a ball as an example. Three-year-old children typically have their arms outstretched when trying to catch a ball. Four-year-olds continue to use this approach, but also open their hands. Neither of these approaches results in many successful catches. Five-year-olds typically hold their arms to the sides of the body and open their hands. This gives them greater flexibility, and they make many successful catches.

Fine Motor Skills

Fine motor skills relate to the use of the hands and fingers to manipulate objects. They are also known as hand-eye skills because they involve the integration of visual and manual abilities. Fine motor skills are required for self-feeding, dressing, and many play activities.

Visual feedback plays an important role in the mastery of these skills. For example, drawing with crayons depends on a constant interchange between seen results and modifications and adjustments in hand and finger movements (Fraiberg, 1977). Manual dexterity is improved through this interchange. The child becomes more efficient at cutting with scissors, brushing teeth, washing hands, and playing with toys. Again, practice and maturation are both important for fine motor skill development (Kellogg, 1970).

Hand Skills

We already discussed handedness in the section pertaining to brain development. Therefore, we will devote this section to discuss the young child's development of art skills. Although adults often dismiss children's art as little more than play, we will soon learn that art skills provide an early foundation for later skills that are vital to academic success.

Preschoolers show an interest in creative expression through drawing with a variety of media. Their drawings may seem primitive to adults, but they are evidence of the integration of visual perception, cognitive skills, and fine motor skills. These early artistic efforts provide the foundation for the acquisition of other skills, such as printing and writing.

Researchers have traced the origins and developmental patterns of artistic abilities in early childhood (Cratty, 1979; Goodnow, 1977; Kellogg & O'Dell, 1967; Taylor & Bacharach, 1981). The sequences they found occur in a general-to-specific manner. A young child does not see the world as an adult does; by preschool, children's artistic endeavors have a freshness and directness that adult artists often try to recapture. When you look at art by modern abstractionists, you can see certain similarities with the productions of young children.

Scribbling is the foundation of artistic abilities. This is the experimentation that children make with some drawing instrument (pencil, crayon, etc.) when they are about two years old.

Consistent practice performing manual dexterity movements enables a child to improve tasks such as brushing their teeth.

Young children have a propensity to scribble on just about any surface. Most adults are not aware that these scribbling experiences are the beginnings of self-expression. Instead, they see the scribbles as disorganized chaos and fail to value and validate the child's efforts.

About twenty basic patterns of scribbling have been catalogued and described (Kellogg & O'Dell, 1967). Compositions range from vertical, horizontal, diagonal, circular, and curving lines to waves and dots. Placement patterns of scribbling also vary. Even at this early age, a child's artwork reflects primitive organization and planning. A child makes progress in scribbling; shapes are implied in the patterns that are produced. These are hints at what will be outlined as circles, squares, crosses, and X's when children are about age three. Young children outline these shapes and learn to recognize and distinguish among them.

Pause and Process:

1. How do males and females differ in their motor skill development?

2. Why are art skills important for development?

HEALTH ISSUES

Nutritional Needs

Nutrition, physical changes, and psychosocial development are closely associated. In infancy, this was evident in the feeding experiences that facilitated a sense of trust. In early childhood, this association is seen in the formation of eating habits, food preferences, and social interaction patterns. It is also evident in the ways that preschoolers explore food and food choices.

Because of their declining growth rates, young children have less demanding appetites than infants (Hamilton & Whitney, 1982). Caregivers usually describe preschoolers as being "picky" about food. This refers not only to what they will and will not eat, but also to the amounts of food they consume.

Preschoolers often will not eat any food that is unfamiliar to them (Birch, 1987). At this stage of life, children are acquiring food preferences. This sometimes causes friction with their parents. For example, some children want only foods that are salty (pretzels, pickles, nuts, chips) or sweet (candy, pastries, cookies) (Birch, McPhee, & Sullivan, 1989). These foods tend to have "empty" calories, so parents may worry whether the preschooler is getting adequate nutrition. They may constantly offer food and even encourage the child to overeat. This can lead to further problems, such as obesity (see subsection below), that exacerbate the original eating problem.

Nutritionists suggest other ways to compensate for poor eating habits (Williams & Caliendo, 1984). First, serving sizes should be smaller than those for adults and older children. Children this age will not be harmed if they eat small amounts of food. Most children, even young infants, regulate their food intake quite satisfactorily (Hamilton & Whitney, 1982). Second, nagging children to eat food they don't want invites a power struggle. Vegetables may be good for children, but if they hate them, it's better to find nutritious substitutes that appeal to them. Third, snacks don't have to be high in sugar and salt. Examples of snack foods that are both nutritional and tasty to most children are celery stuffed with peanut butter or cheese spread, yogurt, puddings, fruit and cheese kabobs, and popcorn.

Although many American children can afford to be picky eaters, approximately twenty million children throughout the world suffer from malnutrition (WHO, 2007). Malnutrition places children at risk for illness, death, and cognitive delays and/or deficits. The World Health Organization postulates that nearly 75 percent of these children could be helped if ready-to-use foods that are specially fortified with nutrients were made available to them.

Obesity

Obesity

A body weight that exceeds by 20 percent what is considered to be appropriate for one's age.

Childhood obesity is of growing concern in the United States, as evidenced by shows such as *Honey, We're Killing the Kids*. **Obesity** is defined as a body mass index (BMI) two standard deviations above the average BMI (WHO, 2007). This condition is believed to affect about 12.4 percent of all preschool-age children in the United States (CDC, 2009).

Being overweight or obese poses many social and psychological consequences to children in early and middle childhood, and beyond (CDC, 2009). Obese children have negative self and body-images. They are also likely to be unpopular. Peers often exclude them from play activities and sometimes reject them altogether (Mendelson & White, 1985; Williams & Stith, 1980). In addition, because eating patterns that are established in childhood usually last a lifetime, children who are overweight or obese are at an increased risk of being overweight or obese as adults (Rolfes & DeBruyne, 1990). Obesity poses serious health risks. It is associated with numerous health issues such as cardiovascular disease, hepatic steatosis (fatty liver), asthma, sleep apnea, and type 2 diabetes (CDC, 2009).

Scientists speculate that obesity is caused by a combination of genetic, behavioral, and environmental factors (CDC, 2009). Some individuals may have a *genetic* predisposition for obesity; however, except for rare genetic disorders, environmental and behavioral factors must come into play for obesity to occur. *Behavioral factors* include caloric intake and physical activity. Television, video games, and computer use seem to contribute to a sedentary lifestyle that precludes physical activity. *Environmental factors* include the influence of family, childcare, and school in helping establish healthy eating and exercise habits.

There are several steps families can take to prevent obesity (CDC, 2009). First, be aware of caloric intake. Avoid sugary drinks and high-calorie/low-nutrient snacks. Eat at home, sitting at the table. Avoid eating in front of the television where it is easy to lose track of what you are eating. Second, lead an active lifestyle. Limit television and other media time. Third, provide healthy role models for eating and exercise to young children. Educate children early about healthy habits. Provide quick, easy, healthy snacks and meals. All of these steps can help prevent obesity.

Illness, Disorders, and Other Concerns

Pediatric psychology

The area of psychology that studies the interactions and relationships among health, illness, physical development, cognitive development, and socioemotional development across the life-span.

Phenomenism

The first stage for understanding of illness "as an external concrete phenomenon that is spatially and temporally remote from the condition of illness."

Contagion

The second stage for understanding of illness as "caused by people or objects that are proximate to, but not touching, the child."

The interactions and relationships among health, illness, physical development, cognitive development, and socioemotional development across the life span are studied in **pediatric psychology** (Bearison, 1998). Researchers in this interdisciplinary field study many important issues in health, including how children understand and cope with illness.

How a child understands illness is dependent upon cognitive development (Bearison, 1998). Bibace and Walsh (1979, 1980, and 1981) conducted a series of classic studies into the stages children go through in understanding illness. During early childhood, understanding of illness is very limited. Two stages of understanding of illness predominate this time period: phenomenism and contagion. **Phenomenism** is the first stage and is described as understanding illness "as an external concrete phenomenon that is spatially and temporally remote from the condition of illness" (Bearison, 1998, p. 679). For example, a young child may say that you can catch the chicken pox from the space shuttle in space. I know that this example seems like nonsense, but such is the reasoning at this stage.

The second stage for understanding illness is called **contagion**. Contagion thinking can be described as understanding illness as "caused by people or objects that are proximate to, but not touching, the child" (Bearison, 1998, p. 679). This means that children believe that you can get sick by being around other sick people, no contact needed. Such thinking applies to all types of illness—colds, flu, or even headaches and heart attacks. About 50 percent of four year olds display this type of thinking.

Although these stages predominate the early childhood years, such thinking may continue into the early school-age years. Additionally, some preschoolers may think at stages beyond these first two. Again, understanding of illness is highly dependent upon cognitive development; hence, as thinking in general develops, so to does an understanding of illness.

Physical Illnesses During Early Childhood

Most of the serious communicable diseases that used to plague childhood are preventable today through immunization. Diphtheria and whooping cough, for instance, were once fatal to many young children but are almost unheard of now in the United States. Most infants are placed on immunization schedules that continue through early childhood. About 80 percent of all American children are fully immunized by their third birthday (Federal Interagency Forum on Child and Family Statistics, 2008).

Although most of the serious diseases are now preventable, young children can still get a variety of illnesses, including upper respiratory diseases such as colds, influenza, and infectious diseases (U.S. Bureau of the Census, 1990a, 1991; WHO, 2007). Preschoolers don't have much resistance to these kinds of diseases because they still lack natural antibody protection and because their organ systems are still maturing. In developing countries, diseases that cause diarrhea, malaria, and pneumonia are of major concern for children (WHO, 2007). Vaccinations, antibiotics, antimalarial medication, clean air and water, breastfeeding, proper nutrition, and insecticide-treated nets for sleeping areas are all needed to help decrease childhood deaths due to these illnesses.

Chronic diseases that are likely to result in death decrease during this time of the life span, although pediatric AIDS is one chronic disease that is advancing rapidly as a leading cause of death among young children (National Center for Health Statistics, 1990). According to the World Health Organization (2007), approximately 2.3 million children worldwide (under the age of fifteen) are infected with HIV. Approximately 1400 more children are infected everyday. Most of these children contact HIV in utero or through breastfeeding; hence, many of these new cases can be prevented through safer delivery and feeding practices and/or antiviral medication.

In the United States, approximately 88 percent of all children have some form of health insurance coverage (Federal Interagency Forum on Child and Family Statistics, 2008). Younger children are more likely to participate in public health insurance programs than older children. Uninsured children are 14 times more likely to lack a primary care physician or clinic than those with health insurance. Regular check-ups and preventative care are important steps in avoiding illness at all stages of development.

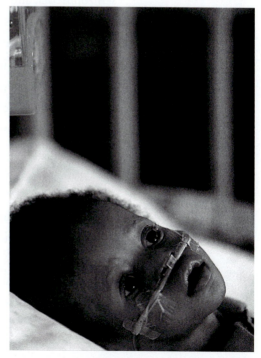

Pediatric AIDS is quickly becoming the leading cause of death among young children.

Mental Disorders During Early Childhood

Mental health is a global aspect to an individual's functioning (SAMHSA, 2003). It has behavioral, cognitive, and socioemotional components and influences on how we function in our daily life. A mental disorder can include harmful behavior, unrealistic thoughts and perceptions, inappropriate emotions, and unpredictable behavior (Hergenhahn, 2005). Mental disorders can range from mild to severe (SAMHSA, 2003). Additionally, mental disorders are often co-morbid, meaning that a person typically suffers from more than one (U.S. Department of Health and Human Services, 1999).

It is estimated that one out of every five children and adolescents suffer from a mental disorder (SAMHSA, 2003 and 2005). Further, approximately 10 percent of all children and adolescents suffer from a serious emotional disturbance that interferes and disrupts their ability to function in everyday life. If you do the math, this means that six million children and adolescents in the United States suffer from a mental disorder. Mental disorders can lead to school struggles, substance abuse, family tension and stress, aggressive behavior, or suicide if untreated.

Mental disorders are diverse and have different causes, symptoms, and treatments (SAMHSA, 2003). Sometimes, we are unaware of the cause. Genetics, injury, viruses, chemical imbalances, and toxins are all biological factors that can cause or trigger a mental disorder. Abuse, stress, or loss of loved ones due to death, divorce, or otherwise are environmental factors that can cause or trigger a mental disorder.

There are many categories of mental disorders. These categories include anxiety disorders, attention deficit/hyperactivity disorder (ADHD), disruptive behavior disorders, eating disorders, learning and communication disorders, affective mood disorders, schizophrenia, and tic disorders. We will highlight different disorders at different stages of the life span. In this chapter, we will focus on ADHD.

Attention deficit/hyperactivity disorder, or ADHD, is predominantly thought to be due to a chemical imbalance in the brain leading to difficulties in regulating attention, impulsivity, and hyperactivity (Fewell & Deutscher, 2002). These children are highly distractible and energetic. They struggle to sit, be still, or behave in the way we expect in a typical school classroom.

Most people do not begin to discuss ADHD until the school-age years. However, there is a push for earlier identification and intervention of ADHD during the preschool years (Fewell & Deutscher, 2002). Perhaps with earlier, accurate identification and intervention, the disorder can come under control prior to entering school. Hence, children will be prepared to learn from day one of kindergarten.

Approximately 5 percent of all children suffer from ADHD (U.S. Department of Health and Human Services, 1999). There are some early signs that parents, child care providers, and preschool teachers can watch for in early childhood: "acts before thinking, changes activities frequently, has a short attention span, fails to focus and follow directions, distracts easily, has difficulty staying on task" (Fewell & Deutscher, 2002, p. 186). Of course all children display these behaviors occasionally. You would want to consider having the child evaluated if the behavior is consistent for at least six months, occurs in multiple settings (e.g., home and daycare), interferes with learning or ability to function, affects relationships and development, is uncontrollable by the child, and cannot be otherwise explained. ADHD can be treated in various ways. Medication and psychosocial interventions can be helpful (Fewell & Deutscher, 2002).

Psychotropic medication

Any medication capable of altering cognition, or behavior.

More and more children are being prescribed **psychotropic medication** for mental disorders (Brown, 2003). However, many of these medications have not been approved by the FDA for use in children due to a lack of research (Brown, 2003; NIMH, 2000). Children's bodies have a different composition than adults and metabolize medication differently than adult bodies. Further, children's brains are developing rapidly, and the affect of psychotropic drugs on these brains is unknown. For this reason, the National Institute of Mental Health (2000) states that children should be prescribed these unapproved medications only when the potential benefits clearly outweigh the potential risks. Medication should always be used in conjunction with psychosocial interventions and be carefully monitored.

Safety Concerns

Accidents claim more lives and cause more injuries to children in the United State between one and four years of age than any other factor (National Center for Health Statistics, 1991, 2007). Most accidental deaths involve a motor vehicle, fires and burns, drowning, or poisoning. Many accidents occur within the home. This indicates that preschoolers need supervision to protect their well-being.

Many home-based injuries are due to the ingestion of harmful substances. Preschoolers are curious and tend to put a lot of substances they are curious about in their mouths. They are also prone to imitate adults who take medicines and pills. Aspirin, pesticides, lead found in paint chips, and petroleum products such as gasoline are common chemical agents that lead to injury and death in young children. Most of these injuries and deaths are preventable.

Children must also be taught to be careful with pets and to avoid wild animals. The Center for Disease Control (2009) urges parents to not allow young children to kiss pets or place animal toys in their mouth because children younger than five are more susceptible to contracting animal diseases than older children. Further, young children should not be allowed to come into contact with cat litters or other areas where pets use the bathroom. Finally, children should be routinely checked for ticks after playing outside. Ticks can carry Lyme disease and Rocky Mountain spotted fever, so they should be removed as soon as possible.

The physical environment must also be considered. Approximately 55 percent of children in the United States live in counties with polluted air (Federal Interagency Forum on Child and Family Statistics, 2008). Ozone and particulate matter that pollute the air can aggravate respiratory systems and increase respiratory problems and symptoms, such as asthma. Clean drinking water can also be of concern, with 10 percent of children in the United States living in communities that fail to meet drinking water health standards. Substandard housing and lead can also be safety concerns and must be considered. Paint with lead should be removed from walls and homes should be checked for safety.

Promoting Wellness

There are many aspects to consider when promoting the wellness of young children. Child care is one area that must be considered. More than 60 percent of all children age six and younger are in child care (Federal Interagency Forum on Child and Family Statistics, 2008). It is important to make certain that this child care is of good quality.

Child abuse is another area of concern. The consequences of abuse can be severe and life-long. Out of every one thousand there are twelve documented cases of child abuse (Federal Interagency Forum on Child and Family Statistics, 2008). Younger children are more likely to be abused than older children. Early detection and intervention is critical for optimal child development.

Economic issues should also be considered when promoting wellness. Approximately 20 percent of all children in the United States, younger than the age of six, live in poverty (Federal Interagency Forum on Child and Family Statistics, 2008). Poverty is especially prevalent among female-householder families (families with an unmarried female as head), with 42 percent of such children living in poverty (compared to only 8 percent of children living with two parents that are married). Additionally, about 12.6 million children (or 17 percent) live in a home where there is a shortage of food. Such economic issues must be addressed in order to promote optimal child development.

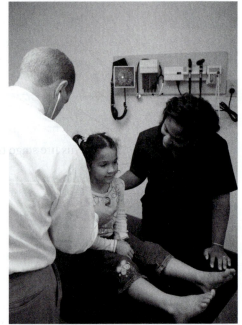

Regular medical check-ups is one way to promote wellness of young children.

Finally, health and safety should be promoted through vaccinations, regular dental and medical check-ups, proper adult supervision, and cleanliness (CDC, 2009). Furthermore, utilizing developmental research more in the creation of public policy, education programs, and intervention programs will help enhance early childhood development across our nation (National Research Council and Institute of Medicine, 2000).

Pause and Process:

1. How is illness understood during early childhood?

2. What issues must be addressed in order to promote health and well-being during early childhood?

COGNITIVE DEVELOPMENT DURING EARLY CHILDHOOD

> ### LEARNING OBJECTIVES:
>
> 1. *Characterize the preoperational stage of cognitive development*
> 2. *Describe information-processing during early childhood*
> 3. *Apply Vygotsky's theory to early childhood cognitive development*
> 4. *Explain language development during early childhood*

Early childhood is a time when children expand their knowledge of the world and develop an attitude of accomplishment. Changes in these years will be the foundation for many future learning experiences. This stage is an exciting time when a child learns to explore the environment in many ways.

This section explores cognitive changes during early childhood, a period that occurs between three to six years after birth. Developmental researchers have concentrated more on this life stage than on any other.

PIAGET'S COGNITIVE DEVELOPMENT THEORY AND THE PREOPERATIONAL STAGE

Preoperational

The kind of thinking young children do when they begin to use mental imagery but are not yet able to use logic; intuition is often used in reaching decisions.

There is a shift in the nature of mental changes at three years of age. Piaget (1967) calls this a change to the **preoperational** mode of thinking. Parents and other caregivers readily recognize that a preschooler thinks differently when compared to an infant. This different way of thinking becomes more noticeable as young children solve problems in their play and daily activities. Their memory and information-processing skills are also more noticeable. Additionally, they show indications of the ability to use elementary logic.

Thought during this new period of mental change focuses on internalizing the environment. Children accomplish this by an increasing use of symbols and mental imagery. They come to rely on representational thought more frequently as they progress through the early childhood stage. Between four and six years of age, children are in transition to the next stage of cognition. They use intuition or hypothesizing to reach decisions. They are increasingly preoccupied with classification and the beginnings of more ordered, logical processing of information.

Preschoolers make judgments and reach conclusions based on their limited understanding of operations and rules. They use a minimal amount of cues and information in doing so. Piaget refers to this as the *intuitive* period of preoperational thought. It is a time when young children are acquiring a knowledge base about things, people, and their environment. Later cognitive functioning will make use of this information.

Mental changes are facilitated by new language skills and perceptual abilities and the changes in brain functioning that occur during early childhood. The preoperational label implies that the child's thought processes are *prelogical* in nature. These prelogical skills lay the foundation for many other, more complex mental changes at later stages of the life span.

Characteristics of Preoperational Thought

Preoperational thought is relatively inflexible. This means that once young children adopt a particular point of view, they have difficulty understanding another one. It also means that young children's thought is dynamically tied to their perception. Preschoolers use sensory information extensively in forming conceptions and reaching conclusions. The maxim "What you see is what you get," is a good way to remember how preschoolers form their ideas of the world. A thing's appearance is often the only means preschoolers use for making judgments or evaluations about that thing.

Piaget uses several concepts to describe the relative rigidity of preschoolers' thought: equation of appearance with reality, egocentrism, centering, irreversibility, inability to solve problems of conservation, preoccupation with classification, animism, and precausal thinking.

Appearance and Reality

Young children define reality almost exclusively as what they see. This characteristic of preoperational thought influences many other aspects of preschool-age cognition. It is generally recognized that preschoolers' thought is bound by their perceptions. They have almost no ability to generalize beyond the obvious or the information at hand (Flavell, 1986; Wadsworth, 2004).

Judgments, decisions, and conclusions are based on what is seen in the world. For example, a young child is shown a car that is colored red. The car is then covered with a special filter that changes its color to black. The filter is then removed to show the red color again. The car is again placed under the filter. When asked to name the color of the car, the child will say that it is black, totally disregarding the reality that the car is actually red and only appears to be black because of the filter. He will do this even though he just saw confirmation that the car is red when the filter was removed. The filter was put back on, and now the car looks black, so it is black as far as he is concerned.

Egocentrism

A cognitive trait that limits a child's understanding of the world to their own perceptions.

Egocentrism

Piaget (1967) believes that the preoperational thought of young children is limited in part by their **egocentrism**. Piaget did not use this word in our usual sense of "selfish" or "conceited." Rather, he used it to describe how young children focus on their own viewpoint and are unable to consider other alternatives. From their perspective, their own vantage point is all that is possible.

Piaget demonstrated the egocentric nature of young children's thoughts in what is now known as the "three mountains experiment" (Piaget & Inhelder, 1967). Preschool-age children were shown a three-dimensional model of three mountains that differed in size and color. The model was placed on a table at which a young child sat on one side. A doll was placed in a chair on an adjacent side of the table. The child was asked to show, by using cardboard cutouts of the mountains models, how the mountains looked to the doll. None of the young children who were the subjects of this experiment were able to do so. They all depicted their own view of the mountains rather than the doll's because they could not understand that an event, object, or situation has a different perspective for someone else.

Young children typically believe that they are the center of their own universe, that things function and happen for their benefit. Appearances fuel this conclusion. For example, a young child on a walk at night might be asked what the moon does. The child will likely explain that the moon follows her everywhere—after all, that is what it appears to be doing. Likewise, a ball does not roll down a hill because it is round or because gravity pulls it. A young child believes it acts this way because he kicked it. This is reason enough for the ball's movement downhill.

Piaget discovered how difficult it is for a child to develop the ability to be knowingly empathic. In early childhood, the individual first learns that each of us has our own interpretation of reality. What must be learned next is that our personal views are not the only representations of reality possible, and certainly not the absolute truth. It is usually a challenge to understand that others have their own views, opinions, problems, perspectives, and knowledge. This understanding will not be completely accomplished by most people until the end of adolescence. In others, it may take even longer to gain an empathic perspective.

Young children begin to overcome their egocentrism and gain a degree of the empathic perspective by the end of early childhood. They start to realize that others see things differently from them and also know or like different things (Flavell, 1985; Hart & Goldin-Meadow, 1984; Taylor, 1988; Wadsworth, 2004).

Critics of Piaget's descriptions of early childhood egocentrism question the conclusiveness of his three mountains experiment (Borke, 1975; Hay et al., 1985). Others have observed that the prosocial behaviors young children demonstrate—such as altruism and sharing—indicate that empathy and responsiveness to others arise earlier than Piaget's schema allows (Leung & Rheingold, 1981; Zahn-Waxler, Radke-Yarrow & Brady-Smith, 1977). Researchers are continually refining our understanding of childhood egocentrism and illuminating how children make adaptations as they become more self-differentiated and socially oriented to others.

Centering

A cognitive trait in early childhood that limits information processing to only one aspect or characteristic rather than several simultaneously.

Centering

Piaget calls another aspect of preoperational thought **centering** (Piaget & Inhelder, 1969). Young children concentrate on only one aspect of an object they see or an activity they do.

They have difficulty in perceiving other aspects or elements simultaneously. When young children are attracted to the color of something, for example, they usually can't consider its size or shape at the same time. They can separate all the yellow buttons, from a large pile of assorted buttons, but the task of separating the yellow wooden round ones is too difficult for them. Because they can handle only one dimension of something at a time, they are capable of making only broad discriminations. The ability to make fine discriminations develops later in the life span.

Irreversibility

Young children typically cannot understand that some operations or processes can be reversed. To a young child, things operate in only one way and that way is irreversible (Piaget, 1967). Some examples will illustrate the **irreversibility** of preschoolers' thinking.

Irreversibility

The inability of young children to comprehend that some processes and operations can be reversed in sequence.

When asked if he has a sister, a preschool-age boy can be expected to reply, "Yes. Her name is Julie." However, when asked if his sister has a brother, the boy replies, "No." A preschooler is shown a blue ball being placed in a cylinder, followed by a green and a yellow one. The child can accurately predict that they will appear from the bottom in that order. However, if the cylinder is rotated to its opposite end, the child cannot understand that the order of appearance will be reversed as the balls appear from this end. Sequential, or serial, reasoning is difficult for young children because they are unable to trace their thought processes backward. Many young children can add or count upward. However, they find subtraction hard to comprehend. This is because subtraction is the reverse of addition and involves reversibility of thought. Similarly, they usually have difficulty understanding how water can be frozen into ice and then melted back into its liquid state.

Reversibility of thought, such as in subtraction, is difficult for young children to comprehend.

Conservation Problems

Conservation

The understanding that the essential characteristics of something are preserved even though it is rearranged in different ways.

Young children cannot understand that something retains the same properties when it is rearranged or reshaped. It is not until middle childhood that they comprehend that its essential properties are preserved, thus mastering the problem of **conservation**.

A trip to the supermarket reveals the prevalence of the problem of conservation even for adults. Manufacturers package similar products in differently shaped containers. A gallon in one type of container may not be recognized as a gallon in another. With the help of labels and an understanding of conservation, adults and older children understand that they can purchase equivalent amounts of a substance in these different containers.

Conservation problems illustrate how preschoolers' perceptions are governed largely by appearances. A classic Piagetian experiment shows that they do not understand that the volume of water is conserved (preserved) when it is poured into a container shaped differently from the original one. The preschooler usually concludes that there is a different amount of water in the new container because the physical appearance of the water has changed owing to the container's different shape. The understanding that the volume is the same is mastered in middle childhood. Comprehending problems of conservation among school-age children is facilitated by their developing abilities to decenter.

Classification

Classification

The cognitive ability to group objects according to traits of similarity or likeness.

The mastery of **classification** skills is a challenge that is accomplished by age six. Centering and egocentrism account for the inflexibility of thinking that prevents younger children from being able to group things according to shared likeness. For example, when young children are given an assortment of plastic shapes (circles, squares, triangles) of different colors and asked to sort them according to likeness, they are unable to do so. Any sorting they do is usually by color rather than shape, especially among older preschool children (Ault, 1983). Similarly, irreversible thinking hampers the ability of young children to move back and forth between various groups to sort them correctly (Siegler, 1998; Wadsworth, 2004).

Sorting different colored shapes according to likeness is a challenge for younger children.

Animism

The belief of young children that all things, including objects are alive.

Animism

Young children believe that all things, including inanimate objects, are alive (Bullock, 1985). This **animism** is a charming aspect of preschool-age thinking. It is often observed when young children are involved in solitary play and talk to their toys using private speech.

When young children bump into a chair, it is not unusual to hear them scold it for being in their way. They believe things fall because they have a life of their own and can move to a different place. In many respects, animism is an extension of egocentrism and prelogical thinking. Young children may use animistic thought to develop hypotheses about a complicated world.

Precausal Thinking

Preschoolers often jump to conclusions. They base their decisions on a limited amount of information or knowledge of circumstances, or on how close one event follows another (Pines, 1983; Pulaski, 1980; Wadsworth, 2004). Young children seem to reason in this manner: If event A causes event B to happen, then whenever event B is observed, event A will follow. For example, a young child may notice that when her mother is asleep (event A), she doesn't wear her glasses (event B). When her mother removes her glasses (event B) during the day to clean them, the child asks, "Is it time for you to go night-night (event A), Mom?" Removing the glasses is associated with going to sleep by the young child, and vice versa. This appears to be an understanding of reversibility. However, it is a type of reasoning based on what is known as **transductive reasoning**, or reasoning from one event to another.

Adults are often amazed at the tall tales and fanciful statements made with certainty by young children. Piaget and Inhelder (1969) describe two aspects of thought that account for **precausal thinking** among preschoolers; their inability to distinguish physical from psychological events, and their belief in an ultimate cause of events— that is, their conviction that there is a reason or explanation for everything. As we have seen, young children have problems differentiating the real from the imagined. For this reason, nightmares are real and fantasy is confused with reality. Intuitive thinking characterizes precausal thinking processes.

Revising Piaget's Findings

Contemporary developmental researchers have found that the children they study do not always behave in the ways reported by Piaget. Many of Piaget's findings have been confirmed when the researchers replicated his methods of studying children (Gelman & Baillargeon, 1983). However, Piaget's approaches are not the only possible for studying changes in individuals' thinking processes over the life span. Contemporary academics have found other ways to study cognitive changes in childhood, and these methods have sometimes yielded results that contradict Piaget's findings (Crain, 2005; Wadsworth, 2004).

One such result is that young children are not as egocentric as Piaget reported. They do understand that an object having a variety of sides (like a house) looks differ-

Transductive reasoning

Seeing a relationship between two objects or events, when in fact no relationship exists.

Precausal thinking

A type of logic unique to young children based on intuition rather than fact.

ent from various angles than one having similar sides (like a ball) (Flavell et al., 1981). Preschoolers also can classify objects if they have had experience with the task and it is not too complicated (Brown et al., 1983). These findings suggest that young children's abilities are not as limited as Piaget believed.

Pause and Process:

1. How would you describe preoperational thought?

2. How is the preoperational stage different from the sensorimotor stage we learned about in chapter three?

INFORMATION-PROCESSING IN EARLY CHILDHOOD

Attention

Attention is selective, involves constructive processing, and has limited capacity (Flavell & Miller, 1998). Infants display the beginnings of understanding attention through shared gazes. Although preschool children have some understanding of attention, it is limited. They often fail to understand that attention is selective. Instead, they often assume that adults will be able to attend to and process any information in the vicinity.

Memory

The ability to process information received from the external environment is an important aspect of cognition. The use of memory is paramount in this process as children gain more experiences with a complex environment. Memory skills improve considerably during early childhood, partly because of the increasing efficiency of the cerebral cortex in storing information. Young children also show improvements in the strategies they use to place such information into their memory (Chance & Fischman, 1987; Schneider & Bjorklund, 1998; Siegler, 1998).

Classification and categorization skills

The ability to use salient features to place objects or constructs into distinct groups.

Rehearsal

Practicing something over and over again.

Two strategies are used increasingly and more efficiently by young children to help them place information into their memories. First, they strive to master **classification and categorization skills** to facilitate learning and the use of memory in information-processing. In recalling words, for example, young children may associate words that rhyme ("sun-fun" and "fat-hat") (Rossi & Wittrock, 1971; Schneider & Bjorklund, 1998; Siegler, 1998). Second, young children learn by **rehearsal**—by doing or saying something repeatedly. For example, when three-year-olds are directed to remember where something is hidden, they look more intently, touch the area, and point to it repeatedly (Wellman, Ritter & Flavell, 1975). Naming objects repeatedly may also assist in the process of memory formation. Parents may quiz a child about what she sees, help her to name it, and ask the child to recall it later (Rosinski, Pellegrini & Siegel, 1977). Preschoolers especially rely on this method of learning when they receive approval for remembering. They become aware that rehearsal improves their ability to use recall (Fabricius & Cavalier, 1989).

Emerging Academic Skills

Although some children learn foundations for academic skills at daycare or preschool, many others learn such skills from their parents or even older siblings. Early academic skills can also be acquired from educational programming (such as *Sesame Street, Between the Lions, or Sid the Science Kid*) or computer programs (such as mathisfun.com, brainpop.com, or specific software programs). Academic skill development is intertwined with cognitive development and language development (Piper, 2003).

Early Mathematic Skills

Culture is very important in determining what mathematical skills are important and need to be learned (Ginsburg, Klein, & Starkey, 1998). Learning the number words and using them to count begins around the age of two. For a while, adult (or older child) help is needed to count things with any accuracy. In fact, the average three-year-old will make a counting mistake 33 percent of the time. A conceptual understanding of what counting means takes longer than simply memorizing the order of the number words.

Counting with conceptual understanding progresses so that by the age of four children have a general conceptual understanding of adding objects or subtracting objects in relation to a group (Ginsburg, Klein & Starkey, 1998). This does not mean that the average four-year-old can do addition and subtraction problems. Instead you can show them an original picture with three cows. You can then show them two other pictures: a picture that still has three cows, and a picture with only two cows. If you asked the child, "Which picture shows that one of the cows left?" he or she would be able to choose the picture with only two cows.

Most three-year-olds do not display a strategy when asked a mathematical question (Ginsburg, Klein & Starkey, 1998). However, across the preschool years, some rudimentary mathematical strategies emerge. An early strategy to emerge is counting. For example, when asked which of two pictures has more tomatoes, most four-year-olds will use counting to answer the question. Another early strategy to emerge is learning to start counting from the larger of two addends. For example, consider the following word problem:

Amy picks four apples from a tree. Then Amy picks three more apples from the tree. How many apples does she have altogether?

A younger child would start counting from one, all the way up to seven. However, an older preschool child would start with the four in mind, and count up three from there. Older preschool children also acquire finger counting for addition and subtraction problems. Surprisingly, older preschool children have two strategies for division problems: consecutive and overlapping (Ginsburg, Klein & Starkey, 1998). For example, consider the following word problem:

Leonardo has five friends. He has ten pencils that he would like to give to them, making sure that each has the same number of pencils. How many pencils will each friend receive?

This division problem could be solved by a young child using either a consecutive strategy or an overlapping strategy (Ginsburg, Klein & Starkey, 1998). In the overlapping strategy, a child could draw five boxes representing the five friends. He or she would then place a tally mark in each box (representing a pencil) until they counted up to ten. In this way, the child could learn that each friend would receive two pencils. The alternative would be the consecutive strategy. With this strategy, the child would distribute the pencils to each friend completely before moving on to the next friend. Early on, this strategy could involve a lot of trial-and-error while trying to figure out how to distribute the total number of pencils equally among the friends.

Early Language Arts Skills

To be successful in our society, a child must learn to read and write. However, how do children come to learn that the strange shapes and lines they see on paper stand for letters? Further, how do they come to know that these letters represent specific sounds in their language? Finally, how do they come to know how to share their thoughts, memories, feelings, or imaginations with the written word? All of these skills typically begin in early childhood.

Phonics

An approach to teaching reading and spelling based upon phonetics, or the sound of letters.

Phonics can be defined as a system "designed to help children use the correspondences between letters and sounds to learn to read and write" (Adams, Treiman & Pressley, 1998). The first step in phonics is to teach that the letters of the alphabet stand for specific sounds. Some letters have only one sound (e.g., the letter B), whereas other letters have more than one sound (e.g., the letter G). Once children know the sounds that letters can make, they can begin sounding out words. Of course, they must learn the language-specific rules during the school-age years (e.g., when "le" is at the end of a two-syllable word, the consonant before the "le" joins it in forming the last syllable, like "candle"). Although phonics is very important for reading development, context is also important in helping young readers decode words that are neither familiar, nor easily sounded out. Additionally, some words must be taught that are neither phonetic nor easily learned through contextual clues. Many of these words, along with high frequency words, are taught in preschool as "sight words."

Writing skills are limited in early childhood. Writing is both a cognitive and motor skill task. Simply holding the pencil (or crayon) and working to make the hand make the desired marks on the paper uses much of the young child's cognitive resources. If a child has to write a story himself, it will be limited and sketchy. However, if a teacher or parent writes a story that the child dictates, the story will be filled with much more information and details.

Metacognition

Knowing how to place information into memory and how to retrieve that information are new skills for preschoolers. Many researchers believe that children do not master this basic

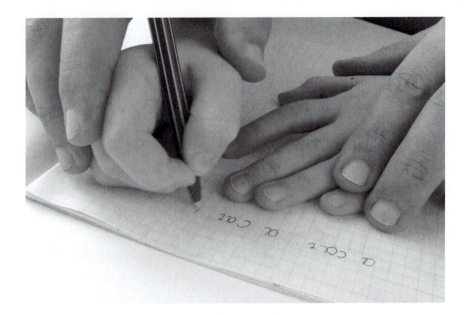

The act of writing is an example of both a cognitive and a motor skill. The child works to make his hand hold and move the pencil to create marks on the paper.

Metacognition

The ability to be aware of and understand the changes occurring in one's own cognitive processes.

skill until they are older (Siegler, 1998; Wellman, 1985). It depends on **metacognition**, or the ability to be aware of, understand, and take note of changes in one's own cognitive processes. Metacognition includes knowing how to pay attention to things to remember them later; what interferes with making one's attention work properly to perform memory storage; and what works well to facilitate the use of one's memory. There is some controversy about whether young children are aware that they can use memory in information-processing. It is clear, however, that in early childhood improvements occur in acquiring skills that help children control what they learn and remember (Brown, 1982; Siegler, 1998).

Pause and Process:

1. How does information-processing develop during early childhood?

2. How is information-processing different in early childhood than in infancy?

OTHER COGNITIVE DEVELOPMENT THEORIES

Vygotsky's Theory

In the first chapter, we learned the foundational concepts for Vygotsky's social-historical theory of cognitive development. The concepts of psychological tools, social-historical context, zone of proximal development, and scaffolding were all introduced. What is important to keep in mind for this chapter is that both Piaget and Vygotsky saw children as active agents in their cognitive development. One of the key distinctive features of Vygotsky's theory is the importance placed upon the social-historical context. Although

Piaget is typically portrayed as viewing children as independent agents out in the world, constructing their own development; Vygotsky viewed children as active, yet highly guided by more mature mentors in the environment.

It is also worth revisiting the key concepts of zone of proximal development and scaffolding from Chapter 1. The **zone of proximal development** is a range of what a child is capable of achieving. At the low end of the range is what the child is capable of achieving independently, whereas the high end represents what the child can achieve with guidance from a mentor. Scaffolding seems to be inherent across cultures. Parents, caregivers, and teachers seem to know to structure tasks in a way that best facilitates learning. With **scaffolding**, intensive help and guidance is given when a new skill is being taught to a child. As the child begins to understand the task and learn the skill, less and less help is given. Ultimately, the child is able to perform the task completely independently. Vygotsky's theory is an area of continued research and will probably continue to impact educational practices for some time.

Theory of Mind

A **theory of mind** is the ability to understand your own mental state, as well as the mental state of others (Dixon, 2003). Furthermore, a theory of mind allows you to understand the connection between mental states and behavior. Mental state refers to your thoughts, knowledge, beliefs, and desires. For example, you know that you do not believe in Santa Clause. However, you may know that your three-year-old niece does believe in Santa Clause. Further, because you know about her beliefs, you may also be able to conjecture her thoughts about Christmas morning. However, a theory of mind takes time to develop.

Henry Wellman has completed a series of studies examining the development of theory of mind. He has also written numerous articles and chapters describing this phenomenon (e.g., Wellman, 1993; Wellman, Cross & Watson, 2001; Wellman & Gellman, 1998; Wellman, Lopez-Duran, LaBounty & Hamilton, 2008). Around the age of two, children begin to understand that people have wants and desires. By the third birthday, this understanding grows to include other mental states, such as thoughts and beliefs. It is at the age of four that children really begin to understand the connection between mental states and behaviors. Children are unable to deceive others until they have a theory of mind. Although most children fully achieve it by the age of four or five, children with older siblings achieve it earlier.

Zone of proximal development

A range of what a child is capable of achieving.

Scaffolding

An instructional strategy in which a learning task is structured whereby a lot of support is offered early on, but as the student begins to learn, less and less support is given.

Theory of mind

The ability to understand your own mental state, as well as the mental state of others.

Pause and Process:

1. Give an example of how a teacher can scaffold learning for children.

2. Why do you think children with older siblings achieve a theory of mind sooner than children without older siblings?

LANGUAGE DEVELOPMENT

In Chapter 3, we discussed language development in infancy. We learned the components of language, theories of language acquisition, and received an overview of language development in these early years. But why do we have language? What function does it serve?

There are various perspectives as to what functions language serves (Piper, 2003). In her book on language development, Piper (2003) integrates the perspectives of several researchers to identify some of the primary functions of language. Some early functions of language include:

- Satisfy needs

- Direct the behaviors of others

- Describe self

- Facilitate social interactions

- Information gathering and sharing

- Play, imagine, and pretend

Later functions of language include:

- Interpretation and integration of experiences

- Expression of cognitive and socioemotional processes

- Organizing communication

These important functions of language necessitate the ability to converse skillfully with others. What makes one individual a good conversationalist and another a boring or inept conversationalist? There are some basic guidelines that allow one to be a competent conversationalist and they begin developing early in childhood.

One important skill to be a competent conversationalist is to be sensitive and empathic to the listener (Piper, 2003). What is the listener's viewpoint? Do they seem to comprehend what you are saying? Is the person even paying attention? Sensitivity to listener needs is a key component to conversational skills. This skill is closely intertwined with cognitive development, and one sees great improvements in this area during the school-age years.

Another important skill is learning to take turns during a conversation (Piper, 2003). Without turn taking, you don't have a conversation, but a monologue. Again, although this skill begins development during infancy (with caretakers taking turns responding to coos), development continues throughout childhood.

There are many other important skills for being a competent conversationalist (Piper, 2003). These skills include use and response to indirect requests, awareness and understanding of relevance, ability to make conversational repairs, and pragmatic adjustments for gender.

Now that we have considered some of the broader, foundational issues of language use, let's consider some specific areas of speech development during early childhood.

Private Speech

Private speech

A speech form prevalent in early childhood in which children talk to themselves or continue to talk even when no one is listening to what they are saying.

One characteristics of language acquisition in early childhood is the use of **private speech**. Piaget (1926) first noted this as a language form in early childhood. He observed that young children frequently talk even when no one is listening to them. He believed that this shows egocentrism in young children—their inability to see things from another's viewpoint. Piaget believed that this type of speech pattern became replaced by other means of self-expression as children developed.

Another interpretation of private speech has been suggested by Vygotsky (1962). Rather than being an indication of egocentrism, private speech, in Vygotsky's view, is used by preschoolers to direct their actions, make plans, and maintain a psychological focus on the present. Again, rather than disappearing, as Piaget suggested, Vygotsky theorized that private speech becomes merely unspoken or sometimes subconscious thought (Berk, 1986; Crain, 2005; Frauenglass & Dias, 1985; Kohlberg, Yaeger & Hjertholm, 1968). Private speech is often observed among preschoolers when they are involved in solitary play. It is also observed when they think "out loud" as they work through situations and learn problem-solving strategies (Crain, 2005; Harris, 1990; Manning, 1990).

The use of private speech is believed to show egocentrism in young children.

Vocabulary

Vocabulary continues to expand rapidly during early childhood (Siegler, 1998). The average three-year-old has a vocabulary of 896 words. By the age of four, vocabulary size increases to an average of 1,540 words. Another jump is seen in vocabulary by the age of five, with an average vocabulary of 2,072 words. Words acquired during this time become more complex with more of the derivatives and inflections acquired (Piper, 2003).

Grammar

Young children learning English as their primary language experience many challenges because English has rather difficult grammar. Parts of speech must be learned, as well as the rules for forming correct sentence structures. This involves comprehending, at an elementary level, such rules as (1) the subject precedes the verb; (2) verbs have different tenses to reflect past, present, and future action; (3) words have different forms in the possessive case; and (4) verbs change form with plural subjects. However, there are many exceptions to these basic rules and they take years to master. Young children are able to place the subject before a verb and the object after it (Clark, 1982). This is the grammatical structure commonly used in English. Infant usage such as "Baby go sleep" is refined into "I'm sleepy, and I want to take a nap." There is limited use of possessive words such as "my" and "mine" at age three, and understanding of the possessive case increases during this period. Verb tenses are learned. Negatives are learned as well. For example, a two-year-old would say when told it is bedtime, "No go!" whereas a four-year-old might say, "I don't wanna go night-night!" Prepositions are difficult and may not be mastered at this time.

Preschoolers often resort to inventing words when forming sentences (Clark, 1982; Piper, 2003). Although they lack the vast vocabulary and cognitive abilities of older individuals, young children strongly desire to communicate so they create words according to their limited knowledge of grammatical structure. For example, they will add an s to a verb, as in "I gots to use the potty," and an er to a noun for a doer, as in "My mom is a good cooker." This type of error is known as overgeneralizing the rules of grammar. Speech in early childhood is abundant with mistakes, but trial-and-error is the means by which young children learn the complexities of language.

Bilingualism

Communicative disorders

Any disorder that impairs one's ability to communicate.

Voice disorders

Persistent difficulties with the quality of voice.

Fluency disorders

Disorders in which a person struggles to communicate smoothly.

The ability to speak more than one language is a cognitive advantage (Piper, 2003). The earlier a child learns a second language, the easier it is for him or her to master it. When a child is raised in a home where two languages are spoken, some confusion may occur between the two languages during early childhood. However, this confusion typically subsides by the end of early childhood. Interestingly, a child raised in a bilingual home will eventually favor one language over the other. It is rare to find balanced bilingualism. Which language dominates is typically determined by which language is dominant in the surrounding environment.

Communicative Disorders

Communicative disorders can range from mild to severe and make either learning or using the language difficult (Piper, 2003). Three of the most common communicative disorders in children involve voice, fluency, and articulation of particular sounds.

Articulation disorders

Disorders in which a person struggles to produce appropriate speech.

Voice disorders are persistent difficulties with the quality of voice (Piper, 2003). They may simply be a nuisance (such as a nasal tone or breathiness) or may make speech unintelligible. **Fluency disorders** disrupt the ability to speak continuously or at a normal rate. Stuttering is one example of a fluency disorder. **Articulation disorders** range from difficulty with specific sounds to severe impairment in the phonological system. Lisping is one example of a mild articulation disorder.

The cause of these communicative disorders varies (Piper, 2003). Sometimes they are due to anatomical abnormalities. Other times they are due to brain injuries. In many cases, however, the cause is unknown. In general, the sooner a communicative disorder is identified and intervention begins, the better the chance of communicative improvement.

Pause and Process:

1. How do Piaget and Vygotsky differ in explaining private speech?

2. How does language develop during early childhood?

GENETICS

LEARNING OBJECTIVES:

1. *Characterize emotional development during early childhood*
2. *Describe understanding of self and others during early childhood*
3. *Explain psychosocial development during early childhood*

Socialization

The process by which individuals are taught to conform to social rules, to acquire personal values, and to develop attitudes typical of their culture.

Early childhood is a time when socialization efforts begin in earnest. **Socialization** is the process by which individuals are taught to conform to social rules, to acquire personal values, and to develop attitudes typical of their culture. A preschooler experiences growing pressures to conform to expectations of "good" behavior. Early childhood is the time when parents start to explore styles of child rearing in earnest. They experiment to find patterns they feel comfortable with and that succeed in achieving the desired results. They encourage their preschooler to develop routines and habits of everyday living. Children at this stage typically must also learn to separate easily and frequently from their parents, especially if they are placed into daycare or a preschool program.

This phase of the life span is also a time when social roles and interaction patterns are first learned and shaped. Children learn to play with others their age in early childhood. As they do so, they experiment in how to relate to others. Most preschoolers like participating with other children in play activities. Several social and mental changes occur in the types of play children engage in at this stage. Play facilitates learning about the social roles found in the child's culture, including appropriate sex-role behaviors. Children experience some conflicts as they learn what is acceptable to both parents and peers.

EMOTIONAL DEVELOPMENT

Key Emotional Development Highlights

Emotional development is intertwined with cognitive development (Siegel, 1999)). As we learned in the last chapter, preschool children enter the preoperational stage of cognitive development. Although preschool children experience increases in attention and memory, they also experience egocentric thought, appearance as reality, animism, and precausal thinking. Hence, this is a period where fears peak and aggression is common. Conversely, it is also a period of increased empathy and gratification delay.

Emotion Regulation

Learning to control one's emotions is a slow and sometimes painful process. During early childhood, controlling emotions is observable in displays of prosocial behavior. Failed attempts at controlling emotions are observable in displays of aggression. Coping with fears is another area that children work with emotion regulation during this phase of the life span. It is these three areas that we will touch upon in this section.

Prosocial Behaviors

Prosocial behaviors

Those behaviors that promote helpfulness and show concern for others, such as altruism or empathy.

Empathy

The ability to comprehend accurately the thoughts, feelings, and actions of others.

Sympathy

The ability to feel the same way that others do; learning to sympathize is the first step toward developing empathy.

Most young children are taught to show some social interest in others. **Prosocial behaviors** are those that promote helpfulness and concern for others. These altruistic behaviors involve an awareness of others' feelings and appropriate reactions to those feelings. Prosocial behavior requires **empathy**, or the ability to comprehend accurately the thoughts, feelings, and actions of others (Burns, 1980; Eisenberg & Fabes, 1998). Empathy differs from **sympathy**, which is the ability to feel the same way that others do, but learning to sympathize is the first step toward developing empathy.

Trying to comfort an upset loved one is prosocial behavior.

As mentioned in our discussion of emotional development in infancy, early empathy may be possible because of the mirror neuron system. Toddlers are also capable of early, if ineffective, attempts at prosocial behavior when trying to comfort an upset loved one. It is common in early childhood to observe empathic responsiveness when children share, comfort, and help each other.

It is unclear what role a parental model plays in facilitating these behaviors in young children. It does appear that when children have opportunities to observe sympathetic behaviors, they tend to behave sympathetically more frequently themselves (Eisenberg & Fabes, 1998; Yarrow, Scott, & Waxler, 1973). Researchers note, however, that sympathetic behaviors are observed throughout infancy and childhood regardless of parental modeling.

Aggression

Aggression

Any hostile act that causes fear in others and leads to forceful contact; may be verbal or physical and directed at people as well as objects.

22. Define aggression.

Psychologists define **aggression** as any hostile action that causes fear and leads to forceful contact with another (Coie & Dodge, 1998; Parke & Slaby, 1983). Aggression can be either verbal or physical or both, and can be directed at people or things. Aggressive behaviors can also be either positive or negative.

During early childhood, verbal aggression increases while physical aggression decreases (Coie & Dodge, 1998). Increases in language ability and the ability to delay gratification may contribute to the decline in physical aggression. Across cultures and socioeconomic groups, boys are more physically and verbally aggressive than girls during the preschool years.

Theorists believe that a wide variety of factors may contribute to aggression (Coie & Dodge, 1998). Genetics, psychobiology, and cognitive processes have all been implicated as contributors to aggression. Other researchers focus on the role of the family environment. They note that children who are treated in harsh, aggressive ways by parents act aggressively toward others. Some attribute the tendency toward aggressive behavior in these children to genetic factors (Ghodsian-Carpey & Baker, 1987). Others stress that an aggressive parent promotes similar behavior in children through modeling (Bandura, 1973; Bandura & Walters, 1963), just as children frequently imitate the violent behavior they see on television (Singer & Singer, 1981). One explanation emphasizes that physical punishment by parents increases a child's aggressiveness (Eron, 1987).

Despite the partial merit of these explanations, it is clear that all young children act aggressively at times. Parents and other caregivers are challenged to teach children to control their aggressive impulses. Research points to the powerful role of reinforcement in helping children learn to act in other ways. Adults give children a confusing message when they spank them for hitting others. If, instead, they positively reinforce prosocial behaviors that are incompatible with aggression, children are likely to learn more beneficial ways to express themselves. Another less damaging way to discourage aggression is to briefly isolate the aggressive child from others. Social learning theory suggests still other alternatives. One is to expose children to models who show appropriate ways for handling the feelings that motivate aggression.

Coping with Fears

Fear

A reaction that involves physical and/or psychological agitation and dreadful anticipation of real or imagined danger to one's safety.

Fear is an emotional response marked by psychological or physical agitation and a dreadful anticipation of actual or imagined danger. We develop fears both by learning and by using our imagination to cope with anxiety. Fears resemble phobias, but are different in nature. A fear may be based on reality, on something that has actually occurred, or stands a good chance of occurring. A phobia, on the other hand, is a compulsive, maladaptive response to relatively harmless and poorly defined stimuli. A fear may serve as the basis of a phobia. For example, a child may be frightened by a large snarling dog. This is a realistic response. But if the child develops a fear of all dogs, even after repeated exposure to the harmless variety, that child has a phobia. Most young children do not develop serious phobias. Those who do may need professional assistance if their reactions interfere with normal functioning.

Most fears of young children relate to the stressfulness of encountering unfamiliar situations and people. Preschoolers have a vivid imagination that fuels an active fantasy life. Their immature level of cognitive functioning does not permit them to easily distinguish between reality and fantasy. Although their interactions with the world are increasing dramatically, they lack the experience to make predictions about the future based on what has occurred in the past. Therefore, they commonly make gross overgeneralizations and jump to conclusions.

Children's fears change as they advance through the preschool stage. One of the most comprehensive examinations of this subject ever conducted was done by Arthur Jersild and Francis Holmes in 1935 (Jersild, 1960). Their findings have been confirmed repeatedly by contemporary investigators (Baurer, 1976; Poznansky, 1973). Young children's fears focus on unpredictable and unknown situations, objects, and events over which they feel they have little control. Studies report that preschoolers show the greatest fear reactions to animals, snakes, the dark, falling, loud noises, and high places. As they gain more experience with the world and advance in cognitive maturation, their fears become more manageable. It is common, however, for early fearful reactions to recur at later stages in the life span, usually in association with major transitions and crises.

A child frightened by a large dog may be the basis of a phobia.

When parents hear children voice their fears and act them out by withdrawing, crying, or trembling, their response is often to regard the fears as irrational (which they are) and to scold the children or become impatient with them. This behavior may promote a sense of guilt rather than alleviate the child's fearfulness.

Children can learn how to overcome their fears (Alexander & Malouf, 1983). Parents and other caregivers can best respond by encouraging children to work through their thoughts about the fearful situation. This helps them to learn to cope successfully, rather than feel guilt about being afraid (Graziano, DeGiovanni & Garcia, 1979). Parents should also encourage children to talk about their fears. This lets them know that they are being taken seriously and have their parents' support. With support, they will learn how to reduce anxiety and gain some degree of mastery over fear-producing stimuli (Eisenberg, 1998). Their self-esteem is heightened in the process.

Delaying Gratification

Delay gratification

The ability to put off something pleasurable and rewarding and work hard in the here and now.

Adults often ask preschoolers to wait for what they want to have right now. The ability to **delay gratification** is desirable to many families. They expect their children to put aside a smaller need satisfied now in exchange for receiving a greater benefit later. This is an important lesson in self-control.

People are able to cope more successfully with difficult situations later in life if they learned to delay immediate gratification in early childhood (Mischel, Shoda & Rodriguez, 1989). For example, researchers identified young children who were highly self-controlled at four years of age. These children were more competent and better able to cope with frustration during middle childhood and adolescence than those who had lower levels of self-control in early childhood. Modeling appears to help preschoolers learn this valuable behavior (Mischel, 1974). Teaching young children to say, "It is good if I wait," also helps them to control their impulsiveness (Toner & Smith, 1977).

Temperament

In earlier chapters, we discussed Thomas and Chess' conceptualization of temperament. If you remember, Thomas and Chess' years of research suggested that there were three basic types of temperament: easy, difficult, and slow-to-warm-up. Although not all infants fit into one of these three categories, most could. However, other conceptualizations of temperament have been proposed (Rothbart & Bates, 1998). In fact, the idea of temperament "types" has been questioned, with a shift toward looking at temperament groups or profiles instead (e.g., Aksan et al., 1999). The idea behind temperament groups emphasizes that although these groups are distinct from one another, there is also great variability within each group.

Regardless of which perspective on temperament you focus on, a clear pattern has emerged showing correlations between specific temperament dimensions and behaviors

(Rothbart & Bates, 2006). Some dimensions of temperament are seen as protective factors against suboptimal behavioral outcomes, whereas others are seen as risk factors for problem behaviors (e.g., Buss & Plomin, 1984; Prior, 1999). For example, a child who is high in negative emotionality is at risk of both internalizing and externalizing behavioral problems. Conversely, low negative emotionality seems to act as a protective factor against internalizing and externalizing behavioral problems.

Attachment

If you remember from Chapter 3, attachment is a strong affectional tie or emotional bond between two individuals (Ainsworth, 1973). Attachment develops from early caregiving interactions and impacts the development of expectations of what to expect in relationships and mental models about self and others (Thomson, 1998). Attachment can be secure or insecure.

Numerous studies have examined the impact of infant temperament on early childhood behavior (see Thomson, 1998, for a review of this research). In general, when you compare a secure child to an insecure child, the secure child is more likely to display the following behaviors and characteristics:

- Lower dependency on preschool teachers

- Higher empathy

- Higher ego resiliency

- Higher self-esteem

- Better emotional health

- More positive mood

- Higher social competence

- Higher compliance

- Better social skills

Hence, secure attachment in infancy is predictive of better outcomes during the preschool years than insecure attachment. We will return to attachment and overall adjustment in Chapter 5.

Pause and Process:

1. Describe aggression and prosocial behavior during early childhood.

2. Given what you have learned about temperament so far in this book, why do you think it would be related to behavioral outcomes such as depression or aggression?

SELF AND OTHERS

Understanding of Self and Others

Self-concept

One's basic ideas about one's inner self.

The process of developing a **self-concept** that began in infancy continues in early childhood. If you remember, the self-concept is a person's ideas about his or her inner self. In late infancy, individuals learn to establish personal boundaries and to differentiate themselves from their parents. In early childhood, they continue to construct elementary notions about their personal identity. Increasingly, young children use their physical characteristics, possessions, and abilities as the basis for constructing their self-concept (Elder, 1989; Harter, 1983, 1998). More importantly, they learn to evaluate their inner selves according to what others tell them about themselves. Children this age see their parents as omnipotent. Parents have the answers to the questions they ask, the power to make things happen that they cannot accomplish, and the ability to protect them from harm. The lessons parents teach a young child about the world and how to act are powerful and lasting. They also deeply affect the child's self-concept.

Gender Identity

Gender identity

One's knowledge of being either male or female.

An important aspect of an individual's self-concept is **gender identity**. This is the knowledge that one is classified as either male or female.

Children first learn gender or sex roles through their parents' and culture's interpretations of masculinity and femininity. In early childhood, reinforcement is used to shape such behaviors. However, innate tendencies also help guide behavior development. Said another way, some sex-role behavior seems largely shaped by the society a child is raised in—such as whether women and girls eat only after the males in the family have been fed. Conversely, some sex-role behavior seems to cut across cultures (and sometimes even species), which hints at an underlying biological tendency—such as males tending to be more physically aggressive than females.

Young children go through a period of rigid stereotypes and ideas about what it means to be male or female. It is helpful to recognize that preschoolers make rigid interpretations of sex-role behaviors because this helps them to understand their own social roles and to organize their behavior accordingly. This rigidity is partly due to the constraints in thought processes that are typical at this age. Young children's reasoning can be primitive and rather inflexible. They base a lot of their notions on concrete cues. Preschoolers typically use visible physical cues to recognize others as either male or female (Bem, 1989). Such cues usually are hairstyles, clothing, and accessories such as hair barrettes. Such limited reasoning means that gender can be changed if the physical cues change. For example, if a preschool child sees a boy dressed like a boy, the preschooler will call him a boy. However, if that same boy is then dressed in girl's clothing, then it is likely that the young preschool child will call

Self-concept such as gender identity classifies whether a child feels that they are either male or female. Cues such as hairstyle and clothing help children determine gender.

him a girl. It is not until around age six that many children have realized that sex roles usually conform to external genitalia. Children with younger, opposite sex siblings will sometimes realize this sooner if they paid attention during diaper changes or baby baths.

The behavioral aspect of children's sex-role development begins at birth when parents are told, "It's a boy!" or "It's a girl!" This immediate classification is made more public by naming a child. Names generally conform to one's biological sex, although in our culture androgynous names can sometimes be given. At any rate, from birth onward, children are channeled into one sex role or the other. They are dressed in clothing and given hairstyles that will help others know whether to treat them as a male or female (Fagot et al., 1985). Girl babies are cuddled more and spoken to softly; boy babies are handled more energetically.

A preschool-age child's knowledge of sex-appropriate role behaviors comes from several sources. The family system is particularly important here. Adults and others in the family system model and reinforce what they consider to be sex-appropriate behavior (Maccoby & Jacklin, 1974). Reinforcement from other same-sex children also promotes sex-appropriate behaviors, especially among boys (Fagot, 1985; Maccoby & Jacklin, 1987).

With time, preschool children will outgrow their rigid ascription to sex-role behaviors and realize that males can cook and be great chefs and females can be firefighters. Sex-role rigid outlooks can be viewed as developmentally appropriate in early childhood and not equivalent with the gender stereotypes adults sometimes hold.

Play

Spotlight

27. Why is play important?

Play, like language, is a primary means by which young children experience socialization. Play is especially pertinent to developing social skills such as prosocial behaviors. It is through play activities with others that young children construct the culture of childhood.

Play is usually seen by adults as recreational, something to keep children busy. But play is much more constructive than most adults realize (Galatzer-Levy & Choler, 1993; Garvey, 1977; Sutton-Smith, 1985; Vandenberg, 1978).

First, play helps children to learn problem-solving skills such as sharing, taking turns, and cooperating. Second, play encourages self-discovery and self-concept formation. The discovery of one's capabilities and limitations, and others' reactions to those capabilities and limitations, during play helps to develop self-definition. Third, repetitive play advances skill mastery and exploration. Fourth, play encourages creativity. Children investigate different approaches as they interact with others and manipulate toys in different ways.

The classic study of children's play was conducted by Parten (1932). Her findings have been confirmed by other investigators who have studied developmental changes in play activities (Barnes, 1971; Harper & Huie, 1985). Parten discovered six categories of play activities in early childhood. They show a progression from general to specific types. A couple of these types were alluded to in chapter three.

An early form of play activity is called **unoccupied play**. A child watches others or engages in seemingly aimless activity such as wandering about. **Solitary play** takes place when children are alone or are playing independently of others. A child makes little attempt to interact with others. **Onlooker play** involves observing others playing. A child asks questions, makes comments, or carries on conversations with others who are actively playing. **Parallel play** is playing alongside others who are doing the same or a different activity. **Associative play** is engaging in a common activity and interacting with others. A child may borrow, lend, share, or influence others' behavior by suggestions. Finally, **cooperative play** is the integration of several children into group play where different roles are assumed. This type of play has an agreed-upon goal or outcome, as when children work together to build a fort.

This progression shows how children's play activities can be expected to change as they grow older (Harper & Huie, 1985). Parallel play dominates among two and three-year-olds. It persists as a primary play form throughout early childhood. Associative play is increasingly observed among three-year-olds. This type of play continues to increase in frequency during early childhood to levels comparable to parallel play. Cooperative play emerges during the third and fourth years and slowly increases thereafter.

It is not uncommon for a child to favor one type of play activity over others. For example, some five-year-olds prefer solitary play activities to associative play activities (Smith, 1978). These children can play at something for hours and be perfectly happy. When playing with other children, they also enjoy the companionship and what they are doing. Piaget (1967) proposes that play changes in conjunction to refinements occurring in cognitive skills.

Dramatic play is another type of activity frequently observed in children at this age. In this form of play, also known as *pretend* or *fantasy play*, children use their imaginations to create characters and project themselves into the activities they fantasize for those characters. Dramatic play begins in late infancy when a child pretends to feed a stuffed animal or doll, for example. In early childhood, dramatic play becomes more complex because young children can create complicated plots and fanciful characters (Rubin et al., 1983).

Unoccupied play

Play that seems random and without purpose.

Solitary play

Children are alone or are playing independently of others.

Onlooker play

Observing others at play.

Parallel play

Playing alongside others who are doing the same or a different activity.

Associative play

Engaging in a common activity and interacting with others.

Cooperative play

The integration of several children into group play where different roles are assumed.

Dramatic play is used by young children to explore behavioral alternatives and options. It may serve as a rehearsal of roles they will assume at some point in their future (Roskos, 1990). Empathy—the ability to project oneself into another's role and approximate what that person feels, perceives, and says—is facilitated by dramatic play.

One of the most common scripts in dramatic play by young children has a simple domestic theme (Garvey, 1977). Young children enjoy playing out scenarios that duplicate home life. By experimenting with playing mother, father, grandmother, or grandfather, children can enhance their empathy skills and further develop their schemas for these roles.

Dramatic play is also a helpful diagnostic tool for therapists. In this context, it is called **play therapy**. Play provides a medium in which children can communicate more easily with professionals, because they lack sophisticated verbal communication skills. Feelings, fears, and fantasies are explored in play therapy and events are replicated from the past.

Another predominant type of play in early childhood, especially among boys, is **rough-and-tumble play** (Humphreys & Smith, 1987). This kind of play involves much physical contact, such as pretend fighting, chasing, pushing, and wrestling. Some adults don't like to see this type of play among children because they equate it with aggressiveness and hostility. Actually, rough-and-tumble play requires more social competence than aggressiveness (Pellegrini, 1987) and it has some benefits. One is that it facilitates use of physical skills. Another is that it may be a variation of cooperative play, which requires negotiation between participants and continual redefinition of rules. Finally, it can teach children problem-solving skills.

Adults often fear that this type of play will escalate into real aggression. Usually, children understand that rough-and-tumble play is just fun. Those who find it hard to relate to others, however, may well see this kind of activity as true aggression rather than a form of fun with no harm intended to anyone (Coie & Kuperschmidt, 1983; Dodge & Frame, 1982).

Play therapy

The use of play to assist a child with psychological, behavioral, or emotional problems.

Rough-and-tumble play

Physically active play.

Family Influences

As mentioned in the introduction to this section, socialization is a process that begins in earnest during early childhood. Parents and significant others in a child's life take an active role in teaching these lessons. The lessons are not usually given by formal instruction. More often they are taught by **modeling**, by allowing a child to observe others' behavior, and by providing directions and interpretations.

Modeling

The process by which behavior is acquired and modified through observing and replicating behavior of others.

A child learns the socialization process by observing the behavior of others.

Children are expected to adopt the rules, behavioral expectations, and boundaries established by their family. They are expected to learn the patterns by which their family system operates. Some psychologists call this kind of learning internalizing behavioral standards promoted by parents and other caregivers. When internalization is completed, a child has the information to judge any action as appropriate and acceptable or inappropriate and unacceptable. Parents must understand that transgression and mistakes are to be expected from young children as they are learning.

We live in a diverse society and different families promote different standards of behavior. Despite the diversity of families today, almost all families teach certain kinds of behaviors and values to children—among them prosocial behaviors, limiting aggression through self-control, delaying gratification, and coping with fears—topics all previously discussed in this chapter.

Divorce is quite prevalent in our society. Although divorce is difficult for all children, age plays a factor as to how the divorce will affect children. Preschoolers are often confused by the changes caused by their parents' divorce. It is difficult for children this age to understand why their father is no longer living with their family. Their reactions include general restlessness, sleep problems, increased aggression, fretfulness/anxiety, regressive behaviors (e.g., bed-wetting), and irritability (Hetherington, Cox & Cox, 1976; Parke & Buriel, 1998; Wallerstein & Kelly, 1975). We will discuss divorce in more detail in Chapter 5.

Parenting Strategies

There are many factors that influence how someone behaves as a parent (Bigner, 1989; Parke & Buriel, 1998). Some factors come from past experiences, whereas others come from more contemporary sources. One of the strongest from the past is a social script for parenting behavior that is formed when we are growing up. This is usually unconscious until parenting is assumed in adulthood. Other factors also are thought to predispose one's future parenting behavior and include (1) cultural influences such as the social group of our family of origin, (2) personality patterns of ourselves and our parents, (3) attitudes about how to behave as a parent, and (4) the model of parenting behavior demonstrated by parents and others that are observed. Factors coming from currently experienced sources include (1) situational influences that occur in the present such as the time of day, the sex of a child, the sex of a parent, and so on; and (2) the goals that are established for childrearing. All of these influence parental behaviors that contribute to the nature of a child's character.

The adults in a family system have much to discuss in defining standards for their parenting behavior patterns. This serves to outline the acceptable patterns in a particular family system for parenting. The central mission is to reach agreement on the significant issues that regulate adults' behavior as parents of young children. For example, these may include (1) what kinds of behaviors are acceptable from young children, (2) what rules and limits should be established, (3) how these can be enforced, (4) what are the consequences of transgressions to rules, (5) what can and cannot be said to communicate with young children, (6) what kinds of equipment do children need to stimulate their development, (7) how can resources be allocated to provide for these, (8) what are acceptable behaviors from both adults and children in a variety of circumstances, (9) how much television should young children watch, or (10) should children be punished for misbehavior and in what ways?

Most mothers and fathers appear to hold similar goals for children (Chilman, 1980). These represent long-term aims that result directly from what parents want to accomplish in their child rearing efforts. Even more global goals are the desires voiced by many parents that their children (1) have a happy and fulfilling life, (2) become a person who functions independently but gets along well with others, and (3) possess skills and competencies that allow effective functioning as an adult in society (Bigner, 1989).

The values, attitudes, and beliefs about goals of child rearing work in association to shape the type of child rearing style parents adopt. Four basic types of child rearing styles have been identified by Baumrind (1967, 1971, and 1991) that are briefly outlined here. It may be helpful to visualize these patterns as lying on a continuum for structure and a continuum for warmth (see Table 4-1 below). The table shows how different parenting

TABLE 4-1	DIFFERENT PARENTING STYLES	

STRUCTURE

WARMTH		High	Low
	High	Authoritative	Permissive
	Low	Authoritarian	Rejecting/neglecting (or uninvolved)

styles are classified based upon the degree to which structure and warmth are evident. The parenting styles are described below.

It is helpful to remember that these are dynamic. They may be adapted in response to situations, age and sex of a child, and so on. It is with such adaptability that a family system maintains equilibrium and homeostasis in parenting patterns.

An adult who believes that parents should be strict with children most likely uses an **authoritarian** style. Adults who practice this approach place a high premium on gaining both immediate and long-range obedience. These parents value "keeping the child in his place … restricting his autonomy, and … assigning household responsibilities to inculcate respect for work" (Baumrind, 1966).

The focus of this parenting style is on controlling a child's behavior. Structure is high, whereas warmth is low. The adult decides what is appropriate child behavior, what rules are to be followed, and enforces consequences to transgressions. Obedience of children is valued highly and obtained in a variety of ways. Frequently, this is accomplished by using physical punishment (such as spanking) and other forceful methods. Little effort is expended by an authoritarian parent to explain the reasoning that underlies rules and regulations. A parent's typical response to a child's questioning of rules may be, "Because I

Authoritarian parenting style

Parents that display discipline, but show little affection.

Baur
Baur *mrind*
Bau

said so." This illustrates the origin of the authoritarian label for this style. The adult is the sole authority in regulating a child's life.

Usually an authoritarian parent evaluates and shapes the behavior of a child according to an absolute standard of appropriate behavior. In many respects, this appears to be based on a perfectionistic notion about acceptable child behavior (Bradshaw, 1988; Miller, 1990). The authoritarian parent's word is law for a child. A parent's actions are always thought to be in the child's best interests.

Parents who practice this style, like all others, firmly believe that their actions express their love and concern

Authoritarian style of parenting is where the parent is the sole authority in regulating a child's life.

for their child. Their goal, like other parents, is to make sure that children are equipped with the abilities to succeed in life and function effectively as adults. This parenting style, however, is not believed to benefit children in the long-run as parents anticipate.

Strict

A classic review of the research on child rearing (Becker, 1964) evaluates the effects of various parenting behaviors on children. It was demonstrated that parental hostility and control, as observed in authoritarian styles, tended to disrupt conscience development. It encouraged hostility, aggressiveness, and resistance to authority in children. More recent research supports this initial research, finding that children with authoritarian parents are indeed aggressive, and that they frequently have low self-esteem and are unhappy (e.g., Silk, et al., 2003).

obedience

Currently, some observers suggest that overreliance on this style of parenting equates to psychological and emotional abandonment of children. This approach to raising children may plant the seeds for a variety of adulthood addictions in individuals who are raised in this manner. Manifestations of this parenting style in adulthood are seen in other ways. These range from difficulties in intimate relationships and work roles to emotional disturbances such as chronic depression and difficulty in making decisions (Forward, 1989; Friel & Friel, 1988; Garbarino, Guttman & Seeley, 1986; Whitfield, 1987).

Permissive style

Parents that are affectionate, but display little discipline.

Adults who approach their parenting behavior using a **permissive style** have different ideas about raising children. With this style, structure is low, whereas warmth is high. They believe that they should respond to their children as individuals. They encourage children's autonomy and help them to learn how to make their own decisions. Parents who adopt this style typically rely on reasoning and manipulation in working with children. They do not usually use overt expressions of parent power to work with children. For example, permissively-oriented parents are not interested in being viewed by a child as an authority figure. Instead, they prefer to be seen as a resource for the child to use in learning to make decisions.

This type of style does not pit adult against child in power struggles and conflicts. Instead, children are given much of the responsibility to learn from their own mistakes. Policies, rules, or limits to a child's behavior are determined by negotiation and consultation. The child's opinion has equal weight with that of the adult. Essentially, a permissively-oriented parent "allows the child to regulate his own activities as much as possible, avoids the exercise of control, and does not encourage him to obey externally defined standards" (Baumrind, 1966).

This style of parenting has received perhaps the same negative review by the public as authoritarian approaches. Children raised by permissive parents are seen as spoiled, unruly, and inconsiderate of others' needs. This approach was popular during the late 1940s through the early 1970s (Bigner, 1972a). It gained popularity as a means that was thought to counteract the negative aspects of authoritarianism. It was promoted by many experts in childrearing including Sigmund Freud, whose theory of personality development was widely adopted in the United States (Bigner, 1989). Research has found, however, that this form of parenting can lead to some problematic outcomes. Children of permissive parents are reported to lack self-control and to be impulsive (Dixon, 2003).

The **rejecting-neglecting parenting style** is the saddest of the parenting styles. With this parenting style, parents are low in both structure and warmth. Children with rejecting-neglecting parents are likely to be aggressive and suffer academic failure (Dixon, 2003).

The **authoritative parenting style** is a compromise between authoritarian and permissive approaches and is seen as the best parenting style for optimal developmental outcomes. With this parenting style, both structure and warmth are high. The authoritative-oriented style emphasizes ways to help children in becoming more autonomous as they grow older. Children are allowed a reasonable degree of latitude in their behavior but are not completely restricted by their parents' authority. When parents enforce limits, they typically resort to whatever lies within their grasp. They use a variety of methods to achieve control over their children's behavior. These may include reasoning, using overt power, or shaping desired behavior by using positive reinforcement.

Limits are used with children but they are labeled as reasonable in what is expected of children. Age of the child often is used in deciding the reasonableness of limits. Baumrind (1966) describes this type of parenting style as when the adult "encourages verbal give and take, sharing with a child the reasoning behind a policy, and soliciting his objections when he refuses to conform."

The benefits of having parents that use an authoritative parenting style are numerous (e.g., Amato & Fowler, 2002; Aunola, Stattin & Nurmi, 2000). For example, children with authoritative parents typically have high academic achievement. They also tend to be self-reliant and responsible.

Rejecting-neglecting parenting style

Parents that display little affection or discipline.

Authoritative parenting style

Parents that display both affection and discipline.

Learning to Be a Sibling

There is a cultural belief that the role and status of children within a family system should be separate from those of adults. This separation frequently is maintained by social power in the relationship between parents and children. Most families establish boundaries and patterns that maintain distance between children's and adults' worlds. A major family developmental task of young children is to learn the sibling roles of a brother or sister.

Being a brother or sister is an important relationship pattern in a family system. The significance of this relationship to individuals often lasts a lifetime (Goetting, 1986; Parke & Buriel, 1998). This relationship may provide many opportunities for learning social skills not available through other means. Researchers also believe that what children learn within their sibling relationships generalizes to interactions with others outside their family system.

Children learn what it means to be a brother or sister through interactions and from instruction provided by parents. The emergence of this role between children creates another microenvironment within a family system. This microenvironment is analogous to other relationship patterns in a family system. Thus, by the end of this family stage, there are at least three distinct microenvironments within a family system. These are based on the relationship between (1) the adults as marriage partners, (2) each adult and each child (the parent-child relationship), and (3) each child and his or her sibling. Each microenvironment is distinct but an integral part of a family system. There are rules that govern the conduct of a sibling relationship, and consequences outline infractions.

Birth order

The order in which children are born in a family.

A hierarchy becomes established in sibling relationships based on who holds the greatest social power. This is usually determined by **birth order**, or whether a child is the first, second, or last-born child. Beginning at this stage, siblings establish social positions based

A hierarchy is established within a sibling relationship. This is usually determined by birth order.

on their order of birth in a family. Parents may contribute to this hierarchy by consciously or unconsciously treating children differently (Sutton-Smith & Rosenberg, 1970). For instance, the oldest child may be assigned more responsibilities than the youngest child.

Researchers have conducted many studies about birth order effects on children's personality development (Goetting, 1986). Researchers consistently find that distinctive personality traits are associated with each birth order position of children in a family system (e.g., Herrera et al. 2003; Sulloway, 2005; Sutton-Smith & Rosenberg, 1970). For example, first-borns are more achievement-oriented and show more responsible behavior traits than later-born children. Middle-born children are found to have lower self-esteem than other children. Last-born children are noted to have charming natures and more advanced social skills than other siblings.

Birth order, however, plays a different role in the relationship between siblings than in individual personality development. Children who have brothers or sisters learn how family relationships are based on social power (Bigner, 1974a,b; Koch, 1956). First-born preschoolers learn to use high-power tactics to achieve social goals with younger siblings. These tactics typically include bossing, making verbal threats, using physical force, and so on. Younger children are not completely at the mercy of an older sibling, however. These children learn to manipulate situations in their favor with other power tactics. These may include sulking, teasing, tattling, harassing, and using verbal or physical aggression. By observing their older sibling, young preschoolers learn how age operates as a factor in social power. Greater age (and implicitly greater experience) is recognized as giving people more social power in relationships.

This knowledge about social power also is used to learn the patterns and boundaries that regulate family sex-roles (Bigner, 1972b; Bigner & Jacobsen, 1980; Koch, 1956). An older sibling frequently serves as a model of behavior for younger siblings. Siblings attribute greater social power to brothers. Sisters are characterized as facilitating social interactions, whereas brothers are noted to be socially disruptive. Sex-role behaviors also are modeled by siblings for each other. Cross-sex and same-sex sibling arrangements facilitate learning and understanding of sex-appropriate behaviors by children.

Having an older sibling helps a preschooler acquire initial meanings and interpretations of family roles. This is seen in preschoolers' descriptions of a "good" or "bad" sibling (Bigner & Jacobsen, 1980). Second-born children use phrases that describe a "good" sibling in positive terms and a "bad" sibling in negative ones. For example, these children describe a "good" brother as someone who helps with chores, plays with the younger sibling, and does not tattle to parents. A "bad" brother is bossy, a pest, uncooperative, and a nuisance in play activities. They describe a "good" sister as nice, loving, and helpful. A "bad" sister destroys toys, talks too much, and doesn't clean up her messes.

Brothers and sisters, then, serve various social functions for individuals. These initial ideas may equip children with a social-psychological template. This serves as a guide for regulating a significant aspect of a family system in which the relationships between children are the principle focus. It also may guide interaction patterns with others from outside the family system (Parke & Buriel, 1998).

THE OUTSIDE WORLD

Friendship and Peers

During early childhood, peer interaction increases in frequency and becomes more multi-faceted (Rubin, Bukowski & Parker, 1998). Play is the main domain in which peer interactions have been researched. In general, play during the preschool years provides young children with a venue in which to learn about social roles and rules. Peer relationships during the preschool years are also characterized by increased prosocial interactions and increased verbal exchanges.

Friendships also begin to emerge during the preschool years. There are developmental changes in how people perceive friendship. Early in childhood, friends are often referred to as momentary playmates (Selman, 1981). Although the title doesn't sound promising, preschool children do treat friends differently from nonfriends (Rubin, Buikowski & Parker, 1998). The focus of the friendship is upon physical objects or activities. Little thought is given to sharing thoughts or feelings. Additionally, children usually choose friends that are similar in physical appearance and behavioral tendencies. This stage in friendship perception is referred to as stage zero, or **momentary playmate**s. In Chapter 5, we will learn about stages one through three in friendship perception development.

Momentary playmates

Temporary playmates, typically because they happen to be in the same physical location.

The Electronic World

The National Research Council and Institute of Medicine (2000) states that "today's children spend more time with media (e.g., television, VCRs, CD players, game systems, computers, among others) than any generation before them" (p. 221). It is estimated that children between the ages of two and four watch an average of three to four hours of television everyday. Even more disturbing is that many parents use the television as an electronic babysitter, leaving young children to watch it alone.

Television provides a medium in which observational learning can occur (Ruble & Martin, 1998). Although some programming, such as *Sesame Street*, may help children learn pre-academic skills, other programming can expose children to harmful images and information. For example, many shows geared toward young children expose children to gender stereotypes. Additionally, children exposed to violence on television tend to behave more aggressively (Attar et al., 1994). Hence, television consumption, along with other media use, should be carefully monitored by caregivers.

Preschool

The benefit of preschool is an area of research that has received a lot of attention lately. Would it be worth the cost to our taxpayers to fund public preschool? It appears that most research says yes, at least for children living in poverty. It appears that the potential bene-fits of preschool outweigh the costs (Barnett & Hustedt, 2003; Bracey & Stellar, 2003).

Preschool education is correlated with better school readiness for kindergarten, better reading and math skills, higher graduation rates from high school, higher college atten-dance, and lower delinquency rates (e.g., Bracey & Stellar, 2003). However, to achieve these outcomes a preschool must be of high quality. A high quality preschool should start at age three, have small class sizes and highly qualified teachers, have involved and sup-portive parents, and have a strong curriculum. Additionally, preschool programs should promote social skills, positive attitudes toward learning, emotional well-being, mental health, and physical health (Stipek, 2006).

Pause and Process:

1. Describe the four parenting styles discussed in this chapter and the developmental outcomes associated with each.

2. How can sibling relationships impact development?

PSYCHOSOCIAL DEVELOPMENT

Developing a Sense of Initiative

30. Describe psychoso-cial development dur-ing early childhood.

Attitude of initiative

A feeling of confidence.

According to Erikson's theory of psychosocial development, many social changes occur during early childhood. These changes relate to the shift in psychosocial focus that takes place at this time of life. In early childhood, an individual's challenge is to develop a healthy *sense of initiative* versus an unhealthy *sense of guilt*. This attitude represents children's further adaptation to their now-enlarging world of experiences and people and reflects their self-confidence in their abilities and powers. The motivation of children this age is to master whatever they encounter—whether that is relationships, objects, or activities.

The **attitude of initiative** translates behaviorally into a focus on action. The curiosity of young children shows an initiative orientation to life. They explore, ask questions, and are constantly active. Initiative is boosted by the attitude of personal autonomy a child acquired during the previous stage of psychosocial development. Now the pervasive psy-chological attitude of "I can!" fully emerges.

Young children's behavior becomes directed toward what Erikson termed "making and making like." This behavioral theme shows up in children's awareness of social roles. Their interest centers on learning the patterns within their family system that regulate behaviors. The circle of significant others now widens to include the entire family group, rather than just the child's parents. These people have a great impact on whether a child learns the healthy or unhealthy attitude for this stage.

If the psychosocial focus becomes centered on guilt rather than initiative, there will be an inhibition of action. Guilt differs from shame, the unhealthy attitude that may have flourished in late infancy. **Shame** is the feeling that one's inner self is exposed as being flawed in some manner. This results in loss of self-esteem. **Guilt** focuses on the pervasive negative aspects of one's behavior. Essentially, guilt is the feeling that one's actions are somehow wrong or bad. This "bad" behavior adds further proof to the conviction that one's inner self is indeed shameful (Burns, 1980/1989).

Shame

The feeling that one's inner self is exposed as being flawed in some manner.

Guilt

Feeling shame and remorse.

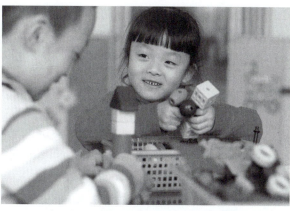

An attitude of initiative is enforced when children learn that their behavior is appropriate.

In Erikson's framework, then, young children develop the attitude of initiative when they learn that their behavior is appropriate. This makes them believe that their inner self is good. They acquire the attitude of guilt when they learn that their behavior is inappropriate. In that case, they perceive their inner self as bad.

These lessons about behavior and self-concept originate from parents, family members, and other caregivers (Erikson, 1950). The unhealthy, inhibiting attitude of feeling guilty about oneself and one's behavior is acquired in several ways. For instance, parents commonly scold children this age when their behavior exceeds established limits. This is not necessarily harmful. Children this age need to know when they have crossed a parentally established boundary or violated a family rule. However, the feeling of guilt is promoted when parents confuse the child's behavior with his or her inner character. If a parent tells a young child *"You're* absolutely the most rotten kid in the world when you hit your brother!" it is only logical for that child to fuse his act with his self-image. When an adult makes this type of negative evaluation, a young child may conclude, "*I* am bad *because* I act this way."

The attitude of guilt becomes deeply ingrained when young children consistently receive negative reinforcement or punishment from adults. This can happen simply because they are behaving with initiative. Parents who seek to restrain their children's active behavior by constantly scolding them for it can encourage guilt rather than initiative. Guilt tends to inhibit learning the value of taking calculated risks, inquisitiveness, and other valuable traits. A child who acquires an attitude of guilt may be hindered in developing to his or her fullest potential in later stages of the life span.

Pause and Process:

1. Why is an attitude of initiative important for optimal development?

2. What is the difference between guilt and shame? Give an example of each.

SUMMARY

1. Growth rates slow during early childhood compared to infancy, and increases in body length and weight are less dramatic. There are characteristic changes in body proportions and appearance. As body fat diminishes, the child's body becomes leaner in appearance.

2. The brain and central nervous system experience the fastest rate of growth among the major body systems in early childhood. The process of myelination of neural tissue accounts for the many advanced abilities observed in young children. Other significant changes include continued hemisphere specialization and hand preference.

3. Muscle and bone growth account for much of the weight gains observed in early childhood. The process of bone ossification continues during this time as well. The primary set of teeth has already erupted by the beginning of this period. Adequate dental care is necessary to maintain their health and that of the developing permanent teeth within the gums.

4. Refinements continue to occur in vision and hearing abilities in early childhood. Advances in motor skills are manifested in the high energy and activity levels of children this age. Refinements also occur in gross motor and fine motor skills. These refinements are attributed to both maturation and environmental influences.

5. Maintaining adequate nutrition for preschool-age children is difficult because they often have a poor appetite and strange, nonnutritious, food preferences. Offering small portions of food and seeing that snacks are nutritious will help young children to eat healthy. Obesity is also on the rise in early childhood and parents should help instill good eating and exercise habits in their children.

6. Understanding of illness during early childhood is limited. During this phase of the life span, they are in the first two stages of understanding illness: phenomenism and contagion. Understanding of illness is dependent upon cognitive development.

7. Most potentially fatal illnesses among young children have been eliminated by immunization in the United States. Less serious illnesses are still common, especially upper respiratory diseases. Mental health is good for the majority of children. However, up to 20 percent of children suffer from a mental disorder. Accidents are the leading cause of death among young children. The majority of these deaths involve a motor vehicle or happen in the home. Adequate supervision may prevent most of these injuries and deaths.

8. The preoperational stage of cognitive development is experienced during early childhood. Cognitive skills are focused on internalizing the environment by an increasing use of mental imagery. Thought during this time of the life span is characterized as inflexible, egocentric, and centered. Children make decisions based on appearances rather than on reality. Preschoolers also have difficulty understanding the principles of conservation and reversibility. Classification skills begin to emerge, as well as precausal thinking, in the later part of this stage. Young children are beginning to master learning skills and to develop strategies for using their memories.

9. Information-processing skills increase during early childhood. Memory strategies improve and early academic skills emerge. The degree to which children have metacognitive skills in early childhood is still open to debate. Vygotsky's social-historical theory and theory of mind are other cognitive theories discussed in the chapter.

10. Language serves several functions. One function is to facilitate social interactions. Conversational skills begin to improve during early childhood. Private

speech is often observed in preschoolers, which will eventually become internalized as thought. Three communicative disorders that may emerge during early childhood are voice disorders, fluency disorders, and articulation disorders.

11. Socialization into appropriate behavioral patterns begins in earnest during early childhood. Parents and other caregivers initiate expectations for behavior, attitudes, and values they wish children to acquire to become effectively functioning future adults. Young children respond best to this instruction when they are reinforced positively in acquiring these behaviors and when adults demonstrate such behaviors for children to model and imitate. Most families in the United States expect children to learn to use prosocial behaviors in interactions such as sharing and being kind; to control their impulses to act aggressively; and to learn to cope with fears and anxieties. These behaviors assist the young child to become an effectively functioning member of the family and society.

12. Young children use play as a tool for learning many important socialization experiences. A developmental sequence is observed in the nature of play activities during early childhood. Play changes from unoccupied and solitary activities that dominate in infancy to associative and cooperative activities that involve more complex social interactions as children get older. Two other types of play are popular among young children: dramatic and rough-and-tumble play. Both involve refinements in social and mental abilities.

13. Parents evolve a parenting style when their oldest child enters this stage. Four styles are commonly found: authoritarian, permissive, rejecting-neglecting, and authoritative. The authoritative parenting style is associated with the best developmental outcomes in children. This style is high in both structure and warmth.

14. Young children may experience the family developmental task of learning to be a sibling. Sibling relationships help children learn social skills that may be transferred to future peer relations. Birth order may influence sibling behavior and personality development.

15. Young children may acquire either a healthy attitude of initiative (a feeling that promotes self-confidence and learning) or an unhealthy attitude of guilt (a feeling that inhibits self-growth), according to Erikson. Either of these attitudes may be promoted by significant others in the family because they are the ones who teach young children about the appropriateness or inappropriateness of their behavior.

SELF-QUIZ

1. What factors impact height and weight increases during early childhood?
2. Describe bone growth during early childhood.
3. What is myelination and why is it important?
4. Define bilateral coordination.
5. Describe eating habits during the preschool years.
6. How prevalent is obesity in early childhood?
7. What are the potential consequences of obesity?
8. What causes obesity and how can we prevent it?
9. What is pediatric psychology?
10. Explain what ADHD is and how a child with the disorder behaves.
11. What stage of Piaget's stages of cognitive development are children in during early childhood?
12. What is egocentrism? How does it limit a child's thinking?
13. What is conservation?
14. Define transductive reasoning and provide an original example.

15. What two memory strategies are prevalent during early childhood?

16. Compare and contrast the overlapping and consecutive math strategies.

17. Why is a solid foundation in phonics important for reading ability?

18. Define theory of mind in your own words.

19. What are some of the functions of language?

20. What makes someone a good conversationalist?

21. What is the difference between sympathy and empathy?

22. Define aggression.

23. Describe early childhood fears.

24. Why is it important for children to learn to delay gratification?

25. What are some positive outcomes associated with secure attachment to parents?

26. What is gender identity?

27. Why is play important?

28. Describe each of Parten's types of play.

29. Explain what factors influence parenting strategies.

30. Describe psychosocial development during early childhood.

TERMS AND CONCEPTS

CHAPTER 5

Middle Childhood

OUTLINE

PHYSICAL DEVELOPMENT DURING MIDDLE CHILDHOOD

- Physical growth
- Motor development
- Health issues

COGNITIVE DEVELOPMENT DURING MIDDLE CHILDHOOD

- Piaget's theory and the concrete operational stage
- Information-processing during middle childhood
- Language development during middle childhood

SOCIAL AND EMOTIONAL DEVELOPMENT DURING MIDDLE CHILDHOOD

- Emotional development
- Self and others
- Psychosocial development

The tempo of developmental changes slows in the period of middle childhood. This stage begins at age six and continues through an individual's twelfth birthday. Motor development becomes more refined and sports become an increasing part of many children's lives during middle childhood. Significant changes occur in cognitive processes and socioemotional skills during this period.

PHYSICAL DEVELOPMENT DURING MIDDLE CHILDHOOD

> *LEARNING OBJECTIVES:*
>
> 1. *Describe physical growth during middle childhood*
> 2. *Explain motor skill development during middle childhood*
> 3. *Awareness of the unique health issues faced in middle childhood*

PHYSICAL GROWTH

Patterns of Growth

Middle childhood is a quiet period for physical growth and changes. The decline in growth rates noted in early childhood becomes even more evident. Growth in middle childhood is often considered the least dramatic and slowest of any stage in the life span.

An average six-year-old weighs about forty-five pounds and is about forty-five inches tall (WHO, 2006). At age ten, this child will weigh about sixty-nine pounds and stand about fifty-four inches tall. There is one exception to this general trend: the growth spurt that occurs about two years before the initiation of puberty. For many children, this prepubertal, or preadolescent, growth spurt takes place between the ages of ten and twelve (Williams & Stith, 1980). Children grow taller and heavier very quickly compared to earlier in middle childhood.

Girls and boys are about the same height during most of middle childhood though girls begin to weigh more than boys at about age nine. Because girls begin puberty earlier than boys, the **prepubertal growth spurt** also begins earlier for them. Thus girls are usually both taller and heavier than boys for about two years toward the end of middle childhood (Tanner, 1978, 1990).

Prepubertal growth spurt

A rapid increase in height and weight preceding puberty (at about age 10 to 12).

Other Body Changes

There is a genetic tendency for females to have a greater proportion of body fat to muscle than males. This difference becomes more noticeable during the latter part of middle childhood. In the first half of this stage, however, there are a few differences in the body contour and proportions of boys and girls.

Body configuration in middle childhood is distinguished by the loss of the prominent "pot belly" of early childhood. There is a general slimming of the body figure in both boys and girls during this time, though toward the end of this stage, girls start to develop a more rounded figure. This comes from the growth of adipose and muscle tissue associated with their approaching puberty.

There are great individual differences in height, weight, and body shape during this time. The differences are so great, in fact, that it is misleading to think in terms of averages for children this age. These physical differences create problems when adults equate them with social or emotional maturity. For example, a child who is much taller and heavier than others the same age might be expected by adults to also act much older (Ames, 1986; Tanner, 1990). This is an example of adult thinking based on appearances instead of reality.

Body configuration and physical changes strongly affect a child's acceptance by peers. School-age children typically select their friends on the bases of external appearance and physical competence (Hartup, 1983; Rubin, Bukowski & Parker, 1998; Williams & Stith, 1980). For example, boys often use such criteria as body size and shape, muscular strength, and athletic ability in choosing their friends. Girls use similar criteria, often, choosing those who are developmentally mature for their age as leaders of groups (Williams & Stith, 1980).

Bone Development

Bone growth and development in middle childhood involve changes in size and composition (Tanner, 1990; Williams & Stith, 1980). These changes are slow in comparison with the rate experienced in infancy and early childhood. Growth slows even more at the end of middle childhood because of the initiation of puberty.

Bones grow at their tips or ends, called epiphyses. This is the type of growth that produces changes in length. They also grow at their outermost edge, known as the

The body configuration changes in middle childhood. A general slimming of the body is seen in both boys and girls, and toward the end of this stage girls start to develop a rounded figure.

perisoteum. This type of growth produces changes in width. As children advance from infancy through adolescence, the soft cartilage at the epiphyses is replaced by hard bone tissue in a process called ossification.

As sex hormone levels increase to prepare the body for puberty, bone development slows. It eventually halts, after the completion of puberty in adolescence. This process occurs at different rates in the various bone groups. For example, most of the bone development of the extremities occurs during the latter part of middle childhood and early adolescence. This development is observed earlier in girls than in boys, in keeping with the earlier ages at which girls begin puberty.

Bone changes during middle childhood are also related to nutrition. Inadequate nutrition delays the ossification process and can even result in bone malformations. Certain physical activities also endanger bone development. For example, ballet dancing to excess and wearing poor-fitting shoes contribute to problems with foot bones.

Muscle Development

A school-age child's strength and greater endurance reflect changes in muscle development. Children this age are able to participate in more strenuous activities for longer periods than younger children. Because they usually enjoy this kind of physical activity, they become more physically fit (Krogman, 1980).

Greater physical activity, then, is associated with advances in muscle development during middle childhood. However, if the muscles of children this age are overused, there may be damage (Williams & Stith, 1980). A condition known as "Little League elbow," for example, can occur from the overuse of the connective tissues involved in throwing objects. Similarly, it is common for children this age to complain of muscular aches and pains around the joints because tendons are stretching to attach muscles to bones.

Changes are observed in the degree and types of physical activity children pursue during this period. The typical six-year-old has a high energy level that translates into much random activity. Children this age apparently move about for the sheer enjoyment of moving. By age twelve, there is less random movement and more control over the body. These and other social and mental changes permit more graceful and coordinated movements (Williams & Stith, 1980).

Physical fitness has many benefits for school-age children. It provides opportunities for social experiences with peers (Williams & Stith, 1980). It stimulates bone growth and ossification (Bailey, 1977). It also seems to improve academic performance (Bailey, 1977) and contributes to a healthy self-concept (Ferguson et al., 1989).

Spotlight

3. What changes occur in dentition during this time?

Dentition

The shedding of one set of teeth and the eruption of another.

Teeth

Dentition is one of the most apparent physical changes of middle childhood. This is the process of shedding existing teeth and erupting new ones. The sixteen primary, or deciduous, teeth that erupted during infancy are lost during the school-age years and twenty-eight permanent teeth erupt to replace them. The first permanent teeth erupt

Bilateral coordination

The cooperative, integrated use of both sides of the body in performing motor acts.

Strength

The ability to exert force.

Flexibility

The freedom to bend or move the body in various directions.

around age six or seven. These are the molars. They do not replace deciduous teeth (there are no molars in the deciduous set), but signal that these are about to be shed. Except for the sets of third molars, or "wisdom teeth", which appear in adolescence or early adulthood, a child should have a complete set of permanent teeth by the end of middle childhood.

Many parents use the folklore of the Tooth Fairy to help children cope with the fears and anxieties of losing teeth. This imaginary figure visits children while they sleep. She collects the lost tooth, which has been placed underneath a pillow, and replaces it with some reward, such as a small amount of money or a special treat. Losing teeth in the first half of middle childhood is often a status symbol for children. It communicates their more mature stature to friends and family. The fanfare associated with losing teeth is diminished by the end of this stage. It is looked upon more as a painful nuisance than a status symbol.

Pause and Process:

1. What is the prepubertal growth spurt?

2. How do bones and muscles develop during middle childhood?

MOTOR DEVELOPMENT

Impulsion

The rate at which body movement begins from a stationary position.

Speed

The rate of movement once the body is in action.

Precision

The dexterity and accuracy of movements.

Coordination

The ability to use various muscle groups together to accomplish specific actions.

Muscular ability and coordination improve considerably during middle childhood. Although physical changes slow down, these changes are important because they lead to more advanced motor skills. School-age children become more adept at activities requiring **bilateral coordination**. This is the ability to use sets of muscles on both sides of the body to perform complex physical acts. Bilateral coordination is observed especially in activities that involve large muscle groups such as those in the arms, legs, and back. The increasing maturation of these muscle groups help children to function more efficiently. The complex skills required for bike riding, for example, are now more easily accomplished.

Changes in motor skills during middle childhood are characterized by steady improvements in coordination and performance. Improvements are particularly noticeable in the following motor skills (Cratty, 1986; Smoll &Schutz, 1990; Williams & Stith, 1980): (1) **strength**, or the ability to exert force, with boys showing greater gripping ability than girls; (2) **flexibility**, or the freedom to bend or move the body in various directions, with girls showing greater flexibility than boys at the trunk, wrists, and legs; (3) **impulsion**, or the rate at which body movement begins from a stationary position, with all school-age children showing steady improvements in reaction time; (4) **speed**, or the rate of movement once the body is in action, with boys improving at the rate of one foot per second faster than girls each year during this stage; (5) **precision**, or dexterity and accuracy of movements, with girls showing greater advances than boys; (6) **coordination**, or the ability to use various muscle groups together to accomplish specific actions (this

Muscular ability and coordination improves during this stage. Riding a bike is now more easily accomplished.

Balance

The ability to maintain equilibrium and stability.

Rhythm

Regular body movements.

Competence

An individual's skills, abilities, and proficiency within a specific domain, such as school, relationships, or sports.

Confidence

Having certainty in one's ability.

Connections

An individual's relationships with others and feelings as though one belongs.

Character

Having a moral compass and integrity.

Caring

Having empathy and concern for others.

factor is associated with precision to produce advances in impulsion); (7) **balance**, or the ability to maintain equilibrium and stability in performing the kind of motor acts typical at this stage (e.g., skating), with girls showing improvements earlier than boys; (8) **rhythm**, or regular body movements, with girls exceeding boys throughout this stage, especially in rhythmic movements involving the feet (e.g., dancing).

It is easy to observe common motor skills in children. Common motor skills that involve the upper body region include printing and writing, playing musical instruments, performing household chores, and using tools. Common motor skills that involve the lower body region include running, skipping, and jumping. Common motor skills that involve the entire body include skating, certain sports, swimming, and bicycle riding. The particular motor abilities and skills that children are expected to acquire in middle childhood generally involve gross- and fine-motor skills that are more complex than those of early childhood.

Sports

A sport can be described as "structured activities with certain rules of engagement" (Theokas, 2009). Although individual sports vary in nature, most provide an opportunity to learn both skills specific to that sport, as well as life skills that can be applied to everyday life (Baron, 2007). Hence, it is widely thought that sport participation can promote healthy development in children and adolescents.

Optimal development can be conceptualized within five categories referred to as the five Cs: **competence**, **confidence**, **connections**, **character**, and **caring** (Lerner et al., 2005; Lerner, Fisher & Weinberg, 2000; Linver, Roth & Brooks-Gunn, 2009). Competence can be described as an individual's skills, abilities, and proficiency within a specific domain, such as school, relationships, or sports. Confidence can be described as having certainty in one's ability. Connections involve an individual's relationships with others and feeling as though one belongs. Character can be thought of as having a moral compass and integrity. Caring can be conceptualized as having empathy and concern for others. Sports can help develop these five domains of healthy development through skill development, adult mentorship, modeling of good sportsmanship, and belonging to a team.

Although sport participation has been associated with positive developmental outcomes, there is also some research that shows that there can be a negative side to sport participation (Gaudreau, Amiot & Vallerand, 2009; Scanlan, 1984; Scanlan, Babkes & Scanlan, 2005). Parents and coaches can place children under extreme stress to perform well. Additionally, injuries, burnout, and delinquency can sometimes plague sport participants.

Despite these potential negative outcomes, sport participation is capable of promoting healthy development if the program is of good quality, the parents and coach are supportive, the coach structures the activity well and provides appropriate praise and direction, and the individual is motivated (Danish, Taylor & Faxio, 2003; Gano-Overway et al., 2009). Further, structured activities besides sports, such as school clubs or religious groups, can offer the same psychological benefits as sport participation. One recent study found that children and adolescents who participated in sports along with other activities achieve better outcomes than children and adolescents who participated only in sports (Linver, Roth & Brooks-Gunn, 2009). Hence, engaging in a broad range of activities appears to offer the best context for development.

Pause and Process:

1. What improvements in motor development are seen during middle childhood?

2. What are the five Cs to healthy development and how are they influenced by sport participation?

HEALTH ISSUES

Nutritional Needs

Nutrition is important to physical well-being in middle childhood. Most of the physical changes we have described so far are affected by nutrition. Children's eating habits and appetites improve as they take up the more demanding physical activities of middle childhood. As their appetites sharpen, their food intake increases. Although most children maintain a healthy weight, obesity is increasing in school-age children (CDC, 2009). Currently, 17 percent of school-age children are considered obese.

Television advertising affects school-age children's nutrition because children pressure parents to buy the products they see on television (Condry, Bence & Scheibe, 1988; Taras et al., 1989). Children this age watch a lot of television. Advertisers design commercials that appeal to children and influence food choices. The food products designed to appeal to children are

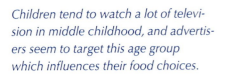

Children tend to watch a lot of television in middle childhood, and advertisers seem to target this age group which influences their food choices.

usually high in sugar, fat, and salt content. Many are snacks that children will eat while watching television. Few offer much true nutrition. Once again, it is imperative for parents to educate their children about proper nutrition and exercise, and to limit the couch time.

Illness, Disorders, and Other Concerns

In Chapter 4, we learned about Bibace and Walsh's (1979, 1980, and 1981) first two stages for understanding illness: phenomenism and contagion. During middle childhood, stages three and four predominate children's thinking. Stage three is called contamination. Contamination can be described as understanding illness as "caused by people, objects, or actions that are external to the child, and it is transmitted by physical contact or harmful action" (Bearison, 1998, p. 679). Although children now have some understanding that their behavior can directly influence whether they get ill or not, they still lack an understanding of the role of bacteria or viruses.

Stage four is called internalization. With internalization thinking, children understand that actions such as breathing in a virus or ingesting food with salmonella can lead to illness. It goes a step beyond contamination thinking because the cause of the illness is seen as internalized inside one's body (Bearison, 1998).

Children typically progress through these two stages during the middle childhood years. Around 60 percent of children display contamination thinking at the age of seven (Bearison, 1998). By the age of eleven, approximately 50 percent of children display internalization thinking. We will discuss the final two stages of understanding illness in Chapter 6.

Physical Illness During Middle Childhood

School-age children generally enjoy better health than preschoolers. Most of the communicable diseases they get are not serious, with the common cold and upper respiratory conditions being most common (Avery, 1989; Starfield et al., 1984). These diseases are spread by contact with other children at school. Immunizations protect most school-age children against the more serious infectious diseases.

Children can also get some infectious diseases because they have not been immunized against them or because no effective vaccine is available. They can also get other minor disorders that affect well-being and school attendance, such as allergies, asthma, or lice.

Accidents are of serious concern during the school-age years, and accidents are the leading cause of death for this age group (Federal Interagency Forum on Child and Family Statistics, 2008; Health United States, 2008). Boys have far more accidents than girls at each stage of development in childhood and adolescence. Accidents can be prevented by adequate supervision and safety restrictions on activities. School-age children are more capable of self-direction than preschoolers, but their judgment is far from adultlike. They still need some supervision.

Mental Health During Middle Childhood

As discussed in Chapter 4, mental health problems plague one in every five children and adolescents (SAMHSA, 2003). Further, one in every ten children suffers from a serious emotional disturbance. Table 5-1 describes some of the mental disorders experienced during childhood (National Institutes of Health, 1997, 1999; SAMHSA, 2003; U.S. Department of Health and Human Services, 1999).

Oppositional defiant disorder (ODD) is a disorder that may lead to conduct disorder if left untreated (AACAP, 1999). ODD is a pattern of behavior in which a child is uncooperative and hostile with authority figures. This behavior is so extreme that it interferes with the child's ability to function in his or her daily life. It is estimated that up to 15 percent of all school-age children struggle with ODD. Its cause is unknown, although it is

Oppositional defiant disorder

A mental disorder characterized by a pattern of disobedience, hostility, and deviant behavior.

TABLE 5-1	DISORDERS EXPERIENCED DURING CHILDHOOD	
DISORDER	**PREVALENCE**	**DESCRIPTION**
Anxiety disorders	13 out of every 100 children & adolescents	Includes phobias, generalized anxiety disorder, obsessive-compulsive disorder, and post-traumatic stress disorder
Severe depression	2 out of every 100 children	Includes negative emotions and thoughts, lack of motivation, and a general sense of ill-being
Attention deficit/hyperactivity disorder	5 out of every 100 children	Includes an inability to sit still, impulsivity, and distractibility
Schizophrenia	5 out of every 1,000 children	Includes delusions, hallucinations, and inappropriate emotions
Conduct disorder	Estimates range from 1 to 4 out of every 100 children and adolescents	Externalizing behavior including verbal assaults, physical aggression, impulsivity, and destructiveness

speculated that both biological and environmental factors influence its onset. ODD is often co-morbid with other mental disorders, such as ADHD, learning disabilities, anxiety disorders, and mood disorders. ODD is often treated with therapy and parent training. Most children show improvement when parents learn and utilize positive parenting techniques.

ODD may lead to conduct disorder.

Promoting Wellness

It is important to continue to monitor children during middle childhood. Many accidents and injuries can be prevented by adult supervision. Additionally, proper nutrition and exercise can promote wellness and prevent obesity. Regular doctor and dental exams can further promote wellness.

Pause and Process:

1. How do children understand illness during middle childhood?

2. What is oppositional defiant disorder and how can it be treated?

COGNITIVE DEVELOPMENT DURING MIDDLE CHILDHOOD

LEARNING OBJECTIVES:

1. *Characterize the concrete operational stage of cognitive development*
2. *Describe information-processing during middle childhood*
3. *Explain language development during middle childhood*

Although physical changes slow down during middle childhood, cognitive and social changes quicken. The cognitive changes are as significant as the social changes experienced in middle childhood. A new stage of thinking emerges as children experience the formal education process. Piaget (1967) refers to this as the period of **concrete operations**. They now base decisions more on fact and logic as they learn to reason. Refinements of mental abilities allow for more advanced functioning. Information-processing skills and language skills also continue to develop during middle childhood.

PIAGET'S COGNITIVE DEVELOPMENTAL THEORY AND THE CONCRETE OPERATIONAL STAGE

Concrete operations

The stage of cognitive development experienced in middle childhood in which thought becomes more logical and based on immediate physical realities and mental imagery abilities become more refined.

School-age children become more sophisticated in their thought processes. Their advanced cognition is obvious when their ways of thinking are contrasted with those of preschoolers. The trend is toward greater use of logic and reasoning based on advanced information-processing skills (Miller, 1986).

Before they enter the stage of cognition that follows preoperational thought, children experience what Piaget (1967) termed the **5-to-7 shift**. This is a transition to what he called prelogical thought. Between five and seven years of age, children use intuition to guess the answers to problems. They do not fully understand the reasoning process behind a solution.

At about age seven or eight, children enter the stage of cognition known as concrete operations. Concrete means children's understanding of their environment is limited to the present and to immediate physical realities. Because of these thought limitations, school-age children have problems with the concepts of past and future. Abstract hypothetical problems are difficult for them to understand and solve.

5-to-7 shift

A transition period in cognitive development between the pre-operational and concrete operations stages; thinking is based more on intuition than logic.

One of the major cognitive accomplishments in middle childhood is the increasing ability to use mental imagery to solve problems. As they acquire this ability, school-age children begin to perform complex operations. These include basic mathematical operations, such as addition, subtraction, multiplication, and division, and classification and grouping. Declining egocentrism throughout this period aids cognitive growth. These advances in cognition are outlined here.

CHARACTERISTICS OF CONCRETE OPERATIONAL THOUGHT

Classification

Decentering

The cognitive ability that allows a school-age child to attend to more than one aspect simultaneously in performing classification operations.

An early aspect of a school-age child's application of operations is the ability to classify objects and events. Children become increasingly adept at employing a mental process known as **decentering**, perhaps because the egocentrism so noticeable in early childhood is weakening (Harter, 1983). Decentering allows a child to attend to more than one detail of an object or event simultaneously. It shows a flexible approach to reasoning.

Preschoolers have difficulty with classification problems because they center on only one attribute of an object or event at a time. They usually sort objects according to their color.

School-age children are able to apply more specific classification schemes to sorting tasks. For example, they recognize that trucks have some of the same attributes as other gasoline-powered vehicles. But they also know that trucks have special features that allow them to perform certain functions other gasoline-powered vehicles cannot do. They can easily distinguish a cow from other four legged animals with tails. They now may group animals according to whether they provide milk or meat. This ability to decenter—to handle several aspects of something simultaneously—allows school-age children to lead more complex mental lives.

Children this age come to enjoy classification problems. They form collections of objects ranging from stamps and coins to bottle caps, mugs, dolls, rocks, seashells, and sport cards. Initially, collections are general and may appear to be worthless junk. A six-year-old is prone to collect anything and everything. However, collections become more specialized and valuable as children's mental operations grow more sophisticated.

Class Inclusion

Class inclusion

A cognitive ability of middle childhood that allows a child to consider the whole as well as its parts in classification operations.

An additional refinement in classification problem solving during middle childhood is known as **class inclusion**. This is the ability to consider simultaneously the whole as well as the parts in grouping objects (Piaget, 1952a). Preschool children cannot do this. They become confused if they are asked, for example, to separate out all the brown wooden beads from an assortment—an assignment school-age children can handle with ease. Preschoolers cannot recognize larger classes of objects such as wooden in this example. They cannot understand that a bead can have both color and texture attributes and be grouped accordingly.

Reversibility

Reversibility

The cognitive ability of school-age children to understand that certain operations can occur in their reverse order (e.g., subtraction is the reverse of addition).

Grasping the concept of **reversibility** allows a child to understand classification operations like class inclusion problems and subtraction. School-age children are able to reverse several classification schemes to sort objects by larger, more inclusive classes. They comprehend that subtraction is the reverse of addition. Their ability to decenter enables them to understand other phenomena—for example, that the whole can be divided into parts and reconstructed into a whole again. Children this age can see how sunlight can be split into its component colors by a prism and then restored to sunlight

Conservation

Horizontal decalage

Unevenness in applying an understanding of conservation problems across different contexts.

In contrast to preschoolers, school-age children understand the idea of conservation (Piaget & Inhelder, 1969). However, they apply it unevenly in the early part of this stage. This unevenness of application is known as **horizontal decalage** (Piaget, 1952b). For example, a school-age child may understand conservation of volume but find conservation of number confusing. By the end of middle childhood, most children have resolved the horizontal decalage difficulty.

Seriation

Seriation is an extension of classification problems that school-age children easily accomplish (Wadsworth, 1971, 2004). This is the ability to scale objects according to various dimensions, such as height or weight. It requires an understanding of the concepts of greater than (>) and less than (<). For example, school-age children can easily solve this problem:

Doll A is taller than (>) Doll B; Doll B is taller than (>) Doll C. Is Doll A taller than (>) or shorter than (<) Doll C?

Understanding Time

Time is an important concept in our culture. Americans' lives tend to be oriented around schedules. Therefore, knowing how to tell time and being familiar with other concepts involving time (days of the week, months of the year) are important skills (Taylor, 1989). Middle-class children have an advantage over poorer children here because clocks are important equipment in middle-class homes. Children from poorer families often have a more difficult time adjusting to a school schedule because a strong sense of time is not emphasized in their households.

Preschoolers are poor judges of time, especially of the duration between events (Levin, 1982; Piaget 1969). Judgment of time spans and knowledge of calendar events improve in middle childhood (Levin, Wilkening & Dembo, 1984). School-age children have a much better grasp of the idea of the future. They can state accurately what day will occur three days from now, for example (Friedman, 1986). However, the ability to work backward in time and an accurate understanding of the concept of past time are not acquired until late adolescence for most individuals.

Understanding the concept of time is an important skill to learn.

Cognitive Style

School-age children evolve a cognitive style that is distinct from that of preschoolers. As we have said, this style is less bound by the egocentrism that leads preschoolers to judge by appearances rather than reality. This is a major accomplishment in middle childhood that leads to higher-level mental functioning.

School-age children use elementary logic to infer reality from situations. This is demonstrated by their ability to solve some types of conservation problems. This mental accomplishment permits them to function effectively in the classroom.

The cognition of school-age children is still limited, however. Just as thinking in early childhood was bound by egocentrism, thinking in middle childhood is bound by cognitive distortions in reasoning. School-age children make many errors in logic as they attempt to understand how their world functions, why people act as they do, and so on.

Cognitive conceit

A characteristic of thought in middle childhood in which individuals perceive situations and people in black-and-white, all-or-nothing.

The all-or-nothing type of reasoning they use is called **cognitive conceit** (Elkind, 1976). It limits their understanding of the complexities of human behavior.

Problems of social cognition illustrate this limitation. School-age children eventually observe a teacher making a mistake. Because of cognitive conceit, they incorrectly conclude that the teacher cannot be trusted to provide correct information. If a teacher is not always right, they think, she must often be wrong. Similarly, a child may reason that because she can give the correct answers on several issues, she is an authority on all issues. This is a type of cognitive distortion that may continue throughout the life span, or it may become resolved at a later life-stage (Burns, 1989).

Pause and Process:

1. How is thinking in the concrete operational stage different from thinking in the preoperational stage?

2. Why may the development of reversibility and seriation be important for academic success during middle childhood?

INFORMATION PROCESSING IN MIDDLE CHILDHOOD

School-age children have many learning experiences, especially in the school system. Individuals are expected to acquire the basic skills our society considers essential for effective functioning during middle childhood. They are also expected to absorb much information about the world of people and things.

Some developmental researchers study the ways that children learn (Bransford, Brown & Cocking, 2000; Brown et al., 1983). This involves trying to understand how a child's mind perceives and processes information from the external world. These researchers have amended Piagetian and learning theory according to what is known about how computers process and logically handle information. However, information-processing researchers emphasize that a human brain is far more complex and sophisticated than any existing computer. Attention, memory, and problem solving are three areas addressed by information-processing research that will be discussed below. However, general developments in information processing seen in middle childhood include better strategies for problem solving or academic skills, increased capacity in working memory, faster information processing, more information processed automatically, and greater control of thinking (referred to as executive functioning in many research articles).

Attention

Compared to preschoolers, school-age children have a better understanding of attention (Flavell & Miller, 1998). They understand that attention is selective and requires processing. They are also able to distinguish between attention and comprehension.

Beyond understanding attention, school-age children possess better attention skills. It is difficult to process information and store it in memory without paying adequate attention. Young children have short attention spans, partly because they are easily distracted (Kaplan, 1990). School-age children show considerable improvement in this area (Flavell, 1985; Flavell & Miller, 1998). Their greater ability to differentiate their attention—that is, to determine the relevance of something—comes partially from instruction by parents and teachers (Small, 1990) and partially from brain development, including myelination.

To perform learning activities, school-age children show improvements in another important cognitive skill: **selective attention** (Enns & Girgus, 1985; Maccoby & Hagen, 1965). This involves tuning out distracting stimulations when performing a particular task. For example, second-grade children find it hard to concentrate on a task while music is playing (Higgins & Turnure, 1984). Sixth-grade children are not so bothered by music in performing the same task. Adolescents may be able to handle even more complex distractions.

Memory

The use of memory to process information has been intensively studied among children. Memory is critical to cognition. Recall allows individuals to compare information newly received with information gained from past experiences.

Researchers know that storage of information in the brain's memory occurs in three phases. First, information is temporarily stored in the **sensory register** (or sensory memory) as it is received from the external world (Hoving et al., 1978; Siegler, 1998). This storage is only for a very brief time, often for less than a second. This form of memory functions at adult levels by the age of five. Second, information is passed into **short-term memory** storage. It remains here for about one minute. It may then be processed into **long-term memory**, where it may remain indefinitely.

It is well recognized that memory in general improves significantly through middle childhood (Siegler, 1998; Williams & Stith, 1980). Memory improvement probably

Selective attention

A cognitive ability to tune out distracting stimulation while performing a task.

Sensory register

The first memory storage location where sensory information is stored in the brain before becoming short- or long-term memory.

Short-term memory

An initial memory storage location in the brain where information remains for about one minute before being erased or placed into long-term memory; recall of information, events, and so on that are relatively recent.

Long-term memory

The final memory location in the brain where information is stored indefinitely; recall of events in the distant past.

occurs for several reasons, including improvements in attention span, brain development, maturation, and strategies for processing information (Siegler, 1998; Wingfield & Byrnes, 1981). In any case, it is known that children discover that verbal strategies assist them to process information into memory (Flavell, Beach & Chinsky, 1966). Through trial-and-error, they find some strategies work better than others (Justice, 1985).

School-age children typically use repetition and rehearsal to place information into memory (Fabricius & Wellman, 1983). They also use chunking, or grouping into one category items that share some attribute. For example, a long list of American presidents may be remembered by grouping all whose last names begin with B, M, and S. Various other mnemonic devices are used by school-age children to help in memory storage. Learning to spell words in English is a challenge. There are many tried-and-true rules to negotiate the spelling irregularities of English. For example, children find this rhyme very helpful for spelling certain words: "i before e except after c, or when sounding like a as in neighbor and weigh."

Scripts

Scripts

An organized series of acts committed to memory (e.g., getting dressed, brushing the teeth).

Researchers have discovered that one reason school-age children become better at memory retrieval is because of improvements they experience in memory organization. One of the more notable organization methods is to develop **scripts**.

A script is formed out of a series of things that occur repeatedly. Frequently, these are routine events in one's daily life. For example, most people develop a repetitious way for brushing their teeth. Instead of intentionally selecting each step in the process every day, they form a "tooth-brushing script" and use it almost automatically. The steps in the process become unconscious—stored in long-term memory for repeated recall (Nelson & Gruendel, 1981; Slackman & Nelson, 1984).

Scripts help children with memory retrieval. An example is a "getting dressed script".

Many scripts are developed during middle childhood because of children's improved memory and more extensive experiences. These range from the mundane, such as "getting dressed scripts," to those that have social significance, such as "parenting scripts" and "spouse scripts." The latter scripts are formed through observation of adults in a family system and are not initiated by an individual until needed later in life. Because all scripts are based on learning, they may be modified and changed in any way at any point in the life span. Before changes can be made, however, a script must be dredged up from the unconscious (Harris & Harris, 1985; Hendrix, 1988; James & Jongeward, 1971).

Metacognition and Metamemory

Metacognition

The ability to be aware of and understand the changes occurring in one's own cognitive processes.

Metamemory

An awareness of the extent of one's memory.

Metacognition is the awareness of the extent of one's knowledge. In middle childhood, many individuals improve in metamemory as well as metacognition. **Metamemory** is the awareness of the extent of what is in one's memory. The degree to which children can comprehend their particular capacity of knowledge and memory has important implications for their academic performance (Holt, 1964; National Research Council, 2000).

School-age children who have high levels of metacognition and metamemory may express more misunderstanding about concepts than others. This is because they are more aware of the extent of their knowledge than children who have lower levels of such awareness. Because they know what information they lack, they understand how to go about getting that information. These children are better students than others. Researchers are discovering ways to help school-age children develop better metacognition and metamemory skills (Cross & Paris, 1988).

Intelligence

Multiple intelligences

A theory in which there are various domains or abilities in which a person can be intelligent.

Linguistic intelligence

Involves the mental abilities in the semantics, syntax, and overall expression of language.

Traditionally, intelligence is defined as "the ability to solve problems and to adapt and learn from experiences" (Santrock, 2008, p. 312). In this traditionalist view, intelligence is conceptualized as a general mental ability. However, not all psychologists or developmentalists conceptualize intelligence in the traditional way. Some view intelligence occurring with various mental abilities (Ferrari & Sternberg, 1998), and these more domain-specific abilities may or may not impact academic success or standardized testing success. Howard Gardner is one such theorist who has developed a theory of **multiple intelligences** (e.g., 1983, 1991 & 1998) or multiple abilities.

Gardner sees intelligence manifested as particular mental abilities (Ferrari & Sternberg, 1998; Gardner, 1993). In other words, you can be smart in different ways. Although his theory is always evolving, eight types of intelligences have been proposed. These types of intelligence are logical, linguistic, spatial, musical, bodily-kinesthetic, naturalistic, interpersonal, and intrapersonal (Bransford, Brown & Cocking, 2000; Hoerr, 2003). A type of intelligence focused upon existential or religious intelligence has also been tentatively proposed.

Linguistic, logical-mathematical, and spatial intelligences most closely resemble the abilities measured by traditional IQ tests. **Linguistic intelligence** involves mental abilities

Logical-mathematical intelligence

Involves mental abilities in pattern recognition, relationships, reasoning, and mathematical operations.

Spatial intelligence

Involves mental abilities in perception of objects and the ability to mentally transform and manipulate these objects.

Interpersonal intelligence

The mental ability to understand one's own emotional self.

Musical intelligence

The mental ability to understand the components of music, such as tone, melody, pitch, and rhythm.

in the semantics, syntax, and overall expression of language (Ferrari & Sternberg, 1998; Gardner, 1983, 1999; Hoerr, 2003; Kail, 2007). **Logical-mathematical intelligence** involves mental abilities in pattern recognition, relationships, reasoning, and mathematical operations. **Spatial intelligence** involves mental abilities in perception of objects and the ability to mentally transform and manipulate these objects.

Interpersonal and intrapersonal intelligences encompass communicative and emotional properties. **Interpersonal intelligence** involves having a really good theory of mind. People high in interpersonal intelligence understand others emotions, intentions, and motivations (Ferrari & Sternberg, 1998; Gardner, 1983, 1999; Hoerr, 2003; Kail, 2007). Additionally, people high in interpersonal intelligence understand how to function well in social relationships Intrapersonal intelligence involves the mental ability to understand one's own emotional self.

Musical, bodily-kinesthetic, and naturalistic intelligences encompass a variety of mental abilities. **Musical intelligence** involves the mental ability to understand the components of music, such as tone, melody, pitch, and rhythm (Ferrari & Sternberg, 1998; Gardner, 1983, 1999; Hoerr, 2003; Kail, 2007). It also involves understanding the ability of music to convey emotion and mood. **Bodily-kinesthetic intelligence** involves the mental ability to control one's body in a purposeful way. For example, dancers are able to tell a story and convey emotions through manipulating their body in dance. **Naturalist intelligence** involves the mental ability to recognize plant and animal life in the environment and the relationships and interconnections between these species. As mentioned above, Gardner has recently proposed the idea of an **existential intelligence**. This type of intelligence involves the mental ability to contemplate the purpose and meaning of life and issues surrounding death and what comes after death.

Traditionally, educational success has measured only a limited number of mental abilities. Further, teaching typically involves strategies that are geared toward a limited

Tone, melody, pitch, and rhythm are the components of music. Music intelligence involves the mental ability to understand these components.

Bodily-kinesthetic intelligence

The mental ability to control one's body in a purposeful way.

Naturalist intelligence

The mental ability to recognize plant and animal life in the environment and the relationships and interconnections between these species.

Existential intelligence

The mental ability to contemplate the purpose and meaning of life and issues surrounding death and what comes after death.

Codified

Math that is written.

18. What is meant by math being codified?

Inventive strategies

Making use of one's own knowledge and current strategies in answering a novel problem.

number of mental abilities. For the last fifteen years, there has been a push in the educational system to teach and assess using a multiple intelligences framework. Preliminary research seems to indicate that students taught using a nontraditional curriculum within the multiple intelligences framework allows students to score well on standardized tests (Hoerr, 2003).

Academic Skills

In the last chapter, we learned about some early academic skills acquired during the preschool years. Some mathematical strategies developed in early childhood include counting, use of fingers in counting, counting on from the higher addend, and the use of overlapping and consecutive strategies in division. Some language arts skills in early childhood include the ability to identify letters of the alphabet, beginning phonics, and early writing.

Mathematical Skills

You are probably not surprised that some basic academic skills are either acquired or further developed during middle childhood. Mathematics is one such area. School-age children are expected to master the basic operations of addition, subtraction, multiplication, and division. Although variations on counting were the predominant strategy for early childhood, more sophisticated skills emerge during middle childhood (Ginsburg, Klein & Starkey, 1998).

The math taught in school is **codified**. Codified can be defined as math that is written, systematically arranged, and guided by explicit rules (Ginsburg, Klein & Starkey, 1998). Such math cannot be learned through exploratory learning; instead it must be taught by formal instruction (sometimes called direct instruction). Once again, what mathematical knowledge is taught depends upon the culture.

As we learned in chapter four, counting strategies continue to evolve so that the early school-age child consistently adds on from the larger addend (Ginsburg, Klein & Starkey, 1998). However, through frequent drills, children eventually store basic number facts into long-term memory (e.g., they will learn that $8 - 5 = 3$ without having to do the counting each time). Drills are often useful in learning addition, subtraction, multiplication, and division facts. They can also be useful in learning conversion facts (e.g., converting inches to centimeters). However, a conceptual understanding should be the foundation upon which to drill.

Much of math is too complicated to be committed to memory via the drill method (Ginsburg, Klein & Starkey, 1998). For these areas of math, algorithms and invented strategies can be useful. An algorithm has been "developed and codified over the course of centuries, {and} produce correct results. When used properly, the algorithm always work" (Ginsburg, Klein & Starkey, 1998, p. 419). For example, $A2 + B2 = C2$ is an algorithm that will always work. **Inventive strategies** are different, however, from algorithms. Inventive strategies make use of one's knowledge and current strategies for help in answering novel problems. For example, a child may know that $5 + 5 = 10$. When faced with the problem $5 + 6 = ?$, she may choose to add $5 + 5$ (which she knows the answer to) and count up one, instead of counting up five from the number six. Exploiting the base 10 system is a very popular inventive strategy.

American children do poorly in these skills compared to children in other countries (Stigler, Lee & Stevenson, 1987). Newer instruction methods are based on what we know about how children in the concrete operations stage of cognitive development learn (Resnick, 1989). They stress cognitive processes rather than memorization and calculation skills. By the end of this period, children should understand fractions, decimals, pre-geometry and pre-algebra knowledge, and conversion between the decimal and standard systems of measurement.

Language Arts Skill

Reading also shows great development during middle childhood. It involves integration of perceptual, attention, and memory skills. Teachers consider many factors in reading instruction: for example, letter size, readability of text material, and the child's knowledge base (Athey, 1983; National Research Council, 2000). Most children enter the first grade knowing the alphabet; some may already know how to sound out words and read easy books. By the end of this period, children should be able to read most books with ease and fluency. When first learning to read, simply sounding out and identifying the words uses most of working memory. It takes time to be able to read and comprehend what one is reading. Reading instruction is based on teaching different reading skills, use of phonics, and different types of comprehension (Jones, 1986; National Research Council, 2000). Phonics is especially important for reading development. Also, the more a child is read to early in childhood, and the more they read independently and with others during middle childhood, the earlier a child is able to read efficiently and for knowledge.

Finally, writing develops by leaps and bounds during middle childhood. Writing also involves the integration of several cognitive skills. Like reading, it is used in many contexts of classroom learning. Classroom writing is less a communication device than a means of evaluating what children have learned. Early during the school-age years, children will often just list everything they have learned in response to an essay question with little organization or coherence. Across middle childhood, children learn to write with thesis statements, introductions, topic sentences, transitional sentences, sum-

At this age the skill of reading is greatly developed.

maries, coherence, and organization. Children also learn how to write informational reports, persuasive arguments, research reports, and other such formats during this time. Of course, these skills continue to be improved upon during adolescence and beyond.

Pause and Process:

1. How does information processing improve during middle childhood?

2. What are sensory memory, short-term memory, and long-term memory?

LANGUAGE DEVELOPMENT

Growing Language Skills

Metalinguistic-awareness

The capacity to use language to analyze, study, and understand language.

Although children are competent communicators with language in early childhood, language skills continue to develop during the school years (Piper, 2003). During the school years, children achieve **metalinguistic-awareness**. Metalinguistic-awareness (or metalinguistic ability) is defined as "the capacity to use language to analyze, study, and understand language" (Hulit & Howard, 1997, p. 247).

During middle childhood, vocabulary continues to grow, though at a slower rate than in early childhood (Hulit & Howard, 1997). Understanding slight variations between words and word choice skills improve. The meaning and definitions of words grow during this time. Children also improve in their ability to understand and use **figurative language** forms, such as similies, proverbs, idioms, and metaphors.

Figurative language

The use of similies, proverbs, idioms, and metaphors.

Language learning during middle childhood often focuses upon mastering the intricacies and rules of the language. Syntax and morphology understanding and use continue to develop (Hulit & Howard, 1997). Early in middle childhood, children are still working to master the exceptions to the general rules of language. For example, they may still occasionally say "childs" instead of "children" or "gooses" instead of "geese." They also begin to learn about rules regarding double negatives in sentences and parts of speech.

Conversational skills, including mastery of pragmatics, continue to improve in middle childhood (Hulit & Howard, 1997). The ability to repair sentences and maintain relevance grows during the school years. The ability to understand the conversational partner's perspective also improves. Finally, the concept of indirect requests, or hinting, in conversation emerges.

Second-Language Acquisition

School bilingualism

The offering of courses in a secondary language in the elementary schools.

In Chapter 4, we discussed bilingualism in early childhood. Most children who are bilingual early in childhood learn the second language in the home. However, many elementary schools offer courses in second language, which is referred to as **school bilingualism** (Piper, 2003). School bilingualism differs from home bilingualism in several ways. For example, language in the home is practical, context-based, and sequential. Language learning in schools is considered "formal, abstract language that is largely decontextualized, logical, and expository" (Piper, 2003, p. 132). Hence, it is more difficult to become bilingual in the school than in the home.

Second-language acquisition is best prior to middle childhood. Research has shown that immigrants to the United States master English grammar as well as natives if they arrive before the age of seven (Siegler, 1998). Children who arrive between the ages of eight and eleven show slight decrements in grammar ability. The downward trend in grammar ability in a second language continues as age increases. By the age of fifteen, grammar ability shows significant negative impacts in comparison to the younger children's mastery.

Pause and Process:

1. What is metalinguistic awareness?

2. How do language skills improve during middle childhood?

SOCIAL AND EMOTIONAL DEVELOPMENT DURING MIDDLE CHILDHOOD

LEARNING OBJECTIVES:

1. *Characterize emotional development during middle childhood*
2. *Describe understanding of self and others during middle childhood*
3. *Explain psychosocial development during middle childhood*

Developmental tasks during this stage center on mastering the basic skills outlined by society for adequate functioning. These include learning to read, write, and calculate (discussed in the last chapter). Other institutions and people now work in association with parents to teach these skills to children. The school becomes a significant cultural world for individuals at this time.

Beyond academic skills, the school environment also encourages children to master personal and social skills. These reflect what Erikson (1950) calls the skills of duty and accomplishment. They play an important role in helping school-age children acquire a healthy sense of industry. Being punctual with assignments, attending meetings, completing projects, and learning behavior routines are examples of these personal and social skills. In addition, school-age children are expected to be more accomplished in relations with peers. This involves learning to function adequately in groups of other children of similar ages. These are the years when society offers opportunities for learning group politics.

School-age children are expected to become more responsible. Families and schools work together to train them to become workers. They learn the work ethic, which stresses personal responsibility, completion of tasks, and initiating work with little direction. By performing work chores at home and at school, school-age children learn the basics of this ethic.

Other activities help school-age children to learn work roles. Participation in youth groups such as Scouts, 4-H, or church organizations fosters social skills. School-age children may also acquire the feeling of accomplishment through instruction in dance, music, art, drama, athletics, or other clubs. These help to foster feelings of self-worth and a positive self-image.

A dramatic developmental change is the increase in social interactions outside the family system. Peer groups become prominent in individual development during middle childhood. A best friend and a group of friends are desired for play activities and interaction. Having the respect of one's peers is a need that increases significantly during this stage.

School is where many developmental challenges of middle childhood take place. Here children learn to work with an authority figure who is not a member of their family system. The school introduces a child to many different peer groups. A child encounters these groups not only in the classroom and on the playground, but also outside the school world. The experiences provided by this environment and culture operate along with the family system in instilling an attitude of industry or inferiority.

Forces in a family system influence an individual's development at this time. Adults adapt their parenting styles to their child's changing nature. The principal adaptation is that they change from being physical to psychological helpers of their child.

A school-age child encounters pressures not previously experienced. These come from peer groups, from the need to learn new skills, from evaluations by teachers and peers, and from very different parental expectations. A child begins to rely on parents in different ways than in early childhood.

Youth programs such as Cub Scouts help children to learn about work roles. They help foster the feeling of self-worth and to have a positive self-image.

EMOTIONAL DEVELOPMENT

Key Emotional Development Highlights

Emotional communication is an area of amazing development during middle childhood. It is during the school-age years that children first understand that it is their cognitive appraisal of experiences or the environment that directly influences what they are feeling (Saarni, Mumme & Campos, 1998). Furthermore, children at this phase of life begin to understand that the same experience or environment may trigger different emotions in different people. Hence, understanding emotions becomes more mature at this time.

Middle childhood also appears to be a time that children experience an increase in their ability to reflect upon subjective experiences, which is directly related to the ability to extrapolate as to the intensity and duration of emotions (Saarni, Mumme & Campos, 1998). The awareness that multiple emotions may be experienced at the same time may develop as early as the preschool years, or in middle childhood. The ability to integrate conflicting emotions probably does not develop until the end of middle childhood.

In summary, the ability to understand one's own emotions, as well as emotions in others, grows during middle childhood. By the end of middle childhood, children are able to navigate emotional communication because they better grasp the cognitive component of emotions, reflect upon emotion-triggering experiences, and understand that emotions may conflict.

Temperament

In Chapter 4, we discussed that temperament can be conceptualized in various ways. A recent study by Janson and Mathiesen (2008) investigated four dimensions of temperament: Sociability, activity level, emotionality, and shyness. They then used statistical modeling to examine how the temperament dimensions cluster together. They found support for five temperament profiles (see Table 5-2).

This study included 921 children and longitudinally studied them from the age of eighteen months until the age of nine. Below are some interesting bits of information that came out of this study.

- At the age of eight or nine, gender differences emerge in temperament profiles.

- Boys are more likely than girls to be classified as confident.

- Girls are more likely than boys to be classified as unremarkable.

- Age impacts which temperament profile is most prevalent.

- Eighteen months: confident profile most prevalent

- Thirty months: uneasy profile most prevalent

- Four to five years: uneasy profile most prevalent

TABLE 5-2	**TEMPERAMENT PROFILES**	
TEMPERAMENT PROFILE	**DESCRIPTION**	**PERCENTAGE WITH TEMPERAMENT PROFILE**
Undercontrolled	High sociability, high activity level, high emotionality, and low shyness	20%
Confident	Low shyness, low emotionality, high activity level, and moderate sociability	23%
Unremarkable	Moderately low levels of sociability, activity level, emotionality, and shyness	22%
Inhibited	Low activity level, low sociability, high shyness, and moderately low levels of emotionality	12%
Uneasy	Moderately high shyness, moderately high emotionality, moderate sociability, and moderate activity level	23%

- Eight to nine years: unremarkable profile most prevalent

- There was moderate stability in temperament across childhood.

- The undercontrolled profile showed the highest degree of externalizing behavior problems.

- The undercontrolled profile, inhibited profile, and uneasy profile showed the highest levels of internalizing behavior problems.

In summary, this study found that temperament is fairly stable from infancy into middle childhood. Further, different profiles are most prevalent at different ages. Finally, certain profiles are more likely to exhibit behavior problems than other profiles.

Attachment

Attachment security in infancy continues to be predictive of behavioral outcomes in middle childhood (Thompson, 1998). A series of studies by Sroufe and colleagues (reviewed by Thompson, 1998) found attachment classification in infancy for boys was predictive of ratings of aggression and passive withdrawal behavior by teachers in elementary school. Additionally, summer camp personnel rated children who were securely attached as infants higher than children who were insecurely attached as infants on the following dimensions:

- Social skills

- Ego resiliency

- Self-esteem

- Self-confidence

- Emotional health

- Social competence

- Friendship development

- Independence

Pause and Process:

1. Describe emotional development during middle childhood.

2. Compare and contrast the temperament "types" discussed in Chapter 3 with the temperament "profiles" in this chapter.

SELF AND OTHERS

24. Define social cognition in your own words.

Social cognition

The skills involved in understanding the dynamics of human social interaction patterns. Self-understanding is also related these skills.

Understanding of Self and Others

Many developmental changes in middle childhood are social and mental in nature. As physical changes diminish, social and mental growth accelerates. The central aspect of social changes among school-age children is a shift to a new psychosocial focus that is both more mature and more self-aware. During this period, individuals refine their self-concept.

Among the skills school-age children are expected to become proficient at are those that involve a basic understanding of interaction patterns and human psychology. Children this age are more and more exposed to people outside their family system for instruction and learning. To cope successfully with many confusing circumstances, they must become adept at **social cognition**.

Social cognition is knowledge of the dynamics of human interaction. This important social skill vastly improves during middle childhood. Social cognition assists school-age children to make sense out of the often chaotic behavior of their peer groups, helps them to understand basic human nature, and promotes self-awareness leading to self-esteem.

Self-Understanding

School-age children advance in self-understanding. This is a significant milestone in helping a child reach decisions about how to behave. It is especially significant in influencing self-concept formation in middle childhood (Damon & Hart, 1982).

Because of their more advanced cognitive abilities, school-age children are more capable than preschoolers of thinking about what kind of person they are (Harter, 1982). As children advance through this stage, they realize that their personalities are composed of different aspects (Harter, 1983). They are able to acknowledge the negative as well as the positive aspects. For example, they know that they are good at spelling, excellent in reading, but weak in math. Admitting faults, areas of weakness, or negative traits is still difficult.

The ability to see their own negative attributes causes school-age children to become increasingly self-critical. This causes a gradual deterioration in positive feelings about the

At this age children have a better understanding of self-concept. They acknowledge the negative and the positive in themselves. They understand that they can be good in spelling and weak in math.

self as they progress through middle childhood (Harter, 1983; Savin-Williams & Demo, 1984). It is common to hear children this age make such self-derogatory comments as "I'm just no good," "I can't do anything right," "Nobody likes me," or "I'm just plain ugly." Most of these critical self-assessments result from comparisons with others their age.

School-age children come to internalize their problems by blaming themselves. Girls, especially, take personal responsibility for their difficulties (Stipek, 1984). This tendency to be so harsh on themselves goes with children's developing ability to take responsibility for their behavior. Another contributing factor is the increasing number of interactions with peers, who are such an important source of self-esteem in middle childhood.

Understanding of Others

In more specific ways, social cognition is the knowledge that other people have thoughts and feelings, personality traits, and reaction styles (Flavell & Ross, 1981). The beginnings of social cognition can be seen in social referencing (discussed in Chapter 3). This is the skill infants use when they look to a parent's emotional expressions (e.g., facial expression) to determine how they should react to something. In early childhood, individuals continue to use these cues—especially facial expressions and voice tone—to determine another's emotional state.

In middle childhood, however, individuals learn that facial expressions are not always reliable indicators of others' emotional states (Bugental, 1986; Flavell, 1985). Children learn around age eight or nine that not only are they expected to control their emotions, but that older people are also very skilled at doing so (Bugental, 1986). At the same time they grasp that people can feign emotional states, they begin to understand teasing, though this behavior is still confusing to children to some extent.

Perhaps the most dramatic insight children learn in middle childhood is that other people are different inside as well as outside. Children begin to comprehend at about age eight that people have personality traits (Schantz, 1983). However, school-age children think in an all-or-nothing manner. Something is either 100 percent one way or another. A person is either all-good or all-bad. They conclude that some personality traits make a person completely good and some traits make a person completely bad.

Once school-age children decide a person has certain traits, they will think about that person almost exclusively in these terms. In many respects, this is similar to the process of stereotyping seen in adults. It is inconceivable to children this age that people possess a mixture of positive and negative traits (Donaldson & Westerman, 1986). It confuses them that personality traits are sometimes contradictory. They have difficulty acknowledging that people do not always behave consistently.

Play and Leisure Time

The power of play is pervasive during middle childhood (Kaplan & Kaplan, 1973). The richness and extensiveness of play reach a zenith during these years. Developmental changes in the types of activities that appeal to school-age children also are observed.

To the uninformed adult, children's play is a useless, time-wasting, attention-consuming activity. To those who have studied children's play, this assumption is inaccurate. Four important contributions of play to development in middle childhood have been identified: (1) it enhances and encourages a child's creativity, (2) it assists a child to learn developmental tasks, (3) it fosters interpersonal relationships with peers, and (4) it bolsters a child's personality and self-concept. Play is a vehicle for modulating stress and reducing tension for school-age children. It enhances their physical development and fosters their social skills. Play provides a context for children's self-exploration as they interact with their environment.

A sequence of changes is seen in middle childhood play activities (Baumeister & Senders, 1989). This is a continuation of the changes that began in early childhood. Generally, there are strong parallels between the types of play children engage in and their increasing orientation to peers during this stage. The ability to interact effectively within a group emerges between ages five and eight. Children these ages demonstrate an increasing ability to tolerate and follow rules, take turns, and share equipment. Between eight and twelve, children pursue more specialized interests and activities. Some frequently observed types of play activities are outlined in Table 5-3.

Other trends are observed in school-age play. First, there is a decline in the types of play involving imagination or fantasy and in those involving action or rough-and-tumble (Baumeister & Senders, 1989). These types of play do not disappear completely in middle childhood, however.

Second, there is a dramatic increase in the types of play involving rules. School-age children enjoy games like tag that allow them to switch roles frequently. At one time a child is "It," and at another time a child is one of those who are chased. This kind of play may help to dismantle the strong egocentrism of early childhood because switching roles promotes the ability to take others' viewpoints (Piaget, 1967).

TABLE 5-3	TYPES OF PLAY ACTIVITIES IN MIDDLE CHILDHOOD	
ACTIVITY	**VALUES FOR CHILDREN**	**EXAMPLES**
Games		
Quiet	Intellectual stimulation; problem solving	Hangman; 20 Questions
Competitive	Social skills; problem solving	Four-square ball
Tags, relays	Energy release; fun; excitement; physical fitness	Chain tag; hide and seek
Team	Group skills; physical fitness	Football; soccer; baseball
Crafts	Creativity; problem solving; personality enrichment	Art; models; weaving; printing
Tricks, puzzles	Problem solving; intellectual skills; curiosity	Connect-the-dots; work searches
Collections	Classification skills; knowledge; information	Stamps; coins; rocks; dolls; models
Symbolic	Communication; imagination; social interaction "Star Wars"; "house"	Superman; Batman; Wonder Women

Third, play becomes increasingly competitive in middle childhood. Many school-age children come to prefer sports activities where there are clear winners and losers. These activities introduce them to complex rules. Television watching and recreational computer-use also become primary recreations. The average child spends around three hours a day watching the television or using the computer for reasons other than school work.

Family Influences

The nature and style of parenting change during middle childhood. One major source that motivates these changes is the child. The developmental tasks and challenges that school-age children experience are entirely different. These are more complex than those of infancy and early childhood. The developmental changes of middle childhood are more social and psychological than physical in nature. Physical skills that are acquired in this period, however, play a significant role in shaping children's self-concepts.

Parenting in middle childhood, as in earlier stages, focuses on helping children to accomplish their essential developmental tasks. However, the tone of interaction and care-giving styles changes. This centers increasingly on parents providing psychological assistance and guidance. Because children change during these years, there are corresponding changes in the ways that parents respond to children's needs. Parents learn that they must respond to or interact with the school-age child differently. Methods and parenting styles that were effective with preschoolers are ineffective with school-age children. Children have new accomplishments and emerging abilities during middle childhood. They may not permit parents to continue a response style or interaction pattern that was appropriate when they were younger. Parents essentially learn that they must now become psychological rather than physical helpers for their school-age children.

Parents help their children with developmental tasks such as tying their shoes.

Changes in the ways that school-age children are disciplined by parents illustrate this process. Parents of preschoolers typically use a variety of control methods. These include isolation, having a child sit in a corner, mild spanking, and so on. These techniques become ineffective in middle childhood. Taking privileges away and reasoning replace the methods used earlier. The methods that are successful with older children place a greater responsibility for behavior management on the child.

Parents begin training children for greater self-control in early childhood. In middle childhood, there is a greater sharing of social power between parents and children. This results in **co-regulation** in which parents exercise general supervision, whereas children gain in moment-to-moment self-regulation (Maccoby, 1984). Parents of school-age children tend to exercise their power mostly when children misbehave in their presence.

Parents of school-age children increasingly use psychological methods of guidance to help children achieve a higher level of self-control. Psychological guidance consists of reassuring children, helping them to recover from social blunders, and giving positive reinforcement for efforts to learn new skills. School-age children continue to need their parents but in ways that are very different from preschoolers.

Increased involvement with peers and the school system calls for parents to release increasing amounts of control over children. School-age children are absent from the home increasingly for longer periods of time. Parents from healthy family systems encourage this as a means of helping children gain independence from the family.

Letting go of school-age children means that parents can be more accepting of the increasing value placed on peers, best friends, and other significant adults. Children this age learn to relate to adults outside the family system. These include teachers, youth group leaders, or religious leaders, for example. Letting go of school-age children means that parents allow children opportunities to interact with other family systems. Children enjoy spending the night at friends' homes, taking weekend camping trips with youth groups, attending summer camp sessions, visiting with grandparents, and so on.

Co-regulation

The shift to greater sharing and balance of social power between parents and children during the Family and School-age Children stage of the family life career.

The expectations that parents hold for school-age children change. This also reflects the shift to co-regulation. For example, a group of parents rank-ordered a series of eight behavior traits in degree of importance for school-age children to have or acquire (Bigner, 1980). The ranking resulted in these traits being considered the most important for children this age: (1) developing social cooperation skills such as being considerate, sharing, or cooperative; (2) being open to experience such as curiosity, creativity, or information gathering skills; and (3) being self-directed by expressing needs, starting activities without being directed, or getting help when needed. These traits may be ideals that parents wish children to have to ensure success in adulthood. These may form the foundation of child rearing goals parents may adopt during this stage of the family life career. Such goals can guide and shape parenting behaviors.

To help children acquire a healthy sense of industry versus inferiority, parents can focus on several aspects in their relationship with children this age: (1) focusing on children's accomplishments, (2) avoiding excessive attention that highlights weaknesses and limitations, and (3) promoting increasing abilities for children to develop self-control.

Divorce Impacts

More than 50 percent of all children in the United States are expected to have a single-parent family experience at some time (Stickle, 2008; Kitson & Morgan, 1990). How this will affect children is a major concern of parents who consider divorce.

Most research regarding divorce addresses two central factors that seem to influence children's adjustment to parents' divorce. These include (1) the age of children at the time of the divorce, and (2) use of available social networks to help children adjust to changes related to their parents' divorce.

Many research studies have focused on the age of children when parents divorce. Findings point to different reactions and adjustment challenges based on this factor alone. Most children, no matter their age at the time of the parents' divorce, find this to be a painful experience. Short-term reactions can be considered as symptoms of grief and mourning. Children experience feelings ranging from anger to depression and guilt. Behavior problems become more common such as noncompliance, aggression, regressive behavior, sleep disturbances, and fearful reactions (Hetherington, Stanley-Hagan & Anders, 1989; Wallerstein, 1983). Apparently, short-term effects are mediated according to the stability of the child's home and school environment following divorce. It is also affected by using social supports available to children to help them cope (Kurdek, 1981).

School-age children react to parents' divorce by feeling hurt, rejected by the absent parent, helpless to make the situation better, and lonely (Wallerstein & Kelly, 1976). Anger also is a common reaction. This is most often directed at one parent in blaming them for causing the divorce and disruption to family life. A common fear among children this age is that they will be abandoned just as their custodial parent has been (Wallerstein, 1987). It is not unusual for children this age to become aligned with one parent or the other following the divorce. When this occurs, anger becomes more intensely directed at the nonaligned parent causing difficulties in their relationship.

The first year is a particularly stressful one for children and adults. Parents are less effective parents (Parke & Buriel, 1998). For example, parents require less mature behavior of their children, show less affection, and are less consistent with discipline during this time. Children's grades and school performance suffer, their behavior becomes more noncompliant, and relationships with both custodial and noncustodial parents become more strained (e.g., Fine, Moreland & Schwebel, 1983; Minuchin & Shapiro, 1983; Parke & Buriel, 1998; Wallerstein, Corbin & Lewis, 1988).

Divorce can have some long-term effects on children (Hetherington, 1989; Parke & Buriel, 1998). Girls whose mothers remain single appear well-adjusted two years after the divorce. They are typically close to their mother and thrive with the added responsibilities of living in a single-parent household. Sons, however, struggle in their relationship with their mother. They are monitored less than boys from intact homes, spend more time with peers, and execute more antisocial behavior. We will learn more about the long-term effects of divorce in Chapter 6.

Children recover more quickly and permanently if parents minimize their interpersonal conflict after the divorce (Wallerstein, 1983). Long-term effects are diminished also when both parents remain involved and try to nurture their relationship with their children (Hetherington, Cox & Cox, 1979; Parke & Buriel, 1998).

Sibling Relationships

Sibling relationships provide a context for learning how to interact with others (Parke & Buriel, 1998). These relationships help children develop social understanding, interpersonal skills, and conflict resolution skills (Eisenberg & Fabes, 1998; Parke & Buriel, 1998). Further, positive sibling relationships may help compensate for negative peer relationships and help prevent problematic outcomes typically associated with negative peer relationships.

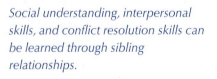

Social understanding, interpersonal skills, and conflict resolution skills can be learned through sibling relationships.

Sibling relationships may provide a context for developing prosocial behavior (Eisenberg & Fabes, 1998). Older siblings sometimes play a caregiver role in monitoring younger sibling behavior and well-being. Such caregiving behavior assists both older and younger children in developing prosocial behavior. Older siblings often display warmth, concern, and kindness when caring for younger siblings. Younger siblings learn to comply with older sibling direction and model the prosocial behavior of their older sibling. Additionally, sibling caregiving relationships provide a context for developing perspective-taking, further assisting in the development of prosocial behavior.

Finally, sibling relationships influence a child's development of self. Older siblings who help care for younger siblings may develop a self-representation of being nurturing or dominating (Harter, 1998). Younger siblings cared for by older siblings may develop a self-representation of being dominated or nurtured.

The Outside World

Entrance into the school signals many changes for a child, the parents, and the family system. The **peer group** becomes an additional socialization agent as children learn the mechanics of **group politics**. This group is also a major source of information children use in constructing their self-concept.

Peers

An individual is a member of several social systems during middle childhood: the family, school, and peer groups. Each is distinct, with its own patterns, rules, and roles. School-age children participate in two separate cultural worlds: that of adults and that of children (Asher & Gottman, 1981; Galzter-Levy & Cohler, 1993).

A peer group consists of children who are of approximately the same age and developmental abilities. Peer groups may be formed spontaneously by children or artificially by adults for children. Children spontaneously form peer groups when they play together on the playground during school recess, for example, or when those who live near each other play together in their neighborhood. Adults artificially form peer groups when they group children together in a classroom, for example. Our schools commonly use age and associated developmental abilities as guides in assigning children to grades (Williams & Stith, 1980).

Peer groups are important agents of socialization. Children learn significant lessons through membership in these groups—lessons that siblings, parents, and teachers cannot teach. These are lessons in group politics, or skills that facilitate successful functioning as a group member. These lessons can last a lifetime.

A peer group functions like any other social system. Patterns and rules of interaction form a code for appropriate behavior. Infractions of rules and patterns result in consequences meant to enforce conformity to the code. A peer group may have its own language and dress styles to promote group identification. During middle childhood, peer groups are often sex-divided. This means that school-age children only include children of the same-sex in their peer group. This tendency decreases in adolescence.

Peer group

A (usually) same-sex group of children of similar ages and developmental abilities that significantly influences social changes in middle childhood.

Group politics

Those social skills that facilitate a child's participation in peer groups.

Spotlight

29. Describe the social hierarchy of peer groups.

Peer groups provide important social-ization lessons that can last a lifetime.

Social hierarchy

An organizational ranking of peers based on how much a child is liked or disliked by others.

Average

A child with a small group of friends, who is neither greatly disliked nor considered popular.

Popular

Children who are liked by many peers.

Neglected

Children who are neglected by peers describe themselves as having no friends.

Rejected

Children who are rejected by peers are disliked and are at risk of many serious problems that include clinical depression.

School-age children begin to establish a degree of organizational order in their peer groups through a **social hierarchy**. This ranking is based on how much a child is liked or disliked by others. This forms the basis of popularity ratings children make of one another. It is important because some children will be well-liked and others will be unpopular. This can determine who the child plays with, how the play occurs, and under what circumstances. School-age children can be expected to construct their self-image and concept on how they are treated by peers.

Most school-age children are considered as **average** in these ratings by others. The greatest concern relates to children who are neglected or rejected by peers (Kupersmidt, 1989; Rubin, Bukowski & Parker, 1998). The proportion of these children is similar to those who are **popular**.

Children who are **neglected** by peers describe themselves as having no friends (Rubin, Bukowski & Parker, 1998). They have an ambiguous status within a peer group because no one likes nor dislikes them. These children may be described as isolated from others. This may or may not be disturbing to them. In many respects, they resemble children who are average in popularity ratings.

Children who are **rejected** by peers are of much greater concern. They are at risk of many serious problems that include clinical depression (Kennedy, Spence & Hensley, 1989; Rubin, Bukowski & Parker, 1998). These children are disliked, sometimes passionately, by peers. If a child is rejected at one grade, there is a high probability that this continues throughout a child's academic career.

A child is rejected by peers usually for behaving in hostile and aggressive ways. The rejected child resembles the stereotype of the class bully. This is a child who picks on other children, preying on those who are weaker physically (French, 1988; MacNeil & Newell, 2004).

However, aggressive behavior alone does not result in rejection by peers. Another group of children is seen as **controversial**. These children, although acting aggressively

Controversial

Children who are liked by many peers, and disliked by many peers.

also have positive traits that are valued by a peer group. Because of the positive traits, these children are not rejected but are liked by some of their peers. The children who are rejected are seen by their peers as lacking any positive traits and acting aggressively.

Rejected children may have difficulties in social cognition not observed in other children. For example, they may act aggressively and are not liked by peers because they lack social skills (Putallaz & Gottman, 1981; Rubin, Bukowski & Parker, 1998). They may interpret accidental behavior of others as intentional, a characteristic of social cognition among much younger children (Dodge & Frame, 1982). This interpretation is thought to provoke their hostility toward others.

More recent research suggests that rejected children lack such important social skills because their rejection deprives them of peer group learning experiences (Kuperschmidt, 1989; Rubin, Bukowski & Parker, 1998). Additionally, rejected children's interpretation of others' aggressiveness as intentional may be correct. Some rejected children are indeed the victims of peers' aggressiveness. These children often are the scapegoats within peer groups but do not usually act aggressively themselves. Other rejected children are victimized but also act aggressively to others. These children are called provocative victims. They seem to provoke hostility from peers that is used to justify their aggressive retaliation.

A child's external physical appearances also can contribute to ratings of likability by peers (Kennedy, 1989; Rubin, Bukowski & Parker, 1998). Children who look differently are likely to be rejected by peers as determined by ratings made both from videotapes and still photographs. These factors may operate to define a child's reputation among peers in middle childhood. School-age children tend to think in an all-or-nothing manner. This is based on global assessments of someone's attributes. A child who is rejected, neglected, or controversial may acquire a label as "difficult," "mean," or "temperamental." A rejected child will learn to expect that others will think of him or her in these terms. Similarly, children who are popular also acquire reputations that are positive. The popular child will learn to expect others to view him or her positively (Waas, 1988). Frequently, a child's reputation remains intact for many years thereafter.

Friendship

In Chapter 4 we were introduced to developmental changes in friendship perception. We learned about stage zero in which friends are considered little more than momentary playmates (Selman, 1981). During the school-age years, children progress through stages one, two, and three. It should be noted here that same-sex friendships are the norm among school-age children (Hartup, 1983).

One-way assistance

The first stage in friendship perception that occurs early in middle childhood where friends must match a child's personal standard.

Stage one of friendship perception is referred to as **one-way assistance** (Selman, 1981). This stage occurs early in middle childhood. In this stage, friends must match a child's personal standard. For example, if a child believes that a friend should be a girl who is the same age, height, and likes soccer, then a person must meet these criteria in order to be considered a friend. A "best friend" would be the person that a child knows the most or is most familiar with, including likes and dislikes.

A "best friend" is considered a stage one friendship. This person is usually the same gender, age, and height, and has the same likes and dislikes.

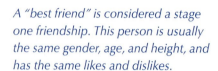

Fair-weather cooperation

The second stage of friendship perception that typically occurs between the ages of eight to ten where ideas of reciprocity and adapting to friends' likes and dislikes govern the early friendship.

Intimate and mutually shared relationships

The third stage of friendship perception that typically occurs at the end of middle childhood, between the ages of ten to twelve where children value the continuity and longevity of friendship.

Stage two of friendship perception is referred to as **fair-weather cooperation** (Selman, 1981). This stage typically occurs between the ages eight to ten. Ideas of reciprocity and adapting to friends' likes and dislikes govern these early friendships. However, these friendships are fragile. There is no sense of long-term commitment and an argument often ends the friendship.

Stage three of friendship perception is referred to as **intimate and mutually shared relationships** (Selman, 1981). This stage typically occurs at the end of middle childhood, between the ages of ten to twelve. Here, children value the continuity and longevity of friendship. Hence, arguments and conflicts are no longer seen as the end to a friendship, but an obstacle to be overcome. Friendships are also viewed as a valuable source of social and emotional support. However, possessiveness and exclusiveness can plague friendships at this stage. These attributes arise from the realization that friendships are complex and challenging to develop and maintain.

School Experiences

Entrance into the school system is a significant event that influences many social and cognitive changes in middle childhood. It is in this setting that a child is introduced to peer groups and exposed to other nonrelated adults who assist in their growth process. Expectations for behavior change yearly as children progress through the school system.

Once the responsibility of the family, children's education is now institutionalized. The school system has gained significance as our culture has become more technologically oriented. Children today are expected to become proficient in basic skills such as reading, writing, and calculation during middle childhood. They are also expected to learn many facts and absorb much information about the world. Parents assume that children will succeed in their learning experiences if they have properly trained teachers who conduct effective educational programs. Of course, parental involvement is key to student success, as is student motivation.

The school system teaches important lessons other than those involving cognition. Because a school is a social system, it has patterns, rules, boundaries, and other factors designed to promote its effectiveness. Children learn many different social lessons within this context, including group politics and prosocial behaviors as taught by peers.

The Electronic World

Television, video games, computers, all these and other forms of media are impacting human development like never before in the history of humankind. Media can be good or bad in terms of human development. For example, computers and the internet can help school-age children complete research papers without ever needing to enter a brick-and-mortar library. Where one of the authors live, the public library offers free, online home-work help so that any child struggling with their studies has a virtual tutor. However, media can also have detrimental effects.

The impact of television on development is the type of media most researched. Often, research in this area offers conflicting results (see Huston & Wright, 1998, for a review of the research). Most studies find a correlation between watching television in childhood and obesity in adolescence. Although most studies infer that television leads to a sedentary lifestyle—hence the increase in obesity—other studies implicate television ads that promote fattening or sugary foods or graze eating while viewing television. Further, although some studies have found that television viewing has no impact on sport or leisure activity participation in middle childhood or adolescence, others have found that heavy television watching decreases participation in such activities.

Whether television viewing impacts academic skills and achievement is also an area of conflicting research (see Huston & Wright, 1998, for a review of the research). Most research indicates that heavy television viewing is correlated with lower levels of time spent reading. Interestingly, children who watch educational programs are more likely to spend time reading, whereas children who watch adult programs or cartoons are less likely to spend time reading. Research seems to indicate that television viewing has little or no impact on homework completion; however, having the television on while doing home-work may result in less concentration and lower learning. In terms of overall academic achievement, it appears that television viewing may interfere with school success when children watch more than four hours a day or thirty hours per week.

Educational programming has been shown to have positive outcomes for children. Shows such as *Sesame Street, Reading Rainbow, Ghostwriter, Barney and Friends,* and *Square One* appear to assist children in learning pre-academic and academic skills (see Huston & Wright, 1998, for a review of the research). For example, counting, reading, writing, math strategies, and prosocial behavior all seem to be promoted by educational programming.

Despite the positive outcomes associated with educational programming, most shows on television fall short of this noble cause. Many shows promote gender stereotypes and the sexualization of girls and women (which we will discuss in our module on adolescence) (APA, 2007; Huston & Wright, 1998; Ruble & Martin, 1998). Violent shows also seem to increase aggression in children and decrease sensitivity toward victims of violence. It is extremely important that parents monitor children's television viewing and watch television with them.

Pause and Process:

1. How does divorce impact school-age children?

2. What is the difference between peer groups and friends?

PSYCHOSOCIAL DEVELOPMENT

Developing a Sense of Industry

Sense of industry

A positive, healthy attitude toward work and the need to master certain basic skills.

School-age children focus on resolving a psychosocial conflict in acquiring a sense of industry versus inferiority. A **sense of industry** is a positive, healthy attitude toward work and the need to master certain basic skills. A healthy attitude toward work means learning to apply oneself to an assigned task. It is an extension of the attitude of initiative acquired in the previous stage, but with this difference: it is expected that what is started will be completed satisfactorily. The family and school systems work together to help children learn this attitude. At home, industry is learned by school-age children as they perform household chores assigned to them by their parents. Parents now enforce higher standards of performance because of the child's advanced abilities. At school, a child acquires industry by completing assigned learning tasks. Children are expected to finish their homework assignments, classroom problems, and more extensive projects.

School-age children learn the work ethic by doing all these things. They learn the association between performance and reward as they are evaluated by parents and teachers. Children may be rewarded with money, privileges, or material goods for performing household chores to standards set by parents.

Essentially, industry is a feeling of pride in one's abilities to do what is expected adequately. This is the basis of the work ethic and an important element of adult success. Our culture expects school-age children to begin learning the principles of right and good conduct in preparation for their future roles as workers and contributors to society.

Sense of inferiority

A pervasive attitude of worthlessness.

The **sense of inferiority** is a pervasive attitude of worthlessness. It is based on negative assessments of oneself, particularly in comparison with others. School-age children adopt this attitude when they conclude they cannot do anything well. This attitude affects their

A child can learn a sense of industry by performing household chores such as washing the dishes.

interactions with other children. School-age children who feel inferior tend to shy away from opportunities to interact with their peers and thus can fail to earn social skills. This is a time of life when others' approval is vastly important. An individual's self-worth is validated by the approval and acceptance of peers. When this is not forthcoming, for whatever reasons, school-age children believe that rejection means they are of lesser value than others.

In Erikson's framework, the theme of psychosocial developmental changes in middle childhood is "making things together." This refers to the more intensive involvement of school-age children with their peers. It is in the group experience that children master many social and mental skills and learn to be productive within their family system, the school, and their peer groups.

Many toys, video and computer games, and youth programs are geared to help children acquire a healthy sense of industry. Dolls or actions figures help children act out themes. Arts, crafts, and hobby kits help kids learn that they can accomplish something if they try. Many educationally-geared computer and video games allow children to collect tokens as individual competencies are mastered. Programs such as the Cub and Boy Scouts, Brownie and Girl Scouts, 4-H, Boys' and Girls' Clubs, and others teach the work ethic by offering merit badges for completing tasks successfully. The uniforms they provide give children a cherished group identity. The family system is involved to help children perform tasks and in activities that promote family interaction. Hence, childhood culture seems geared to assist children in the development of an attitude of industry.

Pause and Process:

   1. How does a sense of industry help a child throughout life?

   2. How does a sense of inferiority hinder a child throughout life?

SUMMARY

1. Middle childhood is a quiet period as far as physical changes are concerned. Body configuration becomes leaner; primary teeth are shed and permanent teeth erupt; bone growth slows; muscle development advances, resulting in greater strength and endurance; and there are steady improvements in coordination and motor skill performance.

2. Sports provide students with the opportunity to learn life skills and maintain physical health. Sports provide an environment in which competence, confidence, connections, character, and caring can all be fostered and developed. Stress from coaches can lead to suboptimal outcomes.

3. Eating habits and appetite improve, and children at this stage have better health than young children. Middle-childhood is also a time where parents must monitor children in order to avoid and prevent accidental injuries.

4. School-age children enter a new stage of cognitive development called concrete operations. Before entering this stage at about seven or eight, they go through a transition period (the five-to-seven shift) when their thinking is based on intuition. The concrete operations stage is characterized by limitation of thought to present physical realities and the increasing ability to use mental imagery in problem solving. Several important cognitive changes take place during middle childhood: (1) classification skills improve because of decentering; (2) class inclusion, or how to consider a whole in relation to its part, is learned; (3) reversible operations such as subtraction are accomplished; (4) most kinds of conservation problems are mastered; (5) seriation tasks, or the scaling of objects according to various dimensions are performed; (6) time is better understood; and (7) a cognitive style that is less bound by egocentrism is formed. Individuals in middle childhood use elementary logic to make inferences, but their reasoning is limited by cognitive conceit, or all-or-nothing thinking.

5. School-age children process information in ways that facilitate the learning experiences required by school systems. They demonstrate their improved abilities to process information in their use of attention and use of memory. School-age children become better at selective attention in gathering information from the environment. Their memory improves significantly and they are better able to recall information when performing cognitive tasks. School-age children use various methods and strategies for memory storage. Many different scripts are formed during this stage to facilitate routines. Other scripts are based on understanding social roles. School-age children show great improvements in metacognition and metamemory. Those who have higher levels of these kinds of awareness perform better in school.

6. Language development includes the emergence of metalinguistic awareness. Children also develop an awareness and use of figurative language. Additionally, conversational skills improve. Finally, children fine-tune their knowledge of the morphology, syntax, and pragmatics during the school years.

7. Emotional communication improves during middle childhood. Temperament profiles and attachment influence developmental outcomes. Five temperament profiles proposed by Janson and Mathiesen (2008) are undercontrolled, confident, unremarkable, inhibited, and uneasy.

8. Social cognition is knowledge of the dynamics of human interaction. It is founded on several skills that improve in middle childhood: understanding of others based on advanced social referencing, self-understanding based on

knowledge of one's strengths and weaknesses; greater willingness to accept responsibility for personal actions, and a positive self-concept based on acquiring a healthy sense of industry that acknowledges both positive and negative aspects of the self.

9. Play serves various functions for school-age children. Play activities in middle childhood follow developmental changes that reflect a child's increasing orientation to peers. Fantasy and rough-and-tumble play declines and activities that use rules and involve competition increase. Television watching takes up much recreational time. Families, siblings, friends, and peers all play a role in socializing children. Divorce has serious short-and long-term effects on children.

10. The fourth stage of psychosocial development proposed by Erikson is experienced in middle childhood. This involves the establishment of a sense of industry versus inferiority. A healthy sense of industry involves a positive attitude toward work, duty, and responsibility. It also requires mastery of the social mental skills considered essential for effective functioning in society. School-age children are influenced by family and school systems, but even more by peer groups in acquiring this attitude. A sense of inferiority is a pervasive attitude of worthlessness, especially in comparison with peers. Either of these attitudes has a profound effect on an individual's perceptions of personal competence.

SELF-QUIZ

1. When does the prepubertal growth spurt occur for most children?
2. How do boys and girls differ in their body composition?
3. What changes occur in dentition during this time?
4. What improvements in motor skills are seen during middle childhood?
5. Give an example for each of the five Cs.
6. What are some positive outcomes related to sport participation?
7. What are some negative outcomes related to sport participation?
8. Explain contamination and internalization in understanding illness.
9. Describe the mental disorders discussed in this chapter.
10. How can health in middle childhood be promoted?
11. Describe concrete-operational thought.
12. How is attention understood during middle childhood?

13. Explain the three phases of memory discussed in this chapter.
14. How does chunking help with memory?
15. Define metamemory.
16. How is intelligence traditionally defined?
17. What are Howard Gardner's proposed areas of multiple intelligences? Define each intelligence in your own words.
18. What is meant by math being codified?
19. What are some math strategies in middle childhood?
20. How is school bilingual education different from home bilingual education?
21. Summarize emotional development during middle childhood.
22. Describe the five temperament profiles proposed by Janson & Mathiesen (2008).
23. What are some positive outcomes in middle childhood associated with having a secure attachment?
24. Define social cognition in your own words.

25. How does self-understanding improve during middle childhood?

26. What are the benefits of play in middle childhood?

27. What are the short-term and long-term impacts of divorce on children?

28. Explain how sibling relationships influence development.

29. Describe the social hierarchy of peer groups.

30. How does the electronic world affect development?

TERMS AND CONCEPTS

Adolescence

Adolescence as a life stage is known only in the United States and other developed countries around the world. It is so accepted here today, however, that it may be surprising to learn that the period between thirteen and eighteen years of age has been recognized as a unique time in the life span merely for the last hundred years.

G. Stanley Hall (1882, 1904) is credited with formalizing the concept of **adolescence** as a developmental stage with its own characteristics and challenges. He was an early proponent of **maturationism**, or the belief that changes in development are due only to heredity; changes result from the execution of genetic programming. Hall based many of his ideas about adolescence on the Darwinian theory of evolution. His global philosophy of developmental change emphasized the concept of *recapitulation*: the idea that the individual's progress through specific stages reflects the social evolution of the human species. Thus he believed that change throughout the life span followed a primitive-to-civilized pattern.

Hall felt that the time between childhood and adulthood was a cultural invention of Western civilization. He characterized this period as one of "storm and stress" that reflected the turbulent growth and rapid change found in modern societies. Hall coined the name for this stage from a Latin word, *adolescere*, meaning "a state of emancipation." This term was applied to slaves in ancient Rome who were not quite freemen but were no longer in servitude.

Most cultures in the world recognize the physical event of puberty as the developmental landmark dividing childhood from full adulthood. Puberty, the process that initiates sexual maturation in humans, begins at about age twelve or thirteen. Many cultures mark this event with ceremonies and initiation rites. Western cultures rarely do so because they see these practices as somewhat primitive.

The anthropologist Margaret Mead investigated adolescence in the South Pacific island cultures of Samoa and New Guinea (1928, 1935). She was particularly interested in the impact of cultural factors on the transition between childhood and adulthood. Mead's studies significantly challenged the universality of Hall's description of adolescence as a time of "storm and stress." In these South Pacific island cultures, Mead found a smooth peaceful transition to adolescence, which she attributed to young people's greater exposure to everyday life. Mead's own work has since been challenged by others, who assert that adolescence in these cultures is, indeed, a stressful experience (Freeman, 1983; Holmes, 1987). This may be a moot point, however, because the notion that adolescence is always stressful in Western cultures is no longer widely accepted.

Nevertheless, several coincidental factors do make these years a distinct period in the life span (Demos & Demos, 1969; Troen, 1985). First, our society has changed from an agrarian one, to one that is technological and urban. This change precipitated many changes in family structure and organization as people moved to cities, adults worked away from home, and children became more involved with others outside their families.

Second, the public school system created institutions in which children were grouped with others of similar ages and segregated from adults. Out of this system a totally new culture of childhood emerged, which eventually led to a new "youth culture" (Kenniston, 1971). The contemporary signs of this youth culture are rock 'n roll and rap music, adolescent dress codes, gang membership, and certain behaviors and attitudes. Instead of a rite of passage into adulthood, our society gives young people the identity of "teenager," with its license to experiment with roles and limits.

Third, technology has changed the outer boundary of adolescence. The period still has its traditional beginning coinciding with the individual's puberty. But when does it end? Originally, Hall envisioned adolescence as a stage of preparation for adulthood. In his day, most people were finished with their education and entering the workforce by age eighteen. But technology has prolonged the educational process in our society. It is common now for people to continue their education well into their twenties or even thirties.

Adolescence today is seen in contradictory terms. On the one hand, it is portrayed as a special time of increased freedom from adult supervision; a time when one comes into one's own as an autonomous person, life is fun, and energy is abundant. On the other hand, it is described as a difficult period marked by conflict with adults, wide swings in emotions, confusion about one's place in the scheme of things, stressful in terms of self-esteem, and rife with dangerous hazards such as pregnancy and substance use. No stage in the life span is without problems and challenges, of course, but adolescence may present more acute challenges than any other stage of the life span for individuals and family systems.

PHYSICAL DEVELOPMENT DURING ADOLESCENCE

> ### *LEARNING OBJECTIVES:*
>
> *1. Describe physical growth during adolescence*
> *2. Awareness of the unique health issues faced in adolescence*

PHYSICAL GROWTH

Adolescence

The fifth stage of the life span, occurring between thirteen and eighteen years of age.

Maturationism

The belief that changes in development are due only to heredity; changes result from the execution of genetic programming.

Puberty

The developmental event occurring in early adolescence in which the sexual organs become functional. It is associated with other significant physical changes in the body.

In contrast with middle childhood, adolescence is a time of physical changes. These changes produce a metamorphosis: an individual goes from child to physical adult. For most individuals, this transformation is completed by age sixteen.

ADOLESCENT GROWTH SPURT   Most of the physical changes commonly associated with adolescence take place in the early part of this stage. During the first four years of adolescence, there is a rapid spurt in growth that is noticeable in almost every aspect of the body, but especially in height and weight. The rate at which these changes occur is comparable to rates seen in the prenatal and infancy stages (Tanner, 1978, 1990). Girls begin their growth spurt typically between the ages of ten and twelve, whereas boys do not generally begin theirs until somewhere between the ages of twelve and fourteen.

Height and Weight Changes   The initiation of **puberty**, the process by which the reproductive organs become functionally mature, signals the beginning of numerous physical and psychological changes. Girls, during their average pubertal period between the ages of ten and fourteen, gain about thirty-eight pounds and ten inches. Boys between twelve and sixteen typically gain about forty-two pounds and also about ten inches (Tanner, 1978, 1990). These changes in height and weight occur sporadically during this four-year period—that is, periods of rapid change are followed by slower periods. The term *spurt* is applied to the periods of most rapid change. During a one-year period, many girls gain about twenty pounds and three inches and many boys gain twenty-six pounds and four inches (Tanner, 1978, 1990).

1. Describe the adolescent growth spurt.

Body Proportions   Growth is asynchronous in adolescence (Katchadourian, 1977). This means that advances in different organ systems take place at different times and at different rates. The extremities (the hands and feet) grow earlier and more rapidly than other areas, giving the young adolescent the appearance of being "all hands and feet." Next the calves of the legs and the forearms begin increasing. This is followed by the trunk area (hips, chest, and shoulders). Most of the gains in height come from growth of the trunk area rather than of the legs.

Internal Organ Systems   Internal organ systems respond to the adolescent growth spurt (Katchadourian, 1977; Thornburg & Aras, 1986). The cardiovascular system—heart, lungs, and blood vessels—increases in capacity. The number of red blood cells increases also, especially in boys, probably because of increasing levels of a male hormone (testosterone) in the blood.

The brain shows significant structural changes right before and during adolescence (NIMH, 2001). If you remember back to brain development during infancy, we learned about how synapses (or connections) are overproduced and then later pruned back. The pruning occurs according to the use-it-or-lose-it principle and helps strengthen used connections while eliminating unused connections. Right before the onset of adolescence, there is a second period of overproduction of gray matter in the prefrontal cortex (Giedd et al., 1999; NIMH, 2001; Rapoport et al., 1999). The prefrontal cortex area of the brain is responsible for many of our higher thinking abilities such as reasoning, organization, planning, working memory, and emotional regulation. For girls, this period of thickening tends to peak at the age of eleven; for boys, it peaks around the age of twelve. After this peak, pruning begins.

There appears to be differing patterns of brain development for gray and white matter. The gray matter is considered our thinking part of our brain, whereas the white matter connects various parts of the brain and nervous system (NIMH, 2001). Research shows that there is a wave of white matter growth flowing from the front of the brain to the back of the brain during childhood. Particularly, connections flourish in the temporal and parietal lobes, which are important for language development and spatial relations. This wave wanes around the age of twelve. It appears that the ability to learn a first or second language is easier during this wave of white matter growth than after it subsides.

Gray matter maturation appears to occur in the opposite direction, beginning at the back of the brain and moving forward (NIMH, 2001). It appears that the frontal lobes are not fully developed until early adulthood. Different processes shift location as these structural developments occur. For example, some forms of emotional processing seem to occur in the amygdala during early adolescence, although adults utilize the frontal lobe. Many developmentalists feel that some of the risky behavior and emotional issues seen during adolescence may be partly contributed to the relatively late development of the frontal cortex.

Skin problems are also associated with adolescence. Facial acne is the most prevalent skin problem, and its incidence increases rapidly during this period. **Acne** is a chronic inflammation of the oil glands and hair follicles located in the facial area. Acne can be triggered by stress and nervousness (AMA, 2006). Some adolescents are more prone to acne (it tends to run in families) and more resistant to treatment than others. Many teenagers get very upset about their acne, some to the point of obsessiveness. They experience loss of self-esteem that can interfere with their social confidence (Roberts & Ludford, 1976).

The one major organ system that decreases in size during adolescence is the lymphoid system, especially the tonsils and adenoids. This may account for the improvement seen in asthma among affected individuals (Katchadourian, 1977). It also may be a contributing factor as to why adolescents experience fewer upper respiratory diseases than school-age children.

Acne

A chronic inflammation of the oil glands and hair follicles located in the facial area.

Sexual Maturation   Puberty, the developmental process by which an individual becomes sexually mature and capable of reproduction, is the physical event most prominently associated with adolescence. The physical changes that take place during puberty are orchestrated by interactions between the central nervous system and the glands of the endocrine system, which produce hormones that regulate the functioning of the body. The *pituitary* is the central gland that coordinates the endocrine system. Its hormone secretions stimulate many other glands in the body to function in particular ways.

When puberty begins, the pituitary stimulates the production of hormones that produce changes in the physical size of the body and its organs. Simultaneously, its hormones stimulate the sex glands to begin producing increasing amounts of hormones. In females, these hormones are estrogen and progesterone (produced by the ovaries). In males, the primary hormone is testosterone (produced within the testicles). These hormones bring sexual organs into mature functioning and produce primary and secondary sexual characteristics.

When does puberty occur? Puberty is experienced by boys and girls in a different maturational sequence and at different ages. Individual differences are also very noticeable in the ages at which this process begins and ends. Both genetics and the environment play a role in the timing of puberty (Mustanki et al., 2004).

FIGURE 6-1   THE MAJOR GLANDS OF THE ENDOCRINE SYSTEM

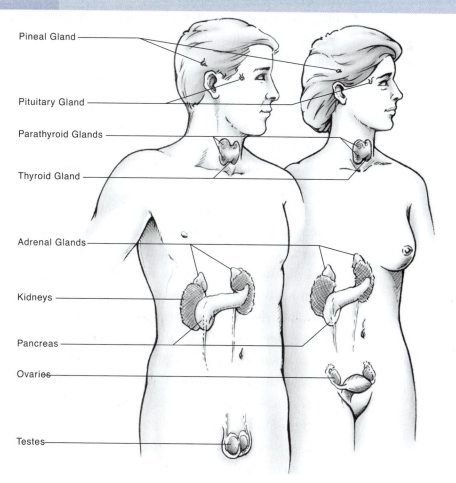

Pineal Gland
Pituitary Gland
Parathyroid Glands
Thyroid Gland
Adrenal Glands
Kidneys
Pancreas
Ovaries
Testes

Secular trend

The trend, inferred from observation of several generations, toward achieving sexual maturity at earlier ages than in the past.

Menarche

The first menstrual period experienced by a girl, marking the beginning of puberty.

There is a worldwide trend known as the **secular trend**, toward earlier puberty. For example, the average age at **menarche** (first period) in Norway in 1840 was seventeen; in 1950, it was thirteen years and four months (Roche, 1979). The secular trend, which has been noted in many other countries, is thought to be due to a few different factors. First, better health due to better nutrition, lower rates of communicable disease infections (due to immunizations), and greater access to health care may contribute to an earlier onset of puberty. Second, lifestyle changes may be leading to earlier puberty. For example, research has shown that a girl that lives in a home with a nonbiological male (such as a stepfather or boyfriend of the mother) tends to have an earlier onset of puberty (Ellis, 2004; Ellis & Garber, 2000; Mustanski et al., 2004). Some recent research has found this to occur in boys as well (Mustanski et al., 2004). Researchers speculate that pheromones may play a part in this phenomenon (Colmenares & Gomendio, 1988; Ellis, 2004). Third, drinking water contaminated by oral contraceptives and other sources of synthetic estrogen may lead to an earlier onset of puberty in females. Because oral contraceptives are designed to not be broken down by the liver, it is excreted in a woman's urine. Waste water treatment plants are not sufficiently designed to remove these synthetic hormones; hence, traces have been found in drinking water throughout the world. In fact, these synthetic hormones have wrecked havoc on fish, reptile, and amphibian populations throughout the world (Guillette, R., 1994; Gyllenhammar, Holm, Eklund & Berg, 2008; Kidd et al., 2007; Todorov et al., 2002; Xu et al., 2008). Finally, a stressful family environment (which includes poverty, family conflict, inadequate parenting, and absence of the biological father) has been linked to early puberty in girls (Doughty & Rodgers, 2000; Kim & Smith, 1998; Moffitt, Caspi, Belsky & Silva, 1992). Later in this chapter we will learn about the risks associated with early puberty.

In the United States, the average girl begins to experience the changes associated with puberty at about ten years of age (Chumlea, 1982; Tanner, 1990). Individual variations are great, however, and the range is typically from eight to eleven years of age (AMA, 2006). Boys begin the process at about age twelve, and their range is from nine to sixteen years of age. Primary and secondary sexual characteristics typically are fully in evidence within two years of the beginning of puberty in both sexes. Besides an individual's sex, puberty is influenced by a person's genetic background and body weight. The age at which menarche occurs differs considerably between unrelated females, but the average time difference between sisters is only about thirteen months, although that between identical twin sisters is a mere three months (Thornburg & Aras, 1986).

Both males and females who are heavier than age-mates tend to begin puberty at earlier ages than those who are thin. The timing of menarche appears to be sensitive to the proportion of fat present in a girl's body. Girls with athletic figures and little body fat menstruate at later ages and more irregularly than others. Girls who are inactive and weigh more begin menstruation earlier (Frisch, 1983).

How do males experience puberty? Body proportions and size generally undergo a rapid increase during adolescence. Puberty also produces rapid changes in the size and functioning of the reproductive organs. There is a sequence that is followed by most males as they become sexually mature. The initial physical changes associated with puberty are very noticeable in boys because the male reproductive organs are visible.

Growth of the testicles usually signals the beginning of puberty for boys. This change precedes growth of the penis, which usually begins at about age twelve. The testicles begin preparations for producing sperm about this same time, though the prostate gland, which produces seminal fluid to convey sperm outside the body, does not function until about age fourteen. Mature, viable sperm are typically produced at about age fifteen (Richardson & Short, 1978). It should be noted that there are considerable variations in the ages at which these events occur.

Pubic hair growth often begins up to two years before the testicles start to increase in size. Hair begins to appear on the chest and in the armpits after the pubic hair has been established. Facial hair changes in texture and growth rate at about this same time, prompting the need for daily shaving. The change to a more masculine deep voice occurs shortly after the completion of pubic hair growth. The characteristic breaks in tone and pitch as this is happening are due to rapid growth of the larynx and thickening of the vocal cords. Boys experience their first ejaculation of semen typically at about age fourteen or fifteen. This typically happens involuntarily during sleep

During puberty, boys gain much body weight, primarily in their muscles. This gives them a different body definition than is observed in girls. Other male body configurations resulting from puberty are a widening of the shoulders, growth of the upper body muscles, and expansion of the rib cage. These give mature males a V-shaped torso above the waist (Chumlea, 1982).

How do females experience puberty? Although growth of the reproductive organs in girls is less observable than it is in boys because these organs are mostly internal, the appearance of certain secondary sex characteristics signals the beginning of puberty in a girl's body (Thornburg & Aras, 1986; AMA, 2006). One of the first indications is enlargement and widening of the hips. As this is happening, the breasts begin to develop. The nipples grow larger and darker before mammary tissue starts to develop. Soon after the initiation of hip and breast enlargement, pubic hair appears.

Hair growth at other locations on the body is associated with the first menstrual period. Hair is lighter in

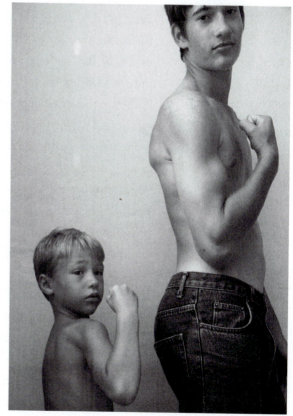

Body weight and muscle is gained during puberty.

pigmentation and softer in texture than in males, except at the armpits and on the legs (because of the practice of shaving these areas). Voice changes are noticeable at this time, but breaks in tone and pitch are uncommon in girls. In both boys and girls, the glands located in the armpits become active at this time, resulting in the production of perspiration and changes in body odor. Similar glands located on the face also begin functioning, sometimes accompanied by acne.

The first indication of sexual maturation is the menarche, or first menstrual period, at about age thirteen (Thornburg & Aras, 1986). The peak of the adolescent growth spurt for girls is associated with the menarche. Menstruation is highly variable in duration and length for about the first year. It is known as *anovulatory* menstruation because regular ovulation, or the production of a viable egg cell during each twenty-eight-day cycle, is not yet occurring. Conception is possible during this time, however, because viable egg cells are sometimes produced.

Menstruation among adolescent girls is sometimes uncomfortable because of cramps. This *dysmenorrhea* may require medical attention if the cramps are painful and limit the girl's activities (Spence & Mason, 1987).

Menarche is a significant physical event for females. It signifies emerging womanhood. However, timing, as our next section will show, is very important.

Off-time

When a person experiences puberty earlier or later than most of his or her same-age peers.

EARLY VERSUS LATE PUBERTY   As we noted earlier, there is considerable variation in the ages at which puberty begins and when the various physical changes associated with it appear. Imagine your reaction if all of your friends have begun the process of sexual maturing, but you have not. Or, imagine that you are well on your way to sexual maturity when most of your friends are still clearly children. When a person experiences puberty earlier or later than most of his or her same-age peers, it is considered **off-time** puberty (as opposed to on-time puberty). Although variations in the rate and timing of puberty are normal, individuals at both extremes experience both advantages and disadvantages from their position.

Sexual maturity brings other changes in addition to the physical. This developmental event transforms an individual socially and psychologically as well. For example, a youth group coordinator once told one of the authors a story about her granddaughter. The youth group was having a dance, and the youth group coordinator brought her then ten-year-old granddaughter (let's call her Adele) to the dance. Adele matured early and had the physical attributes of the average fourteen-year-old girl. Not knowing her age, an older teen boy asked Adele to dance. How do you think she responded? Do you think she did what the typical teenage girl would do and say either "yes," or "no, thank you"? No. Instead, she covered her face and ran into the bathroom crying. The boy was completely confused. Later, when the youth group coordinator explained that Adele was ten, the boy said that he had no idea how young she was and apologized.

What the above story illustrates is that puberty is far more than just physical and that timing is important. Adele had the body of a teenager, but still had the mind and emotional maturity of a child. However, the rest of the world began treating Adele as though she were socially and psychologically older than her age; and, this would impact Adele's development. A year later, Adele was no longer hanging around with the other eleven-year-olds in youth group, but instead with the high school students. Her social circle had changed and she was psychologically more mature than her age-mates. As we will soon see, this can lead to devastating outcomes.

There is a plethora of research on the influence of off-time puberty on developmental outcomes in boys and girls (e.g., Adair & Gordon-Larsen, 2001; Blyth, Simmons & Zakin, 1985; Caspi & Moffitt, 1991; Dick, Rose, Viken & Kaprio, 2000; Duncan et al., 1985; Ge, Conger & Elder, 1996; Ge et al., 2006; Graber, Lewinsohn, Seeley & Brooks-Gunn, 1997; Graber et al., 1998; Jones 1957 and 1965; Kelsey, Gammon & John, 1993; Marshall et al., 1998; McPherson, Sellers, Potter, Bostick & Folsom, 1996; Petersen, 1988; Rudolph, 2008; Sellers et al., 1992; Steinberg, 1987; Susman et al., 2007; Weichold, Silbereisen & Schmitt-Rodermund, 2003; Wellens et al., 1992; Williams & Dunlop, 1999; Wiesner & Ittel, 2002; Wu et al., 1988). Across these studies, the outcomes discussed below were discovered.

Compared to on-time and/or later maturing girls, early maturing girls can experience many problems. The following outcomes have been correlated with early puberty in girls:

- Breast cancer

- Other reproductive system cancers

- Lower self-esteem

- Depression

- Lower coping skills

- Missing school

- Low family and friend support

- Low self-rated health

- Risky sexual behavior

- Teenage pregnancy, with increased rates for miscarriages, stillbirths, and low-birth-weight babies.

- Abortion

- Increased suicide attempts

- Eating disorders

- Substance abuse

- Body dissatisfaction

- Obesity

- Relational aggression

- Risky relationships

- Interpersonal stress

- Externalizing behavior
- Psychopathology
- Lifetime history of adjustment problems

When compared to on-time and/or early maturing girls, late maturing girls are more likely to experience the following:

- Increased self-consciousness
- Thinness
- Increased future academic goals
- Increased lifetime depression rates
- Increased conflict with parents

When compared to on-time or late maturing boys, early maturing boys are more likely to experience the following:

- Early alcohol use
- Increased depression rates
- More major life events
- More emotional reliance on others than on-time maturing boys
- Higher future family goals
- More physical illness
- Increased popularity
- Increased self-image and body satisfaction
- Increased substance abuse
- Increased smoking
- Increased conflict with mothers
- Broad array of antisocial and delinquent behaviors

When compared to on-time or early maturing boys, late maturing boys are more likely to experience the following:

- Lower self-esteem
- Immature behavior
- Feelings of inferiority
- Poorer athletic ability
- Early alcohol use

- More daily hassles
- Depression
- Negative thoughts
- Self-consciousness
- Internalizing behavior problems
- More emotional reliance on others than on-time maturing boys
- Increased tardiness at school
- Lower rates of homework completion
- Increased rates of parental dissatisfaction with grades
- Increased conflict with parents
- Poorer coping skills
- Psychopathology

As the above bulleted lists demonstrate, there are a multitude of problems associated with early or late maturation for both boys and girls. Of course, these are simply outcomes that can happen and steps can be taken to help avoid these outcomes. For example, parental monitoring and social support can help prevent many of these adjustment problems.

Pause and Process:

1. How do males and females physically develop during adolescence?

2. What influences the timing of puberty? What are some potential consequences for off-time puberty?

HEALTH ISSUES

Nutritional Needs

Adults are often amazed at a teenager's capacity for food, especially in contrast to how the same individual ate just a few years earlier. However, the increased need for calories is often met by teenagers eating foods that consist of "empty" calories. The notorious American teenage diet features fast foods and snack foods such as doughnuts, pizza, fries, chips, candies, and burgers. These foods are high in sugar and fat, but deficient in such nutrients as iron, protein, calcium, and zinc. Serious deficiencies in these substances can lead to delayed sexual maturation, stunted growth, and poor skeletal development and organ functioning. They can also adversely affect psychological mood (Steiner, 1990). Nutritional deficiencies are even more serious when a teenage girl becomes pregnant. Improper eating habits can endanger the health and well-being not only of the infant but also of the young mother (Strobino, 1987). Obesity is also a growing concern with 17.6 percent of all adolescents considered obese (CDC, 2009).

The World Health Organization (2008) reports that many individuals are malnourished when they begin adolescence. They may be malnourished due to a lack of food or due to poor eating habits. In fact, it is possible to be overweight or even obese and be malnourished. As mentioned above, lack of nutrition can lead to many physical and psychological issues. At the extreme, malnutrition can lead to serious illness and death. Adolescence is a key time for proper nutrition and exercise, as it acts as the springboard into adulthood. We will discuss eating disorders in the mental health section of this chapter.

Teenagers tend to consume nutrient deficient foods such as hamburgers and fries.

Some teenagers decide to adopt a vegetarian diet. Because of the physical changes that occur during adolescence, the elimination of an entire food group from one's diet can be dangerous (AMA, 2006). It is often helpful for teenagers to meet with a dietitian when beginning a vegetarian diet in order to ensure proper nutrition and learn about possible food combinations. However, research seems to indicate that vegetarian adolescents do a better job of meeting dietary recommendations than nonvegetarian adolescents (Perry et. al, 2002).

Physiologic

The fifth stage for understanding illness; described as the malfunctioning of an internal physiologic organ or process and is explained as a step-by-step sequence of events.

Psychophysiologic

The sixth stage for understanding illness; illness is understood physiologically, but the child also can consider the influence of psychological factors.

ILLNESS, DISORDERS, AND OTHER CONCERNS   In earlier chapters we learned about Bibace and Walsh's (1979, 1980, and 1981) developmental stages for understanding illness. We learned that phenomenism and contagion are how illness is understood in early childhood. We also learned that contamination and internalization are how illness is understood in middle childhood. During adolescence, the final two stages of understanding illness typically emerge.

Physiologic is the fifth stage for understanding illness. **Physiologic** thinking can be described as understanding illness "as the malfunctioning of an internal physiologic organ or process and is explained as a step-by-step sequence of events" (Bearison, 1998). This thinking goes a step beyond the internalization stage by a deeper understanding about the physiological process of illness.

The sixth and final stage is called psychophysiologic. In **psychophysiologic** thinking "illness is understood physiologically, but the child also can consider the influence of psychological factors" (Bearison, 1998). An adolescent at this stage of reasoning will understand that stress can trigger heart attacks, as well as the physiological aspects of a heart attack. It is at this point that a person can begin to approach health and well-being holistically.

Mental Health During Adolescence   Approximately 20 percent of adolescents have a mental disorder of some type (WHO, 2008). Eating disorders are of particular concern during this phase of the life span. Many adolescents are highly self-critical of their bodies. Frantic to achieve a desired body image, they may diet to the point of malnutrition. Some have such a distorted body image that they convince themselves they are obese when objectively they are not (Mellendick, 1983). They feel such low self-esteem in relation to their perceived weight problem that they become vulnerable to serious eating disorders (Button, 1990).

The most common serious eating disorders in adolescence are anorexia nervosa and bulimia nervosa. Both conditions are seen more in teenage girls than in boys. These conditions have serious consequences for the health, well-being, and even the lives of teenagers (Dukes & Lorch, 1989; Phelps & Bajorek, 1991).

Anorexia nervosa is an abnormal fear of obesity that is manifested by distortions of body image and "the relentless pursuit of thinness" (American Psychiatric Association, 1980; Bruch, 1978; SAMHSA, 2003). Its symptoms are excessive weight loss (25 percent of total body weight or more); the cessation of menstruation; a distorted body image—that is, believing that one is seriously overweight when this is not so; obsessive-compulsive preoccupation with dieting; social withdrawal; depression; and feelings of insecurity, loneliness, inadequacy, and helplessness. The typical anorexic is a girl between twelve and twenty years of age who comes from a stable, well-educated, and socially competent family and who is herself bright, well-behaved, and physically attractive (Gilbert & DeBlassie, 1984).

This condition is one of the few psychological disorders that can have fatal consequences if left untreated (SAMHSA, 2003). It begins with dieting to achieve a certain weight level. However, once that level is achieved, an anorexic continues to diet obsessively. Controlling her weight and what she eats has become her central life focus.

The causes of this condition are not clear, although several explanations have been proposed. One is that heavy cultural conditioning convinces adolescent girls that slim figures are essential to attract males (Carruth & Goldberg, 1990). Another explanation is that anorexia is a means to avoid or delay dealing with the many changes associated with puberty. Extreme thinness often stops menstruation and prevents the development of a female body configuration. Finally, some have seen anorexia as a means of rebelling in a passive-aggressive way against strict, overprotective parents. Unable to establish adequate personal boundaries combined with an inability to individuate or attain personal autonomy in normal ways because of parental over-involvement, the anorexic resorts to proving her control of herself by severely controlling her weight (Bruch, 1978; Romeo, 1984).

If left untreated, anorexia can result in death due to starvation. Therapy can involve hospitalization to treat the malnutrition and individual therapy to help the young woman become autonomous in less damaging ways (Beresin, Gordon & Herzog, 1989). Family therapy may be needed to end the extreme enmeshment of the girl with her parents, to improve communication, and to help the family system acquire healthy ways of resolving

Anorexia nervosa

An eating disorder involving complex emotional and body image disturbances that lead to an obsession with limiting dietary intake in order to control body weight. The condition is life-threatening if left untreated.

conflict (Muuss, 1985; Waller, Calam & Slade, 1988). Approximately one out of every one hundred to two hundred adolescent females suffers from anorexia (National Institute of Health, 1999).

Bulimia nervosa involves consuming huge amounts of food and then purging the body by vomiting, using laxatives or enemas, or excessive exercise (Hudson, Pope & Jonas, 1983; Pope et al., 1983, SAMHSA, 2003). The consumption is done in binges, usually to cope with some stressful situation. Like anorexics, bulimics have a distorted body image that leads to an obsession with weight control. Unlike anorexics, however, bulimics know that their behavior is not appropriate. They usually binge and purge in secret to avoid discovery, but they feel much shame and guilt nevertheless.

Bulimia is a common method of achieving weight control among contemporary adolescent girls. Approximately one to three out of every one hundred adolescents suffers from bulimia (National Institute of Health, 1999). It can lead to severe depression, which can result in suicide (Kandel, Raveis & Davies, 1991). Many bulimics are perfectionists with an obsessive desire to control and manage their own and others' lives. They are heavily dependent on others' approval for their self-worth (Pike, 1991).

This condition, like anorexia, responds to psychotherapy and treatment with antidepressant medications. These help bulimics to achieve a better understanding of femininity and healthful ways of dealing with stressful situations (Muuss, 1986; Yager, 1988).

Risky Behavior   The use of drugs among adolescents is one of the greatest health concerns for this age group. Globally, tobacco is used by more than one 150 million adolescents (WHO, 2008). In the United States, 26 percent of all twelfth graders engage in heavy drinking (Federal Interagency Forum on Child and Family Statistics, 2008). Further, 22 percent of twelfth graders report using illegal drugs (Federal Interagency Forum on Child and Family Statistics, 2008). Why would so many adolescents want to use such mood-altering substances when they are at a period of life that our society sees as the best of times? Perhaps there is no simple explanation. Some teenagers seem predisposed to drug use because they observe their parents doing so (Brown, 1989; Kline, Canter & Robin, 1987). Others are susceptible to peer pressure to experiment

Bulimia Nervosa

An eating disorder involving emotional and body image disturbances that lead to intake of large amounts of food that are then purged by vomiting or use of laxatives to control body weight.

Bulimia can sometimes be used to cope with stress.

with drugs (Newcomb, McCarthy & Bentler, 1989; Swaim et al., 1989). Drug use may also have something to do with a lack of adequate parental supervision before and after school (Richardson & Dwyer, 1989) and the nature of relationships within the family system (Brook et al., 1986; Newcomb & Bentler, 1988a, 1988b).

Adolescents do not always perceive drugs as harmful. In reality, teenagers experience harmful effects from drug use in both the short and the long term. Self-destructive behaviors associated with chronic use of these substances include addiction, lack of motivation, and suicide (Sommer, 1984). Drug use begun in adolescence usually continues into adulthood (Kandel et al., 1986; Newcomb & Bentler, 1988). Teenagers who use drugs regularly tend to be in poorer health than their age-mates and to have unstable job and financial conditions, troublesome relationship histories, and emotional depression. Like adults, teenagers use drugs to cope with unhappiness, stress, loneliness, and physical as well as psychological pain. Recent research finds rather serious consequences for even moderate drug use by teenagers. One is that it is highly associated with sexual behaviors that place adolescents at high risk of HIV infection (Keller et al., 1991).

Alcohol   Use of drugs for medicating physical and psychological discomforts is endemic in American culture (Nobles, 1984; Rowe & Rodgers, 1991). Many drugs, in fact, are so widely used that people are surprised to learn they *are* drugs. For example, coffee contains a powerful stimulant, caffeine, which is an addictive drug. Likewise alcohol is a drug that has mood-altering and addictive properties.

Alcohol use among teenagers is so common that some consider it normal, although our society officially defines drinking by those younger than twenty-one as illegal (Newcomb & Bentler, 1989). Nearly 45 percent of high school students have had an alcoholic drink within the past month, according to a comprehensive survey (CDC, 2007). Peer pressure evidently plays a significant role in this behavior.

Tobacco   Although many people don't think of tobacco as a drug, cigarette smoke contains nicotine which is one of the most addictive substances. Smoking is regarded by medical authorities as a serious health hazard (Adeyanju, 1989). Around 20 percent of high school students smoke, although nearly 8 percent use smokeless tobacco (CDC, 2007). Teenagers who use other drugs such as alcohol also tend to smoke cigarettes. Other risk factors are having at least one parent who smokes, a greater tendency than the norm for risk-taking behaviors, and a rebellious personality (Ary & Biglan, 1988; Windle, 1991).

Marijuana   Marijuana ("pot") may symbolize adolescent rebellion against authority and control more than other drugs. Many more adolescents experiment with this drug than use it regularly (Newcomb & Bentler, 1989). For example, a national survey found that although 38 percent of high school students had tried marijuana, 19.7 percent had used it within the last month (CDC, 2007). Those who use marijuana regularly resemble adolescents who use cigarettes and alcohol: they tend to have parents who use drugs as coping mechanisms and who are somewhat rebellious in nature.

The use of marijuana can have adverse affects on the reproductive system. It also impairs motor abilities.

There are both short- and long-term effects of marijuana use on the user's health. The chemical components in marijuana smoke temporarily impair motor abilities and lung functioning, decrease sperm counts in males and interfere with ovulation in females, diminish the responsiveness of the immune system, and contribute to the risk of lung cancer (National Academy of Sciences, 1982). Chronic pot smokers tend to have low motivation and energy, and teenage users may be expected to have problems with school and job performance (Rainone et al., 1987). In addition, violent delinquent behavior is associated with heavy use of marijuana and other illicit drugs among boys (Watts & Wright, 1990).

Sexualization

A person's value comes only from his or her sexual appeal or behavior, to the exclusion of other characteristics; a person is held to a standard that equates physical attractiveness (narrowly defined) with being sexy; a person is sexually objectified—that is, made into a thing for others' sexual use, rather than seen as a person with the capacity for independent action and decision making; and/or sexuality is inappropriately imposed upon a person.

Sexual Activity   Slightly less than half (47.8 percent) of all U.S. high school students have engaged in sexual intercourse (CDC, 2007). Such early sexual behavior is worrisome for several reasons. First, adolescents are not yet emotionally mature enough to handle the aftermath of sexual activity. Second, less than two-thirds of sexually active teens use a condom to prevent sexually transmitted diseases. Third, teenage pregnancy may result from this behavior.

Early sexual behavior is responsible for some scary statistics. Worldwide, adolescents and people in their early twenties account for 45 percent of all new HIV infections (CDC, 2007). Additionally, approximately 11 percent of all births (or sixteen million births) worldwide are to teenage mothers. Furthermore, sexually transmitted disease (STD) rates have increased for adolescents in recent years. According to the Center for Disease Control, "while representing 25 percent of the ever sexually active population, fifteen- to twenty-four-year-olds acquire nearly half of all new STDs." Although condoms can help prevent infections and pregnancy, the one sure way to avoid these outcomes is abstinence (AMA, 2006).

Promoting Wellness   The American Psychological Association (APA) recently had a task force convene to investigate the sexualization of girls in the United States. They released their findings in 2007 in a troublesome report. The APA (2007) defines **sexualization** as the following: "a person's value comes only from his or her sexual appeal or behavior, to the exclusion of other characteristics; a person is held to a standard that equates physical attractiveness (narrowly defined) with being sexy; a person is sexually objectified—that is, made into a thing for others' sexual use, rather than seen as a person with the capacity for independent action and decision making; and/or sexuality is inappropriately imposed upon a person" (p. 1).

In our society, girls are especially inundated with messages from every form of media that they are first and foremost sexual beings (APA, 2007). It isn't hard for girls to begin to base their self-worth on their identity as a sexual being. Parents and peers can further contribute to the sexualization of girls by emphasizing physical appearance and conformity to media messages. Girls can internalize all of these messages and begin to think of themselves as sexual objects to be presented to others for their desires.

Sexualization of girls can lead to serious consequences across various domains (APA, 2007). Obsession with one's appearance can prevent concentrating on academic matters. Mathematical ability and logical reasoning are two areas that research has found are impacted by sexualization. Shame is a common emotion experience by girls and women who have been sexualized. Low self-esteem, eating disorders, and depression are three mental health concerns that research has found to be linked to sexualization. Finally, sexualization can lead to sexual problems in adulthood due to unrealistic expectations or shame.

The impact of sexualization extends beyond the girls who experience it (APA, 2007). Rigid sexual stereotypes are propagated through sexualization. Men may be unable to find a female he considers acceptable (due to unrealistic physical expectations) and establish a healthy relationship (due to treating women as objects). Sexualization contributes to the devaluing of older women who do not meet the young, attractive ideal idolized by our media. Finally, sexualization increases sexism, which is linked to increased rates of sexual harassment and sexual violence, decreased rates of women going into math and science fields, and increased viewership of child pornography.

The sexualization of girls, and society in general, must be fought if health and well-being are to be supported in our adolescents. The APA (2008) has developed specific advice for parents to assist in fighting sexualization of their children. Parents should be aware of what their adolescents are watching and listening to on television and in other forms of media. If their favorite show depicts women as sexual objects, talk about it with them. Increase their awareness of how this is wrong and that both females and males must be valued for traits beyond their physical appearance. Parents should encourage their adolescents to be interested in activities that focus on areas beyond appearance. Sports, religious groups, school clubs, and other extracurricular activities can help youth develop identities that focus on qualities beyond their appearance. Finally, educate adolescents. Appropriate sexual behavior and inappropriate sexual behaviors should be discussed. Ideally, adolescents should feel comfortable discussing sexuality with their parents.

Beyond combating sexualization, there are some other issues to consider in promoting the health and well-being of adolescents. Only 34.7 percent of all adolescents engage in the recommended amount of physical activity each week (CDC, 2007). Further, nearly 25 percent of teens play video games or use a computer for reasons other than schoolwork for more than three hours each day, and 35.4 percent watch television for three or more hours each day. Clearly, steps should be taken to encourage teenagers to spend less time in sedentary activities and more time engaging in physical activities.

Sleep is another area of concern. Adequate sleep is necessary for motivation, mood, attention, learning, and mental health (Dahl, 1999). However, only 31.1 percent of all teenagers regularly obtain the recommended eight hours of sleep each night (CDC, 2007).

The World Health Organization (2008) states that "nearly two thirds of premature deaths and one third of the total disease burden in adults are associated with conditions or behaviors that began in youth, including tobacco use, a lack of physical activity, unprotected sex or exposure to violence." Educating youth about healthy behavior will not only assist achieving a healthy and safe adolescence, but lead to a longer and healthier adult life as well.

Pause and Process:

1. What are some health and behavior concerns during adolescence?

2. What are some consequences of the sexualization of girls?

COGNITIVE DEVELOPMENT DURING ADOLESCENCE

LEARNING OBJECTIVES:

1. Characterize the formal operational stage of cognitive development

2. Describe other ways cognitive abilities develop during adolescence

During adolescence, important changes take place in an individual's cognitive abilities. Thinking and comprehension during early and middle childhood are governed by perceptions. Children use their perceptions of the environment to develop hypotheses about their worlds that they believe are borne out by factual experiences. In adolescence, individuals' understanding of people, events, and circumstances becomes more flexible and abstract reasoning becomes possible.

PIAGET'S COGNITIVE DEVELOPMENTAL THEORY AND THE FORMAL OPERATIONAL STAGE

Piaget (1967) labels adolescence as the period of **formal operations**. Cognitive skills advance during this time as adolescents become increasingly able to use logic and reasoning. They are capable of thinking hypothetically, of using deductive and inductive reasoning to reach conclusions and to solve a variety of problems (Wadsworth, 2004). **Deductive reasoning** is when you begin with the big picture and develop conclusions.

Said another way, you move from the general to the specific with deductive reasoning. **Inductive reasoning** can be defined as "reasoning from specific facts to general conclusions" (Wadsworth, 2004, p. 113). **Hypothetical reasoning** or thought is the ability to think and reason about ideas in the abstract.

The egocentrism that colored an individual's perceptions through childhood lessens. By late adolescence, an individual shows much more flexibility. Thinking is less absolute as teens discover that there are gray areas in many situations where rigid rules fail to apply.

Characteristics of Formal Operational Thought

Formal operations thinking is characterized by hypothetical-deductive reasoning and scientific-inductive reasoning (Piaget, 1972; Wadsworth, 2004). Hypothetical-deductive reasoning allows individuals to work through mathematical and other such problems abstractly. For example, consider the following word problem:

Representatives from eight nations have decided to meet to discuss an international standardized test for graduating college students. The eight nations are China, France, Germany, Italy, Japan, Singapore, Sweden, and the United States. You are the administrative assistant and must develop the seating chart for the meeting. The table is long and rectangular. China must NOT sit across or next to Japan. France must sit next to Germany. Sweden must sit next to Italy and across from Singapore. The United States must be across from Japan. Draw the seating chart.

Hypothetical-deductive reasoning would allow a person to deduce the seating chart from the premises of the problem. Additionally, use of hypothetical-deductive reasoning would allow a person to start with a false premise, yet reason a logical conclusion (Wadsworth, 2004).

In contrast to hypothetical-deductive reasoning, **scientific-inductive reasoning** starts with an observation or thought that generates a hypothesis about something. The person then logically works through the alternatives that are implied as outcomes or conclusions of the hypothesis.

A classic experiment by Inhelder and Piaget (1958) reveals how individuals change their reasoning about the laws of physics by manipulating objects. Shifts in the manner by which hypotheses are generated to explain the physical actions and reactions of objects show how scientific reasoning develops during adolescence. Children and adolescents were given a variety of objects. They were asked to place some in water and explain why certain objects sank while others floated. They were also given different weights to place on a scale or on a pendulum held by a string and challenged to determine what accounted for the speed of the pendulum's swing. Marbles were given to the individuals that they were to roll down an incline and estimate the distance the marbles would roll when reaching a flat surface.

When experimenting with the weights placed on a string pendulum, for example, individuals at all ages were challenged to determine which factor accounts for the pendulum's speed (Ginsburg & Opper, 1979). Several factors must be considered in reaching a solution to this problem: (1) the length of the string, (2) the object's weight, (3) the degree of force used to place the pendulum in motion, and (4) the height from which the object is released.

Children at the preoperational stage were perplexed by this problem. They tended to experiment in a trial-and-error fashion with the various factors. They haphazardly experimented with the different factors. They usually concluded (incorrectly) that it is the force by which an object

Marbles rolling down an incline is an example of a scientific-inductive reasoning test.

is pushed on the pendulum that determines its speed because this *appears* to be the case.

Children at the concrete operations level approached the problem in similar ways. They did not experiment with the various factors systematically, but rather impulsively. However, because thinking at this level of cognitive development involves more mental imagery, they were able to consider several possible solutions before they began experimenting. When experimenting with the different factors, these children were likely to conclude (again, incorrectly) that more than one factor influenced the speed of the pendulum because they varied two factors simultaneously (e.g., the length of the string and the objects weight).

Adolescents of fourteen or fifteen, the age at which one enters the formal operations stage, realized that the solution to the problem could be determined systematically. By experimenting with changes in factors one at a time, these teenagers discovered that only one factor or one combination of factors could affect the pendulum's speed. They generated hypotheses before they began experimenting with making changes in each factor. By reasoning in a scientific manner, they could change one factor, such as the length of the string, while keeping the other factors constant. By methodically experimenting in this fashion, teenagers were able to conclude (correctly) that the string's length is the key factor in determining the speed of a pendulum.

The increasing flexibility in thinking that occurs during adolescence can be seen in other ways. For example, Flavell (1985) proposes that individuals in late adolescence can participate in what is called the **game of thinking**. This requires divorcing oneself from reality and playfully considering various hypothetical possibilities in certain situations. For

Game of thinking

Divorcing oneself from reality and playfully considering various hypothetical possibilities in certain situations.

instance, it is possible for an eighteen-year-old to play the role of "devil's advocate" in discussions of moral issues. In this role, the person suspends his own personal beliefs and assumes, for the sake of argument or to make a conversation more interesting, a position that may be diametrically opposed to what he actually believes. A school-age child would be unable to do this because individuals at the concrete operations level are bound by their perceptions of reality and have great difficulty seeing situations from other vantage points.

Individuals who are developing cognitive skills characteristics at the formal operations level apply these advanced thinking skills to many different types of problems—moral decisions, understanding others, and developing a philosophy of life or a belief system, for example. They first consider all the possible options, alternatives, or avenues for solving a problem or deriving the explanation of a situation. Then they examine each independently and in relation to others to arrive at an acceptable solution.

Cognitive Traits

We gain a better appreciation of adolescents' social behavior when we take their level of cognitive ability into consideration. Like most developmental changes, mature thinking is achieved gradually rather than abruptly. For many individuals, the process continues throughout adulthood (Kohlberg & Gilligan, 1971). For example, only 57 percent of adults forty-five to fifty years old who were presented with the pendulum problem just discussed were successful at solving it. This compares with slightly more than half of the adolescents studied.

Mature thinking styles give people greater freedom to explore possibilities in considering and solving a variety of problems. They make people more empathic and capable of critically examining the values and beliefs they have been taught by others. The ability to disengage oneself from reality to consider numerous possibilities opens avenues that less mature thinking styles restrict or inhibit. These less mature styles are carried from middle childhood into early adolescence, however, and act as barriers or challenges to acquiring the more mature, flexible style that characterizes late adolescence and early adulthood. One cognitive distortion that hinders achievement of fully mature thinking is adolescent egocentrism.

Psychologist David Elkind (1967, 1978) states that the type of cognitive egocentrism observed in adolescence is the essence of adolescence itself. Cognitive egocentrism was first observed in early childhood. Preschoolers are egocentric in that they regard their own perceptual viewpoint as the only means for understanding the operations of the world. This trait somewhat continues to color interpretations of the world throughout middle childhood, though it weakens during this time. However, school-age children still make judgments and interpretations in absolute terms based on appearances and perceptions. This causes them to think in polar extremes: something is either all right or completely wrong; people are treated either fairly or unfairly; something is either 100 percent good or 100 percent bad. Children this age have difficulty perceiving that there is middle ground between these two extremes.

In adolescence, childhood egocentrism gives way to logical thinking. However, even as this is occurring, egocentrism persists, though it manifests itself in new ways.

Pseudostupidity

The tendency of young adolescents to interpret situations in more complex ways than called for.

Imaginary audience

The adolescent egocentric belief that other people are obsessed and consumed with his or her appearance and behavior.

Personal or Invincibility fable

The belief that one is immune from all harm or injury.

Apparent hypocrisy

The considerable incongruence between what they say they believe and how they behave.

1. **Pseudostupidity** is the tendency of young adolescents to interpret situations in more complex ways than called for. This has been termed "reading more into situations than what is intended or implied" or "making mountains out of molehills." Teens can become so overwhelmed by the complexity of issues and the numerous alternatives available for action that they are unable to make any decision. Pseudostupidity produces indecisiveness in some adolescents much of the time, and in most adolescents in some circumstances. For some people, this cognitive distortion continues into adulthood.

2. Young adolescents typically believe that they are the center of everyone's attention or that they are carefully observed by an **imaginary audience**. This belief often makes them overly self-conscious about their appearance. It also convinces them that they can read other people's minds, which leads to another cognitive distortion: *fortune telling* or *jumping to conclusions* (Burns, 1980). This flaw in logical thinking produces negative interpretations based on incomplete or inaccurate information.

3. Young adolescents believe in the **personal** or **invincibility fable** (Elkind, 1974). This is the belief that one is immune from all harm or injury. It leads young adolescents to believe they are special, that bad things can only happen to others, but not to them. This cognitive distortion helps explain the outrageous, extreme, and high-risk behaviors common among young adolescents (e.g., early sexual behavior, drinking, smoking, riding with drivers under the influence of alcohol, riding a motorcycle without a helmet, etc.).

4. Teenagers show a certain degree of **apparent hypocrisy**, meaning there is considerable incongruence between what they say they believe and how they behave. Apparent hypocrisy is often manifested in stubborn arguments with adults, especially parents. For example, young teens can be very critical of parental insensitivity to their needs, yet feel that they do not have to be sensitive to their parents' needs. Their egocentrism leads them to believe they are exempt from rules they believe are valid and important for others to observe.

A major developmental task of adolescence is to overcome the barriers of egocentrism and advance toward more mature ways of reaching decisions (Ginsburg & Opper, 1979). This requires learning to question one's style of thinking. By using more logical thinking processes and gathering information based on fact, an individual achieves more sophisticated levels of formal operations.

Pause and Process:

1. How is the formal operations stage of thinking different from thinking in the concrete operations stage?

2. How may the imaginary audience, invincibility fable, and egocentrism impact the behavior of high school students?

OTHER AREAS OF COGNITIVE DEVELOPMENT IN ADOLESCENCE

Modern cognitive theorists study ways in which cognitive development continues past childhood. Although many areas of information-processing and language skills reach adultlike levels by the end of middle childhood, other areas of cognition continue to develop.

Dialectical Reasoning

Dialectical reasoning

The deliberate coordination of inferences for the purpose of making cognitive progress.

One area that continues to develop is dialectical reasoning. **Dialectical reasoning** can be defined as "the deliberate coordination of inferences for the purpose of making cognitive progress" (Moshman, 1998, p. 961). In plain English, it involves integrating one's assumptions to assist when reasoning through a problem. Argumentation may involve the use of dialectical reasoning. When debating an issue with another, one will often use their beliefs and observations to make a point.

Problem Solving

Problem solving

The development of strategies to overcome an obstacle in order to achieve a goal.

Problem solving is another area that shows continued development across childhood into adolescence (Deloache, Miller & Pierroutsakos, 1998; Siegler, 1998). Problem solving involves developing a strategy to overcome an obstacle in order to achieve a goal. Problem solving involves many aspects of cognitive processes, such as memory, reasoning, metacognition, and perception.

Task analysis

The careful examination of a problem and consideration of what steps will be necessary in order to solve it.

One key component to problem solving is task analysis. **Task analysis** requires you to carefully examine the problem and consider what steps will be necessary in order to solve it (Deloache, Miller & Pierroutsakos, 1998; Siegler, 1998). After task analysis, you must encode. **Encoding** allows you to develop an internal, mental representation of the situation. Finally, your knowledge should be used to assist in addressing the problem and reconciling it.

Encoding

Developing an internal, mental representation of the situation.

There are developmental differences in problem solving strategies and abilities (Deloache, Miller & Pierroutsakos, 1998; Siegler, 1998). Rudimentary forms of problem solving are evident in infancy. Across childhood, the ability to plan a strategy for solving a problem improves. As age increases, the ability to develop and achieve subgoals in assistance to solving the larger problem improves. The ability to choose or develop the most appropriate strategy also improves with age. Finally, with formal operational thought, sophisticated forms of reasoning emerge. Such reasoning allows for better problem solving.

19. What is meant by problem solving?

Moral Reasoning

Up until now, we really haven't discussed moral reasoning. Hence, we will need to back up a bit to childhood in order to understand moral reasoning in adolescence.

Kohlberg describes a model of moral reasoning that is widely accepted among developmental researchers. He believes that children are moral philosophers. A series of related stages is experienced by children in learning moral reasoning. These stages parallel those of cognitive growth. Changes are motivated by maturational factors from within a child's psychology.

Three general levels of moral development are proposed, and each has two substages. Children are able to resolve more complex moral issues as they progress through these levels. The first level is experienced in early childhood and continues throughout most of middle childhood. The second level begins in late middle childhood and continues through adolescence.

Preconventional level

Moral reasoning based upon physical consequences and the power of those in authority.

Level one (ages four to ten) is called the **preconventional level**. Children generally are well behaved during this period. They recognize the meaning of labels such as "good" and "bad." They behave in relation to the physical consequences and the power of those in authority. *Stage one* of this level is demonstrated when children show concern for being punished for wrongdoing. They show unquestioning obedience to those in authority. Children at *stage two* are concerned with good behavior that is associated with primitive utilitarian needs. They will behave well if they receive some personal profit or reward from doing so.

Conventional level

Moral reasoning that consists of conformity to the rules of important groups.

Level two (ages ten and older) is referred to as the **conventional level**. An individual's moral behavior is shown through conformity to rules of important groups, e.g., the family system, peers, the school system. Having allegiances to these are seen as important values for the person. Individuals at *stage three* of this level behave well in order to receive approval from groups. Good behavior is seen as that which helps or pleases others with little attention directed to personal needs. The emphasis is on being "nice." Individuals at *stage four* of this level have a "law and order" orientation. Behaving appropriately is one's duty. Respect is shown for principles or rules that guide appropriate behavior.

The seventh year of life is a watershed period in terms of moral development. Before this time, the ability to reason morally is constrained by a child's egocentrism. After this time, peer group and other social involvements, and a lessening in egocentrism, spur more sophisticated moral reasoning.

Postconventional level

Moral reasoning based upon internalized and personalized values.

The last level is referred to as the **postconventional level** of morality and may be experienced first in adolescence by some individuals (although others never achieve it). Moral decision-making is characterized at this stage first by understanding that rules existing in society are for everyone's benefit. These rules are made by consensus. Reasoning at this level disapproves of individuals practicing a personal code of ethics because this is equivalent to social anarchy. Later at this level, the highest and most idealistic moral reasoning becomes based on standards of universal ethics. These standards often are contradictory in relation to the egocentric standards of ethics of lower levels of moral reasoning. Social dictates such as "Act toward others as you wish to be treated," or "Do no harm," are examples of such universally applied standards. It is at this final level that one makes decisions that guide appropriate behavior based on an individual, personal ethic.

Most young adolescents function at the conventional level of moral reasoning that guides their standards of appropriate behavior. The strict orientation to peer groups as sources of approval and validation of self-worth indicate this level of functioning. Most individuals remain at this level for the remainder of their lives (Shaver & Strong, 1976). Why is this so?

Because the level of a person's moral reasoning parallels their level of cognitive functioning, it should be expected that changes will take place as development progresses. Teenagers usually make shifts to formal operations cognitive skills by performing more abstract, logical reasoning. Researchers find that a person's level of cognition prepares but does not ensure changes to higher levels of moral reasoning (Sobesky, 1983).

Apparently, each particular situation calling for a decision involving what is right or wrong determines the level of moral reasoning that is applied as a guide. The cognitive skills possessed by a person will frame the limits that outline the format of how logical thinking can occur. This is not enough, however, to guarantee continual use of higher levels of moral reasoning.

Moral decisions may be derived from conflicts or dilemmas in which consequences of each choice must be weighed and considered. When the consequences are heavy, it is likely that a lower level of moral reasoning will be applied. As adolescents experiment with moral decision-making, mistakes and errors will take place that help the teen see the consequences of actions. Because behavior at this life stage is experimental, teenagers can be expected to be inconsistent in their behavioral decisions.

It is this discrepancy between high ideals and lower-level moral reasoning in adolescents that is disconcerting to adults (Kohlberg, 1969). For example, some adolescents might reason that it is perfectly acceptable to cheat on examinations because teachers ask "unfair" questions. Such "unfairness" may be thought to lead to lower grades that can prevent them from being accepted to a university. Teenagers at a different level of moral reasoning would not cheat because they know this is academically and morally dishonest. Some might allow others to cheat from their work in order to gain their approval and acceptance.

The difficulty in establishing a personal standard of moral ethics or values is seen in the dilemmas confronting teenagers today. These can involve conflicts between the conventional and postconventional levels of moral reasoning proposed by Kohlberg. Personal standards and values, which involve the highest level of moral reasoning, may not be fully established, if at all, until well into the adulthood years. They reflect what a person believes to be important ideals to attain in daily living.

Are there gender differences? A major difficulty with Kohlberg's model

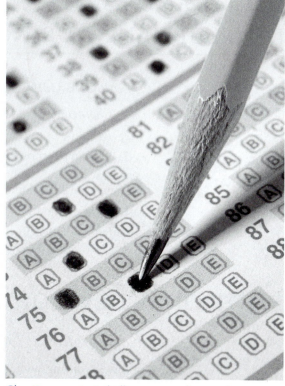

Cheating on a test challenges moral reasoning.

is that it fails to address gender differences, according to Gilligan (1982). Women in our culture are taught to have an orientation in moral reasoning that differs from males. She believes that women are taught to make moral decisions in terms of how interpersonal relationships would be affected. Men learn to base moral reasoning on individual rights, justice, and self-fulfillment. As such, females determine what is right or wrong on caring and concern for others.

A hypothetical problem posed to school-age children by researchers illustrates her views (Garrod, Beal & Shin, 1989). The children were asked how to resolve this problem:

> A porcupine needed a winter home. The only one he could find was sharing one with a family of moles. The moles, who originally thought this was a good idea, eventually wanted the porcupine to leave. This was because his spines kept pricking all the moles, making them uncomfortable.

No differences were found in solutions given by boys' and girls' between six and nine years old. However, ten and eleven year old boys gave responses that involved aggression of the moles against the porcupine, e.g., "They should shoot him." Much more research is needed to establish if males and females differ in moral reasoning.

Pause and Process:

1. What is meant by problem solving?

2. What are Kohlberg's levels of moral reasoning?

SOCIAL AND EMOTIONAL DEVELOPMENT DURING ADOLESCENCE

LEARNING OBJECTIVES:

1. *Characterize emotional development during adolescence*

2. *Describe understanding of self and others during adolescence*

3. *Explain psychosocial development during adolescence*

Socioemotional development in adolescence tends to focus on identity development. Teens wish to know who they are and where their place is in the world. Peers become increasingly important socializers in adolescence, while parents continue to provide social and emotional support.

EMOTIONAL DEVELOPMENT

Key Emotional Development Highlights

Emotions during adolescence is a topic of common discussion. Are adolescents extra moody? Do they return to the temper tantrums seen during the terrible twos?

Emotions do appear to fluctuate more during adolescence, possibly due to hormones (Rosenblum & Lewis, 2003). When hormones stabilize in adulthood, these fluctuations subside. In adolescence, the intensity of positive and negative emotions is not always in proportion to the event triggering the emotion (Steinberg & Levine, 1997). Again, this subsides with time. Emotional regulation improves with development of the frontal lobe of the brain (NIMH, 2001); hence, emotional regulation continues to improve beyond the teenage years. Finally, emotion vocabulary and scripts also show development during adolescence (Saarni, Mumme & Campos, 1998).

Adolescents are able to understand the causes of emotions in others. They are also able to understand that individuals can experience more than one emotion at a time. Finally, they understand that individuals may not always display what emotions they are feeling.

TEMPERAMENT/PERSONALITY   Temperament in infancy is moderately correlated with temperament in adolescence (Wachs & Bates, 2001). Hence, a shy infant is likely to be a shy teenager—though, not always. Parenting behaviors may either assist in the stability of temperament dimensions, or modify them. For example, a difficult temperament infant may display less negative affect and more adaptability if parenting was responsive.

Although we tend to discuss temperament in infancy and childhood, we shift to discussing personality in adulthood. It appears that some aspects of temperament are related to some aspects of adult personality (Caspi et al., 2005; Costa & McCrae, 2001). We will be learning about personality in early adulthood.

ATTACHMENT   Attachment continues to be important to development in adolescence. Adolescents that are securely attached to their parents experience better physical and mental health in comparison to insecurely attached teens (Cooper, Shaver & Collin, 1998). Other studies have found that in comparison to insecurely attached teens, securely attached teens experience higher self-esteem, better peer relationships, higher social competence, and lower levels of psychopathology (e.g., see Thompson, 1998, for a review).

You may be wondering how attachment to parents would impact peer relationships. It all goes back to those mental models we talked about in Chapter 3. If a person believes that he cannot trust others, but that he is competent (i.e., avoidant attachment style), then he may be controlling and bossy in friendships. If a person believes that she is untrustworthy, but that others are competent (i.e., preoccupied attachment style), then she may be clingy and jealous in friendships. Securely attached individuals believe in their self-worth and trust others; hence, they are able to function well, alone or in relationships.

Pause and Process:

1. Why may emotions fluctuate more during adolescence?

2. What are some outcomes associated with secure attachment in adolescence?

SELF AND OTHERS

Understanding of Self and Others

Teenagers become increasingly aware that physical or external attributes are not reliable bases for constructing a self-concept or for judging one's own worth or that of another (O'Mahony, 1989). By adolescence, the self-concept comes to include attitudes, beliefs, roles, and goals (Harter, 1990, 2005; Harter & Monsour, 1992). Adolescents also come to understand that their "self" may vary depending on who they are with and the setting they are in. Because adolescents are now capable of formal operational thought, they are able to think abstractly about their current self and hypothetically about their future self.

Just as self-understanding becomes more abstract in adolescence, understanding of others does as well. By late adolescence, they are generally aware that inner, psychological characteristics are more reliable descriptors for understanding others.

FAMILY INFLUENCES   Parent-child relationships during middle childhood are predictive of parent-child relationships during adolescence (Stickle, 2008). If the relationship has been warm and harmonious during childhood, it will largely continue to be so during adolescence. However, relationships that were conflict-ridden during childhood will most likely be conflict ridden during adolescence. Parents are often a source of support and guidance during adolescence, while allowing adolescents more freedom (Galatzer-Levy & Cohler, 1993).

Blended family

A family unit consisting of an adult male and female couple, one of whom has remarried, and the children of one or both from a previous marriage; a new term for stepfamily.

There really is no "typical" American family. We learned in Chapter 5 that more than 50 percent of all children will live in a single-parent household at some point in time. A little more than 20 percent of all children live in a blended family (Stickle, 2008). A **blended family** is one which includes a step-parent and possibly step-siblings. Additionally, a growing number of children are being raised by grandparents. As you can see, children and adolescents live in a variety of family structures. The next section will discuss what the impact of divorce is on adolescents.

DIVORCE IMPACTS ON ADOLESCENTS
In Chapter 5 we learned about some of the long-term impacts of divorce on children. Although school-age

Parents can offer support and freedom to adolescents.

girls appear to adjust to divorce relatively well if their mothers remain single, this does not remain true during adolescence (Parke & Buriel, 1998). Teenage girls from divorced homes are at increased risk for the following outcomes:

- Mother-daughter conflict

- Noncompliance

- Low self-esteem

- Emotional problems

- Antisocial behavior

- Early sexual behavior and other sexual problems

- Teenage pregnancy (three times more likely)

These difficulties continue into adulthood (Parke & Buriel, 1998). Young women who come from divorced homes are more likely to get pregnant before marriage, marry young, marry unstable husbands, and are more likely to experience divorce themselves. It appears that there is a long-term sleeper effect for the impact of divorce, so although younger girls appear to be coping with the divorce well, the impacts, in fact, lie in wait for the onset of adolescence.

There is further bad news about the long-term impacts of divorce on adolescents—both males and females. Adolescents from divorced homes are more than twice as likely to drop out of high school than high school students from intact homes (Parke & Buriel, 1998). Dropping out of high school has long-term impacts in terms of job prospects and earning potential. The most disturbing statistic, however, is that parental divorce predicts premature death in adulthood (i.e., parental divorce decreases longevity).

THE OUTSIDE WORLD

Peers

An adolescent's first steps toward independence from the family system are explored more thoroughly in the peer group. Peer-orientation is higher in adolescence than in any other time in life (Stickle, 2008). Although parents are still the most important influence on adolescent adjustment, peers are highly influential in daily life. During early adolescence, peers play an increasingly important role in influencing behavior and attitudes. This can be seen, for example, in the styles of dress, musical tastes, use of slang vocabulary, and acceptable behavior patterns promoted among groups.

Peer groups in adolescence serve as a laboratory setting for teens to experiment with behaviors, attitudes, and values. This assists in the identity formation process. As groups shift and change in composition, teens explore their abilities to be leader, follower, activist, rebel, clown, or athlete, for example. The fear that underlies much of the

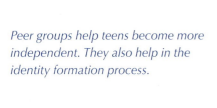

Peer groups help teens become more independent. They also help in the identity formation process.

teenager's concern about acceptance by peers is of being labeled as different from others in some way. Self-confidence is boosted by acceptance by others in early adolescence.

During this time there is an increasing reliance on peers for emotional support. Until recently, it was thought that the peer group increasingly replaced the family system as a source of social and emotional support in adolescence. However, both friends and family offer emotional support. Although psychological closeness to friends grows in adolescence, the family still provides the secure base from which adolescents can venture out into the world with increasing autonomy (Galatzer-Levy & Cohler, 1993).

Parents frequently worry that their child will become more influenced and controlled by friends than by adults during adolescence. However, adolescents typically maintain similar views to their parents in regards to politics, religion, morals, and education (Stickle, 2008).

Peer groups become organized differently in adolescence than in middle childhood. Peer group membership in middle childhood was largely segregated by sex. In adolescence, this characteristic changes as groups become integrated to include both sexes.

Peer groups become major agents of socialization, particularly in early adolescence. It is in the peer group environment that much of the experimentation and exploration occurs that help in identity formation.

Acceptance by others in a group is different in adolescence than in middle childhood. This is a crucial aspect of psychological growth and health for teens. Teenagers look to peers as the major source of validation of their self-worth. Positive self-esteem is evaluated in terms of being accepted by others. Negative self-worth and a sense of alienation is concluded when rejection, lack of acceptance, and being ignored or discounted by others occurs (East, Hess, and Lerner, 1987; Rubin, Bukowski & Parker, 1998).

Most young teens have a high degree of concern, then, about their popularity among friends. This is seen as a gauge that indicates the relative degree of their self-worth. The desire to be recognized by a peer group often is of paramount importance. Although conformity peaks in middle childhood, it is still valued early in adolescence (Galatzer-Levy & Cohler, 1993). Young adolescents often must be willing to forfeit any significant demonstrations of individualism as the price of being accepted by peers.

Crowds

A large mixed-sex group of older children or adolescents who have similar values and attitudes and are known by a common label.

Clique

A smaller group of friends that are similar in appearance, demographics, and activities.

Young teens gravitate toward others whom they perceive as being like themselves (Clasen & Brown, 1985). In this way, various **crowds** form and become labeled and categorized. A crowd can be defined as a large "mixed-sex group of older children or adolescents who have similar values and attitudes and are known by a common label" (Kail, 2007, p. 471). For example, those sharing athletic interests and who participate in sports would make up the "jocks." Although specific categories of cliques vary regionally, typical ones include the populars, nerds, grunges, goths, delinquents, and brains (Stickle, 2008).

A crowd is different from a clique. A crowd is large and all of the individuals may not know each other, whereas a **clique** is a smaller group of friends that are similar in appearance, demographics, and activities (Kail, 2007). Hence, any given crowd may have smaller segments of cliques.

By middle and late adolescence, the qualities used to construct and maintain peer groups become less valued among adolescents. The emphasis shifts from identity formation via experiences within groups to that attained through expressions as an individual. This reflects the developmental changes a teen experiences in reaching self-definition during this stage of the life span.

Dating often begins during adolescence. In general, males and females have different motivations for dating. Females are looking for a companion with which to be psychologically close, whereas males are looking for someone attractive with which to have fun experiences. Of course, there are exceptions to this generality, but it holds for most. Given these different motivations, expectations for the relationship and its longevity are probably different; however, few teens would think to discuss this up front. That said, when a dating relationship ends, lines of communication can become crossed because there is little understanding of the other person's perspective. Despite the confusion and hurt sometimes experienced in teen dating relationships, these relationships do provide a mechanism for learning about what one wants to look for in a future significant other. Additionally, dating relationships help individuals develop dating schemas and scripts that will be used (and continually modified) until marriage.

The Electronic World

Computers and the internet are an ever increasing part of our lives. In fact, it is estimated that 97 percent of high school students and 95 percent of middle school students used computers in 2003 (National Center for Education Statistics, 2005).

Although computers and the internet offer the world at our fingertips, there is some concern about the impact of computers on development. Some educators and developmentalists voice concern that the power of such technology is introduced before students develop the moral fortitude to handle such power responsibly (Monke, 2006). For example, students are purchasing entire research papers online and turning them in as their own

Computers are now a part of life. It remains to be seen how this technology will influence lives in the long term.

work. Cutting and pasting information from websites into one's own paper without quoting the source is rampant. Yet, when students are caught, their typical response is that they didn't know buying papers or cutting and pasting the work of others into their paper was wrong (Chaker, 2003). Clearly, these students learned to use a wonderful and powerful technology before they learned the difference between right and wrong.

Beyond students lacking the morals to use technology responsibly, research indicates that computer use may negatively impact academic achievement (Monke, 2006). Studies have found that as access to home computers increases, standardized test scores decrease (Fuchs & Woessmann, 2004). It is theorized that computers more often distract children and adolescents from studies, rather than facilitating school work.

Because computer technology and the internet is relatively new, it will take time and longitudinal studies in order to ascertain the long-term effects such technology may have on development. However, adolescents, and people in general, may do well to find a balance between living life in the world and life online.

Schools

During early adolescence, most teens make the transition from elementary school to middle school or junior high. This is a significant transition and can be stressful. Middle schools tend to be larger than elementary schools with more students. Crowding may be an issue. Students no longer have one primary teacher, but instead must learn the structure and format required by multiple teachers. Sometimes students may not have books to bring home to study from, or they must learn to utilize teacher online forums for their homework. Finally, adolescents must learn to navigate the world of adolescent peers, classroom changes, more complex lunchrooms, and lockers. Adolescents should be monitored for adjustment struggles during this transitional period so that stressors may be addressed and intervention or help provided if necessary. The same is true for when the teen transitions to high school.

Bullying can also be of concern in school. **Bullying** can be defined as "an aggressive behavior (words, actions, or social exclusion) which intentionally hurts or harms another person; the behavior occurs repetitiously and creates a power imbalance such that it is difficult for the victim to defend him or herself" (MacNeil & Newell, 2004, p. 174). Often, others silently witness these acts of bullying; hence, enabling the perpetrator to continue this evil. Although most children experience bullying occasionally, 10 percent of U.S. and European children are chronically bullied (Kochenderfer & Ladd, 1996; Olweus, 1994).

Although bullying used to occur primarily in or around schools, an increasing number of adolescents are bullied via media (e.g., text messages, social networking sites, etc.). This means that children and adolescent victims that used to be able to find comfort and solace in their homes are now bullied at any time with no reprieve.

Brutus in *Popeye,* Lucy in *Charlie Brown,* Draco Malfoy or Dudley in *Harry Potter,* and Sharpay in *High School Musical* are all famous bullies in cartoons or literature. What are the characteristics of bullies in real life? Research has found that bullies typically come from homes in which some form of abuse occurs (MacNeil & Newell, 2004). Further, bullies tend to have low self-concepts and feel unconnected to their loved ones. Often, the aggressiveness is generational, with parents using aggressive and hostile parenting. Bullies may also have a **hostile attributional bias** in which they are always suspect of the intentions of others and see hostility where there is none. Additionally, they often miss the prosocial overtures of others, while being hypersensitive to hostile and aggressive cues. Male bullies tend to be physically strong and use physical aggression and dominance. Female bullies come in any size and tend to use relational aggression and social dominance (e.g., verbal assaults, gossiping, social exclusion, etc.). In general, physical bullying is more common in elementary and middle school, whereas relational and social bullying is more prevalent in high school (Harris, 2004).

Now that we have a picture of what bullies are like, what are the characteristics of victims? Victims tend to lack social and interpersonal skills (Harris, 2004; MacNeil & Newell, 2004). Further, they are often younger and physically smaller than their aggressors. The lack of friends often makes them lack the social support that could help ward off or buffer the effects of bullies. Victims experience physical and emotional scars. They often withdraw socially, suffer academically, develop anxiety, and experience mental and physical health problems.

Programs aimed at preventing bullying or providing interventions must take a multifaceted approach (Harris, 2004; MacNeil & Newell, 2004). Schools must have a zero-tolerance policy for bullying. Supervision and monitoring at schools must be increased. Witnesses to bullying must be encouraged to report such abuse, as must the victims. Bullies must be taught conflict management skills, whereas victims must be given assertiveness training. Finally, both bullies and victims will probably need psychological counseling.

Work

Many adolescents work part-time. Working can have a positive influence on adolescents (Stickle, 2008). For example, working allows adolescents to develop a sense of the value of

---

Bullying

An aggressive behavior (words, actions, or social exclusion) which intentionally hurts or harms another person; the behavior occurs repetitiously and creates a power imbalance such that it is difficult for the victim to defend him or herself.

Hostile attributional bias

The thinking that bullies are always suspect of the intentions of others and see hostility where there is none.

Spotlight

27. Define hostile attributional bias in your own words.

money. Additionally, working can help adolescents learn about the work culture, responsibility, and the importance of punctuality. However, there can be too much of a good thing. Adolescents who work more than twenty hours a week appear to experience negative outcomes. These negative outcomes include academic struggles, increased substance use, increased delinquency, and increased physical and psychological health issues. Hence, adolescents should consider working part-time, but limit the number of hours.

Work provides for many positive influences such as learning the value of money.

Pause and Process:

1. Describe peer relations during adolescence.

2. What are the characteristics of bullies and victims?

PSYCHOSOCIAL DEVELOPMENT

How Do Teens Acquire a Sense of Identity?

Identity

The fifth attitude proposed by Erikson. Identity is the notion, acquired in adolescence, that the self is composed of different aspects having distinct boundaries that constitute a whole, integrated personality.

Erikson (1950/1964) refers to **identity** formation as the primary psychosocial focus of adolescence. Identity formation involves the acknowledgement that one assumes many different roles in life that represent different aspects of the self. It includes the awareness that one has strengths and weaknesses and different, but related, selves. Adolescents forge a foundational personal identity by psychologically integrating these various aspects or selves into a composite concept of "me" or "I."

A helpful analogy for understanding the process of identity formation is the procedure by which a diamond becomes a gemstone. When first brought from the earth, a diamond looks like a jagged, dirty pebble. The gemstone cutter creates facets by cutting and polishing sides into the diamond that admit light at various wavelengths. When working in an integrated manner, the finished diamond has many facets that operate together to create its brilliant appearance. In the course of identity formation, the adolescent's task is to become aware of the different aspects (facets) of the personality. In doing so, the individual reaches a crossroads in psychosocial development that Erikson describes as a crisis. The challenge is to experience continuity between what the individual has learned about the self from childhood experiences and what she or he anticipates being in the future.

The foundations of the adolescent's attempts to develop an integrated self were laid in previous stages of psychosocial development. The process of determining who one is, what values are important to one, what attitudes one should hold, and what directions one should take in life began in childhood. Children are expected by society to establish some idea of who they are and where they will go in life. Adults often ask them, "What do you want to be when you grow up?" During adolescence, the individual rephrases this question as, "Who am I, and what can I become as an adult?"

Socialization experiences have a broad impact on identity formation in adolescence. Adolescents who have a healthy sense of identity have enjoyed nurturing from family members and others that is associated with emotional warmth. Their parents have set limits for them, valued their autonomy, and encouraged their achievement (Newman & Newman, 1991).

Before they can crystallize their personal identity, adolescents need to establish an identity with a group of peers in early adolescence (Newman & Newman, 1991). In effect, identity is drawn first from tribal experiences. These interactions with peers are similar in some ways to peer group experiences among school-age children. However, the peer group takes on additional functions in adolescence

Teenagers, like school-age children, evaluate themselves according to how their peers evaluate them. In adolescence, peers assume an even more powerful influence as the prime source of self-definition. The peer group becomes both an extension and a representation of the self. Adolescents also enmesh their identities with those of public figures they admire—athletes, movie stars, or musicians, for example.

There are strong similarities between establishing one's personal identity in adolescence and establishing personal autonomy in infancy. The psychosocial task at both stages crucially depends on defining psychological boundaries. This push for autonomy reaches its peak in adolescence, as the teenager demands the freedom to test limits, discover areas of abilities and weakness, and commit mistakes while learning adult skills and problem-solving strategies. Boundaries between the self and parents become more distinct as the adolescent struggles to develop a fully autonomous identity. At the beginning of this process, in early adolescence, the individual tends to shift allegiance from parents almost totally to peers. This creates tensions between the individual and the family system. Peer pressures to conform to established or imagined standards are very high at this time, and boundaries between the self and the peer group are blurred. Acceptance and validation from peers bolsters self-confidence, whereas rejection undermines self-esteem and leads to feelings of alienation.

By late adolescence, experiences with peers have provided important lessons in beliefs, attitudes, and notions about the various aspects of the self. Personal identity crystallizes as the individual becomes capable of drawing boundaries between the self and the social group. Experiences within the family, school, and social systems now bring the adolescent into his or her own as an individual, able to make the connections that provide initial answers to the question, "Who am I, with whom do I belong, and where will I go with my life?"

Role confusion is a disjointed, fragmented concept of the self resulting from the inability to integrate the various aspects of the personality. Erikson believed that a clear

Role confusion

The disjointed, fragmented notion of self resulting from an inability to integrate the various aspects of personality into a unified whole.

idea of personal identity fails to materialize in certain situations—for example, when a teenager's efforts to establish self-identity are punished, thwarted, diminished, or discounted by parents. Boundaries between aspects of the self are blended and blurred and the individual fails to understand how they all work together to create the self.

Before the outcome of this stage is decided between identity formation and role confusion, adolescents may go through one of two phases (Marcia, 1980; Waterman, 1982). Normally, teenagers experiment with roles and behaviors to test out tentative ideas about careers, personal expression, value, beliefs, and so on. This experimentation usually continues throughout the period, eventually leading to a commitment to those ideas that seem to fit the individual best. The process allows adolescents to truly know and own their values, beliefs, and ambitions. Some adolescents, however, do not experience the process of experimentation fully enough to **individuate** from their parents' values, beliefs, and ambitions. The result is **identity foreclosure**, or an aborted attempt at establishing personal identity. When this happens, individuals may make a premature commitment to a lifestyle, occupation, or type of education more to please parents than to fulfill themselves. Identity foreclosure may merely delay identity formation.

The other phase that may delay identity formation is identity moratorium. Some individuals are unable to make a commitment to any role or idea of direction for their lives. Instead, they continually experiment. If they delay making any decision for too long, role confusion may be deeply established.

Waterman (1982) proposes that the sequence of identity formation moves in this fashion: first, young adolescents experience some role confusion as they experiment and discover various aspects of their personalities. Then, they move into identity foreclosure or moratorium. Finally, by the end of adolescence, they achieve an identity. Most individuals achieve an initial outline of their personal identity by the end of adolescence, but others need several more years to complete this process.

After reading this section, you may think that the personal identity that is established by the completion of adolescence is rigidly fixed for life. It is not. Personality and identity can certainly be refined, even redefined, at later stages of the life span. What we mean by the notion of personal identity formation is that a core self-concept is established during adolescence. Other roles and aspects of self are discovered, developed, recognized, and refined, throughout the remainder of the life span, and these become incorporated into the person's core identity. Marriage, parenthood, and career changes are all life-altering events that could further mold an individual's identity during later life stages.

Ethnic Identity

Ethnicity is an aspect of self that must be integrated into one's identity (Stickle, 2008). Although some adolescents embrace their ethnic heritage, others resent it. Those that

Individuation

The process by which an adolescent recognizes and develops his or her personal identity as an individual who is distinct from other family members. It is characterized by developing one's own values and belief systems and having the courage to make decisions and live by these.

Identity foreclosure

The inability to commit to any role or idea of direction for their lives.

value their ethnic identity and incorporate it as part of their identity often feel an emotional connection to their group. In general, these individuals have an easier time integrating the values of their minority culture and dominant culture than those who struggle to achieve an ethic identity.

There are those that feel an emotional connection to their heritage when they incorporate their ethnic identity into their lives.

Pause and Process:

1. Explain the process of identity formation.

2. Why is identity development important?

SUMMARY

1. Adjusting to the many physical changes associated with puberty is a major developmental task of adolescence. Boys experience this process differently and at later ages than girls. Psychological changes are intertwined with physical maturation. Problems can arise when individuals begin puberty either sooner or later than most of their peers.

2. Nutrition is important during adolescence. Obesity and eating disorders are areas of concern during adolescence. Some teenagers decide to adopt a vegetarian diet. Most research indicates that vegetarian teens eat healthier than the average, meat-eating teen.

3. Teenagers develop a complex understanding of illness. Although teens, in general, experience good physical health, risky behaviors may contribute to a premature death down the road. The early sexualization of girls by the media has far reaching negative consequences for girls and society as a whole. In order to promote wellness in teens, we must educate them about the risks of substance use and early sexual behavior. Further, we must educate teens about the importance of sleep, nutrition, and exercise.

4. Some adolescents move from concrete operational thought into formal operational thought during the teen years. Formal operational thought is characterized by hypothetical, deductive, and inductive reasoning. Additionally, egocentrism, pseudostupidity, the imaginary audience, the invincibility fable, and apparent hypocrisy characterize thought at this stage.

5. Dialectical reasoning and problem solving show developmental improvements during adolescence. Further, moral reasoning typically continues to show advancement during the teenage years.

6. Emotional development can be challenging during adolescence. Fluctuations in hormones can lead to intense moods and mood swings. Luckily, these issues subside toward the end of this period.

7. Temperament in adolescence is moderately related to temperament from infancy and childhood. Parenting behaviors either assisted in the continuity of temperament or contributed to its change. Attachment in adolescence is related to numerous areas of well-being and functioning, including psychopathology and peer relations.

8. Understanding of self and others becomes more complex and abstract during adolescence. Parent-child relations continue to be warm and supportive, if they were so during childhood. Divorce increases the risk for numerous problems in adolescence, including teenage pregnancy and antisocial behavior.

9. Peer relationships become more important during the teenage years. Crowds and cliques are common and form based upon similarities between group members. Dating may begin during adolescence, but is complicated due to differing motivations between males and females. Bullying is an area of growing concern in schools and now occurs 24/7 due to online social networking sites and text messaging.

10. The establishment of a sense of personal identity is a major developmental task of adolescence. Identity is based on an understanding that one's self, or personality, is composed of many related aspects. Teens learn about these aspects through experimentation and exploration in a variety of experiences. Role confusion, the diametrical opposite of identity formation, is a fragmented idea of the self that results from the inability to integrate the various aspects of the self into a unified personality.

SELF-QUIZ

1. Describe the adolescent growth spurt.
2. Explain brain development during adolescence.
3. What is the secular trend? What may be contributing to it?
4. Why is the timing of puberty important to development?
5. Explain, in your own words, physiologic and psychophysiologic thinking.
6. Describe anorexia nervosa.
7. What is bulimia and how is it different from anorexia?
8. Characterize substance use (alcohol, tobacco, and drugs) among adolescents.
9. Define the sexualization of girls.
10. What areas of health are of concern in adolescence?
11. Define hypothetical thought in your own words and give an example.
12. Define inductive and deductive reasoning in your own words and provide an example for each.
13. How are hypothetical-deductive reasoning and scientific-inductive reasoning different?
14. What is meant by the game of thinking?
15. How may the imaginary audience impact a teenager's everyday behavior?
16. Define the invincibility fable and describe how it may contribute to risky behavior.
17. Give an example of dialectical reasoning.
18. Provide an example of a time you used dialectical reasoning in an argument or debate.
19. What is meant by problem solving?
20. Describe the levels of moral reasoning development.

21. Describe emotional development in adolescence.

22. How is attachment related to peer relationships?

23. What are some family structures children and adolescents may experience?

24. What are some outcomes related to divorce for adolescents?

25. Explain the differences between crowds and cliques.

26. Why are researchers concerned about computer and internet use by youth?

27. Define hostile attributional bias in your own words.

28. What are some of the effects of being bullied?

29. What are the positive and negative outcomes for working during adolescence?

30. How may identity formation impact the family system?

TERMS AND CONCEPTS

CHAPTER 7

Early Adulthood

OUTLINE

PHYSICAL DEVELOPMENT DURING EARLY ADULTHOOD

- Physical growth
- Health issues

COGNITIVE DEVELOPMENT DURING EARLY ADULTHOOD

- Beyond Piaget's theory
- Information-processing during early adulthood

SOCIAL AND EMOTIONAL DEVELOPMENT DURING EARLY ADULTHOOD

- Emotional development
- Self and others
- Psychosocial development

The period of the life span that we call adulthood has been considered the pinnacle of individual development for many years. To be an adult means that one has arrived at a respected and competent station in life, that one has attained the characteristic we call maturity. The cultural meaning of maturity is completed development. Traditionally, it has been thought that developmental changes cease when one becomes an adult.

This notion is an artifact of past Western civilizations. Until recent historical times, there were two stages in the life span: childhood and adulthood. Childhood was a time of preparing for adulthood that lasted only until an individual reached six or seven years of age. At this age, individuals assumed adult status in their family systems. With this status came new responsibilities, expected behaviors, and appropriate traits. Just attaining adulthood was a significant achievement before the advent of antibiotics, advanced medical care, and advanced sanitation in modern times. Earlier, great numbers of infants and their mothers died of disease and unsanitary living conditions. Artistic works of former periods show adulthood as the more valued and important era in the life span. Even today adulthood is associated with greater social power, influence, and position more so than earlier stages in the life span.

Adulthood was important in former periods.

Philosophical and theoretical changes in the last several decades have prompted a reconsideration of the notion that developmental changes cease at the closure of adolescence. Actually, we know little about changes during this period of the life span, compared to what we know about changes during the stages leading to adulthood.

Because adulthood is the longest period in the typical person's life, it is more easily studied by dividing it into three separate but related stages: early adulthood (eighteen to thirty-nine years), middle adulthood (forty to sixty-five years), and late adulthood (sixty-five years +). We know more about development during late adulthood, than development during early and middle adulthood.

PHYSICAL DEVELOPMENT DURING EARLY ADULTHOOD

LEARNING OBJECTIVES:

1. *Describe physical development during early adulthood*
2. *Awareness of health issues in early adulthood*

PHYSICAL DEVELOPMENT

Adulthood

The period of the life span following adolescence.

We reach our peak of physical well-being in early adulthood. This is the period of greatest strength and good health. Physical **maturity** in height and weight has been reached—in fact, most physical growth ceases before early adulthood begins. Yet there are many physical changes in appearance and in physiology during this stage of the life span.

Body Changes

Maturity

Completion of all growth and developmental changes; associated with attaining adulthood in the past.

Accommodation

Changes made in a personal scheme in order to bring about a better match with reality; in vision, the ability of the eyes to focus quickly and efficiently on objects both near and far away.

Visual acuity

Sharpness of vision.

Presbyopia

Difficulty in accurately perceiving objects that are close.

Presbycusis

The loss of hearing of high-frequency tones.

Periodontal disease

Disease of the gums caused by improper hygiene; it can lead to significant tooth loss.

4. What is periodontal disease?

THE SENSES   The ability of the eyes to accommodate begins changing in this stage. **Accommodation** refers to the dilation and constriction of the pupils to see things at different distances, as well as to the ability of the eyes to focus properly and quickly. There is a gradual loss in accommodation throughout the years of early adulthood (Fozard et al., 1977).

Visual acuity, or sharpness of vision, is at its peak for most people in early adulthood (Spence & Mason, 1987). Men generally have better acuity than women. However, both sexes begin to notice deficiencies in distance perception between ages thirty-five and forty. This results in a condition known as **presbyopia**, meaning difficulty in accurately perceiving objects that are close. People notice this when they find they must hold books and newspapers far away in order to read them. The condition is corrected with reading glasses.

Most young adults who need general vision correction choose contact lenses rather than eyeglasses. Those who need glasses generally begin wearing them by about age twenty-nine. Even people who wear contact lenses develop presbyopia, making reading glasses necessary.

Hearing loss also becomes apparent during this life stage. Typically, it becomes noticeable after age twenty-five, although most adults in their thirties can still hear a whisper (National Center for Health Statistics, 1980). The loss of hearing is most noticeable at high-frequency tones. This results in a condition known as **presbycusis**. Most men experience greater loss of hearing sensitivity than women during adulthood. This may be because greater numbers of them work in noisy occupations for prolonged periods of time.

THE TEETH   Most people retain all their permanent teeth through early adulthood. A small percentage loses all of their upper or lower teeth (Kelly & Harvey, 1979). Tooth loss is more likely among women, partly due to calcium loss during pregnancy. There is a steady increase in filled teeth during early adulthood. The probability of **periodontal disease** also increases. Periodontal disease is an inflammation of the gums and bone tissue surrounding teeth. It results from poor or improper dental hygiene, and genetics may also play a role. If left untreated, this condition can lead to significant tooth loss.

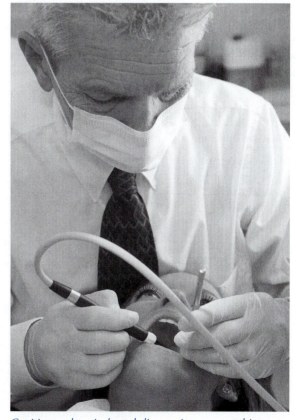

Cavities and periodontal disease increase at this age.

THE CARDIOVASCULAR SYSTEM   As people age, their hearts become more sluggish at pumping blood. This partially explains why people are unable to sustain large work loads for long periods as they get older.

The risk of getting diseases that affect the heart and circulatory system rises throughout early adulthood. Blood pressure rises as part of the natural aging process that begins during this stage. People become more susceptible to **hypertension**, or high blood pressure, at this time (Spence & Mason, 1987). Hypertension is a condition in which the blood vessels become constricted, raising the level of pressure necessary for circulating blood through the body. If untreated, it can lead to heart failure, cerebral hemorrhage (stroke), and related disorders. Hypertension is more common among African Americans and among men of all racial groups.

Hypertension is a silent disease, meaning it has no signs that can be readily observed. Diagnosis requires accurate measurements taken with special equipment. By being aware of the need to have their blood pressure monitored periodically, young adults can begin treatment of the condition long before it becomes serious. Hypertension may be treated by drug therapy, although dietary changes are frequently used as well.

THE LUNGS   The lungs play an important part in the body's ability to sustain exercise and work. They begin to function less efficiently toward the end of early adulthood. Young adults are able to absorb about four and a half times as much oxygen as older adults. The decline in oxygen absorption is partly due to a lowering of the amount of blood pumped to the lungs and partly to losses in the mechanical efficiency of these organs as people age (Timiras, 1972). Throughout adulthood, there is a decline in the amount of air breathed into the lungs. Many people notice this difference at about age forty.

Smoking was long associated with adult status in our culture. This is less so today after multitudes of reports that smoking cigarettes and other tobacco products is associated with heart and lung disease, cancer, and related health disorders (U.S. Department of Health and Human Services, 1987). **Passive smoking**—inhaling air in an area where someone has been smoking—is also hazardous to health.

Since the 1950s, the percentage of adults who smoke has been declining. Today, approximately 21.6 percent of adults smoke (CDC, 2005).

Many people who smoke try to quit. Young adults have greater success than older adults in quitting. Most people stop on their own, although there are many drugs and programs available for those who need help.

THE SKIN   The skin begins to show some signs of aging in early adulthood. Wrinkles appear in the facial area, particularly around the eyes and on the hands. The skin begins to lose its fine texture toward the end of this stage. In early adulthood, most people recover from the acne and related skin disorders that are common in adolescence. The more usual types of skin disorders in young adults are fungal infections (dermatophytosis), especially in the feet, and malignant or benign tumors. Both conditions affect men more than women, perhaps because of differences in working conditions and standards of hygiene (Johnson & Roberts, 1977; Spence & Mason, 1987).

Hypertension

Abnormally high blood pressure caused by constriction of arteries; it increases the likelihood of kidney damage, heart failure, and brain damage via strokes.

Passive smoking

Inhaling air in an area where someone has been smoking.

MUSCULAR STRENGTH AND PHYSICAL PERFORMANCE   People are at their peak muscular strength between ages twenty and thirty. After that, there is a gradual decline until old age, when the decline becomes rapid. Muscular strength differs from work rate. Although muscle strength does not change very noticeable in early adulthood, power output declines after forty, and considerably during middle adulthood (Shock & Norris, 1970; Spence & Mason, 1987).

Pause and Process:

1. How do the heart and lungs change in early adulthood?

2. What problems may occur with the skin in early adulthood?

HEALTH ISSUES

Health in early adulthood is generally very good, though subject to certain hazards. Accidents are a leading cause of death among young adults, but diseases cause numerous health problems (U.S. Bureau of the Census, 1990b). These include upper respiratory infections, flu, and sexually transmitted diseases. Among the last, AIDS is of particular concern among young adults. Other factors that affect health in early adulthood are outlined here.

Stressors

Events that can cause stress reactions.

Stress

The physiological and psychological reactions of an organism to demands placed upon it.

"Type A" personality

Highly competitive, restless, and achievement oriented.

"Type B" personality

A personality that is low in hostility and aggression, and moderately ambitious.

"Type C" personality

Associated with an increased risk for cancer, this personality type tends to be introverted and eager to please.

STRESS   A harsh reality of life is stress. Stress refers to the physiological and psychological reactions of an individual to demands made on him or her. **Stressors** are events that can cause stress. **Stress** in and of itself is not necessarily harmful—in fact, some stress is helpful for motivation (Kobasa, Maddi & Kahn, 1982). However, prolonged severe stress is associated with many negative effects on health and well-being (Selye, 1956). Some of the disorders associated with excessive levels of stress are heart disease, hypertension, migraine headaches, lowered immune system responsiveness, ulcers, gastroenteritis, and asthma (Aldwin, 1994; Denollet et al., 2008; Goleman & Gurin, 1993; Weg, 1983).

Why do some people react more negatively to stress than others? First, personality configuration appears to play a role. People with a **"Type A" personality** seem to be more prone to excessive levels of stress (Rosenman, 1974). These individuals are highly competitive, restless, and achievement-oriented. They often perceive that others are attacking them, and react hostilely. Other people have what is called a **"Type B" personality**, which is diametrically opposite to Type A. **"Type C" personalities** describe individuals that repress their emotions and stress (Cooper & Faragher, 1993). Type A individuals have levels of heart attacks and coronary heart disease that are twice as high as those found in the more easygoing Type Bs. Type A individuals also have higher blood cholesterol levels and higher levels of stress hormones in their blood. Type C personalities show poorer coping with cancer.

Second, stressful life events that occur cumulatively influence reactions (Holmes & Rahe, 1967). Taken singly, many of these events, such as the death of a spouse or divorce, are highly traumatic. When several occur in succession, stressful reactions become much more severe. However, recent research calls in to question whether multiple stressful events in close proximity to each other have a cumulative effect (linear), multiplicative effect, or asymptotic effect (where there is a maximum level that can't be exceeded) (Aldwin, 1994).

Third, the way someone interprets life events influences the reactions. What is distressing to one person may have little effect on another (Chiriboga & Cutler, 1980; Folkman & Lazarus, 1980). How people cope with various levels and sources of stress may, in fact, be the key to modulating the first two factors (personality style and cumulative stressful life events). Regaining a personal sense of control is an important element in coping with stress (Taveris, 1983). Many young adults today are exploring new techniques for regaining this sense of control, such as meditation, blogging, massage, exercise, and diet.

STRESS AMONG COLLEGE STUDENTS   Approximately 30 percent of American college freshman report experiencing substantial stress (National Health Ministries, 2006). Chronic stress can contribute to depression, which we will discuss later in this chapter. Many factors can contribute to stress during college. Lack of regular exercise, substance use, poor diet, weight gain, and use of stimulants (such as caffeine or nicotine) are all unhealthy behaviors that can contribute to stress. Additionally, a lack of social support or failure to establish relatedness in the college environment can contribute to stress. Finally, procrastination, perfectionistic tendencies, becoming a workaholic, and losing one's sense of humor contribute to stress. In the "Promoting Wellness" section of this chapter, we will discuss ways to combat stress.

NUTRITIONAL NEEDS   The number of calories required for normal functioning reaches a plateau in early adulthood. Because physical growth is generally completed in adolescence, the bulk of calories in an adult's diet are used to perform the tasks of daily life and work. Those in excess of what are required for this purpose are metabolized into fat and stored in the body. In both men and women, certain areas of fat storage become more prominent as

Many factors can contribute to stress such as lack of regular exercise, substance use, and a poor diet.

weight is gained in early adulthood. In men, fat tends to accumulate in the abdominal area, whereas in women it accumulates in the abdomen, hips, and thighs.

Contemporary young adults are more health conscious than their predecessors. They recognize the role of diet in promoting well-being. We now know that many health problems that develop in later stages of adulthood can be traced to a poor diet in early adulthood (American Heart Association, 1984). A healthy diet can lower blood serum cholesterol, thus protecting against heart and kidney disease in the later stages of adulthood.

Health and Risky Behavior

Healthy behavior

Any behavior that reduces the susceptibility to disease and enhances physical and psychological function and well-being.

Risky behavior

Any behavior that detrimentally effects health or increases the likelihood of disease, although they typically increase an individual's sense of well-being at the moment.

RISKY BEHAVIOR   What are healthy and risky behaviors? A **healthy behavior** can be defined as any behavior that "can enhance physical and psychological function and well-being, and in some cases, reduce vulnerability to disease and/or slow disease progression" (Leventhal et al., 2001, p. 188). A **risky behavior** can be defined as any behavior that detrimentally effects health or increases the likelihood of disease, although they typically increase an individual's sense of well-being at the moment.

The risky behavior we discussed in the chapter on adolescent physical development continues in early adulthood. In 1995, the CDC sponsored the National College Health Risk Behavior Survey. Results indicated that:

- 27.4 percent drove after drinking alcohol in the last month

- 10.2 percent rarely, if ever, used seat belts

- 10.2 percent had engaged in a physical fight in the last year

- 8.0 percent carried a weapon not related to work in the last month

- 14.0 percent had used marijuana in the last month

- 14.4 percent had used cocaine during their life

- 34.5 percent had six or more sexual partners during their life

- 29.6 percent had used a condom during their last sexual intercourse

- 20.5 percent were overweight

- 26.3 percent ate five or more servings of vegetables and fruits daily

As if the above statistics are not disturbing enough, the CDC (2000) has written a report stating that the United States is experiencing a multiple sexually transmitted disease (STD) epidemic. More than twenty-five diseases are now spread through sexual activity. In the United States, more than sixty-five million people have an STD that is incurable. Each year, more than fifteen million people contract at least one STD, of which 50 percent will be a lifelong infection (Cates, 1999).

Different STDs have different incidence (number of new cases each year) and prevalence (number of people infected) rates (CDC, 2000). More than forty-five million people are infected with herpes, and there are around one million new cases each year. There is no cure for herpes. More than three million people are infected with chlamydia each year in the United States. This disease is highly curable with antibiotics; however, many people do not show any symptoms and fail to receive treatment. Long-term infection can lead to pelvic inflammatory disease and infertility. Gonorrhea, syphilis, HPV, hepatitis B, and trichomoniasis are other STDs that impact the lives of millions of Americans each year. Because STDs can be caught only through risky behavior, these diseases are entirely preventable by making healthy choices.

MENTAL HEALTH   Depression is a mental disorder of serious concern in early adulthood, and throughout the life span. Approximately 9.5 percent of all American adults, or twenty million adults, suffer with depression (NIMH, 2004). In fact, depression is so prevalent that one out of every ten college students has been diagnosed with depression (National Health Ministries, 2006). The median age at which depression manifests is thirty years (NIMH, 2004).

Depression

A disease that involves a person's thoughts, emotions, and feelings.

What is depression? **Depression** is a disease that involves a person's thoughts, emotions, and feelings (NIMH, 2004). Although it is unknown what specifically causes depression, there is evidence that genetic, biochemical, psychological, and environmental factors all may play a role (NIMH, 2009). Signs and symptoms of depression include a persistently sad mood; feelings of helplessness, emptiness, worthlessness, and hopelessness; and loss of interest in engaging in activities that one used to find interesting and enjoyable. In essence, it's a feeling like you are circling down a deep spiral into a bottomless, dark pit from which you can never see yourself escaping.

Although medication and therapy can help most individuals with depression, some suffer so severely and persistently that they consider suicide (Vitiello et al., 2009). In fact, 10.3 percent of all college students have seriously considered attempting suicide (CDC, 1995), and suicide is the second leading cause of death for college students (National

Depression, if left untreated, can lead to suicide. Suicide is the second leading cause of death for college students.

Health Ministries, 2006). In 73 percent of suicide events (suicide ideation or attempt), some interpersonally stressful event had just occurred—such as family conflict or relationship troubles. Most importantly, the sooner an individual seeks help for depression, the better the prognosis for a full recovery.

Infertility

The inability to conceive a child after consistently having intercourse without contraception for at least a year.

HEALTH ISSUES   By and large, young adults are quite healthy. One health problem that may be encountered during early adulthood is infertility. **Infertility** can be defined as "the failure to conceive after a year of regular intercourse without contraception" (www.medterms.com, 2009). Approximately one-third of infertility cases are due to problems with the wife, one-third are due to problems with the husband, and one-third are due to either problems with both spouses or the cause is unknown (NIH, 2009).

Approximately 11.8 percent of married couples in the United States struggle to conceive, whereas 7.4 percent are considered infertile (CDC, 2002). There are several physical reasons why a couple may experience infertility; however, we are going to focus upon the role of stress in the struggle to conceive. Stress in and of itself cannot cause infertility, but its impact can be great in reducing fertility.

When a couple is trying to conceive a child and is unsuccessful, emotional stress can become high (Seibel & McCarthy, 1993). Emotions such as anger, guilt, and isolation can be experienced. Over time, this emotional stress can impact the reproductive system, including causing ovulation problems, fallopian tube spasms, decreased sperm production, or sexual dysfunction resulting in less opportunity for intercourse. Research indicates that stress reduction techniques and therapy can help couples struggling with fertility to conceive. One study found that 34 percent of women previously struggling to conceive a child became pregnant within six months of receiving stress reduction therapy. However, the longer a woman has struggled with fertility, the less likely stress reduction will help in conceiving a child. Beyond stress reduction therapy, support groups also appear to be an effective method in helping couples reduce stress and achieve pregnancy.

PROMOTING WELLNESS   As discussed throughout this chapter, stress and emotions can have serious impacts on all aspects of physical and mental health (Aldwin, 1994; Goleman & Gurin, 1993). What are some ways individuals can decrease and/or manage stress in their lives? Exercise, a healthy diet, avoiding stimulants and drugs, and getting at least seven hours of sleep each night are important steps in managing and limiting stress (National Health Ministries, 2006). Further, time management skills, relaxation techniques, and a healthy social support system can aid in managing stress. If these behaviors are not enough, then counseling can help teach an individual specific techniques for managing daily stress.

Pause and Process:

1. What is stress?

2. Describe the risky behaviors prevalent in early adulthood.

COGNITIVE DEVELOPMENT DURING EARLY ADULTHOOD

LEARNING OBJECTIVES:

1. *Characterize the cognitive development during early adulthood*
2. *Describe information-processing during early adulthood*

In many ways, writing a chapter on cognitive development in early adulthood is difficult. Everything in terms of cognitive processes that was developing throughout childhood is achieved during early adulthood, after which many of these processes decline. Hence, it would be easy to simply say that speed of processing, attention skills, memory, problem-solving, metacognition, and language are all at peak performance during this stage of the life. However, such a view would be far too simplistic. In this section, we will discuss postformal thought, intelligence, and language/communication in terms of technology use.

BEYOND PIAGET'S THEORY: COGNITIVE DEVELOPMENT DURING EARLY ADULTHOOD

Postformal Operational Thought

Postformal operational thought

A possible fifth stage of cognitive development, in early adulthood.

A topic of much debate in cognitive development is whether thinking is basically different among adults than among older adolescents. Even though many adults never achieve the stage of formal operations described by Piaget for adolescence, some researchers suggest that others attain a fifth stage of cognition called **postformal operational thought**.

A classic study illustrates how thought processes change in early adulthood (Perry, 1970). A group of Harvard undergraduates was interviewed during each year of their four-year college career. At their first interview as freshmen, the students expressed the belief that there is only one correct answer to a problem or question. They firmly believed that professors had the duty either to provide the correct answers or assign projects that would lead students to deduce the correct answers. As the students were exposed to classes and learning experiences that provided competing and contradictory opinions, they came to understand that knowledge is relative. No authority figure can provide all the "right" answers on any topic. After discovering this diversity of realities and opinions, the students felt overwhelmed. However, they came to understand that some realities are more credible than others. By the end of their college careers, they saw that they must make choices among the many differing opinions and "right" answers available, and they understood that their choice of "right" answer might apply only to themselves. In comprehending this, they grasped the complexity of decision-making that adults face.

Dialectical thinking

A style of thinking in adulthood in which individuals appear to accept and may even relish contradictions and conflicts in values.

Acquisition period

A shift in cognition seen in childhood and adolescence.

To function as a mature adult may require a shift to what is known as **dialectical thinking** (Riegel, 1973, 1975). This means accepting, and even relishing, contradictions and conflicts in viewpoints. Sorting through these contradictions and considering alternative courses produce intellectual and moral growth.

Not all researchers subscribe to this fifth stage of cognition in adulthood (Schaie & Willis, 1986). The shifts in cognition seen in childhood and adolescence, referred to as the **acquisition period**, are believed to lay the foundation for all the changes in thinking that take place in early adulthood. These thinking abilities assist young adults to choose a career during the achieving period. When individuals make choices from an immense array of possibilities, they gain personal autonomy. This prepares them to move to the next phase—social responsibility—during the middle adult years.

Perhaps the greatest intellectual challenge during early adulthood is learning to accept the uncertainties of life. The choices that must be made in adulthood are sometimes overwhelming, particularly ethical decisions. Young adults may long for the old childhood assurance that life is simple, that right and wrong are obvious. But, after all, the freedom and power to think for one's self, to make one's own choices, and to live with the consequences, was what we all looked forward to as children.

Pause and Process:

1. What is postformal thought?

2. Describe dialectical thinking.

INFORMATION-PROCESSING IN EARLY ADULTHOOD

In general information-processing skills peak during early adulthood. Attention skills are strong, memory is robust, metacognitive skills are solid, and language skills are fully developed. In this section, we will examine some specific developmental aspects of information-processing in early adulthood.

13. Define cognitive style.

COGNITIVE STYLE Cognitive style can be defined as "the intellectual aspects of learning style that represent culturally attuned ways of perceiving, organizing and evaluating information" (Jackson et al., 2003, p. 4). For the purposes of our chapter, you can consider cognitive style as a person's preferred way of learning. In general, people learn better when information is presented to them in the modality (or cognitive style) that they prefer. There are different theories and measures of cognitive style, and there is little consensus as to which constructs of cognitive style are most accurate or how to apply this in the classroom (Reid, 1995). A person's cognitive style may include a preference to perceive and learn information through visual, auditory, haptic (touch and kinesthetic), global/relational (meaningful context), or analytical modalities (Jackson et al., 2003).

MOTIVATION AND LEARNING Motivation is very important for learning in college, as throughout childhood. Motivation is important because it "affects the amount of time that

Intrinsic motivation

A person's internally generated drive to learn because it is inherently enjoyable.

Extrinsic motivation

A person's drive to learn because of what he or she will receive in doing so.

Self-regulated learning

When a person keeps track of what they have learned, what they still need to learn, and have a strategy for how to learn it.

Planning phase

A person sets goals and considers what they already know and what they need to still learn.

Monitoring phase

Maintaining awareness of what is being learned and thinking.

people are willing to devote to learning" (National Research Council, 2000). An environment that promotes motivation for learning provides challenges that incorporate the following:

- Material and assignments are appropriate for the level of knowledge and skills of the learner

- Incorporates social opportunities in which an individual can contribute knowledge

- Learners can see the usefulness and applicability of the material they are being asked to learn

Some motivation is intrinsic, whereas other motivation is extrinsic (for example, see Boggiano & Pittman, 1992; Deci, Koestner & Ryan, 2001; Wigfield & Eccles, 2002). **Intrinsic motivation** is internally generated—a person is driven to learn because learning is inherently enjoyable to him or her. **Extrinsic motivation** is externally generated—a person is driven to learn because of what he or she will receive in doing so (e.g., good grades, stickers, money, avoidance of punishment, etc.). In general, researchers stress the superiority of intrinsic motivation for academic achievement.

Beyond motivation, the ability to regulate what one is learning is also important for academic achievement and life-long learning (Pintrich & Zusho, 2001). **Self-regulated learning** can be defined as "an active, constructive process whereby learners set goals for their learning and then attempt to monitor, regulate, and control their cognition, motivation, and behavior in the service of those goals, guided and constrained by both personal characteristics and the contextual features of the environment (Pintrich & Zusho, 2001, p. 250). Working memory, prior content knowledge, and metacognitive abilities are all important for self-regulation. Theories on self-regulated learning differ in their specifics, but most acknowledge four general areas or phases important to this process: planning, monitoring, control, and reflection.

During the **planning phase**, a person sets goals and considers what they already know and what they need to still learn (Pintrich & Zusho, 2001). This is a time of effortful planning, keeping in mind goals, knowledge, and context. The **monitoring phase** involves an

The reward of receiving a good grade is an example of extrinsic motivation.

Control phase

The period where necessary changes and or adaptations are made in the approach to the learning task.

Reflection phase

The time to judge one's own work, make attributions in regards to the quality of the work, and evaluate the outcomes within the given context.

Crystallized intelligence

Skills acquired through education and socialization such as verbal skills, mathematical skills, inductive reasoning, and interpersonal skills; the ability to recall and use information.

Cognitive flexibility

The ability to shift from one thinking style to another.

Visuomotor flexibility

The ability to shift from familiar to unfamiliar tasks involving hand-eye coordination.

Visualization

The ability to organize and process visual materials.

Fluid intelligence

The ability to perceive relationships, reason logically and abstractly, and form concepts and interpretations.

individual maintaining awareness of what they are learning and thinking. A person is mindful of time management and decides what help may be needed. During the **control phase**, a person decides if changes need to be made in their approach to the learning task and makes necessary adaptations. This can be a phase where a person decides to seek help, renegotiate the task, or give up. A person may also come to realize that they need to increase effort. Finally, the **reflection phase** is a time to judge one's own work, make attributions in regards to the quality of the work, and evaluate the outcomes within the given context.

INTELLIGENCE   Psychologists disagree about the nature of intellectual development in adulthood. There is some evidence that intelligence increases during these years (Bayley & Oden, 1955). Other evidence indicates that intellectual growth peaks in early adulthood and declines thereafter (Bayley, 1970; Baltes & Scahie, 1974). Developmental psychologists suggest that intellectual functioning changes in four areas during early adulthood: (1) **crystallized intelligence**, or skills acquired through education and socialization (e.g., verbal and mathematical skills, inductive reasoning, and interpersonal skills), becomes more refined; (2) **cognitive flexibility**, or the ability to shift from one thinking style to another, improves; (3) **visuomotor flexibility**, or the ability to shift from familiar to unfamiliar tasks involving hand-eye coordination, improves; and (4) **visualization**, or the ability to organize and process visual materials, improves (Baltes & Schaie, 1974).

Researchers report that fluid intelligence reaches its peak between twenty and thirty and declines thereafter (Horn & Donaldson, 1980). **Fluid intelligence** refers to the ability to process information and to make interpretations of events. It differs from crystallized intelligence in being dependent on the functioning and integrity of the nervous system and on one's heredity. It is manifested in speed of thinking, problem-solving ability, and information recall.

LANGUAGE AND COMMUNICATION   Compared to childhood or old age, there is very little research focusing on language development during early adulthood. Instead, most research focusing on language development in relation to young adulthood involves aspects of adult speech and behavior that promote language development in children. The use of direct instruction, modeling, and scaffolding by adults appears to assist in the development of language in childhood (Cazden, 1983). Further, adult use of questions, extending utterances (adding on to what the child has said), and directives appear to assist in language development (Barnes et al., 1983).

Communication via Text-Messaging   Text-messaging is an area of communication that has blossomed in recent years; research on this type of communication is only beginning to catch up. Within this realm of research, older teenagers and young adults are sometimes referred to as the "net generation" (Thurlow, 2003). People text-message for various communicative reasons. Research has categorized these reasons in order to better understand text-messaging (Thurlow, 2003).

As you can see, friendship maintenance is the most common type of text-message (Thurlow, 2003). When you group the above types of messages into two general categories of low intimacy/high transaction orientation and high intimacy/high relational orientation, more than 60 percent of text-messages are of the high intimacy/high relational orientation variety. This means that text-messaging is being used for social interactions as opposed to being used simply as a tool to exchange necessary information.

Ostracism

A social control mechanism used by peer groups to enforce group rules and conformity to behavior standards; it is seen, for example, when children are ignored and rejected on the school playground.

Social communication can be positive or negative. **Ostracism**, or the purposeful ignoring and exclusion of others, can be extremely hurtful to the person being ostracized (Smith & Williams, 2004). Ostracism is associated with lower self-esteem, sense of belongingness, and self-control.

Most ostracism occurs via face-to-face interactions; however, social internet sites such as chat rooms and personal pages can also provide a forum for ostracism. Smith and Williams (2004) recently conducted a study to ascertain whether text-messaging can be used to produce feelings of ostracism. Through a controlled study, participants were either included in a three-way cell phone text-messaging interchange, or excluded after an initial period (the ostracized condition). In comparison with the participants in the controlled condition, participants in the ostracized condition reported a more negative mood, decreased sense of a meaningful existence, and lower self-esteem, self-control, and sense of belonging. Further, they also wrote more provoking text-messages in response to the exclusion. This study shows the power of text-messaging communication.

Beyond the harm that text-messaging can cause through ostracism, provocation, or harassment, a new area of alarm has emerged. Sexting, or text-messaging sexually explicit messages or pictures, is an area of growing concern (www.cyh.com, 2009). Sexting communication can easily become shared communication with the community at large due to the ease of passing the information electronically along or posting it to the internet. When such private communications become public, embarrassment, shame, distress, and humiliation can result. Once this information is public, it can never become private again, and the socioemotional damage can have long-term, devastating effects. Schools, parents, and law enforcement are scrambling to deal with this new form of communication.

Communication via Social Networking Sites   Online social networks can serve a multitude of purposes, and social network theory in relation to the internet is an area of increasing research (Ethier, 2009). "The study of social networks is important because it helps us to better understand how and why we interact with each other, as well as how technology can alter this interaction" (Ethier, 2009, pg. 1). Social networks can be used to help form and persuade opinions, market products or services, influence the reputation of people or companies, and provide a forum for groups to meet and share information.

Many colleges are beginning to provide social network forums for their students (Ethier, 2009). Much like the text-messaging research discussed previously, social network forums can be used for positive or negative communication. The use of buddy lists can increase feelings of exclusion and allow people to estimate how popular (or unpopular) they are. That said, social network communities can be used to create a sense of cohesion and identity among student clubs and majors. They can also be used to decrease one's sense of isolation and provide entertainment.

Online social networking has become the subject of research. Social networks can influence opinions, market products or services, and provide a forum for groups to meet and share information.

A recent study by Kramer and Winter (2008) examined the relationship of extraversion (or outgoingness), self-esteem, self-efficacy, and self-presentation in regards to social networking sites. First, let's explore some of the general information they found in regards to the "typical" social networker. In the study, they found that the average social networker has nearly ninety-two virtual friends and belongs to around twenty-eight groups. Additionally, the typical social networker posts forty-five pictures and will complete 59 percent of available profile fields. On social networking sites, the most popular group categories in order are entertainment, personal data, geography, hobbies and interests, and social life and relationships. More than 98.3 percent of social networkers register with their real name and post their real photo. The majority of photos show the individual's face with either a posing or serious facial expression. Social networkers are also not shy in posting personal information with nearly 33 percent posting their political orientation and 62 percent posting their relationship status.

Now that we have a general description of social networkers, we can see what the Kramer and Winter (2008) study discovered in regards to personality, and other personal characteristics, and social networking. Individuals with a medium score on the extraversion measure participated in the greatest number of groups. Additionally, the higher a person's extraversion score, the more likely they were to post an experimental photo (such as a black and white photo). Self-esteem was not related to the content or style of the social networker's profile, although other studies have found such an association (Banczyk et al., 2008). Participants did display high-efficacy in terms of being able to create a positive impression through self-presentation.

What does all this information mean? Individuals feel that they can control how others perceive them by how they present themselves on social networking sites. That said, most individuals are honest and use real information when creating their profiles. Hence, although social networking sites are often perceived as a virtual world where people can create alternative versions of themselves, most individuals keep it real and enjoy social interaction that is based on reality.

General internet communication   Are there any relationships between internet use, personality, and cognitive style? Well, research in this area of communication is relatively new and more longitudinal studies are needed; however, an initial picture has begun to emerge. Personality does appear to have some relationship to online communication. Extroverted individuals tend to spend more time online and communicate more with e-mail than more introverted individuals (Jackson et al., 2003). The higher an individual is in neuroticism (or emotional instability and high anxiety), the less time they spend online.

Cognitive style, which we discussed earlier in this chapter, also appears to be related to online communication (Jackson et al., 2003). A visual cognitive style is associated with less time spent on the internet. A global/relational cognitive style is associated with more time spent on the internet and more e-mail communications.

Internet use appears to be related to certain demographic characteristics (Jackson et al., 2003). African Americans spend less time online and visit fewer sites than European Americans. In general, the more educated a person is, the more time they spend online. Single adults spend less time online than currently married adults. One study using path analysis (a statistical technique) found that socioeconomic factors and personality factors best predict internet use, cognitive style was not as strongly related.

Pause and Process:

1. What is motivation and why is it important in learning?

2. How is technology influencing communication?

SOCIAL AND EMOTIONAL DEVELOPMENT DURING EARLY ADULTHOOD

LEARNING OBJECTIVES:

1. Characterize emotional development during early adulthood

2. Describe the self in relation to others during early adulthood

3. Explain psychosocial development during early adulthood

Developmentalists have begun to research the many changes that take place in early adulthood. Not everyone experiences these changes at the same rate, but most people between the ages of eighteen and twenty-five follow a predictable pattern.

Like other stages of the life span, adulthood poses unique challenges and tasks. These tasks focus primarily on individuating completely from one's family of origin and creating an independent lifestyle. Social expectations are that individuals at this stage will develop and refine skills and abilities that promote competency or mastery of work related roles; use interpersonal skills to choose a mate and develop a lifestyle based on responsible adult-like behavior; and make the necessary effort to maintain a committed relationship that may include children.

Psychopathology has increased for young adults in recent years. It is speculated that this is partly due to their inability to achieve the expected roles for this phase of life, such as moving out of the parents' home, establishing a career, marriage, and parenthood (Compass, Hinden & Gerhardt, 1995; Seiffge-Krenke, 1998; Seiffge-Krenke, 2006).

EMOTIONAL DEVELOPMENT

Trait

A distinguishing feature or characteristic.

Big five factors personality theory

A theory that posits that there are five super-traits that are the foundation of personality.

Openness

The degree to which a person is comfortable with variety, autonomy, and change.

Conscientiousness

The degree to which a person values and/or needs organization, precision, and self-discipline.

Extroversion

The degree to which a person is outgoing.

Agreeableness

The degree to which a person is trusting, giving, and kind.

Neuroticism

The degree to which a person is insecure, emotional, and anxious.

The areas of the brain responsible for emotional regulation reach maturity in early adulthood. This allows for greater control of emotions. Such emotional control is important, as early adulthood is typically a time for establishing a life-long marriage and beginning a family. In this section of the chapter we will focus upon personality and attachment, both of which play key roles in emotion-related behavior.

PERSONALITY   There are many theories of personality. In this chapter, we are going to focus on a trait theory of personality, called the big five factors personality theory (for example, see Costa & McCrae, 1995; McCrae & Costa, 2006). A **trait** is a disposition or characteristic that has some heritability and produces certain behaviors that are displayed across diverse settings. The **big five factors personality theory** posits that five supertraits lay the foundation for all of our personality possibilities. These five traits are openness, conscientiousness, extraversion, agreeableness, and neuroticism.

Openness can be conceptualized as the degree to which a person is comfortable with variety, autonomy, and change (for example, see Costa & McCrae, 1995; McCrae & Costa, 2006). **Conscientiousness** can be conceptualized as the degree to which a person values and/or needs organization, precision, and self-discipline. **Extroversion** can be conceptualized as the degree to which a person is outgoing, demonstrative, and fun-loving. **Agreeableness** can be conceptualized as the degree to which a person is trusting, giving, and kind. Finally, **neuroticism** can be conceptualized as the degree to which a person is insecure, emotional, and anxious.

Trait theories, in general, have been criticized for overemphasizing traits and underemphasizing the role of the environment in personality development. Most developmentalists believe that personality is the result of complex interactions that include both traits and the environment (Cervone & Mischel, 2002; Mischel, 2004). In chapter eight, we will see which traits tend to change with age, and which tend to stay the same.

ATTACHMENT   Attachment styles play an important role in adult relationships. These attachment styles have their foundations in infancy, where mental models were built based upon parental caregiving and parent/child interaction (Dixon, 2003; Galatzer-Levy & Cohler, 1993). In fact "a central notion of attachment theory is that attachment representation once formed in early childhood, continue to function as a relatively durable template for later relationships throughout adolescence and into adulthood" (Seiffge-Krenke, 2006, p. 865).

Attachment to romantic partners is likely to resemble attachment to parents (Hazen & Shaver, 1987; Steele et al., 1998). Much of the information discussed in this section is based upon the initial research by Bowlby and Ainsworth, and more recent research by Hazen, Shaver, and their colleagues. Let's review the attachment styles introduced in chapter three, with an expanded description of each one's mental model of self and others and their approach to relationships.

Secure attachment:

- Secure attachment style: Trusts self and others and is comfortable in a relationship or out of a relationship. Having parents that were responsive and dependable is related to the development of this attachment style.

Insecure attachment:

- Preoccupied attachment style (a.k.a., resistant attachment style): Has trouble trusting self, and is dependent upon others. This attachment style feels the need to constantly be in a relationship and may display possessiveness and jealousy. Having parents that were inconsistent is related to the development of this attachment style.

- Avoidant attachment style (a.k.a., dismissive attachment style): Trusts self, but has trouble trusting others. Is generally avoidant of close relationships and can be emotionally distant when in a relationship. Having parents that were emotionally dismissive, psychologically distant, or physically unavailable is related to the development of this attachment style.

- Disorganized/disoriented attachment style (a.k.a., unresolved attachment style): Has trouble trusting self and others. Generally struggles in relationships and is at risk for being a victim of domestic violence. Having parents that were neglectful or abusive is related to the development of this attachment style.

Attachment styles are important in adult relationships such as having a romantic partner.

The transition from adolescence to complete independence in adulthood can be difficult. Young adults with a secure attachment to their parents typically report a more emotionally positive transition from adolescence to adulthood than young adults with insecure attachment (for a review see Seiffge-Krenke, 2006). Securely attached individuals seem able to achieve independence in early adulthood more easily, whereas insecure and anxious young adults display lower adjustment and greater distress (Grossman, Grossman & Zimmermann, 1999). More positive interactions are seen in the relationships between securely attached young adults and their parents than in the relationships between insecurely attached young adults and their parents. Adults with a secure attachment to their parents typically value these relationships and believe that this relationship has influenced their life course.

Attachment style greatly impacts one's ability to adjust to the expected tasks in young adulthood, like developing a romantic relationship that will grow into a life-long marriage (Scharf et al., 2004). Securely attached individuals tend to be in longer lasting and more satisfying relationships that exhibit greater trust and commitment than the relationships of insecurely attached individuals (Feeney & Collins, 2007). Further, the romantic relationships of securely attached adults are close and intimate, yet the individuals can maintain a healthy degree of individuality (Shaver, Belsky & Brennan, 2000). When in need of a secure base, individuals with a secure attachment style tend to rely on their romantic partners in adulthood, whereas individuals with an insecure attachment style tend to rely on their parents (Cox et al., 2008). During periods of separation due to work travel, insecurely attached individuals experience greater separation anxiety as exhibited in self-reported stress, cortisol levels (related to physiological stress), and sleeping problems, than securely attached individuals (Diamond, Hicks & Otter-Henderson, 2008). Also, securely attached individuals are more skilled in providing emotional support to their partners than insecurely attached individuals (Rholes & Simpson, 2007).

Beyond romantic relationships, attachment in adulthood is related to numerous other aspects of development and adjustment. For example, adults with insecure attachment tendencies exhibit greater physiological stress and lower levels of self-reported love when listening to an infant cry than adults with secure attachment tendencies (Groh & Roisman, 2009). Such reactions could impact parenting behavior. Attachment also seems to be related to one's religiosity and belief in a loving God (Cassibba et al., 2008). Catholic priests have higher rates of secure attachment than the general population. Additionally, priests and lay Catholics have lower rates of disorganized/disoriented attachment styles than the general population. Several studies have indicated that a secure attachment style and the ability to trust parents in childhood is predictive of the ability to trust and believe in a loving God during adulthood (for example, see Birgegard & Granqvist, 2004; Cassibba et al. 2008). In general, compared to individuals with an insecure attachment style, secure individuals have greater resiliency, self-esteem, emotional control, mental health, coping skills, self-efficacy, and overall positive adaptation (Berman & Sperling, 1991; Hankin, Kassel & Abela, 2005; Miklincer & Shaver, 2007; Scharf et al., 2004).

Pause and Process:

1. What are the big five personality traits?

2. How do the four attachment styles differ in the mental representations of self and others?

SELF WITH OTHERS

Early adulthood is a time of achieving independence from one's parents. It is also a time of establishing a life-long partnership and establishing a family. In this section, we will discuss how young adults go about leaving the parents' home, cohabitation, marriage, career development, and parenthood.

Living Arrangements

Incompletely launched young adults

Young adults who return home to live with their parents.

In-time leavers

Individuals that move out of their parents homes permanently before the age of 25.

Still in the nest

Individuals who are still living at home between the ages of 21 to 25 years, but are actively working towards moving out, and are out by the end of this age-range.

Late leavers

Individuals that are still living at home after the age of 25.

Returners

Young adults who had ventured out to independent living, but subsequently returned to live with their parents at some point between the ages of 21 and 25 years of age.

LEAVING THE NEST   In the chapter on socioemotional development during adolescence, we learned that this period of time can be difficult because adolescents and their parents must strike a new balance between autonomy and relatedness, control and freedom. During the emergence of early adulthood, young adults and their parents must once again seek this balance (O'Conner et al., 1996; Seiffge-Krenke, 2006).

One developmental task that is expected to be completed during early adulthood is moving out of one's parents' home and living independently. Many young adults move out, move back in, and then move back out of their parents' homes (Goldscheider & Goldscheider, 1994; Seiffge-Krenke, 2006; Settersten, 1998). The percentage can vary greatly across ethnicities, cultures, religions, socioeconomic status, and sociohistorical and economic times. Young adults who return home to live with their parents are typically referred to as **incompletely launched young adults**.

Research has indicated four patterns for leaving home and launching an independent life in early adulthood (Seiffge-Krenke, 2006). **In-time leavers** are individuals that move out of their parents homes permanently before the age of twenty-five. Approximately 55 percent of all young adults fall into this category. The average age for a female to move out is twenty-one years, whereas the average age for a male to move out is twenty-three years. Approximately 14 percent of all adults are considered **still in the nest**. These are individuals who are still living at home between the ages of twenty-one to twenty-five years, but are actively working toward moving out, and are out by the end of this age-range. **Late leavers** are those individuals that are still living at home after the age of twenty-five. Approximately 20 percent of young adults fall into the late leavers category. **Returners** are young adults who had ventured out to independent living, but subsequently returned to live with their parents at some point between the ages of twenty-one and twenty-five years of age. Approximately 11 percent of young adults fall into the returner category.

In a study examining these patterns of leaving the nest by Seiffge-Krenke (2006), participants categorized as late leavers and returners shared key demographic characteristics;

26. Explain the four patterns for leaving home and launching an independent life.

hence, these two categories were combined into one general category (late leavers/returners) for statistical analysis. Analysis revealed that there are virtually no differences between in-time leavers, still in the nesters, and late leavers/returners in terms of education level, parents' marital status, number of siblings, socioeconomic status, or gender. Only two participants were unemployed and both were in the late leavers/returners category. Across categories, approximately half of the participants were in an apprenticeship or profession, while the other half was attending college.

So how do individuals in these various patterns of leaving home differ? What predicts how a young adult will time leaving home? One robust finding by Seiffge-Krenke (2006) was the impact of marriage and romantic relationships in terms of leaving the nest. All of the participants in the study that were married were in-time leavers. Further, in-time leavers were more likely to be in a long-term committed relationship than those individuals still at home. In-time leavers predominately had a secure attachment style, whereas late leavers/returners predominately had an avoidant attachment style. Individuals still in the nest were divided in regards to attachment style, with 46 percent classified as secure, 31 percent classified as avoidant, and 23 percent classified as preoccupied.

Another predictor of leaving the home in-time was conflict in the home during adolescence, although this conflict gave way to negotiation in terms of establishing a new balance between autonomy and relatedness. Individuals still in the nest had lower levels of independence during early adulthood, when compared with those that leave in time. Adults that are late leavers/returners have higher levels of mental illness symptoms (as reported by their parents) than in-time or still in the nest individuals. It is speculated that especially rough transitions to independent living may lead to psychopathology.

Cohabitation

Living with a romantic partner prior to marriage.

Cohabitation effect

The increased risk for divorce associated with cohabitation.

COHABITATION   Involvement in a long-term, romantic relationship increases across early adulthood, with 62 percent in such a relationship by age twenty-five (Seiffge-Krenke, 2006). Living with a romantic partner prior to marriage, referred to as **cohabitation**, is an increasingly popular choice among young adults. It is estimated that up to 70 percent of young couples cohabitate in the United States (Bumpass & Lu, 2000; Stanley, Whitton & Markman, 2004). Unfortunately, there are some serious negative consequences to cohabitation.

Couples that cohabitate prior to engagement or marriage report lower marital quality than those that marry prior to living together (Cohan & Kleinbaum, 2002; Stanley et al., 2002). Additionally, couples that cohabitate and then marry are at an increased risk for divorce (Kamp Dush, Cohan & Amato, 2003). In fact, this finding is so robust in the research literature, that it has been coined the **cohabitation effect** (Rhoades, Stanley & Markman, 2009). In comparison to couples that engage or marry prior to living together, cohabiting couples exhibit the following problems:

- Lower marital satisfaction
- Lower relationship quality
- Lower dedication to the spouse and marriage
- Lower interpersonal commitment

- Lower relationship confidence

- More negative communication and interactions

- Increased rates of infidelity

- Cohabiting males are four times more likely to cheat than husbands

- Cohabiting females are eight times more likely to cheat than wives

- Increased rates of aggressive interaction

- Increased rates of domestic violence

- Greater potential for divorce

- Poorer outcomes for children (abuse, problem behavior, poverty, overall welfare)

The above findings are based on numerous research studies (for example see: Kline et al., 2004; Rhoades, Staley & Markman, 2006, 2009; Stanton, 2009; Stets, 1991; Stets & Straus, 1989; Waite & Gallagher, 2000; Wing, 2009; Yllo & Straus, 1981). In summary, young adults may want to think carefully before deciding to live with someone outside of marriage. Cohabitation threatens the future marriage's longevity and quality, increases the risk of violence for women and children, and is detrimental to socioemotional health.

MARRIAGE   Why do people marry? Well, the answer is dependent upon one's religion, ethnicity, culture, and overall socialization. For Christians, the purpose of marriage is to help guide your partner to be closer to God, to be open to procreation, and to use the marriage to glorify God everyday. In a more American, secular sense, marriage is usually based upon love, fulfillment of psychological and financial needs, and parenthood (Brehm, 1992; Cherlin, 1999; Cox, 1990; Steinmetz, Clavan & Stein, 1990). Marriage is correlated with happiness, better health, and increased longevity (Brehm, 1992).

How does one achieve a happy and life-long marriage? First, one should marry someone that they have dated for at least six months and who shares the view that marriage is a life-

There are a variety of beliefs for the purpose of marriage.

long commitment. Second, one must shift his or her self-concept from one of "me" to one of "we." Everyday, efforts should be made to show selflessness and appreciation for your spouse. Third, healthy communication styles must be developed and conflict must be handled in a productive way (Brehm, 1992). Fourth, the marriage must be the primary relationship. Friendships and other family relationships (like sibling or parent relationships) must take a back seat if a marriage is to stay strong and healthy.

Men and women can differ in their communication styles (Brehm, 1992). Women tend to use more self-disclosure in emotional matters. Additionally, women tend to be more expressive (warm and responsive) in their communication style, whereas males are more instrumental (practical). Spouses must come to appreciate and understand each others communication style. Premarital classes can help with this. In general, to improve communication, decrease conflict, and improve marital satisfaction, spouses should do the following (Brehm, 1992; Gottman and colleagues, 1976, 1979, 1994, 1998, 1999):

- Clearly understand the intent and impact of communication

- Validate each others feelings and thoughts

- Discuss problems openly

- Focus on the solvable problems and negotiate agreements and compromise

- Don't assume that the spouse can read your mind

- Avoid mind-reading your spouses intentions, as you may assume more negative intentions

- Turn toward each other in times of distress and nurture affectional ties

- Create a life-story together with shared meaning and history

BECOMING PARENTS   Becoming a parent is a life-altering experience. Once again, one's self-concept must switch from one of "we" (self and spouse), to one of "three" (self, spouse, and child). The transition to parenthood can be both exciting and stressful. The committed marital relationship is the foundation for the new family system.

The Outside World

FRIENDSHIP   The nature and importance of friendships change in early adulthood. Now friends are frequently chosen for the congeniality. The need for group experiences that was declining in late adolescence decreases even more in early adulthood. As individuals focus on developing skills that promote intimate relationships, their social interactions tend to center on one person. As they become involved in a committed relationship, their friendships tend to be with other couples of similar ages and social situations. In the later years of early adulthood, friendships are formed in more complex ways. Regardless, friendships provide a source of support, security, and love (Brehm, 1992).

LEISURE TIME   Leisure activities can provide an opportunity for socialization (Hansen, Dik & Zhou, 2008). During early adulthood, particularly the college-age years, leisure provides a forum for establishing social status, cultivating relationships, and forming a peer reference group (Hansen, Dik & Zhou, 2008; Kleiber & Kelly, 1980). During the college-age years, leisure activities can be completely social in nature (e.g., partying for the sake of hanging out together and having fun). Conversely, leisure time becomes more constricted during the mid and latter part of early adulthood as family and work obligations grow. Hence, a party at work may serve multiple purposes such as social networking with the intention of making career contacts, making a good impression on colleagues, and hanging out with your work friends.

Generation Y

Individuals born after the year 1980.

CAREERS IN EARLY ADULTHOOD   Many young adults today are considered to be part of **Generation Y** (i.e., individuals born after 1980) (Schultz & Schultz, 2010). Within the next couple of years, Generation Y individuals will comprise approximately 50 percent of those who work in the United States. Interestingly, these young adults differ from the preceding generations in what they want and expect in a career.

Silent generation

Individuals born between 1922 and 1945.

Before we discuss what young adults today seek in a career, it would be helpful to describe previous generations' expectations and behaviors. The **Silent Generation** includes individuals born between 1922 and 1945 (Schultz & Schultz, 2010). Most of these individuals have either retired from the workforce or plan to do so in the near future. The Silent Generation valued loyalty, hard work, and respect for authority. Loyalty was seen as a two-way street: employees were loyal to their employers and employers were loyal to their employees. Many individuals in the Silent Generation had only one or two employers, largely because of the importance of loyalty.

Baby boomer generation

Individuals born between 1946 and 1964.

The **Baby Boomer Generation** includes individuals born between 1946 and 1964 (Schultz & Schultz, 2010). Due to the large number of individuals born to this genera-

What is wanted in a career depends upon ones expectations. These expectations vary from one generation to the next.

tion, competition for jobs was intense in their early adulthood. Unfortunately, two related outcomes of this competition were individuals choosing to become workaholics and a decline in time spent with the family.

Generation X includes individuals born between 1965 and 1979 (Schultz & Schultz, 2010). These are the children of the Baby Boomer Generation, and as such, were committed to not becoming workaholics like their parents. This generation values their independence, questions authority, and is skilled in technology.

Now that we know about previous generations of young adults we can learn about Generation Y with a comparative eye. This is a generation that grew up during the big "self-esteem" push in the 1980s. During this time, many school children were shielded from competition and praised for simply trying their hardest. One outcome of this non-competitive, full-of-praise environment is that many Generation Y individuals are self-centered, narcissistic, and expect constant positive feedback from supervisors regardless of actual work produced (McCormack, 2007; Schultz & Schultz, 2010; Zaslow, 2007). These individuals shun the idea of starting at the bottom and working their way up the corporate ladder. Instead, they want to be involved in meaningful, high-end jobs immediately upon graduating from college (Rexrode, 2007; Schultz & Schultz, 2010). Despite all this negative information, Generation Y individuals are enthusiastic and entrepreneurial in the workplace. In contrast to the previous generations discussed, they value leisure time more than money, wish for a flexible schedule, guard against long work hours, disvalue loyalty to their employer, seek creative opportunities, and tend to change jobs every few years. They also seek a career that will allow them to change the world.

Do career interests change substantially between adolescence and middle adulthood? This was a question asked by Low and colleagues (2005) in a review of longitudinal studies. In general, vocational interests in physical, hands-on, or artistic careers are more stable than vocational interests in more clerical, scientific, or social careers. Hence, childhood dreams of certain careers usually do not lead to that career in adulthood, but may for some.

Generation X

Individuals born between 1965 and 1979.

Intimacy versus isolation

The sixth psychosocial attitude described by Erikson; it is developed optimally between eighteen and twenty-four years of age. Intimacy is the ability to have a close and loving relationship with another. Isolation is the refusal to allow oneself to become vulnerable enough to establish intimate relationships.

Pause and Process:

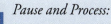

1. What are the dangers associated with cohabitation?

2. Compare and contrast the four generations discussed in terms of work expectations and behaviors.

PSYCHOSOCIAL DEVELOPMENT

Intimacy Versus Isolation

Erikson proposed a normative-crisis model of human development that depicts emotional and social changes as taking place in a sequence. Two stages of psychosocial development are observed in early adulthood, according to Erikson (1950, 1964): (1) a sense of **intimacy versus isolation** is established between eighteen and twenty-four years of age, and

Generativity versus stagnation

The seventh psychosocial attitude described by Erikson; It is developed optimally between twenty-four and fity-four years of age. Generativity is an interest in caring for others and sharing one's knowledge, skills, and information. Stagnation (self-absorption) is directing all one's interest inward to oneself.

30. Why is it important for a person to achieve intimacy instead of social isolation?

(2) a sense of **generativity versus stagnation** (sometimes called generativity versus self-absorption) is established between twenty-four and fifty-four years of age. Because the generativity versus stagnation stage lasts most of middle adulthood, we will discuss this stage in Chapter 8. In this section, we will focus on intimacy versus isolation.

During adolescence, an individual establishes a basic idea of personal identity and settles on an initial direction in life. By accomplishing this central task of adolescence, a person prepares for the next stage in psychosocial development. This occurs in the first years of early adulthood, when an individual is concerned with "losing and finding himself in another," according to Erikson.

During this period of young adulthood, between eighteen and twenty-four, the individual is challenged to learn the skills that will facilitate having an intimate relationship with another person. This is one of the most pressing concerns of young adults. They need to go through a series of experiences in order to learn how to conduct a meaningful adult love relationship. These skills are often learned by observing parental behavior and trial and error.

Through time, individuals learn about themselves and others. They discover what is attractive in others, how and to what degree they should lower barriers to intimacy, when and how they should disclose personal information to another, and how to go about placing trust in another person. The lessons of trust that were learned in infancy are transferred to relationship experiences in adulthood in ways that facilitate the development of intimacy skills.

Social isolation is the principle hazard of inadequate psychosocial development in early adulthood, according to Erikson. It results from an inability to develop a close relationship with another. This can happen because an individual withdraws too soon from his or her peer group, before having opportunities to development close associations. It may also stem from negative relationship experiences that convince the individual that it is emotionally safer not to break down personal boundaries and allow one's self to become vulnerable.

Those who do acquire the skills of intimacy eventually choose a partner for a long-term committed relationship. This relationship serves as the basis for forming a new family system for many people. It is with this partner that an individual now shifts his or her psychosocial focus of the next stage: generativity versus stagnation.

Pause and Process:

1. What is the psychosocial task that should be accomplished in early adulthood? Said another way, which of Erikson's conflicts should be resolved in early adulthood?

2. What can cause social isolation?

SUMMARY

1. Although physical growth was nearly completed in adolescence, individuals experience a variety of physical changes in early adulthood. The eyes gradually lose their ability to focus after about age thirty-five. The likelihood of periodontal disease increases. The heart gradually loses its ability to pump blood efficiently and the risk of cardiovascular disease rises. The lungs begin to work less efficiently as well. The skin begins to show signs of aging. Muscular strength reaches its peak during this period.

2. Health during adulthood is generally very good, though subject to certain hazards. These include high levels of stress over long periods of time, poor diets, and inadequate exercise. Risky behaviors seen in adolescence continue to plague some individuals in early adulthood. According to the CDC (2000), some STDs are at epidemic levels in the United States. Depression and suicide are issues to be aware of and addressed during this phase of life.

3. Intellectual functioning changes in several areas during adulthood. Crystallized intelligence increases, while fluid intelligence declines. Developmental researchers disagree about whether there is a fifth stage of cognitive development called postformal operational thought. Thinking as a mature adult may require a shift to dialectical thinking, or the ability to tolerate uncertainty, contradictions, and conflicts in logic.

4. Motivation and self-regulation are important for learning and academic achievement in college. Extrinsic motivation is dependent upon reward and punishment, whereas intrinsic motivation is internally generated and more powerful. Self-regulated learning allows an individual to keep track of what they are learning and adjust behaviors as needed.

5. Language and communication have been forever altered by the dawn of technology. Text-messaging, social networking sites, and general internet use are increasingly used for social interactions and communications. Although research in this domain is in its infancy, it appears that technology use differs by demographic characteristics, personality, and cognitive style. Further, social and communication interactions using technology may be positive or negative.

6. Personality in early adulthood can be conceptualized as being comprised of five supertraits: openness, conscientiousness, extroversion, agreeableness, and neuroticism. Attachment style in early adulthood is important for overall adjustment to adulthood and the establishment of healthy romantic relationships.

7. Researchers have identified four patterns for young adults to leave their parents' home and establish independent living: in-time leavers, still in the nest leavers, late leavers, and returners. Essentially, individuals in all four categories have similar educational levels, parental marital status, and number of siblings. Factors that impact launching into independent living include committed romantic relationships, support for independence during early adolescence, and conflict in the home during adolescence.

8. Cohabitation prior to engagement or marriage is associated with numerous negative outcomes; including, higher divorce rates, domestic violence, infidelity, and overall lower relationship

quality. Marriage is associated with happiness, better health, and longevity. Healthy communication is important for a marriage to be successful. Becoming parents is a transitional period that may be both exciting and stressful.

9. Generation Y individuals, the majority of which are either in early adulthood or quickly approaching it, will comprise 50 percent of the U.S. workforce within the next couple of years. These individuals tend to be egocentric and expect positive praise regardless of work performance. Further, they desire flexible, limited work hours, and display little employer loyalty. In fact, many Generation Y individuals seek to change jobs/careers every few years in search of personal growth opportunities and creative outlets.

10. The two major psychosocial changes in early adulthood are acquiring a sense of intimacy versus isolation; and beginning efforts to establish a sense of generativity versus stagnation. Acquiring a healthy sense of intimacy between eighteen and twenty-four years equips people with the skills needed to establish and maintain a committed relationship—leading to a happier and more satisfying life.

SELF-QUIZ

1. What is the cultural meaning of maturity?
2. What is the age-range for early adulthood?
3. When do deficiencies in distance perception first become noticeable?
4. What is periodontal disease?
5. Describe changes in muscular strength and physical performance in early adulthood.
6. Describe the three "types" of personalities discussed in the stress section of the chapter and explain how they relate to health.
7. What factors contribute to stress in college students?
8. How do men and women differ in their weight and height changes during early adulthood?
9. Explain what depression is and what are its symptoms?
10. How may stress be related to fertility issues?
11. What is an example of postformal operational thought?
12. How is postformal operational thought different from formal operational thought (discussed in Chapter 6)?
13. Define cognitive style.
14. What do you believe is your predominant cognitive style and why?
15. How are extrinsic motivation and intrinsic motivation different?
16. Why do you think intrinsic motivation is associated with better academic outcomes than extrinsic motivation?
17. Describe the four general phases to self-regulated learning. Provide an example for each phase.
18. What is the nature of intelligence in adulthood?
19. What are the main purposes of communication when text-messaging?
20. Describe the typical person who uses social networking sites.
21. What are some speculations as to why psychopathology in young adults has increased in recent years?
22. What is a trait?
23. Compare and contrast the big five factors of personality discussed in this chapter with the characteristics of temperament discussed in previous chapters.
24. Why is adult attachment predicted by childhood attachment?
25. What are some ways adult attachment style is related to romantic relationships and general well-being?

26. Explain the four patterns for leaving home and launching an independent life.
27. What factors impact when a person moves out of their parents' home?
28. What is the cohabitation effect and why do you think it exists?

29. What are some strategies to make a marriage work?
30. Why is it important for a person to achieve intimacy instead of social isolation?

TERMS AND CONCEPTS

CHAPTER 8

Middle
Adulthood

OUTLINE

PHYSICAL DEVELOPMENT DURING MIDDLE ADULTHOOD

- Theories of biological aging
- Physical growth
- Health issues

COGNITIVE DEVELOPMENT DURING MIDDLE ADULTHOOD

- Beyond Piaget's theory
- Information-processing during middle adulthood

SOCIAL AND EMOTIONAL DEVELOPMENT DURING MIDDLE ADULTHOOD

- Emotional development
- Self and others
- Psychosocial development

The middle adulthood stage is a transitional period. This stage in the life span takes place when people are approximately between the ages forty and sixty-five. During this time, individuals experience both continuity and change in many aspects of their lives. Physical changes signal approaching old age. Roles that have occupied so much of adult life come to a close by the end of this period. These range from reproductive to parenting and work roles. Individuals are challenged to adjust to these and other significant changes in order to make new adaptations of life. Middle age can bring about new perceptions, redefinitions of roles, and different means for achieving personal happiness.

Middle age may be a prime time of life in many respects, but physical changes indicate that the aging process is accelerating. Our culture is prone to **ageism**, or unreasonable and irrational beliefs about aging and older individuals (Neugarten, 1970). When people reach middle age, they notice physical signs of aging in themselves and fear the end of their physical attractiveness.

Many go to great expense to forestall this. Middle-aged Americans sometimes turn to cosmetic surgery to stave off the waning of exterior beauty.

The first physical signs of aging appear during early adulthood. They are not dramatic, however, so people often overlook them. In middle age, the signs multiply rapidly. It is not unusual to find an occasional gray hair in early adulthood, for example. In middle age, people notice many more of these, along with more wrinkled skin, bags under the eyes, a larger waistline, and less attractive muscle tone. Rather than accepting such signs as part of the normal process of getting older, many people determine to hide or reduce them.

Longer life expectancy may also contribute to people's desire to deny the aging process. In earlier eras, people in their fifties and early sixties were considered elderly. Today that is considered relatively young in relation to the amount of time left to live (Perdue & Gurtman, 1990).

PHYSICAL DEVELOPMENT DURING MIDDLE ADULTHOOD

Middle adulthood

The seventh stage of the life span, occurring between 45 and 65 years of age.

LEARNING OBJECTIVES:

1. *Explain the theories of why we age*
2. *Describe physical development during middle adulthood*
3. *Awareness of health issues in middle adulthood*

THEORIES OF BIOLOGICAL AGING

Middle age

A term synonymous with middle adulthood. Middle age can bring about new perceptions, redefinitions of roles, and different means for achieving personal happiness.

Aging is a process that is not well understood (Busse, 1987), though we know it involves a series of complex and interrelated changes. Although this process is largely biological in nature, it also affects psychological and social functioning. With recent advances in the biological sciences, scientists are beginning to unravel this complex process. Some of these questions are being addressed by research: Can aging be prevented? Can the effects of aging be reversed? How far can we push the life expectancy of humans beyond current biological barriers?

Although we do not know why, exactly, the body ages, we do have some theories. In the following paragraphs, we discuss some current theories of why the body ages.

Ageism

Unreasonable or irrational beliefs about aging and older individuals.

Aging

A complex process involving a decline in physiological competence that inevitably increases the incidence and intensifies the effects of accidents, disease, and other forms of environmental stress.

Cellular clock theory

When biological errors in the DNA genetic code accumulate, the cells are unable to function at all and die.

Stochastic processes

The probability of random accidental injury to cellular DNA.

CELLULAR CLOCK THEORY   Some research suggests that aging results from cells becoming defective because of errors in the DNA genetic code (the cellular command molecule located in the nucleus of cells). As cells experience greater numbers of reproductions over time, errors within the DNA chain are inevitable. Thus, aging may result from an accumulation of errors at the cellular level. Ultimately, the **cellular clock theory** asserts that when these biological errors accumulate, the cells are unable to function at all and die (Hayflick, 1980; Lumpkin et al., 1986; Orgel, 1970; Shay & Wright, 2007; Vinters, 2001; Wareham et al., 1987).

Cells are also vulnerable to **stochastic processes**, or the probability of random accidental injury to cellular DNA (from radiation, for example). The likelihood of accidental injury increases with the passage of time, and these mutations are passed on through subsequent cellular reproductions, eventually leading to the death of cells (Comfort, 1970).

FREE-RADICAL THEORY   **Free-radicals** are unstable oxygen molecules that are released when cells metabolize energy (Chandel & Budinger, 2007). These react with other chemicals within cells, interfering with normal cell functioning and damaging DNA (Liu et al., 2007). Cells are usually able to repair the damage that results. However, their ability to repair themselves may be hampered by the aging process itself or by the lack of adequate chemicals to initiate healing. Free-radical damage could lead to numerous diseases, including cancer and neurodegenerative diseases (Katakura, 2006; Vinters, 2001).

MITOCHONDRIAL THEORY   The **mitochondrial theory** is closely related to the free-radical theory. When free-radicals are released in a cell, they can damage the mitochondria (which are responsible for providing energy for cellular growth and repair). When mitochondria cannot properly function, more free-radicals are released, which then further damage the mitochondria. Eventually, mitochondria are unable to perform their jobs as

Aging may be the result of errors in the DNA genetic code, an accumulation of errors at the cellular level.

Free-radicals

Unstable oxygen molecules that are released when cells metabolize energy.

Mitochondrial theory

The inability of the mitochondria to properly function as the cell's powerhouse and failure to provide enough energy for the cell to function. Damage to the mitochondria is caused by free-radicals released into the cell.

Autoimmune responsiveness theory

As people grow older their immune system begins to attack the body's own tissues.

Hormonal stress theory

As the hormone system ages, it is less effective at managing stress.

the cell's powerhouse and fail to provide enough energy for the cell to function properly (Lee & Wei, 2007). Mitochondria defects have been linked to liver problems, dementia, metabolic disorders, and cardiovascular disease (Armstrong, 2007; Davidson & Duchen, 2007; Vinters, 2001).

AUTOIMMUNE RESPONSIVENESS   The efficiency of the body's defense system in protecting tissues against disease declines as people grow older. In young children, the body is protected by the thymus, a gland that is a prime component of the child's immune system. This gland shrinks as a child approaches puberty. The **autoimmune responsiveness theory** suggests that as people grow older their immune system begins to attack the body's own tissues. Aging results from this immune response gone awry. People become more susceptible to conditions such as cancer as they grow older because their immune systems are less efficient at producing antibodies and cells that can destroy cancerous and other abnormal cells (Makinodan, 1977). The autoimmune responsiveness may also explain why death in old age usually comes from internal diseases such as cancer and cardiovascular disorders such as heart attack and stroke. In contrast, death in childhood is usually associated with infectious disease (Timiras, 1972).

HORMONAL STRESS THEORY   When you are stressed, your body releases stress hormones that allow your body to cope with the stressful event. Then, these hormone levels decrease as the stress diminishes. **Hormonal stress theory** posits that as the hormone system ages, it is less effective at managing stress. Indeed, as we age our stress hormones stay elevated for longer periods of time, which weakens the body's immune system. The weakened immune system leaves the body susceptible to illnesses that could normally have been kept at bay (Aldwin, 1994; Epel et al., 2006; Finch & Seeman, 1999; Goleman & Gurin, 1993; Magri et al., 2006).

Pause and Process:

1. What is the cellular clock theory of aging?

2. What are free-radicals? How may they cause aging?

PHYSICAL DEVELOPMENT

Changes in Weight and Height

The trends in physical change that relate to aging first appeared in early adulthood. These continue throughout middle adulthood, with differences between men and women becoming more pronounced, especially regarding weight and height. Men show an average decrease in weight, whereas women add pounds during middle age. These weight change differences between the sexes reflect differences in biological functioning. They also reflect differences in lifestyle (Abraham, 1979).

Most of the internal organs—skeletal muscles, liver, kidneys, and adrenal glands for example—decrease in weight starting in the fifties. The heart is the exception. This organ generally enlarges with age in an attempt to compensate for its declining efficiency (Timiras, 1972).

The trend to declining height that began in early adulthood continues, more rapidly in women than in men. It is caused by shrinkage of the disk material in the spinal column. Height decreases are quite small—almost unnoticeable—during middle adulthood.

Changes in Bodily Systems

Spotlight

6. What changes does the skin experience during middle adulthood?

CHANGES IN SKIN TISSUE   The body organ most often associated with aging is the skin. Its texture, composition, and appearance all change noticeably in middle age (Spence & Mason, 1987). The skin becomes dryer and loses its ability to retain moisture. Therefore, it feels rougher to the touch.

The loss of skin elasticity results in wrinkles, particularly on the neck, face, and hands. There is also a loss of subcutaneous fat, which exacerbates the skin's tendency to fold and wrinkle. One of the most popular types of cosmetic surgery among middle-aged people involves removing wrinkles and skin blemishes associated with aging.

The hair continues to thin and lose its natural pigmentation during middle adulthood. Hairlines of both men and women recede further during these years. Graying and thinning of the hair occurs over the entire body, including the armpits and pubic areas of both men and women, although men tend to become hairier in certain body areas during middle age. The nails, which are actually skin cells, also show signs of aging. Their growth rate declines and they thicken and show color changes.

The incidence of skin conditions and diseases increases throughout middle adulthood. Although fungus diseases are still the most common skin problem, skin tumors increase dramatically during this period (U.S. Bureau of the Census, 1990a, b). These tumors can be benign, precancerous, or cancerous. They are indicative of the aging process as well as environmental conditions such as prolonged and severe exposure to sunlight earlier in life.

Hair thins and hair lines recede during this age.

Osteoporosis

Inflammation of bone tissue causing softness and porous structure; the condition can lead to bone breakage and tooth loss.

THE TEETH AND SKELETAL SYSTEM   The principal change affecting teeth and skeletal system during middle adulthood is osteoporosis. **Osteoporosis** is an inflammation and loss of the bone tissue throughout the body. In the mouth, it causes the bone tissue surrounding the teeth to soften and become more porous. As a result, teeth loosen in their sockets and eventually are lost unless there is intervention (Kart, Metress & Metress, 1978; Spence & Mason, 1987).

Osteoporosis throughout the skeletal system becomes more noticeable during middle adulthood, especially in women. There is a gradual decrease in the rate which new bone tissue forms, but bone absorption continues at a normal rate. Deficiencies in calcium and vitamin D contribute to osteoporosis. When calcium intake is inadequate to supply its needs, the body leaches calcium from bones, which weakens bone structures throughout the body. That is why bone breakage and incomplete healing plague people in old age. Beyond calcium and vitamin D, a decline in estrogen can exacerbate osteoporosis. Increasing weight bearing exercise and ensuring adequate intake of calcium and vitamin D can help slow down bone tissue loss. Hormone replacement therapy (HRT) has come under scrutiny in recent years for links to serious health problems. Such therapy should be carefully considered under the guidance of a competent physician, in which the costs and benefits of HRT are weighed with your personal health history in mind.

People typically experience the first signs of arthritis and rheumatism during middle adulthood. These conditions can occur at earlier stages, but they are generally associated with the aging process. **Arthritis** is an inflammation of a joint area between bone junctions. The two basic types are osteoarthritis and rheumatoid arthritis (Spence & Mason, 1987). Trauma to a joint, chronic obesity, infections, and metabolic disorders are thought to contribute significantly to most forms of osteoarthritis. Rheumatoid arthritis is believed to be some kind of autoimmune response by the body to inflammation in joint areas. As white blood cells invade these areas in overwhelmingly large numbers, the body reacts by forming fibrous tissue around joints. This causes stiffness and soreness and disforms the joints, restricting movement.

Arthritis

Inflammation of the joint area between bone junctions.

Rheumatism

A variety of conditions resulting in stiffness and soreness in tissues associated with bone joints.

Rheumatism describes a variety of conditions that cause stiffness and soreness in the connective tissue associated with the bone joints. Upon rising from bed in the morning, many middle-aged people feel some stiffness in the muscles and joints, making it harder to move about.

Arthritis and rheumatism tend to run in families. Treatment commonly involves use of various anti-inflammatory drugs to reduce swelling and pain.

Atherosclerosis

A cardiovascular disease in which plaques of fatty material form along arterial walls in the body and especially in the heart. This leads to blockage of blood flow and the possibility of clots, increasing the likelihood of heart attack and stroke.

THE CARDIOVASCULAR SYSTEM   The cardiovascular system, which includes the heart and the circulatory system, begins to show the effects of diet, lifestyle, and aging during middle adulthood. Three basic changes may be observed: (1) a decline in the elasticity of the arteries, (2) an increasing accumulation of fatty deposits in the arterial tissues, and (3) a general decline in the ability of the heart to pump blood efficiently.

Two major abnormalities of the cardiovascular system appear with increasing frequency during middle age. They result from the interaction of the aging process with diets that are high in fat and cholesterol (Spence & Mason, 1987). In **atherosclerosis**, plaques of fatty material form along the walls of arteries, blocking and slowing down the flow of blood. As a result, blood clots may form, further contributing to restricted blood flow. In **arteriosclerosis**, commonly called "hardening of the arteries," there is a gradual loss of elasticity in arterial walls throughout the body.

Arteriosclerosis

A condition usually occurring in advanced cases of atherosclerosis in which there is a gradual loss of elasticity in arterial vessels. The end result is high blood pressure or hypertension.

Hypertension

Abnormally high blood pressure caused by constriction of arteries; it increases the likelihood of kidney damage, heart failure, and brain damage via strokes.

Diabetes

The failure of the pancreas gland cells to secrete an adequate amount of an enzyme (insulin) that is essential for metabolizing sugars.

Menopause

The climacteric in females; cessation of all reproductive functions that begins at about age forty-five to forty-eight and is completed by about age fifty-five.

Both of these conditions lead to a reduced blood flow throughout the body, raising the blood pressure. Some increase in blood pressure is natural with age, but these cardiovascular diseases lead to **hypertension**, or abnormally high levels of blood pressure. Hypertension increases the probability of kidney damage, heart attacks, and strokes.

These cardiovascular conditions can be largely controlled through diet, exercise, and drug therapy. Although dietary contributions to cardiovascular diseases begin early in life, the effects do not show up until middle or late adulthood. Diets that are low in fat and sodium and high in fiber appear to give some protection against these conditions, as well as against cancers of the colon and reproductive organs and diabetes (Hausman, 1983; Hausman & Hurley, 1989).

THE DIGESTIVE SYSTEM   The digestive system shows fewer signs of aging than the other organ systems in middle adulthood. Common digestive disturbances in middle age are intestinal obstructions due to ulcerative colitis, absorption problems, gallstones, ulcers in the stomach and duodenum, and hemorrhoids of the lower rectum and anal region.

Gallstones, ulcers, and hemorrhoids result more from poor diet and stress than from the aging process. People who consume a diet high in fat and cholesterol are prone to gallstones. Hemorrhoids can result from a diet high in fat and low in fiber. People subjected to chronically high levels of stress are susceptible to ulcers as well as hemorrhoids (Spence & Mason, 1987). Ulcers are a leading digestive disorder in middle adulthood (U.S. Bureau of the Census, 1990a, b; 1991a, b).

The incidence of **diabetes** increases dramatically during middle age. This condition involves the failure of the pancreas gland cells to secrete an adequate amount of an enzyme (insulin) that is essential for metabolizing sugars. The tendency for diabetes is genetics, but the disease is closely associated with obesity in middle-aged and elderly people (Spence & Mason, 1987).

THE REPRODUCTIVE SYSTEM   Both men and women experience changes in their reproductive organs and sexual functioning during middle adulthood. The changes are perhaps more pronounced among women, because their reproductive functioning ceases at some point during middle age.

Menopause is the term applied to the cessation of reproductive functioning in women (Kelly & Byrne, 1992; Spence & Mason, 1987). This is a gradual process that is completed when ovulation and menstruation cease and hormone levels drop. Most women begin to notice irregular menstrual periods between forty-five and forty-eight years of age. The process is completed by about age fifty-five for most women (Ansbacher, 1983).

The major characteristics of menopause are the cessation of ovulation and menstruation, and a decrease in the production of estrogen. While hormone levels begin to decline, women may experience palpitations, insomnia, hot flashes, chills, headaches, irritability, and anxiety (Burnside, 1976). During menopause, the uterus decreases in weight and the walls of the vaginal tract become thinner (Masters & Johnson, 1966).

Middle-aged men experience changes in sexual functioning more so than in reproductive capacity (Mulligan & Moss, 1991). These changes constitute the **climacteric**. Sperm continue to be produced, but in smaller numbers. There is a gradual degeneration of the reproductive organs and a decline in sexual abilities. The prostate gland enlarges and becomes increasingly coarse as men age. This leads to slower urination. Testosterone levels also diminish with age and are associated with physical changes in the external genitalia.

CHANGES IN SENSATION AND PERCEPTION   Several changes in vision and hearing can be expected during middle age. Common eye symptoms of aging are further loss of accommodation (focusing ability), depigmentation of the iris, declining retinal reflexes, and changes in the lens and cornea (Spence & Mason, 1987). People who did not require reading glasses during the latter part of early adulthood will probably need them sometime during middle adulthood.

Cataracts and **glaucoma** increase in frequency during this stage. Cataracts involve a change in the lens of the eye that renders it opaque to entering light (Fujikado et al., 2004). The condition can be treated with surgery and special glasses or contact lenses (Stifer et al., 2004). Glaucoma is a group of diseases characterized by increases in pressure from within the eyeball (Mok, Lee & So, 2004; Molteno et al., 2006). This condition often damages the optic nerve, causing blindness. It can be controlled by medication and other medical treatment. Because the tendency to both conditions increases in middle age, people should have regular eye examinations when they reach this stage of life.

Hearing loss may become more noticeable during middle adulthood. People often notice a decline in their ability to hear high-frequency sounds or those at the lower ranges. This hearing loss may be more a product of living in a noisy environment for many years than a natural

Climacteric

Decline in sexual functioning among middle-aged men.

Cataracts

A change in the lens of the eye causing it to become opaque to entering light, which reduces vision considerably.

Glaucoma

A group of diseases resulting in increased pressure within the eyeball and leading to blindness if left untreated.

A decline in vision is common at this stage. For example, focusing ability, retinal reflexes, changes in the lens and cornea all are diminished.

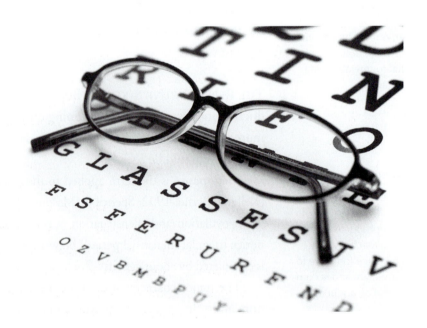

part of the aging process. The threshold at which people can easily detect and understand speech and other sounds also declines throughout this stage (Rowland, 1980).

Pause and Process:

1. How does the body change during middle adulthood?

2. What are some of the changes in the sensory system in middle adulthood?

HEALTH ISSUES

Nutritional Needs

As muscle mass decreases and metabolism slows, middle-aged adults need fewer calories each day. A balanced diet rich in fruits, vegetables, and fiber helps enhance health during this phase of the life span.

PHYSICAL AND MENTAL HEALTH   Most people enjoy a satisfactory state of health during middle adulthood and a general sense of well-being. They adjust to the fact that their bodies are older and function differently and learn how to make compensations.

Health inevitably becomes more compromised, though, as the effects of chronic stress, careless diet and lifestyle, and the wear and tear of life accumulate. To illustrate, among the leading reasons middle-aged people visit a physician are stomach pains and cramps, lower back pain, and hypertension—all of which are symptoms of chronic stress (DeLozier & Gagnon, 1991). Doctor visits increase considerably during middle age as people become more worried about their health and decide to monitor it by having annual examinations.

Mental Health   Post-traumatic stress disorder (PTSD) can be experienced at any stage of the life span. It is an anxiety disorder triggered by witnessing or experiencing a traumatic and terrifying event (NIMH, 2009). Traumatic events can include a sexual assault, an acute life-threatening illness, witnessing a murder, or experiencing an accident. Approximately 8 percent of people in the United States will experience PTSD at some point in their life (U.S. Department of Veteran Affairs, 2009). PTSD is different from acute stress disorder (ASD). ASD is a temporary state of hypervigilance and stress following a traumatic experience, which subsides within a short period of time (NIMH, 2009). PTSD is a disorder that may not appear immediately after a traumatic experience, but once it manifests, it lasts for an extended period of time and interferes with one's ability to function in daily life.

The symptoms of PTSD fall into three general categories: re-experiencing the event, avoidance, and hyperarousal (NIMH, 2009). Re-experiencing the event can occur through nightmares and flashbacks. Avoidance involves social withdrawal and avoiding situations and locations where the traumatic event occurred. Hyperarousal is the experience of always being on alert and waiting for the event to reoccur. An individual may not experience all of these symptoms, but some unique combination of them.

Although any traumatic event can cause PTSD, most of the research has focused on soldiers returning from war. In the general population, 8 percent of men and 20 percent of women will develop PTSD after a traumatic event (U.S. Department of Veteran Affairs, 2009). In any given year, approximately 5.2 million adults in the United States are struggling with PTSD. Different wars have seen different rates of PTSD in soldiers:

- Vietnam soldiers: 30 percent

- Desert Storm soldiers: 10 percent

- Enduring Freedom (Afghanistan) soldiers: 6–11 percent

- Operation Iraqi Freedom soldiers: 12–20 percent

The military is working hard to provide psychological support services to returning soldiers. Recent research has indicated that soldiers who feel that their unit is highly cohesive and has a good leader perceive less stigma and barriers in seeking PTSD care (Wright et al., 2009). Providing PTSD care, working to remove the stigma attached to having a mental disorder, and eliminating barriers will help struggling soldiers heal from their traumatic experiences.

Promoting Wellness   People tend to become more sedentary as they grow older (Sidney, 1981; Timiras, 1972). During middle adulthood, participation in exercise, sports, and general physical activity decreases. A program of mild to moderate exercise in middle age maintains endurance and physical stamina (Schoenborn & Danchik, 1980), prevents excessive weight gain, keeps joints and muscles limber, and aids cardiovascular response.

As throughout the life span, sleep is important to health and well-being in middle adulthood. Sleep problems may begin to manifest during middle adulthood. These problems include difficulties falling asleep, wakeful periods during the night, and decreased amounts of the deepest stage of sleep—all resulting in feeling tired the next day (Abbott, 2003; Alessi, 2007; Ingelsson et al., 2007). Sleep deprivation can also decrease cognitive

Problems arise such as the inability to fall asleep or to stay asleep throughout the night.

processes, mental health, and physical health. Although changes in sleep may be linked to the brain aging, limiting caffeine and alcohol consumption near bedtime, daily exercise, and managing stress can help improve one's chances of getting a good night sleep.

Pause and Process:

1. Describe health in middle adulthood.

2. What is PTSD?

COGNITIVE DEVELOPMENT DURING MIDDLE ADULTHOOD

LEARNING OBJECTIVES:

1. *Characterize cognitive strategies and specialization of knowledge during middle adulthood*

2. *Describe information-processing during middle adulthood*

In this section, we will discuss how there is a shift in middle adulthood from cognitive development to the maintenance of cognitive process and its eventual decline. The idea of experts and how they differ from novices in their cognitive strategies is also discussed. Finally, examples of attention, memory, and intelligence in middle adulthood will be examined.

BEYOND PIAGET'S THEORY: COGNITIVE DEVELOPMENT DURING MIDDLE ADULTHOOD

Selection, optimization, and compensation (SOC) theory

A theory that examines how selection, optimization, and compensation assist individuals in coping with the declines associated with aging. It is often considered a theory of successful aging.

Optimization and Compensation

We will learn in this chapter that during middle adulthood, some aspects of cognitive processes continue to develop, others are maintained, and still others decline. **Selection, optimization, and compensation theory (SOC theory)** stresses that adaptive aging involves maximizing gains and minimizing losses (Baltes, Lindenberger & Staudinger, 1998). With aging, resources shift from promoting growth toward maintenance and the regulation of loss. Behaviors associated with selection include goal specification and identifying new goals when faced with loss. Behaviors associated with optimization include focusing attention, persistence, energy, and effort toward goal obtainment. Behaviors associated with compensation include use of external resources and support, learning new skills, and increasing time and effort in the obtainment of goals.

Growth

Behaviors meant to increase functioning and adaptation.

Maintenance

Behaviors striving to keep functioning at current levels despite declines in processes or ability.

Regulation of loss

Behaviors that allow for reorganization or functioning at lower levels because maintenance is no longer possible.

12. Within SOC theory, describe a behavior or strategy for optimization.

Within SOC theory, **growth** is defined as behaviors meant to increase functioning and adaptation (Baltes, Lindenberger & Staudinger, 1998). **Maintenance** is defined as behaviors striving to keep functioning at current levels despite declines in processes or ability. **Regulation of loss** is defined as behaviors that allow for reorganization of functioning at lower levels because maintenance is no longer possible.

There are four foundational rationales in SOC theory (Baltes, Lindenberger & Staudinger, 1998). First, biological resources decline in quality and amount as people age. For example, our mitochondria become less functional with aging increasing the risk for certain illnesses. Second, the need for culture increases in quality and amount as age increases. For example, as one gets older they may need access to better health care more often. Third, as age increases the efficiency of culture decreases. This means that as a person gets older, the effectiveness of cultural interventions decreases. For example, although we can treat many medical conditions associated with old age, we cannot ultimately stop the aging process or prevent death. Fourth, there is a general lack of cultural support structures for the elderly. Said another way, available cultural resources and support decreases as age increases.

Research has focused on how well the SOC theory can be applied to help promote successful aging (Freund & Baltes, 1998). Findings indicate that use of selection, optimization, and compensation strategies and behaviors is associated with satisfaction with age, decreased emotional loneliness, decreased social loneliness, lack of agitation, and positive emotions.

Personality and subjective assessments are related to one's selection, optimization, and compensation (SOC) scores (Freund & Baltes, 1998). Individuals high in neuroticism have lower SOC scores. Individuals who are highly invested in their life and rate their subjective health highly have high SOC scores. General intelligence is positively correlated with optimization and compensation, but showed no relationships with selection. Hence, certain personal characteristics may influence one's propensity to employ SOC strategies to optimize aging.

EXPERT VERSUS NOVICE KNOWLEDGE

During middle adulthood, many individuals develop expertise within their area of work or hobby. **Expertise** can be defined as having extensive experience, knowledge, and understanding within a specific area of interest (National Research Council, 2000). A

Expert knowledge and experience is usually obtained by middle adulthood.

Expertise

Having extensive experience, knowledge, and understanding within a specific area of interest.

Novice

A person with limited experience, knowledge, or understanding within a specific area of interest.

novice would be someone with limited experience, knowledge, or understanding within a specific area of interest. Experts and novices in a given realm differ in their abilities to problem-solve, remember, and reason in this domain.

Experts differ from novices in their ability to detect meaningful patterns of information (National Research Council, 2000). The detection of these meaningful patterns activates knowledge of corresponding problem-solving strategies and the implications of these strategies. Experts are also better able to "chunk" or group individual pieces of information into meaningful units, and fit this information into a vast network of knowledge. From doctors to chess players, this ability to detect meaningful patterns of information allows experts to outperform novices consistently.

The organization of knowledge is another area that experts differ from novices (National Research Council, 2000). It's not just that experts know more, it is that they structure and store the information in a better organizational framework. Novices typically approach learning new information as a series of facts and information, whereas experts organize specific facts within a web that is organized around major orienting (or core) concepts. Hence, when new facts or information is learned, experts can easily link this new information into the greater web of knowledge. "Within this picture of expertise, 'knowing more' means having more conceptual chunks in memory, more relations or features defining each chunk, more interrelations among the chunks, and efficient methods for retrieving related chunks and procedures for applying these informational units in problem-solving contexts" (National Research Council, 2000, p. 38).

Conditionalized knowledge

The skill experts have in retrieving the specific information that they need for any given problem.

Context and access to knowledge is another realm in which experts differ from novices (National Research Council, 2000). For any given problem, a small part of an expert's knowledge is applicable. For example, an oncologist has an immense amount of knowledge about cancer. However, for any given patient a comparatively small amount of this knowledge is utilized. Hence, experts not only have more knowledge, but they are skilled in accessing the specific information that they need for any given problem. This aspect of expert knowledge and retrieval is referred to as **conditionalized knowledge**.

Merely skilled experts

Expertise that functions largely on routine.

Novices sometimes struggle to retrieve information from memory that is needed to solve a problem. Experts have achieved automatic and fluent retrieval of information from memory (National Research Council, 2000). So not only are they better at retrieving relevant information, they can retrieve this information with great speed and little effort.

Highly competent experts

Experts who exhibit great adaptability, flexibility, and creativity in utilizing their expertise across a variety of situations.

We have just discussed some of the general differences in cognitive processes between novices and experts. Interestingly, there are at least two very different types of experts (National Research Council, 2000). **Merely skilled experts** have expertise that function largely on routine. **Highly competent experts** exhibit great adaptability, flexibility, and creativity in utilizing their expertise across a variety of situations. Merely skilled experts display extensive skills when solving problems and focus on using these skills as quickly and efficiently as possible. Highly competent experts capitalize on solving problems as an opportunity to be creative in their strategies and develop new skills.

Adaptive expertise

An approach to problems that is characterized by flexibility and promotes life-long learning.

Highly competent experts are sometimes said to possess **adaptive expertise**, which is an approach to problems that is characterized by flexibility and promotes life-long learning. Both types of experts monitor their understanding and problem-solving approach and make adjustments as needed.

Pause and Process:

1. What is SOC theory?

2. How do experts and novices differ in their approach to problems?

INFORMATION-PROCESSING IN MIDDLE ADULTHOOD

Crystallized intelligence

Skills acquired through education and socialization such as verbal skills, mathematical skills, inductive reasoning, and interpersonal skills; the ability to recall and use information.

Fluid intelligence

The ability to perceive relationships, reason logically and abstractly, and form concepts and interpretations.

Various researchers have demonstrated an age-related decline in intellectual functioning (Botwinick, 1977). This is attributed to significant declines in information-processing abilities and other skills involving the central nervous system. People appear to learn new things more slowly as they age. This slowdown begins to be noticeable at middle age and continues for the duration of the life span.

Other research suggests that some aspects of intellectual functioning decline, whereas others are maintained or improve (Schaie, 1983). Increases continue to occur in **crystallized intelligence** through the years of middle adulthood. Crystallized intelligence, you may recall, involves cognitive skills, such as verbal reasoning and comprehension and spatial relations, which are acquired through educational experiences. **Fluid intelligence** involves information-processing skills, such as those involved in memory, speed of learning, and mathematical calculation. These skills decline through middle adulthood (Knox, 1977).

There are, however, considerable individual differences in the rates at which both of the processes occur—which suggests that more than the aging process is at work here. An individual's "life complexity" appears to affect how quickly these changes in cognitive functioning take place. Such factors as having an intact marriage and engaging in many social interactions can determine the rate of these processes (Schaie, 1983).

Cognitive style may also change during middle adulthood (Knox, 1977; Labouvie-Vief, 1985, 1986). The style of thinking that emerges during early adulthood emphasizes exploration of options in solving problems. According to Riegel (1973, 1975), mature thinking involves a tolerance of contradictions and conflicts out of the realization that this is how the world functions. In middle adulthood, people rely more on subjectivity and intuition in contrast to the strict logical processing that characterizes earlier adult cognitive style. Middle-aged people incorporate lessons learned from past mistakes into their problem-solving strategies. The ability is especially valuable in ambiguous situations.

We will now turn our attention to some of the specific aspects of information-processing in middle adulthood. We will highlight the areas of attention and memory.

ATTENTION   Selective and divided attention skills peak in adulthood and begin to show decline toward the latter part of middle adulthood. One area that has increased in research interest is the influence of cell phone use on attention and ability to drive effectively. This

Selective and divided attention skills both peak and decline during middle adulthood. The use of cells phones while driving challenges these skills.

research has typically included both young adults and middle-aged adults as participants. One interesting question has been: is there a difference in attention and driving ability if a conversation is occurring between two people in the vehicle (passenger conversations) or if a conversation is occurring on a cell phone (cell phone conversations) (Drews, Pasupathi & Strayer, 2008)? Research findings indicate that driving errors are lower for those engaged in passenger conversations than for those in cell phone conversations. The proposed explanation for this is that when two conversing individuals are in the same vehicle, they have a shared attention and awareness for the traffic and road conditions. This allows for conversation to ebb and flow as needed for the driver. This research helps explain why cell phone conversations quadruple the risk of driving accidents (McEvoy et al., 2005), while the risk of an accident decreases when there is another adult in the vehicle besides the driver (Rueda-Domingo et al., 2004).

Working memory

The workbench of memory where simultaneous cognitive processes can be attended to and handled.

MEMORY   **Working memory** is typically conceptualized as the workbench of memory where simultaneous cognitive processes can be attended to and handled (Baddeley, 1986, 1996; Kemper & Mitzner, 2001). Working memory improves across the life span and peaks during middle adulthood—around age forty-five (Swanson, 1999). Declines in working memory begin toward the latter part of middle adulthood—around age fifty-seven—and continue to decline in late adulthood (Kemper & Mitzner, 2001; Swanson, 1999). Part of the decline in working memory experienced in middle adulthood is attributed to a general decline in information-processing speed (Chaytor & Schmitter-Edgecombe, 2004).

Research investigating the impact of hormones on memory is a growing field. The vast majority of this research has focused upon rodent hormones, brain changes, and memory (Galea et al., 2008). The emerging picture is complex, with level of hormones being an important factor, as well as the observation that hormones impact different parts of the brain and different memory processes in diverse ways. To further complicate matters, hormones have differing influences on males and females. There are two interesting findings worth mentioning here. First, the extended use of oral estrogen (like that in birth control pills and hormone replacement therapy) may negatively impact memory. In research on mice, a medium dose of estrogen decreased **spatial reference memory** (or memory for location and space) (Fernandez & Frick, 2004). Conversely, testosterone has been found to increase memory in castrated rats, including reversing spatial reference memory deficits (Khalil, King & Soliman, 2005). Although this research utilized rodents as research subjects, it is clear that hormones may play an important role in memory—or at least some aspects of memory—in humans. Future research will try to tease apart the complex nature of hormone, brain, and memory interactions.

Spatial reference memory

The aspect of memory that stores information about one's environment and spatial orientation.

INTELLIGENCE   One proposed type of intelligence is **emotional intelligence**, which was first proposed by Salovey and Mayer in 1990. The idea never really became popular until Goleman wrote the book *Emotional Intelligence* in 1995. Emotional intelligence can be thought of as the ability to recognize others' emotions, regulate one's own emotions, and effectively utilize emotions in adaptive and skillful ways (Chapman & Hayslip, 2006). Hence, emotional intelligence is an important and distinct mental ability that allows for smooth interpersonal relationships and social functioning.

Emotional intelligence

The ability to recognize the emotions of others and regulate one's own emotions while effectively utilizing emotions in adaptive and skillful ways.

There is some question as to whether emotional intelligence should be conceptualized as a "type" of intelligence, a cognitive style, or a personality trait (Chapman & Hayslip, 2006). Schaie (2001) has commented that emotional intelligence is a concept that is "somewhere at the intersection between the domains of intelligence and personality" (p. 202). Despite the ambiguity as to what domain emotional intelligence should be categorized, the general theory hypothesizes that emotional intelligence is an ability that increases across childhood, as do other cognitive processes and socioemotional skills (Mayer et al., 2001). What was less known, until recently, was how emotional intelligence develops in adulthood.

A recent study by Chapman and Hayslip (2006) investigated emotional intelligence in young and middle adulthood. Three factors of emotional intelligence were examined: appraising others' emotions (i.e., emotional recognition), optimistic mood regulation (i.e., emotion regulation), and emotion utilization (i.e., emotion use in problem-solving, motivation, and other behaviors). The study found that young and middle-aged adults have similar levels of emotional intelligence in the areas of appraising others' emotions and emotion utilization; however, optimistic mood regulation showed significant increases in middle-aged adults in comparison to younger adults. This means that although some aspects of emotional intelligence appear to be fully developed and stable across early and middle adulthood (emotional recognition and emotion utilization), optimistic mood regulation continues to develop into middle adulthood.

You may recall from earlier in the chapter that crystallized intelligence continues to increase across middle adulthood, whereas fluid intelligence shows decline. Chapman and Hayslip (2006) investigated whether the three components of emotional intelligence were related to crystallized and fluid intelligence. Analysis indicated that crystallized and fluid intelligence are positively correlated, meaning that as crystallized intelligence scores increase, fluid intelligence scores increase. However, there were no correlations between fluid or crystallized intelligence and the three components of emotional intelligence. Based on this study, it appears that a person's emotional intelligence is in no way related to a person's fluid intelligence or crystallized intelligence, further supporting the idea that emotional intelligence is a distinct mental ability.

In summary, emotional intelligence is the ability to function adaptively in interpersonal and social relationships. Emotional intelligence appears to be a distinct mental ability that develops across childhood. Two aspects of emotional intelligence (emotion recognition and emotion utilization) appear to reach maturity in early adulthood, whereas optimistic mood regulation shows increased development into middle adulthood.

Pause and Process:

1. What affect might hormones have on memory?

2. What are the three components of emotional intelligence?

SOCIAL AND EMOTIONAL DEVELOPMENT DURING MIDDLE ADULTHOOD

LEARNING OBJECTIVES:

1. *Characterize emotional development during middle adulthood*
2. *Describe family and social influences during middle adulthood*
3. *Explain psychosocial development during middle adulthood*

21. What does the term sandwich generation mean?

Sandwich generation

The term sometimes used to describe middle-aged individuals, referring to their divided loyalties and responsibilities toward the younger and the older generation within their family systems.

As in all other stages in the life span, middle adulthood has its own unique challenges. These developmental tasks result from physical changes that occur in association with the aging process, environmental pressures, and new obligations prompted by the person's own changes in values and aspirations (Erikson, 1982; Erikson, Erikson & Kivnick, 1986). Developmental tasks in middle adulthood include achieving adult civic and social responsibility, establishing and maintaining an economic standard of living, assisting teenage children to become responsible and happy adults, and developing adult leisure-time activities (Havighurst, 1970). Middle adulthood also includes the tasks of accepting and adjusting to the physiological changes of middle age and adjusting to aging parents.

Middle adulthood can be a particularly challenging time in terms of socioemotional development. Some researchers refer to middle-aged people as the **sandwich generation** because they are often responsible for the care of aging parents while still having some parenting responsibilities for their children. This is a generation "caught" between two others. For some people, reaching middle age brings the new perspective of acting as a bridge between the older and younger generations in an extended family system.

The developmental tasks of middle age not only help people to adjust to this stage of the life span but also prepare them to meet the challenges of old age. Not all these tasks are mastered simultaneously. There are individual differences in the rate of mastery. Some tasks are even put off to the next stage of the life span.

The age at marriage, birth of children, and other life events may determine when individuals confront the developmental tasks of middle age. Because today's young adults are delaying marriage and parenthood, they may confront these tasks at later ages than those given in this chapter.

EMOTIONAL DEVELOPMENT

Transition to Middle Adulthood

Middle age is a transition period between early and late adulthood. It is a time for reassessment and redefinition as changes take place both within the individual and within the family system in which she or he participates. Most people experience a kind of dualism at this time (Chilman, 1968; Chiriboga, 1981; Sherman, 1987). From one viewpoint, this period produces a crisis. People often feel their family is deteriorating because their children are maturing and leaving the home and their own parents are declining. At the same time, they are experiencing initial declines in their own physical well-being and functioning, and witnessing the death of friends and family members in significantly greater numbers than in earlier periods of the life span. There are also significant shifts in parenting, occupation, and family roles. All of these changes are felt as losses, so middle age can be a stressful period.

All these changes force people to reexamine the meaning of their lives, their state of happiness, and the progress they have made toward personal goals. Some researchers believe that this constitutes a midlife transition or crisis (Gould, 1978; Levinson, 1978). Perspectives on life, time, personal happiness, relationships with others, and other important issues change. Many people see middle adulthood as the beginning of the end of life. The future looks more finite. Physical declines that show the signs of aging reinforce these notions. More importantly, however, the change in time perspective spurs people to let go of inefficient or ineffectual ways of coping with stress, solving problems, and interpreting behavior—their own as well as other people's. Thus, the midlife transition can bring about meaningful changes and refinements in aspects of personality that people just discover in themselves or create through new experiences.

From another viewpoint, middle age is the prime of life. People are finally experienced enough to affect change rather than be affected by it. They can take command of their lives. Physical changes are taken in stride as part of the seasoning process. People with this attitude see aging as a positive experience. Like wine, they believe they become better with the passage of time.

Midlife crisis or midlife transition? Popular U.S. culture depicts men as experiencing a midlife crisis in middle adulthood. Some developmental theorists agree with this view, while others do not. First, we will discuss the view that men do experience a midlife crisis; then, we will discuss the criticisms of this view.

New experiences are brought about by midlife transitions. Being middle-aged is considered by some to be the prime of life.

Both Levinson (1978) and Gould (1978) regard middle adulthood as a turbulent time that churns up many confusing, conflicting, and contradictory feelings. These researchers believe, however, that the disturbing questioning that characterizes middle age will produce developmental growth—provided the individuals meet these challenges rather than retreat from them because they feel so threatened.

Levinson and Gould describe early adulthood as the period when people develop initial goals for their lives and determine actions that they hope will secure these goals. Gould believes that individuals must come to terms with their own mortality by the end of middle adulthood. In doing so, they recognize their limitations and weaknesses—which is to say, they fully accept their humanity. They also learn to relinquish the desire to control situations and other people in order to achieve outcomes they wish for strongly. With this comes serenity and acceptance of the nature of life. They learn to go with the flow of life rather than struggling to manipulate what happens and under what circumstances. Ultimately, this leads to a greater acceptance of the certain inevitability of aging and death.

Levinson (1980, 1986) describes middle age as a time when many people start to seriously question the meaning and direction of their lives. Beginning at about age forty, the majority of men in his study had a crucial struggle within themselves and with their environment because of this question. Levinson sees this questioning as a healthy sign of developmental progress. The person undergoing it, however, is more likely to view it as threatening. First reactions may be decisions that others label irrational. From the outside, the decisions do look extreme. From the inside, however, they are seen as necessary to secure desired changes before it is too late. Such decisions can include positive choices such as making a radical occupational change, taking dream vacations, or moving off to some exotic location. Some decisions can be frivolous choices such as dying hair, buying a sports car or motorcycle, or dressing inappropriately for one's age. Finally, some decisions can be emotionally devastating to the self and/or others, such as divorcing after many years of marriage or participating in extramarital sexual affairs. The colloquial expression for such behavior is the middle-age crazies.

Levinson describes a series of transitions that he observed in the men he studied. The midlife crisis involves examining one's own needs in relation to those of others. In early adulthood, needs were prioritized. The men chose either to meet their own needs then or to delay gratification. Most gave certain personal needs low priority. At midlife, they reexamined this ordering. When the reexamination coincided with physical and social changes in their lives, the men often felt pressured to try to accomplish important objectives while they still could. This made them feel conflicted because it was hard to accomplish their personal objectives without compromising the needs of others they loved and valued.

Other developmental researchers question the universality of the midlife crisis (Neugarten & Neugarten, 1987; Rossi, 1980; Schlossberg, 1987). Although not everyone experiences a midlife transition as a crisis, many researchers agree that people do have serious adjustment challenges at some time during this stage of life. Moreover, the changes described by Levinson and Gould can occur earlier in life. The reaction to midlife also seems to differ according to socioeconomic situations (Farrell & Rosenberg, 1981). Midlife may be more stressful for blue-collar workers than for more advantaged middle-class professionals.

Some have critiqued Levinson's idea of a midlife crisis because it ignores "variations in social structure and culture over historical time. Psychosocial transitions were affixed to age as if immutable to institutional change …" (Elder, 1998, p. 944). Some research implies that the midlife transition is a cultural phenomenon specific to societies that recognize middle age as a stage in the life span (Levine, 1980; Rogoff, 2003). One African culture, the Gusii of Kenya, hold a different idea of middle age than Western societies. The men experience only one stage in adult life, that of "warrior," which may last from twenty-five to forty years. Women similarly experience only one stage in adult life, that of "married woman," in recognition of the importance of marriage and procreation for females in this culture. This society apparently has no words for "adolescence," "early adulthood," or "middle age." Transitions in the life span are geared to events rather than to chronological age. Instead of experiencing what our culture labels a midlife transition, Gusii men and women may undergo a spiritual enlightenment in which they recognize their physical limitation for performing work as well as the temporal limits of life. This experience causes them to seek spiritual powers in witchcraft and ritualism to provide help for themselves and their family members against illness or death.

Hence, the idea of a midlife crisis is debatable, whereas the idea of a midlife transition is more palatable to most researchers. However, the midlife transition is far from universal. Instead, a midlife transition is influenced by socioeconomic, cultural, and historical factors.

PERSONALITY AND SELF-CONCEPT   Is personality set by middle adulthood or does it continue to change during this phase of the life span? This is an intriguing question that researchers are still actively researching today. The answer is impacted by which theoretical approach to personality the researcher is utilizing (Srivasta et al., 2003). At present, it appears that some aspects remain stable and others change (Finn, 1986). Those aspects that generally remain stable over the life span are intellectual, cognitive, and self-concept traits. Those that appear to be most subject to alteration are attitudes and interpersonal relationship factors.

In Chapter 7, we learned about the big five factors personality theory. Which factors show change with development and which tend to stay the same? Conscientiousness and agreeableness have been found to increase during early and middle adulthood (Srivasta et al., 2003). Neuroticism decreases during this time frame, most significantly in women. There is a slight decline in openness during adulthood. Extroversion appears to increase slightly in men and decrease slightly in women.

Humans manifest a strong desire to master their environment and achieve self-satisfaction or happiness from infancy, and this desire does not appear to lessen with age. As mentioned previously, middle adulthood is a major period of transition that is self-examination, self-evaluation, and restructuring of self-image. There is a consolidation of the various components of the self at midlife. Both continuity and change in self-concept and personality can be observed as individuals address self-acceptance and self-knowledge during middle adulthood.

Kimmel (1980) describes personality during middle age as more balanced and stable than it was earlier in life. The expansion of the self and interpersonal relations are less demanding and shifting because people have gained experience in coping with stress and dealing with problems. Self-knowledge allows them to deal more effectively with the changes they encounter as part of middle adulthood. However, inflexibility, rigidity, and resistance to creative solutions are equally likely to appear at midlife. Kimmel's conclusions differ considerably from Levinson's research findings about how men react to reaching middle age.

ATTACHMENT   Sometimes when discussing adult attachment, the category we have labeled disorganized/disoriented is called unresolved attachment. If you recall from our previous discussion of attachment styles, the disorganized/disoriented attachment style consists of a mental model in which a person lacks self-worth and struggles to trust others. This attachment style can experience significant difficulties in middle adulthood.

A recent study by Alexander (2009) investigated the relationship between attachment and abuse by multiple partners in adulthood. The study found that women with an unresolved attachment style were more likely to be victimized by multiple partners in adulthood than women with a different attachment classification. Post hoc analysis revealed that women with the unresolved attachment style reported a childhood plagued with parent-child role reversals and exposure to domestic violence.

Although abuse and neglect in childhood are common predictors of unresolved attachment style in children and adults, researchers have begun to investigate if genetics play a role in this particular attachment style (Caspers et al., 2009). A recent study by Caspers and colleagues has discovered that a short 5-HTTLPR allele is correlated with an increased risk for an unresolved attachment style. This research is exciting because attachment has been primarily conceptualized as a process largely social in nature. By demonstrating that genetics may play a role in attachment disposition, researchers will now need to broaden their perspective to study the influence of both relationship experiences and biology.

Pause and Process:

1. Describe Levinson's idea of a midlife crisis.

2. What aspects of personality are likely to change throughout adulthood?

SELF AND OTHERS

Family Influences

PARENTING IN MIDDLE ADULTHOOD   One of the most prominent, as well as early, indications of entrance into this stage of the family life career is when the adult children become completely emancipated. It is this event that can serve as a significant stressor in many family systems causing important shifts in roles, adjustment problems, and emotional crisis.

Family sociologists often refer to this situation as the **empty nest** phase of the family life career that introduces the system into the postparental aspect of family life. Researchers describe this as a transition period for parents as they redefine their image and identity away from parenthood. Their behavior as parents also is redefined in line with the process that began during the previous family life stage (Harkins, 1978).

It is not clear if mothers are more affected than fathers by the empty nest transition. Early studies focused on the adjustments of women to loss of their primary parenting responsibilities. The more frequent finding was that many experienced negative reactions (Bart, 1971, 1975; Spence & Lonner, 1971). The women who were studied usually had been full-time mothers who were not nor had not been employed outside the home. Parenting had been a major responsibility within their family systems. When children became grown and left the home, many reacted by becoming depressed emotionally, feeling lost and unneeded.

Bart (1971) found also that women who rechanneled their activities and energies into new roles made better adjustments than those who did not. These women reacted to the role shift during this stage by entering the work force, enrolling in college, assuming new volunteer activities, or refocusing on their marriages. Subsequent studies have substantiated this finding (Glenn, 1975; Harkins, 1978; Robertson, 1978). Apparently, many women view the experience of the empty nest as a positive time in life. The completion of full-time childrearing responsibilities is seen as liberating. Those who prepare, plan, and anticipate that adjustments will be required also make more positive adjustments to the role shift (Targ, 1979).

Relatively little is known about the reactions of fathers to the empty nest phase. Some fathers seem to have few adjustments to the shift in their parenting responsibilities whereas others find the experience to be painful emotionally (Barber, 1980; Lewis, Feneau & Roberts, 1979; Robinson & Barret, 1986). Men's reactions may depend on how emotionally involved they have been in their role as fathers and with their children. It is possible

Empty nest

The period of the post-parental stage of the family life cycle when a couple phase out their active parenting responsibilities.

that some men may be more vulnerable to negative reactions than women. The principal reason cited by many fathers that is negative in nature is the perception that they have lost an opportunity to be involved in their children's lives. This is in direct contrast to negative reasons cited by women who react to a loss of personal identity when parenting ends.

Most individuals make a successful shift to a lifestyle that does not include children or parenting as a principal focus during middle-age (Kerckhoff, 1976). This adjustment offers opportunities for personal growth and for placing greater emphasis on the committed relation-

Enrolling in college is one way that women can rechannel their activities and energies.

ship that may have been neglected in many respects.

THE MARRIAGE IN MIDDLE ADULTHOOD   Marital satisfaction increases considerably during this stage. As their children become more autonomous during adolescence and early adulthood, many couples begin to find greater satisfaction within their marriage (Olson, 1986). Marital satisfaction at this time of life is as high as among newlyweds. Couples still have disagreements and conflicts, but these are more manageable than earlier, when children absorbed so much attention.

26. What are some roles that grandparents may play in the family system?

BECOMING A GRANDPARENT   Many people assume the new family role of grandparent during this stage of the family life career. It is increasingly common that many will assume this role during their middle-age years (Cherlin & Furstenberg, 1986; Hagestad, 1985; U. S. Bureau of the Census, 1990, 1991). Today, it is increasingly unlikely that this role will overlap with the parenting role as often as it occurred in the past.

The contemporary grandparenting role is ambiguous regarding what this role means and how it functions in a family system (Bengston, 1985; Cherlin & Furstenberg, 1986). This differs considerably from the past when grandparents are thought to have played a vital, active role within a family system. This is thought to have included functions as mentor, role model, caretaker, and repository of wisdom for younger family members.

Today, there is considerable variation as to what this role means and how it is enacted. The popular image of a contemporary grandparent is passive in nature where the companionship characteristics of the role are emphasized (Cherlin & Furstenberg, 1985). This individual is seen to be a loving older person who does not interfere with the functioning of adult children in their parental role. This person sees grandchildren frequently and acts

Becoming a grandparent is a new family role for some.

Remote relationship

A grandparent-grandchildren relationship characterized by infrequent contact governed by behavior that is ritualistic and highly symbolic.

Companionate relationship

A grandparent-grandchildren relationship described as an easygoing, friendly relationship that involves emotionally-satisfying leisure-time.

Involved relationship

A grandparent-grandchildren relationship that focuses on an active role of raising grandchildren and conducting the role as an active caretaker much like a parent.

as a "reserve parent" in times of need, crisis, or emergency. Grandparents are seen to be more actively involved with grandchildren during their infancy and childhood years as caretakers. As children grow older, they are expected to provide more of a recreational or fun-oriented, leisure role in interacting with grandchildren.

A variety of meanings is given to this role by the individuals who assume it. Symbolically, grandparents may attribute several dimensions to their role that include (1) "being there" to act as an element of stability during change and transition for the extended family system, (2) acting as the "family watchdog" to provide care when necessary, (3) serving as family arbitrator during times of family conflict, and (4) serving as the family historian as a bridge between the past, the present, and the future (Bengston, 1985). Other meanings can be attributed to this role as well (see Figure 8-1).

Because this role has no clear guidelines for behavior, individuals usually adapt and create behavioral styles that fit their situation and that of their family system. Three basic grandparenting styles have been identified. These include (1) the **remote relationship**, characterized by infrequent contact with grandchildren governed by behavior that is ritualistic and highly symbolic; (2) the **companionate relationship**, described as an easygoing, friendly relationship that involves emotionally-satisfying leisure-time relationships with grandchildren; and (3) the **involved relationship** that focuses on an active role in raising grandchildren and conducting the role as an active caretaker much like a parent (Cherlin & Furstenberg, 1986).

When researchers have examined the activities of grandparents with grandchildren, a pattern emerges that illustrates the companionate style as one that is practiced more frequently (Cherlin & Furstenberg, 1986) (see Figure 8-2). Pleasurable activities that emphasize expressions of affection toward grandchildren occur more frequently than those involving active caretaking responsibilities such as disciplining children.

FIGURE 8-1	MEANINGS GIVEN TO THE GRANDPARENT ROLE

Biological Renewal "It is through my grandchildren that I feel young again."

Biological Continuity with the Future "It is through these children that I see my life going on in the future." "It's carrying on the family name."

Emotional Self-Fulfillment "I can be and I can do for my grandchildren things I could never do for my own kids. I was too busy with my business to enjoy my kids but my grandchildren are different. Now I have time to be with them."

Resource Person "I take my grandson down to the factory and show him how the business operates—and then, too, I set aside money especially for him."

Extension of Self "She's a beautiful child, and she'll grow up to be a beautiful woman. Maybe I shouldn't, but I can't help feeling proud of that."

Sense of Remoteness from Kin (geographical, age difference) "My grand-daughter is just a baby, and I don't even feel like a grandfather yet."

Source: Adapted from B. L. Neugarten, & K. K. Weinstein (1968). The changing American grandparent. In B. L. Neugarten (Ed.) *Middle age and aging.* Chicago: University of Chicago Press.

FIGURE 8-2	THE ACTIVITIES OF GRANDPARENTS WITH GRANDCHILDREN

Source: *Cherlin, A. J., & Furstenberg, F. F. (1986).* The New American Grandparent, *New York; Basic Books.)*

Percent answering yes

Certain factors appear to influence how this role functions. For example, middle-class individuals often assume more active grandparenting roles than others (Clavan, 1978). Living within close physical distance to one's grandchildren also increases the likelihood of a more active grandparenting role (Cherlin & Furstenberg, 1986). More frequent interactions occur when distances are small. A more remote style is enhanced when distances are great.

Despite the ambiguous nature of this role and sometimes infrequent contact with grandchildren, grandparents appear to influence their grandchildren and the extended family system in several ways (Barranti, 1985) (see Figure 8-3). This can be jeopardized when parents divorce. Grandparental rights are not typically specified when parents divorce, and contact with grandchildren can cease. This is especially the case among paternal grandparents because fathers often have limited visitation and custody rights following divorce (Derdeyn, 1985). However, when parents remarry, children often have access to even more grandparents than before the parental divorce. Little is known about step-grandparent/step-grandchild relationships at this time, however.

FIGURE 8-3   INFLUENCES OF GRANDPARENTS ON FAMILY SYSTEMS

- Accepting behaviors and traits that parents may not be able to tolerate.
- Providing nurturance that parents may not be able to provide.
- Providing instruction in values, ethics, and morals.
- Providing backup support for parents in raising children.
- Providing parents with options for solving interaction problems and conflicts with grandchildren.
- Acting as an equalizer to provide balance within a family system.

Source: Adapted from C. C. R. Barranti (1985). The grandparent/grandchild relationship: Family resource in an era of voluntary bonds. *Family Relations, 34,* 343–352.

CARING FOR AGING PARENTS   A longer life expectancy and other social factors, such as delayed age at first marriage and childbearing, have reshaped the nature of family life. By middle age, parents may have promoted their children into adulthood. However, the expectation continues that they will provide emotional and even financial support for adult children (Aldous, 1987; Troll, 1986).

Caregiving, however, is not restricted to providing support for adult children by middle-aged parents. These individuals also provide care, either through direct means or giving financial support, to aging parents. This is why middle-aged parents are referred to as the "sandwich" or "caught" generation (Hagestad, 1986; Vincent, 1972). Middle-aged parents continue to have ties to the younger and older generations. One of the hazards of being a member of the sandwich or "caught" generation is experiencing a division of one's loyalties. The middle-aged parent is confronted with the dilemma of coping with simultaneous demands from adult children and from aging parents.

Interactions between middle-aged children and their parents are a mixture of problems, benefits, rewards, and difficulties (Alam, 1978). Problems frequently mentioned involve (1) generation gap issues (differences in values, attitudes, and behavior, (2) interference issues (conflicts where both generations attempt to dominate the lives of each other), (3) issues of impatience with the parents' age (health concerns, slower reaction times, and so on), and (4) communication issues (power and dominance concerns). Benefits and rewards of having older parents include (1) the value of having the benefit of their greater experience, wisdom, and knowledge; (2) the reciprocal nature of help available between the two generations; and (3) the value of both younger and older generations to family continuity and effective system functioning.

The arrangements between middle-aged adult children and their parents in providing care and assistance can be stressful and can lead to depression (Cicirelli, 1983). This is especially the situation when role-reversal occurs that accentuates the dependency of elderly parents upon middle-aged adult children. The stressfulness of this situation is manifested in feelings of exhaustion and negativity toward the aging parent. Although the levels of stress are not often excessive, middle-aged children cite feelings of frustration, impatience, and guilt in relation to the elderly parent.

The Outside World

FRIENDSHIP AND PEERS   Friendship patterns change in middle adulthood. Lowenthal and associates (1977) find that friendships among middle-aged people are more complex than those among adolescents and young adults. People at middle age continue to value the same qualities in friendships that they did at earlier ages—namely, reciprocity (sharing), helping, having similar experiences, and ease of communication. Women tend more to choose friends on the basis of reciprocity, whereas men consider similarity with others of prime importance (Johnson, 1989).

Friendships at middle age may reflect some of the personality changes that occur in midlife. People grow more introspective and appreciative of differences in themselves and others by this time of life. Friendships may be especially important to single people as a support system in place of family ties (Lowenthal et al., 1977). Although the frequency of contact with friends diminishes with age, the quality of associations improves considerably (Antonucci, 2001; Cartensen, 1992, 1995). People maintain friendships longer and on a more intimate basis.

LEISURE TIME   Leisure activities are important for mental and physical health (Hansen, Dik & Zhou, 2008). Engagement in leisure activities is correlated with increased self-esteem, marital

While friendships at this stage are more complex the same qualities that were important in adolescence still remain.

28. Describe leisure time in middle adulthood.

satisfaction, life satisfaction, and career involvement. During middle adulthood, leisure is limited due to work and family obligations (Kleiber & Kelly, 1980; Hansen, Dik & Zhou, 2008). Therefore, leisure and socializing are often incorporated into other activities. For example, part of an adults' parenting duties may include taking their children to soccer practices and games, which then also becomes a time to socialize and relax with other parents.

CAREERS IN MIDDLE ADULTHOOD   Middle adulthood is sometimes likened to adolescence because of the interpersonal conflict and inner turmoil that can sometimes occur in both of these periods. These are important processes, however, in stimulating personal growth and integration of various aspects of the individual's self-concept. Vocational development at midlife is characterized by the dual processes of stability and change seen in other areas of development. Career and work roles are examined as part of the midlife transition. Goals are reevaluated in terms of progress made toward vocational objectives determined in early adulthood.

MIDLIFE CAREER CHANGE   It is not uncommon for people to make a career change near the end of early adulthood or the beginning of middle adulthood. Some of these career changes are due to a desire for change; others are due to being forced out of a job (Schultz & Schultz, 2010). For some individuals disenchantment with their work sets in between their mid-forties and mid-fifties (Doering & Rhodes, 1989; Mergenhagen, 1991). Various factors may increase the likelihood of job dissatisfaction occurring.

Job simplification

Work that is repetitive, simplified, and fragmented.

Gender harassment

A workplace environment that is hostile, degrading, or insulting toward one particular gender.

Job simplification—work that is repetitive, simplified, and fragmented—can lead to job dissatisfaction (Schultz & Schultz, 2010). With job simplification, boredom, monotony, and fatigue can quickly develop. Job dissatisfaction can also occur due to ethnic, gender, or sexual harassment. You may be wondering what the difference is between gender harassment and sexual harassment. **Gender harassment** involves a workplace environment that is hostile,

A change in career is common. The reasons vary, for example, a desire for change or being forced out of a job.

Sexual harassment

Unwanted sexual attention.

Ethnic harassment

A workplace environment where verbal assaults are targeted toward individuals because of their ethnicity.

degrading, or insulting toward one particular gender. **Sexual harassment** involves a workplace environment where unwanted sexual attention occurs. **Ethnic harassment** involves a workplace environment where verbal assaults are targeted toward individuals because of their ethnicity. These may include ethnic jokes, slurs, or other offensive comments. Finally, job dissatisfaction may be linked to having an awful supervisor. In fact, surveys have found that 75 percent of employees point to their boss as the worst and most stressful part of their job.

Although some individuals seek a midlife career change due to job dissatisfaction, others do so for more positive reasons. Perhaps they are seeking new challenges or opportunities for growth. Maybe they had always dreamed of owning their own business and now they have the financial ability to do so. This is a period in the life span where individuals focus less on how many years have passed since their birth, and instead focus on how many years are left until their death (Neugarten & Neugarten, 1987). This may explain why middle-aged people feel more pressured to make critical life changes, like career changes, than earlier in adulthood.

Pause and Process:

1. What are some grandparenting styles?

2. What are some reasons individuals may change careers in middle adulthood?

PSYCHOSOCIAL DEVELOPMENT

Generativity Versus Stagnation

As mentioned in Chapter 7, Erikson proposed that the generativity versus stagnation stage begins in early adulthood (around age twenty-four). However, it lasts well into middle adulthood (around age fifty-four), so we are discussing it in this chapter. Most modern psychologists refer to this stage as the generativity versus stagnation stage; however, it is also known as the generativity versus self-absorption stage—as you will see why.

Once a person is in an established relationship, they can begin the process of facing the psychosocial task of generativity versus stagnation. In the productive years of adulthood, people center on establishing a new family system, on achieving progress in their work, on creative efforts, and on community involvement. Parenting and family experiences provide the principal opportunities for most people to explore generativity.

Erikson describes the sense of generativity as "the interest in establishing and guiding the next generation … the absorbing object of a parental kind of responsibility." The central component of generativity is the desire to care for others, by teaching them the skills and knowledge one has learned and passing on to them one's culture and values. Generativity need not be restricted to parenting. It can also be explored by sharing one's self intimately with others in work roles, mentorships (such as Big Brothers or Big Sisters), spiritual parenthood (such as nuns or godparents), or in creative efforts.

The attitude of self-absorption develops when an individual is unwilling or unable to care for others. To be self-absorbed is to treat oneself as one's own infant and pet, according to Erikson. Instead of directing social interest to others, self-absorbed people direct their interest exclusively toward themselves. The self-absorbed person becomes unhealthy and ceases to grow, like a stagnant lake that has no outlet.

PECK'S PSYCHOSOCIAL DEVELOPMENT IN MIDDLE ADULTHOOD   Psychologist Robert Peck (1968) elaborated on Erikson's (1950, 1964) concept of generativity as it is developed during middle adulthood. Erikson proposes that individuals start to explore ways to achieve a sense of generativity in their mid-twenties and continue this task until their mid-fifties. A growing, dynamic individual seeks ways to focus on others, especially those who are younger and may profit from the knowledge the older person has gained in life skills. Peck proposes that during middle age, people focus more on achieving a sense of well-being than on what Erikson labels generativity. This focus includes:

- Valuing wisdom versus valuing physical powers: Physical endurance and stamina begin to decline as individuals experience the aging process more intensely during middle adulthood. Physical attractiveness and abilities were highly valued earlier in life, and people judged others as well as themselves first on these attributes. Now these attributes no longer seem valid as measures of competence. Instead, individuals learn to value knowledge gained from experience in dealing with many different complex problems. This gives them an advantage over younger people.

- Socializing versus sexualizing in human relationships: After experiencing menopause or the climacteric, people come to devalue sexuality as a basis of interpersonal relations. Social skills now take on a greater importance as the focus shifts to relating to others as personalities rather than as sex objects.

- Cathectic flexibility versus cathectic improverishment: Middle-aged people discover the importance of emotional flexibility. Instead of making a heavy emotional investment in one person or one activity, they learn that it is to one's advantage to invest emotion in many people or activities. As parents and friends die, as children leave home, and as they themselves retire from work roles, middle-aged people widen their social support network. Thus they obtain social insurance for times of need.

- Mental flexibility versus mental rigidity: One hazard of growing older is becoming closed-minded to new ideas or solutions. Surviving to this point in the life span often gives people the illusion that their knowledge is complete. However, this attitude stifles growth and promotes stagnation. By remaining open and receptive, people can continue to foster their mental and personal development.

Pause and Process:

1. How can a person express generativity?

2. Compare and contrast Erikson's and Peck's theories about psychosocial development in middle adulthood.

SUMMARY

1. It is interesting to ponder that although we accept aging as a part of life, we do not really understand what causes the body to age. Some theories are focusing upon aging at the cellular level—such as the cellular clock theory and free-radical theory, whereas others focus on a body system, like the hormonal stress theory.

2. Physical changes in middle adulthood focus on the initial effects of aging. Many organ systems show general declines in function and efficiency. The major physical changes at this time of life are a decline in body weight among men and increase among women; various changes in skin tissue, such as increased wrinkling and dryness; gradual declines in visual abilities; increasing occurrence of a variety of conditions such as arthritis, atherosclerosis, arteriosclerosis, hypertension, and minor digestive disturbances.

3. Post-traumatic stress disorder is an anxiety disorder that can develop after experiencing or witnessing a traumatic event. Symptoms of PTSD include hypervigilance, avoidance, and re-experiencing the event. Approximately 8 percent of adults in the United States will experience PTSD at some point during their life.

4. Selection, optimization, and compensation theory strives to assist individuals in aging optimally by teaching strategies that minimize losses and maximize gains. By modifying goal selection, optimizing current functioning levels, and compensating with external support when needed, adults can continue to live happily throughout life.

5. Experts and novices differ in their cognitive abilities. In comparison to novices, experts have a broader knowledge base, organize their knowledge better, and have better retrieval of knowledge. There are two main types of experts with varying degrees of adaptive expertise.

6. Some aspects of information-processing improve while others decline during this stage. Crystallized intelligence continues to grow, whereas fluid intelligence declines. Cognitive style is adapted to involve past experiences and intuition in making decisions.

7. Emotional intelligence is comprised of three main components: emotion recognition, optimistic mood regulation, and emotion utilization. Optimistic mood regulation continues to develop into middle adulthood.

8. Middle adulthood is a transition period in the life span that takes place between forty and sixty-five years of age. Socioemotionally, this stage is characterized by changes in personal and family roles, and intensive self-examination and assessment of personal progress toward life goals.

9. Socioemotional changes at midlife feature shifts in personality and self-concept. The midlife transition offers people the opportunity to reassess their progress toward personal happiness and to change in necessary ways to achieve this. Friendship patterns become more complex during this period. People often examine their work roles in conjunction with the midlife transition. Frequently this results in a career change.

10. Parents have to adjust to the end of their parenting careers with an empty nest. Both men and women may experience difficulties with this change in their role status, but the end of parenting permits couples to refocus their energies on their marriage. Marital satisfaction usually increases when this is done.

11. The new family role of grandparent is often initiated during this stage. The contemporary version of this role is ambiguous, allowing wide differences in structuring. The most commonly observed grandparenting style is companionate: an easygoing, nurturant relationship with grandchildren.

12. Many middle-aged people feel caught between their responsibilities for the younger and the older generations of their family system. Hence, they are known as the sandwich generation.

13. Generativity is an interest in caring for others and sharing one's knowledge, skills, and infor-

mation. As individuals master these psychosocial attitudes, they acquire the ability to respond to life situations and events in mature ways. This leads to greater personal happiness and adjustment, satisfaction with work, and physical health.

SELF-QUIZ

1. What age-range characterizes middle adulthood?

2. What is meant by ageism? What is an example of ageism you have seen?

3. Which theory of aging makes the most sense to you? Provide a reason for your answer.

4. Which theory of aging do you find the least plausible? Provide a reason for your answer.

5. How do height and weight change during middle adulthood?

6. What changes does the skin experience during middle adulthood?

7. Explain what osteoporosis is and how to prevent it.

8. What are the two basic types of arthritis?

9. Explain the difference between atherosclerosis and arteriosclerosis? How do they both contribute to hypertension?

10. What can individuals do during middle adulthood to promote wellness?

11. Within SOC theory, describe a behavior or strategy for selection.

12. Within SOC theory, describe a behavior or strategy for optimization.

13. Within SOC theory, describe a behavior or strategy for compensation.

14. Provide an example of a cognitive process that shows growth, maintenance, and regulation of loss throughout the life span.

15. Explain and provide a unique example for each of the four foundational rationales in SOC theory.

16. How could the ability to detect meaningful patterns of information assist an expert teacher?

17. In what area or activity would you consider yourself an expert (or on your way to becoming an expert)?

18. Which type of surgeon would you want to operate on you: a merely skilled expert or a highly competent expert? Provide reasons for your choice.

19. How does intelligence change in middle adulthood?

20. Explain changes in attention and memory during middle adulthood.

21. What does the term sandwich generation mean?

22. Why is middle adulthood considered a time of transition?

23. What are some criticisms of the idea of a midlife crisis?

24. What new information did you learn about attachment in this chapter?

25. Describe how marriage may change during middle adulthood.

26. What are some roles that grandparents may play in the family system?

27. How does friendship change during middle adulthood? How does it stay the same?

28. Describe leisure time in middle adulthood.

29. What is the difference between gender harassment and sexual harassment?

30. Describe behavioral differences between a person who has achieved generativity versus a person who has fallen into stagnation.

TERMS AND CONCEPTS

TERM	PAGE	TERM	PAGE
Middle age	306	Expertise	316
Middle adulthood	306	Regulation of loss	316
Ageism	307	Maintenance	316
Aging	307	Growth	316
Cellular clock theory	307	Adaptive expertise	317
Stochastic processes	307	Highly competent experts	317
Free-radicals	308	Merely skilled experts	317
Mitochondrial theory	308	Conditionalized knowledge	317
Autoimmune responsiveness theory	308	Novice	317
Hormonal stress theory	308	Fluid intelligence	318
Atherosclerosis	310	Crystallized intelligence	318
Rheumatism	310	Working memory	319
Arthritis	310	Emotional intelligence	320
Osteoporosis	310	Spatial reference memory	320
Menopause	311	Sandwich generation	321
Diabetes	311	Empty nest	327
Hypertension	311	Involved relationship	328
Arteriosclerosis	311	Companionate relationship	328
Glaucoma	312	Remote relationship	328
Cataracts	312	Gender harassment	332
Climacteric	312	Job simplification	332
Selection, optimization, and		Ethnic harassment	333
compensation (SOC) theory	315	Sexual harassment	333

CHAPTER 9

Late Adulthood

OUTLINE

PHYSICAL DEVELOPMENT DURING LATE ADULTHOOD	COGNITIVE DEVELOPMENT DURING LATE ADULTHOOD	SOCIAL AND EMOTIONAL DEVELOPMENT DURING LATE ADULTHOOD
• Physical development • Health issues	• Beyond Piaget's theory • Information-processing during late adulthood	• Emotional development • Self and others • Psychosocial development

When does old age begin? Should this depend on chronological age or a life event such as retirement from work? Although many people maintain that old age is a state of mind, there are several life events that signal the beginning of late adulthood. These are tied to chronology, just as other life events are in previous stages of the life span.

Age sixty-five is considered a milestone and the beginning of late adulthood. Reaching this age generally brings about retirement from work, eligibility for Social Security and Medicare benefits, income tax advantages, reduced fares and admission prices to leisure events, and special purchase or discount privileges. It is projected that by the year 2020, approximately 16.5 percent of the population will be sixty-five years of age or older (up from 4.1 percent in 1900, 8.1 percent in 1950, and 12.4 percent in 2000) (Himes, 2001). This percentage is expected to increase to 20.8 percent by 2060.

Advances in modern medical care, better health practices, improved nutrition, and other factors keep people in better health and living longer today (Himes, 2001). For these and other reasons, the period of late adulthood can be divided into five subcategories based on age by decade (Burnside, Ebersole & Monea, 1979). Please note that originally there were only four subcategories; however, the category of centenarians has been added due to an increasing number of people living past one hundred. These subcategories are described below. Neugarten (1978) was among the first to recognize that not all individuals in late adulthood are disabled or feeble. These age divisions help to create a more realistic and positive impression of the elderly. Upon reading about them, you may conclude correctly that late adulthood comprises a diverse group of individuals. In this respect, it is like every other stage discussed in this text.

The young-old (sixty to sixty-nine years): Society expects people in their sixties to have less energy, responsibility, and independence in adulthood. This expectation demoralizes people and serves as a self-fulfilling prophecy. True, physical strength declines from earlier periods of the life span. Despite this limitation, many individuals in this age bracket are energetic, active in volunteer work, pursue hobbies and interests, lead vigorous lifestyles, and are in a state of good health (Kovar, 1986a, b; Kovar & LaCroix, 1987; Ries & Brown, 1991). Release from work and financial responsibilities gives them the chance to redirect their energies to activities that please them. Self-improvement, sometimes even in the form of entrance into college degree programs, is actively pursued by many people this age.

The middle-aged old (seventy to seventy-nine years): Losses characterize this decade. Deaths of spouses and friends occur more frequently. Health problems become a preoccupation and restrict activities within and outside the home, which can further shrink a person's social world. A significant challenge for people in their seventies is to retain the reintegration of personality accomplished following retirement.

The old-old (eighty to eighty-nine years): People in this age bracket find it increasingly difficult to adapt to the effects of the advanced aging process. Housing and physical space are often obstacles to effective living. People in their eighties become more preoccupied with their memories and interested in relating their past living experiences to others. Health problems become more frequent, severe, and of longer duration. Some people need to be cared for by others, which could be within a family member's home, a nursing home, or some other supervised living situation.

The very old-old (ninety to ninety-nine years): There are far fewer people in this age bracket, so we have very little accurate information about them. Obviously, health problems play a central role in their lifestyles. People in their nineties have very limited physical and social activity, but they appear to be happy, serene, and fulfilled (Bretschneider & McCoy, 1988).

Centenarians (one hundred years and older): Centenarians are a particularly hardy and diverse group of individuals (Duenwald, 2003). They are known for their positive dispositions and lower rates of chronic illness and age-related disabilities that plague their younger, elderly peers. More women than men live to be one hundred; however, men tend to maintain greater health and mental capacity. Although many centenarians avoided smoking and obesity throughout life, others live to be one hundred or more despite suboptimal nutrition, little exercise, environmental toxins, and poor lifestyle choices (such as smoking). A few common themes among centenarians include remaining emotionally close and involved with loved ones throughout life, achieving financial security, and staying mentally active (e.g., reading, writing, and cross word puzzles). Such extreme longevity seems to run in families, hinting that genetics may play a role. Researchers hope to identify the genetic factors that promote such longevity in order to develop drugs that will mimic these genetic effects in others.

There are more women than men in all of the subcategories of late adulthood (Himes, 2001). This difference is because men have higher mortality rates than women throughout life. In general, for every one hundred girls born, one hundred and five boys are born (of course, sex-selection during IVF or abortion can skew these numbers). However, by the age of eighty-five there is a 41:100 ratio—that is for every one hundred women, there are only forty-one men. In general, women can expect to outlive their husbands.

There are also some ethnic differences in terms of the elderly population (Himes, 2001). During the 2000 census, 84 percent of all elderly people were white, non-Hispanic. However, it is projected that the elderly population will become more ethnically diverse over the next fifty years, with 64 percent of the elderly population being considered white, non-Hispanic. It has been speculated that barriers to health care have contributed to earlier mortality rates for African American and Hispanic individuals. Improved access to health care, fertility rates, and immigration will all play a role in the increased diversity of the elderly population in the years to come.

PHYSICAL DEVELOPMENT DURING LATE ADULTHOOD

LEARNING OBJECTIVES:

1. *Describe physical development during late adulthood*
2. *Awareness of health issues in late adulthood*

PHYSICAL DEVELOPMENT

The vast majority of physical changes observed during late adulthood are closely related to the process of advanced aging. Physical functioning and daily activities are curtailed as the organ systems degenerate. Many of the symptoms of organ degeneration appear prominently in middle adulthood, but they become even more pronounced as people progress through late adulthood.

Senescence

The process of aging.

The aging process in late adulthood is termed **senescence**. The general effects of aging combine to make the body's organ systems work less efficiently. For quite a while, people can compensate for the declining efficiency of their organs and the body in general, but the decline becomes dramatic later in this stage.

The discussion of theories of aging in Chapter 8 indicated that various causes have been proposed for aging in human beings. Although no one factor has been identified as being solely responsible for the aging process, researchers note that changes in **collagen** closely parallel changes throughout the body and are associated with the aging process (Spence & Mason, 1987; Timiras, 1972). Collagen, a fibrous protein that is a basic component of connective tissue, is found throughout the body. It is characterized as a large molecule having elastic properties. The flexible nature of collagen allows muscles, blood vessels, tendons, and other organs to transmit tension and experience compression without becoming deformed. We would not be able to move about in a normal way without this important molecule.

Collagen

A fibrous protein that is a basic component of connective tissue.

3. What does senescence mean?

The effects of aging may be closely related to the loss of collagen's elastic properties. This can be observed throughout the body. Calcium salts, for example, begin to be deposited in tissues as people advance in age during middle and late adulthood. This substance contributes to arteriosclerosis or "hardening of the arteries," a condition that causes hypertension, related circulatory system disorders, and eventually death. Collagen changes in heart muscle tissue reduce the ability of this organ to perform properly.

Changes in Weight and Height

The loss of weight in men that begins in middle adulthood continues through late adulthood. Elderly women begin to lose weight in gradual increments during this stage. Decreasing physical activity, less food consumption, lower metabolism, poorer health, and related factors result in a reduction of muscle and tissue mass and hence weight.

Reductions in height also continue into late adulthood for both men and women (Abraham, 1979; Hegner, 1991). This loss in height is caused by compression of the spinal column and the softening of muscle and bone tissue. The changes also result in the characteristically stooped posture, with the head held forward and down from the body, seen in older people.

Changes in Bodily Systems

As the body declines in physical functioning, numerous changes are occurring in bodily systems.

Gingivitis

Inflammation of gum tissue that contributes highly to tooth loss.

THE TEETH   Total loss of teeth occurs in a sizable minority of people between the ages of sixty-five and seventy-four (Cassel, 1990; Kelly & Harvey, 1979). Advanced age is associated with a higher incidence of periodontal disease and **gingivitis**, inflammations of gum tissue that contribute highly to tooth loss. Many of the dental problems of old age, however, are the result of earlier neglect.

Dental problems contribute to poor eating habits that lead to malnutrition. Some elderly people do not get dentures to replace missing teeth for financial reasons; others have poorly fitting dentures. As a result, they may eat only foods that are easy to chew, eliminating many vegetables, fruits, and meats from their diet.

Kyphosis

A "humpback" posture.

Scoliosis

S-curved spinal column.

THE MUSCULAR AND SKELETAL SYSTEMS   The ability to move about becomes more restricted as aging advances because of changes in muscle and bone functioning. Muscles atrophy, reducing strength and restricting movement. Loss of elasticity in muscle tissue reduces flexibility, causing stiffness. Osteoporosis leads to easier bone breakage, **kyphosis** ("humpback" posture), and **scoliosis** (S-curved spinal column). Back pain increases in frequency and intensity, reflecting deterioration of the vertebrae (Hazard, 1990; Meuleman, 1989; Spence & Mason, 1987).

Arthritis and rheumatism are the most prevalent musculoskeletal disorders among the elderly. Other conditions that often cause disability or discomfort at this stage are muscle cramps, bursitis in the shoulder or elbow, and **gout** (a metabolic disorder that results from uric acid crystals forming at joint areas, especially in the feet).

Gout

A metabolic disorder that results from uric acid crystals forming at joint areas, especially in the feet.

THE CARDIOVASCULAR SYSTEM

The effects of aging on the heart and blood vessels that became increasingly apparent in middle adulthood worsen in late adulthood. There is further accumulation of fatty material in the heart muscle and in the arteries (atherosclerosis), the heart valves thicken, and arteriosclerosis (hardening of the arteries) becomes

Muscular and skeletal systems become more restricted.

more pronounced (Schrier, 1990; Spence & Mason, 1987). These conditions cause higher blood pressure, extra stress on the heart, and related cardiovascular problems, although regular exercise has been found to be beneficial in maintaining cardiovascular responsiveness (Thompson, Crist & Osborn, 1990; Van camp & Boyer, 1989).

Decreased cardiac output further jeopardizes the health and well-being of the elderly (Spence & Mason, 1987). The slower heart rate of older people results in a decreased level of oxygen in the blood, which is why elderly people tire more easily and cannot endure stress as well as younger people.

Coronary heart disease increases steadily during late adulthood. It is a leading cause of death at this stage of life. Coronary heart disease stems from a diminished supply of oxygen to the heart muscle through the blood caused by hypertension, atherosclerosis, or coronary aneurysm (ruptured blood vessel in the heart muscle). Over a long period of time, it can lead to heart attack or congestive heart failure.

Emphysema

A condition involving destruction of lung tissue that results in lowered lung elasticity.

Pneumonia

An inflammation of the lungs.

THE RESPIRATORY SYSTEM

The lungs have lowered capacity for inhaling and exhaling air in late adulthood (Horan & Brouwer, 1990; Spence & Mason, 1987). There are three causes of this reduced capacity. First, a change in collagen composition of the lungs causes them to become less elastic and thus less capable of expanding and contracting. Second, the diaphragm and chest muscles that help expand and contract the chest weaken. Third, age-related conditions such as scoliosis reduce chest capacity.

Among the most common serious respiratory conditions among the elderly are cancer of the lungs, **emphysema**, and **pneumonia**. Lung cancer increases considerably during late adulthood; it is associated with chronic conditions such as smoking, pollution, and occupational hazards. Emphysema is a condition involving destruction of lung tissue that results in lowered lung elasticity. People with emphysema have difficulty breathing and moving about freely. Pneumonia is an inflammation of the lungs. It increases in incidence in old age because of decreased lung efficiency, poor circulation, and lowered resistance to infection. Pneumonia is a particular risk for an elderly person who is bedridden for an extended period of time because physical inactivity prevents the lungs from clearing themselves.

THE DIGESTIVE SYSTEM   Digestive problems generally increase through adulthood (Spence & Mason, 1987). In old age, the most commonly reported digestive disorders are constipation, hernia, gallbladder conditions, gastritis (heartburn), and diverticulitis (Drury & Howie, 1979; Whitehead, Drinkwater & Cheskin, 1989).

Constipation and hemorrhoids are frequent complaints of the elderly. Their concern with not having a regular daily bowel movement may be more of a matter of socialization than a true effect of aging, however. Of greater concern for many elderly individuals is the high rate of hemorrhoids and the reliance on laxatives to produce regular bowel movements. This often is related more to dietary practices than to the aging process as well. These conditions may be controlled by adding more fiber to the diet in the form of grain bran, fresh fruits, vegetables, and nuts or by taking dietary supplements containing fiber (Hazard, 1990). In general, between twenty and thirty grams of dietary fiber should be consumed by adults daily for effective control of constipation and hemorrhoids.

Hiatal hernia, a condition in which a portion of the stomach slides up next to the esophagus, is common among the elderly, especially among overweight or obese individuals. Hiatal hernia causes indigestion, gastritis, chest pain, and difficulty in swallowing. It can be treated with therapeutic methods or surgery if severe.

Diverticulitis is an inflammation of a portion of an intestine that causes pain, nausea, and a change in bowel habits. It is usually treated without surgery, unless the affected area of the intestine perforates or ruptures.

Gallbladder problems in old age usually involve gallstones or inflammation of the gallbladder. The gallbladder stores bile from the liver. Gallstones sometimes form from insoluble substances in the bile. They don't cause serious problems unless they block the duct leading from the gallbladder to the intestine. "Gallbladder attacks" are very painful, however, and may be accompanied by nausea and vomiting.

THE GENITOURINARY SYSTEM   Elderly people are susceptible to a variety of disorders in the reproductive organs and the urinary system (kidneys, bladder, and urethra) (Schrier, 1990; Spence & Mason, 1987). As people age, there is a decrease in the blood flow through the kidneys as well as a gradual decrease in the kidneys' efficiency to remove wastes from the blood. Among people of advanced age, urinary **incontinence** (the inability to retain urine in the bladder until voluntarily released) is a very real and embarrassing problem (Ruff & Reaves, 1989).

These changes bring on certain conditions that affect the functioning of the urinary system. Men commonly experience enlargement of the prostate gland, which causes

Hiatal hernia

A condition in which a portion of the stomach slides up next to the esophagus.

Diverticulitis

An inflammation of a portion of an intestine that causes pain, nausea, and a change in bowel habits.

Incontinence

The inability to retain urine in the bladder until voluntarily released.

blockage of the urine flow. This encourages bladder infections and other complications. The most common types of cancer affecting this system in elderly men are cancer of the bladder and of the prostate gland.

Women have more urinary system problems than men throughout life. Bladder infections, such as cystitis, are frequent. In late adulthood, women are at increased risk for problems of the vaginal area, prolapsed uterus, and cancer of the cervix, vulva, and breasts. Breast cancer is a leading cause of death among elderly women (U.S. Bureau of the Census, 2000).

THE BRAIN AND CENTRAL NERVOUS SYSTEM   Several developmental changes in the brain and central nervous system are related to advanced aging (Albert & Killiany, 2001; Spence & Mason, 1987; Vinters, 2001). First, the speed of nerve cell transmission slows with age. Second, brain and nerve cells diminish in number. These two factors, plus decreased transmission of oxygen to the brain, produce the slowing in reaction time that is commonly observed among elderly individuals.

Reaction time affects perception and memory as well as the soundness of various reflexes. Progressively slower reaction times endanger the safety of the elderly people,

FIGURE 9-1	**LOCALIZATION OF CORTICAL FUNCTIONS IN THE FOUR LOBES OF THE LEFT CEREBRAL CORTEX**

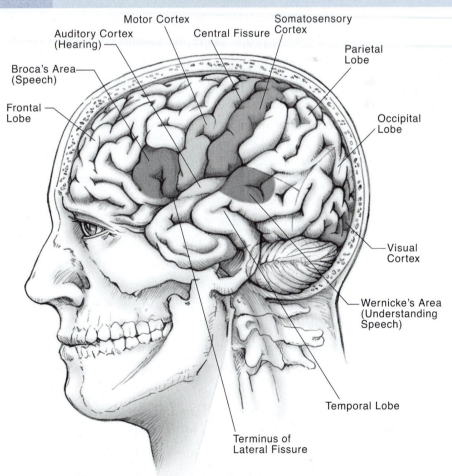

especially when they are driving. Many states now require extra testing for issuance of driver's licenses to the elderly.

Reduced availability of oxygen to the brain can contribute to other conditions that are troublesome to elderly individuals. Sleep disturbances, memory difficulties, and general irritability are related to decreased cerebral blood flow and to changes in the biochemical functioning of the brain in old age (Pollak, Perlick & Linsner, 1990). Insomnia is a frequent complaint among the elderly (Cassel, 1990). There is a general trend to need less sleep as age increases. A newborn infant may sleep about sixteen hours daily, whereas school-age children sleep about ten hours, and adults about eight. Elderly people may be able to sleep only five hours or so a night.

CHANGES IN SENSATION, PERCEPTION, AND MOTOR SKILLS   The ability to adjust and adapt in late adulthood partly depends on the capacity to receive and process information gained through the senses. Elderly people experience sensory deprivation as the sensory organs and the area of the brain that regulate them decline in efficiency. This deprivation has enormous implications for mental alertness and contact with reality.

Vision   Age-related changes in vision during late adulthood include an increase in the threshold of light needed to stimulate retinal cells; a decrease in acuity (sharpness of vision) due to changes in the lens, pupil size, and accommodation (focusing ability); and a decrease in adaptation to dark and light environments (Fozard & Gordon-Salant, 2001; Saxon & Etten, 1978; Spence & Mason, 1987).

Macular degeneration

A decreased blood supply to the retina, causing loss of visual sharpness when looking directly ahead but not in the peripheral vision areas.

Elderly people can expect to experience several eye disorders that can limit visual ability: "specks" in a visual field due to loose cells floating within the vitreous humor of the eyeballs; cataracts; glaucoma; **macular degeneration**, or a decreased blood supply to the retina, causing loss of visual sharpness when looking directly ahead but not in the peripheral vision areas; and drooping eyelids. The risk of blindness increases considerably after age sixty, often because of glaucoma.

Hearing   Perhaps the most significant sensory change during late adulthood is hearing loss. It sometimes leads to a complete withdrawal from social interaction. Hearing handicaps increase considerably with age (Rowland, 1980; Spence & Mason, 1987). About half of all people older than sixty-five have some hearing loss. These losses occur earlier in men than women, perhaps because men were more likely to be exposed to hazardous noise on the job.

The loss of hearing for high-frequency sounds that was first noticed during middle adulthood continues. Loss of hearing in the mid- to low-range frequencies becomes more likely with age. Many elderly people become deaf because of damage to the cochlea hair cells, hardening of the bones, and nerve damage to the structures of the inner ear that transmit sound waves to the brain (Fozard & Gordon-Salant, 2001).

Taste and Smell   Taste and smell perception decline in old age. Many elderly people remark that food tastes bland, and season it heavily with salt, pepper, and other condiments to improve its flavor. This loss of taste is attributed to a decrease in the number of taste buds and to the need for stronger stimulation to taste receptors in the mouth.

Hearing loss is the most significant sensory change during late adulthood.

People do not smell odors as well in late adulthood. This is because of a decrease in the number of nerve fibers in the nose (Saxon & Etten, 1978; Spence & Mason, 1987). This decline has important safety implications. Elderly people sometimes cannot easily smell food that has burned during cooking or smoke from a house fire.

Pause and Process:

1. Why do people see a decrease in height in late adulthood?

2. How do the senses decline in late adulthood?

HEALTH ISSUES

The majority of elderly people are in relatively good health (Kovar, 1986a); although they usually have one or more chronic conditions that require medical attention (DeLozier & Gagnon, 1991). The most common complaints are cardiovascular disease, hypertension, arthritis, hearing impairment, cataracts, glaucoma, and lower back problems.

Elderly people also experience acute illnesses, but less frequently than younger people (U.S. Bureau of the Census, 2000). However, when they do get an acute illness such as influenza, it tends to be more severe and of longer duration than it is among younger people. Elderly people are hospitalized for illness more frequently than younger individuals. Medical expenses play a major role in elderly people's budgets.

Nutritional Needs

The relationship between diet, exercise, and health continues to be strong in late adulthood (Goodwin, 1989; Leventhal et al., 2001). Nutritionists note that many health problems are related to the diets and eating habits of elderly people. These include a lower resistance to disease (Chavance, Herbeth & Fournier, 1989), poor absorption of nutrients (Knox, Kassarkian & Dawson-Hughes, 1991), elevated blood pressure (Lowik, Hoffman & Kok, 1991), and dehydration (Post, 1990). Additionally, diets that are high in fat and protein increase a person's risk for several types of cancer, including colon, uterus, breast, prostate, kidney, and pancreas (Perls, 1999). To decrease a person's risk for developing cancer or heart disease, a diet should emphasize fruit and vegetable consumption.

A NUMBER OF FACTORS WORK AGAINST ADEQUATE NOURISHMENT OF THE ELDERLY: Declining health and general well-being; tooth loss that affects the ability to chew many foods; declines in the senses of taste and smell that affect the enjoyment of food; inadequate fixed incomes that force people to lower food expenditures; physical disabilities that limit shopping and meal preparation; forgetting to eat meals; and loss of appetite (Cain, Reid & Stevens, 1990; Goodwin, 1989; Horwath, 1989; Zheng & Rosenberg, 1989).

Many elderly people erroneously believe they are eating a balanced diet (Fischer, Crockett & Heller, 1991) because they have many misconceptions about nutrition. Malnutrition is not uncommon in late adulthood for this reason (Davies & Carr, 1991). Community nutrition programs promote improved nutrition among the elderly. These services, such as Meals on Wheels, are particularly helpful for the disabled elderly (Manning & Lieux, 1991).

Vitamin and mineral supplements alleviate some nutritional problems among the elderly and improve health (Daly & Sobal, 1990; Perls, 1999). For example, vitamin E is an antioxidant and is believed to impede the development of stroke, heart disease, and Alzheimer's. Selenium is believed to inhibit some forms of cancer. Fiber is thought to have numerous benefits including lower rates of colon cancer and high cholesterol.

Common Illnesses and Disorders

We have already covered many of the common illnesses previously in the chapter in regards to the decline and deterioration in the functioning of physical systems. However, we have yet to discuss cerebrovascular accidents, or strokes. **Strokes** are a leading cause of death among elderly people (Spence & Mason, 1987). A stroke occurs when a blood clot forms and causes a blockage in the amount of blood reaching the brain (Lewis, 1990; Spence & Mason, 1987). The clot can form in an artery of the neck or in the brain. When it does, brain tissue dies from lack of oxygen. An **aneurysm**, or rupture of an artery wall within the brain, can also cause a stroke. In this case, the blood clot forms within the brain.

The severity and damage to the stroke victim's brain varies according to where the hemorrhage or blockage occurred. Some people are only minimally affected; others experience various degrees of paralysis, loss of motor functioning, speech, or combinations of these effects. These effects may or may not last for a lengthy period depending on the severity of injury to brain tissue.

There are some early warning signs for a stroke (Saxon & Etten, 1978). A person may experience sudden, temporary weakness or numbness in the face, arm, or leg. He or she may temporarily have difficulty in speech or vision. Further, a person may experience

Strokes

A cerebrovascular accident occurring when a blood vessel in the brain ruptures or is obstructed by a blood clot.

Aneurysm

A rupture of an artery wall within the brain.

unexplained headaches, dizziness, or a change in personality or mental ability. Most people who have had a stroke in the initial years of late adulthood can expect a limited recovery through occupation, physical, and other kinds of therapy (Lewis, 1990). Occupational therapy is helpful, for example, in assisting stroke patients to develop new patterns of functioning within living environments.

MENTAL HEALTH   One of the greatest fears people have about growing older is that they will lose their mental capacities—in popular terms, become senile. **Senility** is a catch-all term for what many believe are the inevitabilities of old age: loss of mental and emotional abilities to relate to reality, helplessness, and incontinence (Cook & Miller, 1985). Senility is technically referred to as dementia. There are numerous non-Alzheimer dementias that vary in cause and symptoms (Vinters, 2001).

Dementia is a global term for a variety of organic brain disorders related to brain cell impairment (Vinters, 2001). The symptoms of these disorders can include disorientation to time, place, and/or people; memory loss; disturbances in thinking, especially in abstract thinking and reasoning; impairment of judgment; or inappropriate emotional responses (Saxon & Etten, 1978). Symptoms may appear slowly or rather suddenly.

These symptoms are often regarded as idiosyncrasies of the elderly. Actually, people showing these signs are experiencing a type of mental illness that until recently was thought to always be irreversible. Organic brain syndrome occurs in two forms: (1) **acute**, which is reversible in many cases; and (2) **chronic**, which is not reversible. Acute brain syndrome responds to treatment that is directed toward correcting malnutrition, inflammations and infections, and various chemical imbalances in the body. Chronic brain syndrome is permanent and is responsible for many of the mental disorders associated with late adulthood.

One of the more commonly known chronic organic brain disorders is **Alzheimer's disease**. This degenerative disease is an area of active research (Vinters, 2001). Although symptoms can appear during middle adulthood, this condition is much more common

Senility

Marked deterioration in mental organization characterized by confusion, memory loss, information-processing difficulties, and disorientation.

Dementia

A type of organic brain syndrome that is a neuropsychiatric disorder related to brain cell impairment.

Acute

A form of organic brain syndrome that is reversible in many cases.

Chronic

A form of organic brain syndrome that is not reversible.

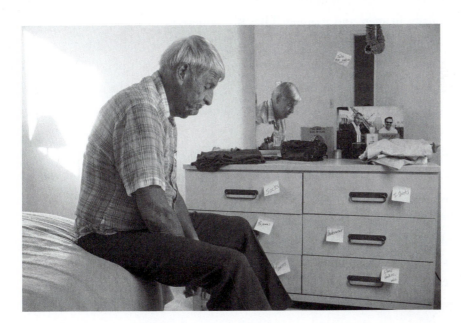

Alzheimer's disease can begin in middle adulthood but is much more common after the age of sixty-five.

Alzheimer's disease

A degenerative chronic brain disorder occurring commonly in late adulthood. It is characterized initially by forgetfulness, later by serious cognitive dysfunction; and eventually by complete loss of mental functioning and death.

after age sixty-five. Although genetics play a role, many other factors may also influence the onset of Alzheimer's disease.

People with Alzheimer's disease seem to follow a certain course. The first sign of the condition is usually forgetfulness. Individuals cannot easily remember where objects are and their short-term memory of recent events is impaired. The next phase is characterized by impaired cognitive functioning. The person is confused, makes inappropriate and irrational decisions, and displays bizarre or eccentric behavior. The final phase is characterized by dementia. The person shows severe disorientation, behavior problems are recurrent, and rage reactions can be common. People in this phase can wander off and become lost or are unable to recognize where they are. Eventually, physical functions diminish so much that people with Alzheimer's disease are unable to provide for their own care and need constant supervision. Death may result from an infection such as pneumonia.

Although Alzheimer's disease is currently considered irreversible, researchers continue to test new drugs and methods to help people cope with its symptoms (Cassel, 1990; Cohen, 1987). Treatments to improve memory include drugs. Researchers are also studying the levels and types of neurotransmitters in the brain and experimenting with ways to alter or improve these.

Many elderly people with Alzheimer's disease eventually need around the clock care. This care can be either provided in the home by loved ones and/or hired nursing staff, or the care can take place in a convalescent home. Care in a twenty-four hour nursing home is costly to families both emotionally and financially. Alzheimer's disease has a devastating effect on the individual experiencing it, but it is also extremely difficult for family members who must watch this physical and psychological deterioration in a loved relative. Religiosity can help family members cope, as they believe that suffering is a process that unites them to Christ and brings them closer to God. There are also support groups devoted to helping family members cope with a loved one's Alzheimer's disease.

Parkinson's disease

A chronic degenerative brain disorder commonly occurring in late adulthood. It is characterized initially by tremors, muscle weakness, and a peculiar gait; then speech becomes slurred; death eventually results from severe brain cell damage.

Dopamine

A neurotransmitter that is responsible for smooth and coordinated movement of the muscles in the body.

Another degenerative brain condition commonly observed in late adulthood is **Parkinson's disease** (National Parkinson Foundation, 2009; Spence & Mason, 1987). It occurs nearly equally in men and women. Like Alzheimer's disease, Parkinson's disease involves brain cell impairment or death over a long period of time that eventually results in the person's death. More specifically, Parkinson's disease is the result of cell impairment and death in the substantia nigra area of the brain. These cells produce the neurotransmitter **dopamine**, which is responsible for smooth and coordinated movement of the muscles in the body. Surprisingly, it is not until 80 percent of these cells have become impaired or died that an individual begins to show the symptoms of Parkinson's disease.

Parkinson's disease is characterized by tremors (shaking) that spread slowly throughout the entire body, sluggish movement, muscle weakness, rigidity, and a peculiar walking gait (National Parkinson Foundation, 2009; Spence & Mason, 1987). Speech becomes slurred and muffled as the disease progresses. Facial expressions may become stiff and handwriting is small and restricted. Depression is also sometimes experienced by individuals with Parkinson's disease.

9. Where are somatic stem cells obtained from?

Embryonic stem cells

Stem cells obtained from human embryos that result in the death of the embryo.

Adult stem cells

Stem cells obtained from patients or donors found in numerous tissues and organ systems, even fat.

Umbilical cord blood and placental stem cells

Stem cells found in the umbilical cord blood and placenta after birth.

Amniotic fluid stem cells

Stem cells found in amniotic fluid.

Somatic stem cells

Another term for adult stem cells.

Equipotentiality

The ability for a cell to develop into any type of cell in the body.

Currently, it is estimated that 1.5 million Americans suffer from Parkinson's disease (National Parkinson Foundation, 2009). There are nearly sixty thousand new cases diagnosed each year. Around 85 percent of diagnosed cases are in individuals older than the age of sixty-five. There is no cure for Parkinson's disease; however, medications that replace or mimic dopamine can be helpful in decreasing the symptoms.

It is difficult to discuss Parkinson's disease and not discuss the issue of stem cell research. This is a topic of much controversy in America today. Sadly, most people engaged in the debate are poorly educated about the types of stem cells and what has been accomplished with this research so far.

A stem cell can be defined as a cell "capable of becoming another more differentiated cell type in the body … they can be used to replace or even heal damaged tissues and cells in the body" (stemcellresearchfacts.com, 2009). There are **embryonic stem cells**, umbilical cord blood stem cells, amniotic fluid stem cells, and **adult stem cells**. The controversy involves embryonic stem cells from which a human embryo must die in order to obtain the initial cells (Elizabeth Johnson, MD, personal communication, 2008). They can also be obtained from miscarried or aborted fetuses. Alternatively, adult stem cells can be obtained from bone marrow, fat, the olfactory bulb, or reprogrammed skin cells without causing any harm to the donor. **Umbilical cord blood and placental stem cells** can be obtained after the birth of a child; and **amniotic fluid stem cells** can be obtained through methods similar to amniocentesis. Stem cells from adults, umbilical cord blood, and amniotic fluid can be grouped under the umbrella term of **somatic stem cells**—allowing them to be easily differentiated from embryonic stem cells (stemcellresearchfacts.com, 2009). Hence, there are many ways to obtain stem cells, of which one is controversial and morally reprehensible to a sizable segment of society.

Some researchers have zeroed in on the use of embryonic stem cells in the development of treatments due to their ability to proliferate and differentiate into many types of cells—referred to as **equipotentiality** (Perin, Geng, & Willerson, 2003). However, in recent years, adult stem cells from the skin have been reprogrammed to have the same equipotentiality. Additionally, some stem cell types in the bone marrow and umbilical cord also show this flexibility (stemcellresearchfacts.org, 2009). Hence, it may be possible to avoid the whole moral and ethical controversy of embryonic stem cells by utilizing certain somatic stem cells instead.

Beyond the ethical/moral debate, there are other reasons that somatic stem cells may be preferable to embryonic stem cells (Elizabeth Johnson, MD, personal communication, 2008; stemcellresearchfacts.com, 2009; The Coalition for Research Ethics, 2008). These are highlighted in Table 9–1 below:

Given the recent breakthroughs using somatic stem cells, it is the hope of many researchers that the debate and controversy of embryonic stem cell research can subside, and more energy and money can be spent on the more fruitful research with somatic stem cells. The question is if taxpayer dollars will indeed be spent funding the research that has produced results in treatments and cures, or if the money will be given to research that has (as of press time) produced only tumors and tissue rejection.

TABLE 9-1	TWO TYPES OF STEM CELLS
EMBRYONIC STEM CELLS	**SOMATIC STEM CELLS**
Difficult to induce growth into the desired cell type or tissue	Some have already begun specialization, so inducing growth into the desired cell type or tissue can be easier
Immunogenic—because the cells come from embryos or fetuses with their own unique DNA, rejection of this donor tissue by the recipient is likely	Not immunogenic—if the stem cells are harvested from the recipients own body (e.g., skin, fat, bone marrow, etc.), rejection is not an issue.
Tumorigenic – tend to produce or promote growth of tumors due to difficulty in controlling their proliferation and growth	Nontumorigenic – Tend not to produce or promote growth of tumors because it is easier to control their growth
No current disease treatments or cures have been developed using embryonic stem cells	Several dozen diseases have been treated or cured using somatic stem cells, including certain cancers, autoimmune diseases, cardiovascular diseases, ocular disorders, immunodeficiencies, neural degenerative diseases and injuries, blood disorders, metabolic disorders, liver disease, and other wounds and injuries.

One final aspect of mental health in late adulthood that must be mentioned is suicide. When people think of suicide, it is typically the image of a teenager tragically taking their own life. Statistically, however, elderly white males have a higher suicide rate than any other age group (Sahyoun, et al, 2001). This rate has increased dramatically in recent years, with a 25 percent jump between 1981 and 1997. Mental health professionals are working to address this growing problem among the elderly.

PROMOTING WELLNESS   Although health behaviors earlier in life have set an elderly person on a certain course, there are still some behaviors that older adults can adopt to improve health and increase longevity. Although sleep becomes difficult in older adulthood, sleeping an average of seven to eight hours can improve mental health and ability (Shoenborn & Danchik, 1980). Not skipping breakfast, controlling weight, and exercising are other activities that improve health. In general, the same health behaviors that are recommended throughout life still apply in late adulthood.

Pause and Process:

1. What causes a stroke?

2. Compare and contrast embryonic stem cells and somatic stem cells.

COGNITIVE DEVELOPMENT DURING LATE ADULTHOOD

LEARNING OBJECTIVES:

1. *Characterize the cognitive development during late adulthood*
2. *Describe information-processing during late adulthood*
3. *Explain changes in language during late adulthood*

Elderly

The term describing individuals in late adulthood who are sixty-five years of age or older.

Late adulthood

The eighth stage of the life span and final stage of adulthood; traditionally, the stage begins at age 65 or retirement from the work force and continues until near-death.

Ageism

Unreasonable or irrational beliefs about aging and older individuals.

Gerontophobia

The unreasonable and irrational fear of the elderly; related to ageism.

Late adulthood is the stage of life in which people are known as the **elderly**. This period of the life span is characterized by declines that occur in association with advanced aging in almost all aspects of development. Old age, or **late adulthood**, extends from age sixty-five until the processes of dying and near-death are initiated. Surprisingly, to many, this stage of the life span is a dynamic period with unique challenges and problems.

Our culture generally promotes youthfulness. No one, we are told, really looks forward to old age or wants to grow old; instead, it is an unfortunate consequence of being human. Our impressions of aging and the aged are based on misleading information and are largely negative, and often times, false. In fact, many individuals look forward to growing old with their spouse and seeing their grandchildren and great-grandchildren born.

Social scientists refer to this negativism about aging and the elderly as **ageism** (Neugarten, 1970) or **gerontophobia** (Kuhn, 1978). Both terms describe an attitude toward the elderly and the aging process that is at best indifferent and at worst unreasonable and filled with irrational fear. This attitude is due in part to historical influences, segregation of the elderly, and lack of positive in-depth experiences with them.

In Asian cultures it is common to have three or more generations living together in a household.

Asian cultures have had decidedly different beliefs about this part of the life span (Martin, 1988). In many of these cultures, such as Japan and Korea, the extended family was the traditional family form, with three or more generations living together in a household. Today, however, the Western model seems to be infiltrating these cultures. Many elderly people no longer expect to live with their children. The Western practice of putting infirm elderly people into nursing homes is no longer unthinkable in many Asian cultures. Most are grappling with the same issues Western cultures face. The elderly group is growing, both numerically and as a percentage of the population, in most advanced societies of the world.

Nevertheless, attitudes about aging and the elderly may be becoming more positive because longevity statistics have convinced younger people that they are likely to survive to an advanced age themselves. Certain structural changes are contributing to this change in thinking. We are no longer a "frontier" society where youth is valued for providing the strength, energy, and force needed to build civilization and industry. We are an advanced society, and thus more ready to appreciate the leadership and wisdom of older people.

Late adulthood presents some formidable challenges to maintaining an active, stimulating mental life. Change in the ability to process information place people of advanced age at a disadvantage, though most are able to compensate for these losses in functioning. Moreover, most elderly people do not suffer from an organic brain condition, which is the prime factor limiting or terminating developmental progress.

BEYOND PIAGET'S THEORY: COGNITIVE DEVELOPMENT DURING LATE ADULTHOOD

Optimization and Compensation

Selection, optimization, and compensation (SOC) theory

A theory that examines how selection, optimization, and compensation assist individuals in coping with the declines associated with aging. It is often considered a theory of successful aging.

In Chapter 8 we learned about **selection, optimization, and compensation theory (SOC theory)**, which stresses that adaptive aging involves maximizing gains and minimizing losses (Baltes, Lindenberger & Staudinger, 1998). Selection refers to the process of choosing appropriate goals. These goals can be behavioral, cognitive, or socioemotional in orientation. Optimization refers to the attention, energy, effort, and persistence given to achieving the selected goal. In optimal conditions, the goal is to achieve one's highest level of ability. Compensation involves mobilizing necessary resources to achieve the goal, particularly in the face of losses or decline. As an individual ages, there is a shift in energy from growth to maintenance and regulation of decline in abilities.

Research using the SOC theoretical framework has found that the focus of goals shifts with age (Freund, 2006). Freund (2006) conducted a study to compare the performance of young adults and older adults in regards to commitment and achievement when performing a sensorimotor task on a computer. The sensorimotor task had two conditions: an optimization condition and a compensation condition. In the optimization condition the stated goal was to perform the task as well as possible. In the compensation condition the stated goal was to prevent losses/decline in the task. Young adults showed greater persistence and motivation in the optimization task, whereas older adults showed greater persistence and motivation in the compensation task. This study supports the idea that goal focus and motivation shift with aging.

Wisdom

Wisdom is not a well-defined or well-understood concept. In fact, until recent years it was a topic that was considered more in the realm of philosophy or theology than psychology. However, wisdom is an area of research that is gaining popularity in human development. Although there is no agreed upon definition of wisdom in human development, a leading theorist in the field conceptualizes it as involving "some balance of intelligence and creativity" (Sternberg & Lubart, 2001, p. 515).

There are three broad categories for approaches to studying and understanding wisdom in human development: **philosophical approaches**, implicit-theoretical approaches, and explicit-theoretical approaches (Sternberg & Lubart, 2001). The philosophical approaches value the history of wisdom discourse in philosophy. They look to the ancient philosophers and analyze their conceptualizations of wisdom.

Implicit-theoretical approaches "search for an understanding of people's folk conceptions of what wisdom is" (Sternberg & Lubart, 2001, p. 501). Here, the goal is to develop a concept of wisdom that is seen as true by the average person, as opposed to some objective, quantifiable construct.

The **explicit-theoretical approaches** largely seek to empirically study wisdom in an objective and scientific way (Sternberg & Lubart, 2001). However, the individual perspectives within this broad category vary in their methodology and conceptualizations of wisdom.

Overall, wisdom is viewed as an important asset in constructing integrity in late adulthood. Wisdom is the perspective the elderly need to understand their own reality and make sense of their lives. It is the product of introspection, and goes far beyond what people learn through education and reading.

Philosophical approaches

Values the history of wisdom discourse in philosophy.

Implicit-theoretical approaches

Approach to the study of wisdom that investigates people's common understanding of wisdom

Explicit-theoretical approaches

Seek to empirically study wisdom in an objective and scientific way.

Pause and Process:

1. How does motivation differ between younger and older adults?

2. What is wisdom?

INFORMATION-PROCESSING IN LATE ADULTHOOD

In middle adulthood we saw that many aspects of information-processing begin to decline. This trend continues in late adulthood. Declines in the speed of cognitive processing are similar to the slowdown in physical development in late adulthood (Birren, Woods & Williams, 1980). These declines parallel the changes taking place in the brain and central nervous system at this time of life. Speed in the ability to process information and in reaction time gradually declines, for example, because of less efficient functioning of the neurological and sensory bases of cognition as well as the desire of elderly people to be accurate (Madden, 2001; Salthouse, 1985).

Attention

Speed of processing and the ability to control what one pays attention to are vital for daily functioning (Rogers & Fisk, 2001; Tun & Lachman, 2008). We already know that processing speed declines as the brain ages, but what about attention? When attention is assessed globally, attention for complex tasks appears to decline over time. However, college-educated adults perform complex attention tasks at levels for individuals who are ten years younger than them, but uneducated. Let us restate this. Have you ever seen the TLC show How to Look *10 Years Younger*? In this show, people who look rather tired and worn for their age are given a complete makeover. By the end of the show, they look ten years younger. Back to attention, the people who went to college have the attention ability of people ten years younger. Pretty cool, huh? This college-effect persists up to the age of seventy-five (Tun & Lackman, 2008). However, this was a study focusing on complex attention measured in a global fashion. Is there a way to tease apart aspects of attention, much like there are different aspects of memory? If so, would these different aspects show the same effects with aging, or differ?

There is evidence to suggest that there are at least two systems devoted to attention in the brain: the **posterior attention system** and the **anterior attention system** (Posner & Peterson, 1990). The posterior attention system includes brain areas such as the posterior parietal cortex and the thalamus (Posner, 1995). This attention system appears to be important for being able to pay attention to visual information, particularly visual space. The anterior attention system includes brain areas such as the prefrontal cortex. This attention system appears to be important for being able to direct and choose what a person wants to pay attention to among a multitude of stimuli. Research using both cognitive tasks and electroencephalogram (EEG) recordings seems to indicate that the aging process affects the anterior attention system more than the posterior attention system (West & Bell, 1997). This would mean that older adults maintain their ability to pay attention to and cognitively process visual information, whereas the ability to focus attention on one particular aspect of a task would show decline.

Not all news is bad news, however, when discussing attention in old age. **Parallel processing** refers to the ability to cognitively process and complete two or more tasks at a time. One study found that older adults outperform young adults in parallel processing when at least one task is automatic (Lien et al., 2006). For example, word recognition is automatic in elderly adults—who have been reading for decades. Older adults are able to complete a word recognition task and another visual or auditory task better than young adults. However, it must be kept in mind that this superior parallel processing in older adults is "restricted to processes for which older adults have greater cumulative experience" (Lien et al., 2006, p. 443). In other words, for older adults to excel in parallel processing, they must be completing tasks that they have been doing for years.

Memory

Among the most striking mental changes are those that affect memory (Poon, 1985). Undoubtedly, these changes are frustrating for both older people and those with whom they interact. A slowing, shrinking brain plays a large role in memory decline.

As individuals progress through late adulthood, they have a harder time recalling more recent events in memory, although maintaining the ability to recall information in the distant past. As they advance in age, elderly people may find that they can describe in intri-

Posterior attention system

Includes the brain areas such as the posterior parietal cortex and the thalamus.

Anterior attention system

Includes the brain areas such as the prefrontal cortex.

Parallel processing

Refers to the ability to cognitively process and complete two or more tasks at a time.

cate detail a high school prom attended sixty years ago, but have difficulty remembering what they had for breakfast that morning.

There may be increasing difficulties with the steps required for processing memory. Usually, three steps are involved in this process: (1) encoding information, (2) storing the information into long-term memory, and (3) retrieving the information for use at a later time. Older people appear to be less efficient in the first step. Encoding is organizing information so that it can be stored in a particular way in the brain (e.g., associating a person's name with an object). Elderly people are also much slower than younger people at retrieving information. Their memory searches take up longer periods of time as they generate and think about alternatives and options. This slowdown is influenced by a person's level of mental activity (Craik, Byrd & Swanson, 1987), for those who remain intellectually stimulated seem to have fewer problems with retrieving information. Hence, if you want to slow down your own memory decline in old age, stay mentally active (e.g., read, do puzzles, write, etc.). The contributions of an enriched lifestyle to maintaining the neurological aspects of mental functioning cannot be overestimated (Hopson, 1984).

Beyond decline in the process of memory, the picture is complex for what specific aspects of memory decline during adulthood. **Episodic memory**, working memory, source memory, and explicit memory all show decline in late adulthood (Backman, Small & Wahlin, 2001). Episodic memory is memory of specific life events. **Working memory** is the workbench where simultaneous cognitive processes can be attended to and handled (Baddeley, 1986, 1996; Kemper & Mitzner, 2001). **Source memory** is the ability to remember where you heard, saw, or learned something. **Explicit memory** is the information that you purposely try to recall, such as when you tell a friend about a movie you just watched.

Semantic memory, or your general knowledge, appears to remain intact. However, it appears that it becomes more difficult to retrieve semantic knowledge in late adulthood (Backman, Small & Wahlin, 2001). **Procedural memory** is knowledge about how to perform certain tasks, like riding a bike, driving a car, or even walking. This type of memory remains largely unchanged with aging (Backman, Small & Wahlin, 2001). **Implicit memory**, or unconscious memory that guides your behavior, thoughts, and feelings, also appears to remain intact. **Primary short-term memory** is the conscious process of keeping information in short-term memory. This aspect of short-term memory appears to remain stable in late adulthood (Backman, Small & Wahlin, 2001).

Intelligence

The aged person is often pictured as forgetful, intellectually slow, and indecisive. IQ scores among people of very advanced age (older than eighty) do show a constant decrease closely associated with the aging process. Scores on the portions of tests that measure problem-solving and speed of performance show a greater decline than scores on the parts that measure verbal skills (Salthouse, 1985). Other information suggests that the lower level of functioning in late adulthood is due more to encountering problems that are new and unfamiliar than to a general diminishment in problem-solving abilities (Labouvie-Vief & Schell, 1982).

Episodic memory

Specific life event memories.

Working memory

The workbench where simultaneous cognitive processes can be attended to and handled.

Source memory

The ability to remember where you heard, saw, or learned something.

Explicit memory

The information that you purposely try to recall, such as when you tell a friend about a movie you just watched.

Semantic memory

General knowledge.

Procedural memory

Knowledge about how to perform certain tasks, like riding a bike or driving a car, or even walking.

Implicit memory

Unconscious memory that guides your behavior, thoughts, and feelings.

Primary short-term memory

The conscious process of keeping information in short-term memory.

A dual-process model of intellectual changes has been proposed to explain what happens to mental functioning in late adulthood (Dixon & Baltes, 1986). This model describes two aspects of intelligence: (1) the mechanics dimension, which resembles fluid intelligence; and (2) the pragmatics dimension, which relates to practical thinking, applying knowledge and skills gained from experience, and wisdom in solving problems of everyday life.

According to this model, elderly people decline in the mechanics dimension because the information that fuels this aspect of intelligence was gained in childhood and has limited usefulness in old age. Pragmatic intelligence, however, is extremely useful at this time of the life span. It can be likened to the wisdom gained from experience. This dimension is much broader in scope than crystallized intelligence. In late adulthood, it enhances the quality of life and may well play an important part in helping elderly individuals achieve the sense of integrity discussed by Erikson.

What about crystallized and fluid intelligence in old age? The trends in cognition that began in middle adulthood continue through the years of late adulthood. Crystallized intelligence skills remain stable or even increase during this stage. As you will recall, these are skills acquired through education, such as verbal comprehension. However, fluid intelligence (involved in processing information) declines during this stage.

Pause and Process:

1. How does attention change in late adulthood?

2. Describe intelligence and the aging process.

LANGUAGE

Changes in Language Skills

One aspect of our language ability is reading. In fact, reading can be quite demanding on our information-processing skills, for we must visually make sense of the written symbols we are seeing, comprehend the words that these symbols make up, assess the syntax and semantics of the sentence, integrate the sentences into a cohesive whole, and consider the context and pragmatics of what has been read (Kemper & Mitzner, 2001). Does aging impact our ability to read? If yes, how and why does aging impact our reading skills?

Working memory, processing speed, and inhibition are three areas that decline in older adulthood. It has been widely researched what role these three areas play in contributing to declines in language-processing tasks such as reading (Kemper & Mitzner, 2001). Working memory can be conceptualized as "where active thinking occurs … Its operation involves combining information coming into sensory memory with information stored in long-term memory and transforming that information into new forms" (Siegler, 1998, p. 67). Working memory is thought to have limited capacity and consists of different components for different types of information and processing (Kemper & Mitzner, 2001; Siegler, 1998). Declines in working memory are correlated with declines in reading (Kemper & Mitzner, 2001). Specifically, declines in working memory appear to impede older adults' ability to keep information in memory for future recall or application.

Beyond declines in working memory, older and younger adults differ in their strategies when reading for comprehension (Kemper & Mitzner, 2001). Although younger and older adults are more similar than different in how they allocate their time when reading a passage, older adults spend less time pausing at sentence boundaries than younger adults. Further, younger adults focus more on new vocabulary words and concepts, whereas older adults rely on the context and connecting new information with old information.

Inhibitory deficit theory suggests that a decline in inhibition plays a primary role in reading decline (Kemper & Mitzner, 2001). Inhibition cognitive processes allow a person to focus on relevant information and ignore irrelevant information. Some research supports this idea showing that older adults get distracted by irrelevant information when reading passages of text. However, other research has failed to support this theory. More research is needed to clarify the role of inhibitory processes in reading.

One interesting, yet controversial, area of research focuses on off-target verbosity. **Off-target verbosity** is the tendency for some older adults to drift to irrelevant topics during conversation (Kemper & Mitzner, 2001). Several areas have been found to be correlated with off-target verbosity, including:

- Lower frontal lobe functioning in the brain
- Psychosocial stress
- Extroverted personality
- Smaller social networks
- Lower social support

Although some research supports the above correlations, other research has not found such results (Kemper & Mitzner, 2001). Similarly, inhibitory deficit theory has been offered as one explanation for off-target verbosity; however it is not the only explanation out there. Alternative theories suggest that perhaps older adults misread cues during conversation or speaking tasks, causing them to engage in more off-target verbosity and monologues about their rich and diverse past.

Elderly-Directed Speech

Elderspeak refers to a style of speech used when speaking with older adults. It is similar to infant-directed speech in which speech is simplified, spoken slowly, and higher in pitch and intonation (Kemper & Mitzner, 2001). Elderspeak is tied to negative stereotypes of the elderly, as well as real communication needs (such as reduced hearing ability).

Elderspeak can lead older adults to develop an "old" identity (Kemper & Mitzner, 2001). This has been correlated with lower levels of self-esteem, cognitive decline, and social isolation.

Inhibitory deficit theory

A theory that examines what aspects of cognitive processing declines with age, and what aspects of cognitive processing remain stable.

Off-target verbosity

The tendency for some older adults to drift to irrelevant topics during conversation.

Spotlight

20. What is the communicative predicament of aging?

Elderspeak

A style of speech used when speaking with older adults. It is similar to infant-directed speech in which speech is simplified, spoken slowly, and higher in pitch and intonation.

These outcomes further increase the use of elderspeak by those around the older person. This nasty downward spiral of communication is referred to as communicative predicament of aging, a term coined by Ryan and colleagues in 1986. Elderspeak is especially noticeable in convalescent homes, where the environment is typically accepting of such speech.

Pause and Process:

1. How is memory related to reading?

2. Explain what off-target verbosity is.

SOCIAL AND EMOTIONAL DEVELOPMENT DURING LATE ADULTHOOD

LEARNING OBJECTIVES:

1. *Characterize emotional development and adjustment during late adulthood*
2. *Describe understanding of self with others during late adulthood*
3. *Explain psychosocial development during late adulthood*

Late adulthood can take up a considerable portion of the individual's life span. One does not immediately become elderly upon reaching sixty-five. Aging is a gradual process and the changes come slowly. Nonetheless, late adulthood is a time of continued decline. This general trend is most noticeable in the physical changes that occur with increasing regularity. The role changes that accompany old age are also very noticeable. These are primarily in work and family roles. Although people are often able to compensate for these declines, adjustments are made more slowly and less frequently as aging advances.

The developmental tasks of late adulthood differ from those of earlier stages of the life span in two fundamental ways. First, there is a focus on the maintenance of one's life and quality of lifestyle rather than on discovery and creativity (Havighurst, 1972). Second, the

Coping with the death of a spouse and shrinking financial resources is a challenge for some.

tasks center on happenings in the person's own life rather than on what is occurring in the lives of others (Hurlock, 1980).

The developmental tasks of late adulthood are vast and varied. People at this stage are challenged to adjust to their increasing dependency upon others, shrinking financial resources that lead to changes in lifestyle and living conditions, and the need to develop new interests (Havighurst, 1972). Furthermore, they may need to cope with the death of a spouse and continue to meet social and civic obligations.

Many people find old age a time of contradictions. On the one hand, they experience deterioration in physical skills and functioning. On the other hand, personal and social growth continues through the years of late adulthood. Thus continuity and change rule even in late adulthood.

Adjusting to changes is a central challenge of social development at this time of life. Most people know that limitations can impede development during their lifetime. Some limitations originate from within, others from the environment. In late adulthood, people become aware of more limitations, but as in all other stages of life, successful adjustment and adaptation can lead to healthy development in late adulthood.

EMOTIONAL DEVELOPMENT

Emotional Adjustment to Aging

Affect intensity, or one's intensity of emotion, is one area of emotional development studied in respect to adulthood and aging (Magai, 2001). Although studies have differed in their results, one rather consistent finding is that older adults report experiencing less intense negative emotions than younger adults. Other studies have found that older adults report lower levels of intensity for both negative and positive emotions. This means that older adults still experience negative and positive emotions, but less intensely.

Beyond intensity, what about frequency of emotions in adulthood? Studies have found that the experience of positive emotions either remain stable or increase across the adult years and remain so until very late adulthood (Magai, 2001). Other studies have found that the experience of negative emotions is highest for younger adults or no difference across adulthood. In summary, older adults are similar to younger adults in their emotional experiences, or experience slightly more positive emotions and less negative emotions.

In comparison with younger adults, older adults appear to be more complex in their emotional experiences (Carstensen et al., 2000; Magai, 2001). This is referred to as **affective complexity**. However, other research indicates that there is an increase in affective complexity between early adulthood and middle adulthood, and then a decline in late adulthood. Affective complexity and emotion regulation has been correlated with healthy coping in adulthood.

Affect intensity

One's intensity of emotion.

Affective complexity

The appearance of older adults having more complex emotional experiences compared with younger adults.

Ego differentiation versus work-role preoccupation

The adjustments that must be made to retirement from work roles.

Body transcendence versus body preoccupation

The necessity of finding happiness and satisfaction in relating to others and in creative or mental endeavors for healthy development to occur.

Ego transcendence versus ego preoccupation

Recognizing and accepting one's impending death by living life as fully as possible and attempting to make life more secure, more satisfying, and more meaningful for those who will survive after one's death.

Integrated

A personality type in late adulthood that may be thought to resemble the sense of integrity described by Erikson.

Armored-defended

A personality type where the individual strives to maintain control over their lives.

PERSONALITY   Personality can be defined as "individual differences in diverse human characteristics, such as traits, goals and motives, emotion and moods, self-evaluative processes, coping strategies, and well-being" (Ryff, Kwan & Singer, 2001, p. 477). There are many theories of personality. In previous adulthood chapters, we focused on the big five traits theory of personality. In this chapter, we are going to learn about some classical theories of personality that focus on older adults.

Peck's Views of Personality Adjustments   Psychologist Robert Peck (1968) extends Erikson's views about psychosocial adjustments in late adulthood (which we will discuss at the end of the chapter). Peck believes that three main adjustments occur in the personality development of elderly people. First, **ego differentiation versus work-role preoccupation** refers to the adjustments that must be made to retirement from work roles. The person must adapt to shifting the primary personal identity away from a work role to other means of self-identity in other roles.

Second, **body transcendence versus body preoccupation** refers to the necessity of finding happiness and satisfaction in relating to others and in creative or mental endeavors for healthy development to occur. Unhealthy development takes place when a person focuses on their bodily concerns and experiences distress due to the increasing decline in physical functioning.

Third, elderly individuals are challenged to master **ego transcendence versus ego preoccupation**. This involves recognizing and accepting one's impending death by living life as fully as possible and attempting to make life more secure, more satisfying, and more meaningful for those who will survive after one's death. The psychosocial tug at this time in life is to be intensely introspective. Although this is important, it cannot become the consuming interest and focus of one's psychological attention at the expense of others who are important in one's life.

Personality Types among the Elderly   Several researchers propose that successful adjustment in late adulthood relates to an individual's personality type (Neugarten, Havighurst & Tobin, 1968; Reichard, Livson & Peterson, 1962). Four basic types are identified in addition to role activities that describe these.

An **integrated** personality type in late adulthood may be thought to resemble the sense of integrity described by Erikson. These individuals are well-adjusted and flexible in their approach to life. Three basic variations can be observed in this pattern: (1) reorganizers are involved in a wide range of activities and rearrange their lives by substituting new roles for those that are terminated, (2) the focused participate in moderate levels of activity and reserve their attention and energies for only a few roles, and (3) the disengaged maintain low levels of activity but attain a high degree of personal satisfaction.

Others have an **armored-defended** personality type. These individuals strive to maintain control of their lives. This is accomplished by implementing various means to defend against anxiety and other threats to one's well-being. Two variations may be observed among such individuals: (1) those who hold-on cling as long as possible to activities typical of middle-aged people such as continuing employment past the time when many others have retired, and (2) those who are constricted or who become withdrawn from activities and people as a defense against the ravages of advanced age.

Others are seen as **passive-dependent** personality types. Two basic variations may be observed: (1) those that are succorance-seeking, or having strong dependency needs on others, and (2) those who are apathetic or having little or no interest in others or in their surroundings. Others are seen as **unintegrated** in personality. These individuals may be described as experiencing dementia. They have poor control of emotional expression and disorganized thought processes.

ATTACHMENT Compared with other stages of the life span, relatively little research has focused on

A shift to avoidant attachment is seen at this stage.

late adulthood and attachment. What little research is out there seems to indicate that there is a shift in attachment style profiles during late adulthood (Magai, 2001). Although the majority of young adults are secure in their attachment style, there is an increase in the avoidant (a.k.a., dismissive) attachment style with age. The rise in avoidant attachment styles in old age may have something to do with an increase in the number of losses during this period. Many elderly individuals have had to cope with the loss of family and friends; a dismissive attachment style may be an adaptation that attempts to help them prepare for future losses.

Armored-defended

A personality type where the individual strives to maintain control over their lives.

Passive-dependent

A personality type with two basic variations that may be observed: (a) those whom are succorance-seeking in having strong dependency needs on others; and (b) those who are apathetic or having little or no interest in others or in their surroundings.

Unintegrated

A personality type where individuals may be described as experiencing dementia.

Pause and Process:

1. Explain how emotions change in late adulthood.

2. Why may attachment change in the elderly?

SELF WITH OTHERS

Leisure Time

Whereas leisure time is constricted in middle adulthood due to family and work obligations, leisure time increases in late adulthood. Retirees are able to appreciate a party for the pure social aspect of it (Hansen, Dik & Zhou, 2008). Like younger adults, older adults enjoy leisure activities such as entertainment, shopping, and gardening. Older adults do differ in terms of leisure interests for more active forms of leisure. Whereas younger and middle age adults see physical, competitive, and outdoor activities as separate interests, older adults do not make such a distinction. It appears that these types of activities converge into one general category for elderly adults.

Moral Development

Values, spirituality, and religiosity are three terms that typically fall into the category of moral development. Earlier in this textbook, we discussed the stages of moral development proposed by Kohlberg, in this section we will discuss what is known about religiosity across the life span.

Values
A person's belief about what is right and what is wrong.

Values can be defined as a person's belief about what is right and what is wrong. Some values are secularly-based, whereas others are derived from one's religion. For example, Hitler had the secularly-based value that a Jew's life was worth little and should be eliminated and that life should be valued only in specific types of people. In contrast, the Judeo-Christian value in the sanctity of all human life is based on their religion. Hence, values can be vastly different dependent upon what they are based.

Spirituality
A sense of connectedness with God (or some other higher spiritual being).

Spirituality can be conceptualized as a sense of connectedness with God (or some other higher spiritual being). **Religiosity** incorporates this spirituality, but includes the additional dimension of living the faith. Said another way, a spiritual person may feel that they have a close relationship with God, but never go to church. A person high in religiosity, however, has both this close relationship with God and acts on this belief by going to church and engaging in other sorts of religious activities. Gallup polls consistently find that most Americans consider religion an important part of their lives.

Religiosity
Incorporates spirituality, but includes the additional dimension of living the faith.

In general, children and adolescents that are raised in families that value social responsibility and compassion internalize these values. These children and adolescents engage in higher levels of volunteerism and show greater compassion for those in need than children not raised in such homes (Flanagan, 2004). Children and adolescents raised by religious parents tend to internalize this belief system (Paloutzian & Park, 2005), especially if the parent-child relationship is good (Dudley, 1999; Ream & Savin-Williams, 2003; Streib, 1999). Numerous research studies (for example, see Cotton et al., 2006; Fehring et al., 1998; King & Benson, 2005; Oser, Scarlett & Butcher, 2006; Ream & Savin, Williams, 2003; Sinha, Cnaan & Gelles, 2007; Youniss, McLellan & Yates, 1999) have examined the impact of religiosity on youth development. Religiosity in adolescence is associated with many positive outcomes, including:

- Meaning and direction in life
- Healthy coping skills
- Higher levels of community service/volunteer work
- Lower drug use, alcohol use, and smoking rates
- Lower delinquency rates

- Lower risk-taking behavior
- Lower rates of premarital sex
- Less depression
- Better grades and less truancy
- Healthier role models
- Greater empathy for those in need

Religion continues to be important and associated with positive outcomes in adulthood. Although it is important to keep in mind that not all Americans consider religion important in their lives, for more than 70 percent of adults it is an important part of their identity and daily living (Brim, 1999). Religiosity typically increases with aging (Wink & Dillon, 2002). Women usually report higher levels of religiosity than men, and African Americans and Latinos report higher levels than European Americans (Idler,

Religion plays an important role for moral development.

2006; Taylor, Chatters & Levin, 2004). Religiosity is associated with better physical health, mental health, longevity, and coping skills (for example, see Gillum & Ingram, 2007; Hummer et al., 2004; Krause, 2006; McCullough & Laurenceau, 2005; Yoon & Lee, 2007). Some research indicates that by increasing meaning in life, religiosity results in a greater sense of well-being (Steger & Frazier, 2005).

Family Influences

Widowhood

A label applied to both men and women who survive the death of a spouse.

Just as adult children must adjust to the death of a parent, many individuals must adjust to the death of a spouse in middle or late adulthood. **Widowhood** is the label applied to both men and women who survive the death of a spouse. Due to differences in life expectancy and death rates, more women become widows than men. Becoming a widow can change a woman's identity, especially if her role as a wife has been a central aspect of her family role. This usually does not hinder a woman's personal development, however. In our culture, there are many alternatives available to women on becoming widows (Anderson, 1984; Houser & Berkman, 1984; Lopata, 1973). Options include remarriage, retraining or education for jobs, reentry into the work force, participating in voluntary organizations and activities, devoting additional time and effort to parenting and grandparenting roles, and so on.

Some of the more pressing needs of women who become widows include (1) expressing grief and experiencing the bereavement process with family and friends; (2) meeting companionship needs, especially if being alone is occurring for the first time in adulthood; (3) being protected from the "good" intentions of people wanting to give advice that is often contradictory in nature; (4) gaining experiences that build self-confidence, personal skills, and competencies; and (5) gaining assistance in reengaging socially with others (Lopata, 1973).

Men who are widowed appear to have different reactions and adjustment issues (Robinson & Barret, 1986; Marshall, 1986). Loneliness and depression may be central problems for middle-aged men because they are less likely than women to have a close, intimate, confidante relationship with someone other than their spouse. These men may experience other difficulties on becoming single at mid or late life. This suggests that these men are poorly prepared to care for themselves (performing household tasks, for example). When widowhood coincides closely with retirement at the end of middle adulthood, losing a spouse tends to destroy plans that have been made for late adulthood involving a couple rather than a single individual. This devastating change in status and situation can be manifested in the high likelihood of suicide observed among men who are widowed (U. S. Bureau of the Census, 1990). Not all men who are widowed react in this manner, however. Healthy ways of adjustment can occur when men become more invested in their grandparenting role or use the experience as a means for initiating personal growth opportunities.

Friendship and Social Support

Friendship and social support continues to be important in late adulthood (for example, see Antonucci, 2001; Carstensen, 1991, 1998, 2006). Friendship provides psychological intimacy and camaraderie. Social support can be emotional in nature (such as holding a person's hand while undergoing kidney dialysis), or instrumental in nature (such as driving a person to doctor appointments). However, the structure of social support networks tends to change in late adulthood.

Socioemotional selectivity theory is a theory that has been developed by Laura Carstensen (e.g., 1991, 1998, 2006) during the past couple of decades. This theory emphasizes that older adults optimize their social networks. They allow peripheral relationships to end, actively end negative relationships, and focus attention and energy on happy, fulfilling relationships. So although older adults may have smaller social networks, they are often filled with rewarding relationships that will stand the test of time.

Adjusting to Retirement

The average person will spend 10–15 percent of their life in retirement. This developmental event that typically occurs in late adulthood is both a process and a significant change in social status (Atchley, 1971, 1976; Dudley, 1991).

29. What six lifestyle patterns did Cox and colleagues find for older adults?

Cox and colleagues (2001) recently identified six lifestyle patterns in older adults:

- Older adults who continue to work full-time
- Older adults that continue to work part-time
- Older adults that retire and become active in volunteer work
- Older adults that retire and become active in recreational/leisure activities

• Older adults that retire and later return to work full-time

Several factors influence when someone will retire (Kovar & LaCroix, 1987). First, the age at which a person is eligible for receiving Social Security benefits influences when many people are able to retire. This age is slowly being increased to sixty-four for early retirement and sixty-seven to receive full Social Security benefits. Second, economic and social conditions influence the decision to continue working or to retire in late adulthood. Third, the ability to do work-related activities is an important determinant of when people retire. Inability to perform certain physical acts required in some jobs—stooping, kneeling, crouching, lifting, carrying, walking, climbing stairs, standing on the feet for extended periods of time—often hastens the decision to retire.

Traditionally, retirement has been viewed as a debilitating experience that people dread. In this view, the work ethic is strongly ingrained in our culture as the primary means for achieving and maintaining identity in adulthood, that retirement becomes equal to social suicide (Beck, 1982; Brubaker, 1990). It is becoming apparent, however, that what people miss when they retire is the income from work rather than the social status and interaction with others (Anrig, 1988; Kirkpatrick, 1989). When people know they will be financially secure during retirement, they frequently are more willing to leave the work force and to do so at earlier ages (Crone, 1990; Flatermayer, 1991).

Many actually look forward to retirement as a time of renewal and personal growth (Palmore & Maeda, 1985). Individuals that retire of their own free will are happier with the transition than individuals that are forced to retire due to health or occupational age limits (Cox et al., 2001). Additionally, individuals that are healthy, well-educated, married, and with a good social support system typically adjust best to retirement (Elovainio et al., 2001; Price & Joo, 2005). Further, individuals who are flexible and develop hobbies, interests, and friendships that are not work related typically adjust best to retirement (Atchley, 2007; Baehr & Bennett, 2007; Cox et al., 2001; Eisdorfer, 1996; Zarit & Knight, 1996). Volunteer work is also related to greater happiness after retirement (Cox et al., 2001).

It is important to make adequate preparations to ensure a sufficient financial base for retirement. Many people start making plans during the latter part of early adulthood or during early middle age for this life change (Bergstrom, 1990; Kirkpatrick, 1989;

Those that develop hobbies and friendships adjust best to retirement.

Weistein, 1991). In general, men spend more time planning for retirement than women (Jacobs-Lawson, Hershey & Neukam, 2005). One important consideration is whether certain employment benefits such as medical and death insurance, disability coverage, annuities, and investments will continue after retirement.

RETIREMENT AS A PROCESS   Although many conceive of retirement as an event (like a birthday party), it is actually a process (Atchley, 1976; Kim & Moen, 2002). According to Atchley (1976), retirement is a process that progresses in stages. Adapting successfully to this significant life event depends on a variety of factors, such as loss of finances, loss of self-esteem, loss of work-related social contacts, loss of meaningful tasks, and loss of a reference group. The stages Atchley describes relate to changes in the retired person's adult social role. The length of time each stage takes and the tasks that need to be accomplished during it differ from person to person. Moreover, not everyone goes through all these stages.

- **Pre-retirement** is composed of two substages. In the first, people have negative attitudes about retirement and see it as an event far into the future. In the second, people realize that retirement is fast approaching and that they must finalize their plans for it if they are to adjust successfully. People may now participate in pre-retirement programs and seminars and seek out others who have already retired for information.

- The **honeymoon phase** immediately follows the formal event marking retirement. Most people feel happy and peaceful initially as they experience the independence of retirement. This is characteristically an active and busy period in which people participate in projects and tasks they have delayed for lack of time.

- The **disenchantment stage** is the aftermath of the honeymoon period. It is a time of emotional depression as people come to realize that they have actually fully withdrawn from a constant and fulfilling social role in their lives. They often feel "at loose ends" with little direction in their lives. They have plumbed the depths of "free time" and are now ready to explore more useful and resourceful ways to spend their days. Many people take up volunteer work, travel, or hobbies as meaningful and enjoyable ways to use their time.

- In the **reorientation stage**, people attempt a more realistic appraisal of their options for the future. Some discover that volunteer activity is too much like actual work, is without meaningful reward, and withdraw from it. Others find that hobbies are boring but find volunteer activity highly rewarding. Finding one's niche and developing routines helps at this time.

- In the **stability stage**, people have a routine of established behaviors. These assist them to cope with other changes taking place in their lives. At this stage of retirement, people have come to accept the new role and personal identity of retiree. In doing so, they acquire a new set of behavioral standards, social norms, and expectations.

Pre-retirement

The period preceding retirement during which a person may make plans and arrangements for his or her retirement.

Honeymoon phase

Immediately following the formal event of retirement, most people feel happy and peaceful initially as they experience the independence of retirement.

Disenchantment stage

In the aftermath of the honeymoon phase, emotional depression settles in as people come to realize that they have actually fully withdrawn from a constant and fulfilling social role in their lives.

Reorientation stage

People attempt a more realistic appraisal of their options for the future.

Stability stage

The routine of established behaviors.

Termination

The last stage which is marked by a role shift from retiree either to being employed again or to being disabled in advanced age.

- The last stage, **termination**, is marked by a role shift from retiree either to being employed again or to being disabled in advanced age. In the latter instance, people can no longer function independently. However, nearly seven million adults return to work after retirement, with about one-third doing so for financial reasons. This means that two-thirds return to work for reasons that are not financial and they report general happiness about this decision (Putnam Investments, 2006).

Pause and Process:

1. What are some adjustments that need to be made when widowed?

2. What are the stages in the retirement process?

PSYCHOSOCIAL DEVELOPMENT

Integrity Versus Despair

The final stage of psychosocial development during the life span described by Erikson (1950, 1964) is the fulfillment, result, and culmination of all preceding stages. Acquiring a **sense of integrity versus a sense of despair** is the challenge of late adulthood.

One achieves a sense of integrity by identifying with all humanity. An individual who acquires the attitude of integrity has come to understand and accept the meaning of life. This person recognizes and values the uniqueness of his or her existence during a particular historical time in a particular culture. Included in this understanding is an acceptance of the temporal limits of life. This acceptance produces serenity at the end of life.

Healthy psychosocial change in old age allows one to complete the integration of the various aspects of the self that has occupied so much developmental attention during the life span. There is wholeness to the self, characterized by acceptance of who one is, how one's life has been lived, the decisions one has made in guiding and directing life changes, and the consequences of these decisions.

Psychosocial development in late adulthood challenges people to reconcile the realities of life with what they had hoped for, dreamed about, or desired. Elderly people spend time reflecting upon and evaluating the course of their lives. They examine the essentials of the self or personality, no longer preoccupied with how they should act and no longer holding false beliefs about what is right or appropriate behavior.

Those who achieve the attitude of integrity attain a stronger sense of satisfaction than they experienced earlier in their life. They see the future as less urgent and everyday temporal existence as more important. For many people at this stage, life is lived for the self rather than for others, as it was in the past.

This period of life is one of renewal. Individuals continue to grow until they die. This new growth is motivated by the courage to face virtues, strengths, weaknesses, and shortcomings.

The attempt to integrate the self at this time of life can also lead to a sense of despair derived from a feeling of loss, disappointment, and deep dissatisfaction with the way one has lived one's life. Elderly people with this attitude feel regret and apology. They fear and dread death. Disgruntlement marks their psychosocial demeanor rather than serenity. They may have a pervasive sense of "If only …" related to intense feelings of remorse about decisions and choices made at crucial points in their life span: "If only I had gone to college, I might have had a better job and been happier in my life," for example, or "If only I hadn't had an abortion, I would have had a child to love and someone to love me right now."

It is a terrible thing to gain such insights about one's life when there is very little time left to make changes that might lead to personal happiness. Despair is psychologically crippling, producing hopelessness, depression, and even desperation.

Most people apparently establish a sense of integrity rather than a sense of despair at this time in life (Neugarten & Neugarten, 1987). This attitude is derived from a sense of satisfaction, apparently not only with decisions made earlier in life, but also with present circumstances. These can include having a sound enough financial base to live decently following retirement and having reasonably good health (Brubaker, 1990). Satisfaction with life in the present also depends on the measure of control an elderly person has of their daily affairs. This is why those who reside in nursing homes often have less positive self-concepts and feel less satisfaction with their lives than elderly people living in their own homes (Kovar, 1988).

Pause and Process:

1. How does a person obtain a sense of integrity?

2. Why might someone obtain a sense of despair?

SUMMARY

1. Late adulthood is the final stage of life span development. It begins at age sixty-five or at retirement and continues until death. Five subcategories of late adulthood are recognized: the young-old (sixty to sixty-nine years), the middle-aged old (seventy to seventy-nine years), the old-old (eighty to eighty-nine years), the very old-old (ninety to ninety-nine years), and the centenarians (one hundred or more years). The developmental tasks of late adulthood focus on adjusting to the aging process and to role changes occurring at this stage of life.

2. Major physical changes in late adulthood are continued reductions in height and weight, dramatic changes in sensory functioning, restricted movement owing to changes in muscle and bone functioning, decreased heart output and rising rates of cardiovascular disease and stroke, decreased elasticity of the lungs, a variety of digestive disorders, increased genitourinary disorders, and less efficient functioning of the brain and central nervous system. Quality of life in late adulthood can be affected positively or adversely by diet, health, and exercise.

3. Two major disorders that can develop during late adulthood are Alzheimer's disease and Parkinson's disease. Both diseases are progressive and involve brain cell impairment and death. Currently, there is no cure for these diseases; however, stem cell research is seen as a hopeful field for the eventual development of a cure. There are two main branches of stem cell research: embryonic stem cells and somatic stem cells. As of the writing of this textbook, embryonic stem cell research has produced no treatments or cures, and is prone to tissue rejection and tumor growth. Conversely, somatic stem cell research has developed dozens of treatments and cures without the controversy surrounding embryonic stem cell research. There is great promise in somatic stem cell research in the future development of treatments and cures for late adulthood diseases and disorders.

4. Research within the framework of selection, optimization, and compensation theory has found that goals and motivations shift across adulthood. Older adults show greater persistence on compensation tasks than younger adults.

5. Wisdom is an area that is gaining attention in human development research. Three broad categories of approaches to wisdom are the philosophical approaches, the implicit-theoretical approaches, and the explicit-theoretical approaches.

6. Two principle cognitive changes occur in late adulthood: a decline in general processing speed and significant decline in some areas of memory. Attention shows decline in some areas. Crystallized intelligence continues to increase or remain stable, whereas fluid intelligence continues to decline during this stage.

7. Language skills are dependent upon the brain, processing speed, memory, and other cognitive processes. We see decline in language abilities as other cognitive processes decline. Two interesting topics of research in language and late adulthood are off-target verbosity and elderspeak.

8. Late adulthood is a time of change and adaptation. Developmental tasks during late adulthood include adjusting to retirement and reduced income, death of a spouse, meeting social and civic obligations, and establishing satisfactory physical living arrangements.

9. Emotional development continues in late adulthood, with the intensity of emotions decreasing, and the experience of positive emotions increasing. Peck theorized that personality goes through three developmental adjustments in late adulthood: ego differentiation versus work-role preoccupation, body transcendence versus body preoccupation, and ego transcendence versus ego preoccupation. There is a shift in attachment style in late adulthood, with more adults developing an avoidant attachment style.

10. Religiosity throughout life is associated with positive outcomes. In adulthood, individuals higher in religiosity seem to have better physical and mental health, longevity, and coping skills.

11. Many individuals will lose a spouse in late adulthood. Men and women typically have different issues that they must deal with during this time of grief. Friendships and social support continue to be important throughout late adulthood, with social networks changing in structure.

12. Retirement is more of a process than a one-time event. Individuals that are financially secure, well-educated, healthy, married, and active in volunteerism or other hobbies adjust best to retirement and experience the greatest satisfaction. After a honeymoon period upon retirement, individuals must seek meaning and validation through volunteer work or hobbies. Eventually, individuals either seek re-employment or complete termination from work activities.

13. Erikson proposes that people develop a sense of integrity versus despair during late adulthood. Integrity is acquired by completing one's personality integration and coming to terms with the way one's life was lived, the decisions that were made, and the consequences of those decisions. Despair may emerge if this evaluation results in feelings of loss, disappointment, and deep dissatisfaction.

SELF-QUIZ

1. How is the population changing in terms of the percentage of older adults?
2. Describe the age divisions for older adults.
3. What does senescence mean?
4. How does weight and height change in late adulthood?
5. Highlight some changes in the muscular and skeletal systems in late adulthood.
6. What changes do we see in the cardiovascular system in late adulthood?
7. What are some early warning signs for a stroke?
8. Explain the course of Alzheimer's disease.
9. Where are somatic stem cells obtained from?
10. What are some medical reasons why somatic stem cells may be preferable to embryonic stem cells?
11. Define ageism in your own words.
12. How is SOC theory important in understanding cognitive changes in late adulthood?
13. Compare and contrast the three approaches to studying wisdom.
14. What can people do to slow down the decline in attention for complex tasks?
15. How do the posterior attention system and the anterior attention system differ in their attentional processes?
16. Describe parallel processing in late adulthood.
17. List the aspects of memory that show decline and the aspects of memory that remain relatively intact.
18. Compare and contrast the dual-process model of intelligence with the idea of fluid and crystallized intelligence.
19. What are some reasons that reading ability declines in late adulthood?
20. What is the communicative predicament of aging?
21. Describe the developmental tasks of late adulthood.
22. What is meant by affect intensity and how does it relate to late adulthood?
23. How is aging related to affective complexity?
24. Describe the four personality types discussed in the chapter (i.e., integrated, armored-defended, passive-dependent, and unintegrated).
25. Why might attachment change in late adulthood?
26. What are values?
27. Explain the difference between spirituality and religiosity.
28. Discuss the issues that women and men face in widowhood.
29. What six lifestyle patterns did Cox and colleagues find for older adults?
30. What factors help determine if an individual achieves a sense of integrity versus a sense of despair?

TERMS AND CONCEPTS

TERM	PAGE	TERM	PAGE
Collagen	341	Parallel processing	356
Senescence	341	Anterior attention system	356
Scoliosis	342	Posterior attention system	356
Kyphosis	342	Episodic memory	357
Gingivitis	342	Working memory	357
Pneumonia	343	Source memory	357
Emphysema	343	Explicit memory	357
Gout	343	Semantic memory	357
Incontinence	344	Procedural memory	357
Diverticulitis	344	Implicit memory	357
Hiatal hernia	344	Primary short-term memory	357
Macular degeneration	346	Elderspeak	359
Aneurysm	348	Off-target verbosity	359
Strokes	348	Inhibitory deficit theory	359
Chronic	349	Affect intensity	361
Acute	349	Affective complexity	362
Dementia	349	Ego differentiation versus work-role preoccupation	362
Senility	349		
Dopamine	350	Body transcendence versus body preoccupation	362
Parkinson's disease	350		
Alzheimer's disease	350	Ego transcendence versus ego preoccupation	362
Equipotentiality	351	Integrated	362
Somatic stem cells	351	Armored-defended	362
Amniotic fluid stem cells	351	Unintegrated	363
Umbilical cord blood and placental stem cells	351	Passive-dependent	363
		Armored-defended	363
Adult stem cells	351	Religiosity	364
Embryonic stem cells	351	Spirituality	364
Gerontophobia	353	Values	364
Ageism	353	Widowhood	365
Late adulthood	353	Pre-retirement	368
Elderly	353	Honeymoon phase	368
Selection, optimization, and compensation (SOC) theory	354	Disenchantment stage	368
		Reorientation stage	368
Explicit-theoretical approaches	355	Stability stage	368
Implicit-theoretical approaches	355	Termination	368
Philosophical approaches	355	Sense of integrity versus a sense of despair	369

CHAPTER 10

The Dusk of Life

OUTLINE

PHYSICAL ASPECTS OF DYING AND DEATH

- What is death?
- Dying trajectories
- Leading causes of death
- Advanced directives
- End of life care

COGNITIVE ASPECTS OF DYING AND DEATH

- Development and understanding death
- Communication during the dying process
- Coping with dying

SOCIOEMOTIONAL ASPECTS OF DYING AND DEATH

- Emotional aspects of death
- Social aspects of death

What is it like to die? Will it hurt? Will I know what is happening to me? Will I lose all control of my behavior and ability to react to my surroundings? Will I know what is happening to me after I die?

Many of us have asked ourselves such questions from time to time. One of the authors had the unfortunate experience of viewing a *Tales from the Crypt* episode way too early in life in which a person died, but was still consciously trapped in his body. This person then suffered the humiliation of hearing the coroner comment about his body and "friends" make derogatory remarks about him at the viewing, without anyone being aware of his consciousness and him being unable to communicate his consciousness. Ultimately, he faced cremation and his final demise. This author has often shuddered at the thought of this character's fate if he had been buried instead of cremated.

All kidding aside, although what happens after death is open to religious beliefs, it is possible to describe what it is like to die. Within this chapter, we will discuss the process of dying, especially as it is experienced by those with a terminal illness who know they are dying. Researchers are just beginning to investigate dying phenomena, so our knowledge about the dying process is in the earliest stages. This information is presented here to provide a better understanding of a process that is difficult not only to research, but also to describe to others by those who are experiencing it.

PHYSICAL ASPECTS OF DYING AND DEATH

LEARNING OBJECTIVES:

1. *Gain awareness of the different definitions of death*
2. *Understand the different trajectories of death*
3. *Explain what the leading causes of death are at different stages of life*
4. *Describe what an advanced directive is and why it is important*
5. *Discuss end of life care*

WHAT IS DEATH?

Death

The cessation of all observable or measurable physical signs of life (physical death); related aspects are social and psychological death.

Death can occur at any point in the life span. This event is most commonly associated with old age, however, and is an anticipated part of late adulthood. For these reasons, the elderly are more aware of, even preoccupied with, death than younger people (Kalish, 1987; Kalish & Reynolds, 1981). The elderly generally are less anxious about death than young adults (Belsky, 1984). When asked how they would spend the last six months of their life, for example, young adults state they would devote the time to doing things they haven't yet done and to traveling. Older people report they would spend the time with family and friends and in contemplation. The elderly seem to fear the process of dying and the pain that is often associated with it rather than death itself (Belsky, 1984; Kimmel, 1980). However, changes in the perception of prescribing pain medication to the dying is allowing for more pain control at the end of life. Although doctors used to shy away from generously prescribing pain medication in general, they now accept that there is little fear in prescribing it to those facing death because developing an addiction to pain medication is not really a concern (Lague, 2000).

Biological Death

Biological death

Historically defined as when the heart stopped beating and respiration ceased, leading to the cessation of brain function.

There is no longer one universally accepted definition of biological death. **Biological death** historically has been defined to take place when a person can no longer breathe independently and the heart stops beating. Until recently, the cessation of respiration and heartbeat resulted in death of the brain and all observable or measurable physical signs of life (Black, 1953; Blank, 2001; Monaghan, 2002; Rubenstein, Cohen & Jackson, 2006). However, advances in medical care have given us the technology for resuscitating heartbeat and respiration, even if the brain is irreparably damaged.

The ability to assist an individual with respiration or electrically restart the heart coincided with the development of immunosuppressant drugs that allows for organ transplantation. Hence, the need for fresh organs for transplant sparked discussion in the mid-1900s about redefining biological death to include brain death (Monaghan, 2002).

Brain death can occur due to injury or disease (Blank, 2001; Monaghan, 2002; Rubenstein, Cohen & Jackson, 2006). Two early problems with which medical personnel grappled, with was how to define brain death and how to actually test for it with any precision. A group commonly referred to as the Harvard Medical School committee created the early criteria to define and diagnose brain death in 1968. These criteria stated that brain death results in the following:

- Unresponsiveness and unreceptivity (lack of consciousness)

- Lack of spontaneous movements or breathing

- Lack of reflexes

Although not part of the official criteria, it was recommended that doctors check for lack of electrical activity in the cerebral cortex (using an EEG) prior to a final judgment of brain death. Additionally, twenty-four hours should be given to see if any improvement is

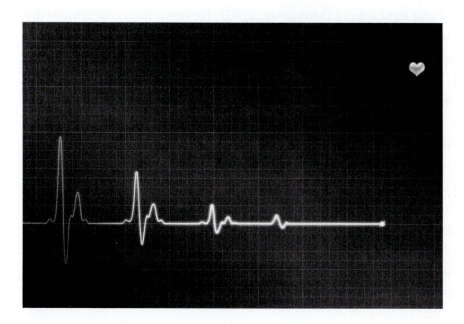

Biological death happens when a person is no longer able to breathe on their own, and their heart stops beating.

shown prior to removal of any life-support machines (Blank, 2001; Monaghan, 2002; Rubenstein, Cohen & Jackson, 2006).

These criteria were electively used by some physicians; however, many physicians still struggled with deciding when to declare someone brain dead and allow organ removal for donation.

The Uniform Determination of Death Act (1980) was the first comprehensive statement developed by governmental agencies, the American Medical Association, and the American Bar Association defining when death can be declared. Below is the definition:

> An individual who has sustained either (1) irreversible cessation of circulatory and respiratory functions, or (2) irreversible cessation of all functions of the entire brain, including the brainstem, is dead. A determination of death must be made in accordance with accepted medical standards (NCCUSL, 1980).

This definition seems to make sense. If your heart is not beating, you are not breathing, and your entire brain is not functioning, you are considered dead. However, proponents of "brain death" balk at this definition because it requires **"whole-brain" death** (Monaghan, 2002). Instead, they seek a **"partial-brain" death** or "cerebral brain" death definition. They seek a definition that would allow for a breathing person who lacks consciousness (presumably permanently) to be considered dead; therefore, allow for organ donation before the blood ceases to pump through the veins. Such partial-brain death can happen when the cerebral cortex loses functionality, but the brain stem continues to function in support of vital functions such as respiration (Blank, 2001; Monaghan, 2002; Rubenstein, Cohen & Jackson, 2006). Such individuals can be referred to being in a persistent vegetative state (PVS) or in a minimal conscious state (MCS).

An international survey that included seventy countries with guidelines about diagnosing brain death found that all of them require irreversible coma and a lack of reflexes associated with brain stem activity (Monaghan, 2002). However, there was considerable variation as to whether cessation of breathing was necessary, how long a patient should be watched for improvement, and how many doctors must concur that the individual is brain dead. Whereas some countries require a confirmatory EEG showing lack of electrical activity in the brain, the United States does not. Hence, a person may be considered dead in one country, yet be considered alive in another.

This redefinition of death that the medical community is currently struggling with will probably persist for the foreseeable future. As with any controversial topic, thorny questions will need to be addressed if movement continues in the direction of allowing for a "partial-brain" death criteria for death (Blank, 2001; Monaghan, 2002; Rubenstein, Cohen & Jackson, 2006). For example, if a person is partially-brain dead, should they be given pain killers as the organs are removed for donation? "Some patients with dead brain stems still have electrical activity in other parts of their brains, and there is no way to test whether the pain perceiving area of the brain still functions" (Mon-

Spotlight

3. How did the Uniform Determination of Death Act define death?

"Whole-brain" death

When the entire brain, including the brain stem, ceases to function.

"Partial-brain" death

A concept that a person should be considered dead if his or her higher cognitive functions no longer function, but parts of the brain still function and maintain physical life.

aghan, 2002, p. 38). Should people in a persistent vegetative state be considered brain dead, because there is little to no hope of them regaining consciousness though the body may function for years in some cases? If yes, should they be given anti-anxiety medications when on the table having their organs removed? Research indicates that people in a persistent vegetative state continue to show physiological emotional responses in reaction to events in their environment (such as a relative's presence) (Dolce et al., 2008). Can you imagine their distress if they realize their death is imminent as their organs are removed? What about individuals in the last stage of Alzheimer's, the profoundly retarded, or anencephalic infants? Should they be considered dead or even have their death hastened by withholding life-sustaining measures such as food? Will parents of the anencephalic infants (those born without most of the brain) be pressured to allow the organs to be harvested immediately and cheated of what little time they have to cradle their child before natural death? Should there be a conscience clause so that individual religious beliefs can be honored even if it runs counter to the medical culture? Finally, how much say should third-party payers have in the determination of death? If a person uses the conscience clause to maintain care for their "dead" loved one, will insurance be required to pay? Such issues make you wish for the days when cessation of heartbeat and breathing were the only criteria for determining death.

Psychological Death

Psychological death refers to the thoughts and emotional reactions experienced by the dying individuals and his or her family and friends. Most people who know they are dying react in particular ways that allow death to function as a developmental event in their life span. We will discuss psychological death in more depth later in this chapter.

Social Death

Social death refers to the institutional and cultural events and processes that relate to a deceased individual, such as the bereavement of family and friends and the funeral. The execution of the deceased person's will is one of the few widely accepted societal events to formally recognize an individual's death. There are few institutionalized practices that accompany someone's death. The funeral or memorial service, although no longer universally practiced in our society, is diverse in form and purposes. We will discuss different religious traditions in dealing with death in the next chapter.

Psychological death

The thoughts and emotional reactions experienced by the dying individuals and his or her family and friends.

Social death

The institutional and cultural events and processes that relate to a deceased individual, such as the bereavement of family and friends and the funeral.

Pause and process:

1. Distinguish between biological death, psychological death, and social death.

2. What is the difference between whole-brain death and partial-brain death.

DYING TRAJECTORIES

Trajectory

A path or pattern that is followed in some particular process.

Dying trajectories

Representations of the duration and shape of the dying process.

Duration

The time the process takes.

Lingering pattern

The person is expected to die, but clings to life for an indeterminate time.

Short-reprieve pattern

The person's death is postponed unexpectedly, but only for a short period of time.

Abrupt-surprise pattern

The person is expected to recover but dies instead.

Suspended-sentence pattern

The person is discharged from medical care and is expected to live for several years.

Entry-reentry pattern

The person experiences steady decline, but is able to remain at home between periods of hospitalization.

Acute phase

A crisis accompanied by high personal stress associated with increasing awareness of the inevitability of death.

Each person experiences death in his or her own way. Death may come suddenly and unexpectedly, as the result of a fatal accident, or it may be a long process, as with terminal diseases such as cancer and AIDS.

A **trajectory** is a path or pattern that is followed in some particular process. **Dying trajectories** differ depending on the circumstances that cause and influence this condition. Researchers outline the process of dying in several ways. For example, Glasser and Strauss (1968) see dying as a passage from being alive to being dead. They refer to dying trajectories as representations of the duration and shape of the dying process. **Duration** refers to the time the process takes, and shape to its rate of progression. Some patterns of dying are of short duration, whereas others are extended. The shape of some dying patterns is a steady decline, whereas that of others alternates between times of decline and times of stability. Glasser and Strauss outlined five dying trajectories:

1. The **lingering pattern** in which the person is expected to die, but clings to life for an indeterminate time.

2. The **short-reprieve pattern** in which the person's death is postponed unexpectedly, but for only a short period of time.

3. The **abrupt-surprise pattern** in which the person is expected to recover but dies instead.

4. The **suspended-sentence pattern** in which the person is discharged from medical care and is expected to live for several years.

5. The **entry-reentry pattern** in which the person experiences steady decline, but is able to remain at home between periods of hospitalization.

Among the terminally ill, dying may be experienced as a series of phases (see Figure 10-1). Three periods have been proposed (Pattison, 1977; Kaufman & Kaufman, 2006):

1. The **acute phase** is a crisis accompanied by high personal stress associated with increasing awareness of the inevitability of death.

2. In the **chronic living-dying phase**, the person adjusts to the idea of approaching death, and experiences a variety of feelings such as grief, fear of the unknown, and isolation.

3. The **terminal period** is characterized by withdrawal from others and general disengagement from the world.

Several researchers report that there are a number of indicators associated with the closeness of death (Bäckman & MacDonald, 2006; Lieberman, 1965; Lieberman & Coplan, 1970; MacDonald, Hultsch & Dixon, 2008; Reigel & Reigel, 1972). These indicators include a decline in the quality of cognitive functioning; a decline in the degree of introspection; a less aggressive self-image; a decline in intelligence test scores; and a decline

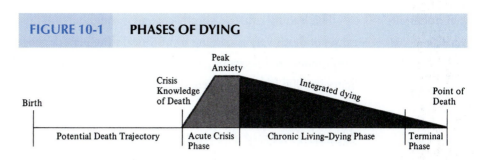

FIGURE 10-1   PHASES OF DYING

Source: From the book, *The Experience of Dying* by E. Mansel Pattison © 1977 by Prentice-Hall, Inc.

in energy. These factors were often observed among people who died within one to three years of a terminal diagnosis.

Terminal decline is the official term used to describe the accelerated cognitive degeneration as elderly individuals approach death (MacDonald, Hultsch & Dixon, 2008). Longitudinal research has found that lower speed of cognitive processing and higher inconsistency of speed are measures predictive of impending death. What is unclear is the nature of the relationships between biological, neurological, and cognitive processes that allow for cognitive measures to predict death (Bäckman & MacDonald, 2006; MacDonald, Hultsch & Dixon, 2008). Bäckman and MacDonald are two developmentalists currently working to develop and test models to help explain the curious relationship between terminal decline and imminent death.

Pause and Process:

1. What is meant by a dying trajectory?

2. Define terminal decline in your own words.

LEADING CAUSES OF DEATH

"When a person's death outshines his life it's a dad blame pity."
    —*Dancing in Cadillac Light* **by Kimberly Willis Holt**

Chronic living-dying phase

The person adjusts to the idea of approaching death, and experiences a variety of feelings such as grief, fear of the unknown, and isolation.

Terminal period

Characterized by withdrawal from others and general disengagement from the world.

The above quote comes from an awarding winning novel for children, which focuses on a young girl's struggle with death and grief. Statistically, most of us will die of the common and expected illnesses that come with aging. However, one out of ten of us will die unexpectedly and suddenly (Lague, 2000). These unexpected, sudden deaths are those that tend to overshadow the person's life. The person is remembered for how they died, not for how they lived.

Further, the deaths of the young are particularly difficult to comprehend. "When the young precede elders in death it is an unnatural event. When children die, it is as if life's promise and potential has been abruptly terminated. We mourn their loss differently from those who have attained maturity and lived a full life" (Jalongo, 2005, p. 46). There is said to be no greater, all-consuming grief than that of a parent losing a child to death (Utne, 2005).

Terminal decline

The official term used to describe the accelerated cognitive degeneration as elderly individuals approach death.

The leading causes of death change throughout the life span. Additionally, the leading causes of death vary according to historical time period, geographical location, ethnicity, and even gender. In this section, we will consider some of the leading causes of death in the United States in 2006 (the most recent data available at press time by the Center for Disease Control).

Death During Prenatal Development

It is extremely difficult to have sound statistics on death during the prenatal period for two reasons. First, it is estimated that approximately 50 percent of zygotes miscarry prior to implantation; hence, many women who have miscarriages never even know they are pregnant (Vorvick, 2009). These early miscarriages can occur either due to natural causes (such as fertilization occurring in the uterus instead of in the fallopian tube) or due to unnatural causes such as the hormones in the birth control pill or "day after" pill. Second, approximately one million pregnancies are electively terminated through abortions each year in the United States; subsequently, it is impossible to know what percentage of those pregnancies would have resulted in natural fetal death (Figa-Talmanca & Repetto, 1988; Guttmacher Institute, 2005).

Of those pregnancies where women know they are pregnant and choose to continue the pregnancy, fetal death is divided into two periods. Unborn babies between conception and nineteen weeks of development are considered miscarried (sometimes called spontaneous abortion). Somewhere between 15–20 percent of all pregnancies miscarry during this period, with most occurring before seven weeks (Vorvick, 2009).

Those twenty weeks or beyond in prenatal development are considered stillborn (sometimes called fetal demise) (Lindsey, 2008). The death rate for stillbirths is approximately 6.9 deaths for every 1000 births, diagnosed by the absence of a heartbeat (Lindsey, 2008). The death rate for elective abortions is approximately 233 deaths for every 1,000 births (Gamble et al., 2008).

The cause of natural death during the prenatal period is unknown in up to 60 percent of all cases (Lindsey, 2008). When the cause can be identified, it can be placed in one of three categories: maternal causes, fetal causes, or placental pathology. The most common cause is chromosomal abnormalities in the baby (Vorvick, 2009). Other fetal causes include infection and congenital abnormalities (such as a heart defect) (Lindsey, 2008; Vorvick, 2009). Maternal causes include advanced maternal age, Rh disease, preeclampsia, hypertension, and diabetes (Lindsey, 2008). Placental causes include cord accidents, hemorrhages, and placental insufficiency. Regardless of the cause, the loss can be overwhelming to the expectant parents, which we will discuss in the section on grief.

Death During Infancy

Congenital anomalies

Birth defects or chromosomal abnormalities that are incompatible with life.

If a child survives until birth, there are several factors that may lead to his or her death before the first birthday. The primary leading cause of death for infants is **congenital anomalies**. These are birth defects or chromosomal abnormalities that are incompatible with life and are responsible for 20.4 percent of infant deaths. A short gestation—or pre-term birth—is the second leading cause of death, responsible for 17.0 percent of infant deaths. Sudden infant death syndrome (SIDS) is the third leading cause of death, responsible for 8.1 percent of infant deaths. Finally, maternal pregnancy complications (5.9 percent) and unintentional injury (4.0 percent) round out the top five leading causes of death in infancy. An unintentional injury is the official term for accidents. Suffocation is the most common cause of unintentional injury deaths, accounting for 73.5 percent of all unintentional deaths.

Death During Early Childhood

Between the ages of one and five, the primary leading cause of death is unintentional injury, accounting for 35.4 percent of all early childhood deaths. Below are the major types of injuries leading to death for this age group:

- Motor vehicle accidents (31.2 percent of all unintentional injury deaths)

- Drowning (27.0 percent of all unintentional injury deaths)

- Fire or burn injuries (12.4 percent of all unintentional injury deaths)

- Suffocation (8.0 percent of all unintentional injury deaths)

- Pedestrian accidents (6.4 percent of all unintentional injury deaths)

Beyond those listed above, falls, being struck, natural/environmental events, poisoning, and firearms are some other categories that also contribute to unintentional injury deaths in early childhood.

Malignant neoplasms

Technical term for cancer.

The second leading cause of death is congenital anomalies, accounting for 10.8 percent of all early childhood deaths. Finally, **malignant neoplasms** (8.9 percent), homicide (7.7 percent), and heart disease (3.4 percent) round out the top five leading causes of death. Malignant neoplasm is the technical term for cancer.

The leading cause of death during early childhood is unintentional injuries such as motor vehicle accidents.

Death During Middle and Late Childhood

Unintentional injury is also the primary leading cause of death between the ages of six and twelve. However, the subcategories and percentages shift slightly for this age group. Below are the major types of injuries leading to death in middle and late childhood:

- Motor vehicle traffic accidents (53.7 percent)

- Drowning (10.5 percent)

- Fire or burn injuries (9.3 percent)

- Other land transportation accidents (such as buses) (5.7 percent)

- Suffocation (4–6 percent)

Beyond the leading causes of unintentional injury deaths listed above, the same sorts of events and occurrences listed in the early childhood section also contribute to these deaths in middle and late childhood (e.g., firearms, falls, and poisoning).

The second leading cause of death in middle and late childhood is malignant neoplasms (16.9 percent). Congenital anomalies (5.8 percent), homicide (5.2 percent), and heart disease (3.5 percent) round out the top five leading causes of death for this age range.

Death During Adolescence

Unintentional injury is the primary leading cause of death in adolescence (44.5 percent). However, as was true in middle and late childhood, the subcategories and percentages shift once again. Below are the subcategories responsible for the most unintentional injury deaths in adolescence:

- Motor vehicle traffic accidents (70.7 percent)

- Poisoning (7.1 percent)

- Drowning (6.5 percent)

- Other land transportation accidents (2.6 percent)

- Suffocation (2.2 percent)

The second leading cause of death in adolescence is homicide (13.7 percent). Sadly, suicide is the third leading cause of death in adolescence (11.0 percent). Finally, malignant neoplasms (6.9 percent) and heart disease (3.6 percent) round out the top five leading causes of death for this stage of the life span.

Death During Early Adulthood

Because the leading causes of death shift between emerging adulthood (eighteen to twenty-five years of age), and the rest of early adulthood (twenty-six to thirty-nine years of age), each substage will be considered separately.

The top five leading causes of death in emerging adulthood are the same as those in adolescence, although the percentages are different. Unintentional injuries account for 45.8 percent of all deaths in emerging adults, with motor vehicle traffic accidents and poisoning accounting for the vast majority of them. Homicide is the second leading cause of death in emerging adulthood, responsible for 16.3 percent of all deaths. Finally, suicide (12.3 percent), malignant neoplasms (4.6 percent), and heart disease (3.4 percent) round out the top five leading causes of death for emerging adults.

For the latter part of early adulthood, unintentional injuries are once again the primary leading cause of death; however, this category accounts for less deaths overall at only 29.9 percent. As in emerging adulthood, motor vehicle traffic accidents and poisoning account for the vast majority of these deaths. Interestingly, the second leading cause of death changes for this age group to malignant neoplasms (11.1 percent). Suicide is still the third leading cause of death (10.7 percent), although heart disease (10.0 percent) becomes a close fourth leading cause of death. Homicide (8.2 percent) is the fifth leading cause of death for those between the ages of twenty-six and thirty-nine.

Death During Middle Adulthood

For the first time since infancy, unintentional injuries are not the leading cause of death. For those between the ages of forty and sixty-five, malignant neoplasms are the primary leading cause of death at 31.5 percent. Heart disease is the second leading cause of death at 21.7 percent. Unintentional injuries drop to the third leading cause of death at just 7.6 percent. Curiously, poisoning edges out motor vehicle traffic accidents as the predominant cause of unintentional injury death. Falls also increase to be the third most likely type of unintentional injury death. Diabetes and cerebrovascular disease tie as the fourth and fifth leading cause of death in middle adulthood, each at 3.6 percent of all deaths. **Cerebrovascular disease** is a category for death related to the blood vessels in the brain, such as a stroke.

Cerebrovascular disease

A category for death related to the blood vessels in the brain such as a stroke.

Death During Late Adulthood

As in early adulthood, the leading causes of death change between the beginning part of late adulthood and the latter part of late adulthood. For this reason, we will consider those between the ages of sixty-five and seventy-five separate from those aged seventy-five and beyond. We will see chronic respiratory disease appear in the top five for the first time, which refers to illnesses such as emphysema, asthma, or chronic obstructive pulmonary disease.

Between the ages of sixty-five and seventy-five, the primary leading cause of death is malignant neoplasms at 34.7 percent. Heart disease comes in second at 23.9 percent. Chronic respiratory disease (7.3 percent), cerebrovascular disease (4.8 percent), and diabetes mellitus (3.9 percent) round out the top five leading causes of death for this age range. You may have noticed that for the first time since birth, unintentional injury is not one of the top five leading causes of death. Indeed, it slips to the sixth position for this age range, accounting for just 2.1 percent of all deaths. However, within this small percentage, motor vehicle traffic accidents and falls nearly tie as the leading cause for such accidental deaths.

For those seventy-five and older, heart disease becomes the primary leading cause of death at 30.5 percent. Malignant neoplasms are the second leading cause of death at 18.3 percent. Cerebrovascular disease (7.2 percent), chronic respiratory disease (5.7 percent), and Alzheimer's disease (5.0 percent) complete the list for the top five leading causes of death. Unintentional injury falls to ninth on the list at 2.1 percent of all deaths, with influenza/pneumonia, diabetes mellitus, and nephritis coming in at sixth, seventh, and eighth respectively. However, of those who die of unintentional injury during this age span, 50.9 percent die due to a fall, whereas 13.5 percent die from a motor vehicle traffic accident.

A Historical Perspective on Causes of Death

We have just learned about the leading causes of death across the stages of the life span. However, it is sometimes interesting to see the leading causes of death from a historical perspective. There have been significant changes in the leading causes of death in the United States since the turn of the twentieth century. Prior to 1900, communicable diseases such as tuberculosis, influenza, and diphtheria were responsible for the majority of deaths (see Table 10-1). By the late 1960s, these diseases accounted for less than 1 percent of all deaths in the United States, quite a shift in statistics. As discussed above, the leading causes of death in mid to late adulthood have shifted from communicable diseases to those classified as chronic degenerative diseases. These include the malignant neoplasms, cardiovascular diseases, chronic respiratory diseases, and cerebrovascular diseases discussed previously.

Changes have also occurred in the place where most individuals die. Prior to 1900, death commonly occurred in the home. Medical care was administered there rather than in a clinic or hospital. As medical technology became more complex, medical care for the dying shifted

TABLE 10-1	THE LEADING CAUSES OF DEATH IN THE UNITED STATES; 1900	
RANK	CAUSES OF DEATH	PERCENTAGE OF ALL DEATHS
1	Influenza and pneumonia	11.8
2	Tuberculosis (all forms)	11.3
3	Gastroenteritis	8.3
4	Diseases of the heart	8.0
5	Vascular lesions affecting the central nervous system	6.2
6	Chronic nephritis	4.7
7	All accidents	4.2
8	Malignant neoplasms (cancer)	3.7
9	Diseases of early infancy	3.6
10	Diphtheria	2.3

Source: National Center for Health Statistics (19830). *Monthly Vital Statistics Report, 37*, No. 13. Washington, DC: U.S. Government Printing Office.

from the home to an institution such as a hospital. This change has affected how families participate in the dying process of a family member, which will be discussed later in this chapter.

> *Pause and Process:*
>
> 1. How do the causes of unintentional injury death change across the life span?
>
> 2. How do you think cognitive processes and emotional control during adolescence contribute to unintentional injury, homicide, and suicide being the top three causes of death during this age span?

ADVANCED DIRECTIVES

Advanced Directives

Advanced directive

A written document explicating what medical measures you would like employed if you lose the capacity to make such decisions. You can also elucidate who you would like to make these decisions for you if you become incapacitated.

Basic nursing care

Basic care provided to all hospital patients (such as food and cleaning of wounds).

An **advanced directive** is a "document that allows you to designate under what conditions you would want life-sustaining treatment to be continued or terminated" (Lague, 2000, p. 139). If you are ninety years old and your heart stops beating, do you want CPR to be administered? If you are thirty-five years old and suffer a heart attack, do you want CPR to be administered? Do you want a respirator if you are unable to breathe on your own? In an advanced directive you can define what treatments you would want administered and what treatments you would want withheld given any specific circumstance or situation (Lague, 2000; McGirt, 2005). Feeding tubes become a complicated ethical and moral issue, because they are not technically a medical treatment (Orr & Meilaender, 2004). Instead, feeding tubes (which provide basic nutritional nourishment) are **basic nursing care** along the same lines as getting a bath or cleaning a wound. No case showcased the issue of feeding tubes and the importance of advance directives like that of Terri Schindler-Schiavo, which is briefly discussed below.

THE TERRI SCHINDLER-SCHIAVO CASE   Terri Schindler-Schiavo was a young woman of twenty-six when she suffered cardiac-respiratory arrest (Terri Schindler-Schiavo Foundation, 2009). The lack of oxygen caused brain damage, although she regained the ability to breathe independently and was otherwise physically healthy.

Terri was not brain dead, in a coma, in a persistent vegetative state, or dying (Terri Schindler-Schiavo Foundation, 2009). No machines were artificially keeping her alive. She required water and food via a feeding tube, but no other medical treatments were needed to sustain her life. Terri showed improvements when she received rehabilitative therapy; however, her husband blocked her therapy and sought to have her feeding tube removed. Even without rehabilitation, she was able to interact with and respond to her environment.

Terri's husband fought in the courts for the right to have Terri's feeding tube removed (Terri Schindler-Schiavo Foundation, 2009). Her family fought heart and soul for this basic

Terri Schindler-Schiavo, by her husbands wishes and court order, was refused food and water. As a result she died of severe dehydration. She did not have an advanced directive in place.

care to be continued. They provided numerous medical affidavits attesting to Terri's physical health and that she could improve with rehabilitation and therapy. It was noted that she had even begun to speak when offered care prior to her husband's ending such treatment.

The courts ultimately ruled to allow the removal of the feeding tube from Terri, who although disabled, was not dying. By refusing her food and water, she slowly died of severe dehydration after thirteen days at the age of forty-one (Terri Schindler-Schiavo Foundation, 2009). This was not withholding medical treatment (she was not dying); instead, it was legally sanctioned omission of basic care, leading to a woman's death. Some consider that murder. In truth, we show more compassion for the pets we euthanize. Even the animals we slaughter for food suffer less in their quick deaths than did Terri Schindler-Schiavo and her family.

This case highlights the importance of having an advanced directive. Terri had no such directive, allowing her husband of about seven years to contradict what her family stated would be her wishes. If you want more information about this case, visit www.terrisfight.org.

Pause and Process:

1. What is an advanced directive?

2. What is the difference between a medical treatment and basic nursing care?

END OF LIFE CARE

"What is a good death? … lack of fear, openness to spirit, and love of community … those same qualities that lie at the heart of a good life."

—Utne, 2005

Spotlight

10. How is palliative care different from hospice care?

There has been a steady increase in the last few decades in the number of people who die in an institution rather than at home. Most deaths occur in a hospital or a nursing home (U.S. Bureau of the Census, 1991b). The manner in which death is managed in these institutions is sometimes criticized as impersonal and callous toward both the dying individual and that person's family. Palliative and hospice care has helped address these criticisms.

Palliative Care

Palliative care

Treatment for those suffering from illness that focuses on pain management, symptom control, and emotional support in the face of stress.

Palliative care is treatment for those suffering from illness that focuses on pain management, symptom control, and emotional support in the face of stress (Center to Advance Palliative Care, 2009). Palliative care can be provided at any point during an illness, whereas hospice care (discussed below) can be provided only to those with less than six months to live. Palliative care also provides emotional support for the family of the ill person.

Hospice Care

Hospice care

Care that is provided in a person's home or hospice home to those with less than six months to live.

Hospice care has emerged in recent years as a humane way to assist dying individuals and their families. The original meaning of hospice was a rest station for weary travelers, or place of healing for those injured in the Crusades during the Middle Ages. Today, hospice care is a way of providing end-of-life care to those with less than six months to live. This care can be provided in the person's home or in a hospice home; however, keep in mind that it has provided many the opportunity to die at home in accordance with their wishes. Palliative care is always a part of hospice care (Center to Advance Palliative Care, 2009).

Within the hospice environment, the dying person is made as peaceful and comfortable as possible (Lague, 2000). Medication to control pain is given only when the person wishes to control the sensations. The dying person's autonomy is carefully respected, and the dignity of the person is uppermost in the minds of the staff providing care.

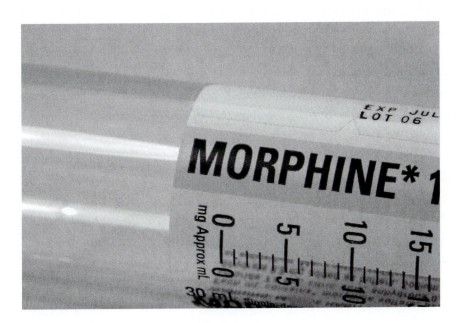

Palliative care focuses on pain management and symptom control.

One of the principal goals of hospice agencies is to help dying people have a "happy death"—one that is typically conceptualized to be as free of pain as possible and in which the dying make major decisions regarding their care and well-being. Further, a happy death usually involves an atmosphere that embraces the value of the dying person, promotes closure and family interactions, and honors religious beliefs (Kehl, 2006).

Hospice agencies also provide support to families after the death. Families given such assistance in working through the bereavement process have been found to manage their grief more effectively and achieve a better adjustment than families whose loved ones died in a hospital (Crawford, 1980).

Physician-assisted suicide

Physician-assisted suicide

When a doctor provides a patient with the means to commit suicide at the patient's request. The doctor provides the lethal dose, but the patient is responsible for actually taking the medication.

Physician-assisted suicide is a topic of growing discussion in the United States today, despite the fact that the majority of medical and nursing associations are against legalizing it. It can be defined as when a doctor provides a patient with the means to commit suicide at the patient's request (Harrigan, 2000).

Oregon was the first state to legalize physician-assisted suicide with the 1997 Death with Dignity Act. People with less than six months to live may request a lethal dose of medication, which two physicians must approve (Yeoman, 2003). You would think that uncontrollable pain would be the leading cause for such requests; remarkably, that has never been cited as the reason for the request (Nightingale Alliance, 2003). Instead, every applicant has cited psychological and social reasons for seeking the lethal dose, with 94 percent citing the loss of independence as the major factor (Nightingale Alliance, 2003; Yeoman, 2003).

Euthanasia

The willful ending of a life that is not a consequence of a disease, illness, or injury.

Non-voluntary euthanasia

A doctor administers a deadly dose of medication without the patient requesting it.

Physician-assisted suicide falls under the broader spectrum of euthanasia. **Euthanasia** is the willful ending of a life that is not a consequence of a disease, illness, or injury (Harrigan, 2000). Voluntary euthanasia is when a patient requests to die and the doctor administers the lethal dose. As mentioned above, physician-assisted suicide is when a patient requests to die, the doctor provides the lethal dose, but the patient is responsible for actually taking the medication. **Non-voluntary euthanasia** is when a doctor administers a deadly dose of medication without the patient requesting it. All three are considered active forms of euthanasia.

There is a long history of euthanasia in the modern world. Euthanizing the socially and physically undesirables was so common in the 1930s in Germany that it was openly discoursed in their medical journals (Harrigan, 2000). Many mentally disabled and physically disabled individuals were victims of nonvoluntary euthanasia, as were individuals of certain ethnic or religious groups.

The Netherlands is one European country with a long history of legal euthanasia (Nightingale Alliance, 2003; Watt, 1994). Studies show that between 50–64 percent of all individuals euthanized in the Netherlands were conducted without the explicit request of patients. Indeed, it is reported that more than ten thousand citizens in the Netherlands carry a "Do Not Euthanize Me" card in their wallet in the event they have the misfortune of needing emergency care. There are growing reports of newborns and infants with disabilities being euthanized without parental request (*Associated Press,* 2005; Nightingale Alliance, 2003). Further, the chronically depressed are considered worthy candidates for physician-assisted suicide. In recent years, 9 percent of all deaths in the Netherlands were due to some form of euthanasia (that is almost one out of every ten deaths). It is wary a weary eye watching the growing problems with euthanasia in the Netherlands (along with other European countries) that people fear the legalization of physician-assisted suicide in the United States.

The arguments for euthanizing or providing physician-assisted suicide to those suffering are often cloaked within the guise that it is the compassionate thing to do, or it is in the public interest. However, one should take pause and wonder how instead of embracing and caring for those who cared for us in our youth, we instead label them a burden and seek to hasten their demise at all cost. Where does this end? Should we model 1930s Germany and also alleviate the burden of caring for those with autism, severe mental retardation, or any slew of other disabilities or disease? Further, although the notion of redefining brain death and legalizing euthanasia and physician-assisted suicide as necessary for the public interest gains momentum, it would behoove us to remain cognizant that public interest has different meaning depending upon the person, group, and society (Sarason, 1986).

Ultimately, as a society, we must ask who has the right to decide what quality of life is an acceptable quality of life, and hence, worthy of life? As it was historically the domain of God (or other believed divinity) to decide when a person's time had come to die (Sarason, 1986), it is now the domain of fallible governments, insurance companies, philosophers, and healthcare providers—giving a whole new meaning to the idea of a "God-complex." Some worry that with the progression of redefining death and the fight to legalize physician-assisted suicide and other forms of euthanasia across the land, things are not boding well for the traditionally disenfranchised groups and for those who need our help and compassion the most.

Pause and Process:

1. What are the various forms of active euthanasia?

2. What is the most common reason the people of Oregon request a physician-assisted suicide?

COGNITIVE ASPECTS OF DYING AND DEATH

LEARNING OBJECTIVES:

1. *Explain how the understanding of death changes with cognitive development.*
2. *Discuss communication strategies for interactions with dying individuals.*
3. *Discuss how an individual copes when facing his or her own death.*

Benjamin Franklin once remarked that the only things certain in life are death and taxes. It is perhaps the certainty of death that motivates us to avoid thinking of it, preparing adequately for it, and understanding its place in the life span. Most people have great difficulty comprehending that one day they will cease to be alive on this planet. The desire for life makes death seem the antithesis of our purposes for living and continuing to deal with the challenges of life. Yet death and dying are as important as birth in the growth and development of an individual.

Dying

The complex process leading to death, characterized by an individual's particular dying trajectory.

Dying and death may be the last taboo topics of discussion in our society. Our ideas about the process of dying, what death is like, what happens after death, the treatment of the body after death, and the reactions of people to someone's death have only recently come to be discussed openly, if still with some trepidation. Covering dying, death, and bereavement in a life span textbook are important for a few reasons. Dying, like being born, is recognized today as a stage in the life span. It is an event that must be faced by everyone someday. It has its own particular developmental tasks, not only for individuals, but for families as well. Dying and death present both with changes that call for a series of adjustments and means for coping with these changes. Our greatest fears often are of things and events that we do not understand. By learning about death and the process of dying, we may humanize this experience and, in turn, further humanize the experience of living (Kimmel, 1980).

UNDERSTANDING DYING AND DEATH

General Awareness and Acceptance of Death

Those who are dying perhaps realize what is happening and accept the inevitability of death. People differ, however, in how they cope with this inevitability. Psychologically, acceptance is a willing embrace of reality. It is awareness of "the way it is," the final step in dealing with the dying process. Liebermann and Coplan (1970) suggest that individuals first confront the issue of personal death in middle age. Elderly people appear to have resolved this issue or are in the process of realizing that death is not so far off. In one sense, this realization is a significant step toward the development of the sense of integrity described by Erikson (1950). The relation between advancing age and fear of impending death is demonstrated graphically in a study by Bengston, Cueller, and Ragan (1977). In middle age, people start to deal with their growing awareness of death, then gradually become less afraid of death through the years of adulthood.

People handle death differently. At the middle age stage people start to deal with their growing awareness of death.

Children may experience dying as a developmental task in different ways, depending upon their age and the cause of their dying.

Individuals can be expected to experience certain needs as part of the dying process, although this process is unique to each individual (Cook & Oltjenbruns, 1989). These needs may be physical, emotional, social, psychological, or spiritual.

DEVELOPMENTAL DIFFERENCES IN ATTITUDES ABOUT DEATH   Our initial attitudes about dying and death are formed in early childhood. These attitudes become modified and refined as our capacity for cognitive functioning improves through the subsequent stages of childhood, adolescence, and adulthood. Socialization processes also affect the manner in which our attitudes are modified throughout the life span. These changes are outlined in this section. You may notice that some of the dates for the studies cited in this section seem quite old. The reason for this is two-fold. First, these studies were well conducted and the findings are still valid. Second, the focus of research on death, dying, and grieving has turned away from studying developmental differences in attitudes about death, and tend to focus more on areas such as terror management, physician-assisted suicide, and the grieving process.

Early childhood   Understanding of death in childhood is dependent upon cognitive development and changes drastically across the years (Children's Grief Network, 2003). Cook and Oltjenbruns (1989) identify four components of young children's understanding of dying and death:

- NONFUNCTIONALITY   This term refers to the cessation of physical functions such as breathing and heart rate. One of the earliest studies of children's concepts of death was performed by Nagy (1948). She found that young children believed that individuals who were dead were capable of some but not all physical activities. This is shown in their belief that dead people are in a sleep state and can be awakened by an adult. Young children's belief in nonfunctionality is not complete, which is attributed to their level of cognitive development. They have animistic concepts, attributing life to inanimate objects. This belief in animism is a normal aspect of preoperational cognitive development in early childhood discussed earlier in this book.

- FINALITY   This term relates to the permanence of death and the understanding that the state cannot be reversed. Psychologist Gerald Koocher (1973, 1974) questioned children ranging in age from six to fifteen years about causes and events related to death and dying. As children grow older, they shift from giving magical and egocentric reasons for death to more abstract, reality-based reasons. Only the younger (preoperational children) believed that "dead things" could be revived. They even told of ways this could occur. None of the older (concrete or formal operational) children believed this. Again, this finding supports Piaget's ideas about animistic thought among young children.

- UNIVERSALITY   This term refers to the fact that everyone will eventually die; no one is exempt from death. Young children have a particularly difficult time understanding this concept. One study reports that about 62 percent of children between two and seven surveyed thought that some people will not die (White, Elsom & Prawat, 1978).

• CAUSALITY   Causality refers to those factors that are responsible for death, such as disease, accident, or injury. Young children's ideas about the causes of death reflect their egocentric understanding of the world. For example, when the young children in Koocher's (1973, 1974) study were asked, "What makes things die?" many responded with statements such as "You can die if you swallow a dirty bug."

Middle childhood   Cook and Oltjenbruns (1989) used the components of the concept of death just discussed to describe how school-age children have modified their cognitive scheme of death. These changes reflect a more advanced level of cognitive development that Piaget labeled concrete operational.

• NONFUNCTIONALITY   School-age children have formed the notion that when people die, they do not have physical functions such as breathing or a heart rate (Nagy, 1948).

• FINALITY   Koochers (1973, 1974) work demonstrates that school-age children understand the finality of death and comprehend that once something is dead, it cannot be brought back to life.

• UNIVERSALITY   When the school-age children in White, Elsom & Prawat's (1978) study were asked, "Do you think that everyone will die someday?" 62 percent of them answered correctly. This compares with 38 percent of the preschool children.

• CAUSALITY   School-age children are able to provide specific examples of what can cause death. This also reflects their level of cognitive functioning. Responses typically are concrete, such as fires, guns, or illnesses (Koocher, 1973, 1974).

Adolescence   Cognition among adolescents is labeled formal operational thought by Piaget. Briefly, thought from adolescence into the years of adulthood is characterized by improving intellectual abilities. These include employing logic and reasoning to reach decisions, flexibility in using abstractions and hypotheses, lessened egocentrism, and increasing use of symbolism. Adolescent thinking has its flaws, however, which may influence thought as well as behavior and may account for some of their risk-taking behaviors. Some flaws in adolescents' thinking stand out: the ideation that they are exempt from danger and rules (the personal fable) and the belief that everyone is paying strict attention to their behavior (the imaginary audience). Because of their advanced abilities in logic and reasoning, adolescents can grasp the notions of eternity, the meaning of life, and mastery of the components of death discussed earlier in this section. Their ability to pose "if, then" situations allows them to ponder such hypothetical questions as, "What are five things you would do if you were told you had six months to live?"

Compared to younger children, high school students are interested in many philosophically oriented questions about dying and death (Cook & Oltjenbruns, 1982). For example, older adolescents apparently understand that dying is a process rather than an event and wonder about how to treat someone who is terminally ill. Adolescents also address ethical issues in their thinking about death as part of their development of formal operational thought patterns. For example, teenage cancer patients are insistent on being honestly dealt with by their caregivers (Orr, Hoffmans & Bennetts, 1984).

The notion that death can occur in adolescence is problematic for most teenagers. Normally, they perceive death as something that can happen to them only in the distant future. Their difficulty in grasping the possibility of their own death can be traced to adolescent flaws in cognitive development such as the personal fable. It is this very inability to conceptualize their own death that allows teenagers with terminal illnesses to cope and use hope as a survival technique (Susman, Pizzo & Poplack, 1981).

Early adulthood   By the time an individual reaches early adulthood, he or she has acquired the basic beliefs, attitudes, and components of our culture's concept of dying and death. Although attitudes toward life generally take a more prominent position in the young adult's thinking, awareness of ideas of death does occur during this time of life. For example, the traditional marriage ceremony includes the vow for commitment "until death do us part," which brings into consciousness the possibility of the loss of a loved one.

The birth of children and parenting them through childhood also brings young adults an awareness of the fragility of life. The loss of a child is a tragedy for a family and involves a very difficult grieving and adjustment process. Some infants and children die of illness,

Adolescents tend to believe that they are exempt from danger and rules. This may be a reason for risk-taking behavior.

birth defects, or accidental injury. Others die before they are born. Similar grief reactions may be experienced when someone has an intentional abortion.

Losses of other kinds can be experienced as symbolic deaths. Young adults learn to deal with the loss of relationships, the termination of jobs, leaving home, and the loss of social roles such as parenting when children are grown. Mastery of these challenges equips them with new skills, maturity, and confidence for facing the challenges of middle and late adulthood. Perhaps these losses also help to prepare them for the physical deaths of family and friends in the future. However, during this period, it is still difficult for most young adults to think about the possibility of their own death (Kastenbaum, 1975, 1977).

Middle adulthood   The midlife transition in the early part of middle adulthood precipitates a change in a person's perception of time. Time is now seen in terms of length left to live rather than in terms of length passed since birth (Neugarten, 1968). This and other changes in perception cause middle-aged people to confront the possibility of their death in the near future. In a deep part of the self, personal death is more of a reality than it was before. Major life changes are often motivated by this awareness.

People begin to experience the aging process more rapidly and in more obvious ways during middle adulthood. Loss is experienced in a variety of ways during this period: the death of friends of similar ages, the death of a spouse, loss of major parenting responsibilities, and retirement from the work force toward the end of this stage. Some people react to the midlife transition with its change in perspectives by discarding goals and behaviors they no longer see as enhancing the self. They may get divorced, change career paths, and discard unhealthy behavior patterns such as addictions in favor of more health-promoting behaviors.

Middle age may be experienced as the time for making a last-ditch effort to achieve personal happiness. Many individuals realize that personal happiness is not to be looked for in external sources or material belongings, but must come from within and has spiritual connections.

Spotlight

19. Define death anxiety in your own words.

Death anxiety

A fundamental fear of death shared by most people.

Late adulthood   The elderly might be expected to be especially fearful of death and to experience high **death anxiety** because of their close proximity to death. Research does not support this assumption. The most common orientation to death among the elderly is not fear but acceptance of its inevitability (Bengston et. al, 1977; Kalish, 1981; Munichs, 1966). Erikson (1950) notes that a fear of death in an elderly person is indicative of the lack of ego integration. An important developmental task at this stage of life—and one that promotes a sense of integrity—is to become less fearful of death. Older people may be less afraid of death than younger people because of its increasing prevalence among their acquaintances. The elderly attend more funerals, read the obituaries more frequently, and visit grave sites more regularly than younger people.

As people progress through late adulthood and experience the effects of the aging process, their impending death is brought more and more to mind. This may account for their preoccupation with preparing a will and disposing of their personal property. They need to be allowed to discuss their views on death and how they wish their own death to be handled.

Pause and Process:

1. How do attitudes toward death change between early childhood and middle childhood?

2. Why do older adults think about death more than younger adults?

COMMUNICATION DURING THE DYING PROCESS

Needs and Concerns of the Dying

Individuals facing impending death experience a variety of needs and concerns. These needs can include physical, emotional, social, psychological, and spiritual needs. It is important to be mindful of the fact that just as grieving is an individualized process, so is the dying process. Said another way, each individual facing death has their own unique set of needs and concerns; we address only the more common and general ones here. The needs discussed in this section do not prescribe an appropriate dying process any more than the needs experienced at any other stage prescribe an appropriate developmental path. Rather, they assist individuals to develop a healthy approach to the end of their life. The following information is based upon the research and findings of Cook & Oltjenbruns (1989).

PHYSICAL NEEDS AND CONCERNS   Two main areas of concern within the physical domain include pain management and body image. Many individuals fear the pain that may infest their body in the final days of life on this planet. As mentioned earlier in this chapter, doctors are more willing than ever to assist in the alleviation of pain through medication and palliative care. With proper medical interventions, pain should be able to be managed for most individuals in their final days. Additionally, just as social and emotional support help mitigate the pain of child birth, so too does such support assist in the pain of dying.

Body image is a bit more difficult to manage in comparison to pain. Body image can be conceptualized as how one sees his or her body and how that body compares to their ideal body image and the bodies of others. The body is often ravaged when succumbing to a terminal illness. Weight drops and bodily function declines. Psychological, physical, and social support can assist dying individuals to cope with these physical changes.

EMOTIONAL NEEDS AND CONCERNS

Emotional needs may focus upon the unknown—what is on the other side of death? There may also be fears of pain or loneliness due to isolation or rejection. Further, a person may be worried about unfulfilled responsibilities.

SOCIAL NEEDS AND CONCERNS

Issues in this domain center upon awareness of impending death. The more aware a person is of their upcoming death, the better he or she can interact with caretakers and express his or her needs. Once an individual becomes aware of their imminent death and accepts it, he or she may become socially withdrawn. Conversely, social isolation may occur due to societal avoidance of death or physical settings (such as a nursing home) that make social interactions more difficult.

Nursing homes may make social interactions more difficult.

PSYCHOLOGICAL NEEDS AND CONCERNS

Dying individuals like to be informed, maintain some sense of control (such as where they will die and how the funeral will be handled), and conduct a life review in which they can find meaning from their journey through life.

SPIRITUAL NEEDS AND CONCERNS

Spiritual and religious beliefs assist many in facing death. Those from various religious convictions often believe that suffering brings them closer to God and is not in vain. Further, religious beliefs can provide a context that gives significance to life.

HOW TO INTERACT WITH SOMEONE WHO IS DYING

If you live long enough, you will eventually experience watching a loved one die. We often feel awkward in this situation, uncertain as to how we should act or what we should say (Lague, 2000). We should keep in mind that people don't want to die alone, and are often desperate for the support and company of family and friends during this last transition in life.

Research has found the following behaviors helpful when interacting with someone who is dying (Lague, 2000):

• Sit close and provide the comfort of holding hands or hugs.

- Allow the conversation pace to be set by the dying person. Silence is okay too.

- Listen to the person non-judgmentally and empathetically. This is not the time to correct any mistakes in his or her memory or knowledge. It is also not the time to tell them that you have heard a particular story one hundred times already, which leads us to the next point.

- Allow the person to reminiscence about their life. Laugh, cry, and ruminate together.

- Support the person to make as many decisions about what should happen after his or her death as possible, if they want.

- Say your goodbyes and express your feelings of love and attachment if possible.

HOW TO SUPPORT A PERSON WHO HAS LOST A LOVED ONE   In the next section, we will discuss grief and mourning in detail. In general, it is best to allow the grieving individual to set the course of discourse. Listen. Never say that you understand what they are going through; everyone experiences grief differently. Offer actual, practical help, such as cooking a meal, making phone calls, or watching the kids. Often, the little things mean the most.

Pause and Process:

1. What are some of the needs and concerns of the dying?

2. How should you interact with a dying person?

COPING WITH DYING AND DEATH

Death anxiety, or fear of death, is a fundamental feeling shared by almost all individuals, according to existential philosophers and psychologists. These scholars believe that people search for meaning to their lives. The choice of life over death, or vice versa, is always possible for individuals throughout the life span. According to this view, choosing death is the ultimate freedom, but death remains threatening because it destroys the person's known existence and renders life meaningless (May, 1958).

The fear of death is deeply ingrained in Western culture (Haoward & Scott, 1965). Death is commonly regarded as a defeat and as a separation from loved ones. For others, it is seen as a journey home to be with their God. In general, death represents the unknown to many individuals.

Kübler-Ross' Stages of Dying

The psychiatrist Elizabeth Kübler-Ross has made one of the most significant contributions to the field of **thanatology** (the study of dying, death, and grief). She interviewed people who knew they had a terminal illness, such as cancer, and these individuals provided her with insights about the death process among those who are aware of their impending death.

Thanatology

The study of dying, death, and grief.

Kübler-Ross (1969) identified five stages experienced by people going through the process of dying: *denial, anger, bargaining, depression,* and *acceptance.* All these stages are not experienced by everyone who is dying, nor are they always experienced in the sequence Kübler-Ross outlined. People may shift from one stage to another during this involved and complex process.

Denial, the first stage in this model, is characterized by the unwillingness to accept the diagnosis of impending death. A common reaction is, "No, not me. It can't be true." Some people believe that a mistake has been made in the diagnostic tests or that someone else's records were confused with their own. Some react by seeking opinions from other physicians—which, even if the diagnosis is accurate, is a good step to make.

Denial is the first stage of dealing with dying and death.

In the second stage, initial attempts to cope with the idea of impending death are replaced by feelings of anger. People rage, "Why me?" These harsh feelings are directed at anyone who is accessible; including family, friends, and medical personnel. Such reactions are understandable, according to Kübler-Ross, because the person feels cheated of the basic right to life and is resentful of what seems to be a cruel twist of fate.

Kübler-Ross calls the next stage bargaining. The person decides that anger is an ineffective means for securing additional time to live. What may work instead, the person now reasons, are requests addressed to God and to medical personnel for help in postponing death. The person tries to strike a deal by agreeing to be good, to dedicate remaining time to service to others in exchange for a lifting of the death sentence. Kübler-Ross sees this stage as a positive step toward coping with the stress of dying.

When people begin to show signs of a great sense of loss, Kübler-Ross notes, they are experiencing another step in the dying process she labels depression. She describes two types of depressive reactions: **reactive depression**, or feelings of loss and disfigurement of the body from surgery or from the ravages of disease; and **preparatory depression**, or beginning to prepare for death by grieving for the separation from loved ones. Kübler-Ross notes that preparatory depression is often silent and calls for quiet demonstrations of reassurance from others. Reactive depression is often verbalized and requires visible signs of "cheering up" from others.

Reactive depression

Feelings of loss and disfigurement of the body from surgery or from the ravages of disease.

Preparatory depression

Beginning to prepare for death by grieving for the separation from loved ones.

The final stage is acceptance. At this time the person is almost without expression of negative feelings. Neither depression, anger, or grief is evident. The person has become reconciled to the inevitability of death. There is general fatigue and weakness. The stage is characterized by efforts to contemplate death with a "certain degree of quiet expectation." Kübler-Ross believes that at this stage the dying person has come to terms with his or her approaching death, but family members have not. There is a discrepancy between where the dying individual is and where loved ones are in the process.

A number of criticisms have been directed at this model of dying. Several investigators have questioned the validity of these stages for all dying persons, as well as the sequence that Kübler-Ross outlines (Hinton, 1963; Lieberman, 1965; Metzger, 1980; Schulz & Aderman, 1974). Kübler-Ross based her model on data from subjective interviews with people who were terminally ill. Other investigators used more objective methods to collect data. All who have studied the terminally ill individuals observe that they experience depression prior to death, but only Kübler-Ross describes a series of stages in a sequence that culminates with death. For example, Kastenbaum (1975) suggests exploration of ethnic differences in people who are dying; personality types and styles that may influence coping with dying; the effects of age and developmental level of the dying; and so on. The model described by Kübler-Ross does not adequately address such issues; however, it did provide an excellent start on this area of research.

Pause and Process:

1. What is death anxiety?

2. Explain the stages of dying.

SOCIOEMOTIONAL ASPECTS OF DYING AND DEATH

LEARNING OBJECTIVES:

1. *Describe the stages of grief and complicated grief*
2. *Explain American death rituals, the role of religion, and cultural-historical perspectives on death*

Death can occur at any point in the life span. When death is not accidental or unexpected, people experience changes and events that help to prepare them for the end of their life. These may be the death of associates or friends, a chronic illness, and other occurrences. For example, one of the authors watched one of her children stare death in the face at the tender age of ten. Luckily, the child lived; however, the lesson of the fragility of life has never been forgotten.

Neugarten (1968b) points out that people shift their perception of time in the middle years of life from "time since birth" to "time left to live." Perhaps this realization prepares individuals for the approach of death long before it usually occurs.

EMOTIONAL ASPECTS OF DEATH

A person's attitude often predicts or guides behavior. Attitudes are acquired as a person grows and progresses through the various stages of the life span. An individual is socialized to have certain feelings, values, and beliefs by parents, peer groups, and the culture at large. These are communicated through a variety of methods, such as books, television, movies, and events in the family and community. Hence, the emotional aspects of death are intertwined with social influences.

Many people's impressions about death come from first-hand experiences. These influence both current and future understanding and feelings about death. In a report by Kübler-Ross and Worden (1977) of the results of a questionnaire completed by 5,274 individuals who attended workshops and lectures on dying and death, the average age at first contact with a death experience was 11.4 years. For almost half the respondents, the death of a grandparent was the first death experience. Next, was the death of a parent, friend, or other family member. Sadness and grief were the most frequently mentioned reactions. Confusion, denial, and shock were also frequent reactions.

Grief

The natural or expected response to personal loss; often used interchangeably with bereavement.

Bereavement

A term used interchangeably with grief to describe a natural or expected response to personal loss.

Mourning

The socially prescribed ways of expressing grief.

The Experience of Grief and Loss

When a person we love or feel close to dies, our reaction is painful and very emotional. We experience this death as one of the most stressful events in life. **Grief** and **bereavement** are terms that are used interchangeably to refer to the normal response to the loss of someone or something that is important to us. **Mourning** describes the socially prescribed ways people display grief (Pine, 1976).

All of us experience a number of losses as part of our growth and development throughout the life span and we often react to them by grieving. For example, people may

Bereavement refers to the normal response of the loss of someone.

experience grief when they move from one location to another, lose their job or valuable possessions, or get divorced. Some of these losses are more painful than others. Reactions to them vary, not only in degree and nature, but also in duration (Kimmel, 1980).

Theories of grief and loss often describe people's reactions in terms of the degree of their attachment to the object lost (Bowlby, 1980; Freud, 1917). Because of our psychological makeup, we human beings form strong attachments to others as well as to things. Need fulfillment has a strong emotional base and motivates much human behavior. Separation from the object (person or thing) that fulfills such emotional needs causes a variety of distressing reactions and generates anxiety.

Although dealing with the death of any loved one is difficult, it is said that the death of a child is particularly difficult. Although people expect young parents to experience grief after the death of an infant from conditions such as sudden infant death syndrome (SIDS), parents also suffer loss of a child through miscarriage, stillbirth, or even abortion. Below, we will discuss the loss of the very young and the grief such loss triggers. Then, we will move on to the grief process experienced in reaction to all losses, whether the deceased is a fetus, child, or adult.

Miscarriage

Miscarriage

The natural loss of an embryo, usually before the tenth week of pregnancy.

Miscarriage, also known as spontaneous abortion, is the loss of an unborn child before it is viable (officially defined as before twenty weeks of prenatal development) (Lindsey, 2008). As discussed in the first section, a miscarriage can be caused by a variety of factors, such as fetal factors or maternal factors. It is particularly frustrating and devastating because it, by and large, cannot be predicted or prevented

Both parents experience grief after a miscarriage (Belkin, 1985; Borg & Lasker, 1981; Leitar, 1986). The intensity of grief is not determined by the amount of time that has passed since conception. Rather, it depends on the meaning the couple attributed to the pregnancy, their motivation to become parents, and the values and status of parenthood in the couple's culture. Tragically, many young couples undergoing this experience do not receive adequate support and understanding from either the medical community or their social networks (Leff, 1987). The medical community is guilty of great insensitivity when it places a woman whose miscarriage requires hospitalization on the maternity floor—sometimes even in the same room with women who have just delivered a healthy baby. Although this practice is changing, its once routine use is a statement about society's ignorance of the effects of a miscarriage on couples.

Guilt is a common reaction in women who have miscarried (Seibel & Graves, 1980). They erroneously personalize what has happened, blaming themselves for not exercising enough, working too long and hard, or eating the "wrong" kinds of food. Because many women connect the ability to reproduce with their femininity and personal competence, a miscarriage may make them feel like failures. A miscarriage also motivates many couples to rush into initiating another pregnancy without allowing sufficient time for physical and psychological healing. Community support groups or church ministries may help couples to work through their grief successfully before they attempt another pregnancy.

Stillbirth and neonatal death

Sometimes a fetus dies inside the mother's uterus and is not expelled from the mother's uterus until the normal time for delivery. This is known as **stillbirth** (twenty plus weeks of prenatal development) (Lindsey, 2008). When a newborn dies immediately after birth, it is called **neonatal death**. Both classes of death are known as **perinatal deaths**, because they occur in relation to birth. The frustrating aspect of these deaths is that they frequently happen for unexplainable reasons.

Society tends to discount the effect that a stillbirth or death of a newborn has on parents because it is commonly believed that people do not develop a significant attachment to their offspring before birth. Those who have experienced such a loss disagree. They find them very hard to accept because they have developed an attachment to the child during prenatal development, even though it may be less intense than the attachment parents feel toward an older child.

A perinatal death constitutes a crisis for the young couple, especially in their marriage relationship. Many women blame themselves. Men, too, sometimes feel guilty or responsible for the death in some way. If the couple has a history of losses of this nature, the situation is exacerbated. Counseling may be necessary to work through the grief and save the marriage (Leff, 1987; Wing et al., 2001).

Sudden infant death syndrome (SIDS)

Sometimes an infant dies suddenly for no apparent reason. It is impossible to describe the shock of discovering a child dead in its crib when hours or minutes before it was in apparent good health.

SIDS is the third leading cause of death among infants in their first year of life. It used to be the leading cause; however, public education about laying an infant to sleep on their back without pillows and blankets has helped lower the incidence some. That said, even after years of intensive study, researchers and medical providers continue to debate the causes of SIDS (ACOG, 2005; Bass, Kravath & Glass, 1986; Mackintosh, 1982).

Although it is known that the immediate cause of SIDS is the cessation of the infant's breathing; the million dollar question is why the infant ceases to breathe. As mentioned above, sleeping on the stomach, having soft bedding, or sleeping with pillows and blankets contributed to the high incidence of SIDS. However, infants continue to die of SIDS without these contributing factors. One possible cause of SIDS (and there is probably more than just one cause) is a condition known as **idiopathic protracted apnea** (Naeye, 1980). Idiopathic protracted apnea is an interruption in breathing during sleep. It is thought to be caused by a disturbance in the functioning of neurotransmitters within those areas of the brain that regulate breathing and other functions (Sahni, Fifer & Myers, 2007). For some reason, a chemical imbalance may occur, causing breathing to stop and not to be resumed. Other proposed explanations include a genetic propensity for SIDS, viral infections, enzyme abnormalities, or reactions to medications.

There are some risk factors that increase the likelihood of SIDS. Exposure to second hand smoke is a risk factor for SIDS (ACOG, 2005). Infants should never be around an individual smoking or near clothing or furniture that smells of cigarette smoke. Low birthweight infants are at an increased risk of SIDS, as are infants that suffer from sleep apnea. Infants who have siblings that have died from SIDS are also at risk for SIDS themselves.

As previously discussed, there are a few steps that can be taken to try to prevent SIDS (ACOG, 2005). Avoidance of soft bedding, blankets, and pillows is an important step in preventing SIDS, as is placing the infant to sleep on the back. Allowing the infant to fall asleep using a pacifier seems to lower the risk of SIDS. Not smoking during pregnancy and avoiding second hand smoke after birth help prevent SIDS. Additionally, sleeping under a ceiling fan may help prevent SIDS. The unexpected death of an infant causes grief reactions that are very hard to resolve (Cook & Oltjenbruns, 1989). Parental reactions range from shock to denial, guilt, anger, and self-reproach. It is not unusual for the young parents to assume full responsibility for this type of death, though they rarely have anything for which to blame themselves. Many parents are subjected to homicide investigations by the police and social service agency officials. Because child abuse is so common in our society, this is a necessary precaution. However, it adds a great deal more stress to an already devastating situation.

One of the more comprehensive studies about the effects of sudden infant death upon family members finds the following (DeFrain & Ernst, 1978): (1) Sudden infant death was the most severe crisis ever experienced by parents in the study. (2) It required about six months for the family to recover to earlier levels of functioning. (3) It took about sixteen months for the adults to regain the level of personal happiness they enjoyed prior to the death. (4) Most adults experienced feelings of personal guilt as well as physiological and psychological disorders while they were grieving. (5) Within two and a half years, 60 percent of the families had moved from the residence where the infant's death occurred.

Many couples find the support they need by participating in groups designed to assist them, some of which are sponsored by the National SIDS Foundation (Williamson, 1986). As the public becomes more educated about the unpredictability of SIDS, attitudes are changing. People are less likely to blame parents for causing SIDS (Chng, 1982).

Stages of grief and mourning

Many do not realize that there is a difference between grief and the grieving process. Grief is the term used to express the raw emotion associated with loss, whereas the grieving process is the means of coping with grief (Leming & Dickinson, 2006). Emotions associated with grief include a sense of hopelessness, meaninglessness, helplessness, and complete and utter pain and suffering. The grieving process can encompass several stages and one learns to muddle through and manage a life without their loved one.

One must keep in mind that there are many faces to the grieving process. Grieving has emotional, cognitive, cultural, sociological, spiritual, and physical components (Attig, 1991; Leming & Dickinson, 2006). Whereas grief is a passive emotion in which the inflicted has had no choice in partaking, the grieving process provides a means through which grief can be actively addressed.

At the heart of any grieving process is the coping of the loss of a relationship (Leming & Dickinson, 2006). There is now only a "me" instead of a "we," and this shatters one's sense of self. There is no one "right" way to grieve; it is a highly individualized process.

Models of grieving describe not only the stages that individuals go through in reaction to some type of loss, but also the manifestations of grief during those stages (Brasted & Callahan, 1984; Jacobs et al., 1987; James & Cherry, 1988; Spangler & Demi, 1988). One of the primary conclusions of such models is that grieving is a complex, multidimensional process that takes varying periods of time and is experienced with varying degrees of intensity. Its manifestations are physical, emotional, and behavioral. Below, we will examine two different models for the stages of grief. You will notice that there is considerable overlap between the two models; yet, some noticeable differences as well.

The Grief Wheel

Grief wheel

A model of the grieving process described by Spangler and Demi.

Spangler and Demi (1988) present one of the more easily understood models of the grief process (see Figure 10-2). Called the **grief wheel**, it parallels to a certain degree the stages of dying described by Kübler-Ross (1969). The difference is that this model describes grief reactions to any kind of loss and is therefore applicable to people who are affected by the death of a close friend or relative.

According to the grief wheel model, the life path theoretically proceeds in a fairly uneventful manner until, at some point, a loss of some type is experienced. Then there is a period of personal decline and disorganization, until finally, the grieving person is reconciled to the loss and achieves a redefinition of life. The steps in the grieving process of this model are outlined briefly here:

1. *Shock*   The first reaction to loss is shock or confusion and denial. These intrapsychic (emotional and psychological) reactions are health-promoting at this time because they protect people against the initial severity of the loss. The outward manifestations range from the common reaction of crying to symptoms ordinarily associated with depression, such as loss of appetite and sleep disturbances.

2. *Protest*   This next step is characterized by further symptoms of depression, such as guilt and fear. Anger is a prominent outward expression of grief. As people allow themselves to experience the pain of their loss, their adjustment and recovery are enhanced.

3. *Disorganization*   This is the low point of dealing with grief, the "bottoming out" period during which most people must either accept the reality of their loss or continue to function in a disorganized manner. Apathy and withdrawal are hallmarks of

FIGURE 10-2   THE "GRIEF WHEEL" REPRESENTATION OF THE BEREAVEMENT PROCESS

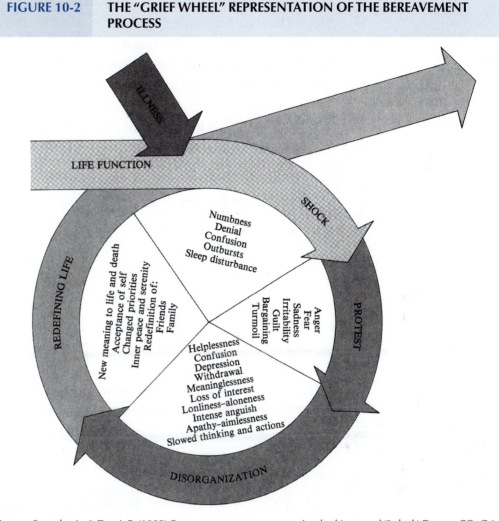

Source: Spangler, J., & Demi, E. (1988) *Bereavement support groups: Leadership annual* (3rd ed.) Denver, CO: Grief Education Institute.

the attempt to draw on inner resources to deal with the grief. Depression may be fully symptomized at this time. Toward the end of this step, people desire to recover the object of their loss. This may explain why people who are grieving have a strong preoccupation with what or whom they have lost. For those who have lost a loved one through death, this preoccupation may be manifested by frequent visits to the grave site, keeping the person's room and belongings exactly as they were when the person died, or being reluctant to discard anything that belonged to the person.

4. *Redefining life*   Almost all theories of grief address the notion that emotional attachment to the love object must be severed for recovery from the loss to be completed. Freud (1917) terms this final aspect **grief work**. It is at this stage that people accept the reality of their loss and begin the business of rebuilding their lives. In order for them to do so, however, they must take the time to be introspective, to fully experience the pain of the loss. Then feelings are freed and they come to terms with a life that does not include the lost person (Worden, 1982). People at the early

Grief work

The stage in which people accept the reality of their loss and begin the business of rebuilding their lives.

part of this step may appear to be emotionally sterile and closed off to relationships. Then they begin to feel again and to come to terms with reality, which enhances recovery. They reassess and redefine personal priorities and goals. Upon completion of this step, the life path or function recovers to the point where it was at the time of the loss. In fact, for those who fully experience grief and use it as an opportunity for personal growth, the model suggests that functioning resumes at a level greater than that known prior to the loss. In other words, adversity has been turned to self-enhancement.

Although this model is useful for understanding the grief process, several cautions should be issued for clarification (Bugen, 1979). First, the stages are not sequential—people may move forward and then regress to an earlier stage, and intrapsychic reactions from more than one stage can be experienced simultaneously. Second, components of the stages tend to blend or overlap; there are often no definite beginnings or endings in time. It is possible for people to spend an indefinite period at each stage as they work through their grief. Third, this model fails to allow for individual differences in the process of grieving. Finally, some people never progress through all the stages of this model and adjust completely to their loss. For them, full recovery may require professional help.

SEVEN BEHAVIORS AND FEELINGS IN THE GRIEVING PROCESS   Kavanaugh (1972) identified seven behaviors and emotions associated with the grieving process, which may be experienced by individuals coping with grief (Leming & Dickinson, 2006). These seven behaviors and emotions are similar in nature to Kübler-Ross's stages of the dying process. We will discuss Kavanaugh's seven components to the grieving process below.

1. *Shock and denial*   Although unexpected deaths are often devastating, even expected deaths can lead to a period of shock and denial. There is a feeling of surrealism and disbelief. The shock provides a sort of safe place to function in until denial sets in for a person. Although often conceived of as a negative process, denial can be adaptive for short periods of time when dealing with death. Denial provides an escape from the feelings of loneliness and devastation that a death can

The shock of a death is the precursor to denial.

cause. Death causes multiple disruptions and problems that must be dealt with—for example, the loss of a husband may mean the loss of a primary breadwinner, best friend, lover, and father of their children. With denial, each of these individual losses can be addressed slowly and separately as cognitive coping ability allows (Leming & Dickinson, 2006).

2. *Disorganization*   In many ways, the period of disorganization after a death can be perceived as a period of existential crisis. The death has caused the person to feel a sense of meaninglessness, purposelessness, and loss of identity. There is a pervading feeling of disconnect with reality and death is somewhat viewed as preferable to life (Leming & Dickinson, 2006).

3. *Volatile reactions*   Emotions run high during this stage of grief. With the loss of identity suffered during disorganization, a sense of being attacked or facing utter destruction can set in. Such "under siege" feelings may be experienced and expressed as anger, horror, resentment, or dread. Some individuals may even go through a period of experiencing feelings of hatred toward their deceased loved one. Other objects of such negative emotions include doctors, God, friends, family members, clergy members, or funeral personnel. Occasionally, negative emotions may become internalized and manifest themselves as physical symptoms, such as headaches or stomach issues (Leming & Dickinson, 2006).

4. *Guilt*   When the emotions associated with grief are internalized, more than just physical symptoms may emerge. In fact, the feeling of guilt is one common manifestation from the internalization of resentment, anger, or trepidation (Leming & Dickinson, 2006). Depression, anxiety, or self-loathing may result.

    Guilt is far from rare when coping with the death of a loved one. Cognitive dissonance in regards to why a loved one had to die while you still live may develop. One way to cope with such cognitive dissonance is to blame the victim. Blaming the victim allows an individual to mitigate the experience of guilt by transferring the negative emotions to either the person who has died or to someone who may (at least in the grieving individual's mind) have prevented the death (Leming & Dickinson, 2006).

5. *Loss and loneliness*   As denial wanes, the reality of loss edges into the grieving person's consciousness. As the grieving individual resumes daily life, the loss of the loved one is experienced at a whole new level. Holidays, traditions, and regular social outings become a regular reminder of the person's death. The grieving individual may recognize the void in his or her life and encounter loneliness. This loneliness may manifest itself as emotions of self-pity, depression, or woe. Even loved ones that were abusive, cruel, or emotionally unavailable are missed, because anyone is better than no one.

    The experience of loss and loneliness in the grief process is ultimately unavoidable. Some individuals may seek refuge again in denial. Others may unwisely seek refuge in shallow or superficial "replacement" marriages, friendships, or relationships. However, genuine relationships alone will help provide any long-term release from loss and loneliness (Leming & Dickinson, 2006).

6. *Relief*   Sometimes in the midst of the grieving process, a sense of relief is experienced. It is not uncommon for someone who has watched a loved one slowly die to think to him or herself, "at least they are at peace now," and experience relief. Occasionally, these feelings of relief can trigger guilt. However, it is important to realize that this relief is not due to negative feelings toward the deceased, but due to an end of suffering and a search for peace and growth in the future (Leming & Dickinson, 2006).

7. *Reestablishment*   Reestablishment is concerned with regaining a sense of purpose and meaning in life, a new sense of normalcy. This process takes time and a person may not even be aware that they are on the path of reestablishment until it is complete and he or she has time to reflect upon the time between the death and the present (Leming & Dickinson, 2006).

It is important to realize that these seven behaviors and feelings neither occur in a linear nor mutually exclusive fashion. A person experiencing relief may suddenly be plunged back into the experience of guilt and loss, then retreat back into denial until he or she is ready to once again deal with the death. The process of grief is highly individualized and no two people grieve in exactly the same manner (Leming & Dickinson, 2006). Bereavement is a messy emotional, cognitive, behavioral, social, and spiritual process; however, as the cliché goes, whatever doesn't kill us makes us stronger in the end.

Tasks of mourning

Spotlight

28. List and describe the four tasks of mourning.

Sometimes, the mourning process is conceptualized as having four necessary tasks that must be addressed before closure can occur (Leming & Dickinson, 2006). These tasks emphasize the necessarily active nature of the mourning process and assert that these tasks must be completed in order for reestablishment to develop. These four tasks, based upon research by the National Institute of Health, include the following:

1. Accept that the loss is real

2. Suffer through the emotional turmoil and misery of grief

3. Adapt to daily life without the deceased

4. Redirect the emotional energy once focused upon the deceased loved one and that relationship to a new and viable relationship

ACCEPTANCE THAT THE LOSS IS REAL   When a death is expected, we can engage in anticipated or preparatory grieving. However, when a death occurs unexpectedly, the reality of the

Viewing photographs of the deceased may help one accept the loss of a loved one.

situation and loss can take some time to accept (Leming & Dickinson, 2006). Viewing the body, talking about the person and his or her death, viewing photographs of the deceased, looking upon the deceased's personal belongings, and passing on these belongings to friends and loved ones are all activities that can assist in this task of mourning.

EXPERIENCE THE PAIN OF GRIEF   The pain of grief is both physical and emotional (Leming & Dickinson, 2006). Tears, deep, soul-wrenching sobbing, headaches, stomach pains, and the like may all be experienced during this task of mourning.

ASSUME NEW SOCIAL ROLES   Someone must assume the social roles previously occupied by the deceased (Leming & Dickinson, 2006). Some social roles include hosting the yearly Thanksgiving meal for the family, organizing family reunions, being the fix-it handyman, or being the fun grandparent who takes the grandkids fishing and camping every summer. Redesignating these social roles is necessary for this task of mourning.

REINVEST IN NEW RELATIONSHIPS   The energy that was previously invested in the relationship with the now deceased person must be redirected during this task of mourning (Leming & Dickinson, 2006). This does not mean that one stops loving the person who has died, but that as humans we crave social interactions and emotional connections. To make relationships work, they require energy, and the energy once devoted to the previous relationship can now be invested in a different relationship.

Factors affecting the grief process

Researchers have identified at least four factors that influence how the grief process is experienced and affect its duration and intensity (Cook & Oltjenbruns, 1989). These are briefly outlined here.

SEX   Researchers find that men and women differ in their reactions to death, especially to the death of a spouse (Galatzer-Levy & Cohler, 1993). After the death of a spouse, women experience more health problems than men (Parkes & Brown, 1972; Sanders, 1979), as well as more death anxiety, feelings of anger, social isolation, depersonalization, and symptoms of depression. Women also feel a greater sense of abandonment after a spouse's death than men do (Glick et al., 1974). Despite all of these problems experienced by women, overall, men have more difficulty adjusting to the death of a spouse than women (Galatzer-Levy & Cohler, 1993). Whereas women feel abandoned, men feel that they have lost a part of themselves. Men take longer to ultimately adjust to life without their soul mate.

Reactions to children's deaths are also dissimilar for men and women. Mothers tend to have a more extreme reaction to the death of a newborn child than fathers do (Peppers & Knapp, 1980; Wing et al., 2001). They also experience more difficulty during the first year following the child's death as they attempt to cope with the holidays, the child's birthday, and the anniversary of the child's death (Cook, 1983; Wing et al., 2001).

There are several speculations as to why men and women differ in their reaction to a child's death, and to grief in general (Wing et al., 2001). Attachment differences between a mother/child and father/child relationship may lead to differences in grief when a loss of the child is experienced. Sex differences in how one orients his or herself to stress and coping in general may lead to sex differences in grieving. Finally, gender roles and social norms and expectations may lead to sex differences in the emotional expression of grief.

AGE   Although painful for both children and adults, expressing bereavement differs with age and level of development (Kaufman & Kaufman, 2006). Because children conceptualize death differently than adults, their reactions are also different (Goldman, 1998; Kaufman & Kaufman, 2006). Young children experience grief even when they do not have an accurate understanding of death. They show physical and psychological manifestations of grief, as discussed in the models of grieving; however, the forms are more appropriate to a child's level of development. For example, bedwetting, regressive overdependent-type behaviors, aggressiveness, temper tantrums, and exaggerated death fantasies are not uncommon (Elizur & Kaffman, 1983). Generally, reactions to grief are intense in young children.

School-age children have a somewhat more refined concept of death than preschoolers, and thus a different pattern of grief. Their reactions to the death of a parent range from feelings of guilt to a desire to protect the surviving parent (Berlinsky & Biller, 1982; Ikeman et al., 1987; Kaffman & Elizur, 1979). One out of five bereaving children shows significant problems two years after a parent's death (Kaufman & Kaufman, 2006). Reactions to the death of a sibling include fears related to illnesses, a desire to learn more about death, and inappropriate acting-out behaviors (Kock-Hatten, 1986; Spinette, Swarner & Sheposh, 1981). Dealing with a death during childhood or the teenage years can increase the risk for academic problems, depression, social withdrawal, anxiety, and a variety of behavioral problems (Kaufman & Kaufman, 2006).

Adolescents might be expected to follow the more adult grief reaction pattern described by Lamers (1978). However, researchers find that behavioral problems occur if adolescents are not encouraged to deal with their grief in an open manner (Aubrey, 1977; Shoor & Speed, 1976). This suggests that adolescents may be helped in their recovery process when they are treated more like adults than children (e.g., by recognizing their ability to participate in funerals or memorial services).

Adult mourning is characterized by the realization that significant social interaction is lost by the death and may vary according to the mourner's personality (e.g., the degree of maturity versus immaturity) (Gut, 1974). When Catherine Sanders (1980a) studied the bereavement of forty-five adults who had lost a spouse, she found differences between the younger (less than sixty-three years) and older (more than sixty-five years) people. Younger surviving spouses showed greater grief for as long as eighteen months after the death of a spouse, but older spouses demonstrated more aggravated reactions. Among people this age, it is probably harder to regain optimism and feelings of belonging.

Sanders (1980b) also reports different intensities of grief according to the age and relationship of the deceased. The parents of a child who has died show greater grief reactions than people who have lost a spouse or an older parent. This researcher reports that frequent church attendees were less likely to respond with great outward pessimism, but showed more repressed bereavement responses. Most interesting was the finding of no differences in bereavement intensities between those adults whose loved one died after a chronic illness and those whose loved one died suddenly and unexpectedly. Additionally, middle-aged people show greater declines in health status than young adults or the elderly (Perkins & Harris, 1990). They may be more vulnerable to the hazards placed on their health by bereavement than the young or the old because of the multiple types of stresses in their lives.

Those that are more vulnerable to a loss tend to center their lives and well-being around their relationship with a significant other.

PERSONALITY   In general, those who have a dependent personality are more vulnerable to a difficult grief reaction than others (Gut, 1974; Parkes & Brown, 1972). These individuals generally rely on significant others for approval, have a low tolerance for frustration, and have high levels of anxiety. They tend to center their emotional lives and well-being around their relationship with a significant other. When this person dies or is otherwise lost from their life, they are likely to experience severe depression, a lengthy bereavement, and a less optimistic prognosis for recovery.

CULTURE   Cultural guidelines for appropriate grieving behavior tell people how to express their grief. For example, our culture as a whole generally tends to prescribe that mourning the dead should be done in private.

Some funeral homes or mortuaries even provide what is termed a "grieving room" for family members. This room may be fitted with a large window covered by a mesh curtain so the family can view the funeral but the audience cannot view the family. The intent is to protect the family's privacy during the highly emotional event of their loved one's funeral. Exceptions to this practice of private mourning can be found, however. Some African-American subcultures, for example, permit unrestrained emotional reactions at funerals (Charmaz, 1980).

Family rituals

Rituals are used by a culture to formalize certain events and to give them meaning. We have a variety of rituals that recognize birth and other life events. Birthdays, for instance, are recognized in a ritualized manner by celebrations, special cakes, making a wish before blowing out the cake candles, and singing "Happy Birthday." These rituals are known to virtually everyone in the United States (a very small percentage of religious groups reject the birthday ritual).

A number of rituals are associated with death, although the United States seems to be currently experiencing a crisis in regards to death rituals. These rituals have traditionally assisted families and friends to formally recognize the close of their relationship as it had been known with the person who has died. Rituals are important because they promote acceptance of death rather than denial. They also are important because they help people to express feelings in nonverbal ways, which facilitates the bereavement process (Conley, 1987).

A fading, yet perhaps best-known, ritual associated with death is the funeral or memorial service. This ritual serves certain functions for families and friends. It recognizes the person's life; sanctions public mourning of the person's death; facilitates the bereavement process; allows the functioning of social support networks such as kinship groups to the immediate family; and establishes new social statuses for both the person who has died (the deceased) and those who survive (the bereaved) (Charmaz, 1980; Fulton, 1987).

Traditionally, other rituals accompany the funeral or memorial service. These may include internment of the ashes in a respectful manner; having a military tribute; throwing a fistful of dirt on the person's casket as it is lowered into the ground; participating in a wake prior to the funeral; selecting certain pieces of clothing for the deceased person's burial; placing mementos in the person's casket before the burial; viewing the person's body as it lies in state; and releasing helium-inflated balloons at the conclusion of the funeral to symbolize the release of the person's spirit through death.

Customarily, other rituals may follow the funeral or memorial service: the reading of the person's will; sorting through and disposing of the dead person's personal effects; voluntary removal of a wedding ring by the widow or widower; visiting the grave and supervising the installation of the headstone; and responding to gestures of sympathy made by family and friends. All of these traditional rituals are thought to help people in their grief work.

Grief therapy

At some time in our lives, most of us will feel called upon to provide support for someone who is grieving some loss. Fortunately, most people are able to successfully accomplish their grief work. However, it is useful to know some general guidelines when called upon to help someone in this process. Cook and Oltjenbruns (1989) suggest that anyone who wants to provide support to a grieving person should:

1. Give the person permission to grieve by listening and providing appropriate supportive statements.

2. Support the grief work in ways that are meaningful to the person.

3. Encourage expressions of grief by appropriately recognizing them.

4. Support the person's acceptance of the loss by acting as a mirror of reality.

5. Listen as the person shares his or her grief work.

6. Share any information known about the normal grief responses and process.

7. Assist in ways that are meaningful to the person, such as helping with housework and taking care of children.

All of these gestures show care, concern, and sympathy for the surviving person's well-being and assist that person through the grief process. Sometimes, however, people need professional assistance because their grieving is blocked or inhibited or because they are "stuck" at one step in the grief process. **Grief therapy** consists of specific psychotherapeutic methods for helping people move toward recovery (James & Cherry, 1988). Besides individual therapy work with a professional, self-help books and support groups can greatly aid people to deal with a difficult grieving process. In the next section, we will explore a type of grief, **complicated grief**, which may require such intervention.

Grief therapy

Professional counseling specifically aimed at helping individuals who experience difficulty in completing their grief process.

Complicated grief

Grief that involves an adjustment disorder or interferes with a person's ability to function in everyday life.

Helping children cope with loss

A child's stage of development (cognitively and socioemotionally) greatly influences his or her ability to recognize the finality of death and the grief response (Bagshaw, 1998; Graham, 2004). A child's adaptive capacities are challenged when facing a loss. Protective factors such as a sense of purpose and problem-solving abilities are taxed. A child's resiliency is tested in ways never before imagined. Social support is of paramount importance.

When children are coping with a death, be it a pet, a classmate, or a relative, it is important to answer their questions honestly. It is best to follow a grieving child's lead and to respect his or her process of coping (Jalongo, 2005).

Programs, such as Seasons for Growth, have been developed to help children cope with loss due to death or divorce (Graham, 2004). Individual bereavement counseling is also an option. The goal is to assist the child to adapt to the loss by recognizing emotions,

Children face many challenges when they suffer a loss. It is important to be supportive during this time.

appropriately sharing and expressing emotions, reducing a sense of isolation, and teaching healthy problem-solving, decision-making, and coping strategies.

Below are some strategies for helping a child to express and work through grief (Children's Grief Network, 2006; Cunningham, 2009; Graham, 2004; Kaufman & Kaufman, 2006):

- Art therapy

- Mime

- Role-playing

- Stories

- Discussion

- Playdough

- Music

- Journaling

- Doll or puppet play

- Poetry

- Creating a family tree

- Memory boxes or collages

- Creating a loss timeline

- Children's stories about death and grieving

- Bibliotherapy

The goal is to express emotions and to develop a new sense of normalcy (Graham, 2004). To have healthy grief, a child must be provided the opportunity to express their loss in a meaningful way (Kaufman & Kaufman, 2006). Research has shown that grief programs and social support groups promote positive outcomes for children and adolescents dealing with loss. Some outcomes include a more positive attitude, a greater sense of happiness, better communication and coping skills, and a lower sense of isolation.

Complicated grief and bereavement counseling: Sometimes the grieving process becomes blocked or unresolved. When grief is not being actively dealt with and is interfering with one's ability to function in daily life, complicated grief could be the cause. It is as though there is a wall between a person's grief and mind, and counseling can help break the wall down (Children's Grief Network, 2006).

Complicated grief may develop for several reasons (Children's Grief Network, 2006; Kaufman & Kaufman, 2006). Contributing factors include: a sudden or traumatic death (such as homicide or suicide); a social stigma attached to the death (such as AIDS or abortion); when a person has experienced multiple losses within a short window of time; if the relationship with the deceased was conflict-ridden; or when there is a lack of social support to assist with grieving. Therapy can help individuals of all ages work through their complicated grief and learn to be happy again.

Pause and Process:

1. What is the difference between grief and the grieving process?

2. What are the tasks of grieving?

SOCIAL ASPECTS OF DEATH

American death rituals

Although there is no set standard that all Americans prescribe to in terms of a death ritual, there tends to be a common process most Americans experience. Funerals and memorial services serve multiple purposes following the death of a loved one (Dickinson & Leming, 2008). First, they provide a means of disposing of the body. Second, family and friends are provided a forum in which to remember and reminisce about the person's life. Third, seeing the body or casket assists in accepting the reality of the death. Fourth, the funeral or memorial service is a rite of passage, after which, mourners are expected to return to their daily life and tasks.

Most Americans (79 percent) choose to have a traditional ground burial (Dickinson & Leming, 2008). Cremation, although growing in popularity, is chosen by 21 percent of Americans. Regardless, our cultural norms require that the deceased be treated with dignity and regard; burials and internment of ashes fulfill this norm (Leming & Dickinson, 2006; Lynch, 2007).

Children benefit emotionally by being allowed to participate in the death rituals, such as eulogies, writing the obituary, or attending the funeral (Kaufman & Kaufman, 2006; Leming & Dickinson, 2006). Once again, children's questions should be answered honestly, but at their level (i.e., you don't need to go into the intricate details of how the person died). Children often provide emotional support to the grieving adults (Jalongo, 2005; Leming & Dicksonson, 2006).

Death rituals are in a time of transition in America (Basler, 2004; Whalen, 1990). There is a movement toward "green" burials. **Green burials** and graveyards work to support the environment while still respecting the deceased. Examples include using biodegradable caskets and integrating forests and conservation efforts with graveyards.

There is also a move toward "quicky" funerals (Whalen, 1990). A current fad includes drive-up windows at funeral homes through which mourners can quickly view the body and sign the condolence book (the culture of convenience at its finest). Other places offer time-share cemetery plots, where the body is placed and mourned for a specified amount of time, after which that body is disposed of and the plot is made available for the next fresh body (scary, but true).

Green burials

The use of biodegradable caskets and integrating forests and conservation efforts with graveyards.

Religious traditions

In the previous section, we discussed the bare bones of the death rituals in America. However, many religious traditions offer richer and more intricate death rituals (Whalen, 1990). We will highlight just a few here.

The Hindu people traditionally have a ceremony called the Shraddha (Whalen, 1990). The body is washed, clothed in a shroud covered with flowers, and carried to a pyre. A male relative lights the fire and engages in reciting sacred verses as he walks around the body. The body must be cremated so that the spirit moves on to its next life. After

Religious traditions regarding death are varied. For example, the Hindu ceremony called the Shraddha calls for the body to be washed, clothed in a shroud and covered in flowers. It is then carried to a pyre to be cremated.

three days pass, the ashes are collected and temporarily buried. About a week and a half later, the ashes are retrieved and placed in a sacred river. The son of the deceased recites prayers and invokes the spirits and support of ancestors (which is one reason why male babies are desired more than female babies).

Whereas the Hindu and Buddhists embrace cremation, Muslims and Baha'i forbid it (Whalen, 1990). People of the Muslim and Baha'i faith bury the body shortly after death. In some Muslim communities, the cultural norm is for women to wail at the funeral loudly in a show of their grief.

The Catholic Church has funeral rites laid out in the Order of Christian Funerals. The focus is upon the person's soul entering purgatory or heaven (Johnson, 1994). In the Catholic faith, purgatory can be conceptualized as "a temporary state of purification for those destined for heaven but not yet totally free from the effects of sin and selfishness" (Whalen, 1990, p. 153). Additionally, the Church recognizes that this is a time of terrible grief for family and friends and works to help them in their suffering. Below we will discuss the three steps of the Catholic funeral rite, in which the family and friends are encouraged to help. These steps help provide a process of support and healing for the bereaved (Johnson, 1994).

The first step in a Catholic funeral is a **vigil** (Johnson, 1994). The vigil can take place in a funeral parlor, a home, or a church. The body may or may not be there, it is open to personal preferences. The vigil is short in duration and focuses mainly on prayer, although readings and music are also included.

The second step in a Catholic funeral is the funeral liturgy, which takes place at a Catholic church (Johnson, 1994). This liturgy (which includes readings and a homily) may take place within a mass or on its own. The body may or may not be present, depending on personal preferences. There is not, however, any eulogy. The focus is on God's love and mercy and the promise of eternal life. "You're supposed to console and strengthen the community in their loss, not to dwell on somebody's past accomplishments in the face of the great equalization of death" (Johnson, 1994, p. 89).

The third and final step in the Catholic funeral is the **rite of committal**. Here, the person's body or ashes is sprinkled with holy water, possibly incensed, and placed in its final resting place.

Although we have touched upon the religious death rituals for the Hindu, Muslim, Buddhist, Baha'i, and Catholic faiths, these are just the tip of the iceberg. Judaism, Protestant faiths, Mormons, and Freemasons all have their own religious death traditions that offer comfort during a time of distress and loss (Whalen, 1990).

Historical and cultural perspectives on death

We cannot begin to do justice to the rich history and diversity of death perspectives and traditions in this small space. From the mummification of Egyptians to the Viking kings set afloat on burning ships, cultures across history have found ways to show respect to the dead and send them on their journey to the afterlife (Whalen, 1990).

Vigil

The first step in a Catholic funeral that may take place in a funeral parlor, a home, or a church. The vigil is short in duration and focuses mainly on prayer, although readings and music are also included.

Rite of committal

The third and final step in a Catholic funeral where the person's body or ashes is sprinkled with holy water, possibly incensed, and placed in its final resting place.

Although culture shapes death rituals, death can shape culture. The black death of the Middle Ages brought about a child's rhyme that is still popular today: Ring around the rosies, a pocketful of posies, ashes, ashes, we all fall down. "The meaning of the rhyme was that life could be unimaginably beautiful—and the reality unbearably horrible" (Cantor, 2001, p. 40). The bubonic plague killed around one-third of Western Europe's population and contributed to shifts in politics and religion that are still evident in the culture today. Hence, death shapes life as much as life shapes death.

Pause and Process:

1. What does the traditional American death ritual entail?

2. What are some religious traditions in regard to death?

SUMMARY

1. The definition of death has changed from earlier times to reflect advances in medical technology used to sustain life. Dying is understood today to be the final stage of the life span, a process in which certain steps are taken to prepare for impending death. Death can occur at any point of the life span for reasons related to age and developmental stage of the individual. The leading causes of death changed during the twentieth century (from infections to chronic degenerative diseases), as has the place where death usually occurs (from the home to an institution).

2. There are different dying trajectories and phases of death. Each trajectory and phase has its own characteristics and issues that must be addressed. Terminal decline is the curious occurrence that cognitive declines can predict impending death.

3. Advance directives allow you to dictate what medical interventions and treatment you would want if incapacitated. The Terri Schindler-Schiavo case highlighted the importance of writing down your wishes in the event that some tragic accident or illness happens.

4. End of life care is better than ever. Pain can be managed more than in the past, and palliative and hospice care help address the dying person's physical, emotional, psychological, social, and spiritual needs. Physician-assisted suicide is gaining momentum in the United States; however, it may prove a slippery slope as we watch our European nations report its use on newborns without parental consent and the mentally ill who cannot possibly give informed consent.

5. Attitudes about dying and death are formed early in the life span but are modified as individuals experience refinements in their cognitive abilities and develop maturity. Attitudes about dying and death among older individuals differ from those of children and adolescents. Many life events in adulthood assist people to prepare for their own eventual death. By learning to cope with change and loss throughout the years of adulthood, individuals may come to have less death anxiety in late adulthood.

6. Most individuals experience dying as a process. This process varies from person to person. The

stages that many people go through before death happens are highly individualistic. That said, Kübler-Ross offered a theory for five stages of facing death that is useful in understanding certain stages that an individual may experience.

7. Grief and bereavement are interchangeable terms that refer to the normal response to personal loss. Mourning refers to the ways people express grief.

8. One hazard of pregnancy is the chance of loss through miscarriage, stillbirth, or SIDS. Because these are unanticipated events, they are highly problematic to parents and other family members. Parents' grief reactions include anger, guilt, confusion, preoccupation with thoughts of the child, sadness, loss of appetite, sleeping disorders, and irritability. Participation in community support groups or church ministry groups may assist parents to work through their grief.

9. Grieving is a process that involves several stages characterized by internal and external behaviors. There is no set duration or intensity for bereavement, but grief recovery is a realistic goal. Factors that influence the grief process include the person's sex, age, personality, and cultural background. Social rituals help people in their grieving process. Some of these are associated with the funeral or memorial services, whereas others take place afterward. When people are unable to resolve their grief on their own, specialized therapy aimed at alleviating blocks to progress toward recovery can be very helpful.

10. The traditional, generic death ritual in America is a funeral or memorial service. This ritual assists individuals to accept the death and find closure. Different religions have different rites. Death has shaped history and death rites vary across time and culture.

SELF-QUIZ

1. What was the historical definition of biological death? How has this definition changed in recent decades?

2. Explain the Harvard Medical School criteria for declaring someone dead.

3. How did the Uniform Determination of Death Act define death?

4. What is the difference between whole-brain death and partial-brain death?

5. Describe what is meant by psychological death and social death.

6. What are the leading causes of death across the childhood and adolescent years?

7. What are the leading causes of death across the adult years?

8. Explain how the Terri Schindler-Shiavo case taught the American public about the importance of having an advanced directive.

9. What characterizes a "good death"?

10. How is palliative care different from hospice care?

11. Describe developmental changes in attitudes toward death.

12. What are some of the physical needs and concerns of the dying?

13. Explain the emotional needs and concerns of the dying.

14. Describe the social needs and concerns of the dying.

15. What are some of the psychological needs of the dying?

16. Discuss the spiritual needs and concerns of the dying.

17. What are some suggestions on how to interact with a dying person?

18. How can you support a person in mourning?

19. Define death anxiety in your own words.

20. Describe the stages of dying.

21. Explain what is meant by bereavement.

22. What is the difference between grief and mourning?

23. Clarify the distinction between a miscarriage and a stillbirth.

24. Define what is meant by neonatal death.

25. List the factors associated with contributing to SIDS.

26. Describe the stages of the grief wheel.

27. Explain the seven behaviors and feelings involved in the grieving process.

28. List and describe the four tasks of mourning.

29. Describe and characterize the developmental differences in bereavement across the life span.

30. How do the traditional American death rituals compare with some of the religious death rituals described in this chapter?

TERMS AND CONCEPTS

Glossary

Abrupt-surprise pattern   The person is expected to recover but dies instead.

Accommodation   Changes made in a personal scheme in order to bring about a better match with reality; in vision, the ability of the eyes to focus quickly and efficiently on objects both near and far away.

Acne   A chronic inflammation of the oil glands and hair follicles located in the facial area.

Acquisition period   A shift in cognition seen in childhood and adolescence.

Active genotype-environment correlation   An environment that the child seeks due to genetic preferences.

Acute   A form of organic brain syndrome that is reversible in many cases.

Acute phase   A crisis accompanied by high personal stress associated with increasing awareness of the inevitability of death.

Adaptive expertise   An approach to problems that is characterized by flexibility and promotes life-long learning.

Adaptive features   Those features that are conducive to survival in a given environment, whatever those features may be.

Adaptive reflexes   This group of reflexes aids the neonate to locate and obtain food, thus helping to ensure its survival.

Adolescence   The fifth stage of the life span, occurring between thirteen and eighteen years of age.

Adult stem cells   Stem cells obtained from patients or donors found in numerous tissues and organ systems, even fat.

Adulthood   The period of the life span following adolescence.

Advanced directive   A written document explicating what medical measures you would like employed if you lose the capacity to make such decisions. You can also elucidate who you would like to make these decisions for you if you become incapacitated.

Affect intensity   One's intensity of emotion.

Affective complexity   The appearance of older adults having more complex emotional experiences compared with younger adults.

Afterbirth   The final stage of labor which involves the expulsion of the placenta and the membranes as well as any remaining amniotic fluid from a woman's uterus.

Age of viability   The point in prenatal development where the baby stands a chance of surviving outside of the womb.

Ageism   Unreasonable or irrational beliefs about aging and older individuals.

Aggression   Any hostile act that causes fear in others and leads to forceful contact; may be verbal or physical and directed at people as well as objects.

Aging   A complex process involving a decline in physiological competence that inevitably increases the incidence and intensifies the effects of accidents, disease, and other forms of environmental stress.

Agreeableness   The degree to which a person is trusting, giving, and kind.

Alzheimer's disease   A degenerative chronic brain disorder occurring commonly in late adulthood. It is characterized initially by forgetfulness, later by serious cognitive dysfunction; and eventually by complete loss of mental functioning and death.

Amniocentesis   The withdrawal of a sample of amniotic fluid (which includes the baby's sloughed off skin cells) from the mother's uterus.

Amniotic fluid stem cells   Stem cells found in amniotic fluid.

Aneurysm   A rupture of an artery wall within the brain.

Animism   The belief of young children that all things, including objects, are alive.

Anorexia nervosa   An eating disorder involving complex emotional and body image disturbances that lead to an obsession with limiting dietary intake in order to control body weight. The condition is life-threatening if left untreated.

Anoxia   Oxygen starvation of tissues.

Anterior attention system   Includes the brain areas such as the prefrontal cortex.

Apgar score   An evaluation method for assessing the health status of a newborn.

Apparent hypocrisy   The considerable incongruence between what they say they believe and how they behave.

Armored-defended   A personality type where the individual strives to maintain control over their lives.

Arteriosclerosis   A condition usually occurring in advanced cases of atherosclerosis in which there is a gradual loss of elasticity in arterial vessels. The end result is high blood pressure or hypertension.

Arthritis   Inflammation of the joint area between bone junctions.

Articulation disorders   Disorders in which a person struggles to produce appropriate speech.

Association   The ability to form a connection between a stimuli and a response.

Associative play   Engaging in a common activity and interacting with others.

Atherosclerosis   A cardiovascular disease in which plaques of fatty material form along arterial walls in the body and especially in the heart. This leads to blockage of blood flow and the possibility of clots, increasing the likelihood of heart attack and stroke.

Attachment   A strong affectional tie or emotional or emotional bond between two individuals.

Attachment theory   Intense emotional tie between two individuals, such as an infant and a parent.

Attention deficit/hyperactivity disorder   A disorder that causes children to be highly distractible and energetic. It is caused by a chemical imbalance in the brain leading to difficulties in regulating attention, impulsivity, and hyperactivity.

Attitude of initiative   A feeling of confidence.

Authoritarian parenting style   Parents that display discipline, but show little affection.

Authoritative parenting style   Parents that display both affection and discipline.

Autoimmune responsiveness theory   As people grow older their immune system begins to attack the body's own tissues.

Autonomy   Refers to establishing personal boundaries and self-differentiation from things and others.

Autosomes   A single chromosome; any one of the forty-six chromosomes found in the nucleus of a human cell.

Average   A child with a small group of friends, who is neither greatly disliked nor considered popular.

Avoidant-insecure attachment style   An infant does not seem to care if the mother leaves or returns.

Axon   Takes information from the neuron away to be sent to other neurons.

Babinski reflex   Named for its discoverer, this reflex occurs when the sole of the baby's foot is stroked along the outer edge. In response, the neonate's toes spread wide in a fanning action, relax somewhat, curl forward tightly closed, and return to their original position.

Baby blues   Feelings of sadness and exhaustion that over 70 percent of women experience the first week or two after birth.

Baby boomer generation   Individuals born between 1946 and 1964.

Balance   The ability to maintain equilibrium and stability.

Basic nursing care   Basic care provided to all hospital patients (such as food and cleaning of wounds).

Basic processes   "Frequently used, rapidly executed, memory activities such as association, generalization, recognition, and recall. They are among the building blocks of cognition, in the sense that all more complex cognitive activities are built by combining them in different ways."

Basic trust   The sense that others are predictable and can be relied on.

Bereavement   A term used interchangeably with grief to describe a natural or expected response to personal loss.

Big five factors personality theory   A theory that posits that there are five super-traits that are the foundation of personality.

Bilateral coordination   The coordinated, integrated use of both sides of the body in performing motor acts.

Bioecological theory   A theory by Bronfenbrenner that emphasizes the nested environments that influence human development.

Biological age   How old an individual's body is based on health.

Biological death   Historically defined as when the heart stopped beating and respiration ceased, leading to the cessation of brain function.

Birth order   The order in which children are born in a family.

Blended family   A family unit consisting of an adult male and female couple, one of whom has remarried, and the children of one or both from a previous marriage; a new term for stepfamily.

Bodily-kinesthetic intelligence   The mental ability to control one's body in a purposeful way.

Body transcendence versus body preoccupation   The necessity of finding happiness and satisfaction in relating to others and in creative or mental endeavors for healthy development to occur.

Braxton-Hicks contractions   Practice contractions by the uterus.

Breech   When a child is upside down for delivery, with the bottom being delivered first.

Bulimia   An eating disorder involving emotional and body image disturbances that lead to intake of large amounts of food that are then purged by vomiting or use of laxatives to control body weight.

Bullying   An aggressive behavior (words, actions, or social exclusion) which intentionally hurts or harms another person; the behavior occurs repetitiously and creates a power imbalance such that it is difficult for the victim to defend him or herself.

Caring   Having empathy and concern for others.

Cataracts   A change in the lens of the eye causing it to become opaque to entering light, which reduces vision considerably

Cell body   Contains the parts of the cell to keep it alive and functioning (such as the nucleus).

Cellular clock theory   When biological errors in the DNA genetic code accumulate, the cells are unable to function at all and die.

Centering   A cognitive trait in early childhood that limits information processing to only one aspect or characteristic rather than several simultaneously.

Cephalic presentation   Head first delivery.

Cephalocaudal growth pattern   Changes occur in the head region of the body, both internally and externally in advance of those occurring toward the abdominal region.

Cerebrovascular disease   A category for death related to the blood vessels in the brain such as a stroke.

Character   Having a moral compass and integrity.

Childproofing   Arranging and adapting housing and physical space (e.g., by capping electrical outlets) to meet safety concerns for infants.

Chorionic villus sampling   A procedure by which chorionic villi (hairlike structures that are the predecessors of the placenta) are removed and analyzed to determine if genetic disease is present.

Chromosomal disorder   A disorder due to a chromosomal abnormality or defect.

Chromosomes   A collection of genes contained within a cell nucleus; the total number per cell is constant for each species, with humans having forty-six in each cell, except for the gametes, which have twenty-three.

Chronic   A form of organic brain syndrome that is not reversible.

Chronic living-dying phase   The person adjusts to the idea of approaching death, and experiences a variety of feelings such as grief, fear of the unknown, and isolation.

Chronological age   The number of years that have passed since an individual's birth (or conception in some cultures).

Circular reactions   Actions that occur by chance and then are repeated and modified through practice.

Class inclusion   A cognitive ability of middle childhood that allows a child to consider the whole as well as its parts in classification operations.

Classical conditioning   The pairing of a neutral stimulus with an unconditioned stimulus in order to achieve a desired response.

Classification   The cognitive ability to group objects according to traits of similarity or likeness.

Classification and categorization skills   The ability to use salient features to place objects or constructs into distinct groups.

Client-centered therapy   Also known as person-centered therapy, it is a non-directive approach to therapy based upon humanistic theory. This approach believes that the client has the necessary inner resources to cope with his or her problems.

Climacteric   Decline in sexual functioning among middle-aged men.

Clique   A smaller group of friends that are similar in appearance, demographics, and activities.

Codified   Math that is written.

Codominance   Occurs when both alleles are fully expressed.

Cognition   Those processes, such as perception, thinking, reasoning, and problem solving, by which one comes to know and understand the world.

Cognitive conceit   A characteristic of thought in middle childhood in which individuals perceive situations and people in black-and-white, all-or-nothing.

Cognitive domain   Changes in intellectual or mental functioning.

Cognitive flexibility   The ability to shift from one thinking style to another.

Cohabitation   Living with a romantic partner prior to marriage.

Cohabitation effect   The increased risk for divorce associated with cohabitation.

Cohort   A group of individuals having a statistical factor (as age or class membership) in common in a demographic study.

Collagen   A fibrous protein that is a basic component of connective tissue.

Colostrum   The first liquid secreted by the mammary glands, full of antibodies and nutrition.

Communicative disorders   Any disorder that impairs one's ability to communicate.

Companionate relationship   A grandparent-grandchildren relationship described as an easy-going, friendly relationship that involves emotionally-satisfying leisure-time.

Competence   An individual's skills, abilities, and proficiency within a specific domain, such as school, relationships, or sports.

Complicated grief Grief that involves an adjustment disorder or interferes with a person's ability to function in everyday life.

Conception The fertilization of an ovum by a sperm cell.

Concrete operations The stage of cognitive development experienced in middle childhood in which thought becomes more logical and based on immediate physical realities and mental imagery abilities become more refined.

Conditionalized knowledge The skill experts have in retrieving the specific information that they need for any given problem.

Confidence Having certainty in one's ability.

Congenital anomalies Birth defects or chromosomal abnormalities that are incompatible with life.

Connections An individual's relationships with others and feelings as though one belongs.

Conscientiousness The degree to which a person values and/or needs organization, precision, and self-discipline.

Conservation The understanding that the essential characteristics of something are preserved even though it is rearranged in different ways.

Contagion The second stage for understanding of illness as "caused by people or objects that are proximate to, but not touching, the child."

Continuous variation When a trait or variation is distributed on a continuum or spectrum.

Control group The group that receives the placebo.

Control phase The period where necessary changes and or adaptations are made in the approach to the learning task.

Controversial Children who are liked by many peers, and disliked by many peers.

Conventional level Moral reasoning that consists of conformity to the rules of important groups.

Cooperative play The integration of several children into group play where different roles are assumed.

Cooperatively The willingness to play with one another.

Coordination The ability to use various muscle groups together to accomplish specific actions.

Co-regulation The shift to greater sharing and balance of social power between parents and children during the Family and School-age Children stage of the family life career.

Correlational research The study of relationship existence between two or more variables.

Co-sleeping Parents and children sleep in the same bed.

Crawling Locomotion with the abdomen on a surface.

Creeping Locomotion by moving the hands and knees with the abdomen off the surface.

Cross-sectional A research design that compares measurements or observations of some particular trait or behavior between groups of people of different ages at the same time.

Crowds A large mixed-sex group of older children or adolescents who have similar values and attitudes and are known by a common label.

Cruising Walking using the assistance of objects or people.

Crystallized intelligence Skills acquired through education and socialization such as verbal skills, mathematical skills, inductive reasoning, and interpersonal skills; the ability to recall and use information.

Curvilinear relationship In this type of correlation, two variables increase or decrease together up to a point, then switch to a negative correlation where one variable increases while the other decreases.

Death anxiety A fundamental fear of death shared by most people.

Death   The cessation of all observable or measurable physical signs of life (physical death); related aspects are social and psychological death.

Decentering   The cognitive ability that allows a school-age child to attend to more than one aspect simultaneously in performing classification operations.

Deciduous teeth   The primary or first set of sixteen teeth that erupt when an infant is between five and seven and one half months of age.

Deductive reasoning   Beginning with the big picture and developing conclusions.

Delay gratification   The ability to put off something pleasurable and rewarding and work hard in the here and now.

Dementia   A type of organic brain syndrome that is a neuropsychiatric disorder related to brain cell impairment.

Dendrites   Receives information from other neurons.

Dentition   The shedding of one set of teeth and the eruption of another.

Deoxyribonucleic acid (DNA)   A complex molecule composed of four basic nucleotides that is the carrier of genetic inheritance.

Dependent variable   A variable that is measured in an experimental study; the outcome of an experimental study.

Depression   A disease that involves a person's thoughts, emotions, and feelings.

Descriptive research   Research that seeks to describe a phenomenon.

Developmental tasks   The unique characteristics and tasks that help define each stage of life span.

Diabetes   The failure of the pancreas gland cells to secrete an adequate amount of an enzyme (insulin) that is essential for metabolizing sugars.

Dialectical reasoning   The deliberate coordination of inferences for the purpose of making cognitive progress.

Dialectical thinking   A style of thinking in adulthood in which individuals appear to accept and may even relish contradictions and conflicts in values.

Difficult temperament   The resisting of physical handling, crying inconsolably, and showing irregular sleeping and eating patterns.

Discontinuous variation   When a trait or variation can be placed into distinct categories.

Disenchantment stage   In the aftermath of the honeymoon phase, emotional depression settles in as people come to realize that they have actually fully withdrawn from a constant and fulfilling social role in their lives.

Disorganized/disoriented attachment style   An infant that lacks a cohesive strategy in coping with the strange situation.

Diverticulitis   An inflammation of a portion of an intestine that causes pain, nausea, and a change in bowel habits.

Dominant   A gene from one parent that controls or suppresses the influence of the complementary (recessive) gene from the other parent in the offspring.

Dopamine   A neurotransmitter that is responsible for smooth and coordinated movement of the muscles in the body.

Double-blind study   An experiment where neither the researcher nor the participants are aware of who is receiving the actual treatment or who is receiving the placebo.

Doula   A professional labor coach.

Duration   The time the process takes.

Dying   The complex process leading to death, characterized by an individual's particular dying trajectory.

Dying trajectories   Representations of the duration and shape of the dying process.

Easy temperament   A baby who is adaptable, cheerful and happy, and responsive to others and situations.

Ectopic   A pregnancy that develops in a location outside the uterus.

Ego   The rational part of our psyche which tries to balance the needs of the id and superego.

Ego differentiation versus work-role preoccupation The adjustments that must be made to retirement from work roles.

Ego transcendence versus ego preoccupation Recognizing and accepting one's impending death by living life as fully as possible and attempting to make life more secure, more satisfying, and more meaningful for those who will survive after one's death.

Egocentrism A cognitive trait that limits a child's understanding of the world to their own perceptions.

Elderly The term describing individuals in late adulthood who are sixty-five years of age or older.

Elderspeak A style of speech used when speaking with older adults. It is similar to infant-directed speech in which speech is simplified, spoken slowly, and higher in pitch and intonation.

Embryo The name of the developing individual during the embryonic period.

Embryonic period The two weeks after conception until around eight weeks after conception.

Embryonic stem cells Stem cells obtained from human embryos that result in the death of the embryo.

Emotional intelligence The ability to recognize the emotions of others and regulate one's own emotions while effectively utilizing emotions in adaptive and skillful ways.

Emotions Subjective feelings such as love or joy that help to define our existence as human beings.

Empathy The ability to comprehend accurately the thoughts, feelings, and actions of others.

Emphysema A condition involving destruction of lung tissue that results in lowered lung elasticity.

Empty nest The period of the post-parental stage of the family life cycle when a couple phase out their active parenting responsibilities.

Encoding Developing an internal, mental representation of the situation.

Entry-reentry pattern The person experiences steady decline, but is able to remain at home between periods of hospitalization.

Epigenetic information A characteristic of developmental changes meaning that changes that are currently observed were determined by those that occurred earlier in time, and changes that follow will be influenced by the ones currently being observed.

Episodic memory Specific life event memories.

Equipotentiality The ability for a cell to develop into any type of cell in the body.

Ethnic harassment A workplace environment where verbal assaults are targeted toward individuals because of their ethnicity.

Ethnographic research A specific type of naturalistic research largely used in anthropology, education, and cultural studies.

Ethology The field of inquiry that studies the biological bases of behavior patterns in animals and humans.

Euthanasia The willful ending of a life that is not a consequence of a disease, illness, or injury.

Evocative genotype-environment correlation An environment in which the child elicits certain environments or behaviors due to his or her genetics.

Evolutionary theory Those theories of developmental change that are founded on Darwin's theory of evolution; these theories stress the role of biological factors in the individual's adaptation to the environment.

Existential intelligence The mental ability to contemplate the purpose and meaning of life and issues surrounding death and what comes after death.

Experimental group The group that receives the experimental treatment.

Experimental research Seeks to establish cause and effect relationships.

Experimenter bias The influence of the experimenter's expectations or behavior in an experiment.

Expertise   Having extensive experience, knowledge, and understanding within a specific area of interest.

Explicit memories   Conscious memories that can be visualized as well as provide a verbal account.

Explicit memory   The information that you purposely try to recall, such as when you tell a friend about a movie you just watched.

Explicit-theoretical approaches   Seek to empirically study wisdom in an objective and scientific way.

Exploratory play   Object oriented play.

Extrinsic motivation   A person's drive to learn because of what he or she will receive in doing so.

Extroversion   The degree to which a person is outgoing.

Fair-weather cooperation   The second stage of friendship perception that typically occurs between the ages of eight to ten where ideas of reciprocity and adapting to friends' likes and dislikes govern the early friendship.

Family systems theory   The approach that theorizes that families operate as a system in the ways they make decisions and take actions that govern behavior, help the group meet its goals, and enable the group to maintain stability over time.

Fast-mapping   A language skill used by young children; the meaning of a new word is acquired by comparing it with one that is familiar.

Fear   A reaction that involves physical and/or psychological agitation and dreadful anticipation of real or imagined danger to one's safety.

Fertilization   The penetration of the ovum by a sperm cell.

Fetal alcohol syndrome   A disorder that may include physical abnormalities and cognitive deficits due to a mother drinking alcohol during pregnancy.

Fetal medicine   Any medical intervention or care directed at the developing, in utero individual.

Fetal period   The phase of prenatal development that spans from eight weeks after conception to birth (at around forty weeks).

Fetal surgery   Surgery that is conducted while the child is still developing prenatally.

Fetus   The name of the developing individual beginning in the ninth week after conception until birth.

Figurative language   The use of similies, proverbs, idioms, and metaphors.

Fine motor skills   Those motor acts that require the use of small muscle groups and hand-eye coordination.

Fitness   How well an individual is suited for his or her environment and the ability to survive and reproduce.

5-to-7 shift   A transition period in cognitive development between the preoperational and concrete operations stages; thinking is based more on intuition than logic.

Fixation   Occurs when attempts to satisfy needs at a certain stage of personality development are continually frustrated.

Flexibility   The freedom to bend or move the body in various directions.

Fluency disorders   Disorders in which a person struggles to communicate smoothly.

Fluid intelligence   The ability to perceive relationships, reason logically and abstractly, and form concepts and interpretations.

Formal operations   The fourth stage of cognitive development proposed by Piaget that commences in adolescence; thought is characterized as less rigid, more flexible, and less dependent on perceptions and past experiences.

Free-radicals   Unstable oxygen molecules that are released when cells metabolize energy.

Game of thinking   Divorcing oneself from reality and playfully considering various hypothetical possibilities in certain situations.

Gender harassment   A workplace environment that is hostile, degrading, or insulting toward one particular gender.

Gender identity   One's knowledge of being either male or female.

Generation X   Individuals born between 1965 and 1979.

Generation Y   Individuals born after the year 1980.

Generativity versus stagnation   The seventh psychosocial attitude described by Erikson; It is developed optimally between twenty-four and fifty-four years of age. Generativity is an interest in caring for others and sharing one's knowledge, skills, and information. Stagnation (self-absorption) is directing all one's interest inward to oneself.

Genes   The basic agents of heredity from one generation of humans to the next.

Genetic imprinting   The repression or expression of a gene or chromosome in an offspring that is dependent upon which parent it is inherited from.

Genotype   The total genetic makeup of an individual.

Germinal period   The phase of prenatal developing lasting from conception until implantation in the uterus (around ten to fourteen days).

Gerontophobia   The unreasonable and irrational fear of the elderly; related to ageism.

Gingivitis   Inflammation of gum tissue that contributes highly to tooth loss.

Glaucoma   A group of diseases resulting in increased pressure within the eyeball and leading to blindness if left untreated.

Goodness-of-fit   How adaptable a child's environment is to his or her temperament.

Gout   A metabolic disorder that results from uric acid crystals forming at joint areas, especially in the feet.

Green burials   The use of biodegradable caskets and integrating forests and conservation efforts with graveyards.

Grief   The natural or expected response to personal loss; often used interchangeably with bereavement.

Grief therapy   Professional counseling specifically aimed at helping individuals who experience difficulty in completing their grief process.

Grief wheel   A model of the grieving process described by Spangler and Demi.

Grief work   The stage in which people accept the reality of their loss and begin the business of rebuilding their lives.

Gross motor skills   Those motor acts that require the use of large muscle groups.

Group politics   Those social skills that facilitate a child's participation in peer groups.

Growth   Behaviors meant to increase functioning and adaptation.

Guilt   Feeling shame and remorse.

Habituation/dishabituation   An experimental technique that allows researchers to measure recognition in babies.

Hand skills   The ability to explore and manipulate a wide variety of objects with the hands.

Healthy behavior   Any behavior that reduces the susceptibility to disease and enhances physical and psychological function and well-being.

Hiatal hernia   A condition in which a portion of the stomach slides up next to the esophagus.

Highly competent experts   Experts who exhibit great adaptability, flexibility, and creativity in utilizing their expertise across a variety of situations.

Hitching   Crawling or creeping backward using the buttocks rather than the hands and knees.

Holophrases   An early speech form used by infants in which single words convey a wide number of meanings.

Honeymoon phase   Immediately following the formal event of retirement, most people feel happy and peaceful initially as they experience the independence of retirement.

Horizontal decalage   Unevenness in applying an understanding of conservation problems across different contexts.

Hormonal stress theory   As the hormone system ages, it is less effective at managing stress.

Hospice care   Care that is provided in a person's home or hospice home to those with less than six months to live.

Hostile attributional bias   The thinking that bullies are always suspect of the intentions of others and see hostility where there is none.

Human development   The changes that occur in individuals between conception and death.

Hypertension   Abnormally high blood pressure caused by constriction of arteries; it increases the likelihood of kidney damage, heart failure, and brain damage via strokes.

Hypothesis   Generically, hypothesis means educated guess. A hypothesis should come from a theory, be a statement, and be testable.

Hypothetical reasoning   The ability to think and reason about ideas in the abstract.

Id   The drives that seek gratification of elemental needs for food, water, sex, and warmth.

Identity   The fifth attitude proposed by Erikson. Identity is the notion, acquired in adolescence, that the self is composed of different aspects having distinct boundaries that constitute a whole, integrated personality.

Identity foreclosure   The inability to commit to any role or idea of direction for their lives.

Idiopathic protracted apnea   An interruption in breathing during sleep.

Imaginary audience   The adolescent egocentric belief that other people are obsessed and consumed with his or her appearance and behavior.

Imitation   The basic process of a newborn being capable of immediately imitating your behavior.

Implantation   Occurs when the zygote burrows into the uterus.

Implicit memories   Unconscious memories that influence our behavior.

Implicit memory   Unconscious memory that guides your behavior, thoughts, and feelings.

Implicit-theoretical approaches   Approach to the study of wisdom that investigates people's common understanding of wisdom

Impulsion   The rate at which body movement begins from a stationary position.

Incomplete dominance   Occurs when one allele is not completely dominant over the second allele.

Incompletely launched young adults   Young adults who return home to live with their parents.

Incontinence   The inability to retain urine in the bladder until voluntarily released.

Independent variable   A variable that is controlled and/or manipulated.

Individual difference   Any quality, trait, or characteristic that distinguishes one person from others.

Individuation   The process by which an adolescent recognizes and develops his or her personal identity as an individual who is distinct from other family members. It is characterized by developing one's own values and belief systems and having the courage to make decisions and live by these.

Inductive reasoning   Reasoning from specific facts to general conclusions.

Infant-directed speech   Speech that is more accentuated and of a higher pitch.

Infantile amnesia   The inability to remember much about the first two or so years of life after birth.

Infertility   The inability to conceive a child after consistently having intercourse without contraception for at least a year.

Information-processing   How information is represented, processed, and applied in reference to memory constraints at any given age.

Informed consent   Providing research participants with enough information about a study that they can knowledgeably agree or disagree to participate.

Inherited disorder   A disorder or disease that develops due to a gene mutation, chromosomal problem, or other genetic factor.

Inhibitory deficit theory   A theory that examines what aspects of cognitive processing declines with age, and what aspects of cognitive processing remain stable.

Institutional Review Board (IRB)   A committee that evaluates whether a research study is ethical and allowed to be conducted.

Integrated   A personality type in late adulthood that may be thought to resemble the sense of integrity described by Erikson.

Interpersonal intelligence   The mental ability to understand one's own emotional self.

Intimacy versus isolation   The sixth psychosocial attitude described by Erikson; it is developed optimally between eighteen and twenty-four years of age. Intimacy is the ability to have a close and loving relationship with another. Isolation is the refusal to allow oneself to become vulnerable enough to establish intimate relationships.

Intimate and mutually shared relationships   The third stage of friendship perception that typically occurs at the end of middle childhood, between the ages of 10 to twelve where children value the continuity and longevity of friendship.

In-time leavers   Individuals that move out of their parents homes permanently before the age of twenty-five.

Intrinsic motivation   A person's internally generated drive to learn because it is inherently enjoyable.

Inventive strategies   Making use of one's own knowledge and current strategies in answering a novel problem.

Involved relationship   A grandparent-grandchildren relationship that focuses on an active role of raising grandchildren and conducting the role as an active caretaker much like a parent.

Irreversibility   The inability of young children to comprehend that some processes and operations can be reversed in sequence.

Job simplification   Work that is repetitive, simplified, and fragmented.

Kyphosis   A "humpback" posture.

Labor   The process by which the cervix is opened prior to birth and the fetus is moved from the uterus through the birth canal; accomplished by means of contractions of the uterus, which increase in strength, duration, and frequency as delivery nears.

Laboratory studies   Allow for better variable control and manipulation than naturalistic studies.

Language   "A system of abstract symbols and rule-governed structures, the specific conventions of which are learned."

Language Acquisition Device (LAD)   An innate brain structure proposed by Chomsky that regulates the means by which an individual learns language.

Lanugo   A fine down-like hair covering the baby's body.

Late adulthood   The eighth stage of the life span and final stage of adulthood; traditionally, the stage begins at age sixty-five or retirement from the work force and continues until near-death.

Late leavers   Individuals that are still living at home after the age of twenty-five.

Life history   All the changes experienced by a living organism, from its conception to its death.

Lightening   Occurs when the fetus' head drops down into the pelvis.

Lingering pattern   The person is expected to die, but clings to life for an indeterminate time.

Linguistic intelligence   Involves the mental abilities in the semantics, syntax, and overall expression of language.

Logical-mathematical intelligence   Involves mental abilities in pattern recognition, relationships, reasoning, and mathematical operations.

Longitudinal design   A study that makes repeated measurements or observations of the same individuals over an extended period of time.

Long-term memory   The final memory location in the brain where information is stored indefinitely; recall of events in the distant past.

Macular degeneration   A decreased blood supply to the retina, causing loss of visual sharpness when looking directly ahead but not in the peripheral vision areas.

Maintenance   Behaviors striving to keep functioning at current levels despite declines in processes or ability.

Malignant neoplasms   Technical term for cancer.

Maturationism   The belief that changes in development are due only to heredity; changes result from the execution of genetic programming.

Maturity   Completion of all growth and developmental changes; associated with attaining adulthood in the past.

Meconium   A newborn's first bowel movement.

Meiosis   The process by which the gametes (sperm and ova) are produced in the male testicles and the female ovaries.

Menarche   The first menstrual period experienced by a girl, marking the beginning of puberty.

Menopause   The climacteric in females; cessation of all reproductive functions that begins at about age forty-five to forty-eight and is completed by about age fifty-five.

Mental health   A state of psychological well-being in which an individual is able to behave according to cultural standards.

Merely skill experts   Expertise that functions largely on routine.

Meta-analysis   The data from numerous studies on a particular topic are synthesized and analyzed.

Metacognition   The ability to be aware of and understand the changes occurring in one's own cognitive processes.

Metalinguistic-awareness   The capacity to use language to analyze, study, and understand language.

Metamemory   An awareness of the extent of one's memory.

Microgenetic studies   A study that only lasts a matter of days or weeks.

Middle adulthood   The seventh stage of the life span, occurring between forty-five and sixty-five years of age.

Middle age   A term synonymous with middle adulthood. Middle age can bring about new perceptions, redefinitions of roles, and different means for achieving personal happiness.

Miscarriage   The unwanted ending of a pregnancy, usually within the first three months of pregnancy.

Mitochondrial theory   The inability of the mitochondria to properly function as the cell's powerhouse and failure to provide enough energy for the cell to function. Damage to the mitochondria is caused by free-radicals released into the cell.

Mitosis   The splitting of each chromosome in the body cell to form a new pair.

Modeling   The process by which behavior is acquired and modified through observing and replicating the behavior of others.

Momentary playmates   Temporary playmates, typically because they happen to be in the same physical location.

Monitoring phase   Maintaining awareness of what is being learned and thinking.

Moro reflex   This reflex is associated with a sudden change in movement or support of the newborn. If a neonate is raised or lowered suddenly or if support of its head is released, the baby responds by raising its arms upward very quickly and curling its fingers. Moving of the legs accompanies these reflex motions.

Morphemes   Meaningful units of speech.

Mourning   The socially prescribed ways of expressing grief.

Multifactorial disorder   A disorder that results from the interaction of genetics with the environment.

Multiple intelligences   A theory in which there are various domains or abilities in which a person can be intelligent.

Multiple regression   A statistical method that allows researchers to predict one variable based on the values of other variables.

Musical intelligence   The mental ability to understand the components of music, such as tone, melody, pitch, and rhythm.

Mutation   A change in the chemical structure of the gene or genes and can occur during cell division or as a result of environmental influences.

Myelin   A fatty material deposited around axons.

Myelinated   A layer of fat that can surround the axon.

Naturalist intelligence   The mental ability to recognize plant and animal life in the environment and the relationships and interconnections between these species.

Naturalistic observation method   A method of conducting research on human development that usually occurs in the "real" world where behavior happens spontaneously.

Needs hierarchy   A person's need to satisfy certain basic needs before they attempt to realize self-actualization.

Negative correlation   As one variable increases, the other decreases.

Neglected   Children who are neglected by peers and describe themselves as having no friends.

Neonatal death   Death of a baby during the neonatal period (birth to two weeks of age).

Neuron   The information processing cell of the nervous system.

Neuroticism   The degree to which a person is insecure, emotional, and anxious.

Neurotransmitters   Chemical messengers that carry information to other neurons.

Non-voluntary euthanasia   A doctor administers a deadly dose of medication without the patient requesting it.

Novice   A person with limited experience, knowledge, or understanding within a specific area of interest.

Obesity   A body weight that exceeds by 20 percent of what is considered to be appropriate for one's age.

Observational learning   Learning that occurs through observing others.

Observer bias   Different accounts given by people who observe the same event.

Off-target verbosity   The tendency for some older adults to drift to irrelevant topics during conversation.

Off-time   When a person experiences puberty earlier or later than most of his or her same-age peers.

One-way assistance   The first stage in friendship perception that occurs early in middle childhood where friends must match a child's personal standard.

Onlooker play   Observing others at play.

Openness   The degree to which a person is comfortable with variety, autonomy, and change.

Operant conditioning   The use of reinforcers and punishers to control behavior.

Operational definition   How a variable is defined in a measurable way.

Oppositional defiant disorder   A mental disorder characterized by a pattern of disobedience, hostility, and deviant behavior.

Organogenesis   The formation of organs during the embryonic period.

Osteoporosis   Inflammation of bone tissue causing softness and porous structure; the condition can lead to bone breakage and tooth loss.

Ostracism   A social control mechanism used by peer groups to enforce group rules and conformity to behavior standards; it is seen, for example, when children are ignored and rejected on the school playground.

Overextension   When a child applies the meaning of a word too broadly.

Overlaps   When a word is underextended on some occasions and overextended on other occasions.

Palliative care   Treatment for those suffering from illness that focuses on pain management, symptom control, and emotional support in the face of stress.

Palmar (hand) and plantar (foot) grasping reflex   These reflex movements are produced by touching or stroking the palm of the newborn's hands or the soles of its feet. Both fingers and toes curl in the grasping manner in response. The strength of these reflexes is remarkable.

Parallel play   Playing alongside others who are doing the same or a different activity.

Parallel processing   Refers to the ability to cognitively process and complete two or more tasks at a time.

Parkinson's disease   A chronic degenerative brain disorder commonly occurring in late adulthood. It is characterized initially by tremors, muscle weakness, and a peculiar gait; then speech becomes slurred; death eventually results from severe brain cell damage.

"Partial-brain" death   A concept that a person should be considered dead if his or her higher cognitive functions no longer function, but parts of the brain still function and maintain physical life.

Passive genotype-environment correlation   An environment in which the child passively receives an environment.

Passive smoking   Inhaling air in an area where someone has been smoking.

Passive-dependent   A personality type with two basic variations that may be observed: (a) those whom are succorance-seeking in having strong dependency needs on others; and (b) those who are apathetic or having little or no interest in others or in their surroundings.

Peak experiences   The feeling of great joy, ecstasy, and cosmic identification with the whole universe.

Pediatric psychology   The area of psychology that studies the interactions and relationships among health, illness, physical development, cognitive development, and socioemotional development across the life-span.

Peer group   A (usually) same-sex group of children of similar ages and developmental abilities that significantly influences social changes in middle childhood.

Perceptual skill   The ability to perceive through sight and sound; especially those skills related to motor skill development, such as depth perception and pattern perception, that emerge in infancy.

Perfection principle   An internalized judge or parent figure guiding the person's behavior according to social and moral ideals.

Perinatal deaths   A term that includes deaths from twenty weeks gestation to four weeks after birth.

Perinatology   Concerned with the detection and treatment of illness in developing individuals before birth.

Periodontal disease   Disease of the gums caused by improper hygiene; it can lead to significant tooth loss.

Permissive style   Parents that are affectionate, but display little discipline.

Personal or Invincibility fable   The belief that one is immune from all harm or injury.

Personality   The inner behavior that represents the true inner self as well as to outward actions manifesting that inner self.

Phenomenism   The first stage for understanding illness "as an external concrete phenomenon that is spatially and temporally remote from the condition of illness."

Phenotype   The traits and characteristics such as hair color, skin color, and behavior that can be observed.

Philosophical approaches   Values the history of wisdom discourse in philosophy.

Phonemes   The simplest and most elementary sounds in speech, or the building blocks of speech.

Phonics   An approach to teaching reading and spelling based upon phonetics, or the sound of letters.

Physical (biological) domain   Changes in the body or physical appearance.

Physician-assisted suicide   When a doctor provides a patient with the means to commit suicide at the patient's request. The doctor provides the lethal dose, but the patient is responsible for actually taking the medication.

Physiologic The fifth stage for understanding illness; described as the malfunctioning of an internal physiologic organ or process and is explained as a step-by-step sequence of events.

Placebo An inert or innocuous substance used especially in controlled experiments testing the efficacy of another substance (as a drug).

Planning phase A person sets goals and considers what they already know and what they need to still learn.

Play therapy The use of play to assist a child with psychological, behavioral, or emotional problems.

Pleasure principle Attraction to those things which are enjoyable and repelled by those things that produce discomfort.

Pneumonia An inflammation of the lungs.

Polygenic process The interaction of alleles from more than one gene.

Popular Children who are liked by many peers.

Positive correlation As one variable increases, the other variable increases.

Positive regard Characterized as being warm, genuine, and giving total attention and acceptance to the client.

Postconventional level Moral reasoning based upon internalized and personalized values.

Posterior attention system Includes the brain areas such as the posterior parietal cortex and the thalamus.

Post-formal operational thought A possible fifth stage of cognitive development, in early adulthood.

Postpartum depression The feelings of sadness and exhaustion persist or even worsen past the two week mark.

Postpartum psychosis When a woman is afraid to be left alone with the baby and has thoughts of hurting herself or the baby.

Pragmatics The ability to adjust speech in socially and culturally appropriate ways.

Precausal thinking A type of logic unique to young children based on intuition rather than fact.

Precision The dexterity and accuracy of movements.

Preconventional level Moral reasoning based upon physical consequences and the power of those in authority.

Prediction A statement of what somebody thinks will happen in the future.

Premature baby A baby who weighs five and one half pounds or less at birth and has a gestational age of less than thirty-seven weeks.

Preoccupied-insecure attachment An infant is terribly upset when the mother leaves and is inconsolable when she returns.

Preoperational The kind of thinking young children do when they begin to use mental imagery but are not yet able to use logic; intuition is often used in reaching decisions.

Preparatory depression Beginning to prepare for death by grieving for the separation from loved ones.

Prepubertal growth spurt A rapid increase in height and weight preceding puberty (at about age ten to twelve).

Pre-retirement The period preceding retirement during which a person may make plans and arrangements for his or her retirement.

Presbycusis The loss of hearing of high-frequency tones.

Presbyopia Difficulty in accurately perceiving objects that are close.

Primary emotions Emotions which are present at birth or shortly thereafter. They are believed to be hard-wired into the brain and serve an adaptive purpose.

Primary short-term memory The conscious process of keeping information in short-term memory.

Private speech A speech form prevalent in early childhood in which children talk to themselves or continue to talk even when no one is listening to what they are saying.

Problem solving   The development of strategies to overcome an obstacle in order to achieve a goal.

Procedural memory   Knowledge about how to perform certain tasks, like riding a bike or driving a car, or even walking.

Prosocial   A growing sense of others (e.g. comforting other children who seem sad or worried).

Prosocial behaviors   Those behaviors that promote helpfulness and show concern for others, such as altruism or empathy.

Proximodistal growth pattern   Changes happen first in the center, innermost area of the body and then move outward to the ends of extremities.

Pruning   The elimination of unnecessary excess neuron connections between millions of neuron cells over time.

Pseudostupidity   The tendency of young adolescents to interpret situations in more complex ways than called for.

Psychological age   Based upon an individual's adaptive capacities in relation to their chronological age.

Psychological death   The thoughts and emotional reactions experienced by the dying individuals and his or her family and friends.

Psychopathology   The branch of medicine dealing with the causes and processes of mental disorders.

Psychophysiologic   The sixth stage for understanding illness; illness is understood physiologically, but the child also can consider the influence of psychological factors.

Psychosocial crisis   A central problem that the person is expected to master in order to make healthy progress to the next stage.

Psychotropic medication   Any medication capable of altering cognition, or behavior.

Puberty   The developmental event occurring in early adolescence in which the sexual organs become functional. It is associated with other significant physical changes in the body.

Punishers   Are meant to decrease the behaviors they follow.

Quickening   The first detection by mother of movements made by a fetus.

Randomly assigned   Assignment of research participants to groups in an experimental study by chance.

Reactive depression   Feelings of loss and disfigurement of the body from surgery or from the ravages of disease.

Reality principle   According to Freud, the tendency to behave in ways that are consistent with reality.

Recall   The basic process of a newborn being capable of recalling observed behavior experiences.

Recessive   A gene from one parent whose influence is repressed by the complementary (dominant) gene from the other parent in the offspring.

Recognition   Awareness or recollection of having seen something before.

Reflection phase   The time to judge one's own work, make attributions in regards to the quality of the work, and evaluate the outcomes within the given context.

Reflexes   A response controlled by the autonomic nervous system, over which an individual has no willful control.

Regulation of loss   Behaviors that allow for reorganization or functioning at lower levels because maintenance is no longer possible.

Rehearsal   Practicing something over and over again.

Reinforcers   Are meant to increase the behavior they follow.

Rejected   Children who are rejected by peers are disliked, and are at risk of many serious problems that include clinical depression.

Rejecting-neglecting parenting style   Parents that display little affection or discipline.

Religiosity   Incorporates spirituality, but includes the additional dimension of living the faith.

Remote relationship   A grandparent-grandchildren relationship characterized by infrequent contact governed by behavior that is ritualistic and highly symbolic.

Reorientation stage   People attempt a more realistic appraisal of their options for the future.

Returners   Young adults who had ventured out to independent living, but subsequently returned to live with their parents at some point between the ages of twenty-one and twenty-five years of age.

Reversibility   The cognitive ability of school-age children to understand that certain operations can occur in their reverse order (e.g., subtraction is the reverse of addition).

Rheumatism   A variety of conditions resulting in stiffness and soreness in tissues associated with bone joints.

Rhythm   Regular body movements.

Risky behavior   Any behavior that detrimentally effects health or increases the likelihood of disease, although they typically increase an individual's sense of well-being at the moment.

Rite of committal   The third and final step in a Catholic funeral where the person's body or ashes is sprinkled with holy water, possibly incensed, and place in its final resting place.

Role confusion   The disjointed, fragmented notion of self resulting from an inability to integrate the various aspects of personality into a unified whole.

Rooting reflex   This is a searching reflex motion that helps the neonate to locate a breast or bottle nipple. It occurs when the baby's cheeks are stroked or the corner of its mouth is touched. The response is "rooting," in which the baby turns its head in the direction of the stimulation, and as it does so, opens its mouth. The baby's tongue begins to move forward and backward in its mouth.

Rough-and-tumble play   Physically active play.

Sample   A subset of a population.

Sandwich generation   The term sometimes used to describe middle-aged individuals, referring to their divided loyalties and responsibilities toward the younger and the older generation within their family systems.

Scaffolding   An instructional strategy in which a learning task is structured whereby a lot of support is offered early on, but as the student begins to learn, less and less support is given.

Schema   Any consistent, reliable pattern or plan of interaction with the environment.

School bilingualism   The offering of courses in a secondary language in the elementary schools.

Science   The marriage of rationalism and empiricism that provides a mechanism allowing for understanding the world within a system of checks and balances.

Scientific method   A series of steps that scientists from any field use as a process to test theories and gain knowledge within their field.

Scientific-inductive reasoning   Starting with an observation or thought that generates a hypothesis about something.

Scoliosis   S-curved spinal column.

Scripts   An organized series of acts committed to memory (e.g., getting dressed, brushing the teeth).

Secondary emotions   Emotions that develop during the second year or so after birth, as cognitive development advances. They can be a blend of two or more primary emotions, culturally-specific, or self-conscious/self-evaluative in nature.

Secular trend   The trend, inferred from observation of several generations, toward achieving sexual maturity at earlier ages than in the past.

Secure attachment style   An infant misses their mother when she leaves the room and greets her upon returning.

Selection, optimization, and compensation (SOC) theory   A theory that examines how selection, optimization, and compensation assist individuals in coping with the declines associated with aging. It is often considered a theory of successful aging.

Selective attention   A cognitive ability to tune out distracting stimulation while performing a task.

Self-actualization   A person's drive to achieve their personal full potential.

Self-awareness A child's use of self-referencing pronouns, using their own name, and occasionally labeling themselves by sex and age.

Self-concept One's basic ideas about one's inner self.

Self-regulated learning When a person keeps track of what they have learned, what they still need to learn, and have a strategy for how to learn it.

Semantic memory General knowledge.

Semantics The ability to express meaning through language.

Senescence The process of aging.

Senility Marked deterioration in mental organization characterized by confusion, memory loss, information-processing difficulties, and disorientation.

Sense of industry A positive, healthy attitude toward work and the need to master certain basic skills.

Sense of inferiority A pervasive attitude of worthlessness.

Sense of integrity versus a sense of despair The final psychosocial attitude proposed by Erikson; it is developed in late adulthood. Integrity is characterized by completion of the task of integrating the various aspects of the self-concept and identity and evaluation of one's life as having been a meaningful and fulfilling experience. Despair is characterized by a feeling of loss, disappointment, and deep dissatisfaction with the way one's life was lived.

Sensory register The first memory storage location where sensory information is stored in the brain before becoming short- or long-term memory.

Sequential design A compromise that minimizes the disadvantages of both cross-sectional and longitudinal designs.

Seriation A cognitive ability that allows objects to be scaled according to various dimensions (e.g., large to small).

Sex chromosomes The twenty-third pair of chromosomes which determines a person's gender.

Sexual harassment Unwanted sexual attention.

Sexualization A person's value comes only from his or her sexual appeal or behavior, to the exclusion of other characteristics; a person is held to a standard that equates physical attractiveness (narrowly defined) with being sexy; a person is sexually objectified—that is, made into a thing for others' sexual use, rather than seen as a person with the capacity for independent action and decision making; and/or sexuality is inappropriately imposed upon a person.

Shame The feeling that one's inner self is exposed as being flawed in some manner.

Shame and doubt Refers to the belief that one is unable to be autonomous and that one's inner self is basically flawed and defective.

Short-reprieve pattern The person's death is postponed unexpectedly, but only for a short period of time.

Short-term memory An initial memory storage location in the brain where information remains for about one minute before being erased or placed into long-term memory; recall of information, events, and so on that are relatively recent.

Significant others Those people who are singularly important at each particular stage of a person's psychosocial development.

Silent generation Individuals born between 1922 and 1945.

Slow-to-warm-up temperament The display of quiet activity levels, somewhat fussy, and wary around others and situations.

Social age Based upon social norms and expectations in relation to what an individual "should" be doing at a specific chronological age.

Social cognition The skills involved in understanding the dynamics of human social interaction patterns. Self-understanding is also related to these skills.

Social death The institutional and cultural events and processes that relate to a deceased individual, such as the bereavement of family and friends and the funeral.

Social hierarchy   An organizational ranking of peers based on how much a child is liked or disliked by others.

Social norms   Expectations in a given society about how an individual should behave, feel, and think.

Social policy   Typically, a government policy regarding a social issue.

Social referencing   When infants look at their parents' faces and behavior for information about something.

Social smile   Smiling in response to social stimulation from others.

Socialization   The process by which individuals are taught to conform to social rules, to acquire personal values, and to develop attitudes typical of their culture.

Sociobiology   The study of the biological bases of social behavior.

Sociocultural theory   A theory that cognitive development is dependent upon social interactions.

Socioemotional domain   Changes in emotion, personality, and relationships.

Socioemotional selectivity theory   A theory that as age increases, so does the desire to be more selective in one's social relationships, optimizing positive interactions.

Solitary play   Children are alone or are playing independently of others.

Somatic stem cells   Another term for adult stem cells.

Source memory   The ability to remember where you heard, saw, or learned something.

Spatial intelligence   Involves mental abilities in perception of objects and the ability to mentally transform and manipulate these objects.

Spatial reference memory   The aspect of memory that stores information about one's environment and spatial orientation.

Speech   Orally expressed language.

Speed   The rate of movement once the body is in action.

Spina bifida   A birth defect in which the tissue surrounding the spinal cord does not properly close during prenatal development

Spirituality   A sense of connectedness with God (or some other higher spiritual being).

Stability stage   The routine of established behaviors.

Startle reflex   This reflex is most often elicited by loud noises and unexpected, sudden touching of the newborn's trunk area.

Still in the nest   Individuals who are still living at home between the ages of twenty-one to twenty-five years, but are actively working towards moving out, and are out by the end of this age-range.

Stillbirth   Death of a fetus before birth due to any one of several reasons.

Stochastic processes   The probability of random accidental injury to cellular DNA.

Stranger wariness   Or stranger anxiety, which is observable around six months of age.

Strength   The ability to exert force.

Stress   The physiological and psychological reactions of an organism to demands placed upon it.

Stressors   Events that can cause stress reactions.

Strokes   A cerebrovascular accident occurring when a blood vessel in the brain ruptures or is obstructed by a blood clot.

Structural equation modeling   A model that is developed to explain patterns of relationships among variables.

Sucking reflex   The sucking reflex is closely associated with both the rooting and swallowing reflexes. It is produced when the soft palate in the baby's mouth is stimulated.

Sudden infant death syndrome (SIDS)   A condition of unknown cause resulting in the sudden and unexpected death of an infant.

Superego   Functions to control and override the id's attempts to express basic drives in ways that are socially unacceptable.

Suspended-sentence pattern   The person is discharged from medical care and is expected to live for several years.

Swimming reflex   This unusual reflex occurs when the neonate is submerged on its abdomen in water. The baby holds its breath and makes swimming motions with both arms and legs.

Symbolic play   Using objects in a pretend fashion (e.g. like tea parties).

Sympathy   The ability to feel the same way that others do; learning to sympathize is the first step toward developing empathy.

Synapses   The tiny gaps between neurons.

Syntax   The rules for making grammatical sentences.

Task analysis   The careful examination of a problem and consideration of what steps will be necessary in order to solve it.

Temperament   A baby's general approach to the world and behavioral orientation.

Teratogen   Anything that can cause abnormal development.

Teratology   A branch of science that studies the causes, mechanisms, and patterns of abnormal development.

Terminal decline   The official term used to describe the accelerated cognitive degeneration as elderly individuals approach death.

Terminal period   Characterized by withdrawal from others and general disengagement from the world.

Termination   The last stage which is marked by a role shift from retiree either to being employed again, or to being disabled in advanced age.

Thanatology   The study of dying, death, and grief.

Theoretical eclecticism   The approach of investigating the varied models and concepts and choosing the best to apply to a particular issue.

Theory   A collection of ideas used to explain observations.

Theory of mind   The ability to understand your own mental state, as well as the mental state of others.

Time-series analysis   A study of the same variable across time.

Tonic neck reflex   This reflex usually occurs when the neonate is placed on its back. The arms, legs, and head move to a characteristic "fencing" position in which the arm and leg on one side are extended, while those on the other side are flexed. The baby's head turns to one side, usually in the direction of its extended limbs.

Toxemia   An acute hypertensive disease of pregnancy characterized by high blood pressure, retention of body fluids, and the presence of protein in the urine.

Trait   A distinguishing feature or characteristic.

Trajectory   A path or pattern that is followed in some particular process.

Transductive reasoning   Seeing a relationship between two objects or events, when in fact no relationship exists.

Transverse   When a child is sideways during labor (requires either that the child is physically moved to the head-down position, or delivered C-section).

"Type A" personality   Highly competitive, restless, and achievement oriented.

"Type B" personality   A personality that is low in hostility and aggression, and moderately ambitious.

"Type C" personality   Associated with an increased risk for cancer, this personality type tends to be introverted and eager to please.

Umbilical cord blood and placental stem cells   Stem cells found in the umbilical cord blood and placenta after birth.

Underextension   When a child limits the meaning of the word too narrowly.

Unintegrated   A personality type where individuals may be described as experiencing dementia.

Unoccupied play   Play that seems random and without purpose.

Values   A person's belief about what is right and what is wrong.

Variables   Anything that can vary.

Vernix caseosa A thick, cold cream-like substance covering the baby's skin. It serves to protect the skin and lubricate the fetus for passage through the birth canal.

Vernix The lubricating, creamlike substance that has formed during the fetal period.

Vestigial reflexes Several reflexes present at birth that seem to be relics of adaptive experiences sometime in our vast evolutionary past.

Vigil The first step in a Catholic funeral that may take place in a funeral parlor, a home, or a church. The vigil is short in duration and focuses mainly on prayer, although readings and music are also included.

Visual acuity Sharpness or clarity of vision

Visualization The ability to organize and process visual materials.

Visuomotor flexibility The ability to shift from familiar to unfamiliar tasks involving hand-eye coordination.

Voice disorders Persistent difficulties with the quality of voice.

Walking reflex Step-like motions of the legs occur reflexively when the neonate is held in an upright position and allowed to touch a flat surface with its feet. The legs respond by flexing alternately as if the child is walking.

"Whole-brain" death When the entire brain, including the brain stem, ceases to function.

Widowhood A label applied to both men and women who survive the death of a spouse.

Working memory The workbench of memory where simultaneous cognitive processes can be attended to and handled.

Zone of proximal development The range between what a child can accomplish alone and what can be accomplished with assistance.

Zygote The name of the developing individual during the germinal period.

References

Abraham, S. (1979). Weight and height of adults 18–74 years of age, United States 1971–1974. *Vital and Health Statistics, Series 11, No. 211.* DHEW Publication No.(PHS) 79–1659.

Abraham, S. (1979). Mean weight in pounds of adults 18–74 years by age and sex: United States, 1971–1974. *Vital and Health Statistics, Series 11, No. 211.* DHEW Publication No. (PHS) 799–1659.

Acredolo, L. P., & Goodwyn, S. (1988). Symbolic gesturing in normal infants. *Child Development, 59,* 450–466.

Acredolo, L. P., & Hake, J. K. (1982). Infant perception. In B. B. Wolman (Ed.), *Handbook of developmental psychology.* Englewood Cliffs, NJ: Prentice Hall.

Ad Hoc Committee of the Harvard Medical School. (1968). A definition of irreversible coma: Report of the Ad Hoc Committee of the Harvard Medical School to Examine the Definition of Brain Death. *Journal of the American Medical Association, 205,* 337–340.

Adams, C. G., & Turner, B. F. (1985). Reported change in sexuality from young adulthood to old age. *Journal of Sex Research, 21,* 126–141.

Adeyanju, M. (1990). Adolescent health status, behaviors, and cardiovascular disease. *Adolescence, 25,* 155–169.

Ainsworth, M. (1973). The development of infant-mother attachment. In B. Caldwell & H. Riciuti (Eds.), *Review of child development research.* Vol. 3. Chicago: University of Chicago Press.

Ainsworth, M. (1977). Attachment theory and its utility in cross-cultural research. In P. Leiderman, S. Tulkin, & A. Rosenfield (Eds.), *Culture and infancy: Variations in the human experience.* New York: Academic Press.

Ainsworth, M. D. S., Blehar, M. C., Waters, E., & Wall, S. (1978). *Patterns in attachment: A psychological study of the strange situation.* Hillsdale, NJ: Erlbaum.

Alam, S. E. (1978). The aging parent and the adult child. *Journal of Home Economics, 71,* 26–28.

Albert, M. S., & Killiany, R. J. (2001). Age-related cognitive change and brain-behavior relationships. In J. E. Birren & K. W. Schaie (Eds.), *Handbook of the psychology of aging.* San Diego, CA: Academic Press.

Aldous, J. (1978). *Family careers: Developmental change in families.* New York: Wiley.

Aldous, J. (1987). Family life of the elderly and the near-elderly. *Journal of Marriage and the Family, 49,* 227–234.

Aldwin, C. M. (1994). *Stress, coping, and development: An integrative perspective.* NY: The Guilford Press.

Alessandri, S., & Wozniak, R. (1989). Perception of the family environment and interfamilial agreement in belief concerning the adolescent. *Journal of Early Adolescence, 9,* 67–81.

Alexander, J. F., & Malouf, R. E. (1983). Problems in personality and social development. In P. Mussen (Ed.), *Handbook of child psychology.* Vol. 4. New York: Wiley.

Allegeier, E. R., & Murnen, S. K (1985). Perceptions of parents as sexual beings: Pocs & Godow revisited. *Siecus Reports, 13,* 11–12.

Allport, G. W. (1961). *Pattern and growth in personality.* New York: Holt, Rinehart, Winston.

American Association of Retired Persons. (1986). *A profile of older Americans.* Washington, DC: American Association of Retired Persons.

American Cancer Society. (1988). *Cancer facts and figures.* New York: American Cancer Society.

American College of Obstetricians and Gynecologists (2005). *Your pregnancy and birth* (4th ed.). Washington, DC: The American College of Obstetricians and Gynecologists and Meredith Books.

American Heart Association. (1984). *Eating for a healthy heart: Dietary treatment for hyperlipidemia.* Dallas, TX: American Heart Association.

American Psychiatric Association. (1980). *Diagnostic and statistical manual of mental disorders* (3rd ed.). Washington, DC: American Psychiatric Association.

Ames, L. B. (1986). Ready or not. *American Educator, 10,* 30–34.

Anastasi, A. (1958). Heredity, environment, and the question "how." *Psychological Review, 65,* 197–208.

Anderson, D. (1987). Family and peer relations of gay adolescents. *Adolescent Psychiatry, 14,* 162–178.

Anderson, T. (1984). Widowhood as a life transition: Its impact on kinship ties. *Journal of Marriage and the Family, 46,* 105–114.

Andrew, E., Clancy, K., & Katz, M. (1980). Infant feeding practices of families belonging to a prepaid group practice health care plan. *Pediatrics, 65,* 978–987.

Anglin, J. M. (1977). *Word, object, and conceptual development.* New York: Norton.

Anrig, G., Jr. (1988). How to retire early and comfortably. *Money, 17(12),* 58–60.

Ansbacher, R. (1983). Median age for menopause. *Medical Aspects of Human Sexuality, 17,* 143.

Antonucci, T. C. (2001). Social relations: An examination of social networks, social support, and sense of control. In J. E. Birren & K. W. Schaie (Eds.), *Handbook of the psychology of aging.* San Diego, CA: Academic Press.

Aries, P. (1962). *Centuries of childhood* (Translated by R. Baldick). New York: Knopf.

Ary, D. V., & Biglan, A. (1988). Longitudinal changes in adolescent cigarette smoking behavior: Onset and cessation. *Journal of Behavioral Medicine, 11,* 361–382.

Asher, S., & Gottman, J. (Eds.). (1981). *The development of children's friendships.* New York: Cambridge University Press.

Ashner, L., & Meyerson, M. (1990). *When parents love too much: What happens when parents won't let go.* New York: William Morrow.

Aslin, R. N. (1987). Motor aspects of visual development in infancy. In P. Salapatek & L. Cohen (Eds.), *Handbook of infant perception.* Vol. 1. New York: Academic Press.

Astin, A. (1977). *Four critical years.* San Francisco: Josey-Bass.

Atchley, R. C. (1971). Retirement and work orientation. *The Gerontologist, 2,* 29–32.

Atchley, R. C. (1976). *The sociology of retirement.* Cambridge, MA: Schenkman.

Athey, I. (1983). Language development factors relating to reading development. *Journal of Educational Research, 76,* 197–203.

Attie, I., & Brooks-Gunn, J. (1989). Development of eating problems in adolescent girls. *Developmental Psychology, 25,* 70–79.

Aubrey, R. R. (1977). Adolescents and death. In E. R. Prichard et al., (Eds.), *Social work with the dying patient and family* (pp. 131–145). New York: Columbia University Press.

Auerbach-Fink, S. (1978). Mothers' expectations of child care. *Young Children, 32,* 12–21.

Aukett, R. (1988). Gender differences in friendship patterns. *Sex Roles, 19,* 57–63.

Ault, R. (1983). *Children's cognitive development* (2nd ed.) New York: Oxford University Press.

Avery, M. E. (1989). *Pediatric medicine.* Baltimore: Williams and Wilkins.

Babchuck, N., Peters, G., Hoyt, D., & Kaiser, M. (1979). The voluntary associations of the aged. *Journal of Gerontology, 34,* 579–587.

Babladelis, G. (1987). Young persons' attitudes toward aging. *Perceptual and Motor Skills, 65,* 553–554.

Backett, L. (1986). *Mothers and fathers.* New York: St. Martin's Press.

Backman, L., Small, B. J., & Wahlin, A. (2001). Age and memory: Cognitive and biological perspectives. In J. E. Birren & K. W. Schaie (Eds.), *Handbook of the psychology of aging.* San Diego, CA: Academic Press.

Bailey, D. A. (1977). The growing child and the need for physical activity. In R. Smart & M. Smart (Eds.), *Readings in child development and relationships* (2nd ed.). New York: Macmillan.

Bailey, G. W. (1989). Current perspectives on substance abuse in youth. *Journal of the American Academy of Child and Adolescent Psychiatry, 28,* 151–162.

Baillargeon, R. (1987). Object permanence in 3 1/2 and 4 1/2 month old infants. *Developmental Psychology, 23,* 655–664.

Baltes, P. B., Lindenberger, U., & Staudinger, U. M. (1998). Life-span theory in developmental psychology. In W. Damon & R. M. Lerner (Eds.), *Handbook of child psychology (Vol. 1): Theoretical models of human development* (5th ed.). NY: John Wiley & Sons, Inc.

Baltes, P., & Schaie, K. (1974). Aging and the IQ: The myth of the twilight years. *Psychology Today, 7,* 35–40.

Baltes, P. B., & Smith, J. (1990). Toward a psychology of wisdom and its ontogenesis. In R. J. Sternberg (Ed.), *Wisdom: Its nature, origins, and development.* NY: Cambridge University Press.

Bandura, A. (1973). *Aggression: A social learning analysis.* Englewood Cliffs, NJ: Prentice Hall.

Bandura, A. (1977). *Social learning theory.* Englewood Cliffs, NJ: Prentice Hall.

Bandura, A. (1986). *Social foundations of thought and action.* Englewood Cliffs, NJ: Prentice Hall.

Bandura, A. (1989). Human agency in social cognitive theory. *American Psychologist, 44,* 1175–1184.

Bandura, A., & Walters, R. H. (1963). *Social learning and personality development.* New York: Holt, Rinehart, and Winston.

Banks, M. S., & Salapatek, P. (1983). Infant visual perception. In M. M. Haith & J. Campos (Eds.), *Handbook of child psychology.* Vol. 2. New York: Wiley.

Baptiste, D. A., Jr. (1987). The gay and lesbian stepparent family. In F. Bozett (Ed.), *Gay and lesbian parents.* New York: Praeger.

Barber, C. E. (1980). Gender differences in experiencing the transition to the empty nest. *Family Perspective, 14,* 87–95.

Barglow, P., Vaughn, B., & Molitor, N. (1987). Effects of maternal absence due to employment on the quality of infant-mother attachment in a low-risk sample. *Child Development, 58,* 945–954.

Barling, J. (1990). *Employment, stress, and family functioning.* Chichester, England: John Wiley.

Barnes, K. E. (1971). Preschool play norms: A replication. *Developmental Psychology, 5,* 99–103.

Barnes, G., & Welte, J. (1988). Predictors of driving while intoxicated among teenagers. *Journal of Drug Issues, 18,* 367–384.

Barranti, C. C. R. (1985). The grandparent/grandchild relationship: Family resource in an era of voluntary bonds. *Family Relations, 34,* 343–352.

Barrera, M., & Maurer, D. (1981). Discrimination of strangers by the three month old. *Child Development, 52,* 558–563.

Barret, R. L., & Robinson, B. L. (1990). *Gay fathers.* Lexington, MA: DC Heath.

Bart, P. (1971). Depression in middle age women. In V. Gornick & B. Moran (Eds.), *Women in sexist society.* New York: Basic Books.

Bart, P. (1975). The loneliness of the long distance mother. In J. Freeman (Ed.), *Women: A feminist perspective.* Palo Alto, CA: Mayfield.

Bass, M., Kravath, R., & Glass, L. (1986). Death-scene investigation in sudden infant death. *New England Journal of Medicine, 315,* 100–105.

Baughman, E. (1971). *Black Americans.* New York: Academic Press.

Baumeister, R., & Senders, P. (1989). Identity development and the role structure of children's games. *Journal of Genetic Psychology, 150,* 19–37.

Baumrind, D. (1966). Effects of authoritative parental control on child behavior. *Child Development, 37,* 887–907.

Baumrind, D. (1967). Child care practices anteceding three patterns of preschool behavior. *Genetic Psychology Monographs, 75,* 43–88.

Baumrind, D. (1971). *Current patterns of parental authority.* Developmental Psychology Monographs, 4(1).

Baurer, D. H. (1976). An exploratory study of developmental changes in children's fears. *Journal of Child Psychology and Psychiatry, 17,* 69–74.

Bayley, N. (1969). *Bayley scales of infant development.* New York: Psychological Corporation.

Bayley, N. (1970). Development of mental abilities. In P. Mussen (Ed.), *Carmichael's manual of child psychology.* (3rd ed.). Vol. 1. New York: Wiley.

Bayley, N., & Oden, M. (1955). The maintenance of intellectual ability in gifted adults. *Journal of Gerontology, 10,* 91–107.

Beattie, M. (1987). *Codependent no more.* New York: Harper/Hazelden.

Beattie, M. (1989). *Beyond codependency and getting better all the time.* San Francisco, CA: Harper & Row.

Beck, S. (1982). Adjustment to and satisfaction with retirement. *Journal of Gerontology, 37,* 616–624.

Beck, M. (1990). *The geezer boom.* Newsweek, Special edition Winter/Spring, 63–68.

Beck, R., & Beck, S. (1989). The incidence of extended households among middle-aged black and white women. *Journal of Family Issues, 10,* 147–168.

Becker, W. (1964). Consequences of different kinds of parental discipline. In M. Hoffman & L. Hoffman (Eds.), *Review of child development research,* Vol. 1. New York: Russell Sage.

Becvar, R. J., & Becvar, D. S. (1982). *Systems theory and family therapy: A primer.* New York: University Press of America.

Belgrave, L. L. (1990). The relevance of chronic illness in the everyday lives of elderly women. *Journal of Aging and Health, 2,* 475–481.

Belkin, L. (1985). *Counseling and support following miscarriage.* New York Times (June 6), 20.

Bell, R. Q. (1968). A reinterpretation of the direction of effects in studies of socialization. *Psychological Review, 75,* 81–95.

Bell, R. Q. (1971). Stimulus control of parent or caretaker behavior by offspring. *Developmental Psychology, 4,* 63–72.

Bell, R. R. (1981). Friendships of women and men. *Psychology of Women Quarterly, 5,* 402–417.

Bell, A. P., & Weinberg, M. S. (1978). *Homosexualities: A study of diversity among men and women.* New York: Simon and Schuster.

Belsky, J. (1978). The effects of day care: A critical review. *Child Development, 49,* 929–949.

Belsky, J. (1981). Early human experience: A family perspective. *Developmental Psychology, 17,* 3–23.

Belsky, J. (1984). *The psychology of aging: Theory and research and practice.* Monterey, CA: Brooks/Cole.

Belsky, J. (1988). The "effects" of infant day care reconsidered. *Early Childhood Research Quarterly, 3,* 235–273.

Belsky, J. (1990). Child care and children's socioemotional development. *Journal of Marriage and the Family, 52,* 885–903.

Belsky, J. (1990). Parental and nonparental child care and children's socioemotional development: A decade in review. *Journal of Marriage and the Family, 52,* 885–903.

Belsky, J., & Rovine, M. J. (1988). Nonmaternal care in the first year of life and the security of infant-parent attachment. *Child Development, 59,* 157–168.

Belsky, J., Lang, M. E., & Rovine, M. (1985). Stability and change in marriage across the transition to parenthood: *A second study. Journal of Marriage and the Family, 47,* 855–865.

Belsky, J., Robins, E., & Gamble, W. (1984). The determinants of parental competence: Toward a contextual theory. In M. Lewis (Ed.), *Beyond the dyad.* New York: Plenum.

Belsky, J., Spanier, G. B., & Rovine, M. (1983). Stability and change in marriage across the transition to parenthood. *Journal of Marriage and the Family, 45,* 567–577.

Belsky, J., Steinberg, L. D., & Walker, A. (1982). The ecology of day care. In M. Lamb (Ed.), *Nontraditional families: Parenting and child development.* Hillsdale, NJ: Erlbaum.

Belsky, J. K. (1988). *Here tomorrow: Making the most of life after fifty.* New York: Ballantine Books.

Bengston, V. (1985). Diversity and symbolism in grandparental roles. In V. Bengston & J. Robertson (Eds.), *Grandparenthood.* Beverly Hills, CA: Sage.

Bem, S. (1989). Genital knowledge and gender constancy in preschool children. *Child Development, 60,* 649–662.

Bengston, V. (1975). Generation and family effects in value socialization. *American Sociological Review, 40,* 358–371.

Bengston, V. L., Cuellar, J. B., & Ragan, P. K. (1977). Stratum contrasts and similarities in attitudes toward death. *Journal of Gerontology, 32,* 76–88.

Bengston, V., Dowd, J., Smith, D., & Inkeles, A. (1975). Modernization, modernity, and perceptions of aging: A cross-cultural study. *Journal of Gerontology, 30,* 688–695.

Bengston, V. L., Rosenthal, C. J., & Burton, L. M. (1990).Families and aging: Diversity and heterogeneity. In R. H. Binstock & L. George (Eds.), *Handbook of aging and the social sciences* (3rd ed.). San Diego, CA: Academic Press.

Benoliel, J. Q. (1975). Childhood diabetes: The commonplace in living becomes uncommon. In A. L. Strauss & B. G. Glaser (Eds.), *Chronic illness and the quality of life.* St. Louis, MO: Mosby.

Beresin, E. V., Gordon, C., & Herzog, D. B. (1989). The process of recovering from anorexia nervosa. *Journal of the American Academy of Psychoanalysis, 17,* 103–130.

Bergstrom, L. R. (1990). Retiring with security. *Security Management, 34,* 97–100.

Berk, L. E. (1986). Private speech: Learning out loud. *Psychology Today,* (May), 34–42.

Berlinsky, E., & Biller, H. B. (1982). *Parental death and psychological development.* Lexington, MA: Lexington Books.

Berman, A. L. (1986). Helping suicidal adolescents: Needs and responses. In C. A. Cort & J. M. McNell (Eds.), *Adolescence and death* (pp. 151–166). New York: Springer.

Bernard, J. (1981). The good provider role: Its rise and fall. *American Psychologist, 36,* 1–12.

Berndt, T., Hawkins, J., & Hoyle, S. (1986). Changes in friendship during a school year: Effects on children's and adolescents' impressions of friendship and sharing with friends. *Child Development, 57,* 1284–1297.

Bernstein, B. E. (1978). Generational conflict and the family. *Adolescence, 13,* 751–754.

Bertenthal, B, & Campos, J. (1987). New directions in the study of early experience. *Child Development, 58,* 560–567.

Bianchi, S. M., & Spain, D. (1986). *American women in transition.* New York: Russell Sage Foundation.

Bieber, I., Dain, H., Dince, P., Drellich, M., Grand, H.,Gundlach, R., Kremer, M., Rifkin, A., Wilbur, C., & Bieber, T. (1962). *Homosexuality: A psychoanalytical study.* New York: Basic Books.

Bigner, J. J. (1972a). Parent education in popular literature: 1950–1970. *Family Coordinator, 21,* 313–319.

Bigner, J. J. (1972b). Sibling influence on sex-role preference of young children. *Journal of Genetic Psychology, 121,* 271–282.

Bigner, J. J. (1974a). A Wernerian developmental analysis of children's descriptions of siblings. *Child Development, 45,* 317–323.

Bigner, J. J. (1974b). Second-born's discrimination of sibling role concepts. *Developmental Psychology, 10 ,* 564–573.

Bigner, J. J. (1980). *Preliminary report: Development of social competencies in children.* Ft. Collins, CO: Colorado State University Experiment Station.

Bigner, J. J. (1989). *Parent-child relations: An introduction to parenting* (3rd ed.). New York: Macmillan.

Bigner, J. J., & Bozett, F. W. (1989). Parenting by gay fathers. *Marriage and Family Review, 14,* 155–176.

Bigner, J. J., & Jacobsen, R. B. (1980). Children's perceptions of "goodness" and "badness" in sibling roles. *Home Economics Research Journal, 8,* 274–280.

Bigner, J. J., & Jacobsen, R. B. (1989a). The value of children to gay and heterosexual fathers. *Journal of Homosexuality, 18,* 163–172.

Bigner, J. J., & Jacobsen, R. B. (1989b). Parenting behaviors of homosexual and heterosexual fathers. *Journal of Homosexuality, 18,* 173–186.

Bigner, J. J., Jacobsen, R. B., & Heward, L. (1987). *Developmental changes in the value of children for adults.* Unpublished manuscript.

Bigner, J. J., Jacobsen, R. B., & Miller, J. A. (1982). The value of children for farm families. *Psychological Reports, 50,* 793–794.

Bigner, J. J., Jacobsen, R. B., & Phelan, G. K. (1981). Cultural correlates of parent-nonparent stereotypes: A multivariate analysis. *Home Economics Research Journal, 9,* 184–192.

Binstock, R. H. (1987). Health care: Organization, use, and financing. In G. Maddox (Ed.), *Encyclopedia of aging.* New York: Springer.

Birch, L. L. (1987). Children's food preferences: Developmental patterns and environmental influences. *Annals of Child Development, 4,* 171–208.

Birch, L. L., McPhee, L., & Sullivan, S. (1989). Children's food intake following drinks sweetened with sucrose or aspartame: Time course effects. *Physiology and Behavior, 45,* 387–395.

Birnholz, J., & Benacerraf, B. (1983). The development of human fetal hearing. *Science, 222,* 516–518.

Birren, J. E., Kinney, D. K., Schaie, K. W., and Woodruff, D. S. (1981). *Developmental psychology.* Boston: Houghton Mifflin.

Birren, J. E., & Schaie, K. W. (Eds.) (2001). *Handbook of the psychology of aging.* San Diego, CA: Academic Press.

Birren, J. E., Woods, A., & Williams, M. (1980). Behavioral slowing with age: Causes, organization, and consequences. In L. Poon (Ed.), *Aging in the 1980s.* Washington, DC: American Psychological Association.

Black, C., & DeBlassie, R. R. (1985). Adolescent pregnancy: Contributing factors, consequences, treatment, and plausible solutions. *Adolescence, 47,* 671–678.

Black, H. (1953). *Black's law dictionary* (4th ed.). St. Paul, MN: West.

Blakeslee, S. (1986). Rapid changes seen in young brain. *New York Times, June 24,* C1, C10.

Blank, R. H. (2001). Technology and death policy. In G. E. Dickinson & M. R. Leming, (Eds.), *Dying, death, and bereavement* (10th ed.). NY: McGraw-Hill.

Blau, Z. S. (1973). *Old age in a changing society.* New York: Franklin Watts.

Blieszner, R., & Alley, J. (1990). Family caregiving for the elderly: An overview of resources. *Family Relations, 39,* 97–102.

Block, C., Norr, K., Meyering, S., Norr, J., & Charles, A. (1981). Husband gatekeeping in childbirth. *Family Relations, 30,* 197–204.

Blood, R. O., & Wolfe, D. M. (1960). *Husbands and wives: The dynamics of married living.* New York: Free Press.

Bloom, B. S. (1964). *Stability and change in human characteristics.* New York: Wiley.

Bloom, L. (1970). *Language development: Form and function in emerging grammar.* Cambridge, MA: MIT Press.

Bloom, L., & Lahey, M. (1978). *Language development and language disorders.* New York: Wiley.

Bloom, M. V. (1987). Leaving home: A family transition. In J. & S. Bloom-Feshbach (Eds.), *The psychology of separation and loss: Perspectives on development, life transitions, and clinical practice.* San Francisco: Josey-Bass.

Blumberg, R. L., & Winch, R. F. (1977). Societal complexity and familial complexity: Evidence for the curvilinear hypothesis. *American Journal of Sociology, 77,* 898–920.

Blumenfield, M., Levy, N. B., & Kaufman, D. (1978). The wish to be informed of a fatal illness. *Omega, 9,* 323–326.

Bohannan, P. (1970). The six stations of divorce. In P. Bohannan (Ed.), *Divorce and after.* New York: Doubleday.

Boivin, M., & Begin, G. (1989). Peer status and self-perception among early elementary school children: The case of the rejected children. *Child Development, 60,* 591–596.

Bok, S. (1976). Personal directions for the care at the end of life. *The New England Journal of Medicine, 295,* 367–368.

Boldt, M. (1982). Normative evaluations of suicide and death: A cross generational study. *Omega, 13,* 145–157.

Borg, S., & Lasker J. (1981). *When pregnancy fails: Families coping with miscarriage, stillbirth, and infant death.* Boston: Beacon Press.

Borhek, M. V. (1988). Helping gay and lesbian adolescents and their families: A mother's perspective. *Journal of Adolescent Health Care, 9,* 123–128.

Borke, H. (1975). Piaget's mountains revisited: Change in the egocentric landscape. *Developmental Psychology, 12,* 185–191.

Bornstein, M., & Sigman, M. (1986). Continuity in mental development from infancy. *Child Development, 57,* 251–274.

Boss, P. (1980). Normative family stress: Boundary changes across the life span. *Family Relations, 29,* 445–452.

Botwinick, J. (1977). Intellectual abilities. In J. E. Birren & K. Schaie (Eds.), *Handbook of the psychology of aging.* New York: Van Nostrand.

Boukydis, C., & Burgess, R. (1982). Adult physiological response to infant cries: Effects of temperament of infant, parental status, and gender. *Child Development, 53,* 1291–1298.

Bower, T. (1975). Infant perception of the third dimension and object concept development. In L. Cohen & P. Salapatek (Eds.), *Infant perception: From sensation to cognition.* Vol. 2. New York: Academic Press.

Bower, T. (1976). Repetitive processes in child development. *Scientific American, 235,* 38–47.

Bower, T. (1977). *A primer of infant development.* San Francisco: Freeman.

Bowlby, J. (1952). *Maternal care and mental health.* Monograph Series No. 2. Geneva: World Health Organization.

Bowlby, J. (1969). *Attachment and loss: Attachment* (Vol. 1). NY: Basic Books.

Bowlby, J. (1980). *Attachment and loss: Loss, sadness, and depression.* (Vol. 3). New York: Basic Books.

Bowlby, J. (1982). Attachment and loss: Retrospect and prospect. *American Journal of Orthopsychiatry, 52,* 664–678.

Bowman, M. L. (1990). Coping efforts and marital satisfaction: Measuring marital coping and its correlates. *Journal of Marriage and the Family, 52,* 463–474.

Boyden, T., Carroll, J., & Maier, R. (1984). Similarity and attraction in homosexual males: The effects of age and masculinity-femininity. *Sex Roles, 10,* 939–948.

Boysson-Bardies, B., Sagart, L., & Durand, C. (1984). Discernible differences in the babbling of infants according to target language. *Journal of Child Language, 11,* 1–15.

Bozett, F. W., & Sussman, M. B. (1989). Homosexuality and family relations: Views and research issues. *Marriage and Family Review, 14,* 1–8.

Brackbill, Y. (1977). Long-term effects of obstetrical anesthesia on infant autonomic function. *Developmental Psychology, 10,* 529–535.

Brackbill, Y., Adams, G., Drowell, D. H., & Gray, M. L. (1966). Arousal levels in neonates and preschool children under continuous auditory stimulation. *Journal of Experimental Child Psychology, 4,* 178–188.

Bradbard, M. R., & Endsley, R. C. (1986). Sources of variance in young working mothers' satisfaction with child care. In S. Kilmer (Ed.), *Advances in early education and day care.* Vol. 4. Greenwich, CT: JAI.

Bradshaw, J. (1988). *Bradshaw on: The family.* Deerfield Beach, FL: Health Communications.

Bransford, J. D., Brown, A. L., & Cocking, R. R. (Eds.) (2000). *How people learn: Brain, mind, experience, and school* (Expanded ed.). Washington, DC: National Academy Press.

Brasted, W. S., & Callahan, E. J. (1984). Review article: A behavioral analysis of the grief process. *Behavioral Therapy, 15,* 529–543.

Bratcher, W. (1982). The influence of the family on career selection: A family systems perspective. *Personnel and Guidance Journal, October,* 87–91.

Brazelton, T. B. (1969). *Infants and mothers: Differences in development.* New York: Delacorte.

Brazelton, T. B. (1978). Introduction. In A. J. Sameroff (Ed.), Organization and stability of newborn behavior: A commentary on the Brazelton Neonatal Behavior Assessment Scale. *Monographs of the Society for Research in Child Development, 43* (177), 1–13.

Brazelton, T. B. (1987). Behavioral competence in the newborn infant. In G. B. Avery (Ed.), *Neonatalogy: Pathophysiology and management of the newborn.* (Pp. 379–399). Philadelphia: Lippincott.

Brehm, S. S. (1992). *Intimate relationships* (2nd ed). NY: McGraw-Hill, Inc.

Bretschneider, J. G., & McCoy, N. L. (1988). Sexual interest and behavior in healthy 80 to 102-year-olds. *Archives of Sexual Behavior, 17,* 109–129.

Bridges, K. (1930). A genetic theory of emotions. *Journal of Genetic Psychology, 37,* 514–527.

Bridges, K. (1932). Emotional development in early infancy. *Child Development, 3,* 324–341.

Broccolo, A. (1989). How to select the right nursing home. *Family Safety and Health, 48,* 7–13.

Brock, D. W. (2006). How much is more life worth? In G. E. Dickinson & M. R. Leming, (Eds.), *Dying, death, and bereavement* (10th ed.). NY: McGraw-Hill.

Broderick, C. (1979). *Marriage and the family.* Englewood Cliffs, NJ: Prentice Hall.

Brody, E. (1981). Women in the middle and family help to older people. *The Gerontologist, 21,* 471–480.

Brody, E. B., & Brody, N. (1976). *Intelligence.* New York: Academic Press.

Brody, J. (1990). *Preventing children from joining yet another unfit generation.* New York Times, May 24, B14.

Broman, S. (1986). Obstetric mediation: A review of the literature on outcomes in infancy and childhood. In M. Lewis (Ed.), *Learning disabilities and prenatal risk.* Urbana, IL: University of Illinois Press.

Bronfenbrenner, U. (1977a). Nobody home: The erosion of the American family. *Psychology Today, 10* (May), 41–47.

Bronfenbrenner, U. (1977b). Toward an experimental ecology of human development. *American Psychologist, 32,* 513–531.

Bronfenbrenner, U., & Morris, P. A. (1998). The ecology of developmental processes. In W. Damon & R. M. Lerner (Eds.), *Handbook of child psychology (Vol. 1): Theoretical models of human development* (5th ed.). NY: John Wiley & Sons, Inc.

Brook, J., Whiteman, M., Gordon, A., & Cohen, P. (1986). Some models and mechanisms for explaining the impact of maternal and adolescent characteristics on adolescent stage of drug use. *Developmental Psychology, 22,* 460–467.

Brooke, V. (1989). Nursing home life: How elders adjust. *Geriatric Nursing, 10,* 66–74.

Brooks, R., & Obrzut, J. (1981). Brain lateralization: Implications for infant stimulation and development. *Young Children, 26,* 9–16.

Brooks-Gunn, J., & Furstenberg, F. (1990). Coming of age in the era of AIDS: Puberty, sexuality, and contraception. *Milbank Quarterly, 68,* 59–84.

Brooks-Gunn, J., & Petersen, A. (1983). *Girls at puberty.* New York: Plenum.

Brooks-Gunn, J., & Ruble, D. (1982). The development of menstrual-related beliefs and behavior during adolescence. *Child Development, 53,* 1567–1577.

Brooks-Gunn, J., Boyer, C., & Hein, K. (1988). Preventing HIV infection and AIDS in children and adolescents. *American Psychologist, 43,* 958–964.

Brophy, J. (1986). Teacher influences on student achievement. *American Psychologist, 41,* 1069–1077.

Brown, A. (1982). Learning and development: The problems of compatibility, access, and induction. *Human Development, 25,* 89–115.

Brown, A., Bransford, J., Ferrarar, R., & Campione, J. (1983). Learning, remembering, and understanding. In P. Mussen (Ed.), *Handbook of child psychology* (4th ed.). Vol. 3. New York: Wiley.

Brown, J. M., O'Keefe, J., Sanders, S., & Baker, B. (1986). Developmental changes in children's cognition to stressful and painful situations. *Journal of Pediatric Psychology, 11,* 343–357.

Brown, R. A. (1973). *First language.* Cambridge: Harvard University Press.

Brown, S. (1989). Life events of adolescents in relation to personal and parental substance abuse. *American Journal of Psychiatry, 146,* 484–489.

Brown, S. L., & Booth, A. (1996). Cohabitation versus marriage: A comparison of relationship quality. *Journal of Marriage and Family, 58,* 668–678.

Brubaker, T. H. (1990). Families in later life. *Journal of Marriage and the Family, 52,* 959–982.

Bruch, H. (1978). *The golden cage: The enigma of anorexia nervosa.* Cambridge, MA: Harvard University Press.

Bruner, J. (1971). *The relevance of education.* New York: Norton.

Bruner, J. (1983). *Child's talk.* New York: Norton.

Bruner, J., Olver, R., & Greenfield, P. (1966). *Studies in cognitive growth.* New York: Wiley.

Buell, S. J., & Coleman, P. D. (1979). Dendritic growth in the aged human brain and failure of growth in senile dementia. *Science, 206,* 854–856.

Bugen, L. A. (1979). *Death and dying: Theory/research/practice.* Dubuque, IA: William C. Brown.

Bugental, D. B. (1986). Unmasking the "polite smile:" Situational and personal determinants of managed affect in adult-child interaction. *Personality and Social Psychology Bulletin, 12,* 7–16.

Bullock, M. (1985). Animism in childhood thinking: A new look at an old question. *Developmental Psychology, 21,* 217–226.

Bullock, M., & Lutkenhaus, P. (1988). The development of volitional behavior in the toddler years. *Child Development, 59,* 664–675.

Bumpass, L. L. (1984). Children and martial disruption: A replication and update. *Demography, 21,* 71–81.

Bumpass, L. L., & Lu, H. H. (2000). Trends in cohabitation and implications for children s family contexts in the United States. *Population Studies, 54,* 29–41.

Burden, D. S. (1986). Single parents and the work setting: The impact of multiple job and home life responsibilities. *Family Relations, 35,* 37–44.

Burger, S., Miller, B., & Mauney, B. (1986). *A guide to management and supervision of nursing homes.* Springfield, IL: Charles C. Thomas.

Burns, D. D. (1980). *Feeling good: The new mood therapy.* New York: William Morrow and Co., Inc.

Burns, D. D. (1989). *The feeling good handbook: Using the new mood therapy in everyday life.* New York: William Morrow.

Burnside, I. M., Ebersole, P., & Monea H. E. (Eds.). (1979). *Psychological caring through the life cycle.* New York: McGraw-Hill.

Burt, R. D., Vaughan, T. L., & Daling, J. R. (1988). Evaluating the risks of Cesarean section: Low Apgar score in repeat C-section and vaginal deliveries. *American Journal of Public Health, 78,* 1312–1314.

Busse, E. W. (1987). Primary and secondary aging. In G. Maddox (Ed.), *The encyclopedia of aging.* New York: Springer.

Butler, L. (1989). Sexual problems in the elderly, II: Men's vs. women's. *Geriatrics, 44,* 75–82.

Butler, R. N. (1963). The life review: An interpretation of reminiscence in the aged. *Psychiatry, 26,* 65–76.

Button, R. (1990). Self-esteem in girls aged 11–12: Baseline findings from a planned prospective study of vulnerability to eating disorders. *Journal of Adolescence, 13,* 407–413.

Cahan, S., & Cohen, M. (1989). Age versus schooling effects on intelligence development. *Child Development, 60,* 1239–1249.

Cain, W. S., Reid, F., & Stevens, J. C. (1990). Missing ingredients: Aging and the discrimination of flavor. *Journal of Nutrition for the Elderly, 9,* 3–9.

Cairns, R. B. (1998). The making of developmental psychology. In W. Damon & R. M. Lerner (Eds.), *Handbook of child psychology (Vol. 1): Theoretical models of human development* (5th ed.). NY: John Wiley & Sons, Inc.

Caldwell, M., & Peplau, L. (1984). The balance of power in lesbian relationships. *Sex Roles, 10,* 587–599.

Caldwell, B. M., Wright, C., Honig, A., & Tannenbaum, J. (1970). Infant day care and attachment. *American Journal of Orthopsychiatry, 40,* 397–412.

Calhoun, L. G., & Selby, J. W. (1980). Voluntary childlessness, involuntary childlessness, and having children: A study of social perceptions. *Family Relations, 29,* 181–183.

Callari, E. S. (1986). *A gentle death: Personal caregiving to the terminally ill.* Greensboro, N.C.: Tudor.

Cameron, E. (1988). Old, needy, and black. *Nursing Times, August 10,* 38.

Campbell, D., Bunker, V. W., & Thomas, A. J. (1989). Selenium and vitamin E status of healthy and institutionalized elderly subjects: Analysis of plasma, erthyrocytes and platelets. *British Journal of Nutrition, 61,* 221–225.

Candib, L. M. (1989). Point and counterpoint: Family life cycle theory: A feminist critique. *Family Systems Medicine, 7,* 473–487.

Cantor, N. F. (2001). Studying the Black Death. In G. E. Dickinson & M. R. Leming, (Eds.), *Dying, death, and bereavement* (10th ed.). NY: McGraw-Hill.

Cantor, P. (1977). Suicide and attempted suicide among students: Problem, prediction, and prevention. In P. Cantor (Ed.), *Understanding a child's world.* New York: McGraw-Hill.

Cantor, D., Fischel, J., & Kaye, H. (1983). Neonatal conditionability: A new paradigm for exploring the use of interoceptive clues. *Infant Behavior and Development, 6,* 403–413.

Caputo, D. V., & Mandell, W. (1970). Consequences of low birth weight. *Developmental Psychology, 3,* 363–383.

Carey, S. (1978). The child as word learner. In M. Halle, J. Bresnan, & G. Miller (Eds.), *Linguistic theory and psychological reality.* Cambridge, MA: MIT Press.

Carey, R. G., & Posavac, E. J. (1978). Attitudes of physicians on disclosing information to and maintaining life for terminal patients. *Omega, 9,* 67–77.

Carroll, J., & Rest, J. (1982). Moral development. In B. Wolman (Ed.), *Handbook of human development.* Englewood Cliffs, NJ: Prentice Hall.

Carruth, B. R., & Goldberg, D. L. (1990). Nutritional issues of adolescents: Athletics and the body image mania. *Journal of Early Adolescence, 10,* 122–140.

Carter, D., & Welch, D. (1981). Parenting styles and children's behavior. *Family Relations, 30,* 191–195.

Carver, C. S., & Gaines, J. G. (1987). Optimism, pessimism, and postpartum depression. *Cognitive Therapy and Research, 11,* 449–462.

Cassady, G., & Strange, M. (1987). The small-for-gestational age (SGA) infant. In G. B. Avery (Ed.), *Neonatology: Pathophysiology and management of the newborn.* (pp. 299–331). Philadelphia: Lippincott.

Cassel, C. K. (Ed.). (1990). *Geriatric medicine.* New York: Springer-Verlag.

Cassidy, J. (1986). The ability to negotiate the environment: An aspect of infant competence as related to quality of attachment. *Child Development, 57,* 121–134.

Cataldo, C., & Whitney, E. (1986). *Nutrition and diet therapy: Principles and practices.* St. Paul, MN: West Publishing Co. Center for Disease Control. (1991).

Cernoch, J., & Porter, R. (1985). Recognition of maternal axillary odors by infants. *Child Development, 56,* 1593–1598.

Chance, P., & Fischman, J. (1987). The magic of childhood. *Psychology Today, 21* (May), 48–60.

Chand, I., Crider, D., & Willets, F. (1975). Parent-youth disagreement as perceived by youth: A longitudinal study. *Youth and Society, 6,* 365–375.

Charmaz, K. (1980). *The social reality of death: Death in contemporary America.* Reading, MA: Addison-Wesley.

Chasnoff, I. J. (1988). *Drugs, alcohol, pregnancy, and parenting.* Hingham, MA: Kluwer.

Chatters, L. M. (1988). Subjective well-being evaluations among older blacks. *Psychology and Aging, 3,* 184–190.

Chavance, M., Herbeth, B., & Fournier, C. (1989). Vitamin status, immunity, and infections in an elderly population. *European Journal of Clinical Nutrition, 43,* 827–833.

Cherlin, A., & Furstenberg, F. (1986). *The new American grandparent: A place in the family.* New York: Basic Books.

Cherry, L., & Lewis, M. (1976). The preschool teacher-child dyad: Sex differences in verbal interaction. *Child Development, 46,* 532–535.

Chilman, C. (1968). Families in development at mid-stage of the family life cycle. *Family Coordinator, 17,* 297–312.

Chilman, C. (1980). Parental satisfactions, concerns, and goals for their children. *Family Relations, 29,* 339–345.

Chilman, C. (1983). *Adolescent sexuality in a changing American society* (2nd ed.). New York: Wiley.

Chiriboga, D., & Cutler, L. (1980). Stress and adaptation: Life span perspectives. In L. W. Poon (Ed.), *Aging in the 1980s.* Washington, DC: American Psychological Association.

Chiriboga, D. (1981). The developmental psychology of middle age. In J. Howells (Ed.), *Modern perspectives in the psychiatry of middle age.* New York: Bruner/Mazel.

Chiriboga, D., & Cutler, L. (1980). Stress and adaptation: Life span perspectives. In L. W. Poon (Ed.), *Aging in the 1980s.* Washington, DC: American Psychological Association.

Chisholm, J. S. (1983). *Navajo infancy: An ethological study of child development.* New York: Aldine.

Chitwood, D. G., & Bigner, J. J. (1980). Young children's perceptions about old people. *Home Economics Research Journal, 8,* 369–374.

Chng, C. (1982). Sudden infant death syndrome: An inexplicable tragedy for the family. *Family Perspective, 16,* 123–128.

Choi, J. W. (1978). Exercise and participation in sports among persons 20 years of age and over. *Advance Data from Vital and Health Statistics, No. 19,* March 15.

Chomsky, N. (1957). *Syntactic structures.* The Hague: Mouton.

Chomsky, N. (1959). A review of B. F. Skinner's Verbal behavior. *Language, 35,* 26–58.

Chomsky, N. (1965). *Aspects of a theory of syntax.* Cambridge, MA: MIT Press.

Chomsky, N. (1968). *Language and mind.* New York: Harcourt, Brace, Jovanovich.

Chomsky, N. (1975). *Reflections on language.* New York: Pantheon Books.

Chown, S. (Ed.). (1972). *Human aging.* Baltimore: Penguin.

Chugani, H., & Phelps, M. (1986). Maturational changes in cerebral function in infants determined by FDG positron emission tomography. *Science, 231,* 840–843.

Chumlea, W. C. (1982). Physical growth in adolescence. In B. Wolman (Ed.), *Handbook of developmental psychology.* Englewood Cliffs, NJ: Prentice Hall.

Cicirelli, V. (1983). Adult children and their elderly parents. In T. Brubaker (Ed.), *Family relationships in later life.* Beverly Hills, CA: Sage.

Claperede, E. (1912). Jean Jacques Rousseau et la conception functionelle de l'enfance. *Revue de Metaphysique et de Morale, 20,* 391–416.

Clapp, G. (1988). Television: Today's most important socializer? In G. Clapp (Ed.), *Child study research.* Lexington, MA: Lexington Books.

Clark, E. V. (1982). The young word maker: A case study of innovation in the child's lexicon. In E. Warner & L. Gleitman (Eds.), *Language acquisition: The state of the art.* Cambridge, England: Cambridge University Press.

Clark, D. (1988). *As we are.* Boston, MA: Alyson Publications.

Clarke, J. I., & Dawson, C. (1989). *Growing up again: Parenting ourselves, parenting our children.* Minneapolis, MN: Hazelden.

Clarke-Stewart, K. A. (1984). Day care: A new context for research and development. In M. Perlmutter (Ed.), Parent-child interactions and parent-child relations in child development: *The Minnesota symposium on child psychology.* Vol. 17. Hillsdale, NJ: Erlbaum.

Clarke-Stewart, K. A. (1988). Parents effects on children's development: A decade of progress? *Journal of Applied Developmental Psychology, 9,* 41–84.

Clarke-Stewart, K. (1989). Infant day care: Maligned or malignant? *American Psychologist, 44,* 266–273.

Clasen, D., & Brown, B. (1985). The multidimensionality of peer pressure in adolescence. *Journal of Youth and Adolescence, 14,* 451–468.

Clavan, S. (1978). The impact of social class and social trends on the role of grandparent. *Family Coordinator, 27,* 351–357.

Clemens, A. W., & Axelson, L. J. (1985). The not-so-empty nest: Return of the fledgling adult. *Family Relations, 34,* 259–264.

Clinton, H. R. (1990). *In France, day care is every child's right.* New York Times, April 7, 25.

Cohan, C. L., & Kleinbaum, S. (2002). Toward a greater understanding of the cohabitation effect: Premarital cohabitation and marital communication. *Journal of Marriage and Family, 64,* 180–192.

Cohen, E. (2005). What living wills won't do. In G. E. Dickinson & M.R. Leming, (Eds.), *Dying, death, and bereavement* (10th ed.). NY: McGraw-Hill.

Cohen, G. (1987). Alzheimer's disease. In G. Maddox (Ed.),The encyclopedia of aging. New York: Springer. Comfort, A. (1976). *A good age.* New York: Crown.

Cohen, D., & Zigler, E. (1977). Federal day care standards: Rationale and recommendations. *American Journal of Orthopsychiatry, 47,* 456–465.

Cohen, J., Coburn, K., & Pearlman, J. (1980). *Hitting our stride: Good news about women in their middle years.* New York: Delacorte.

Coie, J. D., & Kuperschmidt, J. B. (1983). A behavioral analysis of emerging social status in boys' groups. *Child Development, 54,* 1400–1416.

Coleman, J. (1961). *The adolescent society.* Glencoe, IL: Free Press.

Coleman, M., & Ganong, L. H. (1985). Remarriage myths: Implications for the helping professions. *Journal of Counseling and Development, 64,* 116–120.

Coleman, M., & Ganong, L. H. (1990). Remarriage and stepfamilies. *Journal of Marriage and the Family, 52,* 925–940.

Colligan, R. C., & Offord, K. P. (1990). MacAndrew versus MacAndrew: The relative efficacy of the MAC and the SAP scales for the MMPI in screening male adolescents for substance abuse. *Journal of Personality Assessment, 55,* 708–716.

Colombo, J. (1982). The critical period concept: Research, methodology, and theoretical issues. *Psychological Bulletin, 91,* 260–275.

Comer, J., & Schraft, C. (1980). Working with black parents. In R. Abidin (Ed.), *Parent education and intervention handbook.* Springfield, IL: Charles C. Thomas.

Comfort, A. (1970). Biological theories of aging. *Human Development, 13,* 127–139.

Condon, W. S., & Sander, L. W. (1974). Synchrony demonstrated between movements of the neonate and adult speech. *Child Development, 45,* 456–462.

Condon, J. T., & Watson, T. L. (1987). The maternity blues: Exploration of a psychological hypothesis. *Acta Psychiatrica Scandinavia, 76,* 164–171.

Condry, J., Bence, P., & Scheibe, C. (1988). Nonprogram content of children's television. *Journal of Broadcasting and Electronic Media, 32,* 255–269.

Conley, B. H. (1987). Funeral directors as first responders. In E. J. Dunne, J. L. McIntosh, & K. Dunne-Maxim (Eds.), *Suicide and its aftermath: Understanding and counseling pediatric illness* (pp. 171–181). New York: Norton.

Cook, J. A. (1983). A death in the family: Parental bereavement in the first year of life. *Suicide and Life Threatening Behavior, 13,* 42–61.

Cook, S. (1985). Experimenting on social issues: The case of school desegregation. *American Psychologist, 40,* 452–460.

Cook, A. S., & Oltjenbruns, K. A. (1982). A cognitive developmental approach to death education for adolescents. *Family Perspective, 16,* 9–14.

Cook, A. S., & Oltjenbruns, K. A. (1989). *Dying and grieving: Life span and family perspectives.* New York: Holt, Rinehart, Winston.

Cook, T. H., & Miller, N. (1985). The challenge of Alzheimer's disease. *American Psychologist, 40,* 1245–1250.

Coopersmith, S. (1967). *The antecedents of self-esteem.* San Francisco: Freeman.

Corbin, C. (1980). The physical fitness of children. In C. Corbin (Ed.), *A textbook of motor development.* Dubuque, IA: W. C. Brown.

Cordell, A., Parke, R., & Sawin, D. (1980). Fathers' views of fatherhood with special reference to infancy. *Family Relations, 29,* 331–338.

Coverman, S., & Sheley, J. (1986). Change in men's housework and childcare time, 1965–1975. *Journal of Marriage and the Family, 48,* 413–422.

Cowan, C., Cowan, P., Heming, G., Garrett, E., Coysh, W., Curtis-Boles, H., Boles, A. (1985). Transitions to parenthood: His, hers, and theirs. *Journal of Family Issues, 6,* 451–482.

Cowgill, D. (1986). *Aging around the world.* Belmont, CA: Wadsworth.

Cox, F. D. (1990). *Human intimacy: Marriage, the family, and its meaning* (5th ed.). St. Paul, MN: West.

Cox, H. (1977). Eastern cults and western culture: Why young Americans are buying oriental religions. *Psychology Today, July,* 43–47.

Cox, H. (Ed.) (2006). *Annual editions: Aging* (18th ed.). Dubuque, IA: McGraw-Hill/Dushkin.

Cox, M. J., Owen, M. T., Lewis, J., Riedel, C., Scalf-McIver, L., & Suster, A. (1985). Intergenerational influences on the parent-infant relationship in the transition to parenthood. *Journal of Family Issues, 6,* 543–564.

Cozby, P. C. (2001). *Methods in behavioral research* (8th ed.). NY: McGraw Hill.

Craik, F., Byrd, M., & Swanson, J. (1987). Patterns of memory loss in three elderly samples. *Psychology and Aging, 21,* 79–86.

Crain, W. C. (2005). *Theories of development: Concepts and applications* (5th ed.). Englewood Cliffs, NJ: Prentice Hall.

Cratty, B. J. (1986). *Perceptual and motor skill development in infants and children* (3rd ed.). Englewood Cliffs, NJ: Prentice Hall.

Crawford, J. K. (1980). The role of hospice services in family members' adjustment to death. Unpublished master's thesis, University of Nebraska.

Crilly, R. G., Willems, D. A., & Trenholm, K. J. (1989). Effect of exercise on postural sway in the elderly. *Gerontology, 35,* 137–145.

Crockett, W., & Hummert, M. (1987). Perceptions of aging and the aged. In K. Schaie & K. Eisdorfer (Eds.), *Annual review of gerontology and geriatrics.* Vol. 7. New York: Springer.

Crone, T. M. (1990). The aging of America: Impacts on the marketplace and workplace. *Business Review, May 1,* 3.

Crook, C. (1978). Taste perception in the newborn infant. *Infant Behavior and Development, 1,* 52–69.

Crook, C., & Lipsett, L. (1976). Neonatal nutritive sucking: Effects of taste stimulation on sucking rhythm and heart rate. *Child Development, 47,* 518–522.

Crosby, J. (1985). *Reply to myth: Perspectives on intimacy.* New York: Wiley.

Cross, D., & Paris, S. (1988). Developmental and instructional analyses of children's metacognition and reading comprehension. *Journal of Educational Psychology, 80,* 131–142.

Crouter, A., MacDermid, S., McHale, S., & Perry-Jenkins, M. (1990). Parental monitoring and perceptions of children's school performance and conduct dual--and single-earner families. *Developmental Psychology, 26,* 649–657.

Crouter, A., Perry-Jenkins, M., Huston, T., & McHale, S. (1987). Processes underlying father involvement in dual-earner and single-earner families. *Developmental Psychology, 23,* 431–441.

Csikszentimihalyi, M., & Larson, R. (1984). *Being adolescent: Conflict and growth in the teenage years.* New York: Basic Books.

Cuber, J. F., & Haroff, P. B. (1965). *Sex and the significant Americans.* Baltimore: Penguin Books.

Cumming, E. (1963). Further thoughts on the theory of disengagement. *International Social Science Journal, 15,* 377–393.

Cumming, E., & Henry, W. E. (1961). *Growing old.* New York: Basic Books.

Cunningham, F. G., MacDonald, P. C., & Gant, N. F. (1989). *Williams' obstetrics* (18th ed.). Norwalk, CN: Appleton & Lange.

Cutler, S. (1977). Aging and voluntary association participation. *Journal of Gerontology, 32,* 470–479.

Cutler, W., Garcia, C., & McCoy, N. (1987). Perimenopausal sexuality. *Archives of Sexual Behavior, 16,* 225–234.

Daly, M. P., & Sobal, J. (1990). Vitamin/mineral supplement use by geriatric outpatients in the United Kingdom. *Journal of Nutrition for the Elderly, 10,* 55–60.

Damon, W. (1983). Self-understanding and moral development from childhood to adolescence. In W. Kurtines & J. Gewirtz (Eds.), *Morality, moral behavior, and moral development.* New York: Wiley.

Damon, W., & Hart, D. (1982). The development of self-understanding from infancy through adolescence. *Child Development, 53,* 841–864.

Damon, W., & Lerner, R. M. (1998). *Handbook of child psychology (Vol. 1): Theoretical models of human development* (5th ed.). NY: John Wiley & Sons, Inc.

Dannemiller, J., & Stephens, B. (1988). A critical test of infant pattern preference models. *Child Development, 59,* 210–216.

Davidoff, J. B. (1975). *Differences in visual perception: The individual eye.* New York: Academic Press.

Davidson, J. K., & Darling, C. A. (1988). The stereotype of single women revisited: Sexual practices and sexual satisfaction among professional women. *Health Care for Women International, 9,* 317–322.

Davies, L., & Carr, K. (1991). Warning signs for malnutrition in the elderly. *Journal of the American Dietetic Association, 91,* 1413–1420.

Dawson, D. A., & Cain, V. S. (1990). Child care arrangements: United States, 1988. *Advance Data From Vital and Health Statistics, No. 187.* Hyattsville, MD: National Center for Health Statistics.

Dawson, D., & Hendershot, G. (1987). Aging in the Eighties: Functional limitations of individuals age 65 and over. *Advance Data from Vital and Health Statistics, No. 133, June 10.* DHHS Publication No. (PHS) 87–1250. Hyattsville, MD: U. S. Public Health Service.]

Deaux, K. (1985). Sex and gender. *Annual Review of Psychology, 36,* 49–81.

DeCasper, A. J., & Carstens, A. A. (1981). Contingencies of stimulation: Effects on learning and emotion in neonates. *Infant Behavior and Development, 4,* 19–35.

DeFrain, J. (1979). Androgynous parents tell who they are and what they need. *Family Coordinator, 28,* 237–243.

DeFrain, J., & Ernst, L. (1978). The psychological effects of sudden infant death syndrome on surviving family members. *Family Practitioner, 6,* 985–988.

DeLozier, J. E., & Gagnon, R. O. (1991). National ambulatory medical care survey: 1989 summary. *Advance Data From Vital and Health Statistics, No. 203.* Hyattsville, MD: National Center for Health Statistics.

deMonteflores, C., & Schultz, S. (1978). Coming out: Similarities and differences for lesbians and gay men. *Journal of Social Issues, 34,* 59–72.

Demos, J., & Demos, V. (1969). Adolescence in historical perspective. *Journal of Marriage and the Family, 31,* 632–638.

Dennis, W., & Dennis, M. (1940). The effect of cradling practices upon the onset of walking in Hopi children. *Journal of Genetic Psychology, 56,* 77–86.

Derdeyn, A. (1985). Grandparent visitation rights: Rendering family dissension more pronounced. *American Journal of Orthopsychiatry, 55,* 277–287.

DeVito, J. (1970). *The psychology of speech and language.* New York: Random House.

deVos, S. (1990). Extended family living among older people in six Latin American countries. *Journal of Gerontology, 45,* 87–94.

DeVries, M. W., & Sameroff, A. J. (1984). Culture and temperament: Influence on infant temperament in three East African societies. *American Journal of Orthopsychiatry, 54,* 83–96.

Dickinson, G. E. & Leming, M. R., (Ed.) (2008). *Dying, death, and bereavement* (10th ed.). NY: McGraw-Hill.

Dick-Reed, G. (1944). *The principles and practice of natural childbirth.* New York: Harper.

Dickson, S., & Parke, R. D. (1988). Social referencing in infancy: A glance at fathers and marriage. *Child Development, 59,* 506–511.

DiClemente, R. J. (1990). The emergence of adolescents as a risk group for human immunodeficiency virus infection. *Journal of Adolescent Research, 5,* 7–17.

Dixon, R., & Baltes, P. (1986). Toward life span research on the functions and pragmatics of intelligence. In R. Sternberg & R. Wagner (Eds.), *Practical intelligence: Nature and origins of competence in the everyday world.* New York: Cambridge University Press.

Dixon Jr., W. E. (2003). *Twenty studies that revolutionized child psychology.* Upper Saddle River, NJ: Prentice Hall.

Dodge, K., & Frame, C. (1982). Social cognitive biases and deficits in aggressive boys. *Child Development, 53,* 620–635.

Doering, M. R., & Rhodes, S. R. (1989). Changing careers: A qualitative study. *Career Development Quarterly, 37,* 316–322.

Dohrenwend, B. S., & Dohrenwend, B. P. (1974). *Stressful life events: Their nature and effects.* New York: Wiley.

Donaldson, S., & Westerman, M. (1986). Development of children's understanding of ambivalence and causal theories of emotions. *Developmental Psychology, 22,* 655–662.

Douglas, K., & Arenberg, D. (1978). Age changes, cohort differences, and cultural changes on the Guilford-Zimmerman Temperament Survey. *Journal of Gerontology, 33,* 737–747.

Dowd, J. (1975). Aging as exchange: A preface to theory. *Journal of Gerontology, 30,* 584–594.

Dowd, J. (1980). Exchange rates and old people. *Journal of Gerontology, 35,* 596–602.

Dowd, J. (1984). Beneficence and the aged. *Journal of Gerontology, 39,* 102–108.

Dowd, J., & Tronick, E. Z. (1986). Temporal coordination of arm movements in early infancy: Do infants move in synchrony with adult speech? *Child Development, 57,* 772–776.

Dreeben, R., & Gamoran, A. (1986). Race, instruction, and learning. *American Sociological Review, 51,* 660–669.

Dreyer, P. H. (1982). Sexuality during adolescence. In B. Wolman (Ed.), *Handbook of developmental psychology.* Englewood Cliffs, NJ: Prentice Hall.

Drury, T. F., & Howie, L. J. (1979). Prevalence of selected chronic digestive conditions. *Vital and Health Statistics, Series 10, No. 123,* DHEW Publication No.(PHS) 79–1558.

Dubrow, E., & Tasak, J. (1989). The relation between stressful life events and adjustment in elementary school children: The role of social support and social problem-solving skills. *Child Development, 60*, 1412–1424.

Dudley, D. L. (1991). Coping with retirement: Stress and lifechange. *Cupa Journal, 42*, 1–4.

Dukes, R. L., & Lorch, B. D. (1989). The effects of school, family, self-concept, and deviant behavior on adolescent suicide ideation. *Journal of Adolescence, 12*, 239–251.

Dunphy, D. (1963). The social structure of urban adolescent peer groups. *Sociometry, 26*, 230–246.

Duvall, E. (1977). *Marriage and family development.* 5th ed. Philadelphia: Lippincott.

Duvall, E. M., & Miller, B. (1985). *Marriage and family development* (6th ed.). New York: Harper & Row.

Dyer, E. (1963). Parenthood as crisis: A restudy. *Journal of Marriage and the Family, 25*, 196–201.

Eakins, P. S. (1986). *The American way of birth.* Philadelphia: Temple University Press.

East, P., Hess, I., & Lerner, R. (1987). Peer social support and adjustment in early adolescent peer groups. *Journal of Early Adolescence, 7*, 135–163.

Eaton, W. O., & Ennis, L. R. (1986). Sex differences in human motor activity level. *Psychological Bulletin, 100*, 19–28.

Eder, R. A. (1989). The emergent personalist: The structure and content of 3 1/2, 5 1/2, and 7 1/2-year-olds' concepts of themselves and other persons. *Child Development, 60*, 1218–1229.

Eggerman, S., & Dustin, D. (1985). Death orientation and communication with the terminally ill. *Omega, 16*, 255–265.

Eisele, J., Hertsgaard, D., & Light, H. (1986). Factors related to eating disorders in young adolescent girls. *Adolescence, 21*, 283–290.

Eisenberg, N. (1989). The development of prosocial values. In N. Eisenberg, J. Reykowski, & E. Staub (Eds.), *Social and moral values: Individual and social perspectives.* Hillsdale, NJ: Erlbaum.

Eisenberg, N., Wolchik, S. A., Hernandez, R., & Pasternack, J. (1985). Parental socialization of young children's play: A short-term longitudinal study. *Child Development, 56*, 1506–1514.

Elder, G. (1962). Structural variations in the childrearing relationship. *Sociometry, 25*, 233–245.

Elder, G. H. (1998). The life course and human development. In W. Damon & R. M. Lerner (Eds.), *Handbook of child psychology (Vol. 1): Theoretical models of human development* (5th ed.). NY: John Wiley & Sons, Inc.

Elia, E. A. (1991). Exercise and the elderly. *Clinics in Sports Medicine, 10*, 141–147.

Elizur, E., & Kaffman, M. (1983). Factors influencing the severity of childhood bereavement reactions. *American Journal of Orthopsychiatry, 53*, 669–676.

Elkind, D. (1967). Egocentrism in adolescence. *Child Development, 38*, 1024–1038.

Elkind, D. (1974). *Children and adolescents: Interpretative essays on Jean Piaget.* New York: Oxford University Press.

Elkind, D. (1976). *Child development and education.* New York: Oxford University Press.

Elkind, D. (1978). Understanding the young adolescent. *Adolescence, 13*, 127–134.

Elkind, D. (1981). *The hurried child.* Reading, MA: Addison-Wesley.

Elkind, D. (1987). *Miseducation.* New York: Knopf.

Ellis, L., Ames, M. Peckham, W., & Burke, D. (1988). Sexual orientation of human offspring may be altered by severe maternal stress during pregnancy. *Journal of Sex Research, 25*, 152–157.

Eng, L., & O'Laughlin, M. (1989). The next generation. *San Francisco Examiner, June 24*, 58.

Enns, J. T., & Girgus, J. S. (1985). Developmental changes in selective and integrative visual attention. *Journal of Experimental Child Psychology, 40*, 319–337.

Entwisle, D. R., & Alexander, K. L. (1987). Long-term effects of Cesarean delivery on parents' beliefs and children's schooling. *Developmental Psychology, 23*, 676–682.

Entwisle, D., & Doering, S. G. (1980). *The first birth.* Baltimore, MD: Johns Hopkins University Press.

Erikson, E. (1950). *Childhood and society.* New York: Norton.

Erikson, E. (1964). *Insight and responsibility.* New York: Norton.

Erikson, E. (1982). *The life cycle completed.* New York: Norton.

Erikson, E., Erikson, J., & Kivnick, H. (1986). *Vital involvement in old age.* New York: Norton.

Eron, L. (1987). The development of aggressive behavior from the perspective of a developing behaviorism. *American Psychologist, 42*, 435–442.

Espenshade, T. (1984). *Investing in children: New estimates of parental expenditures.* Washington, DC: Urban Institute Press.

Espino, D. V., Neufeld, R. R., Mulvihill, M., & Libow, L. S. (1988). Hispanic and non-Hispanic elderly on admission to the nursing home: A pilot study. *The Gerontologist, 28*, 821–827.

Evans, M. A., Esbenson, M., & Jaffe, C. (1981). Expect the unexpected when you care for a dying patient. *Nursing, 11*, 55–56.

Eveleth, P. B., & Tanner, J. M. (1976). *Worldwide variation in human growth.* Cambridge, England: Cambridge University Press.

Everitt, A. V. (1976). Conclusion: Aging and its hypothalamic-pituitary control. In A. V. Everitt & J. A. Burgess (Eds.), *Hypothalamus, pituitary, and aging.* Springfield, OH: Charles C. Thomas.

Fabricius, W., & Cavalier, L. (1989). The role of causal theories about memory in young children's memory strategy choice. *Child Development, 60*, 298–308.

Fabricius, W., & Wellman, H. (1983). Children's understanding of retrieval cue utilization. *Developmental Psychology, 19*, 15–21.

Fagan, J. F., & McGrath, S. K. (1981). Infant recognition memory and later intelligence. *Intelligence, 5*, 121–130.

Fagot, B. (1978). The influence of sex of child on parental reactions to toddler children. *Child Development, 49*, 459–465.

Fagot, B. (1985). Beyond the reinforcement principle: Another step toward understanding sex-role development. *Developmental Psychology, 21*, 1097–1104.

Fagot, B., Hagan, R., Leinbach, M., & Kronsberg, S. (1985). Differential reactions to assertive and communicative acts of toddler boys and girls. *Child Development, 56*, 1499–1505.

Fairchild, T. N. (1986). Suicide prevention. In T. N. Fairchild (Ed.), *Crisis intervention strategies for school-based helpers* (pp. 321–369). Springfield, IL: Charles C. Thomas.

Faltermayer, E. (1991). Ready to retire: Decisions galore. *Fortune, 124(10)*, 137–140.

Fantz, R. I. (1958). Pattern vision in young infants. *Psychological Record, 8*, 43–47.

Fantz, R. I. (1961). The origin of form perception. *Scientific American, 36*, 66–72.

Fantz, R. I., Fagan, J. F., & Miranda, S. B. (1975). Early visual selectivity. In L. B. Cohen & P. Salapatek (Eds.), *Infant perception: From sensation to cognition.* Vol. 1. New York: Academic Press.

Farley, R., & Allen, W. R. (1987). *The color line and the quality of life in America.* New York: Russell Sage Foundation.

Farrell, M., & Rosenberg, S. (1981). *Men at midlife.* Boston: Auburn.

Fasteau, M. F. (1975). *The male machine.* New York: McGraw-Hill.

Faust, M. S. (1960). Developmental maturity as a determinant of prestige of adolescent girls. *Child Development, 31*, 173–186.

Fay, R. E., Turner, C. F., Klasen, A., & Gagnon, J. (1989). Prevalence and patterns of same-gender sexual contact among men. *Science, 243*, 338–348.

Feather, N. T. (1980). Values in adolescence. In J. Adelson (Ed.), *Handbook of adolescent psychology.* New York: Wiley.

Feldman, H. (1981). A comparison of intentional parents and intentionally childless couples. *Journal of Marriage and the Family, 43*, 593–600.

Feldman, S., & Gehring, T. (1988). Changing perceptions of family cohesion and power across adolescence. *Child Development, 59*, 1034–1045.

Feldman, S., & Nash, S. (1979). Sex differences in responsiveness to babies among mature adults. *Developmental Psychology, 15*, 430–436.

Feldman, S., & Quatman, T. (1988). Factors influencing age expectations for adolescent autonomy: A study of early adolescents and their parents. *Journal of Early Adolescence, 8*, 325–343.

Ferguson, K., Yesalis, C., Pomrehn, P., & Kirkpatrick, M. (1989). Attitudes, knowledge, and beliefs as predictors of exercise intent and behavior in schoolchildren. *Journal of School Health, 59,* 112–115.

Fernandez, E. (1989). *Coming out is hard to do.* San Francisco Examiner, June 20, 47.

Fine, M. A., Moreland, J. R., & Schwebel, A. (1983). Long-term effects of divorce on parent-child relationships. *Developmental Psychology, 5,* 703–714.

Finn, S. (1986). Stability of personality self-ratings over 30 years: Evidence for an age/cohort interaction. *Journal of Personality and Social Psychology, 50,* 813–818.

Fischer, K. W. (1987). Relations between brain and cognitive development. *Child Development, 58,* 623–632.

Fischer, C. A., Crockett, S. J., & Heller, K. E. (1991). Nutrition knowledge, attitudes, and practices of older and younger elderly in rural areas. *Journal of the American Dietetic Association, 91,* 1398–1404.

Fitting, M., Rabins, P., Lucas, M. J., Eastham, J. (1986). Caregivers for demented patients: A comparison of husbands and wives. *Gerontologist, 26,* 248–252.

Flavell, J. H. (1985). *Cognitive development* (2nd ed). Englewood Cliffs, NJ: Prentice Hall.

Flavell, J. H. (1986). The development of children's knowledge about the appearance-reality distinction. *American Psychologist, 41,* 418–426.

Flavell, J., & Ross, L. (1981). *Social cognitive development: Frontiers and possible futures.* Cambridge, England: Cambridge University Press.

Flavell, J. (1985). *Cognitive development* (2nd ed.). Englewood Cliffs, NJ: Prentice Hall.

Flavell, J., Beach, D., & Chinsky, J. (1966). Spontaneous verbal rehearsal in memory tasks as a function of age. *Child Development, 37,* 283–299.

Flavell, J., Flavell, E., Green, F., & Wilcox, S. (1981). The development of three spatial perspective-taking rules. *Child Development, 52,* 356–368.

Fleming, A. S., Ruble, D. N., Flett, G. L., & Shaul, D. L. (1988). Postpartum adjustment of first-time mothers: Relations between mood, maternal attitudes, and mother-infant interactions. *Developmental Psychology, 24,* 71–81.

Folkman, S., & Lazarus, R. (1980). An analysis of coping in a middle-aged community sample. *Journal of Health and Social Behavior, 21,* 219–239.

Forrest, J. D., & Singh, S. (1990). The sexual and reproductive behavior of American women, 1982–1988. *Family Planning Perspectives, 22,* 206–214.

Forward, S. (1989). *Toxic parents: Overcoming their hurtful legacy and reclaiming your life.* New York: Bantam Books.

Fozard, J. L., & Gordon-Salant, S. (2001). Changes in vision and hearing with aging. In J. E. Birren & K. W. Schaie (Eds.), *Handbook of the psychology of aging.* San Diego, CA: Academic Press.

Fozard, J., Wolf, E., Bell, B., McFarland, A., & Podosky, S.(1977). Visual perception and communication. In J. Birren & K. Schaie (Eds.), *Handbook of the psychology of aging.* New York: Van Nostrand Reinhold.

Fraiberg, S. (1977). *Insights from the blind: Comparative studies of blind and sighted infants.* New York: Basic Books.

Frankenburg, W. K., & Dodds, J. (1967). The Denver developmental screening test. *Journal of Pediatrics, 71,* 181–191.

Frankenburg, W. K., Frandal, A., Sciarillo, W., & Burgess, D. (1981). The newly abbreviated and revised Denver Developmental Screening Test. *The Journal of Pediatrics, 99,* 995–999.

Frauenglass, M., & Diaz, R. (1985). Self-regulatory functions of children's private speech: A critical analysis of recent challenges to Vygotsky's theory. *Developmental Psychology, 21,* 357–364.

Freeman, D. (1983). *Margaret Mead and Samoa.* Cambridge, MA: Harvard University Press.

French, D. (1988). Heterogeneity of peer-rejected boys: Aggressive and nonaggressive subtypes. *Child Development, 59,* 976–985.

Freud. S. (1917). Mourning and melancholia. In J. Strachey (Ed.), *The standard edition of the complete psychological works of Sigmund Freud.* London: Hogarth Press.

Freudenberger, H., & Richelson, G. (1980). *Burnout: The high cost of high achievement.* New York: Anchor/Doubleday.

Fried, P. A., Watkinson, B., Dillon, R. F., & Dulberg, C. S. (1987). Neonatal neurological status in a low-risk population after prenatal exposure to cigarettes, marijuana, and alcohol. *Journal of Developmental and Behavioral Pediatrics, 8,* 318–326.

Friedman, W. (1986). The development of children's knowledge of temporal structure. *Child Development, 57,* 1386–1400.

Friedrich, O. (1983). What do babies know? *Time, August 15,* 52–59.

Friel, J., & Friel, L. (1988). *Adult children: The secrets of dysfunctional families.* Deerfield Beach, FL: Health Communications.

Frisch, R. E. (1983). Fatness, puberty, and fertility: The effects of nutrition and physical training on menarche and ovulation. In J. Brooks-Gunn & A. Petersen (Eds.), *Girls at puberty: Biological and psychosocial aspects.* New York: Plenum.

Frodi, A., & Lamb, M. (1978). Sex differences in responsiveness to infants: A developmental study of psychophysiological and behavioral responses. *Child Development, 49,* 1182–1188.

Froggatt, K. (2006). A survey of end-of-life care in care homes. In G. E. Dickinson & M. R. Leming, (Eds.), *Dying, death, and bereavement* (10th ed.). NY: McGraw-Hill.

Fromm, E. (1970). *The art of loving.* New York: Bantam.

Fulton, R. (1987). Death, grief, and the funeral. In M.A. Morgan (Ed.), *Bereavement: Helping the survivors* (pp. 123–126). London, Ontario: King's College.

Furstenberg, F. F. (1983). The life course of children of divorce: Marital disruption and parental contact. *American Sociological Review, 52,* 656–668.

Gaddis, A., & Brooks-Gunn, J. (1985). The male experience of pubertal change. *Journal of Youth and Adolescence, 14,* 61–69.

Galatzer-Levy, R. M. & Cohler, B. J. (1993). *The essential other: A developmental psychology of the self.* New York: Basic Books.

Galper, M. (1978). *Coparenting: Sharing your child fully.* Philadelphia: Running Press.

Galvin, K. M., & Brommel, B. J. (1986). *Family communication: Cohesion and change.* Glenview, IL: Scott, Foresman.

Gamoran, A. (1989). Rank, performance, and mobility in elementary school grouping. *Sociological Quarterly, 30,* 109–123.

Gannon. J. P. (1989). *Soul survivors: A new beginning for adults abused as children.* New York: Prentice Hall Press.

Garbarino, J. (1980). Changing hospital childbirth practices: A developmental perspective on prevention of child maltreatment. *American Journal of Orthopsychiatry, 50,* 588–597.

Garbarino, J., Guttman, E., & Seeley, J. W. (1986). *The psychologically battered child: Strategies for identification, assessment, and intervention.* San Francisco: Jossey-Bass.

Gardner, J. M., & Karmel, B. (1984). Arousal effects on visual preference in neonates. *Developmental Psychology, 20,* 374–377.

Gardner, D. B. (1979). *Preventing childhood accidents.* Ft. Collins, CO: Commercial Printing.

Gardner, H. E. (1998). Extraordinary cognitive achievements (ECA): A symbol systems approach. In W. Damon & R. M. Lerner (Eds.), *Handbook of child psychology (Vol. 1): Theoretical models of human development* (5th ed.). NY: John Wiley & Sons, Inc.

Garn, S., Sandusky, S., Nagy, J., & Trowbridge, F. Negro-caucasoid differences in permanent tooth emergence at a constant income level. *Archives of Oral Biology, 18,* 609–615.

Garrod, A., Beal, C., & Shin, P. (1989). The development of moral orientation in elementary school children. Paper presented at the biennial meeting of the Society for Research in Child Development, Kansas City.

Garvey, C. (1977). *Play.* Cambridge, MA: Harvard University Press.

Geary, D. (1989). A model for representing gender differences in the pattern of cognitive abilities. *American Psychologist, 44,* 1155–1156.

Geber, M. (1958). The psychomotor development of African children in the first year, and the influence of maternal behavior. *Journal of Social Psychology, 47,* 185–195.

Gee, A. S. (1978). Understanding cohabitation: Implications for home economists. *Journal of Home Economics, 13,* 38–42.

Gelman, R., & Baillargeon, R. (1983). A review of some Piagetian concepts. In P. Mussen (Ed.), *Handbook of child psychology* (4th ed.). Vol. 3. New York: Wiley.

General Mills Corp. (1981). *Raising children in contemporary America.* Minneapolis, MN: General Mills.

George, L. K., & Weiler, S. J. (1981). Sexuality in middle and late life. *Archives of General Psychiatry, 38,* 919–923.

Gerard, H. (1983). School desegregation. *American Psychologist, 38,* 869–877.

Gesell, A., & Ames, L. B. (1947). The development of handedness. *Journal of Genetic Psychology, 70,* 155–175.

Gesell, A. & Ilg, F. (1946). *The child from five to ten.* New York: Harper & Row.

Gesell, A., & Thompson, H. (1929). Learning and growth in identical infant twins: An experimental study by the method of co-twin control. *Genetic Psychology Monographs, 6,* 1–124.

Ghodsian-Carpey, J., & Baker, L. (1987). Genetic and environmental influences on aggression in 4 to 7-year-old twins. *Aggressive Behavior, 13,* 173–186.

Gibson, E. (1969). *Principles of perceptual learning and development.* New York: Appleton-Century-Crofts.

Gibson, R. C. (1986). Older black Americans. *Generations, 10,* 35–39.

Gibson, E., & Walk, R. D. (1960). *The visual cliff. Scientific American, 202,* 64–71.

Gilbert, E., & DeBlassie, R. (1984). Anorexia nervosa: Adolescent starvation by choice. *Adolescence, 19,* 839–846.

Gilchrist, L. D., Schinke, S. P., & Maxwell, J. S. (1987). Life skills counseling for preventing problems in adolescence. *Journal of Social Service Research, 10,* 73–84.

Gilford, R. (1984). Contrasts in marital satisfaction throughout old age: An exchange theory analysis. *Journal of Gerontology, 39,* 325–333.

Gilligan, C. (1982). *In a different voice: Psychological theory and women's development.* Cambridge, MA: Harvard University Press.

Ginsburg, H., & Opper, S. (1979). *Piaget's theory of intellectual development* (2nd ed.). Englewood Cliffs, NJ: Prentice Hall.

Glaser, K. (1978). The treatment of depressed and suicidal adolescents. *American Journal of Psychotherapy, 32,* 252–269.

Glass, J. (1983). Prebirth attitudes and adjustment to parenthood: When "preparing for the worst" helps. *Family Relations, 32,* 377–386.

Glasser, B. G., & Strauss, A. L. (1965). *Awareness of dying.* Chicago: Aldine.

Glasser, B. G., & Strauss, A. L. (1968). *Time for dying.* Chicago: Aldine.

Glenn, N. D. (1975). Psychological well-being in the postparental stage: Some evidence from national surveys. *Journal of Marriage and the Family, 37,* 105–110.

Glenn, N. D., & McLanahan, S. (1981). The effects of offspring on the psychological well-being of older adults. *Journal of Marriage and the Family, 41,* 409–421.

Glenn, N. D., & Weaver, C. N. A note on family situation and global happiness. *Social Forces, 57,* 960–967.

Glenwick, D. S., & Mowrey, J. D. (1986). When parent becomes peer: Loss of intergenerational boundaries in single parent families. *Family Relations, 35,* 57–62.

Glick, P., & Lin, S. (1986). More young adults are living with their parents: Who are they? *Journal of Marriage and the Family, 48,* 107–112.

Glick, I., Weiss, R., & Parkes, C. (1974). *The first year of bereavement.* New York: Wiley.

Goetting, A. (1982). The six stations of remarriage: Developmental tasks of remarriage after divorce. *Family Relations, 31,* 213–222.

Goetting, A. (1986). The developmental tasks of siblingship over the life cycle. *Journal of Marriage and the Family, 48,* 703–714.

Goldberg, H. (1976). *The hazards of being male: Surviving the myth of masculine privilege.* New York: Nash.

Goldfarb, W. (1945). Effects of psychological deprivation in infancy and subsequent adjustment. *American Journal of Psychiatry, 102,* 18–33.

Goleman, C. (1986). Major personality study finds that traits are mostly inherited. *New York Times, (July 29),* 17–18.

Goleman, D., & Gurin, J. (Eds.) (1993). *Mind body medicine: How to use your mind for better health.* NY: Consumer Reports Books.

Gonzalez-Mena, J. (1986). Toddlers: What to expect. *Young Children, 42,* 85–90.

Goodenough, F. (1939). A critique of experiments on raising the IQ. *Educational Methods, 19,* 73–79.

Goodnow, J. (1977). *Children drawing.* Cambridge, MA: Harvard University Press.

Goodwin, J. S. (1989). Social, psychological, and physical factors affecting the nutritional status of elderly subjects: Separating cause and effect. *American Journal of Clinical Nutrition, 50,* 1201–1210.

Gordon, S. (1981). Preteens are not latent, adolescence is not a disease. In L. Brown (Ed.), *Sex education.* New York: Plenum.

Gottfried, A., Gottfried, A., & Bathurst, K. (1988). Maternal employment, family environment, and children's development: Infancy through the school years. In A. Gottfried & A. Gottfried (Eds.), *Maternal employment and children's development: Longitudinal research.* New York: Plenum.

Gould, R. (1978). *Transformations: Growth and change in adult life.* New York: Simon and Schuster.

Gould, L. A. (1990). Cardiovascular health and sexual function. *Medical Aspects of Human Sexuality, 24,* 27–29.

Graham, C. (1991). Exercise and the aging. *Diabetes Forecast, 44,* 34–40.

Graham, J. W., Marks, G., & Hansen, W. B. (1991). Social influence processes affecting adolescent substance use. *Journal of Applied Psychology, 76,* 291–298.

Graziano, A., DeGiovanni, I. S., & Garcia, K. A. (1979). Behavioral treatment of children's fears: A review. *Psychological Bulletin, 86,* 804–830.

Greenberg, M., & Morris, N. (1974). Engrossment: The newborn's impact on the father. *American Journal of Orthopsychiatry, 44,* 520–531.

Greenberger, E., & Steinberg, L. D. (1986). When teenagers work. New York: Basic Books. Grinder, R. (1973). *Adolescence.* New York: Wiley.

Greenleaf, P. (1978). *Children through the ages.* New York: McGraw-Hill.

Greyson, B., & Stevenson, I. The phenomenology of near death experiences. *American Journal of Psychiatry, 137,* 1193–1196.

Grinder, R. (1973). *Adolescence.* New York: Wiley.

Grotevant, H. D., & Cooper, C. R. (1985). Patterns of interaction in family relationships and the development of identity exploration in adolescence. *Child Development, 56,* 415–428.

Grotevant, H. D., & Cooper, C. R. (1986). Individuation in family relationships. *Human Development, 29,* 82–100.

Gullotta, T. P., Adams, G. R., & Alexander, S. J. (1986). *Today's marriages and families.* Monterey, CA: Brooks/Cole.

Gut, E. (19974). Some aspects of adult mourning. *Omega, 5,* 323–342.

Guttman, D. (1969). *The country of old men: Cross-cultural studies in the psychology of later life.* Ann Arbor, MI: Institute of Gerontology, University of Michigan-Wayne State.

Guttman, D. (1977). The cross-cultural perspective. In J. E. Birren & K. Schaie (Eds.), *Handbook of the psychology of aging.* New York: Van Nostrand.

Hagestad, G. (1985). *Continuity and connections.* In V. Bengston & J. Robertson (Eds.), Grandparenthood. Beverly Hills, CA: Sage.

Hagestad, G. (1986). *The family: Women and grandparents as kin keepers.* In A. Pifer & L. Bronte (Eds.), Our aging society. New York: Norton.

Haith, M. M. (1980). *Rules that babies look by: The organization of newborn visual activity.* Hillsdale, NJ: Erlbaum.

Hall, G. S. (1882). *The moral and religious training of children.* Princeton Review, 26–48.

Hall, G. S. (1904). *Adolescence.* Vols. 1 and 2. New York: D. Appleton & Co.

Halpern, D. (1989). The disappearance of cognitive gender differences: What you see depends on where you look. *American Psychologist, 44,* 1156–1158.

Halpern, H. W. (1990). *Cutting loose: An adult's guide to coming to terms with your parents.* New York: Simon & Schuster.

Halpert, E. (1991). Aspects of a dilemma of middle age: Whether or not to place aged, failing parents in a nursing home. *The Psychoanalytic Quarterly, 60,* 426–435.

Halverson, H. M. (1931). An experimental study of prehension in infants by means of systematic cinema records. *Genetic Psychology Monographs, 10,* 107–286.

Hamill, P. V. (1977). NCHS Growth curves for children. *Vital Health Statistics, Series 11,* No. 165. (DHEW Publication No. 78–1650). Washington, DC: U. S. Government Printing Office.

Hamilton, E., & Whitney, E. (1982). *Nutrition: Concepts and controversies* (2nd ed.). St. Paul, MN: West Publishing.

Handler, E. (1973). Expectations of day care parents. *Social Service Review, 47,* 266–277.

Hannson, R., Nelson, R., Carver, M., NeeSmith, D., Dowling, E., Fletcher, W., & Suhr, P. (1990). Adult children with frail elderly parents: When to intervene? *Family Relations, 39,* 153–158.

Hansen, D. A., & Hill, R. (1964). Families under stress. In H. Christensen (Ed.), Handbook of marriage and the family. Chicago: Rand-McNally.

Hanson, S. (1986a). Healthy single parent families. *Family Relations, 35,* 125–132.

Hanson, S. (1986b). Single custodial fathers. In S. Hanson & F. W. Bozett (Eds.), *Dimensions of fatherhood.* Beverly Hills, CA: Sage.

Hanson, S. L., Myers, D. R., & Ginsburg, A. (1987). The role of responsibility and knowledge in reducing teenage out-of-wedlock childbearing. *Journal of Marriage and the Family, 49,* 241–256.

Hapgood, C. C., Elkind, G. S., & Wright, J. J. (1988). Maternity blues: Phenomena and relationship to later postpartum depression. *Australian and New Zealand Journal of Psychiatry, 22,* 299–306.

Harkins, E. (1978). Effects of empty nest transition on self-report of psychological and physical well-being. *Journal of Marriage and the Family, 40,* 549–556.

Harkins, E. (1978). Effects of empty nest transition on self-report of psychological and physical well-being. *Journal of Marriage and the Family, 40,* 549–556.

Harlow, H. (1958). The nature of love. *American Psychologist, 13,* 673–685.

Harlow, H., Harlow, M., & Hansen, E. (1963). The maternal affectional system of rhesus monkeys. In H. Rheingold (Ed.), *Maternal behavior in animals.* New York: Wiley.

Harper, L., & Huie, K. (1985). The effects of prior group experience, age, and familiarity on the quality of organization of preschoolers social relations. *Child Development, 56,* 704–717.

Harper, L. V., & Sanders, K. M. (1978). Preschool children's use of space: Sex differences in outdoor play. In M. Smart & R. Smart (Eds.), *Preschool children: Development and relationships.* New York: Macmillan.

Harris, A., & Harris, T. (1985). *Staying OK.* New York: Harper & Row.

Harris, K. R. (1990). Developing self-regulated learners: The role of private speech and self-instructions. *Educational Psychologist, 25,* 38–45.

Harris, M. (1985). The three career life. *Money, May,* 108–110.

Harry, J. (1982). Decision-making and age differences among gay male couples. *Journal of Homosexuality, 8,* 9–21.

Hart, L., & Goldin-Meadow, S. (1984). The child as a nonegocentric art critic. *Child Development, 55,* 2122–2129.

Hart, N. A., & Keidel, G. C. (1979). The suicidal adolescent. *American Journal of Nursing, 79,* 80–84.

Harter, S. (1982). Children's understanding of multiple emotions: A cognitive developmental approach. In W. Overton (Ed.), *The relationship between social and cognitive development.* Hillsdale, NJ: Erlbaum.

Harter, S. (1983). Developmental perspectives on the self-system. In P. Mussen (Ed.), *Handbook of child psychology,* Vol. 4. New York: Wiley.

Hartup, W. (1983). Peer relations. In P. Mussen (Ed.), *Handbook of child psychology,* Vol. 4. New York: Wiley.

Hartup, W. (1989). Social relationships and their developmental significance. *American Psychologist, 44,* 120–126.

Hatton, C. L., Valente, S. M., & Rink, A. (1977). *Suicide: Assessment and intervention.* New York: Appleton-Century-Crofts.

Hatwell, Y. (1987). Motor and cognitive functions of the hand in infancy and childhood. *International Journal of Behavioral Development, 10,* 509–526.

Hausman, P. (1983). *Foods that fight cancer: A diet and vitamin program that protects the entire family.* New York: Rawson Associates.

Hausman, P., & Hurley, J. B. (1989). *The healing foods: The ultimate authority on the curative power of nutrition.* Emmaus, PA: Rodale Press.

Havighurst, R. (1964). Stages of vocational development. In H. Borrow (Ed.), *Man in a world at work.* Boston: Houghton Mifflin.

Havighurst, R. J. (1972). *Developmental tasks and education* (3rd ed.). New York: David McKay.

Havighurst, R. F., & Albrecht, R. (1953). *Older people.* New York: Longmans, Green.

Havighurst, R. F., Neugarten, B. L., & Tobin, S. S. (1968). Disengagement and patterns of aging. In B. L. Neugarten (Ed.), *Middle age and aging.* Chicago: University of Chicago Press.

Hay, D., Murray, P., Cecire, S., & Nash, A. (1985). Social learning of social behavior in early life. *Child Development, 56,* 43–57.

Hayflick, L. (1974). Cyrogerontology. In M. Rockstein (Ed.), *Theoretical aspects of aging.* New York: Academic Press.

Hayflick, L. (1977). The cellular base for biological aging. In C. E. Finch & L. Hayflick (Eds.), *Handbook of the biology of aging.* New York: Van Nostrand.

Hayflick, L. (1980). The cell biology of aging. *Scientific American, 242,* 58–65.

Hazard, W. R. (Ed.). (1990). *Principles of geriatric medicine and gerontology* (2nd ed.). New York: McGraw-Hill.

Heaney, R. P. (1989). Nutritional factors in bone health in elderly subjects: Methodological and contextual problems. *American Journal of Clinical Nutrition, 50,* 1182–1187.

Heddescheimer, J. C. (1976). Multiple motivations for mid-career changes. *Personnel and Guidance Journal, 55,* 109–111.

Hegner, B. R. (1991). *Geriatrics: A study of maturity* (5th ed.). Albany, NY: Delmar.

Heibeck, T. H., & Markman, E. M. (1987). Word learning in children: An examination of fast mapping. *Child Development, 58,* 1021–1034.

Hein, K. (1989). AIDS in adolescent: Exploring the challenge. *Journal of Adolescent Health Care, 10,* 10S–35S.

Heller, M. (1986). Commuter marriages: A growing necessity for many couples in academe. *The Chronicle of Higher Education, 31.*

Helson, R., & Moane, G. (1987). Personality change in women from college to midlife. *Journal of Personality and Social Psychology, 53,* 176–186.

Hendrix, H. (1988). *Getting the love you want: A guide for couples.* New York: Henry Holt.

Herek, G. (1985). On doing, being, and no being: Prejudice and the social construction of sexuality. *Journal of Homosexuality, 12,* 135–151.

Hergenhahn, B. R. (2000). *An introduction to the history of psychology* (3rd ed.). NY: Wadsworth Publishing.

Herman, E. (1976). Senile hypophyseal syndromes. In A. V. Everitt & J. A. Burgess (Eds.), *Hypothalamus, pituitary, and aging.* Springfield, OH: Charles C. Thomas.

Hess, E. H. (1962). Ethology: An approach toward the complete analysis of behavior. *In New Directions in Psychology.* Vol. 1. New York: Holt, Reinhart, & Winston.

Hess, E. (1972). Imprinting in a natural laboratory. *Scientific American, 226,* 24–31.

Hess, R. D., & Camara, K. A. (1979). Post-divorce family relationships as mediating factors in the consequences of divorce for children. *Journal of Social Issues, 35,* 79–96.

Hetherington, E. M. (1972). Effects of father absence on personality: Development in adolescent daughters. *Developmental Psychology, 7,* 313–321.

Hetherington, E. M. (1979). Divorce: A child's perspective. *American Psychologist, 34,* 851–859.

Hetherington, E. M., Cox, M., & Cox, R. (1976). Divorced fathers. *Family Coordinator, 25,* 417–427.

Hetherington, E. M., Cox, M., & Cox, R. (1979). Family interaction and the social, emotional, and cognitive development of children following divorce. In C. Vaughn & T. B. Brazelton (Eds.), *The family: Setting priorities.* New York: Science and Medicine Publications.

Hetherington, E. M., Stanley-Hagan, M., & Anderson, E. R. (1989). Marital transitions. *American Psychologist, 44,* 303–312.

Higgins, A., & Turnure, J. (1984). Distractibility and concentration of attention in children's development. *Child Development, 55,* 1799–1810.

Hill, E., & Dorfman, L. (1982). Reaction of housewives to the retirement of their husbands. *Family Relations, 31,* 195–200.

Himes, C. L. (2001). Elderly Americans. In H. Cox (Ed.), *Annual editions: Aging* (18th ed.). Dubuque, IA: McGraw-Hill/Dushkin.

Hine, V. H. (1979). Dying at home: Can families cope? *Omega, 10,* 175–187.

Hinton, J. M. (1963). The physical and mental distress of dying. *Quarterly Journal of Medicine, 32,* 1–21.

Hirschman, C., & Hendershot, G. (1979). Trends in breast-feeding among American mothers. *Vital and Health Statistics, Series 23 (3),* DHEW Publication No. (PHS) 79–1979.

Hobbins, J., & Mahoney, M. (1974). In utero diagnosis of hemoglobinopathies: Technic for obtaining fetal blood. *New England Journal of Medicine, 290,* 1065–1067.

Hobbs, D. (1965). Parenthood as crisis: A third study. *Journal of Marriage and the Family, 27,* 367–372.

Hobbs, D., & Wimbish, J. (1977). Transition to parenthood by black couples. *Journal of Marriage and the Family, 39,* 677–689.

Hodges, W. F., Tierney, C. W., & Buchsbaum, H. K. (1984). The cumulative effect of stress on preschool children of divorced and intact families. *Journal of Marriage and the Family, 46,* 611–617.

Hoff-Ginsberg, E. (1986). Function and structure in maternal speech: The relation to the child's development of syntax. *Developmental Psychology, 22,* 155–163.

Hoffman, L. (1977). Changes in family roles, socialization, and sex differences. *American Psychologist, 32,* 644–657.

Hoffman, L. (1979). Maternal employment. *American Psychologist, 34,* 859–865.

Hoffman, L. (1986). Work, family, and the child. In M. Pallak & R. Perloff (Eds.), *Psychology and work: Productivity, change, and employment.* Washington, DC: American Psychological Association.

Hoffman, L. (1989). Effects of maternal employment in the two-parent family. *American Psychologist, 44,* 283–293.

Hoffman, L. W., & Manis, J. D. (1979). The value of children in the United States: A new approach to the study of fertility. *Journal of Marriage and the Family, 41,* 583–596.

Hogan, D. (1980). The transition to adulthood as a career contingency. *American Sociological Review, 45,* 261.

Holden, C. (1983). OTZ cites financial disaster of Alzheimer's. Science, 233, 839–841.

Holland, J. (1973). *Making vocational choices: A theory of careers.* Englewood Cliffs, NJ: Prentice Hall.

Holmes, L. D. (1987). *Quest for the real Samoa: The Mead-Freeman controversy and beyond.* South Hadley, MA: Bergin & Garvey.

Holmes, T. H., & Rahe, R. H. (1967). The social readjustment scale. *Journal of Psychosomatic Research, 11,* 213–218.

Holt, J. (1964). *How children fail.* New York: Pitman.

Hooker, E. (1969). *Final report of the task force on homosexuality.* Bethesda, MD: National Institute of Mental Health.

Hopkins, J., Campbell, S. B., & Marcus, M. (19870. Role of infant-related stressors in postpartum depression. *Journal of Abnormal Psychology, 96,* 237–241.

Hopkins, J., Marcus, M., & Campbell, S. B. (1984). Postpartum depression: A critical review. *Psychological Bulletin, 95,* 498–515.

Hopson, J. A. (1984). A love affair with the brain: PT conversation with Marian Diamond. *Psychology Today, 18,* 62.

Horan, M. A., & Brouwer, A. (Eds.). (1990). *Gerontology: Approaches to biomedical and clinical research.* London: Edward Arnold.

Horn, J. L., & Donaldson, G. Y. (1980). Cognitive development in adulthood. In D. G. Brim & J. Kagan (Eds.), *Constancy and change in human development.* Cambridge, MA: Harvard University Press.)

Horowitz, A., & Shindelman. (1983). Reciprocity and affection: Past influences on present caregiving. *Journal of Gerontological Social Work, 5,* 5–20.

Horwath, C. C. (1989). Chewing difficulty and dietary intake in the elderly. *Journal of Nutrition for the Elderly, 9,* 17–25.

Households and families. (1985). *Family Economics Review, 1,* 19–20.

Houseknecht, S. (1979). Childlessness and marital adjustment. *Journal of Marriage and the Family, 41,* 249–265.

Houseknecht, S. (1987). Voluntary childlessness. In M. B. Sussman & S. K. Steinmetz (Eds.), *Handbook of marriage and the family.* New York: Plenum.

Houser, B. B., & Berkman, S. L. (1984). Aging parent/mature child relationships. *Journal of Marriage and the Family, 46,* 295–299.

Hoving, K., Spencer, T., Robb, K., & Schulte, D. (1978). Developmental changes in visual information processing. In P. Ornstein (Ed.), *Memory development in children.* Hillsdale, NJ: Erlbaum.

Howard, A., & Scott, R. (1965). Cultural values and attitudes toward dying. *Journal of Existentialism, 6,* 161–174.

Howes, C. (1990). Can the age of entry and the quality of infant child care predict adjustment in kindergarten? *Developmental Psychology, 26,* 292–303.

Howes, C., & Stewart, P. (1987). Child's play with adults, toys, and peers: An examination of family and child care influences. *Developmental Psychology, 23,* 423–430.

Howes, C., Rodning, C., Galluzzo, D., & Myers, L. (1988). Attachment and child care: Relationships with mother and caregiver. Early *Childhood Research Quarterly, 3,* 403–316.

Hoy, E. A., Sykes, D. J., Bill, J. M., & Halliday, H. L. (1991). The effects of being born of very-low-birth-weight. *Irish Journal of Psychology, 12,* 182–197.

Hrdy, S. B. (1999). *Mother nature: Maternal instincts and how they shape the human species.* NY: Ballantine Books.

Hubel, D. H., & Weisel, T. N. (1970). The period of susceptibility to the physiological effects of unilateral eye closure in kittens. *Journal of Physiology, 206,* 419–436.

Hudson, J., Pope, H., & Jonas, J. (1983). Treatment of bulimia with antidepressants: Theoretical considerations with clinical findings. In A. Stunkard & E. Stellar (Eds.), *Eating and its disorders.* New York: Ravan Books.

Hulit, L. M. & Howard, M. R. (1997). *Born to talk: An introduction to speech and language development* (2nd ed.). Needham Heights, MA: Allyn & Bacon.

Humphreys, A. P., & Smith, P. K. (1987). Rough and tumble friendship and dominance in school children: Evidence for continuity and change with age in middle childhood. *Child Development, 58,* 201–212.

Hunt, M. (1974). *Sexual behavior in the 1970s.* Chicago: Playboy Press.

Hunt, R. J. (1988). Incidence of tooth loss among elderly Iowans. *American Journal of Public Health, 78,* 1330–1336.

Hunter, F. T., & Younis, J. (1982). Changes in functions of three relations during adolescence. *Developmental Psychology, 18,* 806–811.

Hurlock, E. (1980). *Developmental psychology* (5th ed.). New York: McGraw-Hill.

Husain, S., & Vandiver, T. (1984). *Suicide in children and adolescents.* New York: SP Medical and Scientific Books.

Ikeman, B., Block, R., Avery, J., Niedra, R., Sulman, J., Tretowsky, S., & Yorke, E. (1987). Grief work with children: Access, clinical issues, community advocacy. In M. A. Morgan (Ed.), *Bereavement: Helping the survivors* (pp. 105–119). London, Ontario: King's College.

Ilg, F. L., & Ames, L. B. (1955). *Child behavior.* New York: Harper & Brothers.

Illingworth, R. (1975). *The development of the infant and young child* (6th ed.). London: Churchill Livingstone.

Inhelder, B., & Piaget, J. (1958). *The growth of logical thinking from childhood to adolescence.* New York: Basic Books.

Institute for Social Research. (1985). *Time, goods, and well-being.* Ann Arbor, MI: University of Michigan Press.

Izard, C., Huebner, R., Resser, D., McGinness, G., & Doughterty, L. (1980). The young infant's ability to produce discrete emotional expressions. *Developmental Psychology, 16,* 132–140.

Izard, C., Hembree, E., Doughterty, L., & Spizziri, C. (1983). Changes in two to nineteen month old infants' facial expressions following acute pain. *Developmental Psychology, 19,* 418–426.

Izard, C., Hembree, E., & Huebner, R. (1987). Infants' emotion expressions to acute pain: Developmental change and stability of individual differences. *Developmental Psychology, 23,* 105–113.

Jacklin, C. (1989). Female and male: Issues of gender. *American Psychologist, 44,* 127–133.

Jacobs, L. (1980). Variations in penile tumescence during sex activity. *Medical Aspects of Human Sexuality, 14,* 11.

Jacobs, S. C., et al. (1987). Attachment theory and multiple dimensions of grief. *Omega, 18,* 41–52.

Jacobsen, R. B. (1971). An exploration of parental encouragement as an intervening variable in occupational-educational learning of children. *Journal of Marriage and the Family, 33,* 174–182.

Jacobsen, R. B., Bigner, J. J., & Hood, S. (1991). Black versus white single parents and the value of children. *Journal of Black Studies, 21,* 302–312.

Jacobson, S. W. (1979). Matching behavior in the young infant. *Child Development, 50,* 425–430.

Jahoda, M. (1982). *Employment and unemployment: A social-psychological perspective.* Cambridge: Cambridge University Press.

Jalongo, M. R. (2005). Editorial: On behalf of children. In G. E. Dickinson & M. R. Leming, (Eds.), *Dying, death, and bereavement* (10th ed.). NY: McGraw-Hill.

James, J. W., & Cherry, F. (1988). *The grief recovery handbook.* New York: Harper & Row.

James, M., & Jongeward, D. (1971). *Born to win.* New York: Addison-Wesley.

Jensen, A. (1969). How much can we boost IQ and scholastic achievement? *Harvard Educational Review, 39,* 1–123.

Jersild, A. (1960). *Child psychology* (5th ed.). Englewood Cliffs, NJ: Prentice Hall.

John-Roger, & McWilliams, P. (1990). *You can't afford the luxury of a negative thought.* Los Angeles, CA: Prelude Press.

Johnson, M. A. (1989). Variables associated with friendship in an adult population. *Journal of Social Psychology, 129,* 379–384.

Johnson, M. T., & Roberts, J. (19778). Prevalence of dermatological disease among persons 1–74 years of age: United States. *Advance Data from Health and Vital Statistics, No. 4,* January 26.

Johnson, V., & Pandina, R. J. (1991). Effects of the family environment on adolescent substance use, delinquency, and coping styles. *American Journal of Drug and Alcohol Abuse, 17,* 71–88.

Jones, B. (1986). Quality and equality through cognitive instruction. *Educational Leadership, April,* 4–11.

Jones, G., & Smith, P. (1984). The eyes have it: Young children's discrimination of age in masked and unmasked facial photographs. *Journal of Experimental Child Psychology, 38,* 328–337.

Jones, H. (1957). The later careers of boys who were early- or late-maturing. *Child Development, 28,* 113–128.

Jones, H., & Bayley, N. (1950). Physical maturing among boys as related to behavior. *Journal of Educational Psychology, 41,* 129–148.

Jones, H., & Mussen, P. (1958). Self-conceptions, motivations, and interpersonal attitudes of early and late-maturing girls. *Child Development, 29,* 491–501.

Jones, W. (1979). Grief and involuntary career change: Its implications for counseling. *Vocational Guidance Quarterly, 27,* 196–201.

Jones, D. C., Bloys, N., & Wood, M. (1990). Sex roles and friendship patterns. *Sex Roles, 23,* 133–139.

Jorgensen, S. R., & Sonstegard, J. S. (1984). Predicting adolescent sexual and contraceptive behavior: An application and test of the Fishbein model. *Journal of Marriage and the Family, 46,* 43–55.

Judson, F. N. (1989). What do we really know about AIDS control? *American Journal of Public Health, 79,* 878–882.

Jussim, L. (1989). Teacher expectations: Self-fulfilling prophecies, perceptual biases, and accuracy. *Journal of Personality and Social Psychology, 57,* 469–480.

Justice, E. (1985). Categorization as a preferred memory strategy. *Developmental Psychology, 21,* 1105–1110.

Jylha, M., & Jokela, J. (1990). Individual experiences as cultural: A cross-cultural study on loneliness among the elderly. *Aging and Society, 10,* 295–306.

Kach, J. A., & McGhee, 1982). Adjustment to early parenthood: The role of accuracy of preparenthood experiences. *Journal of Family Issues, 3,* 375–388.

Kachigan, S. K. (1986). *Statistical analysis: An interdisciplinary introduction to univariate and multivariate methods.* NY: Radius Press.

Kaffman, M., & Elizur, E. (1979). Children's bereavement reactions following death of the father. *International Journal of Family Therapy, 1,* 203–229.

Kagan, J. (1970). The determinants of attention in the infant. *American Scientist, 58,* 298–306.

Kagan, J. (1972). Do infants think? *Scientific American, 226,* 74–82.

Kagan, J. (1984). *The nature of the child.* New York: Basic Books.

Kagan, J., Reznick, J. S., Clarke, C., Snidman, N., & Garcia-Coll, C. (1984). Behavioral inhibitions to the unfamiliar. *Child Development, 55,* 2212–2225.

Kalish, R. (1963). An approach to the study of death attitudes. *American Behavioral Scientist, 6,* 68–80.

Kalish, R. (1981). *Death, grief, and caring relationships.* Monterey, CA: Brooks/Cole.

Kalish, R. (1987). Death. In G. L. Maddox et al., (Eds.), *The encyclopedia of aging.* New York: Springer.

Kalish, R., & Reynolds, D. (1976). *Death and ethnicity: A psychocultural study.* Los Angeles, CA: University of California Press.

Kalish, R., & Reynolds, D. (1981). *Death and ethnicity: A psychological study.* Farmington, N. Y.: Baywood.

Kalnins, I., & Bruner, J. (1973). Infant sucking to change the clarity of a visual display. In L. Stone, H. Smith, & L. B. Murphy (Eds.), *The competent infant: Research and commentary.* New York: Basic Books.

Kamin, L. J. (1974). *The science and politics of IQ.* Potomac, MD: Erlbaum.

Kamp Dush, C. M., Cohan, C. L., & Amato, P. R. (2003). The relationship between cohabitation and marital quality and stability: Change across cohorts? *Journal of Marriage and Family, 65,* 539–549.

Kandel, D. B., Davies, M., Karus, D., & Yamaguchi, K. (1986). The consequences in young adulthood of adolescent drug involvement. *Achives of General Psychiatry, 43,* 746–754.

Kandel, D. B., Raveis, V. H., & Davies, M. (1991). Suicidal ideation in adolescence: Depression, substance use, and other risk factors. *Journal of Youth & Adolescence, 20,* 289–309.

Kaplan, B. J. (1986). A psychobiological review of depression during pregnancy. *Psychology of Women Quarterly, 10,* 35–48.

Kaplan, H., & Dove, H. (1987). Infant development among the Ache of East Paraguay. *Developmental Psychology, 23,* 190–198.

Kaplan, P. (1990). *Educational psychology for tomorrow's teacher.* St. Paul, MN: West Publishing Co.

Kaplan, F., & Kaplan, T. (1973). *The power of play.* Garden City, NJ: Anchor Press.

Kaplan, S., Nessbaum, M., Skomoronsky, P., Shenker, I., & Ramsey, P. (1980). Health habits and depression in adolescence. *Journal of Youth and Adolescence, 9,* 299–304.

Kart, C., Metress, E. S., & Metress, J. F. (1978). *Aging and health: Biologic and social perspectives.* Menlo Park, CA: Addison-Wesley.

Kastenbaum, R. J. (1975). Is death a life crisis? On the confrontation with death in theory and practice. In N. Datan & L. Ginsberg (Eds.), *Life-span developmental psychology: Normative life crises.* New York: Academic Press.

Kastenbaum, R. J. (1977). Death and development through the life span. In H. Feifel (Ed.), *New meanings of death.* New York: McGraw-Hill.

Kastenbaum, R. J. (1986). *Death, society, and human experience* (3rd ed.). Columbus, OH: Charles E. Merrill.

Kastenbaum, R. J., & Aisenberg, R. (1972). *The psychology of death.* New York: Springer.

Katch, B. (1981). Fathers and infants: Reported caregiving and interaction. *Journal of Family Issues, 2,* 275–296.

Katchadourian, H. A. (1977). *The biology of adolescence.* San Francisco: Freeman.

Katchadourian, H. A. (1985). *Fundamentals of human sexuality* (4th ed.). New York: Holt, Rinehart, Winston.

Kaufman, K. R. & Kaufman, N. D. (2006). And then the dog died. In G. E. Dickinson & M.R. Leming, (Eds.), *Dying, death, and bereavement* (10th ed.). NY: McGraw-Hill.

Kehl, K. A. (2006). Moving toward peace. In G. E. Dickinson & M. R. Leming, (Eds.), *Dying, death, and bereavement* (10th ed.). NY: McGraw-Hill.

Keller, W. D., Hildebrandt, K. A., & Richards, M. E. (1985). Effects of extended father-infant contact during the newborn period. *Infant Behavior and Development, 8,* 337–350.

Keller, S. E., Bartlett, J. A., Schleifer, S. J., & Johnson, R. L. (1991). HIV-relevant sexual behavior among a healthy inner-city heterosexual adolescent population in an endemic area of HIV. *Journal of Adolescent Health, 12,* 44–48.

Kellett, J. M. (1991). Sexuality of the elderly. *Sexual and Marital Therapy, 6,* 147–160.

Kelley, K., & Byrne, D. (1992). *Exploring human sexuality.* Englewood Cliffs, NJ: Prentice Hall.

Kellogg, R. (1970). *Analyzing children's art.* Palo Alto, CA: Mayfield.

Kellogg, R., & O'Dell, S. (1967). *The psychology of children's art.* San Francisco: CRM.

Kelly, A. (1988). Gender differences in teacher-pupil interactions: A meta-analytic review. *Research in Education, 39,* 1–23.

Kelly, J. E., & Harvey, C. R. (1979). Basic dental examination findings of persons 1–74 years. *Vital and Health Statistics, Series 11,* No. 214. DHEW Publication No. (PHS) 79–1662.

Kemper, S., & Mitzner, T. L. (2001). Language production and comprehension. In J. E. Birren & K. W. Schaie (Eds.), *Handbook of the psychology of aging.* San Diego, CA: Academic Press.

Kennedy, J. (1989). Determinants of peer social status: Contributions of physical appearance, reputation, and behavior. Paper presented at the annual meeting of the Society for Research in Child Development, Kansas City.

Kennedy, E., Spence, S., & Hensley, R. (1989). An examination of the relationship between childhood depression and social competence among primary school children. *Journal of Child Psychology and Psychiatry, 30,* 561–573.

Kennedy, M. M. (1980). *Office politics: Seizing power, wielding clout.* Chicago: Follett.

Kennedy, M. M. (1982). *Salary strategies: Everything you need to know to get the salary you want.* New York: Rawson, Wade.

Kennedy, M. M. (1985). *Office warfare: Strategies for getting ahead in the aggressive 80s.* New York: Macmillan.

Kennell, J., Slyter, H., & Klaus, M. (1970). The mourning response of parents to the death of a newborn infant. *New England Journal of Medicine, 283,* 344–349.

Kenniston, K. (1971). *Youth and dissent: The rise of a new opposition.* New York: Harcourt, Brace, Jovanovich.

Kerckhoff, R. L. (1976). Marriage and middle age. *Family Coordinator, 20,* 5–11.

Kessen, W., Haith, M. M., & Salapatek, P. (1970). Infancy. In P. Mussen (Ed.), *Carmichael's manual of child psychology* (3rd ed.). Vol. 1. New York: Wiley, 1970.

Ketcham, C. J., & Stelmach, G. E. (2001). Age-related declines in motor control. In J. E. Birren & K. W. Schaie (Eds.), *Handbook of the psychology of aging.* San Diego, CA: Academic Press.

Kett, J. (1977). *Rites of passage: Adolescence in America.* New York: Basic Books.

Kimball, M. (1989). A new perspective on women's math achievement. *Psychological Bulletin, 105,* 198–214.

Kimmel, DC (1980). *Adulthood and aging.* (2nd ed.). New York: Wiley.

Kinard, E. M., & Reinherz, H. (1986). Effects of marital disruption on children's school aptitude and achievement. *Journal of Marriage and the Family, 48,* 285–294.

Kinsey, A. C., Pomeroy, W. B., & Martin, C. E. (1948). *Sexual behavior in the human male.* Philadelphia: Saunders.

Kinsey, A. C., Pomeroy, W. B., Martin, C. E., & Gebhard, P. H. (1953). *Sexual behavior in the human female.* Philadelphia: Saunders.

Kirkpatrick, D. (1989). Will you be able to retire? *Fortune, 120*(3), 56–59.

Kitson, G. C., Babri, K. B., & Roach, M. J. (1985). Who divorces and why. *Journal of Family Issues, 6,* 255–294.

Kitson, G. C., & Morgan, L. A. (1990). Consequences of divorce. *Journal of Marriage and the Family, 52,* 913–924.

Kitzinger, S. (1983). *The complete book of pregnancy and childbirth.* New York: Knopf.

Klaus, M., & Kennell, J. H. (1976). *Maternal-infant bonding.* St. Louis, MO: Mosby.

Kline, G. H., Stanley, S. M., Markman, H. J., Olmos-Gallo, P. A., St. Peters, M., Whitton, S. W., et al. (2004). Timing is everything: Pre-engagement cohabitation and increased risk for poor marital outcomes. *Journal of Family Psychology, 18,* 311–318.

Kline, R. B., Canter, W. A., & Robin, A. (1987). Parameters of teenage alcohol use: A path analytic conceptual model. *Journal of Consulting and Clinical Psychology, 55,* 521–528.

Klinnert, M. D., Emde, R., Butterfield, P., & Campos, J. (1986). Social referencing: The infant's use of emotional signals from a friendly adult with mother present. *Developmental Psychology, 22,* 427–432.

Knaub, P. K., Hanna, S. L., & Stinnett, N. (1984). Strengths of remarried families. *Journal of Divorce, 7,* 41–55.

Knox, A. (1977). *Adult development and learning.* San Francisco: Josey-Bass.

Knox, T. A., Kassarkian, Z., & Dawson-Hughes, B. (1991). Calcium absorption in elderly subjects on high and low-fiber diets: Effect of gastric acidity. *American Journal of Clinical Nutrition, 53,* 1480–1487.

Kobasa, S., Maddi, S., & Kahn, S. (1982). Hardiness and health: A prospective study. *Journal of Personality and Social Psychology, 42,* 168–177.

Koblinsky, S. A., & Todd, C. M. (1989). Teaching self-care skills to latchkey children: A review of research.

Koch, H. (1956). Sissiness and tomboyishness in relation to sibling characteristics. *Journal of Genetic Psychology, 88,* 231–244.

Koch-Hattem, A. (1986). Siblings' experience of pediatric cancer: Interviews with children. *Health and Social Work, 11,* 107–117.

Kohlberg, L. (1966). Development of moral character and moral ideology. In M. Hoffman & L. Hoffman (Eds.), *Review of child development research.* Vol. 1. New York: Russell Sage.

Kohlberg, L. (1969). Stage and sequence: The cognitive-developmental approach to socialization. In D. Goslin (Ed.), *Handbook of socialization theory and research.* Chicago: Rand McNally.

Kohlberg, L. (1984). *Essays on moral development,* Vol. 2. San Francisco: Harper & Row.

Kohlberg, L., & Gilligan, C. (1971). The adolescent as a philosopher: The discovery of the self in a postconventional world. *Daedalus, Fall,* 1051–1086.

Kohlberg, L., Yaeger, J., & Hjertholm, E. (1968). Private speech: Four studies and a review of theories. *Child Development, 39,* 817–826.

Kolata, G. (1986). Obese children: A growing problem. *Science, 232,* 20–21.

Kolata, G. (1987). Associations or rules in acquiring language? *Science, 237,* 133–134.

Kolb, B. (1989). Brain development, plasticity, and behavior. *American Psychologist, 44,* 1203–1212.

Koocher, G. P. (1973). Childhood, death, and cognitive development. *Developmental Psychology, 9,* 369–375.

Koocher, G. P. (1974). Talking with children about death. *American Journal of Orthopsychiatry, 44,* 405–411.

Kopp, C. (1982). Antecedents of self-regulation. *Developmental Psychology, 18,* 199–214.

Korner, A. (1971). Individual differences at birth: Implications for early experience and later development. *American Journal of Orthopsychiatry, 41,* 608–619.

Kourany, R. F. (1987). Suicide among homosexual adolescents. *Journal of Homosexuality, 13,* 111–117.

Krogman, W. M. (1980). *Child growth.* Ann Arbor, MI: University of Michigan Press.

Kovar, M. G. (1986a). Aging in the eighties. *Advance Data From Vital and Health Statistics, No. 115.* DHHS Publication No. (PHS) 86–1250. Hyattsville, MD: Public Health Service.

Kovar, M. G. (1986b). Aging in the eighties: Age 65 years and over and living alone: Contacts with family, friends, and neighbors. *Advance Data From Vital and Health Statistics, No. 116, May 9.* DHHS Publication No. (PHS) 86–1250. Hyattsville, MD: U. S. Public Health Service.

Kovar, M. G. (1988). Aging in the eighties: People living alone—two years later. *Advance Data From Vital and Health Statistics, No. 149, April 4.* DHHS Publication No. (PHS) 88–1250. Hyattsville, MD: U. S. Public Health Service.

Kovar, M. G., & LaCroix, A. Z. (1987). Aging in the eighties: Ability to perform work-related activities. *Advance Data From Vital and Health Statistics, No. 136.* DHHS Publication No. (PHS) 87–1250. Hyattsville, MD: Public Health Service.

Kowles, R. V. (1985). *Genetics, society, and decisions.* Columbus, OH: Charles Merrill.

Kozma, A., & Stones, M. J. (1983). Prediction of happiness. *Journal of Gerontology, 38,* 626–628.

Kreutler, P. A. (1980). *Nutrition in perspective.* Englewood Cliffs, NJ: Prentice Hall.

Kriesberg, L. (1970). *Mothers in poverty: A study of fatherless families.* Chicago: Aldine.

Krogman, W. M. (1980). *Child growth.* Ann Arbor, MI: University of Michigan Press.

Kubler-Ross, E. (1969). *On death and dying.* New York: Macmillan.

Kubler-Ross, E., & Worden, J. W. (1977). Attitudes and experiences of death workshop attendees. *Omega, 8,* 91–106.

Kuhn, M. (1978). Insights on aging. Journal of Home Economics, 71, 18–20.

Kupersmidt, J. (1989). Socially rejected children: Bullies, victims, or both? Paper presented at the annual meeting of the Society for Research in Child Development, Kansas City.

Kurdek, L. A. (1981). An integrative perspective on children's divorce adjustment. *American Psychologist, 36,* 856–866.

Kurdek, L. (1989). Relationship quality in gay and lesbian cohabiting couples: A 1-year follow-up study. *Journal of Social and Personal Relationships, 6,* 39–59.

Labaree, D. (1987). Politics, markets, and the compromised curriculum. *Harvard Educational Review, 57,* 483–494.

Labouvie-Vief, G., & Schell, D. (1982). Learning and memory in later life. In B. Wolman (Ed.), *Handbook of developmental psychology.* Englewood Cliffs, NJ: Prentice Hall.

Labouvie-Vief, G. (1985). Intelligence and cognition. In J. E. Birren & K. Schaie (Eds.), *Handbook of the psychology of aging* (2nd ed.). New York: Van Nostrand.

Labouvie-Vief, G. (1986). Modes of knowledge and the organization of development. In M. Commons, L. Kohlberg, F. Richards, & J. Sinnot (Eds.), *Beyond formal operations 3: Models and methods in the study of adult and adolescent thought.* New York: Praeger.

Lagercrantz, H., & Slotkin, T. A. (1986). *Scientific American, 254(4),* 100–107.

Lamanna, M. A., & Reidmann, A. (1988). *Marriages and families: Making choices and facing change* (3rd ed.).Belmont, CA: Wadsworth Publishing Co.

Lamaze, F. (1958). *Painless childbirth: Psychoprophylactic method.* New York: Harper & Row.

Lamb, M., & Goldberg, W. (1982). The father-child relationship. In L. Hoffman et al., (Eds.), *Parenting.* Hillsdale, NJ: Erlbaum Associates.

Lamb, M. E., Hwang, C. P., Broberg, A., & Bookstein, F. (1988). The effects of out of home care on the development of social competence in Sweden: A longitudinal study. *Early Childhood Research Quarterly, 3,* 379–402.

Lang, A., & Brody, E. (1983). Characteristics of middle-aged daughters and help to their elderly parents. *Journal of Marriage and the Family, 45,* 193–202.

LaRossa, R. (1986). *Becoming a parent.* Beverly Hills, CA: Sage Publications.

LaRossa, R., & LaRossa, M. (1981). *Transition to parenthood.* Beverly Hills, CA: Russell Sage Foundation.

Larsen, E. (1985). *Stage II recovery.* San Francisco: Harper & Row.

Larsen, E. (1987). *Stage II relationships: Love beyond addiction.* San Francisco, CA: Harper & Row.

Laury, G. V. (1981). Difficulty in reaching orgasm by aging men. *Medical Aspects of Human Sexuality, 15,* 29, 32.

Laury, G. V. (1982). Ejaculatory changes in aging men. *Medical Aspects of Human Sexuality, 16,* 136, 145.

Leboyer, F. (1976). *Birth without violence.* New York: Knopf.

Leff, P. (1987). Here I am, Ma: The emotional impact of pregnancy loss on parents and health-care professionals. *Family Systems Medicine, 5,* 105–114.

Leifer, M. (1980). *Psychological effects of motherhood: A study of first pregnancy.* New York: Praeger.

Leitar, E. (1986). Miscarriage. In T. Rando (Ed.), *Parental loss of a child.* Champaign, IL: Research Press.

LeMasters, E. E. (1957). Parenthood as crisis. *Marriage and Family Living, 19,* 352–355.

LeMasters, E. E. (1974). *Parents in modern America* (Rev. ed.). Homewood, IL: Dorsey.

LeMasters, E. E. (1983). Parents in contemporary America: *A sympathetic view* (4th ed.). Homewood, IL: Dorsey.

Lennenberg, E. H. (1969). On explaining language. *Science, 164,* 635–643.

Lerner, J. V., & Galambos, N. L. (1985). Maternal role satisfaction, mother-child interaction, and child temperament: A process model. *Developmental Psychology, 21,* 1157–1164.

Lerner, M. (1980). When, why, and where people die. In E. S. Shneidman (Ed.), *Death: Current perspectives* (pp. 87–106). Palo Alto, CA: Mayfield.

Lerner, R. M. (1998). Theories of human development: Contemporary perspectives. In W. Damon & R. M. Lerner (Eds.), Handbook of child psychology (Vol. 1): *Theoretical models of human development* (5th ed.). NY: John Wiley & Sons, Inc.

Lerner, R. M., Karson, M., Meisels, M., & Knapp, J. R. (1975). Actual and perceived attitudes of late adolescents and their parents: The phenomenon of the generation gap. *Journal of Genetic Psychology, 126,* 195–207.

Lester, B., Hoffman, J., & Brazelton, T. B. (1985). The rhythmic structure of mother-infant interaction in term and preterm infants. *Child Development, 56,* 15–27.

Leung, E., & Rheingold, H. (1981). Development of pointing as a social gesture. *Developmental Psychology, 17,* 215–220.

LeVay, S. (1991). A difference in hypothalamic structure between heterosexual and homosexual men. *Science, 253,* 1034.

Leventhal, H., Rabin, C., Leventhal, E. A., & Burns, E. (2001). Health risk behaviors and aging. In J. E. Birren & K. W. Schaie (Eds.), *Handbook of the psychology of aging.* San Diego, CA: Academic Press.

Levin, I. (1982). The nature and development of time concepts in children: The effects of interfering cues. In W. Friedman (Ed.), *The developmental psychology of time.* New York: Academic Press.

Levin, I., Wilkening, F., & Dembo, Y. (1984). Development of time quantification: Integration and nonintegration of beginnings and endings in comparative durations. *Child Development, 55,* 2160–2172.

Levine, R. (1980). Adulthood among the Gusii of Kenya. In N. J. Smelser & E. H. Erikson (Eds.), *Themes of work and love in adulthood.* Cambridge, MA: Harvard University Press.

Levinson, D., et. al. (1978). *The seasons of a man's life.* New York: Ballentine.

Levinson, D. (1980). Toward a conception of the adult life course. In N. J. Smelser & E. Erikson (Eds.), *Themes of work and love in adulthood.* Cambridge, MA: Harvard University Press.

Levinson, D. (1986). A conception of adult development. *American Psychologist, 41,* 3–13.

Levy, J. C., & Deykin, E. Y. (1989). Suicidality, depression, and substance abuse in adolescence. *American Journal of Psychiatry, 146,* 1462–1467.

Levy, M. H. (1988). Pain control research in the terminally ill. *Omega, 18,* 265–275.

Lewis, C., Battistich, V., & Schaps, E. (1990). School-based primary prevention: What is an effective program? *New Directions for Child Development, Winter,* 35–59.

Lewis, C. B. (Ed.). (1990). *Aging: The health care challenge* (2nd ed.). Philadelphia: F. A. Davis.

Lewis, M. (1987). Social development in infancy and early childhood. In J. Osofsky (Ed.), *Handbook of infant development.* New York: Wiley.

Lewis, R., Feneau, P., & Roberts, C. (1979). Fathers and the postparental transition. *Family Coordinator, 28,* 514–520.

Lieberman, M. A. (1965). Psychological correlates of impending death: Some preliminary observations. *Journal of Gerontology, 20,* 181–190.

Lieberman, M. A., & Coplan, A. S. (1970). Distance from death as a variable in the study of aging. *Developmental Psychology, 2,* 71–84.

Lindsey, R. (1987). Colleges accused of bias to stem Asians' gain. *New York Times, January 25,* 10.

Loehlin, J., Lindzey, G., & Spuhler, J. (1975). *Race differences in intelligence.* San Francisco: Freeman.

Logan, B. N. (1991). Adolescent substance abuse prevention: An overview of the literature. *Family and Community Health, 13,* 25–36.

Logan, D. (1980). The menstrual experience in 23 foreign countries. *Adolescence, 15,* 247–256.

Lomax, R. G. (2001). *Statistical concepts: A second course for education and the behavioral sciences* (2nd ed.). Mahwah, NJ: Lawrence Erlbaum Associates, Publishers.

Lopata, H. Z. (1973). *Widowhood in an American city.* Cambridge, MA: Schenkman.

Lorenz, K. (1965). *Evolution and modification of behavior.* Chicago: University of Chicago Press.

Lowenthal, M. F., Thunher, M., & Chirigoa, D. (1977). *Four stages of life.* San Francisco: Josey-Bass.

Lowik, M. R. H., Hofman, Z., & Kok, F. J. (1991). Nutrition and blood pressure among elderly men and women. *Journal of the American College of Nutrition, 10,* 149–153.

Lowrey, C. R., & Settle, S. A. (1985). Effects of divorce on children: Differential impact of custody and visitation patterns. *Family Relations, 34,* 455–463.

Lumpkin, C., Jr., McClung, J., Pereira-Smith, O., & Smith, J. (1986). Existence of high abundance antiproliferative mRNAs in senescent human diploidfibroblasts. *Science, 232,* 393–395.

Lynch, T. (2007). Into the oblivion. In G. E. Dickinson & M. R. Leming, (Eds.), *Dying, death, and bereavement* (10th ed.). NY: McGraw-Hill.

Maccoby, E. (1980). *Social development: Psychological growth and the parent-child relationship.* New York: Harcourt Brace Jovanovich.

Maccoby, E. (1984). Middle childhood in the context of the family. In W. Collins (Ed.), *Development during middle childhood: The years from six to twelve.* Washington, DC: National Academy of Sciences.

Maccoby, E. (1990). Gender and relationships: A developmental account. *American Psychologist, 45,* 513–520.

Maccoby, E., & Jacklin, C. (1974). *The psychology of sex differences.* Stanford, CA: Stanford University Press.

Maccoby, E., & Hagen, J. (1965). Effect of distraction upon central versus incidental recall: Developmental trends. *Journal of Experimental Child Psychology, 2,* 280–289.

Maccoby, E., & Jacklin, C. N. (1987). Gender segregation in childhood. In *Advances in child development and behavior.* Vol. 20. New York: Academic Press.

Mace, D. (Ed.) (1983). *Prevention in family services: Approaches to family wellness.* Beverly Hills, CA: Sage.

MacEwen, K. E., & Barling, J. (1991). Effects of maternal employment experiences on children's behavior via mood, cognitive difficulties, and parenting behavior. *Journal of Marriage and the Family, 53,* 635–644.

Mackintosh, E. (1982). Mysteries. *Science, 82,* 108.

Mackintosh, N. J. (1983). *Conditioning and associative learning.* Oxford: Clarendon Press.

Macklin, E. (1987). Alternative family forms. In M. B. Sussman & S. K. Steinmetz (Eds.), *Handbook of marriage and the family.* New York: Plenum.

Macrae, J., & Herbert-Jackson, E. (1976). Are behavioral effects of infant day care program specific? *Developmental Psychology, 12,* 269–270.

Madden, D. J. (2001). Speed and time of behavioral processes. In J. E. Birren & K. W. Schaie (Eds.), *Handbook of the psychology of aging.* San Diego, CA: Academic Press.

Maddox, G. L. (1968). Persistence of life style among the elderly: A longitudinal study of patterns of social activity in relation to life satisfaction. In B. L. Neugarten (Ed.), *Middle age and aging.* Chicago: University of Chicago Press.

Magai, C. (2001). Emotions over the life span. In J. E. Birren & K. W. Schaie (Eds.), *Handbook of the psychology of aging.* San Diego, CA: Academic Press.

Maier, H. W. (1965). *Three theories of child development.* New York: Harper & Row.

Makinodan, T. (1977). Immunity and aging. In C. E. Finch & L. Hayflick (Eds.), *Handbook of the biology of aging.* New York: Van Nostrand.

Malinak, D. P., Hoyt, M. F., & Patterson, V. (1979). Adults' reactions to the death of a parent: A preliminary study. *American Journal of Psychiatry, 136,* 1152–1156.

Mancini, J., & Bleiszner, R. (1991). Aging parents and adult children: Research themes in intergenerational relations. In A. Booth (Ed.), *Contemporary families: Looking forward, looking back.* Minneapolis, MN: National Council on Family Relations.

Mandell, F., McAnulty, E., & Reese, R. M. (1980). Observations of parental response to sudden unanticipated infant death. *Pediatrics, 65,* 221–224.

Manning, B. H. (1990). Task-relevant private speech as a function of age and sociability. *Psychology in the Schools, 27,* 365–372.

Manning, C., & Lieux, E. (1991). Volunteer labor contribution in nutrition programs for the elderly. *Journal of Nutrition for the Elderly, 10,* 5–10.

Marcia, J. E. (1980). Identity in adolescence. In J. Adelson (Ed.), *Handbook of adolescent psychology* (pp. 159–187).New York: Wiley.

Marciano, T. (1979). Male influences on fertility: Needs for research. *Family Coordinator, 28,* 561–568.

Markusen, E., Owen, G., Fulton, R., & Bendiksen, R. (1978). SIDS: The survivor as victim. *Omega, 84,* 277–283.

Margolin, G., Huster, G., & Glueck, C. J. (1991). Blood pressure lowering in elderly subjects: A double-blind cross-over study of omega-3 and omega-6 fatty acids. *American Journal of Clinical Nutrition, 53,* 562–566.

Maris, R. (1985). The adolescent suicide problem. *Suicide and Life Threatening Behavior, 15,* 91–109.

Markides, K. S., & Krause, N. (1986). Older Mexican Americans. *Generations, 10,* 31–34.

Markman, E. M., & Wachtel, G. F. (1988). Children's use of exclusivity to constrain the meanings of words. *Cognitive Psychology, 20,* 121–157.

Marlatt, G., Baer, J., Donovan, D., & Kivlahan, D. (1988). Addictive behaviors: Etiology and treatment. *Annual Review of Psychology, 39,* 223–252.

Marshall, S., & Smith, J. (1987). Sex differences in learning mathematics: A longitudinal study with item and error analysis. *Journal of Educational Psychology, 79,* 372–381.

Marshall, V., (1986). A sociological perspective on aging and dying. In V. Marshall (Ed.), *Later life: The social psychology of aging.* Beverly Hills, CA: Sage.

Martin, L. G. (1988). The aging of Asia. *Journal of Gerontology, 43,* 99–113.

Martin, A. D., & Hetrick, E. S. (1988). The stigmatization of the gay and lesbian adolescent. *Journal of Homosexuality, 15,* 163–183.

Martin, J. (1987). The impact of AIDS on gay male sexual behavior patterns in New York City. *American Journal of Public Health, 75,* 493–496.

Martinez, G., & Nalezwinski, J. (1981). 1980 update: The recent trend in breast-feeding. *Pediatrics, 67,* 260–263.

Martocchio, B. C. (1986). Agendas for quality of life. *The Hospice Journal, 2,* 11–21.

Maslow, A. (1968). *Toward a psychology of being.* Princeton, NJ: Van Nostrand.

Maslow, A. (1970). *Motivation and personality* (2nd ed.). New York: Harper & Row.

Masters, W. H., & Johnson, V. E. (1966). *Human sexual response.* Boston: Little, Brown.

Masters, W. H., & Johnson, V. E. (1970). *Human sexual inadequacy.* Boston: Little, Brown.

Masters, W. H., & Johnson, V. E. (1979). *Homosexuality in perspective.* Boston: Little, Brown.

Masters, W. H., Johnson, V. E., & Kolodny, R. C. (1985). *Human sexuality* (2nd ed.). Boston: Little, Brown.

Maultsby, H. (1979). Rational rules for making rules. *Interaction, 7,* 3–4.

Maurer, D., & Maurer, C. (1988). *The world of the newborn.* New York: Basic Books.

Mauritzen, J. (1988). Pastoral care for the dying and bereaved. *Death Studies, 12,* 111–122.

May, R. (1958). Contributions to existential psychotherapy. In R. May, E. Angel, & H. F. Ellenberger (Eds.), *Existence: A new dimension in psychiatry and psychology.* New York: Basic Books.

McCandless, B. (1970). *Adolescents: Behavior and development.* New York: Holt, Rinehart, & Winston.

McCann, I., & Holmes, D. (1984). Influence of aerobic exercise on depression. *Journal of Personality and Social Psychology, 46,* 1142–1147.

McCarthy, M. (1991). Family caregivers of the frail elderly: Impact of caregiving on their health and implications for interventions. *Family and Community Health, 14,* 48–55.

McCartney, K. (1984). Effect of quality of day care environment on children's language development. *Developmental Psychology, 20,* 244–260.

McClearn, G. (1964). Genetics and behavior development. In M. Hoffman and L. Hoffman (Eds.), *Review of child development research.* Vol. 1. New York: Russell Sage.

McClearn, G. (1970). Genetic influences on behavior and development. In P. Mussen (Ed.), *Carmichael's manual of child psychology* (pp. 39–76). Vol. 1. New York: Wiley.

McClearn, G. E., & Vogler, G. P. (2001). The genetics of behavioral aging. In J. E. Birren & K. W. Schaie (Eds.), *Handbook of the psychology of aging.* San Diego, CA: Academic Press.

McClelland, D., Constantian, C., Regalado, D., & Stone, C. (1978). Making it to maturity. *Psychology Today, 18(June),* 42.

McClelland, K. A. (1982). Adolescent subculture in the schools. In T. Field et al., (Eds.), *Review of human development.* New York: Wiley.

McCoy, N., Cutler, W., & Davidson, J. (1985). Relationships among sexual behavior, hot flashes, and hormone levels in perimenopausal women. *Archives of Sexual Behavior, 14,* 385–394.

McCubbin, H. I. (1979). Integrating coping behavior in family stress theory. *Journal of Marriage and the Family, 41,* 237–244.

McCubbin, H. I., & Patterson, J. M. (1983). Family stress and adaptation to crisis: A double ABCX model of family behavior. In D. H. Olson & B. C. Miller (Eds.), *Family Studies Review Yearbook.* Vol. 1. Beverly Hills, CA: Sage Publications.

McGrory, A. (1978). *A well model approach to the care of the dying client.* New York: McGraw-Hill.

McKim, M. (1987). Transition to what? New parents' problems in the first year. *Family Relations, 36,* 22–25.

McNally, J. W., & Mosher, W. D. (1991). AIDS-related knowledge and behavior among women 15–44 years of age: United States, 1988. *Advance Data from Vital and Health Statistics, No. 200.* Hyattsville, MD: National Center for Health Statistics.

McNeil, K. J., LeBlanc, E. M., & Joyner, M. (1991). The effect of exercise on depressive symptoms in the moderately depressed elderly. *Psychology and Aging, 6,* 487–491.

McNemar, Q. (1940). A critical examination of the University of Iowa studies of environmental influence upon the IQ. *Psychological Bulletin, 37,* 63–92.

McWhirter, D., & Mattison, A. (1984). *The male couple: How relationships develop.* Englewood Cliffs, NJ: Prentice Hall.

McWilliams, J-R., & McWilliams, P. (1990). *Life 101: Everything we wish we had learned about life in school—but didn't.* Los Angeles, CA: Prelude Press.

Mead, M. (1928). *Coming of age in Samoa.* New York: William Morrow & Co., Inc.

Mead, M. (1935). *Sex and temperament in three primitive societies.* New York: William Morrow & Co., Inc.

Mead, M., & MacGregor, F. (1951). *Growth and culture: A photographic study of Balinese children.* New York: Putnam.

Mellendick, G. (1983). Nutritional issues in adolescence. In A. Hoffman (Ed.), *Adolescent medicine.* Reading, MA: Addison-Wesley.

Meltzhoff, A. N., & Moore, M. K. (1977). Imitation of facial and manual gestures by human neonates. *Science, 198,* 75–78.

Meltzhoff, A. N., & Moore, M. K. (1979). Interpreting "imitative" responses in early infancy. *Science, 205,* 217–219.

Meltzhoff, A. N., & Moore, M. K. (1983). Methodological issues in studies of imitation: Comments on McKenzie & Over and Koepke et al. *Infant Behavior and Development, 6,* 103–108.

Menaghan, E. G., & Parcel, T. L. (1990). Parental employment and family life: Research in the 1980s. *Journal of Marriage and the Family, 52,* 1079–1098.

Mendelson, B., & White, D. (1985). Development of self-body in overweight youngsters. *Developmental Psychology, 21,* 90–97.

Mercier, L. R., & Berger, R. M. (1989). Social service needs of lesbian and gay adolescents: Telling it their way. *Journal of Social Work and Human Sexuality, 8,* 75–95.

Meredith, N. V. (1969). Body size of contemporary groups of eight-year-old children studied in different parts of the world. *Monographs of the Society for Research in Child Development, 34,* Whole No. 1.

Mergenhagen, P. (1991). Doing the career shuffle. *American Demographics, 13,* 42–47.

Messer, D. J., McCarthy, M. E., McQuiston, S., MacTurk, R. H., Yarrow, L. J., & Vietze, P. M., (1986). Relation between mastery behavior in infancy and competence in early childhood. *Developmental Psychology, 22,* 366–372.

Mattessich, P., & Hill, R. (1987). Life cycle and family development. In M. Sussman & S. Steinmetz (Eds.), *Handbook of marriage and the family.* New York: Plenum.

Metzger, A. M. (1980). A Q-methodological study of the Kubler-Ross stage theory. *Omega, 10,* 291–301.

Meuleman, J. (1989). Osteoporosis and the elderly. *Medical Clinics of North America, 73,* 1455–1460.

Meyer, K. (1987). The work commitment of adolescents: Progressive attachment to the work force. *Career Development Quarterly, 36,* 140–147.

Miller, A. (1990). *For your own good: Hidden cruelty in childrearing and the roots of violence.* New York: The Noonday Press.

Miller, B. C., & Moore, K. A. (1990). Adolescent sexual behavior, pregnancy, and parenting: Research through the 1980s. *Journal of Marriage and the Family, 52,* 1025–1044.

Miller, C. A. (1987). A review of maternity care programs in western Europe. *Family Planning Perspectives, 19,* 207–211.

Miller, J., Williamson, E., Glue, J., Gordon, Y., Grudzinskas, J., & Sykes, A. (1980). Fetal loss after implantation: A prospective study. *The Lancet, 83,* 554–556.

Miller, M. (1978). Geriatric suicide: The Arizona study. *Gerontologist, 18,* 488–496.

Miller, S. A. (1988). Parents' beliefs about children's cognitive development. *Child Development, 59,* 259–286.

Miller, S. (1986). Certainty and necessity in the understanding of Piagetian concepts. *Developmental Psychology, 22,* 3–18.

Miller, P., & Aloise, P. (1989). Young children's understanding of the psychological causes of behavior: A review. *Child Development, 60,* 257–285.

Miller, P., Danaher, D., & Forbes, D. (1986). Sex-related strategies for coping with interpersonal conflict in children aged five to seven. *Developmental Psychology, 22,* 543–548.

Miller, V., Onotera, R. T., & Deinard, A. S. (1984). Denver developmental screening test: Cultural variations in southeast Asian children. *Journal of Pediatrics, 104,* 481–482.

Miller-Jones, D. (1989). Culture and testing. *American Psychologist, 44,* 360–366.

Millstein, S. (1989). Adolescent health: Challenges for behavioral scientists. *American Psychologist, 44,* 837–843.

Millstein, S. (1990). Risk factors for AIDS among adolescents. *New Directions for Child Development, Winter,* 3–15.

Mindel, C. H., & Vaughn, C. E. (1978). A multidimensional approach to religiosity and disengagement. *Journal of Gerontology, 33,* 103–108.

Minix, N. A. (1987). Drug and alcohol prevention education: A developmental social skills approach. *The ClearingHouse, 61,* 162–165.

Minuchin, P. P., & Shapiro, E. K. (1983). The school as a context for social development. In E. Hetherington (Ed.), *Handbook of child psychology,* Vol. 4. New York: Wiley.

Mischel, W. (1974). Processes in delay of gratification. In L. Berkowitz (Ed.), Advances in experimental psychology. Vol. 7. New York: Academic Press.

Mischel, W., Shoda, Y., & Rodriguez, M. (1989). Delay of gratification in children. *Science, 244,* 933–938.

Mohs, R., Breitner, J., Silverman, J., & Davis, K. (1987). Alzheimer's disease. *Archives of General Psychiatry, 44,* 405–408.

Molloy, D. W., Richardson, L. D., & Grilly, R. G. (1988). The effects of a three-month exercise program on neuropsychological function in elderly institutionalized women: A randomized controlled trial. *Age and Aging, 17,* 303–309.

Monaghan, P. (2002). The unsettled question of brain death. In G. E. Dickinson & M. R. Leming, (Eds.), *Dying, death, and bereavement* (10th ed.). NY: McGraw-Hill.

Montemayer, R. (1983). Parents and adolescents in conflict: All families some of the time and some families most of the time. *Journal of Early Adolescence, 3,* 83–103.

Montemayer, R. (1986). Family variation in parent-adolescent storm and stress. *Journal of Adolescent Research, 1,* 15–31.

Moody, H. R. (1984). Can suicide on grounds of old age be ethically justified? In M. Tallmer, et al., (Eds.), *The life-threatened elderly* (pp. 64–92). New York: Columbia University Press.

Moody, R. A. (1975). *Life after life.* New York: Bantam.

Moore, K. L. (1988). *The developing human: Clinically oriented embryology* (4th ed.). Philadelphia: Saunders.

Moore, S., & Rosenthal, D. A. (1991). Adolescent invulnerability and perceptions of AIDS risk. *Journal of Adolescent Research, 6,* 164–180.

Mor-Barak, M. E., & Miller, L. S. (1991). Social networks, life events, and health of the poor, frail elderly: A longitudinal study of the buffering versus the direct effects. *Family and Community Health, 14,* 1–14.

Morbidity and Mortality Weekly Report (MMWR). (1985, June 21). Suicide —U.S., 1970–1980.

Morgan, V., & Dunn, S. (1988). Cameleons in the classroom: Visible and invisible children in nursery and infant classrooms. *Educational Review, 40,* 3–12.

Morisey, P. G. (1990). Black children in foster care. In S. M. Logan, E. M. Freeman, & R. G. McRoy (Eds.), *Social work practice with black families.* New York: Longman.

Morley, J. E. (1990). Anorexia in older patients: Its meaning and management. *Geriatrics, 45,* 59–65.

Morrison, D. (1985). Adolescent contraceptive behavior: A review. *Psychological Bulletin, 98,* 538–568.

Morrison, R. S., & Meier, D. E. (2004). Palliative care. In G. E. Dickinson & M. R. Leming, (Eds.), *Dying, death, and bereavement* (10th ed.). NY: McGraw-Hill.

Mosher, W. D. (1990). Use of family planning services in the United States: 1982 and 1988. *Advance Data from Vital and Health Statistics, No. 184.* Hyattsville, MD: National Center for Health Statistics.

Mosher, W. D., & Pratt, W. F. (1990). Contraceptive use in the United States, 1973–88. *Advance Data from Vital and Health Statistics, No. 182.* Hyattsville, MD: National Center for Health Statistics.

Moskowitz, B. (1978). The acquisition of language. *Scientific American, 239,* 92–108.

Mounts, N., Lamborn, S., & Steinberg, L. (1989). Relations between family processes and school achievement in different ethnic contexts. Paper presented at the biennial meeting of the Society for Research in Child Development, Kansas City.

Mulligan, T. (1990). Chronic disease and impotence in the elderly. *Medical Aspects of Human Sexuality, 24,* 33–34. National Center for Health Statistics.

Mulligan, T., & Moss, C. (1991). Sexuality and aging in male veterans: A cross-sectional study of interest, ability, and activity. *Archives of Sexual Behavior, 20,* 17–25.

Munnichs, J. (1966). *Old age and finitude.* Basel, Switzerland: Karger.

Murdock, G. P. (1949). *Social structure.* New York: Macmillan.

Murphy, J. M., & Gilligan, C. (1980). Moral development in late adolescence and adulthood: A critique and reconstruction of Kohlberg's theory. *Human Development, 23,* 77–104.

Murray, S. F., Dolby, R. M., Nation, R. L., & Thomas, D. B. (1981). Effects of epidural anesthesia on newborns and their mothers. *Child Development, 52,* 71–82.

Murstein, B., Chalpin, M., Heard, K., & Vyse, S. (1989). Sexual behavior, drugs, and relationship patterns on a college campus over thirteen years. *Adolescence, 24,* 125–139.

Mussen, P., & Jones, M. (1957). Some conceptions, motivations and interpersonal attitudes of late and early-maturing boys. *Child Development, 28,* 242–256.

Muuss, R. E. (1985). Adolescent eating disorder: Anorexia nervosa. *Adolescence, 20,* 525–536.

Muuss, R. E. (1986). Adolescent eating disorder: Bulimia. *Adolescence, 21,* 257–267.

Myers, B. (1982). Early intervention using Brazelton training with middle-class mothers and fathers of newborns. *Child Development, 53,* 462–472.

Nader, P. R., Wexler, D. B., Patterson, T. L., & McKusick, L. (1989). Comparison of beliefs about AIDS among urban, suburban, incarcerated, and gay adolescents. *Journal of Adolescent Health Care, 10,* 413–418.

Naeye, R. (1980). Sudden infant death. *Scientific American, 242,* 56–62.

Nagy, M. (1948). The child's theories concerning death. *Journal of Genetic Psychology, 73,* 3–27.

National Academy of Sciences. (1982). *Marijuana and health.* Washington, DC: National Academy Press.

National Association of State Boards of Education (1990). *Code blue: Uniting for healthier youth.* Alexandria, VA: National Association of State Boards of Education.

National Center for Health Statistics (1980). Basic data on hearing levels of adults. *Vital and Health Statistics, Series 11, No. 215.*

National Center for Health Statistics (1986). Maternal weight gain and the outcome of pregnancy, United States, 1980. *Vital Statistics (DHHS Publication No. 86–1922).* Washington, DC: U. S. Government Printing Office.

National Center for Health Statistics. (1990). Advance report of final mortality statistics, 1988. *Monthly Vital Statistics Report, 39(7).* Hyattsville, MD: U. S. Public Health Service.

National Center for Health Statistics. (1990). *Annual summary of births, marriages, divorces, and deaths: United States, 1989. Monthly Vital Statistics Report, Vol. 38 (13).* Hyattsville, MD: Public Health Service.

National Center for Health Statistics. (1991). Births, marriages, divorces, and deaths for 1990. *Monthly Vital Statistics Report, 39(12).* Hyattsville, MD: U. S. Public Health Service.

National Committee for Citizens in Education (NCCE). (1986). Don't be afraid to start a suicide prevention program in your school. *Network for Public Schools, Winter Holiday,* 1–4.

National Institute on Drug Abuse (NIDA). (1987). Cocaine use remains steady, other drug use declines among high school seniors. *NIDA Notes, 2(2),* 1.

National Research Council (2000). *How people learn: Brain, mind, experience, and school* (Expanded ed.). Washington, DC: National Academy Press.

National Research Council and Institute of Medicine (2000). *From neurons to neighborhoods: The science of early childhood development.* Committee on Integrating the Science of Early Childhood Development. Jack P. Shonkoff and Deborah A. Phillips, eds. Board on Children, Youth, and Families, Commission on Behavioral and Social Sciences and Education. Washington, DC: National Academy Press.

Nelson, K. (1978). How children represent knowledge of their world in and out of language: A preliminary report. In R. Siegler (Ed.), *Children's thinking: What develops.* Hillsdale, NJ: Erlbaum.

Nelson, K., Rescorla, L., Gruendel, J., & Benedict, H. (1978). Early lexicons: What do they mean? *Child Development, 49,* 960–968.

Nelson, K., & Gruendel, J. (1981). Generalized event representations: Basic building blocks of cognitive development. In M. E. Lamb & A. Brown (Eds.), *Advances in developmental psychology,* Vol. 1. Hillsdale, NJ: Erlbaum.

Nelson, N. M., Enkin, M. W., Saigal, S., Bennett, K. J., Milner, R., & Sackett, D. L. (1980). A randomized clinical trial of the Leboyer approach to childbirth. *New England Journal of Medicine, 302,* 655–660.

Nelson-LeGall, S., & Gumerman, R. (1984). Children's perceptions of helpers and helper motivation. *Journal of Applied Developmental Psychology, 5,* 1–12.

Neugarten, B. (1968). The awareness of middle age. In B. L. Neugarten (Ed.), *Middle age and aging.* Chicago: University of Chicago Press.

Neugarten, B. (1968). Adult personality: Toward a psychology of the life cycle. In B. L. Neugarten (Ed.), *Middle age and aging.* Chicago: University of Chicago Press.

Neugarten, B. (1970). The old and the young in modern societies. *American Behavioral Scientist, 14,* 18–24.

Neugarten, B. (1973). Personality change in later life: A developmental perspective. In C. Eisdorfer & M. P. Lawton (Eds.), *The psychology of adult development and aging.* Washington, DC: American Psychological Association.

Neugarten, B. (1978). *The wise of the young-old.* In R. Gross, B. Gross, & S. Seidman (Eds.), *The new old: Struggling for decent aging.* Garden City, NY: Doubleday-Anchor.

Neugarten, B. L., Havighurst, R. J., & Tobin, S. S. (1968). Personality and patterns of aging. In B. L. Neugarten (Ed.), *Middle age and aging.* Chicago: University of Chicago Press.

Neugarten, B. L., & Moore, J. W. (1968). The changing age-status system. In B. L. Neugarten (Ed.), *Middle age and aging.* Chicago: University of Chicago Press.

Neugarten, B., & Neugarten, D. (1987). The changing meanings of age. *Psychology Today, 21,* 29–33.

Newberger, C. M., Milnicoe, L. H., & Newberger, E. H. (1986). *The American family in crisis: Implications for children.* New York: Year Book Medical Publishers.

Newcomb, M. D., & Bentler, P. M. (1988a). The impact of family context, deviant attitudes, and emotional distress on adolescent drug use: Longitudinal latent-variable analyses of mothers and their children. *Journal of Research in Personality, 22,* 154–176.

Newcomb, M. D., & Bentler, P. M. (1988b). Impact of adolescent drug use and social support on problems of young adults: A longitudinal study. *Journal of Abnormal Psychology, 97,* 64–75.

Newcomb, M. D., & Bentler, P. M. (1989). Substance use and abuse among children and teenagers. *American Psychologist, 44,* 242–248.

Newcomb, M. D., Fahy, B., & Skager, R. (1990). Reasons to avoid drug use among teenagers: Associations with actual drug use and implications for prevention among different demographic groups. *Journal of Alcohol and Drug Education, 36,* 53–81.

Newcomb, M. D., McCarthy, W. J., & Bentler, P. M. (1989). Cigarette smoking, academic lifestyle, and social impact efficacy: An eight-year study from early adolescence to young adulthood. *Journal of Applied Social Psychology, 19,* 251–281.

Newman, P. R., & Newman, B. M. (1991). *Development through life: A psychosocial approach* (5th ed.). Pacific Grove, CA: Brooks/Cole.

NICHD Early Child Care Research Network. (2001). Nonmaternal care and family factors in early development: An overview of the NICHD Study of Early Child Care. *Journal of Applied Developmental Psychology, 22,* 457–492.

Nobles, W. W. (1984). Alienation, human transformation and adolescent drug use: Toward a reconceptualization of the problem. *Journal of Drug Issues, 14,* 243–252.

Noelker, L., & Wallace, R. (1985). The organization of family care for impaired elderly. *Journal of Family Issues, 6,* 23–44.

Norton, A. J., & Glick, P. C. (1986). One parent families: A social and economic profile. *Family Relations, 35,* 356–361.

Norton, A. J. (1983). Family life cycle: 1980. *Journal of Marriage and the Family, 45,* 267–275.

Noyes, R. (1980). Attitude change following near death experiences. *Psychiatry, 43,* 234–242.

Noyes, R., & Clancy, J. (1977). The dying role: Its relevance to improved medical care. *Psychiatry, 40,* 41–47.

Noyes, R., & Kletti, R. (1977). Panoramic memory: A response to the threat of death. *Omega, 8,* 181–194.

Nunnally, J. C. (1973). Research strategies and measurement methods for investigating human development. In J. R. Nesselroade and H. W. Reese (Eds.), *Life span developmental psychology* (pp. 87–110). New York: Academic Press.

Nye, F. I. (1957). Child adjustment in broken and in unhappy, unbroken homes. *Marriage and Family Relations, 19,* 356–361.

O'Connor, S., Vietze, P. Sherrod, K., Sandler, H., & Alteneier, W. (1980). Reduced incidence of parenting inadequacy following rooming-in. *Pediatrics, 66,* 176–182.

O'Mahony, J. (1989). Development of thinking about things and people: Social and nonsocial cognition during adolescence. *Journal of Genetic Psychology, 150,* 217–224.

O'Neill, N., & O'Neill, G. (1972a). *Open marriage: A new lifestyle for couples.* New York: Evans & Co.

O'Neill, B., & O'Neill, G. (1972b). Open marriage: A synergic model. *Family Coordinator, 21,* 403–409.

O'Rand, A. M., & Krecker, M. L. (1990). Concepts of the life cycle: Their history, meanings, and use in the social sciences. *Annual Review of Sociology, 16,* 241–262.

Oates, D. S., & Heinicke, C. M. (1985). Prebirth prediction of the quality of the mother-infant interaction: The first year of life. *Journal of Family Issues, 6,* 523–542.

Oetting, G. R., & Beauvais, F. (1991). Orthogonal cultural identification theory: The cultural identification of minority adolescents. *International Journal of Addictions, 25,* 655–685.

Ogborn, W. F. (1933). *Recent social trends in the United States.* New York: McGraw-Hill.

Okun, B. (1984). *Working with adults: Individual, family, and career development.* Monterey, CA: Brooks/Cole.

Olson, D. H., & McCubbin, H. I. (1983). *Families: What makes them work?* Beverly Hills, CA: Sage Publications.

Olson, D. H., McCubbin, H., Barnes, H. L., Larsen, A. S., Muxen, M. J., & Wilson, M. A., (1983). *Families: What makes them work.* Beverly Hills, CA: Sage.

Olson, D. H., Sprenkle, D., & Russell, C. (1979). Circumplex model of marital and family systems I: Cohension and adaptability dimensions, family types, and clinical applications. *Family Process, 18,* 3–28.

Olson, D. H. (1986). What makes families work? In S. Van Zandt et al., (Eds.), *Family strengths 7: Vital connections.* Lincoln, NE: Center for Family Strengths, University of Nebraska.

Orgel, L. (1970). The maintenance of the accuracy of protein synthesis and its relevance to aging: A correction. *Proceedings of the National Academy of Science, 67,* 1476.

Orr, D. P., Hoffmans, M. A., & Bennetts, G. (1984). Adolescents with cancer report their psychological needs. *Journal of Psychosocial Oncology, 2,* 47–59.

Osgood, N. J. (1989). Aging in America: Preventing suicide in the elderly. *Medical Aspects of Human Sexuality, 23,* 27–29.

Overpeck, M. D., & Moss, A. J. (1991). Children's exposure to environmental cigarette smoke before and after birth: Health of our nation's children, United States, 1988. *Advance Data From Vital and Health Statistics. No. 202.* Hyattsville, MD: National Center for Health Statistics.

Overton, W. F. (1998). Developmental psychology: Philosophy, Concepts, and Methodology. In W. Damon & R. M. Lerner (Eds.), Handbook of child psychology (Vol. 1): *Theoretical models of human development* (5th ed.). NY: John Wiley & Sons, Inc.

Padawer, J. A., Fagan, C., Janoff-Bulman, R., Strickland, B. R., & Chorowski, M. (1988). Women's psychological adjustment following emergency Cesarean versus vaginal delivery. *Psychology of Women Quarterly, 12,* 25–34.

Palmore, E. (1975). *The honorable elders.* Durham, NC: Duke University Press.

Palmore, E., & Maeda, D. (1985). *The honorable elders revisited: A revised cross-cultural analysis of aging in Japan.* Durham, NC: Duke University Press.

Parcel, G., Simons-Morton, B., O'Hara. N., Baranowski, T., Kolbe, L., & Bee, D. (1987). School promotion of healthful diet and exercise behavior: An integration of organizational change and social learning theory interventions. *Journal of School Health, 57,* 150–156.

Parke, R. (1979). Perspectives on father-infant interaction. In J. D. Osofsky (Ed.), *Handbook of infant development.* New York: Wiley.

Parke, R., & Sawin, D. (1976). The father's role in infancy: A reevaluation. *Family Coordinator, 25,* 365–371.

Parke, R., & Tinsley, B. (1987). Family interaction in infancy: In J. Osofsky (Ed.), *Handbook of infant development.* New York: Wiley.

Parke, R. D., & Slaby, R. G. (1983). The development of aggression. In P. H. Mussen (Ed.), *Handbook of child psychology.* Vol. 4. New York: Wiley.

Parker, W. A. (1980). Designing an environment for childbirth. In B. L. Blum (Ed.), *Psychological aspects of pregnancy, birthing, and bonding.* New York: Human Sciences Press.

Parkes, C. M. (1975). Determinants of outcome following bereavement. *Omega, 6,* 303–323.

Parkes, C. M., & Brown, R. J. (1972). Health after bereavement: A controlled study of young Boston widows and widowers. *Psychosomatic Medicine, 34,* 449–461.

Parmalee, A. H., & Stern, E. D. (1972). Development of states in infants. In C. Clemente, D. Purpura, & F. Mayer (Eds.), *Sleep in the maturing nervous system.* New York: Academic Press.

Parmelee, A. H., Jr., & Sigman, M. (1983). Perinatal brain development and behavior. In P. Mussen (Ed.), *Handbook of child psychology. Vol. 2. Infancy and developmental psychobiology.* New York: Wiley.

Parsons, J., Adler, T., & Kaczala, C. (1982). Socialization of achievement attitudes and beliefs: Parental influences. *Child Development, 53,* 310–321.

Parten, M. B. (1932). Social participation among preschool children. *Journal of Abnormal and Social Psychology, 27,* 243–269.

Pasley, K., & Ihinger-Tallman, M. (1987). *Remarriage.* Beverly Hills, CA: Sage.

Patten, B. M. (1976). *Patten's human embryology: Elements of clinical development.* New York: McGraw-Hill.

Patterson, J., & McCubbin, H. (1983). Chronic illness: Family stress and coping. In C. Figley & H. McCubbin (Eds.), *Stress and the family: Coping with catastrophe.* Vol. 2. New York: Bruner/Mazel.

Pattison, E. M. (1977). The dying experience. In E. M. Pattison (Ed.), *The experience of dying.* Englewood Cliffs, NJ: Prentice Hall.

Peck, R. D. (1968). Psychological developments in the second half of life. In B. L. Neugarten (Ed.), *Middle age and aging.* Chicago: University of Chicago Press.

Pedersen, G., & Mehl, L. (1979). Some determinants of maternal attachment. *American Journal of Psychiatry, 135,* 1168–1173.

Pellegrini, A. D. (1987). Rough and tumble play: Developmental and educational significance. *Educational Psychologist, 22,* 23–32.

Pelletier, K. R. (1993). Between mind and body: Stress, emotions, and health. In D. Goleman & J. Gurin (Eds.), *Mind body medicine: How to use your mind for better health.* NY: Consumer Reports Books.

Pennington, S. B. (1987). Children of lesbian mothers. In F. W. Bozett (Ed.), *Gay and lesbian parents.* New York: Praeger.

Peppers, L., & Knapp, R. (1980). Maternal reactions to involuntary fetal-infant death. *Psychiatry, 43,* 155–159.

Peppers, L. G., & Knapp, R. S. (1980). *Motherhood and mourning: Perinatal death.* New York: Praeger.

Perdue, C. W., & Gurtman, M. B. (1990). Evidence for the automaticity of ageism. *Journal of Experimental Social Psychology, 26,* 199–206.

Peretz, A., Neve, J., & Desmedt, J. (1991). Lymphocyte response is enhanced by supplementation of elderly subjects with selenium enriched yeast. *American Journal of Clinical Nutrition, 53,* 1323–1329.

Perkins, H. W., & Harris, L. B. (1990). Family bereavement and health in adult life course perspective. *Journal of Marriage and the Family, 52,* 233–242.

Perlmutter, M. (1987). Aging and memory. In K. W. Schaie & K. Eisdorfer (Eds.), *Annual review of gerontology and geriatrics.* Vol. 7. New York: Springer.

Perry, W. G., Jr. (1970). *Forms of intellectual and ethical development in the college years: A scheme.* New York: Holt, Rinehart, Winston.

Peskin, H. (1967). Pubertal onset and ego functioning. *Journal of Abnormal Psychology, 72,* 1–15.

Peskin, H. (1973). Influence of the developmental schedule of puberty on learning and ego functioning. *Journal of Youth and Adolescence, 2,* 273–290.

Petersen, A. C. (1988). Adolescent development. *Annual Review of Psychology, 39,* 583–607.

Peterson, G. W., & Rollins, B. C. (1987). Parent-child socialization. In B. Sussman & S. Steinmetz (Eds.), *Handbook of marriage and the family.* New York: Plenum.

Pfannenstiel, J., & Seltzer, D. (1989). New parents as teachers: Evaluation of early parent education programs. *Early Childhood Research Quarterly, 4,* 1–18.

Phelps, L., & Bajorek, E. (1991). Eating disorders of the adolescent: Current issues in etiology, assessment, and treatment. *School Psychology Review, 20,* 9–22.

Phillips, J. L., McCartney, K., & Scarr, S. (1987). Child care quality and children's social development. *Developmental Psychology, 23,* 537–543.

Phillips, D. A. (Ed.) (1987). *Quality in child care: What does research tell us?* Washington, DC: National Association for the Education of Young Children.

Piaget, J. (1926). *The language and thought of the child.* New York: Harcourt, Brace Jovanovich.

Piaget, J. (1932). *The moral judgment of the child.* London: Kegan Paul, Trench, & Trubner.

Piaget, J. (1952a). *The child's conception of number.* New York: Humanities Press.

Piaget, J. (1952b). *The origins of intelligence in children.* New York: International Universities Press.

Piaget, J. (1967). *Six psychological studies.* New York: Random House.

Piaget, J. (1969). *The child's conception of time.* New York: Basic Books.

Piaget, J. (1972). Intellectual evolution from adolescence to adulthood. *Human Development, 15,* 1–12.

Piaget, J., & Inhelder, B. (1969). *The psychology of the child.* New York: Basic Books.

Piaget, J., & Inhelder, B. (1967). *The child's concept of space.* (F. Langdon & E. Lunzer, Trans.). New York: Norton.

Piernot, C. (1978). Parental expectations of day care centers. Unpublished Master's thesis, Colorado State University.

Pike, K. M. (1991). Mothers, daughters, and disordered eating. *Journal of Abnormal Psychology, 100,* 198–204.

Pine, V. R. (1976). Grief, bereavement, and mourning: The realities of loss. In V. R. Pine et al., (Eds.), *Acute grief and the funeral* (pp. 105–114). Springfield, IL: Charles C. Thomas.

Pines, M. (1983). Can a rock walk? *Psychology Today, 17(November),* 46–54.

Piper, T. (2003). *Language and learning: The home and school years* (3rd ed.). Upper Saddle River, NJ: Merrill Prentice Hall.

Pleck, J. (1985). *Working wives/working husbands.* Beverly Hills, CA: Sage.

Pollak, C. P., Perlick, D., & Linsner, J. P. (1990). Sleep problems in the community elderly as predictors of death and nursing home placement. *Journal of Community Health, 15,* 123–133.

Pollock, M. L., Carroll, J. F., & Graves, J. E. (1991). Injuries and adherence to walk/jog and resistance training programs in the elderly. *Medicine and Science in Sports and Exercise, 23,* 1194–1199.

Poon, L. W. (1985). Differences in human memory with aging: Nature, causes, and clinical implications. In J. E. Birren & K. Schaie (Eds.), *Handbook of the psychology of aging* (2nd ed.). New York: Van Nostrand.

Pope, H., Hudson, J., Jonas, J., & Yurgelun-Todd, D. (1983). Bulimia treated with imipramine: A placebo controlled, double-blind study. *American Journal of Psychiatry, 140,* 554–558.

Porter, L., Miller, R. H., & Marshall, R. (1986). Neonatal pain cries: Effects of circumcision on acoustic features and perceived urgency. *Child Development, 57,* 790–802.

Post, S. G. (1990). Nutrition, hydration, and the demented elderly. *Journal of Medical Humanities, 11,* 185–191.

Poznansky, E. O. (1973). Children with excessive fears. *American Journal of Orthopsychiatry, 43,* 428–438.

Prevention Research Center. (1986). *Prevention index '86: A report card on the nation's health.* Emmaus, PA: Rodele.

Price-Bonham, S., & Addison, S. (1978). Families and mentally retarded children: Emphasis on the father. *Family Coordinator, 27,* 221–230.

Protinsky, H., & Shilts, L. (1990). Adolescent substance use and family cohesion. *Family Therapy, 17,* 173–175.

Pruett, K. D. (1987). *The nurturing father.* New York: Warner.

Pulaski, M. (1980). *Understanding Piaget* (revised and expanded edition). New York: Harper & Row.

Putallaz, M., & Gottman, J. (1981). Social skills and group acceptance. In S. Asher & J. Guttman (Eds.), *The development of children's friendships.* New York: Cambridge University Press.

Quilligan, E. J. (1983). *Pregnancy, birth, and the infant.* NIH Publication No. 82–2304. Washington, DC: U. S. Government Printing Office.

Quinn, P., & Allen, K. R. (1989). Facing challenges and making compromises: How single mothers endure. *Family Relations, 38,* 390–395.

Rabin, A. (1965). Motivation for parenthood. *Journal of Projective Techniques, 29,* 405–411.

Radke-Yarrow, M., Zahn-Waxler, C., & Chapman, M. (1983). Children's prosocial dispositions and behavior. In M. E. Hetherington (Ed.), *Handbook of child psychology.* Vol. 4. New York: Wiley.

Rainone, G., Deren, S., Fleinman, P., & Wish, E. (1987). Heavy marijuana users not in treatment: The continuing search for the "pure" marijuana user. *Journal of Psychoactive Drugs, 19*, 353–359.

Reading, J., & Amateo, E. S. (1986). Role deviance or role diversification: Reassessing the psychosocial factors affecting the parenthood decision of career-oriented women. *Journal of Marriage and the Family, 48*, 255–260.

Reichard, S., Livson, F., & Peterson, P. G. (1962). *Aging and personality.* New York: Wiley.

Rescorla, R. A. (1987). A Pavlovian analysis of goal-directed behavior. *American Psychologist, 42*, 119–129.

Resnick, L. (1989). Developing mathematical knowledge. *American Psychologist, 44*, 162–169.

Rest, J. (1983). Morality. In P. Mussen (Ed.), *Handbook of child psychology, Vol. 3.* New York: Wiley.

Reznick, J. S., Kagan, J., Snidman, N., Gersten, M., Baak, K., & Rosenberg, A. (1986). Inhibited and uninhibited children: A follow-up study. *Child Development, 57*, 660–680.

Rheingold, H. (1966). Development of social behavior in human infants. In H. Stevenson (Ed.), The concept of development. *Monographs of the Society for Research in Child Development, 31*, Whole. No. 107.

Rheingold, H. (1985). Development as the acquisition of familiarity. *Annual Review of Psychology, 36*, 1–17.

Rhoades, G. K., Stanley, S. M., & Markman, H. J. (2006). Pre-engagement cohabitation and gender asymmetry in marital commitment. *Journal of Family Psychology, 20*, 553–560.

Ribble, M. (1943). *The rights of infants.* New York: Columbia University Press.

Rice, M. L. (1982). Child language: What children know and how. In T. Field et al. (Eds.), *Review of human development.* New York: Wiley.

Richards, L. N. (1989). The precarious survival and hard-won satisfactions of white single-parent families. *Family Relations, 38*, 396–403.

Richards, M., Boxer, A., Petersen, A., & Albrecht, R. (1990). Relation of weight to body image in pubertal girls and boys from two communities. *Developmental Psychology, 26*, 313–321.

Richardson, D., & Short, R. (1978). Time of onset of sperm production in boys. *Journal of Biosocial Science, 5*, 15–25.

Richardson, J., Dwyer, K. (1989). Substance use among eighth-grade students who take care of themselves after school. *Pediatrics, 84*, 556–566.

Ricks, S. (1985). Father-infant interactions: A review of empirical research. *Family Relations, 34*, 505–511.

Riegel, K. (1973). Dialectic operations. The final period of cognitive development. *Human Development, 16*, 346–370.

Riegel, K. (1975). Adult life crisis: A dialectical interpretation of development. In N. Datan & H. Ginsberg (Eds.), *Life span developmental psychology: Normative life crises.* New York: Academic Press.

Riegel, K., F., & Riegel, R. M. (1972). Development, drop, and death. *Developmental Psychology, 6*, 306–319.

Rierdan, J., & Koff, E. (1980). The psychological impact of menarche: Integrative versus disruptive changes. *Journal of Youth and Adolescence, 9*, 49–58.

Ries, P. (1991). Characteristics of persons with and without health care coverage: United States, 1989. *Advance Data from Vital and Health Statistics, No. 201.* Washington, DC: U. S. Government Printing Office.

Ries, P., & Brown, S. (1991). Disability and health: Characteristics of persons by limitation of activity and assessed health status. *Advance Data From Vital and Health Statistics, No. 197. DHHS Publication No. (PHS)91–1250.* Hyattsville, MD: National Center for Health Statistics.

Ring, K. (1980). *Life at death: A scientific investigation of the near death experience.* New York: William Morrow.

Ringwalt, C. L., & Palmer, J. H. (1990). Differences between white and black youth who drink heavily. *Addictive Behaviors, 15*, 455–460.

Risman, B. J. (1986). Can men "mother?" Life as a single father. *Family Relations, 35*, 95–102.

Rizzo, T., & Corsaro, W. (1988). Toward a better understanding of Vygotsky's process of internalization: Its role in the development of the concept of friendship. *Developmental Review, 8*, 219–237.

Roberts, J. (1975). Eye examination findings among children and youths aged 12–17 years: United States. *Vital and Health Statistics, Series 11, No. 157. DHEW Publication No. (HRA) 76–1639.* Washington, DC: U. S. Government Printing Office.

Roberts, J., & Ahuja, E. M. (1975). Hearing sensitivity and related medical findings among youth 12–17 years: United States. *Vital and Health Statistics, Series 11, No. 154. DHEW Publication No. (HRA) 76–1637.* Washington, DC: U. S. Government Printing Office.

Roberts, J., & Rowland, M. (1978). Refraction status and motility defects of persons 4–74 years. *Vital and Health Statistics, Series 11, No. 206.* Hyattsville, MD: National Center for Health Statistics.

Roberts, J., & Ludford, J. (1976). Skin conditions of youth aged 12–17: United States. *Vital and Health Statistics, Series 11, No. 157. DHEW Publication No. (HRA) 76–1639.* Washington, DC: U. S. Government Printing Office.

Roberts, P., & Newton, P. (1987). Levinsonian studies of women's adult development. *Psychology and Aging, 2*, 154–163.

Robertson, J. F. (1978). Women in mid-life crisis: Reverberations and support networks. *Family Coordinator, 27*, 375–382.

Robinson, B., & Barret, R. L. (1986). *The developing father: Emerging roles in contemporary society.* New York: Guilford Press.

Roche, A. F. (1979). Secular trends in stature, weight, and maturation. In A. F. Roche (Ed.), Secular trends in growth, maturation, and development of children. *Monographs of the Society for Research in Child Development, 44*, 3–27.

Roche, J. (1986). Premarital sex: Attitudes and behavior by dating stage. *Adolescence, 81*, 107–121.

Rodin, J. (1986). Aging and health: Effect of the sense of control. *Science, 233*, 1217–1276.

Rodman, H., & Cole, C. (1987). Latchkey children: A review of policy and resources. *Family Relations, 36*, 101–105.

Roffwarg, H., Muzio, J., & Dement, W. (1966). Ontogenetic development of the human sleep-dream cycle. *Science,152*, 604–619.

Rogers, C. R. (1961). *On becoming a person.* Cambridge, MA: Riverside Press.

Rogers, W. A., & Fisk, A. D. Understanding the role of attention in cognitive aging research. In J. E. Birren & K. W. Schaie (Eds.), *Handbook of the psychology of aging.* San Diego, CA: Academic Press.

Rogoff, B. (2003). *The cultural nature of human development.* NY: Oxford University Press.

Rolfes, S., & DeBruyne, L. (1990). *Life span nutrition.* St. Paul, MN: West Publishing Co.

Rollins, B., & Cannon, K. (1974). Marital satisfaction over the family life cycle: A reevaluation. *Journal of Marriage and the Family, 36*, 271–282.

Rollins, B., & Feldman, H. (1970). Marital satisfaction over the family life cycle. *Journal of Marriage and the Family, 32*, 20–28.

Romeo, F. (1984). Adolescence, sexual conflict, and anorexia nervosa. *Adolescence, 19*, 551–555.

Roscoe, B., & Peterson, K. (1989). Age-appropriate behaviors: A comparison of three generations of females. *Adolescence, 23*, 39–46.

Roosa, M. W. (1984). Maternal age, social class, and the obstetric performance of teenagers. *Journal of Youth and Adolescence, 13*, 365–374.

Rose, S. A., & Wallace, I. F. (1985). Visual recognition memory: A predictor of later cognitive functioning in preterms. *Child Development, 56*, 843–852.

Rosel, N. (1978). Toward a social theory of dying. *Omega, 9*, 49–55.

Rosenfeld, A., & Stark, E. (1987). The prime of our lives. *Psychology Today, 21*, 62–72.

Rosenman, R. (1974). The role of behavioral patterns and neurogenic factors on the pathogenesis of coronary heart disease. In R. Eliot (Ed.), *Stress and the heart.* New York: Futura.

Rosenthal, R., & Jacobson, L. (1968). *Pygmalion in the classroom.* New York: Holt, Rinehart, & Winston.

Rosenthal, P. A., & Rosenthal, S. (1984). Suicidal behavior by preschool children. *American Journal of Psychiatry, 141*, 520–525.

Rosett, J., & Sander, L. (1979). Effects of maternal drinking on neonatal morphology and state regulation. In J. Osofsky (Ed.), *Handbook of infant development.* New York: Wiley.

Rosinski, R., Pellegrini, J., & Siegel, A. (1977). Developmental changes in the processing of pictures and words. *Journal of Experimental Child Psychology, 23*, 382–391.

Roskos, K. (1990). A taxonomic view of pretend play activity among 4 and 5-year-old children. *Early Childhood Research Quarterly, 5*, 495–500.

Ross, C. E., Mirowsky, J., & Goldsteen, K. (1990). The impact of the family on health: The decade in review. *Journal of Marriage and the Family, 52*, 1059–1078.

Ross, C. P. (1985). Teaching children the facts of life and death: Suicide prevention in the schools. In M. L. Peck, N. L. Faberow, & R. E. Litman (Eds.), *Youth suicide* (pp. 147–169). New York: Springer.

Ross, H., & Lollis, S. (1987). Communication within infant social games. *Developmental Psychology, 23*, 241–248.

Rossi, A. (1968). Transition to parenthood. *Journal of Marriage and the Family, 30*, 26–39.

Rossi, A. S. (1977). A biosocial perspective on parenting. *Daedalus, 106*, 1–31.

Rossi, A. (1980). Aging and parenthood in the middle years. In P. Baltes & O. Brim (Eds.), *Life-span development and behavior.* Vol. 3. New York: Academic Press.

Rossi, S., & Wittrock, M. (1971). Developmental shifts in verbal recall between mental ages two and five. *Child Development, 42*, 333–340.

Rotenberg, K., & Sliz, D. (1988). Children's restrictive disclosure to friends. *Merrill-Palmer Quarterly, 34*, 163–184.

Routh, D. K., Schroeder, C. S., & O'Tuama, L. A. (1974). Development of activity level in children. *Developmental Psychology, 10*, 163–168.

Rowe, D.C., & Rodgers, J. L. (1991). Adolescent smoking and drinking: Are they "epidemics?" *Journal of Studies on Alcohol, 52*, 110–117.

Rowe, G. P., & Meredith, W. H. (1982). Quality in marital relationships after twenty-five years. *Family Perspectives, 16*, 149–155.

Rowland, M. (1980). Basic data on hearing levels of adults, 25–74 years: United States, 1971–1975. *Vital and Health Statistics, Series 11, No. 215.* DHEW Publication No. (PHS) 80–1663.

Rubin, K. H., Fein, G. G., & Vandenberg, B. (1983). Play. In M. Hetherington (Ed.), *Handbook of child development* (4th ed.). New York: Wiley.

Rubin, K. H., Maioni, T. L., & Hornung, M. (1976). Free play behaviors in middle and lower class preschoolers: Parten and Piaget revisited. *Child Development, 47*, 414–419.

Ruff, C. C., & Reaves, E. L. (1989). Diagnosing urinary incontinence in adults. *The Nurse Practitioner, 14*, 8–15.

Russell, C. S. (1974). Transition to parenthood: Problems and gratifications. *Journal of Marriage and the Family, 36*, 294–301.

Rutter, M. (1979). Protective factors in children's responses to stress and disadvantage. In M. Kent & J. Rolf (Eds.), *Primary prevention of psychopathology, Vol. 3.* Hanover, NH: University Press of New England.

Rutter, M. (1980). *Changing youth in a changing society.* Cambridge, MA: Harvard University Press.

Rutter, M. (1981). Social-emotional consequences of day care for preschool children. *American Journal of Orthopsychiatry, 51*, 4–28.

Rutter, M. (1983a). School effects on pupil progress: Research findings and policy implications. *Child Development, 54*, 1–29.

Rutter, M. (1983b). Stress, coping, and development: Some issues and some questions. In N. Garmezy & M. Rutter (Eds.), *Stress, coping, and development in children.* New York: McGraw-Hill.

Rutter, M. (1984). Resilient children. *Psychology Today, 18*, 57–65.

Rutter, M. (1985). Resilience in the face of adversity: Protective factors and resistance to psychiatric disorder. *British Journal of Psychiatry, 147*, 598–611.

Ryan, R., & Lynch, J. (1989). Emotional autonomy versus detachment: Revising the vicissitudes of adolescence and young adulthood. *Child Development, 60*, 340–356.

Ryff, C. D., Kwan, C. M. L., & Singer, B. H. (2001). Personality and aging: Flourishing agendas and future challenges. In J. E. Birren & K. W. Schaie (Eds.), *Handbook of the psychology of aging.* San Diego, CA: Academic Press.

Sacher, G. A. (1977). Life table modifications and life prolongation. In C. E. Finch & L. Hayflick (Eds.), *Handbook of the biology of aging.* New York: Van Nostrand.

Sager, S. J., Steer, H., Crohn, H., Rodstein, E., & Walker, E. (1980). Remarriage revisited. *Family and Child Mental Healthy Journal, 6*, 19–33.

Sahyoun, N.R., Lentzner, H., Hoyert, D., & Robinson, K. N. (2001). Trends in causes of death among the elderly. In G. E. Dickinson & M.R. Leming, (Eds.), *Dying, death, and bereavement* (10th ed.). NY: McGraw-Hill.

Salmon, C. F., & Salmon, F. C. (1978). Housing the elderly. *Journal of Home Economics, 71*, 23–35.

Salthouse, T. (1985). Speed of behavior and its implications for cognition. In J. E. Birren & K. W. Schaie (Eds.), *Handbook of the psychology of aging* (2nd ed.). New York: Van Nostrand.

Saluter, A. F. (1989). Changes in American family life. *Current Population Reports, Series P–23, No. 163.* Washington, DC: U. S. Bureau of the Census.

Saluter, F. (1989). Singleness in America. In Studies in marriage and the family. *Current Population Reports, Series P–23, No. 162.* Washington, DC: Bureau of the Census.

Sameroff, A. J. (1968). The components of sucking in the human newborn. *Journal of Experimental Child Psychology, 6*, 607–623.

Sanchez-Ayendez, M. (1988). Puerto Rican elderly women: The cultural dimension of social support networks. *Women & Health, 14*, 239–244.

Sanders, C. M. (1979). A comparison of adult bereavement in the death of a spouse, child, and parent. *Omega, 10*, 217–232.

Sanders, C. M. (1980a). Comparison of younger and older spouses in bereavement outcomes. *Omega, 10*, 217–232.

Sanders, C. M. (1980b). A comparison of adult bereavement in the death of a spouse, child, and parent. *Omega, 10*, 303–322.

Sanik, N. M., & Mauldin, T. (1986). Single versus two parent families: A comparison of mothers' time. *Family Relations, 35*, 53–56.

Sarason, S. B. (1977). *Work, aging, and social change: Professionals and the one life-one career imperative.* New York: Free Press.

Sassen, G. (1980). Success anxiety in women: A constructivist interpretation of its source and significance. *Harvard Educational Review, 50*, 13–24.

Satir, V. (1972). *Peoplemaking.* Palo Alto, CA: Science and Behavior Books.

Saunders, C. (1978). Terminal care. In C. A. Garfield (Ed.), *Psychosocial care of the dying patient* (pp. 22–33). New York: McGraw-Hill

Savin-Williams, R. (1979). Dominance hierarchies in groups of early adolescents. *Child Development, 50*, 923–935.

Savin-Williams, R. (1980). Dominance hierarchies in groups of middle to late adolescent males. *Journal of Youth and Adolescence, 9*, 75–85.

Savin-Williams, R. (1988). Theoretical perspectives accounting for adolescent homosexuality. *Journal of Adolescent Health Care, 9*, 95–104.

Savin-Williams, R. (1989). Gay and lesbian adolescents. *Marriage and Family Review, 14*, 197–216.

Savin-Williams, R., & Demo, D. (1984). Developmental change and stability in adolescent self-concept. *Developmental Psychology, 20*, 1100–1110.

Savin-Williams, R., & Small, S. A. (1986). The timing of puberty and its relationship to parent and parent perceptions of family interactions. *Developmental Psychology, 22*, 342–348.

Sawin, D., & Parke, R. (1979). Fathers' affection stimulation and caregiving behaviors with newborn infants. *Family Coordinator, 28*, 509–513.

Saxon, S. V., & Etten, M. J. (1978). *Physical change and aging.* New York: Tiresias Press.

Saxton, L. (1990). *The individual, marriage, and the family* (7th ed.). Belmont, CA: Wadsworth.

Scanzoni, L., & Scanzoni, J. (1976). *Men, women, and change: A sociology of marriage and the family.* New York: McGraw-Hill.

Scanzoni, L., & Scanzoni, J. (1981). *Men, women, and change* (2nd ed.). New York: McGraw-Hill.

Schneider, S. G., Farberow, N. L., & Kruks, G. N. (1989). Suicidal behavior in adolescent and young adult gay men. *Suicide and Life-Threatening Behavior, 19*, 381–394.

Scarf, M. (1980). *Unfinished business: Pressure points in the lives of women.* Garden City, NY: Doubleday.

Scarr, S. (1984). *Mother care/Other care.* New York: Basic Books.

Scarr, S., Phillips, D., & McCartney, K. (1989). Working mothers and their families. *American Psychologist, 44*, 1402–1409.

Schachter, F. f. (1981). Toddlers with employed mothers. *Child Development, 52,* 958–964.

Schaffer, H., & Emerson, P. E. (1964). The development of social attachments in infancy. *Monographs of the Society for Research in Child Development, 29,* Whole No. 3.

Schaie, K. W. (1983). The Seattle longitudinal study: A twenty-one year exploration of psychometric intelligence in adulthood. In K. W. Schaie (Ed.), *Longitudinal studies of adult psychological development.* New York: Guilford Press.

Schaie, K. W., & Willis, S. (1986). *Adult development and aging* (2nd ed.). Boston: Little, Brown.

Schantz, C. U. (1983). Social cognition. In P. Mussen (Ed.), *Handbook of child psychology, Vol. 3.* New York: Wiley.

Schlossberg, N. (1987). Taking the mystery out of change. *Psychology Today, 21,* 74–75.

Schmidt, D. F., & Boland, S. M. (1986). Structure of perceptions of older adults: Evidence for multiple stereotypes. *Psychology and Aging, 1,* 255–260.

Schneider, E., Vining, E., Hadley, E., & Farnham, S. (1986). Recommended dietary allowances and the health of the elderly. *New England Journal of Medicine, 314,* 157–160.

Schoenborn, C. A., & Danchik, K. M. (1980). Health practices of young adults. *Advance Data from Vital and Health Statistics, No. 64.* Hyattsville, MD: National Center for Health Statistics.

Schrier, R. W. (1990). *Geriatric medicine.* Philadelphia: Saunders.

Schultz, D. & Schultz, S. E. (2010). *Psychology and work today* (10th ed.). Old Tappan, NJ: Prentice Hall.

Schulz, R., & Aderman, D. (1974). Clinical research and the stages of dying. *Omega, 5,* 137–143.

Schuster, C. S. (1986). Intrauterine development. In C. S. Schuster & S. S. Ashburn (Eds.), *The process of human development.* Boston: Little, Brown.

Schwarz, J., Strickland, R., & Krolick, G. (1974). Infant day care: Behavioral effects at preschool age. *Developmental Psychology, 10,* 502–506.

Sears, R., Maccoby, E., & Levin, H. (1957). *Patterns of child rearing.* New York: Harper & Row.

Sebald, H. (1981). Adolescents' concepts of popularity and unpopularity, comparing 1960 with 1976. *Family Coordinator, 18,* 361–371.

Seccombe, K., Ryan, R., & Austin, C. D. (1987). Care planning: Case managers' assessment of elders' welfare and caregivers' capacity. *Family Relations, 36,* 171–175.

Seibel, M., & Graves, W. (1980). The psychological implications of spontaneous abortion. *Reproductive Medicine, 24,* 161–165.

Seibel, M. M. & McCarthy, J. A. (1993). Infertility, pregnancy, and the emotions. In D. Goleman & J. Gurin (Eds.), *Mind body medicine: How to use your mind for better health.* NY: Consumer Reports Books.

Siegler, R. S. (1998). *Children's Thinking* (3rd ed.). Upper Saddle River, NJ: Prentice Hall.

Selman, R. (1981). The child as friendship philosopher. In. S. Asher & J. Gottman (Eds.), *The development of children's friendships.* New York: Cambridge University Press.

Selman, R., Beardslee, W., Schultz, L., Krupa, M., & Podorefsky, D. (1986). Assessing adolescent interpersonal negotiation strategies: Toward the integration of structural and functional models. *Developmental Psychology, 22,* 450–459.

Seltzer, G. B., Begun, A., Seltzer, M. M., & Krauss, M. W. (1991). Adults with mental retardation and their aging mothers: Impacts of siblings. *Family Relations, 40,* 310–317.

Selye, H. (1956). *The stress of life.* New York: McGraw-Hill.

Serock, K., Seefeldt, C., Jantz, R., & Galper, A. (1977). As children see old folks. *Today's Education, March-April,* 70–73.

Settles, B. H. (1987). A perspective on tomorrow's families. In M. Sussman and S. Steinmetz (Eds.), *Handbook of marriage and the family.* New York: Plenum.

Shaffer, J. B. (1978). *Humanistic psychology.* Englewood Cliffs, NJ: Prentice Hall.

Shanas, E., Townsend, P., Wedderburn, D., Fries, H., Milhoj, P., & Stejouwer, J. (1968). *Old people in three industrial societies.* New York: Atherton.

Shantz, C. (1983). Social cognition. In J. Flavell & E. Markman (Eds.), *Handbook of child psychology* (4th ed.). Vol. 3. New York: Wiley.

Shaughnessy, P. W. (1989). Quality of nursing home care: Problems and pathways. *Generations, 13,* 17–25.

Shaver, J., & Strong, W. (1976). *Facing value decisions: Rationale-building for teachers.* Belmont, CA: Wadsworth.

Sheehy, G. (1976). *Passages: Predictable crises of adulthood.* New York: Dutton.

Sheehan, N., & Nuttall. (1988). Conflict, emotion, and personal strain among family caregivers. *Family Relations, 37,* 92–98.

Sheehy, G. (1976). *Passages: Predictable crises of adult life.* New York: Dutton.

Sherman, E. (1987). *Meaning in mid-life transitions.* Albany, NY: State University of New York Press.

Shirley, M. (1931). *The first two years.* Vol 2. Minneapolis: University of Minnesota Press.

Shock, N. (1977). Biological theories of aging. In J. E. Birren & K. W. Schaie (Eds.), *Handbook of the psychology of aging.* New York: Van Nostrand.

Shock, N. W., & Norris, A. H. (1970). Neuromuscular coordination as a factor in age change in muscular exercise. In E. Jokl & E. Brunner (Eds.), *Physical activity and aging.* Vol. 4. Basel, Switzerland: S. Karger.

Shoenborn, C. A., & Danchik, K. M. (1980). Health practices among adults. *Advance Data From Vital and Health Statistics, No. 64,* November 4.

Shonkoff, J. (1984). The biological substrate and physical health in middle childhood. In W. Collins (Ed.), *Development during middle childhood.* Washington, DC: National Academy Press.

Shoor, M., & Speed, M. H. (1976). Death, delinquency, and the mourning process. In R. Fulton (Ed.), *Death and identity.* Bowie, MD: Charles Press.

Shore, C. (1986). Combinatorial play, conceptual development, and early multiword speech. *Developmental Psychology, 22,* 184–190.

Shostak, A. (1987). Singlehood. In M. B. Sussman & S. K. Steinmetz (Eds.), *Handbook of marriage and the family.* New York: Plenum.

Shulman, N. (1975). Life cycle variations in patterns of close relationships. *Journal of Marriage and the Family, 37,* 813–821.

Sidney, K. (1981). Cardiovascular benefits of physical activity in the exercising aged. In E. Smith & R. Serfass (Eds.), *Exercise and aging: The scientific basis.* Hillsdale, NJ: Enslow.

Siegal, D. (1990). Women's reproductive changes: A marker, not a turning point. *Generations, 14,* 31–32.

Siegel, D. J. (1999). *The developing mind: Toward a neurobiology of interpersonal experience.* NY: The Guilford Press.

Siegel, K., & Tuckel, P. (1984). Rational suicide and the terminally ill cancer patient. *Omega, 15,* 263–269.

Siegler, R. S. (1986). *Children's thinking.* Englewood Cliffs, NJ: Prentice Hall.

Silverstone, B., & Hyman, H. K. (1976). *You and your aging parents.* New York: Pantheon.

Simon, M. (1959). Body configuration and school readiness. *Child Development, 30,* 493–512.

Singer, J., & Singer, D. (1981). *Television, imagination, and aggression: A study of preschoolers.* Hillsdale, NJ: Erlbaum.

Singh, S., Forrest, J. D., & Torres, A. (1989). *Prenatal care in the United States.* New York: Alan Guttmacher Institute.

Skinner, B. F. (1938). *The behavior of organisms.* New York: Appleton-Century-Crofts.

Skinner, B. F. (1948). *Walden two.* New York: Macmillan.

Skinner, B. F. (1957). *Verbal behavior.* New York: Appleton-Century-Crofts.

Skinner, B. F. (1971). *Beyond freedom and dignity.* New York: Knopf.

Slackman, E., & Nelson, K. (1984). Acquisition of an unfamiliar script in story form by young children. *Child Development, 55,* 329–340.

Slavin, R. (1987). Ability grouping and student achievement in elementary schools: A best-evidence synthesis. *Review of Educational Research, 57,* 293–336.

Sluckin, W., Herbert, M., & Sluckin, M. (1983). *Maternal bonding.* Oxford, England: Blackwell.

Small, M. (1990). *Cognitive development.* San Diego, CA: Harcourt Brace Jovanovich.

Smith, C., & Lloyd, B. (1978). Maternal behavior and perceived sex of infant: Revisited. *Child Development, 49,* 1263–1265.

Smith, P. K. (1978). A longitudinal study of social participation in preschool children: Solitary and parallel play reexamined. *Developmental Psychology, 14*, 517–523.

Smith, T. (1981). Adolescent agreement with perceived maternal and paternal educational goals. *Journal of Marriage and the Family, 43*, 85–93.

Smock, P. J. (2000). Cohabitation in the United States: An appraisal of research themes, findings, and implications. *Annual Review of Sociology, 26*, 1–20.

Smoll, F. L., & Schutz, R. W. (1990). Quantifying gender differences in physical performance: A developmental perspective. *Developmental Psychology, 26*, 360–370.

Snarey, J. (1985). Cross-cultural universality of social-moral development: A critical review of Kohlbergian research. *Psychological Bulletin, 97*, 202–232.

Snarey, J., Reimer, J., & Kohlberg, L. (1985). Development of social-moral reasoning among kibbutz adolescents: A longitudinal cross-cultural study. *Developmental Psychology, 21*, 2–18.

Snyder, J., Dishion, T., & Patterson, G. (1986). Determinants and consequences of associating with deviant peers during preadolescence and adolescence. *Journal of Early Adolescence, 6*, 29–43.

Sobesky, W. (1983). The effects of situational factors on moral judgments. *Child Development, 54*, 575–584.

Sokolov, Y. N. (1969). The modeling properties of the nervous system. In M. Coles & I. Maltzman (Eds.), *A handbook of contemporary Soviet psychology.* New York: Basic Books.

Solomon, G. F. (1991). Psychosocial factors, exercise, and immunity: Athletes, elderly persons, and AIDS patients. *International Journal of Sports Medicine, 12*, 250–255.

Sommer, B. (1984). The troubled teen: Suicide, drug use, and running away. *Women & Health, 9*, 117–141.

Sommer, R. (1988). Two decades of marijuana attitudes: The more it changes, the more it is the same. *Journal of Psychoactive Drugs, 20*, 67–70.

Sorce, J., Emde, R., Campos, J., & Klinnert, M. (1985). Maternal emotional signaling: Its effect on the visual cliff behavior of 1-year-olds. *Developmental Psychology, 21*, 195–200.

Sorensen, R. C. (1973). *The Sorensen report: Adolescent sexuality in contemporary America.* New York: World Publishing.

Spangler, J., & Demi, E. (1988). *Bereavement support groups: Leadership manual.* (3rd ed.). Denver, CO: Grief Education Institute.

Spanier, G. (1983). Married and unmarried cohabitation in the United States: 1980. *Journal of Marriage and the Family, 45*, 277–288.

Spence, A. P., & Mason, E. B. (1987). *Human anatomy and physiology* (3rd ed.). Menlo Park, CA: Benjamin/Cummings.

Spence, D., & Lonner, T. (1971). The "empty nest:" A transition within motherhood. *Family Coordinator, 19*, 369–375.

Spence, D. A., & Wiener, J. M. (1990). Nursing home length of stay patterns: Results from the 1985 national nursing home survey. *The Gerontologist, 30*, 16–24.

Spence, J. T., & Helmreich, R. L. (1978). *Masculinity and femininity: Their psychological dimensions, correlates, and antecedents.* Austin, TX: University of Texas Press.

Spiker, C. (1966). The concept of development: Relevant and irrelevant issues. In H. W. Stevenson (Ed.), Concept of development (pp. 40–54). *Monographs of the Society for Research in Child Development, 31*, Whole No. 107.

Spinette, J., Swarner, J., & Sheposh, J. (1981). Effective parental coping following the death of a child from cancer. *Journal of Pediatric Psychology, 6*, 251–263.

Spirito, A., Hart, K., Overholser, J., & Halverson, J. (1990). Social skills and depression in adolescent suicide attempters. *Adolescence, 25*, 543–552.

Spitz, R. (1945). Hospitalism. In O. Fenichel et al. (Eds.), *The psychoanalytical study of the child.* Vol. 1. New York: International Universities Press.

Sroufe, L. A. (1985). Attachment classification from the perspective of infant-caregiver relationships and infant temperament. *Child Development, 56*, 1–14.

Sroufe, L. A., & Waters, E. (1976). The ontogenesis of smiling and laughter: A perspective on the organization of development in infancy. *Psychological Review, 83*, 173–189.

Sroufe, L. A., & Wunsch, J. (1972). The development of laughter in the first year of life. *Child Development, 43*, 1326–1344.

Stanley, S. M., Amato, P. R., Johnson, C. A., & Markman, H. J. (2006). Premarital education, marital quality, and marital stability: Findings from a large, random, household survey. *Journal of Family Psychology, 20*, 117–126.

Stanley, S. M., & Markman, H. J. (1992). Assessing commitment in personal relationships. *Journal of Marriage and Family, 54*, 595–608.

Stanley, S. M., Markman, H. J., & Whitton, S. W. (2002). Communication, conflict and commitment: Insights on the foundations of relationship success from a national survey. *Family Process, 41*, 659–675.

Stanley, S. M., Rhoades, G. K., & Markman, H. J. (2006). Sliding vs. deciding: Inertia and the premarital cohabitation effect. *Family Relations, 55*, 499–509.

Stanley, S. M., Whitton, S. W., & Markman, H. J. (2004). Maybe I do: Interpersonal commitment and premarital or nonmarital cohabitation. *Journal of Family Issues, 25*, 496–519.

Staples, R., & Mirande, A. (1980). Racial and cultural variations among American families: A decennial review of the literature on minority families. *Journal of Marriage and the Family, 42*, 887–903.

Starfield, B., Katz, H., Gabriel, A., Livingston. G., Benson, P., Hankin, J., Horn, S., & Steinwachs, D. (1984). Morbidity in childhood — a longitudinal view. *The New England Journal of Medicine, 310*, 824–829.

Starling, B. P., & Martin, A. C. (1990). Adult survivors of parental alcoholism: Implications for primary care. *The Nurse Practitioner, 15*, 16–23.

Steckel, A. (1987). Psychosocial development of children of lesbian parents. In F. W. Bozett (Ed.), *Gay and lesbian parents.* New York: Praeger.

Steinberg, L. (1987). Impact of puberty on family relations: Effects of pubertal status and pubertal timing. *Developmental Psychology, 23*, 451–460.

Steinberg, L. (1988). Reciprocal relation between parent-child distance and pubertal maturation. *Developmental Psychology, 24*, 122–128.

Steiner, H. (1990). Defense styles in eating disorders. *International Journal of Eating Disorders, 9*, 141–151.

Steinmetz, S. (1988). *Duty bound: Elder abuse and family care.* Newbury Park, CA: Sage.

Steinmetz, S., & Stein, K. F. (1988). Traditional and emerging families: A typology based on structures and functions. *Family Science Review, 1*, 103–114.

Steinmetz, S., Clavan, S., & Stein, K. F. (1990). *Marriage and family realities: Historical and contemporary perspectives.* New York: Harper & Row.

Steinmetz, S. K., Clavan, S., & Stein, K. F. (1990). *Marriage and family realities: Historical and contemporary perspectives.* New York: Harper & Row.

Stenback, A. (1980). Depression and suicidal behavior in old age. In J. E. Birren & R. B. Sloan (Eds.), *Handbook of mental health and aging* (pp. 616–652). Englewood Cliffs, N. J.: Prentice-Hall.

Stern, L. (1985). *The structures and strategies of human memory.* Homewood, IL: Dorsey.

Sternberg, R. J. (1987). The uses and misuses of intelligence testing: misunderstanding meaning, users over-rely on scores. *Education Week, September 23*, 22.

Sternberg, R. J. (Ed.) (1990). *Wisdom: Its nature, origin, and development.* NY: Cambridge University Press.

Sternberg, R. J., & Lubart, T. I. (2001). Wisdom and creativity. In J. E. Birren & K. W. Schaie (Eds.), *Handbook of the psychology of aging.* San Diego, CA: Academic Press.

Sternglanz, S., Gray, J., & Murakami, M. (1977). Adult preferences for infantile facial features: An ethological approach. *Animal Behavior, 25*, 108–115.

Stevens-Long, J. (1979). *Adult life: Developmental processes.* Palo Alto, CA: Mayfield.

Stevens-Long, J. (1988). *Adult life* (3rd ed.). Palo Alto, CA: Mayfield.

Stevenson, H., Azuma, H., & Hazkuta, K. (Eds.). (1986). *Child development and education in Japan.* New York: Freeman.

Stevenson, H., Lee, S.-Y., & Stigler, J. (1986). Mathematics and achievement of Chinese, Japanese, and American children. *Science, 231*, 693–699.

Stigler, J., Lee, S.-Y., & Stevenson, H. (1987). Mathematics classrooms in Japan, Taiwan, and the United States. *Child Development, 58*, 1272–1285.

Stinnett, N., Walters, J., & Kaye, E. (1984). *Relationships in marriage and the family,* 2nd ed. New York: Macmillan.

Stinnett, N., Walters, J., & Stinnett, N. (1991). *Relationships in marriage and the family* (3rd ed.).New York: Macmillan.

Stipek, D. (1984). Sex differences in children's attributions of success and failure on mathematics and spelling tests. *Sex Roles, 11,* 969–981.

Stockdale, D., Hegland, S., & Chiaromonte, T. (1989). Helping behaviors: An observational study of preschool children. *Early Childhood Research Quarterly, 4,* 533–544.

Stockman, L., & Graves, C. S. (1990). *Adult children who won't grow up: How to finally cut the cord that binds you.* Rocklin, CA: Prima Publishing & Communications.

Streib, G. F. (1977). Changing roles in later years. In R. A. Kalish (Ed.), *The later years: Social applications of gerontology.* Monterey, CA: Brooks/Cole.

Streissguth, A. P., Burr, H. M., Sampson, P. D., Darby, B. L., & Martin, DC (1989). IQ at age 4 in relation to maternal alcohol use and smoking during pregnancy. *Developmental Psychology, 25,* 3–11.

Strobino, D. (1987). *The health and medical consequences of adolescent sexuality and pregnancy: A review of the literature in risking the future.* Vol. 2. Washington, DC: National Academy Press.

Suitor, J., & Pillemer, K. (1988). Explaining intergenerational conflict when adult children and elderly parents live together. *Journal of Marriage and the Family, 50,* 1037–1047.

Sullivan, T., & Schneider, M. (1987). Development and identity issues in adolescent homosexuality. *Child and Adolescent Social Work Journal, 4,* 13–24.

Sullivan-Bolyai, J., Hull, H. F., Wilson, C., & Corey, L. (1983). Neonatal herpes simplex virus infection in King County, Washington: Increasing incidence and epidemiologic correlates. *Journal of the American Medical Association, 250,* 3059–3062.

Super, D. E. (1957). *The psychology of careers.* New York: Harper.

Super, D. E. (1963). *Career development: Self-concept theory.* New York: College Entrance Examination Board.

Surra, C. A. (1990). Research and theory on mate selection and premarital relationships in the 1980s. *Journal of Marriage and the Family, 52,* 844–865.

Susman, E. J., Pizzo, P. A., & Poplack, D. G. (1981). Adolescent cancer: Getting through the aftermath. In P. Ahmed (Ed.), *Living and dying with childhood cancer* (pp. 99–117). New York: Elsevier.

Sutton-Smith, B. (1985). The child at play. *Psychology Today, 19 (October),* 64–65.

Sutton-Smith, B., & Rosenberg, B. G. (1970). *The sibling.* New York: Holt, Rinehart, & Winston.

Suzuki-Slakter, N. (1988). Elaboration and metamemory during adolescence. *Contemporary Educational Psychology, 13,* 206–220.

Swaim, R., Oetting, E., Edwards, R., & Beauvais, F. (1989). Links from emotional distress to adolescent drug use: A path model. *Journal of Consulting and Clinical Psychology, 57,* 227–231.

Sweet, J. A., & Bumpass, L. L. (1987). *American families and households.* New York: Russell Sage Foundation.

Swyer, P. R. (1987). The organization of perinatal care with particular reference to the newborn. In G. B. Avery (Ed.), *Neonatology: Pathophysiology and management of the newborn.* Philadelphia: Lippincott.

Tan, L. E. (1985). Laterality and motor skills in four-year-olds. *Child Development, 56,* 119–124.

Tanner, J. M. (1978/1990). *Foetus into man: Physical growth from conception to maturity.* Cambridge: Harvard University Press.

Taras, H., Sallis, J., Patterson, T., Nader, P., & Nelson, J. (1989). Television's influence on children's diet and physical activity. *Developmental and Behavioral Pediatrics, 10,* 176–180.

Targ, D. (1979). Toward a reassessment of women's experience at middle age. *Family Coordinator, 28,* 377–382.

Tautermannova, M., (1973). Smiling in infants. *Child Development, 44,* 701–704.

Taveris, C. (1983). *Anger: The misunderstood emotion.* New York: Simon & Schuster.

Taylor, M. (1988). Conceptual perspective taking: Children's ability to distinguish what they know from what they see. *Child Development, 59,* 703–718.

Taylor, R. J., Chatters, L. M., Tucker, M. B., & Lewis, E. (1990). Developments in research on black families: A decade review. *Journal of Marriage and the Family, 52,* 993–1014.

Taylor, M., & Bacharach, V. (1981). The development of drawing rules: Meta-knowledge about drawing influences performances on nondrawing tasks. *Child Development, 52,* 373–375.

Taylor, E. (1989). Time is not on their side. *Time, February, 27,* 74.

Teachman, J. (2003). Premarital sex, premarital cohabitation and the risk of subsequent marital dissolution among women. *Journal of Marriage and Family, 65,* 444–455.

Tennov, D. (1979). *Love and limerance.* New York: Stein & Day.

Thelen, E. (1981). Rhythmical behavior in infancy: An ethological perspective. *Developmental Psychology, 17,* 237–257.

Thelen, E. (1986). Treadmill elicited stepping in seven month old infants. *Child Development, 57,* 1498–1506.

Thomas, A. (1986). Gender differences in satisfaction with grandparenting. *Psychology and Aging, 1,* 215–219.

Thomas, A., & Chess, S. (1984). Genesis and evolution of behavioral disorders: From infancy to early adult life. *American Journal of Psychiatry, 141,* 1–9.

Thomas, A., & Chess, S. (1987). Roundtable: What is temperament? *Child Development, 58,* 505–529.

Thomas, A., Chess, S., & Birch, H. G. (1968). *Temperament and behavior disorders in childhood.* NY: New York University Press.

Thomas, L. (1979). Causes of midlife change from high status careers. *Vocational Guidance Quarterly, 27,* 202–208.

Thomas, R. M. (1979). *Comparing theories of child development.* Belmont, CA: Wadsworth.

Thompson, M., Alexander, K., & Entwisle, D. (1988). Household composition, parental expectations, and school achievement. *Social Forces, 67,* 424–451.

Thompson, R. F., Crist, D. M., & Osborn, L. A. (1990). Treadmill exercise electocardiography in the elderly with physical impairments. *Gerontology, 36,* 112–118.

Thornburg, H. D., & Aras, Z. (1986). Physical characteristics of developing adolescents. *Journal of Adolescent Research, 1,* 47–78.

Thorndike, E. L. (1898). Animal intelligence: An experimental study of the associative processes in animals. *Psychological Review, 2* (Supplement No. 8).

Tienda, M., & Angel, R. (1982). Headship and household composition among blacks, Hispanics, and other whites. *Social Forces, 61,* 508–531.

Timiras, P. S. (1972). *Developmental physiology and aging.* New York: Macmillan.

Tobin, J., Wu, D., & Davidson, D. (1989). *Preschools in three cultures: Japan, China, and the United States.* New Haven, CT: Yale University Press.

Tobin-Richards, M., Boxer, A., & Petersen, A. (1983). The psychological significance of pubertal change: Sex differences in perceptions of self during early adolescence. In J. Brooks-Gunn & A. Petersen (Eds.), *Girls at puberty.* New York: Plenum.

Tognoli, L. (1980). Male friendship and intimacy across the life span. *Family Relations, 29,* 273–297.

Tomasello, M., Mannle, S., & Kruger, A. (1986). Linguistic environment of 1 to 2-year old twins. *Developmental Psychology, 22,* 641–653.

Toner, I., & Smith, R. (1977). Age and verbalization in delay maintenance behavior in children. *Journal of Experimental Child Psychology, 24,* 123–128.

Tower, R. (1987). *How schools can help combat student drug and alcohol abuse.* Washington, DC: NEA Professional Library.

Trevathan, W. (1983). Maternal "en face" orientation during the first hour after birth. *American Journal of Orthopsychiatry, 53,* 92–99.

Troen, S. K. (1985). Technological development and adolescence: The early twentieth century. *Journal of Early Adolescence, 5,* 429–440.

Troll, L. E. (1986). Parents and children in later life. *Generations, 10,* 23–25.

Trotter, R. (1983). Baby face. *Psychology Today, 17(8),* 14–20.

Trotter, R. (1987). You've come a long way, baby. *Psychology Today, 21(5),* 34–45.

Turner, R., & Avison, W. (1985). Assessing risk factors for problem parenting: The significance of social support. *Journal of Marriage and the Family, 47,* 881–892.

U. S. Bureau of the Census. (1983). *Current population report.* Washington, DC: U. S. Government Printing Office.

U. S. Bureau of the Census (1989). Changes in American family life. *Current Population Reports, Series P–23, No. 163.* Washington, DC: U. S. Government Printing Office.

U. S. Bureau of the Census. (1989). Studies in marriage and the family: Singleness in America, single parents and their children, married-couple families with children. *Current Population Reports, Series P–23(162).* Washington, DC: U. S. Government Printing Office.

U. S. Bureau of the Census (1990a) *Statistical abstract of the United States* (110th ed.). Washington, DC: U. S. Government Printing Office.

U. S. Bureau of the Census. (1990b). Household and family characteristics: March 1990 and 1989. *Current Population Reports, Series P–20, No. 447.* Washington, DC: U. S. Government Printing Office.

U. S. Bureau of the Census. (1991a). Cohabitation, marriage, marital dissolution, and remarriage: United States, 1988. *Advance Data, No. 194. DHHS Publication No. (PHS) 91–1250.* Washington, DC: U. S. Government Printing Office.

U. S. Bureau of the Census (1991b). *Statistical abstract of the United States* (111h ed.). Washington, DC: U. S. Government Printing Office.

U. S. Bureau of Labor. (1986). *Consumer expenditure survey, 1982–1983. Bulletin No. 2246.* Washington, DC: U. S. Government Printing Office.

U. S. Department of Agriculture. Updated estimates of the cost of raising a child, 1987. *Family Economic Review, 4,* 36–37.

U. S. Department of Health and Human Services (1987). *Smoking and health: A national status report* (HHS/PHS/CDC Publication No. 87–8396). Washington, DC: U. S. Government Printing Office.

U. S. Senate, Special Committee on Aging. (1986). *Aging America: Trends and projections.* Washington, DC: U. S. Government Printing Office.

Utne, N. (2005). To live with no regrets. In G. E. Dickinson & M.R. Leming, (Eds.), *Dying, death, and bereavement* (10th ed.). NY: McGraw-Hill.

Vaillant, G. E. (1977). *Adaptation to life.* Boston: Little, Brown.

Van Camp, S. P., & Boyer, J. L. (1989). Cardiovascular aspects of aging. *Physician and Sports Medicine, 17,* 120–125.

Vandell, D. L., Henderson, V. K., & Wilson, K. S. (1988). A longitudinal study of children with day-care experiences of varying quality. *Child Development, 59,* 1286–1293.

Vandenberg, B. (1978). Play and development from an ethological perspective. *American Psychologist, 33,* 724–739.

Veevers, J. E. (1973). The social meanings of parenthood. *Psychiatry, 36,* 291–310.

Vega, W. A. (1990). Hispanic families in the 1980s: A decade of research. *Journal of Marriage and the Family, 52,* 1015–1024.

Vega, W. A., Patterson, T., Sallis, J., Nader, P., Atkins, C., & Abramson, I. (1986). Cohesion and adaptability in Mexican-American and Anglo families. *Journal of Marriage and the Family, 48,* 857–867.

Verbrugge, L. M. (1977). The structure of adult friendship choices. *Social Forces, 56,* 576–597.

Verbrugge, L. M. (1979). Multiplexity in adult friendships. *Social Forces, 57,* 1286–1309.

Vetere, V. (1982). The role of friendship in the development and maintenance of lesbian love relationships. *Journal of Homosexuality, 8,* 51–65.

Vincent, C. (1972). An open letter to the "caught" generation. *Family Coordinator, 21,* 143–146.

Vinters, H. V. (2001). Aging and the human nervous system. In J. E. Birren & K. W. Schaie (Eds.), *Handbook of the psychology of aging.* San Diego, CA: Academic Press.

Vogt, W. P. (1993). *Dictionary of statistics and methodology: A nontechnical guide for the social sciences.* Newbury Park, CA: SAGE Publications.

von Bertalanffy, L. (1974a). General systems theory and psychiatry. In S. Arieti (Ed.), *American handbook of psychiatry, Vol. 1* (2nd ed.). New York: Basic Books.

von Bertalanffy, L. (1974b). *General systems theory.* New York: Braziller.

von Hofsten, C. (1983). Catching skills in infancy. *Journal of Experimental Psychology, 9,* 75–85.

von Hofsten, C., & Fazel-Zandy, S. (1984). Development of visually guided hand orientation in reaching. *Journal of Experimental Child Psychology, 38,* 208–219.

Voydanoff, P. (1990). Economic distress and family relations. *Journal of Marriage and the Family, 52,* 1099–1115.

Vurpillot, E. (1968). The development of scanning strategies and their relation to visual differentiation. *Journal of Experimental Child Psychology, 6,* 632–650.

Vygotsky, L. S. (1962). *Thought and language.* Cambridge, MA: MIT Press.

Vygotsky, L. S. (1978). *Mind in society: The development of higher psychological processes.* Cambridge, MA: Harvard University Press.

Waas, G. (1988). Social attributional biases of peer-rejected and aggressive children. *Child Development, 59,* 969–975.

Wadsworth, B. (1971). *Piaget's theory of cognitive development.* New York: David MacKay.

Wadsworth, B. J. (2004). *Piaget's theory of cognitive and affective development* (5th ed.). NY: Pearson Education, Inc.

Walbroehl, G. S. (1988). Effects of medical problems on sexuality in the elderly. *Medical Aspects of Human Sexuality, 22,* 56–57.

Walford, R (1983). *Maximum life span.* New York: Norton.

Walker, A. J. (1985). Reconceptualizing family stress. *Journal of Marriage and the Family, 47,* 827–838.

Walker, A. J., Pratt, C. C., Martell, L. K., & Martin, S. K. (1991). Perceptions of aid and actual aid in intergenerational caregiving. *Family Relations, 40,* 318–323.

Walker, B. A., & Mehr, M. (1983). Adolescent suicide—a family crisis: A model for effective intervention by family therapists. *Adolescence, 18,* 285–292.

Waller, G., Calam, R., & Slade, P. (1988). Family interaction and eating disorders: Do family members agree? *British Review of Bulimia and Anorexia Nervosa, 3,* 33–40.

Wallerstein, J. S. (1983). Children of divorce: The psychological tasks of the child. *American Journal of Orthopsychiatry, 53,* 230–243.

Wallerstein, J. S. (1987). Children of divorce: Report of a ten-year follow-up of early latency-age children. *American Journal of Orthopsychiatry, 57,* 199–211.

Wallerstein, J., & Blakeslee, S. (1989). *Second chances.* New York: Ticknor & Fields.

Wallerstein, J., Corbin, S., & Lewis, J. (1988). Children of divorce: A 10-year study. In E. Hetherington & J. Arasteh (Eds.), *Impact of divorce, single parenting, and stepparenting.* Hillsdale, NJ: Erlbaum.

Wallerstein, J. S., & Kelly, J. B. (1975). The effects of parental divorce: Experiences of the preschool child. *Journal of the American Academy of Child Psychiatry, 14,* 600–616.

Wallerstein, J. S., & Kelly, J. B. (1976). The effects of parental divorce: Experiences of the child in later latency. *Journal of the American Academy of Child Psychiatry, 15,* 257–269.

Wallerstein, J. S., & Kelly, J. B. (1980). Effects of divorce on the visiting father-child relationship. *American Journal of Psychiatry, 137,* 1534–1539.

Wareham, K., Lyon, M., Glenister, P., & Williams, E. (1987). Age-related reactivation of an X-linked gene. *Nature, 327,* 725–727.

Waterman, A. S. (1982). Identity development from adolescence to adulthood: An extension of theory and a review of research. *Developmental Psychology, 18,* 341–358.

Watson, J. B. (1924). *Behaviorism.* New York: Norton.

Watson, R. (1983). Premarital cohabitation vs. traditional courtship: Their effects on subsequent marital adjustment. *Family Relations, 32,* 139–147.

Wattenberg, B. (1984). *The good news is bad news.* New York: Simon & Schuster.

Wattleton, F. (1987). American teens: Sexually active, sexually illiterate. *Journal of School Health, 57,* 379–380.

Watts, W. D., & Wright, L. S. (1990). The relationship of alcohol, tobacco, marijuana, and other illegal drug use to delinquency among Mexican-American, Black, and White adolescent males. *Adolescence, 25,* 171–181.

Weatherly, D. (1964). Self-perceived rate of physical maturation and personality in late adolescence. *Child Development, 35,* 1197–1210.

Weg, R. (1983). Changing physiology of aging. In D. Woodruff & J. E. Birren (Eds.), *Aging: Scientific perspectives and social issues.* Monterey, CA: Brooks/Cole.

Wegscheider-Cruse, S. (1985). *Choicemaking.* Pompano Beach, FL: Health Communications.

Weinberg, A. D., Engingro, P. F., & Miller, R. L. (1989). Death in the nursing home: Senescence, infection, and other causes. *Journal of Gerontological Nursing, 15,* 12–17.

Weiner, A. S. (1977). Cognitive and social-emotional development in adolescence. *Journal of Pediatric Psychology, 2,* 87–92.

Weisfeld, G. E. (1982). The nature-nurture issue and the integrating concept of function. In B. B. Wolman (Ed.), *Handbook of developmental psychology.* Englewood Cliffs, NJ: Prentice Hall.

Weisman, A. D. (1972). *On dying and denying.* New York: Behavioral Publications.

Weistein, S. (1991). Retirement planning should be done now. *The Practical Accountant, 24,* 28–35.

Wellen, C. (1985). Effects of older siblings on the language young children hear and produce. *Journal of Speech and Hearing Disorders, 50,* 84–99.

Weller, R. H., & Bouvier, L. F. (1983). *Population: Demography and policy.* New York: St. Martin's Press.

Wellman, B. (1932). The effects of preschool attendance upon intellectual development. *Journal of Experimental Education, 1,* 48–69.

Wellman, H. M. (1985). The origins of metacognition. In D. Forrest-Pressley, G. McKinnon, & T. Waller (Eds.), *Cognition, metacognition, and performance.* New York: Academic Press.

Wellman, H. M., Ritter, K., & Flavell, J. H. (1975). Deliberate memory behavior in the delayed reactions of very young children. *Developmental Psychology, 11,* 781–787.

Wenger, J. E. (1989). Finding a nursing home. *Diabetes Forecast, July 1,* 78.

Werner, E. E. (1984). Resilient children. *Young Children, 24,* 686–692.

Werner, E. E., & Smith, R. (1982). *Vulnerable but not invincible: A study of resilient children.* New York: McGraw-Hill.

Werner, P., Middlestadt-Carter, S., & Crawford, T. (1975). Having a third child: Predicting behavioral intentions. *Journal of Marriage and the Family, 37,* 348–358.

Wertlieb, D., Weigel, C., & Felstein, M. (1989). Stressful experiences, temperament, and social support: Impact on children's behavior symptoms. *Journal of Applied Developmental Psychology, 10,* 487–505.

Wertlieb, D., Weigel, C., Springer, T., & Feldstein, M. (1987). Temperament as a moderator of children's stressful experiences. *American Journal of Orthopsychiatry, 57,* 234–245.

West, J. R. (1986). *Alcohol and brain development.* London: Oxford University Press.

Whisnant, L., Brett, E., & Zegans, L. (1975). Implicit messages concerning menstruation in commercial educational materials prepared for young adolescent girls. *Journal of Psychiatry, 132,* 815–820.

White, S. H. (1975). Commentary. In L. B. Miller & J. L. Dyer, (Eds.), Four preschool programs: Their dimensions and effects. *Monographs of the Society for Research in Child Development, 40,* 168–170.

White, T. G. (1982). Naming practices, typicality, and underextension in child language. *Journal of Experimental Child Psychology, 33,* 324–346.

White, L. K., & Booth, A. (1985). The quality and stability of remarriages: The role of stepchildren. *American Sociological Review, 50,* 689–698.

White, C. B. (1982). A scale for the assessment of attitudes and knowledge regarding sexuality in the aged. *Archives of Sexual Behavior, 11,* 491–502.

White, E., Elsom, B., & Prawat, B. (1978). Children's conceptions of death. *Child Development, 49,* 307–311.

Whitehead, W. E., Drinkwater, D., & Cheskin, L. J. (1989). Constipation in the elderly living at home: Definition, prevalence, and relationship to lifestyle and health status. *Journal of the American Geriatrics Society, 37,* 423–430.

Whitfield, C. L. (1987). *Healing the child within: Discovery and recovery for adult children of dysfunctional families.* Deerfield Beach, FL: Health Communications.

Whitney, E., & Hamilton, E. (1987). *Understanding nutrition* (4th ed.). St. Paul, MN: West Publishing Co.

Wilcox, B. L., Millstein, S. G., & Gardner, W. (1990). Protecting adolescents from AIDS. *New Directions for Child Development, Winter,* 71–75.

Wilkie, C., & Ames, E. (1986). The relationship of infant crying to parental stress in the transition to parenthood. *Journal of Marriage and the Family, 48,* 545–550.

Williams, H. (1983). *Perceptual and motor development.* Englewood Cliffs, NJ: Prentice Hall.

Williams, E. R., & Caliendo, M. A. (1984). *Nutrition: Principles, issues, and applications.* New York: McGraw-Hill.

Williams, J. W., & Stith, M. (1980). *Middle childhood: Behavior and development* (2nd ed.). New York: Macmillan.

Williams, S. R. (1989). *Nutrition and diet therapy* (6th ed.). St. Louis, MO: Times Mirror/Mosby College Publishing.

Williamson, P. (1986). National Sudden Infant Death Syndrome Foundation. In T. Rando (Ed.), *Parental loss of a child.* Champaign, IL: Research Press.

Wilson, E. O. (1975). *Sociobiology: The new synthesis.* Cambridge, MA: Harvard University Press.

Wilson, E. O. (1978). *On human nature.* Cambridge, MA: Harvard University Press.

Wilson, R. S. (1985). Risk and resilience in early mental development. *Developmental Psychology, 21,* 795–805.

Windle, M. (1991). The difficult temperament in adolescence: Associations with substance use, family support, and problem behaviors. *Journal of Clinical Psychology, 47,* 310–315.

Wingfield, A., & Byrnes, D. (1981). *The psychology of human memory.* New York: Academic Press.

Winick, M., & Brasel, J. (1977). Early malnutrition and subsequent brain development. *Annals of the New York Academy of Science, 300,* 280–282.

Winterton, M. (1991). Strategies for promoting physical fitness. *Nursing Clinics of North America, 26,* 855–890.

Wise, T. (1978). Variations in male orgasm. *Medical Aspects of Human Sexuality, 12,* 72.

Wolff, P. H. (1966). The causes, controls, and organization of behavior in the neonate. *Psychological Issues, 5,* 496–503.

Wolff, P. (1969). The natural history of crying and other vocalizations in early infancy. In B. Foss (Ed.), *Determinants of infant behavior.* Vol. 4. London: Methuen.

Woods, L. N., & Emery, R. E. (2002). The cohabitation effects on divorce: Causation or selection? *Journal of Divorce and Remarriage, 37,* 101–119.

Worden, J. W. (1982). *Grief counseling and grief therapy.* New York: Springer

Yager, J. (1988). The treatment of eating disorders. *Journal of Clinical Psychiatry, 49,* 18–25.

Yamamoto, K., Soliman, A., Parsons, J., & Davies, O.L. (1987). Voices in unison: Stressful events in the lives of children in six countries. *Journal of Child Psychology and Psychiatry, 28,* 855–864.

Yang, R. K., Zweig, A. R., Douthitt, T. C., & Federman, E. J. (1976). Successive relationships between maternal attitudes during pregnancy, analgesic medication during labor and delivery, and newborn behavior. *Developmental Psychology, 12,* 6–14.

Yarrow, M., Scott, P., & Waxler, C. (1973). Learning concern for others. *Developmental Psychology, 8,* 240–260.

Yeaworth, R. C., York, J., Hussey, M. A., Ingle, M. E., & Goodwin, T. (1980). The development of an adolescent life change event scale. *Adolescence, 15,* 91–97.

Yonas, A., Granrud, C. E., & Pettersen, L. (1985). Infants' sensitivity to relative size information at distance. *Developmental Psychology, 21,* 161–167.

Young, C. (1991). Alcohol, drugs, driving, and you: A comprehensive program to prevent adolescent drinking, drug use, and driving. *Journal of Alcohol and Drug Education, 36,* 20–25.

Zahn-Waxler, C., Radke-Yarrow, M., & Brady-Smith, J. (1977). Perspective-taking and prosocial behavior. *Developmental Psychology, 13,* 87–88.

Zelazo, P. (1983). The development of walking: New findings and old assumptions. *Journal of Motor Behavior, 15,* 99–137.

Zelnik, M., & Kim, Y. (1982). Sex education and its association with teenage sexual activity, pregnancy, and contraceptive use. *Family Planning Perspectives, 14,* 117–126.

Zheng, J. J., & Rosenberg, I. H. (1989). What is the nutritional status of the elderly? *Geriatrics, 44,* 57–44.

Zill, N., & Rogers, C. C. (1988). Recent trends in the well-being of children in the United States and their implications for public policy. In A. J. Cherlin (Ed.), *The changing American family and public policy.* Washington, DC: Urban Institute Press.

Zimet, G. D., Hillier, S. A., Anglin, T. M., & Ellick, E. (1991). Knowing someone with AIDS: The impact on adolescents. *Journal of Pediatric Psychology, 16,* 287–294.

Zinker, J.C., & Fink, S. l. (1966). The possibility of psychological growth in a dying person. *Journal of General Psychology, 74,* 185–199.

Zuckerman, B., Frank, D., Hingson, R., AMaro, H., Levenson, S. M., Kayne, J., Parker, S., Vinci, R., Aboagye, K., Fried, L., Cabral, H., Timperi, R., & Bauchner, H. (1989). Effects of maternal marijuana and cocaine use on fetal growth. *The New England Journal of Medicine, 320,* 762–768.

Zuger, B. (1989). Homosexuality in families of boys with effeminate behavior: An epidemiological study. *Archives of Sexual Behavior, 18,* 155–166.

Zuger, B. (1989). Homosexuality in families of boys with effeminate behavior: An epidemiological study. *Archives of Sexual Behavior, 18,* 155–166.

Photo Credits

Chapter 1: CMPS, 1; iStockphoto, 2; iStockphoto, 3; iStockphoto, 4; iStockphoto, 11; iStockphoto, 13; iStockphoto, 17; AP Wide World Photos, 21; Library of Congress, 25; iStockphoto, 26; Shutterstock images, 31; AP Wide World Photos, 33; iStockphoto, 45; AP Wide World Photos, 47.

Chapter 2: iStockphoto, 53; iStockphoto, 58; iStockphoto, 63; Shutterstock images, 65; iStockphoto, 66; Courtesy of T. Grayson, 68; iStockphoto, 70; iStockphoto, 73; iStockphoto, 78; Courtesy of T. Grayson, 81; iStockphoto, 83; iStockphoto, 87; iStockphoto, 92.

Chapter 3: iStockphoto, 99; iStockphoto, 100; iStockphoto, 103; iStockphoto, 105: iStockphoto, 107; iStockphoto, 109; Shutterstock images, 110; iStockphoto, 115; iStockphoto, 116; Courtesy of J. James, 121; iStockphoto, 124; iStockphoto, 126; iStockphoto, 132; iStockphoto, 134.

Chapter 4: iStockphoto, 141; iStockphoto, 144; Shutterstock, 145; iStockphoto, 148; AP Wide World Photos, 151; Shutterstock, 154; iStockphoto, 158; iStockphoto, 159; iStockphoto, 164; iStockphoto, 167; iStockphoto, 170; Shutterstock images, 172; iStockphoto, 176; iStockphoto, 178; iStockphoto, 181; iStockphoto, 183; iStockphoto, 187.

Chapter 5: iStockphoto, 193; iStockphoto, 195; iStockphoto, 198; iStockphoto, 200; iStockphoto, 202; iStockphoto, 205; iStockphoto, 208; iStockphoto, 210; iStockphoto, 212; iStockphoto, 215; iStockphoto, 219; iStockphoto, 222; iStockphoto, 224; iStockphoto, 226; iStockphoto, 228; iStockphoto, 231.

Chapter 6: iStockphoto, 235; iStockphoto, 241; iStockphoto, 246; iStockphoto, 248; iStockphoto, 250; iStockphoto, 254; iStockphoto, 259; iStockphoto, 262; iStockphoto, 264; iStockphoto, 266; iStockphoto, 268; iStockphoto, 271.

Chapter 7: iStockphoto, 275; iStockphoto, 276; iStockphoto, 277; iStockphoto, 280; iStockphoto, 282; iStockphoto, 286; iStockphoto, 289; iStockphoto, 292; iStockphoto, 296; iStockphoto, 298.

Chapter 8: iStockphoto, 305; iStockphoto, 307; iStockphoto, 309; iStockphoto, 312; iStockphoto, 314; iStockphoto, 316; iStockphoto, 319; Corbis, 323; iStockphoto, 327; iStockphoto, 328; iStockphoto, 331; iStockphoto, 332.

Chapter 9: iStockphoto, 339; iStockphoto, 343; iStockphoto, 347; Getty Images, 349; iStockphoto, 353; iStockphoto, 360; iStockphoto, 363; iStockphoto, 365; iStockphoto, 367.

Chapter 10: iStockphoto, 375; iStockphoto, 377; iStockphoto, 383; AP Wide World Photos, 388; iStockphoto, 389; iStockphoto, 392; iStockphoto, 395; iStockphoto, 398; iStockphoto, 400; iStockphoto, 402; iStockphoto, 404; iStockphoto, 408; iStockphoto, 411; iStockphoto, 413; iStockphoto, 416; iStockphoto, 418.

Index